THE LOGIC OF SOCIAL HIERARCHIES

The Logic of Social Hierarchies

Edited by
EDWARD O. LAUMANN
PAUL M. SIEGEL
ROBERT W. HODGE
University of Michigan

MARKHAM PUBLISHING COMPANY / Chicago

MARKHAM SOCIOLOGY SERIES
Robert W. Hodge, Editor

Adams, *Kinship in an Urban Setting*
Adams, *The American Family: A Sociological Interpretation*
Appelbaum, *Theories of Social Change*
Farley, *Growth of the Black Population: A Study of Demographic Trends*
Filstead, ed., *Qualitative Methodology: Firsthand Involvement with the Social World*
Laumann, Siegel, and Hodge, eds., *The Logic of Social Hierarchies*
Zeitlin, ed., *American Society, Inc.: Studies of the Social Structure and Political Economy of the United States*

Library of Congress Catalog Card Number: 76-111977
Standard Book Number: 8410-4009-5

Acknowledgements

"On the Origin of Inequality Among Men" is reprinted from *Essays in the Theory of Society* by Ralf Dahrendorf, with the permission of the publishers, Stanford University Press. © 1968 by the Board of Trustees of Leland Stanford Junior University

"Developmental Trends in the Structure of Small Groups" is reprinted from an article in *Sociometry* (February 1953) by C. Heinicke and Robert F. Bales, and is published here with permission of the original publisher, the American Sociological Association.

"Class, Status, Party," *From Max Weber: Essays in Sociology,* edited and translated by H. H. Gerth and C. Wright Mills, is reprinted by permission. Copyright 1946 by Oxford University Press, Inc.

"Caste, Class and Slavery: The Taxonomic Problem," by Edmund R. Leach, is reprinted from *Caste and Race: Comparative Approaches,* edited by Anthony de Reuck and Julie Knight, with permission of the original publisher, J. and A. Churchill, Ltd. (1967).

"Organized Dependency Relations," by Arthur L. Stinchcombe, is reprinted from a chapter in *Handbook of Organizations,* edited by James March, with permission of the original publisher, Rand McNally and Company. Copyright 1965.

"Feudalism as a Type of Society," by Marc Bloch, is reprinted from a chapter in *Feudal Society,* Vol. 2, translated by L. A. Manyon, with permission of the original publisher, University of Chicago Press. Copyright 1964.

"America's Unique Class Politics: The Interplay of Labor, Credit and Commodity Markets," by Norbert Wiley, is reprinted from an article in *American Sociological Review,* 32 (August 1967), with permission of the original publisher, the American Sociological Association.

"Some Principles of Stratification," by Kingsley Davis and Wilbert E. Moore, is reprinted from an article in *American Sociological Review,* 10 (April 1945), with permission of the original publisher, the American Sociological Association.

"Recent Trends in Family Income" is excerpted from *Income Distribution in the United States* (1960 Census Monograph) by Herman P. Miller (Washington, D.C.: U.S. Government Printing Office, 1966).

"The Corporation: How Much Power? What Scope?" by Carl Kaysen, is reprinted by permission of the publisher from Edward S. Mason, ed., *The Corporation in Modern Society* (Cambridge, Mass.: Harvard University Press). Copyright 1959, by the President and Fellows of Harvard College.

"Organizational Control Structure," by Arnold S. Tannenbaum and Robert L. Kahn, is reprinted from an article in *Human Relations,* Vol. 10, no. 2 (1957), with permission of the original publisher, Plenum Publishing Company, Ltd.

"The Ruling Class" is reprinted from *The Ruling Class* by Gaetano Mosca. Copyright, 1939, McGraw-Hill, Inc. Used with permission of McGraw-Hill Book Company.

"The Higher Circles" is from *The Power Elite,* by C. Wright Mills. Copyright © 1956 by Oxford University Press, Inc. Reprinted by permission.

"A Critique of the Ruling Elite Model," by Robert A. Dahl, is reprinted from an article in *American Political Science Review*, 52 (June 1958), with permission of the original publisher, the American Political Science Association.

"Ascription in Modern Societies" was originally published in *Sociological Inquiry*, Vol. 38, no. 2 (Spring 1968).

"The Immigrants' Progress and the Theory of the Establishment" is excerpted from *The Protestant Establishment* by E. Digby Baltzell, and is reprinted here with permission of the original publisher, Random House, Inc. Copyright 1964.

"Full Citizenship for the Negro American" is excerpted with permission of The Macmillan Company from *Sociological Theory and Modern Society* by Talcott Parsons. Copyright © 1967 by The Free Press, a division of The Macmillan Company.

"Minorities and the Process of Stratification," by Beverly Duncan and Otis Dudley Duncan, is reprinted from an article in *American Sociological Review*, 33 (June 1968), with permission of the original publisher, the American Sociological Association.

"Income and Education" is excerpted from *Income Distribution in the United States* (1960 Census Monograph) by Herman P. Miller (Washington, D.C.: U.S. Government Printing Office, 1966).

"The Role of Economic Dominants in Community Power Structure," by Robert O. Schulze, is reprinted from an article in *American Sociological Review*, 23 (February 1958), with permission of the original publisher, the American Sociological Association.

"The Boys and the Total Institution" is excerpted from *English Public Schools* by Ian Weinberg. Reprinted by permission of the publishers, Atherton Press, Inc. Copyright © 1967, Atherton Press, Inc., New York. All rights reserved.

"Sponsored and Contest Mobility and the School System," by Ralph H. Turner, is reprinted from an article in *American Sociological Review*, 25 (December 1960), with permission of the original publisher, the American Sociological Association.

"Deference" is reprinted from a chapter by Edward A. Shils in *Social Stratification: Sociological Studies, I*, edited by J. A. Jackson, with permission of the original publisher, Cambridge University Press. Copyright 1968.

"Some Conditions of Obedience and Disobedience to Authority," by Stanley Milgram, is reprinted from an article in *Human Relations*, Vol. 18, no. 1 (1965), with permission of the original publisher, Plenum Publishing Company, Ltd.

"Class Consciousness and Class Structure" is excerpted from *The Psychology of Social Classes: A Study of Class Consciousness* by Richard Centers (Princeton University Press, 1949). Reprinted by permission of Princeton University Press.

"Continuities in Theories of Status Consistency and Cognitive Dissonance" is reprinted from an article by James A. Geschwender in *Social Forces*, 46 (December 1967), with permission of the original publisher, University of North Carolina Press.

"The Domestic Cycle and the Distribution of Power in Turkish Villages," by Paul Stirling, is reprinted from a chapter in *Mediterranean Countrymen*, edited by Julian Pitt-Rivers, with permission of the original publisher, Mouton & Co. (1963).

"What Social Class Is in America" is reprinted from *Social Class in America* by W. Lloyd Warner, Marchia Meeker, and Kenneth Eells. Copyright 1949 by Science Research Associates, Inc. Reprinted with permission of Harper & Row, Publishers, Inc.

"The Decline and Fall of Social Class," by Robert A. Nisbet, is excerpted from *Pacific Sociological Review*, 2 (Spring 1959), and is reprinted here with permission of the original publisher.

"The Subcultures of the Working Class, Lower Class and Middle Class" is reprinted with permission of The Macmillan Company from *The Urban Villagers* by Herbert J. Gans. © 1962 by the Free Press of Glencoe, a division of The Macmillan Company.

"Status, Conformity, and Innovation" is excerpted from *Social Behavior, Its Elementary Forms* by George C. Homans. © 1961 by Harcourt Brace Jovanovich, Inc., and reprinted with their permission.

"Social Class, Speech Systems and Psycho-therapy," by Basil Bernstein, is excerpted from an article in *British Journal of Sociology*, 15 (March 1964), and is reprinted here with permission of the original publishers, Routledge & Kegan Paul Ltd. and the London School of Economics.

"Evolution in Process" is reprinted from *Mankind Evolving* by Theodosius Dobzhansky, with permission of the original publisher, Yale University Press. Copyright © 1962, by Yale University.

"Do American Women Marry Up?" by Zick Rubin, is reprinted from an article in *American Sociological Review,* 33 (October 1969), with permission of the original publisher, the American Sociological Association.

"Social Class, Mental Illness, and American Psychiatry: An Expository Review," by S. M. Miller and Elliott G. Mishler, is reprinted from an article in *Milbank Memorial Fund Quarterly,* 37 (April 1959), with permission of the original publisher.

"The Shifting Role of Class in Political Attitudes and Behavior," by Philip E. Converse, is reprinted from *Readings in Social Psychology,* edited by E. E. Maccoby, T. M. Newcomb, and E. L. Hartley. Copyright 1947, 1952, © 1958 by Holt, Rinehart, and Winston, Inc. Reprinted by permission of Holt, Rinehart, and Winston, Inc.

"On the Evolution of Social Stratification and the State," by Morton H. Fried, is reprinted from *Culture in History,* edited by S. Diamond, with permission of the original publisher, Columbia University Press. Copyright 1960.

"Privilege and Poverty: Two Worlds on One Planet," by Nathan Keyfitz, is excerpted from an article in *Bulletin of the Atomic Scientists,* 22 (March 1966), and is reprinted here with permission of the original publisher, Educational Foundation for Nuclear Science.

"Miners and Agrarian Radicalism," by James Petras and Maurice Zeitlin, is reprinted from an article in *American Sociological Review,* 32 (August 1967), with permission of the original publisher, the American Sociological Association.

"The Trend of Occupational Mobility in the United States," by Otis Dudley Duncan, is reprinted from an article in *American Sociological Review,* 30 (August 1965), with permission of the original publisher, the American Sociological Association.

"On the Cost of Being a Negro," by Paul M. Siegel, was originally published in *Sociological Inquiry,* 35, no. 1 (Winter 1965).

"Aid to the Poor and Social Exchange," by Gerald D. Suttles and David Street, is excerpted from working paper #110, Center for Organization Studies, University of Chicago, January 1969.

"The Youth Ghetto," by John Lofland, is abridged from the *Journal of Higher Education,* 39 (March 1968). Copyright © 1968 by the Ohio State University Press and reprinted by permission.

Preface

Faced with the burgeoning theoretical and research-oriented literature on social inequality, the editors, as teachers of courses on social stratification, were faced with the increasingly difficult task of bringing together for our students a diverse range of source materials that have appeared in a variety of professional journals, books and unpublished manuscripts in various disciplines. While a number of anthologies in the past several years have attempted to compile some of these materials, we were dissatisfied with them on various grounds, primarily because they neglected one or more areas of the field that we felt deserved more systematic attention.

We have, consequently, attempted to create a systematic introduction to the field by presenting brief introductory essays followed by selections from the relevant literature. Bibliographies are included to aid the student who is interested in a particular issue and wishes to explore it in greater depth. Our criteria for selecting articles for inclusion have stressed current empirical and theoretical work in the field. As a result, some 55 percent of the articles were published after 1965 and 75 percent after 1960. Despite this emphasis on contemporary treatments, the classical statements are justly represented by sociologists such as Weber and Mosca and representative papers on the controversy over the Davis-Moore functional theory of stratification.

In addition, the editors have included methodologically sophisticated selections that demonstrate the relevance of methods courses to the analysis of important social issues. This enables the student to acquire a more sophisticated grasp of the meaning of social inequality than is often afforded him in other collections. We have, however, edited these selections to insure that they do not presume too much technical background. As mentioned before, each general section is introduced by a provocative essay that *articulates* rather than merely summarizes the selections included, relating them to more general considerations. Finally, the editors have attempted to broaden the conventional perspective on social stratification and inequality (which emphasizes societal and community-level analyses) by including articles on status phenomena in small groups and formal organizations. The social psychological processes concomitant and consequent to stratification and inequality have also been emphasized by including such authors as Homans, Milgram, Geschwender, Bernstein, Converse, and Lofland.

From some points of view, our selection of readings may be criticized for failing to include much "comparative" material—i.e., studies of the stratification systems of societies other than the United States. In our view, the comparative method ideally implies the comparison of two or more objects by means of measurements taken in identical ways and analyzed by similar techniques. The inclusion of materials from diverse countries without explicit comparisons or of dissimilar materials from diverse countries that are inherently noncomparable simply does not meet this definition of the comparative method. Many of the studies that meet this stringent criterion are either easily accessible elsewhere or are too technical and too long to justify inclusion in a reader of this kind. At the expense of omitting some conventional comparative studies, we have been able to cover more intensively a variety of topics which have been neglected in recent compilations—for instance, status crystallization, the emergence of status differentiation in small groups, social psychological aspects of status, and status and power in formal organizations.

The introductory sections of this volume were drafted while Robert W. Hodge was a Simon Senior Research Fellow in the Department of Social Anthropology and Sociology at the Victoria University of Manchester during 1969–70. He is grateful to the late Lord Simon of Wythenshawe for the support made possible through the Simon Fund, as well as to Lady Simon and the staff of Broomcroft Hall for providing pleasant accommodations for the year. The other residents of the Hall provided many evenings of entertaining and lively conversation. The hospitality and intellectual stimulation extended by many members of the staff and their wives, but especially by Bryan and Sue Roberts, David and Mary Weir, and Peter and Sheila Worsley, is gratefully acknowledged. The support and friendship of three other temporary members of the staff—Ann K. Allen, Dick Atkinson, and Margie Hall—made the months in Manchester particularly rewarding and memorable; they cannot be repaid for the lessons in life and sociology they gave, but one hopes that friends like these have been partially repaid in kind.

As is customary with such things, the time and effort spent in hammering out a coherent perspective from our divergent orientations and theoretical predilections (i.e., the Parsonsian vs. the "Chicago School") and of performing the more mundane tasks of obtaining authors' and publishers' permissions to use their materials greatly exceeded our wildest initial estimates. We are especially indebted to our research assistants, Paula Pelletier and Jane Hood, who over the past year have contributed so much to simplifying our task by collating relevant materials and extracting the appropriate permissions from publishers and authors. Jane Hikel has ably assisted us in typing manuscripts.

In the course of our collaboration, we have learned much from each other. We hope that the result will prove of value to others.

Edward O. Laumann
Paul M. Siegel
Robert W. Hodge

Contents

I

Social Differentiation

The maintenance of any social system requires the continuous and successful performance of a variety of activities. There is no known social system in which every member performs exactly the same pattern of activities. Thus, in addition to obvious differences among individuals (such as age and sex), members of a social system become differentiated according to the patterns of activities they regularly perform. These diverging activity patterns become routinized into social roles—"standard" sets of activities and expectations about them. The capacity of individuals to perform different social roles does not correspond well to biological differences in age, sex, and heredity. Every social system is confronted, then, with the problem of allocating persons to social roles. Lacking a biologically determined solution, societies have evolved many alternative mechanisms for allocating persons to roles.

The observable histories of industrializing and industrialized nations, as well as comparative analyses of peoples whose social institutions do not embody the concept of nationhood, make clear that there has been a general evolutionary tendency for societies to develop increasingly complex forms of differentiation. The emerging patterns of differentiation appear at both the inter- and intra-institutional levels. Thus

even in agriculture, the organization of production has been more and more disassociated from the family. Not only have new institutional forms emerged, but old ones have themselves become internally more differentiated. While the economic and political responsibilities of the family have been assumed by business enterprises and public administration, the continued need for families to relate to the larger society has generated both a more complex family life cycle and a greater variety of family forms. No longer may family members be sorted out solely by sex and their reproductive capacity. Now their responsibilities to each other are more finely gauged, both formally and informally, by whether they are in or out of school, in or out of the labor force, recognized or not recognized as legal adults, and so forth. Correspondingly, families pass through a more complex life cycle and are presented with a greater variety of alternatives, especially those hinged on the work involvements of husband and wife at the various stages of childrearing.

The development of social differentiation is of central importance to our understanding of social stratification because every axis of the former is at least a potential dimension of the latter. Given that one or more properties of social objects are util-

1

ized to distribute them to various groups, there is always the possibility that the features used to distinguish one object from another will become not just distinguishing marks, but marks of distinction. In this event, the objects, and the groups into which they fall, will be both differentiated and differentially valued. Thus social differentiation *may* be transformed into social inequality.

Although there is clearly a connection between social differentiation and social inequality, the nature of that association is neither fully known nor fully understood. In part this deficiency stems from the fact that our records of the evolution of man and society are mute on the issues at stake: we have no certain knowledge of how social inequality came to be imposed upon social differentiation. Consequently, social philosophers and social theorists have had to rely upon speculative reconstructions of the origins of inequality in society. In the paper reprinted in this section, Ralf Dahrendorf supplies a critical analysis of one such reconstruction, that associated with the functional theory of stratification.

Lacking a firm historical knowledge of the emergence of social differentiation and inequality, there is an alternative to relying upon speculation and theoretical imagination and the piecemeal evidence from archaeology. One can conduct experimental studies of the development of role differentiation and of differential evaluations in small groups. Not only can the applicability in particular settings, and hence the generality, of propositions generated by the historical record be tested in this way, but such studies can also provide important guides for interpreting incomplete historical information and principles upon which to base theoretical speculations. The paper by Heinicke and Bales demonstrates some important features of the evolution of social differentiation in small groups. Plainly, the generalization of these principles to larger groups and to entire societies will be legitimate only insofar as they pertain to the generic properties of all social systems. The chance of isolating such general features of human behavior has made the study of small groups exciting to some, while others —particularly those who espouse situationally determined theories of behavior—have judged such investigations to be largely irrelevant to our understanding of society.

REFERENCES

Adams, Robert McC.
  1960 The Evolution of Urban Society. Chicago: Aldine.
Farrag, Abdelmegid M.
  1964 "The occupational structure of the labor force: Patterns and trends in selected countries." Population Studies 18: 17-34.
Galle, Omer R.
  1963 "Occupational composition and the metropolitan hierarchy: The inter- and intra-metropolitan division of labor." American Journal of Sociology 69: 260-269.
Parsons, Talcott.
  1966 Societies: Evolutionary and Comparative Perspectives. Englewood Cliffs, New Jersey: Prentice-Hall.
Sahlins, Marshall and Elman R. Service (eds.).
  1960 Evolution and Culture. Ann Arbor: University of Michigan Press.
Steward, Julian H.
  1955 Theory of Culture Change: The Methodology of Multilinear Evolution. Urbana: University of Illinois Press.

CHAPTER 1

On the Origin of Inequality Among Men

RALF DAHRENDORF

Even in the affluent society, it remains a stubborn and remarkable fact that men are unequally placed. There are children who are ashamed of their parents because they think that a university degree has made them "better." There are people who decorate their houses with antennas without having the television sets to go with them, in order to convince their neighbors that they can afford television. There are firms that build their offices with movable walls because the status of their employees is measured in square feet and an office has to be enlarged when its occupant is promoted. There are clerical workers whose ambition it is to achieve a position in which they not only can afford, but are socially permitted to own, a two-tone car. Of course, such differences are no longer directly sustained by the force of legal sanction, which upholds the system of privilege in a caste or estate society. Nevertheless, our society— quite apart from the cruder gradations of property and income, prestige and power—is characterized by a multitude of differences of rank so subtle and yet so penetrating that one cannot but be skeptical of the claim one sometimes hears that a leveling process has caused all inequalities to disappear. It is no longer usual to investigate the anxiety, suffering, and hardship that inequalities cause among men—yet there are suicides because of poor examination results, divorces based on "social" incompatibility, crimes occasioned by a feeling of social inequality. Throughout our society, social inequality is still turning men against men.

These remarks are not meant as a plea for equality. On the contrary, I shall later agree with Kant, who called "inequality among men" a "rich source of much that is evil, but also of everything that is good." (104: 325.) Yet the extreme effects of inequality may give a general idea of the problem that concerns me. Diderot has our sympathy when he states in his article "Société" in the *Encyclopédie*:

> There is no more inequality between the different stations in life than there is among the different characters in a comedy: the end of the play finds all the players once again in the same position, and the brief period for which their play lasted did not and could not convince any two of them that one was really above or below the other. (92: 208.)

But the life of men in society is not merely a comedy, and the hope that all will be equal in death is a feeble consolation for most. The question remains: Why is there inequality among men? Where do its causes lie? Can it be reduced, or even abolished altogether? Or do we have to accept it as a necessary element in the structure of human society?

I shall try to show that historically these were the first questions asked by sociology. By surveying the various attempts to answer them a whole history of sociological thought might be written, and I shall at least give some indication of how this may be so. So far, however, as the problem of inequality itself is concerned, this history has achieved little more than to give it a different name: what was called in the eighteenth century the origin of inequality and in the nineteenth the formation of classes, we describe today as the theory of social stratification—all this even though the original problem has not changed and no satisfactory solution to it has been found. In this essay I shall attempt a new explanation of the old problem, one that in my opinion will take us a few steps beyond the present state of our thinking.

II

The younger a branch of scholarship is, the more concerned are its historians to pursue its origins back at least as far as Greek antiquity. Historians of sociology are no exception to this rule. But if one regards the problem of inequality as a key to the history of sociology, it can be clearly shown not only that Plato and Aristotle were definitely not sociologists, but also why they were not. It is always awkward to ascribe to an academic discipline a precise date of birth, but this discussion may help us to date the beginnings of sociology with reasonable plausibility.

In 1792, a gentleman by the name of Meiners, described as a "Royal British Councillor and *rite* teacher of worldly wisdom in Göttingen," wrote some reflections on "the causes of the inequality of estates among the most prominent European peoples." His results were not especially original:

> In all times inequality of natures has unfailingly produced inequality of rights. . . . If the negligent, the lazy, the untrained, and the ignorant were to enjoy equal rights with those who display the corresponding virtues, this would be as unnatural and unjust as if the child had rights equal to those of the adult, the weak and cowardly woman rights equal to those of the strong and courageous man, the villain the same security and respect as the meritorious citizen. (108: 41.)

Meiners's reflections are a version, highly characteristic of his time, of an ideology that to the present day, and with only minor refinements, is invoked by all societies that are worried about their survival to reassure themselves of the justice of their injustices. By repeating in a simplified form the errors of Aristotle, such societies assert a preestablished harmony of things natural and social, and above all a congruence of natural differences between men and social differences between their positions. It was Aristotle, after all, who said:

> It is thus clear that there are *by nature* free men and slaves, and that servitude is agreeable and just for the latter. . . . Equally, the relation of the male to the female is *by nature* such that one is superior and the other inferior, one dominates and the other is dominated. . . . With the barbarians, of course, the female and the dominated have the same rank. This is because they do not possess a naturally dominating element. . . . This is why the poets

say, "It is just that Greeks rule over barbarians," because the barbarian and the slave are *by nature* the same. (97: 1254b, 1252a.)

Now this is just the attitude that makes impossible a sociological treatment of the problem, i.e., an explanation of inequality in terms of specifically social factors expressed in propositions capable of being empirically tested.

So far, I have talked about social inequality as if it were clear what is meant by this notion. Obviously, this is a somewhat optimistic assumption. The lathe operator and the pipe fitter, the general and the sergeant, the artistically gifted child and the mechanically gifted child, the talented and the untalented, are all pairs of unequals. Yet these inequalities are evidently themselves rather unequal, and have to be distinguished from one another in at least two respects. First, we must distinguish between inequalities of natural capability and those of social position; second, we must distinguish between inequalities that do not involve any evaluative rank order and those that do. If we combine these two approaches, four types of inequality emerge, all of which we shall have to discuss. In relation to the individual there are (1) *natural differences of kind* in features, character, and interests, and (2) *natural differences of rank* in intelligence, talent, and strength (leaving open the question of whether such differences do in fact exist). Correspondingly, in relation to society (and in the language of contemporary sociology) there are (3) *social differentiation* of positions essentially equal in rank, and (4) *social stratification* based on reputation and wealth and expressed in a rank order of social status.[1]

Our interest here is primarily in inequalities of the stratification type. On the question of what these are, or, more technically speaking, how they can be measured, no consensus has so far been reached, nor has a suggestion been offered that would make a con-

---

[1] The distinction between natural and social inequalities can be found in Rousseau; indeed, it constitutes the core of his argument. "I perceive two kinds of inequality among men: one I call natural or physical . . . ; the other might be called moral or political." (111: 39.) The distinction between social stratification and social differentiation, by contrast, has only recently been made unambiguously, for example by Melvin M. Tumin (119) and Walter Buckley (98). Yet this distinction is no less important than the other, as the attempt to explain social stratification in terms of social differentiation shows.

sensus possible. I am accordingly making an arbitrary decision here when I distinguish the distributive area of stratification—the explicandum of our theoretical discussion—from nondistributive inequalities such as those of power.[2] According to this distinction, wealth and prestige belong to the area of stratification, even if they are assembled to a considerable extent by one person; property and charisma, by contrast, are nondistributive. How wealth and prestige relate to each other, and especially whether they are mutually convertible and can therefore be reduced to one concept, one single "currency" of social stratification, is an important technical question that I cannot go into here.[3]

III

Aristotle was concerned as we are here to examine the origin of the fourth type of inequality, social stratification. However, by trying to explain social stratification—as so many authors of antiquity, the Christian middle ages, and modern times did after him—in terms of assumed natural differences of rank between men, he missed precisely that type of analysis which we should today describe as sociology. In consequence, his analysis subjects a potentially sociological problem to assumptions that transcend the realm of social fact and defy the test of historical experience. That this attitude helped to delay the birth of sociology by more than twenty centuries is perhaps no great loss, considering the political consequences of so unhistorical an explanation. I believe that Rousseau was right, for all his polemical tone, when he argued that it did not make sense

> to investigate whether there might not be an essential connection between the two inequalities [the natural and the social]. For it

---

[2] For what has here been called "distributive" and "nondistributive" one could also use the terms "intransitive" and "transitive" (in the grammatical sense). Transitive or nondistributive inequalities are the creators of the more passive intransitive or distributive ones.

[3] A possible currency of this kind might be the (structured) "chances of participation"—or, in Weber's terms, "life chances"—that we acquire by virtue of our positions.

would mean that we must ask whether rulers are necessarily worth more than the ruled, and whether strength of body and mind, wisdom, and virtue are always found in the same individuals, and found, moreover, in direct relation to their power or wealth; a question that slaves who think they are being overheard by their masters may find it useful to discuss, but that has no meaning for reasonable and free men in search of the truth. (111: 39.)[4]

This is Rousseau's argument in his prize essay of 1754 on "The Origin of Inequality among Men and Whether It Is Legitimated by Natural Law." Unlike his earlier essay of 1750 on "The Moral Consequences of Progress in the Arts and Sciences," this essay was not awarded the prize of the Dijon Academy. I do not know why the judges preferred the essay of "a certain Abbé Talbert" (as one editor of Rousseau's work describes him); but conceivably they began to feel uneasy about the radical implications of their own question. For the new meaning given by Rousseau and his contemporaries to the question of the origin of inequality involved a revolution in politics as well as intellectual history.

The pivotal point of the Aristotelian argument—if I may use this formula as an abbreviation for all treatments of the problem before the eighteenth century—was the assumption that men are by nature unequal in rank, and that there is therefore a natural rank order among men. This presupposition collapsed in the face of the assumption of natural law that the natural rank of all men is equal. Politically, this meant that together with all other hierarchies, the hierarchies of society also lost their claim to unquestioning respect. If men are equal by nature, then social inequalities cannot be established by nature or God; and if they are

---

[4] Clearly Aristotle and numerous thinkers between his time and the revolutionary period had important sociological insights; one need only mention the way Aristotle relates social strata to political constitutions in the *Politics*. Nor would it be correct to charge Aristotle with having naïvely asserted the congruence of natural and social inequalities. But Aristotle (to say nothing of Plato) and all others down to the eighteenth century lacked what one might call pervasive "sociological thinking," i.e., an unwavering sense of the autonomously social (and thus historical) level of reality. Such thinking required a radical break with the undisputed constants of earlier epochs, a break that first became general in the age of the great revolutions. For this reason one may well derive the birth of sociology from the spirit of revolution.

not so established, then they are subject to change, and the privileged of today may be the outcasts of tomorrow; it may then even be possible to abolish all inequalities. A straight road leads from such reflections to the Declaration of the Rights of Man and Citizen of 1789: "Men are born and remain free and equal in rights. Social differences, therefore, can only be based on general utility."

In terms of intellectual history, the same process meant that the question of the origin of inequality was now phrased in a new and different, i.e. sociological, manner. If men are by nature equal in rank, where do social inequalities come from? If all men are born free and equal in rights, how can we explain that some are rich and others poor, some respected and others ignored, some powerful and others in servitude? Once the question was posed in these terms, only a sociological answer was possible.[5] With good reason, then, Werner Sombart and others have seen the beginnings of sociology in the works of those authors who first tried to give a sociological answer to this question—notably the French *philosophes,* the Scottish moral philosophers and political economists, and the thinkers of the German Enlightenment in the second half of the eighteenth century.[6]

IV

The first sociological explanation of the origin of inequality proved disappointing, though for a century it reappeared in a suc-

[5] Historically, therefore, one necessary condition of the sociological mode of inquiry into the origin of inequality was the assumption of the natural equality (equality of rank) of all men. But here as so often what was historically necessary is logically superfluous: once the question of the origin of inequality is posed in a sociological way (i.e., without recourse to natural inequalities), its answer has nothing to do with whether or not men are by nature equal or unequal. Thus the difficult philosophical question of the natural rank of men can be set aside here as irrelevant to the truth or falsity of sociological explanations of social stratification. We rule out only explanations based on the assumed congruence, or tendency to congruence, of the natural and social rank orders.

[6] Few historians of sociology have taken up Sombart's reference to the Scottish moral philosophers and their attack on natural law (116); apart from a recently published dissertation (103), only William C. Lehmann has elaborated on it (105, 106). Parallel developments on the Continent are described even more rarely. One can write the history of sociology in many ways, of course; but it seems to me that the origin of inequality would be far from the worst central theme.

cession of new forms. It consisted in a figure of thought, which may be demonstrated by further reference to Rousseau's prize essay.

As we have seen, Rousseau begins by assuming the natural equality of men. In the style of his time, he then projects this assumption into history and constructs a pre-social original state in which there was complete equality of all, where no one was superior to anyone else in either rank or status. Inequality, he argues, came about as a result of leaving the state of nature; it is a kind of original sin, which he links with the emergence of private property. How private property itself came into existence, Rousseau does not explain; instead, he confines himself to a statement as obscure as it is concrete: "The first man who fenced in an area and said, 'This is mine,' and who found people simple enough to believe him, was the real founder of civil society." (111: 66.)

Not all of Rousseau's contemporaries, even those who shared most of his assumptions, accepted the one-sidedness of his explanation or his evaluation of the process he described. Adam Ferguson's *History of Civil Society* (1767) and John Millar's *Origin of the Distinction of Ranks* (1771) come quite close to Rousseau in assuming a natural state of equality and ascribing to property the crucial part (Millar) or at least an important part (Ferguson) in destroying this natural state. But both of them regard the fact that men have learned "to strive for riches and admire distinctions," and thus to differentiate according to income and prestige, not as a curse but as a step toward the civilization of "civil society." (See 102: II, 2, 3.)

Even further removed from Rousseau the romantic utopian are Schiller's Jena lectures of 1789, "On the First Human Society"; the title is a clear, if implicit, reference to Kant's essay on the "Probable Beginning of Human History," which in turn referred explicitly to Rousseau's essay (see 112: 322, 325). Schiller praises the "abolition of equality of status" as the step that enabled man to leave the "tranquil nausea of his paradise" (112: 600–601). But the assumption of an original state of equality, and the explanation of the origin of inequality in terms of private property, remained unchallenged from Rousseau to Lorenz von Stein and Karl Marx.[7]

---

[7] Obviously these men's arguments were not as simple as this account may suggest. The most unambiguous emphasis on property as a cause of inequality is found in

For many writers between 1750 and 1850, and for their public, the explanation of inequality in terms of private property remained politically attractive. A society without private property is at least conceivable; and if the idea of equality is associated with this notion, the abolition of private property may become the supreme goal of political action. Indeed, it can be argued that two great revolutions have been abetted to no small extent by the association of inequality with private property, one by Rousseau's dream of reestablishing the original, natural equality of man, the other by Marx's dream of a communist society. Attractive as this explanation may be to some people, however, and though it represents an undeniable methodological advance over the Aristotelian argument, it does not stand the test of historical experience.

To be sure, private property was never completely abolished in the Soviet Union. Nevertheless, the disappointment of the Webbs and other Socialist visitors in the 1930's, caused by the evident inequalities of income and rank in the Soviet Union, may be taken as an experimental refutation of the thesis of Rousseau and Millar, Ferguson and Schiller, Stein and Marx. In the Soviet Union, in Yugoslavia, in Israel, and wherever else private property has been reduced to virtual insignificance, we still find social stratification. Even if such stratification is prevented for a short period from manifesting itself in differences of possessions and income (as in the *kibbutzim* of Israel), the undefinable yet effective force of prestige continues to create a noticeable rank order. If social inequality were

---

Rousseau, Millar, Stein, and Marx. Millar displays a nice historical concreteness on this point: "The invention of taming and pasturing cattle gives rise to a more remarkable and permanent distinction of ranks. Some persons, by being more industrious or more fortunate than others, are led in a short time to acquire more numerous herds and flocks." (109: 204.) Property here has a very definite sociological sense which becomes even clearer in Stein (118: 275): "Class formation is that process by which the distribution of property leads to a distribution of spiritual rights, goods, and functions among the individual members of society, such that the attributes of persistence and fixity are transferred from property to social position and function." This means that property both causes inequality and stabilizes it socially; as Ferguson aptly puts it, "Possessions descend, and the luster of family grows brighter with age." (102: 166.)

The other authors mentioned here do not give property quite the same prominence; in varying degrees they invoke the division of labor, the motive of conquest, and natural differences in rank between men. Rousseau and Marx are unrivaled in their radical insistence on property as the sole cause of social inequality.

really based on private property, the abolition of private property
would have to result in the elimination of inequality. Experience
in propertyless and quasi-propertyless societies does not confirm
this proposition. We may therefore regard it as disproved.[8]

V

Stein and Marx are only marginal members of the group of writers who, by explaining the origin of stratification in terms of property, contributed to the emergence of sociology. Both Stein and
Marx (and, to a lesser extent, Ferguson and several political economists of the late eighteenth century) mention a second factor in
addition to property, one that came to dominate the discussion of
the formation of classes, as our problem was now called, throughout the second half of the nineteenth century and the beginning
of the twentieth. This factor was the division of labor.

As early as the 1870's Engels, in his *Anti-Dühring*, had developed
a theory of class formation on the basis of the division of labor. The
subsequent discussion, however, is associated preeminently with
the name of Gustav Schmoller. It began with the famous controversy between Schmoller and Treitschke over Schmoller's essay on
"The Social Question and the Prussian State"—a controversy that
is of interest to us here because it raised once again the question
of whether a sociological science was possible. Against Schmoller,
Treitschke argued (one would be tempted to say a century too late,
if this were not characteristic of the whole of German history) for
a congruence of natural and social rank orders. Schmoller (with
arguments often no less curious) tried to explain the formation of
classes by the division of labor.

Schmoller's essays on "The Facts of the Division of Labor" and

---

[8] The scientific significance of Communism can hardly be overestimated in this
context, though it provides yet another example of the human cost of historical experiments. For almost two centuries, property dominated social and political thought:
as a source of everything good or evil, as a principle to be retained or abolished. Today we know (though we do not yet have the most rigorous sort of proof) that the
abolition of property merely replaces the old classes with new ones, so that from
Locke to Lenin the social and political significance of property has been vastly overestimated.

"The Nature of the Division of Labor and the Formation of Classes," published in 1889 and 1890, prompted Karl Bücher's polemical Leipzig inaugural lecture of 1892 on "The Division of Labor and the Formation of Social Classes," which was later extended and modified in his book *The Emergence of Economy*. This in turn was attacked not only by Schmoller, but by Emile Durkheim in his *Division of Labor in Society*. Durkheim also discussed at some length Georg Simmel's "On Social Differentiation," which had appeared in 1890 in Schmoller's *Staatswissenschaftliche Forschungen*. Schmoller greeted Durkheim gladly in a review "as one striving to the same end, although he has not convinced us altogether," and continued to pursue the subject and his thesis. After Schmoller's death in 1917, however, both the subject and his view of it found few friends—only Pontus Fahlbeck and (with reservations) Franz Oppenheimer and Joseph Schumpeter come to mind—before they were forgotten, at which point, of course, the dispute remained unresolved.

Many of the issues that came up in the course of this prolonged debate cannot be discussed here, either because they lead us too far from our subject or because they are merely historical curiosities. Notable among the other issues was Simmel's and Durkheim's discussion of the relation between the division of labor and social integration.[9] Among the historical curiosities is Schmoller's theory of the genetics of special abilities acquired by the progressive division of labor. Bücher rightly attacked this theory repeatedly and

---

[9] For Simmel and Durkheim, and to some extent for Bücher and even Schmoller, the division of labor was the main concern, and class formation merely one of its aspects. There would certainly be a point in reexamining the origin of inequality of the differentiation type as well as inequality of the stratification type. The main question is whether the division of labor is based on the natural differences among men (between man and woman, adult and child, etc.), or whether it might be explained by purely social factors (such as technical development). As with stratification, one of the problems of the division of labor is whether it is a universal phenomenon, or a historically developed and therefore at least potentially ephemeral one (as Marx as well as Schmoller and Bücher believed). The consequences of the division of labor, too, require a reexamination that goes beyond Durkheim's at many points. I mention these problems to show that in confining ourselves to explanations of class formation by the division of labor, we are considering only a small segment of the sociological debate of the turn of the century.

violently, without succeeding in forcing out of Schmoller more than very minor concessions. Yet Schmoller's position, especially in his early papers of 1889 and 1890, contains elements of a theory of class formation that has to be taken quite seriously, if only because in a new (but not very different) form it seems to play a certain role in contemporary sociology.

According to Schmoller's theory, class formation (that is, inequality of rank) is based on the fact that occupations are differentiated. However one may wish to explain the division of labor itself— Schmoller explains it in terms of the exchange principle, Bücher in terms of property (and neither regards it as universal)—differentiation precedes the stratification of social positions. "The emergence of social classes always depends in the first instance on an advance in the division of labor within a people or a nation." (114: 74.) Or even more clearly: "The difference in social rank and property, in prestige and income, is merely a secondary consequence of social differentiation." (See 114: 29.)

Schmoller later modified his position without disavowing the principles on which it rested (see 23: 428ff). It must be admitted, however, that the crucial arguments against his views were not made in the literature of the time. To state them, we must remember the distinction between social differentiation and social stratification introduced above.

Since we tend, particularly in modern society, to associate social rank with occupational position, one might be led to suspect that differences of rank are in fact based on the differentiation of occupations. On the contrary, it must be emphasized that the notion of differentiation does not in itself imply any distinctions of rank or value among the differentiated elements. From the point of view of the division of labor (the "functional organization" of industrial sociology), there is no difference in rank between the director, the typist, the foreman, the pipe fitter, and the unskilled laborer of an enterprise: these are all partial activities equally indispensable for the attainment of the goal in question. If in fact we do associate a rank order (or "scalar organization") with these activities, we do so as an additional act of evaluation, one that is neither caused nor explained by the division of labor; indeed, the same activities may be evaluated quite differently in different societies. What we have, then, is a rank order (i.e., a social stratification) of activities that in functional terms are merely differentiated in kind.[10]

Schmoller seems to have sensed this gap in his argument when, in later editions, he suddenly inserted a "psychological fact" between the division of labor and the formation of classes: "the need for human thought and feeling to bring all related phenomena of any kind into a sequence, and estimate and order them according to their value." (23: 428–29.) However factual this fact may be, that Schmoller felt compelled to introduce it serves as further evidence that social differentiation and social stratification cannot explain each other without some intermediate agency.

VI

This conclusion played an important part in the third major historical phase of sociological theorizing about the origin of inequality: the American discussion of the theory of social stratification. Since Talcott Parsons first published his "Analytical Approach to the Theory of Social Stratification" in 1940, there has been an unceasing debate over the so-called "functional" theory of social stratification. Almost all major American sociologists have taken part in this debate, which—unknown though it still is on the Continent—represents one of the more significant contributions of American sociology toward our understanding of social structures.

The chief immediate effect of Parsons's essay of 1940 was to acquaint American sociologists with the idea of a theory of social stratification. The largely conceptual paper published by Parsons's disciple Kingsley Davis in 1942 was also mainly preparatory in character. The discussion proper did not begin until 1945, when Davis and Wilbert E. Moore published "Some Principles of Stratification."

---

[10] One difficult question remains unresolved here: whether there are two different kinds of coordination of partial activities—one "functional," which merely follows "inherent necessities" and completes the division of labor, and one "scalar," which produces a rank order founded on other requirements.

Both Rousseau and his successors and Schmoller and his adherents had regarded inequality as a historical phenomenon. For both, since there had once been a period of equality, the elimination of inequality was conceivable. Davis and Moore, by contrast, saw inequality as a functional necessity in all human societies—i.e., as indispensable for the maintenance of any social structure whatever —and hence as impossible to eliminate.

Their argument, at least in its weaknesses, is not altogether dissimilar to Schmoller's. It runs as follows. There are in every society different social positions. These positions—e.g. occupations—are not equally pleasant, nor are they equally important or difficult. In order to guarantee the complete and frictionless allocation of all positions, certain rewards have to be associated with them—namely, the very rewards that constitute the criteria of social stratification. In all societies, the importance of different positions to the society and the market value of the required qualifications determine the unequal distribution of income, prestige, and power. Inequality is necessary because without it the differentiated (occupational) positions of societies cannot be adequately filled.

Several other writers, among them Marion J. Levy and Bernard Barber, have adopted this theory more or less without modification. But it has been subjected to severe criticism, and despite several thoughtful replies by the original authors, some of the criticisms seem to be gaining ground. The most persistent critic, Melvin M. Tumin, has presented two main arguments against Davis and Moore (in two essays published in 1953 and 1955). The first is that the notion of the "functional importance" of positions is extremely imprecise, and that it probably implies the very differentiation of value that it allegedly explains. The second is that two of the assumptions made by Davis and Moore—that of a harmonious congruence between stratification and the distribution of talent, and that of differential motivation by unequal incentives—are theoretically problematical and empirically uncertain.

This second argument was bolstered in 1955 by Richard Schwartz, whose analysis of two Israeli communities showed that it is in fact possible to fill positions adequately without an unequal distribution of social rewards (115). Buckley charged Davis and Moore in 1958 with confusing differentiation and stratification; unfortunately, however, his legitimate objection to the evaluative undertones of the notion of "functional importance" led in the end to an unpromising terminological dispute. Since then, criticism of the functional theory of stratification has taken two forms. Some critics have followed Dennis Wrong, who in 1959 took up Tumin's suggestion that Davis and Moore had underestimated the "dysfunctions" of social stratification, i.e., the disruptive consequences of social inequality (122); the conservative character of the functional theory has been emphasized even more clearly by Gerhard Lenski (107). Other critics have raised methodological objections, questioning the value of a discussion of sociological universals that ignores variations observed in the workings of real societies.[11]

But the significance of the American debate on stratification is only partly to be found in its subject matter. In this respect, its main conclusion would seem to be that social inequality has many functions and dysfunctions (that is, many consequences for the structure of societies), but that there can be no satisfactory functional explanation of the origin of inequality. This is because every such explanation is bound either to have recourse to dubious assumptions about human nature or to commit the *petitio principii* error of explanation in terms of the object to be explained. Yet this discussion, like its historical predecessors, has at several points produced valuable propositions, some of them mere remarks made in passing. With the help of these propositions, let us now attempt to formulate a theory of social stratification that is theoretically satisfactory and, above all, empirically fruitful.[12]

[11] The origin of inequality has been only one of several subjects of dispute in the American debate on stratification. Davis and Moore, for example, after their first few pages, turn to the empirical problems of the effect and variability of stratification. Their critics do much the same thing. But the dispute was ignited by the "functional explanation of inequality": its substantive justification, its scientific fruitfulness, and its political significance. The dispute, which still continues, may be seen as a commentary on the subterranean conflicts in American sociology.

[12] The concentration of my historical account of discussions of inequality on three epochs and positions—property in the eighteenth century, division of labor in the nineteenth, and function in the twentieth—rests on my conviction that these are the

The very first contribution to the American debate on stratification, the essay by Parsons, contained an idea which, although un-
tenable in Parsons's form, may still advance our understanding of
the problem. Parsons tries to derive the necessity of a differentiated
rank order from the existence of the concept of evaluation and its
significance for social systems. The effort to formulate an ontological proof of stratification is more surprising than convincing—as
Parsons himself seems to have felt, for in the revised version of his
essay, published in 1953, he relates the existence of a concept of
evaluation to the mere probability, not the necessity, of inequality.[13] In fact, Parsons's thesis contains little more than the suggestion, formulated much more simply by Barber, that men tend to
evaluate themselves and the things of their world differently (26: 2).
This suggestion in turn refers back to Schmoller's "psychological
assumption" of a human tendency to produce evaluative rank orders, but it also refers—and here the relation between evaluation
and stratification begins to be sociologically relevant—to Durkheim's famous proposition that "every society is a moral community." Durkheim rightly remarks that "the state of nature of the
eighteenth-century philosophers is, if not immoral, at least amoral"
(100: 394). The idea of the social contract is nothing but the idea

---

most important stages in the discussion of the subject. But historically this account
involves some questionable simplifications. As early as 1922, Fahlbeck (101: 13–15)
distinguished four explanations of inequality: (1) "differences in estate are exclusively the work of war and conquest in large things, force and perfidy in little ones";
(2) "in property and its differential distribution" can be found "the real reason for
all social differences"; (3) "the origin and raison d'être of classes" can be traced to
"the connections with the general economic factors of nature, capital, and labor";
and (4) "classes are a fruit of the division of labor." (Fahlbeck favors the last.) To
these we should have to add at least the natural-differences explanation and the functional explanation. All six notions found support, at times side by side in the same
works, and all six would have to be taken into account in a reasonably complete historical account of the problem. It is another question whether such an account would
advance our knowledge.

13 Parsons 1940 (110: 843): "If both human individuals as units and moral evaluation are essential to social systems, it follows that these individuals *will be* evaluated
as units." And 1953 (96: 387): "Given the process of evaluation, *the probability is*
that it will serve to differentiate entities in a rank order of some kind." (My emphases.) In both cases, as so often at those points of Parsons's work where classification is
less important than conceptual imagination and rigor of statement, his argument is
remarkably weak.

of the institution of compulsory social norms backed by sanctions. It is at this point that the possibility arises of connecting the concept of human society with the problem of the origin of inequality —a possibility that is occasionally hinted at in the literature but that has so far gone unrealized.[14]

Human society always means that people's behavior is being removed from the randomness of chance and regulated by established and inescapable expectations. The compulsory character of these expectations or norms[15] is based on the operation of sanctions, i.e., of rewards or punishments for conformist or deviant behavior. If every society is in this sense a moral community, it follows that there must always be at least that inequality of rank which results from the necessity of sanctioning behavior according to whether it does or does not conform to established norms. Under whatever aspect given historical societies may introduce additional distinctions between their members, whatever symbols they may declare to be outward signs of inequality, and whatever may be the precise content of their social norms, the hard core of social inequality can always be found in the fact that men as the incumbents of social roles are subject, according to how their roles relate to the dominant expectational principles of society, to sanctions designed to enforce these principles.[16]

[14] An attempt in this direction has recently been made by Lenski, but his approach and the one offered here differ significantly in their para-theoretical and methodological presuppositions.

[15] Since expectations, as constituent parts of roles, are always related to concrete social positions, whereas norms are general in their formulation and their claim to validity, the "or" in the phrase "expectations or norms" may at first seem misleading. Actually, this is just a compressed way of expressing the idea that role expectations are nothing but concretized social norms ("institutions").

[16] A similar idea may be found at one point in the American discussion of stratification—as distinguished, perhaps, from Othmar Spann's biology-based argument (117: 293), "The law of stratification of society is the ordering of value strata," which might seem superficially similar—in a passing remark by Tumin (119: 392). "What does seem to be unavoidable," Tumin says, "is that differential prestige shall be given to those in any society who conform to the normative order as against those who deviate from that order in a way judged immoral and detrimental. On the assumption that the continuity of a society depends on the continuity and stability of its normative order, some such distinction between conformists and deviants seems inescapable." It seems to me that the assumption of a "continuity and stability of the normative order" is quite superfluous; it shows how closely Tumin remains tied to the functional approach.

Let me try to illustrate what I mean by some examples which, however difficult they may seem, are equally relevant. If the ladies of a neighborhood are expected to exchange secrets and scandals with their neighbors, this norm will lead at the very least to a distinction between those held in high regard (who really enjoy gossip, and offer tea and cakes as well), those with average prestige, and the outsiders (who, for whatever reasons, take no part in the gossiping). If, in a factory, high individual output is expected from the workers and rewarded by piecework rates, there will be some who take home a relatively high paycheck and others who take home a relatively low one. If the citizens (or better, perhaps, subjects) of a state are expected to defend its official ideology as frequently and convincingly as possible, this will lead to a distinction between those who get ahead (becoming, say, civil servants or party secretaries); the mere followers, who lead a quiet but somewhat anxious existence; and those who pay with their liberty or even their lives for their deviant behavior.

One might think that individual, not social, inequalities are in fact established by the distinction between those who for essentially personal reasons (as we must initially assume, and have assumed in the examples) are either unprepared for or incapable of conformism and those who punctiliously fulfill every norm. For example, social stratification is always a rank order in terms of prestige and not esteem, i.e., a rank order of positions (worker, woman, resident of a certain area, etc.), which can be thought of independently of their individual incumbents. By contrast, attitudes toward norms as governed by sanctions seem to be attitudes of individuals. There might therefore seem to be a link missing between the sanctioning of individual behavior and the inequality of social positions. This missing link is, however, contained in the notion of social norm as we have used it so far.

It appears plausible to assume that the number of values capable of regulating human behavior is unlimited. Our imagination permits the construction of an infinite number of customs and laws. Norms, i.e., socially established values, are therefore always a selection from the universe of possible established values. At this point, however, we should remember that the selection of norms always involves discrimination, not only against persons holding sociologically random moral convictions, but also against social positions that may debar their incumbents from conformity with established values.

Thus if gossip among neighbors becomes a norm, the professional woman necessarily becomes an outsider who cannot compete in prestige with ordinary housewives. If piecework rates are in force in a factory, the older worker is at a disadvantage by comparison with the younger ones, the woman by comparison with men. If it becomes the duty of the citizen to defend the ideology of the state, those who went to school before the establishment of this state cannot compete with those born into it. Professional woman, old man, young man, and child of a given state are all social positions, which may be thought of independently of their individual human incumbents. Since every society discriminates in this sense against certain positions (and thereby all their incumbents, actual and potential), and since, moreover, every society uses sanctions to make such discrimination effective, social norms and sanctions are the basis not only of ephemeral individual rankings but also of lasting structures of social positions.

The origin of inequality is thus to be found in the existence in all human societies of norms of behavior to which sanctions are attached. What we normally call the law, i.e., the system of laws and penalties, does not in ordinary usage comprise the whole range of the sociological notions of norm and sanction. If, however, we take the law in its broadest sense as the epitome of all norms and sanctions, including those not codified, we may say that the law is both a necessary and a sufficient condition of social inequality. There is inequality because there is law; if there is law, there must also be inequality among men.

This is, of course, equally true in societies where equality before the law is recognized as a constitutional principle. If I may be allowed a somewhat flippant formulation, which is nevertheless seriously meant, my proposed explanation of inequality means in the case of our own society that all men are equal *before* the law but they are no longer equal *after* it: i.e., after they have, as we put it, "come in contact with" the law. So long as norms do not exist, and insofar as they do not effectively act on people ("before the law"), there is no social stratification; once there are norms that impose inescapable requirements on people's behavior and once their actual behavior is measured in terms of these norms ("after the law"), a rank order of social status is bound to emerge.

Important though it is to emphasize that by norms and sanctions we also mean laws and penalties in the sense of positive law, the introduction of the legal system as an illustrative *pars pro toto* can itself be very misleading. Ordinarily, it is only the idea of punishment that we associate with legal norms as the guarantee of their compulsory character.[17] The force of legal sanctions produces the distinction between the lawbreaker and those who succeed in never coming into conflict with any legal rule. Conformism in this sense is at best rewarded with the absence of penalties. Certainly, this crude division between "conformists" and "deviants" constitutes an element of social inequality, and it should be possible in principle to use legal norms to demonstrate the relation between legal sanctions and social stratification. But an argument along these lines would limit both concepts—sanction and stratification—to a rather feeble residual meaning.

It is by no means necessary (although customary in ordinary language) to conceive of sanctions solely as penalties. For the present argument, at least, it is important to recognize positive sanctions (rewards) as both equal in kind and similar in function to negative sanctions (punishments). Only if we regard reward and punishment, incentive and threat, as related instruments for maintaining social norms do we begin to see that applying social norms to human behavior in the form of sanctions necessarily creates a system of inequality of rank, and that social stratification is therefore an

---

17 Possibly this is a vulgar interpretation of the law, in the sense that legal norms (which are after all only a special case of social norms) probably have their validity guaranteed by positive as well as negative sanctions. It may be suspected, however, that negative sanctions are preponderant to the extent to which norms are compulsory—and since most legal norms (almost by definition) are compulsory to a particularly great extent, behavior conforming to legal norms is generally not rewarded.

immediate result of the control of social behavior by positive and negative sanctions. Apart from their immediate task of enforcing the normative patterns of social behavior, sanctions always create, almost as a by-product, a rank order of distributive status, whether this is measured in terms of prestige, or wealth, or both.

The presuppositions of this explanation are obvious. Using eighteenth-century concepts, one might describe them in terms of the social contract (*pacte d'association*) and the contract of government (*pacte de gouvernement*). The explanation sketched here presupposes (1) that every society is a moral community, and therefore recognizes norms that regulate the conduct of its members; (2) that these norms require sanctions to enforce them by rewarding conformity and penalizing deviance.

It may perhaps be argued that by relating social stratification to these presuppositions we have not solved our problem but relegated its solution to a different level. Indeed, it might seem necessary from both a philosophical and a sociological point of view to ask some further questions. Where do the norms that regulate social behavior come from? Under what conditions do these norms change in historical societies? Why must their compulsory character be enforced by sanctions? Is this in fact the case in all historical societies? I think, however, that whatever the answers to these questions may be, it has been helpful to reduce social stratification to the existence of social norms backed by sanctions, since this explanation shows the derivative nature of the problem of inequality. In addition, the derivation suggested here has the advantage of leading back to presuppositions (the existence of norms and the necessity of sanctions) that may be regarded as axiomatic, at least in the context of sociological theory, and therefore do not require further analysis for the time being.

To sum up, the origin of social inequality lies neither in human nature nor in a historically dubious conception of private property. It lies rather in certain features of all human societies, which are (or can be seen as) necessary to them. Although the differentiation of social positions—the division of labor, or more generally the multiplicity of roles—may be one such universal feature of all societies, it lacks the element of evaluation necessary to explain distinctions of rank. Evaluative differentiation, the ordering of social positions and their incumbent scales of prestige or income, is effected only by the sanctioning of social behavior in terms of normative expectations. Because there are norms and because sanctions are necessary to enforce conformity of human conduct, there has to be inequality of rank among men.

VIII

Social stratification is a very real element of our everyday lives, much more so than this highly abstract and indeed seemingly inconsequential discussion would suggest. It is necessary, then, to make clear the empirical relevance of these reflections, or at least to indicate what follows from this kind of analysis for our knowledge of society. Such a clarification is all the more necessary since the preceding discussion is informed, however remotely, by a view of sociology as an empirical science, a science in which observation can decide the truth or falsity of statements. What, then, do our considerations imply for sociological analysis?

First, let us consider its conceptual implications. Social stratification, as I have used the term, is above all a system of distributive status, i.e., a system of differential distribution of desired and scarce things. Honor and wealth, or, as we say today, prestige and income, may be the most general means of effecting such a differentiation of rank, but there is no reason to assume that it could not be effected by entirely different criteria.[18] As far as legitimate power is concerned, however, it has only one aspect that can be seen as affecting social stratification, namely patronage, or the distribution of power as a reward for certain deeds or virtues. Thus to explain differences of rank in terms of the necessity of sanctions is not to explain the power structure of societies;[19] it is rather to explain stratification in

[18] Honor and wealth (or prestige and income) are general in the sense that they epitomize the ideal and the material differences in rank among men.

[19] Thus the theory advanced here does not explain the origin of power and of inequalities in the distribution of power. That the origin of power also requires explanation, at least in a para-theoretical context, is evident from the discussion of the

terms of the social structure of power and authority (using these terms to express Weber's distinction between *Macht* and *Herr-schaft*). If the explanation of inequality offered here is correct, power and power structures logically precede the structures of social stratification.[20]

It is hard to imagine a society whose system of norms and sanctions functions without an authority structure to sustain it. Time and again, anthropologists have told us of "tribes without rulers," and sociologists of societies that regulate themselves without power or authority. But in opposition to such fantasies, I incline with Weber to describe "every order that is not based on the personal, free agreement of all involved" (i.e., every order that does not rest on the voluntary consensus of all its members) as "imposed," i.e., based on authority and subordination (121: xiii, 27). Since a *volonté de tous* seems possible only in flights of fancy, we have to assume that a third fundamental category of sociological analysis belongs alongside the two concepts of norm and sanction: that of institutionalized power. Society *means* that norms regulate human conduct; this regulation is guaranteed by the incentive or threat of sanctions; the possibility of imposing sanctions is the abstract core of all power.

---

universality of historicity of power (see below). What an explanation of inequalities of power might look like is hard to say; Heinrich Popitz suggests that the social corollaries of the succession of generations are responsible for such inequalities.

20 This conclusion implies a substantial revision of my previously published views. For a long time I was convinced that there was a strict logical equivalence between the analysis of social classes and constraint theory, and between the analysis of social stratification and integration theory. The considerations developed in the present essay changed my mind. I have now come to believe that stratification is merely a consequence of the structure of power, integration a special case of constraint, and thus the structural-functional approach a subset of a broader approach. The assumption that constraint theory and integration theory are two approaches of equal rank, i.e., two different perspectives on the same material, is not so much false as superfluous; we get the same result by assuming that stratification follows from power, integration from constraint, stability from change. Since the latter assumption is the simpler one, it is to be preferred.

This conclusion may also be seen as opposing the "synthesis" of "conservative" and "radical" theories of stratification proposed by Lenski (108). It seems to me that this synthesis is in fact merely a superficial compromise, which is superseded at important points by Lenski himself: "The distribution of rewards in a society is a function of the distribution of power, not of system needs." (108: 63.)

I am inclined to believe that all other categories of sociological analysis may be derived from the unequal but closely related trinity of norm, sanction, and power.[21] At any rate, this is true of social stratification, which therefore belongs on a lower level of generality than power. To reveal the explosiveness of this analysis we need only turn it into an empirical proposition: the system of inequality that we call social stratification is only a secondary consequence of the social structure of power.

The establishment of norms in a society means that conformity is rewarded and deviance punished. The sanctioning of conformity and deviance in this sense means that the ruling groups of society have thrown their power behind the maintenance of norms. In the last analysis, established norms are nothing but ruling norms, i.e., norms defended by the sanctioning agencies of society and those who control them. This means that the person who will be most favorably placed in society is the person who best succeeds in adapting himself to the ruling norms; conversely, it means that the established or ruling values of a society may be studied in their purest form by looking at its upper class. Anyone whose place in the coordinate system of social positions and roles makes him unable to conform punctiliously to his society's expectations must not be surprised if the higher grades of prestige and income remain closed to him and go to others who find it easier to conform. In this sense, every society honors the conformity that sustains it, i.e., sustains its ruling groups; but by the same token every society also produces within itself the resistance that brings it down.

Naturally, the basic equating of conformist or deviant behavior with high or low status is deflected and complicated in historical

[21] This is a large claim, which would justify at least an essay of its own. For our present purposes only two remarks need be added. First, the three categories are obviously disparate. Sanction is primarily a kind of intermediate concept (between norm and power), although as such it is quite decisive. Norm has to be understood as anterior to power, just as the social contract is anterior to the contract of government (this may help as a standard of orientation). Second, we must ask whether the "elementary category" of social role can also be derived from the trinity norm-sanction-power. I tend to think it can, at least insofar as roles are complexes of norms concretized into expectations. Beyond that, however, the question is open.

societies by many secondary factors. (In general, it must be emphasized that the explanation of inequality proposed here has no immediate extension to the history of inequality or the philosophy behind it.) Among other things, the ascriptive character of the criteria determining social status in a given epoch (such as nobility or property) may bring about a kind of stratification lag: that is, status structures may lag behind changes in norms and power relations, so that the upper class of a bygone epoch may retain its status position for a while under new conditions. Yet normally we do not have to wait long for such processes as the "*déclassement* of the nobility" or the "loss of function of property" which have occurred in several contemporary societies.

There are good reasons to think that our own society is tending toward a period of "meritocracy" as predicted by Michael Young, i.e., rule by the possessors of diplomas and other tickets of admission to the upper reaches of society issued by the educational system. If this is so, the hypothesis of stratification lag would suggest that in due course the members of the traditional upper strata (the nobility, the inheritors of wealth and property) will have to bestir themselves to obtain diplomas and academic titles in order to keep their position; for the ruling groups of every society have a tendency to try to adapt the existing system of social inequality to the established norms and values, i.e., their own. Nevertheless, despite this basic tendency we can never expect historical societies to exhibit full congruence between the scales of stratification and the structures of power.[22]

IX

The image of society that follows from this exceedingly general and abstract analysis is in two respects non-utopian and thereby

[22] The variability of historical patterns of stratification is so great that any abstract and general analysis of the kind offered here is bound to mislead. The criteria, forms, and symbols of stratification vary, as does their meaning for human behavior, and in every historical epoch we find manifold superimpositions. The question of what form stratification took in the earliest known societies is entirely open. This is but one of the many limitations of the present analysis.

anti-utopian as well.[23] On the one hand, it has none of the explicit
or concealed romanticism of a revolutionary utopia *à la* Rousseau
or Marx. If it is true that inequalities among men follow from the
very concept of societies as moral communities, then there cannot
be, in the world of our experience, a society of absolute equals. Of
course, equality before the law, equal suffrage, equal chances of education, and other concrete equalities are not only possible but in
many countries real. But the idea of a society in which all distinctions of rank between men are abolished transcends what is sociologically possible and has a place only in the sphere of poetic imagination. Wherever political programs promise societies without class
or strata, a harmonious community of comrades who are all equals
in rank, the reduction of all inequalities to functional differences,
and the like, we have reason to be suspicious, if only because political promises are often merely a thin veil for the threat of terror and
constraint. Wherever ruling groups or their ideologists try to tell us
that in their society all men are equal, we can rely on George Orwell's suspicion that "some are more equal than others."

The approach put forward here is in yet another sense a path out
of utopia. If we survey the explanations of inequality in recent
American sociology—and this holds for Parsons and Barber as it
does for Davis and Moore—we find that they betray a view of society from which there is no road leading to an understanding of the
historical quality of social structures. In a less obvious sense this is
also true, I think, of Rousseau and Marx; but it is more easily de-
monstrable by reference to recent sociological theory.[24] The American functionalists tell us that we ought to look at societies as entities functioning without friction, and that inequality among men

[23] The following para-theoretical discussion is *inter alia* a criticism of Lenski's
oversimple dichotomy between "conservative" and "radical" theories of stratification.
Our approach is "radical" in assuming the dominant force of power structures, but
"conservative" in its suspicion that the unequal distribution of power and status cannot be abolished. Other combinations are conceivable.

[24] The assumption that history follows a predetermined and recognizable plan is
static, at least in the sense in which the development of an organism into an entelechy
lacks the historical dimension of openness into the future. For this reason, and because of the static-utopian notion of an ultimate state necessarily connected with
such a conception, a lack of historicity might also be imputed to Rousseau and Marx.

(since it happens to exist) abets this functioning. This point of view, however useful in other ways, may then lead to conclusions like the following by Barber: "Men have a sense of justice fulfilled and of virtue rewarded when they feel that they are fairly ranked as superior and inferior by the value standards of their own moral community." (98: 7.) Even Barber's subsequent treatment of the "dysfunctions" of stratification cannot wipe out the impression that the society he is thinking of does not need history anymore because everything has been settled in the best possible way already: everybody, wherever he stands, is content with his place in society, and a common value system unites all men in a big, happy family.

It seems to me that whereas an instrument of this kind may enable us to understand Plato's Republic, it does not describe any real society in history. Possibly social inequality has some importance for the integration of societies. But another consequence of its operation seems rather more interesting. If the analysis proposed here proves useful, inequality is closely related to the social constraint that grows out of sanctions and structures of power. This would mean that the system of stratification, like sanctions and structures of institutionalized power, always tends to its own abolition. The assumption that those who are less favorably placed in society will strive to impose a system of norms that promises them a better rank is certainly more plausible and fruitful than the assumption that the poor in reputation and wealth will love their society for its justice.

Since the "value system" of a society is universal only in the sense that it applies to everyone (it is in fact merely dominant), and since, therefore, the system of social stratification is only a measure of conformity in the behavior of social groups, inequality becomes the dynamic impulse that serves to keep social structures alive. Inequality always implies the gain of one group at the expense of others; thus every system of social stratification generates protest against its principles and bears the seeds of its own suppression. Since human society without inequality is not realistically possible and the complete abolition of inequality is therefore ruled out, the intrinsic explosiveness of every system of social stratification confirms the general view that there cannot be an ideal, perfectly just, and therefore non-historical human society.

This is the place to recall once again Kant's critical rejoinder to Rousseau, that inequality is a "rich source of much that is evil, but also of everything that is good." There is certainly reason to regret that children are ashamed of their parents, that people are anxious and poor, that they suffer and are made unhappy, and many other consequences of inequality. There are also many good reasons to strive against the historical and therefore, in an ultimate sense, arbitrary forces that erect insuperable barriers of caste or estate between men. The very existence of social inequality, however, is an impetus toward liberty because it guarantees a society's ongoing, dynamic, historical quality. The idea of a perfectly egalitarian society is not only unrealistic; it is terrible. Utopia is not the home of freedom, the forever imperfect scheme for an uncertain future; it is the home of total terror or absolute boredom.[25]

[25] These last paragraphs contain in highly abridged form—and in part imply—two arguments. One is that the attempt to realize a utopia, i.e., a society beyond concrete realization, must lead to totalitarianism, because only by terror can the appearance of paradise gained (of the classless society, the people's community) be created. The other is that within certain limits defined by the equality of citizenship, inequalities of social status, considered as a medium of human development, are a condition of a free society.

CHAPTER 2

Developmental Trends in the Structure of Small Groups

C. HEINICKE and ROBERT F. BALES

It is a common observation that newly formed groups tend in the course of time to develop relatively stable patterns of interaction. The development of stability is by no means inevitable, however, as we are reminded by the cases of groups which disintegrate soon after formation, or continue for a long period in a state of inner turmoil. The course of structural development in new groups seems to depend not simply upon changes in conditions which are inevitably linked with time, but upon conditions which may be different from the very first, either in the original composition of the group or in the situation which they face.

In the present study[1] we attempt to develop a preliminary conception of some of the factors underlying structural change in small groups. The basic ideas grow out of experience in the observation of groups under laboratory conditions, out of deduction from findings we regard as already fairly well established, and out of inductive exploration of our data. The data reported include measures of various aspects of interaction and ratings of members by each other in a number of newly formed, "initially leaderless" discussion groups during a series of meetings under reasonably constant laboratory conditions. There was no experimental variation of external conditions, but rather an attempt to keep them as constant as possible. We find that groups formed in this fashion nevertheless show measurable differences in their very early structure. Whatever their source, these differences in initial structure seem to be associated with later differences in developmental trends.

As research becomes more refined one hopes to measure and take account of those factors which he cannot control. In setting up the groups we hoped that we would learn to make some useful distinctions as to

[1] The data at Northwestern University were collected by Christoph Heinicke as part of a basic research project supported by the Office of Naval Research and directed by Dr. Robert L. French. The authors would like to express their indebtedness to Dr. French and also to Carol Bell and Dr. Kermit Rhode who were members of the project. The Harvard study was facilitated by the Laboratory of Social Relations and supported by funds from The RAND Corporation, Santa Monica, California. For the work at Harvard we are particularly grateful for the stimulation and suggestions of Philip E. Slater, Research Assistant in the Laboratory of Social Relations.

31

structure types which we could measure and take into account, even if we could not control them. We hoped to get an idea of what "natural developmental trends" we would have to take into account in experimental designs that call for repeated meetings of groups. We hoped to provide some basis for deciding how long to hold groups together for given experimental purposes, and what types of observations we needed in order to assure ourselves that we had succeeded in setting up groups of the type we intended. Finally we hoped that the observations would assist us in formulating more precise hypotheses as to the factors related to structural development which we could subject to experimental control and variation.

PROCEDURE

Since some groups were studied at Northwestern University, (4) and some at Harvard University, and since the procedures differed slightly, they will be described separately below.

Procedure at Northwestern
Subjects and Groups

Six groups of five subjects each were made up of male students in elementary psychology classes. At the time volunteers were called for, the classes were told that the object of the study was to ascertain the opinions of groups of undergraduates on a series of problems of psychological interest, that each group would meet at the same time once per week for six successive weeks, and that participation would satisfy the course requirement for service as an experimental subject. The final selection of subjects was then made essentially at random from those volunteers whose free period permitted their being scheduled with a group, and who did not know anyone already scheduled for the group.

Discussion Problems

At each session a group was given the task of discussing a problem of human relations and writing to the hypothetical protagonist a letter embodying its conclusions and recommendations. Six problems were used, a different one for each session of a group. Their order of presentation was partially counterbalanced for different groups by treating the problems as letters in a six-by-six Latin square.

Criteria governing the design of the problems were interest-value for students, and the presence of genuine value conflicts which would insure some disagreement and render impossible any solution with reference to objective factual standards. Earlier trials of the problems indicated that they met both requirements. An abbreviated description of one of the problems follows:

> While overseas Allen has had an affair with an English girl, and feels obliged on his return to tell his wife; but he hesitates because of her strong feelings about infidelity. (Adapted from Deutsch (3).)

Instructions to Subjects

When members of a group had assembled in the experimental room for the first scheduled meeting, they were asked to seat themselves about a round table, and to put on different colored coats which would serve to identify them to one another. After some introductory remarks, mimeographed descriptions of the problem for that day were passed out, and the problem was read aloud by the experimenter. Subjects were then told that they would have 40 minutes in which to discuss the problem, arrive at agreement and write up their recommendations, and that they could not dispose of the problem by referring it to someone else, e.g. a psychiatrist. They were informed, further, that they were one of six groups who would be competing for a group prize. Each member of the group giving the best performance during the six week period would receive additional points toward his psychology grade and two dollars in cash. The subjects were told that evaluation of their performance would involve ratings of the written solutions with reference to completeness with which relevant considerations were taken into account, realism in assessing these, and cogency of expression.

The sessions were sound recorded and interaction was recorded by an observer behind a one-way mirror. The subjects were not told about the sound recording or the one-way mirrors. Presumably the only observations were made by the experimenter who remained in the room after giving the instructions.

At the end of the session subjects were asked to record their general impressions of the meeting, and to say nothing about the nature of the study to other people.

At subsequent meetings the initial procedure described above was progressively abbreviated. Following the final session, subjects filled out a questionnaire concerning various aspects of their experience. The nature of the experiment was then explained and discussed with them.

Status Rankings and Questionnaire Data

After each session the interaction observer and the experimenter who handled the groups ranked members of the group for leadership displayed during the session. The median correlation between the two observers for the 36 sessions was .90. In a previous experiment involving 18 one-session groups, the members of each of which ranked one another for leadership immediately after the session, the rankings by the group had shown a median correlation of .90 with rankings given by the interaction observer. It seemed reasonable to conclude, therefore, that the latter's ranking would indicate reliably the way in which group members would rank each other if given the opportunity. This opportunity was not given during the first five sessions for fear the procedure might disturb the course of group development; but at the end of the sixth session the subjects did rank one another as a part of a longer questionnaire.

The questionnaire aimed to secure reactions of the subjects to the situation, as a possible basis for further insight into processes of group development. Interspersed among other questions were the following:

Q. 8. Considering all six sessions, which member of the group would you say stood out most definitely as a leader in the discussion? How would you rank the others? Include yourself.

Q. 14. Which member of the group did the most to guide the discussion and keep it moving? Which was next in this respect?

Q. 20. Which member of the group contributed the best ideas for solving the problem? Which was next best in this respect?

Performance Ratings

The letters setting forth the problem solutions were typed, coded for identification, and rated in random order by two observers using a 20-point scale. The main criteria were "realism", cogency of expression, and how many facets of the problem were taken into account in the solution. The correlation between the 36 ratings given by the two raters was .59. Group performance was measured by averaging the two observers' ratings. Application of the Spearman-Brown formula to estimate reliability of the combined ratings yielded a coefficient of .74.

Procedure at Harvard

Subjects and Groups

A preliminary analysis of the Northwestern data indicated that probably most of the important changes had occurred by the fourth session. Because of the difficulty of getting all the subjects of a group back six times, it was decided to run only four groups for four sessions.

The groups were again composed of male undergraduates, but rather than using course students, volunteers were obtained from the Student Employment Service, and were paid the prevailing student rates. As at Northwestern, it was insured that the subjects did not know each other.

Finally, primarily for statistical reasons, the group size was increased from five to six. It was felt this would make little difference in a study of the development of structure, and yet give us certain statistical advantages; e.g. in testing the significance of rho.

Discussion Problems

The problems were again of a human relations sort. Although still primarily value-centered, the problems contained many more facts, and were thus considerably longer. Aside from providing more substance for the discussion, the additional facts tended to embed the value conflict and thus make it less obvious. An attempt was made to match the formal structure of the problems, and as far as possible to equalize the kind of interaction likely to be produced. To further eliminate any remaining problem differences, the order of presentation again followed a Latin Square design.

Instructions to Subjects

Although some differences should be noted between the Northwestern and Harvard instructions, they were again of a minor sort. First of all, before the first session the subjects were told a few things about the nature of the experiment including the characteristics and purpose of the one-way screen. The microphones were pointed out and the subjects were told that the sessions would be sound recorded. After this introduction, they were informed that they would have seven minutes to read the case at the end of which time the experimenter would take the cases out of the room. The subjects were asked to summarize the solution orally rather than write it. Finally, there was no offer of a prize or other extra inducement. It would seem that the prize made little difference to the Northwestern groups.

Status Rankings and Questionnaire Data

It will be remembered that the Northwestern groups were not asked any specific questions until the end of the experiment. For the Harvard groups on the other hand it was decided to pass out a questionnaire at the end of each session. This included the following items:

1. A 12 point rating scale on which the subject checked how well satisfied he was with the quality of the group solution to the problem.
2. A request to rank order the individuals in his group (including himself) on the following items:
   a. Who contributed the best ideas for solving the problem?
   b. Who did the most to guide the discussion and keep it moving effectively?

3. A series of four questions asking each individual whom he liked, disliked, and felt neutral toward among other members of the group.

4. A corresponding series of four questions asking each individual to guess how the other members felt toward him.

5. A list of 60 statements sometimes made about groups. The subject was asked to check any statement which he felt applied to this session of his group. Examples are:
   a. This group needs more information to do its job properly.
   b. The atmosphere in this group is pleasant and congenial.

At the end of the fourth session certain additional questions were asked. The only one of interest here is the question which was also asked the Northwestern groups at the end of their last session:

> Considering all the sessions, which member of the group would you say stood out most definitely as a leader in the discussion? How would you rank the others? Include yourself. (This provided the data for the so-called overall status rankings.)

Interaction Observations

At both Northwestern and Harvard the interaction of subjects was observed and categorized by two observers behind one-way mirrors. Table 1 shows the categories used. On the left is the set used at Harvard, developed by Bales, and described in previous publications.[2] On the right is the set used at Northwestern with certain categories grouped to show the correspondence with Bales' set. The Northwestern categories were developed independently from a previous 32 category list taken from Bales. In both sets of observations the behavior was recorded in terms of the "surface" meaning it presumably had in common for the person who made the contribution and the person it was directed toward. "Who-to-whom" was recorded in each case as well as category of the act. The scoring at Northwestern differed from that at Harvard however, in that at Northwestern larger units were used: a given contribution or speech was categorized only once, as one unit, unless the speaker's intent changed during the course of the speech. According to Bales' method used at Harvard, the contribution is broken down into single simple sentence units or acts, and a continuing speech by a single member may produce a number of scores all in the same category.

Reliability of categorization was determined at each place by comparing the records of two trained observers who scored simultaneously but independently. For each observer the raw number of scores obtained in a given

---

2 See Bales, R. F., *Interaction Process Analysis*, Cambridge, Mass., Addison Wesley Press, 1950. See also item (2) under References.

single category was listed for the series of sessions (or sub-periods). A Pearson correlation was then computed between the series of the two observers. The resulting coefficients are presented with the category descriptions in Table 1 except in the cases of certain categories which yielded too few scores to make this analysis dependable. Coefficients for these categories

TABLE 1

CATEGORIES USED IN INTERACTION OBSERVATION AND RELIABILITIES OBTAINED

Categories by Sections	Harvard	r	Northwestern	r
A. POSITIVE REACTIONS	1 Shows Solidarity	—	Shows Solidarity	—
	2 Shows Tension Release	.90	Shows Tension Release[1]	.97
	3 Agrees	.88	Agrees	.95
B. ATTEMPTED ANSWERS	4 Gives Suggestion	.90	Gives Solution Requests Action	.92 .90
	5 Gives Opinion	.76	Gives Opinion	.93
	6 Gives Orientation	.86	Gives Orientation Gives Information[2]	.91 .78
C. QUESTIONS	7 Asks for Orientation			
	8 Asks for Opinion	.74	Asks Question	.80
	9 Asks for Suggestion			
D. NEGATIVE REACTIONS	10 Disagrees	.79	Disagrees	.94
	11 Shows Tension	—	Shows Tension Goes Out of Field	— —
	12 Shows Antagonism	—	Shows Antagonism	—
	Categories 1 + 2 Categories 10 + 11 + 12	.84 .86	Categories 1 + 2 Categories 10 + 11 + 12	.93 .93

[1] The Northwestern category list included another category designed to score conversation not directly concerned with the problem, but not really Out of Field in nature. It showed the same trends over time as Tension Release and had a reliability of .93.

[2] The correspondence between these two categories and Bales' category No. 6 is not so exact as for some of the other pairings.

as grouped with their adjacent categories are given at the bottom of the table.

At Northwestern the coefficients obtained ranged from .78 to .97, with a median of .91. At Harvard they ranged from .74 to .90 with a median of .86.

A similar analysis of inter-observer agreement as to the direction of interaction (who-to-whom) was carried out separately for each of the pair relations in the group. The coefficients at Northwestern ranged from .69 to .98, with a median of .90. At Harvard the range was from .62 to .98, with a median of .91. At Northwestern the reliability figures are based on 14 of the total 36 sessions. At Harvard reliability figures are based on all of the sessions, plus 16 other five man sessions scored by the same two observers (Bales and Heinicke) for another purpose, with each session broken into three parts. The N is thus much larger for the Harvard figures (96 as compared to 14) and this probably accounts for the appearance of somewhat lower reliability. Over all, we consider the reliability to be satisfactory for interpretation of results, and a fair sample of the reliability which can be obtained from this method of interaction scoring. We feel confident that these figures can be improved somewhat by further training.

ANALYSIS OF RESULTS

General Trends in Interaction

Figure 1 compares the interaction trends for the Harvard and Northwestern groups. Although there are differences in absolute amounts, the *trends* are generally very much the same for the two sets of groups. Most of the differences in absolute amounts are probably due to the difference in size of unit used in observation, though some may be due to the fact that the Harvard case problems contained many more "facts". It will be noticed that the Northwestern groups are generally lower in the "task-oriented" categories (giving orientation, opinion, and suggestion), and generally higher on agreement and disagreement. It is known that the "long speeches" of members tend to fall in the task-oriented categories. The method of scoring used for the Harvard groups broke these long speeches up into simple sentences, whereas the method used at Northwestern assigned only one score unless the category changed. Thus the difference between the groups on the balance between task-oriented and social-emotional categories is probably largely an artifact of scoring methods. This should be kept in mind in the later presentation of rates combining Harvard and Northwestern data. Comparisons in terms of absolute rates should be avoided, and attention

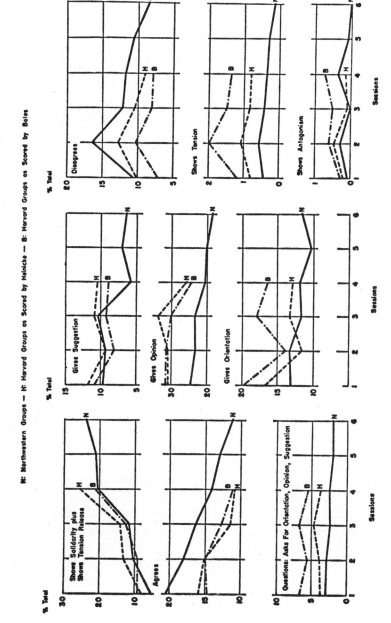

Figure I: TRENDS IN INTERACTION OVER SIX SESSIONS

N: Northwestern Groups — H: Harvard Groups as Scored by Heinicke — B: Harvard Groups as Scored by Bales

should be focused on changes in rates through time, which are not seriously affected by the scoring differences.

Figure 1 also compares the two observers for the Harvard groups. Again there are some differences in absolute amounts, but no serious differences in trends. Finally, it may be noted that where trends can be discerned the two extra sessions of the Northwestern groups continue the trends in the same direction, thus justifying to some extent our assumption that four sessions would give us about as good an idea of major trend developments as six sessions. Since the present study is concerned primarily with developmental trends, the general correspondence in trends seems to justify pooling the data of the Northwestern and Harvard groups, and gives us some assurance that the trends we describe are reliable under similar but not identical conditions.

The rates by categories as they change over the four sessions for the pooled raw data on both Northwestern and Harvard groups are shown in Table 2. Most single category trends are not statistically significant. By larger groupings, however, there are highly significant trends. There is a trend toward decreasing rates in the task-oriented categories (giving orientation, giving opinion, and giving suggestion) and a concomitant rise in the social-emotional categories. Negative reactions are low in the first session, show a sharp rise in the second session, and thereafter decrease again. Positive reactions as a whole show a minor rise through the first three sessions, and then a larger rise in the fourth. There are two kinds of trends within the area of positive reactions, however. Overt showing of agreement shows a steady and significant downward trend, which is counteracted by a sharply rising trend of showing solidarity and tension release (largely joking and laughing). In other words there is a marked shift from the more neutral and tentative task-oriented "agreement" to the more affectively-charged types of Positive Reactions.

Described more globally, and with a little more interpretation, it appears that on the average these groups started in session 1 with a heavier emphasis on task-oriented types of interaction, with inhibition of the more affective types of reaction and with low rates of overt negative reactions. In session 2, however, overt negative reactions show a sharp rise, task-oriented activities begin to decline, and positive reactions, while maintaining their level, show a shift toward greater affect. It appears that session 2 is, on the average, the session of greatest conflict. In sessions 3 and 4 the shift toward greater affect and less emphasis on task-oriented activities continues,

TABLE 2

INTERACTION TRENDS OVER TIME FOR NORTHWESTERN AND HARVARD GROUPS COMBINED

Categories	Percentage Rates[1] by Session				Level of Significance[2]
	1	2	3	4	
1 + 2	8.0	9.8	12.1	21.0	**
3	18.2	16.8	14.9	12.7	**
4	10.1	8.9	10.0	6.9	
5	28.0	26.8	26.5	22.1	
6	15.6	13.4	14.1	13.7	
7 + 8 + 9	4.3	3.9	3.9	3.7	
10	9.2	13.9	10.5	10.1	
11	.7	1.1	.8	.8	
12	.1	.6	.2	.6	
A	26.9	27.1	27.8	33.9	**
B	54.6	49.7	51.3	43.4	
C	4.3	3.9	3.9	3.7	
D	10.5	16.0	11.8	12.0	**
A — D	15.0	6.8	14.5	19.8	**

[1] Whenever percentage measures were analyzed in this study, an angular transformation was used. (6) This involves converting percentages to the angles having the sine equal to the square root of the percentage. The transformation is appropriate in those cases where the totals on which the percentages are based, are fairly equal. The latter was insured to a sufficient extent by having the discussion last for about 40 minutes. The percentages shown do not always add to 100 percent. Partially this is due to the use of the arc sine transformation, but largely it is due to the omission of one of the Northwestern categories. See footnote 1, Table 1.

[2] Throughout this study one asterisk will be used to stand for the .05, two for the .01, and three for the .001 level of significance. Wherever an asterisk appears *between* two numbers it indicates that they differ significantly. Wherever no asterisk appears the differences are not significant.

but the negative reactions drop and the positive reactions rise. It appears that the groups have gone through some sort of "crisis".[3]

Although these data are of interest in themselves without further breakdown, it turned out that additional light could be thrown on the meaning of the interaction rates and other measures by the introduction of the concept of a "degree of structure" with which groups end their meetings. For present purposes we use the concept to refer mainly to the degree to which the

---

[3] The supposed mechanisms are elaborated in detail in Bales (2).

members agree on where each one stands in the status hierarchy of the group. We shall speak of this as the degree of "status consensus". In this paper we largely ignore the qualitative differentiation of roles, which is certainly of prime importance in any detailed understanding of the "structure" of groups.[4]

Through the use of member ratings of each other we were able to distinguish between groups which ended their sessions or meetings with a High degree or a Low degree of status consensus. The next section deals with the problem of how this division was made and later sections attempt to show how this distinction enabled us to clarify and sharpen the general picture obtained from the pooled interaction rates.

DIVISION OF SAMPLE INTO HIGH AND LOW STATUS-CONSENSUS GROUPS

Since the concept of status is very general in nature, many specific operational definitions seem plausible. Our questionnaire data include member rankings of each other on "Who had the best ideas", and "Who did the most to guide the group" as well as a ranking on "Who stood out most definitely as leader". These ratings were available for both Northwestern and Harvard groups for the final session.

We should like to have status ratings for each session of each group as well as for the final session. For the Harvard groups we have the members' "idea" and "guidance" ranking for each session, whereas for the Northwestern groups we have observer ratings on leadership for each session, but no members' "idea" and "guidance" ranking except after the last session. Fortunately, all of these measures seem to be highly intercorrelated and we can take advantage of this fact to obtain roughly comparable status ratings for each session.

For the Northwestern groups after the final sessions the "idea ranking", correlates highly and significantly with the "leadership ranking", with a median rho of .875. The median rho for the correlation between "guidance ranking" and "leadership ranking" after these last sessions was also .875. For the Harvard groups the "idea ranking" after *each* session correlates with the "leadership ranking" after the final session with a median rho of .700, while the median rho for the correlation between "guidance ranking" on each of the four sessions and the "leadership ranking" was .872. Furthermore, for the Harvard groups the "idea ranking" and the "guidance ranking"

---

[4] The problem of the qualitative differentiation of roles and its relation to the developmental trends discussed in the present paper will be treated in another paper now in preparation. A beginning in this direction is contained in Bales (2).

for each of the four sessions correlate highly with each other with a median rho of .893. Finally, as reported above, it had been shown previously at Northwestern that rankings assigned by interaction observers after each session correlated with members' own final "leadership rankings" with a median rho of .900.

It seems a fair assumption that all of these measures are tapping the same broad factor, and that an acceptble general term for it is "status". On this assumption we can obtain roughly comparable status rankings of the members for each session of each group as well as strictly comparable measures for the final session of each. For the separate sessions of the Northwestern groups we use the observer's ratings. For the separate sessions of the Harvard groups we use the combined rankings on "best ideas" and "guidance". By comparing the rankings for individual sessions with the over-all rankings on leadership given at the end of the final session we can trace the course of changes in the status structure of each group through its series of sessions.

The above measures give status rankings for the members. Now what can we use as a measure of status-*consensus*? To illustrate in terms of an example: after the last session the members are asked to rank each other in term of "leadership". One can determine the extent to which they agree that No. 5 (identification number) ranks first, No. 1 is second, No. 4 is third, and this might be called a measure of status-*consensus*. M. G. Kendall (5) has reported a statistic, W, for indicating the degree of agreement in such a matrix of ranks. It is called the *Coefficient of Concordance* and is computed by the following formula:[5]

$$W = \frac{12S}{m^2(n^3 - n)}$$

where S equals the sum of the squares of the deviation of the column totals from the mean of these column totals, n equals the number of individuals (listed as the designations of columns), and m equals the number of individuals doing the ranking (listed as the designations of rows). Putting it in words, W is simply the ratio of the observed amount of deviation of the column totals from their mean to the maximum amount of column deviation possible for a given size matrix. When the agreement is perfect (that is, the observed column deviations are at a maximum), then W is equal to one; when there is no agreement, the column totals are all the same and W equals

---

[5] If there are many ties in the matrix of ranks, a correction is necessary. See Kendall (5) page 82.

zero. Using W as a measure then, we may define status-consensus as follows: a group is said to have a High degree of Consensus in the status rankings of members by each other as W of a matrix of these rankings approaches the value of 1 and to have a Low degree of Status-Consensus as W approaches a value of 0.

We are now in a position to divide our total sample into High and Low groups for further analysis. Using the W on the "leadership" ratings at the end of the last session as the index, a group was put in the High classification if its W was .500 or above and into the Low classification if its W was .499 or below. It turned out that one of the Harvard groups, and three of the Northwestern groups fall into the High status consensus classification, the six others were Low. A W of .500 was chosen as the dividing criterion because there seemed to be a gap in the distribution, and also because the secondary criteria of division noted below gave the same result.

For the Harvard groups it was possible to compute W indices on the "idea rankings" and "guidance rankings" made by the members at the end of each session. The two W's for each session were then averaged to obtain a single measure. This measure for the first session is considerably above .500 for the one High group, and below .500 for all three Low groups. Apparently the High group started high, and the Low groups started low. This is of considerable interest in relation to future studies. One may be able to differentiate High and Low groups at the end of the first session, and so predict something about their later developmental trends, since as we shall see, these trends seem to differ for the two types of groups.

Since we can not obtain a W for all of our groups, we fall back on another measure: the correlation of the status ranking of members for each session with their final ranking of each other on "leadership". It turns out that the correlation between the first session status ranking and the final "leadership ranking" is always above .800 for the High groups and always below .800 in the case of the Low groups. The first session status ranks then seem to be better predictors of the final ratings for the High groups than the Low groups. Finally, if we compute for each group the correlations between each of its session rankings and its final "leadership ranking", we find that the median rho for the High groups is .933 while the figure for the Low group is only .680. The difference between these median rho's is significant at the .01 level.[6] In other words, each of the session rankings

---

[6] Here as elsewhere in the paper the problem of independence was considered in computing the level of significance.

of the High groups on the average is a better predictor of the final status rankings than for the Low groups.

In summary, we have noted that the High groups have a W of .500 or higher both on the overall ratings and probably on the ratings of the first session. The extent of correlation between individual session rankings and the final "leadership rankings" is also higher for the High groups. This difference between High and Low groups is especially evident in the first session.

Before moving into the analysis and partially in anticipation, let us briefly examine the possible implications of the division into High and Low status consensus. First, it should be noted that the nature of the task (which lacks a clear criterion of successful solution other than group agreement) and the fact that the groups are initially leaderless tends to make it very important whether or not the members of the group can work out a satisfactory set of social-emotional relationships to each other. And surely an important aspect of this social-emotional set of problems is the settlement of problems of relative status or prestige as between members. One can also think of these as problems of "power" and "leadership". These terms are not all synonymous, but as a first approximation we lump these problems together as status problems.

One would expect that those groups which could arrive at a common (though perhaps unspoken) agreement as to the relative status of members would show a shorter period of overt disagreement and other negative reactions. That is, the lack of status consensus may be one important underlying factor associated with the degree of social-emotional conflict on the overt level.

Finally it seems reasonable to suppose that those groups which can solve adequately their problems of relative status will be more "efficient" in some sense, and also more "satisfied". The rest of the analysis will attempt to elaborate these general notions in terms of certain specific hypotheses.

HYPOTHESES ABOUT HIGH VERSUS LOW GROUPS

Hypothesis 1—*The developmental trends of groups initially high in status consensus show a decrease and then a gradual increase in status consensus, while those initially low in status consensus show a much less regular trend.*

Using the extent of correlation between individual session status rankings and the over-all status ranks as the best index of the trend of status consensus available for both Harvard and Northwestern groups, the High and Low groups are compared in Table 3. Even though available only for the Harvard groups, the average of the "idea" and "guidance" W's is also presented.

TABLE 3
TRENDS IN STATUS CONSENSUS OF HIGH AND LOW GROUPS

Indices of Status-Consensus	N	Types of Structure	Weekly Sessions			
			1	2	3	4
Mean rho between Session and Over-all Status Ranks:	4	High	.961 *	.822	.861	.914
	6	Low	.397 *	.638	.465	.529
Mean W on Sessions. Harvard Groups only:	1	High	.808	.552	.628	.736
	3	Low	.358	.401	.332	.395

In general the picture given by the two indices is similar. The High groups start with a relatively high status-consensus, drop in the second session, and then increase again regularly to the final session. The Low groups start low, increase, decrease, and increase in a zig-zag pattern. The difference in patterns may be visualized more clearly by reference to Figure 2.

It will be remembered that the Northwestern groups met for six sessions. If we compare the average rho between the session rank and the final "leadership rank" for the last two sessions with the corresponding average rho for the first four sessions, we find that there was a further slight increase in the last two sessions for the High groups. (See Table 4.) The structure trend for the High groups seems to show a significant decrease from the first to the second session and a gradual increase from there on to the last session.

While the High groups show a "crisis and recovery" trend, the pattern for the Low groups is one of continual fluctuation. There is a significant increase in status consensus from the first to the second session, then a decrease from the second to the third, and then again an increase from the third to the fourth session. Finally, using just the Northwestern data again, we find a decrease in the last two sessions when compared with the first four. (See Table 4.) For the *Northwestern* groups the difference between the mean rho's for the High and Low groups during the *first* four sessions does not reach significance. The difference between the means for the *last* two sessions is however significant at the .01 level. (See Table 4.)

In summary, the High groups show a dip and then a gradual increase in status-consensus while the comparable trend for the Low groups is much less consistent. It seems quite clear that the two trends differ from each other.

Hypothesis 2—*Groups with High as well as Low initial status-consensus go through a period of overt social emotional conflict, but in the High groups this conflict is more sharply focussed in time and in terms of the status rank of the people involved.*

Figure 2

TRENDS IN STATUS-CONSENSUS FOR HIGH AND LOW GROUPS

(Data from Table 3)

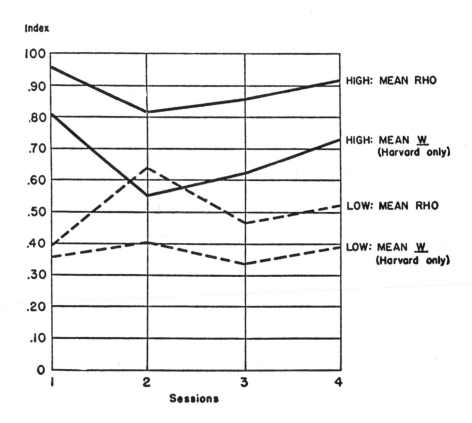

TABLE 4

CONTRASTING STRUCTURE OF HIGH AND LOW STATUS-CONSENSUS GROUPS
IN FIRST FOUR AND LAST TWO SESSIONS
NORTHWESTERN GROUPS ONLY

Index of Structure	Type of Structure	First Four Sessions	Last Two Sessions
Mean Rho between Session and Over-all Status Rank	High	.893	.900 **
	Low	.507	.400

We now re-examine the interaction trends. Examination of Table 5 reveals that for the High groups the social emotional conflict was highest in the second session. An overall index of the social emotional balance

TABLE 5

MEAN PERCENTAGE OF GROUP INTERACTION IN VARIOUS CATEGORIES
AND COMBINATION OF CATEGORIES IN SUCCESSIVE SESSIONS
HIGH GROUPS ONLY

Categories		Weekly Sessions				Level of Significance for total trend from session to session
		1	2	3	4	
	1 + 2	6.1	7.4	15.2	18.4	**
	3	17.7	16.4	14.7	12.6	
	4	9.0	10.2	9.1	9.0	
	5	27.2	27.4	23.7	23.3	
	6	16.8	12.1	13.8	12.6	
	7 + 8 + 9	4.2	3.4	2.9	3.5	
	10	12.8	17.8	11.4	11.2	
	11	.18	.49	.45	.47	
	12	.06	.20	.01	.44	
A	Positive Reactions	24.6	24.2 *	30.3	31.1	
B	Attempted Answers	53.9	50.2	47.6	45.4	
C	Questions	4.2	3.4	2.9	3.5	
D	Negative Reactions	13.3	18.7	11.9	12.6	
A — D		10.5 *	2.7 **	16.2	17.5	*

The reader is reminded that the percentages shown do not add to 100, for the reasons explained in footnote 1, Table 2

(Positive Reactions minus Negative Reactions, or A per cent—D per cent) shows a significant drop from the first to the second session, and a significant increase from the second to the third session. The various components of the index are also given in Table 5. It should be noted that D per cent is made up mostly of category 10 (disagreement), and that categories 11 and 12 show the same trends as category 10. Also of interest is the fact that categories 4 and 5 tend to show the same trend as D per cent. Finally, it will be noticed that agreement shows a steady but non-significant drop in the first four sessions.

Turning now to Table 6 and the trends for the Low Groups, it should be noted first of all that there are no significant differences for the A per cent— D per cent index. Furthermore, the A per cent shows a significant decrease from session two to three.

The other indices seem to fit the general picture of increased conflict

TABLE 6

MEAN PERCENTAGE OF GROUP INTERACTION IN VARIOUS CATEGORIES
AND COMBINATION OF CATEGORIES IN SUCCESSIVE SESSIONS
LOW GROUPS ONLY

Categories	Weekly Sessions				Level of Significance for total trend from session to session
	1	2	3	4	
1 + 2	9.4	11.5	10.4	22.9	**
3	18.5	17.1	15.0	12.8	**
4	10.9	8.1 *	10.5 *	5.7	**
5	28.6	26.5	28.5 **	21.3	*
6	14.9	14.3	14.3	14.5	
7 + 8 + 9	4.4	4.3	4.6	3.8	
10	7.2	11.6	10.0	9.5	
11	1.3	1.6	1.1	1.1	
12	.12	.61	.22	.60	
A Positive Reactions	28.5	29.1 *	26.1	35.9	
B Attempted Answers	55.3	49.3	53.9	42.2	
C Questions	4.4	4.3	4.6	3.8	
D Negative Reactions	8.7 *	14.3	11.7	11.6	
A — D	18.8	10.4	13.4	21.3	

See footnote 1, Table 5.

starting in the second session. Note the significant increase for D per cent from session one to two in spite of the fact that the W index at the *end* of this session is higher than at the end of the first. The fact that the trends in the Low groups for suggestion and opinion reach a high point in session three seems to fit into the picture of continued conflict in session three. That is, when groups are having trouble reaching agreement, there may be a tendency to initiate more and more suggestions and opinions. The fact that the correlation between giving suggestion and showing disagreement for the whole sample is .743 (significant at the .01 level) fits in with this interpretation. The correlation between the amount of opinion and disagreement is not significant, however. On the other hand, although not significant, the High groups also initiated the most opinion and suggestion during the session in which they showed the most disagreement.

Further confirmation is presented by the Northwestern groups for which we have data on two additional sessions. Table 7 compares the first four sessions, pooled, with the last two sessions, pooled. While little if any change was taking place in the Low group trend during the last two sessions, the High groups showed a significant increase in solidarity and tension release,

TABLE 7

MEAN PERCENTAGE OF GROUP INTERACTION IN VARIOUS CATEGORIES AND
COMBINATION OF CATEGORIES FOR THE FIRST FOUR VERSUS THE
LAST TWO SESSIONS OF THE NORTHWESTERN GROUPS

Categories	Type of Structure	First Four Sessions		Last Two Sessions
A — D	High	9.9	**	26.3
	Low	16.0		19.4
D	High	16.0	*	8.9
	Low	11.6		11.5
3	High	15.3	**	9.7
	Low	15.8		15.1
1 + 2	High	11.6	***	27.5
	Low	13.5		17.9
4	High	8.9		4.8
	Low	8.3		9.3
5	High	23.2	*	17.0
	Low	23.6		22.2

a significant decrease in the amount of negative social interaction, and a significant decrease in the amount of suggestion and opinion. The concomitant decline of the latter two categories and the negative categories (D per cent), seems further to fit the interpretation that the degree of consensus is reflected in the amount of suggestion and opinion.

What about the fact that the amount of agreement also declines? Does this not contradict the implication that a high state of consensus was reached in the High Northwestern groups during the last two sessions? It will be remembered that for the first four sessions both the High and Low groups showed a decline in overt agreement, although this trend was significant only for the Low groups (See Tables 4 and 5). It appears to us that a low rate of showing agreement can mean either that a state of conflict exists, and there is in fact little agreement in the underlying structural state, or it can mean that a high state of consensus in the underlying structural state has been reached so that there is little need for the overt expression of agreement. In other words, the rate of agreement taken alone is ambiguous. This is true of any of the rates taken alone.[7] Any given rate must be interpreted in conjunction with the total body of evidence covering the underlying structural state of the system. In this case, a drop in the rate of showing agreement coupled with a drop in showing disagreement, tension, and antagonism, and a rise in showing tension release and solidarity suggests an underlying structural state of growing consensus, with less need for routine guidance of the process by *signs* of agreement and disagreement, and more time for positive affective rewards which in a sense have become an expression of the existing state of consensus. On the other hand, a drop in the rate of agreement, *without* a corresponding drop in the rate of showing disagreement, tension, and antagonism, coupled with a rise in showing tension-release and solidarity suggests an underlying state of growing difficulty in consensus, with the tensions being "bled off" by tension release and attempts to improve the situation but with the underlying difficulty still unresolved.

Not only does the amount of social-emotional conflict tend to be focussed for the High groups in the second session, but it also tends to involve mainly the top status individuals. Computing the per cent of the total disagreement (category 10) expressed by the two individuals who received the two top status rankings at the end of the session, we find that their mean per cent in the High groups is considerably higher during the second session than in the other three sessions. The trend for the Low groups was not significant. (See Table 8.)

---

[7] As discussed at length in Bales, R. F., *Interaction Process Analysis*, pp. 117-122.

TABLE 8

MEAN EXTENT[1] OF DISAGREEMENT BETWEEN THE TWO TOP STATUS INDIVIDUALS

Type of Structure	Sessions				Significance level of total trend
	1	2	3	4	
High	5.0	30.8	6.9	11.2	*
Low	17.8	10.6	3.2	3.6	

[1] Extent was expressed as the ratio of the amount of disagreement between the two top individuals to the total amount of disagreement expressed by the group during the session.

In summary, the social emotional conflict of the High groups is focussed in the second session and shows a steady decline from there on. Furthermore, a large share of the disagreement during this session is taking place between the two top status individuals. The high point of social emotional conflict for the Low groups is less focussed both in time, and in terms of the individuals involved.

Hypothesis 3—*After passing the "crisis", the high status individuals in the High groups initiate less and less overt interaction in certain categories highly associated with status.*

It will be remembered that we have status rankings available for each session. We can also rank order the people in a group in terms of the amount which they initiated or received in a particular category during a particular session. We can then correlate the status ranks of each of the sessions with each of the category ranks. Finally, we can average all the rho's for a particular category to determine the average association between this category and status.

We are now in a position to see whether or not the high status people in the High groups tend to decrease their performance of these activities as the group meets again. Table 9 shows the changes in extent of association between status rank and category rank for those five categories which on the whole correlated highest with status. It will be seen that for the High groups there is a decrease in the extent of association between status and type of activity for each of the first five categories shown: Total initiated, total received, agreement received, suggestion initiated, and opinion initiated. For three of the categories this trend is significant. The Low groups on the other hand show no consistent or significant trends.

In summary then, the high status people in the High groups do tend

TABLE 9

CHANGES IN THE MEAN EXTENT OF ASSOCIATION (Rho) BETWEEN THE STATUS
RANKINGS AND CERTAIN CATEGORIES[1]

Categories	Type of Structure	Weekly Sessions				Level of Significance of Total Trend
		1	2	3	4	
Total	High	.975	.971	.661	.554	**
Initiated	Low	.588	.431	.440	.602	
Total	High	.875	.932	,796	.807	
Received	Low	.593	.498	.690	.469	
Agreement	High	.950	.862	.782	.833	
Received	Low	.436	.671	.704	.664	
Suggestion	High	.993	.782	.382	.636	*
Initiated	Low	.588	.471	.726	.545	
Opinion	High	.946	.922	.586	.672	*
Initiated	Low	.448	.578	.469	.481	

[1] The analysis of variance was originally performed on the z equivalents of rho (See Snedecor, (6)). At the suggestion of F. Mosteller the computations were done on the raw rho's as well. It was felt that this procedure was more justifiable even though the results turned out to be the same. The raw mean rho's are reported here. The reader should not interpret these coefficients too literally, but rather concentrate on the differences in mean rho under various conditions.

to initiate less in the categories of activity most closely associated with high status, that is, the association between these activities and status decreases through time. It should be noted, however, that the average association between these activities and status is in each case significantly higher for the High groups. (See Table 10.) In other words, although the high status people in the High groups slacken off in their status associated activities as the group meets again and again, on the average they still perform them relatively more frequently than the high status people in the Low groups.

Further evidence supporting Hypothesis 3, is given in Figure 3. Shown here are the changes over time in the per cent of total activity initiated by each of the status ranks. For example, for the High groups, during the first session the Number 1 man in terms of status for that session initiated 32.8 per cent of the total activity. In the fourth session on the other hand the

TABLE 10

AVERAGE EXTENT OF ASSOCIATION (Rho) BETWEEN STATUS AND CERTAIN CATEGORIES
FOR HIGH AND LOW GROUPS

Categories	Mean Rho for High Groups	Mean Rho for Low Groups	Significance Level of Difference
Total Initiated	.790	.515	**
Total Received	.853	.563	***
Agreement Received	.857	.619	*
Suggestion Initiated	.700	.583	*
Opinion Initiated	.781	.494	*

Number 1 man for the session initiated only 22.5 per cent of the total
interaction. Of special interest is the fact that the major changes for the
High groups occurs from the second to the third session. It will be remembered that the second session was the period of lowest status-consensus and
highest social emotional conflict for High groups. Furthermore, it was seen
that the top two status people exchanged the most disagreement during this
session. It seems, therefore, that for the High groups, once the point of
maximum conflict has been passed, the Number 1 status person tends to
relax and to give up some of his activity-time to others. In the Low groups
(not illustrated) the Number 1 status person actually increases his participation from the first session on to the third, when his activity is highest of
the four sessions.

These trends in total initiation and especially the drop from the second
to the third session throw further light on the High group trends in Table 8.
If the Number 1 man shows the greatest drop in total initiation from session
two to session three, his performance of status associated activities ought
also to show the greatest decrease from session two to three. Translating
this into rank order correlation coefficients, one would expect that the average
extent of association between each of the status associated activities and
status will be higher in session one and two than in session three and four.
Table 10 contrasts the mean rho for the first two sessions with the mean
rho for the last two sessions. It will be seen that in each case there is a drop

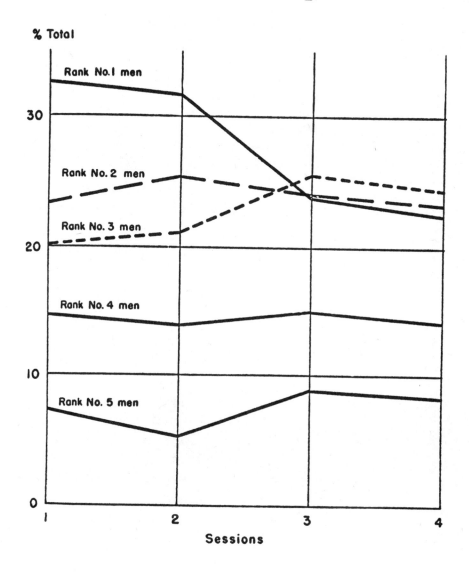

MEAN PERCENTAGE OF TOTAL ACTIVITY
INITIATED BY VARIOUS STATUS RANKS
HIGH GROUPS ONLY

and that for four of the categories this change is significant. As one might expect, the greatest drops occur in the initiation categories. Thus while playing a less important role in terms of initiating certain activities, the high status individuals show less change in their roles of receiving activity. Although what one initiates will to a great extent determine what one receives, in general one has less control over what one receives than what one initiates.

Further inspection of Figure 3 reveals that while the trends in amounts of interaction for the Number 1, 2 and 3 men for the High groups tend to overlap in the later sessions, the trends for the Number 4 and 5 men are quite separate and show no significant changes. That is, Number 2 and especially Number 3 whose trend change is almost significant, seemed to be taking over most of the activity that Number 1 has dropped. The status rankings support this picture. An examination of the status rankings of the High groups for successive sessions (see Table 12) reveals that while the top three men are shifting positions, the fourth and fifth tend to retain their position. That is, in the High groups, once a man finds himself in the number 4 or 5 position he is likely to stay there. The changes take place among the higher status men. To examine these shifts in terms of a measure, let us say that if a man is Number 1 during the first session, and Number 2

TABLE 11

MEAN RHO BETWEEN STATUS AND CERTAIN CATEGORIES
FOR FIRST TWO VERSUS SECOND TWO SESSIONS
HIGH GROUPS ONLY

Categories	Mean Rho for First Two Sessions	Mean Rho for Second Two Sessions	Significance Level of Difference
Total Initiated	.973	.607	***
Total Received	.904	.802	
Agreement Received	.906	.808	
Suggestions Initiated	.888	.509	**
Opinion Initiated	.934	.629	**

during the second session, this is considered a shift of one, if he is Number 3, this is a shift of 2, etc. In the High groups the average number of shifts for the first three men is markedly and significantly higher than for the last two men, as shown in Table 12. For the Low groups the picture is different. In general the number of shifts is greater, and involves the lower status positions as well as the higher.

TABLE 12

MEAN NUMBER OF STATUS SHIFTS DURING FIRST FOUR MEETINGS FOR THE FIRST THREE AND THE LAST TWO STATUS POSITIONS[1]

Type of Structure	Mean Number of Status Shifts		
	For First Three Status Positions		For Last Two Status Positions
High	.972	***	.250 ***
Low	1.232		1.486

[1] The final status ratings were used for separating the first three and the last two status positions.

Hypothesis 4—*The High groups are in general more satisfied both with their group and with the groups' solutions of the problems than the Low groups.*

Unfortunately data on satisfaction were available only for the Harvard groups. For these groups two independent measures were obtained. One consisted of a Guttman scale of .91 reproducibility derived from the opinion check list relating to satisfaction with the group. The scale was made up of the following items, and was originally constructed from data on groups other than those reported here:

1. The atmosphere in this group is pleasant and congenial.
2. There is plenty of freedom to talk in this group.
3. I am well satisfied with my position in this group.
4. The morale of this group at this point is high.
5. This is one of the best groups I have worked in.

The score here ranged from 0 to 5. The other was a check on a 12-point scale in answer to the question: "How satisfied were you with the solution to the problem". In Table 12 the means of the individual ratings for the four sessions of the one Harvard High group (a total of 24 ratings), are compared with means of the 72 ratings made by the Harvard Low groups. Both measures show the difference and both are highly significant. It seems

TABLE 13

MEAN SATISFACTION RATINGS OF HIGH AND LOW STRUCTURE GROUPS
HARVARD ONLY

Satisfaction	Type of Group Structure		Significance Level of Difference
	High	Low	
Mean Guttman Scale Rating	4.04	2.58	***
Mean Rating Scale Rating	10.04	7.92	***

clear that as far as the Harvard groups are concerned,[8] individuals taking part in sessions of the High status-consensus group were more satisfied both with their group and the solutions to the problems than the members of the Low status-consensus groups.

One additional finding is of interest here. For the three Harvard Low groups the average rho between status and a popularity ranking shows a consistent and significant (.01) decline. The mean rho's are .806 for the first session, .390 for the second, .238 for the third, and .031 for the fourth session. The popularity ranking was based on how many total positive socio-metric choices a person received. It would seem that in the Low groups the amount of negative affect expressed toward the high status people increases through time. Not only are the members more dissatisfied than those belonging to High groups, but they also seem to become increasingly hostile toward their leaders.[9] Unfortunately sufficient data were not available to make a similar analysis for the High groups.

Hypothesis 5—*The High groups are more "efficient" than the Low groups*

While the satisfaction data were available only for the Harvard groups, the data to support this hypothesis are available only for the Northwestern groups. It will be remembered that for the Northwestern groups the written solution of each session of each group was rated by two raters in terms of certain criteria. (See section on Northwestern procedure.) Also available for each session was the duration in seconds of the total discussion. "Efficiency" was measured by the ratio of the productivity rating (average for

---

[8] The comparison involves very few groups, hence this finding must be tentative. Since the collection of the data here analyzed, however, further analysis of new data strongly supports the finding.

[9] This, we believe, is one of the most important mechanisms in the structural change of groups. Our data concerning the role structure will be presented in greater detail in later papers.

the two raters) to the length of the discussion in seconds. Multiplying the ratios by a constant, we find that the mean ratio for the High group is 20.0 while the mean ratio for the Low group is 12.8. This difference is just significant at the .05 level.

DISCUSSION

No variables were explicitly manipulated in this study and the number of cases is small, consequently one can not be too confident in the interpretation of the findings. However, if this exploratory study is to stimulate further research into the factors affecting the development of structure in small groups, some of the more general implications should be pointed out.

Since the picture for the High groups seems clearer, let us discuss these results first. These groups had developed a high degree of status consensus by the end of the first session. During the second session, not only did the status consensus decline, but a somewhat different hierarchy emerged. In the course of this session the social emotional conflict reaches a peak and most of the disagreement is expressed between the two top status members. This increased overt struggle between the two top men, taken together with a general picture of increased conflict and a decline in status consensus lends plausibility to the interpretation that some kind of "status struggle" is taking place in the second session of the High groups. That is, the hierarchy which emerged in the first session is somehow challenged during the second session. After the second session, however, the challenge is apparently dealt with successfully. The old structure again emerges (rho of session status rankings with overall status rankings increases), the measure of status consensus increases, the general social-emotional picture becomes more positive, and the top status individuals play a much less active role in any disagreement that takes place.

A more detailed examination of the roles of these top status individuals throws further light on the general trend. During the first two sessions the Number 1 man plays a very active part. Apparently he must perform actively if he is to establish his position initially and then defend it. He is high on the initiation of suggestion and opinion, receives a lot of disagreement as well as agreement, and during the second session takes an active part in the struggle for status, presumably defending his top position. Having secured his position, however, he can, so to speak, "let up" in the third and fourth sessions, and thus permit others to play a more active role without losing his status. It is of interest, however, that he still receives the most responses, and especially receives a large portion of agreement. It appears that his opinions and suggestions tend to be accepted and he no longer has to do much to win his point. People in general look to him for approval (they address their remarks and suggestions to him), and they tend to accept his decisions.

A passage from W. F. Whyte's memorandum (8) referring to the gang analyzed in *Street Corner Society* seems appropriate here:

"It is my observation that interaction can be patterned and still have no resemblance to [the] stereotype of autocratic leadership. Take, for example, Doc in the Norton's Gang as described in my *Street Corner Society*. Doc gave the impression of being quite unaggressive in that he did not often come out with ideas for action for the group. On the contrary, there were many occasions when members of the group would suggest actions that the group subsequently carried out. But note this important point. The suggestions were always made to Doc and were not acted upon positively unless Doc gave at least his acquiescence. I observed that activity involving the whole group would be initiated either through the acceptance by Doc of suggestions presented by others or by proposals directly from Doc to the group. I observed further that Doc tended to respond favorably most often to members of the group close to him in prestige, while suggestions of members of less importance were often passed over."

Relevant to the last observation is the fact that in the High group the Number 3 man took over most of the activity that the Number 1 man dropped in the third and fourth session. (See Figure 3 and the data on status reversals in Table 12.)

We have then a picture of the development of a status structure which permits the reaching of consensus on *task* problems. The Number 1 man (and possibly Numbers 2 and 3) have become, after the crisis, the main source for determining when something is "right". There is little need for a lot of overt expression of agreement—only a few statements made by the "right" people need to be agreed to. As it turned out, the agreement decreased significantly during the 5th and 6th session only for the High groups. When the status problem is settled, we may suppose, less time has to be spent in discussion which is essentially a thinly disguised attempt to change generalized status positions. Perhaps the solution of the status problem (whatever makes it possible in the first place) is mainly responsible for the higher satisfaction and higher efficiency found among the High groups.

The picture for the Low groups is much less clear. Little status consensus emerges by the end of the first session. Whatever hierarchy emerges appears to be challenged during the second session as overt negative reactions increase. The overt conflict during the session, however, may result in a clearer hierarchy by the end of the session. The measure of status consensus is higher at the end of the second session for the Low groups than at the end of the first, but is still probably no higher than that of the High groups at the crisis. In the third session there is still another change in the nature of the hierarchy and the degree of status consensus decreases. Perhaps this third session is roughly analogous to the second session of the High groups. It appears that the status hierarchy which emerged by the end of the second session is challenged in the third, but a new status structure is not successfully established. This interpretation is much less clearly supported here than when applied to the High groups.

It seems fairly clear, however, that the Low groups never adequately solve the problem of status consensus. The fact that members at all levels continue to shift status positions may possibly be associated with the low degree of efficiency and satisfaction found in these groups. On the whole the Low groups are characterized by a failure to develop a pattern of relationships for deciding who stands where, and whose solutions are apt to be "right". Rather they tend to express more and more dislike of the top status members on the sociometric choices, and depose them one after another.

One could, of course, assume that the Low groups represent a kind of junk category which in actuality has in it many different kinds of trends. Even if this is true it would be of interest to know that groups which initially have difficulty in organizing show a greater variety of trends and attempts to organize than those which do not have this initial difficulty. On the other hand, the evidence suggests that even groups with a high degree of initial status consensus have internal strains which tend to result in a "crisis".

Summary

Various aspects of the development of status structure were studied in a number of newly formed initially leaderless groups during a series of meetings under reasonably constant laboratory conditions. The subjects were asked to discuss and solve a human relations problem within a period of about 40 minutes. The successive meetings of ten small groups of undergraduate students were observed using Bales' interaction category system. Observer ratings and subjects' ratings of each other were also available as sources of data.

To analyze the developmental trends of the groups, they were divided into a High and Low status-consensus classification. The analysis of trends was organized in terms of five main hypotheses, all of which receive substantial support from the data:

Hypothesis 1—The developmental trends of groups initially High in status consensus show a decrease and then a gradual increase in status consensus, while those initially Low in status consensus show a much less regular trend.

Hypothesis 2—Groups with High as well as Low initial status-consensus go through a period of overt social emotional conflict, but in the High groups this conflict is more sharply focussed in time and in terms of the status of the people involved.

Hypothesis 3—After passing the "crisis", the high status individuals in the High groups initiate less and less overt interaction in certain categories highly associated with status.

Hypothesis 4—The High groups are in general more satisfied both with their group and with the groups' solutions of the problems than the Low groups.

Hypothesis 5—The High groups are more "efficient" than the Low groups.

The findings were discussed in more general terms. It is hoped that this study will provide a basis for exploring further the factors which effect the development of structure in groups.

REFERENCES

1. Bales, R. F. *Interaction Process Analysis*. Cambridge, Mass., Addison-Wesley Press, 1950.
2. Bales, R. F. "The Equilibrium Problem in Small Groups", in Parsons, T., Bales, R. F., and Shils, E. A., *Working Papers in the Theory of Action*, Chapter IV. Glencoe, Ill., The Free Press, 1952.
3. Deutsch, M. "An Experimental Study of the Effects of Co-operation and Competition upon Group Process," *Human Relations*, 1949, 2, 199-231.
4. Heinicke, C. M. *The Development of Structure in Small Groups of Men*, Master's Dissertation, Northwestern University, 1950.
5. Kendall, M. G. Rank Correlation Methods. London, Charles Griffin and Co., 1948.
6. Snedecor, G. W. Statistical Methods. Ames, Iowa, The Iowa State College Press, 1950.
7. Taylor, F. Kräupl, "Quantitative Evaluation of Psycho-Social Phenomena in Small Groups," *J. Ment. Sci.*, 1951, 97, 690-717.
8. Whyte, W. F. "The Analysis of Group Discussion." Unpublished memorandum.

II

Types of Stratification

Social inequalities between groups exist within all known societies, but there is still wide variation in the methods of defining these groups, their criteria for membership, and the means, if any, by which one may move from group to group within the society. There are, of course, innumerable bases of group formation including age, sex, race, residence, religious affiliation, kinship, interest, and so forth (e.g., see Suttles, 1968). In addition, there is an equally large number of ways in which these groups may be stratified once they are formed. They may differ in economic reward, level of education, control over resources (including other groups), command of deference, etc. The particular ways in which groups are differentiated, the criteria by which they are stratified, and the interrelationships between the various dimensions of both differentiation and stratification serve to define different types of stratification systems.

Among the various dimensions of social inequality, three have been especially important in theoretical treatments of the bases of stratification. The reason for their importance is obvious: they form the bases of inequality in three important subsectors of society. (1) The economic subsector. Some social groups plainly have command or control over a much wider range and quantity of resources than do others. Although there are many types of resources, the three types most frequently involved are property (including land, machines, and human capital), specialized technical knowledge, and of course, accumulated wealth, which is a useful resource only when it may be converted either into property or the technical knowledge necessary to secure property or insure its growth. *Economic stratification* refers to inequalities that arise because of group differences in access to capital resources. (2) The political subsector. Persons and social groups vary extensively in their ability to obtain the conformity of others to their wills in situations where those very same others are desirous of some other course of events. *Political stratification* concerns the differential ability of groups or persons to impose their commands in the face of opposition. Coercion and the threat of coercion are doubtless the most important bases of power in this sense, though crude displays of force are generally avoided because obedience to commands backed by differential power are secured through the legal, charismatic or traditional authority associated with their source (cf. Weber, 1947). Regimes established by unconstitutional means are often violent because their control is secured only through continuous

63

use of force, reprisal, and threats rather than through the voluntary submission of the populace because of a general popular belief in their legitimacy. Even popular revolutions headed by a single, charismatic figure are seldom stable, at least until the forces of opposition have been eliminated or the new regime has been co-opted by old interests and further revolt chilled by creation of a chain of command reflecting realistic political resources. (3) The social subsector. Neither economic nor political stratification depends ultimately upon the evaluations persons and groups have of each other: either you have a competitive advantage or you don't and either you can back your command with force or you can't. Whether either form of inequality is approved is irrelevant to its exercise. We know, however, that inequalities in the estimates that groups and individuals make of each other emerge in the course of social interaction and exchange. *Social stratification* rests on the differential evaluations of social honor or esteem accorded various groups in a society; any commodity or quality which is differentially valued can, therefore, be a basis of social stratification because groups can be sorted out according to the amounts they have or whether they have it or not.

Economic, political and social facets of stratification are, in a theoretical sense, independent of each other because knowledge about a group's location on any one of these dimensions *logically* implies nothing about its location on the others. Nevertheless, these features of inequality are *statistically* associated so that those groups which control capital are also likely to exercise oligarchic control over violence and to receive deference from others. The degree or extent to which these dimensions of inequality are intercorrelated determines how *crystallized* a society is and how integrated its stratification system is. Where there is a perfect correspondence between these several aspects of inequality, the stratification system is *unidimensional:* he who owns, rules; he who rules, is well regarded; he who is well regarded, owns. When, however, the economic, political and social positions of groups and persons are less than perfectly correlated, the stratification system is multi-dimensional and, typically, behavior in various situations comes to be guided by diverse systems of inequality. The relative preponderance of any one of these forms of inequality over the others becomes apparent only in the event that they come into conflict with each other, i.e., when the norms governing their applicability and legitimacy in specific situations are conflicting or inconsistent. Some theories of stratification maintain that one of these dimensions of inequality is the root cause of all other forms of inequality. Marxists, for example, attribute the crucial role to ownership of the means of production and political and socioreligious equalitarianism are seen as important mechanisms of social control whereby real (and unfairly gained) inequalities in material well-being are sustained.

Not only may societies differ in the relative emphasis which they accord economic, political and social stratification and the extent to which these dimensions of inequality are intermingled, but they may also differ in the units or groups which are stratified, as well as the means of movement between them. The selections by Leach, Stinchcombe and Bloch reveal the diversity in the units of stratification in different types of societies. Leach makes a special attempt to give careful definition to the key characteristics of certain of these units.

The dimensions of social inequality outlined above are, of course, the subject of Weber's now famous discussion included as the first selection in this section. The continuing relevance of these distinctions is clearly revealed in Wiley's analysis of the political consequences of stratification in the United States.

REFERENCES

Bell, Daniel.
  1966 "Notes on the post-industrialized society —Part I." The Public Interest 6 (Winter).
  1967 "Notes on the post-industrialized society —Part II." The Public Interest 7 (Spring).
Benóit-Smullyan, Emile.
  1944 "Status, status types, and status interrelationships," American Sociological Review 9: 151-161.
Goldthorpe, John H.
  1964 "Social stratification in industrial society." Pp. 97-122 in Paul Halmos (ed.), The Development of Industrial Society. The Sociological Review, Monograph No. 8.
Hsu, F. L. K.
  1963 Clan, Caste and Club. Princeton, New Jersey: D. Van Nostrand.
Kimberly, James.
  1970 "The emergence and stabilization of stratification in simple and complex social systems: Some implications of small group research." Social Inquiry 40 (Spring).
Lewis, Oscar.
  1958 Village Life in Northern India. Urbana: University of Illinois Press.
Marx, Karl.
  n.d. "The Communist Manifesto." In Selected Works of Marx and Engels, 2 Vols. New York: International Publishers.
  n.d. "The Eighteenth Brumaire of Louis Bonaparte." In Selected Works of Marx and Engels, 2 vols. New York: International Publishers.
Marx, Karl and Friedrich Engels.
  1939 The German Ideology. New York: International Publishers.
Ossowski, Stanislaw.
  1963 Class Structure in the Social Consciousness. London: Routledge & Kegan Paul.
Parsons, Talcott.
  1970 "Some further thoughts on the action theory of stratification." Sociological Inquiry 40 (Spring).
Stinchcombe, Arthur L.
  1962 Agricultural enterprise and rural class relations. American Journal of Sociology 67: 165-176.
Suttles, Gerald D.
  1968 The Social Order of the Slum: Ethnicity and Territory in the Inner City. Chicago: University of Chicago Press.
van den Berghe, Pierre L.
  1958 "The dynamics of racial prejudice." Social Forces 73: 138-141.
Weber, Max.
  1947 The Theory of Social and Economic Organization. Translated by A. M. Henderson and Talcott Parsons. New York: Oxford University Press.

CHAPTER 3

Class, Status, Party

MAX WEBER

1: Economically Determined Power and the Social Order

Law exists when there is a probability that an order will be upheld by a specific staff of men who will use physical or psychical compulsion with the intention of obtaining conformity with the order, or of inflicting sanctions for infringement of it.* The structure of every legal order directly influences the distribution of power, economic or otherwise, within its respective community. This is true of all legal orders and not only that of the state. In general, we understand by 'power' the chance of a man or of a number of men to realize their own will in a communal action even against the resistance of others who are participating in the action.

'Economically conditioned' power is not, of course, identical with 'power' as such. On the contrary, the emergence of economic power may be the consequence of power existing on other grounds. Man does not strive for power only in order to enrich himself economically. Power, including economic power, may be valued 'for its own sake.' Very frequently the striving for power is also conditioned by the social 'honor' it entails. Not all power, however, entails social honor: The typical American Boss, as well as the typical big speculator, deliberately relinquishes social honor. Quite generally, 'mere economic' power, and especially 'naked' money power, is by no means a recognized basis of social honor. Nor is power the only basis of social honor. Indeed, social honor, or prestige, may even be the basis of political or economic power, and very frequently has been. Power, as well as honor, may be guaranteed by the legal order, but, at least normally, it is not their primary source. The

* Wirtschaft und Gesellschaft, part III, chap. 4, pp. 631-40. The first sentence in paragraph one and the several definitions in this chapter which are in brackets do not appear in the original text. They have been taken from other contexts of Wirtschaft und Gesellschaft.

here describe how after this initial displacement the importance of the vernacular steadily progressed under the influence of the broadening administrative tasks of state and church, hence as the language of administration and of the sermon. I may, however, add one more word about the economic determination of modern language conflicts.

Today quite considerable pecuniary and capitalist interests are anchored in the maintenance and cultivation of the popular language: the interests of the publishers, editors, authors, and the contributors to books and periodicals and, above all, to newspapers. Once Polish and Latvian newspapers existed, the language fight conducted by governments or ruling strata of another language community had become as good as hopeless, for reasons of state are powerless against these forces. And to the interests in profits of the capitalist another material interest of great weight has to be added: the bilingual candidates in competing for office throw their bilingualism into the balance and seek to lay claim upon as large an area of patronage as possible. This occurred among the Czechs in Austria with their surplus of intellectual proletariat bred *en masse*. The tendency as such is old.

The conciliar, and at the same time nationalist, reaction against the universalism of the papacy in the waning Middle Ages had its origin, to a great extent, in the interests of the intellectuals who wished to see the prebends of their own country reserved for themselves and not occupied by strangers *via* Rome. After all, the name *natio* as a legal concept for an organized community is found first at the universities and at the reform councils of the church. At that time, however, the linkage to the national language *per se* was lacking; this linkage, for the reasons stated, is specifically modern.

If one believes that it is at all expedient to distinguish national sentiment as something homogeneous and specifically set apart, one can do so only by referring to a tendency toward an autonomous state. And one must be clearly aware of the fact that sentiments of solidarity, very heterogeneous in both their nature and their origin, are comprised within national sentiments.

legal order is rather an additional factor that enhances the chance to hold power or honor; but it cannot always secure them.

The way in which social honor is distributed in a community between typical groups participating in this distribution we may call the 'social order.' The social order and the economic order are, of course, similarly related to the 'legal order.' However, the social and the economic order are not identical. The economic order is for us merely the way in which economic goods and services are distributed and used. The social order is of course conditioned by the economic order to a high degree, and in its turn reacts upon it.

Now: 'classes,' 'status groups,' and 'parties' are phenomena of the distribution of power within a community.

2: Determination of Class-Situation by Market-Situation

In our terminology, 'classes' are not communities; they merely represent possible, and frequent, bases for communal action. We may speak of a 'class' when (1) a number of people have in common a specific causal component of their life chances, in so far as (2) this component is represented exclusively by economic interests in the possession of goods and opportunities for income, and (3) is represented under the conditions of the commodity or labor markets. [These points refer to 'class situation,' which we may express more briefly as the typical chance for a supply of goods, external living conditions, and personal life experiences, in so far as this chance is determined by the amount and kind of power, or lack of such, to dispose of goods or skills for the sake of income in a given economic order. The term 'class' refers to any group of people that is found in the same class situation.]

It is the most elemental economic fact that the way in which the disposition over material property is distributed among a plurality of people, meeting competitively in the market for the purpose of exchange, in itself creates specific life chances. According to the law of marginal utility this mode of distribution excludes the non-owners from competing for highly valued goods; it favors the owners and, in fact, gives to them a monopoly to acquire such goods. Other things being equal, this mode of distribution monopolizes the opportunities for profitable deals for all those who, provided with goods, do not necessarily have to exchange them. It increases, at least generally, their power in price wars with those who, being propertyless, have nothing to offer but their services in native form or goods in a form constituted through their own labor, and who above all are compelled to get rid of these products in order barely to subsist. This mode of distribution gives to the propertied a monopoly on the possibility of transferring property from the sphere of use as a 'fortune,' to the sphere of 'capital goods'; that is, it gives them the entrepreneurial function and all chances to share directly or indirectly in returns on capital. All this holds true within the area in which pure market conditions prevail. 'Property' and 'lack of property' are, therefore, the basic categories of all class situations. It does not matter whether these two categories become effective in price wars or in competitive struggles.

Within these categories, however, class situations are further differentiated: on the one hand, according to the kind of property that is usable for returns; and, on the other hand, according to the kind of services that can be offered in the market. Ownership of domestic buildings; productive establishments; warehouses; stores; agriculturally usable land, large and small holdings—quantitative differences with possibly qualitative consequences—; ownership of mines; cattle; men (slaves); disposition over mobile instruments of production, or capital goods of all sorts, especially money or objects that can be exchanged for money easily and at any time; disposition over products of one's own labor or of others' labor differing according to their various distances from consumability; disposition over transferable monopolies of any kind—all these distinctions differentiate the class situations of the propertied just as does the 'meaning' which they can and do give to the utilization of property, especially to property which has money equivalence. Accordingly, the propertied, for instance, may belong to the class of rentiers or to the class of entrepreneurs.

Those who have no property but who offer services are differentiated just as much according to their kinds of services as according to the way in which they make use of these services, in a continuous or discontinuous relation to a recipient. But always this is the generic connotation of the concept of class: that the kind of chance in the *market* is the decisive moment which presents a common condition for the individual's fate. 'Class situation' is, in this sense, ultimately 'market situation.' The effect of naked possession *per se,* which among cattle breeders gives the non-owning slave or serf into the power of the cattle owner, is only a forerunner of real 'class' formation. However, in the cattle loan and in the naked severity of the law of debts in such communities, for the first time mere 'possession' as such emerges as decisive for the fate of the individual. This is very much in contrast to the agricultural communities based on labor. The creditor-debtor relation becomes the basis of 'class situations' only in those cities where a 'credit market,' however primitive, with rates of interest increasing according to the extent of dearth and a factual monopolization of credits, is developed by a plutocracy. Therewith 'class struggles' begin.

Those men whose fate is not determined by the chance of using goods or services for themselves on the market, e.g. slaves, are not, however, a 'class' in the technical sense of the term. They are, rather, a 'status group.'

3: Communal Action Flowing from Class Interest

According to our terminology, the factor that creates 'class' is unambiguously economic interest, and indeed, only those interests involved in the existence of the 'market.' Nevertheless, the concept of 'class-interest' is an ambiguous one: even as an empirical concept it is ambiguous as soon as one understands by it something other than the factual direction of interests following with a certain probability from the class situation for a certain 'average' of those people subjected to the class situation. The class situation and other circumstances remaining the same, the direction in which the individual worker, for instance, is likely to pursue his interests may vary widely, according to whether he is constitutionally qualified for the task at hand to a high, to an average, or to a low degree. In the same way, the direction of interests may vary according to whether or not a *communal* action of a larger or smaller portion of those commonly affected by the 'class situation,' or even an association among them, e.g. a 'trade union,' has grown out of the class situation from which the individual may or may not expect promising results. [Communal action refers to that action which is oriented to the feeling of the actors that they belong together. Societal action, on the other hand, is oriented to a rationally motivated adjustment of interests.] The rise of societal or even of communal action from a common class situation is by no means a universal phenomenon.

The class situation may be restricted in its effects to the generation of essentially *similar* reactions, that is to say, within our terminology, of 'mass actions.' However, it may not have even this result. Furthermore, often merely an amorphous communal action emerges. For example, the 'murmuring' of the workers known in ancient oriental ethics: the moral disapproval of the work-master's conduct, which in its practical significance was probably equivalent to an increasingly typical phenomenon of precisely the latest industrial development, namely, the 'slow down' (the deliberate limiting of work effort) of laborers by virtue of tacit agreement. The degree in which 'communal action' and possibly 'societal action,' emerges from the 'mass actions' of the members of a class is linked to general cultural conditions, especially to those of an intellectual sort. It is also linked to the extent of the contrasts that have already evolved, and is especially linked to the *transparency* of the connections between the causes and the consequences of the 'class situation.' For however different life chances may be, this fact in itself, according to all experience, by no means gives birth to 'class action' (communal action by the members of a class). The fact of being conditioned and the results of the class situation must be distinctly recognizable. For only then the contrast of life chances can be felt not as an absolutely given fact to be accepted, but as a resultant from either (1) the given distribution of property, or (2) the structure of the concrete economic order. It is only then that people may react against the class structure not only through acts of an intermittent and irrational protest, but in the form of rational association. There have been 'class situations' of the first category (1), of a specifically naked and transparent sort, in the urban centers of Antiquity and during the Middle Ages; especially then, when great fortunes were accumulated by factually monopolized trading in industrial products of these localities or in foodstuffs. Furthermore, under certain circumstances, in the rural economy of the most diverse periods, when agriculture was increasingly exploited in a profit-making manner. The most important historical example of the second category (2) is the class situation of the modern 'proletariat.'

4: Types of 'Class Struggle'

Thus every class may be the carrier of any one of the possibly innumerable forms of 'class action,' but this is not necessarily so. In any case, a class does not in itself constitute a community. To treat 'class' conceptually as having the same value as 'community' leads to distortion. That men in the same class situation regularly react in mass actions to such tangible situations as economic ones in the direction of those interests that are most adequate to their average number is an important and after all simple fact for the understanding of historical events. Above all, this fact must not lead to that kind of pseudo-scientific operation with the concepts of 'class' and 'class interests' so frequently found these days,

and which has found its most classic expression in the statement of a talented author, that the individual may be in error concerning his interests
but that the 'class' is 'infallible' about its interests. Yet, if classes as such
are not communities, nevertheless class situations emerge only on the
basis of communalization. The communal action that brings forth class
situations, however, is not basically action between members of the
identical class; it is an action between members of different classes. Communal actions that directly determine the class situation of the worker
and the entrepreneur are: the labor market, the commodities market,
and the capitalistic enterprise. But, in its turn, the existence of a capitalistic enterprise presupposes that a very specific communal action exists
and that it is specifically structured to protect the possession of goods
per se, and especially the power of individuals to dispose, in principle
freely, over the means of production. The existence of a capitalistic enterprise is preconditioned by a specific kind of 'legal order.' Each kind of
class situation, and above all when it rests upon the power of property
per se, will become most clearly efficacious when all other determinants
of reciprocal relations are, as far as possible, eliminated in their significance. It is in this way that the utilization of the power of property in the
market obtains its most sovereign importance.

Now 'status groups' hinder the strict carrying through of the sheer
market principle. In the present context they are of interest to us only
from this one point of view. Before we briefly consider them, note that
not much of a general nature can be said about the more specific kinds
of antagonism between 'classes' (in our meaning of the term). The great
shift, which has been going on continuously in the past, and up to our
times, may be summarized, although at the cost of some precision: the
struggle in which class situations are effective has progressively shifted
from consumption credit toward, first, competitive struggles in the commodity market and, then, toward price wars on the labor market. The
'class struggles' of antiquity—to the extent that they were genuine class
struggles and not struggles between status groups—were initially carried
on by indebted peasants, and perhaps also by artisans threatened by debt
bondage and struggling against urban creditors. For debt bondage is the
normal result of the differentiation of wealth in commercial cities, especially in seaport cities. A similar situation has existed among cattle
breeders. Debt relationships as such produced class action up to the time
of Cataline. Along with this, and with an increase in provision of grain
for the city by transporting it from the outside, the struggle over the

means of sustenance emerged. It centered in the first place around the provision of bread and the determination of the price of bread. It lasted throughout antiquity and the entire Middle Ages. The propertyless as such flocked together against those who actually and supposedly were interested in the dearth of bread. This fight spread until it involved all those commodities essential to the way of life and to handicraft production. There were only incipient discussions of wage disputes in antiquity and in the Middle Ages. But they have been slowly increasing up into modern times. In the earlier periods they were completely secondary to slave rebellions as well as to fights in the commodity market.

The propertyless of antiquity and of the Middle Ages protested against monopolies, pre-emption, forestalling, and the withholding of goods from the market in order to raise prices. Today the central issue is the determination of the price of labor.

This transition is represented by the fight for access to the market and for the determination of the price of products. Such fights went on between merchants and workers in the putting-out system of domestic handicraft during the transition to modern times. Since it is quite a general phenomenon we must mention here that the class antagonisms that are conditioned through the market situation are usually most bitter between those who actually and directly participate as opponents in price wars. It is not the rentier, the share-holder, and the banker who suffer the ill will of the worker, but almost exclusively the manufacturer and the business executives who are the direct opponents of workers in price wars. This is so in spite of the fact that it is precisely the cash boxes of the rentier, the share-holder, and the banker into which the more or less 'unearned' gains flow, rather than into the pockets of the manufacturers or of the business executives. This simple state of affairs has very frequently been decisive for the role the class situation has played in the formation of political parties. For example, it has made possible the varieties of patriarchal socialism and the frequent attempts—formerly, at least—of threatened status groups to form alliances with the proletariat against the 'bourgeoisie.'

5: Status Honor

In contrast to classes, *status groups* are normally communities. They are, however, often of an amorphous kind. In contrast to the purely economically determined 'class situation' we wish to designate as 'status situation' every typical component of the life fate of men that is determined by a specific, positive or negative, social estimation of *honor*. This honor may be connected with any quality shared by a plurality, and, of course, it can be knit to a class situation: class distinctions are linked in the most varied ways with status distinctions. Property as such is not always recognized as a status qualification, but in the long run it is, and with extraordinary regularity. In the subsistence economy of the organized neighborhood, very often the richest man is simply the chieftain. However, this often means only an honorific preference. For example, in the so-called pure modern 'democracy,' that is, one devoid of any expressly ordered status privileges for individuals, it may be that only the families coming under approximately the same tax class dance with one another. This example is reported of certain smaller Swiss cities. But status honor need not necessarily be linked with a 'class situation.' On the contrary, it normally stands in sharp opposition to the pretensions of sheer property.

Both propertied and propertyless people can belong to the same status group, and frequently they do with very tangible consequences. This 'equality' of social esteem may, however, in the long run become quite precarious. The 'equality' of status among the American 'gentlemen,' for instance, is expressed by the fact that outside the subordination determined by the different functions of 'business,' it would be considered strictly repugnant—wherever the old tradition still prevails—if even the richest 'chief,' while playing billiards or cards in his club in the evening, would not treat his 'clerk' as in every sense fully his equal in birthright. It would be repugnant if the American 'chief' would bestow upon his 'clerk' the condescending 'benevolence' marking a distinction of 'position,' which the German chief can never dissever from his attitude. This is one of the most important reasons why in America the German 'clubby-ness' has never been able to attain the attraction that the American clubs have.

6: Guarantees of Status Stratification

In content, status honor is normally expressed by the fact that above all else a specific *style of life* can be expected from all those who wish to belong to the circle. Linked with this expectation are restrictions on 'social' intercourse (that is, intercourse which is not subservient to economic or any other of business's 'functional' purposes). These restrictions may confine normal marriages to within the status circle and may lead to complete endogamous closure. As soon as there is not a mere individual and socially irrelevant imitation of another style of life, but an agreed-upon communal action of this closing character, the 'status' development is under way.

In its characteristic form, stratification by 'status groups' on the basis of conventional styles of life evolves at the present time in the United States out of the traditional democracy. For example, only the resident of a certain street ('the street') is considered as belonging to 'society,' is qualified for social intercourse, and is visited and invited. Above all, this differentiation evolves in such a way as to make for strict submission to the fashion that is dominant at a given time in society. This submission to fashion also exists among men in America to a degree unknown in Germany. Such submission is considered to be an indication of the fact that a given man *pretends* to qualify as a gentleman. This submission decides, at least *prima facie,* that he will be treated as such. And this recognition becomes just as important for his employment chances in 'swank' establishments, and above all, for social intercourse and marriage with 'esteemed' families, as the qualification for dueling among Germans in the Kaiser's day. As for the rest: certain families resident for a long time, and, of course, correspondingly wealthy, e.g. 'F. F. V., i.e. First Families of Virginia,' or the actual or alleged descendants of the 'Indian Princess' Pocahontas, of the Pilgrim fathers, or of the Knickerbockers, the members of almost inaccessible sects and all sorts of circles setting themselves apart by means of any other characteristics and badges . . . all these elements usurp 'status' honor. The development of status is essentially a question of stratification resting upon usurpation. Such usurpation is the normal origin of almost all status honor. But the road from this purely conventional situation to legal privilege, positive or negative, is easily traveled as soon as a certain stratification of the social order has in fact been 'lived in' and has achieved stability by virtue of a stable distribution of economic power.

7: 'ETHNIC' SEGREGATION AND 'CASTE'

Where the consequences have been realized to their full extent, the status group evolves into a closed 'caste.' Status distinctions are then guaranteed not merely by conventions and laws, but also by *rituals.* This occurs in such a way that every physical contact with a member of any caste that is considered to be 'lower' by the members of a 'higher' caste is considered as making for a ritualistic impurity and to be a stigma which must be expiated by a religious act. Individual castes develop quite distinct cults and gods.

In general, however, the status structure reaches such extreme consequences only where there are underlying differences which are held to be 'ethnic.' The 'caste' is, indeed, the normal form in which ethnic communities usually live side by side in a 'societalized' manner. These ethnic communities believe in blood relationship and exclude exogamous marriage and social intercourse. Such a caste situation is part of the phenomenon of 'pariah' peoples and is found all over the world. These people form communities, acquire specific occupational traditions of handicrafts or of other arts, and cultivate a belief in their ethnic community. They live in a 'diaspora' strictly segregated from all personal intercourse, except that of an unavoidable sort, and their situation is legally precarious. Yet, by virtue of their economic indispensability, they are tolerated, indeed, frequently privileged, and they live in interspersed political communities. The Jews are the most impressive historical example.

A 'status' segregation grown into a 'caste' differs in its structure from a mere 'ethnic' segregation: the caste structure transforms the horizontal and unconnected coexistences of ethnically segregated groups into a vertical social system of super- and subordination. Correctly formulated: a comprehensive societalization integrates the ethnically divided communities into specific political and communal action. In their consequences they differ precisely in this way: ethnic coexistences condition a mutual repulsion and disdain but allow each ethnic community to consider its own honor as the highest one; the caste structure brings about a social subordination and an acknowledgment of 'more honor' in favor of the privileged caste and status groups. This is due to the fact that in the caste structure ethnic distinctions as such have become 'functional' distinctions within the political societalization (warriors, priests, artisans that are politically important for war and for building, and so on). But even pariah people who are most despised are usually apt to continue cultivating in some manner that which is equally peculiar to ethnic and to status communities: the belief in their own specific 'honor.' This is the case with the Jews.

Only with the negatively privileged status groups does the 'sense of dignity' take a specific deviation. A sense of dignity is the precipitation in individuals of social honor and of conventional demands which a positively privileged status group raises for the deportment of its members. The sense of dignity that characterizes positively privileged status groups is naturally related to their 'being' which does not transcend itself, that is, it is to their 'beauty and excellence' (καλο-κἀγαϑια). Their kingdom is 'of this world.' They live for the present and by exploiting their great past. The sense of dignity of the negatively privileged strata naturally refers to a future lying beyond the present, whether it is of this life or of another. In other words, it must be nurtured by the belief in a providential 'mission' and by a belief in a specific honor before God. The 'chosen people's' dignity is nurtured by a belief either that in the beyond 'the last will be the first,' or that in this life a Messiah will appear to bring forth into the light of the world which has cast them out the hidden honor of the pariah people. This simple state of affairs, and not the 'resentment' which is so strongly emphasized in Nietzsche's much admired construction in the *Genealogy of Morals,* is the source of the religiosity cultivated by pariah status groups. In passing, we may note that resentment may be accurately applied only to a limited extent; for one of Nietzsche's main examples, Buddhism, it is not at all applicable.

Incidentally, the development of status groups from ethnic segregations is by no means the normal phenomenon. On the contrary, since objective 'racial differences' are by no means basic to every subjective sentiment of an ethnic community, the ultimately racial foundation of status structure is rightly and absolutely a question of the concrete individual case. Very frequently a status group is instrumental in the production of a thoroughbred anthropological type. Certainly a status group is to a high degree effective in producing extreme types, for they select personally qualified individuals (e.g. the Knighthood selects those who are fit for warfare, physically and psychically). But selection is far from being the only, or the predominant, way in which status groups are formed: Political membership or class situation has at all times been at least as frequently decisive. And today the class situation is by far the predominant factor, for of course the possibility of a style of life expected for members of a status group is usually conditioned economically.

8: Status Privileges

For all practical purposes, stratification by status goes hand in hand with a monopolization of ideal and material goods or opportunities, in a manner we have come to know as typical. Besides the specific status

honor, which always rests upon distance and exclusiveness, we find all
sorts of material monopolies. Such honorific preferences may consist
of the privilege of wearing special costumes, of eating special dishes
taboo to others, of carrying arms—which is most obvious in its consequences—the right to pursue certain non-professional dilettante artistic
practices, e.g. to play certain musical instruments. Of course, material
monopolies provide the most effective motives for the exclusiveness of a
status group; although, in themselves, they are rarely sufficient, almost
always they come into play to some extent. Within a status circle there
is the question of intermarriage: the interest of the families in the
monopolization of potential bridegrooms is at least of equal importance
and is parallel to the interest in the monopolization of daughters. The
daughters of the circle must be provided for. With an increased inclosure
of the status group, the conventional preferential opportunities for special
employment grow into a legal monopoly of special offices for the members. Certain goods become objects for monopolization by status groups.
In the typical fashion these include 'entailed estates' and frequently also
the possessions of serfs or bondsmen and, finally, special trades. This
monopolization occurs positively when the status group is exclusively entitled to own and to manage them; and negatively when, in order to
maintain its specific way of life, the status group must *not* own and
manage them.

The decisive role of a 'style of life' in status 'honor' means that status
groups are the specific bearers of all 'conventions.' In whatever way it
may be manifest, all 'stylization' of life either originates in status groups
or is at least conserved by them. Even if the principles of status conventions differ greatly, they reveal certain typical traits, especially among
those strata which are most privileged. Quite generally, among privileged
status groups there is a status disqualification that operates against the
performance of common physical labor. This disqualification is now
'setting in' in America against the old tradition of esteem for labor.
Very frequently every rational economic pursuit, and especially 'entrepreneurial activity,' is looked upon as a disqualification of status. Artistic
and literary activity is also considered as degrading work as soon as it is
exploited for income, or at least when it is connected with hard physical
exertion. An example is the sculptor working like a mason in his dusty
smock as over against the painter in his salon-like 'studio' and those
forms of musical practice that are acceptable to the status group.

9: Economic Conditions and Effects of Status Stratification

The frequent disqualification of the gainfully employed as such is a direct result of the principle of status stratification peculiar to the social order, and of course, of this principle's opposition to a distribution of power which is regulated exclusively through the market. These two factors operate along with various individual ones, which will be touched upon below.

We have seen above that the market and its processes 'knows no personal distinctions': 'functional' interests dominate it. It knows nothing of 'honor.' The status order means precisely the reverse, viz.: stratification in terms of 'honor' and of styles of life peculiar to status groups as such. If mere economic acquisition and naked economic power still bearing the stigma of its extra-status origin could bestow upon anyone who has won it the same honor as those who are interested in status by virtue of style of life claim for themselves, the status order would be threatened at its very root. This is the more so as, given equality of status honor, property *per se* represents an addition even if it is not overtly acknowledged to be such. Yet if such economic acquisition and power gave the agent any honor at all, his wealth would result in his attaining more honor than those who successfully claim honor by virtue of style of life. Therefore all groups having interests in the status order react with special sharpness precisely against the pretensions of purely economic acquisition. In most cases they react the more vigorously the more they feel themselves threatened. Calderon's respectful treatment of the peasant, for instance, as opposed to Shakespeare's simultaneous and ostensible disdain of the *canaille* illustrates the different way in which a firmly structured status order reacts as compared with a status order that has become economically precarious. This is an example of a state of affairs that recurs everywhere. Precisely because of the rigorous reactions against the claims of property *per se,* the 'parvenu' is never accepted, personally and without reservation, by the privileged status groups, no matter how completely his style of life has been adjusted to theirs. They will only accept his descendants who have been educated in the conventions of their status group and who have never besmirched its honor by their own economic labor.

As to the general *effect* of the status order, only one consequence can be stated, but it is a very important one: the hindrance of the free de-

velopment of the market occurs first for those goods which status groups
directly withheld from free exchange by monopolization. This monopolization may be effected either legally or conventionally. For example, in
many Hellenic cities during the epoch of status groups, and also originally
in Rome, the inherited estate (as is shown by the old formula for indic-
tion against spendthrifts) was monopolized just as were the estates of
knights, peasants, priests, and especially the clientele of the craft and
merchant guilds. The market is restricted, and the power of naked property *per se,* which gives its stamp to 'class formation,' is pushed into the
background. The results of this process can be most varied. Of course,
they do not necessarily weaken the contrasts in the economic situation.
Frequently they strengthen these contrasts, and in any case, where stratification by status permeates a community as strongly as was the case
in all political communities of antiquity and of the Middle Ages, one can
never speak of a genuinely free market competition as we understand
it today. There are wider effects than this direct exclusion of special
goods from the market. From the contrariety between the status order
and the purely economic order mentioned above, it follows that in
most instances the notion of honor peculiar to status absolutely
abhors that which is essential to the market: higgling. Honor abhors
higgling among peers and occasionally it taboos higgling for the members of a status group in general. Therefore, everywhere some status
groups, and usually the most influential, consider almost any kind of
overt participation in economic acquisition as absolutely stigmatizing.

With some over-simplification, one might thus say that 'classes' are
stratified according to their relations to the production and acquisition
of goods; whereas 'status groups' are stratified according to the principles
of their *consumption* of goods as represented by special 'styles of life.'

An 'occupational group' is also a status group. For normally, it successfully claims social honor only by virtue of the special style of life which
may be determined by it. The differences between classes and status
groups frequently overlap. It is precisely those status communities most
strictly segregated in terms of honor (viz. the Indian castes) who today
show, although within very rigid limits, a relatively high degree of indifference to pecuniary income. However, the Brahmins seek such income in many different ways.

As to the general economic conditions making for the predominance
of stratification by 'status,' only very little can be said. When the bases of
the acquisition and distribution of goods are relatively stable, stratifica-

tion by status is favored. Every technological repercussion and economic transformation threatens stratification by status and pushes the class situation into the foreground. Epochs and countries in which the naked class situation is of predominant significance are regularly the periods of technical and economic transformations. And every slowing down of the shifting of economic stratifications leads, in due course, to the growth of status structures and makes for a resuscitation of the important role of social honor.

10: Parties

Whereas the genuine place of 'classes' is within the economic order, the place of 'status groups' is within the social order, that is, within the sphere of the distribution of 'honor.' From within these spheres, classes and status groups influence one another and they influence the legal order and are in turn influenced by it. But 'parties' live in a house of 'power.'

Their action is oriented toward the acquisition of social 'power,' that is to say, toward influencing a communal action no matter what its content may be. In principle, parties may exist in a social 'club' as well as in a 'state.' As over against the actions of classes and status groups, for which this is not necessarily the case, the communal actions of 'parties' always mean a societalization. For party actions are always directed toward a goal which is striven for in planned manner. This goal may be a 'cause' (the party may aim at realizing a program for ideal or material purposes), or the goal may be 'personal' (sinecures, power, and from these, honor for the leader and the followers of the party). Usually the party action aims at all these simultaneously. Parties are, therefore, only possible within communities that are societalized, that is, which have some rational order and a staff of persons available who are ready to enforce it. For parties aim precisely at influencing this staff, and if possible, to recruit it from party followers.

In any individual case, parties may represent interests determined through 'class situation' or 'status situation,' and they may recruit their following respectively from one or the other. But they need be neither purely 'class' nor purely 'status' parties. In most cases they are partly class parties and partly status parties, but sometimes they are neither. They may represent ephemeral or enduring structures. Their means of attaining power may be quite varied, ranging from naked violence of any sort to canvassing for votes with coarse or subtle means: money, social influence, the force of speech, suggestion, clumsy hoax, and so on to the rougher or more artful tactics of obstruction in parliamentary bodies.

The sociological structure of parties differs in a basic way according to the kind of communal action which they struggle to influence. Parties also differ according to whether or not the community is stratified by status or by classes. Above all else, they vary according to the structure of domination within the community. For their leaders normally deal with the conquest of a community. They are, in the general concept which is maintained here, not only products of specially modern forms of domination. We shall also designate as parties the ancient and medieval 'parties,' despite the fact that their structure differs basically from the structure of modern parties. By virtue of these structural differences of domination it is impossible to say anything about the structure of parties without discussing the structural forms of social domination *per se.* Parties, which are always structures struggling for domination, are very frequently organized in a very strict 'authoritarian' fashion. . .

Concerning 'classes,' 'status groups,' and 'parties,' it must be said in general that they necessarily presuppose a comprehensive societalization, and especially a political framework of communal action, within which they operate. This does not mean that parties would be confined by the frontiers of any individual political community. On the contrary, at all times it has been the order of the day that the societalization (even when it aims at the use of military force in common) reaches beyond the frontiers of politics. This has been the case in the solidarity of interests among the Oligarchs and among the democrats in Hellas, among the Guelfs and among Ghibellines in the Middle Ages, and within the Calvinist party during the period of religious struggles. It has been the case up to the solidarity of the landlords (international congress of agrarian landlords), and has continued among princes (holy alliance, Karlsbad decrees), socialist workers, conservatives (the longing of Prussian conservatives for Russian intervention in 1850). But their aim is not necessarily the establishment of new international political, i.e. *territorial,* dominion. In the main they aim to influence the existing dominion.*

* The posthumously published text breaks off here. We omit an incomplete sketch of types of 'warrior estates.'

CHAPTER 4

Caste, Class and Slavery: The Taxonomic Problem

EDMUND R. LEACH

O NE might be forgiven for supposing, from the programme of this symposium, that underlying it is the assumption that any form of rigid social hierarchy is a form of oppression. "Racism"—that is, the exploitation of ethnic difference as a badge of social inferiority—is, by implication, a monstrous affair and "caste difference" belongs to the same order of social phenomena. Indeed, our chairman, Professor Myrdal, is one of those who have equated colour bar segregation in the Southern States of the United States with caste difference. And because colour bar segregation in the United States developed out of an institution of chattel slavery there is a tendency in some quarters to think that the words "caste", "race" and "slavery" are all very much of a muchness. If we add to this the Marxist notion of a class war, we have a whole series of words which are quite deplorably confused. I do not think we shall make matters any better if we try to establish artificial definitions, for the words "caste", "class", "slavery" and "race" all have a long history of ambiguity. In common parlance the meanings overlap. But at the beginning of a symposium such as this it may be useful to try to indicate some of the sources of this ambiguity. "Race" is a problem for others; my commission is to try to distinguish the three key words "caste", "class" and "slavery". I will discuss them one by one and then see how they fit together.

The most general of these words is "class", so let me take it first. Classification is an essential element of the thinking process as such. We are already conceptualizing human beings as belonging to social classes as soon as we distinguish males from females or parents from children. Of course this is *not* what we mean when we talk about social class but it shows that we need to be careful. Classes are not things which exist "out there", they are not a part of God's truth; they are mental configurations. But whose mental configurations? Are social classes invented by the Registrar General, by politicians, by social scientists or simply by general public opinion? It would take a month of Sundays to give a satisfactory answer to such a question ... the only point I want to make here is that different kinds of people mean totally different things when they talk about social class and anyone who wants to understand sociological or political arguments on this theme needs to keep this ambiguity constantly in mind.

Three varieties of the concept of social class seem especially relevant. First there is what one might call the "degenerate Marxist view". Society as a whole is viewed as a battleground between the *haves* and the *have-nots*, the ruling class and the proletariat. Class membership depends upon the individual's position in the socio-economic scale, more particularly on whether he is an employer or a worker. Important aspects of this kind of model are: (*a*) it is taken for granted that members of a socio-economic class have an intrinsic tendency to act corporately in support of class interests; (*b*) the structure is presumed to be unstable—in due time the lower exploited class will inevitably overthrow its oppressors; (*c*) the class war thesis implies a two-tiered model: there is no room for a neutral middle class and everyone must take sides either with the oppressors or with the oppressed.

Secondly, I would distinguish a "degenerate Max Weber view". Here the two-tiered class war is replaced by an elaborate hierarchy of professional status groups. It is assumed that social class is determined by occupation rather than by control over economic resources. It is again assumed that members of a class tend to act corporately in support of class interests. This scheme is an equilibrium model, not a self-destructive revolutionary model. The "Marxist" and the "Weberian" conceptions both suppose that classes are distinct without much cross-cutting of categories. In other words, each social class has a kind of sub-culture of its own within the wider whole. Up to a point, this last detail is empirically verifiable. In England, for example, we can readily distinguish social groups employing different verbal vocabularies with different accents and maintaining modes of life which are really quite distinct from those of other groups with which they are in close territorial contact. But how do these "sub-culture classes" fit into the concepts of the class war or the status hierarchy? It is very difficult to say. What is quite clear is that while the sub-culture groups certainly "exist", awareness of their existence is a very subjective matter. Their boundaries are *not* sharply defined and only very rarely can members of such a class be tricked into displaying corporate solidarity. Yet in some ways this third very ill-defined type of class concept, the "degenerate culture group view", has much more practical relevance than the highly artificial constructs of the politicians and the sociologists. Ask yourself the simple question: "How do *I* recognize others who are of the same class as myself?" You do not enquire about their finances or their occupation; you respond directly to the way they talk, the sort of standards of life they maintain, the interests they display. The Registrar General's class categories are based strictly on income and on the assumption that everyone who is in the same kind of job leads the same kind of life. This may be good enough as a rough and ready measure for the purposes of an advertising campaign, but it does not correspond to social reality. The people whom *I* recognize as "*my* social class" have an extremely wide range of incomes and engage in a very wide range of occupations, and conversely the people who have similar incomes to myself or who engage in similar occupations to myself are by no means necessarily "of the same social class" . . . *in the sub-culture sense.*

One reason why the sub-culture type of class is important is that members of the same sub-culture tend to intermarry and this means that any cultural attribute of such a class becomes hereditary. Consequently those sub-culture classes which have a traditional concern for the conservation of assets perpetuate themselves not merely as sub-cultures but also as units of political and economic power. It is here, of course, that we get a tie-up with the other models. In the Marxist scheme the landed gentry and the *bourgeoisie* both show a concern for the conservation of assets which is lacking among the proletariat. The decision as to whether a middle-class individual will choose to support the oppressors or the oppressed depends upon whether or not he possesses hereditable capital assets.

Let me sum up this section: A general way of life, a sub-culture, tends to be hereditary because (*a*) individuals from the same sub-culture tend to intermarry, and (*b*) parents bring up their children to imitate themselves. When politicians talk about social class they are not thinking of people who share a general way of life so much as corporate groups which have differing degrees of privilege and unequal access to productive resources. Where there exists a "sub-culture class" which possesses exclusive privileges it is certainly likely to act corporately in such a way as to make those privileges hereditary. There can thus be *some* situations in which the "economic-interest social class" of the politician is *also* "a sub-culture class". But the two types of social classification are intrinsically quite different and we need to remember this. Reference-group statements of the kind "X and Y are of the same social class" are often, perhaps usually, highly ambiguous. We should also remember that the Marxist concept of "the class war" has its Utopian counterpart "the classless society". The latter concept seems to me a purely religious idea comparable to the notion of "life after death". It may signify something for the devout but in strictly semantic terms it can mean nothing whatever.

Let me now say something about "caste". In contemporary

literature we meet with the word "caste" in two quite different contexts. On the one hand it is a word used without any particular geographical limitation to denote a type of class system in which hierarchy is very sharply defined and in which the boundaries between the different layers of the hierarchy are rigidly fixed. A "ruling class" may be described as a *caste* when the fact of class endogamy is strikingly obvious and when the inheritance of privilege has become narrowly restricted to members of that "caste" in perpetuity. This kind of situation is likely to arise when the ruling group is distinguished from the inferior group or groups by *wide* differences of standard of living or by other easily recognized labels. Obvious examples are the colour bar situation in the Southern States of the United States and in South Africa, where ideas of social class, hierarchy and privilege are conveniently supported by visible differences of skin colour in the population.

The *other* use of the word "caste" is to define the system of social organization found in traditional India and surviving to a large extent to the present day. I myself consider that, as sociologists, we shall be well advised to restrict the use of the term *caste* to the Indian phenomenon only. In what follows I shall therefore ignore the fact that some writers mean by caste only a special form of class hierarchy.

The endogamy of English social classes is a tendency only and the groups so formed are ill-defined and unnamed; in India, on the other hand, endogamy is a basic principle. This has the consequence that all members of "my sub-caste" (*jāti*) are my kinsmen and, *vice versa*, all my kinsmen are members of my sub-caste. The sub-caste groups thus formed are clearly defined. Each individual is born into a particular named group which is the same as that of both his parents and he or she remains a member of that group throughout life.

The terminology is tricky. In India these endogamous groups of kin which lead a distinctive way of life are usually known as *jāti*. But the word *jāti* is also used for other groups which are not of this

distinctive endogamous kind. English writers sometimes refer to
the endogamous kin groups as castes and sometimes as sub-castes.
I will here call them sub-castes. The membership of a single sub-
caste is hardly likely to number more than a few thousand. All
members will usually live within a restricted area and share a
distinctive religious cult.

Within India as a whole there are a vast number of such sub-
castes but within any one local area there are not likely to be more
than about twenty. Within such a local area each individual will be
able to identify members of his own sub-caste and to arrange all
other sub-castes known to him in some kind of hierarchy. There is
unlikely to be complete agreement between different informants
on the details of this hierarchy, but there will be fairly general
consensus in terms of two frames of reference. On the one hand
sub-castes are ranked according to their ritual purity, with
Brahmans at the top and "untouchables" at the bottom; on the
other they are ranked according to their political–economic status
in the local (traditional) feudal order, with landlords at the top,
free tenants below, "tied" tenants below that and landless
labourers at the bottom, with certain artisan groups such as
blacksmiths somewhere in the middle.

The two frames are not entirely coincident and it is easier for a
group to raise its economic status than to improve its ritual
respectability, but nevertheless there is a broad correspondence.
Landlords tend to be members of "clean" or "very clean" sub-
castes; landless labourers tend to be members of "untouchable"
sub-castes, as do also the "tied" tenants who are commonly
required to fulfil ritual services (such as temple drumming) as part
of their feudal duty. In order to justify this grading of sub-castes in
terms of ritual purity informants will usually refer to the model
provided by the four *varna* of ancient literature. This classical
model is a binary scheme based on the following principles. Human
beings are either within society or outside it; if they are within
society they are either superior persons (twice-born) or ordinary
persons; if they are twice-born they are either holy men (Brah-

mans) or secular men; if they are twice-born secular men they are either princes or merchants.

This ancient classification provided a five-layered model of Brahmans (priests), Kshatriya (princes), Vaishya (merchants), Shudra (ordinary people) and polluted outsiders. The advantages of education and political and economic power were an exclusive privilege of the top three grades—the twice-born.

In the classical literature this social system is presented to us as one of complete inflexibility. The first essential of moral duty is that of resignation and acceptance. The individual gains personal merit by fulfilling the tasks which are proper to the station into which he has been born. The humblest and most menial polluted individual can thus be just as virtuous as the most saintly Brahman priest: the rewards for virtue will come in the next life.

Even today Indian ethical theory declares that moral rules differ widely between different castes and sub-castes. There are no universal principles of right and wrong. A man has a duty to accept the rules of his own caste. It is a sin to imitate the behaviour of others even when the others rank high in the hierarchy of public esteem.

Since modern India does not have a feudal type of political structure one might suppose that the logic of the *varṇa* scheme has no relevance to present conditions, but in fact it is still used as an explanatory device to show why sub-castes are felt to stand in a hierarchy of intrinsic purity. In particular, sub-castes are allocated to one or other of three major divisions: (*i*) Brahmans (*ii*) clean non-Brahmans and (*iii*) polluted non-Brahmans, and these three categories are treated as approximately the equivalent of the *varṇa* types: twice-born Brahman, Shudra and "untouchable". This classification is based principally on occupation. Each sub-caste is associated with a "traditional occupation" along with the theory that, in the ancient feudal system, the members of that sub-caste alone could (and must) fulfil the functions of that particular occupation. Such traditional occupations are felt to differ in their intrinsic purity. For example, it is polluting to touch carcases of dead creatures and in consequence all members of any sub-caste which is associated with this polluting activity, such as leather-workers or fishermen, are felt to be relatively impure as compared with, say, the members of a sub-caste of vegetarian rice farmers.

In former times sub-castes belonging to the Shudra and "outsider" groups were the feudal serfs of the twice-born landlords. But the servile status of the inferior groups was ambivalent. It carried rights as well as duties. The Shudra were (in general) persons of tenant status who held their land in return for an obligation to perform feudal services of an artisan type for the landlords. The "outsider" groups were feudal dependants of the landlords in a *more* servile status. The latter were seldom actual tenants of land but they had the right to employment as agricultural labourers in return for performing polluting menial services. They also had the *right* to receive support from their superior landlords in times of famine and these rights could be very important.

At the beginning of the nineteenth century the British administrators tended to interpret the status of these servile outsiders as that of *slavery* and in the enthusiasm for abolishing slavery which prevailed in the 1820's, the *legal* rights of the feudal lords over their servile dependants were abolished. This "liberation" of the servile sub-castes did not in fact improve their economic status. It may indeed have made it much worse. It had consequences for the very poor rather similar to those of the enclosure acts in seventeenth and eighteenth century England.

This brings me to *slavery*. This is a term used in the most loose manner to describe all kinds of conditions of servile status. We get very confused about this because we have ideological reactions to the word "freedom", which we think of as something both desirable and attainable. What we really mean by *freedom* is debatable, but the concept came into European thought as an antithesis to that of *slavery*. Free men were those who were *not* slaves, though of course their "freedom" depended on the fact that there were slaves to do the dirty work! In reality social man can never be absolutely free and the age-old core of all political arguments is the problem of how to decide just how much un-freedom he must be prepared to accept. "Slavery" tends to be a political propaganda word used by those who object to one form of un-freedom while tacitly accepting another.

It is possible to distinguish certain major types of un-free status which have at different times been labelled as "slavery".

At one extreme there is pure chattel slavery of the type which prevailed in colonial Latin America and also in the Southern States of the United States in the eighteenth and early nineteenth centuries. Here the rights of the master over his slave were indistinguishable from the rights he would exercise over a cow or a dog. It should be emphasized that *this* form of slavery has historically been somewhat unusual though it has cropped up in other situations, notably in ancient Athens and in other parts of the ancient classical world.

At the opposite extreme we meet with various institutions which are sometimes labelled debt-slavery or bond-slavery. In this system an individual mortgages his person as guarantee for a debt. The bond-slave remains a human being in the fullest sense and it is by no means clear to me why institutions of this kind should be considered objectionable; indeed they only become objectionable when Europeans for reasons of their own label them as "slavery". It is very significant that in a great many societies where institutions of this kind have been closely studied, it is found that the status of the "bond-slave" in respect of his master is very close indeed to that of a "son-in-law".

In between these two extremes of the chattel slave whose servility is quite involuntary and the bond-slave whose servility is optional, we meet with a whole range of variations, some of which are described in the literature as "slavery" and some as "serfdom". The most common features of such un-freedom are that the slave or serf is under an obligation to pursue a certain type of occupation in a particular place and that parts of the fruits of his labour accrue to the "owner" of the slave, and that his or her marital arrangements are made under the control of the "owner". But within this limiting definition we meet with very great variation in the degree of free enterprise which the "slave" may undertake. Further, it is important to recognize that in the overall hierarchy, a slave is not necessarily at the bottom. In the seraglio of the Ottoman sultans all the women, and there were about 2,000 of them, were "slaves". Although the life prospects of some of these women were undoubtedly precarious, their status was certainly not low and one or other of them was destined to be the mother of the next Sultan! Likewise, all the administrative officers of the Turkish Empire were legally in the status of slave.

The ambiguities of this particular word are indeed so confusing that sociologists might be well advised to eliminate it from their discussions altogether. When one tries to understand the literature on this topic, two cross-cutting variables often prove to be relevant. Of anyone who is alleged to be a "slave" we need to ask not only "Is his position high or low in the total hierarchy?" but also "Does he have recognized kinship links with persons other than his master?" In many social systems a good working definition of a slave would be "a man or woman who has no recognized kin outside his owner's family (*familia*)".

Let me sum up. Class, Caste, Slavery ... each of these words is liable to carry overtones which suggest the exploitation of the underprivileged by the overprivileged. In the context of this symposium we need to be on our guard against initial prejudices of this sort. Marxism has so infected our thinking that we not only take it for granted that it is in the nature of modern society that there should be a class struggle but we are also inclined to believe that unqualified equality, unqualified freedom and the utopia of a classless society are sensible political goals for all right-thinking men. May I urge you most strongly to draw a distinction between political slogans and sociological categories? Freedom and classlessness are political ideas; they have no place in sociological analysis, which must necessarily be concerned with social constraints and status differences. The word *slavery* (as we use it today) suggests that we can readily distinguish between social constraints which are morally justifiable and those which are not. I deny this. If we call a particular Soviet institution a "slave labour camp" we are saying it is bad; if we call a rather similar English institution an "open prison" we are saying it is good. This is simply prejudice. We need to analyse the forms of un-freedom but if we are to do this sensibly we should keep away from contentious labels. Likewise with *class*. *Of course* we think of society as made up of classes; we can even demonstrate that, up to a point, these classes have objective existence; but it is a mistake to think that such classes must *inevitably* be arranged as strata in a hierarchy. Because some very important social classes possess political and economic privilege it does not follow that this is the *only* principle in terms of which classes may be formed. And as an anthropologist I would urge my sociological colleagues to pay more attention to endogamy and less to economic factors when they are considering these matters.

Most members of this symposium share a common European liberal ethic. We assume that men are born equal. We must remember that this is a judgement and not a fact. Social systems different from our own rest on different assumptions. In particular, systems of the feudal type (taking feudal in a wide sense) have presupposed that men are born unequal and that the individual's prime moral duty is to fulfil the duties which are proper to his natural station. In such systems the Protestant ethic of self-improvement—the aspiration to rise from Private to Field Marshal—is tantamount to grievous sin. The traditional Indian caste order was a feudal system in this sense and we only invite confusion if we use the word *caste* in contexts where differential status is open to challenge.

In colour bar situations such as those found in South Africa and the southern United States the privileged whites assert that it is the "natural condition" of the Negroes that they should be in an inferior status, and this valuation, as well as the emphasis on status group endogamy, is certainly reminiscent of Indian caste. But there are also great differences. In the South African and American situations members of the "inferior" group do *not* accept their inferiority and on that account the total situation becomes one of oppression, so much so that the dominant white group virtually has to take up arms to protect itself against the revolutionary ferment among the Negroes. Revolts of the underprivileged have occurred in India also, but to suggest that the Indian caste order is simply a complicated kind of colour bar situation with all its attendant forms of tyranny and exploitation is grossly misleading. The converse is likewise true. Within India itself the relation between the residue of the old caste order and the newly emergent class order is one of great complexity and great sociological importance. This relationship needs close analysis but we shall certainly fog the whole issue if we use our basic category words in such a way that *caste* appears to be nothing more than a peculiarly ossified form of *class*.

CHAPTER 5

Organized Dependency Relations and Social Stratification

ARTHUR L. STINCHCOMBE

The study of social stratification in modern society has moved in the direction of the study of allocation processes in stratification systems rather than problems of *class relations,* which were the classical concerns. That is, the tendency is to ask how prestige is distributed among occupations rather than how men with "superior" occupations treat men with "inferior" ones; or to ask what social class power elites are drawn from, rather than what powerful people can get others to do; or to ask whether America is becoming a middle-class society, rather than whether all classes are now obliged to treat everyone as if he were middle class. Rates of social mobility are studied, rather than comparing what men get in terms of deference, submission, and privileges when they are socially mobile. The main exceptions to this trend occur—for good reasons—in monographs like Bendix's *Work and Authority in Industry* (1956) or Dahrendorf's *Class and Class Conflict in Industrial Society* (1959), which treat the stratification system in relation to the organizational life of the society. The reasons for the close relation between organizational life and class relations will become clearer if a few conceptual problems are discussed first.

An organization, like other social groups, is something of a "community of fate."

That is, either through psychological mechanisms like identification or through reward systems, an aggregate becomes a group to the degree that damage to the collectivity (or its members) is "bad" for the individual, and success of the collectivity is "good." But an organization differs from other communities of fate in that it is deliberately designed to reward people in such a way that they are better off if some specialized purpose is achieved, and worse off (punished, wages lowered, careers cut off, or honor smirched) if the purpose is not achieved. A community of fate is more binding to the degree to which its members are *dependent* on the group for all their satisfactions. If children could choose their parents, they would not as often develop dependency relations with them.

Organizations are among the groups where the community of fate is shared *among unequals* (families are, of course, another). Furthermore, these unequals are in different social classes, and are often not psychologically intimately identified with one another. Outside organizations, the social classes tend to be segregated from one another, in residence, in cultural milieu, in circles of friends, in marriage. Organizational activity is in fact the main place where social classes *meet* on a continuous basis. Just as studies of the relations between generations would be almost without body unless families and schools were studied, the relations between classes disappear from studies of stratification not explicitly concerned with the analysis of organizations.

The upper classes occupy the higher positions within organizations (in modern society, largely because class position is derived from organizational position; in ascriptive societies, because the derivation is the other way around).[26] In general, the fate of the organizational elite is more closely tied to the fate of the organization than is that of their "inferiors." This is so for several reasons. In the first place, organizational prestige is translated quite directly into personal prestige of the elite. Hopkins full professors are held in high regard as much for the merit of Johns Hopkins as for their personal accomplishments, if only because most of the people who admire them are incapable of judging their accomplishments. Elite value commitments are often, for various reasons, more directly related to organizational goals than are commitments of subordinates, and there is also the matter of elite appropriation of money and other profits of the organization.

This implies that a central variable in the relations between subordinates and superiors, and consequently between the classes of society, is the degree of dependency of the inferiors on the organization. For if the inferiors are not dependent (while the superiors almost always are), then the superiors are dependent on the consent of the inferiors. The more the subordinate's needs

and wants are met by the organization, the more the superior controls the flow of these satisfactions, and the less the subordinate could meet these needs elsewhere, the less the upper classes have to court the subordinate's consent and compliance. To take extreme examples, a senator is surely a member of the upper classes in prestige, money, and power, and so is a general. But a senator meets the lower classes in a situation in which his fate is tied to the fate of the party organization, while theirs is only if he can convince them that it is. He meets the lower classes as a supplicant for their support of his organization in a context where the alternative organization they might support is all too obvious. The general meets the lower classes in a context in which the alternatives to obedience are unpleasant, where he controls most of the sources of those little gratifications that make life bearable. It hardly needs emphasis that the rhetoric and etiquette of relations between the classes are different when they meet at election time than when they meet on a military post.

The problem having been posed, this section will proceed as follows. First, some of the main conditions that determine the degree of dependency of inferiors in different types of organizations will be outlined, and a few examples of organizations, on the basis of these conditions, will be ranked by the degree of dependency of inferiors. Then, a case of the change in class relations that followed upon a change in the degree of dependency in economic organizations analyzed in detail by Weber, namely, class relations on the large landed estates of eastern Germany, will be treated.

What sort of factors, then, influence the degree of dependence of superiors on inferiors, or the degree of independence of inferiors? The following seven seem to be of the greatest importance:

1. The capacity of inferiors to organize in opposition to superiors. This capacity in turn is dependent on the structure of communications channels among inferiors and their capacity to recruit and protect a competent leadership. Urbanism, literacy, the concentration of large numbers of inferiors together in urban slums or agricultural

---

[26] But also because authority relations within an organization create "human relations problems" if the subordinates have higher outside status than superordinates. Two excellent documentations are Whyte (1948) with women giving orders to men and Bidwell (1961) with uneducated officers and noncoms giving orders to professionals who were enlisted men. Such status discrepancies are more serious if the organization is a continuing one than if it is temporary. One of Udy's results (1961) is a demonstration that temporary organizations (in his terminology, those with "low specification") need not be closely related to the statification system of the society, while continuing ones do.

villages, all tend to increase their organizational capacity. And very often in the first stages of organization, a leadership trained in other groups (such as the Methodist lay leaders in the British labor movement) or disaffected elements of the old elite are important.

2. The existence and availability of alternative sources for the satisfaction of needs now met by the superiors. Particularly if organizations compete for the services of inferiors by offering comparable terms of employment, tenancy, etc., the power of any one superior is reduced.

3. The vesting of interests of inferiors by a stable and efficient enforcement system, so that the status and rewards of inferiors are not precarious. Jobs protected by effective craft norms, peasant property defended in courts of law, tenure policies of universities supported both by civil courts and by faculty opinion, all increase the independence of inferiors.

4. All three of the above variables depend in part on the content of laws and the efficiency of their enforcement. Freedom of organization and propaganda, freedom of movement to alternative employers by labor, forbidding of blacklists to keep alternatives open, defense of freeholds in the king's court rather than in manorial courts, all are attempts, generally more or less successful, to control the degree of dependence by law.

5. The degree of institutionalized dependence of superiors on inferiors, especially by devices of free competitive election. The relation between dictatorship (that is, lack of elections) and oppression is so obvious that we usually use them as synonyms, and in this case the folk wisdom embedded in the language is quite correct.

6. It is apparently inherent in some kinds of tasks that there are alternatives available to inferiors. Any complex task requiring initiative, responsible operative decision, or sustained attention automatically provides the opportunity for "conscientious withdrawal of efficiency." Thus intensive agriculture on highly valuable land presents the possibility of a slowdown and waste of crucial resources by labor more forcibly than more extensive agriculture on cheap

land. (Often land is cheap not because of low productivity, but because it was obtained by conquest rather than free sale.) And apparently the kind of discipline required of inferiors on valuable land is more easily obtained by tenancy arrangements than by employment of agricultural labor. (For a summary of some of the evidence, see Stinchcombe, 1961, pp. pp. 169–172. See also Weber, 1924, p. 24.) Factory labor is apparently not efficiently done with unfree or coerced labor (compare Weber's discussion described above), nor can unfree agricultural labor generally stand comparison with wage labor unless it is very much cheaper per hour.

7. The nature of the ideology of superiors. Ideologies differ on the question of how independent inferiors ought to be, on whether or not it is right to use power that falls into one's hands. It is naturally difficult to assess the importance of this factor, but it seems that elites raised as Protestants or Jews differ from those raised as Catholics, that elites raised in democratic countries differ from those raised in aristocratic countries, that elites raised in traditional landholding plantation or feudal families differ from those raised in bourgeois families.[27] Protestants, democrats, bourgeois are less likely to believe in their right to use all means to reduce inferior classes to dependence, and given the same values on other variables, seem actually to exercise their powers less. (The most extensive analysis of the effect of ideology on authority relations is Bendix, 1956.) On the other hand, the reduction of Jews in Nazi concentration camps to complete dependence clearly reflected ideological pressures.

Table 2 presents an impressionistic ranking of some organizations along the dimension of the degree of dependence of inferiors on superiors. To turn to the example under the "old regime" in East German rural areas (see especially Weber, 1924, pp. 444–507. A good summary in English is Bendix, 1960, pp. 13–41. See also Wunder-

---

[27] For example, see André Siegfried's statement of the great effect of large, noble landed property on elections and the small effect of large, bourgeois property (1913, p. 304).

TABLE 2

IMPRESSIONISTIC RANKING OF ORGANIZATIONS BY THE DEGREE OF DEPENDENCE OF
INFERIORS ON SUPERIORS

Dependence of Inferiors	Organizations	Main Factor Making Inferiors Less Dependent than Those in Organizations Immediately Above on the List
HIGH	1. Concentration camps in Nazi Germany	
	2. American slavery, "humane custodial" prisons	Ideology of superiors more humane
	3. South American slavery, feudal hereditary subjection	Vesting of interests, defended (sporadically) by king and church
	4. Modern armies in garrison, capitalist plantations with wage labor	Certain restricted alternatives open, generally at specified re-enlistment or contract-renewal times
to	5. Armies in combat, intensive agriculture, factory labor	Much more open to "conscientious withdrawal of efficiency"
	6. Craft production, universities with respect to faculty	Vesting of interests more common and organizations more powerful, and even more opportunity for damage by "soldiering"
	7. Oligarchic unions and other oligarchic voluntary associations	More freedom to withdraw support without penalty
LOW	8. Elected officials in democracies	More institutionalized dependence of superiors through election
	9. Elected officials in voluntary associations with many factions	Freedom to withdraw and institutionalized dependence of superiors

lich, 1961, *passim*) the normal cottager received housing, garden space, and pasturage for an animal or two from his lord, who was also quite often the official local government; even if the lord was not endowed with strictly feudal powers, he and his fellow landlords dominated the courts, administration, and legislatures of the local areas. The cottager was quite completely dependent on his lord, since police power and power over his house and food were concentrated in the lord, and the cottager had relatively little chance to move if he offended him. It was quite a normal practice for cottagers to be "paid" for their work on the lord's land by giving them a share of the grain at threshing time, and the lord made "contributions" in time of need. To some degree, then, the cottagers shared in the lord's prosperity and suffered a bad season with him. It is common to call this combined situation of community of fate and greatly unequal power a "patriarchal"

system, since it is very similar to that in patriarchal families.

Neither in the culture of hierarchical conservatism that was prevalent among the upper class,[28] nor in the practical power situation, was there any substantial limita-

---

[28] In such a situation it is very hard to tell what the culture of the subordinated population is. When there is a relatively high density of interaction among the peasantry in large agricultural towns, as in Spain, southern Italy, or Sicily, many periodic rebellions with a millennial anarchistic egalitarian ideology develop, quite often with strong traditionalistic elements around the edges. Events similar to the so-called church and king rebellion, in which a more or less mythical superior would have stopped exploitation before ("if he only knew"), are frequent features of such situations. Another alternative, for some reason, seems to be the rule of local villages by gangsters in the service of local rich men. These rebellions (or the wars of each against all) are not, of course, any more the "real" expression of the culture of the subordinates than the more usual situation of dull, apathetic fatalism. On the rebellions of Spain and southern Italy, see Hobsbawm (1959).

tion of the lord's authority to a defined sphere. All privileges of a cottager were "by the grace of his lord."

As the Prussian nobility started having to compete with the bourgeoisie and the cultured elite (who claimed fame and power by virtue of their *Bildung*) for power and prestige, they needed more returns from their enterprises. The unification of Germany and industrialization opened up new opportunities in the cities for migrants from rural areas. By the turn of the century, the patriarchal organizations were essentially bourgeois enterprises with patriarchal ideology. As an index of the capitalistic nature of these enterprises, by this time forced sales for debt of large properties were more common than for small, and the reasons for failure were those typical of commercial enterprises: weakness of capital structure and changes in the market. Forced sales of small properties were still those characteristic of subsistence agriculture: foreclosures of debts for consumption, deaths in the family, and the like (Weber, 1897, especially the table on p. 18).

The change in opportunities for the workers reduced their dependence on their lords. The lords meanwhile could no longer "afford" to share their prosperity, particularly that derived from capital improvements on the land, for they needed the returns to stay solvent and to maintain their position in Berlin. Wage labor was therefore substituted more and more for cottagers whose subsistence was guaranteed and who shared in the harvest. Both the dependence of the workers and the community of fate between themselves and their lord, the very bases of patriarchal authority, were eroded by these processes. With practical freedom to move and less to gain by staying, the German agricultural laborers left the land in great numbers, being more and more replaced by Polish and Russian seasonal wage labor.

With the institution of the Weimar Republic after World War I (for this period, see especially Wunderlich, 1961), the rights and duties enforced by the government changed as well. Collective bargaining and written contracts were imposed to erode dependency relations; workers were organized into socialist unions and given political and judicial rights; and ideological disagreement over the rights of landlords and the duties of workers became institutionalized.

In summary, then, over the course of a half-century or so, the organizational context in which the social classes met in eastern Germany changed from a patriarchal environment into one in which landed entrepreneurs who still believed in patriarchal rule confronted a relatively independent labor force represented by a socialist government. Class conflict had developed from whatever ambivalent feelings in the private opinions of subordinates might be inferred to the recognized and institutionalized method of deciding the distribution of returns.

REFERENCES

Banfield, E. *The moral basis of a backward society.* Glencoe, Ill.: Free Press, 1958.

Bendix, R. *Work and authority in industry.* New York: Wiley, 1956.

Bendix, R. *Max Weber: an intellectual portrait.* Garden City, N.Y.: Doubleday, 1960.

Bidwell, C. The young professional in the army. *Amer. sociol. Rev.,* 1961, 26, 360–372.

Dahrendorf, R. *Class and class conflict in industrial society.* Stanford, Calif.: Stanford Univer. Press, 1959.

Hobsbawm, E. J. *Primitive rebels.* Manchester, Eng.: Manchester Univer. Press, 1959. Published in the U.S. as *Social bandits and primitive rebels.*

Siegfried, A. *Tableau politique de la France de l'ouest sous la troisième république.* Paris: Colin, 1913.

Stinchcombe, A. L. Agricultural enterprise and rural class relations. *Amer. J. Sociol.,* 1961, 67, 165–176.

Udy, S. Technical and institutional factors in production organization. *Amer. J. Sociol.,* 1961, 67, 247–260.

Weber, M. *Gesammelte Aufsätze zur Sozial- und Wirtschaftsgeschichte.* Tübingen: Mohr, 1924.

Whyte, W. F. *Human relations in the restaurant industry.* New York: McGraw-Hill, 1948.

Wunderlich, F. *Farm labor in Germany.* Princeton: Princeton Univer. Press, 1961.

CHAPTER 6

Feudalism as a Type of Society

MARC BLOCH

1 HAS THERE BEEN MORE THAN ONE FEUDALISM?

IN the eyes of Montesquieu, the establishment of 'feudal laws' was a phenomenon *sui generis*, 'an event which happened once in the world and which will perhaps never happen again'. Voltaire, less experienced, no doubt, in the precise formulation of legal definitions, but a man of wider outlook, demurred. 'Feudalism', he wrote, 'is not an event; it is a very old form which, with differences in its working, subsists in three-quarters of our hemisphere.'[1] Modern scholarship has in general rallied to the side of Voltaire. Egyptian feudalism, Achaean feudalism, Chinese feudalism, Japanese feudalism—all these forms and more are now familiar concepts. The historian of the West must sometimes regard them with a certain amount of misgiving. For he cannot be unaware of the different definitions which have been given of this famous term, even on its native soil. The basis of feudal society, Benjamin Guérard has said, is land. No, it is the personal group, rejoins Jacques Flach. Do the various exotic versions of feudalism, which seem to abound in universal history today, conform to Guérard's definition or to Flach's? The only remedy for these uncertainties is to go back to the origins of the problem. Since it is obvious that all these societies, separated by time and space, have received the name 'feudal' only on account of their similarities, real or supposed, to Western feudalism, it is the characteristics of this basic type, to which all the others must be referred, that it is of primary importance to define. But first it is necessary to dispose of some obvious instances of the misuse of a term which has made too much noise in the world not to have undergone many perversions.

In the system which they christened 'feudalism' its first godfathers, as we know, were primarily conscious of those aspects of it which conflicted with the idea of a centralized state. Thence it was a short step to describing as feudal every fragmentation of political authority; so that a value judgment was normally combined with the simple statement of a fact. Because sovereignty was generally associated in the minds of these writers

[1] *Esprit des Lois*, XXX, I; Voltaire, *Fragments sur quelques révolutions dans l'Inde*, II (ed. Garnier, XXIX, p. 91).

with fairly large states, every exception to the rule seemed to fall into the category of the abnormal. This alone would suffice to condemn a usage which, moreover, could scarcely fail to give rise to intolerable confusion. Occasionally, indeed, there are indications of a more precise notion. In 1783 a minor municipal official, the market-watchman of Valenciennes, denounced as responsible for the increase in the price of foodstuffs 'a feudality of great country landlords'.[1] How many polemists since then have held up to public obloquy the 'feudalism' of bankers or industrialists! Charged with more or less vague historical associations, the word with certain writers seems to suggest no more than the brutal exercise of authority, though frequently it also conveys the slightly less elementary notion of an encroachment of economic powers on public life. It is in fact very true that the identification of wealth—then consisting mainly of land —with authority was one of the outstanding features of medieval feudalism. But this was less on account of the strictly feudal character of that society than because it was, at the same time, based on the manor.

Feudalism, manorial system—the identification here goes back much farther. It had first occurred in the use of the word 'vassal'. The aristocratic stamp which this term had received from what was, after all, a secondary development, was not strong enough to prevent it from being occasionally applied, even in the Middle Ages, to serfs (originally closely akin to vassals properly so called because of the personal nature of their dependence) and even to ordinary tenants. What was then only a kind of linguistic aberration, especially frequent in somewhat incompletely feudalized regions like Gascony or Leon, became a more and more widespread usage, as familiarity with genuine vassalage faded. 'Everyone knows', wrote Perreciot in 1786, 'that in France the subjects of lords are commonly called their vassals.'[2] Similarly it became customary, in spite of etymology, to describe as 'feudal rights' the burdens to which peasant holdings were subject. Thus when the men of the Revolution announced their intention to destroy feudalism, it was above all the manorial system that they meant to attack. But here again the historian must interpose. Though an essential element in feudal society, the manor was in itself an older institution, and was destined to last much longer. In the interests of sound terminology it is important that the two ideas should be kept clearly separate.

Let us therefore try to bring together in broad outline what we have learned about European feudalism, in the strict sense of the word, from its history.

[1] G. Lefebvre, Les paysans du Nord, 1924, p. 309.

[2] For example, E. Lodge, 'Serfdom in the Pyrenees', in Vierteljahrschr. für Soz. und W. G., 1905, p. 31; Sanchez-Albornoz, Estampas de la vida en Leon, 2nd ed., p. 86, n. 37; Perreciot, De l'état-civil des personnes, II, 1786, p. 193, n. 9.

2 THE FUNDAMENTAL CHARACTERISTICS OF
EUROPEAN FEUDALISM

The simplest way will be to begin by saying what feudal society was not. Although the obligations arising from blood-relationship played a very active part in it, it did not rely on kinship alone. More precisely, feudal ties proper were developed when those of kinship proved inadequate. Again, despite the persistence of the idea of a public authority super-imposed on the multitude of petty powers, feudalism coincided with a profound weakening of the State, particularly in its protective capacity. But much as feudal society differed from societies based on kinship as well as from those dominated by the power of the State, it was their successor and bore their imprint. For while the characteristic relationships of personal subjection retained something of the quasi-family character of the original companionage, a considerable part of the political authority exercised by innumerable petty chiefs had the appearance of a usurpation of 'regalian' rights.

European feudalism should therefore be seen as the outcome of the violent dissolution of older societies. It would in fact be unintelligible with-out the great upheaval of the Germanic invasions which, by forcibly uniting two societies originally at very different stages of development, disrupted both of them and brought to the surface a great many modes of thought and social practices of an extremely primitive character. It finally developed in the atmosphere of the last barbarian raids. It involved a far-reaching restriction of social intercourse, a circulation of money too sluggish to admit of a salaried officialdom, and a mentality attached to things tangible and local. When these conditions began to change, feudal-ism began to wane.

It was an unequal society, rather than a hierarchical one—with chiefs rather than nobles; and with serfs, not slaves. If slavery had not played so small a part, there would have been no need for the characteristically feudal forms of dependence, as applied to the lower orders of society. In an age of disorder, the place of the adventurer was too important, the memory of men too short, the regularity of social classifications too uncertain, to admit of the strict formation of regular castes.

Nevertheless the feudal system meant the rigorous economic subjection of a host of humble folk to a few powerful men. Having received from earlier ages the Roman *villa* (which in some respects anticipated the manor) and the German village chiefdom, it extended and consolidated these methods whereby men exploited men, and combining inextricably the right to the revenues from the land with the right to exercise authority, it fashioned from all this the true manor of medieval times. And this it did partly for the benefit of an oligarchy of priests and monks whose task it was to propitiate Heaven, but chiefly for the benefit of an oligarchy of warriors.

As even the most perfunctory comparative study will show, one of the most distinctive characteristics of feudal societies was the virtual identity of the class of chiefs with the class of professional warriors serving in the only way that then seemed effective, that is as heavily armed horsemen. As we have seen, of the societies where an armed peasantry survived, some knew neither vassalage nor the manor, while others knew them only in very imperfect forms—as in Scandinavia for example, or the kingdoms of north-western Spain. The case of the Byzantine Empire is perhaps even more significant because its institutions bore the stamp of a much more conscious directing ·thought. There, after the anti-aristocratic reaction of the eighth century, a government which had preserved the great administrative traditions of the Roman period, and which was furthermore concerned to provide itself with a strong army, created tenements charged with military obligations to the State—true fiefs in one sense, but differing from those of the West in that they were peasant fiefs, each consisting of a small farm. Thenceforth it was a paramount concern of the imperial government to protect these 'soldiers' properties', as well as small-holdings in general, against the encroachments of the rich and powerful. Nevertheless there came a time towards the end of the eleventh century when the Empire, overwhelmed by economic conditions which made independence more and more difficult for a peasantry constantly in debt, and further weakened by internal discords, ceased to extend any useful protection to the free farmers. In this way it not only lost precious fiscal resources, but found itself at the mercy of the magnates, who alone were capable thereafter of raising the necessary troops from among their own dependants.

In feudal society the characteristic human bond was the subordinate's link with a nearby chief. From one level to another the ties thus formed— like so many chains branching out indefinitely—joined the smallest to the greatest. Land itself was valued above all because it enabled a lord to provide himself with 'men' by supplying the remuneration for them. We want lands, said in effect the Norman lords who refused the gifts of jewels, arms, and horses offered by their duke. And they added among themselves: 'It will thus be possible for us to maintain many knights, and the duke will no longer be able to do so.'[1]

It remained to devise a form of real property right suitable for the remuneration of services and coinciding in duration with the personal tie itself. From the solution which it found for this problem, Western feudalism derived one of its most original features. While the 'men of service' who surrounded the Slav princes continued to receive their estates as outright gifts, the fief of the Frankish vassal, after some fluctuations of policy, was in theory conceded to him only for the term of his life. For among the highest classes, distinguished by the honourable profession of arms,

[1] Dudo of Saint-Quentin, ed. Lair (*Mém. Soc. Antiquaires Normandie*, XXIII), III 43–4 (933).

relationships of dependence had assumed, at the outset, the form of contracts freely entered into between two living men confronting one another.
From this necessary personal contact the relationship derived the best part
of its moral value. Nevertheless at an early date various factors tarnished
the purity of the obligation: hereditary succession, natural in a society
where the family remained so strong; the practice of enfeoffment which
was imposed by economic conditions and ended by burdening the land
with services rather than the man with fealty; finally and above all, the
plurality of vassal engagements. The loyalty of the commended man
remained, in many cases, a potent factor. But as a paramount social bond
designed to unite the various groups at all levels, to prevent fragmentation
and to arrest disorder, it showed itself decidedly ineffective.

Indeed in the immense range of these ties there had been from the first
something artificial. Their general diffusion in feudal times was the legacy
of a moribund State—that of the Carolingians—which had conceived the
idea of combating social disintegration by means of one of the institutions
born of that very condition. The system of superposed protective relationships was certainly not incapable of contributing to the cohesion of the
State: witness, the Anglo-Norman monarchy. But for this it was necessary
that there should be a central authority favoured, as in England, not only
by the fact of conquest itself but even more by the circumstance that it
coincided with new material and moral conditions. In the ninth century
the forces making for disintegration were too strong.

In the area of Western civilization the map of feudalism reveals some
large blank spaces—the Scandinavian peninsula, Frisia, Ireland. Perhaps
it is more important still to note that feudal Europe was not all feudalized
in the same degree or according to the same rhythm and, above all, that it
was nowhere feudalized completely. In no country did the whole of the
rural population fall into the bonds of personal and hereditary dependence.
Almost everywhere—though the number varied greatly from region to
region—there survived large or small allodial properties. The concept of
the State never absolutely disappeared, and where it retained the most
vitality men continued to call themselves 'free', in the old sense of the
word, because they were dependent only on the head of the people or his
representatives. Groups of peasant warriors remained in Normandy, in the
Danelaw, and in Spain. The mutual oath, strongly contrasting with the
oaths of subordination, survived in the peace associations and triumphed
in the communes. No doubt it is the fate of every system of human
institutions never to be more than imperfectly realized. Capitalism was
unquestionably the dominant influence on the European economy at the
beginning of the twentieth century; yet more than one undertaking continued to exist outside it.

Returning to our feudal map, we find between the Loire and the Rhine,
and in Burgundy on both banks of the Saône, a heavily shaded area which,

in the eleventh century, is suddenly enlarged by the Norman conquests of England and southern Italy. All round this central nucleus there is an almost regular shading-off till, in Saxony and especially in Leon and Castile, the stippling becomes very sparse indeed. Finally the entire shaded area is surrounded by blank spaces. In the most heavily shaded zone it is not difficult to recognize the regions where the regularizing influence of the Carolingians had been most far-reaching and where also the mingling of Romanized elements and Germanic elements—more pronounced here than elsewhere—had most completely disrupted the structure of the two societies and made possible the growth of very old seeds of territorial lordship and personal dependence.

3 A CROSS-SECTION OF COMPARATIVE HISTORY

A subject peasantry; widespread use of the service tenement (i.e. the fief) instead of a salary, which was out of the question; the supremacy of a class of specialized warriors; ties of obedience and protection which bind man to man and, within the warrior class, assume the distinctive form called vassalage; fragmentation of authority—leading inevitably to disorder; and, in the midst of all this, the survival of other forms of association, family and State, of which the latter, during the second feudal age, was to acquire renewed strength—such then seem to be the fundamental features of European feudalism. Like all the phenomena revealed by that science of eternal change which is history, the social structure thus characterized certainly bore the peculiar stamp of an age and an environment. Yet just as the matrilineal or agnatic clan or even certain types of economic enterprise are found in much the same forms in very different societies, it is by no means impossible that societies different from our own should have passed through a phase closely resembling that which has just been defined. If so, it is legitimate to call them feudal during that phase. But the work of comparison thus involved is clearly beyond the powers of one man, and I shall therefore confine myself to an example which will at least give an idea of what such research, conducted by surer hands, might yield. The task is facilitated by the existence of excellent studies which already bear the hall-mark of the soundest comparative method.

In the dark ages of Japanese history we dimly perceive a society based on kinship groups, real or fictitious. Then towards the end of the seventh century of our era, under Chinese influence a system of government is founded which strives (exactly as the Carolingians did) to maintain a kind of moral control over its subjects. Finally, about the eleventh century, the period begins which it has become customary to call feudal and whose advent seems (in accordance with a pattern with which we are now familiar) to have coincided with a certain slackening of commercial activity. Here, therefore, as in Europe, 'feudalism' seems to have been preceded by two very different forms of social organization; and, as with us, it was profoundly influenced by both. The monarchy, though it had less connection than in Europe with the feudal structure proper—since the chains of vassalage terminated before reaching the Emperor—subsisted, in law, as the theoretical source of all power; and there also the fragmentation of political authority, which was fostered by very old habits, was held to be a consequence of encroachments on the State.

Above the peasantry a class of professional warriors had arisen. It was in these circles that ties of personal dependence developed, on the model furnished by the relations of the armed retainer with his chief; they were thus, it appears, marked by a much more pronounced class character than European 'commendation'. They were hierarchically organized, just as in Europe; but Japanese vassalage was much more an act of submission than was European vassalage and much less a contract. It was also more strict, since it did not allow plurality of lords. As these warriors had to be supported they were granted tenements closely resembling the fiefs of the West. Sometimes even, on the pattern of our *fiefs de reprises*, the grant was purely fictitious and involved in fact lands which had originally belonged to the patrimony of the pretended recipient. These fighting-men were naturally less and less willing to cultivate the soil, though as in Europe there were to the end exceptional cases of peasant 'vavasours'. The vassals therefore lived mainly on the rents from their own tenants. There were too many of them, however—far more, apparently, than in Europe—to admit of the establishment for their benefit of real manors, with extensive powers over the people. Few manors were created, except by the baronage and the temples, and being widely scattered and having no demesne, they recalled the embryonic manors of Anglo-Saxon England rather than those of the really manorialized regions of the West. Furthermore, on this soil where irrigated rice-fields represented the prevailing form of agriculture, the technical conditions were so different from European practice that the subjection of the peasantry assumed correspondingly different forms.

Although far too brief, of course, and too absolute in its appraisal of the contrasts between the two societies, it seems to me that this outline nevertheless enables us to reach a fairly firm conclusion. Feudalism was not 'an event which happened once in the world'. Like Europe—though with inevitable and deep-seated differences—Japan went through this phase. Have other societies also passed through it? And if so, what were the causes, and were they perhaps common to all such societies? It is for future works to provide the answers. I should be happy if this book, by suggesting questions to students, were to prepare the way for an inquiry going far beyond it.

CHAPTER 7

America's Unique Class Politics: The Interplay of the Labor, Credit and Commodity Markets

NORBERT WILEY

American political life, both historically and at present, has proven unusually resistant to economic interpretation, either by the Classical Liberal or the Marxist versions of economic determinism. Instead, political scholars have placed heavy reliance on a variety of non-economic factors, the most recent being those of alienation, mass society and status protest. However, in this paper we argue that a great deal of American political life can be explained economically, in terms of class conflict, if revisions are made in class theory. Accordingly, a multi-dimensional theory of class conflict, based on the work of Max Weber, is presented, using the dimensions of the credit and commodity markets along with the usual dimension of the labor market. This theory is then applied to three political problems: (1) the relation between agrarian and labor protest in the 19th century; (2) the contemporary radical right; and (3) the current Negro protest movement.

THE broad features of American political history have always been something of a puzzle for political sociologists. This country is probably the most fully developed case of capitalist democracy, yet throughout much of its history there has been an undercurrent of volatile radicalism in the agrarian heartland. The tradition of agrarian radicalism becomes especially difficult to interpret when compared to the much less radical political history of the urban proletariat for, while the small agrarian capitalists have often pursued socialist objectives, the urban workers have usually clung to non-socialist trade unions and political parties. From the viewpoint of Marxian political sociology, the United States has rightly been called "exceptional," for the facts do not easily permit an economic interpretation.[1]

If Marxism has proved inadequate, the other major economic theory of politics, classical liberalism, has not been better. This theory assumes that the economic and political systems operate on the market principle, and that the economic market is the basis for political life. Pure competition, however, has never characterized the American economy, let alone the political order, and the course of history has brought a steady decline in the importance of market controls. Thus the theory of economic determinism, whether Marxist or Liberal, has not provided a useful interpretation of American political history.[2]

Revision of a paper read at the annual meeting of the American Sociological Association, August, 1966. For assistance at various stages in the preparation of this paper I am especially indebted to William H. Form, as well as to David L. Westby, Peter Rossi and Hans Gerth. In addition, the comments of Donald Warren and Madeline Karmel on an earlier draft are much appreciated.

[1] The "exception", of course, is mainly from the point of view of Western European history. From the vast literature on this question, a convenient discussion of labor history is Walter Galenson, "Why the American Labor Movement is not Socialist", *American Review*, 1 (Winter, 1961), pp. 1–19. A more general discussion of the American political tradition is Louis Hartz, *The Liberal Tradition in America*, New York: Harcourt, Brace, 1955.

[2] The classic treatment of the decline of market controls in the American economy is Adolf A. Berle, Jr. and Gardiner C. Means, *The Modern Corporation and Private Property*, New York: Macmillan, 1932. The neo-liberal position, that some kind of self-balancing political system exists despite the decline in market controls, is criticized

In the absence of a workable economic theory, some political sociologists have attempted major interpretations with purely social theories. Perhaps the most important of these are the theory of status politics, as found in the writings of Richard Hofstadter and Seymour Lipset, and the theory of mass society, as stated, for example, by William Kornhauser. These theories have not been presented as alternatives to economic theories, but as supplements. Yet they have often been proposed to explain precisely those problems which proved inexplicable by the economic theories, so the effect is nearly one of mere substitution. While neither of the social theories have been fully developed or tested, it is our opinion that they do not help a great deal in interpreting American politics, either historical or contemporary.[3]

It is the argument of this paper that economic theories have not been adequately explored, and that the two alternatives of Marxism and utilitarian liberalism have acted as an intellectual strait jacket.[4] Specifically, it is our thesis that if one takes a broader view of economic class conflict than usual, the major features of American politics can be adequately understood in class terms. We will begin by presenting a revised conception of economic class and class conflict. Then we will make some interpretations of American political history, and finally discuss some contemporary problems. The review of American politics will be short and sketchy and is intended to give only a rough idea of how the frame of reference might be applied.

THE CONCEPTS OF CLASS AND CLASS CONFLICT

Many contemporary sociologists use the

concept of economic class in an oversimplified and ambiguous way.[5] Typically, it is regarded as unidimensional and is measured by position in the labor market, often being specified simply as blue collar vs. white collar or manual vs. non-manual. Sometimes it is defined as a hierarchy of incomes, and here the emphasis is on purchasing power and how it affects the person's "life chances." Both of these formulations, occupation and income, are ambiguous because they are not clearly distinguished from status (prestige). The occupational hierarchy, however objectively economic it may seem, is really a hierarchy of occupational prestige; indeed the category of "occupational level" is often used interchangeably as an indicator of either class or status. Similarly, the income hierarchy, except at its highest levels, is a hierarchy of consumer purchasing power, and consumption is the arena in which status is determined, not class.

To make a clear distinction between class and status, it is necessary that classes be considered in some kind of economic relationship to each other. Dahrendorf feels that this relationship is basically one of conflict, and believes that any other conception is faulty.[6] We think his assumption is unnecessary, and that the form of the relationship can be left unspecified, so long as the content is one of economic and not prestige interchange. The most famous example of an economic theory of class is, of course, that of Marx, for whom the main class relationship was between property owners and workers, with the focus of the relationship being the price of labor. However simplistic that picture may be, the classes are in an objective economic relationship in a way that is not so of occupational strata or income levels. In the century that has passed since Marx's analysis, the categories of owners and workers have become even more complex and subdivided than

in C. Wright Mills, *The Power Elite*, New York: Oxford University Press, 1959, chapter 11. The contrasting positions of Mills and David Riesman are discussed in William Kornhauser, " 'Power Elite' or 'Veto Groups'," which appears in Reinhard Bendix and Seymour Martin Lipset, eds., *Class, Status, and Power*, New York: The Free Press, 1966, pp. 210–218.

[3] William Kornhauser, *The Politics of Mass Society*, New York: The Free Press, 1959; Richard Hofstadter, "The Pseudo-Conservative Revolt", in Daniel Bell, ed., *The Radical Right*, Garden City, New York: Doubleday, 1964, pp. 75–95; and Seymour Martin Lipset, "The Sources of the 'Radical Right'", in Daniel Bell, *op. cit.*, pp. 307–371.

[4] The straitening effects of these two theories

have been moral too, as C. Wright Mills was so passionately aware. See, for example, his chapter "On Reason and Freedom", in *The Sociological Imagination*, New York: Grove Press, 1959.

[5] A useful criticism of class conceptions appears in Ralf Dahrendorf, "Some Recent Theories of Class Conflict in Modern Societies", in his *Class and Class Conflict in Industrial Society*, Stanford University Press: Stanford, California, 1959, pp. 72–116.

[6] Dahrendorf, *op. cit.*, p. 76.

they were during Marx's time, and the structure of economic interest groups yields to no simple conception of duality or hierarchy. But if the economic order is complex, the theory of class should be revised to take account of these complexities.

The value of visualizing classes in their economic relationships is not just in maintaining the analytic separateness of the class order. The greater importance is in making class theory a useful instrument for understanding the relations between economic and political life. If classes are conceived in a way which emphasizes their economic interests, especially opposed interests, the connections between these interests and political action are more likely to be found.

That such a theory can be developed and that complexity need not be a barrier is suggested by the complex and imaginative developments that have been brought to bear on the theory of status itself in recent years. Status is now viewed as a variable containing many dimensions and many relations among these dimensions. Such notions as status consistency, status conflict, nonhierarchical relations, degrees of status closure and channels of mobility suggest the richness of analysis that has been brought to this idea. Yet in the writings of Max Weber, who has been the inspiration for much of status theory, there are the elements of a much more complex and serviceable theory of class than is currently in use.

In Weber's view, as it appears in his essay on "Class, Status and Party," economic class is multidimensional, and there are as many bases for class differentiation as there are forms of competitive relationship in the economy. It is true that he gave a great analytic emphasis to the dimension of the labor market and the struggle over the price of labor, for that issue has been most salient during the industrialization of Western Europe. Accordingly, he distinguished those who live by exploiting capital property from those who live by selling services and made further distinctions within each of those two major classes. He was also concerned, however, with the relations between debtors and creditors, buyers and sellers, and landlords and tenants, and he recognized the possibility that economic classes might be formed along the dimensions of the credit and commodity markets

as well as the labor market. In speaking of the history of European class conflict he points out that, "the struggle in which class situations are effective has progressively shifted from consumption credit toward, first, competitive struggles in the commodity market and, then, toward price wars on the labor market".[7] It seems clear, then, that Weber visualized the economic class system as a constellation of related dimensions, any one of which might become the major focus of class conflict under the right historical conditions.

Weber did not pay much attention to the relations among these three areas of class conflict or to the possibility of a historical reversal, which might again make debtor and consumer protest central. But from the viewpoint of the 1960s, and especially in the United States, it is obvious that economic struggles are not confined to the issue of the price of labor and that the future will bring even more complexity in the class order.

We will follow Weber in distinguishing three major dimensions of the class system: (1) the labor market, which is the source of the conflict among occupational and property-owning groups, (2) the credit or money market, which is the basis for the conflict between debtors and creditors, and (3) the commodity market, which is the basis for the conflict between buyers and sellers, and landlords and tenants. Accordingly, anyone who participates in all three markets is a member of three distinct economic classes and may participate in class conflict along three distinct axes. These three lines of con-

---

[7] Hans H. Gerth and C. Wright Mills, *From Max Weber*, New York: Oxford University Press, 1958, p. 185 in the essay "Class, Status, Party". This well-known essay is usually seen as a critique of Marx in which the influences of status and party are added to that of class with the result that economic determinism is conditioned by non-economic factors. However, the point in the essay that I am singling out suggests a second, and perhaps equally important critique of Marx. This point is that class conflict, even after the industrial revolution, is by no means confined to the labor market, and thus the influence of class conflict, even within its limits, is more complex than Marx visualized. Both of these elements in Weber—his careful awareness of such non-economic forces as religious values and status communities, and his appreciation for complex economic influences—are important in his analysis of almost any problem, although his American reputation seems to be based mainly on his analyses of non-economic influences.

flict are not equally important at any one time in the industrialization process or in the business cycle, nor do distinct interest groups always form around each issue. Nevertheless, all three conflicts are deeply imbedded in capitalism, and the historic problems of economic ethics—those of usury, the just price and the living wage—are manifested squarely in the three markets.[8]

Weber's perspective permits the invention of a number of new class concepts, and, if our intention were the formal development of this theory, we would systematically draw out these concepts. Instead, our purpose is to analyze American politics, and we will concentrate on concepts that serve this purpose. One such concept is that of inconsistencies in the class order itself, apart from any inconsistencies that might exist in the status order. Class inconsistency can exist either for the individual or for the system. Beginning with individual inconsistency, this pattern will be defined in relation to its opposite, the consistent pattern.

There are two consistent sets of class attributes, the propertied and the non-propertied. The propertied set is that of employer-creditor-seller; the non-propertied that of employee-debtor-buyer. All other sets entail a mixture of the propertied and the non-propertied, or non-membership in one or more markets, or membership on both the propertied and non-propertied sides in one or more markets, or some combination of these. It will be assumed that all sets, other than the two consistent ones, are likely to involve a conflict of economic interest for the person, and it is in this sense that we refer to them as inconsistent. The extent of inconsistency reflects the degree to which the three axes of class conflict divide a population at different points, and to that extent a society will have a built-in source of cross-pressures.

It might be asked if conflict of economic interest cannot exist also within the "consistent" sets of propertied and non-propertied. Certainly this always exists to some extent, but we are assuming that at the level of the individual it will usually be easier to find harmony among a "consistent" than among an "inconsistent" set of class interests. However, if, in the society as a whole, there are substantial conflicts of interest among debtors, workers and buyers, or among creditors, employers and sellers, we will refer to this situation as class inconsistency within the system.[9] The two types of class inconsistency, individual and systematic, are independent of each other to some extent, but if there is a great deal of individual inconsistency it will tend to create inconsistency at the systematic level also. If, for example, the debtors are a different group from the workers, the two sets of interests will be more likely to diverge and conflict. Also, if there is a rentier-creditor group different from the employer group, a systematic

---

[8] Dahrendorf's theory of class is constructed especially for *industrial* societies, whether capitalist or socialist, while the theory we will develop from Weber is meant to apply mainly to *capitalist* societies, whether industrial or non-industrial. A second difference is that Dahrendorf combines the two notions of class and power (or economic and political power) under the broader notion of authority (in associations), while we go in the opposite direction and, not only retaining the distinction between the economic and the political, make additional distinctions within the category of class. On the point in question see Dahrendorf, *op. cit.*, pp. 165–173. For the understanding of American life in particular, we think our direction is more useful than Dahrendorf's.

[9] The distinction between individual and systematic consistency might be applied to conceptions of *status* consistency as well. In most status consistency studies it is assumed that no matter how much inconsistency there is at the level of individuals, the prestige standards themselves remain firm and compatible. The assumption is questionable.

More generally, there are two important ways in which the present theory differs from the theory of status consistency, as developed by Gerhard Lenski and others. (1) We are concerned only with objective economic dimensions of stratification. Status consistency theory is concerned with a mixture of economic and prestige dimensions—specifically, occupation, income, education and ethnicity, in Lenski's original formulation—although the two economic dimensions are approached from a prestige point of view. (2) Status consistency theory, with its reliance on firm and clear prestige standards, assumes a great deal of harmony and consensus in society between the rich and the poor, the high and the low. Without this consensus, there would be no exact prestige standards against which to measure individual status profiles. On the assumption of conflict, the theory breaks down. On the other hand, the present theory does not disallow either consensus or conflict, just so long as the economy keeps going and there is no outright revolution.

Lenski's original statement appears in "Status Crystallization: A Non-Vertical Dimension of Social Status," *American Sociological Review*, 19 (August, 1954), pp. 405–413.

conflict of interest is likely to appear on the propertied side.

A society with a systematic inconsistency in its class structure may have political qualities which derive from this inconsistency, just as an individual with inconsistent class interests may find his political interests affected by this situation. This expanded conception of class allows one to see various combinations of class interests and conflict and to frame new hypotheses concerning class and politics.

Class Conflict in American History. Central to the history of class conflict in America is the paradox previously mentioned. The most vigorous class action, particularly in political life, has come from small agrarian capitalists, especially the wheat farmers of the Great Plains, while the urban workers, with their clearer class interest and stronger organizational potential, have been less militant. To describe these phenomena in Weber's terms, a distinction must be made among varieties of class interests. The farmers were pursuing their class interests in the credit and commodity markets and not in the labor market, for the most important class memberships of American farmers were as debtors and sellers. Being farm owners they were neither employees, nor, to any important extent, employers. Thus American class conflict has gone on largely outside the labor market, and the relative tranquility of the urban workers has given our history an unusual distribution of class action.[10]

The problem of the American worker's lack of attraction to socialism can be examined more sharply if we distinguish among types of socialism. Within our frame of reference there are three pure forms of socialism: debtor, consumer and proletariat socialism. The common feature is that in each case the government controls the relevant market in the interest of the poorer class.[11]

With debtor socialism, government owns or controls credit institutions; with consumer socialism, the distribution of commodities; and with proletariat socialism, capital property. The agrarian radicals, even when most militant, as at certain times and places during the Populist Movement, were by no means complete socialists. They wanted elements of debtor and commodity socialism but not proletariat socialism, even though some Populist literature made vague demands in that direction. Certainly the Populists showed no interest in having themselves placed on collective farms.[12]

---

serviceable to think of "socialism" as a name for a family of related economies, differing in the way they blend the foregoing three variables. Then the question becomes one of finding the political and economic consequences of different varieties of socialism.

In any event, we are ignoring the preceding dilemmas to introduce the notion of sectoral socialism. Each deprived interest group—consumers, debtors and workers—will, analytically speaking, want a different kind of sectoral socialism. The net political response from below will depend partly on how much overlap there is among the three deprived classes and how badly deprived they are. Of course, the three issues of ownership, control and equality are still present for these types.

[12] Populism has been subject to a good bit of controversy by recent historians over both factual and interpretive questions. Our entry into this area, despite the intellectual risks, is to show that this frame of reference may have a broad interpretive value for historical as well as contemporary politics.

For several decades, American historians have made heavy use of class theory, in the broad sense, to interpret such pivotal questions as Jacksonian Democracy, the Civil War, and the whole reform tradition from the early stirrings of Populism through the New Deal. But, finding difficulty in applying Marxist and European categories to American experience, these conceptions of class have usually been *ad hoc* constructions, built to fit whatever particular problem or period might be at issue. Charles A. Beard's work is an example of this tendency. Much of the impact of Richard Hofstadter's book on *The Age of Reform,* New York: Vintage, 1960, which is at the center of the recent Populism controversy, is that he circumvents the typically unwieldy versions of class theory to introduce *status protest* in his analyses of Populism and Progressivism. To many readers this shift in analysis reduced the class heroes of Populism and Progressivism to the status of cranky petit bourgeoisie. The whole point of my paper, though, is that American political analysis, including historical analysis, need not choose between unwieldy class and pure status theories, but should find new class theories that will, at the same time, provide a better grounding for status theories.

---

[10] We are referring mainly to class action in the political order. In the economic order as such workers have probably been more militant than farmers.

[11] The term "socialism," just as "capitalism," is a word of many disputed meanings. This question of definition seems to range over three issues: (a) how much government *ownership* need be present, (b) how much government *control* there should be, as against private planning or market controls, and (c) how much *equality* there should be in incomes and living standards. It is probably more

On the other hand, the American government has taken its strongest socialist actions, limited as they are, along the line of commodity socialism by providing a variety of cheap or free services in the health, education and welfare areas. Not the least of the commodity controls has been the provision of price supports for the farmers. Debtor socialism has been less developed, and proletarian socialism, with the outright nationalization of capital property, least of all. Of course the impact of any socialistic measure, on any of the three dimensions, is not only in government control but in the question of which class benefits, and from this point of view the meaning of existing government controls in the United States is quite controversial.

The problem of the urban worker can now be restated as follows: why has the urban working class not supported proletarian socialism? Social thinkers have answered this question in a variety of ways, and several special American conditions which had a subduing effect on the working class have been cited. Our perspective suggests a new factor, or perhaps a new way of looking at something long recognized. *The United States has had a highly inconsistent class structure with a largely different subordinate class along each dimension of class conflict.*[13] This has disunified American radicalism, for the militant debtor class has been in conflict of interest with the proletarian class. The main class issue of the farmers was that of

credit and commodity prices; the main issue of the workers was wages and working conditions. The two streams of radicalism were at odds over membership, class interest, and therefore organizational and political programs.

In the technical terms of this paper, the farmers and workers both had inconsistent sets of class attributes, for the farmers lacked a clear interest in the labor market and the workers lacked interest in the credit market. This individual inconsistency was so widespread, and structured in such a way, that there was a clash between debtor and worker needs. For instance, inflation, while it would have relieved farmer debt and increased farmer selling power, would have meant little more than increased commodity prices for the urban workers.

This conflict was not entirely clear at the time, for both groups identified themselves under the heading of "producing classes" and both identified their opponent as big business, the plutocracy or the "money power". Yet the two sections of the producing class were quite distinct in their relation to property, and the concessions they wanted from their common enemy were also distinct, if not incompatible.[14] From the point of view

---

Other items in the Populism controversy are C. Vann Woodward, "The Populist Heritage and the Intellectuals," *American Scholar,* 29 (Winter, 1959–1960), pp. 55–72; Norman Pollack, *The Populist Response to Industrial America,* New York: W. W. Norton, 1962; and the following symposium that appears in *Agricultural History,* 39 (April, 1965), Norman Pollack, "Fear of Man: Populism, Authoritarianism, and the Historian," pp. 58–67; Oscar Handlin, "Reconsidering the Populists," pp. 68–74; Irwin Unger, "Critique of Norman Pollack's 'Fear of Man'," pp. 75–80; and J. Rogers Hollingsworth, "Populism: The Problem of Rhetoric and Reality," pp. 81–85.

[13] Concerning the many other factors that have been proposed to account for the weakness of American socialism, see Hartz, *op. cit.,* Galenson, *op. cit.,* and Seymour M. Lipset, *Agrarian Socialism,* Berkeley, California: The University of California press, 1959, p. 2. In terms of the present scheme, it might be added, Lipset's concept of agrarian socialism is a mixture of debtor and consumer socialism.

[14] If this conflict of interest was not entirely clear at the time, it was by no means entirely unclear either, especially to some of the leading spokesmen for labor. Samuel Gompers, who headed the young American Federation of Labor at the time, refused cooperation with the Populists on the grounds that they were "employing farmers", who would divert labor from its own interests. See Samuel Gompers, "Organized Labor in the Campaign", in George B. Tindall, "A Populist Reader," New York: Harper and Row, 1966, pp. 185–191. Daniel De Leon, who headed the Socialist Labor Party, the major socialist party of the time, similarly viewed farmers as capitalists, asserting that "Silver bugs and gold bugs are capitalistic bugs . . . Both kinds are social vermin and should be exterminated." Quoted in Howard H. Quint, *The Forging of American Socialism,* Indianapolis: Bobbs-Merrill, 1964, p. 217. On the other hand, the Knights of Labor, or what was left of it at this time, supported Populism and had many farmers as members. Our point, then, is that workers and their spokesmen, whether for or against Populism, had an oversimplified and misleading picture of the structure of class interests.

[15] This was a complex election, with regional as well as class variation. Bryan's farm support was strong only in the South and in the states west of the Mississippi, in the one-crop and silver mining areas of the country. McKinley drew farm as well as urban support in the rest of the country. It is not

of big business, a divide and conquer strategy was built into the American class system, and this is nowhere seen more clearly than in the critical 1896 Presidential election in which the farmers backed Bryan and inflation while the workers supported McKinley and the tariff.[15]

We are saying, then, that the absence of urban support for socialism was due partly to the centrality of the agrarian reform movement in American politics. During industrialization, the American farmer displayed a militancy not seen in the farmers of any other industrializing nation of the time. In England, for example, the decline of small agriculture and the enclosure movement preceded industrialization. In the United States, however, small agriculture grew with early industrialization, and a large agrarian class was available to spearhead the protest movement. The industrial revolution increased the consistency of the class structure in England, while it decreased it in the United States. The normal response of a consistent lower class, centered around proletarian interests, is socialism; the normal response of an inconsistent lower class, centered around several inconsistent interests, is something more diffuse and less radical than socialism. This diffuseness is well illustrated by the American case, for the strength of the agrarian protest blurred the class consciousness and the political interest of the American lower classes generally, weakened both lines of radicalism, and gave business interests a working control of the federal government until 1932.[16]

---

certain that McKinley carried the vote of the urban workers, as opposed to the urban middle class, even in the Northern cities where he ran strongest, nor is it clear how many worker votes he received due to the widespread employer and banker intimidation. What is clear is that if Bryan, the more radical candidate, had received strong worker support, he would have won the election, and the big business hegemony of the next few decades probably would not have come about. On the 1896 election see Paul W. Glad, *McKinley, Bryan, and the People,* Philadelphia: J. B. Lippincott, 1964; Stanley L. Jones, *The Presidential Election of 1896,* Madison, Wisconsin: University of Wisconsin Press, 1964; William Diamond, "Urban and Rural Voting in 1896," *American Historical Review,* 46 (January, 1941), pp. 281–305.

[16] It is often observed that the "absence of feudalism" inhibited the growth of class consciousness and, by that account, prevented radical political protest in the United States. Louis Hartz, *op.*

CONTEMPORARY RIGHT-WING MOVEMENTS

The question of the radical right is one of the most investigated and least illuminated matters in political sociology.[17] The question of why these groupings appeared, or reappeared, after World War II, and what social forces support them is still unclear. There are difficulties at the more elementary level of political classification as well. Do these groups have enough in common to be placed in the same category, do their programs share anything more than anti-Communism, does the support of each tend to come from the same segments of the population, or at least the same general social forces? The changes in the radical right, from the early 1950s to the middle 1960s, have not made analysis any easier, for the right's orientation has shifted from the anti-Communism of Senator McCarthy, to the crusade against welfare state legislation of the John Birch Society, and finally to the anti-desegregation position of the Southern groups that backed Goldwater. These ideological shifts seem to have brought substantial shifts in the sources of popular support. Considering the complexities of this question, it does not seem likely that any single theory would be able to explain it.[18]

---

cit., for example, makes much of this. But we think an important step is missing in this argument. For the absence of feudalism *permitted a strong market agriculture,* and this in turn had political effects which, in their net impact, were non-radical. Looking at this from another point of view, two important peculiarities of American political history, the militancy of agriculture and the non-militancy of labor, are interpreted as two facets of the same process in our frame of reference.

[17] This is due to the complexity of the problem and the difficulty of doing research with secret and semi-secret groups. The same thing can be said about research into National Socialism in Germany. For a review and evaluation of this research see Andrew G. Whiteside, "The Nature and Origins of National Socialism", *Journal of Central European Affairs,* 17 (April, 1957), pp. 48–73. Much of the research into the American radical right is found in the three following collections: Bell, *op. cit.;* Earl Latham, ed., *The Meaning of McCarthyism,* Boston: D. C. Heath, 1965; and *The Journal of Social Issues,* 19 (April, 1963), the entire issue of which is devoted to articles on "American Political Extremism in the 1960's".

[18] The shifts in orientation and support from the McCarthy to the John Birch Society periods are discussed in several of the essays in Bell, *op. cit.,* especially Seymour Martin Lipset, "Three Decades of the Radical Right: Coughlinites, Mc-

The hypothesis we will submit is an attempt to clarify only one factor, one that arises from the class system, which may push people toward right-wing groups. No doubt it interacts with other factors, and its influence may not be the statistically most important at any one time, but we think it is a continuously predisposing factor. This hypothesis is built on a paper by Martin Trow entitled "Small Businessmen, Political Tolerance, and Support for McCarthy".[19] Trow shows, from a sample survey of Bennington, Vermont, that small businessmen supported McCarthy more strongly than did either manual workers or the salaried middle class. More importantly, he shows that certain economic attitudes, which appeared most frequently among the small business group, were good predictors of pro-McCarthy attitudes. These were attitudes of hostility toward both big business and labor unions. Trow calls this set of attitudes "19th century liberalism", and he reasons that people holding this backward-looking view probably feel unrepresented by any of the major pressure groups and political parties of contemporary life. It follows that they might have been especially attracted to the negativism and opposition to powerful institutions which McCarthy expressed.[20]

Trow's research finds a source of support for McCarthy in the secular decline of small business, pressed between labor unions and big business, and the generalized economic hostility which this decline brought about. This interpretation is extended and translated into our frame of reference in the following hypothesis: *People with inconsistent class attributes are especially prone to support right-wing groups.* It will be recalled that there are two consistent sets of attributes, the propertied set of employer-creditor-seller and the non-propertied set of employee-debtor-buyer. All others are inconsistent. Small businessmen along with farmers are the classic mixed types, for while both make their living by selling, they also do capital buying from powerful sellers, and their incomes are often affected as much by buying as by selling. In addition, they are often heavily in debt and may be employers of labor, at least sporadically. Both groups, consequently, are afflicted with economic cross-pressures and cannot identify their interests with either big business or labor unions.

If the political disaffection of small businessmen is due to the mechanism we have described, it should be possible to find other forms of this mechanism in other segments of the population which exhibit a similar tendency toward the right wing. For example, a factor of this kind may be operating among some manual workers. The strong response of manual workers to McCarthy and some of the other right-wing groups has been difficult to explain, since these groups often oppose labor unions and welfare state legislation. Their response cannot be attributed to the greater intolerance or authoritarianism of manual workers, since there is some doubt that they are more intolerant on political matters.[21] But beyond that, it has

Carthyites and Birchers", pp. 373–446. Goldwater's support is analyzed in Irving Crespi, "The Structural Basis for Right-Wing Conservatism: The Goldwater Case", *Public Opinion Quarterly,* 29 (Winter, 1965–66, pp. 523–543. Governor Wallace's support in the Wisconsin presidential primary of 1964 is analyzed in Michael Rogin, "Wallace and the Middle Class: The White Backlash in Wisconsin", *Public Opinion Quarterly,* 30 (Spring, 1966), pp. 98–108.

In Lipset's earlier essay, entitled "The Sources of the 'Radical Right'", in Bell, *op. cit.,* pp. 307–371, he presented the theory of status politics, not only as an explanation for the whole range of McCarthy's support, but as a means of accounting for a whole series of intolerant political movements, beginning with the Know-Nothings of the 1850's. In that essay he used primarily qualitative analysis and remained at the macroscopic level, but in his later essay on "Three Decades," which is quantitative and microscopic, he finds that the available data on attitudes toward McCarthy do not support the status politics theory. Whatever this might mean for the historical applications of the status politics theory, it strongly suggests that no single-factor theory will explain the whole complex of phemonena labelled the "radical right".

[19] In the *American Journal of Sociology,* 64 (November, 1958), pp. 270–281.

[20] Support for Trow's hypothesis appears in

Raymond E. Wolfinger, Barbara Kaye Wolfinger, Kenneth Prewitt, and Sheilah Rosenhack, "America's Radical Right: Politics and Ideology", in David E. Apter, ed., *Ideology and Discontent,* New York: The Free Press of Glencoe, 1964, pp. 262–293. Wolfinger *et al.* used Trow's questions and found that the "19th century liberals" in a sample of people who attended a Christian Anti-Communism Crusade "Anti-Communism School" were considerably more "estranged from conventional means of political expression" than the rest of the sample. *Ibid.* p. 284.

[21] See Seymour Martin Lipset, "Democracy and Working-Class Authoritarianism," *American So-*

been shown that political intolerance and support for right-wing groups have only a weak relationship to each other.[22]

Our hypothesis predicts that workers who have a stake in capital property in some respect would be drawn to the right wing. This could take the form of a second job, or a wife's job, in small business, a sales "route," or part-time farming, or it could be some sort of direct capital investment in neighborhood real estate or corporate securities. Such people might be moving socially, up or down, or they might just be carrying two jobs or lines of economic activity, with no thought of mobility. In any case, they are in a mixed class position, on the nonpropertied side in the labor market and on the propertied side in the commodity or credit market. The investment might be an extremely modest one, or even only in the planning stage, and still affect the class attachments and political actions of these people.

It follows that such people might experience much the same cross pressures as the small businessman or farmer in relation to big business and labor and to the two major political parties. This group of workers might also be quite Republican, despite their political uneasiness, opposed to welfare state legislation, attached to the Protestant Ethic and religiously fundamentalistic.[23] In a re-

cent paper, Lipset reviewed four major polls on McCarthyism and concluded that among manual workers, especially the Republican ones, support for McCarthy increased with income. He suggests that "Perhaps the higher-income people within lower occupational or educational strata were precisely those who were most drawn to an ideology that attacked as pro-Communist both liberal lower-class-based politics and moderate, conservative old upper-class-elitist groups".[24] We would add that perhaps these higher income manual workers were often responding to the mixed class pressures of my hypothesis.

Turning to the category of retired people, especially those living on small incomes, it is not difficult to see how they might experience economic cross pressures and react irrationally. They are no longer attached to organized labor or any other occupational group, and upon retirement their class interests shift entirely to the credit and commodity markets.

Finally let us consider the salaried middle class. This group was among the weakest supporters of McCarthy but it seems to be giving stronger support, relatively speaking, to the John Birch Society.[25] On the face of it, this group is consistently on the non-

---

ciological Review, 24 (August, 1959), pp. 484–501; S. M. Miller and Frank Riessman, " 'Working-Class Authoritarianism': A Critique of Lipset", British Journal of Sociology, 12 (September, 1961), pp. 263–276; Lewis Lipsitz, "Working-Class Authoritarianism: A Re-Evaluation", American Sociological Review, 30 (February, 1965), pp. 103–109.

[22] This is one of the main findings in Trow, op. cit. A similar finding appears in Robert Sokol, "The Radical Right: A Panel Study of McCarthyism and Birchism", unpublished paper read at the annual meeting of the American Sociological Association, August, 1966.

[23] It might seem that people who are ideologically estranged from the major political parties would remain aloof from party participation and voting, but this does not necessarily follow. Participation could come from the desire not to waste a vote, from the feeling that there is no alternative outlet, or even from the desire to "bore from within". Many of Goldwater's followers in 1964, for example, seemed to be very much inside the Republican Party, even though they may have been ideological outsiders.

The relation between attachment to the radical right and partisan activity involves another issue that deserves comment. In his essay entitled "Toward an Explanation of McCarthyism", Nelson W. Polsby considers a series of variables usually

thought to be correlated with support for McCarthy and finds that the strongest correlate by far is simply attachment to the Republican Party. From this he concludes that McCarthyism was primarily a political phenomenon rather than a response to some more diffuse social strain. One difficulty with his conclusion arises from the nature of the particular Gallup Poll he chose to analyze. From the many national polls in which Gallup asked questions about McCarthy, Polsby chose a relatively late one, dated April 6, 1954, in which support for McCarthy, at 31 percent favorable, was lower than in any other Gallup Poll. It may be that if he had chosen a more representative poll from among those mentioned in footnote 12 of his article, the Republican support would have been lower. This is on the assumption that his Republican supporters would tend to be the last to desert him.

Lipset, in his "Three Decades" article, raises the more serious question of how many of these pro-McCarthy Republicans were former Democrats, and the data he presents show that there were a significant number of these. Polsby's article appears in Nelson W. Polsby, Robert A. Dentler and Paul A. Smith, Politics and Social Life, Boston: Houghton Mifflin, 1963, pp. 809–824.

[24] From Lipset's "Three Decades" article in Bell, op. cit., p. 402.

[25] Ibid., p. 430.

propertied side, just as manual workers are. Yet there are many small, and some large, investors in this group. More importantly, it is the salaried middle class that often becomes psychologically identified with the interests of big business. The result is that people who are typically employee-debtor-buyers may perceive themselves as employer-debtor-buyers. Thus they place themselves in the class position not of big business, but of small business, and evidently experience many of the political pressures of the old middle classes.

People in all of these positions—farmers, manual workers, retirees, and even the salaried middle class—thus may sometimes find themselves under the same kind of class pressures that Trow singled out for the case of small business. There is good reason to expect unusual political consequences from these situations, for they do not present clear cues for conventional political action. When class attachments are inconsistent, there is no single source of pressure, no clear source of trouble and no reasonable target. Pursuit of class interest becomes ambiguous, not only because class interests are scattered, but because *there is no class enemy*. All the powerful groups are, in some respect, enemies, and no single form of opposition will give emotional, let alone rational, satisfaction. It is not surprising if the political response carries a hostility toward all major institutions and suggests comparison with the clinical condition of paranoia at times.[26]

It is the mixed position in particular that produces what C. Wright Mills called the inability to see the relation between private troubles and public issues.[27] More generally, it follows that the people caught between bureaucracies and class interests are a greater source of irrationality than the people solidly located within bureaucracies. Mannheim argued that the growth of rational bureaucracy decreases the political rationality of the ordinary person employed within a bureaucracy.[28] As he put it, the growth of functional rationality decreases substantive rationality. This may be true for the response to crisis situations, such as characterized Europe between the two World Wars, but in non-crisis situations, such as post-war United States, it is apparently the mixed-class types, without a solid bureaucratic attachment, who are most pressured into the irrational political response.[29]

This hypothesis is not incompatible with many of the social and psychological theories of the right wing. Many of the mixed-class types are, for example, in a mixed status position as well, and much of the status instability in the United States is the social expression of an underlying class inconsistency, as with the worker-landlord or worker-farmer.[30] And, of course, status inconsistency, with its resentments and frustrations, would intensify the frustrations of an underlying economic inconsistency.

Similarly, there is a kind of alienation in not being clearly attached to any of the powerful bureaucracies, but this form of alienation comes, not from the growth of bureaucracy and mass society, but from the unevenness of this growth.[31]

These social and psychological factors, then, may move in the same direction as the underlying economic cross pressures. But they are mediating and not originating forces, and they are usually brought into play by the class base.

---

[26] Richard Hofstadter, in his *The Paranoid Style in American Politics and Other Essays*, New York: Alfred A. Knopf, 1965, observes that a quasi-paranoid political style appears not only in the contemporary right wing but in a series of political movements, of various ideological orientations, going back into early American history. If this style is especially characteristics of the United States, and Hofstadter does not make that assertion, it might be due to the strains that come from the historical inconsistencies in the American class structure.

[27] See, for example, his "Mass Society and Liberal Education", in Irving Louis Horowitz, ed., *Power, Politics and People*, New York: Ballantine Books, 1963, p. 370.

[28] Karl Mannheim, *Man and Society in an Age of Reconstruction*, London: Routledge & Kegan Paul Ltd., 1960, p. 58.

[29] We are again borrowing from Trow, *op. cit.* He makes approximately the same point, but in a less general way, in comparing the salaried middle class and small businessmen in Nazi Germany and the United States.

[30] Status "instability" or "inconsistency" refers here to the state in which a person's honor or prestige fluctuates from one situation to the next, whatever the reason. Inconsistency of rank on different prestige dimensions, e.g. the Negro doctor, is only one of several possible reasons for this. Inconsistency of rank or position on the same dimension or family of dimensions, as with our "class inconsistents," is another.

[31] Kornhauser, *op. cit.*, chapter 13.

Throughout this section we have drawn on the notion of individual class inconsistency. This was in contrast to the previous section where the major concept was systematic class inconsistency at the level of social structure. This shift in emphasis reflects a shift in the political importance of these two factors in the last seventy years or so. During this period, the United States class system has become progressively more consistent on the structural level as the labor unions and big business have grown, as the old middle classes have declined as an interposing force between business and labor, and as the major political parties have taken clearer class positions. During this time the incidence of individual inconsistency also declined, mainly because of the decline of the old middle class. The result, though, is that the remaining class inconsistents are in a much more ambiguous and free-floating class position than they were during the earlier period, when they had the stability of numbers and less powerful opposition. Their economic interest is not as clear as before, so they are less likely to pursue interest politics and more likely to vent general resentments on the entire institutional system.[32] This does not mean, however, that as the old middle classes decline still further this general source of right-wing support will disappear, for the other mixed-class types that we discussed are not declining.

THE NEGRO PROTEST MOVEMENT

Like the previous problems we considered, the Negro protest movement is difficult to define in traditional political categories. It is not simply a case of class conflict, for even though Negroes are typically in a consistent lower class situation, some Negroes of all classes are on the one side, just as some whites of all classes are on the other. Nor is it purely a case of racial or status conflict, for the issues are not empty status symbols; they are solidly economic and cut into all spheres of economic life. In fact, it is this very economic diffuseness, this spilling over beyond the familiar category of jobs and

---

[32] Perhaps this shift in the structure of class interests relates to the question of why the liberal ideals and many of the leaders of Populism and Progressivism went so incredibly sour during the period between the two World Wars.

working conditions, in combination with the status issue, which makes the Negro revolution unique in our political history.

It is illuminating to regard the economic side of this movement as a special form of class conflict in the commodity market, in other words as a conflict between buyers and sellers, landlords and tenants, government agencies and commodity recipients. The concrete grievances of Negroes often center around the need for commodities, which they either cannot afford or are not permitted to buy or rent, and much of the non-violent action, such as sit-ins, has been an attempt to obtain forbidden commodities and to secure complete freedom within this market. When these actions have been most militant, as in the rioting and store looting of recent summers or the rent strikes in some urban slums, the economic side of the conflict has been squarely in the commodity market.

This is not to say that the major economic disabilities of Negroes are in the commodity market, even when this market is conceived quite broadly. Certainly unemployment, low wages and other labor market troubles are the Negroes' most serious economic problem. But sometimes the response is incommensurate with the stimulus, because something mediates. The commodity market in the United States is the economic area most saturated with status and symbolic values, and the pure status conflict or "tribal" confrontation between Negroes and whites finds issues in the commodity market more easily than in other areas. Commodity protests define the interaction of status and class conflict in this case. This response, moreover, is in line with what might be expected from a people with only a marginal allegiance to the working class and a predominantly "lumpenproletariat" mentality.

This leads to a theoretical question about the lumpenproletariat generally. I think it is a mistake to regard this bottom-of-the-heap group as declassed or lacking in class interest. This may be true in labor market terms, but if we consider that the extreme poor are always buyers and almost always debtors, we can see a distinct class interest in these other areas. What the lumpenproletariat lack is not class interest or economic grievances. They lack organization, and the self-respect and political commitment that can come only from organization. If they could organize around their existing class interests, no one would make the mistake of saying they are without class or objective political interest.

The organization of propertyless elements for purposes of collective action has usually centered around type of job and place of work. But the Negro protest movement is showing that this organization can occur outside of the labor market, on other bases. There are indications that the Negro poor can now be organized and made a political force more easily than the white poor, for the Negroes have found an organizational weapon lacking to the whites. This weapon is skin color itself, and it is backed up by the residential ghetto with its many small organizations, its grapevines and other communication networks. Color and segregation give a unity and an organizational potential which the white poor do not have. We are not saying these mechanisms are a sufficient condition for the Negro protest movement. Rather, they are organizational resources which are intensifying a movement which began for quite different reasons. Negro organization is building on these unifying bases, much as the industrial labor unions were built on the unifying elements of the factory itself and its working conditions. But the Negro response, by virtue of the resources it has to work with, has been drawn to the commodity market. This is the area of most visible grievance, most degrading deprivation, and, above all, most unifying resentment.

The special class orientation and organizational needs of Negroes help explain why they have been drawn to ethnic solidarity and black nationalism in a way that other American ethnic groups were not. Broadly speaking, the labor movement has been the vehicle of protest for most other American ethnic groups. But because of the Negroes' rural backgrounds, marginal employment situation and the discrimination in the unions themselves, this vehicle of protest has not been available to Negroes. Accordingly, as a larger proportion of Negroes enter the stable working class, one might expect their protest to lose its emphasis on the commod-

ity market, on racial unity, and to merge with the labor movement generally.[33]

The Negro revolution, then, can be visualized as a combination of status conflict and mixed class conflict, with the primary class dimension being in the commodity market up until now. From another point of view, this revolution resembles the tradition of agrarian radicalism, for while both movements are forms of economic class conflict, they operate largely outside the labor market and are not explicable from a narrowly Marxist viewpoint.

CONCLUSION

In this paper we have tried to develop the Weberian theory of class and class conflict, relating it to selected problems of American politics. The central argument can be stated as follows: because of the special way in which industrialization occurred in the United States, there has been an unusual degree of inconsistency in the economic class structure, and, with important transformations, this pattern has persisted and has led to several political patterns of uniquely American quality. To explain these patterns, political sociology needs a more comprehensive economic theory than presently exists. The prevailing economic theories of Marxism and utilitarian liberalism were invented during a period of relatively uncomplicated economic life and were shaped especially by British experience.[34] Clearly, the economic

---

[33] The Newark and Detroit riots of the summer of 1967 occurred after these lines were written. In these riots commodity protests were carried to their violent extreme, and it is now more important than ever that the predominantly white labor movement accept the problem of the Negroes as basically a labor market problem. Without the strong political and economic support of organized labor, the Negro protest has no workable channel of expression.

[34] There are some indications that automation in the United States, in the long run, will drastically reduce the number of people needed in the labor force. This would decrease the importance of the labor market, and increase that of the commodity market, in the class order. Presumably these changes would, in due course, register in the system of pressure groups and politics. A suggestion of what kind of changes this could bring is given by the AFL-CIO's Industrial Union Department's successes in winning contracts for some thousands of tenants in Chicago's slums.

influences on politics are now extremely complex, and it would be unfortunate if the importance of economic factors were not fully recognized merely because the available theories were obsolete. It is our opinion that a more adequate theory can be developed, along the lines suggested in this paper, from the ideas of Max Weber. Once this has been done, a better framework will be available for the interpretation of such non-economic factors as status conflict, religion, psychological tensions and the like.

III

On the Sources of Inequality

Once a particular pattern of division of societal labor has emerged within a society or group, it is faced with a new dilemma: once you have the positions, they must be filled. If the society cannot find a procedure for allocating individuals to the differentiated roles and replacing deceased or mobile incumbents, it must necessarily undergo further change in the division of labor. Thus, a society or group will avoid this kind of change by the very step of employing some procedure to fill the positions in its existing division of labor. Regardless of the particular method employed, once a society has operated under a particular division of labor for a time (of the order of a generation or so), it will be reluctant to undergo change merely because of the unknown levels of risk and uncertainty which change entails. Even a "better" method is unattractive—why use chemical fertilizer when dung suffices?

Frequently the division of labor is preserved by attaching differential rewards to social positions, thus maintaining a particular pattern of social differentiation by creating social inequality. This happens, for example, when some roles require training and practice but others do not. Under these circumstances, the unequal requirements for entering the several roles are matched by unequal rewards for their performance.

The degree of inequality in the rewards is, in theory, just large enough to attract a sufficient number of competent persons to undertake the training and practice necessary to fill the roles, and not so large that more persons will be attracted to training and practice than there are roles to be filled. Thus, according to the functional theory of stratification developed by Davis and Moore in their now classic paper reprinted in this section, the maintenance of certain types of social differentiation requires that positions be differentially rewarded.

Once social inequality arises to preserve social differentiation, societies have a new locus in which change can take place and a new source of resistance to change. Once differential rewards have come to be associated with differentiated positions, change can take the form of reassigning rewards to positions. And once rewards have been employed to recruit individuals into positions, some individuals will oppose both change in the division of labor—which threatens the existence of their positions—and change in the assignment of rewards to positions, because both pose direct, real, and personal threats.

The claim that social differentiation per se is the cause of social inequality has been extremely controversial. No one, of course, has ever observed a society which is neither differentiated nor inequalitarian. Furthermore, if one omits the possibility of considering abstract ideal groups as stratified and limits the meaning of inequality to the differential reward or evaluation of actual groups, inequality cannot exist in the absence of differentiation: for two actual groups to be unequal in reward or social evaluation, they must be distinguishable on some ground. In this view, then, differentiation is closely bound to inequality both logically and empirically. It is impossible to have inequality without differentiation, so observed inequality logically implies differentiation. There is no society that is neither differentiated nor inequalitarian (and probably we would hesitate to call such a group, even if we could imagine it, a social system). Thus, the empirical question is whether differentiation must be regarded *only* as a necessary condition of inequality or *both* as a necessary and sufficient condition of inequality. The existence of even one situation where differentiation exists without social inequality would resolve the issue. Some have argued that the Israeli kibbutz (see Spiro, 1963; Schwartz, 1955) closely approximates this case, but the evidence supporting this contention is not wholly convincing. For the most part, then, empirical observations have provided no basis for rejecting the generalization that all societies are both differentiated and inequalitarian in some generic sense, but the question of how particular differences are converted into particular forms of inequality remains.

Although the differentiation of real groups must occur before they may be stratified, is it not possible that they were differentiated only so they could subsequently be stratified? Many bases of differentiation in modern societies (and we expect in primitive societies as well) are useful precisely because they simultaneously differentiate and stratify people. Tests of intelligence, of physical prowess, and, indeed, of personality itself serve to set aside the normal from the abnormal and, in so doing, hold up for disapprobation those made suspect by the unusual character of their performance. (In this context, we leave open the question of whether or not the too intelligent, too physically fit and too well adjusted are subjected to the same disapprobation by their location at the opposite extremes.) Thus, there is the distinct possibility that *conceptions* about inequality are an important determinant of the differentiation upon which objective inequalities rest. Also, there remains the question of how the several forms of inequality and differentiation are interrelated. The functional theory of stratification accounts for only a very limited range of phenomena. It helps us to understand why there is inequality at all, but it tells us nothing about why inequality takes the form it does. Furthermore, the functional theory does not help us at all to understand *stratification* in the sense of intergenerational transmission of wealth, power and status. These and other issues are raised and discussed in the papers by Wrong and Moore.

Often, it is charged that the functional theory of stratification is *inherently* static insofar as it contributes only to our understanding of the maintenance of the status quo. We would put the matter differently: the functional theory is not inherently static, it simply does not seek to explain anything more than why social inequality, in preserving the division of labor, will itself be maintained *in an unchanging environment*. Functional theorists admit that when the environment changes, this stability will break down, but they contend that the theory is not concerned with what happens in the face of exogenous environmental change.

Although a theory cannot be faulted for failing to accomplish something it does not set out to do, a single, coherent and comprehensive theory of interrelated phenomena is usually preferable to several disjoint explanations of various features of the same phenomena. Thus, in the final analysis, a theory of stratification which has no dynamic aspect is likely to give way to a more comprehensive scheme that enables one to understand not only how societies pass from one form of stratification to another, but also the conditions under which a particular regime of inequality will be stable. Marxian analysis, which is reviewed in the article by Ossowski included in this section, provides a very important point of departure for understanding how various types of social inequality are created, maintained and ultimately transformed. The maintenance of social systems requires continuous exchange between its constituent groups, as well as between the physical environment and the social structure. New modes of exploiting the physical environment may alter the relationships between groups or, for that matter, old relationships may falter because their productivity has been weakened through exhaustion of the resources they were designed to exploit. Whenever an unequal exchange between groups emerges, there will be a tendency on the part of one group to retain its advantage over the other: the mere act of maintaining existing inequalities may itself require the introduction of new inequalities and either the system will be transformed or the creation of new conflicts of interest will undermine it. These and other ideas are part of the Marxian corpus which continues to offer a unique and critical perspective on social stratification.

REFERENCES

Birnbaum, Norman.
  1969 The Crisis of Industrial Society. New York: Oxford University Press.
Buckley, Walter.
  1958 "Social stratification and the functional theory of social differentiation." American Sociological Review 28: 805-808.
Dahrendorf, Ralf.
  1959 Class and Class Conflict in Industrial Society. Stanford: Stanford University Press.
Davis, Kingsley.
  1959 "The abominable heresy: A reply to Dr. Buckley." American Sociological Review 24: 82.
Huaco, George A.
  1963 "A logical analysis of the Davis-Moore theory of stratification." American Sociological Review 28: 801-803.
Lichtheim, George.
  1961 Marxism: An Historical and Critical Study. New York: Praeger.

Schwartz, Richard D.
  1955 "Functional alternatives to inequality." American Sociological Review 20: 772-782.
Spiro, Melford E.
  1963 Kibbutz: Venture in Utopia. New York: Schocken Books.
Stinchcombe, Arthur L.
  1963 "Some empirical consequences of the Davis-Moore theory of stratification." American Sociological Review 28: 805-808.
  1968 "Marxian functionalism: Functional arguments in a system of unequal power." Pp. 93-98 in Constructing Social Theories. New York: Harcourt, Brace and World.
Sweezy, Paul M.
  1942 The Theory of Capitalist Development. New York: Oxford University Press.
Tumin, Melvin M.
  1953 "Some principles of stratification. A critical analysis." American Sociological Review 18: 387-393.

CHAPTER 8

Some Principles of Stratification

KINGSLEY DAVIS and WILBERT E. MOORE

IN A PREVIOUS PAPER some concepts for handling the phenomena of social inequality were presented.[1] In the present paper a further step in stratification theory is undertaken—an attempt to show the relationship between stratification and the rest of the social order.[2] Starting from the proposition that no society is "classless," or unstratified, an effort is made to explain, in functional terms, the universal necessity which calls forth stratification in any social system. Next, an attempt is made to explain the roughly uniform distribution of prestige as between the major types of positions in every society. Since, however, there occur between one society and another great differences in the degree and kind of stratification, some attention is also given to the varieties of social inequality and the variable factors that give rise to them.

Clearly, the present task requires two different lines of analysis—one to understand the universal, the other to understand the variable features of stratification. Naturally each line of inquiry aids the other and is indispensable, and in the treatment that follows the two will be interwoven, although, because of space limitations, the emphasis will be on the universals.

Throughout, it will be necessary to keep in mind one thing—namely, that the discussion relates to the system of positions, not to the individuals occupying those positions. It is one thing to ask why different positions carry different degrees of prestige, and quite another to ask how certain individuals get into those positions. Although, as the argument will try to show, both questions are related, it is essential to keep them separate in our thinking. Most of the literature on stratification has tried to answer the second question (particularly with regard to the ease or difficulty of mobility between strata) without tackling the first. The first question, however, is logically prior and, in the case of any particular individual or group, factually prior.

THE FUNCTIONAL NECESSITY OF STRATIFICATION

Curiously, however, the main functional necessity explaining the universal presence of stratification is precisely the requirement faced by any society of placing and motivating individuals in the social structure. As a functioning mechanism a society must somehow distribute its members in social positions and induce them to perform the duties of these positions. It must thus concern itself with motivation at two different levels: to instill in the proper individuals the desire to fill certain positions, and, once in these positions, the desire to perform the duties attached to them. Even though the social order may be relatively static in form, there is a continuous process of metabolism as new individuals are born into it, shift with age, and die off. Their absorption into the positional system must somehow be arranged and motivated. This is true whether the system is competitive or non-competitive. A competitive system gives greater importance to the motivation to achieve positions, whereas a non-competitive system gives perhaps greater importance to the mo-

[1] Kingsley Davis, "A Conceptual Analysis of Stratification," *American Sociological Review*. 7: 309-321, June, 1942.

[2] The writers regret (and beg indulgence) that the present essay, a condensation of a longer study, covers so much in such short space that adequate evidence and qualification cannot be given and that as a result what is actually very tentative is presented in an unfortunately dogmatic manner.

tivation to perform the duties of the positions; but in any system both types of motivation are required.

If the duties associated with the various positions were all equally pleasant to the human organism, all equally important to societal survival, and all equally in need of the same ability or talent, it would make no difference who got into which positions, and the problem of social placement would be greatly reduced. But actually it does make a great deal of difference who gets into which positions, not only because some positions are inherently more agreeable than others, but also because some require special talents or training and some are functionally more important than others. Also, it is essential that the duties of the positions be performed with the diligence that their importance requires. Inevitably, then, a society must have, first, some kind of rewards that it can use as inducements, and, second, some way of distributing these rewards differentially according to positions. The rewards and their distribution become a part of the social order, and thus give rise to stratification.

One may ask what kind of rewards a society has at its disposal in distributing its personnel and securing essential services. It has, first of all, the things that contribute to sustenance and comfort. It has, second, the things that contribute to humor and diversion. And it has, finally, the things that contribute to self respect and ego expansion. The last, because of the peculiarly social character of the self, is largely a function of the opinion of others, but it nonetheless ranks in importance with the first two. In any social system all three kinds of rewards must be dispensed differentially according to positions.

In a sense the rewards are "built into" the position. They consist in the "rights" associated with the position, plus what may be called its accompaniments or perquisites. Often the rights, and sometimes the accompaniments, are functionally related to the duties of the position. (Rights as viewed by the incumbent are usually duties as viewed by other members of the community.) However, there may be a host of subsidiary rights and perquisites that are not essential to the function of the position and have only an indirect and symbolic connection with its duties, but which still may be of considerable importance in inducing people to seek the positions and fulfil the essential duties.

If the rights and perquisites of different positions in a society must be unequal, then the society must be stratified, because that is precisely what stratification means. Social inequality is thus an unconsciously evolved device by which societies insure that the most important positions are conscientiously filled by the most qualified persons. Hence every society, no matter how simple or complex, must differentiate persons in terms of both prestige and esteem, and must therefore possess a certain amount of institutionalized inequality.

It does not follow that the amount or type of inequality need be the same in all societies. This is largely a function of factors that will be discussed presently.

THE TWO DETERMINANTS OF POSITIONAL RANK

Granting the general function that inequality subserves, one can specify the two factors that determine the relative rank of different positions. In general those positions convey the best reward, and hence have the highest rank, which (a) have the greatest importance for the society and (b) require the greatest training or talent. The first factor concerns function and is a matter of relative significance; the second concerns means and is a matter of scarcity.

Differential Functional Importance. Actually a society does not need to reward positions in proportion to their functional importance. It merely needs to give sufficient reward to them to insure that they will be filled competently. In other words, it must see that less essential positions do not compete successfully with more essential ones. If a position is easily filled, it need not be heavily rewarded, even though important. On the other hand, if it is important but hard to fill, the reward must be high enough to get it filled anyway. Functional importance is therefore a necessary but not a sufficient cause of high rank being assigned to a position.[3]

Differential Scarcity of Personnel. Practically all positions, no matter how acquired, require some form of skill or capacity for performance. This is implicit in the very notion of position, which implies that the incumbent must, by virtue of his incumbency, accomplish certain things.

There are, ultimately, only two ways in which a person's qualifications come about: through inherent capacity or through training. Obviously, in concrete activities both are always necessary, but from a practical standpoint the scarcity may lie primarily in one or the other, as well as in both. Some positions require innate talents of such high degree that the persons who fill them are bound to be rare. In many cases, however, talent is fairly abundant in the population but the training process is so long, costly, and elaborate that relatively few can qualify. Modern medicine, for example, is within the mental capacity of most individuals, but a medical education is so burdensome and expensive that virtually none would undertake it if the position of the M.D. did not carry a reward commensurate with the sacrifice.

If the talents required for a position are abundant and the training easy, the method of acquiring the position may have little to

[3] Unfortunately, functional importance is difficult to establish. To use the position's prestige to establish it, as is often unconsciously done, constitutes circular reasoning from our point of view. There are, however, two independent clues: (a) the degree to which a position is functionally unique, there being no other positions that can perform the same function satisfactorily; (b) the degree to which other positions are dependent on the one in question. Both clues are best exemplified in organized systems of positions built around one major function. Thus, in most complex societies the religious, political, economic, and educational functions are handled by distinct structures not easily interchangeable. In addition, each structure possesses many different positions, some clearly dependent on, if not subordinate to, others. In sum, when an institutional nucleus becomes differentiated around one main function, and at the same time organizes a large portion of the population into its relationships, the *key* positions in it are of the high-

do with its duties. There may be, in fact, a virtually accidental relationship. But if the skills required are scarce by reason of the rarity of talent or the costliness of training, the position, if functionally important, must have an attractive power that will draw the necessary skills in competition with other positions. This means, in effect, that the position must be high in the social scale—must command great prestige, high salary, ample leisure, and the like.

How Variations Are to Be Understood. In so far as there is a difference between one system of stratification and another, it is attributable to whatever factors affect the two determinants of differential reward—namely, functional importance and scarcity of personnel. Positions important in one society may not be important in another, because the conditions faced by the societies, or their degree of internal development, may be different. The same conditions, in turn, may affect the question of scarcity; for in some societies the stage of development, or the external situation, may wholly obviate the necessity of certain kinds of skill or talent. Any particular system of stratification, then, can be understood as a product of the special conditions affecting the two aforementioned grounds of differential reward.

MAJOR SOCIETAL FUNCTIONS AND STRATIFICATION

Religion. The reason why religion is necessary is apparently to be found in the fact that human society achieves its unity primarily through the possession by its members of certain ultimate values and ends in common. Although these values and ends are subjective, they influence behavior, and their integration enables the society to operate as a system. Derived neither from inherited nor from external nature, they have evolved as a part of culture by communication and moral pressure. They must, how-

est functional importance. The absence of such specialization does not prove functional unimportance, for the whole society may be relatively unspecialized; but it is safe to assume that the more important functions receive the first and clearest structural differentiation.

ever, appear to the members of the society to have some reality, and it is the role of religious belief and ritual to supply and reinforce this appearance of reality. Through belief and ritual the common ends and values are connected with an imaginary world symbolized by concrete sacred objects, which world in turn is related in a meaningful way to the facts and trials of the individual's life. Through the worship of the sacred objects and the beings they symbolize, and the acceptance of supernatural prescriptions that are at the same time codes of behavior, a powerful control over human conduct is exercised, guiding it along lines sustaining the institutional structure and conforming to the ultimate ends and values.

If this conception of the role of religion is true, one can understand why in every known society the religious activities tend to be under the charge of particular persons, who tend thereby to enjoy greater rewards than the ordinary societal member. Certain of the rewards and special privileges may attach to only the highest religious functionaries, but others usually apply, if such exists, to the entire sacerdotal class.

Moreover, there is a peculiar relation between the duties of the religious official and the special privileges he enjoys. If the supernatural world governs the destinies of men more ultimately than does the real world, its earthly representative, the person through whom one may communicate with the supernatural, must be a powerful individual. He is a keeper of sacred tradition, a skilled performer of the ritual, and an interpreter of lore and myth. He is in such close contact with the gods that he is viewed as possessing some of their characteristics. He is, in short, a bit sacred, and hence free from some of the more vulgar necessities and controls.

It is no accident, therefore, that religious functionaries have been associated with the very highest positions of power, as in theocratic regimes. Indeed, looking at it from this point of view, one may wonder why it is that they do not get *entire* control over their societies. The factors that prevent this are worthy of note.

In the first place, the amount of technical competence necessary for the performance of religious duties is small. Scientific or artistic capacity is not required. Anyone can set himself up as enjoying an intimate relation with deities, and nobody can successfully dispute him. Therefore, the factor of scarcity of personnel does not operate in the technical sense.

One may assert, on the other hand, that religious ritual is often elaborate and religious lore abstruse, and that priestly ministrations require tact, if not intelligence. This is true, but the technical requirements of the profession are for the most part adventitious, not related to the end in the same way that science is related to air travel. The priest can never be free from competition, since the criteria of whether or not one has genuine contact with the supernatural are never strictly clear. It is this competition that debases the priestly position below what might be expected at first glance. That is why priestly prestige is highest in those societies where membership in the profession is rigidly controlled by the priestly guild itself. That is why, in part at least, elaborate devices are utilized to stress the identification of the person with his office—spectacular costume, abnormal conduct, special diet, segregated residence, celibacy, conspicuous leisure, and the like. In fact, the priest is always in danger of becoming somewhat discredited—as happens in a secularized society—because in a world of stubborn fact, ritual and sacred knowledge alone will not grow crops or build houses. Furthermore, unless he is protected by a professional guild, the priest's identification with the supernatural tends to preclude his acquisition of abundant wordly goods.

As between one society and another it seems that the highest general position awarded the priest occurs in the medieval type of social order. Here there is enough economic production to afford a surplus, which can be used to support a numerous and highly organized priesthood; and yet the populace is unlettered and therefore credulous to a high degree. Perhaps the most extreme example is to be found in the Buddhism of Tibet, but others are encountered in the Catholicism of feudal Europe, the Inca regime of Peru, the Brahminism of India, and the Mayan priesthood of Yucatan. On the other hand, if the society is so crude as to have no surplus and little differentiation, so that every priest must be also a cultivator or hunter, the separation of the priestly status from the others has hardly gone far enough for priestly prestige to mean much. When the priest actually has high prestige under these circumstances, it is because he also performs other important functions (usually political and medical).

In an extremely advanced society built on scientific technology, the priesthood tends to lose status, because sacred tradition and supernaturalism drop into the background. The ultimate values and common ends of the society tend to be expressed in less anthropomorphic ways, by officials who occupy fundamentally political, economic, or educational rather than religious positions. Nevertheless, it is easily possible for intellectuals to exaggerate the degree to which the priesthood in a presumably secular milieu has lost prestige. When the matter is closely examined the urban proletariat, as well as the rural citizenry, proves to be suprisingly god-fearing and priest-ridden. No society has become so completely secularized as to liquidate entirely the belief in transcendental ends and supernatural entities. Even in a secularized society some system must exist for the integration of ultimate values, for their ritualistic expression, and for the emotional adjustments required by disappointment, death, and disaster.

Government. Like religion, government plays a unique and indispensable part in society. But in contrast to religion, which provides integration in terms of sentiments, beliefs, and rituals, it organizes the society in terms of law and authority. Furthermore, it orients the society to the actual rather than the unseen world.

The main functions of government are, internally, the ultimate enforcement of norms, the final arbitration of conflicting interests, and the overall planning and direction of society; and externally, the handling of war and diplomacy. To carry out these functions it acts as the agent of the entire people, enjoys a monopoly of force, and controls all individuals within its territory.

Political action, by definition, implies authority. An official can command because he has authority, and the citizen must obey because he is subject to that authority. For this reason stratification is inherent in the nature of political relationships.

So clear is the power embodied in political position that political inequality is sometimes thought to comprise all inequality. But it can be shown that there are other bases of stratification, that the following controls operate in practice to keep political power from becoming complete: (a) The fact that the actual holders of political office, and especially those determining top policy must necessarily be few in number compared to the total population. (b) The fact that the rulers represent the interest of the group rather than of themselves, and are therefore restricted in their behavior by rules and mores designed to enforce this limitation of interest. (c) The fact that the holder of political office has his authority by virtue of his office and nothing else, and therefore any special knowledge, talent, or capacity he may claim is purely incidental, so that he often has to depend upon others for technical assistance.

In view of these limiting factors, it is not strange that the rulers often have less power and prestige than a literal enumeration of their formal rights would lead one to expect.

Wealth, Property, and Labor. Every position that secures for its incumbent a livelihood is, by definition, economically rewarded. For this reason there is an economic aspect to those positions (e.g. political and religious) the main function of which is not' economic. It therefore becomes convenient for the society to use unequal economic returns as a principal means of controlling the entrance of persons into positions and stimulating the performance of their duties. The amount of the economic return therefore becomes one of the main indices of social status.

It should be stressed, however, that a position does not bring power and prestige *because* it draws a high income. Rather, it draws a high income because it is functionally important and the available personnel is for one reason or another scarce. It is therefore superficial and erroneous to regard high income as the cause of a man's power and prestige, just as it is erroneous to think that a man's fever is the cause of his disease.[4]

The economic source of power and prestige is not income primarily, but the ownership of capital goods (including patents, good will, and professional reputation). Such ownership should be distinguished from the possession of consumers' goods, which is an index rather than a cause of social standing. In other words, the ownership of producers' goods is properly speaking, a source of income like other positions, the income itself remaining an index. Even in situations where social values are widely commercialized and earnings are the readiest method of judging social position, income does not confer prestige on a position so much as it induces people to compete for the position. It is true that a man who has a high income as a result of one position may find this money helpful in climbing into another position as well, but this again reflects the effect of his initial, economically advantageous status, which exercises its influence through the medium of money.

In a system of private property in productive enterprise, an income above what an individual spends can give rise to possession of capital wealth. Presumably such possession is a reward for the proper management of one's finances originally and of the productive enterprise later. But as social differentiation becomes highly advanced and yet the institution of inheritance persists, the phenomenon of pure ownership, and reward for pure ownership, emerges. In such a case it is difficult to prove that the position is functionally important or that the scarcity involved is anything other than extrinsic and accidental. It is for this reason, doubtless,

that the institution of private property in productive goods becomes more subject to criticism as social development proceeds toward industrialization. It is only this pure, that is, strictly legal and functionless ownership, however, that is open to attack; for some form of active ownership, whether private or public, is indispensable.

One kind of ownership of production goods consists in rights over the labor of others. The most extremely concentrated and exclusive of such rights are found in slavery, but the essential principle remains in serfdom, peonage, encomienda, and indenture. Naturally this kind of ownership has the greatest significance for stratification, because it necessarily entails an unequal relationship.

But property in capital goods inevitably introduces a compulsive element even into the nominally free contractual relationship. Indeed, in some respects the authority of the contractual employer is greater than that of the feudal landlord, inasmuch as the latter is more limited by traditional reciprocities. Even the classical economics recognized that competitors would fare unequally, but it did not pursue this fact to its necessary conclusion that, however it might be acquired, unequal control of goods and services must give unequal advantage to the parties to a contract.

Technical Knowledge. The function of finding means to single goals, without any concern with the choice between goals, is the exclusively technical sphere. The explanation of why positions requiring great technical skill receive fairly high rewards is easy to see, for it is the simplest case of the rewards being so distributed as to draw talent and motivate training. Why they seldom if ever receive the highest rewards is also clear: the importance of technical knowledge from a societal point of view is never so great as the integration of goals, which takes place on the religious, political, and economic levels. Since the technological level is concerned solely with means, a purely technical position must ultimately be subordinate to other positions that are religious, political, or economic in character.

Nevertheless, the distinction between ex-

---

[4] The symbolic rather than intrinsic role of income in social stratification has been succinctly summarized by Talcott Parsons, "An Analytical Approach to the Theory of Social Stratification," *American Journal of Sociology.* 45:841-862, May, 1940.

pert and layman in any social order is fundamental, and cannot be entirely reduced to
other terms. Methods of recruitment, as well
as of reward, sometimes lead to the erroneous
interpretation that technical positions are
economically determined. Actually, however,
the acquisition of knowledge and skill cannot
be accomplished by purchase, although the
opportunity to learn may be. The control of
the avenues of training may inhere as a sort
of property right in certain families or classes,
giving them power and prestige in consequence. Such a situation adds an artificial
scarcity to the natural scarcity of skills and
talents. On the other hand, it is possible for
an opposite situation to arise. The rewards
of technical position may be so great that a
condition of excess supply is created, leading
to at least temporary devaluation of the
rewards. Thus "unemployment in the learned
professions" may result in a debasement of
the prestige of those positions. Such adjustments and readjustments are constantly occurring in changing societies; and it is always
well to bear in mind that the efficiency of a
stratified structure may be affected by the
modes of recruitment for positions. The social
order itself, however, sets limits to the inflation or deflation of the prestige of experts:
an over-supply tends to debase the rewards
and discourage recruitment or produce revolution, whereas an under-supply tends to
increase the rewards or weaken the society
in competition with other societies.

Particular systems of stratification show
a wide range with respect to the exact position of technically competent persons. This
range is perhaps most evident in the degree
of specialization. Extreme division of labor
tends to create many specialists without high
prestige since the training is short and the
required native capacity relatively small. On
the other hand it also tends to accentuate
the high position of the true experts—scientists, engineers, and administrators—by increasing their authority relative to other
functionally important positions. But the
idea of a technocratic social order or a
government or priesthood of engineers or
social scientists neglects the limitations of
knowledge and skills as a basic for performing social functions. To the extent that the
social structure is truly specialized the prestige of the technical person must also be
circumscribed.

VARIATION IN STRATIFIED SYSTEMS

The generalized principles of stratification
here suggested form a necessary preliminary
to a consideration of types of stratified systems, because it is in terms of these principles
that the types must be described. This can
be seen by trying to delineate types according
to certain modes of variation. For instance,
some of the most important modes (together
with the polar types in terms of them) seem
to be as follows:

(a) *The Degree of Specialization.* The
degree of specialization affects the fineness
and multiplicity of the gradations in power
and prestige. It also influences the extent to
which particular functions may be emphasized in the invidious system, since a given
function cannot receive much emphasis in
the hierarchy until it has achieved structural
separation from the other functions. Finally,
the amount of specialization influences the
bases of selection. Polar types: *Specialized,
Unspecialized.*

(b) *The Nature of the Functional Emphasis.* In general when emphasis is put on
sacred matters, a rigidity is introduced that
tends to limit specialization and hence the
development of technology. In addition, a
brake is placed on social mobility, and on
the development of bureaucracy. When the
preoccupation with the sacred is withdrawn,
leaving greater scope for purely secular preoccupations, a great development, and rise
in status, of economic and technological positions seemingly takes place. Curiously, a
concomitant rise in political position is not
likely, because it has usually been allied with
the religious and stands to gain little by the
decline of the latter. It is also possible for
a society to emphasize family functions—as
in relatively undifferentiated societies where
high mortality requires high fertility and kinship forms the main basis of social organization. Main types: *Familistic, Authoritarian
(Theocratic* or sacred, and *Totalitarian* or
secular), *Capitalistic.*

(c) *The Magnitude of Invidious Dif-ferences*. What may be called the amount of social distance between positions, taking into account the entire scale, is something that should lend itself to quantitative measurement. Considerable differences apparently exist between different societies in this regard, and also between parts of the same society. Polar types: *Equalitarian, Inequalitarian*.

(d) *The Degree of Opportunity*. The familiar question of the amount of mobility is different from the question of the comparative equality or inequality of rewards posed above, because the two criteria may vary independently up to a point. For instance, the tremendous divergences in monetary income in the United States are far greater than those found in primitive societies, yet the equality of opportunity to move from one rung to the other in the social scale may also be greater in the United States than in a hereditary tribal kingdom. Polar types: *Mobile* (open), *Immobile* (closed).

(e) *The Degree of Stratum Solidarity*. Again, the degree of "class solidarity" (or the presence of specific organizations to promote class interests) may vary to some extent independently of the other criteria, and hence is an important principle in classifying systems of stratification. Polar types: *Class organized, Class unorganized*.

EXTERNAL CONDITIONS

What state any particular system of stratification is in with reference to each of these modes of variation depends on two things: (1) its state with reference to the other ranges of variation, and (2) the conditions outside the system of stratification which nevertheless influence that system. Among the latter are the following:

(a) *The Stage of Cultural Development*. As the cultural heritage grows, increased specialization becomes necessary, which in turn contributes to the enhancement of mobility, a decline of stratum solidarity, and a change of functional emphasis.

(b) *Situation with Respect to Other Societies*. The presence or absence of open conflict with other societies, of free trade relations or cultural diffusion, all influence the class structure to some extent. A chronic state of warfare tends to place emphasis upon the military functions, especially when the opponents are more or less equal. Free trade, on the other hand, strengthens the hand of the trader at the expense of the warrior and priest. Free movement of ideas generally has an equalitarian effect. Migration and conquest create special circumstances.

(c) *Size of the Society*. A small society limits the degree to which functional specialization can go, the degree of segregation of different strata, and the magnitude of inequality.

COMPOSITE TYPES

Much of the literature on stratification has attempted to classify concrete systems into a certain number of types. This task is deceptively simple, however, and should come at the end of an analysis of elements and principles, rather than at the beginning. If the preceding discussion has any validity, it indicates that there are a number of modes of variation between different systems, and that any one system is a composite of the society's status with reference to all these modes of variation. The danger of trying to classify whole societies under such rubrics as *caste, feudal,* or *open class* is that one or two criteria are selected and others ignored, the result being an unsatisfactory solution to the problem posed. The present discussion has been offered as a possible approach to the more systematic classification of composite types.

CHAPTER 9

The Functional Theory of Stratification: Some Neglected Considerations

DENNIS H. WRONG

The functional theory of stratification advanced by Davis and Moore attempts to explain the universality and the necessity of inequality in societies with a complex division of labor, a task that is independent of efforts to explain the division of labor itself or the intergenerational perpetuation of inequalities along family lines. The theory is so general, however, that it excludes none of the Utopian models of "classless societies" proposed by Western thinkers and, its critics to the contrary notwithstanding, says nothing whatsoever about the range of inequality and the determinants of the range in concrete societies. The theory appears to understate the degree to which positions are inherited by failing to view societies in long-range historical perspective. In common with the arguments of its critics, it also ignores the possible disruptive consequences of mobility and equality of opportunity, a theme notably neglected by American sociologists.

NEARLY fifteen years after its original publication, the issues raised by Kingsley Davis and Wilbert E. Moore in their article "Some Principles of Stratification"[1] are still being debated by sociologists. Critics of the authors' thesis have succeeded in showing that there are a great many things about stratification that Davis and Moore have failed to explain, but they have not succeeded in seriously denting the central argument that unequal rewards are

---

[1] *American Sociological Review*, 10 (April, 1945), pp. 242–249. An extended and revised version of the theory which, as Davis has complained, the critics have largely ignored appears in Kingsley Davis, *Human Society*, New York: Macmillan, 1949, pp. 366–378.

functionally necessary in any and all societies with a division of labor extending much beyond differences in age and sex. On the other hand, the extreme abstractness and limited relevance of the Davis-Moore theory to the concrete historical world have been only partially recognized by its authors and their critics alike. Moreover, several of the theory's assumptions have yet to be made explicit and a number of additional implications have been ignored by participants in the debate.

THE DEFINITION OF STRATIFICATION

Walter Buckley's criticism of the Davis-Moore theory largely centers on the question of how stratification should be defined.[2] He accuses Davis and Moore of confusing *social differentiation*, the existence of specialized roles or of a division of labor, with *social stratification*, which he defines as a system of unequally privileged groups, membership in which is determined by the intergenerational transmission of roles, or of opportunities to attain them, through kinship affiliation. Davis has replied that what is or is not to be called stratification is purely a terminological question provided that a distinction is clearly made between the hierarchy of unequally rewarded roles and the way in which particular individuals are recruited in each generation to fill them.[3] Three relevant types of social organization, however, should be distinguished:

First, there is the existence of role differentiation or division of labor itself, irrespective of whether or how the roles are ranked and their incumbents unequally rewarded. This is what is usually called *social differentiation*. Its causes and consequences, as Durkheim's famous study illustrates, can be discussed independently of the logically separable questions of how and why "horizontal" or "lateral" differences in position are transformed into "vertical" differences in rank.

Second, there are the unequal rewards distributed among the various roles making up the division of labor. The Davis-Moore theory tries to explain the ubiquity and inevitability of unequal rewards wherever role differentiation is highly developed.

Third, there is the tendency, a result of kinship loyalties, for roles and opportunities to attain them to be passed on from one generation to the next, giving rise to enduring classes or strata monopolizing certain roles and exhibiting a greater or lesser degree of solidarity and a common style of life.

Buckley accuses Davis and Moore of confusing the second and third types of social organization, but he himself confuses the first and second. The Davis-Moore theory, if it achieves nothing else, surely provides sound arguments for regarding the existence of a hierarchy of roles as a problem in its own right. Consider that Buckley's terminology would require him to describe an army which recruited all of its officers from the lower ranks as a differentiated but non-stratified organization. And the same description would apply to the Catholic Church, where celibacy rules prevent the intergenerational transmission of roles. Admittedly, these types of hierarchy differ in important respects from hereditary class systems; if the term "stratification" is to be confined to the latter, however, another term is needed to distinguish armies, celibate priestly orders, and other bureaucracies from pre-civilized tribal societies, collegial bodies, parliaments, and similar non-hierarchical social structures.[4] But Davis and Moore are concerned with hierarchy or inequality *per se:* such a distinction is only tangentially relevant to their argument.

THE FUNCTIONAL NECESSITY OF STRATIFICATION

What the critics of the Davis-Moore theory fundamentally object to is that in their view "the theory implies an assumption that any scheme of stratification is somehow the best that could be had, that the prevailing distribution of rewards comes into being somehow because it is 'functionally necessary.' "[5] The charge, repeated in some form

---

[2] "Social Stratification and the Functional Theory of Social Differentiation," *American Sociological Review*, 23 (August, 1958), pp. 369–375.

[3] "The Abominable Heresy: A Reply to Dr. Buckley," *American Sociological Review*, 24 (February, 1959), pp. 82–83.

[4] They might usefully be called *ladder hierarchies* to distinguish them from *class hierarchies*.

[5] Richard L. Simpson, "A Modification of the Functional Theory of Social Stratification," *Social Forces*, 35 (December, 1956), p. 132.

by all of the critics, that Davis and Moore are "defending" or "justifying" the *status quo*, any *status quo*, rests on finding this implication in the theory. Yet it is not a logically correct implication, although it has never been explicitly disavowed by the authors.

All that the Davis-Moore theory actually asserts is that *if* the more important, highly skilled, and physically and psychologically demanding positions in a complex division of labor are to be adequately filled both from the standpoint of numbers and of minimally efficient performance, *then* there must be *some* unequal rewards favoring these positions over others. This proposition rests on certain assumptions about human nature. The important thing to note, however, is that it in no way denies that a particular distribution of rewards prevailing in a given historical society may vastly exceed the minimum inequalities necessary to maintain a complex division of labor.[6] Nor does it deny that some roles that are unimportant, unskilled, and pleasurable may be highly rewarded, provided only that they do not compete so successfully with roles possessing the opposite attributes that they reduce the quantity or the quality of candidates for the latter below some minimum level.[7] Nothing in their theory requires Davis and Moore to disagree with Tumin's claim that the "sacrifices" made by those who undergo professional training are over-rewarded,[8] nor with Simpson's contention that such roles as personal servant or kept woman may be highly rewarded although they make little contribution to society. Davis and Moore are committed solely to the view that there must be unequal rewards; *how* unequal these need to be or how strictly they must be apportioned according to functional importance and skill are separate questions the answers to which are not deducible from the theory.

The particular scale of unequal rewards prevailing in a society is likely so to shape people's expectations and sense of distributive justice that they will oppose efforts to alter it, even though no general sociological principle rules out the feasibility of a viable society in which the range of inequality might be far narrower. Notions of "fair price," "deserved recognition," and "proper return for services" may be invoked to protest increased taxation of large incomes, the imposition of wage cuts on manual workers, or even changes in wage and salary differentials between occupations differing in skill, responsibility, and traditional prestige.

Belief in the *legitimacy* of the existing scale of rewards, however, should be distinguished from the *power* possessed by threatened groups to resist any reduction in the size of their shares. The incumbents of the more functionally important and skilled roles are able to fight back by threatening withdrawal of their services if faced with a proposed distribution of rewards. This follows directly from the Davis-Moore principle viewed from a somewhat different perspective from that of its authors. Significantly, Davis and Moore have not formulated their theory in a way that focuses attention on the power element in stratification: they argue that unequal rewards are necessary to attract individuals into the more important and skilled positions yet neglect to observe that once these positions have been filled their very importance and dependence on scarce skills gives their incumbents the power not only to insist on payment of expected rewards but even to demand larger ones. This power is inherent in the positions. The unequal rewards in wealth and prestige "attached to" the positions also give their incumbents greater opportunities to influence the general distribution of rewards in society and to protect or augment their own privileges. A further consideration is that the incumbents of the most highly-rewarded

---

[6] Davis and Moore recognize the independent variability of the *scale of rewards*, or what they call "the magnitude of invidious differences," in listing it as a distinct "mode of variation" of stratified systems. *Op. cit.*, pp. 248–249. See also the very lucid discussion by Ralph Ross and Ernest van den Haag in *The Fabric of Society*, New York: Harcourt, Brace, 1957, pp. 121–122.

[7] "Actually a society does not need to reward positions in proportion to their functional importance. It merely needs to give sufficient reward to insure that they will be filled competently." And, it should be added, in sufficient numbers. Davis, *Human Society*, p. 368.

[8] Melvin M. Tumin, "Some Principles of Stratification: A Critical Analysis," *American Sociological Review*, 18 (August, 1953), p. 390. Davis replies that Tumin ignores the "onerous necessity of studying," but no such defense is required to uphold his theory. Davis, "Reply," *Ibid.*, p. 396.

roles are relatively few in number, which, as Michels and Mosca have taught us, facilitates collective organization and solidarity, preconditions for the effective exercise of social power.

Yet the history of left-wing parties and of labor movements in modern times demonstrates that the more numerous but individually less powerful occupants of the less-rewarded positions may organize to offset the initial power advantage of the privileged. By doing so they have succeeded often enough in effecting a redistribution of rewards in their favor. But the difficulties in organizing and maintaining solidarity among relatively poor, uneducated, apolitical, and geographically scattered majorities are formidable. That is why, as G. L. Arnold writes of the industrial worker, " 'Solidarity' is for him what 'honor' was to the feudal order, and 'honesty' for the bourgeois: a claim which is felt as absolute because the existence of the individual depends on it." [9]

Reformist and revolutionary governments striving to alter the existing scale of rewards have often been forced to modify their egalitarian programs when confronted with the resistance of privileged groups. The threat or reality of a flight of capital has sometimes been employed to compel moderation of the policies of governments committed to greater economic equalization. The British Labor Party was forced to make concessions to the medical profession when socializing health services in England. Even unorganized lower strata may by passive resistance and what Veblen called "calculated withdrawal of efficiency" succeed at least in slowing up the pace of drastic changes imposed on them by centralized authorities: the Soviet regime from its earliest days repeatedly has made concessions to the peasants in the interests of higher agricultural productivity and has also found it expedient to restore "capitalist" incentives and wage differentials in industry.

These examples illustrate the eternal difficulties faced by reformers and Utopians in "making the leap from history into freedom." The progressive departure from egalitarian practices in the Soviet Union since the Revolution may indicate the "functional necessity" of maintaining a certain scale of unequal rewards in societies in the early stages of capital accumulation.[10] But neither the resistance aroused by efforts to modify existing inequalities in any society nor the possible need for wide inequalities in societies experiencing rapid industrialization justifies the conclusion that a more equal distribution of rewards is in principle incompatible with the maintenance of a complex division of labor.

Freud, in observing the social pathology of everyday life, spoke of a "narcissism with respect to minor differences," and students of bureaucratic organization confirm its reality when they report the immense significance people often attach to the door which is used to enter the place of work, the size and location of desks, the exact shade of cordiality of the boss's salutation, and so on. But can *all* differences, even those that are trivial in comparison with the inequalities we usually have in mind when discussing historical class systems, be abolished? Davis and Moore answer in the negative; a simple negative answer is all that their theory implies and all that any sociologist is entitled to mean in characterizing a "classless society" as a "sociological monstrosity" or a "contradiction in terms." [11]

It is worth noting that most egalitarian reformers in Western history have been concerned with narrowing the range of inequality and creating wider equality of *opportunity* rather than with the establishment of total equality of *condition:* the abolition of any system of unequal rewards altogether. And those who have favored the latter, notably sectarian Christian communists and Israeli *Kibbutznikim,* have been willing to pay the price set by Davis and Moore; foregoing the advantages of an elaborate division of labor and permanent commitment to an agrarian way of life. Marx relegated the achievement of his ideal society based on the principle "from each according to his quality, to each according to his need" to the "higher phase" of communism when the state will have

[9] G. L. Arnold, "Collectivism Reconsidered," *British Journal of Sociology,* 6 (March, 1955), p. 9.

[10] Barrington Moore, Jr., *Political Power and Social Theory,* Cambridge: Harvard University Press, 1958, p. 137.

[11] E. Digby Baltzell, *Philadelphia Gentlemen: The Making of a National Upper Class,* Glencoe, Ill.: Free Press, 1958, pp. 1, 396.

withered away, an economy of abundance will have been realized, and a division of labor will no longer be necessary.[12] However difficult it may be to imagine technological innovations radical enough to make possible such a society,[13] there is nothing in its conception that violates the Davis-Moore principle. Moreover, the Marxist slogan refers only to *material* rewards. By recognizing different kinds of rewards, Davis and Moore do not rule out the possibility of a differentiated society in which complete income equality exists provided only that inequality of "psychological income" remains.[14]

The Davis-Moore theory, then, is formulated at so high a level of generality that it fails to rule out the "funetional" viability of the major Utopian models of egalitarian societies which have been advanced by visionary thinkers since Medieval times and even earlier. Although this may be regarded as evidence of the theory's undeniable validity, one may be disposed to conclude that, like other generalizations about the "universal functional prerequisites" of societies, it explains so little about concrete class structures, social inequalities, and the ways in which they arise and change, that the theory's value is limited.

Yet by recognizing, if only implicitly, the separability of types of reward, the Davis-Moore theory is superior to other functionalist theories of stratification which tend to subsume all rewards under prestige or "differential evaluation."[15] Such theories require the questionable assumption that there is a single value-consensus in society. But there are always roles which *must* carry high material rewards to attract people to them in compensation for their abysmally low prestige—for example, hangmen, prostitutes, professional criminals. The independent variability of types of reward also helps to account for social change: that wealth or power can be gained in certain roles, even though their very existence may be deplored by prevailing mores and the resulting prestige judgments, encourages the spread of new activities, the rise of "new men" to foster them, and ultimately the development of new values, ideologies, and prestige rankings imposed by ascendant classes.

To avoid the "fallacy of misplaced concreteness," the Davis-Moore theory must be challenged on the ground of its psychological assumptions. Tumin is the only critic who has done so.[16] He suggests that motives other than desire for the prestige and material rewards attached to important and skilled roles might be institutionalized and might ensure competent role performance at less cost to society than unequal rewards. He mentions "joy in work" and "social duty" as possibilities. However, as Davis has pointed out in his rejoinder, Tumin blurs the distinction between prestige and esteem, between incentives for striving to attain positions and incentives for conscientiously fulfilling their duties once they have been attained. The motives Tumin mentions conceivably might induce people to carry out properly the duties of their positions, but, even if men were angels, the need for some selective system to allocate them to these positions in the first place would still exist. That exactly the right number of would-be doctors needed by society would feel an inner call to cure the ill at exactly the right time, or that individuals, however beneficent their intentions, would spontaneously distribute them-

[12] Marx's view is stated most succinctly in *The Critique of the Gotha Programme*, Part I, Point 3, any edition.

[13] And, barring the Malthusian problem which Marxists have notoriously slighted, it is not so difficult to imagine as it once was in view of the prospects of automation. As Meyer remarks: "Marx and Engels . . . had an idealized and quite premature conception of modern industrial society as a push-button shop, without realizing the complex technical demands such a society would make." Alfred G. Meyer, *Marxism: The Unity of Theory and Practice*, Cambridge: Harvard University Press, 1954, p. 81. See also Barrington Moore, *loc. cit.*

[14] Thus Walter Buckley is in error in suggesting that the Davis-Moore theory asserts that "some persons' incomes must always be greater or less than others.' " "A Rejoinder to Functionalists Dr. Davis and Dr. Levy," *American Sociological Review*, 24 (February, 1959), pp. 84–85. Tumin (*op. cit.*, p. 392) has noted the possibility of emphasizing one type of reward "to the virtual neglect of others."

[15] See, e.g., Talcott Parsons, "A Revised Analytical Approach to the Theory of Social Stratification," in R. Bendix and S. M. Lipset, editors, *Class, Status, and Power*, Glencoe, Ill.: Free Press, 1953, pp. 92–128; Bernard Barber, *Social Stratification*, New York: Harcourt, Brace, 1957, pp. 1–16.

[16] "Some Principles of Stratification: A Critical Analysis," *loc. cit.*, p. 391.

selves among positions in exactly the right proportions, to put it mildly, is an improbable supposition.

Tumin's point that sociology should not "shut the door on inquiry into alternative possible social arrangements"[17] is well-taken, but he fails to propose any alternative to the Davis-Moore positional reward mechanism for recruiting individuals to their roles.[18] If we overlook the probability that the tendency to make invidious comparisons both of unlike tasks ("prestige") and of performances of like tasks ("esteem") is rooted in the very nature of the self, we may concede that intrinsic job satisfaction and social duty might ensure high levels of performance in a static society where roles are ascribed at birth. But this does not appear to be what Tumin has in mind.

THE PROBLEM OF EQUALITY OF OPPORTUNITY

Davis and Moore see stratification as a sorting mechanism allocating the more talented and ambitious individuals to the more socially important and demanding roles by means of differential rewards which serve as incentives. Their model, as several critics have noted, is a special case of the market mechanism or price system of classical economic theory. And just as the conditions for

the "perfect" functioning of the market mechanism are never met by actual economies, so the stratification system never fully performs its imputed social function in actual societies.

In *Human Society* Davis has attempted to modify the theory to take into account the evident fact that differential rewards do not function as a selective mechanism for talent and industry when roles are ascribed to individuals at birth.[19] His arguments, which have been largely ignored by his critics, are worth examining in some detail. He begins by observing that the institution of the family limits the operation of the stratification system by giving to the children of the incumbents of roles in one generation relatively or absolutely greater opportunities to attain the same roles in the next generation. He shows in an analysis of the Indian caste system, however, that, despite its overwhelming emphasis on inherited status, the system cannot entirely preclude individual mobility because of caste fertility and mortality differentials, eventual changes in the physical environment giving rise to new roles and destroying old ones, and a number of other considerations.[20] He reiterates the distinction between the hierarchy of positions and the way in which individuals are recruited to them, pointing out that "the low estate of the sweeper castes in India, as compared with the priestly castes, cannot be explained by saying that sons of sweepers become sweepers and the sons of Brahmins become Brahmins." Since "there is a tendency for sweepers to have a low status in every society," Davis concludes that "the functional necessity behind stratification seems to be operative at all times, despite the concurrent operation of other functions."[21]

Now this argument actually does no more than assert that *over time but not necessarily "at all times"* differential rewards will operate as a selective mechanism. It lacks, but requires, a distinction analogous to that between the short-run and the long-run in economic analysis. By neglecting to make this distinction explicit the degree to which highly rewarded roles may be filled almost exclu-

---

[17] "Reply to Kingsley Davis," *American Sociological Review*, 18 (December, 1953), p. 672.

[18] Earlier in his original article Tumin suggests that "a system of norms could be institutionalized in which the idea of threatened withdrawal of services . . . would be considered as absolute moral anathema." This observation, in common with his proposed motives for conscientiousness, indicates his exclusive concern with behavior *after* the various roles in a division of labor have been filled. But Davis and Moore are concerned with explaining how they come to be filled in the first place. As I have previously argued, they neglect the power to secure and enhance their rewards which accrues to role-incumbents once they have been recruited and trained. Tumin, however, makes the reverse error. In a later article, "Rewards and Task-Orientations," *American Sociological Review*, 20 (August, 1955), pp. 419–423, Tumin also overlooks this crucial distinction, contending that parents perform their child-rearing tasks with dedication in the absence of expectations of unequal rewards; but, even if this be the case, motives for having children and for caring for them once they are born may be of a different order. And there is no assurance, of course, that people will reproduce at the rate which is optimal for society.

[19] *Op. cit.*, pp. 369–370.

[20] *Ibid.*, pp. 382–385.

[21] *Ibid.*, p. 370. See also Davis, "Reply," *op. cit.*, p. 395.

sively by ascription "in the short-run" or "at any given time" is understated. Where inheritance of positions generally prevails, the existence of a system of unequal positional rewards favoring the important and skilled roles, far from reflecting a "functional necessity" that is currently "operative," can be understood only with reference to the past, to the events which shaped the system at the time when the society was developing a differentiated social structure.

Thus we arrive at the paradoxical conclusion that the Davis-Moore theory, especially when it is applied to rigid caste societies, is often a better theory of social origins than of contemporary functioning—an odd conclusion indeed in view of the anti-historical bias of functional explanations. The high estate of Brahmins can, in terms of the theory, be explained only if we assume that the promise of unequal rewards was once necessary to attract men to the priesthood before the hierarchy of positions had hardened into a hierarchy of hereditary strata. The truth of Schumpeter's assertion, alien to the spirit of functional analysis, is thus confirmed: "Any theory of class structure, in dealing with a given historical period, must include prior class structures among its data; and . . . any general theory of classes and class formation must explain the fact that classes coexisting at any given time bear the marks of different centuries on their brow. . . ."[22]

Schumpeter, like Davis, insists on the ubiquity of mobility, even in relatively stagnant societies where legal and customary barriers between classes appear to be impassable. However, as in all of his writings, including his technical economic works, Schumpeter's approach is fundamentally historical: he clearly differentiates between a cross-sectional or short-run view of economies and social structures and a long-run view that takes into account changes in the position of families and firms within stable structures and, ultimately, changes in the structures themselves. Schumpeter sees the lineal family rather than the individual as

[22] Joseph A. Schumpeter, *Imperialism and Social Classes*, New York: Meridian Books, 1955, p. 111. Schumpeter's brilliant essay on social classes, first published in German in 1926, encompasses nearly all of the issues raised by the participants in the debate over the functionalist theory of stratification, including those raised by the present writer.

the "true unit" of class and of mobility within and between classes; it may take generations for the representatives of a family line to inch their way upwards in the class hierarchy to the point where an apparently secure hereditary class position is achieved. By looking at mobility in terms of family lines and generations, Schumpeter avoids the rival errors of viewing class position as entirely hereditary and immobile, on the one hand, and, on the other, of regarding existing inequalities as reflections of the actual distribution of ability and effort in the population. Lacking a truly historical perspective, the Davis-Moore theory, even in Davis' revised version of it, leaves itself open to the charge of committing the latter error, although Davis' later qualifications implicitly take into account time and change as crucial variables.

American sociologists often stress the "dysfunctions" of the inequalities of opportunity that result from the inheritance of positions. When able and energetic individuals are prevented from competing for the most important and highly rewarded positions, the "efficiency" or "productivity" of society is alleged to suffer. This argument is a major one used by the critics of the Davis-Moore theory. Davis and Moore, however, themselves accept the argument when they insist that the function of unequal rewards is to allocate talent to the positions where it is most needed and answer their critics by claiming that this function can never be entirely suppressed. Yet for some important roles requiring subtle skills and character traits hereditary ascription may actually be a more efficient way of recruiting candidates. Some administrative and leadership roles are perhaps best filled by those who are "to the manner born," who have been subjected to a process of character-molding beginning in infancy and preparing them for later assumption of their roles. Obviously this does not apply to activities requiring genuinely scarce genetic aptitudes, for example mathematics and music. But such roles are largely technical and are usually, as Davis and Moore point out, less highly rewarded than administrative positions—religious, economic, or political—requiring "skill in handling people" or "capacity to make decisions," qualities which probably do not depend on rare genetic talents falling outside the range of endowment of the average man.

It is strange how insistence on the alleged "inefficiency" of unequal opportunities often leads sociologists to stress genetic endowment, the importance of which they are disposed to minimize in other connections. I suspect that this argument is another instance of the dangerous proclivity of contemporary social scientists to find "factual" or "instrumental" reasons for supporting views they ultimately favor on ethical grounds.[23] Nevertheless it is true, in a society with a growing population and an expanding economy, that barriers to full equality of opportunity may lead to shortages in the *supply* of candidates for important positions.[24] But this situation, clearly applicable to engineers, physical scientists, doctors, and other professionals in the United States today, does not necessarily imply deficiencies in the role-performance of those who are the beneficiaries of unequal opportunities. Nor should it be generalized to apply to all social orders where inequality of op-

portunity prevails, notably to static agrarian societies with caste-like stratification systems. The proponents of the view that inequality of opportunity is "dysfunctional" fail to distinguish between its effects when the *shape* or *profile* of the stratified occupational system is changing and under conditions where *pure mobility* alone is at issue.[25]

In hereditary class societies the desire for esteem rather than for prestige must suffice to motivate individuals to perform their roles competently.[26] Monopolizing the positions carrying high rewards, a ruling stratum is always subject to the temptation to become absentee owners embracing the values of Veblen's leisure class which make a virtue of "functionless" activity and elevate what have previously been viewed as rewards for performance into criteria of worth in their own right. One of the patterns of conspicuous leisure described by Veblen is precisely the phenomenon noted by Richard Simpson: the creation by the privileged of new positions—servants, footmen, courtesans, and the like, whose function is to serve as lackeys catering to the most trivial wants of their masters. Davis and Moore note the existence of reward for "pure ownership," but add in a phrase with curious evolutionist overtones that it "becomes more subject to criticism as social development proceeds toward industrialization."[27]

It cannot be assumed, however, that a hereditary ruling class always degenerates into a "decadent" leisure class in the Veble-

---

[23] Paul Kecskemeti, "The Psychological Theory of Prejudice," *Commentary*, 18 (October, 1954), pp. 359–366; also Bruno Bettelheim, "Discrimination and Science," *Commentary*, 21 (April, 1956), pp. 384–386; and Dennis H. Wrong, "Political Bias and the Social Sciences," *Columbia University Forum*, 2 (Fall, 1959), pp. 28–32.

[24] Actually, societies face three distinct problems in "allocating" and motivating their members: the number of candidates for important roles must be sufficient; their talents and aptitudes, innate or previously acquired, must not fall below a certain level; and once they have been trained and have assumed their roles they must be induced to do their best. A solution to one of these problems is not necessarily a solution to the others.

If we wished to raise the intellectual level of the American academic profession, for example, two exactly opposite policies might prove effective. We might stop paying professors anything at all with the result that only men with a genuine love of learning and a profound dedication to the pursuit of truth would be willing to become mendicant scholars. Or we might raise professorial salaries so that the academy could compete with business and the highly-paid professions in attracting able and ambitious men. Both of these policies might lead to greatly improved academic performance, but only the second would ensure an adequate supply of would-be professors to staff American colleges and universities. I am indebted for this (I hope) fanciful example to Russell Kirk, *Academic Freedom: An Essay in Definition*, Chicago: Regnery, 1955, pp. 170–171.

[25] For the concept of *shape* or *profile* of stratification, see Pitirim A. Sorokin, *Social Mobility*, New York: Harper, 1927, pp. 36 ff. For the concept of *pure mobility*, see Natalie Rogoff, *Recent Trends in Occupational Mobility*, Glencoe, Ill.: Free Press, 1953, pp. 30–31; also Ross and van den Haag, *op. cit.*, Chapter 10, which contains an excellent general theoretical discussion of the different factors affecting mobility.

[26] This is not, of course, strictly true: important political, bureaucratic, and military roles may be filled only from the ranks of a hereditary upper class but not all members of the class fill such roles. Thus prestige incentives may be effective in inducing feudal princes to strive to become and to remain the King's first minister, Junker landlords to seek to be generals, etc. This situation necessitates the familiar distinction between the "elite," those necessarily few men who possess actual decision-making powers, and the "ruling class," the larger stratum from which the elite is recruited.

[27] *Op. cit.*, p. 247.

nian sense. Clearly, there have been hereditary aristocracies deeply imbued with an
ethos of honor, responsibility, and *noblesse
oblige* serving to motivate conscientious
role-performance. Hereditary upper classes
may even exhibit a stronger sense of duty
and accountability to society than *arriviste*
elites precisely because of their awareness
that they are the recipients of "unearned"
privileges which can only be justified by
continuous effort.[28] Which model—Veblenian
leisure class or responsible aristocracy—
characterizes a hereditary class is a matter
of the particular historical context.

Although American social scientists have
stressed the "dysfunctions" for society of inequality of opportunity, they have also been
highly sensitive to the negative consequences
for the *individual* of vertical mobility, upward or downward. But they have been
extraordinarily remiss in exploring systematically the disintegrative effects for *society*
of high rates of mobility, as well as the
dangers posed by full equality of opportunity to other cherished values. Scores of
books and articles have been written attributing neurosis, criminality, and demoralization to the competitiveness allegedly inspired
by intense mobility strivings in a society
which holds out the promise of high rewards
to those who rise to the top.[29] But one can

cite few writings by Americans which deal
directly with the negative consequences for
the social structure of rapid mobility [30]—
apart from Davis' argument, echoed by other
functionalists, that the requirements for family solidarity set limits to complete equality
of opportunity. However, a number of non-
sociologists, many of them English, have recently become concerned with the question
of just how much mobility and equality of
opportunity a modern society can stand.[31]
Will the trend towards the replacement of

---

[28] Baltzell, *op. cit.*, pp. 4–5. C. Wright Mills has
suggested that the way of life of Veblen's leisure
class is probably more characteristic of the *nouveau
riche*, specifically of the self-made millionaires whose
antics loomed so large on the American scene when
Veblen was writing, than of established hereditary
aristocracies. See his "Introduction to the Mentor
Edition," Thorstein Veblen, *The Theory of the
Leisure Class,* New York: Mentor, 1953, p. xiv.

[29] This was, in fact, a major theme, if not *the*
major theme, of the most widely read works of
American social science and social criticism in the
1930s and early 1940s. Representative are Karen
Horney, *The Neurotic Personality of Our Time,*
New York: Norton, 1937; Robert S. Lynd,
Knowledge for What? Princeton: Princeton University Press, 1939, esp. Chapter 3; Robert K.
Merton, "Social Structure and Anomie," *American
Sociological Review,* 3 (October, 1938), pp. 672–
682. Treatments of American society in the books
of Margaret Mead, Ruth Benedict, Lawrence Frank,
Abram Kardiner, Elton Mayo, and others also
stress this theme. Most of these writers fail to
distinguish between the effects of competition *per se*
and of competition under conditions where full
equality of opportunity is manifestly absent. Merton,

however, explicitly attributes the "strain towards
anomie" he finds in American life to the "contradiction between cultural emphasis on pecuniary ambition and the social bars to full opportunity," but it
is far from certain that the deviant and anomic
responses he describes would disappear in an industrial society which successfully removed all
major barriers to opportunity. In fact the cultural
emphasis on success might very well be enhanced
under such circumstances.

[30] The only examples I have found of American
sociologists who have made the general point that
rapid mobility may be "dysfunctional," as distinct
from noting particular unpleasant consequences of
recent mobility in analyses of ethnic prejudice or
of "McCarthyism," are Baltzell, *loc. cit.*, and Seymour Martin Lipset and Reinhard Bendix, *Social
Mobility in Industrial Society,* Berkeley: University
of California Press, 1959, pp. 260–265, 285–287. Lipset and Bendix mention the neglect of this topic by
American sociologists and refer to an article by
Melvin M. Tumin, "Some Unapplauded Consequences of Social Mobility in a Mass Society,"
Social Forces, 36 (October, 1957), pp. 32–37. This
article, however, is chiefly concerned with the "unapplauded" consequences of status discrepancies
between high occupational position and low ethnic
or kinship status, and of mobility defined in terms
of consumption gains alone.

[31] See Paul Kecskemeti, *Meaning, Value and
Communication,* Chicago: University of Chicago
Press, 1952, pp. 268–274; David Potter, *People of
Plenty,* Chicago: University of Chicago Press, 1954,
pp. 103–110; Peregrine Worsthorne, "The New
Inequality," *Encounter,* 7 (November, 1956), pp.
24–34; C. A. R. Crosland, *The Future of Socialism,*
New York: Macmillan, 1957, Chapter 10; Ross and
van den Haag, *op. cit.*, pp. 126–127, 132–134;
Michael Young, *The Rise of the Meritocracy,*
London: Thames and Hudson, 1958, *passim;* Raymond Williams, *Culture and Society, 1780–1950,*
London: Chatto and Windus, 1958, pp. 331–332. Of
these writers only Young is a professional sociologist
by background and his entire book argues the un-
desirability of a society in which full equality of
opportunity is institutionalized; see the review of
his volume by Charles Curran in *Encounter,* 12
(February, 1959), pp. 68–72, which makes precisely
the Davis-Moore point that such a society is impossible because of man's "philo-progenitive" impulses.

class hierarchies by ladder hierarchies [32] in industrial societies eliminate the evils (or, if preferred, the "dysfunctions") which have been so widely attributed to inherited class privileges? Considering the charges of ideological bias which have been bandied about by both sides in the debate over the Davis-Moore theory, it is worth noting that in England staunch conservatives and confirmed socialists alike have raised this question. The following doubts have been expressed by at least two or more of the writers cited in notes 30 and 31:

1. Might not a self-made elite owing its position to demonstrated merit alone be even more intolerant and self-righteous in its attitude toward the lower strata than an elite owing its position largely to birth? [33]

2. Would not those who failed to achieve high positions feel even more guilt-ridden, demoralized, and alienated than at present if their failure were truly owing to proven lack of objective ability rather than to "accidents of birth" or "not knowing the right people," excuses which can now be employed as rationalizations for failure?

3. Is it really desirable that the lower strata should consist only of those who are genuinely inferior, thus depriving their ranks of a leaven of able and aggressive individuals to lead and represent them in conflicts of interest with the more highly-placed groups and to contribute variety and liveliness to their social experience?

Let us ignore the extreme case of a brutal centralized totalitarianism which, as George Orwell has suggested, may actually be more compatible with a social structure resembling a ladder hierarchy than with a regime of hereditary social classes. Whether rapid mobility and full equality of opportunity in a democratic industrial society have the effects described above depends on a number of conditions, of which the major ones probably are the cultural value placed on upward mobility, the range of inequality or what I have called "the scale of unequal rewards," and the rate of economic expansion and technical progress. These factors of course are only partially independent of one another.

If the price of failure to rise socially—or even of downward mobility—is not too great, if a definite floor and ceiling are institutionalized to confine inequalities within tolerable limits, and if the general standard of living is high, then upward mobility, as David Potter has suggested, may come to be viewed as "optional rather than obligatory" and equality of opportunity need not produce a monolithic elite ruling over an inert mass. A diversified value system which recognizes and honors human qualities other than functional intelligence and single-minded ambition will be more likely to flourish.

Potter, David Riesman, W. H. Whyte, and others have noted the decline of the Protestant Ethic, the relaxation of the success-drive, and the new importance of leisure as opposed to work in American life. There are also signs, however, that the decline of strong aspirations to occupational mobility has coincided with an increase of status-seeking in leisure pursuits and consumption behavior.[34] Davis and Moore and others who

---

[32] See note 4, above.

[33] "The Party is not a class in the old sense of the word. It does not aim at transmitting power to its own children, as such; and if there were no other way of keeping the ablest people at the top, it would be perfectly prepared to recruit an entire new generation from the ranks of the proletariat. In the crucial years, the fact that the Party was not a hereditary body did a great deal to neutralize opposition. The older kind of Socialist, who had been trained to fight against something called 'class privilege,' assumed that what is not hereditary cannot be permanent. He did not see that the continuity of an oligarchy need not be physical, nor did he pause to reflect that hereditary aristocracies have always been shortlived, whereas adoptive organizations such as the Catholic Church have sometimes lasted for hundreds or thousands of years. The essence of oligarchical rule is not father-to-son inheritance, but the persistence of a certain world-view and a certain way of life, imposed by the dead upon the living. A ruling group is a ruling group so long as it can nominate its successors. The Party is not concerned with perpetuating its blood but with perpetuating itself. Who wields power is not important, provided that the hierarchical structure remains always the same." George Orwell, *1984*, New York: Harcourt, Brace, 1949, pp. 210–211. Too many American sociologists resemble Orwell's "the older kind of Socialist" in their views on stratification. Confusion of biological continuity with permanency of structure is particularly marked in Buckley's article, *op. cit.*, pp. 370–371.

[34] See Tumin, "Some Unapplauded Consequences of Social Mobility in a Mass Society," *loc. cit.* I have ignored in this paper the different types of mobility: occupational, status, consumption, etc. For a discussion of these, see Lipset and Bendix, *op. cit.*, pp. 269–277; also Lipset and Hans L. Zetterberg, "A

have theorized about the limits to equality in human societies have been chiefly concerned with the relationship of unequal rewards and mobility to the functional division of labor; the newer forms of "status panic" raise questions of a cultural and psychological nature which fall outside the scope of theories that focus primarily on social structure.

Finally, if economic expansion and technical progress continue to change the shape of occupational stratification, producing "automatic" upward mobility by reducing the number of workers needed in low-status positions, the combination of hierarchy and equality of opportunity will be less likely to generate social tensions.[35]

All of the dimensions of hierarchy—the range of inequality, the shape of the hierarchical structure, the amount of mobility, and the ways in which each of these is changing—are empirically interdependent and jointly produce particular social consequences, although they can and must be analytically distinguished. American sociol-

---

Comparative Study of Social Mobility, Its Causes and Consequences," *Prod*, 2 (September, 1958), pp. 7–11. The fact that England has traditionally possessed a steeper status hierarchy than the United States and one in which status distinctions are much more sharply drawn probably accounts for the greater misgivings of English social analysts about the advantages of equality of opportunity *per se.*

[35] Inequalities of power are probably increasing as modern society becomes more bureaucratized at the same time that "consumer equality" is becoming more marked. For perceptive discussions of this trend, see Worsthorne, *op. cit.*, and Arnold, *op. cit.*; also G. L. Arnold, *The Pattern of World Conflict*, New York: Dial, 1955, pp. 130–131.

ogists, reflecting the values of their own society, have been preoccupied with the amount of mobility to the neglect of the other dimensions.

CONCLUSION

If the inducement of unequal rewards is required to encourage men to convert their talents into skills, exercise their skills conscientiously, and undertake difficult tasks, it is also the case that, having won their rewards, they will use their superior power, wealth, and prestige to widen still further existing inequalities in their favor. And they are likely to do so even when their chances of passing on differential advantages to their children are strictly limited. Thus there may *never* be a correspondence between the existing scale of unequal rewards and the minimum scale required to maintain the social order—although democratic government and the organization of the lower strata to countervail the initial power superiority of the elite may stabilize or even narrow the existing scale. But conflicts between unequally rewarded groups and a sense of injustice on the part of the less privileged may be just as endemic in society as the necessity for unequal rewards itself. This of course is the central insight of the Marxist tradition. Sociologists pay lip-service to the theoretical obligation to stress both the integrative and the divisive effects of social arrangements. The obligation applies with special force to discussions of stratification. Power, justice, and social necessity are perhaps ultimately incommensurable.

CHAPTER 10

But Some Are More Equal than Others

WILBERT E. MOORE

A review of the "functional theory of stratification" indicates some neglect of dysfunctions and other dynamic elements in systems of social inequality, but does not find the critics persuasive on the possibility of eliminating inequality. In behavioral terms inequality is seen as deriving from the probability of differential valuation of performance, qualities (a prospective view of performance) and achievements (a retrospective view of performance). In structural terms these variables are seen as modes of access to positions, but positional differentiation is independently linked to inequality of rewards. Although equity strains inhere in any system of differential rewards, there is no reason to suppose that an equalitarian system would be free from such strains, as fairness and complete equality are scarcely synonymous and equalitarianism as a value is rather restrictive in its context of applicability.

THE theoretical controversy ever the interpretation of social inequality is one of the most enduring disputes in contemporary sociology. Now nearing the end of a second decade since the publication of the essay by Davis and Moore [1] and more

---

The title of course is borrowed from George Orwell's *Animal Farm,* New York: Harcourt, Brace, 1954.

† The present essay is partially derived from a joint work with Arnold S. Feldman, *Order and*

Change in Industrial Societies, now in preparation. I also benefited from critical comments by my collaborator, but accept sole responsibility for the present formulation.

[1] Kingsley Davis and Wilbert E. Moore, "Some Principles of Stratification," *American Sociological Review,* 10 (April, 1945), pp. 242–249.

than two decades since the original version of an essay by Parsons,[2] the debate continues, with an important and extensive critical commentary by Tumin[3] as the most recent major statement on the issues. It would be naively arrogant to suppose that the present attempt to review and clarify the analysis of inequality will be taken as definitive, for the issues are empirical but also semantic, theoretical but also ideological. It is even possible, though by no means certain, that the controversy prompts useful inquiry as well as providing the pleasure of polemics to participants and their partisans.

The recent statement by Tumin and earlier ones by the same author[4] and by others[5] chiefly question the *necessary* universality of social inequality, although not its empirical ubiquity, and additionally raise questions concerning the "dysfunctions" of stratification. My current view is that the Davis-Moore position was incomplete, resulting in some overstatement (as noted by Simpson[6]) and some neglect of dysfunc-

tions. These criticisms have already been noted by Davis.[7] In addition, I should specifically reject any stable equilibrium version of "functionalism" as both incorrect and extrinsic to the position that social inequality is a necessary feature of any social system.[8] For example, constructive innovation is an intrinsic feature of industrial societies and of those seeking to become such —or whose leaders are seeking that goal, if one feels required to avoid anthropomorphism. This disequilibrating behavior is almost certain to be differentially rewarded, and is certainly "functional" by any of the proposed meanings or nuances of the term save only the connotation of stasis. The "functional theory of stratification" maintained only that positions of unequal importance would be unequally rewarded, and was silent, regretably but not criminally, on the subject of systemic changes.

By use of the term "stratification" the Davis-Moore position also implied that clearcut and consistent statuses attributable to individuals could be generalized into categories for individuals of "similar" status, and the categories ranked as "strata." The utility of such summations and classifications is subject to empirical test: do the "operational" definitions of generalized status and, say, class have predictive value for social variables not included in the definition? If status inconsistency is widespread and "class" variables have weaker predictive power than the separate definitional components, such as occupation, income, and education, then this empirical situation is clearly a relevant set of specifications about the characteristics of inequality in a society. If "class" is not a very useful analytical tool as applied to contemporary complex societies, this tells us a good deal about those societies. It does not, by any stretch of theoretical imagination or empirical confrontation, tell us that those societies are "equalitarian."

[2] Talcott Parsons, "An Analytical Approach to the Theory of Social Stratification," *American Journal of Sociology*, 45 (May, 1940), pp. 841–862. See also "A Revised Analytical Approach to the Theory of Social Stratification," in Reinhard Bendix and Seymour M. Lipset, *Class, Status and Power*, Glencoe, Ill.: Free Press, 1953, pp. 92–128.

[3] Melvin M. Tumin with Arnold S. Feldman, *Social Class and Social Change in Puerto Rico*, Princeton: Princeton University Press, 1961, especially Chap. 29, "Theoretical Implications." This chapter is by the senior author alone.

[4] Tumin, "Some Principles of Stratification: A Critical Analysis," *American Sociological Review*, 18 (August, 1953), pp. 387–394; Tumin, "Obstacles to Creativity," *Review of General Semantics*, 11 (Summer, 1954), pp. 261–271; Tumin, "Rewards and Task Orientations," *American Sociological Review*, 20 (August, 1955), pp. 419–423; Tumin, "Some Disfunctions of Institutional Imbalance," *Behavioral Science*, 1 (July, 1956), pp. 218–223; Tumin, "Competing Status Systems," in Arnold S. Feldman and Wilbert E. Moore, eds., *Labor Commitment and Social Change in Developing Areas*, New York: Social Science Research Council, 1960, Chap. 15.

[5] See Richard L. Simpson, "A Modification of the Functional Theory of Stratification," *Social Forces*, 35 (December, 1956), pp. 132–137; Richard D. Schwartz, "Functional Alternatives to Inequality," *American Sociological Review*, 24 (December, 1959), pp. 772–782; Leonard Reissman, *Class in American Society*, Glencoe, Ill.: Free Press, 1959, pp. 69–94.

[6] Simpson, *loc. cit.*

[7] See Davis, "Reply to Tumin," *American Sociological Review*, 18 (August, 1953), pp. 394–397.

[8] A close approximation to the original Davis-Moore position, and with some resemblance to the present one, is that of Bernard Barber, *Social Stratification*, New York: Harcourt, Brace, 1957, especially Chaps. 1–4. Barber, however, does appear to deal only with a stable equilibrium model.

Although Davis and Moore were fairly explicit in equating "social stratification" with unequal rewards, that now appears unfortunate. I have some sympathy for Buckley's criticism [9] on this point. Thus part of the difficulty in the continuing controversy has been semantic; and part has been empirical, in the sense that the clarity of class identification and its predictive value are questions of fact.

The single issue to which the present remarks are addressed is whether social inequality is a necessary feature of social systems. It is thus not a theoretical (to say nothing of ideological) defense of "social stratification" in the limited sense of clearly identifiable social categories, mutually exclusive, hierarchically ranked, and in sum exhaustive of all members of society. The proposition that every social system must exhibit manifestations of social inequality *permits no inference whatsoever* concerning the consistency of ranking from one context of action to another, the empirical reference for "general social status," or the empirical validation of "social classes."

What we are dealing with, then, is the elementary circumstance that inequality is ubiquitous in human societies, which is not in dispute and at least partial explanation of this universal phenomenon, which is in dispute. The explanation presented here reiterates the thesis that "functional differentiation" of positions will inevitably entail unequal rewards, and adds the thesis that differences in performance must be expected to be and will be differentially valued. The legitimacy of this kind of analysis, or its potential relation to questions of status consistency and "stratification" in the narrow sense, scarcely needs defense. To conclude, as does Buckley, that the functional theory "promotes an insuperable discontinuity in sociological research" [10] is simply tendentious.

ELEMENTARY PROCESSES OF SOCIAL VALUATION

In his attempt to construct an equalitarian system, Tumin concedes the necessity of differentiating normative compliance from deviance. This concession, however, has far-reaching implications. Even in social contexts in which equality may be the norm or expectation, compliance with expectations is not automatically assured, and failure to adhere to that or any other relevant norm will be the basis for a negative valuation of *performance*.

All social relationships governed by norms (and which ones are not?) are likely to provide a scale of approximations to and departures from ideal conduct. *Qualities* also are likely to be differentially valued, perhaps as indicative of probable or expected performance. And *achievements*, a retrospective view of performances, are likely to be evaluated unless all social relationships are to be viewed as transitory and memories abolished.

This "behavioral" view of the process of social valuation involves gradations with reference to "ideals." But there is no reason to suppose that the ideal is the same for every person in every context of action. Positional gradation, too, is governed by norms, and one must have a strong urge to believe in the power of evil to view all such norms as maliciously imposed by persons of privilege.

Positional gradation may be taken as the basic feature of social inequality from a "structural" view. From that point of view the properties of individuals that prompt valuation—performance, qualities, and achievements—constitute modes of *access* to positions.[11] Valuation itself confers a status, however transitory or enduring it may be. However, once statuses are institutionalized, that is, are endowed with normatively sanctioned role requirements, they will have ranking attributed to them and to their in-

---

[9] Buckley's principal criticism of the Davis-Moore position is the use of the term "social stratification," which he would limit to hereditary social strata. See Walter Buckley, "Social Stratification and the Functional Theory of Social Differentiation," *American Sociological Review*, 23 (August, 1958), pp. 369–375.

[10] *Ibid.*, p. 375.

[11] A small conceptual point may be noted here. Parsons, in his revised essay, uses qualities, performances, and possessions as the properties of individuals subject to differential valuation. This appears less satisfactory than the distinction between access to positions and rewards to their incumbents—both of which are somewhat more extensive than Parsons' formulation would indicate.

cumbents *ex officio* somewhat independently of mode of access. For example, in the extreme case, a position may be filled by drawing lots, and yet confer prestige on its incumbent. (Perhaps "luck" may be a valued quality.)

Social differentiation is a universal and necessary fact of social existence. The Davis-Moore "functional" interpretation of inequality rested on the unequal functional importance of positions and the unequal supply of talents for filling them. That interpretation, unlike most functional analyses, was explicitly evolutionary, and like many had possible rationalistic overtones. Tumin essentially skirts the issues of importance and talents, but rejects the evolutionary explanation, for which he substitutes the view that stratification is an anachronistic survival maintained by self-perpetuating power. (That revolutionary polities establish new modes of social stratification escapes his attention.) Between those two modes of appeal to inferential evidence there is little basis of proof, and the argument must shift to other grounds.

Tumin would not abolish functional differentiation, but only differential rewards. He would declare all positions of equal value, and the sole basis of differential valuation that of "conscientiousness." Short of universal and perfect skill in instantaneous psychiatric diagnosis, I suggest that the judgment of subjective intention would promptly lead to judgments of qualities, achievements, and, especially, performance. Esteem,[12] in other words, would become the single permissible mode of evaluation or reward.

To accomplish the almost-termination of inequality, Tumin has a large and unfilled set of tasks: (1) to make all tasks equal in difficulty and in various other "intrinsic" qualities, lest elements of positional prestige creep in; (2) to achieve coordination of specialized activities without resort to graded authority: (3) and, of course, to equalize all material or financial rewards and prevent any form of differential accumulation.

The *attributes* of positions, the role re-

quirements, may include power and influence. Thus the giving of orders, providing instruction, setting goals and procedures, creative innovation, "exemplary" conduct in the strict sense may all follow from "superior" positions in various groups and organizations. The counterparts are obedience, learning, emulation, imitation, deference, and so on. These actions bear witness to the acceptance of the normative system and the legitimacy of the role performances of the superior. It is, I suggest, impossible to imagine a social system totally lacking in these manifestations of inequality.

Unless intrinsic task equalization is accomplished, it would seem extremely unlikely that equality of rewards—or rather, permitting only esteem-rewards—would be institutionalized by any conceivable system of socialization. This would require a somewhat greater extension of martyrdom than any religious system has yet achieved, and religious martyrs expect future rewards. I believe that Tumin has become entrapped by an ideological position that I see no reason to accept: namely, that equality is intrinsically more equitable than inequality. The practice of equal rewards for unequal performance does not immediately recommend itself as either functionally or ethically superior to the contrary scandal of unequal rewards for equal performance. (In order to maintain the view that inequality is *ipso facto* iniquitous, Tumin consistently emphasizes unequal rewards, systematically avoids unequal demands, such as the exceptional effort required for acceptable performance in some roles or the responsibility-costs of power.)

THE PROBLEM OF REWARDS

The possible rewards for unequal performance or performance in unequal positions are not only self-esteem, the approval of significant others, "fame," and so on, but may include differential allocations of any scarcities such as disposable time and material goods or money. Now it is especially material or financial rewards (the two are not the same) that most upset Tumin about social inequality, and it is in fact theoretically imaginable to have a viable social order without substantial purchasing-power

---

[12] See Davis, "A Conceptual Analysis of Stratification," *American Sociological Review*, 7 (June, 1942), pp. 309–321.

differentials. Income equalization might well heighten the differentials in other attributes and rewards for superior positions. Unless a market system of distribution permitting consumer choice is to be entirely abandoned, the way consuming units use their income would still probably result in invidious valuation. And it would be exceptionally difficult to prevent other sources and forms of inequality from being used instrumentally to gain a disproportionate share of scarcities.

Indeed, modes of access, attributes, and rewards of positions are all subject to possible instrumental use in the same or other contexts of action. This is one clear source for the presumed pressure for status consistency.[13] The degree to which consistency prevails, however, is not impressive in any industrial society, and especially in those with pluralistic institutional systems. Fragmentation [14] of even nominally singular statuses into incomparable analytical subsystems—for example, an administrator's involvement with occupational peers, in a structure of authority, and in the labor market—should more than offset tendencies to status coalescence. Even income, the one "universal solvent," has early limits in determining "worth" in non-economic contexts and in others it may be a necessary but not sufficient means of social placement and valued performance.

Where the contexts of social differentiations are fragmented and comparability among them minimal because of the absence of an adequate mode of mensuration, a remaining common denominator such as income may take on a special significance. But that significance arises only when a uniform standard is sought, and the occasions for doing so may be rather limited. Tumin's position here is compounded of several empirical errors: (a) a class system "really exists"; (b) it is posited upon only one dominant "phase" of social life, the economic, which is associated with (the cause of?) prestige and power; (c) other worthwhile human endeavors are given something

less than their "due" because the economy has "invaded" other institutional areas. Not only does this entail an exaggeration of status comparability in industrial societies, but it leads to a perception of status anxieties more pervasive than any evidence indicates. Tumin's convictions concerning the evils of inequality provoke him into constructing a "minor handbook of a scoundrel's guide to how to disguise inequality," [15] which includes many of the actual characteristics of social differentiation in modern societies. The implication that obfuscation of a "general social status" represents a conspiracy is supported by no known evidence. One might just as properly view social systems characterized by complex role differentiation as conspiring against the sociologist's attempt to impose on them a simplified structure of "social stratification."

The instrumental use of elements of inequality outside their original context is only one of the intrinsic strains in stratification systems. Privilege may seek to perpetuate itself, speaking elliptically. That is, a privileged group may seek to guard its position for its "own kind," even by changing the modes of access—for example, by emphasis on irrelevant qualities such as lineage or graduation from a particular school. Being comprised of mortal members, no privileged group can literally "perpetuate itself" except by some form of recruitment. If the forms of recruitment are contrary to other values and norms—for example, relevant performance criteria or equality of opportunity—equity strains will become intensified.

To maintain that social inequality is an essential feature of social systems not only has no implications for tidy and rectilinear ranking, as noted previously, but also does not rule out value inconsistency, "dysfunctions," strain, conflict, and change. These too are empirical characteristics of social systems, perfectly integrated models being only analytical constructs of dubious utility. Certainly the proponents of the "functional theory" of inequality seem to have been less impeded in their analysis by ideological orientations than have some of the critics.[16]

---

[13] See Parsons' revised essay, previously cited.

[14] For a discussion of the process of status fragmentation in industrial societies, see Feldman, "The Interpenetration of Firm and Society," in International Social Science Council, *Social Implications of Technological Change*, Paris, 1962, pp. 179–198.

[15] "Theoretical Implications," p. 502.

[16] This is the position taken by Davis. See "The

THE MEANING OF EQUALITARIANISM

A final critical note must be added concerning the interpretation of every manifestation of inequality as contrary to the avowed value of equality, attributed to American and at least some other industrial societies.[17] Now neither inconsistency in values nor inconsistency between ideals and practice would be a surprising empirical finding, but the conclusion must be approached with some caution. Ideals as well as behavioral norms are subject to limitation by the contexts of social action. This is an elementary fact of social organization and its recognition is surely incumbent on any social analyst. An interesting and possibly significant basis of comparison through time and space would be the contexts in which, on the one hand, *common* rights and duties are the norm, and, on the other, unequal valuation of performance and position is the expectation. In other words, what are the rights of men generally and what are the rights of social units differentially?

Absolute equality may be a kind of vague and unspecified dream for the millennial future of socialist states, but certainly has been espoused by few of the ideologists of the Western democracies and cannot be taken as an established social value: equality before the law and the state, perhaps; and, later, equality of opportunity for unequal rewards, but not an absence of evaluative differentiation and consequent position. It is not even true that "all men are equal in the sight of God," unless one hastens to add, as in George Orwell's *Animal Farm*, "but some are more equal than others."

One would have to be naive indeed to suppose that income inequality has no implications for "equality before the law." It does not follow that measures to increase legal equality stem from a bad conscience about income inequality or appear solely as a diversionary tactic so that income inequality will be tolerated without revolt. Similarly, as long as the family is a primary agency of attitude-formation in children, existing differentials in social privileges may well have negative implications for equality of opportunity. But this is an empirical insight—of considerable importance—not something that is true by definition. It is even true, as Tumin maintains, that existing "systems" of social stratification tend to waste talents and real or potential skills. It does not follow that an equalitarian system would optimize their utilization. The measures to tap talents are likely to be directed toward openness rather than flatness of social positions, and diversity rather than uniformity of rewards.

Equalitarianism may indeed provide an instrumental "value" for social critics, both lay and professional, who seek to extend its application. Their efforts may bear some fruit, such as the extension of social as against private income in such fields as health and education. Yet the needs for the one or the talents for the other are not equally distributed, and it is thus opportunities and not results that are equalized.

Equity strains are evident in most contexts of social inequality, and involve questions of "proper" rewards to the "right" people. It is extremely unlikely that any system of inequality will be institutionalized and provided with a rationale in social values adequate to prevent discontent. Such strains are likely to produce changes, and in some situations a possible change may be toward equality. In most situations the more likely change is toward a restructuring of access, attributes, and rewards. Fairness is simply not a synonym for equality, and no amount of sentimentalizing about the worthiness of all men will make it so.

Abominable Heresy: A Reply to Dr. Buckley," *American Sociological Review*, 24 (February, 1959), pp. 82–83.

[17] See Tumin, "Theoretical Considerations," pp. 493, 497–498, 510–511.

CHAPTER 11

The Marxian Synthesis

STANISLAW OSSOWSKI

The Doctrine of Marx in the History of Social Ideas

THE MID-NINETEENTH century saw the birth and development of the comprehensive theoretical system of Marx and Engels. This system aimed at achieving a synthesis of the problems of sociology, economics, philosophy and history, in which general propositions of the type encountered in natural science would provide the foundation for concrete historical conceptions, and in which the most abstract principles and metaphysical assumptions would provide a starting-point for deductions leading to practical conclusions in the sphere of political and economic activity.

If one measures the significance of a theoretical work by the scope of its social consequences, one must regard the Marxian system as one of unusual importance. For a century, writers and men of action fighting for a new order have been reared on the ideas contained in this system. These ideas have shaped the social consciousness of the most active sections of the working class in Europe and beyond and have provided the justification and theoretical foundation for many social programmes. They have constituted the sources of energy for the revolutionary movement by spreading the belief that the realization of revolutionary aims and designs is guaranteed by incontrovertible laws of history.

But the works of Marx and Engels have yet another significance, in that they achieved a great synthesis in the history of thought. There has been a general tendency in the Marxist camp to over-estimate the originality of particular views propounded by

Marx. In almost all his fundamental basic ideas the author of *Das Kapital* had his forerunners. Lenin aptly defined the three sources of the Marxist system: German philosophy, English political economy and French utopian socialism. But these three do not by any means exhaust the cultural heritage which found expression in the works of such absorptive writers. To outline the history of Marx's predecessors, one would also have to mention writers whose work was not directly known to Marx, such as Babeuf, who in a letter to Chades Germain of 28 July, 1795, on the eve of the *Plebeian Manifesto*, formulated *inter alia* the idea of *la loi barbare dictée par les capitaux*.

The originality of the founders of Marxism and the epoch-making role of Marxist theory consist in the bold deduction of far-reaching consequences from assumed ideas; on the development of ideas of varying origin into a coherent system; on the association of theoretical conceptions with a programme of action, with an analysis of historical events and with a vision of the future; and on the achievement of a great synthesis of various trends in theoretical thought and ideological currents. In this regard, the writings of Marx form some sort of immense lens which concentrates the rays coming from different directions, and which is sensitive both to the heritage of past generations and to the creative resources of modern science.

Since Lenin's death we have been wont to associate Marxism not with the metaphor of a lens but with that of an optical device which, as far as post-Marxian theory is concerned, lets through only the rays coming from one direction. This is one of the reasons why as a rule both the followers of Marx and his opponents fail to appreciate the whole varied range of the connexions which link his doctrines with the general history of European thought.

These connexions in Marx's theory appear quite clearly in his analysis of the concept of social structure, that is to say in his concept of class. In choosing a heading for this chapter I had in mind this particular synthesis of the various ways of conceiving social structure, rather than the overall synthesis of the Marxian *Weltanschaung*.

The Concept of Social Class in Marxian Doctrine

The concept of social class is something more than one of the fundamental concepts of Marxian doctrine. It has in a certain sense become the symbol of his whole doctrine and of the political programme that is derived from it. This concept is expressed in the terms 'class standpoint' and 'class point of view', which in Marxist circles used until recently to be synonymous with 'Marxist standpoint' or 'Marxist point of view'. In this sense 'class standpoint' simply meant the opposite of 'bourgeois standpoint'.

According to Engels,[1] Marx effected a revolutionary change in the whole conception of world history. For Marx, so Engels maintained, had proved that 'the whole of previous history is a history of class struggles, that in all the simple and complicated political struggles the only thing at issue has been the social and political rule of social classes'.

The concept of social class is also linked with what Engels in the same article calls the second great discovery of Marx, to which he attaches so much importance in the history of science – the clarification of the relationship that prevails between capital and labour. Finally, it may be said that the concept of social class is bound up with the entire Marxian conception of culture as the superstructure of class interests.

The role of the class concept in Marxian doctrine is so immense that it is astonishing not to find a definition of this concept, which they use so constantly, anywhere in the works of either Marx or Engels. One might regard it as an undefined concept of which the meaning is explained contextually. But in fact one has only to compare the various passages in which the concept of social class is used by either writer to realize that the term 'class' has for them a variable denotation: that is, that it refers to groups differentiated in various ways within a more inclusive category, such as the category of social groups with common economic interests, or the category of groups whose members share economic conditions that are identical in a certain respect. The sharing of permanent economic interests is a particularly important characteristic of social classes in Marxian doctrine, and for this reason it has been easy to overlook the fact that although it is, in the Marxian view, a *necessary condition* it does not constitute a *sufficient condition* for a valid definition of social class.

Marx left the problem of producing a definition of the concept of social class until much later. The manuscript of the third

[1] ME, Vol. II, p. 149; the quotation comes from F. Engels, *Karl Marx*.

volume of his *magnum opus, Das Kapital,* breaks off dramatically at the moment when Marx was about to answer the question: 'What constitutes a class?' We do not know what answer he would have given if death had not interrupted his work. Nor do we know whether he would have attempted to explain the discrepancies in his earlier statements.

After the death of Marx, Engels did not take up the question which the manuscript of *Das Kapital* left unanswered. Lenin's later definition, which has been popularized by Marxist text-books and encyclopaedias, links two different formulations but fails to explain how we are to regard them. Does the author see them as two equivalent definitions and does he link them in order to give a fuller characteristic of the designate of the concept of class? Or is the conjunction of the two formulations essential because the characteristics given in one of them are not necessarily conjoint to the characteristic given in the second? Independently of this, such metaphorical expressions as the 'place in the historically determined system of social production' may be variously interpreted and Lenin's definition is sufficiently loose to be applicable to all the shades of meaning found in the term 'class' as used by Marx and Engels.[1] Bucharin's definition,[2] which is also intended to reflect the Marxian conception of social class, affords room for even wider possibilities of interpretation, and it is only Bucharin's classification of social classes that enables one to grasp the denotation assigned by the author to the concept of social class.[3]

In using the concept of class based on economic criteria, Marx sometimes restricts the scope of this concept by introducing psychological criteria. An aggregate of people which satisfies the economic criteria of a social class becomes a class in the full mean-

[1] 'Classes are large groups of people which differ from each other by the place they occupy in a historically determined system of social production, by their relation (in most cases fixed and formulated in law) to the means of production, by their role in the social organization of labour and, consequently, by the dimensions and method of acquiring the share of social wealth of which they dispose. Classes are groups of people one of which can appropriate the labour of another owing to the different places they occupy in a definite system of social economy.' (V.I. Lenin, *A Great Beginning,* in *The Essentials of Lenin* in Two Volumes, London, Lawrence & Wishart, 1947, p. 492.)

[2] N. Bucharin, *Historical Materialism, A System of Sociology,* London, 1926, p. 267 (English translation).

[3] *Ibid.* pp. 282–4.

ing of this term only when its members are linked by the tie of class consciousness, by the consciousness of common interests, and by the psychological bond that arises out of common class antagonisms.[1] Marx is aware of the ambiguity and makes a terminological distinction between *Klasse an sich* and *Klasse für sich*, but he does not in general make much further use of these more narrowly defined concepts.

Marx sometimes uses a different term to denote a class which is not a class in the fullest sense because it lacks psychological bonds. For instance, he sometimes uses the term 'stratum'; on other occasions he avoids using a more general term and confines himself to the name of a specified group such as the 'small peasantry'. At times he may even call certain classes which are conscious of their class interests 'fractions' of a more inclusive class. In the case of capitalists and landowners, for instance, Marx sometimes sees them as two separate classes, at others as two fractions of a single class, the bourgeoisie.

All these discrepant uses of the term 'class' were probably the less important for Marx because, according to his theory, further social development would render them obsolete. This was to result from the growth of the social consciousness and from the predicted disappearance of the difference between the *Klasse an sich* and the *Klasse für sich* as well as from the progressive process of class polarization in the social structure.

The matter can however be put in a different way. We may take it that Marx, instead of providing a definition of social class which would make it possible to fix the scope of this concept, is giving

[1] Cf. the following passages:

'The separate individuals form a class in so far as they have to carry on a common battle against another class.' (K. Marx and F. Engels, *The German Ideology* (The Marxist-Leninist Library, Volume XVII, London, Lawrence & Wishart, 1940, pp. 48–49). 'The organization of the proletarians into a class, and consequently into a political party.' ('Manifesto of the Communist Party', ME ,Vol. I, p. 41.) 'In so far as millions of families live under economic conditions of existence that separate their mode of life, their interests and their culture from those of the other classes, and put them in hostile opposition to the latter, they form a class. In so far as there is merely a local interconnection among these small-holding peasants, and the identity of their interests begets no community, no national bond and no political organization among them, they do not form a class. They are consequently incapable of enforcing their class interest.' (ME, Vol. I, p. 303; quotation from K. Marx), Bonaparte represented the most numerous class of the French society at that time, the small-holding (*Pazzellen*) peasants' (ME, Vol. I, p. 302; quotation from 'The Eighteenth Brumaire of Loui Bonaparte').

the model of a social class, the ideal type which is to be fully
realized in the future, in the last stage of the development of the
capitalist system. In the period in which Marx wrote, the industrial proletariat of Western Europe was approximating to the
ideal type of a social class. Other social groups separated on the
basis of economic criteria could be called classes only to a greater
or lesser extent, and could approximate to the ideal type only in
some respects. Hence endeavours to apprehend them by means of
conceptual categories with sharply-drawn boundaries of application must lead to confusion.

However that may be, one should, when considering the
Marxian conception of class structure, remember that the component elements of this structure are confined to those groups
which Marx calls 'classes' when contrasting them with 'strata',
in which 'the identity of their interests (those of the members of a
"stratum") begets no unity, no national union and no political
organization'.

As we shall see below, the Marxian concept of social class
involves certain conceptual complications which are more than a
matter of terminology.

Interpretations of Class Structure in Marxian Conceptions

It has already been said that the works of Marx and Engels
constitute a sort of lens which focuses the manifold trends in
European thought. So far as the problems discussed in previous
chapters are concerned, all three schemes of social structure
which were described there are to be found in Marx's conceptions,
as well as a new mode, peculiar to himself, of conceiving the class
system derived from the intersection of three dichotomic divisions.

The Basic Dichotomy

Marx and Engels are above all the inheritors of the dichotomic
perceptions found in folklore and of the militant ideology of
popular revolutions. Reading their works, one never loses sight
of the age-old conflict between the oppressing classes and the
oppressed classes. I have already mentioned the dichotomic perceptions of the drama of history that appear in the Communist

Manifesto and in Engels' work written three years earlier. The reader will recall the two-fold way of conceiving human relations within the social structure in terms of a dichotomic division: the manifold polar division of the various oppressor and oppressed classes in earlier societies gives way to a single all-inclusive dichotomy. According to the forecast of the Communist Manifesto, the capitalist society was to achieve this dichotomy in full in the penultimate act of the drama, in the period that precedes the catastrophe. In approximating to such a dichotomy, the social structure of the capitalist world would then be nearing its end.

According to the founders of Marxian doctrine, the society in which they lived was characterized by a tendency to develop in the direction indicated above. In this society Marx discerned 'the inevitable destruction of the middle bourgeois classes and of the so-called peasant estate'.[1] In Engels' version, the era marked the accomplishment of 'the division of society into a small, excessively rich class and a large, propertyless class of wage-workers'.[2] The workers' rising in Paris on 22 June, 1848, was regarded by Marx as 'the first great battle . . . between the two classes that split modern society . . . the war of labour and capital'.[3]

Two Conceptions of the Intermediate Classes

Marx the revolutionary and Marx the dramatist of history developed a dichotomic conception of a class society. Marx the sociologist was compelled in his analysis of contemporary societies to infringe the sharpness of the dichotomic division by introducing intermediate classes. He could not overlook the 'mass of the nation . . . standing between the proletariat and the bourgeoisie'.[4] These intermediate classes were a very important element in the pictures of his own era given us by Marx in his historical studies. Sometimes he speaks of 'intermediate strata' when giving a narrower definition of a social class. Elsewhere the

[1] ME, Vol. 1, p. 75; quotation from K. Marx, *Wage, Labour and Capital*.
[2] ME, Vol. 1, p. 73; quotation from F. Engel's Introduction to Marx's *Wage, Labour and Capital*.
[3] ME, Vol. 1, pp. 147, 148; quotations from K. Marx, *The Class Struggles in France, 1848–1850*.
[4] *Ibid.* p. 137.

term 'middle estate' appears, although in this context it does not denote an institutionalized group such as the French *tiers état*.

There is such a variety of social statuses and economic positions in these intermediate classes that it is difficult to confine them within a uniform scheme. The term 'intermediate classes' suggests a scheme of gradation. And in fact one sometimes finds in Marx's writings the conception of the intermediate classes as groupings of individuals occupying an intermediate position in the economic gradation in respect of their relation to the means of production, or to the variety of their social roles and sources of income. For instance, in the *Address of the Central Community to the Communist League*, written by Marx and Engels in 1850, the petit bourgeoisie includes the small capitalists, whose interests conflict with those of the industrialists. And again, in his *The Civil War in France*, Marx refers to the 'liberal German middle class, with its professors, its capitalists, its aldermen and its penmen,'.[1] Here he conceives of the middle class in the sense in which the term is used in England or the United States. A capitalist – that is to say an owner of the means of production – may belong to one class or another depending on the amount of capital he owns. One should however bear in mind that Marx is not thinking here of 'high society' nor of rows and columns in statistical tables. For him the amount of capital owned by an individual is associated with separate class interests.

It was not, however, this conception of an intermediate class that was incorporated in the set of basic concepts in the Marxian analysis of the capitalist society. In constructing his theoretical system, Marx set up the foundation for another conception of the class which occupies the intermediate position between the class of capitalists and the proletariat. This conception was not in fact formulated in its final form by either Marx or his pupils. It is nevertheless related to the scheme of class structure of the capitalist society that is characteristic for Marx and Marxism, a scheme in which three social classes correspond to three kinds of relations to the means of production.

In this scheme the intermediate class, which Marx usually calls the 'petit bourgeoisie' regardless of whether reference is being made to urban or rural dwellers, is determined by the simul-

[1] ME, Vol. 1, p. 447: quotation from the *Second Address of the General Council of the International Working Men's Association on the Franco-Russian War*.

taneous application of two criteria. Each of these criteria taken separately forms the basis for a dichotomic division of social classes, although in a different way. One criterion is the ownership of the means of production. This is a criterion which, in a dichotomic scheme, divides society into propertied and propertyless classes. The second criterion is work, which, however, in contradistinction to Saint-Simon's conception, does not include the higher managerial functions in capitalist enterprises. We have come across this second criterion in the dichotomic scheme as well. It divides society into working classes and idle classes. In this conception, the intermediate class consists of those who belong to both the overlapping categories; those who possess their own means of production and themselves make use of them.

Marxism applies still another version of this trichotomous division, a version which is usually not differentiated from the former one. In it the first criterion of division (the ownership of the means of production) remains the same. On the other hand, the second criterion is not work but the fact of not employing hired labour. In this version, the intermediate class is more narrowly defined than in the earlier one. It does not include all those working people who possess their own means of production but only those who work on their own account without employing hired labour. According to this version, a wealthy farmer who employs two or three regular hired labourers, or who has smallholders working for him in exchange for an advance in cash or kind, is included in the class of rural capitalists. In the first version the petit bourgeoisie includes two strata; those who work in their own work-shops and employ hired labour, and those who do not employ such labour. Sociologically speaking, the first version is more suited to describe some conditions, the second more suited to others; thus it depends on various circumstances which need not be discussed here. The combination of the two versions gives two functionally differentiated intermediate classes, as the diagram on the next page shows.

From the viewpoint of the Marxian assumptions concerned with the tendencies of development in capitalism, the position of the petit bourgeoisie, which is intermediate between the two basic classes, is sometimes interpreted in yet another way. The petit bourgeoisie is said to belong to the propertied class so far as present conditions are concerned, to the proletariat with regard

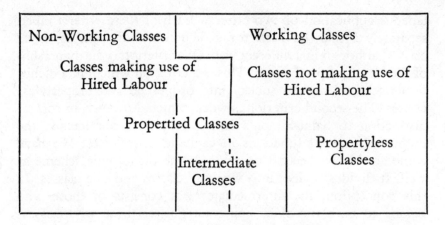

to its future prospects. Thus not only the craftsman but also the small-holder are potential proletarians.[1]

There is also an economic gradation that corresponds to this trichotomous scheme. The capitalist class is that class which owns large-scale means of production or at least sufficient to make possible the employment of hired labour; the petit bourgeoisie consists of those who dispose of the means of production on a modest scale; while the proletariat is in principle the class that owns no means of production whatsoever. In this functional scheme, however, it is not the degree of wealth that determines the boundaries between classes but the social roles, namely their relation to the means of production, work and their relation to the hiring of labour. In the scheme of gradation referred to earlier, on the other hand, the middle class could also include *rentiers*, the owners of small industrial establishments and other capitalists with property not exceeding the limits of 'moderate wealth'.

A strict observance of functional economic criteria in distinguishing the three classes – capitalists, petit bourgeoisie, and proletariat – leads, however, to conflicts with sociological criteria. For instance, an engineer would in his capacity as hired labour in a capitalistic establishment have to be included amongst the proletariat, as would a doctor employed in a private sanatorium. As we know, Marx associated the concept of the proletariat with the

[1] Cf. Engels: *The Peasant Question in France and Germany*, ME, Vol, I. pp. 384, 395. Bucharin, in developing Marx's theory of social classes, differentiates the category of classes intermediate between the two basic classes in a different way than is done in our scheme; he distinguishes intermediate classes, transition classes and classes of mixed types. (*op. cit.*, pp. 283–4).

conception of a fundamental dichotomy. The proletarian is a man who is unprotected from the extremes of exploitation by any special qualifications which would prevent him from being replaced by another worker with equal physical strength. According to Marx's intentions, this criterion would exclude the engineer or doctor from the class of the proletariat.

Moreover, according to the Marxian assumption that a class is united by the common interests of its members in great social conflicts, yet another factor may help to correct a scheme based on 'relations to the means of production'. For instance, the salary of the engineer employed by the capitalist includes a portion of the 'surplus value' produced by the workers and appropriated by the capitalist.

In summing up our discussion of this classical Marxian scheme of social roles in relation to the various ways of conceiving the social structure which were discussed earlier, we may consider it as an overlapping of a dichotomic view and a scheme of gradation. In this conception the intermediate class is determined by the boundaries of the two basic and antagonistic classes. It is separated from the others by virtue of the fact that these two basic classes are divided against each other, not by one single criterion, but by two or three criteria to which correspond class-groupings of varying extensions. The intermediate class is made up of people who are connected with each of the two basic classes but in differing respects. This connexion exists both in the logical sense (characteristics which enter into the definition of two basic classes) and in the sociological sense. At the same time, as I have already pointed out, the petit bourgeoisie, as determined by its peculiar 'relations to the means of production', occupies a central position in the trichotomous economic gradation (the extent of ownership of the means of production).

A Trichotomous Functional Scheme without an Intermediate Class

With Marx the revolutionary, the dichotomic conception of social structure is dominant. With Marx the theorist, we sometimes have to deal not only with the trichotomous scheme with a middle class between the two opposing classes but also with a scheme which is inherited from bourgeois economics. This is the trichotomous functional scheme of Adam Smith. This scheme appears rarely in the works of Marx and Engels,[1] but its importance is increased by the fact that it is the starting-point of the last chapter of the third volume of *Das Kapital,* the chapter which is devoted exclusively to an analysis of classes in modern society. This uncompleted chapter, entitled 'Classes', opens with the words:

'The owners merely of labour-power, owners of capital, and land-owners, whose respective sources of income are wages, profit and ground-rent, in other words, wage-labourers, capitalists and land-owners, constitute then three big classes of modern society based upon the capitalist mode of production'.[2]

And a little further on, when he is dealing with the question 'What constitutes a class?' Marx again takes precisely this conception of the social structure as his starting-point.

In the dichotomic conception and in the trichotomous Marxian conception which I have discussed earlier the emphasis is placed on human relationships. In Smith's conception, on the other hand, the viewpoint of an economist rather than of a sociologist is dominant. The main stress falls on the relations of people to things. Clear economic categories, that is criteria concerned with relationships to things, leave no place in the social structure for the intermediate classes which a sociologist cannot overlook. In Adam Smith's scheme those who own their own means of production and yet work themselves do not form a separate class but belong to two or three classes simultaneously.

'It sometimes happens, indeed, that a single independent workman has stock sufficient both to purchase the materials of his work and to maintain himself till it be completed. He is both master and workman, and enjoys the whole produce of his own labour, or the whole value which it adds to the materials upon which it is bestowed. It includes what are usually two distinct revenues, belonging to two distinct persons, the profits of stock, and the wages of labour.'[3]

[1] Cf. *Ludwig Feuerbach and the End of Classical German Philosophy* (ME, Vol. II, p. 356); Marx's letter to Engels of April 30, 1868 (K. Marx and F. Engels, *Selected Correspondence,* Moscow, Foreign Languages Publishing House, n.d., pp. 245–50).

[2] K. Marx, *Capital,* Vol. III, Moscow Foreign Languages Publishing House, 1959, p. 862.

[3] *op. cit.,* Vol. I, Everyman's Library, p. 58.

Marx considers this point in the third volume of *Das Kapital*, and even accords it conditional approval.[1]

Thus we find two different trichotomous schemes of social structure in Marx, to both of which may be applied the definition of class as a group determined by the relation to the means of production. In the first case (capitalists, petit bourgeoisie, proletariat), the various classes have correspondingly *various relationships to the means of production*. In the second case (landowners, owners of capital and those who own nothing but their own labour), the classes are determined by the *relation to the various means of production*, the capacity to work being regarded here as a category of the means of production.

A Multi-Divisional Structure

A functional scheme can contain more than three classes, as we saw with Madison. In Marx's writings a direct formulation which would conceive of social structure in terms of such a multi-divisional scheme is nowhere to be found. But if we bring together statements made in various works we find that even an image of this kind can be derived from his works. In his *German Ideology* we find the bourgeoisie and the class of the large industrialists set against each other as classes of different and in a certain respect even opposite social functions; for the interests of the bourgeoisie are contained within national boundaries, while the large industrialists form a cosmopolitan class on an international scale.[2] In his *Class Struggles in France* Marx shows us how the class interests of the French financial aristocracy clash with those of the industrial bourgeoisie.[3] Marx attributes to the financial

---

[1] 'When an independent labourer – let us take a small farmer, since all three forms of revenue may here be applied – works for himself and sells his own product, he is first considered as his own employer (capitalist), who makes use of himself as a labourer, and second as his own landlord, who makes use of himself as his own tenant. To himself as wage-worker he pays wages, to himself as capitalist he gives the profit, and to himself as landlord he pays rent. Assuming the capitalist mode of production and the relations corresponding to it to be the general basis of society, this subsumption is correct, in so far as it is not thanks to his labour, but to his ownership of the means of production (. . .) that he is in a position to appropriate his own surplus labour.' *Capital*, Vol. III, Lawrence & Wishart, London, 1960, p. 853.

[2] K. Marx and F. Engels, *The German Ideology*, Lawrence and Wishart, 1939, pp. 24–26.

[3] 'The mania to get rich not by production, but by pocketing the already available wealth of others'. *The Class Struggles in France 1848–1850*, ME, Vol. I, pp. 128–29.

aristocracy the 'desire to enrich themselves not by production but by cleverly appropriating to themselves riches that already exist', and calls them ironically 'the *lumpenproletariat* on the heights of bourgeois society'.[1] Apart from these two rival classes, **Marx** mentions the petit bourgeoisie which is removed from political power. A year or so later, in his description of the same society in *The Eighteenth Brumaire*, Marx once again shifts the line dividing the bourgeoisie into two antagonistic factions. This antagonism, for which the ideological superstructure was the conflict between Orleanists and Legitimists, is seen as the outcome of the competition between capital and ownership of land.[2] These factions, based on the ownership of different types of wealth, are the two basic classes from Adam Smith's scheme.

If we now take the class differentiation of the rural population, as it is presented for instance by Engels in the introduction to his work *The Peasant Wars in Germany*,[3] and if we do not overlook the *lumpenproletariat* – which is not a 'class' according to the Marxian definition but a 'stratum' – 'a mass sharply differentiated from the industrial proletariat'[4] – a stratum which can play a specific role in social movements – we obtain an image in which the capitalist society is functionally differentiated into seven, eight or even nine classes or strata.

The Overlapping of Viewpoints

In his character of revolutionary, economist and sociologist, Marx inherited all three basic types of conceiving the class structure which are encountered in the history of European thought. These are the dichotomic scheme, the scheme of gradation and the functional scheme. At the same time he introduced a characteristic way of conceiving this structure, by intersecting two or three dichotomic divisions. It is this latter way that has come to be regarded as the classic Marxian scheme, although Marx does not employ it when he is discussing the concept of class in the last pages of his greatest work.

We have noted in Marx's writings two versions of this classic

[1] *The Class Struggles in France 1848–1850*, ME, Vol. I, p. 131.
[2] K. Marx, *The Eighteenth Brumaire of Louis Bonaparte*, ME, Vol. I, pp. 247–53.
[3] F. Engels, Prefatory Note to *The Peasant War in Germany*, ME, Vol. I, pp. 584–86.
[4] *The Class Struggles in France 1848–1850*, ME, Vol. I, p. 142.

Marxian scheme, and also an explicit formulation of Adam Smith's trichotomous functional scheme; there is also an implied multi-class version of a functional scheme which recalls that of Madison. Thus it may be maintained that the works of Marx and Engels contain at least six different ways of conceiving the structure of contemporary capitalist societies. The definition of a social class which refers to the relations to the means of production is just as applicable to the classic Marxian scheme as it is to the schemes of Adam Smith and of Madison.

The schemes may differ, but this does not involve contradictory assumptions. The dichotomic aspect of the Marxian theory of classes indicates the direction in which capitalist societies will develop; seen in this perspective the multi-divisional schemes are intended to refer to transitory phenomena. But even without a reference to trends of development the Smithian scheme cited in the third volume of *Das Kapital* and elsewhere need not run counter to the basic dichotomy. It is sufficient to group landowners and owners of capital in a single more inclusive 'superior' category of 'propertied classes' and to set them against 'those who own nothing but their own labour' as the 'propertyless class'. The trichotomous scheme of gradation may be reconciled with the dichotomic conception by treating the middle class as a grouping resulting from overlapping class extensions or as one determined by the boundaries of the two opposite classes.

We may still seek other explanations. In the Marxian image of capitalist society the dichotomy refers to the classes that participate in capitalist production, which, it should be noted, is not the only form of production in existing capitalist societies. The dichotomy is a basic scheme for the Marxian model of a capitalist society, with its two large classes which appear '*à l'interieur de l'atelier capitaliste*', as Labriola puts it. But this dichotomous class-division of capitalist society is not inconsistent with the existence of other social groups, so long as one accepts the view that other forms of relations of production and their corresponding classes have survived from the past within this society. The dichotomic scheme is intended to characterise capitalist society with regard to its dominant and peculiar form of relations of production, while the multi-divisional scheme reflects the actual social structure.[1]

[1] 'Dire que le capitalisme est caractérisé par l'organisation autoritaire de la fabrique et la division en classes – capitalistes et salariés – qui en découle, ce n'est

Adam Smith's scheme brings out other problems than does the Marxian scheme based on two or three criteria of division. The petit bourgeoisie which occupies such an important position in the Marxian sociological analysis of the French society of that time is not sufficiently important from the viewpoint of certain economic problems for Adam Smith to differentiate it in his functional scheme. Adam Smith does not, however, overlook the existence of the petit bourgeoisie: he describes them as people who, on the basis of certain economic criteria, belong simultaneously to two or three of the classes differentiated in his image of the social structure. This is not incompatible with the classic Marxian scheme, in which the petit bourgeoisie, as an intermediate class, is connected with the proletariat by one criterion, and with the capitalist class by a second.

The founders of Marxian doctrine found this image of the social structure convenient for certain theoretical and practical purposes, while another might serve better for other purposes.

Two Categories of the Class Struggle

It must not be forgotten that the use of the same terms in describing reality in its different aspects and in formulating generalizations made from different viewpoints can lead to misunderstandings. It is easy to overlook the fact that the concept of the class struggle, the basic concept for Marxian doctrine, comprises two different categories of historical process. The first includes liberation struggles within the framework of the perennial conflict between the oppressing classes and the oppressed classes; the second includes struggles between classes competing for power in a society with a multi-divisional structure. It is not often perceived that the class struggles referred to in the first chapter of the *Communist Manifesto* are social conflicts of a kind different

---

pas nier qu'avec le capitalisme survivent d'autres régimes économiques. (. . . Si Marx) s'occupait des deux grandes classes qui existent à l'intérieur de l'atelier capitaliste, il ne pouvait pour cela supprimer d'un trait de sa plume autoritaire petite bourgeoisie, groupes professionnels et autres métiers inclassables'. (Arturo Labriola: *Karl Marx – L'économiste – Le socialiste*, Paris 1909, p. 185–86). Sorel points out that Marx frequently confuses logical constructions with his descriptions of actual phenomena, and conjectures that Marx did not always realize the abstract character of his theory of classes.

from those mentioned by Engels in his introduction to a new posthumous edition of Marx's *Class Struggles in France*.

In the *Communist Manifesto* we read:

'The history of all hitherto-existing society is the history of class struggles. Freeman and slave, patrician and plebeian, lord and serf, guildmaster and journeyman, in a word, oppressor and oppressed, stood in constant opposition to one another, carried on an uninterrupted, now hidden, now open fight.'

In Engels' introduction, on the other hand, we find quite another picture of the class struggle:

'All revolutions up to the present day have resulted in the displacement of one definite class rule by another; but all ruling classes up to now have been only small minorities in relation to the ruled mass of the people . . . the common form of all these revolutions was that they were minority revolutions. Even when the majority took part, it did so – whether willingly or not – only in the service of a minority.'[1]

I have cited these two well-known passages to show that both those who, while regarding the class struggle as the driving force of history, treat the history of class struggles at times as if it consisted exclusively of the conflict between an oppressed majority and a minority of exploiters and at other times as if it consisted exclusively of conflicts between minority classes competing for power could appeal to the example of the classics of Marxism.

It is as well to realize this point, for this duality is linked with tendencies to still greater simplification in presenting historical events. An instance of this may be found in the tendency to regard the so-called 'premature liberation movements', such as the peasants' or workers' insurrections in the periods preceding the full triumph of the bourgeoisie, as if they had no other significance in history than that conferred on them by their participation in the struggles between classes occupying superior positions in the social structure and competing for power. One of the leading Marxists of contemporary France, Garaudy, ascribes a reactionary role to the French Communists of the 18th century, on the grounds that their activities weakened the offensive strength of

[1] ME, Vol. I, pp. 113–14; the quotation comes from F. Engels' Introduction to Karl Marx's *The Class Struggles in France, 1848–1850*.

the bourgeoisie in its struggle with the feudal lords.[1] Writing forty years earlier, Jaurés would appear to have given a similar evaluation of the conspiracy of Babeuf.

The Sharpness of Class Divisions and The Class Interpretation of Cultural Phenomena

It would seem that in the very assumption that class struggles are the driving force of history, two different views concerning causal relationships are intertwined.

The first of these views holds that the driving force of history consists of struggles between an oppressed class and an oppressor class. The second maintains that it comes from struggles between classes with different interests. Among Marx's predecessors, the first view recalls Babeuf, the second Madison or Ricardo. In the first case, the basic phenomenon adduced in causal explanations is the appropriation of the 'surplus value' and the oppression of man by man. In the second it is the antagonisms of class interests, antagonisms which are not confined to situations in which the appropriation of the 'surplus value' is involved.

It is true that in his conception of history Marx undoubtedly assumes that the necessary condition for the existence of all class division is the existence of an exploited class and that the dichotomic division of society into exploited and exploiters is the source of all class divisions. And this additional assumption, which emerges even more clearly in Engels' writings, gives precedence to the first of the two views mentioned above. On the other hand, in the concrete historical studies of both Marx and Engels, the second view takes precedence and class struggles are interpreted more broadly.

This elasticity in the interpretation of basic concepts is not unconnected with the practical significance of Marxian doctrine as a weapon of revolution. It is no accident that one can single out several different ways of conceiving social structure in the writings of Marx and Engels. Nor is it accidental that such varied

---

[1] 'Toute doctrine qui tend alors à diviser le Tiers-Etat en mettant au premier plan les conflits nés de l'inégalité des fortunes, diminue la force offensive de cette classe contre le féodalité et joue par consequent un rôle de frein, un rôle réactionnaire. Les utopies socialistes jouent alors ce rôle et n'ont par conséquent qu'un caractère négative et rétrograde'. R. Garaudy, *Les source françaises du socialisme scientifique*, Paris 1949, p. 29.

trends of thought have intermingled in the Marxian theory of social class, including trends flowing from the dichotomic view of society, the heritage of folklore and the revolutionary movements on the one side, and on the other side from the scheme of Adam Smith. For the concept of social class to perform the role which it did in the history of Marxism and during the social changes of the last century, it had to satisfy seemingly contradictory requirements. A synthesis of the different aspects of the class structure was necessary for this doctrine, which sees in the class struggle the driving force of history and the justification for its political programme, which seeks the explanation of all historical processes in class antagonisms, and gives a class interpretation to all cultural phenomena.

Because of its militant programme, this doctrine must emphasize in the strongest possible way the sharpness of class divisions and the asymmetry of relations in the social structure. The scheme of gradation and the dichotomic scheme are constructed in terms of asymmetrical relations. The sharpest class division is achieved by this dichotomic conception, in which the division of two classes is the only division.[1] In the scheme of gradation this sharpness is weakened by the introduction of intermediate classes; and the clarity of class contours is still further blurred as the number of classes in the social structure increases. This is particularly so when the number of social classes is not clearly fixed, and when it is possible to distinguish five or at other times six or eight classes.

The dichotomic view is the most convenient for the tasks which the Marxian doctrine was to carry out, because of the sharpness of the asymmetrical divisions. On the other hand, a large number of social classes is an assumption which is needed for the 'class interpretation' of the complicated processes of history and the whole variety of cultural phenomena. This interpretation, which ascribes a many-sided significance to class divisions and draws all spheres of spiritual life into the orbit of the class struggle, cannot

---

[1] In this context is is worth recalling Sorel's view:
'Les propagandistes socialistes ne peuvent se resoudre à subordonner leur conceptions des classes aux faits, qui nous montrent une excessive complexité de la structure sociale; sans la division dichotomique il leur serait impossible de faire comprendre l'idée revolutionnaire, de même que sans la déscription d'un idéal futur ils ne pourraient faire pénétrer dans les masses la notion de la catastrophe morale. Autre chose est faire de la science sociale et autre chose est former les consciences'. Sorel, *op. cit.*, p. 188.

be confined within a dichotomic structure. If all political or religious struggles are to be interpreted as class struggles, if we are
to correlate the various literary and artistic trends with underlying
class relations, if we are to look for a reflexion of class interests
and class prejudices in moral norms, then we must make use of a
greater number of classes than the two basic ones in the *Communist Manifesto.*

IV

The Distribution of Values, Status, Wealth, and Power

Knowing the potential for economic, political and social stratification in any society tells one nothing, of course, about the actual degree of empirically observed inequality in these areas. The selections in this section provide descriptive accounts of the extent of various types of inequality in modern, industrial societies. Pineo and Porter present the results of the most detailed occupational prestige study yet published; Laumann and House discuss variations in living room styles as expressions of differences in personal value orientations and status locations: Miller provides the details of income distribution in the United States and summarizes recent changes; Kaysen reviews the dominance of markets by massive corporations and its ramifications elsewhere in society; while Tannenbaum and Kahn address problems engendered by the internal distribution of control within organizations among various groups of participants rather than their external impact. Many observations could be made in addition to those distributional aspects of inequality covered by the articles reprinted here. It would be hopeless in a brief introduction to review all the relevant characteristics which have been arbitrarily excluded

by virtue of the particular selections we have made. However, it is possible to place the materials at hand into comparative and temporal perspective.

Values and status. We know, of course, that the occupational prestige structure observed in contemporary Canada could not possibly characterize either the developing countries or, indeed, Canada itself in the not very distant past. Historically, some occupations—such as midwives and blacksmiths—have disappeared, while others—e.g., airplane pilots and computer technicians—have been created to meet the changing technology of industrial production and the changing demands of the public. Similarly, a major concomitant of economic development is the transformation of an agrarian occupational structure into an urban industrial structure, a change which expands the relative number of professional, semiskilled, and service workers at the expense of agricultural employment and traditional handicrafts. Thus, since the occupational structures of developing nations differ so dramatically from those of developed countries, and there have been substantial shifts in occupational structures even in advanced nations, there have been corresponding changes in the distribution of prestige. A shift in the occupational *structure* (creation of new positions and elimination of old ones) or occupational *distribution* (the relative numbers in several occupational groups whose content is unchanging) necessarily implies some corresponding change in any prestige hierarchy superimposed upon occupational categories.

But what about those occupational categories that remain historically unchanged and that are shared by nations at various stages of industrialization and modernization? A comparison of these categories reveals a picture of massive stability and constancy rather than one of substantial change. By and large, the prestige accorded to similar occupations in diverse nations is virtually identical whether the nations involved are Western or non-Western, democratic or Communistic, advanced or retarded, largely agrarian or primarily urban. Of course, some small differences can be detected, but largely, they appear to be unsystematic deviations. There is a possibility that the occupational prestige structures of developing nations, differing in small and random ways from those observed in developed countries, are converging to the occupational evaluations common among advanced nations. The evidence on this point, however, is less than convincing and difficult to muster because of the fundamental similarity between nations in the prestige rankings of the occupations they share in common (see Hodge, Treiman and Rossi, 1966).

The available evidence also supports several other important generalizations about occupational prestige ratings. (1) There appears to be a very substantial temporal stability in the prestige ratings of occupations. At least in the United States, where we have studies dating back to 1925, there has been no fundamental rearrangement of the occupational prestige hierarchy, though particular, detailed occupations may have shifted slightly in their relative positions (see Hodge, Siegel, and Rossi, 1966). (2) Different groups, whether they are defined by occupational status or by other social characteristics such as age, sex, education and place of residence, tend to evaluate the prestige of occupations in virtually the same way (see Reiss, 1961; Siegel, 1970). Empirical studies leave no doubt that the prestige evaluations of occupations are an important part of the *common* or shared value system in contemporary societies. This generalization applies in both developed and developing nations, though there is some reason to suspect that the small differences that can be detected are accentuated to some extent in the economically less advanced countries. (3) The prestige accorded to occupations conforms very closely to the average educational attainment and income level of their incumbents. Thus, respondents appear to take into account both the training required to pursue an occupation and the rewards received from performing it when assigning prestige ratings.

We know less about changes in the personal and social characteristics associated with status accruing through interpersonal behavior and public impression management (see Goffman, 1959) than we know about occupational prestige. Of course, the history of fashion and architecture reveals something of the changing expression of status through life styles but unfortunately, it fails to provide substantial material bearing upon the distribution of life styles. A fair guess would be that the variety of acceptable life styles has correspondingly expanded with the levels of consumption among diverse social groups. We know from expenditure studies that the proportion of income allocated to basic necessities (housing and food) declines, as income rises, and thus more funds are available, both relatively and absolutely, for expressions of individual taste.

Income and wealth. In the past four decades, there has been a modest income revolution in the United States. Real income for all portions of the population has risen, but there have been moderate shifts in its distribution. Fundamentally, the shares of total income received by upper-income groups, particularly the upper five and ten percent, have been substantially redistributed to middle-income groups, especially the upper two-fifths. This revolution has not, however, had any impact upon lower-income groups. The share of total income received by those in the lowest fifth of the income distribution has not changed in any important way. Of course, these lower-income families have experienced rises in real income, but the proportion of their share has been unaffected. The shift toward greater equality in income distribution has been effected almost wholly by decreasing inequality at the top.

Disparities in income in underdeveloped countries are as wide as those observed in developed countries. If anything, the disparities between the extremes may be wider; in any case, the overall inequality tends to be greater as wealth is concentrated primarily in the hands of a few landholding or ruling families while great masses of rural laborers and underemployed urban dwellers live at subsistence levels (see Lenski, 1966; Treiman, 1970). Needless to say, there are exceptions to this generalization, which is only statistical in nature.

Power. It is much easier to study the distributional aspects of wealth, income, occupational prestige, educational attainment and even material cultural artifacts than to study the distribution of power. While there is a fair degree of agreement about what is being measured and about comparability of the measurements on different elements of a population and, to a lesser degree, on different societies in regard to wealth, income, etc., the study of the distribution of power in small groups, communities and societies is replete with unresolved controversies regarding the meaning of power and the units in terms of which it may be measured (see Lasswell and Kaplan, 1950; Mills, 1956; Emerson, 1962; Dahl, 1961; Parsons, 1963a, 1963b; Keller, 1963). A central difficulty is that, in essence, power seems to refer to an asymmetric *relationship* between two actors or collectivities in which the "intent" or desire of one becomes the basis of the behavior of the other, who would not otherwise have acted in that way. In this sense, a power or, more generally, control relationship is always a process—that is, a time-ordered sequence of events in which the intent of A leads to communicative acts directed to B, which leads to the intent of B which leads to behavior of B which may or may not fulfill A's intent. Thus, there is no way to tell by looking at an individual by himself how much power he has.

A power structure is a situation in which there is a relatively high and stable likelihood of certain alters being controlled by certain others. The introduction of the notion of "likelihood" suggests that power structures involve two fundamental aspects —first, a *historical* aspect in which the control of one individual or group over another has been successfully exercised in the past in specific situations, and second, a *potential* aspect in which such successful control is more or less likely to occur in the future in situations which may or may not closely correspond to the specific situations of the past. These two aspects may result in quite different pictures of power distributions although it is usually assumed that one can infer the potential power structure from the history of the system in question and by determining who controls the bases of power.

But a further difficulty arises because there are disagreements among theorists and empirical investigators regarding the scope of the definition. Some wish to restrict the meaning of power to the ability of a power holder to mobilize negative sanctions (especially physical force and coercion or the threat of its employment) in order to elicit compliance from others. As a result, they tend to focus particularly on the analysis of the power of the "State" and its agents in relation to its subjects or citizens. Other theorists expand the definition to include all situations in which there is a reasonably high probability that certain specific commands (or all commands) from a given source, (whether an individual or a group) will be obeyed by a given person or group regardless of the basis on which this probability is secured (see Weber, 1947). In this more inclusive formulation, the bases of power may derive from a variety of different sources ranging from control over facilities, information or social approval desired by others (for example, material goods or money, the professional advice of a doctor who possesses a "monopoly" on information about an individual's health or well-being, or the social approval of a valued associate) to control over negative sanctions (e.g., physical punishment) (see Homans, 1961; Emerson, 1962; Blau, 1964).

In addition, the manner and range in which a powerholder may be constrained in employing these bases of power are manifold. The area to which its use is restricted is sometimes called the "scope" of a power domain. For example, a despot may have no important limits placed on the contexts in which he may exercise his power resources while the occupant of a bureaucratic office may have only very specific spheres of authority in which he may mobilize his power resources to reward or punish his subordinate. In short, there are two sources of variance in the exercise of power: the bases of power and the scope of their employment. As scholars vary considerably in the degree to which they consider each of these sources in their analyses, it is hardly surprising that there is relatively little consensus among investigators regarding empirical descriptions of power distributions in local communities (see Hunter, 1953; Dahl, 1961; Polsby, 1959, 1962; Spinrad, 1965) or national societies (see Berle and Means, 1932; Mills, 1956; Kornhauser, 1959, 1961; Keller, 1963; Lenski, 1966). The resulting controversies over whether communities or societies have highly centralized power distributions, i.e., the power or ruling elite model, or relatively dispersed power distributions, i.e., the structural pluralist model in which a number of groups compete for determinative influence over given decisions, arise at least in part from the different research and measurement strategies employed and the aspects of the concept of power the investigators choose to emphasize as crucial.

REFERENCES

Anderson, C. Arnold, and Mary Jane Bowman.
1953   "The vanishing servant and the contemporary status system of the American South." American Journal of Sociology 59: 215-230.

Berle, Adolf A., and Gardiner C. Means.
1932   The Modern Corporation and Private Property. New York: Macmillan.

Blau, Peter M.
1964   Exchange and Power in Social Life. New York: Wiley.

Dahl, Robert.
1961   Who Governs? Democracy and Power in American Life. New Haven: Yale University Press.

Duncan, Otis Dudley.
1961   "A socioeconomic index for all occupations. Properties and characteristics of the socioeconomic index." Pp. 109-161 in Albert J. Reiss, Jr. et al., Occupations and Social Status. New York: Free Press.

Emerson, Richard M.
1962   "Power-dependence relations." American Sociological Review 27: 31-41.

Goffman, Erving.
1959   The Presentation of Self in Everyday Life. New York: Anchor Books.

Hodge, Robert W., Paul M. Siegel, and Peter H. Rossi.
1966   "Occupational prestige in the United States: 1925-1963." Pp. 322-334 in Reinhard Bendix and Seymour M. Lipset (eds.), Class, Status, and Power. 2d ed. New York: Free Press.

Hodge, Robert W., Donald J. Treiman, and Peter H. Rossi.
1966   "A comparative study of occupational prestige." Pp. 309-321 in Reinhard Bendix and Seymour M. Lipset (eds.), Class, Status, and Power. 2d ed. New York: Free Press.

Homans, George C.
1961   Social Behavior: Its Elementary Forms. New York: Harcourt, Brace and World.

Hunter, Floyd.
1953   Community Power Structure. Chapel Hill, North Carolina: University of North Carolina Press.

Inkeles, Alex, and Peter H. Rossi.
1956   "National comparisons of occupational prestige." American Journal of Sociology 61: 329-339.

Keller, Suzanne.
1963   Beyond the Ruling Class. New York: Random House.

Kolko, Gabriel.
1962   Wealth and Power in America: An Analysis of Social Class and Income Distribution. New York: Praeger.

Kornhauser, William.
1959   Politics in Mass Society. New York: Free Press.
1961   " 'Power elite' or 'veto groups?' " in Seymour M. Lipset and Leo Lowenthal (eds.), Culture and Social Character. New York: Free Press.

Kuznets, Simon.
1966   Modern Economic Growth: Rate, Structure and Spread. New Haven: Yale University Press.

Lampman, Robert.
1962   The Share of Top Wealth-Holders in National Wealth: 1922-1956. Princeton: Princeton University Press.

Lasswell, H. D., and A. Kaplan.
1950   Power and Society. New Haven: Yale University Press.

Laumann, Edward O.
1965   "Subjective social distance and urban occupational stratification." American Journal of Sociology 71: 26-36.

Lenski, Gerhard.
1966   Power and Privilege: A Theory of Social Stratification. New York: McGraw-Hill.

Mills, C. Wright.
1956   The Power Elite. New York: Oxford University Press.

National Bureau of Economic Research.
1955   Business Concentration and Price Policy: A Conference of the Universities National Bureau. New York: National Bureau of Economic Research.

Parsons, Talcott.
1957   "The distribution of power in American society." World Politics 10.
1960   Structure and Process in Modern Societies. New York: Free Press.
1963a   "On the concept of political power." Proceedings of the American Philosophical Society 107.
1963b   "On the concept of influence." Public Opinion Quarterly 27: 37-62.

Polsby, Nelson W.
1959   "Three problems in the analysis of community power." American Sociological Review 24: 796-803.
1962   "Community power: Some reflections on the research literature." American Sociological Review 27: 838-841.

Reiss, Albert J., Jr.
1961   Occupations and Social Status. New York: Free Press.

Siegel, Paul M.
1970   "Occupational prestige in the Negro subculture." Sociological Inquiry 40.

Spinrad, William.
1965   "Power in local communities." Social Problems 12: 335-356.

Treiman, Donald J.
1970   "Industrialization and social stratification." Sociological Inquiry 40.

Veblen, Thorstein.
1953   The Theory of the Leisure Class. New York: The New American Library.

Warner, W. Lloyd, Darab B. Unwaller and John H. Trimm (eds.).
1967   The Emergent American Society: Large Scale Organizations. New Haven: Yale University Press.

Weber, Max.
1947   The Theory of Social and Economic Organization. Translated and Edited by A. M. Henderson and Talcott Parsons. New York: Oxford University Press.

CHAPTER 12

Occupational Prestige in Canada*

PETER C. PINEO and JOHN PORTER

Interest in the public evaluation or social ranking of occupations stems from the theory of social stratification, and from the need for a standardized indicator of social class or measure of socio-economic status. A subsidiary interest has been the need in industrial societies to recruit specialized manpower.

This manpower interest has meant that occupational ranking has often been done by special and restricted populations, such as school children or college students. It has also meant that the occupations to be ranked were over-weighted with high-prestige and professional occupations. These two facts raise questions about the relevance for general stratification analysis of the occupational prestige data so far available.

Exceptions are the few instances where occupations have been ranked by national samples. The first of these was the 1947 ranking of 88 occupations, by the National Opinion Research Centre (NORC), employing old quota sampling techniques and based on a national sample of adults and youths. One of its major findings was that with small variation between the major sub-groupings there was a remarkable consistency in the prestige of occupations, enough to indicate a general ranking consensus for the society. Since 1947 there have been many studies of occupational ranking in both industrialized and developing countries, but only two of these, by Svalastoga[1] in Denmark and Carlsson[2] in Sweden, were truly national studies. Others have been extremely limited. For example, in the Hall-Jones study in the United Kingdom the rankers came mainly from the membership of white collar trade unions.[3] Thus despite the fact that there have been many studies of occupational prestige only a few can be considered to have measured a national consensus, and very few are really comparable with each other.

The present study, in addition to being the first national study of occupational prestige for Canada, was also designed to make rigorous U.S.-Canadian comparisons. We hope, therefore, it will be a contribution not only to Canadian sociology but also to comparative studies.

We can claim only minimal credit for the complexity and ingenuity of the research design, which we will outline briefly. In 1962 NORC decided to undertake a much more ambitious study of occupational prestige than any so far. Their plan has two stages. One was an exact replication of the NORC 1947 study, using the same questions, occupational titles, and sampling methods, with the object of seeing if the prestige of occupations had changed since that time. The main finding of this replication, published in 1964,[4] was that there was a high degree of stability in occupational prestige over time, represented by a Pearsonian correlation coefficient of .99. For the second stage, NORC designed a study in which a national sample of adults would rank 200 occupations. It is this second stage, with the necessary adaptations in design, which we have replicated in Canada.

The research design which we adapted

required all respondents to rank 204 occupational titles. Although occupation is undoubtedly the principal element entering into a person's status there are other elements, such as the place or "situs" in which he works, ethnicity, and religion. For this reason sub-samples of respondents were required to rank 72 industries and corporations, 36 ethnicities, and 21 religions. As well as the ranking of occupations the interview elicited social background characteristics of the respondents, their spouses, their parents, and information relating to work experience, mobility, attitudes to education, and inter-ethnic relations.

Because of our interest in a comparative study we sought to minimize changes, but some important ones could not be avoided. There had to be changes in the occupational titles to make them representative of the Canadian labour force. We ended up with 174 titles common to the U.S. and Canadian studies, including 13 U.S. titles which required only slight changes; for example, "state governor" became "provincial premier" and "member of the United States House of Representatives" became "Member of the Canadian House of Commons." We increased the number of primary occupations and also took into consideration the regionality of occupations to discover differences in ranking and differences in knowledge about occupations. ("Whistle punk" and "cod fisherman" are examples). We also added, at the suggestion of Oswald Hall, two nonexistent occupations, "biologer" and "archaeopotrist," to see what proportion would respond "don't know." We felt that if a large proportion of the sample declined to rank non-existent occupations or specifically regional occupations it would indicate that the ranking task was being taken seriously.

When the changes in the occupational titles were completed we felt that ours were more representative of the Canadian labour force than the U.S. study was of the U.S. labour force. However, managerial and professional occupations were still overrepresented. We had much less difficulty in choosing industries to be ranked. We kept a good number of the U.S. titles and added

others more appropriate to Canada. For names of, firms we chose the Canadian names of subsidiaries of U.S. firms, as well as names of specific Canadian firms, and we included publicly and privately owned companies, and firms in different sectors of the economy. For ethnicities and religions we chose all the major Canadian census titles.

The second major adaptation for Canada was to make the study bilingual by ensuring satisfactory translations of the occupational titles so that the stimulus would be nearly the same in English and French. In any language occupations have emotionally charged words to describe them, "soda jerk" and "grease monkey," for example. Moreover, masculine and feminine gender gave some trouble. Since the entire ranking task was an evaluative one, obviously extreme care had to be taken in the translations. Our occupational titles were initially translated by a bilingual social scientist whose mother tongue is French. The translations were then given to two others to rate on a four-point scale of being satisfactory translations, and to suggest improvements; changes were made in the light of their suggestions. As we now try to explore French-English differences, however, we wish we had spent more time on this problem.

Since each respondent would rank from three to four hundred titles, some relatively easy method was required. Each title stimulus was printed in English and French on a one-third size I.B.M. stub card, colour coded for each ranking task and prepunched with a case number and a stimulus number. The ranking task required the respondent to sort the cards on a ladder of "social standing." The ladder had nine boxes into which the cards could be sorted, from high social standing at the top to low at the bottom. After sorting, the cards were put in special envelopes corresponding to the place on the ladder into which the cards had been sorted. When they were returned they were fed into a reproducer and the data on them, including the order into which they had been sorted, converted onto full-size cards for subsequent processing.

The fieldwork was done by a commercial firm which was considered to be the most competent in Canada. Because of our comparative interest we had to keep sampling procedures as close as possible to those of the U.S. study. The sample maintained by the firm appeared to be quite similar to the U.S. sample used by NORC, the chief difference was that there was no listing of households in advance so that for our study interviewers counted off an interval as they walked a predetermined path in order to choose households. It seems to be normal practice for Canadian firms to permit interviewers to substitute households in the case of no one at home or refusals, while the preferred method and the one employed by NORC was to use frequent call-backs to get a completion rate of about 80 percent. We would not allow substitutions and worked out a system of three, and in some cases four, call-backs.

Interviewers were assigned six cases in each of 237 sampling units. We were hoping for a completion rate which would give us a case base of 1,000. The field work began in April 1965: six weeks later it became apparent that the 70 percent completion rate we had expected was not going to be achieved. It was in fact 55 percent. The main cause of the low completion rate appeared to be refusals. Obviously such a low completion rate was not satisfactory and so we designed a second wave of interviewing which required going back to a sample of the sampling units and having interviewers call back twice more on the non-respondents in those sampling units. This kept the study in the field until December. The completion rate was brought up to 64.3 percent. We ended up with a national sample of 793 cases.

In checking the adequacy of our fieldwork we found it possible to make 12 comparisons between our study data and the census. One would expect no more than one or two of these comparisons to fail to show good fit with the census if the sampling and interviewing were perfect. In fact, of the 12 checks, 8 failed to show sufficient similarity between the sample and the census. We must conclude that our sample is biased and we have attempted some weighting procedures to correct for this.

The source of the discrepancies is most probably our inadequate completion rate. The largest source of loss is in the acceptance of refusals. Our refusal rate is 30 percent, while it is as low as 7 or 8 percent in contemporary U.S. studies.

Our sample is sufficiently representative of the country on the following variables: province, religious affiliation, occupation, labour force status. It is only slightly biased on three variables: sex, country of birth, and mother tongue. Of these, two were in fact variables upon which the sample was built—province and sex—so that some consistency with the census was guaranteed for those two variables.

Our sample fails to match the census on the following variables: age, marital status, official language, years of schooling, and size of community of residence. Middle aged, married people are over-represented. Some correction for the fact that we interviewed only one adult in three-generation households reduces this distortion. The sample is also composed of more bilingual people, more farmers, and more highly educated people than can be explained by sampling fluctuation alone. We appear to have had the most difficulty in obtaining interviews from the non-family individuals in the urban or suburban working class.

The bias in the sample seemed to us to be of such a magnitude that some attempt to remove it through weighting procedures was mandatory. A weighting to correct for three-generation households produces so few changes in the rankings of occupations that the correlation between weighted and unweighted scores is .999. It may be safely ignored. We attempted two other weighting systems but neither improved the fit between the sample and the census.

The ranking question went as follows:

> Now let's talk about jobs. Here is a ladder with nine boxes on it, and a card with the name of an occupation on each. Please put the card in the box at the *top* of the ladder if you think that occupation has the highest possible social standing.
>
> Put it in the box at the *bottom* of the

ladder if you think it has the lowest possible social standing.

If it belongs somewhere in between, just put it in the box that matches the social standing of the occupation.

Interviewers were instructed to repeat these instructions if the respondent showed uncertainty. They were told in their instructions that they were not to explain what the words *social standing* meant. Synonyms such as prestige, respect, or regard were specifically disallowed. Rather they were to repeat the words *social standing* in various ways, as in "Well, you probably think some jobs have higher standing than others. If you think this is one of those then place it . . ." and so on. The interviewers were also instructed never to explain the nature of any job the respondent did not recognize. Rather respondents were to be allowed to place the card to the side and it eventually ended up in an envelope marked "Don't Know."

After the respondent had sorted the first card given him he was given the rest of the pile and the interviewer said:

Here are some more cards with names of occupations. Just put them in the boxes on the ladder which match the social standing they actually have. If you want to you can change your mind about where an occupation belongs and move its card to a different box.

After the sorting was completed the interviewer was instructed to encourage the respondent to make any changes he wanted and also to attempt once again to sort any which he had placed in the "Don't Know" pile.

In French, the crucial words "social standing" became *"position social."* Since this ranking question came right at the beginning of the interview it was not contaminated by previous questions, as was the case with the NORC 1947 study.

We, of course, inherited this question from the NORC study. Once again there is some of the ambiguity noted in the 1947 NORC[5] question where the respondent was asked to give his *personal* opinion of the *general standing* that an occupation had. The question still does not make the path completely clear for a respondent who

feels his personal judgment of the social standing of a job is at variance with that of the community at large. It may be difficult for any question to do so satisfactorily. Do we want him to report his own opinion of the job's standing, or his opinion of the general community evaluation of the job? Presumably the question is workable because cases of this discontinuity between personal evaluation and perceived community evaluation are rare. In a later ranking task, the specifications to interviewers make it clear that the respondent should ignore his own opinion if it is at variance with that of the community at large. We suspect that the inclusion of this new rule for the later ranking, which is the ranking of ethnicities, may have influenced the sort of advice given by our interviewers to respondents who found difficulty in any of the ranking tasks.

We can now present some initial findings: the occupational prestige scores for the national sample and for its English and French components; some differences between English and French; and the occupational prestige of the major census classifications. We are planning a detailed analysis of the survey data, but the following represents some of the major problems the study was designed to investigate.

The appendix table arranges the occupations in alphabetical order within socioeconomic groupings. The eight-level classification plus one other for farmers in much like those used in studies of social mobility. The scores are a transformation of the mean which makes it adopt a range from 0 to 100 for rough comparison with earlier, published prestige scores. We point out a few results that struck us as interesting.

The highest score given (89.9) was to Provincial Premier. The French gave this occupation an extraordinarily high score (93.6). As can be seen, federal political occupations ranked highly also. We may question, therefore, the view that what has been described as a decline of political skill in Canada can be attributed to "a relative loss in the attractiveness and prestige of politics as compared to other vocations."[6]

Professional occupations ranked highly,

particularly physician, university professor, county court judge, and lawyer. Moreover, these occupations relative to others are homogeneously judged to be high as measured by the standard deviation. Artistic occupations are not ranked particularly highly, for example, ballet dancer, jazz musician, musician, musician in a symphony orchestra, sculptor, and T.V. star. In spite of the stereotype of French Canadians as placing greater value on artistic pursuits than on others, the French ranked all of the artistic occupations, except jazz musician, lower than did the English. The lowest ranked occupations were newspaper peddler and garbage collector. For Canada we introduced several farming titles which ranked fairly close to each other, except for farm labourer and hog farmer, the latter probably affected by the word "hog." Attention is drawn to eight titles at the end of the table which are not labour force titles. Our nonexistent occupations ranked reasonably well, but the "don't know" response was high, that is 44 percent for "archaeopotrist" and 30 percent for "biologer." The only other occupations which equalled these two in "don't know" responses were those which we had included for their regionality, for example "whistle punk" and "troller." It is interesting that "Occupation of my family's main wage earner" was right in the middle of the range. Someone who lives on relief has no prestige at all.

Earlier Canadian information suggests, as do Inkeles and Rossi's cross-national comparisons,[7] that there would be a high correlation between the ranking of occupations in Canada and in the U.S. The original Tuckman data[8] (1947), based on the ranking of 25 occupations by 379 college students and 40 job applicants at a Jewish vocational service, produced correlations with U.S. rankings (NORC, 1963) of .96 over nineteen occupations. Blishen's scale developed from the 1951 Canadian Census, using a combination of education and income as the measure of occupational rank, correlated with U.S. prestige scores, from the 1947 study, at a similarly high level (r =.94). Blishen also reports that, over

eighteen occupations, his scale correlated .91 with the Tuckman scores.[9]

A major question answered by our survey is whether, with a substantial improvement in the quality of the data, the correlation between the rankings in the U.S. and Canada increases or decreases from the .96 which Tuckman's scores produced. Our study is an improvement on Tuckman's in many respects: it ranks a longer and more representative list of occupations, it is based on a proper sample of the whole country, it uses a ranking question which is more acceptably worded. Had the correlation between the rankings produced in our study and that of the recent NORC study been smaller than any previous ones some questioning of the hypothesis of identical rankings in all industrialized nations would be appropriate. In fact, the correlation was higher: it went up from .96 to .98.[10]

So far, findings are limited to an initial search for basic differences in ratings. We have been concerned with two kinds of differences. There is the traditional problem of describing the prestige hierarchy. We can compare the ranking of occupations in other countries with Canada, and of subgroups within Canada, such as French with English Canada. The second problem is the study of the total amount of prestige given the occupational system as a whole. In this case we look for tendencies in a country or a sub-group to rate all jobs systematically higher, suggesting that, within that group, work itself has a greater prestige. Additional differences in the level of ranking may also be found for subclasses of occupations.

Our vague hypothesizing went something like this: cross-national comparisons led us to expect high correlations between the U.S. and Canada and between English and French Canada in the rating of occupations. However, in respect to differences in the level of ranking we expected the U.S. to be higher than Canada. That is the total amount of prestige put into the system or more correctly into the 174 matching occupations would be greater. Theoretically it could be anticipated that as the process of industrialization advances the prestige of work and occupations associated with a high level of industrialization would increase. This condition would seem functionally appropriate to provide a fit between the value system, the motivation of actors and socialization to occupational roles in a more complex economy. This is the central manpower problem for industrial societies at present.

One of the interesting findings in comparing the NORC 1963 rankings with NORC 1947 (it will be recalled the latter was a replication of the former) was that in the U.S. there was a slight increase in the average prestige given jobs between the two points in time.[11] Since Canada is less industrialized than the U.S., and has a labour force with a much lower level of education, we anticipated Canada would put much less prestige into the occupational structure than did the U.S. and that similarly French-Canada would put even less than English-Canada. We were therefore surprised to discover that the Canadian rankings on the average were two points higher on the 10-point scale than those in the U.S.

It is clear we must do a great deal of thinking and tabulating before we can interpret this Canadian-U.S. difference. It could be something as trivial as the fact that our study had a higher refusal rate than the U.S. study, although we doubt this is the explanation.

There may be more than one reason for differing amounts of prestige in the occupational world. It occurs to us there may be a deferential element in the Canadian rankings derived from the elitist value pattern suggested by Lipset[12] as being important in Canadian society. The tendency in Canada to rate jobs higher is greatest for the professional and semiprofessional categories of jobs where, on the average, the jobs are ranked about 4 points higher than the U.S. Elitist values do not account for all the difference. The tendency for Canadian ratings to be higher is found to some degree throughout the whole list of occupations; they average 2.4 points higher for the white-collar jobs and 1.4 points higher for the blue-collar jobs.

The difference between our occupational rankings and others in Canada are much as we expected. In over twenty occupations in common with Tuckman's study our scores correlated .93 with his. In a study by Robson, a sample of Canadian undergraduates ranked some of the original NORC titles. These ratings and ours over 31 matching titles produced a correlation of .96. With Blishen's scale based on the 1951 census our ratings correlate .93 when the comparison is restricted to 57 very closely matching titles and .88 when the comparison includes another 73 titles which are relatively poor matches. These correlations

Table 1. English-French Differences in Evaluation of Occupations

Occupational Category	Number of Occupational Titles with Higher Prestige Score Given by:	
	English	French
Professional	12	9
Proprietors, managers and officials, large	12	3
Semiprofessional	22	7
Proprietors, managers and officials, small	10	13
Clerical and sales	6	17
Skilled	9	18
Semiskilled	11	23
Unskilled	4	14
Farmer	2	4

may be compared to the multiple correlation of income and education on prestige of .91 found by Duncan in the U.S.[13]

Some French-English differences in the ranking of jobs were pointed out in the discussion of the table of occupational rankings where scores for the two groups are given separately. Calculations based on these scores suggest some distinctiveness in ratings of French-speaking respondents. Overall, the prestige hierarchy in French Canada differs slightly from that in English Canada and in the U.S.: the French rankings correlated with the English Canadian rankings .95.

The tendency for jobs to be rated higher in Canada than in the U.S. is true of both French and English Canada, but the French show an additional tendency in

**Table 2. Twenty Occupational Titles with Greatest Differences in Ranking
by Respondents Interviewed in English and French**

English Title	English Score	French Score	French Title
Apprentice to a master craftsman	38.9	18.0	Apprenti
Protestant minister	71.7	53.7	Pasteur protestant
Timber cruiser	36.1	53.1	Estimateur forestier
Whistle punk	14.3	29.4	Siffleur (forestage)
Department head in city government	74.5	60.4	Chef de départment dans l'administration municipale
Advertising executive	59.4	46.5	Membre de la direction d'un agence de publicité
Bill collector	26.8	38.4	Agent de collection
Ballet dancer	51.6	40.7	Danseur ou Danseuse de ballet
Lunchroom operator	29.2	39.9	Propriétaire d'un casse-croute
Physicist	79.9	69.3	Physicien
Social worker	57.4	47.4	Travailleur social
Typesetter	40.0	49.9	Typographe
Quarry worker	24.4	34.0	Ouvier dans une carrière
Construction labourer	24.4	33.8	Manoeuvre dans l'industrie de la construction
Troller	26.3	16.9	Pêcheur à la cuiller
T.V. Star	67.7	58.7	Vedette de la télévision
Musician in a symphony orchestra	58.0	49.3	Musicien dans un orchestre symphonique
Paper-making machine tender	29.5	38.2	Préposé à une machine à faire le papier
Locomotive engineer	50.9	42.2	Conducteur de locomotive
Farm labourer	19.6	27.9	Ouvrier agricole

their rankings not to sort the jobs into the very highest and the very lowest categories to the extent that the English Canadians and U.S. respondents do. Table 1 shows this tendency. For blue-collar jobs and for clerical, sales, and small managerial jobs the French rankings tend to be higher and for the superior white-collar jobs they tend to be lower. This pattern is similar to that found for lower income groups by Hall and Jones in Great Britain, and Reiss, et al., in the U.S.[14] and might be interpreted as a self-enhancing manner of ranking the occupations; jobs to which blue-collar workers can reasonably aspire are slightly upgraded and those which are unattainable are slightly downgraded. We would not have been surprised to have found the overall Canadian ranking showing such a pattern.

A major problem in our analysis will be to determine the extent to which the French-English differences or French-U.S. differences are because of translations. Table 2 contains the occupational titles for which the French-English differences are greatest. Some of the differences are probably due to translation and we are having all our translations rated for adequacy by several bilingual judges. "Whistle punk," for example, is rated lower by the English; the word "punk" may have too negative a connotation which is absent in the French version "siffleur."

One of the important products of a public ranking of occupations is the basic material to construct a scale of socioeconomic status. The NORC 1947 rankings have been widely used in this way in the United States and to some extent in Canada. The theoretical support for the use of rankings

Table 3. Occupational Prestige Scores by Major Census Classifications

Census Major Occupation Group	Number of Titles	Mean Score	Standard Deviation
Owners and managers	27	60.38	15.71
Professional occupations	46	64.11	10.95
Clerical occupations	14	37.46	7.23
Sales occupations	11	36.99	12.91
Service and recreation occupations	23	37.17	15.92
Transport and communications	13	41.72	12.83
Farmers and farm workers	6	34.98	10.01
Loggers and related workers	3	27.87	11.25
Fishermen, trappers and hunters	2	23.50	0.32
Miners, quarrymen and related workers	5	33.12	7.22
Craftsmen, production process workers	43	36.55	8.00
Labourers, n.e.s.	3	21.47	6.02

of occupations made by a representative cross section of the society is that class is a subjective phenomenon experienced by actors in a social system. Class is also analysed by objective criteria such as income, property, and so forth, selected by investigators and considered as independent of the evaluations of actors. As we have seen there is a high correlation between occupations ranked subjectively and objectively on such criteria as income and education. We feel these two approaches are complementary and necessary to the understanding of the structure of stratification.

One of our aims would be to establish prestige levels for a much greater proportion of the labour force than has been previously possible. We are, of course, faced with the problem of matching our titles with census titles, but we feel that we can do that sufficiently well to relate our rankings to a wide range of objective attributes of occupations derived from census data. Sociologists have long been critical of the way in which occupations have been treated in the Canadian census, particularly of the major categories, sociologically meaningless, into which they are arranged: now we feel that we have some empirical

justification for this criticism.

Table 3 shows the mean occupational rank of those occupations falling into each of the major census codes. Table 4 similarly arranged these occupations into sociologically common-sense socioeconomic status categories which are also the classifications of the Appendix table. A good coding system produces homogeneous categories. In each table the standard deviation of the prestige scores for the occupations within each category is given as a test of homogeneity. If we restrict the analysis to categories with at least five occupations in them and arbitrarily define homogeneity by a standard deviation of less than 10, only three of the nine possible census categories are homogeneous while seven of the nine socioeconomic status categories are.

A good coding system must also differentiate, as it will do if the categories are homogeneous. The socioeconomic status classification shows almost a clear gradient from professional to unskilled in the means for each category. The exception is the almost identical score of "clerical and sales" occupations and "skilled" occupations. Many have doubted the justification of the nonmanual-manual dichotomy so

Table 4. Occupational Prestige Scores by Socioeconomic Categories

Occupational Title	Number of Titles	Mean Score	Standard Deviation
Professional	21	72.04	8.16
Proprietors, managers and officials, large	15	70.42	12.99
Semiprofessional	29	57.73	8.29
Proprietors, managers and officials, small	23	48.79	8.91
Clerical and sales	23	38.57	8.90
Skilled	27	38.76	6.98
Semiskilled	34	32.91	7.71
Unskilled	18	23.46	6.23
Farmer	6	34.98	10.01

frequently used in sociological research. In a highly industrialized society at least, there are many white-collar occupations which have less prestige than many skilled blue-collar occupations. The census shows a much less satisfactory pattern. If the analysis is confined to those categories with at least five occupations the socioeconomic status classifications cover a much wider range of occupational prestige than do the census categories, that is 23.46 to 72.04 for the SES classifications, compared to 33.1 to 64.1 for the census categories. The SES classifications separate "skilled," "semi-skilled," and "unskilled" whereas the census lumps them all together under "Craftsmen, Production Process Workers." The differences in the prestige levels of manual workers justifies their being subdivided. Quite meaningless from the point of view of stratification theory is the census category "owners and managers." Its occupations range in their scores from 31.6 to 89.9 or 60 percent of the entire theoretical prestige hierarchy and 80 percent of the actual. The use of such a category for the tabulation of census data is sociologically absurd; it is extraordinarily difficult to find any defensible reason for it. Only slightly less absurd are the "service and recreation" and the "transport and communications" categories. In some respects these last two constitute families of occupations, but they have little relevance to stratification. Sociologists have sought in vain for a relationship between census occupational cate-gories and the structural categories of sociology, and it is all the more distressing because it is sociology more than the other social sciences which could make the most use of the mass of census and other macro data.

NOTES

*Revision of a paper presented to the Canadian Association of Sociology and Anthropology, Sherbrooke, Quebec, June, 1966. Financial assistance for this project came from Canada Council, Department of Labour, Department of Citizenship and Immigration, McConnell Foundation, Social Science Research Council, and Carleton University. We are very much indebted to the National Opinion Research Centre for making available the necessary materials for us to replicate their study in Canada, and for their advice. We should also like to acknowledge the help of Ann Kitchen and Kathleen Kelly, our research assistants.

[1]K. Svalastoga, Prestige, Class and Mobility (Copenhagen: 1959).

[2]G. Carlsson, Social Mobility and Class Structure (Gleerup/Lund: 1958).

[3]John Hall and D. Caradog Jones, "The Social Grading of Occupations," British Journal of Sociology I (March, 1950).

[4]R. W. Hodge, P. M. Siegel, and P. H. Rossi, "Occupational Prestige in the United States, 1925-1963," American Journal of Sociology (November, 1964), 286-302.

[5]"Jobs and Occupations: A Popular Evaluation," Opinion News, IX (September, 1947).

[6]John Meisel, "The Stalled Omnibus: Canadian Parties in the 1960's," Social Research, XXX (Autumn 1963), 386.

[7]A. Inkeles and P. H. Rossi, "National Comparisons of Occupational Prestige," American

Journal of Sociology, LXI (January, 1956).

[8]J. Tuckman, "Social Status of Occupations in Canada," *Canadian Journal of Psychology, 1* (June, 1947).

[9]B. R. Blishen, "The Construction and Use of an Occupational Class Scale," in B. R. Blishen, *et al.,* eds., *Canadian Society* (Toronto: 1964).

[10]The N.O.R.C. rankings were supplied to us on a confidential basis and we are not, therefore, in a position to comment extensively, at this time, on Canadian-U.S. differences.

[11]Hodge, Siegel, and Rossi, "Occupational Prestige in the United States, 1925-1963."

[12]S. M. Lipset, *The First New Nation* (New York: 1963), Chap. 7.

[13]Otis Dudley Duncan, "A Socio-Economic Index for All Occupations" in Albert J. Reiss, Jr., *Occupations and Social Status* (New York: 1961), 124.

[14]Hall and Jones, "The Social Grading of Occupations," 42-43; Reiss, *Occupations and Social Status,* 183.

Appendix. Occupational Prestige Scores by Occupational Classes

Occupational Title	National N = 793		National English N = 607		National French N = 186	
	Score	S.D.	Score	S.D.	Score	S.D.
Professional						
Accountant	63.4	19.2	62.9	19.4	65.4	18.4
Architect	78.1	18.3	77.6	18.4	79.6	17.9
Biologist	72.6	20.9	73.4	20.2	69.7	23.0
Catholic priest	72.8	25.5	71.5	25.0	77.2	26.6
Chemist	73.5	19.3	73.3	18.8	73.9	21.1
Civil engineer	73.1	19.0	72.6	18.8	75.1	19.3
County Court judge	82.5	18.6	81.0	18.6	87.4	17.7
Druggist	69.3	20.0	68.5	19.8	72.0	20.5
Economist	62.2	22.3	63.0	21.6	59.5	24.2
High school teacher	66.1	20.7	67.8	20.0	60.4	22.2
Lawyer	82.3	16.7	81.6	17.0	84.4	15.5
Mathematician	72.7	20.1	73.7	20.1	69.5	19.9
Mine safety analyst	57.1	20.5	57.2	20.5	56.6	20.8
Mining engineer	68.8	20.5	68.6	20.1	69.3	21.6
Physician	87.2	15.9	87.5	16.1	86.1	15.2
Physicist	77.6	21.4	79.9	20.0	69.3	24.1
Protestant minister	67.8	26.3	71.7	23.0	53.7	32.1
Psychologist	74.9	20.3	76.0	19.6	71.3	22.2
Public grade school teacher	59.6	20.5	59.8	20.8	58.8	19.2
University professor	84.6	17.3	86.1	16.9	79.9	17.7
Veterinarian	66.7	21.3	66.7	20.9	66.6	22.5
Semiprofessional						
Airline pilot	66.1	20.5	67.4	19.9	61.6	21.8
Author	64.8	21.7	65.8	21.7	61.4	21.6
Ballet dancer	49.1	26.2	51.6	25.2	40.7	27.6
Chiropractor	68.4	22.0	67.2	21.6	72.2	22.9
Commercial artist	57.2	20.5	58.1	20.4	54.1	20.6
Computer programmer	53.8	21.6	53.6	21.2	54.8	22.9
Disc jockey	38.0	23.1	38.2	23.0	37.3	23.6
Draughtsman	60.0	20.6	59.9	20.4	60.0	21.1
Funeral director	54.9	23.7	55.2	22.8	53.7	26.5
Jazz musician	40.9	24.5	40.9	24.3	41.2	25.2
Journalist	60.9	20.0	62.3	19.5	56.4	21.0
Medical or dental technician	67.5	21.7	66.7	21.8	70.0	21.4
Musician	52.1	22.9	53.7	22.5	46.6	23.2
Musician in a symphony orchestra	56.0	23.0	58.0	22.1	49.3	25.0
Physiotherapist	72.1	19.4	72.3	19.0	71.3	20.6
Playground director	42.8	22.3	43.1	21.7	41.8	24.1
Professional athlete	54.1	24.2	54.5	24.3	52.9	23.9
Professionally trained forester	60.0	20.6	60.4	19.9	58.9	22.8
Professionally trained librarian	58.1	21.7	58.5	21.2	56.7	23.1
Registered nurse	64.7	21.4	66.1	20.8	59.9	22.5
Research technician	66.9	19.1	67.1	19.1	66.1	19.2
Sculptor	56.9	23.6	58.0	23.5	53.5	23.9
Social worker	55.1	24.0	57.4	23.2	47.4	25.2
Surveyor	62.0	20.4	60.6	20.1	66.9	20.7
T.V. announcer	57.6	21.6	57.9	21.4	56.5	22.4
T.V. cameraman	48.3	21.4	47.8	21.0	49.9	22.6
T.V. director	62.1	21.5	63.1	21.4	58.9	21.7
T.V. star	65.6	26.8	67.7	25.9	58.7	28.6
YMCA director	58.2	21.8	59.2	21.0	54.5	24.4

Occupational Prestige Scores by Occupational Classes (cont.)

Occupational Title	National		National English		National French	
	Score	S.D.	Score	S.D.	Score	S.D.
Proprietors, Managers and Officials, Large						
Administrative officer in federal Civil Service	68.8	20.1	69.9	19.6	64.9	21.6
Advertising executive	56.5	21.8	59.4	21.2	46.5	20:9
Bank manager	70.9	19.3	72.1	19.4	67.1	18.5
Building contractor	56.5	19.3	56.4	18.9	56.7	20.7
Colonel in the army	70.8	22.0	71.6	21.3	68.4	24.2
Department head in city government	71.3	21.3	74.5	19.5	60.4	23.7
General manager of a manufacturing plant	69.1	19.2	70.4	18.5	64.9	20.8
Mayor of a large city	79.9	20.4	80.6	20.2	77.5	20.7
Member of Canadian Cabinet	83.3	19.9	84.2	18.8	80.4	22.9
Member of Canadian House of Commons	84.8	18.8	84.9	18.4	84.5	20.2
Member of Canadian Senate	86.1	21.1	86.0	20.8	86.1	22.3
Merchandise buyer for a department store	51.1	19.3	52.7	19.0	45.5	19.3
Owner of a manufacturing plant	69.4	21.3	69.8	20.6	67.9	23.4
Provincial Premier	89.9	18.1	88.7	19.1	93.6	13.3
Wholesale distributor	47.9	20.5	49.1	19.9	43.6	22.0
Proprietors, Managers and Officials, Small						
Advertising copy writer	48.9	20.6	48.3	19.8	50.9	22.8
Beauty operator	35.2	20.9	34.4	20.3	37.9	22.6
Construction foreman	51.1	20.0	50.4	19.7	53.3	20.8
Driving instructor	41.6	21.6	40.0	20.9	46.9	23.2
Foreman in a factory	50.9	19.3	49.2	18.6	56.8	20.4
Government purchasing agent	56.8	21.6	56.9	21.0	56.2	23.4
Insurance claims investigator	51.1	20.1	50.8	20.1	52.0	20.2
Job counsellor	58.3	20.7	58.7	20.0	56.8	23.0
Livestock buyer	39.6	21.5	40.6	20.6	36.1	24.2
Lunchroom operator	31.6	21.4	29.2	20.3	39.9	23.2
Manager of a real estate office	58.3	20.9	58.8	20.7	56.8	21.8
Manager of a supermarket	52.5	20.2	52.7	20.0	51.9	20.6
Member of a city council	62.9	21.4	64.7	20.3	57.1	24.0
Motel owner	51.6	23.5	50.9	21.7	53.8	28.0
Owner of a food store	47.8	21.3	49.7	20.8	41.7	21.9
Public relations man	60.5	19.4	60.3	19.2	61.4	20.2
Railroad ticket agent	35.7	21.1	36.5	20.6	33.0	22.5
Sawmill operator	37.0	21.7	36.4	21.4	38.9	22.5
Service station manager	41.5	20.4	42.5	18.9	38.1	24.5
Ship's pilot	59.6	22.7	59.6	22.4	59.7	23.5
Superintendent of a construction job	53.9	20.4	55.3	20.4	49.0	19.5
Trade union business agent	49.2	21.0	48.6	20.9	51.1	21.3
Travel agent	46.6	20.7	45.0	19.5	52.0	23.5
Clerical and Sales						
Air hostess	57.0	21.1	55.7	21.0	61.0	20.7
Bank teller	42.3	21.0	42.4	20.1	41.9	24.0

Occupational Prestige Scores by Occupational Classes (cont.)

Occupational Title	National		National English		National French	
	Score	S.D.	Score	S.D.	Score	S.D.
Clerical and Sales (cont.)						
Bill collector	29.4	21.5	26.8	21.1	38.4	20.4
Bookkeeper	49.4	20.2	50.0	20.1	47.3	20.7
Cashier in a supermarket	31.1	21.4	30.5	21.1	33.0	22.1
Clerk in an office	35.6	20.3	35.0	19.8	37.8	22.1
File clerk	32.7	21.2	31.5	20.4	36.7	23.1
IBM keypunch operator	47.7	21.5	46.5	21.0	51.9	22.8
Insurance agent	47.3	19.7	46.6	19.1	49.7	21.5
Manufacturer's representative	52.1	19.1	51.7	19.0	53.5	19.1
Post office clerk	37.2	21.9	37.2	21.6	36.9	22.8
Real estate agent	47.1	21.1	46.2	20.1	49.8	23.9
Receptionist	38.7	20.9	39.7	20.4	35.5	22.1
Sales clerk in a store	26.5	19.7	26.6	19.4	25.9	20.7
Shipping clerk	30.9	20.1	30.7	19.3	31.7	22.7
Stenographer	46.0	20.2	44.6	19.6	50.6	21.5
Stockroom attendant	25.8	19.2	24.9	18.8	29.0	20.1
Telephone operator	38.1	22.0	37.6	21.7	39.9	23.0
Telephone solicitor	26.7	23.0	28.3	23.2	21.7	21.6
Travelling salesman	40.2	21.1	38.8	21.0	45.1	20.6
Truck dispatcher	32.2	20.4	32.1	20.1	32.7	21.2
Typist	41.9	20.7	41.1	20.1	44.7	22.4
Used car salesman	31.2	21.0	30.4	20.0	34.0	24.0
Skilled						
Airplane mechanic	50.3	22.4	49.3	22.1	53.4	23.1
Baker	38.9	20.5	38.8	20.1	39.4	22.1
Bricklayer	36.2	21.6	36.0	21.3	36.9	22.6
Butcher in a store	34.8	20.2	34.7	19.7	35.0	21.6
Coal miner	27.6	22.1	26.2	21.9	32.3	22.4
Cook in a restaurant	29.7	21.0	28.9	21.3	32.3	19.8
Custom seamstress	33.4	20.3	33.7	19.3	32.5	23.3
Diamond driller	44.5	21.7	44.8	21.4	43.2	22.5
Electrician	50.2	20.5	49.5	20.5	52.3	20.4
House carpenter	38.9	20.7	38.7	20.3	39.4	22.1
House painter	29.9	19.4	29.0	19.0	33.0	20.4
Locomotive engineer	48.9	22.2	50.9	21.7	42.2	22.7
Machinist	44.2	21.9	44.0	21.9	45.0	22.0
Machine set-up man in a factory	42.1	21.4	41.9	21.5	42.6	21.4
Mucking machine operator	31.5	20.5	30.3	20.3	35.1	20.5
Plumber	42.6	20.8	42.7	20.7	42.4	21.5
Power crane operator	40.2	20.7	39.8	20.7	41.4	21.0
Power lineman	40.9	21.2	41.8	20.3	37.5	24.3
Pumphouse engineer	38.9	21.8	40.6	21.6	33.3	21.7
Railroad brakeman	37.1	20.9	37.5	20.8	35.9	21.2
Railroad conductor	45.3	21.8	44.5	21.2	48.2	23.5
Saw sharpener	20.7	20.1	19.6	19.1	24.6	22.9
Sheet metal worker	35.9	20.5	36.8	19.9	32.5	22.6
T.V. repairman	37.2	20.4	36.5	20.2	39.3	20.9
Tool and die maker	42.5	22.2	44.1	21.8	36.7	22.6
Typesetter	42.2	20.5	40.0	19.6	49.9	21.4
Welder	41.8	21.5	41.4	21.3	43.2	22.2

Occupational Prestige Scores by Occupational Classes (cont.)

Occupational Title	National		National English		National French	
	Score	S.D.	Score	S.D.	Score	S.D.
Semiskilled						
Aircraft worker	43.7	21.6	43.6	21.6	43.9	21.8
Apprentice to a master craftsman	33.9	23.1	38.9	21.9	18.0	19.5
Assembly line worker	28.2	20.4	27.6	20.3	30.4	20.8
Automobile repairman	38.1	20.8	36.9	20.2	41.9	22.2
Automobile worker	35.9	21.2	34.4	20.6	41.3	22.2
Barber	39.3	20.2	38.9	19.6	40.4	22.2
Bartender	20.2	19.5	19.4	19.5	22.8	19.2
Book binder	35.2	20.1	33.5	19.6	41.0	20.8
Bus driver	35.9	21.3	35.8	21.9	36.1	19.2
Cod fisherman	23.4	21.0	24.8	21.0	18.6	20.5
Firefighter	43.5	24.4	44.2	24.5	41.4	23.8
Fruit packer in a cannery	23.2	20.7	22.0	20.3	27.6	21.4
Logger	24.9	21.3	25.4	20.9	23.2	22.5
Longshoreman	26.1	21.1	26.5	21.0	24.9	21.5
Loom operator	33.3	19.7	32.3	19.3	36.4	20.7
Machine operator in a factory	34.9	22.2	33.1	21.7	41.1	23.0
Newspaper pressman	43.0	20.6	44.3	20.2	38.4	21.2
Oil field worker	35.3	21.9	34.6	21.6	37.5	22.7
Oiler in a ship	27.6	21.2	26.3	20.2	31.7	23.7
Paper making machine tender	31.6	20.4	29.5	19.8	38.2	20.8
Policeman	51.6	23.0	52.1	23.0	49.9	22.9
Private in the army	28.4	22.9	29.6	23.5	24.4	20.4
Production worker in the electronics industry	50.8	23.0	50.4	22.7	52.2	23.7
Professional babysitter	25.9	22.5	25.2	22.3	28.5	23.1
Quarry worker	26.7	22.3	24.4	21.3	34.0	23.8
Sewing machine operator	28.2	19.9	26.7	19.2	33.1	21.3
Steam boiler fireman	32.8	21.1	33.9	21.0	29.0	21.0
Steam roller operator	32.2	20.7	32.0	20.2	32.7	22.3
Steel mill worker	34.3	20.6	35.2	20.9	31.2	19.1
Textile mill worker	28.8	19.5	28.6	19.5	29.7	19.6
Timber cruiser	40.3	22.6	36.1	21.5	53.1	21.3
Trailer truck driver	32.8	22.0	31.8	21.7	36.5	22.4
Troller	23.6	20.7	26.3	20.9	16.9	18.8
Worker in a meat packing plant	25.2	20.3	24.3	19.7	28.3	22.1
Unskilled						
Carpenter's helper	23.1	20.0	22.5	20.0	24.9	19.8
Construction labourer	26.5	22.7	24.4	22.1	33.8	23.1
Elevator operator in a building	20.1	20.7	21.8	20.9	14.4	18.8
Filling station attendant	23.3	20.3	22.2	19.7	27.7	22.1
Garbage collector	14.8	20.0	15.0	20.3	13.8	18.9
Hospital attendant	34.9	24.9	34.2	24.2	37.6	26.8
Housekeeper in a private home	28.8	23.5	28.5	24.1	30.0	21.2
Janitor	17.3	19.1	16.3	18.5	20.8	21.0
Laundress	19.3	20.1	19.3	19.8	19.6	21.3
Mailman	36.1	23.0	36.2	23.0	35.8	23.3
Museum attendant	30.4	21.8	31.5	21.2	26.9	23.1
Newspaper peddler	14.8	19.0	14.3	18.7	16.5	20.1

Occupational Prestige Scores by Occupational Classes (cont.)

Occupational Title	National		National English		National French	
	Score	S.D.	Score	S.D.	Score	S.D.
Unskilled (cont.)						
Railroad sectionhand	27.3	21.8	25.7	21.7	32.6	21.5
Taxicab driver	25.1	20.3	24.3	19.8	27.8	21.7
Waitress in a restaurant	19.9	19.4	19.1	19.0	22.6	20.3
Warehouse hand	21.3	18.3	20.2	18.1	25.1	18.7
Whistle punk	18.4	21.2	14.3	18.7	29.4	23.4
Worker in a dry cleaning or laundry plant	20.8	19.6	20.3	19.4	22.4	19.9
Farmer						
Commercial farmer	42.0	22.3	41.7	22.0	42.9	23.3
Dairy farmer	44.2	22.9	43.3	22.4	47.3	24.5
Farm labourer	21.5	22.0	19.6	21.7	27.9	22.0
Farm owner and operator	44.1	23.7	44.8	23.2	41.7	25.5
Hog farmer	33.0	23.6	31.3	23.5	38.8	23.1
Part time farmer	25.1	22.4	26.6	22.3	20.1	21.9
Not in Labour Force						
Archaeopotrist	63.7	23.9	64.7	22.5	59.7	28.4
Biologer	64.2	24.1	66.0	22.8	57.8	27.4
Occupation of my family's main wage earner	50.9	25.1	50.3	24.5	53.0	27.0
Occupation of my father when I was 16	42.5	25.6	42.6	25.2	42.2	26.8
Someone who lives off inherited wealth	45.8	31.5	45.8	31.9	46.0	30.2
Someone who lives off property holdings	48.7	25.9	46.9	25.4	54.4	26.7
Someone who lives off stocks and bonds	56.9	27.9	56.7	28.0	57.5	27.8
Someone who lives on relief	7.3	15.9	7.2	15.5	7.8	17.4

Living Room Styles and Social Attributes: The Patterning of Material Artifacts in a Modern Urban Community*

EDWARD O. LAUMANN and JAMES S. HOUSE

Over the past seventy years, many writers have commented on the importance of studying the material artifacts with which individuals and families surround themselves in order to gain insight into the ways by which people express their personalities, facilitate their pursuit of personal and social goals, and symbolize their status position in society. Many theorists have attempted to go beyond the obvious fact that material artifacts typically serve utilitarian or functional needs for individuals and groups to consider why most artifacts seem to be elaborated in design or decoration far beyond the modest dictates of strict utility. Such theorists range from those anthropologists who suggest that certain fundamental panhuman expressive needs for aesthetic expression and aesthetic delight are fulfilled by the embellishment of objects[1] to certain rather more cynical sociologists who emphasize the role that non-utilitarian elaboration of objects plays in facilitating the invidious comparison of individuals and groups, particularly in the more "advanced" societies. With regard to this last point, we might note Veblen's (1953) classic work on the theory of the leisure class, which was especially directed to analyzing the significance of the conspicuous consumption of time and goods in interpreting the status behavior of the leisure and working (industrial) classes.

While somewhat oversimplifying the general picture, the subsequent sociological research tradition on material style of life may be characterized as falling into two broad categories or camps.[2] On the one hand, writers in what might be termed the tradition of social commentary and criticism have typically acknowledged their deep indebtedness to Veblen[3] and have updated his commentary. In a society in which leisure and consumption have become increasingly central in the lives of individuals, these writers view style of consumption as a primary means of asserting and/or validating social status and identity. Thus, the style and quality of the exterior and interior of a person's home are viewed as pawns in a Goffmanesque game of impression management (Goffman, 1959). This process has been chronicled in its most extreme forms among those newly arrived in (or still striving for) more prestigious social positions, e.g., the new "suburbanites" or the rising young "Organization man." (See Seeley, et al., 1956: esp. Ch. 3; Whyte, 1956; esp. Part VII.)

On the other hand, writers of a more methodologically sophisticated and "objective" bent, such as F. Stuart Chapin (1935) and William Sewell (1940), have confined their attention to an evaluation of the potential utility of using, let us say, selected living room furnishings to predict the relative socio-economic status or family income of the household. The possible significance of differences in taste and styles of decor (given comparable economic positions) in serving expressive functions for the individual's personality or in symbolizing the individual's social location and conception of his social position have often been ignored on the grounds of being too "subjective" to sustain rigorous analysis.[4] Thus, the first camp is very rich in social insight and interpretation of contemporary society, but often lacks convincing empirical tests of its propositions; while the second is methodologically more rigorous, but limited in the scope and application of its findings.

In this paper we wish to show that it is possible and fruitful to bring more rigorous empirical methods to bear on some of the theoretical speculations of the "social commentary tradition." We will employ for this purpose some new techniques for multivariate statistical analysis. This is thus an exploratory effort at empirical measurement and analysis of one aspect of individuals' "styles of life," which hopefully will suggest both the need for and the difficulty of further research in this area. More specifically, we seek to explore the relationship of social attributes and attitudes (including social status and social mobility) to the manner in which persons furnish their living rooms.

The living room (in addition to the front exterior of the home) is clearly the most appropriate source of data for examining the ways in which individuals express their actual (or desired) social identities in their homes. Goffman (1959: Ch. 3) makes the distinction between the front (public) and rear (private) regions of behavior in impression management: "The performance of an individual in a front region may be seen as an effort to give the appearance that his activity in the region maintains and embodies certain standards." (Goffman, 1959: 107.) A crucial part of the front region is the "setting," i.e., "the fixed sign-equipment in such a place" (Goffman, 1959: 107). The living room is the area where "performances" for guests are most often given, and hence the "setting" of it must be appropriate to the performance.

Thus we expect that more than any other part of the home, the living room reflects the individual's conscious and unconscious attempts to express a social identity. Its decor, in contrast to that of other rooms, is most likely to reflect decisions made on criteria of taste and style, rather than purely economic grounds.

There are at least two points of view as to how the "criteria of taste and style" are acquired or chosen. On the one side is Veblen's notion of the standard-setting function of the leisure class in establishing matters of taste and style in consumption:

> The leisure class stands at the head of the social structure in point of reputability; and its manner of life and its standards of worth therefore affords [sic] the norm of reputability for the community. The observance of these standards, in some degree of approximation, becomes incumbent upon all classes lower in the scale. In modern civilized communities the lines of demarcation between social classes have grown vague and transient, and wherever this happens the norm of reputability imposed by the upper class extends it coercive influence with but slight hindrance down through the social structure to the lowest strata. The result is that the members of each stratum accept as their ideal of decency the scheme of life in vogue in the next higher stratum, and bend their energies to live up to that ideal. (Veblen, 1953: 70.)

Noteworthy here is the fact that Veblen assumed a monolithic or singular leisure class that effectively monopolized the canons of reputability and enjoyed a general consensus on what these canons should be at a particular point in time. His argument would seem to imply that traditionally high-status "persons" should be the ultimate arbiters of taste in home decorations and, therefore, that those striving for or recently arriving in the top status group should eagerly adopt the style of those who are already well-established there. Furthermore, he would expect that innovation in style should be the exclusive province of such a top group.

In contrast, more recent social commentators such as David Riesman (1953) and

William H. Whyte, Jr. (1956), have seen the most transient people (both geographically and socially mobile) as those most sensitive (because of their hypothesized other directedness) to the changes in the canons of consumption. And such canons are in Riesman's view bound to be transient in a modern consumption-oriented society. From this perspective the socially and geographically mobile will shun the life style of the "traditional aristocracy" for one which partakes of the latest fashions and fads. These fashions and fads are set more often by the class of "tastemakers" (Lynes, 1954), i.e., advertising men, designers, etc., rather than the "leisure class." Such an explanation would be consistent with such phenomena as the life style of the so-called "jet set," and the rapid acceptance of pop art.

Given the rich, but diffuse and impressionistic nature of previous theoretical speculation, our empirical effort must be clearly exploratory. Basically our analysis will seek to answer the following questions:

(a) Are clear patterns of decor evident in the living rooms of families in an urban area, and can they be meaningfully characterized?

(b) How are social status and other aspects of social identity (religion, ethnicity, values, etc.) related to style of decor?

(c) Is there a clear upper-class style of life, and how have the canons of this style disseminated themselves through the stratification system (particularly among those who are upwardly mobile)?

SOURCE OF THE DATA

During the spring and summer of 1966, interviewers from the University of Michigan Detroit Area Study conducted 85-minute interviews with a probability sample of 1,013 native-born, white men between the ages of 21 and 64, living in the greater metropolitan area of Detroit.[5] Midway through the interview, the respondent was asked to fill out a self-administered questionnaire taking approximately ten minutes

to complete. During this interval, the interviewer noted the contents and characteristics of the living room on a 53-item checklist inventory. In most cases, the interviewer was merely to check the list if a given object(s) was to be found in the living room. The objects *had* to be seen in the living room itself—the fact that the object might be found in some other room in the house did not result in a "check" for present. For example, nearly all households possessed a television set, but it was checked only if it was actually in the living room. As we shall see, the presence of the television set in the living room is associated with relatively low-income households. Many higher-income families put the television set in another room, which often is specially designed for television viewing. In 11.5 percent of the households, the relevant information could not be collected because the interview was conducted in another part of the house and the interviewer did not have an opportunity to observe the living room. Consequently, the results reported below are based on only 897 cases.

DATA ANALYSIS

THE SMALLEST SPACE ANALYSIS

First, we wanted to see if certain clusters of objects seemed to occur together more frequently than others in our respondents' living rooms, and whether these clusters constituted meaningful styles of decor. Second, we hoped to look at the social correlates of these styles.

We, therefore, coded each object or attribute as present (1) or absent (0) and then correlated these attributes with each other (using the ϕ coefficient). The resulting 53 x 53 matrix of correlations showed the degree to which any given object tended to be found in the same living room with each of the other objects. For example, the presence of modern furniture is highly correlated with the presence of sculpture and abstract painting, indicating that people with modern furniture often have sculpture and abstract paintings in their living rooms.

We then used a technique called smallest

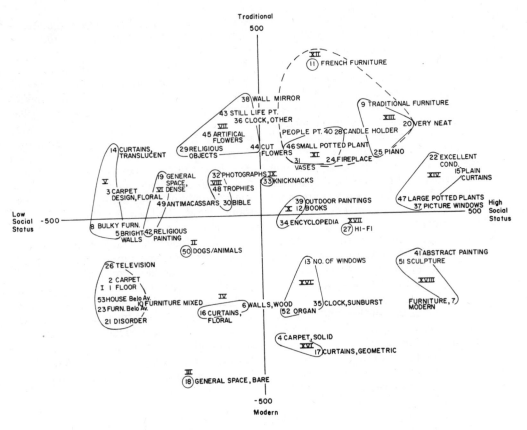

FIGURE 1. Graphic Portrayal of the Best 2-Space Solution for Living Room Objects.
(Source: Table 1)

space analysis to transform the information in the correlation matrix into a graphic representation of how living room characteristics covary.[6] This technique takes account of the whole correlation matrix simultaneously and tries to map the 53 objects into an m-dimensional Euclidean space such that the following condition is satisfied:

(1) Distance (A,B) $\leq$ distance (A,C),
whenever $r_{AB} \geq r_{AC}$.

That is, object A will be nearer to B than it is to C when the correlation of A with B is greater than the correlation of A with C. The higher the positive correlation between two variables the closer they will be in the m-dimensional space; the higher the negative correlation the farther apart they will be. (Thus in Figure 1, sculpture, abstract painting and modern furniture appear close together, but far away from antimacassars and French furniture.)

To the extent that condition (1) above is not satisfied in all cases, the geometric portrayal of the correlation matrix is inaccurate. The degree of inaccuracy is expressed by the "coefficient of alienation." Smallest space analysis tries to arrange the points in a space with the smallest possible number of dimensions, while keeping the coefficient of alienation low.

In this analysis a good fit was obtained in a five-dimensional space.[7] However, we found that the basic arrangement of the points in the two dimensional space was not greatly altered in the higher dimensionalities.[8] Since it is also easier to visualize and interpret the results in two dimensions, we present data for that solution. Figure 1 shows how our 53 variables arranged themselves in this space. Clusters of objects which are most often found together are circled and designated by Roman numerals.

INTERPRETATION OF THE SPACE

While the coordinate axes in Figure 1 are themselves essentially arbitrary, the configuration of points remains the same no matter where the axes are placed. The coordinates, however, can help us in understanding the underlying dimensions of this configuration of points. Visual inspection of Figure 1 suggests that the ordering of points along the first axis is in terms of social status or family income. More speculatively, the second axis seems to order objects roughly along a dimension of modern vs. traditional style of decor. Thus, French and traditional furniture, wall mirrors, pianos, flowers and vases all appear near the top of this dimension and are generally associated with traditional decor. Likewise, the cluster of modern furniture, sculpture and abstract paintings is near the bottom of the second dimension, along with sunburst clocks and solid carpets—all elements of modern decor.

We tried to validate and extend these intuitions by relating an object's position on these dimensions to the correlation of the presence of that object with other socioeconomic and attitudinal variables. Thus we asked if the presence of objects that are near the positive end of our first dimension is highly positively correlated with measures like income, education and occupation; while the presence of objects near the negative end is negatively correlated with these measures. Likewise, are objects near the top of the second dimension highly correlated with indicators of "traditional" values, like frequency of church attendance or "devotionalism"? Table 1 presents the results of correlating an object's position on each axis with the correlation between this object and socioeconomic or attitudinal measures.

One can readily see from this table that the first axis of the solution is highly related to measures of family income, occupational status, and educational attainment of husband and wife (rows 1-4). Although family income appears to be related quite strongly to the first axis, it is still moderately related to the second axis where high family income, occupational status, and educational attainment tend to be associated with the more "traditional" objects (positive end of the second axis in the 2nd space) and lower family income, etc., with "modern" objects.

Clearly then the ordering of objects along the first axis is a function of the ability to pay for them. We will contend that the second (vertical) axis orders attributes along a dimension of modern vs. traditional decor. Each quadrant of the space in Figure 1 seems to have an intuitive substantive meaning. Roughly, there appear to be four distinguishable styles of decor: (1) high-status modern (i.e., clusters XVI, XVII, and XVIII); (2) higher-status traditional (i.e., clusters XI, XII, and XIII); (3) low-status traditional (i.e., clusters V, VI, VII, and VIII); and (4) low-status modern (i.e., clusters I, II, III, and IV). The last pattern seems more the result of impoverishment than real stylistic preference.

Since the second axis is also highly correlated with income, we have partialed out the effects of income in the third column of Table 1. Here it becomes very clear that our "traditional" axis is strongly associated with attitudinal measures of traditionalism in two areas: (1) religion and (2) conceptions of marital roles. "Traditional" objects tend to be found in the homes of persons who are Catholic, "devotional" (in Lenski's sense of the word) and frequent church attenders. Hence our notion of "traditionalism" has a strong religious flavor to it. But people with "traditional" homes are also highly likely to hold "traditional" views about marriage—to feel that husbands and wives should stick to masculine and feminine tasks (as traditionally defined), respectively, and not share in household chores or decision-making. There is also a less marked tendency for traditional decor to be found in the homes of the upwardly mobile.

Table 1. Product-moment Correlations of the Coordinates of the Best 2-Space Solutions with Selected Socioeconomic and Attitude Characteristics

Characteristics	Smallest Space Coordinates 2-Space		
	First Axis	Second Axis	Second Axis (Income Partialed)
1. Total family income	.846	.468	
2. Occupational status	.798	.437	
3. Educational attainment of respondent	.814	.310	
4. Educational attainment of wife	.749	.315	
5. Religious preference of respondent	.363	.261	.558
6. Religious preference of wife	.287	.243	.441
7. Subjective ethnic identification	.245	.252	.427
8. Frequency of church attendance	.428	.553	.416
9. Devotionalism	.113	.495	.443
10. Preference to marry some religion	.471	.521	.342
11. Political party preference	.681	.386	.000
12. Father-son intergenerational mobility	.534	.466	.205
13. Father-in-law—son-in-law intergenerational mobility	.697	.533	.298
14. Traditionalism in marital role relations	+.542	.193	.629

Significance levels (for r and partial r's):   r $\geq$ .273, p $<$ .05;   r $\geq$ .354, p $<$ .01.

1. The "total family income" refers to the total income earned or received by all members of the household and not merely to the respondent's personal income. Eight intervals of family income were coded, ranging from under $3,000 to $25,000 and over.

2. The "occupational status" of the respondent was coded in the 2-digit Index of Socioeconomic Status, as described by Otis Dudley Duncan, "A Socioeconomic Index for All Occupations," in Albert J. Reiss, Jr., *Occupations and Social Status* (New York: Free Press of Glencoe, 1961), esp. 109-161, 263-275.

3. "Educational attainment" was coded in 8 categories, ranging from 0-8 grades to 17 years or more (graduate training).

4. Same as Note 3 above.

5. The "religious preference" of the respondent was coded "1" for Protestant and "2" for Catholic. Jews and those with other or no religious preference were deleted from the analysis.

6. Same as Note 5 above.

7. The "subjective ethnic identification" of the respondent refers to his self-reported identification with a nationality group. Southern and eastern European nationalities were assigned low numbers, while northwest European nationalities were assigned higher numbers.

8. The "frequency of church attendance" refers to the number of times per month the respondent went to church. Six categories of church attendance were coded, ranging from never to more than once a week.

9. "Devotionalism" refers to the sum of the respondent's answers to two questions treated as dichotomies:

Q116. When you have decisions to make in your everyday life, do you ask yourself what God would want you to do—often, sometimes, never?

Q117. Which of these describes most accurately how often you yourself pray? Alternatives ranged from more than once a day to never.

10. "Preference to marry within the same religion" refers to the respondent's answer to Question 114:
"Many people feel that—all things considered—it is better to marry someone of the same religion as oneself. Other people do not agree. What is your view on this?"

11. The "political party preference" of the respondent was coded "1" for strong Democratic party preference to "7" for strong Republican party preference, with "independents" being coded "4".

12. "Father-son intergenerational mobility" was measured in the following manner: "The son's (respondent's) Index of Socio-economic Status (see Note 2 above) was subtracted from the father's index and 100 was added. Consequently, downwardly mobile respondents had scores below 100, intergenerationally stationary respondents had scores approximately equal to 100, while upwardly mobile respondents had scores in excess of 100."

13. "Father-in-law—son-in-law (respondent) mobility" was measured in the same way as described in Note 12 above.

14. "Traditionalism" in marital roles is measured by the sum of a respondent's responses to the following items (each on a 4-point scale from strongly disagree to strongly agree):

QS2. A wife should not expect her husband to help around the house after he's home from a hard day's work.

QS5. Most of the important decisions in the life of the family should be made by the man of the house.

QS13. In general, husbands and wives should both share in deciding matters that are important to the family's future.

THE MSA ANALYSIS

To this point we have looked at the data in a highly aggregated form. This has proved useful in demonstrating that we can meaningfully characterize, the styles of decor of living rooms in an urban area, and further, that these styles are determined in part by income and, in part, by a tendency toward more "modern" or "traditional" ways of thinking. Since these conclusions were based on a complex manipulation of the original data, we sought to further validate them and extend our analysis by use of another new multivariate technique: multi-dimensional scalogram analysis. This technique is similar to SSA discussed above, except that it maps people (rather than objects) into a Euclidean space according to the attributes they possess. The basic idea is that (ideally) if a person has modern furniture his position in the space is to be closer to that of *every* other person with modern furniture than it is to that of *any* person who does not have modern furniture. Using a computer routine, the MSA tries to satisfy the basic condition for a number of variables simultaneously.[9]

Since the computer routine for this technique will handle only a limited number of persons and variables, we had to choose a small subset of both. (This has the advantage of allowing a more microscopic analysis of the social correlates of taste.) Since high-income people have the greatest discretionary power in decorating their homes and since one of our original interests was Veblen's idea of the standard-setting function of the "upper classes," we randomly chose 41 respondents from those (N = 186) with an income of $15,000 or more, and a list of seventeen attributes which the SSA showed to be characteristic of higher-income households but to vary along the modern traditional dimension. Table 2 gives a listing of these items arranged in order of their location on the traditional-modern dimension. The number in the parenthesis refers to the number of the cluster in which the object appears in Figure 1. Each respondent could then be characterized by the pattern of objects he had present in his living room. The MSA program plotted the 41 respondents into a 2-dimen-

Table 2. Distribution of the Seventeen Living Room Objects or Attributes by the Three Types of Decor, Arranged in the Order Given by the Second Axis of the Best 2-Space: Percent Distribution

Living Room Object/Attribute	Location on 2nd Axis	Types of Decor Percent Having Each Object		
		Traditionals (N = 9)	Mixed (N = 17)	Moderns (N = 15)
1. Traditional furniture (XIII)	293	100	0	0
2. Still-life paintings (VII)	270	11	41	0
3. Paintings with human subjects (XI)	222	67	53	13
4. Candleholders (XI)	220	77	65	0
5. Piano (XIII)	153	67	35	0
6. Vases (XI)	150	33	53	20
7. Fireplace (XI)	134	67	71	20
8. Plain curtains (XIV)	112	55	41	33
9. Knickknacks (IX)	88	22	65	67
10. Large potted plants (XIV)	24	22	41	40
11. Space, dense (VI)	−105	22	35	7
12. Abstract paintings (XVIII)	−107	11	29	20
13. Sunburst clock (modern) (XVI)	−124	11	24	7
14. Modern furniture (XVIII)	−236	0	65	87
15. Solid carpet (XV)	−332	0	0	13
16. Curtains with geometric designs (XV)	−375	0	0	20
17. Space, bare (III)	−454	33	29	13

sional solution, with a coefficient of contiguity (λ) of .95, indicating a very acceptable fit.[10]

The 2-dimensional solution placed subjects in such a way that a group with clearly modern decor and one with clearly traditional decor emerged at opposite ends of the first dimension, with a group in the middle with mixed decor. The respondents were consequently divided into three groups for further analysis. We obtained a set of 9 respondents with traditional decor, 15 with modern decor and 17 with mixed decor. Table 2 shows the percentage of cases in each of the three groups who had a given object or attribute. The defining attributes of the modern and traditional groups become clear in this table, with the mixed group being characterized by the presence of both traditional and modern objects. Thus, the multi-dimensional scalogram analysis of person-types substantially confirms the conclusions regarding the reality of styles of decor that we drew from the smallest space analysis.

LIVING ROOM STYLES IN RELATION TO SOCIAL ATTRIBUTES

We will now turn to a consideration of how living room style relates to social attributes within this upper-income stratum. Table 3 presents a summary of the differences between the modern, traditional, and mixed groups on selected aspects of achieved and ascribed status. The groups show no significant differences in age or present levels of achieved status, i.e., income and education (cf. lines 1, 2, and 3 of Table 3).

In the lower part (lines 4, 5, and 6) of the table, a clear pattern of results emerges. The "moderns" tend to be upwardly mobile in terms of father-son occupational mobility (see footnote 12, Table 1, for a description of the measurement), Catholic, and descendants of the "New Migration" (southern and eastern Europeans). The "traditionals" are non-mobile Protestants and descendants of the members of the "Old Migration" (northwest European), that is, a part of the "Protestant Establish-

ment." Generally, the "mixed" group stands somewhere between the moderns and traditionals with respect to these characteristics.

The difference in mean mobility score between the moderns and traditionals is quite striking and clearly significant (p. < .05, two-tailed test). It appears that the "mixed" group is as mobile as the moderns; however, when the data are looked at another way, greater upward mobility is found in the modern group. The median mobility score for the sample of 41 cases in the analysis is 123. If we look at the *proportion* of cases in each group *above the median*, we again see our more usual pattern of results with the mixed group intermediate between the traditionals and moderns: 12.5 percent of the traditionals, 52.9 percent of the "mixed" group, and 66.7 percent of the moderns are above the median in mobility.

Differences in religious and ethnic composition of the three groups are also clear. These variables are highly related in that all Protestants in this subsample are part of the "Old Migration," while persons of French, Irish, and German origin are the only potentially Catholic members of the "Old Migration." The other southern and eastern European nationalities, which we have grouped into the "New Migration," are predominantly Catholic, except for several eastern European Jews. Excluding the Jews and persons with no religious preference, we find that Protestants comprise 83 percent of the "traditionals", 50 percent of the "mixed" group, and 43 percent of the "moderns" (Fisher's exact test, p. = .107).

Considering ethnicity, we find that the descendants of the "Old Migration" constitute 78 percent of the "traditionals," 88 percent of the "mixed" group, and 47 percent of the "moderns" (Fisher's exact test, p. = .118, for traditionals and moderns). In ethnicity and religion, the mixed group is clearly very mixed, containing a larger number of persons who violate the general tendency for Catholicism to be associated with the "New Migration." Specifically, in the mixed group, we find 38 percent of the cases are Catholic descendants of the Old

Table 3. Summary of the Differences among the Three Types of Decor on Selected Socioeconomic and Attitudinal Characteristics

| Characteristics* | Types of Decor | | | Type of Test | Level of Significance |
	Traditional (1)	Mixed (2)	Modern (3)		
1. Average occupational status	71.1	(71.2)	64.1	t-test	nonsign.
2. Average educational attainment	6.33	(5.71)	5.27	t-test	about .15, one-tailed
3. Average age	41.2	(48.8)	41.3	t-test	nonsign.
4. Protestant-Catholic religious preference	Prot.	(split)	Cath.	Fisher's exact	about .107
5. National origin	"Old Migration"	(split)	"New Migration"	Fisher's exact	about .118
6. Intergenerational mobility (average)	100.5	(124.9)	123.0	t-test	about .025, one-tailed
7. Per cent above the median for upward mobility	12.5	52.9	66.7	chi-square	p < .02
	Combined, Traditional-Modern		Mixed		
8. Party preference	Definite party preference		Independent	chi-square	less than .05

*See footnotes to Table 1 for description of measures employed in rows 1-8.

Note: All tests in rows 1-7 involved the traditional vs. the modern group only. In row 8, the traditionals and moderns are combined and compared with the mixed group.

Migration; the traditionals contain no such persons and the modern group only one.

LIVING ROOM STYLES AND POLITICAL ATTITUDES

A very intriguing and unexpected finding emerges when we look at the relationship between living room decor and political party identification. We might expect that traditionals would be Republicans and moderns Democrats, with the mixed group falling in between. Party identification was measured on a seven-point scale, ranging from strong Republican to strong Democrat, with the midpoint being an independent inclining neither toward the Republican or Democratic party. When the means of the three groups are compared, all three fall into the "independent" range (3-5) on our scale, with the traditionals and moderns having almost identical averages and the

mixed group falling somewhat more toward the Republican end of the scale. But if we look at the data in terms of who expresses a party preference and who does not (i.e., say they are independents), the relationship becomes more meaningful. In the mixed group, 50 percent of the respondents assert they are political independents, while the percentage of independents is only 33.3 percent and 7 percent in the traditional and modern groups respectively (p < .05, chi-square test corrected for continuity).

From these data, it appears that people who manifest a consistent life style in their living room decor also express a consistent and, relatively speaking, a more extreme political view of the world than those who manifest mixed tastes in decor. Note that it is the consistency of the decor and ideology and not the type of decor and ideology that is relevant here.

Because the above findings were based

on a small number of cases, a replication was performed with a new sample of 59 persons with incomes of $15,000 or more. Every finding reported, except that regarding party preference, was substantially confirmed (i.e., all results were in the same direction as reported above although levels of significance were sometimes higher and sometimes lower). Thus, we have derived a very stable picture of the social correlates of traditional and modern decor of a metropolitan area. Our initial finding regarding political attitudes must remain a tantalizing hypothesis, as no differences in proportion of independents or party-identifiers appeared in the replication.

DISCUSSION

The MSA results substantially confirm the SSA findings, while at the same time uncovering an interesting contradiction in regard to the social correlates of traditional vs. modern decor. Clearly, the modern-traditional dimension constitutes perhaps the major source of variation in the decor of upper-income homes. However, there is no one style that is clearly dominant, both modern and traditional decor being represented, the former in somewhat larger numbers.

Judging from their social attributes, it would appear that the "traditionals" in the MSA represent the established upper class, that is they tend to be white, Anglo-Saxon, Protestants who were *not* recently upwardly mobile in this generation. In contrast, the "moderns" are generally upwardly mobile in this generation, and from non-Anglo-Saxon (often southern and eastern European), Catholic origins—they constitute the *nouveaux riches*. And they appear to be responding more to the newly emerging decorative norms in our society and not to the norms of the established upper classes. In this they resemble Riesman's (1953) notion of the other-directed individuals.

The MSA would indicate that although those striving for and achieving status in our society do *conform* to certain decorative standards, they are not those of the traditional American elites. We must, how-

ever, recall that in our SSA analysis of the total sample, upwardly mobile, non-Anglo-Saxon Catholics seemed to be adopting *traditional* styles of decor. This presents the paradox of the "noveaux riches" of our MSA sample behaving in complete opposition to the total population of persons who are most similar to the nouveaux riches in social attributes (i.e., upwardly mobile, Catholic, non-Anglo-Saxon).

This paradox may be partially an artifact of the number and types of items on our checklist, particularly the intermingling of religious and traditional concerns in defining our second axis. But it may also mean that there is some truth in the notions of both Veblen and the more recent social commentators like Riesman and Whyte.

Veblen posited that the traditional elite would set the consumption norms for society and would be emulated by those below. Our SSA results would indicate that generally this is true, especially among those who are upwardly mobile, Catholic and non-Anglo-Saxon. However, the nouveaux riches of our MSA analysis who are really "making it" for the first time behave quite differently. Here the notions of Riesman, Whyte and Edward Sapir (1931) seem more illuminating. The nouveaux riches have a strong need to validate their newly found status, yet they are not accepted socially by the traditional upper classes (see Warner, 1953, on the lack of association between the "upper upper" and "lower upper" classes). Since their associations do not clearly validate their position, they turn to conspicious consumption. However, conspicious consumption must be done with "taste" if it is to validate one's claims to high status in respects other than mere money. Hence the nouveaux riches, in their other-directedness, seek to discover what are the latest and most *chic* norms of consumption.

Discovery of such norms is easy in a society that possesses a class of professional taste-makers (e.g., architects, interior decorators, fashion designers) and taste-setting media (ranging from *Better Homes and Gardens* through the *New Yorker*). Normative consumption trends are also evident in the styles of decor adopted by business and government for their new offices and stores. In all cases, the norms today favor modern decor. The nouveaux riches, then, spurn the style of the traditional upper class in favor of the newer fashions. This serves a double purpose: (1) to establish their tastefulness and hence status, while (2) symbolically showing their disdain of the "snobby" traditionals.

The rest of the population does not follow the path of the nouveaux riches partly because status validation may be somewhat less of a problem for them, and partly because they are less likely to be in touch with the people or mass media that propagate the latest trends. As the nouveaux riches become established, and modern norms of consumption become more clearly modal, we may expect the upwardly mobile at all levels to adopt modern styles. But by then the nouveaux riches may have moved on to newer styles.

Naturally these speculations and conclusions must be offered very tentatively indeed. Several qualifications (and suggestions for improving subsequent research) arising out of the character of our data and methods of analysis should be noted. First, although we attempted to include many types of objects in our inventory, there remains a fundamental crudity in our categorization of these objects. Our pretesting experience with the inventory of objects revealed that the interviewers were not capable of making very refined distinctions in stylistic and qualitative features of a number of objects without an investment of special training that could not be undertaken given the limited time available. Knickknacks, for example, are highly heterogeneous in stylistic and quality connotations —a Woolworth hobnail milk glass or ten-cent-store figurine (low status traditional) is very different from a Steuben Glass owl or dolphin (high-status modern) or from Royal Doulton and Hummel figures (high-status traditional). Such distinctions were often beyond the untutored grasp of our interviewers. It is interesting to note that the crude category "knickknacks" falls *between* the low and high status traditional

clusters and toward the middle of the traditional-modern axis in Figure 1. In the MSA, knickknacks are found in all three groups—though in all probability there are quite different types of objects in each. Future research ought to try to delineate the dimensions along which style differences are of interest (e.g., modern vs. traditional, colorful vs. subdued, ornate vs. functional, etc.) and build a checklist of objects aimed at delineating just such distinctions. This, of course, entails the construction of hypotheses as to why such dimensions of style are important as indicators of social attributes or attitudes.

Secondly, our sample of attributes seems to contain many more indicators of traditional decor than of modern (33 attributes in the upper quadrants vs. 20 in the lower). Furthermore, the traditional objects are fairly evenly distributed along the status dimension, while the modern objects are clustered at the upper and lower extremes. This may reflect the realities of middle class decor (in line with our above interpretations), but it may also reflect our failure carefully to select and differentiate the objects in our checklist. The distribution of objects along posited stylistic dimensions should receive greater attention in future studies.

Nevertheless, the techniques appear to yield sufficiently plausible and promising results that further work obtaining more refined and elaborate data would be amply justified. Certainly they afford a means of examining some of the more subtle hypotheses regarding people's life styles with greater objectivity and precision than hitherto has been possible.

CONCLUSION

We have shown that it is possible to characterize in a meaningful way the styles of interior decoration found in the living rooms of homes in a metropolitan area. The choice of a styles of decor is rather strongly related to the achieved and ascribed statuses of the individuals, and to their attitudes and behavior in other areas of life. That is, people with traditional decor are also more traditional in their behavior and attitudes regarding religion and marital role definitions. Finally we have tried to indicate how these data reflect on the theories of Veblen and other social commentators regarding the establishment and dissemination of norms for styles of life and consumption.

NOTES

*Paper read at the 64th Annual Meetings, American Sociological Association, San Francisco, California, August 1969. We are indebted to Dr. Howard Schuman, Director of the Detroit Area Study, and Miriam Sonn, a graduate student participant in the study, for their contributions in the design of the interview checklist, and to Terry Gleason, I.S.R., for his helpful comments on the statistical aspects of the analysis. Acknowledgment is also due to the students and teaching assistants too numerous to mention by name who assisted in all phases of the design and execution of the study. The total study and this analysis were aided by grants from the Horace H. Rackham School of Graduate Studies, University of Michigan, the National Institute of Mental Health (MH-13464-01) and the National Science Foundation (GS-1929).

[1]For example, Melville Herskovits (1955: 234, 266) observes:

> The search for beauty is universal in human experience. Its innumerable forms have sprung from the play of the creative imagination, and afford some of the deepest satisfactions known to man. To understand how closely integrated with all of life, and how expressive of a way of living art can be, is again not easy for members of the highly specialized societies of Euro-american culture, where we are confronted with the effect of compartmentalization. . . .
> . . . in all societies the aesthetic impulse finds expression in terms of beauty laid down in the traditions of the people. . . . No art . . . is haphazard or chaotic. It is the expression of the desire for beauty that finds fulfillment in the application of technical skill through sanctioned form, in terms of the patterned perception and imaginative resources of the artistically endowed members of every society.

See also, Clyde Kluckhohn (1960).

[2]For a selected bibliography, see Edward Sapir (1931: 139-44); F. Stuart Chapin (1935:373-97); William H. Sewell (1940); A. L. Kroeber and Jane Richardson (1940); Allison Davis, Burleigh B. Gardner, and Mary R. Gardner (1941); Erving Goffman (1951: 294-304); David Riesman (1953: 94-102, 141-49, 168-88, 240-46, 260-71, 330-45); Thomas Ford Hoult (1954: 324-28); Russell Lynes (1954); Buford H. Junker (1955); James A. Davis (1955); William H. Whyte (1956: 295-448); John R. Seeley, R. Alexander Sim, and Elizabeth W. Loosely (1956: esp. Chapter 3); Jurgen Ruesch and Weldon Kees (1956: 132-59); Herbert J. Gans (1962: 181-87); James N. Porter, Jr. (1967: 255-65).

Of course, as noted above, there is voluminous anthropological literature, beginning with Franz Boas, cataloging material artifacts of primitive peoples and discussing their significance in understanding the cultures of these peoples. On the whole, however, the issues addressed, such as the diffusion of objects and the determination of culture areas, are not directly of relevance to the concerns of this paper although they do bear some indirect relevance. Cf. Herskovits (1955); Kluckhohn (1960); Frank M. LeBar (1964: 335-50); Horace Miner (1956: 503-7); Harold E. Driver and Karl Schuessler (1957: 655-63).

[3]For example, see C. Wright Mills' introduction to Veblen (1953: vi-xix).

[4]For one exception to this generalization, see James A. Davis (1955). Davis had respondents make judgments about the social status and some other attributes of the owners of pictured living rooms, a complementary approach to the problem in this paper. His study is flawed methodologically because 15 of the 23 pictures he used contained people who often provided stronger status cues than the living room itself. His most interesting finding in relation to the present paper was that the ability to judge the status of living rooms (i.e., "sensitivity to generalized status order of symbols") is associated with *expectancy* of change in social context or status, but not necessarily with actual past histories of social mobility. (Davis, 1955: 113.) The lack of association between actual mobility and status sensitivity seems counter to generally accepted beliefs and the findings of this paper. But his findings are still generally consistent with explanations offered for the greater sensitivity of the socially mobile (cf. results of MSA analysis and discussion below).

[5]A multi-stage probability sample of dwelling units of that part of the Detroit SMSA that was tracted in 1950 plus some small additions made to take into account recent suburban population growth was drawn. Within each dwelling unit having one or more eligible respondents, one person was drawn at random for interview. A total of 985 actual interviews was obtained, of which 28 have been double-weighted, yielding a final set of 1,013 cases for use in analysis. These 1,013 cases represent 80 percent of the eligible households sampled. Refusals to grant interviews

accounted for 13.9 percent of the eligible households (N = 1,271); another 6.4 percent was lost because no one had been found home after 6 calls (5.5 percent) or for other reasons.

For further details concerning the sampling design and sample completion rates, the interested reader may write Professor Howard Schuman, Director, Detroit Area Study, University of Michigan, for a copy of Working Paper #1, Project #938, "Sampling Memorandum for 1965-66 Detroit Area Study," January, 1967.

[6]For a more detailed exposition of the statistical analysis and a description of the available computer programs, see Louis Guttman (1968); James C. Lingoes (1966a; 1965a: 183-84; 1965b: 487; 1966b: 75-76); Edward O. Laumann and Louis Guttman (1966: 169-78); Louis Guttman (1967: 71-82).

[7]The coefficients of alienation for solutions in one, two, three, four and five dimensions were: .464, .324, .240, .189, .154 respectively. The coefficient of alienation is described in detail in Lingoes (1966a); and Guttman (1968). Guttman notes that a coefficient of .15 indicates an acceptable fit. Briefly, one may describe the computation of the coefficient in the following way: The normalized phi is defined as the ratio of the sum of the squared differences between the distances as calculated from the coordinate system and the same distances permuted to maintain the rank-order of the original coefficients (otherwise known as the rank-images) over twice the sum of the squared distances (calculated from the coordinates), or

$$\phi = \frac{\displaystyle\sum_{i=1}^{n}\sum_{j=1}^{n}(d_{ij}-d_{ij}{}^{*})^{2}}{2\displaystyle\sum_{i=1}^{n}\sum_{j=1}^{n}d_{ij}{}^{2}}, \text{ where } i \neq j.$$

The coefficient of alienation, then, is equal to:

$$\sqrt{1-(1-\phi)^{2}}$$

The smaller the coefficient, the better the fit.

[8]To assure ourselves on this point, we turned to a new technique developed by Terry Gleason (1969: 1) (cf. Schönemann, 1966) for comparing the similarity of two configurations of points "by rotating one by an orthogonal transformation until it matches the other as closely as possible according to a least squares criterion." In this case

we compared our two-dimensional solution with the first two dimensions of the five-dimensional solution. As we expected, the two configurations of points were highly similar and had a relatively low (for this number of points) coefficient of configurational dissimilarity (see Gleason, 1969: 3-4, for the computational formula).

[9]See James C. Lingoes (1966c: 76-78) for a description of the specific computer program employed and for citations to the relevant literature on the method. Also see James C. Lingoes (1966d).

Lingoes and Guttman have briefly described the objectives of the program in the following way:

MSA-I . . . starts with a purely qualitative characteristic function denoting presence or absence, but produces a Euclidean space into which person-types can be mapped in such a way as to require a minimum number of coordinates to partition subjects by categories over all items simultaneously under the constraint of contiguity. In essence, a contiguous zone is determined for each category of each item by use of a notion of "outer-points," as follows.

Given a trial set of coordinates for representing the observed types as points in an m-dimensional Euclidean space, each item is regarded as a partition of this space. The points belonging to a given category of an item will generally not fall into a single contiguous zone at this stage. For each point *not* belonging to the category, there is a closest point that does belong to the category; such a closest point is a trial outer-point of the category. An "inner-point" of a category is a point belonging to that category that is not an outer-point. The set of points belonging to a category, i.e., all its outer- and inner-points, is considered to be contiguous if each inner-point is closer to some outer-point of the *same* category of the same item.

The degree of contiguity produced by a given set of trial coordinates is inverse to the extent to which inner-points are further from the respective closest outer-points of alternatives. Using Louis Guttman's absolute value principle, a coefficient of contiguity is defined which is to be maximized by the iterations of our computer alogrithm. This coefficient, denoted by λ, varies between $-$ and $+1$. Perfect contiguity obtains when $\lambda = +1$. Unlike the coefficient of monotonity used in smallest space analysis, the coefficient of contiguity has no *a priori* assumptions of order.

See James C. Lingoes and Louis Guttman. Note for our application that an "item" is a living room object and the two "categories" of the item are "presence" or "absence".

[10]See footnote 9 for a description of this coefficient.

REFERENCES

Chapin, F. Stuart.
  1935 Contemporary American Institutions: A Sociological Analysis. New York: Harper and Brothers, esp. Chapter 19.

Davis, Allison, Burleigh B. Gardner, and Mary R. Gardner.
  1941 Deep South: A Social Anthropological Study of Caste and Class. Chicago: University of Chicago Press.

Davis, James A.
  1955 Living Rooms as Symbols of Status: A Study in Social Judgment. Unpublished doctoral dissertation, Harvard University.

Driver, Harold E., and Karl Schuessler.
  1957 Factor analysis of ethnographic data. American Anthropologist 59 (August): 655-663.

Gans, Herbert J.
  1962 The Urban Villagers: Group and Class in the Life of Italian-Americans. New York: Free Press of Glencoe, esp. pp. 181-187.

Gleason, Terry C.
  1969 "Users write-up for COMPARE." Mimeographed Paper. Ann Arbor: The Institute for Social Research.

Goffman, Erving.
  1951 Symbols of class status. British Journal of Sociology 2 (December): 294-304.
  1959 The Presentation of Self in Everyday Life. New York: Anchor Books.

Guttman, Louis.
  1967 The development of nonmetric space analysis: A letter to Professor John Ross. Multivariate Behavioral Research 2:71-82.
  1968 A general nonmetric technique for finding the smallest Euclidean space for a configuration of points. Psychometrika 33 (December): 469-506.

Herskovits, Melville J.
  1955 Cultural Anthropology: An Abridged Version of Man and His Works. New York: Alfred A. Knopf.

Hoult, Thomas Ford.
  1954 Experimental measurement of clothing as a factor in some social ratings of selected men. American Sociological Review 19 (June): 324-328.

Junker, Buford H.
  1955 Room Compositions and Life Styles: A Sociological Study in Living Rooms and Other Rooms in Contemporary Dwellings. Unpublished doctoral dissertation, University of Chicago.

Kluckhohn, Clyde.
  1960 Mirror for Man. New York: McGraw-Hill; Premier Books.

Kroeber, A. L., and Jane Richardson.
  1940 Three centuries of women's dress fashions: A qualitative analysis. Anthropological Records 2, No. 2.

Laumann, Edward O., and Louis Guttman.
  1966 The relative associational contiguity of occupations in an urban setting. American Sociological Review 31 (April): 169-178.

LeBar, Frank M.
  1964 A household survey of economic goods on Romonum Island, Truk. Pp. 335-350 in Ward H. Goodenough (ed.), Explorations in Cultural Anthropology: Essays in Honor of George P. Murdock. New York: McGraw-Hill.

Lenski, Gerhard.
  1953 The Religious Factor. Garden City, New York: Doubleday Anchor Books.

Lingoes, James C.
  1965a An IBM-7090 program for Guttman-Lingoes smallest space analysis—I. Behavioral Science 10:183-184.
  1965b An IBM-7090 program for Guttman-Lingoes smallest space analysis—II. Behavioral Science 10:487.
  1966a New computer developments in pattern analysis and nonmetric techniques. I.B.M. Journal.
  1966b An IBM-7090 program for Guttman-Lingoes smallest space analysis—III. Behavioral Science 11: 75-76.
  1966c An IBM-7090 program for Guttman-Lingoes multidimensional scalogram analysis—I. Behavioral Science 11.
  1966d The Multivariate Analysis of Qualitative Data. Paper presented at the Conference on Cluster Analysis of Data. New Orleans, Louisiana, December 9-11. Mimeograph paper, University of Michigan.

Lingoes, James C., and Louis Guttman.
    An IBM-7090 program for Guttman-Lingoes multidimensional scalogram—I. Mimeograph paper, University of Michigan.

Lynes, Russell.
  1954 The Tastemakers. New York: Harper and Brothers.

Miner, Horace.
  1956 Body ritual among the nacirema. American Anthropologist 58:503-507.

Porter, James N., Jr.
  1967 Consumption patterns of professors and businessmen: A pilot study of conspicuous consumption and status. Sociological Inquiry 37 (Spring): 255-265.

Riesman, David.
1953 The Lonely Crowd. Garden City, New York: Doubleday Anchor Books.
Ruesch, Jurgen, and Weldon Kees.
1956 Nonverbal Communication: Notes on the Visual Perception of Human Relations. Berkeley and Los Angeles: University of California Press.
Sapir, Edward.
1931 Fashion: Encyclopedia for the Social Sciences, Vol. VI. New York: Macmillan, pp. 139-144.
Schönemann, Peter H.
1966 A generalized solution of the orthogonal procrustes problem. Psychometrika 31: 10.
Seeley, John R., R. Alexander Sim, and Elizabeth W. Loosely.
1956 Crestwood Heights: A Study of the Culture of Suburban Life. New York: Basic Books, esp. Chapter 3.
Sewell, William H.
1940 The construction and standardization of a scale for the measurement of the socio-economic status of Oklahoma farm families. Stillwater, Oklahoma: Oklahoma Agricultural and Mechanical College, Agricultural Experiment Station, Technical Bulletin No. 9.
Veblen, Thorstein.
1953 The Theory of the Leisure Class. New York: The New American Library. Originally published by Macmillan, 1899.
Warner, W. Lloyd.
1953 American Life. Chicago: University of Chicago Press.
Whyte, William H.
1956 The Organization Man. Garden City, New York: Doubleday Anchor Books.

CHAPTER 14
Recent Trends in Family Income

HERMAN P. MILLER

INTRODUCTION

Few statistics reveal as much about the operation of an economy as do those on income distribution. Although the levels of living that are possible in any society are prescribed by the size of the national product, a given output can be distributed in many different ways. It can provide palaces for live kings and pyramids for dead ones, but hovels and hunger for the mass of mankind; or it can be widely distributed and provide reasonably uniform levels of living for all.

In view of the complex questions that income statistics are used to answer, it would be surprising indeed if the data were easy to collect or to interpret. The difficulties of measurement and interpretation are attested to by Simon Kuznets, who, after plowing this field for a lifetime, has called measures of income distribution " . . . preliminary informed guesses. . . ."[1] and by Dorothy S. Brady, who has referred to income statistics in general as " . . . deficient in both quantity and quality."[2]

These judgments, however, can be made about all statistics. The more one knows about a set of numbers the less likely he is to be entirely satisfied with them. Numbers at best provide a very thorny path to the truth. Thus, the income statistician may find himself in a position not too different from that of Stephen Crane's "Wayfarer."

The wayfarer,
Perceiving the pathway to truth,
Was struck with astonishment.
It was thickly grown with weeds.
"Ha," he said,

"I see that no one has passed here
In a long time."
Later he saw that each weed
Was a singular knife.
"Well," he mumbled at last,
"Doubtless there are other roads."

As the story unfolds, the numerous and serious shortcomings of income statistics will be discussed in some detail. It would be a mistake, however, to dwell on the limitations of the data, for although there are still many unanswered questions, much more is now known about income distribution than ever before. The primary purpose of this monograph is to summarize and synthesize the information. It has been collected from many sources, but principally from the results of the past three decennial censuses, the annual surveys conducted by the Bureau of the Census since 1945, and data published by the Office of Business Economics of the Department of Commerce. The available data permit us to answer questions that would have been regarded as impossible to answer only a generation ago. We can now quantify with some degree of certainty the annual changes in the distribution of income among families (using several different definitions of income and the family), changes in the composition of lower and upper income groups, and the amount and direction of income changes among occupations and industries. We can also shed light on a host of other important economic questions.

To begin with, we might examine the widely held opinion that incomes in the United States are gradually becoming more evenly distributed. This view is held by prominent economists and is shared by influential writers and editors. Arthur F. Burns stated in 1951 that the " . . . transformation in the distribution of our national income . . . may already be counted as one of the great social revolutions of history."[3] Paul Samuelson remarked in 1961 that there are studies which suggest that " . . . the American income pyramid is becoming less unequal."[4] Several major stories on this subject have appeared in *The New York Times,* and the editors of *Fortune* announced in 1953 that "Though not a head has been raised aloft on a pikestaff, nor a railway station seized, the U.S. has been for some time now in a revolution."[5]

What are the facts about trends in the inequality of income distribution in the United States? Few would question that real incomes have risen for most of the population; or that even those who have been left behind enjoy a far higher level of living than most people in other parts of the world. Despite the generally high levels of living, we remain concerned about income shares.

Has there been any narrowing of this gap between the rich and the poor? If we stick to the figures, the answers are clear, unambiguous, and contrary to widely held beliefs. The statistics show no appreciable change in income shares for nearly 20 years. The heart of the story is told in table 1, which was obtained by ranking families and unrelated individuals from lowest to highest according to income and cumulating the amount of income each received. The table shows the percent (or share) of the total income paid out each year that went to each fifth of the families and individuals, and to the top 5 percent. The share received by the top 5 percent is large because their incomes were so much larger than those of others. In 1962, families and individuals in the top 5 percent on the average received $17,200 or more, whereas those in the lowest 20 percent made $2,900 or less (about $55 a week).

During the depression of the thirties there was a distinct drop in the share of the income received by the upper income groups. In 1929, the last year of the prosperous twenties, the top 5 percent received 30 percent of the income. Their share, which dropped regularly during the depression, amounted to about one-fourth of the income at the time we entered World War II. The decline continued during the war years and in 1944 their share dropped to 21 percent. Since that time there has been no significant change in the percent of income received by the top 5 percent, and a similar trend applies to the top 20 percent.

At the bottom of the income scale, the data show that in 1935-1936 the lowest 20 percent of the families and individuals received only 4 percent of the income, and that in 1944 their share rose to 5 percent, where it has remained ever since. The stability of the shares received by each of the other quintiles is equally striking.

These figures hardly support the view held by many Americans that incomes in our society are becoming more evenly distributed. The changes that took place— ending about a quarter of a century ago— involved in large measure a redistribution of income among families in the top and middle brackets. Although the share received by the lowest income groups increased slightly during the war, since then it has not changed.[6]

PROBLEMS OF INTERPRETATION

The stability of income shares shown in table 1 does not necessarily imply a stability of economic welfare; it is conceivable that a proportional increase in everybody's real income means more to the poor than to the rich. How can we compare the utility of a loaf of bread to the man who is starving, with the utility of another Cadillac to the man who already has three? Exact comparisons cannot be made; yet many people believe that satisfying the most urgent and basic needs of the poor implies some leveling up in the comforts of life, even though income shares have rmained constant.

To cite further and similar examples, it is likely that the extension of government services which provide better housing,

Table 1.—Percent Distribution of Families and Unrelated Individuals, by Family Personal Income Received by Each Fifth and by the Top 5 Percent, for Selected Years, 1929 to 1962

Income rank	1962	1961	1960	1944	1941	1935-36	1929
Families and unrelated individuals							
Total	100	100	100	100	100	100	100
Lowest fifth	5	5	5	5	4	4 ⎫	13
Second fifth	11	11	11	11	10	9 ⎭	
Middle fifth	16	16	16	16	15	14	14
Fourth fifth	23	23	23	22	22	21	19
Highest fifth	46	46	45	46	49	52	54
Top 5 percent	20	20	20	21	24	27	30
Families							
Total	100	100	100	100	100	100	(NA)
Lowest fifth	6	6	6	6	5	4	(NA)
Second fifth	12	12	12	12	10	9	(NA)
Middle fifth	17	17	17	16	16	14	(NA)
Fourth fifth	23	22	22	22	22	21	(NA)
Highest fifth	43	43	43	44	48	52	(NA)
Top 5 percent	18	18	18	20	24	27	(NA)

NA: Not available.

Source: Data for families and individuals from U.S. Bureau of the Census, *Historical Statistics of the United States: Colonial Times to 1957,* p. 166, and *Survey of Current Business,* April 1964, p. 8. Data for families for 1960–62 computed from *Survey of Current Business,* April 1964, p. 6; and for 1935–36, 1941, and 1944 from Selma F. Goldsmith, *et al.,* "Size Distribution of Income Since the Mid-Thirties," *Review of Economics and Statistics,* February 1954, p. 9.

more adequate medical care, and improved educational facilities has been of more benefit to low-income families than to those with higher incomes. And the increase in paid vacations has surely brought a more equal distribution of leisure time—a good that is almost as precious as money. Furthermore, improved working conditions, including air conditioning, better lighting, mechanization of routine work, and the like, have undoubtedly benefited more manual workers than those in higher paid and more responsible positions.

When allowance is made for these and other factors, it may well be that some progress has been made during recent years in diminishing the inequality of levels of living. But we do not know how much allowance to make, and our judgments could be wrong. Moreover, most opinions

regarding changes in inequality, including those held by professional economists, are based on statistical measures of income rather than on philosophic concepts. With all their limitations, the income figures may well serve as a first approximation of changes in welfare.

The picture presented in table 1 is further complicated by taxes. The figures shown are for income before taxes. Since families in the higher income groups pay a large share of the taxes, their share would be smaller on an after-tax basis. It is smaller, but not by as much as one might suppose. In recent years the top 5 percent received 20 percent of the income before taxes, and about 18 percent of the income after Federal individual income tax payments were deducted.[7] Since the graduated income tax falls more heavily on the upper income groups than do most other major tax measures, it is not surprising that their share of the income is decreased when individual income tax payments are deducted. This tax, however, accounts for only 37 percent of the $124 billion collected in 1962 by Federal, State, and local governments from all sources.[8] Many of the other taxes—the sales tax, for example—are paid disproportionately by the lower income groups. Taking into account all tax payments, the equalization of income as a result of taxation would be less than that shown for the Federal individual income tax alone.[9]

Still restricting our attention to the interpretation of results shown in table 1, numerous other problems come to mind—problems centering largely on the definition of the income-receiving unit, on the accounting period over which income is cumulated, on concepts of income, and on the accuracy of the underlying data.[10]

To begin with definitions, the income-receiving unit shown in table 1 is the family or the unrelated individual. The family is defined as a group of two or more persons related by blood, marriage, or adoption, and living together. The income of the family is the combined total received by all family members during the calendar year. An unrelated individual is defined as a person (other than an inmate of an institution) who is not living with relatives. These persons are called unattached individuals in statistics compiled by the OBE. For all practical purposes the terms are interchangeable.

When these definitions are examined critically a host of problems emerge. Since the end of World War II, a very sharp increase has taken place in the number of older people who maintain their own households rather than share living quarters with children or other relatives. This type of living arrangement has been made possible, for the most part, by the small measure of financial independence provided by the Social Security System, and by the prosperous conditions of the postwar years.

For the income statistician, the increasing tendency for older people to continue to maintain their own households creates serious problems. Today there are porportionately far more unrelated individuals than there were in the forties. These groups typically have very low incomes; thus their inclusion in the distribution tends to increase its inequality, since it creates relatively large numbers of units with little or no income at the bottom of the distribution. Therefore, even though the definition of the income-receiving unit has remained constant over time, changes in living arrangements of the population may have produced variations in the statistics. The impact of this change is minimized considerably by showing figures for families alone rather than for families and individuals combined. Table 1 shows that trends in income distribution for families alone are almost identical with those for families and individuals combined. Other methods of reducing the impact of changes in living arrangements on the measure of income concentration are described near the end of this chapter.

Closely related to the definition of the income-receiving unit is the accounting period covered by the figures. Simon Kuznets has referred to the classification of families by their income in a single year as the major limitation of income statistics for purposes of measuring income inequality.[11]

Family income is defined as the combined receipts of all members of a family during a calendar year. Since the family includes only those persons living together at the time of the survey, some obvious distortions may arise. For example, a widow who has been supported by her husband during the year preceding the survey would be tabulated as an unrelated individual without income if she happened to be living alone at the time of the survey. Newly married couples who had been living with and supported by their parents during the preceding year would also appear at the bottom of the distribution. Here, of course, there is a dual problem—a change in family status, plus the fact that income is counted for only a single year. For a young family, low income has a significance entirely different from that for a middle-aged family.

Turning now to the income concept itself, we find that it presents several important limitations that complicate interpretation. The figures in table 1 represent money and nonmoney income; in this respect they are much more complete than the census figures, which relate only to cash receipts. Since it is not feasible in a census to try to collect information on imputed income, the data necessary for adjustment were not available. However, much of what is counted as nonmoney income in table 1 is included, not because it provides a more realistic portrayal of the funds available for consumption or saving by the average family, but for the sake of consistency with the national income accounts.[12]

Few would argue about adding the value of nonmoney food or housing received by farmers or farm laborers. These items, however, accounted for only a little more than $3 billion of a total of about $25 billion of nonmoney income included in the aggregate that underlies the distribution for 1960 shown in table 1. About $11 billion of the total represents imputed interest (largely the value of free banking services received by the owners of checking accounts, and the estimated amount that policy holders would receive if insurance companies distributed their property income), and about $6 billion is imputed rental income assumed to have been received by nonfarm homeowners who served as their own landlords.[13]

Money income includes the items usually thought of as income: cash wages and salaries; net income (after expenses) from self-employment; and cash income from other sources such as interest, dividends, net rental income, Social Security and unemployment benefits, private pensions, public assistance, and regular contributions for support from persons not living in the household.

Both the family personal income concept (used in table 1) and the money income concept exclude imputed income from paid vacations, fringe benefits, and from many other receipts not normally counted as income. These concepts also exclude capital gains and losses, which have become more important during recent years for the upper income groups. While income from this source is of prime importance in many individual cases, it does not have a major impact on the overall income curve because it represents only about 2.5 percent of total family personal income. An attempt made in 1958 to adjust the distribution of family personal income to include capital gains and losses showed that there was little if any change in the share of the aggregate received by each of the four lowest quintiles, and that the share received by the top 5 percent increased only slightly—from 19.9 percent to 20.3 percent.[14]

DISTRIBUTION BY INCOME LEVELS, 1929 TO 1962

Since the depression of the thirties the increase in the aggregate and average family income has been widespread throughout the population, resulting in a general movement of families up the income scale. There have, of course, been many exceptions. The aged, uneducated, and unskilled have not moved ahead as fast as the others; but even for these groups the sharp edge of poverty has been blunted.[15]

The more typical picture, especially during the postwar years, has been one of gradually rising family incomes due not only to the full-time employment of chief breadwinners, but also to the rising tendency for families to send secondary workers into the labor market. These factors, combined with the increasing productivity of American industry, have caused a persistent drop in the number and proportion of families at the lower income levels, and a corresponding increase in the middle and upper levels. Although part of the rise is due to an inflation of dollar values, even after adjustments are made for price changes, there has been a very marked increase in real family income.

The extent of the increase can be seen most dramatically in a single statistic. In 1929, at the height of the prosperous twen-

Table 2.—Families and Unrelated Individuals, by Family Personal Income Level, for Selected Years, 1935 to 1962

Family personal income level		1962	1961	1960	1959	1958	1957	1956	1955	1954	1953	1952	1951	1950	1947	1946	1944	1941	1935-36
Families and unrelated individuals:																			
Number	millions	57.9	57.3	56.1	55.3	54.6	53.7	52.9	52.2	51.2	50.5	50.2	49.5	48.9	44.7	43.3	40.9	41.4	38.4
Percent		100.0	100.0	100.0	100.0	100.0	100.0	100.0	100.0	100.0	100.0	100.0	100.0	100.0	100.0	100.0	100.0	100.0	100.0
Under $2,000		12.0	12.9	13.1	13.6	14.1	14.2	14.6	15.8	17.5	16.9	17.8	18.7	23.2	24.9	26.4	30.5	58.9	77.7
$2,000 to $3,999		18.3	19.4	19.8	20.7	22.2	22.1	23.1	25.4	27.0	26.6	28.2	31.0	34.2	38.2	40.1	40.3	32.1	17.5
$4,000 to $5,999		20.4	21.3	21.7	22.3	23.9	24.3	25.8	26.1	25.7	26.3	27.3	26.4	24.0	20.6	19.5	17.3	6.8	3.3
$6,000 to $7,499		14.1	14.1	14.1	14.1	13.9	14.1	13.6	13.3	12.3	12.6	11.6	10.7	7.9	7.0	5.9	5.5	{ 0.9	{ 0.6
$7,500 to $9,999		15.7	14.7	14.5	14.0	12.6	12.6	11.6	10.0	9.2	9.4	8.2	6.8	5.6	4.8	4.0	3.4		
$10,000 to $14,999		12.3	11.1	10.6	9.6	8.5	8.0	7.2	5.9	5.2	5.2	4.1	3.8	3.1	2.7	2.5	1.7	{ 1.3	{ 0.9
$15,000 and over		7.2	6.5	6.2	5.7	4.8	4.7	4.1	3.5	3.1	3.0	2.8	2.6	2.0	1.8	1.6	1.3		
Average (mean) income		$7,262	$6,930	$6,819	$6,615	$6,284	$6,238	$6,007	$5,640	$5,356	$5,389	$5,122	$4,904	$4,444	$4,126	$3,940	$3,614	$2,209	$1,631
Aggregate income	billions	$420.4	$397.0	$382.3	$365.8	$343.3	$334.6	$317.4	$294.2	$274.0	$272.2	$257.2	$242.7	$217.3	$184.6	$170.7	$147.7	$91.4	$62.7
Percent		100.0	100.0	100.0	100.0	100.0	100.0	100.0	100.0	100.0	100.0	100.0	100.0	100.0	100.0	100.0	100.0	100.0	100.0
Under $2,000		1.8	2.1	2.1	2.3	2.5	2.6	2.7	3.2	3.9	3.7	4.0	4.4	6.1	7.2	8.0	10.0	27.9	45.4
$2,000 to $3,999		7.7	8.5	8.9	9.5	10.8	10.8	11.8	13.9	15.4	15.0	16.8	19.2	23.1	27.8	30.4	33.2	40.1	28.7
$4,000 to $5,999		14.1	15.3	15.9	16.9	18.9	19.2	21.3	23.0	23.8	24.2	26.2	26.4	26.0	24.0	23.8	23.0	15.5	10.3
$6,000 to $7,499		13.0	13.6	13.9	14.4	14.8	15.1	15.2	15.8	15.3	15.6	15.1	14.7	11.8	11.3	9.9	10.1	{ 3.5	{ 3.2
$7,500 to $9,999		18.6	18.2	18.3	18.1	17.2	17.4	16.5	15.1	14.7	14.9	13.5	11.8	10.8	10.0	8.7	8.8		
$10,000 to $14,999		20.2	19.2	18.6	17.3	16.3	15.5	14.4	12.5	11.6	11.6	9.4	9.3	8.4	7.7	7.5	5.7	{ 13.0	{ 12.4
$15,000 and over		24.6	23.1	22.3	21.5	19.5	19.4	18.1	16.5	15.3	15.0	15.0	14.2	13.5	12.0	11.7	10.0		
Families:																			
Number	millions	46.9	46.2	45.4	44.8	44.1	43.7	43.4	42.7	41.8	41.1	40.8	40.4	39.8	37.0	35.9	33.3	32.9	30.4
Percent		100.0	100.0	100.0	100.0	100.0	100.0	100.0	100.0	100.0	100.0	100.0	100.0	100.0	100.0	100.0	100.0	100.0	100.0
Under $2,000		6.9	7.5	7.4	7.8	8.0	8.2	8.4	9.3	10.7	9.9	10.7	11.3	15.6	17.3	18.5	22.0	53.2	74.1
$2,000 to $3,999		14.4	15.6	16.0	16.9	18.7	18.6	19.9	22.6	24.7	24.1	26.2	29.8	34.1	39.5	42.2	43.4	36.2	20.3
$4,000 to $5,999		20.6	21.8	22.6	23.6	25.7	26.3	28.5	29.3	29.1	29.8	31.3	30.3	27.9	23.9	22.7	20.3	8.0	3.8
$6,000 to $7,499		16.0	16.2	16.3	16.5	16.4	16.6	16.0	15.7	14.6	15.1	13.8	12.8	9.4	8.3	6.9	6.6	{ 1.1	{ 0.7
$7,500 to $9,999		18.6	17.5	17.4	16.7	15.1	15.1	13.7	11.9	11.1	11.3	9.8	8.2	6.8	5.8	4.8	4.1		
$10,000 to $14,999		14.8	13.5	12.8	11.6	10.3	9.7	8.6	7.0	6.3	6.3	4.9	4.6	3.8	3.2	2.9	2.1	{ 1.5	{ 1.1
$15,000 and over		8.7	7.9	7.5	6.9	5.8	5.5	4.9	4.2	3.5	3.5	3.3	3.0	2.4	2.0	2.0	1.5		
Average (mean) income		$8,151	$7,797	$7,667	$7,435	$7,065	$6,992	$6,706	$6,303	$5,994	$6,041	$5,737	$5,477	$4,969	$4,574	$4,369	$4,027	$2,437	$1,784
Aggregate income	billions	$382.2	$360.1	$347.8	$332.9	$311.7	$305.3	$290.7	$268.9	$250.3	$248.4	$233.9	$221.4	$197.7	$169.3	$156.7	$134.1	$80.2	$54.3
Percent		100.0	100.0	100.0	100.0	100.0	100.0	100.0	100.0	100.0	100.0	100.0	100.0	100.0	100.0	100.0	100.0	100.0	100.0
Under $2,000		1.0	1.2	1.2	1.3	1.4	1.5	1.6	1.8	2.3	2.1	2.4	2.7	4.1	5.0	5.6	7.0	24.2	41.5
$2,000 to $3,999		5.4	6.2	6.5	7.1	8.3	8.3	9.3	11.3	12.7	12.4	14.2	16.9	21.0	26.2	29.3	32.4	41.4	30.5
$4,000 to $5,999		12.7	14.1	14.8	15.9	18.2	18.8	21.0	23.1	24.2	24.5	27.0	27.3	27.5	25.2	25.0	24.4	16.7	10.9
$6,000 to $7,499		13.2	14.0	14.3	14.9	15.5	15.8	16.0	16.7	16.3	16.7	16.1	15.6	12.5	12.0	10.5	10.9	{ 3.8	{ 3.4
$7,500 to $9,999		19.7	19.3	19.4	19.3	18.4	18.5	17.6	16.1	15.7	16.0	14.4	12.5	10.7	10.7	9.3	8.6		
$10,000 to $14,999		21.7	20.6	20.0	18.5	17.5	16.6	15.4	13.5	12.5	12.4	10.1	10.0	9.0	8.3	8.0	6.2	{ 13.9	{ 13.7
$15,000 and over		26.3	24.6	23.8	23.0	20.7	20.5	19.1	17.5	16.3	15.9	15.8	15.0	14.4	12.6	12.3	10.5		

Source: Family data for 1955-62 from Jeannette M. Fitzwilliams, "Size Distribution of Income in 1963," *Survey of Current Business*, April 1964, p. 6; and for 1935-36, 1941, 1944, 1946, 1947, and 1950-54 from U.S. Bureau of the Census, *Historical Statistics of the United States: Colonial Times to 1957*, p. 164.

ties, 31 percent of the families and individuals had incomes under $2,000. Using the same dollar standard, adjusted for price changes, we find that 32 years later only 12 percent of the families and individuals had incomes this low. This decrease clearly means that there has been a very sharp drop in the proportion of persons living at near-subsistence levels, and that for millions of people *absolute* want has been eliminated.

Numerous studies have been made of trends in the overall distribution of families by income levels, and the factors associated with these trends are reasonably well known. The summary data permit a comparison of figures from two of the major sources of information on the subject—the Census and OBE estimates. Tables 2 and 3 show the OBE data in current and constant dollars, respectively.

One dramatic change shown by these figures is a precipitous drop in the proportion of families and individuals with incomes under $40 a week (less than $2,000 a year). During the depression of the 1930's about 3 out of every 4 families and individuals received incomes less than this; by 1941, the proportion had dropped to 3 out of 5, and by 1950, to 1 out of 4. In 1962 only 1 of each 8 were receiving incomes this low.

Another view of this same change may be had in terms of share of all incomes received by families and individuals with incomes below $2,000 per year. During the thirties, this group received nearly half of all incomes, and its share fell to about 1 in 4 by the start of World War II, and to about 1 in 50 in 1962.

It is true that the change in the value of the dollar during the last 30 years makes it hard to extricate the real change from the apparent change, but the figures suggest strongly, as does other information to be dealt with later, that there has been an impressive decline in the proportion of families and individuals at the lowest income levels.

During the same period, equally impressive changes were taking place at the other end of the income scale among the top income groups. During the thirties, and even as recently as 1941, only 1 percent of the families in these groups had incomes over $10,000. By 1950, the proportion had increased fivefold, and in 1962, nearly one-fifth of the families and individuals were in this income class. In terms of aggregate income, this top class received only one-eighth of the total in the prewar period, compared with 45 percent in 1962.

The figures in table 3 on income distribution, adjusted for price changes, show that

Table 3.—Percent Distribution of Families and Unrelated Individuals by
Family Personal Income Level in 1962 Dollars, for Selected Years, 1929 to 1962

Family personal income level (1962 dollars)	1962	1961	1960	1959	1947	1941	1929
Families and unrelated individuals							
Millions	58.6	57.3	56.1	55.3	44.7	41.4	36.1
Percent	100	100	100	100	100	100	100
Under $2,000	12	12	13	13	16	27	31
$2,000 to $3,999	19	19	19	20	28	29	39
$4,000 to $5,999	21	22	22	22	26	22	15
$6,000 to $7,999	18	18	18	18	14	12	7
$8,000 to $9,999	11	11	11	11	7	4	3
$10,000 to $14,999	12	11	11	10	6⎤	6	5
$15,000 and over	7	7	6	6	3⎦		

Source: Jeannette M. Fitzwilliams, "Size Distribution of Income in 1962," *Survey of Current Business*, April 1963, p. 15.

although some of the preceding analysis must be modified, the basic conclusions are substantially unchanged. Starting at the bottom, we find that even during the boom of the twenties about one-third of the families and individuals had incomes under $2,000. This proportion dropped to about one-fourth (27 percent) at the outbreak of World War II, but was only 12 percent in 1962. Thus, in a third of a century, the proportion of families and individuals with real incomes under $2,000 had been reduced by about two-thirds. During the same period, there was also a significant bulge in the proportions in the middle and upper income levels. In 1962, for example, the $6,000 to $10,000 income group contained nearly three-tenths of the total, compared with only one-tenth in the prewar period. The purchasing power of this middle income group rose proportionately. The top income class—$10,000 and over—has also had a fourfold rise since the depression.

NOTES

[1]Simon Kuznets, "Economic Growth and Income Inequality," *American Economic Review* (March, 1955), p. 4.

[2]Dorothy S. Brady, "Research on the Size Distribution of Income," *Studies in Income and Wealth,* Vol. 13 (New York: National Bureau of Economic Research, 1951), p. 4.

[3]Arthur F. Burns, *Looking Forward,* 31st Annual Report of the National Bureau of Economic Research, p. 4.

[4]Paul Samuelson, *Economics,* 5th ed. (New York: McGraw-Hill Book Co., 1961), p. 114.

[5]The Changing American Market, Editors of *Fortune* (1953), p. 52.

[6]For an entirely different view of trends in income distribution see Gabriel Kolko, *Wealth and Power in America* (New York: Praeger, 1962). Kolko concludes that "A radically unequal distribution of income has been characteristic of the American social structure since at least 1910, and despite minor year-to-year fluctuations in the shares of the income-tenths, no significant trend toward income equality has appeared" (p. 13). This conclusion is based on data for 1910 to 1937 prepared by the National Industrial Conference

Board and for 1941 to 1959 by the Survey Research Center of the University of Michigan. Kolko states that the NICB data are the best material on income distribution by tenths for the period prior to 1941. This statement is very questionable. The NICB data were considered so poor by a panel of experts, including Selma F. Goldsmith and Simon Kuznets, that they were excluded from U.S. Bureau of the Census, *Historical Statistics of the United States: Colonial Times to 1957,* even though they had appeared in the earlier version of that book, *Historical Statistics of the United States, 1789-1945.* The figures for 1929 and 1935-1936 shown in table 1 are thought to be much more reliable than those used by Kolko.

An examination of the figures used by Kolko shows that the share of income received by the highest tenth of income recipients dropped from 38 and 39 percent in 1921 and 1929, to 34 percent in 1927 and 1941, to 29 percent in 1958. He dismisses the figures for 1921 and 1929 without further explanation as representing exceptional years. He then concludes that the difference between the prewar and postwar figures can be eliminated when the latter are "corrected to allow for their exclusion of all forms of income in kind and the very substantial understatement of income by the wealthy." The figures in table 1 include many types of income in kind and they have also been adjusted for underreporting of income. They do not include various items that accrue primarily to the wealthy which Kolko thinks should be added, notably expense accounts and undistributed profits. Also excluded from the concept and not mentioned by Kolko are various types of fringe benefits such as life insurance, medical care, health insurance and pension plans, as well as government services, which have been increasing rapidly in recent years and are widely distributed throughout the population. A study published in 1954 by Selma F. Goldsmith and her colleagues showed that incomes were more equally distributed in the postwar period than in 1929, even when allowance is made for undistributed corporate profits [Selma F. Goldsmith *et al.,* "Size Distribution of Income Since the Mid-Thirties," *Review of Economics and Statistics* (February, 1954), p. 20]. A more recent study shows that the addition of capital gains to the distribution increases the share received by the wealthiest 5 percent by only a fraction of a percentage point [Maurice Liebenberg and Jeannette M. Fitzwilliams, "Size Distribution of Personal Income, 1957-60," *Survey of Current Business* (May 1961), p. 14].

[7]Selma F. Goldsmith *et al.,* "Size Distribution of Income Since the Mid-Thirties," *Review of Economics and Statistics* (February 1954), p. 132; and *Survey of Current Business* (April 1964), p. 8.

[8]U.S. Bureau of the Census, *Statistical Abstract of the United States: 1964,* p. 416.

[9]For figures showing taxes paid as a percent of income by income class in 1958, see Tax Foundation, *Allocation of the Tax Burden by Income Class* (New York, 1960), p. 17. This source shows no variation in the percent of income paid in federal, state, and local taxes for each income class below $15,000. In each class, about one-fifth of the income was paid in taxes.

[10]Only brief reference to the conceptual problems associated with the interpretation of statistics on income distribution is made here. For a more complete discussion, see Dorothy S. Brady, "Research on the Size Distribution of Income," *Studies in Income and Wealth*, Vol. 13 (New York:

National Bureau of Economic Research, 1951).

[11]Kuznets, "Economic Growth," p. 3.

[12]See U.S., Office of Business Economics, *Income Distribution in the United States* (1953), p. 20.

[13]Based on data of the Office of Business Economics.

[14]Maurice Liebenberg and Jeannette M. Fitzwilliams, "Size Distribution of Personal Income, 1957-60," *Survey of Current Business* (May 1961), pp. 12-15.

[15]For an eloquent description of poverty in the United States, see Michael Harrington, *The Other America* (New York: Macmillan, 1962).

CHAPTER 15

The Corporation: How Much Power?
What Scope?

CARL KAYSEN

The proposition that a group of giant business corporations, few in number but awesome in aggregate size, embodies a significant and troublesome concentration of power is the cliché which serves this volume as a foundation stone. I propose here to analyze this proposition, both to trace out what I consider its valid content to be, and to reflect briefly on its possible implications for social action. Let me anticipate my conclusion on the first point by saying that its familiarity is no argument against its truth.

The power of any actor on the social stage I define as the scope of significant choice open to him. Accordingly, his power over others is the scope of his choices which affect them significantly. Our fundamental proposition thus asserts that a few large corporations exert significant power over others; indeed, as we shall see, over the whole of society with respect to many choices, and over large segments of it with respect to others. It is worth noting that this sense of "power" is not that in which we speak of the "power" of a waterfall or a fusion reaction, or any other transformation in a fully deterministic system; rather it is appropriate to a social system in which we see human actors, individually or in organized groups, as facing alternative courses of action, the choice among which is not fully determined without reference to the actors themselves.

We usually demonstrate the concentration of power in a small number of large corporate enterprises by showing what part of various total magnitudes for the whole economy the largest enterprises account for. The statistics are indeed impressive: I list a few of the more striking below.[1]

213

(1) There are currently some 4.5 million business enterprises in the United States. More than half of these are small, unincorporated firms in retail trade and service. Corporations formed only 13 per cent of the total number; 95 per cent of the unincorporated firms had fewer than twenty employees.

(2) A recent census survey covered all the firms in manufacturing, mining, retail and wholesale trade, and certain service industries: in total some 2.8 million. These firms employed just under 30 million persons. The 28 giant firms with 50,000 or more employees — just 0.001 per cent of the total number — accounted for about 10 per cent of the total employment. The 438 firms with 5000 or more employees (including the 28 giants) accounted for 28 per cent of the total. In manufacturing, where large corporations are characteristically more important than in the other sectors covered, 263,000 firms reported just over 17 million employees: 23 giants with 50,000 or more employees reported 15 per cent of the total, 361 with 5000 or more, just under 40 per cent.

(3) The most recent compilation of the corporation income-tax returns showed 525,000 active nonfinancial corporations reporting a total of $413 billion of assets. The 202 corporations in the largest size class — each with assets of $250 million or more — owned 40 per cent of this total.

(4) The last survey of the National Science Foundation reported some 15,500 firms having research and development laboratories. The largest 7 among them employed 20 per cent of the total number of technical and scientific personnel in the whole group, and accounted for 26 per cent of the total expenditures on research and development. The largest 44, all those with 25,000 or more employees in total, accounted for 45 per cent of the total number of technicians and scientists, and more than 50 per cent of the total expenditures.

(5) The one hundred companies that received the largest defense contracts over the period July 1950–June 1956 received nearly two thirds of the total value of all defense contracts during the period. The largest ten contractors accounted for just short of one third of the total value of all contracts. These were General Motors, General Electric, American Telephone and Telegraph, and seven large aircraft manufacturers.

Large corporations are not of the same importance in all sectors of the economy.[2] In agriculture they are of no importance; in service, trade, and construction, proprietorships and partnerships and small corporations that are essentially similar in all but legal form predominate. Conversely, activity in the utility, transportation, mining, manufacturing, and financial sectors is overwhelmingly the activity of corporations, and predominantly that of corporate giants. The share of total business accounted for by corporations in these sectors ranged from 85 per cent for finance to 100 per cent of utilities; by contrast it was between 50 and 60 per cent for trade and construction, less than 30 per cent in service, and less than 10 per cent in agriculture. The five sectors in which large corporations predominate produced 51 per cent of the total national income, and 57 per cent of the privately-produced national income. Moreover, the strategic importance of these sectors as compared with trade and service — the largest part of the small-business part of the economy — is greater than their contribution to national income would indicate. The relative share of giant corporations in these sectors was larger than in the economy as a whole. The corporate income-tax returns for 1955 showed the relative importance of the largest corporations, as in the accompanying table.

Many more figures similar to these could be added to the

The Relative Share of Giant Corporations in Various Sectors
of the United States Economy.

| | All corporations | | Corporations with assets of $250 million or more | |
Sector	Number (thousands)	Assets (billions of dollars)	Number	Proportion of assets of all corporations (percentage)
Manufacturing	124.2	201.4	97	42
Mining *	9.7	13.3	5 (19)	17 (32)
Public utilities	4.8	62.9	56	72
Transportation	21.9	43.5	30	61
Finance	214.6	474.9	218	46

* The figures in parentheses show the number and share of corporations with assets of $100 million or more, since the number of mining corporations in the largest size class is so small.

list. They show clearly that a few large corporations are of overwhelmingly disproportionate importance in our economy, and especially in certain key sectors of it. Whatever aspect of their economic activity we measure — employment, investment, research and development, military supply — we see the same situation. Moreover, it is one which has been stable over a period of time. The best evidence — though far from complete — is that the degree of concentration has varied little for the three or four decades before 1947; more recent material has not yet been analyzed. Further, the group of leading firms has had a fairly stable membership, and turnover within it is, if anything, declining.[3] We are thus examining a persistent situation, rather than a rapidly changing one, and one which we can expect to continue into the future.

Disproportionate share alone, however, is not a valid basis for inferring power as I have defined it. In addition, we must consider the range of choice with respect to significant decisions open to the managers of the large corporation. The disproportionate share of the sun in the total mass of our solar system would not justify the ascription to it of "power" over the planets, since in the fully-determinate gravitational system the sun has no choice among alternative paths of motion which would change the configuration of the whole system. Though the relative weight of the sun is great, its range of choice is nil, and it is the product of the two, so to speak, which measures "power." It is to an examination of the managers' range of choice that we now turn.

Our economy is organized on a decentralized, competitive basis. Each business firm, seeking higher profit by providing more efficiently what consumers want, is faced by the competition of others, seeking the same goal through the same means. Coordination and guidance of these activities is the function of the system of markets and prices. These form the information network that tells each manager what is and what is not currently profitable, and, in turn, registers the effects of each business decision, of changes in consumers' tastes, and the availability and efficiency of productive factors. Ideally, in a system of competitive markets, the signals would indicate only one possible course for any particular manager consistent with profitability. Nor would this depend on the degree to which the manager was committed to the goal of profit-maximization; margins between costs and prices would be so narrow as to make bankruptcy the alternative to "correct" choices. In practice, of course, no real firm functions in markets operating with the sureness, swiftness, and freedom from frictions that would eliminate the discretion of management entirely and make the firm merely an instrument which registered the forces of the market. But firms operating in highly competitive markets are closely constrained by market pressures, and the range of economic decision consistent with survival and success that is open to them is narrow.

By contrast, there exist much less competitive markets in which firms are insulated from these compulsions and the range of discretionary choice in management decisions is correspondingly widened. There is a wide variety of situations which can confer such market power on firms. In practice, the most important is large size relative to the market: the situation in which a few large firms account for all or nearly all of the supply. Large size relative to the market is associated with large absolute size of firm. Other reasons, including barriers to the entry of new firms into the market provided by product differentiation and advertising, by patents, by control over scarce raw materials, or by collusive action of existing firms, or by government limitation of competition, are also significant, but they are of less importance than the oligopolistic market structure common in those sectors of the economy that are dominated by large firms.

In manufacturing, nearly two-thirds of the identifiable markets, accounting for about 60 per cent of the value of manufacturing output, showed significant elements of oligopoly; they were especially important in the durable-goods and capital-equipment fields. In mining, the proportion of identifiable markets with oligopolistic structures was much higher, but since the largest mining industry — bituminous coal — is unconcentrated, these accounted for less than 25 per cent of total mineral output. Public utilities, transportation, and finance are all subject to more or less direct government regulation, of more or less effectiveness. But the underlying market structures in these areas are either monopolistic, as in electric and gas utilities and telephone communication, or oligopolistic, as in transportation and finance.[4] Thus, typically, the large corporation in which we are interested operates in a situation in which the constraints imposed by market forces are loose, and the scope for managerial choice is considerable. It is this scope combined with the large relative weight of the giant corporation that defines its economic power; it is substantially on its economic power that other kinds of power depend.

The powerful firm can use its power primarily to increase its profit over what it could earn in a competitive market: the traditional economic view of the drawback of market power has been the achievement of monopoly profit by the restriction of supply. But it need not do so. While the firm in the highly competitive market is constrained to seek after maximum profits, because the alternative is insufficient profit to insure survival, the firm in the less competitive market can choose whether to seek maximum profit or to be satisfied with some "acceptable" return and to seek other goals. Further, the firm in a competitive market must attend more closely to immediate problems, and leave the long future to take care of itself; while the firm with considerable market power necessarily has a longer time-horizon, and takes into account consequences of its decisions reaching further into the future. This in turn increases the range of choice open to it, for the future is uncertain, and no single "correct" reading of it is possible. Many courses of action may be consistent with reasonable expectations of the future course of events. The more dominant the position of any particular firm in a single market, the further into the future will it see the consequences of its own choices as significant, and correspondingly, the wider will be its range of significant choice. The width of choice and the uncertainty of consequences combine to rob the notion of maximum profit of its simplicity; at the minimum of complexity, the firm must be viewed as seeking some combination of anticipated return and possible variation, at the same time perhaps safeguarding itself against too much variation. But even this is too simple. In the absence of the constraints of a competitive market, the firm may seek a variety of goals: "satisfactory" profits, an "adequate" rate of growth, a "safe" share of the market, "good" labor relations, "good" public relations, and so forth, and no particular combination need adequately describe the behavior of all large firms with significant market power.

The large corporations with which we are here concerned characteristically operate many plants and sell and buy in many markets. Their power in some markets can be used to reinforce their power in others; their large absolute size, and the pool of capital at their command, adds something to their power in any particular market which is not explained simply by the structure of that market. In the extreme, the operations of the firm in a particular market can be completely or almost completely insensitive to its economic fortunes in that market, and thus the range of choice of decisions with respect to it may be widened far beyond that possible to any firm confined within its boundaries. Absolute size has to a certain extent the same effect in respect to the operations of any particular short time-period: the impact of likely short-period losses or failures may bulk insufficiently large to form a significant constraint on action.

We have spoken so far of the powers of choice of the corporation and the management interchangeably. By and large, this is justified. Corporate management is typically — in the reaches of business we are examining — an autonomous center of decision, organizing the affairs of the corporation and choosing its own successors. While stockholders are significant as part of the environment in which management operates, they exercise little or no power of choice themselves. The views of stockholders, as reflected in their willingness to hold or their desire to dispose of the corporation's stock, are certainly taken into account by management, but only as one of a number of elements which condition their decisions. The ideology of corporate management which describes them as one among a number of client groups whose interests are the concern of management — labor, consumers, and the "public" forming the others — is in this particular realistic.

How does the giant corporation manifest its power? Most directly, in economic terms, the noteworthy dimensions of choice open to it include prices and price-cost relations, investment, location, research and innovation, and product character and selling effort. Management choice in each of these dimensions has significance for the particular markets in which the firm operates, and with respect to some of them, may have broader significance for the economy as a whole.

Prices and price-cost relations, in turn, show at least four important aspects. First is the classic question of the general level of prices in relation to costs: are profits excessive? Second, and perhaps more important, is the effect of margins on the level of costs themselves. Where the pressure of competition does not force prices down to costs, costs themselves have a tendency to rise: internal managerial checks alone cannot overcome the tendency to be satisfied with costs when the over-all level of profit is satisfactory. Third, there is the problem of interrelations among margins on related products: does the price of Chevrolet bear the same relation to its costs as the price of a Cadillac, or is there a tendency to earn more in the long run on resources converted into the one than into the other? This form of distortion of price-cost relations is common in the multiproduct firm, and can coexist with a modest average profit margin. Finally, there are the interrelations, both directly within a single firm and indirectly through labor and product markets, of prices and wages. Where price increases are the response to wage increases which in turn respond to price increases, the pricing policy of a firm or group of firms can be an inflationary factor of some importance. This has been the case in the steel industry in the postwar period.[5] A related problem is the behavior of prices in the face of declining demand. When a group of firms can raise prices relative to wages although unused capacity is large and increasing, they make a contribution to aggregate instability, in this case in a deflationary rather than an inflationary direction. Here again the steel industry provides a recent example.

The investment decisions of large firms are of primary importance in determining the rates of growth of particular industries, and where the role of these industries in the economy is a strategic one, their impact may be much wider. Again we may point to the steel industry. Overpessimism about expansion in the early postwar period contributed to the continuing bottleneck in steel that was apparent until the 1957 recession. In the twenties, the slowness with which aluminum capacity was expanded led to recurrent shortages in that market. The speed, or slowness, with which investment in nuclear-fueled electric power generation is now going forward, even with the aid of considerable government subsidy, is again the product of the decisions of a relatively small number of major power producers. This is not to argue that the pace chosen is the wrong one, but simply to indicate a choice of possible broad significance, lying in large part in the hands of a few corporate managements.

A particular kind of investment decision, the consequences of which may reach far into the future and beyond the specific firm or industry involved, is the decision about location. Where new plants are placed both in regional terms and in relation to existing centers of population affects the balance of regional development and the character of urban and suburban growth. Characteristically, it is the large multiplant enterprise which has the widest set of alternatives from among which to choose in making this decision; smaller firms are tied closely to their existing geographic centers.

Even more far reaching are the choices of large enterprises in respect to innovation. Decisions as to the technical areas which will be systematically explored by research and development divisions and decisions as to what scientific and technical novelties will be translated into new products and new processes and tried out for economic viability have very deep effects. Ultimately, the whole material fabric of society, the structure of occupations, the geographic distribution of economic activity and population are all profoundly affected by the pattern of technical change. Not all significant technical change springs from the activities of organized research and development departments, but they do appear to be of increasing importance. And the disproportionate share of a few large corporations in this sphere is greater than in any other. Here again, I am not arguing that the decisions now taken on these matters are necessarily inferior to those which would result from some different distribution of decision-making power, but only pointing to the locus of an important power of choice.

It is worth remarking, on a lower level of generality, that the concentration of the power of choice with respect to new products and new models of old products in a few hands has a significance which is enhanced by the large role which producers' initiative plays in determining consumers' choices in our economy. Whether the extent and character of advertising and selling in our economy is something idiosyncratically American, or simply a product of the high average level of income combined with its relatively equal distribution, it is clear that the importance of these institutions adds to the importance of the producers' power of choice in respect to product change and new products. Further, selling and advertising are likewise relatively highly concentrated, and both the pervasiveness of "sales talk" in the media of communication and the relatively large amounts of its income our rich society spends on all kinds of durable goods give decisions in the sphere of product character and selling techniques a wide impact.

The significance of the economic choices that are made by the powerful large firm can be summed up in terms of their effects on the achievement of four basic economic goals: efficiency, stability, progressiveness, and equity. Economic efficiency means producing the most of what consumers want with available supplies of resources. It involves not only the idea of technical efficiency — for example, performing any particular technical operation with the cheapest combination of inputs required for a unit of output — but the more subtle idea of not producing less of any one particular good in relation to others, and conversely, more of another, than consumers' desires indicate. In more concrete terms, whenever one particular good is priced high in relation to its costs, while another one is priced low, then too much of the second and too little of the first tends to be produced in relation to consumers' demands. When the price-cost margin on a product remains high over a period of time, this is an indication of economic inefficiency. So is continued price discrimination, in the sense in which we defined it above. In addition, of course, the lack of competitive pressure on margins may lead to inefficiency in the simpler sense as well: not producing the actual goods with the minimum amount of resources possible. The exercise of market power thus leads frequently to economic inefficiency.

Stability of output and employment at high levels, and, perhaps a little less important, of price levels, is an economic goal which is generally given great weight. The exercise of pricing discretion can contribute to destabilizing forces both in upswings and downswings of activity. As we argued before, there are examples of wage-price spirals in which a significant upward push on wage levels in general, and thus on price levels, is exercised by particular pricing decisions. The maintenance of margins in the face of declining demand is less clear and striking in its effects, but it probably makes a net contribution to further destabilization in comparison with some moderate decline. On the other hand, it is clear that stable prices and wages are far more desirable than continuous declines in both in the face of declining aggregate demand; and thus the choice typically made by the powerful firm may be less than the best but considerably better than the worst possible one.

When we come to test the economic decisions of the large firm against the standard of progressiveness, we find that we can say little that is unequivocal. That large firms spend heavily on research and development is clear. That some industries in which the application of improved techniques and growth of output of new products is spectacular are industries — such as chemicals, oil, electronics — dominated by large firms is also clear. But when we try to look deeper, obscurity replaces clarity. Is the present degree of dominance of large firms a necessary condition of the amount of progress experienced, or even a sufficient condition? Are larger firms more effective, per dollar of expenditures, in producing new ideas and new methods than smaller ones are, and over what size range is this true? Should corporations spend on research and development much more or much less than they now spend? Should the incentives of the market be allowed more or less control than they now have of the whole chain of sequential and interrelated processes from the first observation of a new natural phenomenon or the first conception of a new scientific idea to the introduction into the market of a new product or the application on the production line of a new technology? These are all questions to which well-informed and competent students do not give the same answer, if indeed they give any. However, it is enough for our present purpose to say that there are specific examples of the importance for technical progress of competition, and particularly of the kind of competition represented by new and small firms that are not heavily committed to present products and processes, in sufficient number to cast doubt on the universal correctness of the judgments of powerful dominant firms.[6] While we cannot assert that these judgments are likely to be always wrong, we also cannot say that they need no corrective. When technical change can take the spectacularly wasteful forms that it has achieved recently in the automobile industry, in which new products, introduced at considerable production and marketing expense, are not cheaper to produce, cheaper to operate, nor more durable than those they supplant, and their increase in serviceability, functional efficiency, or even aesthetic appeal is at best debatable, it is hard to deny that "progress" and "free choice in the marketplace" both become phrases of rather dubious content. All the potential gain in productive efficiency in the automobile industry over the last decade, and probably more, has gone into "more" product rather than into cost savings and price reductions. This result is the product of decisions of a small number of managements — perhaps only one — and it underlines the appropriateness of raising the question of whether there is not too much power in the hands of those responsible for the choice.

The standard of equity is at least as slippery as that of progressiveness, although for different reasons. While the importance of equity in the sense of a fair distribution of the income of society as a goal is undeniable, equity itself is not measurable by any economic standard. We have long since abandoned reliance on the notion that the reward of the marketplace is necessarily a "fair" reward, even when the market functions effectively and competitively. Indeed, some of our interferences with the functioning of markets are justified on equity grounds, reflecting our social dissatisfaction with the income distribution resulting from the unchecked operation of the market. But, although little exists in the way of comprehensive standards of equity which command wide acceptance, certain specific judgments are possible. "Excessive" property incomes are suspect: high profits based on monopoly power are widely subject to criticism. Where market power is translated into sustained high profits, the result can be described as inequitable as well as inefficient. Further, where management decision translates a portion of the high profits into high salaries, bonuses, stock options, and generous pension plans for itself, the imputation of unfairness is strengthened. These are recorded as views that command fairly wide agreement, not as economically inevitable conclusions nor necessary moral judgments. It may be that the equally high incomes of crooners and .400 hitters are logically open to as much criticism; in fact, however, they are not so much criticized.

Any discussion of equity moves rapidly from an economic to what is essentially a political view, since equity is ultimately a value problem whose social resolution is of the essence of politics. When we make this move, a new order of equity problems connected with the power of the large firm appears. This is the problem of the relation between the large enterprise and the host of small satellite enterprises which become its dependents. These may be customers bound to it by a variety of contractual relations, such as the service stations bound to the major oil companies who are their suppliers (and frequently their landlords and bankers as well), or the automobile dealers connected with the manufacturers by franchise arrangements. Or they may be customers without explicit contractual ties, yet nonetheless dependent on the maintenance of "customary" relations with large suppliers of their essential raw material, as has been the case with small fabricators of aluminum and steel products, whose business destinies have been controlled by the informal rationing schemes of the primary producers in the frequent shortage periods of the postwar decade. Or they may be small suppliers of large firms: canners packing for the private brands of the large chain grocers, furniture or clothing manufacturers producing for the chain department stores and mail-order houses, subcontractors producing for the major military suppliers. In any case, these small firms are typically wholly dependent on their larger partners. It is worth noting that this dependence may be consistent with a fairly competitive situation in the major product market of the large purchaser, or even the over-all selling market of the large supplier, provided the particular submarket in which the transactions between large and small firm occur is segmented enough to make it costly and risky for the small firm to seek new sources or outlets.

All these relations present a double problem. First, is the treatment which the dependent firms experience "fair" in the concrete: Have there been cancellations of dealers' franchises by major automobile manufacturers for no cause, or, worse, in order to transfer them to firms in which company executives had an interest? Have aluminum companies "favored" their own fabricating operations at the expense of independent fabricators during periods of short supply? [7] Second, and more fundamental, is what might be called the procedural aspect of the problem. Whether unfair treatment by large firms of their small clients abounds, or is so rare as to be written off as the vagary of a few executives, the question of whether it is appropriate for the large firm to possess what amount to life-and-death powers over other business remains.

And the same question arises more broadly than in respect to the patron-client relations of large firms and their dependent small suppliers and customers. All of the areas of decision in which powerful managements have wide scope for choice, with effects reaching far into the economy, that we discussed above raise the same question. Not the concrete consequences of choice measured against the economic standards of efficiency, stability, progressiveness, and equity, but the power and scope of choice itself is the problem. This view of the problem may appear somewhat abstract, and even be dismissed as a piece of academic fussiness: if the outcomes are in themselves not objectionable, why should we concern ourselves with the process of decision which led to them; and, if they are, why not address ourselves to improving them directly? But so to argue ignores the point that choice of economic goals is itself a value choice, and thus a political one; and that direct concern with the loci of power and constraints on its use may legitimately rank in importance as political goals with the attainment of desired economic values. If the regime of competition and the arguments of *laissez-faire* ever commended themselves widely, it has been primarily on political rather than economic grounds. The replacement of the all-too-visible hand of the state by the invisible hand of the marketplace, which guided each to act for the common good while pursuing his own interests and aims without an overt show of constraint, was what attracted general ideological support to the liberal cause. The elegance of the optimum allocation of resources which Walras and Pareto saw in the ideal competitive economy by contrast has remained a concept of importance only to the most academic economist. When the invisible hand of the competitive market is, in turn, displaced to a significant extent by the increasingly visible hand of powerful corporate management, the question "Quo warranto?" is bound to arise, whatever decisions are in fact made. And the fact is that the power of corporate management is, in the political sense, irresponsible power, answerable ultimately only to itself. No matter how earnestly management strives to "balance" interests in making its decisions — interests of stockholders, of employees, of customers, of the "general public," as well as the institutional interests of the enterprise — it is ultimately its own conception of these interests and their desirable relations that rules. When the exercise of choice is strongly constrained by competitive forces, and the power of decision of any particular management is narrow and proportioned to the immediate economic needs of the enterprise, the political question of the warrant of management authority and its proper scope does not arise. When, as we have argued, the scope of choice is great and the consequences reach widely into the economy and far into the future, the problem of the authority and responsibility of the choosers is bound to become pressing.

The market power which large absolute and relative size gives to the giant corporation is the basis not only of economic power but also of considerable political and social power of a broader sort. Some of the political power of large business is of course the product of group action to defend group interests and, in this sense, presents no problems peculiar to large business, except perhaps the problem of the large availability of funds and certain nonpurchasable resources of specialized talent and prestige in support of its interest. That we pay, in the form of percentage depletion, an outrageous subsidy to the oil and gas business (which goes to many small producers as well as to the giant integrated oil firms) is a phenomenon of no different order than that we pay nearly equally outrageous ones to farmers. On the other hand, it is money rather than votes which supports the one, and votes rather than money which support the other; and the latter situation is, as the former is not, in accord with our professed political morality. More special to the position of the large firm is the power in both domestic and foreign affairs which the large oil companies have by virtue of their special positions as concessionaires — frequently on a monopoly basis in a particular country — in exploiting the oil of the Middle East and the Caribbean. Here the large firms exercise quasi-sovereign powers, have large influence on certain aspects of the foreign policy of the United States and the Atlantic Alliance, and operate in a way which is neither that of public government nor that of private business. While the oil companies are the most spectacular examples of the involvement of strong American companies with weak foreign governments in areas which are important to national policy, they are not the only ones, and other examples could be cited.

Perhaps the most pervasive influence of big business on national politics lies in the tone of the mass media. Both because of the influence of advertising — itself heavily concentrated in the largest firms, and the big-business character of many publishing and broadcasting enterprises, the political tone of the media is far from reflecting even approximately the distribution of attitudes and opinions in the society as a whole. But an influence may be pervasive without thereby being powerful, and the importance of this state of affairs is open to argument.

It is when we step down from the level of national politics to the state and local levels that the political power of the large corporation is seen in truer perspective. The large national-market firm has available to it the promise of locating in a particular area or expanding its operations there, the threat of moving or contracting its operations as potent bargaining points in its dealings with local and even state political leaders. The branch manager of the company whose plant is the largest employer in a town or the vice-president of the firm proposing to build a plant which will become the largest employer in a small state treats with local government not as a citizen but as a quasi-sovereign power. Taxes, zoning laws, roads, and the like become matters of negotiation as much as matters of legislation. Even large industrial states and metropolitan cities may face similar problems: the largest three employers in Michigan account for probably a quarter of the state's industrial employment; in Detroit the proportion is more nearly a third. At this level, the corporation's scope of choice, its financial staying power, its independence of significant local forces are all sources of strength in dealing with the characteristically weak governments at the local and often at the state levels.

The broader social power which the high executives of large corporations exercise — in part in their own positions, in part in their representative capacity as "business leaders" — is more difficult to define and certainly less definite than the kind of political power and economic power discussed above. Yet it is no less important, and to the extent that it is linked to the economic power of the large firm — a point to which I return immediately below — no less relevant to our discussion. One aspect of this broad power to which we have already referred is the position that corporate management occupies as taste setter or style leader for the society as a whole. Business influence on taste ranges from the direct effects through the design of material goods to the indirect and more subtle effects of the style of language and thought purveyed through the mass media — the school of style at which all of us are in attendance every day. Further, these same business leaders are dominant social models in our society: their achievements and their values are to a large extent the type of the excellent, especially for those strata of society from which leaders in most endeavors are drawn. This, more shortly stated, is the familiar proposition that we are a business society, and that the giant corporation is the "characteristic," if not the statistically typical, institution of our society, and, in turn, the social role of high executives is that appropriate to leading men in the leading institution.

How much is this kind of social power, as well as the political power discussed above, connected with the market power of giant firms? Is it simply a consequence of their economic power, or does it depend on deeper elements in our social structure? These are questions to which any firm answer is difficult, in part because they can be interpreted to mean many different things. To assert that any diminution in the underlying power of large firms in the markets in which they operate would lead to a corresponding decrease in their social and political power appears unwarranted; so does the assertion that universally competitive markets would end the social and political power of business. But there are important connections. Part of the power of the business leaders comes from the size of the enterprises they operate and the number of people they influence directly as employees, suppliers, customers; absolute size, in turn, is highly correlated with relative size and market power. Freedom in spending money is connected with both absolute size, and the security of income which market power provides. The initiative in the complex processes of taste formation might shift away from smaller and more competitive businesses toward other institutions to a substantial extent; and the ability of firms to spend large resources on shaping demand would be lessened by reductions in their market power. Thus diminution of the economic power of large firms would have a more-than-trivial effect on their power in other spheres, even if we cannot state firmly the law that relates them.

The reasons for concern about the social and political power of business are also worth consideration, since they are not obviously the same as those which the concentrated economic power of large corporations raise. There are two aspects of this question which appear worth distinguishing. The first is the already-mentioned point of the irresponsibility of business power. Its exercise with respect to choices which are themselves far from the matters of meeting the material needs of society that are the primary tasks of business further emphasizes this point. The process of selection of business leaders may be adaptive with respect to their performance of the economic function of business; there is no reason to expect that it should be with respect to the exercise of power in other realms. In short, why should we entrust to the judgment of business leaders decisions of this kind, when we have neither a mechanism for ratifying or rejecting their judgments and them, nor any reason to believe them particularly suited to make these judgments? Second, we can go further than merely to raise the question of whether the training and selection of business leaders qualifies them to make the kinds of decisions and exercise the kinds of power we have discussed. In some quite important respects, it is clear that business values and business attitudes are dysfunctional in meeting our national needs. This is true both with respect to the many problems which we face in our international relations, and with respect to important domestic problems as well. If we look on our economic relations with the underdeveloped nations, especially those of Asia and Africa, as primarily tasks of business firms to be met through the market under the stimulus of market incentives, supported to some extent by special subsidies, it appears unlikely that we will succeed in achieving our political and security goals. If our attitudes toward other governments are heavily colored by ideological evaluations of the kind of economic organization they favor, from the standpoint of our own business ideology, our world problems will be made no easier. And in the domestic sphere, there is a range of problems from education to metropolitan organization and urban renewal which cannot be dealt with adequately if viewed in business perspectives and under business values.

We can sum up these points by saying that the position of big businesses and their leaders contributes significantly to our being a "business society." Do we want to be? Can we afford to be?

These rhetorical questions indicate clearly enough my own view on whether or not we should try to limit or control the power of large corporate enterprise. The crucial question, however, is whether such power can be limited or controlled. Broadly, there are three alternative possibilities. The first is limitation of business power through promoting more competitive markets; the second is broader control of business power by agencies external to business; the third, institutionalization within the firm of responsibility for the exercise of power. Traditionally, we have purported to place major reliance on the first of these alternatives, in the shape of antitrust policy, without in practice pushing very hard any effort to restrict market power to the maximum feasible extent. I have argued elsewhere that it is in fact possible to move much further than we have in this direction, without either significant loss in the over-all effectiveness of business performance or the erection of an elaborate apparatus of control.[8] While this, in my judgment, remains the most desirable path of policy, I do not in fact consider it the one which we will tend to follow. To embark on a determined policy of the reduction of business size and growth in order to limit market power requires a commitment of faith in the desirability of the outcome and the feasibility of the process which I think is not widespread. What I consider more likely is some mixture of the second and third types of control. Business itself has argued vehemently that a corporate revolution is now in process, which has resulted in a redirection of business goals and conscious assumption of responsibility in broad social spheres. This theme has been put forward by academic writers as well.[9] To whatever extent such a "revolution" has taken place, it does not meet the need for the institutionalization of responsibility which the continued exercise of wide power demands. It is not sufficient for the business leaders to announce that they are thinking hard and wrestling earnestly with their wide responsibilities, if, in fact, the power of unreviewed and unchecked decision remains with them, and they remain a small, self-selecting group.[10] Some of the more sophisticated accounts of the revolutionary transformation of business identify business as a "profession" in the honorific sense, and imply that professional standards can be relied on as a sufficient social control over the exercise of business power, as society does rely on them to control the exercise of the considerable powers of doctors and lawyers. This is a ramifying problem which we cannot here explore; it is sufficient to remark that there is, at least as yet, neither visible mechanism of uniform training to inculcate, nor visible organization to maintain and enforce, such standards; and, further, that even if business decisions in the business sphere could be "professionalized" and subject to the control of a guild apparatus, it seems less easy to expect that the same would be true of the exercise of business power in the social and political spheres.

Some likely directions of development of explicit control can be seen in the kinds of actions which now provoke Congressional inquiry, and the suggestions which flow from such inquiries. Concern with the wage-price spiral has led to Congressional investigation of "administered prices" and to suggestions that proposed price and wage changes in certain industries be reviewed by a public body before becoming effective. A combination of the increase of direct regulation of some of the economic choices of powerful firms with an increase in public criticism, and perhaps even institutionalized public discussion of the choices which are not explicitly controlled, appears probable. Such a program will, in effect, do by a formal mechanism and systematically what is currently being done in a somewhat haphazard way by Congressional investigation. On the whole, it is this which has been the active front. The development of mechanisms which will change the internal organization of the corporation, and define more closely and represent more presently the interests to which corporate management should respond and the goals toward which they should strive is yet to begin, if it is to come at all.

Chapter 5. The Corporation: How Much Power? What Scope?

1. The sources for the figures quoted are listed in order below.

Total business population: 1956, 4.3 million; 1954, 4.2 million, whence my current estimate. See U. S. Department of Commerce, Bureau of the Census, *Statistical Abstract of the United States 1957* (Washington, D. C., 1957), p. 482.

Corporate share and size distribution: U. S. Department of Commerce, Office of Business Economics, *Survey of Current Business* (April 1955); figures refer to January 1, 1952, for share, and January 1, 1947, for size distribution. If anything, the figures understate the numerical preponderance of small unincorporated enterprises today.

The census figures refer to 1954. See U. S. Department of Commerce, Bureau of the Census, *Company Statistics 1954*, Bulletin CS-1 (Washington, D. C., 1958).

Asset holding of large corporations: U. S. Treasury, Internal Revenue Service, *Statistics of Income, Part 2 1955* (Washington, D. C., 1958), Table 5, pp. 41ff.

Research and Development Expenditures: U. S. National Science Foundation, *Science and Engineering in American Industry* (Washington, D. C., 1956).

Defense Contracts: "100 Companies and Affiliates Listed According to Net Value of Military Prime Contract Awards, July 1950–June 1956." Department of Defense, Office of Assistant Secretary of Defense (Supply and Logistics), mimeo release dated 10 April 1957.

For a fuller but slightly dated discussion, see M. A. Adelman, "The Measurement of Industrial Concentration," *The Review of Economics and Statistics*, 23: 269–296 (1951), reprinted in *Readings in Industrial Organization and Public Policy*, ed. R. B. Heflebower and G. W. Stocking (Homewood, Ill., 1958).

2. The figures on the relative importance of corporations come from R. A. Gordon, *Business Leadership in the Large Corporation* (Washington, D. C., 1946), p. 14, and Appendix A. These figures refer to 1939; no more recent ones are available and they almost certainly understate the relative importance of corporations. The shares of the sectors in national income are calculated from the figures for national income by industrial origin for 1956 given in *Statistical Abstract of the U. S. 1957*, p. 300. The shares of large corporations in asset holdings of all corporations are from the *Statistics of Income, Part 2, 1955*, table 5, pp. 41ff.

3. See Adelman, "The Measurement of Industrial Concentration," S. Friedland, "Turnover and Growth of the Largest Industrial Firms, 1906–1950," *Review of Economics and Statistics* (February, 1957), and J. F. Weston, *The Role of Mergers in the Growth of Large Firms* (Los Angeles, 1953).

4. These estimates are taken from Carl Kaysen and D. F. Turner, "Antitrust Policy, an Economic and Legal Analysis" (to be published by Harvard University Press, Cambridge, Mass.). See chap. ii and the appendices. The figures are based on data for 1954 for manufacturing, and on scattered years for other industries.

5. See Otto Eckstein, "Inflation, the Wage-Price Spiral, and Economic Growth," *The Relationship of Prices to Economic Stability and Growth*, papers submitted by panelists appearing before the Joint Economic Committee, 85 Cong., 2 Sess. (Washington, D. C., March 1958).

6. See R. Maclaurin, *Innovation and Invention in the Radio Industry* (New York, 1949); A. A. Bright, Jr., *The Electric Lamp Industry* (New York, 1949); C. Kaysen, *United States v. United Shoe Machinery Co.* (Cambridge, Mass., 1956); J. Jewkes *et al.*, *The Sources of Invention* (London, 1958).

7. See, on automobiles, the *Hearings* on Automobile Marketing Practices before the Interstate and Foreign Commerce Committee of the Senate, 84 Cong., 2 Sess. On aluminum, see the *Hearings* before Subcommittee No. 3 of the Select Committee on Small Business, House of Representatives, 84 Cong., 1 Sess. (1956) and the *Hearings* before the same Subcommittee, 85 Cong., 1 and 2 Sess. (1958).

8. See Kaysen and Turner, "Antitrust Policy."

9. A. A. Berle, Jr., *The Twentieth Century Capitalist Revolution* (New York, 1954); A. D. H. Kaplan, *Big Enterprise in a Competitive System* (Washington, D. C., 1954), and A. D. H. Kaplan, J. Dirlam, and R. Lanzilloti, *The Pricing Policy of Big Business* (Washington, D. C., 1958).

10. See E. S. Mason, "The Apologetics of Managerialism," *Journal of Business, University of Chicago*, 31: 1 (1958).

CHAPTER 16

Organizational Control Structure

ARNOLD S. TANNENBAUM and ROBERT L. KAHN

MUCH interest of late has been focused on the importance of the control function in organizations. Cartwright has pointed out that 'a major deficiency of our theories of group psychology and of social psychology generally is that we have been soft on power', and he has reviewed a number of studies that demonstrate the importance of this variable in interpersonal situations (1). Some effects of varying conditions of control within an organization have been discussed by Worthy, who points out that delegation of control to local autonomous groups within a large organization has a favorable effect on morale (8). A recent experiment performed by the Human Relations Program of the Survey Research Center has likewise demonstrated the effects of differing conditions of organizational control on the involvement and satisfaction of employees within a business organization.[2]

The results of these studies emphasize the importance of control as a social-psychological variable, especially for the understanding of organizations. There are a number of reasons for this importance. First of all, by definition, control is the capacity to manipulate available means for the satisfaction of needs (4). Control is basic to the distribution of rewards and punishments within the organization. What a person gets out of an organization depends in part on who controls the available stock of rewards within the organization, or, more generally, on who determines the way in which the organization shall operate. Control processes, of course, are an essential aspect of the functioning of an organization. They help circumscribe idiosyncratic individual actions and keep them conformant with the rational plan of the organization. Organizations require conformity and the integration of diverse processes. It is the function of control to see that organizational requirements are properly met, and the ultimate goals of the organization achieved.

Control has further social-psychological significance because of its association with types of political systems. Democracy is described as control by the citizens and their representatives. Dictatorship can be characterized as a highly centralized system of control, with ultimate power concentrated in one or a few persons. Oligarchy and *laissez-faire*, communism and fascism, refer to different systems of control, to the distribution of control among people in different social positions, and to the extent to which the behavior of an individual is subject to the control of others.

1. The authors would like to thank Angus Campbell, James K. Dent, Eugene Jacobson, and Daniel Katz for their helpful comments concerning this paper.
2. This work was begun under the general direction of Daniel Katz, and was directed by Nancy C. Morse and Everett Reimer. The authors would like to acknowledge this study in particular for laying the ground-work for many of the ideas discussed in the present article. For a brief relevant description of this project see N. C. Morse, E. Reimer, and A. S. Tannenbaum (5).

Control, as a social-psychological variable, is important for another reason. Psychological predispositions to types of control systems are developed early in life. The infant's behavior is controlled by persons upon whom he is extremely dependent, and the process of socialization involves the imposition of controls by parents, teachers, and other 'authority figures'. In this growing-up process, a pattern of responses to control is developed. Control takes on an emotional meaning.

Control, then, is important as a variable because it relates to the satisfaction of important human needs, because it has broad social and political implications, and because it has acquired an emotional meaning for people. A very general notion upon which this investigation is based states that differences in control systems within organizations will make for numerous and widespread differences in the functioning of those organizations.

It is our objective in this paper to illustrate a descriptive technique for the study of organizational control structure. Although this method is largely in an exploratory stage, it nevertheless helps clarify certain aspects of control in organizations. It appears further to suggest new dimensions of importance.

The data represented below are taken from a study of membership participation in four local unions. The unions chosen for study are of the industrial type, are within a size range of 300–850 members, and are located in Michigan. They were chosen to differ in their level of membership participation as measured by attendance at meetings (regular and special), member activities at these meetings (such as raising and seconding motions, asking questions, etc.), involvement in committee work, and voting in union elections. The locals are assigned fictitious names, and are called, in the order of their level of membership participation: National, Sergeant, Ensign, and Walker.[3]

We shall be interested below in exploring the control characteristics of these locals as they relate to participation, and shall discuss tentatively the relationships among aspects of control, ideology, and uniformity behavior in unions.

THE CONTROL GRAPH

We have chosen to represent the control structure of our locals in terms of a general schema that we have called the 'control graph'. The horizontal axis of this graph represents a scale of hierarchical levels in an organization. In many local unions this scale would run from the rank-and-file members at the low end through various office levels to the president at the high end. (In a business organization, it might include the employees at one end; various supervisory groups at intermediate levels; and the board of directors, or president of the board, at the other end.)

The vertical axis of the control graph represents the amount of control instituted by these various hierarchical levels. This may vary from none to a very great deal of control. Thus, 'having a great deal of control' means that persons at the hierarchical level under consideration determine in large degree the specific actions and policies of the organization. 'Having no control' on this dimension means that *all* persons

---

3. Participation in the four locals was measured by means of a written questionnaire administered to a random sample of about 150 members in each local. The rank order of locals obtained in this way corresponds to independent judgment made by international officers.

at a given level have no 'say' or influence in determining the policies and actions of the organization.

We can now create a curve by plotting and connecting the points that show the amount of control characteristic of each hierarchical level. One can conceive of such control curves assuming various shapes and levels. For example, one curve may have a negative slope, indicating that the amount of control instituted at successive levels increases as one goes up the hierarchy. Such a curve might be a relatively straight line, indicating regular increases in control from one level to the next (*Figure 1*), or it might have a positive or negative acceleration. In some organizations, there may be very little increase in the degree to which the various levels institute control until the top of the organization is reached; there a great increase takes place. This type of organization is controlled by only a few individuals (*Figure 2*). It is conceivable too, for the curve to decline as one moves up the hierarchy. An organization in which the leader has little power relative to the body politic would yield such a picture (*Figure 3*). A curve of this kind does not necessarily identify a figurehead or ineffective leader. This shape of curve applies also to an organization where individuals at the lower levels *as a group* have more control than the individuals at the uppermost level, even though these may be active and effective leaders.

Some organizations may be characterized by a relatively flat curve. Such a curve may be *low* and flat, indicating a very low degree of control throughout the organization. A *laissez-faire* or anarchic situation, for example, would be described in these terms (dotted line in *Figure 4*). On the other hand, a flat curve might be high on the vertical axis, indicating that people at all levels in the organization have a great deal of influence (solid line in *Figure 4*). The difference between these two flat curves, one low and one high, illustrates a general postulate concerning control curves, that the shape of the curve may remain constant while the general height of the curve varies. In other words, the *relative* power of different hierarchical levels might be the same in two organizations that nevertheless differed greatly in the absolute amounts of control exercised. Important differences in organizational functioning would be expected to accompany such variations in the general height of the control curve, despite the fact that the shape of the curves remained the same.

Control curves give us, by implication, a good deal of information about an organization. It can be seen from the preceding diagrams that the height and shape of the control curves tell us something about how control is distributed in an organization and also something about the *total amount of control* that is instituted in that organization. This latter dimension, total control, is indicated by the general height of the control curve, or more properly by the area under the curve. It is to a large degree independent of the shape of the curve. Total control may vary while the general shape of the curve remains the same. On the other hand, the general shape of the curve may vary while total control remains constant.

Data on total control, together with information on the distribution of control within the organization, should provide an effective method of describing important aspects of the control structure in an organization. For example, a high flat curve suggests that many persons in the organization have a lot of 'say' on many issues. A low flat curve indicates that no one has much to say about any issue. In the former we have the picture of an active, relatively strong organization eliciting the involvement and participation of a large segment of its members. The latter implies

Figures 1–4
The Control Graph—Types of Control Curve

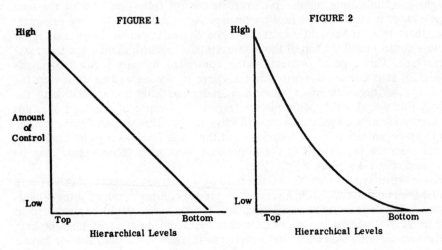

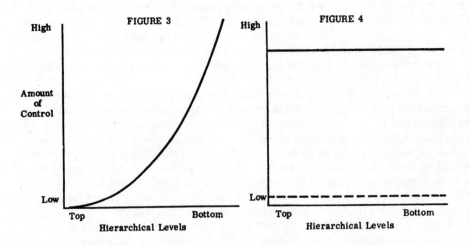

a relatively weak, inactive, *laissez-faire* organization. In the extreme case there is question as to whether or not the agglomeration of persons involved in such a situation can be called an organization at all.

In order to derive control curves for the locals studied in the present research, the amount of control instituted by individuals at varying levels in the union hierarchy was ascertained. The hierarchical levels include the membership at the low end, the president at the high end, and the executive board and bargaining committee somewhere between.[4] We have operationalized control at these various levels by asking judgments of our sample of respondents. This means, of course, that we are measuring control in terms of member-perceptions rather than by more objective means. We are making the assumption that an accurate picture of control in these locals can be derived as an average of *all* the members' judgments. The validity of this assumption remains to be tested fully, but in the present instance it received some confirmation from the observations of the authors and the judgments of international officers. The four questions employed in this connection are:

1. 'In general, how much do you think the president has to say about how things are decided in this local?'
2. 'In general, how much do you think the executive board has to say about how things are decided in this local?'
3. 'In general, how much do you think the plant bargaining committee has to say about how things are decided in this local?'
4. 'In general, how much do you think the membership has to say about how things are decided in this local?'

Each of these questions was answered by checks on a five-point scale ranging from 'a great deal of say' to 'no say at all'. *Figure 5* represents the control curves for the four locals based on the data from the above questions.

A number of comparisons are possible from these curves (p. 132).

1. within-local differences in the extent to which various hierarchical levels exercise control,
2. between-local differences in the extent to which any given hierarchical level exercises control,
3. between-local differences in the general shape of the curves,
4. between-local differences in total control—the general height of the curves.[5]

In the following discussion, it will not be possible to explore in detail each of these potential lines of analysis. We will attempt, however, to include in our observations points illustrative of all four types of comparison.

An examination of the curves tells us immediately that within each local the several hierarchical levels appear to institute different amounts of control, although the differences are more marked in some locals than in others. In order to evaluate more precisely which of these visible differences represents significant increments of control, statistical tests were performed on the differences between the amount of

---

4. It is obvious that we are not dealing with equal scale units along the abscissa, and that the ordering of executive board and bargaining committee is somewhat arbitrary. While it is clear that these groups fall between the president and the membership, their relative positions are uncertain.

5. This is operationalized in the present study simply by adding the amount of control for all of the groups—the membership, executive board, etc.—in each local.

FIGURE 5

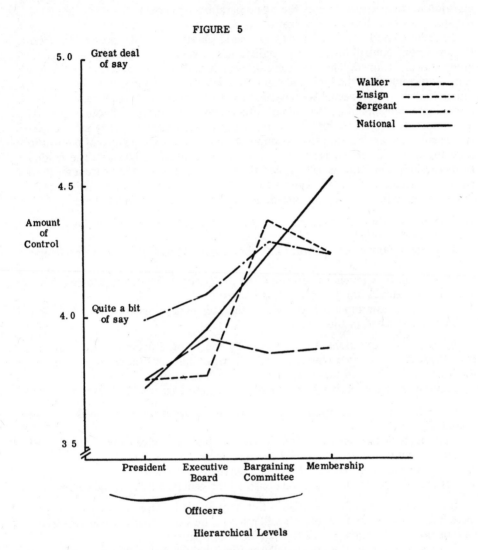

CONTROL CURVES OF FOUR UNION LOCALS BASED ON MEAN SCORES
OF RATINGS ON HOW MUCH SAY VARIOUS PERSONS AND GROUPS HAVE
IN HOW THINGS ARE DECIDED IN THE LOCAL *

* The means are based on N's of about 150 in each local.

control exercised by the membership of a local and the amount exercised by each of the officer levels—president, executive board, and bargaining committee. In National, the membership as a whole has a significantly greater amount of control than either the bargaining committee, executive board, or the president.[6] In Ensign, the membership as a whole is significantly higher than the executive board and the president, but does not differ significantly from the bargaining committee. In Walker, the membership does not differ significantly from any other group, but a suggestive difference exists between the membership as a whole and the president. In Sergeant, the membership is significantly higher than the president, but it does not differ from the other groups in the local.

An examination of the curves for between-local differences in the amount of control exercised by a given hierarchical level calls attention to some differences that offer corroboration of information obtained earlier by observation and from the comments of international officers. For example, the sharpest contrast between locals is that between the amount of control exercised by the membership in National, the local highest in member-participation, and that exercised in Walker, the local lowest in participation. National had been cited by international officers as a local in which the membership was especially active in decision-making.

A similar comparison can be made in terms of the amount of control exercised by local presidents. Sergeant stands out among the four locals as having the most influential president. This is substantiated by direct observation of this officer, by the reference of the international officers to his 'tight political machine', and by his election to seven successive terms of office. At the time of this measurement no other local president had served more than a year.

Comparisons in the shape and height of the four curves can be discussed simultaneously to some advantage. The curves for Walker and Sergeant are both relatively flat, but the amount of *total control* in these two locals differs sharply. Sergeant is high in total control, while Walker is relatively low. National stands out as having a relatively steep curve. It is the only local where no other group ranks above the membership in amount of control. In Ensign and Sergeant the bargaining committee ranks first and in Walker the executive board ranks first, although these within-local differences are not significant. While a definitive characterization of the four locals should not be attempted on the basis of these data alone, National appears to conform most closely to the 'democratic' model, while Walker more closely approximates the *laissez-faire* model. Sergeant's high total control with lower membership control suggests a kind of oligarchy or 'élite' government, while Ensign appears to conform least to previously discussed prototypes.[7]

Although the membership as a whole ranks high on the control curves, this does not imply that each member individually has more influence than each officer individually. The average member, though part of a group having a great deal of influence in the local, is very markedly less influential than the president, for example. The power of the membership is distributed among a large number of people; that of the president is in the possession of one person. Moreover, although

6. The t-test for paired differences was employed here. The 5 per cent level of confidence is accepted as a criterion of significance. Differences at between the 5 and 10 per cent levels are referred to as suggestive.

7. It should be remembered that these classifications are inferred *from* the curves and are not the basis *for* the curves. The essential element in our discussion is the curve itself and not the types associated with it.

in one local the membership is the single most powerful group and in the other three the second most powerful group, the membership cannot be considered (except perhaps in National) to be more influential than the other groups *combined*. The above data seem to suggest that, while the membership does have very high influence in each of these locals, the officers (including the president, executive board, and bargaining committee) *as a group* might have more. Their influence would be dominant if the officers were to act in a concerted manner, as a single tight-knit group.

THE APPLICATION OF CONTROL CURVES

Many questions and hypotheses relating control to other functions in organizations have been proposed in the literature. For example, how does control relate to conformity behavior, to participation, to leadership characteristics, to the ideology or philosophy of an organization? What effects do such variables have on the control structure of an organization, and in what ways are they affected by that structure? The limited sample of four locals of course precludes any definitive answer to such questions; however, by way of illustrating the application of control graphs, a number of tentative conclusions are suggested.[8]

The control graphs suggest that some current hypotheses about organizations might be sharpened if they were stated in terms of specific dimensions of control (such as its hierarchical distribution or the total amount of control instituted by all hierarchical levels), rather than in more global terms. For example, let us take a question around which conflicting hypotheses have been generated: what are the implications of inter-organizational conflict on control processes within the opposing organizations? One school of thought maintains that 'Continued . . . antagonism between corporations and unions prevents the latter from sinking into bureaucratic sloth. Merely to survive, the union must remain vital, democratic and militant' (2). On the other hand, we have the widely held belief that conflict between organizations may lead to the tightening of control by the leadership.

The data of the present study suggest that conflict between organizations is related to the total amount of control exercised in these organizations, but not necessarily to the hierarchical distribution of that control (see *Table 1*, p. 135). The rank order of the four locals with respect to amount of conflict with management is identical with their rank order on total control, but apparently unrelated to the slope of the control curve (i.e. distribution of control).[9]

On the basis of these data, we might hypothesize that the most immediate effect of conflict with management is to increase the amount of control within the local. The rationale for this hypothesis might be developed along these lines: conflict does not necessarily imply *who* should exercise control, but merely that control should be exercised. Conflict increases the organizational problems implicit in idiosyncratic behavior. This may serve as an incentive for concentrating control in the hands of a few *or* for increasing the total amount of control in the organization in other ways. The important thing is that the organization be more tightly and 'efficiently'

---

8. A. Tannenbaum discusses more thoroughly the rationale and implications of the relationships sketched in this section in (7). See also a forthcoming book by the authors.

9. The ordering of locals with respect to union-management conflict was done *a priori*, on the basis of information obtained from company and union officers.

controlled. During conflict (or certain other crises), there may be a greater sensitization to and acceptance of control *throughout* the organization, not merely at the lowermost levels. We are therefore led to the hypothesis that inter-organizational strife will create an increase in *total control*—but not necessarily exerted at the top of the organization. The distribution of this control in time of crisis is determined by other factors, as it is in more restful periods.

What factors do determine the distribution of control? One general view states that the specific external functions that the union performs have an important effect on how control is structured within the union. For example, Hoxie argues that 'business unions', which strive exclusively toward the achievement of such specific 'bread-and-butter' goals as higher wages, shorter hours, and pensions, tend to emphasize internal discipline and autocratic control (3). Howe and Widick make the complementary suggestion that unions that are interested in broader social functions and problems (political action, the general welfare of the community, organizing the unorganized) tend to be democratically controlled (2).

In the present study, members were questioned directly regarding their level of interest in eight different issues, each of which had been judged by the authors to represent either 'broad' or 'bread-and-butter' goals. Member-responses were combined to form indices of interest level in each type of goal. Evidence from these data, summarized in *Table 1*, lends some support to the hypothesis that an interest in broad and general goals for the union may be correlated with the observance of democratic procedures (positive sloped curve). However, interest on the part of the union in bread-and-butter issues does not appear to be correlated, positively or negatively, with democratic procedures. This no doubt reflects the fact that a union may have an interest in *both* types of goal; an interest in broad issues does not imply lack of interest in bread-and-butter problems.

A final example of the application of control curves can be given brief mention here, with a summary of the relevant data in *Table 1*. This involves the phenomenon of conformity or uniformity of attitudes and behaviors in unions. Uniformity was measured in this study in terms of the inverse of the variance on a number of items chosen *a priori* to reflect union norms. These items include perceived norms about voting, attending meetings, and helping out on strikes; the frequency of sanctions against members for failure to perform the above functions; the intensity of member-involvement in the union, and the alacrity with which members utilize union channels for the expression of grievances. Uniformity, like inter-organizational conflict, appears to be associated with total amount of control, rather than with

TABLE 1   RANK ORDER OF LOCALS ON CERTAIN ASPECTS OF THEIR CONTROL STRUCTURE AND OTHER VARIABLES

Local	Degree of positive slope of control curve	Subscription of members to broad goals	Total amount of control	Uniformity behavior	Extent of union-management conflict	Subscription of members to bread-and-butter goals
National	1	1	2	2	2	2·5
Ensign	2	3	3	3	3	4
Sergeant	3	2	1	1	1	1
Walker	4	4	4	4	4	2·5

the distribution of control within the local. Thus, in the present sample, greatest uniformity is found in Sergeant, which ranks first in total control; there is least uniformity in Walker, which ranks last.

FURTHER IMPLICATIONS AND QUESTIONS

The above discussion is intended to illustrate briefly the application of control curves to testing relationships between aspects of control and other organizational factors. Some further implications and questions relating to the use of these curves are summarized below.

1. The curves characterize in terms of two continuous variables a number of organizational types that have hitherto been treated as important but discrete. Such concepts as democracy, autocracy, and *laissez-faire* as distinct types or classes of control structure are brought into a single schema. We are thus provided with a unitary way of looking at these types, and at the same time working with the many variations between these extremes. A democratic control structure in unions might be diagrammed as a control curve having particular shape. This curve would be high for the rank-and-file and relatively low for persons in the upper hierarchy. The autocratic model, on the other hand, might present a somewhat different picture. This curve would be low for the rank-and-file and relatively high for those at the top of the hierarchy. *Laissez-faire* involves still another picture—one that is low for all levels of the hierarchy; no one has any appreciable control over the organization. The converse of *laissez-faire* would be described by means of a curve high at all points along the hierarchy. This would be a highly regulated type of organization, perhaps characterized by a large amount of internal political activity and clique-formation. Although such a control pattern would seem to be as interesting and important in its implications as *laissez-faire*, it has been neglected in social studies. Needless to say, the infinite variations between these extremes are also of interest; it seems likely that a full understanding of control in organizations will come, not alone through studies of democracy, autocracy, and *laissez-faire* as pure types, but through studies that examine the full range of control patterns in organizations.

2. The control curves of course emphasize the importance of control in organizations, and provide a means of taking a more holistic view of it. Studies of leadership, influence, and power in organizations can be made within such a framework. Leadership, for example, is not simply the influence of one isolated person by another, but a process in which the persons involved are placed at various points on the organizational control curve. It can be expected that such leadership processes and behaviors will be affected by the positions of the actors on this curve, and also by the general shape of the curve itself. Some research data already available point in this general direction. For example, Pelz finds that a leader is effective with his subordinates to the extent that the leader himself has influence in the organizational hierarchy (6).

Questions in this area that deserve further investigation include the following: What effect does varying the relative power positions of leaders and followers have on leadership processes? What implications do varying shapes of control curves have on leader-follower behavior? Is there an optimum curve for achieving maximum leadership effectiveness, and for other criteria of organizational functioning?

Is the supervisor in an organization high in total control confronted by a set of role requirements different from those of the supervisor in an organization that is relatively low in total control?

3. The control curve presents a picture of the control distribution in an organization. Organizational control, however, is a more fluid and dynamic process than is suggested by the control curves, which reflect the situation at a given point in time. The question of alignments and coalitions is one that should be considered. For example, one group may be lower than another in the amount of control it can institute in the organization, but it might add to its effective control by aligning with a third group. Groups might do this on a temporary basis relative to a specific issue, or they might form a more permanent faction or clique. If some rough assumptions about the additive properties of control can be tentatively accepted, certain judgments about the effects of various types of alignments might be made. For example, in an organization with an extremely steep curve, one group may be so powerful that no combination of opposing groups can overpower it. In an organization with a relatively flat curve the balance of power may be so delicate that any shift in the alignment of sub-groups may change radically the control situation. Such an approach leads into the intricate question of political processes in organizations, and suggests that an investigation of such processes could be carried out with the use of control curves.

4. One might speculate about the psychology of control in connection with these curves. One analysis of interest would entail plotting the control curves for all the organizations to which a given individual belongs: his work, his social groups, his family, etc. From this we can derive a control profile for the individual. These profiles can be expected to vary considerably from person to person, with some rather extreme types being manifest. One, for example, would be the individual who has relatively little control in any of the organizations to which he belongs. Another, and perhaps more rare type, is the individual who has relatively high control in all of the organizations to which he belongs. Still others will have differing degrees of control in the various types of organizations and groups to which they belong. An analysis of the psychological correlates of such differing patterns of control for individuals should be extremely rewarding. Their entire psychology, their way of looking at life, their general attitudes, their aspirations and levels of satisfaction would be expected to differ markedly.[10]

5. There are, of course, many questions with regard to the use of the control curves as an analytical technique. These refer to methodological as well as theoretical difficulties:

(a) The units of measurement are problematical. Scaling of equal units along both the abscissa and ordinate would be ideal. This has not as yet been done, and is complicated by the fact that organizational hierarchies do not conform to simple statistical assumptions.

(b) The relationship between the actual control structure of an organization and the structure as perceived by its members and leaders requires further exploration. An accurate measure of the actual control structure is by far the more difficult to

---

10. The data of the present research suggest the hypothesis that active union members differ from inactive members on this control profile; actives tending more in the direction of greater control in the organizations to which they belong, while inactives tend in the direction of lower control.

obtain. Although we have assumed that the measures employed in the present study accurately reflect the control picture as it actually exists, we recognize the need to test this assumption.

(c) There are aspects of control in organizations that appear to have broad implications, but are not fully reflected in the control graphs as they are presently drawn. The graphs do not give information about the mechanisms by which control is exercised, although these may modify greatly the effects of a given level or amount of control. For example, control may be exercised through the dispensation of rewards, the institution of sanctions, or through combinations of these. In organizations and political systems, control may be exercised directly, or indirectly through the employment of agents or representatives. While the graphs are designed to describe the *amount* of control that individuals at various hierarchical levels exercise, they do not describe the means through which this control is exercised.

(d) These curves may be better diagrammed in terms of specific areas of control rather than in terms of general (global) control in the organization. If specific areas are used, a satisfactory way of integrating these to provide an overall picture must be developed.

(e) The curves discussed above are based on what we have called *active* control. The actor is doing the controlling. Curves can also be drawn in terms of *passive* control. In these cases the actor is *being* controlled. The relationship between these two types of control needs further investigation. It would be informative in examining the control structure of an organization to consider simultaneously the passive control curve (the extent to which persons at various levels in the hierarchy *are controlled*) and the active control curve (the extent to which they *are doing the controlling*). An infinite number of variations are possible but a number of prototypes might be chosen for special study. For example, is the autocratic model one where *active* control is great at the top of an organization and small at the lower levels, and where the slope of the passive control curve presents the reverse picture?

Does the democratic model imply a reversal of the above curves? Is 'responsible leadership' distinguished from 'autocratic leadership' by the fact that the former has *both* high active and passive control? Is the 'responsible' leader, in other words, controlled as well as controlling? The president of a republic, for example, has considerable power (active control) but in turn he is also subject to many constraints (passive control). The leader in a dictatorship, on the other hand, may have a great deal of power, but relatively few constraints. The implications of the various shapes of active and passive control curves and the combinations of such' curves deserve further investigation.

(f) A type of hypothetical curve might be plotted describing the amount of control and the distribution of control that is *desired* by the membership. This may or may not correspond to the *actual* control structure. If these two curves, actual and desired, were superimposed, the discrepancies between them (perhaps best thought of in terms of the area between them) would be expected to have an important bearing on membership participation, involvement, and loyalty to the organization. In an organization where the actual control curve differs sharply from the desired curve, the area between these curves is great, and we would predict a corresponding degree of dissatisfaction, frustration, and disaffection among the members. Contrast this with a second hypothetical organization having the same actual control structure but in which the desired control curve corresponds more closely to the actual curve. We would predict for this organization a greater degree of membership satisfaction and loyalty.

We have only begun to think about this problem, but past psychological research suggests the importance of discrepancies between what individuals want and what they get. Although the actual distribution of control appears to have direct implications for the satisfaction of members, the *difference* between the actual and desired curves may make an additional contribution to our understanding of the implications of control.

While the control graph is primarily descriptive, it has both conceptual and operational advantages. It helps one think about the process of control and it offers specific operational indices for characterizing and measuring aspects of control in organizations. It opens up to the process of scientific testing a number of hypotheses that have been discussed primarily in speculative terms.

REFERENCES

1. CARTWRIGHT, DORWIN. 'Toward a Social Psychology of Groups.' Presidential address delivered before the Society for the Psychological Study of Social Issues, Cleveland, Ohio, 5 September 1953.
2. HOWE, IRVING, and WIDICK, B. J. *The UAW and Walter Reuther*. New York: Random House, 1949.
3. HOXIE, R. F. *Trade Unionism in the United States*. (2nd ed.) New York: Appleton, 1923.
4. KNICKERBOCKER, I. 'Leadership: a Conception and Some Implications.' *J. soc. Issues*, Vol. IV, pp. 23–40, Summer 1948.
5. MORSE, N. C., REIMER, E., and TANNENBAUM, A. S. 'Regulation and Control in Hierarchical Organizations.' *J. soc. Issues*, Vol. VII, No. 3, pp. 41–8, 1951.
6. PELZ, DONALD C. 'Leadership within a Hierarchical Organization.' *J. soc. Issues*, Vol. VII, No. 3, pp. 49–55, 1951.
7. TANNENBAUM, A. S. 'Control Structure and Union Functions.' *Amer. J. Sociol.*, Vol. LXI, No. 6, pp. 536–45, May 1956.
8. WORTHY, JAMES C. 'Factors Influencing Employee Morale.' *Harv. Busin. Rev.*, Vol. XXVIII, pp. 61–73, January 1950.

V

The Formation of Elites

As the readings in previous sections have indicated, there is no single basis of social stratification in complex societies. Instead, there are several forms of inequality, each associated with different institutional complexes within the society. For example, there is the well known stratification of universities in the United States. A mere handful of the several thousand institutions of higher learning can be singled out as particularly prominent and prestigious. The list of such elite institutions would include a few old, largely secularized private institutions, such as Harvard, Princeton and the University of Chicago, and the largest and best financed public institutions, such as the Universities of California (Berkeley), Michigan (Ann Arbor), and Wisconsin (Madison). At least in the recent past, such a list (about which agreement could be obtained from scholars in diverse fields) would have been notable for its exclusion of any institution located in the South and of any parochial institution maintaining strong religious connections to any faith, but especially the Catholic (see Berelson, 1960; Cartter, 1966). These prominent institutions are seen as the seats of higher learning in America; their reputation and position are justified by their standards of academic excellence. The men who staff them and the men and women they teach are thought of as the educational elite in the United States, an elite which can, of course, be subdivided into a variety of professional elites dominating their respective fields. There is another hierarchy of colleges ranged in terms of excellence in undergraduate education and the post-baccalaureate careers of their alumni (see Knapp and Greenbaum, 1953). The fact that such a list would only partially overlap with the list of elite universities serves to emphasize the fact that there is no single basis of inequality even within an institutional complex.

The case of educational elites is illustrative of the stratification that can be found in most areas of institutional life; each institutional complex is dominated by its own particular elite. The criteria of elite membership may, of course, vary from one complex to another. In education, a combination of past and current performance contributes to the relative standing of both individuals and the institutions they represent. In business, corporate size and, probably, growth as well as product type and quality are central to the stratification of firms, while the esteem in which particular men are held probably rests on criteria such as educational background (i.e., the prestige of schools they attended) as well as on criteria relevant to performance rec-

249

ord. In general, however, there is a constraint to stratify the key positions (and the men holding them) within an institutional complex by means of the same criteria as the various specific institutions forming the complex are stratified. Thus, if the best company has the most sales, the best salesman makes the most sales; and if the best professor is the one whose scholarly productivity is of the highest quality (rather than, say, quantity), then the best university is the one whose faculty's aggregate production has the highest overall quality. What is problematic about elites and elite institutions is whether the institutions make the men or the men make the institutions (see Zuckerman, 1970).

Within each institutional sphere, elites are further divided by the nature of their institutional loyalties. The difference between the orientations of locals—whose orientation is circumscribed by their own particular town, company or institution—and *cosmopolitans*—whose orientation is more global in scope, and focuses upon a constituency which is not bounded by the doors of any particular organization—represents, in part, the resolution effected when conflicting demands are made upon limited resources of time and energy (see Gouldner, 1957-58).

Reference, once again, to the educational front suffices to illustrate the point. Inevitably, there is pressure within departments to devote considerable energy to the execution of administrative detail. Those committed to such tasks also accumulate a certain degree of informal power if for no reason other than that they know the administrative routines necessary for getting things done. Involvement in administration never ends and each detail completed is replaced by several more to be done. The horizons of involvement also widen, since there is a tendency to recruit those who have successfully fullfilled their departmental responsibilities into the higher administration and to the elected faculty posts. Unlike industrial products, time devoted to one activity cannot be rehabilitated and used again elsewhere. Administrative activity competes with scholarly responsibilities

for one's attention. Some choose to commit themselves to professional activities rather than to the management of any particular institution. Through the breadth of their own knowledge and their research contributions, they seek to gain professional recognition and prominence. Because professional activities are typically organized at the national or regional level, those with strong professional involvements develop less circumscribed and more cosmopolitan outlooks than those whose activities are restricted to the confines of local institutions.

Most students of elite formation and structure have been especially concerned with two issues. The first of these concerns the amount of specialization in elite structure, the extent to which different spheres of activity are dominated by different persons, and the degree in which eminence and control achieved in one sphere of activity carry over into other realms of social life (see Keller, 1963). The second concern presumes that elites are specialized and focuses upon the ways in which different elites are interlocked into a potentially cohesive and unified power and sociometric structure. The selections reprinted here deal mainly with the latter question and, indeed, come to quite different conclusions about the applicability of the ruling elite model to American Society either locally or nationally. The first issue is, however, addressed more directly in the selections by Baltzell and Schulze, which have been placed in the following section since, in examining the conditions under which social and managerial elites are also engaged in national and local politics, they are more directly concerned with modes of access to power.

REFERENCES

Aron, Raymond.
    1950 "Social structure and the ruling class."
          Parts I and II. British Journal of Sociology 1:1-17; 126-144.

Banfield, Edward C.
1961   Political influence. New York: Free
        Press.
Berelson, B.
1960   Graduate Education in the United
        States. New York: McGraw-Hill.
Bottomore, T. B.
1964   Elites and Society. New York: Basic
        Books.
Bradley, Donald S., and Mayer N. Zald.
1966   "From commercial elite to political ad-
        ministrator: The recruitment of the
        mayors of Chicago." American Journal
        of Sociology 71:153-167.
Cartter, Allan C.
1966   An Assessment of Quality in Graduate
        Education. Washington: American
        Council on Education.
Dahl, Robert.
1961   Who Governs? Democracy and Power
        in an American City. New Haven: Yale
        University Press.
Gouldner, Alvin W.
1957-   "Cosmopolitans and locals: Toward an
   58   analysis of latent social roles." Parts I
        and II. Administrative Science Quarter-
        ly 2:281-306; 444-480.
Hawley, Amos H.
1963   "Community power and urban renewal
        success." American Journal of Sociology
        68:422-431.
Hunter, Floyd.
1953   Community Power Structure. Chapel
        Hill: University of North Carolina Press.
Janowitz, Morris.
1961   The Professional Soldier: A Social and
        Political Portrait. Glencoe, Ill.: Free
        Press.
1964   The Military in the Political Develop-
        ment of New Nations: An Essay in
        Comparative Analysis. Chicago: Uni-
        versity of Chicago Press.

Keller, Suzanne
1963   Beyond the Ruling Class: Strategic Elites
        in Modern Society. New York: Random
        House.
Knapp, R. H. and J. H. Greenbaum.
1953   The Younger American Scholar: His
        Collegiate-Origins. Chicago: University
        of Chicago Press.
Kornhauser, William.
1959   Politics in Mass Society. New York:
        Free Press.
Polsby, Nelson W.
1959   "Three problems in the analysis of com-
        munity power." American Sociological
        Review 24:796-803.
1962   "Community power: Some reflections
        on the recent literature." American So-
        ciological Review 27:838-841.
Rosenberg, Hans.
1958   Bureaucracy, Aristocracy and Autoc-
        racy: The Prussian Experience 1600-
        1815. Cambridge: Harvard University
        Press.
Rossi, Peter H.
1957   "Community decision making." Admin-
        istrative Science Quarterly 1:415-443.
Thrupp, Sylvia L.
1948   The Merchant Class of Medieval Lon-
        don, 1300-1500. Chicago: University of
        Chicago Press.
Warner, W. Lloyd, and James C. Abegglen.
1955   Big Business Leaders in America. New
        York: Atheneum Books.
Zald, Mayer N.
1969   "The power and functioning of boards
        of directors: A theoretical synthesis."
        American Journal of Sociology 75:97-
        111.
Zuckerman, Harriet.
1970   "Stratification in American science." So-
        ciological Inquiry 40 (Spring).

CHAPTER 17

The Ruling Class

GAETANO MOSCA

1. Among the constant facts and tendencies that are to be found in all political organisms, one is so obvious that it is apparent to the most casual eye. In all societies—from societies that are very meagerly developed and have barely attained the dawnings of civilization, down to the most advanced and powerful societies—two classes of people appear—a class that rules and a class that is ruled. The first class, always the less numerous, performs all political functions, monopolizes power and enjoys the advantages that power brings, whereas the second, the more numerous class, is directed and controlled by the first, in a manner that is now more or less legal, now more or less arbitrary and violent, and supplies the first, in appearance at least, with material means of subsistence and with the instrumentalities that are essential to the vitality of the political organism.

In practical life we all recognize the existence of this ruling class (or political class, as we have elsewhere chosen to define it).[1] We all know that, in our own country, whichever it may be, the management of public affairs is in the hands of a minority of influential persons, to which management, willingly or unwillingly, the majority defer. We know that the same thing goes on in neighboring countries, and in fact we should be put to it to conceive of a real world otherwise organized—a world in which all men would be directly subject to a single person without relationships of superiority or subordination, or in which all men would share equally in the direction of political affairs. If we reason otherwise in theory, that is due partly to inveterate habits that we follow in our thinking and partly to the exaggerated importance that we attach to two political facts that loom far larger in appearance than they are in reality.

The first of these facts—and one has only to open one's eyes to see it—is that in every political organism there is one individual

---

[1] Mosca, *Teorica dei governi e governo parlamentare*, chap. I.

252

who is chief among the leaders of the ruling class as a whole and stands, as we say, at the helm of the state. That person is not always the person who holds supreme power according to law. At times, alongside of the hereditary king or emperor there is a prime minister or a major-domo who wields an actual power that is greater than the sovereign's. At other times, in place of the elected president the influential politician who has procured the president's election will govern. Under special circumstances there may be, instead of a single person, two or three who discharge the functions of supreme control.

The second fact, too, is readily discernible. Whatever the type of political organization, pressures arising from the discontent of the masses who are governed, from the passions by which they are swayed, exert a certain amount of influence on the policies of the ruling, the political, class.

But the man who is at the head of the state would certainly not be able to govern without the support of a numerous class to enforce respect for his orders and to have them carried out; and granting that he can make one individual, or indeed many individuals, in the ruling class feel the weight of his power, he certainly cannot be at odds with the class as a whole or do away with it. Even if that were possible, he would at once be forced to create another class, without the support of which action on his part would be completely paralyzed. On the other hand, granting that the discontent of the masses might succeed in deposing a ruling class, inevitably, as we shall later show, there would have to be another organized minority within the masses themselves to discharge the functions of a ruling class. Otherwise all organization, and the whole social structure, would be destroyed. .

2. From the point of view of scientific research the real superiority of the concept of the ruling, or political, class lies in the fact that the varying structure of ruling classes has a preponderant importance in determining the political type, and also the level of civilization, of the different peoples. According to a manner of classifying forms of government that is still in vogue, Turkey and Russia were both, up to a few years ago, absolute monarchies, England and Italy were constitutional, or limited, monarchies, and France and the United States were

classed as republics. The classification was based on the fact
that, in the first two countries mentioned, headship in the state
was hereditary and the chief was nominally omnipotent; in the
second two, his office is hereditary but his powers and prerogatives are limited; in the last two, he is elected.

That classification is obviously superficial. Absolutisms
though they were, there was little in common between the manners in which Russia and Turkey were managed politically, the
levels of civilization in the two countries and the organization of
their ruling classes being vastly different. On the same basis, the
regime in Italy, a monarchy, is much more similar to the regime
in France, a republic, than it is to the regime in England, also a
monarchy; and there are important differences between the
political organizations of the United States and France, though
both countries are republics.

As we have already suggested, ingrained habits of thinking
have long stood, as they still stand, in the way of scientific
progress in this matter. The classification mentioned above,
which divides governments into absolute monarchies, limited
monarchies and republics, was devised by Montesquieu and was
intended to replace the classical categories of Aristotle, who
divided governments into monarchies, aristocracies and democracies. What Aristotle called a democracy was simply an
aristocracy of fairly broad membership. Aristotle himself was
in a position to observe that in every Greek state, whether
aristocratic or democratic, there was always one person or more
who had a preponderant influence. Between the day of Polyb-
ius and the day of Montesquieu, many writers perfected Aristotle's classification by introducing into it the concept of "mixed"
governments. Later on the modern democratic theory, which
had its source in Rousseau, took its stand upon the concept that
the majority of the citizens in any state can participate, and in
fact *ought* to participate, in its political life, and the doctrine of
popular sovereignty still holds sway over many minds in spite
of the fact that modern scholarship is making it increasingly
clear that democratic, monarchical and aristocratic principles
function side by side in every political organism. We shall not
stop to refute this democratic theory here, since that is the task
of this work as a whole. Besides, it would be hard to destroy in
a few pages a whole system of ideas that has become firmly rooted

in the human mind.   As Las Casas aptly wrote in his life of
Christopher Columbus, it is often much harder to unlearn than
to learn.

3. We think it may be desirable, nevertheless, to reply at this
point to an objection which might very readily be made to our
point of view.   If it is easy to understand that a single individual
cannot command a group without finding within the group a
minority to support him, it is rather difficult to grant, as a constant and natural fact, that minorities rule majorities, rather
than majorities minorities.   But that is one of the points—so
numerous in all the other sciences—where the first impression
one has of things is contrary to what they are in reality.   In
reality the dominion of an organized minority, obeying a single
impulse, over the unorganized majority is inevitable.   The power
of any minority is irresistible as against each single individual in
the majority, who stands alone before the totality of the organized minority.   At the same time, the minority is organized for
the very reason that it is a minority.   A hundred men acting
uniformly in concert, with a common understanding, will triumph
over a thousand men who are not in accord and can therefore be
dealt with one by one.   Meanwhile it will be easier for the
former to act in concert and have a mutual understanding simply
because they are a hundred and not a thousand.   It follows that
the larger the political community, the smaller will the proportion
of the governing minority to the governed majority be, and the
more difficult will it be for the majority to organize for reaction
against the minority.
However, in addition to the great advantage accruing to them
from the fact of being organized, ruling minorities are usually so
constituted that the individuals who make them up are distinguished from the mass of the governed by qualities that give
them a certain material, intellectual or even moral superiority;
or else they are the heirs of individuals who possessed such
qualities.   In other words, members of a ruling minority regularly have some attribute, real or apparent, which is highly
esteemed and very influential in the society in which they live.

4. In primitive societies that are still in the early stages of
organization, military valor is the quality that most readily

opens access to the ruling, or political, class. In societies of advanced civilization, war is the exceptional condition. It may be regarded as virtually normal in societies that are in the initial stages of their development; and the individuals who show the greatest ability in war easily gain supremacy over their fellows— the bravest become chiefs. The fact is constant, but the forms it may assume, in one set of circumstances or another, vary considerably.

As a rule the dominance of a warrior class over a peaceful multitude is attributed to a superposition of races, to the conquest of a relatively unwarlike group by an aggressive one. Sometimes that is actually the case—we have examples in India after the Aryan invasions, in the Roman Empire after the Germanic invasions and in Mexico after the Aztec conquest. But more often, under certain social conditions, we note the rise of a warlike ruling class in places where there is absolutely no trace of a foreign conquest. As long as a horde lives exclusively by the chase, all individuals can easily become warriors. There will of course be leaders who will rule over the tribe, but we will not find a warrior class rising to exploit, and at the same time to protect, another class that is devoted to peaceful pursuits. As the tribe emerges from the hunting stage and enters the agricultural and pastoral stage, then, along with an enormous increase in population and a greater stability in the means of exerting social influence, a more or less clean-cut division into two classes will take place, one class being devoted exclusively to agriculture, the other class to war. In this event, it is inevitable that the warrior class should little by little acquire such ascendancy over the other as to be able to oppress it with impunity.

Poland offers a characteristic example of the gradual metamorphosis of a warrior class into an absolutely dominant class. Originally the Poles had the same organization by rural villages as prevailed among all the Slavic peoples. There was no distinction between fighters and farmers—in other words, between nobles and peasants. But after the Poles came to settle on the broad plains that are watered by the Vistula and the Niemen, agriculture began to develop among them. However, the necessity of fighting with warlike neighbors continued, so that the tribal chiefs, or voivodes, gathered about themselves a certain number of picked men whose special occupation was the bearing of arms. These warriors were distributed among the various rural communities. They were exempt from agricultural duties, yet they received their share of the produce of the soil, along with the other members of the community. In early days their position was not considered very desirable, and country dwellers sometimes waived exemption from agricultural labor in order to avoid going to war. But gradually as this order of things grew stabilized, as one class became habituated to the practice of arms and military organization while the other hardened to the use of the plow and the spade, the warriors became nobles and masters, and the peasants, once companions and brothers, became villeins and serfs. Little by little the warrior lords increased their demands to the point where the share they took as members of the community came to include the community's whole produce minus what was absolutely necessary for subsistence on the part of the cultivators; and when the latter tried to escape such abuses they were constrained by force to stay bound to the soil, their situation taking on all the characteristics of serfdom pure and simple.

In the course of this evolution, around the year 1333, King Casimir the Great tried vainly to curb the overbearing insolence of the warriors. When peasants came to complain of the nobles, he contented himself with asking whether they had no sticks and stones. Some generations later, in 1537, the nobility forced all tradesmen in the cities to sell such real estate as they owned, and landed property became a prerogative of nobles only. At the same time the nobility exerted pressure upon the king to open negotiations with Rome, to the end that thenceforward only nobles should be admitted to holy orders in Poland. That barred townsmen and peasants almost completely from honorific positions and stripped them of any social importance whatever.[1]

We find a parallel development in Russia. There the warriors who formed the druzhina, or escort, of the old knezes (princes descended from Rurik) also received a share in the produce of the mirs (rural peasant communities) for their livelihood. Little by little this share was increased. Since land abounded and workers were scarce, the peasants often had an eye to their advantage and moved about. At the end of the sixteenth century, accordingly,

[1] Mickiewicz, *Les Slaves*, vol. I, leçon XXIV, pp. 376–380; *Histoire populaire de Pologne*, chaps. I–II.

the czar Boris Godunov empowered the nobles to hold peasants
to their lands by force, so establishing serfdom.   However, armed
forces in Russia were never composed exclusively of nobles.
The muzhiks, or peasants, went to war as common soldiers under
the droujina.   As early as the sixteenth century, Ivan the Terrible established the order of strelitzes which amounted practically
to a standing army, and which lasted until Peter the Great
replaced it with regiments organized along western European
lines.   In those regiments members of the old druzhina, with an
intermixture of foreigners, became officers, while the muzhiks
provided the entire contingent of privates.[1]

Among peoples that have recently entered the agricultural
stage and are relatively civilized, it is the unvarying fact that
the strictly military class is the political, or ruling, class.   Sometimes the bearing of arms is reserved exclusively to that class,
as happened in India and Poland.   More often the members of
the governed class are on occasion enrolled—always, however,
as common soldiers and in the less respected divisions.   So
in Greece, during the war with the Medes, the citizens belonging
to the richer and more influential classes formed the picked corps
(the cavalry and the hoplites), the less wealthy fought as peltasts
or as slingers, while the slaves, that is the laboring masses,
were almost entirely barred from military service.   We find
analogous arrangements in republican Rome, down to the period
of the Punic Wars and even as late as the day of Marius; in
Latin and Germanic Europe during the Middle Ages; in Russia,
as just explained, and among many other peoples.   Caesar notes
repeatedly that in his time the backbone of the Gallic armies was
formed by cavalrymen recruited from the nobility.   The Aedui,
for example, could not hold out against Ariovistus after the
flower of their cavalry had been killed in battle.

5. Everywhere—in Russia and Poland, in India and medieval
Europe—the ruling warrior classes acquire almost exclusive
ownership of the land.   Land, as we have seen, is the chief source
of production and wealth in countries that are not very far
advanced in civilization.   But as civilization progresses, revenue
from land increases proportionately.   With the growth of
population there is, at least in certain periods, an increase in

[1] Leroy-Beaulieu, *L'Empire des tzars et les Russes*, vol. I, pp. 338 f.

rent, in the Ricardian sense of the term, largely because great centers of consumption arise—such at all times have been the great capitals and other large cities, ancient and modern. Eventually, if other circumstances permit, a very important social transformation occurs. Wealth rather than military valor comes to be the characteristic feature of the dominant class: the people who rule are the rich rather than the brave.

The condition that in the main is required for this transformation is that social organization shall have concentrated and become perfected to such an extent that the protection offered by public authority is considerably more effective than the protection offered by private force. In other words, private property must be so well protected by the practical and real efficacy of the laws as to render the power of the proprietor himself superfluous. This comes about through a series of gradual alterations in the social structure whereby a type of political organization, which we shall call the "feudal state," is transformed into an essentially different type, which we shall term the "bureaucratic state." We are to discuss these types at some length hereafter, but we may say at once that the evolution here referred to is as a rule greatly facilitated by progress in pacific manners and customs and by certain moral habits which societies contract as civilization advances.

Once this transformation has taken place, wealth produces political power just as political power has been producing wealth. In a society already somewhat mature—where, therefore, individual power is curbed by the collective power—if the powerful are as a rule the rich, to be rich is to become powerful. And, in truth, when fighting with the mailed fist is prohibited whereas fighting with pounds and pence is sanctioned, the better posts are inevitably won by those who are better supplied with pounds and pence.

There are, to be sure, states of a very high level of civilization which in theory are organized on the basis of moral principles of such a character that they seem to preclude this overbearing assertiveness on the part of wealth. But this is a case—and there are many such—where theoretical principles can have no more than a limited application in real life. In the United States all powers flow directly or indirectly from popular elections, and suffrage is equal for all men and women in all the states of the

Union. What is more, democracy prevails not only in institutions but to a certain extent also in morals. The rich ordinarily feel a certain aversion to entering public life, and the poor a certain aversion to choosing the rich for elective office. But that does not prevent a rich man from being more influential than a poor man, since he can use pressure upon the politicians who control public administration. It does not prevent elections from being carried on to the music of clinking dollars. It does not prevent whole legislatures and considerable numbers of national congressmen from feeling the influence of powerful corporations and great financiers.[1]

In China, too, down to a few years ago, though the government had not accepted the principle of popular elections, it was organized on an essentially equalitarian basis. Academic degrees gave access to public office, and degrees were conferred by examination without any apparent regard for family or wealth. According to some writers, only barbers and certain classes of boatmen, together with their children, were barred from competing for the various grades of the mandarinate.[2] But though the moneyed class in China was less numerous, less wealthy, less powerful than the moneyed class in the United States is at present, it was none the less able to modify the scrupulous application of this system to a very considerable extent. Not only was the indulgence of examiners often bought with money. The government itself sometimes sold the various academic degrees and allowed ignorant persons, often from the lowest social strata, to hold public office.[3]

In all countries of the world those other agencies for exerting social influence—personal publicity, good education, specialized training, high rank in church, public administration, and army— are always readier of access to the rich than to the poor. The rich invariably have a considerably shorter road to travel than the poor, to say nothing of the fact that the stretch of road that the rich are spared is often the roughest and most difficult.

---

[1] Jannet, *Le istituzioni politiche e sociali degli Stati Uniti d'America*, part II, chap. X f.

[2] Rousset, *À travers la Chine*.

[3] Mas y Sans, *La Chine et les puissances chrétiennes*, vol. II, pp. 332–334; Huc, *L'Empire chinois*.

6. In societies in which religious beliefs are strong and ministers of the faith form a special class a priestly aristocracy almost always arises and gains possession of a more or less important share of the wealth and the political power. Conspicuous examples of that situation would be ancient Egypt (during certain periods), Brahman India and medieval Europe. Oftentimes the priests not only perform religious functions. They possess legal and scientific knowledge and constitute the class of highest intellectual culture. Consciously or unconsciously, priestly hierarchies often show a tendency to monopolize learning and hamper the dissemination of the methods and procedures that make the acquisition of knowledge possible and easy. To that tendency may have been due, in part at least, the painfully slow diffusion of the demotic alphabet in ancient Egypt, though that alphabet was infinitely more simple than the hieroglyphic script. The Druids in Gaul were acquainted with the Greek alphabet but would not permit their rich store of sacred literature to be written down, requiring their pupils to commit it to memory at the cost of untold effort. To the same outlook may be attributed the stubborn and frequent use of dead languages that we find in ancient Chaldea, in India, and in medieval Europe. Sometimes, as was the case in India, lower classes have been explicitly forbidden to acquire knowledge of sacred books.

Specialized knowledge and really scientific culture, purged of any sacred or religious aura, become important political forces only in a highly advanced stage of civilization, and only then do they give access to membership in the ruling class to those who possess them. But in this case too, it is not so much learning in itself that has political value as the practical applications that may be made of learning to the profit of the public or the state. Sometimes all that is required is mere possession of the mechanical processes that are indispensable to the acquisition of a higher culture. This may be due to the fact that on such a basis it is easier to ascertain and measure the skill which a candidate has been able to acquire—it is easier to "mark" or grade him. So in certain periods in ancient Egypt the profession of scribe was a road to public office and power, perhaps because to have learned the hieroglyphic script was proof of long and patient study. In modern China, again, learning the numberless characters in

Chinese script has formed the basis of the mandarin's education.[1]
In present-day Europe and America the class that applies the
findings of modern science to war, public administration, public
works and public sanitation holds a fairly important position,
both socially and politically, and in our western world, as in
ancient Rome, an altogether privileged position is held by lawyers.
They know the complicated legislation that arises in all peoples
of long-standing civilization, and they become especially powerful
if their knowledge of law is coupled with the type of eloquence
that chances to have a strong appeal to the taste of their
contemporaries.

There are examples in abundance where we see that long-
standing practice in directing the military and civil organization
of a community creates and develops in the higher reaches of the
ruling class a real art of governing which is something better than
crude empiricism and better than anything that mere individual
experience could suggest.   In such circumstances aristocracies of
functionaries arise, such as the Roman senate, the Venetian
nobility and to a certain extent the English aristocracy.
Those bodies all stirred John Stuart Mill to admiration
and certainly they all three developed governments that were
distinguished for carefully considered policies and for great
steadfastness and sagacity in carrying them out. This art of
governing is not political science, though it has, at one time or
another, anticipated applications of a number of the postulates
of political science. However, even if the art of governing has
now and again enjoyed prestige with certain classes of persons
who have long held possession of political functions, knowledge
of it has never served as an ordinary criterion for admitting to
public offices persons who were barred from them by social station.
The degree of mastery of the art of governing that a person
possesses is, moreover, apart from exceptional cases, a very difficult thing to determine if the person has given no practical
demonstration that he possesses it.

7. In some countries we find hereditary castes. In such cases
the governing class is explicitly restricted to a given number of

[1] This was true up to a few years ago, the examination of a mandarin covering
only literary and historical studies—as the Chinese understood such studies, of
course.

families, and birth is the one criterion that determines entry into the class or exclusion from it. Examples are exceedingly common. There is practically no country of long-standing civilization that has not had a hereditary aristocracy at one period or another in its history. We find hereditary nobilities during certain periods in China and ancient Egypt, in India, in Greece before the wars with the Medes, in ancient Rome, among the Slavs, among the Latins and Germans of the Middle Ages, in Mexico at the time of the Discovery and in Japan down to a few years ago.

In this connection two preliminary observations are in point. In the first place, all ruling classes tend to become hereditary in fact if not in law. All political forces seem to possess a quality that in physics used to be called the force of inertia. They have a tendency, that is, to remain at the point and in the state in which they find themselves. Wealth and military valor are easily maintained in certain families by moral tradition and by heredity. Qualification for important office—the habit of, and to an extent the capacity for, dealing with affairs of consequence—is much more readily acquired when one has had a certain familiarity with them from childhood. Even when academic degrees, scientific training, special aptitudes as tested by examinations and competitions, open the way to public office, there is no eliminating that special advantage in favor of certain individuals which the French call the advantage of *positions déjà prises.* In actual fact, though examinations and competitions may theoretically be open to all, the majority never have the resources for meeting the expense of long preparation, and many others are without the connections and kinships that set an individual promptly on the right road, enabling him to avoid the gropings and blunders that are inevitable when one enters an unfamiliar environment without any guidance or support.

The democratic principle of election by broad-based suffrage would seem at first glance to be in conflict with the tendency toward stability which, according to our theory, ruling classes show. But it must be noted that candidates who are successful in democratic elections are almost always the ones who possess the political forces above enumerated, which are very often hereditary. In the English, French and Italian parliaments we frequently see the sons, grandsons, brothers, nephews and sons-in-law of members and deputies, ex-members and ex-deputies.

In the second place, when we see a hereditary caste established in a country and monopolizing political power, we may be sure that such a status de jure was preceded by a similar status de facto. Before proclaiming their exclusive and hereditary right to power the families or castes in question must have held the scepter of command in a firm grasp, completely monopolizing all the political forces of that country at that period. Otherwise such a claim on their part would only have aroused the bitterest protests and provoked the bitterest struggles.

Hereditary aristocracies often come to vaunt supernatural origins, or at least origins different from, and superior to, those of the governed classes. Such claims are explained by a highly significant social fact, namely that every governing class tends to justify its actual exercise of power by resting it on some universal moral principle. This same sort of claim has come forward in our time in scientific trappings. A number of writers, developing and amplifying Darwin's theories, contend that upper classes represent a higher level in social evolution and are therefore superior to lower classes by organic structure. Gumplowicz we have already quoted. That writer goes to the point of maintaining that the divisions of populations into trade groups and professional classes in modern civilized countries are based on ethnological heterogeneousness.[1]

Now history very definitely shows the special abilities as well as the special defects—both very marked—which have been displayed by aristocracies that have either remained absolutely closed or have made entry into their circles difficult. The ancient Roman patriciate and the English and German nobilities of modern times give a ready idea of the type we refer to. Yet in dealing with this fact, and with the theories that tend to exaggerate its significance, we can always raise the same objection—that the individuals who belong to the aristocracies in question owe their special qualities not so much to the blood that flows in their veins as to their very particular upbringing, which has brought out certain intellectual and moral tendencies in them in preference to others.

[1] *Der Rassenkampf.* This notion transpires from Gumplowicz's whole volume. It is explicitly formulated in book II, chap. XXXIII.

Among all the factors that figure in social superiority, intellectual superiority is the one with which heredity has least to do. The children of men of highest mentality often have very mediocre talents. That is why hereditary aristocracies have never defended their rule on the basis of intellectual superiority alone, but rather on the basis of their superiorities in character and wealth.

It is argued, in rebuttal, that education and environment may serve to explain superiorities in strictly intellectual capacities but not differences of a moral order—will power, courage, pride, energy. The truth is that social position, family tradition, the habits of the class in which we live, contribute more than is commonly supposed to the greater or lesser development of the qualities mentioned. If we carefully observe individuals who have changed their social status, whether for better or for worse, and who consequently find themselves in environments different from the ones they have been accustomed to, it is apparent that their intellectual capacities are much less sensibly affected than their moral ones. Apart from a greater breadth of view that education and experience bring to anyone who is not altogether stupid, every individual, whether he remains a mere clerk or becomes a minister of state, whether he reaches the rank of sergeant or the rank of general, whether he is a millionaire or a beggar, abides inevitably on the intellectual level on which nature has placed him. And yet with changes of social status and wealth the proud man often becomes humble, servility changes to arrogance, an honest nature learns to lie, or at least to dissemble, under pressure of need, while the man who has an ingrained habit of lying and bluffing makes himself over and puts on an outward semblance at least of honesty and firmness of character. It is true, of course, that a man fallen from high estate often acquires powers of resignation, self-denial and resourcefulness, just as one who rises in the world sometimes gains in sentiments of justice and fairness. In short, whether a man change for the better or for the worse, he has to be exceptionally level-headed if he is to change his social status very appreciably and still keep his character unaltered. Mirabeau remarked that, for any man, any great climb on the social ladder produces a crisis that cures the ills he has and creates new ones that he never had before.[1]

[1] *Correspondance entre le comte de Mirabeau et le comte de La Marck*, vol. II, p. 228.

Courage in battle, impetuousness in attack, endurance in resistance—such are the qualities that have long and often been vaunted as a monopoly of the higher classes. Certainly there may be vast natural and—if we may say so—innate differences between one individual and another in these respects; but more than anything else traditions and environmental influences are the things that keep them high, low or just average, in any large group of human beings. We generally become indifferent to danger or, perhaps better, to a given type of danger, when the persons with whom we daily live speak of it with indifference and remain cool and imperturbable before it. Many mountaineers or sailors are by nature timid men, yet they face unmoved, the ones the dangers of the precipice, the others the perils of the storm at sea. So peoples and classes that are accustomed to warfare maintain military virtues at the highest pitch.

So true is this that even peoples and social classes which are ordinarily unaccustomed to arms acquire the military virtues rapidly when the individuals who compose them are made members of organizations in which courage and daring are traditional, when—if one may venture the metaphor—they are cast into human crucibles that are heavily charged with the sentiments that are to be infused into their fiber. Mohammed II recruited his terrible Janizaries in the main from boys who had been kidnapped among the degenerate Greeks of Byzantium. The much despised Egyptian fellah, unused for long centuries to war and accustomed to remaining meek and helpless under the lash of the oppressor, became a good soldier when Mehemet Ali placed him in Turkish or Albanian regiments. The French nobility has always enjoyed a reputation for brilliant valor, but down to the end of the eighteenth century that quality was not credited in anything like the same degree to the French bourgeoisie. However, the wars of the Republic and the Empire amply proved that nature had been uniformly lavish in her endowments of courage upon all the inhabitants of France. Proletariat and bourgeoisie both furnished good soldiers and, what is more, excellent officers, though talent for command had been considered an exclusive prerogative of the nobility. Gumplowicz's theory that differentiation in social classes depends very largely on ethnological antecedents requires proof at the very least. Many facts to the contrary readily occur to one—

among others the obvious fact that branches of the same family often belong to widely different social classes.

8. Finally, if we were to keep to the idea of those who maintain the exclusive influence of the hereditary principle in the formation of ruling classes, we should be carried to a conclusion somewhat like the one to which we were carried by the evolutionary principle: The political history of mankind ought to be much simpler than it is. If the ruling class really belonged to a different race, or if the qualities that fit it for dominion were transmitted primarily by organic heredity, it is difficult to see how, once the class was formed, it could decline and lose its power. The peculiar qualities of a race are exceedingly tenacious. Keeping to the evolutionary theory, acquired capacities in the parents are inborn in their children and, as generation succeeds generation, are progressively accentuated. The descendants of rulers, therefore, ought to become better and better fitted to rule, and the other classes ought to see their chances of challenging or supplanting them become more and more remote. Now the most commonplace experience suffices to assure one that things do not go in that way at all.

What we see is that as soon as there is a shift in the balance of political forces—when, that is, a need is felt that capacities different from the old should assert themselves in the management of the state, when the old capacities, therefore, lose some of their importance or changes in their distribution occur—then the manner in which the ruling class is constituted changes also. If a new source of wealth develops in a society, if the practical importance of knowledge grows, if an old religion declines or a new one is born, if a new current of ideas spreads, then, simultaneously, far-reaching dislocations occur in the ruling class. One might say, indeed, that the whole history of civilized mankind comes down to a conflict between the tendency of dominant elements to monopolize political power and transmit possession of it by inheritance, and the tendency toward a dislocation of old forces and an insurgence of new forces; and this conflict produces an unending ferment of endosmosis and exosmosis between the upper classes and certain portions of the lower. Ruling classes decline inevitably when they cease to find scope for the capacities through which they rose to power, when they can no longer render the social services which they once rendered, or when their talents and the services they render lose in importance in the social environment in which they live. So the Roman aristocracy declined when it was no longer the exclusive source of higher officers for the army, of administrators for the commonwealth, of governors for the provinces. So the Venetian aristocracy declined when its nobles ceased to command the galleys and no longer passed the greater part of their lives in sailing the seas and in trading and fighting.

In inorganic nature we have the example of our air, in which a tendency to immobility produced by the force of inertia is continuously in conflict with a tendency to shift about as the result of inequalities in the distribution of heat. The two tendencies, prevailing by turn in various regions on our planet, produce now calm, now wind and storm. In much the same way in human societies there prevails now the tendency that produces closed, stationary, crystallized ruling classes, now the tendency that results in a more or less rapid renovation of ruling classes.

The Oriental societies which we consider stationary have in reality not always been so, for otherwise, as we have already pointed out, they could not have made the advances in civilization of which they have left irrefutable evidence. It is much more accurate to say that we came to know them at a time when their political forces and their political classes were in a period of crystallization. The same thing occurs in what we commonly call "aging" societies, where religious beliefs, scientific knowledge, methods of producing and distributing wealth have for centuries undergone no radical alteration and have not been disturbed in their everyday course by infiltrations of foreign elements, material or intellectual. In such societies political forces are always the same, and the class that holds possession of them holds a power that is undisputed. Power is therefore perpetuated in certain families, and the inclination to immobility becomes general through all the various strata in that society.

So in India we see the caste system become thoroughly entrenched after the suppression of Buddhism. The Greeks found hereditary castes in ancient Egypt, but we know that in the periods of greatness and renaissance in Egyptian civilization political office and social status were not hereditary. We possess an Egyptian document that summarizes the life of a high army officer who lived during the period of the expulsion of the Hyksos. He had begun his career as a simple soldier. Other documents show cases in which the same individual served successively in army, civil administration and priesthood.[1]

The best-known and perhaps the most important example of a society tending toward crystallization is the period in Roman history that used to be called the Low Empire. There, after several centuries of almost complete social immobility, a division between two classes grew sharper and sharper, the one made up of great landowners and high officials, the other made up of slaves, farmers and urban plebeians. What is even more striking, public office and social position became hereditary by custom before they became hereditary by law, and the trend was rapidly generalized during the period mentioned.[2]

On the other hand it may happen in the history of a nation that commerce with foreign peoples, forced emigrations, discoveries, wars, create new poverty and new wealth, disseminate knowledge of things that were previously unknown or cause infiltrations of new moral, intellectual and religious currents. Or again—as a result of such infiltrations or through a slow process of inner growth, or from both causes—it may happen that a new learning arises, or that certain elements of an old, long forgotten learning return to favor so that new ideas and new beliefs come to the fore and upset the intellectual habits on which the obedience of the masses has been founded. The ruling class may also be vanquished and destroyed in whole or in part by foreign invasions, or, when the circumstances just mentioned arise, it may be driven from power by the advent of new social elements who are strong in fresh political forces. Then, naturally, there comes a period of renovation, or, if one prefer, of revolution, during which individual energies have free play and certain individuals, more passionate, more energetic, more intrepid or merely shrewder than others, force their way from the bottom of the social ladder to the topmost rungs.

Once such a movement has set in, it cannot be stopped immediately. The example of individuals who have started from nowhere and reached prominent positions fires new ambitions,

---

[1] Lenormant, Maspero, Brugsch.

[2] Marquardt, *Manuel des antiquités romaines;* Fustel de Coulanges, *Nouvelles recherches sur quelques problèmes d'histoire.*

new greeds, new energies, and this molecular rejuvenation of the ruling class continues vigorously until a long period of social stability slows it down again. We need hardly mention examples of nations in such periods of renovation. In our age that would be superfluous. Rapid restocking of ruling classes is a frequent and very striking phenomenon in countries that have been recently colonized. When social life begins in such environments, there is no ready-made ruling class, and while such a class is in process of formation, admittance to it is gained very easily. Monopolization of land and other agencies of production is, if not quite impossible, at any rate more difficult than elsewhere. That is why, at least during a certain period, the Greek colonies offered a wide outlet for all Greek energy and enterprise. That is why, in the United States, where the colonizing of new lands continued through the whole nineteenth century and new industries were continually springing up, examples of men who started with nothing and have attained fame and wealth are still frequent —all of which helps to foster in the people of that country the illusion that democracy is a fact.

Suppose now that a society gradually passes from its feverish state to calm. Since the human being's psychological tendencies are always the same, those who belong to the ruling class will begin to acquire a group spirit. They will become more and more exclusive and learn better and better the art of monopolizing to their advantage the qualities and capacities that are essential to acquiring power and holding it. Then, at last, the force that is essentially conservative appears—the force of habit. Many people become resigned to a lowly station, while the members of certain privileged families or classes grow convinced that they have almost an absolute right to high station and command.

A philanthropist would certainly be tempted to inquire whether mankind is happier—or less unhappy—during periods of social stability and crystallization, when everyone is almost fated to remain in the social station to which he was born, or during the directly opposite periods of renovation and revolution, which permit all to aspire to the most exalted positions and some to attain them. Such an inquiry would be difficult. The answer would have to take account of many qualifications and exceptions, and might perhaps always be influenced by the personal preferences of the observer. We shall therefore be careful not to venture on any answer of our own. Besides, even if we could reach an undebatable conclusion, it would have a very slight practical utility; for the sad fact is that what the philosophers and theologians call free will—in other words, spontaneous choice by individuals—has so far had, and will perhaps always have, little influence, if any at all, in hastening either the ending or the beginning of one of the historical periods mentioned.

CHAPTER 18

The Higher Circles

C. WRIGHT MILLS

THE powers of ordinary men are circumscribed by the everyday worlds in which they live, yet even in these rounds of job, family, and neighborhood they often seem driven by forces they can neither understand nor govern. 'Great changes' are beyond their control, but affect their conduct and outlook none the less. The very framework of modern society confines them to projects not their own, but from every side, such changes now press upon the men and women of the mass society, who accordingly feel that they are without purpose in an epoch in which they are without power.

But not all men are in this sense ordinary. As the means of information and of power are centralized, some men come to occupy positions in American society from which they can look down upon, so to speak, and by their decisions mightily affect, the everyday worlds of ordinary men and women. They are not made by their jobs; they set up and break down jobs for thousands of others; they are not confined by simple family responsibilities; they can escape. They may live in many hotels and houses, but they are bound by no one community. They need not merely 'meet the demands of the day and hour'; in some part, they create these demands, and cause others to meet them. Whether or not they profess their power, their technical and political experience of it far transcends that of the underlying population. What Jacob Burckhardt said of 'great men,' most Americans might well say of their elite: 'They are all that we are not.'[1]

The power elite is composed of men whose positions enable them to transcend the ordinary environments of ordinary men and women; they are in positions to make decisions having major consequences. Whether they do or do not make such decisions is less important than the fact that they do occupy such pivotal positions: their failure to act, their failure to make decisions, is itself an act that is often of greater consequence than the decisions they do make. For they are in command of the major hierarchies and organizations of modern society. They rule the big corporations. They run the machinery of the state and claim its prerogatives. They direct the military establishment. They occupy the strategic command posts of the social structure, in which are now centered the effective means of the power and the wealth and the celebrity which they enjoy.

The power elite are not solitary rulers. Advisers and consultants, spokesmen and opinion-makers are often the captains of their higher thought and decision. Immediately below the elite are the professional politicians of the middle levels of power, in the Congress and in the pressure groups, as well as among the new and old upper classes of town and city and region. Mingling with them, in curious ways which we shall explore, are those professional celebrities who live by being continually displayed but are never, so long as they remain celebrities, displayed enough. If such celebrities are not at the head of any dominating hierarchy, they do often have the power to distract the attention of the public or afford sensations to the masses, or, more directly, to gain the ear of those who do occupy positions of direct power. More or less unattached, as critics of morality and technicians of power, as spokesmen of God and creators of mass sensibility, such celebrities and consultants are part of the immediate scene in which the drama of the elite is enacted. But that drama itself is centered in the command posts of the major institutional hierarchies.

1

The truth about the nature and the power of the elite is not some secret which men of affairs know but will not tell. Such men hold quite various theories about their own roles in the sequence of event and decision. Often they are uncertain about their roles, and even more often they allow their fears and their hopes to affect their assessment of their own power. No matter how great their actual power, they tend to be less acutely aware of it than of the resistances of others to its use. Moreover, most American men of affairs have learned well the rhetoric of public relations, in some cases even to the point of using it when they are alone, and thus coming to believe it. The personal awareness of the actors is only one of the several sources one must examine in order to understand the higher circles. Yet many who believe that there is no elite, or at any rate none of any consequence, rest their argument upon what men of affairs believe about themselves, or at least assert in public.

There is, however, another view: those who feel, even if vaguely, that a compact and powerful elite of great importance does now prevail in America often base that feeling upon the historical trend of our time. They have felt, for example, the domination of the military event, and from this they infer that generals and admirals, as well as other men of decision influenced by them, must be enormously powerful. They hear that the Congress has again abdicated to a handful of men decisions clearly related to the issue of war or peace. They know that the bomb was dropped over Japan in the name of the United States of America, although they were at no time consulted about the matter. They feel that they live in a time of big decisions; they know that they are not making any. Accordingly, as they consider the present as history, they infer that at its center, making decisions or failing to make them, there must be an elite of power.

On the one hand, those who share this feeling about big historical events assume that there is an elite and that its power is great. On the other hand, those who listen carefully to the reports of men apparently involved in the great decisions often do not believe that there is an elite whose powers are of decisive consequence.

Both views must be taken into account, but neither is adequate. The way to understand the power of the American elite lies neither solely in recognizing the historic scale of events nor in accepting the personal awareness reported by men of apparent decision. Behind such men and behind the events of history, linking the two, are the major institutions of modern society. These hierarchies of state and corporation and army constitute the means of power; as such they are now of a consequence not before equaled in human history—and at their summits, there are now those command posts of modern society which offer us the sociological key to an understanding of the role of the higher circles in America.

Within American society, major national power now resides in the economic, the political, and the military domains. Other institutions seem off to the side of modern history, and, on occasion, duly subordinated to these. No family is as directly powerful in national affairs as any major corporation; no church is as directly powerful in the external biographies of young men in America today as the military establishment; no college is as powerful in the shaping of momentous events as the National Security Council. Religious, educational, and family institutions are not autonomous centers of national power; on the contrary, these decentralized areas are increasingly shaped by the big three, in which developments of decisive and immediate consequence now occur.

Families and churches and schools adapt to modern life; governments and armies and corporations shape it; and, as they do so, they turn these lesser institutions into means for their ends. Religious institutions provide chaplains to the armed forces where they are used as a means of increasing the effectiveness of its morale to kill. Schools select and train men for their jobs in corporations and their specialized tasks in the armed forces. The extended family has, of course, long been broken up by the industrial revolution, and now the son and the father are removed from the family, by compulsion if need be, whenever the army of the state sends out the call. And the symbols of all these lesser institutions are used to legitimate the power and the decisions of the big three.

The life-fate of the modern individual depends not only upon the family into which he was born or which he enters by marriage, but increasingly upon the corporation in which he spends the most alert hours of his best years; not only upon the school where he is educated as a child and adolescent, but also upon the state which touches him throughout his life; not only upon the church in which on occasion he hears the word of God, but also upon the army in which he is disciplined.

If the centralized state could not rely upon the inculcation of nationalist loyalties in public and private schools, its leaders would promptly seek to modify the decentralized educational system. If the bankruptcy rate among the top five hundred corporations were as high as the general divorce rate among the thirty-seven million married couples, there would be economic catastrophe on an international scale. If members of armies gave to them no more of their lives than do believers to the churches to which they belong, there would be a military crisis.

Within each of the big three, the typical institutional unit has become enlarged, has become administrative, and, in the power of its decisions, has become centralized. Behind these developments there is a fabulous technology, for as institutions, they have incorporated this technology and guide it, even as it shapes and paces their developments.

The economy—once a great scatter of small productive units in autonomous balance—has become dominated by two or three hundred giant corporations, administratively and politically interrelated, which together hold the keys to economic decisions.

The political order, once a decentralized set of several dozen states with a weak spinal cord, has become a centralized, executive establishment which has taken up into itself many powers previously scattered, and now enters into each and every crany of the social structure.

The military order, once a slim establishment in a context of distrust fed by state militia, has become the largest and most expensive feature of government, and, although well versed in smiling public relations, now has all the grim and clumsy efficiency of a sprawling bureaucratic domain.

In each of these institutional areas, the means of power at the disposal of decision makers have increased enormously; their central executive powers have been enhanced; within each of them modern administrative routines have been elaborated and tightened up.

As each of these domains becomes enlarged and centralized, the consequences of its activities become greater, and its traffic with the others increases. The decisions of a handful of corporations bear upon military and political as well as upon economic developments around the world. The decisions of the military establishment rest upon and grievously affect political life as well as the very level of economic activity. The decisions made within the political domain determine economic activities and military programs. There is no longer, on the one hand, an economy, and, on the other hand, a political order containing a military establishment unimportant to politics and to money-making. There is a political economy linked, in a thousand ways, with military institutions and decisions. On each side of the world-split running through central Europe and around the Asiatic rimlands, there is an ever-increasing interlocking of economic, military, and political structures.[2] If there is government intervention in the corporate economy, so is there corporate intervention in the governmental process. In the structural sense, this triangle of power is the source of the interlocking directorate that is most important for the historical structure of the present.

The fact of the interlocking is clearly revealed at each of the points of crisis of modern capitalist society—slump, war, and boom. In each, men of decision are led to an awareness of the interdependence of the major institutional orders. In the nineteenth century, when the scale of all institutions was smaller, their liberal integration was achieved in the automatic economy, by an autonomous play of market forces, and in the automatic political domain, by the bargain and the vote. It was then assumed that out of the imbalance and friction that followed the limited decisions then possible a new equilibrium would in due course emerge. That can no longer be assumed, and it is not assumed by the men at the top of each of the three dominant hierarchies.

For given the scope of their consequences, decisions—and indecisions—in any one of these ramify into the others, and hence top decisions tend either to become co-ordinated or to lead to a commanding indecision. It has not always been like this. When numerous small entrepreneurs made up the economy, for example, many of them could fail and the consequences still remain local; political and military authorities did not intervene. But now, given political expectations and military commitments, can they afford to allow key units of the private corporate economy to break down in slump? Increasingly, they do intervene in economic affairs, and as they do so, the controlling decisions in each order are inspected by agents of the other two, and economic, military, and political structures are interlocked.

At the pinnacle of each of the three enlarged and centralized domains, there have arisen those higher circles which make up the economic, the political, and the military elites. At the top of the economy, among the corporate rich, there are the chief executives; at the top of the political order, the members of the political directorate; at the top of the military establishment, the elite of soldier-statesmen clustered in and around the Joint Chiefs of Staff and the upper echelon. As each of these domains has coincided with the others, as decisions tend to become total in their consequence, the leading men in each of the three domains of power—the warlords, the corporation chieftains, the political directorate—tend to come together, to form the power elite of America.

2

The higher circles in and around these command posts are often thought of in terms of what their members possess: they have a greater share than other people of the things and experiences that are most highly valued. From this point of view, the elite are simply those who have the most of what there is to have, which is generally held to include money, power, and prestige—as well as all the ways of life to which these lead.[3] But the elite are not simply those who have the most, for they could not 'have the most' were it not for their positions in the great institutions. For such institutions are the necessary bases of power, of wealth, and of prestige, and at the same time, the chief means of exercising power, of acquiring and retaining wealth, and of cashing in the higher claims for prestige.

By the powerful we mean, of course, those who are able to realize their will, even if others resist it. No one, accordingly, can be truly powerful unless he has access to the command of major institutions, for it is over these institutional means of power that the truly powerful are, in the first instance, powerful. Higher politicians and key officials of government command such institutional power; so do admirals and generals, and so do the major owners and executives of the larger corporations. Not all power, it is true, is anchored in and exercised by means of such institutions, but only within and through them can power be more or less continuous and important.

Wealth also is acquired and held in and through institutions. The pyramid of wealth cannot be understood merely in terms of the very rich; for the great inheriting families, as we shall see, are now supplemented by the corporate institutions of modern society: every one of the very rich families has been and is closely connected—always legally and frequently managerially as well—with one of the multi-million dollar corporations.

The modern corporation is the prime source of wealth, but, in latter-day capitalism, the political apparatus also opens and closes many avenues to wealth. The amount as well as the source of income, the power over consumer's goods as well as over productive capital, are determined by position within the political economy. If our interest in the very rich goes beyond their lavish or their miserly consumption, we must examine their relations to modern forms of corporate property as well as to the state; for such relations now determine the chances of men to secure big property and to receive high income.

Great prestige increasingly follows the major institutional units of the social structure. It is obvious that prestige depends, often quite decisively, upon access to the publicity machines that are now a central and normal feature of all the big institutions of modern America. Moreover, one feature of these hierarchies of corporation, state, and military establishment is that their top positions are increasingly interchangeable. One result of this is the accumulative nature of prestige. Claims for prestige, for example, may be initially based on military roles, then expressed in and augmented by an educational institution run by corporate executives, and cashed in, finally, in the political order, where, for General Eisenhower and those he represents, power and prestige finally meet at the very peak. Like wealth and power, prestige tends to be cumulative: the more of it you have, the more you can get. These values also tend to be translatable into one another: the wealthy find it easier than the poor to gain power; those with status find it easier than those without it to control opportunities for wealth.

If we took the one hundred most powerful men in America, the one hundred wealthiest, and the one hundred most celebrated away from the institutional positions they now occupy, away from their resources of men and women and money, away from the media of mass communication that are now focused upon them— then they would be powerless and poor and uncelebrated. For power is not of a man. Wealth does not center in the person of the wealthy. Celebrity is not inherent in any personality. To be celebrated, to be wealthy, to have power requires access to major institutions, for the institutional positions men occupy determine in large part their chances to have and to hold these valued experiences.

3

The people of the higher circles may also be conceived as members of a top social stratum, as a set of groups whose members know one another, see one another socially and at business, and so, in making decisions, take one another into account. The elite, according to this conception, feel themselves to be, and are felt by others to be, the inner circle of 'the upper social classes.'[4] They form a more or less compact social and psychological entity; they have become self-conscious members of a social class. People are either accepted into this class or they are not, and there is a qualitative split, rather than merely a numerical scale, separating them from those who are not elite. They are more or less aware of themselves as a social class and they behave toward one another differently from the way they do toward members of other classes. They accept one another, understand one another, marry one another, tend to work and to think if not together at least alike.

Now, we do not want by our definition to prejudge whether the elite of the command posts are conscious members of such a socially recognized class, or whether considerable proportions of the elite derive from such a clear and distinct class. These are matters to be investigated. Yet in order to be able to recognize what we intend to investigate, we must note something that all biographies and memoirs of the wealthy and the powerful and the eminent make clear: no matter what else they may be, the people of these higher circles are involved in a set of overlapping 'crowds' and intricately connected 'cliques.' There is a kind of mutual attraction among those who 'sit on the same terrace'—although this often becomes clear to them, as well as to others, only at the point at which they feel the need to draw the line; only when, in their common defense, they come to understand what they have in common, and so close their ranks against outsiders.

The idea of such ruling stratum implies that most of its members have similar social origins, that throughout their lives they maintain a network of informal connections, and that to some degree there is an interchangeability of position between the various hierarchies of money and power and celebrity. We must, of course, note at once that if such an elite stratum does exist, its social visibility and its form, for very solid historical reasons, are quite different from those of the noble cousinhoods that once ruled various European nations.

That American society has never passed through a feudal epoch is of decisive importance to the nature of the American elite, as well as to American society as a historic whole. For it means that no nobility or aristocracy, established before the capitalist era, has stood in tense opposition to the higher bourgeoisie. It means that this bourgeoisie has monopolized not only wealth but prestige and power as well. It means that no set of noble families has commanded the top positions and monopolized the values that are generally held in high esteem; and certainly that no set has done so explicitly by inherited right. It means that no high church dignitaries or court nobilities, no entrenched landlords with honorific accouterments, no monopolists of high army posts have opposed the enriched bourgeoisie and in the name of birth and prerogative successfully resisted its self-making.

But this does *not* mean that there are no upper strata in the United States. That they emerged from a 'middle class' that had no recognized aristocratic superiors does not mean they remained middle class when enormous increases in wealth made their own superiority possible. Their origins and their newness may have made the upper strata less visible in America than elsewhere. But in America today there are in fact tiers and ranges of wealth and power of which people in the middle and lower ranks know very little and may not even dream. There are families who, in their well-being, are quite insulated from the economic jolts and lurches felt by the merely prosperous and those farther down the scale. There are also men of power who in quite small groups make decisions of enormous consequence for the underlying population.

The American elite entered modern history as a virtually unopposed bourgeoisie. No national bourgeoisie, before or since, has had such opportunities and advantages. Having no military neighbors, they easily occupied an isolated continent stocked with natural resources and immensely inviting to a willing labor force. A framework of power and an ideology for its justification were already at hand. Against mercantilist restriction, they inherited the principle of *laissez-faire;* against Southern planters, they imposed the principle of industrialism. The Revolutionary War put an end to colonial pretensions to nobility, as loyalists fled the country and many estates were broken up. The Jacksonian upheaval with its status revolution put an end to pretensions to monopoly of descent by the old New England families. The Civil War broke the power, and so in due course the prestige, of the ante-bellum South's claimants for the higher esteem. The tempo of the whole capitalist development made it impossible for an inherited nobility to develop and endure in America.

No fixed ruling class, anchored in agrarian life and coming to flower in military glory, could contain in America the historic thrust of commerce and industry, or subordinate to itself the capitalist elite—as capitalists were subordinated, for example, in Germany and Japan. Nor could such a ruling class anywhere in the world contain that of the United States when industrialized violence came to decide history. Witness the fate of Germany and Japan in the two world wars of the twentieth century; and indeed the fate of Britain herself and her model ruling class, as New York became the inevitable economic, and Washington the inevitable political capital of the western capitalist world.

4

The elite who occupy the command posts may be seen as the possessors of power and wealth and celebrity; they may be seen as members of the upper stratum of a capitalistic society. They may also be defined in terms of psychological and moral criteria, as certain kinds of selected individuals. So defined, the elite, quite simply, are people of superior character and energy.

The humanist, for example, may conceive of the 'elite' not as a social level or category, but as a scatter of those individuals who attempt to transcend themselves, and accordingly, are more noble, more efficient, made out of better stuff. It does not matter whether they are poor or rich, whether they hold high position or low, whether they are acclaimed or despised; they are elite because of the kind of individuals they are. The rest of the population is mass, which, according to this conception, sluggishly relaxes into uncomfortable mediocrity.[5]

This is the sort of socially unlocated conception which some American writers with conservative yearnings have recently sought to develop.* But most moral and psychological conceptions of the elite are much less sophisticated, concerning themselves not with individuals but with the stratum as a whole. Such ideas, in fact, always arise in a society in which some people possess more than do others of what there is to possess. People with advantages are loath to believe that they just happen to be people with advantages. They come readily to define themselves as inherently worthy of what they possess; they come to believe themselves 'naturally' elite; and, in fact, to imagine their possessions and their privileges as natural extensions of their own elite selves. In this sense, the idea of the elite as composed of men and women having a finer moral character is an ideology of the elite as a privileged ruling stratum, and this is true whether the ideology is elite-made or made up for it by others.

In eras of equalitarian rhetoric, the more intelligent or the more articulate among the lower and middle classes, as well as guilty members of the upper, may come to entertain ideas of a counter-elite. In western society, as a matter of fact, there is a long tradition and varied images of the poor, the exploited, and the oppressed as the truly virtuous, the wise, and the blessed. Stemming from Christian tradition, this moral idea of a counter-elite, composed of essentially higher types condemned to a lowly station, may be and has been used by the underlying population to justify harsh criticism of ruling elites and to celebrate utopian images of a new elite to come.

The moral conception of the elite, however, is not always merely an ideology of the overprivileged or a counter-ideology of the underprivileged. It is often a fact: having controlled experiences and select privileges, many individuals of the upper stratum do come in due course to approximate the types of character they claim to embody. Even when we give up—as we must—the idea that the elite man or woman is born with an elite character, we need not dismiss the idea that their experiences and trainings develop in them characters of a specific type.

* See below, FOURTEEN: The Conservative Mood.

Nowadays we must qualify the idea of elite as composed of higher types of individuals, for the men who are selected for and shaped by the top positions have many spokesmen and advisers and ghosts and make-up men who modify their self-conceptions and create their public images, as well as shape many of their decisions. There is, of course, considerable variation among the elite in this respect, but as a general rule in America today, it would be naïve to interpret any major elite group merely in terms of its ostensible personnel. The American elite often seems less a collection of persons than of corporate entities, which are in great part created and spoken for as standard types of 'personality.' Even the most apparently free-lance celebrity is usually a sort of synthetic production turned out each week by a disciplined staff which systematically ponders the effect of the easy ad-libbed gags the celebrity 'spontaneously' echoes.

Yet, in so far as the elite flourishes as a social class or as a set of men at the command posts, it will select and form certain types of personality, and reject others. The kind of moral and psychological beings men become is in large part determined by the values they experience and the institutional roles they are allowed and expected to play. From the biographer's point of view, a man of the upper classes is formed by his relations with others like himself in a series of small intimate groupings through which he passes and to which throughout his lifetime he may return. So conceived, the elite is a set of higher circles whose members are selected, trained and certified and permitted intimate access to those who command the impersonal institutional hierarchies of modern society. If there is any one key to the *psychological* idea of the elite, it is that they combine in their persons an awareness of impersonal decision-making with intimate sensibilities shared with one another. To understand the elite as a social class we must examine a whole series of smaller face-to-face milieux, the most obvious of which, historically, has been the upper-class family, but the most important of which today are the proper secondary school and the metropolitan club.[6]

5

These several notions of the elite, when appropriately understood, are intricately bound up with one another, and we shall use them all in this examination of American success. We shall study each of several higher circles as offering candidates for the elite, and we shall do so in terms of the major institutions making up the total society of America; within and between each of these institutions, we shall trace the interrelations of wealth and power and prestige. But our main concern is with the power of those who now occupy the command posts, and with the role which they are enacting in the history of our epoch.

Such an elite may be conceived as omnipotent, and its powers thought of as a great hidden design. Thus, in vulgar Marxism, events and trends are explained by reference to 'the will of the bourgeoisie'; in Nazism, by reference to 'the conspiracy of the Jews'; by the petty right in America today, by reference to 'the hidden force' of Communist spies. According to such notions of the omnipotent elite as historical cause, the elite is never an entirely visible agency. It is, in fact, a secular substitute for the will of God, being realized in a sort of providential design, except that usually non-elite men are thought capable of opposing it and eventually overcoming it.*

The opposite view—of the elite as impotent—is now quite popular among liberal-minded observers. Far from being omnipotent, the elites are thought to be so scattered as to lack any coherence as a historical force. Their invisibility is not the invisibility of secrecy but the invisibility of the multitude. Those who occupy the formal places of authority are so check-mated—by other elites exerting pressure, or by the public as an electorate, or by constitutional codes—that, although there may be upper classes, there is no ruling class; although there may be men of power, there is no power elite; although there may be a system of stratification, it

---

* Those who charge that Communist agents have been or are in the government, as well as those frightened by them, never raise the question: 'Well, suppose there are Communists in high places, how much power do they have?' They simply assume that men in high places, or in this case even those in positions from which they might influence such men, do decide important events. Those who think Communist agents lost China to the Soviet bloc, or influenced loyal Americans to lose it, simply assume that there is a set of men who decide such matters, actively or by neglect or by stupidity. Many others, who do not believe that Communist agents were so influential, still assume that loyal American decision-makers lost it all by themselves.

has no effective top. In the extreme, this view of the elite, as weakened by compromise and disunited to the point of nullity, is a substitute for impersonal collective fate; for, in this view, the decisions of the visible men of the higher circles do not count in history.*

Internationally, the image of the omnipotent elite tends to prevail. All good events and pleasing happenings are quickly imputed by the opinion-makers to the leaders of their own nation; all bad events and unpleasant experiences are imputed to the enemy abroad. In both cases, the omnipotence of evil rulers or of virtuous leaders is assumed. Within the nation, the use of such rhetoric is rather more complicated: when men speak of the power of their own party or circle, they and their leaders are, of course, impotent; only 'the people' are omnipotent. But, when they speak of the power of their opponent's party or circle, they impute to them omnipotence; 'the people' are now powerlessly taken in.

More generally, American men of power tend, by convention, to deny that they are powerful. No American runs for office in order to rule or even govern, but only to serve; he does not become a bureaucrat or even an official, but a public servant. And nowadays, as I have already pointed out, such postures have become standard features of the public-relations programs of all men of power. So firm a part of the style of power-wielding have they become that conservative writers readily misinterpret them as indicating a trend toward an 'amorphous power situation.'

But the 'power situation' of America today is less amorphous than is the perspective of those who see it as a romantic confusion. It is less a flat, momentary 'situation' than a graded, durable structure. And if those who occupy its top grades are not omnipotent, neither are they impotent. It is the form and the height of the

---

* The idea of the impotent elite, as we shall have occasion to see, in ELEVEN: The Theory of Balance, is mightily supported by the notion of an automatic economy in which the problem of power is solved for the economic elite by denying its existence. No one has enough power to make a real difference; events are the results of an anonymous balance. For the political elite too, the model of balance solves the problem of power. Parallel to the market-economy, there is the leaderless democracy in which no one is responsible for anything and everyone is responsible for everything; the will of men acts only through the impersonal workings of the electoral process.

gradation of power that we must examine if we would understand the degree of power held and exercised by the elite.

If the power to decide such national issues as are decided were shared in an absolutely equal way, there would be no power elite; in fact, there would be no *gradation* of power, but only a radical homogeneity. At the opposite extreme as well, if the power to decide issues were absolutely monopolized by one small group, there would be no gradation of power; there would simply be this small group in command, and below it, the undifferentiated, dominated masses. American society today represents neither the one nor the other of these extremes, but a conception of them is none the less useful: it makes us realize more clearly the question of the structure of power in the United States and the position of the power elite within it.

Within each of the most powerful institutional orders of modern society there is a gradation of power. The owner of a roadside fruit stand does not have as much power in any area of social or economic or political decision as the head of a multi-million-dollar fruit corporation; no lieutenant on the line is as powerful as the Chief of Staff in the Pentagon; no deputy sheriff carries as much authority as the President of the United States. Accordingly, the problem of defining the power elite concerns the level at which we wish to draw the line. By lowering the line, we could define the elite out of existence; by raising it, we could make the elite a very small circle indeed. In a preliminary and minimum way, we draw the line crudely, in charcoal as it were: By the power elite, we refer to those political, economic, and military circles which as an intricate set of overlapping cliques share decisions having at least national consequences. In so far as national events are decided, the power elite are those who decide them.

To say that there are obvious gradations of power and of opportunities to decide within modern society is not to say that the powerful are united, that they fully know what they do, or that they are consciously joined in conspiracy. Such issues are best faced if we concern ourselves, in the first instance, more with the structural position of the high and mighty, and with the consequences of their decisions, than with the extent of their awareness or the purity of their motives. To understand the power elite, we must attend to three major keys:

I. One, which we shall emphasize throughout our discussion of each of the higher circles, is the psychology of the several elites in their respective milieux. In so far as the power elite is composed of men of similar origin and education, in so far as their careers and their styles of life are similar, there are psychological and social bases for their unity, resting upon the fact that they are of similar social type and leading to the fact of their easy intermingling. This kind of unity reaches its frothier apex in the sharing of that prestige that is to be had in the world of the celebrity; it achieves a more solid culmination in the fact of the interchangeability of positions within and between the three dominant institutional orders.

II. Behind such psychological and social unity as we may find, are the structure and the mechanics of those institutional hierarchies over which the political directorate, the corporate rich, and the high military now preside. The greater the scale of these bureaucratic domains, the greater the scope of their respective elite's power. How each of the major hierarchies is shaped and and what relations it has with the other hierarchies determine in large part the relations of their rulers. If these hierarchies are scattered and disjointed, then their respective elites tend to be scattered and disjointed; if they have many interconnections and points of coinciding interest, then their elites tend to form a coherent kind of grouping.

The unity of the elite is not a simple reflection of the unity of institutions, but men and institutions are always related, and our conception of the power elite invites us to determine that relation. Today in America there are several important structural coincidences of interest between these institutional domains, including the development of a permanent war establishment by a privately incorporated economy inside a political vacuum.

III. The unity of the power elite, however, does not rest solely on psychological similarity and social intermingling, nor entirely on the structural coincidences of commanding positions and interests. At times it is the unity of a more explicit co-ordination. To say that these three higher circles are increasingly co-ordinated, that this is *one* basis of their unity, and that at times—as during the wars—such co-ordination is quite decisive, is not to say that the co-ordination is total or continuous, or even that it is very sure-footed. Much less is it to say that willful co-ordination is the sole or the major basis of their unity, or that the power elite has emerged as the realization of a plan. But it is to say that as the institutional mechanics of our time have opened up avenues to men pursuing their several interests, many of them have come to see that these several interests could be realized more easily if they worked together, in informal as well as in more formal ways, and accordingly they have done so.

6

It is not my thesis that for all epochs of human history and in all nations, a creative minority, a ruling class, an omnipotent elite, shape all historical events. Such statements, upon careful exami-nation, usually turn out to be mere tautologies,[7] and even when they are not, they are so entirely general as to be useless in the attempt to understand the history of the present. The minimum definition of the power elite as those who decide whatever is decided of major consequence, does not imply that the members of this elite are always and necessarily the history-makers; nei-ther does it imply that they never are. We must not confuse the conception of the elite, which we wish to define, with one theory about their role: that they are the history-makers of our time. To define the elite, for example, as 'those who rule America' is less to define a conception than to state one hypothesis about the role and power of that elite. No matter how we might define the elite, the extent of its members' power is subject to historical variation. If, in a dogmatic way, we try to include that variation in our ge-neric definition, we foolishly limit the use of a needed conception. If we insist that the elite be defined as a strictly coordinated class that continually and absolutely rules, we are closing off from our view much to which the term more modestly defined might open to our observation. In short, our definition of the power elite can-not properly contain dogma concerning the degree and kind of power that ruling groups everywhere have. Much less should it permit us to smuggle into our discussion a theory of history.

During most of human history, historical change has not been visible to the people who were involved in it, or even to those

enacting it. Ancient Egypt and Mesopotamia, for example, endured for some four hundred generations with but slight changes
in their basic structure. That is six and a half times as long as the
entire Christian era, which has only prevailed some sixty generations; it is about eighty times as long as the five generations of the
United States' existence. But now the tempo of change is so rapid,
and the means of observation so accessible, that the interplay of
event and decision seems often to be quite historically visible, if
we will only look carefully and from an adequate vantage point.

When knowledgeable journalists tell us that 'events, not men,
shape the big decisions,' they are echoing the theory of history as
Fortune, Chance, Fate, or the work of The Unseen Hand. For
'events' is merely a modern word for these older ideas, all of which
separate men from history-making, because all of them lead us to
believe that history goes on behind men's backs. History is drift
with no mastery; within it there is action but no deed; history is
mere happening and the event intended by no one.[8]

The course of events in our time depends more on a series of
human decisions than on any inevitable fate. The sociological
meaning of 'fate' is simply this: that, when the decisions are innumerable and each one is of small consequence, all of them add up
in a way no man intended—to history as fate. But not all epochs
are equally fateful. As the circle of those who decide is narrowed,
as the means of decision are centralized and the consequences of
decisions become enormous, then the course of great events often
rests upon the decisions of determinable circles. This does not
necessarily mean that the same circle of men follow through from
one event to another in such a way that all of history is merely
their plot. The power of the elite does not necessarily mean that
history is not also shaped by a series of small decisions, none of
which are thought out. It does not mean that a hundred small
arrangements and compromises and adaptations may not be built
into the going policy and the living event. The idea of the power
elite implies nothing about the process of decision-making as such:
it is an attempt to delimit the social areas within which that process, whatever its character, goes on. It is a conception of who is
involved in the process.

The degree of foresight and control of those who are involved
in decisions that count may also vary. The idea of the power elite

does not mean that the estimations and calculated risks upon which decisions are made are not often wrong and that the consequences are sometimes, indeed often, not those intended. Often those who make decisions are trapped by their own inadequacies and blinded by their own errors.

Yet in our time the pivotal moment does arise, and at that moment, small circles do decide or fail to decide. In either case, they are an elite of power. The dropping of the A-bombs over Japan was such a moment; the decision on Korea was such a moment; the confusion about Quemoy and Matsu, as well as before Dienbienphu were such moments; the sequence of maneuvers which involved the United States in World War II was such a 'moment.' Is it not true that much of the history of our times is composed of such moments? And is not that what is meant when it is said that we live in a time of big decisions, of decisively centralized power?

Most of us do not try to make sense of our age by believing in a Greek-like, eternal recurrence, nor by a Christian belief in a salvation to come, nor by any steady march of human progress. Even though we do not reflect upon such matters, the chances are we believe with Burckhardt that we live in a mere succession of events; that sheer continuity is the only principle of history. History is merely one thing after another; history is meaningless in that it is not the realization of any determinate plot. It is true, of course, that our sense of continuity, our feeling for the history of our time, is affected by crisis. But we seldom look beyond the immediate crisis or the crisis felt to be just ahead. We believe neither in fate nor providence; and we assume, without talking about it, that 'we'—as a nation—can decisively shape the future but that 'we' as individuals somehow cannot do so.

Any meaning history has, 'we' shall have to give to it by our actions. Yet the fact is that although we are all of us within history we do not all possess equal powers to make history. To pretend that we do is sociological nonsense and political irresponsibility. It is nonsense because any group or any individual is limited, first of all, by the technical and institutional means of power at its command; we do not all have equal access to the means of power that now exist, nor equal influence over their use. To pretend that 'we' are all history-makers is politically irresponsible because it obfuscates any attempt to locate responsibility for the consequential decisions of men who do have access to the means of power.

From even the most superficial examination of the history of the western society we learn that the power of decision-makers is first of all limited by the level of technique, by the *means* of power and violence and organization that prevail in a given society. In this connection we also learn that there is a fairly straight line running upward through the history of the West; that the means of oppression and exploitation, of violence and destruction, as well as the means of production and reconstruction, have been progressively enlarged and increasingly centralized.

As the institutional means of power and the means of communications that tie them together have become steadily more efficient, those now in command of them have come into command of instruments of rule quite unsurpassed in the history of mankind. And we are not yet at the climax of their development. We can no longer lean upon or take soft comfort from the historical ups and downs of ruling groups of previous epochs. In that sense, Hegel is correct: we learn from history that we cannot learn from it.

For every epoch and for every social structure, we must work out an answer to the question of the power of the elite. The ends of men are often merely hopes, but means are facts within some men's control. That is why all means of power tend to become ends to an elite that is in command of them. And that is why we may define the power elite in terms of the means of power—as those who occupy the command posts. The major questions about the American elite today—its composition, its unity, its power— must now be faced with due attention to the awesome means of power available to them. Caesar could do less with Rome than Napoleon with France; Napoleon less with France than Lenin with Russia; and Lenin less with Russia than Hitler with Germany. But what was Caesar's power at its peak compared with the power of the changing inner circle of Soviet Russia or of America's temporary administrations? The men of either circle can cause great cities to be wiped out in a single night, and in a few weeks turn continents into thermonuclear wastelands. That the facilities of power are enormously enlarged and decisively centralized means that the decisions of small groups are now more consequential.

But to know that the top posts of modern social structures now permit more commanding decisions is not to know that the elite who occupy these posts are the history-makers. We might grant that the enlarged and integrated economic, military, and political structures are shaped to permit command decisions, yet still feel that, as it were, 'they run themselves,' that those who are on top, in short, are determined in their decisions by 'necessity,' which presumably means by the instituted roles that they play and the situation of these institutions in the total structure of society.

Do the elite determine the roles that they enact? Or do the roles that institutions make available to them determine the power of the elite? The general answer—and no general answer is sufficient —is that in different kinds of structures and epochs elites are quite differently related to the roles that they play: nothing in the nature of the elite or in the nature of history dictates an answer. It is also true that if most men and women take whatever roles are permitted to them and enact them as they are expected to by virtue of their position, this is precisely what the elite need *not* do, and often do not do. They may call into question the structure, their position within it, or the way in which they are to enact that position.

Nobody called for or permitted Napoleon to chase *Parlement* home on the 18 *Brumaire*, and later to transform his consulate into an emperorship.[9] Nobody called for or permitted Adolf Hitler to proclaim himself 'Leader and Chancellor' the day President Hindenburg died, to abolish and usurp roles by merging the presidency and the chancellorship. Nobody called for or permitted Franklin D. Roosevelt to make the series of decisions that led to the entrance of the United States into World War II. It was no 'historical necessity,' but a man named Truman who, with a few other men, decided to drop a bomb on Hiroshima. It was no historical necessity, but an argument within a small circle of men that defeated Admiral Radford's proposal to bomb troops before Dienbienphu. Far from being dependent upon the structure of institutions, modern elites may smash one structure and set up another in which they then enact quite different roles. In fact, such destruction and creation of institutional structures, with all their means of power, when events seem to turn out well, is just what is involved in 'great leadership,' or, when they seem to turn out badly, great tyranny.

Some elite men *are*, of course, typically role-determined, but others are at times role-determining. They determine not only the role they play but today the roles of millions of other men. The creation of pivotal roles and their pivotal enactment occurs most readily when social structures are undergoing epochal transitions. It is clear that the international development of the United States to one of the two 'great powers'—along with the new means of annihilation and administrative and psychic domination—have made of the United States in the middle years of the twentieth century precisely such an epochal pivot.

There is nothing about history that tells us that a power elite cannot make it. To be sure, the will of such men is always limited, but never before have the limits been so broad, for never before have the means of power been so enormous. It is this that makes our situation so precarious, and makes even more important an understanding of the powers and the limitations of the American elite. The problem of the nature and the power of this elite is now the only realistic and serious way to raise again the problem of responsible government.

CHAPTER 19

A Critique of the Ruling Elite Model

ROBERT A. DAHL

A great many people seem to believe that "they" run things: the old families, the bankers, the City Hall machine, or the party boss behind the scene. This kind of view evidently has a powerful and many-sided appeal. It is simple, compelling, dramatic, "realistic." It gives one standing as an inside-dopester. For individuals with a strong strain of frustrated idealism, it has just the right touch of hard-boiled cynicism. Finally, the hypothesis has one very great advantage over many alternative explanations: It can be cast in a form that makes it virtually impossible to disprove.

Consider the last point for a moment. There is a type of quasi-metaphysical theory made up of what might be called an infinite regress of explanations. The ruling elite model *can* be interpreted in this way. If the overt leaders of a community do not appear to constitute a ruling elite, then the theory can be saved by arguing that behind the overt leaders there is a set of covert leaders who do. If subsequent evidence shows that this covert group does not make a ruling elite, then the theory can be saved by arguing that behind the first covert group there is another, and so on.

Now whatever else it may be, a theory that cannot even in principle be controverted by empirical evidence is not a scientific theory. The least that we can demand of any ruling elite theory that purports to be more than a metaphysical or polemical doctrine is, first, that the burden of proof be on the proponents of the theory and not on its critics; and, second, that there be clear criteria according to which the theory could be disproved.

With these points in mind, I shall proceed in two stages. First, I shall try to clarify the meaning of the concept "ruling elite" by describing a very simple form of what I conceive to be a ruling elite system. Second, I shall indicate what would be required in principle as a simple but satisfactory test of any hypothesis asserting that a particular political system is, in fact, a ruling elite system. Finally, I shall deal with some objections.

A SIMPLE RULING ELITE SYSTEM

If a ruling elite hypothesis says anything, surely it asserts that within some specific political system there exists a group of people who to some degree exercise power or influence over other actors in the system. I shall make the following assumptions about power.[1]

1. In order to compare the relative influence of two actors (these may be individuals, groups, classes, parties, or what not), it is necessary to state the scope of the responses upon which the actors have an effect. The statement, "A has more power than B," is so ambiguous as to verge on the meaningless, since it does not specify the scope.

2. One cannot compare the relative influence of two actors who always perform identical actions with respect to the group influenced. What this means as a practical matter is that ordinarily one can test for differences in influence only where there are cases of differences in initial preferences. At one extreme, the difference may

mean that one group prefers alternative A and another group prefers B, A and B being mutually exclusive. At the other extreme, it may mean that one group prefers alternative A to other alternatives, and another group is indifferent. If a political system displayed complete consensus at all times, we should find it impossible to construct a satisfactory direct test of the hypothesis that it was a ruling elite system, although indirect and rather unsatisfactory tests might be devised.

Consequently, to know whether or not we have a ruling elite, we must have a political system in which there is a difference in preferences, from time to time, among the individual human beings in the system. Suppose, now, that among these individuals there is a set whose preferences regularly prevail in all cases of disagreement, or at least in all cases of disagreement over key political issues (a term I propose to leave undefined here). Let me call such a set of individuals a "controlling group." In a full-fledged democracy operating strictly according to majority rule, the majority would constitute a controlling group, even though the individual members of the majority might change from one issue to the next. But since our model is to represent a ruling elite system, we require that the set be *less than a majority in size*.

However, in any representative system with single member voting districts where more than two candidates receive votes, a candidate *could* win with less than a majority of votes; and it is possible, therefore, to imagine a truly sovereign legislature elected under the strictest "democratic" rules that was nonetheless governed by a legislative majority representing the first preferences of a minority of voters. Yet I do not think we would want to call such a political system a ruling elite system. Because of this kind of difficulty, I proposed that we exclude from our definition of a ruling elite any controlling group that is a product of rules that are actually followed (that is, "real" rules) under which a majority of individuals could dominate if they took certain actions permissible under the

"real" rules. In short, to constitute a ruling elite a controlling group must not be *a pure artifact of democratic rules*.

A ruling elite, then, is a controlling group less than a majority in size that is not a pure artifact of democratic rules. It is a minority of individuals whose preferences regularly prevail in cases of differences in preference on key political issues. If we are to avoid an infinite regress of explanations, the composition of the ruling elite must be more or less definitely specified.

SOME BAD TESTS

The hypothesis we are dealing with would run along these lines: "Such and such a political system (the U.S., the U.S.S.R., New Haven, or the like) is a ruling elite system in which the ruling elite has the following membership." Membership would then be specified by name, position, socioeconomic class, socioeconomic roles, or what not.

Let me now turn to the problem of testing a hypothesis of this sort, and begin by indicating a few tests that are sometimes mistakenly taken as adequate.

The first improper test confuses a ruling elite with a group that has a high *potential for control*. Let me explain. Suppose a set of individuals in a political system has the following property: there is a very high probability that if they agree on a key political alternative, and if they all act in some specified way, then that alternative will be chosen. We may say of such a group that it has a *high potential for control*. In a large and complex society like ours, there may be many such groups. For example, the bureaucratic triumvirate of Professor Mills would appear to have a high potential for control.[2] In the City of New Haven, with which I have some acquaintance; I do not doubt that the leading business figures together with the leaders of both political parties have a high potential for control. But a potential for control is not, except in a peculiarly Hobbesian world, equivalent to actual control. If the military leaders of this country and their subordinates agreed that it was desirable, they could most assuredly establish a military dictatorship of the most overt sort; nor would they need the aid of leaders of business corporations or the executive branch of our government. But they have not set up such a dictatorship. For what is lacking are the premises I mentioned earlier, namely agreement on a key political alternative and some set of specific implementing actions. That is to say, a group may have a high potential for control and a *low potential for unity*. The actual *political effectiveness* of a group is a function of its potential for control *and* its potential for unity. Thus a group with a relatively low potential for control but a high potential for unity may be more politically effective than a group with a high potential for control but a low potential for unity.

The second improper test confuses a ruling elite with a group of individuals who have more influence than any others in the system. I take it for granted that in every human organization some individuals have more influence over key decisions than do others. Political equality may well be among the most utopian of all human goals. But it is fallacious to assume that the absence of political equality proves the existence of a ruling elite.

The third improper test, which is closely related to the preceding one, is to generalize from a single scope of influence. Neither logically nor empirically does it follow that a group with a high degree of influence over one scope will necessarily have a high degree of influence over another scope within the same system. This is a matter to be determined empirically. Any investigation that does not take into account the possibility that different elite groups have different scopes is suspect. By means of sloppy questions one could easily seem to discover that there exists a unified ruling elite in New Haven; for there is no doubt that small groups of people make many key decisions. It appears to be the case, however, that the small group that runs urban redevelopment is not the same as the small group that runs public education, and neither is quite the same as the two small groups that run the two parties. Moreover the small group that runs urban redevelopment with a high degree of unity would almost certainly disintegrate if its activities were extended to either education or the two political parties.

A PROPOSED TEST

If tests like these are not valid, what can we properly require?

Let us take the simplest possible situation. Assume that there have been some number—I will not say how many—of cases where there has been disagreement within the political system on key political choices. Assume further that the hypothetical ruling elite prefers one alternative and other actors in the system prefer other alternatives. Then unless it is true that in all or very nearly all of these cases the alternative preferred by the ruling elite is actually adopted, the hypothesis (that the system is dominated by the specified ruling elite) is clearly false.

I do not want to pretend either that the research necessary to such a test is at all easy to carry out or that community life lends itself conveniently to strict interpretation according to the requirements of the test. *But I do not see how anyone can suppose that he has established the dominance of a specific group in a community or a nation without basing his analysis on the careful examination of a series of concrete decisions.* And these decisions must either constitute the universe or a fair sample from the universe of key political decisions taken in the political system.

Now it is a remarkable and indeed astounding fact that neither Professor Mills nor Professor Hunter has seriously attempted to examine an array of specific cases to test his major hypothesis.[3] Yet I suppose these two works more than any others in the social sciences of the late few years have sought to interpret complex political systems essentially as instances of a ruling elite.

To sum up: The hypothesis of the existence of a ruling elite can be strictly tested only if:

1. The hypothetical ruling elite is a well defined group.
2. There is a fair sample of cases involving key political decisions in which the preferences of the hypothetical ruling elite run counter to those of any other likely group that might be suggested.
3. In such cases, the preferences of the elite regularly prevail.

DIFFICULTIES AND OBJECTIONS

Several objections might be raised against the test I propose.

First, one might argue that the test is *too weak*. The argument would run as follows: If a ruling elite *doesn't* exist in a community, then the test is satisfactory; that is, if every hypothetical ruling elite is compared with alternative control groups, and in fact no ruling elite exists, then the test will indeed show that there is no minority whose preferences regularly prevail on key political alternatives. But—it might be said —suppose a ruling elite *does* exist. The test will not *necessarily* demonstrate its existence, since we may not have selected the right group as our hypothetical ruling elite. Now this objection is valid; but it suggests the point I made at the outset about the possibility of an infinite regress of explanations. Unless we use the test on every possible combination of individuals in the community, we cannot be certain that there is not some combination that constitutes a ruling elite. But since there is no more *a priori* reason to assume that a ruling elite does exist than to assume that one does not exist, the burden of proof does not rest upon the critic of the hypothesis, but upon its proponent. And a proponent must specify what group he has in mind as his ruling elite. Once the group is specified, then the test I have suggested is, at least in principle, valid.

Second, one could object that the test is *too strong*. For suppose that the members of the "ruled" group are indifferent as to the outcome of various political alternatives. Surely (one could argue) if there is another group that regularly gets its way in the face of this indifference, it is in fact the ruling group in the society. Now my reasons for wishing to discriminate this case from the other involve more than a mere question of the propriety of using the term "ruling elite," which is only a term of convenience. There is, I think, a difference of some theoretical significance between a system in which a small group dominates over another that is opposed to it, and one in which a group dominates over an indifferent mass. In the second case, the alternatives at stake can hardly be regarded as "key political issues" if we assume the point of view of the indifferent mass; whereas in the first case it is reasonable to say that the alternatives involve a key political issue from the standpoint of both groups. Earlier I refrained from defining the concept "key political issues." If we were to do so at this point, it would seem reasonable to require as a necessary although possibly not a sufficient condition that the issue should involve actual disagreement in preferences among two or more groups. In short, the case of "indifference vs. preference" would be ruled out.

However, I do not mean to dispose of the problem simply by definition. The point is to make sure that the two systems are distinguished. The test for the second, weaker system of elite rule would then be merely a modification of the test proposed for the first and more stringent case. It would again require an examination of a series of cases showing uniformly that when "the word" was authoritatively passed down from the designated elite, the hitherto indifferent majority fell into ready compliance with an alternative that had nothing else to recommend it intrinsically.

Third, one might argue that the test will not discriminate between a true ruling elite and a ruling elite together with its satellites. This objection is in one sense true and in one sense false. It is true that on a series of key political questions, an apparently unified group might prevail who would, according to our test, thereby constitute a ruling elite. Yet an inner core might actually make the decisions for the whole group. However, one of two possibilities must be true. Either the inner core and the front men always agree at all times in the decision process, or they do not. But if they always agree, then it follows from one of our two assumptions about influence that the distinction between an "inner core" and "front men" has no operational meaning; that is, there is no conceivable way to distinguish between them. And if they do not always agree, then the test simply requires a comparison at those points in time when they disagree. Here again, the advantages of concrete cases are palpable, for these enable one to discover who initiates or vetoes and who merely complies.

Fourth, it might be said that the test is either too demanding or else it is too arbitrary. If it requires that the hypothetical elite prevails in *every single case,* then it demands too much. But if it does not require this much, then at what point can a ruling elite be said to exist? When it prevails in 7 cases out of 10? 8 out of 10? 9 out of 10? Or what? There are two answers to this objection. On the one hand, it would be quite reasonable to argue, I think, that since we are considering only key political choices and not trivial decisions, if the elite does not prevail in *every* case in which it disagrees with a contrary group, it cannot properly be called a ruling elite. But since I have not supplied an independent definition of the term "key political choices," I must admit that this answer is not wholly satisfactory. On the other hand, I would be inclined to suggest that in this instance as in many others we ought not to assume that political reality will be as discrete and discontinuous as the concepts we find convenient to employ. We can say that a system approximates a true ruling elite system, to a greater or lesser degree, without insisting that it exemplify the extreme and limiting case.

Fifth, it might be objected that the test I have proposed would not work in the most obvious of all cases of ruling elites, namely in the totalitarian dictatorships. For the control of the elite over the expression of opinion is so great that overtly there is no disagreement; hence no cases on which to base a judgment arise. This objection is a fair one. But we are not concerned here with totalitarian systems. We are concerned with the application of the techniques of modern investigation to American communities, where, except in very rare cases, terror is not so pervasive that the investigator is barred from discovering the preferences of citizens. Even in Little Rock, for example, newspaper men seemed to have had little difficulty in finding diverse opinions; and a northern political scientist of my acquaintance has managed to complete a large number of productive interviews with White and Negro Southerners on the touchy subject of integration.

Finally one could argue that even in a society like ours a ruling elite might be so influential over ideas, attitudes, and opinions that a kind of false consensus will exist—not the phony consensus of a terroristic totalitarian dictatorship but the manipulated and superficially self-imposed adherence to the norms and goals of the elite by broad sections of a community. A good deal of Professor Mills' argument can be interpreted in this way, although it is not clear to me whether this is what he means to rest his case on.

Even more than the others this objection points to the need to be circumspect in interpreting the evidence. Yet here, too, it seems to me that the hypothesis cannot be satisfactorily confirmed without something equivalent to the test I have proposed. For once again either the consensus is perpetual and unbreakable, in which case there is no conceivable way of determining who is ruler and who is ruled. Or it is not. But if it is not, then there is some point in the process of forming opinions at which the one group will be seen to initiate and veto, while the rest merely respond. And we can only discover these points *by an examination of a series of concrete cases where key decisions are made:* decisions on taxation and expenditures, subsidies, welfare programs, military policy, and so on.

It would be interesting to know, for example, whether the initiation and veto of alternatives having to do with our missile program would confirm Professor Mills' hypothesis, or indeed any reasonable hypothesis about the existence of a ruling elite. To the superficial observer it would scarcely appear that the military itself is a homogeneous group, to say nothing of their supposed coalition with corporate and political executives. If the military alone or the coalition together is a ruling elite, it is either incredibly incompetent in administering its own fundamental affairs or else it is unconcerned with the success of its policies to a degree that I find astounding.

However I do not mean to examine the evidence here. For the whole point of this paper is that the evidence for a ruling elite, either in the United States or in any specific community, has not yet been properly examined so far as I know. And the evidence has not been properly examined, I have tried to argue, because the examination has not employed satisfactory criteria to determine what constitutes a fair test of the basic hypothesis.

NOTES

[1]See Robert A. Dahl, "The Concept of Power," *Behavioral Science* 2 (July 1957): 201-215.

[2]C. Wright Mills, *The Power Elite* (New York: Oxford University Press, 1956).

[3]Mills, *Power Elite;* Floyd Hunter, *Community Power Structure* (Chapel Hill: University of North Carolina Press, 1953).

VI

Access to Status, Wealth, and Power

In a population whose structure consists of differentiated roles and positions ranged in hierarchies of inequality according to their differential evaluation and the extent to which they partake of valued attributes, the problem of stratification consists in the degree to which and the mechanisms by which the positions and attributes of fathers affect the positions and attributes of their sons. Some positions are attained by virtue of being born into the appropriate social category—one is born a male or a Negro, one is middle-aged by virtue of having been born some time previously, one's parental Nationality makes one of English descent and his parental affiliation makes him Episcopalian—and these positions can be changed only with some difficulty. One *may* be born to positions of wealth, status or power, but in modern societies most individuals attain these goals by achieving positions that provide access to them. Thus, our interest shifts to the process of attaining the positions which confer access. In particular, we focus upon the processes of occupational achievement since, in modern societies, occupations and the qualities necessary to gain them are the major source of access to status, wealth,

and power for most individuals. The role of ascriptive positions—positions attained by birth—may be either to facilitate or to hinder the achievement of desirable positions through their effect on intergenerational transmission of advantage. Or they may serve directly as the criteria upon which positions and their desiderata are distributed.

The relevance of one's occupational origins to one's final occupational destination is a well established feature of modern societies. Much of the gross correlation between the achievement of sons and their fathers is, of course, due to the intervening factor of the son's education, which is an important determinant of his occupational attainment, and is in part determined by his father's socioeconomic position. Thus, even if origin exerted no direct influence on destination, the two would still be correlated by virtue of their linkage through son's education. As it turns out empirically, education is not a sufficient linkage to account for the entire correlation of father's occupational attainment and his son's occupational attainment.

Although the features of social mobility in modern societies sketched in the forego-

Figure 1

Father's Education → Father's Occupational SES → Son's Education → Occupational SES of Son's First Full-time Job → Occupational SES of Son's Current Job

ing paragraph have been known for some time (see Glass, et al., 1954; Carlsson, 1958; Anderson, 1961), they have only recently been subjected to more precise measurement and explicitly evaluated in a causal framework. This new work, primarily based on data for the United States collected in March, 1962, from a large, national sample of men aged 20-64, is reported in Blau and Duncan's *The American Occupational Structure* (1967) and in subsequent papers by Duncan and his students elaborating the basic findings. Although several reports from this study have been included in the present collection (see the article by Duncan and Duncan in this section and that by Duncan in the section on "The Dynamics of Change in Stratification Systems"), the highly technical character of much of the study makes it impossible to give a full report upon it in the present context. We can, however, provide a brief description of the most important conclusions in this introductory statement, referring the reader to the relevant sources for technical detail and documentation.

The basic variables employed in the Blau-Duncan study may be arrayed in the causal sequence set out in Figure 1. This arrangement is meant primarily to indicate the *temporal* sequence of the variables in question; it does not, for example, imply that the variables form a simple causal chain wherein the association between any pair of variables would be entirely explained by the variables separating them in the chain. Taking the temporal ordering of the variables as a causal one, there are two ways of expositing the interrelationships suggested by the sequence. First, reading from right to left in the sequence, we may let the causally most proximate variables account for as much variation as possible, accumulating explained variance as we read backwards through the causal chain. Thus, via tech-

niques of correlation and multiple regression, we find that 29 percent of the variance in the current occupational socioeconomic status (SES) of sons may be attributed to variation in son's first job. Adding in the effects of the son's education raises the explained variance by another 13 points to 42 percent. Incorporating father's occupational SES again raises the explained variance but by only one percent. Once father's occupational SES is in the analysis, only a negligible additional contribution is made by father's education. In all, the four antecedents of son's occupational SES identified here account for 43 percent of the variation in son's occupational SES. Occupational attainment is thus by no means completely determined by the variables identified here, since over half of the variation in current occupational SES is unexplained.

Although the total variance explained must necessarily remain unchanged, there is a second way of decomposing the variation in son's current occupational SES. This is accomplished by reading from left to right in the sequence, letting the initial and causally most distant variables account for as much variation as possible in current occupational SES. Thus, for example, we find that 10 percent of the variation in son's current occupation is already determined by variation in father's educational attainment. To be sure, we know from our previous decomposition that much of this influence is *transmitted through intervening variables*. Together, however, the two analyses reveal not only that there is a substantial common variation in father's education and son's occupational SES, but also that virtually all of the common variation is transmitted via other variables rather than being directly associated with father's educational attainment. Put another way, changing the variation in father's education would not greatly affect the variation in son's occupational attainment *except* insofar as changing the variation in father's education would change the variation in father's occupational SES and son's educational attainment. Moving on in the diagram from father's education, an additional 8 percent of the variation in son's current occupational SES is attributable to father's occupational SES. Thus, in all, only 18 percent of the variation in occupational attainment is due *in any sense* to socioeconomic origins. This figure not only reveals precisely how intergenerationally fluid socioeconomic status has been in the recent past, but also reveals exactly how much room is left for the operation of individual achievement and chance factors in the determination of occupational mobility. We take it that most observers would concur with our judgment that this figure is substantial.

The relevance of educational attainment to occupational destination is no less clear in the present analysis than in the previous one. Adding son's education, after allowance for father's education and father's occupational SES, still raises the explained variation in son's occupational SES by 20 points to 38 percent. Finally, the SES of one's point of entry into the labor force makes a further contribution to variation in current occupational SES. Even though the full impact of socioeconomic background and educational attainment have been previously established. SES of first full-time job raises the explained variation in current occupational SES by 5 percent to the total, already known from the first decomposition of 43 percent.

Adding variables to the model analyzed here does not alter in any fundamental way the conclusions drawn from the preceding analysis. Occasionally, the effects of one variable upon another are more completely specified by inclusion of a new variable, but the variation in current occupational SES which can be explained is not materially affected by considerations of further factors. For example, intelligence is plainly correlated with occupational attainment, yet inclusion of son's IQ in the analysis hardly alters the explained variation. The reason for this is that son's education is already acting (partially) as a surrogate for son's IQ: including intelligence in the analysis, then, lowers the effects assigned to education. However, the effects assigned above to education tend only to be evenly divided with IQ; the joint effects of education and IQ are not appreciably greater than the effects of education alone (see Duncan, 1968a). Similarly, inclusion of mother's education barely raises the proportion of the variation in son's education which can be explained over that explained by father's occupational SES and father's education alone, and has no appreciable effect at all on son's occupational SES once son's education is in the picture. Mother's education does, however, account for part of the variation which would be assigned to father's education in a model of the determinants of son's education which did not take mother's education into account (see Blau and Duncan, 1967: 188-191). The roles of size of family of origin and broken homes are similar: including them does not substantially raise the explanatory or predictive power already achieved by the variables discussed above, but they do further specify the effects of socioeconomic background upon son's career, especially upon son's education (see B. Duncan, 1967; Duncan and Duncan, 1969). Careful re-analysis (see Duncan, Featherman and Duncan, 1968) of data initially employed by Crockett (1962) fails to turn up any substantial unique effect of achievement motivation upon occupational attainment. As is the case with many other variables mentioned herein, achievement motivation has a significant weight in an analysis of current occupational SES largely at the expense of variables already included in the basic analysis, notably education, and adds little to the explained variation.

Even so dramatic and potentially disruptive an experience as military service appears to have no important impact upon subsequent career development. Once allowance has been made for the superior fitness, both mental and physical, of veterans (who are selected into the service on these criteria), one is unable to detect any appreciable difference between their occupational or economic destinations and those of non-veterans. Military service does little, in American society, but retard one's civilian career development by the length of military service, a substantial burden for which our young men who fulfill their military obligations receive no adequate compensation. Social stratification within the military appears to depart in some interesting ways from the patterns of stratification observed in the civilian society. The difference between the two systems may be succinctly put: ascribed statuses are of continuing relevance to one's position in civilian life, but are of no relevance to one's attainment within the military. To be sure, military rank and the prestige attributed to one's military occupational specialty are *correlated* with such ascribed characteristics as race, region of birth and father's occupational SES. However, once an allowance has been made for pre-military educational attainment and for measured intellectual capacity, these associations disappear. Thus, one's achievement within the military depends in a *direct* way only upon one's premilitary civilian achievements. However, one's achievements within the military have no appreciable consequence for one's subsequent civilian career path. Indeed, on return to civilian life the ascriptive features of one's background which proved of little consequence within the service resume their importance. The military is, then, a kind of attic to society where (a) constraints imposed by one's background are relaxed, (b) attainment is governed by performance, and (c) unfortunately, achievement has, in the main, no important future consequences. (This discussion has been based almost entirely upon the unpublished doctoral dissertation of William M. Mason, which is, for all practical purposes, the sole sound basis for understanding the interrelationships between military and civilian stratification.)

With a few notable exceptions, neither ethnicity nor religious affiliation proves to be an occupational or economic advantage or handicap. To be sure, there are well-known differences between the average income and occupational SES of various ethnic and religious groups (see Glenn, 1967). These differences are, however, primarily attributable to differences between the groups in educational attainment and socioeconomic origins (see Duncan and Duncan on ethnicity reprinted in this section; Warren, 1970, for religion). There are, however, some important exceptions to these generalizations. Even relative to their education and origins, Mexican-Americans are underachievers, presumably because of discriminatory practices that close certain occupational and economic opportunities to them. Jews, on the other hand, are well known to be overachievers relative to their origins and education, a fact which, oddly enough, is usually traced to familial or motivational characteristics, rather than to structural considerations (such as the concentration of Jewish people in self-employed, enterpreneurial activities which gives them greater freedom to follow pro-Jewish employment practices and the high degree of Jewish in-group marriage which provides a familial basis for such practices). At least in America, overachievement and success tend to be linked in popular ideology (and social science fiction) to individual drive and initiative whereas underachievement and failure are related to discrimination and other handicaps rather than to idleness and stupidity. But, whatever the correct interpretation, there is little question that by virtue of their ethno-religious membership, the Jews do experience a real advantage (which probably accounts also for the relative overachievement of largely Jewish ethnic minorities such as Russian immigrants).

There is no substance, however, to the frequently alleged socioeconomic differences between Protestants and Catholics. The differences between Protestants taken as a whole and Catholics are trivial both for the nation as a whole and within most regions. In addition, where economic and occupational differences can be documented, they are reducible to small differentials in educational attainment, which are not attributable to differences in context or content produced by the parochial school system, and to socioeconomic background. While the Protestant-Catholic distinction has no important socioeconomic consequences, it is still an important determinant of political and religious belief and behavior. Differentiation between the various Protestant groups is, however, of greater socioeconomic import, for there is some evidence which suggests that the more prestigious Protestant denominations (Episcopalians, Presbyterians, Unitarians) squeeze noticeably higher economic and occupational rates of returns from their educational investments (see Gockel, 1969). Mean differences between the several Protestant groups in income and occupation are, however, primarily due to differences in background and education (see Warren, 1970).

Unlike religion and ethnicity, however, race remains a very salient factor in socioeconomic attainment. Even though allowance is made for size of family of origin, broken families and socioeconomic origins, there is a significant educational cost in being a Negro in American society, both in the quantity and quality of education. This burden, of course, not only carries over into the occupational and economic spheres, but is augmented by additional racial barriers specific to those areas (see Duncan, 1969). Unfortunately, space does not permit us to discuss the full socioeconomic constraints imposed upon our Negro citizens.

Comparative and temporal generalization of the results discussed above is at best tenuous, since readings on the relevant variables are simply unavailable. Despite the significant changes which have taken place in the occupational *distribution*, there has probably been no really important shift in the *degree of association* between father's and son's occupational SES or prestige in the past half century. There may have been an extremely modest deterioration in the association between educational attainment, occupational attainment and personal income in the recent past; but these declines are modest at best and are surely overshadowed by the significant movements of the educational distribution toward high school graduation as the norm, of the occupational distribution toward rel-

atively greater concentration in professional and scientific jobs, and of the income distribution toward greater equality. Thus, in the recent past, there do not appear to have been any substantial changes in the United States in either the degree of stratification (i.e., intergenerational similarity of father's and son's occupations) or the degree of crystallization (i.e., level of association between different facets of social status and inequality) (see Duncan, 1968b).

Comparative generalization is, if anything, more difficult than the documentation of recent historical changes. There are, in fact, no adequate comparative studies. The only study *within* the United States with comparable data on *different* communities suggests that the stratification systems of smaller places may, in fact, be somewhat more crystallized than that observed in larger cities (see Lane, 1968). A similar conclusion is suggested by the analysis of intergenerational occupational mobility according to the size of place of current residence (see Duncan, 1968b). What social processes might account for these variations by city size remains, however, unspecified. Documenting differences in the mobility and stratification systems of industrial nations is made difficult by lack of comparability between the data available from different countries. Despite claims to the contrary (see Lipset and Bendix, 1959; Svalastoga and Carlsson, 1961), there is reason to believe that there is somewhat less intergenerational mobility in western Europe than in the more economically advanced countries, to wit, Australia, Canada, the United States, and possibly New Zealand. The full basis for this claim cannot be advanced here, but it is based on (1) the discovery of certain flaws of a statistical and technical nature in previous analyses of available data and (2) the unpublished results of studies still in progress.

The selections incorporated in this section augment the conclusions reached by Duncan and his associates in two ways. First, they address somewhat more general issues, providing the broader setting in which the work outlined above may be placed. Second, they focus in several instances upon particular groups, the importance of which can, of course, go undetected in national studies covering the entire socioeconomic spectrum. The continued relevance of ascriptive normative standards, even in modern societies such as the United States, is ably demonstrated by Mayhew, while the selections from Baltzell and Parsons discuss the details and implications of their operation in status associations along religious lines and in race relations. Duncan and Duncan demonstrate that the socioeconomic origins of various foreign-born and second-generation groups largely account for their socioeconomic outcomes, while Miller reviews the major correlates of income in the contemporary United States. Schulze, emphasizing the potential ability of corporate officials to dominate local political and cultural activities, suggests how certain historical changes in the nature of business and management (viz., recruitment of non-local, temporary executives by absentee controlled firms rather than local talent to local family firms) restrict their full, legitimate community participation to matters required by performance of their occupational duties.

REFERENCES

Anderson, C. Arnold.
1961   "A skeptical note on the relation of vertical mobility to education." American Journal of Sociology 66:560-570.

Anderson, C. Arnold, J. C. Brown, and M. J. Bowman.
1952   "Intelligence and occupational mobility." Journal of Political Economy 60:218-239.

Blau, Peter M., and Otis Dudley Duncan.
1967   The American Occupational Structure. New York: Wiley.

Burt, Cyril.
1961   "Intelligence and social mobility." British Journal of Statistical Psychology 14:3-24.

Carlsson, Gösta.
1958   Social Mobility and Class Structure. Lund, Sweden: Gleerup.

Crockett, Harry J., Jr.
1962   "Achievement motive and differential

occupational mobility in the United States." American Sociological Review 27:191-204.

Dogan, Mattei.
1961   "Political ascent in a class society: French deputies 1870-1958." In Dwaine Marvick (ed.), Political Decision-Makers. New York: Free Press.

Duncan, Beverly.
1967   "Education and social background." American Journal of Sociology 72:363-372.

Duncan, Otis Dudley.
1968a "Ability and achievement." Eugenics Quarterly 15:1-11.
1968b "Social stratification and mobility: Problems in the measurement of trend." In W. E. Moore and E. B. Sheldon (eds.), Indicators of Social Change. New York: Russell Sage.
1969   "Inheritance of poverty or inheritance of race." In Daniel P. Moynihan (ed.), On Understanding Poverty: Perspectives from the Social Sciences. New York: Basic Books.

Duncan, Otis Dudley, and Beverly Duncan.
1969   "Family stability and occupational success." Social Problems 16:273-285.

Duncan, Otis Dudley, David L. Featherman, and Beverly Duncan.
1968   Socioeconomic Background and Occupational Achievement: Extensions of a Basic Model. Final Report. Project Number 5-0074 (EO-191) Contract Number OE-5-85-072. Bureau of Research. Office of Education. United States Department of Health, Education, and Welfare.

Featherman, David L.
1969   The Socioeconomic Achievement of White Married Males in the United States, 1957-1967. Unpublished doctoral dissertation, University of Michigan.

Glass, David V., et al.
1954   Social Mobility in Britain. London: Routledge and Kegan Paul.

Glenn, Norvall D.
1967   "Religious preference and worldly success: Some evidence from national surveys." American Sociological Review 32:73-82.

Gockel, Galen L.
1969   "Income and religious affiliation: A regression analysis." American Journal of Sociology 74: 632-647.

Goldstein, Sidney.
1969   "Socioeconomic differentials among religious groups in the United States." American Journal of Sociology 74:612-631.

Hauser, Philip M.
1965   "Demographic factors in the integration

of the Negro." Daedalus (Fall): 847-877.

Hauser, Robert M.
1969 "Schools and the stratification process." American Journal of Sociology 74:587-611.

Hodge, Robert W., and Patricia Hodge.
1965 "Occupational assimilation as a competitive process." American Journal of Sociology 71:249-264.

Kelsall, R. K.
1955 Higher Civil Servants in Britain, from 1870 to the Present Day. London: Routledge and Kegan Paul.

Lane, Angela.
1968 "Occupational mobility in six cities." American Sociological Review 33:740-749.

Laumann, Edward O.
1966 Prestige and Association in an Urban Community. Indianapolis: Bobbs-Merrill.

Lipset, Seymour M., and Reinhard Bendix.
1959 Social Mobility in Industrial Society. Berkeley and Los Angeles: University of California Press.

Mason, William M.
1969 "The impact of military service on the subsequent civilian attainment of Post-World War II American veterans." Proceedings of the American Statistical Association, Social Statistics Section: 418-429.
1970 On the Socioeconomic Effects of Military Service. Unpublished doctoral dissertation. University of Chicago.

Sewell, W. H., A. O. Haller, and A. Portes.
1969 "The educational and early occupational attainment process." American Sociological Review 34:82-92.

Svalastoga, Kaare.
1965 Social Differentiation. New York: David McKay.

Svalastoga, Kaare, and Gösta Carlsson.
1961 "Social stratification and social mobility in Scandinavia." Sociological Inquiry 31:23-46.

Taeuber, Alma F., et al.
1966 "Occupational assimilation and the competitive process: A reanalysis." American Journal of Sociology 72:273-285.

Warren, Bruce.
1970 "Socioeconomic achievement and religion: The American case." Sociological Inquiry 40 (Spring).

CHAPTER 20

Ascription in Modern Societies

LEON MAYHEW

In our critical analysis of sociological theories, we often fail to distinguish what a conceptual scheme takes for granted from what it takes to be problematic. We sometimes even castigate the author of a theoretical scheme for failing to accept the existence of what he actually takes for granted. Thus, Talcott Parsons has been faulted on numerous occasions for "underestimating" the significance of conflict in social life. In his concern for order, it is said, he overlooks the fundamental cleavages and struggles that stimulate movement and change in society. Without judging the ultimate value of Parsonian analysis of conflict, I think it is safe to assert that Parsons has not overlooked the significance of conflict. Indeed, it is precisely because he sees conflict and potential conflict as ever present that he insists that the existence of order in social life is problematic, even awesome.[1] Those who do not admire his account of conflict would more accurately say that they do not believe he has made the sources and forms of conflict sufficiently problematic.

There is a parallel problem in the Parsonian treatment of ascription in social structure. It would be absurd to allege that Parsons is unaware of the significance of ascription; at the same time he has tended to treat ascription as a given and to take as problematic the *breakdown* of ascription. His theory of social change is above all a theory of differentiation, an account of how social structures and institutions that are ascriptively fused with one another come to break apart and then to reunite in more complex ways.[2] His contributions to the analysis of differentiation are extraordinarily valuable and he has used them with great sensitivity and insight. At the same time he has not (despite his occasional papers on race relations, age and sex, and community structure), incorporated the systematic study of ascription into his most precise and global formulations of the theory of social system. Again, for the sake of accurate statement let it be understood that the global theory does not ignore ascription; the problem of how ascription comes to break down is one of its principal concerns. Nevertheless, the sources of ascription, the functions of ascription and, even more important, the consequences of residual ascriptive elements in highly differentiated societies, lack a sufficiently clear and adequate status in the grand conceptual scheme. The aim of this paper is to begin to find a proper theoretical home for these phenomena.

This paper is intended as a contribution to the growing recognition that tradition and modernity are not mutually exclusive conceptual opposites.[3] An adequate theory of

---

[2]Talcott Parsons, "Some Considerations on the Theory of Social Change," *Rural Sociology*, 26 (1961), pp. 219-239.

[3]Joseph Gusfield, "Tradition and Modernity: Misplaced polarities in the Study of Social Change," *American Journal of Sociology*, 72 (January, 1967), pp. 351-362. See also Reinhard Bendix, "Tradition and Modernity Reconsidered," *Comparative Studies in Society and History*, April, 1967 and Arthur L. Stinchcombe, "Social Structure and Organization," in J. G. March (ed.), *Handbook of Organizations*, New York: Rand McNally, 1965. For an excellent example of empirical work in this vein see James C. Abegglen, *The Japanese Factory*, Glencoe, Ill.: The Free Press, 1958.

---

[1]Talcott Parsons, *et al.*, eds., *Theories of Society*, New York: The Free Press of Glencoe, 1961, pp. 30-79.

modern society must not treat social evolution as a process of the breakdown of ascription and its replacement by differentiated social arrangements. The most extreme version of this idea is illustrated by the sort of mass society theory that imagines a totally atomized population bound only by calculated impersonal markets and bureaucracies. Modernization does involve the breakdown of ascription but, at the same time, it also involves mechanisms which use and incorporate traditional ascriptive elements and solidarities. In many individual instances sociologists have recognized this fact, but such recognition seems to have been coerced by empirical discoveries rather than predicted by sociological theory.

FOCI OF ASCRIPTION
IN PARSONIAN THEORY:
EARLY WORK

For Parsons, "ascription" refers to *the fusion of intrinsically separate functions in the same structural unit.* Thus, if the family household is both the center of child rearing and kinship functions on the one hand, and the basic organized producing unit in the economy on the other, then we would speak of ascription. In this context "intrinsically separate functions" mean functions that *can only achieve high levels of performance in different and somewhat incompatible structural settings.*[4] In our examples the structures that are effective in socializing children are based on quite different premises than the structures that are effective in producing a rational exchange of economic goods. The former presupposes intense loyalties, permanent commitments and personalistic relations and the latter is founded on the strict calculation of fluctuating impersonal interests.

This approach to the meaning of "ascription" reflects Parsons' recent macro-functional and evolutionary concerns. Originally, of course, ascription was one pole of one of the pattern variable dichotomies; indeed the concept of ascription had a more elaborate and problematic status in the pattern variable version of social system theory than it does in the current evolutionary apparatus. Treated as a pattern variable, "ascription" refers to *the classification of objects,* in this case social objects, *according to their qualities or attributes.* Actors can, in dealing with other actors, give rewards and punishments primarily on the basis of other's past, present or future performances, or they can act on the basis of others' given attributes, such as age or membership in a group.[5] Ascribed status is a part of any social system because of the universality of certain biological and physical exigencies of the human condition. Every human being has an age, a sex, a position in a reproductive chain, and a physical location in space and time. In many contexts we cannot help but respond to the physical presence or absence of others, the physical capacities associated with their age or their capacity to bear children. Further, reproductive chains form a universal relational network which provides a very convenient structure for defining basic social responsibilities. Thus, both sheer physical attributes and fixed biological relationships are universally used to define some basic social statuses. As long as infant dependency makes primary socialization a need, as long as humans engage in sexual reproduction, as long as social control ultimately requires physical access to persons in space, so long will some ascriptive foci remain in social structures. Given the elemental significance of some biological and physical attributes, it is not surprising that these ascriptive foci are elaborated into larger social structures such as kinship, ethnic groupings and the territorial community.[6]

Because the ascription-achievement pattern variable (subsequently changed to *quality-performance*) refers not to the classification of motivational orientations but to the classification of the treatment of other actors, this pattern variable (along with universalism-particularism), has a special part to play in the classification of social structures. The cross classification of ascription-achievement and universalism-particularism produces a four-fold table defining four

---

[4]Parsons, "Some Considerations on the Theory of Social Change," *op. cit.* Also see Talcott Parsons and Neil Smelser, *Economy and Society,* New York: The Free Press, 1956, pp. 246-274.

[5]Talcott Parsons, *The Social System,* Glencoe, Ill.: The Free Press, 1951, pp. 63-65.
[6]*Ibid.,* pp. 170-177.

basic types of value systems. Thus the combination of universalism and achievement produces a value position exemplified in the American ethos with its emphasis on the achievement of goals according to a universalistically defined set of rules of competition. On the other hand, value systems stressing ascription and particularism tend to produce a social structure closely tied to the positions of actors in classificatory schemes and fixed relational networks,[7] such as the Indian caste system.

We can see from this brief account of the treatment of ascription in *The Social System* that, even in this phase of his work, Parsons thought of ascriptive structures as basic reference points from which differentiation in society takes place. As Parsons has himself pointed out, it would be a mistake to underestimate the continuity between the pattern variable system and the newer macro-functional evolutionary apparatus.[8] There is a direct and explicit formal connection between the achievement-ascription pattern variable, which is the basic dichotomy for analysing the structure of social systems in the earlier work, and the dichotomy between structural fusion and structural differentiation which has become so important in the recent evolutionary studies. This connection is readily apparent if we restate in structural terms what it means to categorize another actor in terms of his qualities. To view another actor in relation to his attributes is to view him in relation to a set of structural positions and group memberships which do not define his potential performance. In other words, he is treated entirely with reference to his fixed position in an established social structure.

The pattern variable specificity-diffuseness is also closely connected to structural ascription. It is by adopting attitudes of specificity that actors segregate their specialized roles. To respond to another in a diffuse way is to respond to a set of diverse characteristics, many of which derive from his embedding in a variety of ascriptive structures.

Indeed, all of the pattern variables can be

shown to relate to ascription in some way. However, as Parsons produced further elaborations of the relations between the pattern variables and macro-functional concepts the analysis became more and more complicated. First, in *Working Papers in the Theory of Action,* Parsons came to the conclusion that the performance or achievement potential of objects becomes most relevant to actors during the goal attainment phase of their interaction. Ascription is especially important during the phase of latent tension management. Further, actors must take special account of the *specific* characteristics of objects during the initial adaptive phases of interaction but a more *diffuse* characterization of objects is appropriate during integrative phases.[9] In this stage of the development of his scheme Parsons was especially interested in motivational analysis and in the connections and convergences between his own analysis of motivation in the social system and Bales' work on functional phases in problem solving groups. His initial work on the correspondences between pattern variables and functions reflected that preoccupation.

Later, in "Pattern Variables Revisited" he came to see that these links between functional problems and pattern variables outlined above are only a special case and that the full range of associations between functions and pattern variables is more diverse and differentiated.[10] The appropriate pattern variable choice for an actor in a given functional context depends upon a variety of factors at various levels. In the new formulation, actors in a given sub-system of action must adopt pattern variable choices according to the type of adaptive exigencies faced by the sub-system, the character of the objects dealt with by the sub-system, the special needs of the actors in the sub-system, and the specialized functional contribution of the sub-system to the larger system of which it is a part. For example, performance and specificity, with their connotations of *differentiation,* are primarily connected with problems of task management, goal seeking, and relations with the

[7]*Ibid.*, pp. 106 ff.
[8]Talcott Parsons, "Pattern Variables Revisited: A Response To Robert Dubin," *American Sociological Review*, 25 (August, 1960), pp. 467-482.

[9]Talcott Parsons, Robert F. Bales and Edward A. Shils, *Working Papers in the Theory of Action,* Glencoe, Ill.: The Free Press, 1953, p. 182.
[10]Parsons, "Pattern Variables Revisited," *op. cit.*

environment. Quality and diffuseness, with their connotations of *ascription*, are primarily appropriate for dealing with broad social emotional problems and problems of group stability, integration and meaning.

FOCI OF ASCRIPTION IN PARSONIAN THEORY: RECENT WORK

In Parsons' recent evolutionary work ascription has become *the base state from which evolution occurs in the form of continuing differentiation and re-integration*. In this scheme relatively little attention is paid to ascription as a phenomenon in its own right. However, a few of his theoretical papers bear on the problem quite directly. In one section of *Theories of Society* Parsons classifies the basic ascriptive solidarities from which evolution occurs.[11] The first category is *kinship*. Initially all social structures are fused with the fundamental structure of kinship and all functions are located in kin groupings and relationships. From this perspective the process of evolution initially involves pulling some functions out of their ascriptive embedding in kinship structures. Two extensions of kinship-like ties constitute the next two categories of ascription. The first is *ethnic solidarity* which involves the extension of a familial type of loyalty to a much larger group of culturally or genetically similar persons. The second is the *primary group* which represents the extension into other spheres of life of the sort of groups and relationships found in the kin context. The final ascriptive focus of social structure is the *territorial grouping*. Even though human beings are quite mobile in space, all human action has a territorial reference and for this reason all social organization is ultimately grounded in groups with a territorial reference.[12]

These ascriptive features of social life may become attenuated by differentiation and technological advance, but none may be eliminated from the structure of society, for each represents an ineluctable exigency of social functioning.[13] In this sense, Parsons recognizes that ascription will be a part of the structure of even the most modern and highly differentiated society.

In his most systematic attempt to account for the continuation of ascriptive elements in differentiated contexts,[14] Parsons points out that even highly differentiated and specialized groups cannot avoid the full range of functional problems. Thus, even highly specialized economic units face political exigencies and, for this reason, business firms might make use of non-economic criteria in recruiting persons to positions of top leadership. Concrete institutions are linked to each other because they all share a common set of functional exigencies which limit their specialization. Business firms must meet political exigencies and they cannot neglect the fact that workers have a family life outside of the work context; political units cannot be exclusively concerned with effectiveness, ignoring legitimacy and the economic allocation of resources; persons in professional roles cannot be entirely economic in their orientations for they must respond to the special pattern-maintenance functions of professional roles.

It is important to note that this line of attack on the problem of ascription does not retreat from the idea that given orientations in the actor are appropriate to given functional contexts. Rather it insists on the multifunctional character of any given concrete context. This approach represents a translation to the macrofunctional level of Parsons' historic and continuing insistence that social evolution does not produce a complete transformation of all social life to the *Gesellschaftlich* orientations of specificity, affective neutrality, universalism, achievement and self interest. All concrete social units must deal with problems of integration and tension management and with other problems that require a continuation of *Gemeinschaftlich* orientations in some contexts. Since these orientations are likely to support responding to others in terms of their statuses and their diffuse qualities,

---

[11]Parsons *et al.*, *Theories of Society, op. cit.*, pp. 242-244.

[12]Talcott Parsons, "The Principal Structures of Community," in *Structure and Process in Modern Society*, Glencoe, Ill.; The Free Press, 1960, pp. 250-279.

[13]*Ibid.*, pp. 277-278.

[14]Parsons, *Theories of Society, op. cit.*, pp. 53-56.

there will always be limitations on differentiation and specialisation in social systems.

In sum, throughout his career Parsons has recognized the force and staying power of the ascriptive elements of social structure. He recognizes limits to differentiation and sees these limits as deriving from several inescapable exigencies of social action and social organization. At the same time he believes that the course of social evolution is best described as a process of greater and greater adaptation to the environment and that adaptation occurs through a progressive differentiation of systems of social action. As this differentiation occurs, the functions of ascription become limited to a circumscribed sector of social life. Ascription, and its associated orientations in the actor, survive only where ascription as such contributes to the solution of problems of integration, socialization, and tension management.

CRITIQUE

The strategic misstep in Parsons' approach to ascription lies in his persistent attempts to link ascription to particular functions. In contrast, this paper argues that *various forms of ascription contribute to the solution of all of the functional problems faced by social systems.* Any attempt to associate ascription (and its related orientations in the actor) to particular functional contexts is misguided and can only obscure the residual staying power of ascription in contemporary society. Worse, such attempts impede analysis of the consequences of ascription in contemporary society, particularly the impact of ascription on the relations between the institutional sectors of society and the role of ascription in hindering social action.

Of course, Parsons is correct within the context of his own *broadly* comparative and *broadly* evolutionary concerns. The sociological literature is cluttered with irrelevant attacks upon Parsons that fail to appreciate the broadly comparative aims of his work. Thus, Parsons has written of the relative isolation of the nuclear family in American society.[15] This view has been attacked on the basis of empirical research showing that some Americans do visit their relatives, and on some occasions, call upon them for aid. Obviously the question is not whether contact with extended kin is more than zero; the question is whether such contact is less than in relatively undifferentiated societies. The existence of a pattern of contact between relatives does not make the American kinship system an essential replica of the kinship systems of aboriginal Australia.

Similarly, in his evolutionary studies, Parsons has made a number of valid points about the adaptive potential of differentiation. Modern American society clearly has more adaptive potential, in the evolutionary sense, than primitive Australian society. Further, this adaptive capacity is, in large measure, a product of a long series of differentiations, each of which involved a breakdown of ascription and structural fusion. All of Parsons' "evolutionary universals" constitute breakdowns of ascription in social and cultural structure: *stratification* breaks down the system of equal status found in any structure entirely bound to kinship and kinship obligation, thus paving the way for differentiated leadership as well as other kinds of specialization. *"Cultural legitimation"* means the development of clear boundaries for a society vis-à-vis other societies through the institutionalization of clear symbolization of the definition of the "we," thus permitting the development of a "societal community" and, in so doing, increasing the capacity of the society to incorporate large numbers of members. *Bureaucracy,* with its concept of "office," involves the strict differentiation of political roles from other roles, and with bureaucracy comes a great increase in the capacity of society to mobilize human and natural resources. The *market* emancipates economic resources from such ascriptive bonds as kinship, political loyalty, and detailed religious obligations. A *specialized and abstract legal system* eliminates the ascription of integrative norms to political bargaining or diffuse, detailed religious norms, thus permitting society to deal with problems of coordination and integration in their own terms. Finally, *the democratic*

---

[15]Talcott Parsons, "The Kinship System of the Contemporary United States," in *Essays in Sociological Theory,* Glencoe, Ill.: The Free Press, 1954, pp. 177-196.

association increases the political and integrative capacity of society by freeing political loyalty from attachment to given leaders independent of their performance. All of these evolutionary universals involve the breakdown of ascription, emancipating or mobilizing resources so as to permit large populations spread over wide territorial areas to develop complex, highly differentiated, productive, and yet solidary societies. Such societies can be seen as maximizing the evolutionary potential of the human organism.[16]

In my opinion this analysis is an important contribution to sociological theory. But it is *broadly* evolutionary and *broadly* comparative. Analysis of the fundamental evolutionary breakthroughs that permit new forms of society to develop should not blind us to the actual structure and functioning of contemporary society. We cannot view contemporary society as a mere opposite of traditional society, nor can we see the traditional elements of modern society as mere functionless vestiges of an earlier era. Ascriptive elements of a variety of types retain their vitality and they function as an integral component of modern social structure. The course of evolution neither eliminates nor isolates ascriptive elements of social structure; their meaning may change and their mode of integration with the larger society may become altered, but their real impact is never eliminated.

Parsons has repeatedly recognized and acknowledged the importance and necessity of ascription in all societies. The purpose of this paper is to develop the implications of this recognition and to emphasize that ascription is not limited to any one of the functional requisites of social systems.

THE FUNCTIONS OF ASCRIPTION

The source of the staying power and functional capacity of ascription can be summed up in three words: it is cheap. Ascription involves using an existent, pre-established structure as a resource rather than creating a new specialized structure for the same purpose. We may state, as a gen-

eral hypothesis, that *a specialized structure will not be created unless it will be sufficiently productive to justify the costs involved in creating and maintaining it.* The development of a new structure to deal with a pressing problem consumes time and attention. Thus, the development of an organizational apparatus to cope with one problem limits the resources available to cope with other problems. Paradoxically, specialization in one area of problems encourages the use of, (indeed the search for), convenient or cheap techniques for handling other problems. In traditional or primitive settings "convenient" may be a more appropriate term to describe the function of ascription, but the important point here is that even after the transition to rational, deliberate, calculating orientations, ascription retains its capacity to provide low cost solutions to the myriad problems facing an organization. Indeed, such a rational and calculating attitude may lead to the *deliberate adoption* of an ascriptive technique.

A concrete illustration will clarify this point: Consider a business firm faced with the problem of recruiting and maintaining a labor force. A complex modern firm confronts a variety of problems which reflect the variety in the occupational roles represented in the firm. For some positions there will be chronic shortages while for other positions there will be only relatively slow normal attrition. The problem of severe shortages will be more salient and a great deal of time and energy will be devoted to specialized techniques for expanding the firm's range of purview over potential labor in these categories. Local and even national news media will be used, special recruitment trips might be made to search for potential talent, internal training programs may be adopted and special efforts might be expended to integrate new ethnic groups into the labor force. All of these policies have clear implications for ascription; all of them tend to attack the various ascriptive ties which bind occupational roles to residential location, to given statuses in the organization, and to ethnic status.

On the other hand, for those positions subject only to normal replacement, it will be easier to rely on natural flows of labor input. Preoccupied with more pressing problems, the personnel department will fill

---

[16]Talcott Parsons, "Evolutionary Universals in Society," *American Sociological Review*, 29 (June, 1964), pp. 339-357.

easily fillable vacancies in the easiest possible way. What are these "natural flows of labor input"? In large measure, the ordinary process of recruitment is tied to networks of primary group affiliation and informal contacts. Information about possible job openings passes by word of mouth, from relative to relative, neighbor to neighbor, friend to friend, through ethnic groups, social strata and other segments of the community. Here the implications for ascription are different; rather than working to break ascription down, such a process serves to reproduce the established structure of the community in the labor force of the business firm.

Even when energy is being expended on conscious recruitment, management will not overlook the possibility of using ascriptive channels to the labor market. In fact, such channels may be assiduously cultivated and protected as "inside tracks" to scarce resources. After all, the problem of a personnel manager is not to find the best possible people to fill available positions; he seeks to fill positions with qualified applicants at *minimum cost to the organization.*

Herein lies the Achilles heel of the approach to functional problems through the pattern variables. From one perspective it would seem that the rational personnel director would employ persons on the basis of their performance potential rather than on the basis of any ascriptive qualifications, and so he would, *given an established array of candidates.* The approach to functional problems through the pattern variables seems to imply an additive approach; we sum the appropriate actions of a personnel manager over an array of given alters with whom he interacts. It is true that when he interacts with a given alter he will, if he is rational, respond to alter's performance potential. But from an organizational point of view his problem is not to deal sequentially with a set of candidates; his problem is to generate a labor force for the organization. This is a different problem and one that may lead him to adopt as an *economical organizational strategy,* a technique for recruiting personnel which depends heavily on established social structures, including all of their ascriptive elements.

We might note that departments of soci-

ology face a similar problem. They seek to recruit the best possible staff of professional sociologists and, to that end, they seek to employ the brightest young sociologists entering the market from the graduate schools each year. Given a number of competitive applicants for a single position, departments will make their choice on the basis of an assessment of the potential quality of the applicants' performance rather than an assessment of the prestige of their school of origin or their academic sponsors. On the other hand, few departments could afford the expense of actually examining the total output of all of the graduate schools in the country. It is more economical to select a relatively small sample of prestige schools and to recruit from those schools more or less exclusively. On an actuarial basis it is probable that high prestige schools will produce higher quality candidates. Of course this technique works to the disadvantage of the best graduates of some urban state universities and other schools with lower status, and to this extent a variety of ascriptive factors operate in the talent market in the field of sociology. The point is that it is not direct prejudice (read quality orientation) that is operating here; rather it is the *indirectly* ascriptive effect of a decision based upon the perfectly rational economic grounds that it is inexpensive to utilize established social structures.

Similar considerations apply to the political organization of community activity. Attempts to mobilize support for organized, goal-directed group activity at minimum cost may bring the top leadership of a movement to rely on the recruitment of established resources of leadership and loyalty. In consequence, when these resources are ascriptively defined, the structure of the entire movement often comes to be permeated by ascriptive relationships. Consider *sponsorship* as a device for obtaining organizational support for activity. Suppose a group wishes to operate a series of boys' clubs throughout a city in order to instil in the boys respect for and commitment to the community. Such a group could organize centrally and bureaucratically to gain the necessary funds, obtain leadership and implement the program. An alternative strategy would be to secure the cooperation of other organizations in the community who are willing to sponsor clubs. Churches, schools, veterans groups, playgrounds and other groups may be willing to provide some of the necessary funds and leadership and to undertake the operation of the clubs in particular neighborhoods and groups. The latter strategy risks the possibility that sponsoring organizations might subvert the goals of the movement. A sponsor might seize upon this opportunity as a means of obtaining partial support for a purely athletic program without reference to any of the larger community goals envisioned by the founders of the movement. Bureaucratic theory would suggest that an independent centralized apparatus would be more likely to insure close control over the activities of the movement. But sponsorship has one overwhelming advantage; it is very cheap. It permits an organization to hook into an established social structure in order to gain access to a target population

Turning now from these discursive examples to a more systematic analysis of the functions of ascription, let us examine in turn each of Parsons' four functional prerequisites of a society,—adaptation, goal attainment, integration and pattern maintenance. As the following exposition will show, these four functions may be derived from cross-classifying two dimensions of system problems. Problems may derive from sources *internal* or *external* to the system. Some problems concern the development of resources and these may be called "*instrumental*" problems. Other problems involve the application or expenditure of resources and these may be termed "*consummatory*." The cross-classification of these two distinctions produce the four system problems. The relation of the four functions to the two distinctions will be further defined as each of the functions is examined in turn. The general form of the relationship is given by Table I.[18] For each func-

TABLE I

	Instrumental	Consummatory
External	Adaptation	Goal-attainment
Internal	Pattern-maintenance	Integration

and to make use of established patterns of leadership and control. In this sense, sponsorship is a very adaptive mechanism. It is not hard to see why such organizations as the Boy Scouts of America use sponsorship as a means of gaining access to and tapping the resources of the local community. At the same time it is clear that sponsorship is a device that reflects the constraints of ascription. Whatever ascriptive elements of race or class or wealth are involved in the structure of the neighborhood, the church or the voluntary organization will be reproduced in the structure of any movement which relies on sponsorship as a device.[17]

tional requisite we shall examine the contribution of ascription to its fulfillment. In this way we will be able to identify the types of ascription that have great staying power in the face of differentiation and modernization, and we will be in a position to examine the structural consequences of the continuation of those forms of ascription in the infrastructure of modern society.

ADAPTATION

Adaptation is the external instrumental function of social systems. Adaptation is external in the sense that it involves relating the system to an environment and it is instrumental in the sense that it involves, not the pursuit of particular environmental goals, but the *development of generalized means* for pursuing a variety of goals and

[17] These ideas on sponsorship were developed by the author in collaboration with Phillip Kunz. For further elaboration and a detailed application see Phillip Kunz, "Sponsorship as an Organizational Device: The Case of the Boy Scouts of America," unpublished doctoral dissertation, The University of Michigan, 1967.

[18] Talcott Parsons, "General Theory in Sociology," in Robert K. Merton, *et al.*, eds., *Sociology Today: Problems and Prospects*, New York: Basic Books, 1959, pp. 3-38, at pp. 4-8.

for meeting a variety of environmental conditions as they fluctuate and evolve over time. The key word in this definition is "generalized." Systems increase their adaptive capacities by developing generalized facilities that are uncommitted to any particular use. Adaptive facilities are mobile. Thus, a market economy is a very adaptive allocative mechanism for it does not tie down resources; it frees resources for use toward any goal that is sufficiently economic to pay for itself.

If the key to adaptation is mobility it would seem that ascription could not be adaptive for it involves ascribing resources to particular structural locations. For example, to ascribe a man's economic role to his race is to restrict the use of his capacities as mobile resources in the social system. Hence, in a broad sense ascription is not adaptive and we would expect ascription to break down as a social system develops its adaptive capacities.

However, in one specific sense ascription is adaptive. Ascription functions as a generalized resource for a unit in a social system *when access to a given resource provides the unit with access to an extensive pool of resources* (or to a broad range of resources), *by virtue of ascriptive links between resources.*

To cite a homely example, it is better to use a baby sitter who has a number of sisters who also sit. If one can establish a relationship with a family of baby sitters he is more likely to be able to obtain a sitter on any given night; he can obtain a sitter on shorter notice, (and this is the essence of adaptation); he can find a sitter with less expenditure of energy. This is a far better situation than establishing a relationship with a single girl, especially if she is pretty and courting. Further, the arrangement with sisters will be more enduring for, as one sister goes away to college or marries, a replacement reaches the age of responsibility. A relationship with a family is not so adaptive as some more differentiated arrangements, such as baby sitting pools or professional sitting services, but it is more adaptive than a connection with a single isolated girl, and it is less costly than differentiated arrangements. It is less costly because the development of a differentiated professional baby sitting service requires the outlay of capital and continuing expenditure of overhead which are *unlikely to be overbalanced by economies of scale*. It has also been suggested that ascriptively bound pools of labor are less costly because they provide a more exploitable resource and some empirical studies suggest this to be true, but this has become a very technical question.[19] Suffice it to say that in some situations ascription can become a source of cheap labor for some entrepreneurs because of restrictions on competition but what we are emphasizing here is the fact that ascription is a cheap *access route* to resources for all operative units.

Some readers may wonder why the term "ascription" is appropriate for the use of a group of sisters as baby sitters. After all, the employer is not bound to use only those sisters, sisters are not bound to work for the employer or to work only as baby sitters, and no norms enforce this arrangement. Nevertheless, "ascription" is an appropriate label for the arrangement because its effect is to reproduce in one functional context the structural patterns of another functional setting. In this example, kinship patterns are reproduced in the patterning of a set of employment relations. This necessarily restricts someone else's opportunity to become a baby sitter. The example, of course, is trivial, but the principle is not, for the thrust of the whole argument is that ascription is built into structures and the relations between structures; it is not always a matter of negative orientations towards the qualities of other actors.

GOAL ATTAINMENT

Goal attainment is the external consummatory function, external in that it refers to relating the system to its environment and consummatory in that it involves not the

---

[19] For an introduction to this controversy see Gary Becker, *The Economics of Discrimination,* Chicago: University of Chicago Press, 1957; Robert W. Hodge and Patricia Hodge, "Occupational Assimilation as a Competitive Process," *American Journal of Sociology,* 71 (November, 1965), p. 263; Alma F. Taeuber, *et al.,* "Occupational Assimilation and the Competitive Process," *American Journal of Sociology,* 72 (November, 1966), pp. 273-285, Paul M. Siegel, "On the Costs of Being a Negro," *Sociological Inquiry,* 35 (Winter, 1965), pp. 41-57.

development of generalized instrumental resources but *organization for the effective pursuit of particular system goals.* The key word in this definition is "effective." Systems are well equipped for goal attainment when they are organized to control performances in order to bring them to bear on collective goals. In this sense, capacity for goal attainment refers to a system's ability to organize the effective expenditure of political energy. Energy is expended ineffectively when it is dissipated on diffuse goals, when it is diverted to internal power struggles, or when it is bound to traditional or irrational techniques. Thus, bureaucracy, as described by Weber, is especially well suited to goal attainment for it organizes political control hierarchically in order to facilitate the rational pursuit of specific goals and avoids the ascription of decision-making to internal politics.

If the key to goal attainment is political effectiveness, it would seem that ascription could not be functional, for ascription involves binding political motivation to particularistic loyalties, rather than incorporating it within rationally organized goal-seeking organizations. Parsons has discussed bureaucracy and the democratic association as evolutionary universals tending to free political organization from fixed loyalties which operate independently of performance.[20] Again, in a broad sense, we would expect ascription to decline as systems develop organizational techniques for controlling the expenditure of political energies and for marshalling them in the effective pursuit of collective goals, but, again, ascription can be shown to have goal attainment functions in particular contexts.

Under certain conditions ascription provides inexpensive access to usable political loyalties. We frequently observe that rational administrators avoid the creation of bureaucratic organization or constrain the development of free floating democratic political markets and instead attach their goals to available organizational resources. Sponsorship, as described above, is an example of this technique. Colonial administration provides an even more clear cut illustration. Indeed, colonialism is an ex-

cellent example of the exploitation of the functional capacities of ascription in the economic and political realm. As Rupert Emerson has said apropos of colonial administration: "To produce gold, coffee or rubber or to build jails or roads is a far easier assignment than to transform the inner structure of old and close-knit communities."[21] In consequence the colonialist is quite willing to tie his productive efforts and his political control to this "inner structure of old and close-knit communities," to utilize them as ready made channels of economic and political access. One wonders whether his indigenous nationalist and modernizing successors, beset by overwhelming productive problems and fierce political squabbles, can afford to do otherwise, despite the long run drawbacks of the strategy for the building of integrated nation states.

By the same token, ascriptive solidarities continue to have potential in modern societies. In a competitive political situation, an aspirant for office is unlikely to attempt to fragment his ethnic support for the sake of principle; and, if successful in gaining office, is unlikely to refuse continued opportunities to mobilize ethnic political machines on behalf of collective goals.

INTEGRATION

Integration, the third function, is internal and consummatory. Goal attainment and adaptation are problems in relation to an environment, but integration involves relating the constituent units of a system to each other. Integration is a consummatory function in the sense that it involves not the development of general facilities and resources of stability such as value commitment or emotional therapy, but *the confrontation and solution of given coordinative problems.* Integration may be defined as the prevention of the mutual interference of the units of a system with each other. Such interference may arise from conflict, from the breakdown of mutual expectations, or from a lack of complementarity of performances. Differentiation increases the com-

---

[20]Parsons, "Evolutionary Universals," *op. cit.,* pp. 347-349, 353-356.

[21]Rupert Emerson, *From Empire to Nation: The Rise to Self-Assertion of Asian and African Peoples,* Boston: Beacon Press, 1960, p. 40.

plexity of integrative problems because with greater variety of types of activity and problems of mutuality, complementarity and coordination are exacerbated. Given complex coordinative problems, reflecting the technical exigencies of a variety of complicated activities, integration can be performed most adequately when specialized integrative systems are allowed to deal with integrative problems in their own terms, without political interference or the imposition of a sacred and immobile tradition. Thus, Parsons has spoken of the emergence of secular, specialized legal systems as an evolutionary universal in advanced societies.[22] Such a system permits the continuous elaboration, specification and modification of normative obligations in response to emergent integrative exigencies. By contrast, an integrative system founded on a network of fixed statuses and the traditional mutual obligations attached to these statuses is inflexible and incapable of progressive elaboration. The ascriptive solidarities of a highly ramified kinship system illustrate such a status-bound integrative system.

The continuing integrative potential of ascriptive solidarities is a very complicated aspect of modern society but, broadly speaking, the integrative capacity of such solidary ties depends on the extent to which they extend across other types of structural divisions in society. Kin-based integrative systems do not rest entirely on the solidarity they produce within segments of the community. If this were so, kinship would be merely a segmenting and divisive influence. The integrative capacity of kin ties depends on the existence of cross-cutting ties that create overlapping solidary segments. Maternal, paternal and affinal ties overlap as do kin ties and village or territorial loyalties, creating a network of obligations and sentiments that cross cuts any particular basis of segmentation.

This integrative mechanism is not limited to segments of a social system; it can also link differentiated spheres. When group membership cross cuts units of potential conflict some persons must necessarily experience role conflict and will be constrained to seek workable solutions. The cross-

cutting group memberships need not be of an ascriptive type but if they are ascriptive they have no less integrative potential. Indeed, if the memberships are inescapable it is all the more difficult to solve the problem by choosing one loyalty over another.

Integration through cross-cutting loyalties also leads to the solution of integrative problems in their own terms for it encourages direct confrontation of problems at the grass roots level by persons with detailed knowledge of the ramifications of the difficulties. Specialized integrative systems, such as systems of courts, can deal with coordinative problems in the abstract, and, by virtue of this abstraction can escape the distorting pressures of special interests and the inflexibility of established tradition. This is certainly a helpful contribution to the establishment of institutional frameworks. However, the same abstraction can prevent clear articulation of the practical aspects of problems as they appear at lower operative levels in the system. At those levels neutrality and constructive coordination are maintained by the existence of persons whose interests transcend a given problem. Cross-cutting ascriptive ties can be one source of this mechanism. Perhaps the creation of bureaucratic organization throughout a society increases its unity and collective capacity by creating goal-directed organizations to cross cut traditional particularistic loyalties, but the reverse process is equally significant. Bureaucratic organizations are linked by cross-cutting particularistic ties. We are prone to interpret these ties in terms of such concepts as the power elite, and illegitimate influence, but, as a generic phenomenon, they have a much broader significance. The links between relatives or school-mates in positions of power consolidate the position of a dominant elite but they also mitigate integrative strains between differentiated interests within an elite. Further, such diverse phenomena as ethnic ties across political parties, kin ties across social strata, particularistic political loyalties across formal government bureaucracies, and primary group ties between the agents of social control and their subjects are examples of cross-cutting integrative ties in modern society.[23]

[22]Parsons, "Evolutionary Universals," *op. cit.*, pp. 350-353.

[23]See James S. Coleman, *Community Conflict*, New York: The Free Press, 1957, and Robin

PATTERN MAINTENANCE

The final functional prerequisite is internal and consummatory. It refers to a problem in maintaining relations between units within the system, but whereas "integration" refers to the problem of meeting specific coordinative problems and conflicts, "pattern maintenance" refers to the problem of *developing generalized resources for dealing with internal disturbance of all kinds.* In social systems the requisite of pattern maintenance is met through the development of mechanisms to insure the maintenance of commitment to general patterns of normative order. Thus, stable values insure continuity in the normative order and in patterns of mutual expectations and provide a focus for the inculcation of generalized loyalty and commitment to the society. The contribution of ascription to pattern maintenance is less problematic in Parsonian theory. The kin organized society is both a model of ascriptive organization and an example of heavy stress on pattern maintenance. Kinship provides a fixed pattern of relationships between statuses to which a structure of obligations and expectations can be attached. Further, because of the intimate involvement of kinship and the family, kinship provides a convenient locus for inculcating commitments to the group and its obligations. All obligation can be cast meaningfully in the language of loyalties to *primary groups.*

In his recent essays on evolution, Parsons seems to have become more interested in the weaknesses of ascription as a device for pattern maintenance and these weaknesses are closely related to the strengths.

The problem in attaching commitment to primary ties lies in the limited range of these ties. In relatively small groups, or in societies composed only of small independent communities, kinship obligation may be sufficient, but the evolution of larger more complex societies requires the differentiation of membership loyalties from their embedding in small scale groups. It requires a sense of the "we" that extends to a larger societal community and an order of values that extends to the legitimation of differentiated political institutions.[24]

Nevertheless, as in the case of the other functional requisites, social evolution does not render the pattern maintenance potential of ascription obsolete. Insofar as commitments to the larger societal community can be attached to the values and commitments inculcated in primary groups the individual's attachment to the larger society will be correspondingly deep and strong. If disloyalty to the society is also disloyalty to family, ethnic group, community, friendship circle and other small scale units, the overall structure of solidarity is more firmly grounded. The logic of cost and convenience still holds. If other small scale structures can do the job of inculcating values and commitments, supporting value systems, and engaging in emotional therapy to soothe the stresses endemic in a demanding social system, it is not economic to attempt to replace these units with a differentiated system which limits itself to the support of societal level commitments and values. Indeed, if the value system of a society supports pluralism, religious freedom, and privacy, then that society is largely dependent on the capacity of smaller solidary units to produce commitment to solidarity in the larger society.

THE CONDITIONS OF ASCRIPTIVE FUNCTIONS

If the foregoing analysis is correct then ascription may contribute to the solution of each of the functional problems of social systems. On the other hand ascription may impede performance of each of the functions. Further, by specifying the mechanism by which ascription may support the various functional exigencies the groundwork has been laid for stating the conditions under which ascription will be functional and disfunctional in a modern differentiated society.

The adaptive potential of ascription rests upon the existence in ascriptively defined groups of *a range of usable talents and capacities.* If an ascriptively defined group is so cut off from the larger society as to fail to develop any of the requisite capacities and skills to perform roles in that society then ascription cannot contribute to adaptation. The cheapness of ascriptive routes to resources is only a bargain if the resources

---

Williams, *American Society,* New York: Alfred A. Knopf, 1951, p. 531.
[24] *Ibid.,* pp. 345-346.

are usable. The capacities of members of ascriptively defined groups are *crucial in direct proportion to the levels of skill required in performing societal roles.* Thus, as long as there is a vast demand for relatively unskilled labor, ascriptively defined groups can be tapped even though these groups are socially and culturally isolated. But the more the requirements of economic performance become upgraded the more *low capacity* becomes a condition impeding the adaptive function of ascription.

The potential of ascription for goal attainment rests upon the existence of an *effective leadership structure* within ascriptively defined groups and an *articulation* of that leadership structure with the political organization of the larger society. The political loyalties of the members of ascriptively defined groups are not manipulable unless there is both a structure for effectively mobilizing them in concrete situations and some definite links between the political leadership of the larger society and its constituent ascriptive groups. The more centralized and totalitarian the political organization of a society and the more it has direct access to each citizen, the less dependent it is upon political leadership within its constituent solidary groups. Indeed, such groups constitute a potential threat to central authority. On the other hand, the more a political system depends upon coordinating a diverse array of interests and solidary groups the more serious becomes the *political isolation* of any group.

The integrative potential of ascription rests upon the existence of *cross-cutting ties of solidarity* within the society. The more a group is socially isolated from participation in the larger society the less the likelihood that cross-cutting ties of an integrative character will develop. In some instances cross-cutting memberships and loyalties are built into traditional social structure. Marriage arrangements may create loyalties that cross cut mother's kin group and father's kin group or kin groups and local communities. With the rise of voluntary associations these ascriptively defined traditional dual loyalties become less important and the *restricted participation* of the members of any ascriptively defined group will have more serious consequences.

Finally, the potential of ascription for pattern maintenance presupposes that persons in ascriptively defined locations are not so isolated that their socialization fails to *extend the horizons of their social consciousness* to the larger society. Regional groups, ethnic and religious groups, or castes may fail to inculcate loyalties and identities beyond the immediate group. This is not a serious weakness with respect to pattern maintenance if the structure of the larger society consists in a loose confederation of such groups. But, when the society rests upon political and economic organization which presumes a consolidated nation, *limited horizons* within ascriptively defined groups becomes a serious functional problem.

In sum, a modern differentiated society may contain a number of impediments to the functional potential of ascription. If any group's participation becomes so ascribed as to isolate its members from the larger society then ascription cannot have the various functions described earlier. In particular, if a group is characterized by low capacity, political isolation, restricted participation, or limited horizons then ascribed membership in that group will be dysfunctional. However, this argument has two edges, for when an ascriptively defined group comes to have a range of usable capacities, well developed political leadership which is integrated with the polity at the societal level, extensive participation in a variety of roles, and extended horizons of loyalty, then ascription can come to play an important functional role within a highly differentiated society. This is a very important theoretical point for it weighs against the tendency to argue that participation breaks down ascription. We must argue against a unilinear model of evolution which would suppose that ascription and differentiation are mutually exclusive. On the contrary, the extensive participation of ascriptively defined groups in differentiated roles and institutions does not simply break down ascription; *it insinuates ascriptive elements into the institutional structure of modern society* in complex and variegated ways.

By way of illustration of the empirical importance of this point, quotation of a recent comment on the political development of Indian society is in order. According to Joseph Gusfield, "India appears to be approaching and entering a phase in which modernization will be directed and implemented by persons whose loyalties and ideologies are considerably more traditionalized than has been true in the past decades." [25] As I understand Gusfield, this phenomenon is not to be understood as an evolutionary reversal but as a natural consequence of the extended participation of various Indian traditional groups. The structure and functioning of modern and modernizing societies is not to be understood as a product of the mere elimination of ascriptive or traditional elements but as a consequence of the modification of these elements and their incorporation into a differentiated institutional structure.

THE CLASSIFICATION OF IMPEDIMENTS AND REMEDIES

The foregoing discursive account of impediments to the functions of ascription masked the underlying dimensions of the problem. The four impediments described above merely illustrate four general types of problems of ascription which can be produced by the cross classification of two

defined group can contribute to functional processes only if they meet two conditions of effective participation in the larger society. On the one hand, both commitments and interests must attain some degree of consistency with the values and goals of the larger system, and on the other hand these commitments and interests must have sufficient range and variety to permit widespread participation in the range of differentiated activity present in a modern society. *Low capacity* illustrates a problem of the horizontal range of realistic elements and *restricted participation* illustrates the problem of horizontal range of normative commitments. On the vertical side, *political isolation* is a problem of the vertical consistency of interests and *limited horizons* a problem of the vertical integration of loyalties. These dimensions and their illustrative examples are shown in Table II.[26]

Note that each of the cells in Table I refers to an impediment to one of the functions in the familiar A-G-I-L series. The adaptive functions of ascription rest upon capacities and interests which permit participation in a variety of roles. The integrative function of ascription is founded upon actual participation in, commitment to, and identification with a variety of institutional

TABLE II
IMPEDIMENTS TO ASCRIPTIVE FUNCTIONS

	Problems of Horizontal Range and Variety	Problems of Vertical Consistency
Normative Factors: Commitments, Loyalties and Identities	Restricted Participation (I)	Limited Horizons (L)
"Realistic" Factors: Interests and Capacities	Low Capacity (A)	Political Isolation (G)

theoretical axes. The first axis derives from the distinction between normative commitments, identities and loyalties on the one hand and "realistic" interests and capacities on the other. The second axis refers to the distinction between vertical consistency and horizontal range and variety. Differently stated, both the *normative* commitments and the *realistic* situation of a given ascriptively

roles. The potential contributions of ascriptive organization to goal attainment is

[26]Readers familiar with the normal pattern in four-fold functional tables will note that Table II does not present the usual order of functions. Table II is organized around problems of integrating ascriptively defined groups into a larger differentiated society. Hence, the two integrative dimensions of organic solidarity (A-I) and mechanical solidarity (G-L), which in the normal table are presented as diagonals, are presented as the vertical dimensions of the table in order to emphasize two major aspects of integration.

[25]Gusfield, "Tradition and Modernity," *op. cit.,* p. 361.

dependent upon the articulation of societal goals and the political structure of ascriptive groups. Finally, the potential of ascriptive organization for the function of pattern maintenance depends upon the development of links between particularistic loyalties and commitment to the larger society.

The correspondence between the paradigm of functional prerequisites and the paradigm of barriers to the functions of ascription provides a clue to the classification of remedies to these barriers. Pattern-maintenance and Adaptation are both *instrumental* problems and their solution depends upon the development of generalized facilities and capacities. Integration and Goal Attainment are *consummatory* problems whose reference is actual goal directed activity by actors who can effectively participate in social systems. Accordingly, it is not surprising that there are two main classes of remedies for impediments to the utilization of ascriptive organization. These two classes focus around two prominent universals in the evolutionary development of modern society, mass education and the citizenship-civil rights complex. Mass education tends to remove barriers to the *instrumental* functions of ascription. Ascriptive organization becomes more usable when ascriptively defined groups are subject to education which provides usable skills and widens the horizons of the social world. The institutionalization of civil rights for citizens facilitates the participation and political organization of ascriptive groups and, in this way, removes the impediments to the *consummatory* functions of ascription. The citizenship-civil rights complex includes such institutions as universal suffrage, the legal protection of economic rights, and the legal elimination of sumptuary privileges.

Mass education and the institutionalization of citizenship are usually viewed as *attacks* upon ascription and in a general sense this is an accurate view. But the burden of my argument is that these trends operate selectively; certain constraints upon capacity and participation are eliminated but, paradoxically, *the removal of these limitations increases the usability of the internal organization of ascriptive groups.* In consequence the complex modern society increases its complexity by involving lower level solidary organization in the structure of differentiated institutions.

CONCLUSION

If the preceding analysis is correct, the evolutionary model of society involves several dangers. Insofar as our concerns are *broadly* comparative and *broadly* evolutionary the model of increasing differentiation is very productive. But the study of contemporary modern societies must not be allowed to founder on the assumption that differentiation eliminates ascription.

Such an assumption is particularly inappropriate to the study of the relations between institutions. Parsons' major contribution to this area is his development of the paradigms for double interchanges between institutional sectors of society. The exchange paradigms presume that as institutional sectors become differentiated from each other their continuing integration with each other becomes problematic. The solution to this problem lies in the emergence of exchanges between separated institutional spheres and, in the framework of Parsonian analysis, regulated interinstitutional exchange is the major form of institutional integration in modern society.

This conceptual scheme fails to facilitate analysis of the myriad institutional links which rest on more direct interpenetrations between societal sectors. The impact of racial segregation is a good example of such structured links between institutions. Given a minimum level of integration of the Negro in society through education (albeit inferior) and participation (albeit limited), then restrictions on Negro participation in some institutional spheres are directly reproduced in others. Residential segregation becomes translated into de facto school segregation; school segregation affects educational quality and hence preparation for economic roles; racially determined choices of close associates affect the flow of information about and access to economic and social opportunities. All of these phenomena derive from the fact that organizations utilize established structural locations and networks because of low cost and convenience. Nor can we suppose that improvement of mass education or civil rights laws would rectify these problems for they are deeply rooted in the infra-structures of society. To emphasize the differentiated character of modern institutions and neglect their grounding in persistent networks of ascriptive relationships is to court the danger of prematurely concluding that modern society has solved its problems.

CHAPTER 21

The Immigrants' Progress and the Theory of the Establishment

E. DIGBY BALTZELL

Several years ago an Englishman, visiting America for the first time, remarked to an editor of *Harper's* magazine that nobody had prepared him for his quick discovery that this was not an Anglo-Saxon nation.[1] Although he had long been aware of our multinational, racial and religious origins in the abstract, he simply had not visualized the heterogeneity of our population in general, nor the heterogeneity of the persons of talent and ability in leadership positions. Hollywood, of course, portrays America to people all over the world. Yet the personalities of our screen stars, well-publicized representatives of the American rags-to-riches dream, had done little to dissuade him of our over-all Protestant and Anglo-Saxon ancestry. A brief look at the original names of some of our more famous, pseudo Anglo-Saxon, Hollywood heroes was indeed a revelation. A sample of the Warner Brothers stable of stars, for instance, included Doris Kapplehoff, Larry Skikne, Bernie Schwartz, Mladen Sekulovish, Marie Tomlinson Krebs, Frances Gumm, and Arthur Gelien; among the famous at 20th Century-Fox were Max Showalter, Virginia McMath, Mitzi Gerber, Balla Wegier, Claudette Chauchoin and Ethel Zimmerman; at MGM were Vito Farinola, Joseph Meibes, Tula Finklea and Spengler Arlington Brough; stars at Columbia included Dianne Laruska, Judy Tuvim, Gwyllyn Ford, Margarita Carmen Cansino, Aldo Da Re and Vincent Zoino; while Zalma Hedrick, Donna Mullenger, Sarah Fulks, Ella Geisman, Issur Danielovitch, Daniel Kaminsky, Dino Crocetti and Joseph Levitch were among the leaders at Paramount.* Just as the original names of these famous stars suggest the ethnic diversity of talent in modern America, so their assumed names attest to the Anglo-Saxon ideal which still persists in our culture. For, in spite of the fact that some forty million immigrants of diverse religious and ethnic origins came to America in the course of the nineteenth and early twentieth centuries, we were a predominantly Anglo-Saxon-Protestant people for almost the first two-thirds of our history. Thus our earliest cultural traditions—in language and literature as well as in our legal, political and religious institutions—were modeled on those of seventeenth- and eighteenth-century England. And, above all, our upper class has always been overwhelmingly Anglo-Saxon and Protestant in both origins and values. The "Sixty Families" or the "Four Hundred," the "Rich and the Well-Born," the "Harvard Man," the "Senator," the "Diplomat," the "Socialite," and the "Man of Distinction in the Executive Suite" are all continuing symbols of this Anglo-American ideal which the Hollywood stars, regardless of their own ethnic origins, have tended to perpetuate. The uncomfortable paradox of American society in the twentieth century is that it has tried to combine the democratic ideal of equality of opportunity in an ethnically diverse society with the persistent and conservative traditions of an Anglo-Saxon caste ideal at the top.

THE IMMIGRANTS' PROGRESS

The WASP upper class remained more or less in control of the American elite throughout the first three decades of this century. This was perhaps inevitable, and, as it served to maintain a continuity of tradition at the level of leadership, it was a healthy thing for society as a whole. In the meantime, however, new ethnic families were gradually establishing themselves on the ladder of economic, political and social mobility. By and large this was a three-generational process. The members of the first generation, long used to a subservient and fixed status in the Old Country, clung to their traditional ways, deferred to their "betters," and gradually built up rich ethnic islands in the poorer neighborhoods of our large metropolitan areas. They protected themselves from the strange and often hostile ways of the native Americans by settling along the "Irish Riviera" in South Boston, the "Chinatowns," "Little Italies," or "Ghettos" in New York's Lower East Side and many another booming industrial and commercial city; their language, their patriarchal and familistic mores, and especially their religion, remained that of their ancient ancestors. Economically, they were predominantly unskilled laborers, domestic servants or small entrepreneurs serving the other members of their own communities.

These ethnic islands were, of course, located in the heart of some of the worst slums in the nation, if not in the world. In the Twentieth Congressional District of New York, which sent La Guardia to Congress, some 250,000 people of twenty-seven nationalities, each in its own enclave, were crowded into one square mile. While a vast majority of the foreign-born lived out their lives as best they could, many of their children became delinquents and some of the parents sought an explanation for their suffering in such ideologies as socialism and communism.

But leveling ideologies of the socialist variety have never had a wide appeal to the vest majority of ambitious Americans. As the traditional ways to wealth and respec-

tability in business or the professions were more or less monopolized by Protestant Americans of older stock, many of the more talented and ambitious members of minority groups found careers in urban politics, in organized crime, or, for those of the Catholic faith, in the hierarchy of the Church. Of the two largest minority groups, the Irish and the Italian, the former tended to dominate both the Church and the urban political machines which, except in the City of Philadelphia, were largely responsible for keeping the Democratic Party alive during the years of Republican rule between the Civil War and the New Deal. This dominance of the Church and politics by the Irish may have been one of the factors that led the more overambitious members of the Italian community (the vast majority of whom were solid and law-abiding citizens) into the ranks of organized crime.

While the second and third generations of hyphenated-Americans supplied outstanding leaders in urban politics, the Church and in organized crime, there were at the same time many men who came to the fore in the fields of business, entertainment, and in the arts and sciences. Yet even though they supplied an invigorating talent to the leadership of the nation as a whole, hyphenated-Americans, regardless of occupation or accomplishment, remained more or less isolated from the Protestant establishment. They were too often stereotyped as members of a class of non-Anglo-Saxon immigrants who filled the urban slums of the nation.

But the position of the newer immigrants as a whole was gradually improving. Before the First World War, for example, the center of gravity of the newer immigrants was in the first generation ethnic islands. Between the two wars, however, their sons and grandsons gradually improved their economic positions. As further immigration was cut off in the twenties, by the end of the thirties the center of gravity moved to the second generation. Although the majority were still members of the laboring classes, many had moved up a notch (this was reflected by the increase during the twenties of advertisements for white-collar jobs stating that "no Catholics or Jews need apply"). As this second generation now knew the language, had been educated in the public schools, and had assimilated American values of democracy, self-respect and equal opportunity, they were ready to move into the mainstream of American life. And they found support in the Democratic Party, which, in the 1930's, moved out from local machine politics and onto the national stage under the leadership of Franklin D. Roosevelt.

While the New Deal served to bridge the gap between the immigrants and their children and the mainstream of American life and leadership, the Second War and the postwar boom hastened the process. By the middle of the 1950's, the descendants of immigrants to the urban slums were increasingly affluent, college educated and members of the great middle class. The center of gravity was now in the third generation.

THE THIRD GENERATION AND THE TRIPLE MELTING POT

Just what kind of Americans are these members of the third generation? In their attempt to answer this question, social scientists have developed the theory of the "triple melting pot."[2] According to this theory, ethnic and nationality groups are being Americanized, in the third and fourth generation, within three main religious communities—Catholic, Protestant and Jewish. Religious pluralism is replacing the ethnic pluralism of the earlier era. The process is somewhat as follows: prosperity in the expanding postwar economy has allowed large numbers to move out of their traditional ethnic neighborhoods and occupations. This has meant suburban residence, attendance at suburban schools along with older-stock neighbors, and the consequent need for new means of self-identification (especially for children). And this has produced a rapid increase in church and synagogue affiliation. Thus the Jewishness (ethnic) of the urban ghettos,

and even in the areas of second settlement like the Bronx or along the upper West Side, is now being translated into the new Judaism of the synagogue-centered suburbia (Nathan Glazer estimates that whereas 75 percent of the children in the Bronx during the thirties were receiving no Jewish training, in the suburbs of the fifties, almost 75 percent report attendance at Sunday Schools).[3] And similarly, the one suburban Catholic church has replaced the Irish, Polish and Italian churches and institutions which characterized the downtown neighborhoods. In short, the Italian-, Polish-, Russian- or Irish-American of the urban, first- and second-generation minorities, has now given way to the Protestant-, Catholic- and Jewish-American sense of self-identity in our postwar suburban era. While the American electorate, for instance, would not elect an obviously Irish American to the White House in 1928, they were apparently less prejudiced about the dangers of a Catholic American being sent there in 1960.

THE JEWISH MELTING POT AND THE CLASS STRUCTURE

Within each of the three religious communities which make up the triple melting pot there are, of course, several class levels. And mobility within these class systems is one of the major instruments of assimilation. Just as the middle-class Baptist or Methodist is likely to join a suburban Presbyterian church in the course of his rise to a position of elite affluence, and the move on to an Episcopal church in order to assimilate into the upper class, so the Orthodox East European Jew rises out of the ghetto and joins a Conservative synagogue uptown or out in a largely Jewish suburb, and perhaps eventually finds a Reform congregation even more congenial to his tastes as he moves into a predominately German-Jewish upper-class community.

There are, of course, highly complex class systems within every Catholic community in America, marked by Polish, Italian and Irish parishes, neighborhoods and associations, and led by the Church hierarchy and perhaps a few first families like the Fitzgeralds, Kennedys and Curleys of Boston. This chapter, however, will concentrate on the nature of the rather highly organized and rigid class system which developed within the Jewish community after the Civil War. The Jewish class system, in fact, has gone through three historical periods, depending on the size and composition of the Jewish community itself, and on the reactions of the gentile community.[4]

The first Jews in America arrived at New Amsterdam from the Dutch West Indies, in 1654, and a slow flow continued throughout the Colonial period. By the time of our first census, in 1790, some two thousand Jews were spread throughout the colonies. They were mostly merchants who had come from the West Indies and England and consequently were not marked off as a visible community. There were no rabbis in America during this period when, in fact, only five percent of the population as a whole (in contrast to some 70 percent today) were church-affiliated. Even where there was a sense of community, as in the Sephardic congregations in Newport or Philadelphia, the small number of Jewish merchants spent most of their time with non-Jews, which fostered intermarriage and assimilation (there was a shortage of Jewish females at this time). This was especially true at the highest levels of society, where Jews were part of the merchant establishment. This, then, was the classic period of aristocratic assimilation, and even today there are leading families within the old-stock and Protestant upper class, some of whose ancestors were prominent Jews during the Colonial period. This process of assimilation continued into the early part of the nineteenth century, when immigration was at a low point because of War and depression in this country and because of the Napoleonic conflicts in Europe.

But immigration picked up after 1820. And an increasing number of Jews came to America during the 1840's and 1850's, along with other immigrants from Germany. Although many of them were considered German rather than Jewish and therefore were assimilated immediately, the American-Jewish community had grown to some 150,000 persons by the time of the Civil War. In contrast to the merchants from the West Indies and England who predominated in the Colonial period, most of the new immigrants from Germany were peddlers seeking opportunities to rise in the world. Fortunately, these pre-Civil War decades were marked by the opening of the West and the rapid growth of small-town America. Thus many Jews became pioneers, first-family founders, and leading citizens in small towns all over the nation, often within one generation of their landing. The integration of the Jews in San Francisco in the years immediately following the discovery of gold in 1849 was more or less characteristic of many other American cities in this second, and predominately German, period of immigration.

Perhaps the most important demographic factors affecting the position of the Jews during this second period was their relatively small number and wide dispersion throughout the land. As of 1880, there were Jewish communities in all states, in 173 towns and cities, with no concentration in any particular part of the country (Jews made up about 3 percent of the population of New York City in 1880, as against 30 percent in 1920 and almost 40 percent today).

These numerous German-Jewish communities centered around the synagogue and the family. Though members were of all classes, they were for the most part middle-class entrepreneurs. Those who became prominent in civic and business affairs formed an elite; they were not barred from belonging to prominent clubs and associations, and many were accepted socially by the best gentile society, some assimilating through marriage. This was especially true before the Civil War, when, for instance, the president of the most prominent men's club in Philadelphia was a member of a Jewish family and head of his synagogue. At the same time, Moses Lazarus—father of Emma, whose poem adorns the Statue of Liberty—was one of the founders of New York's patrician

Knickerbocker Club, while Joseph Seligman was a founder of the Union League during the Civil War. Even as late as the 1870's, when young Louis D. Brandeis was welcomed into the best Boston society, Jews still belonged to the best clubs in many cities, and a leading society journal could feature the news of a fashionable "Hebrew Wedding" in New York's Orthodox Thirty-fourth Street Synagogue.[5]

Perhaps the most important feature of this second historical period was the development of an affluent and highly aristocratic German-Jewish upper class.[6] Although the more famous family dynasties such as the Lehmans, Warburgs, Schiffs, Strauses, Loebs, Morgenthaus, Ochses, Sulzbergers, Seligmans and Guggenheims eventually settled in New York, they formed a national upper class composed of small local aristocracies in the larger cities, linked together by intercity marriage alliances. Strict class and religious endogamy was characteristic of this class which was based largely on famous founders who came to America during the forties and fifties and made their fortunes in banking, merchandising and mining. The eminent banking house of Kuhn, Loeb & Company, founded in the middle of the century by Abraham Kuhn and Solomon Loeb, typified the dynastic proclivities of this aristocracy. The senior partner during the free-booting Morgan era, Jacob Schiff, came to America from Frankfurt am Main after the Civil War and married one of Solomon Loeb's daughters; Paul M. Warburg, of a Hamburg banking family, married another daughter; and his brother, Felix Warburg, married Jacob Schiff's daughter. These banking families were also intermarried with the Strauses, who along with the Gimbels and Rosenwalds were among the great mercantile families in the nation.

To summarize, the second historical period of the Jewish adjustment to the American environment included a largely Americanized series of German-Jewish communities, dispersed throughout the nation and headed at the elite level by an intercity aristocratic establishment. As anti-Semitism was only sporadic and idiosyncratic,

many individuals still participated at the top levels of gentile society, some being assimilated completely through marriage or conversion and others through membership in exclusive clubs and associations. But all this was changed by the flood tide of immigrants from Eastern Europe who came to America after 1880, when a third period of adjustment began.

This new immigration, as we have seen, changed the whole character of American society. It also had a profound influence on the nature of the Jewish community. Just as the Catholic peasant from Italy, Sicily, Poland and Czechoslovakia brought quite different customs, values and traditions to the New World than the earlier, Protestant immigrants from Northern Europe, so the Jews from Russia and Poland were also very different from the Sephardic and German Jews who were already established here as of 1880. It is no wonder that the majority of established citizens, both gentile and Jew, were frankly appalled at this tidal wave of new immigrants, possessed as they were of such alien ways. "One can understand," wrote Nathan Glazer, "the feelings of dismay of the earlier German Jewish immigrants as the Russian Jewish immigration, which had spurted upwards at the beginning of the 1880's, showed no signs of abating, and indeed grew larger. It is as if a man who has built himself a pleasant house and is leading a comfortable existence suddenly finds a horde of impecunious relatives descending upon him."[7]

This horde of impecunious relatives swelled the American-Jewish community to over four million persons by the end of the 1920's, almost 80 percent of whom were, by this time, of East European origin. But far more than the increased size of the community was involved. First, there was the concentration of East European Jews in our large cities, especially along the Eastern Seaboard. Thus by 1916, a majority of American Jewry were living in the five cities of New York, Philadelphia, Boston, Chicago and Baltimore (while there were 250,000 Jews in all America in 1880, by 1916, 350,000 were living in New York's Lower East Side alone). Moreover, while the majority of German Jews had been middle class and self-employed, the newer immigrants were largely wage workers concentrated in one industry, garment manufacture. This increase in the size and concentrated location of the newer immigrants, as well as their lower-class occupational pattern, was bound to creat unfavorable stereotypes and stimulate anti-Semitism.

And these stereotypes which intensified anti-Semitism now applied to the whole Jewish community. Thus the term "kike," first coined by German Jews as a derogatory stereotype applying to the new Russian immigrants, was now used by gentiles when referring to Jews in general, the cultivated and Americanized German as well as the impoverished and alien garment workers on the Lower East Side. This was, of course, a terrible shock to the established Jews, especially the cultivated elite, some of whom became anti-Semitic themselves. For "the outraged 'German' Jew saw, shuffling down the gangplank, himself or his father, stripped of the accessories of respectability," writes Oscar Handlin, a leading contemporary historian of immigration. "This was what he had escaped from, been Americanized away from; he did not like its catching up with him. . . . It was distasteful to incur the ill-feeling of one's fellow citizens on account of these unattractive new Jews; and this unattractiveness, it was frequently pointed out, was 'not so much a matter of religion, but of race and of habits.' "[8]

This new situation might well have precipitated a caste division within the American-Jewish community. For, after all, the differences in "race and habits" as between the newer "Russian" and the older "German" Jews were far greater than the cultural gulf dividing the Americanized German Jews from their gentile neighbors. And indeed there were tendencies toward caste, but the forces of aristocratic assimilation finally won out, and mainly for two reasons. First, increased anti-Semitism among gentiles created new and rigid caste barriers which now excluded all Jews, as well as convinced Christians of Jewish origins, from communal or associational participation in the larger gentile society, especially at the elite level. At the same time, and partly in reaction to new caste barriers raised by the gentiles, a majority of the most influential Jewish leaders within the established upper class, acting on their own ancient traditions of *noblesse oblige,* took the lead in insisting on the rights of Jews to seek refuge in this country, then assisted them in adjusting to their new life here, and eventually assimilated them into all levels of the American-Jewish community.

This process of aristocratic assimilation within the Jewish community went through several stages. In the first place, as the nineteenth century came to a close, almost all the charitable resources of the established community went toward aiding the new immigrants from Eastern Europe. And each year the amounts raised and the number of contributors increased. In Philadelphia, for example, the United Hebrew Charities, which raised some $15,000 dollars from about seven hundred contributors in 1870, increased its efforts to raise over $50,000 from more than eight thousand contributors by 1894. These charitable efforts within the established German-Jewish community continued and expanded throughout the early decades of the present century. At the same time, so-called Russian organizations played a larger and larger role in charitable giving, until the two groups, German and Russian, eventually merged. Again taking Philadelphia as an example of a nationwide trend, it was right after the First War that the Federation of Jewish Charities carried on its first combined campaign (over fifty German and Russian agencies cooperated), which set a pattern that has continued down to the present.

The changing patterns of charitable giving, even more so among Jews than among gentiles, are often excellent indexes of change within the elite and the upper-class structures. Thus, while the German-Jewish elite were bearing the main charitable burden at the turn of the century, they were also setting up various caste defenses against the ugliness of the urban melting pot. In much the same way as their gentile peers, they were forming their own exclusive clubs and neighborhoods as well as a series of exclusive summer colonies along the Jersey shore. They also built, in the manner of the Episcopalian gentry, new Reform synagogues, uptown, out in the suburbs and down at the shore. What was happening, in other words, was that both the old-stock gentile and Jewish upper classes, once organized along familistic and communal lines, were now becoming more formal and associational. This was because of the swelling of their ranks as a result of the great expansion of wealth at the turn of the century and the consequent need for formalized institutional ways of assimilating new men and families into the ranks of their respective upper classes. At the same time these exclusive institutions served to protect both upper classes from the rest of the population.

But just as the elite Russian Jews were assimilated into the new and combined charitable organizations after the First War, so the German upper class gradually let down its caste barriers and admitted leading members of the newer immigrant groups into its ranks. In Philadelphia, the leading Jewish country club as well as the most exclusive men's club in the center of the city were both founded and dominated by old-stock German-Jewish families well into the 1930's. By the end of the Second World War, however, these clubs had absorbed leading members of the new Russian-Jewish elite. And today, although there still remains a certain sense of caste superiority among the elder generation of old-stock Jewish families, the members of the younger generation are tending to blend on the basis of common affinity of culture, manners and wealth, rather than on ethnic origins alone.

At this point, I think, it is appropriate to stress the fact that the strength of the American-Jewish community—its low crime, delinquency and divorce rates, for example, as well as its members' extraordinary accomplishments—is at least partly due to its well-articulated class system which, at the same time, has always been combined with both the aristocratic and opportunitarian ideals of assimilation and mobility.

THE ELITE AND THE MARGINAL MAN

Winston Churchill once said that in any hierarchical situation there is all the difference in the world between the number one man and number two, three, four and the rest. Thus, while most Americans are living within and moving up the class hierarchy within each of our larger religious communities, there exists today an important qualitative difference in the nature of social relationships at the very top levels of society. In other words, while there are upper-, middle- and lower-class levels *within the Protestant, Catholic* and *Jewish communities,* there are Protestants, Catholics and Jews *within the elite.* To put it another way, class tends to replace religion (and even ethnicity and race) as the independent variable in social relationships at the highest levels of our society (see Diagram I).

And this difference as between the elite and the rest of society is more pronounced in the third, as against the first and second generations. Whereas, for instance, Mayor John Francis Fitzgerald was an "FIF (First Irish Family) within the Boston Catholic community, his son-in-law became a member of the national elite, both as a multimillionaire businessman and Ambassador to the Court of St. James. While the second generation was still emotionally rooted in a *marginal culture,* the third generation had produced a marginal man. This same marginality characterized the lives of Baruch, La Guardia and Weinberg, because of their elite positions. While Weinberg, for instance, was very naturally led into such intimate relationships as cruising in Maine with Charles Dickey because of their common elite positions at Goldman-Sachs and J. P. Morgan respectively, the majority of Jewish employees at Goldman-Sachs, even at quite high levels, led their private lives entirely within Jewish communities (and probably had not even met their gentile counterparts at the Morgan firm). And similarly, part of the tragedy of La Guar-

Diagram I

The Triple Melting Pot
and the Class System, 1900 and 1950

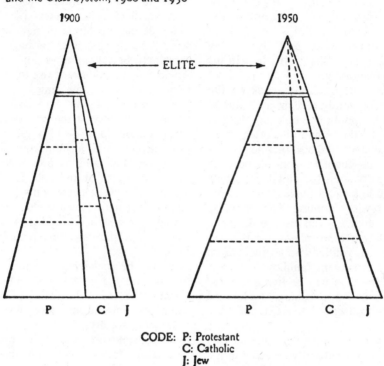

CODE: P: Protestant
       C: Catholic
       J: Jew

dia's life was that, though he had led a rich and convivial social life among his artistic and professional friends of Italian and Jewish extraction while he was a rising young lawyer in Greenwich Village, when he went to Washington, and later when he became Mayor of New York, he was forced by his functional position of leadership either to lead a social life within the elite or to have no social life at all.

The functional necessity that elite members associate with each other regardless of background or religion (or race, as the complications in the lives of such eminent Americans as Ralph Bunche or Marian Anderson attest to), is paralleled in many other areas of life. In residential patterns, for instance, the lower-class Jew will live within an entirely Jewish neighborhood, the middle-class Jew in a predominately, but not wholly, Jewish suburb, while the elite Jew will more likely be found in an almost predominately gentile neighborhood. In New York City, while elite Jews have lived on the gentile East Side of Central Park for some years now, most of the leaders within the Jewish community will be found on the West Side of the Park. And in the fashionable suburbs, especially in the postwar exurbs, gentiles and Jews live as neighbors within elite class enclaves rather than in religious neighborhoods. One would imagine, for instance, that Jacob Schiff's grandson John Mortimer Schiff, who is married to George F. Baker's granddaughter and lives in the fashionable neighborhood of Oyster Bay, on Long Island, would have most of his primary social relationships with his gentile neighbors and in-laws.

The marginal elite member also has to face the problem of club membership. John Mortimer Schiff, as befitting his residence in Oyster Bay, is a member of the best gentile sporting and golfing clubs out on the Island. In town, however, where he is a senior partner, like his father and grandfather before him, in Kuhn, Loeb & Company and a civic leader of some distinction, he does not belong to any of the more patrician men's clubs—even those which his brother-in-law and Oyster Bay neighbor George F. Baker, Jr., lists in his *Who's Who* biography.

This elite pattern also extends to the socialization of children at school and at college. While public schools are largely neighborhood schools, and thus often ethnically homogeneous, the best pirvate schools cater to a class clientele from all parts of the city and its suburbs, and increasingly tend to include a small nucleus of children from elite Jewish families. The boarding school is, of course, even a more powerful class-assimilating atmosphere for the minority of Jewish youths who go there from wealthy and prominent families. Similarly, the sons of the elite will be living in a far more class-bound atmosphere at Harvard than at the College of the City of New York.

Finally, of course, the class-limited way of life at the top is naturally reflected in the frequency of intermarriages and religious conversions. Thus Baruch, La Guardia and Schiff all married gentiles, as did one of Sidney Weinberg's sons. Though most elite Jews do not go so far as religious conversion and prefer to live a secular social life outside synagogue or church, one has the definite impression that those who do become Christians prefer the Episcopalian communion, as well as the manners of the communicants, to other Protestant denominations. It is interesting that in Philadelphia, where Quakers tend to be among the city's elite, one often meets Friends of Jewish origins, especially at the more or less one-class suburban meeting houses (while the powerful man of affairs usually converts to the Episcopal ritual, the intellectual convert today—both gentile and Jew—prefers the studied absence of ritual in the Quaker or Unitarian services).

The theory of the triple melting pot, then, must be modified at the elite level in order to take into account the overwhelm-ing factor of class. While in the third generation and at most class levels there is a return to ethnic and religious roots, centered in the suburban synagogue and church, there is a reversal of this trend today at the top levels of national leadership. And the pinch of prejudice will increasingly be felt as more and more non-Anglo-Saxon Protestants rise to this level of society. At the same time, it should be emphasized that this important of class makes the theory of the persistence of the Anglo-Saxon Ideal—which many sociologists have seen as an important modifying factor in the melting-pot theory—even more important at the elite level than at other social-class levels. This is of course because the nation's leadership is still dominated by members of the WSP upper class, the primary source and carrier of this ideal.

While the social organization of the triple melting pot serves quite effectively in assimilating the descendants of the more recent immigrants into most levels of our pluralistic society, there is, at the same time, constant pressure at the top levels of leadership today, which is increasingly composed of hyphenated-Americans of the third generation, to assimilate *all* talented and powerful men, regardless of their origins or religious convictions, into the mainstream of traditional authority by ultimately rewarding them with the dignity, security and family honor implied and nourished by membership in an establishment.

THE TRIPLE MELTING POT AND THE THEORY OF THE ESTABLISHMENT

In order to sharpen and elaborate the theory of the establishment, I have attempted to conceptualize, in a series of logical models shown in Diagram II, the past and possible future relationships between the three main ethnic-religious groupings in American society and the two variables of stratification: *social* power (position and power in the functional hierarchy of politics, business, religion, art, etc.) and *social status* (family posi-

Diagram II
The Establishment and
the Triple Melting Pot

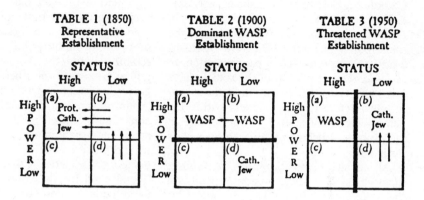

TABLE 1 (1850)
Representative
Establishment

TABLE 2 (1900)
Dominant WASP
Establishment

TABLE 3 (1950)
Threatened WASP
Establishment

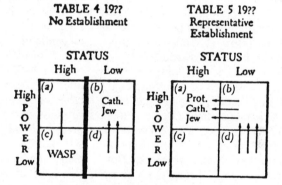

TABLE 4 19??
No Establishment

TABLE 5 19??
Representative
Establishment

KEY CONCEPTS: Elite: Boxes a and b (High Functional Power)
Upper Class: Boxes a and c (High Social Status)
Establishment: Box a (Power, Status and Authority)
WASP: White-Anglo-Saxon-Protestant
Caste: Status without Authority (Box c)
Aristocracy: Status with Authority (Box a)

tion and prestige in the social-class hierarchy). Diagram II, in other words, conceptualizes the logically possible relationships between Protestants (WASPs), Catholics and Jews and the social organization of leadership. The *elite* concept, then, refers to those *individuals* at the top of the social power hierarchy (Diagram II, Boxes a and b); the *upper-class* concept refers to those *families* at the top of the social-status hierarchy (Boxes a and c); and the *establishment* refers to those leaders within the elite whose families also belong, or are in the process of belonging, to the upper class (Box a).

All social organizations are, of course, hierarchical. For social action depends on the differential distribution of power as between classes and individuals. The essential problem of social order, in turn, depends not on the *elimination* but the *legitimation* of social power. For power which is not legitimized (Box b) tends to be either coercive or manipulative. Freedom, on the other hand, depends not on doing what one wants but on wanting to do what one ought because of one's faith in long-established authority. An establishment (Box a), then, is composed of families who carry traditional authority deriving from the past, and present, power of their members. Both Franklin Roosevelt and Fiorello La Guardia, for instance, has power because of their personal qualities and functional positions. The Roosevelt family, however, possessed the kind of established authority which was denied the family of La Guardia.

This is not to say that all leaders in a changing society should be members of the establishment (Box a). They definitely should not. For new men (Box b) are always needed in every generation. The trouble comes when whole classes of new men, because of the accidents of ancestry, are denied the opportunity of translating their power and talent into some sort of family authority. But caste not only denies the families of new men access to established authority; caste also weakens established authority itself because it tends to alienate its supposed beneficiaries by emphasizing their rights to privilege (Box c) rather than their *duties* to lead (Box a). Both the Roosevelt family's continual assumption of leadership and the continuous assimilation of men like La Guardia and Weinberg into the ranks of the upper class tend to strengthen the establishment's authority. On the other hand, both when the established fail to lead and when leaders fail to become established, authority is in grave danger of degenerating into authoritarianism, and an organic social order becomes an atomized horde of fearful, alienated and manipulated individuals. The most difficult and delicate problem faced by democratic societies is that of balancing the liberal need for the continuous circulation of individual elites (Box b) with the conservative need for maintaining a continuity of family authority (Box a).

It is the theory of the establishment, then, that the processes of history may be conveniently conceptualized in terms of classes of men and their families circulating counterclockwise on the logical model outlined in Diagram II. When the cycle is complete, and is working without the corruptions of caste, the accomplishments and power of individual leaders are translated into family prestige and the continuity of established authority is maintained. From this point of view American leadership has gone through three more or less distinct periods.

In the first period, from the nation's founding and roughly through the first half of the nineteenth century, positions in the establishment were open to all white men, regardless of ethnic origins (Diagram II, Table 1). Thus, although there was a great deal of anti-Catholicism and fear of "Popery," individual Catholics were assimilated into the upper class on the basis of achievement and manners. The famous anti-Catholic riots in Philadelphia during the 1840's were really anti-Irish, and there was little or no antipathy toward middle-class German Catholics and certainly none toward the few distinguished Catholics who belonged to the upper class. At this time many leading families of Irish and Catholic origins became converts and passed on to their descendants solidly established positions in the Eastern Seaboard upper class. This was the case, for example, for such leading members of the Protestant establishment in Philadelphia as the Drexels of banking eminence (originally Austrian Catholics) or the descendants of George Gordon Meade, Lincoln's choice to lead the Union forces at Gettysburg, who was baptized an Episcopalian at the time of the Civil War, though his ancestors had been staunch Catholics in Ireland and in Philadelphia at the time of the Revolution. And this same pattern of accepting men on their merits and manners and assimilating their families into the establishment was followed, as we have seen, in the case of the Jews. The power of aristocratic assimilation which existed at this time, for example, was implied in a recently published history of the Philadelphia Assemblies—annual balls, attendance at which still marks a family's inclusion within the innermost circles of Philadelphia's upper class and which have been held continuously since George Washington was one's dancing partner. Thus the author of this history was proud to write that "there are on the Subscribers' List of the Assemblies today, families of the following racial strains: English, Welsh, Irish, French, German, Dutch, Swiss, Italian, Spanish, Portuguese, Swedish, and Polish."[9] (What he meant was that the impeccable WASP establishment in the city of Philadelphia was composed of families whose ancestors included Spanish, Portuguese, German and Polish Jews, Irish, French and Italian Catholics, as well as Protestants from all these nations and dominated by those from the British Isles.) In this first historical period, then, the American establishment, though rooted in a mercantile upper class which was exclusive, proud, uniform in manners and certainly less patronizingly democratic in its treatment of the rest of the population than is the case today, was nevertheless still representative of the ethnic and religious composition of the white population.

But all this was to change after the Civil War, when the ethnic composition of American society was radically altered by the new immigration. This second historical period, which reached its peak somewhere between 1900 and the First World War, was marked by an associationally exclusive establishment of White-Anglo-Saxon-Protestants who dominated the leadership of the nation. Here it is only necessary to emphasize that the WASP establishment during this period was still representative of the elite, even though it was increasingly less representative of the population as a whole (Diagram II, Table 2). For this reason the establishment still possessed authority. In other words, it is not necessary, in the short run at least, that an upper class be representative of the whole people. In fact upper-class families are not recruited from the population at all but only from its leadership. The elite, on the other hand, must in the long run reflect and draw on the pool of national talent which inevitably resides in all classes. This is especially true where the people are literate and where a considerable majority have an opportunity for education. As of 1900, there was an authoritative establishment even though there was a more or less closed caste line drawn at the elite level which excluded those hyphenated-Americans of the Catholic and Jewish communities.

The significant difference in the structure of leadership in America in the third, as against the second, historical period is the fact that the caste line is now drawn in a status rather than a power sense, or, as it were, right down the middle of the elite (Diagram II, Table 3). In other words, our open class system has continued to work quite well and has produced a more or less ethnically representative elite. Our status system, on the other hand, has failed to keep pace. The WASP establishment has been forced to share its power while at the same time continuing to hoard its social privileges. In a very important sense, we now have in America, at the elite level of leadership, a *caste-ridden, open-class society*. And the consequent pressure upon the upper class to open its doors to the most talented and polished descendants of the newer immigrants has increased tremendously. For example, whereas the great expansion of the public school system in the first half of the twentieth century was useful in preparing the children of immigrants to rise within the confines of their particular ethnic community, the present boom among the college educated is producing quite different patterns of mobility and attitudes toward the melting pot. For the polished graduate of Harvard in the third generation will surely not be content either to remain within the confines of his Ethno-religious community, or to remain forever a marginal man.

At this time it is hard to see how the dynamic tension between the pressures of caste exclusion and of aristocratic assimilation which is now characteristic of the nation's leadership will finally be resolved. Today the situation is an ambivalent one. In the long run, there are two logically possible alternatives: either the WASP establishment will eventually develop into a closed caste, protecting its way of life and privileges while gradually abdicating from its position of leadership (Diagram II, Table 4), or a new aristocracy will emerge with the energy and ability to absorb the most prominent and polished families in the nation, regardless of their ethnic origins or religious convictions (Diagram II, Table 5). These strictly logical alternatives are, of course, only polar tendencies, and reality will fall somewhere in between.

THE TENDENCY TO CASTE

History is a graveyard of classes which have preferred caste privileges to leadership. The Roman republic, for instance, eventually passed into a democratic despotism largely because the old senatorial aristocracy, in spite of the attempted reforms of the two Gracchi, gradually degenerated into a caste that was unable to successfully absorb the class of Knights, or newly rich urban businessmen and Tocqueville pointed out how the British learned from, while the French followed, this Roman precedent. In this country, the eventual decline of the Federalist aristocracy at the beginning of the nineteenth century was, among other things, due to its leaders' failure to learn from the examples of Rome and Paris. While Jefferson and his followers did everything to capture the immigrants' vote, Harrison Gray Otis and the Federalist leaders at the Hartford Convention of 1812, "blind to the realities of pluralist politics to the last gasp, urged a constitutional amendment to bar naturalized citizens from elective and civil office."[10] The Republican establishment today may also have failed to learn from history.

There are always tendencies toward the caste position (Diagram II, Box c) within any upper class. There are, for example, the well-bred expatriates who live abroad and consider everything American rather common and vulgar; there are the patrician clubmen who so often specialize in genealogy, getting on club admission committees and keeping people out; and there is the growing class of gentlemen-farmers in America, many of them expatriated down on the Eastern shore in Maryland or in the beautiful hunting country around Middleburg, Virginia. One was recently offered an opportunity to reflect on the caste-psychology of this kind of American when, soon after the 1960 Presidential election, a group a Middleburg gentlemen-farmers attempted to block the Kennedy family from membership in the local hunt club.

But perhaps of greater importance as factors in the decline of the establishment than those persons who have, as it were, resigned from the American experiment is the ever increasing number of business gentlemen who are more interested in success and the protection of their privileged way of life than in leading the community as a whole. They are the successful lawyers who would not consider an appointment to the local bench, or even the Supreme Court (the Philadelphia bar abounds with Proper Protestants while the bench is conspicuous, in recent years, by their absence); they are the favored ones who would not think of dirtying their hands in politics or encouraging their sons to do so. This mood was shown recently in Philadelphia when the exposure of a series of voting frauds rocked the complacency of the city. Thus when the leading local newspaper asked a group of the city's most distinguished citizens to comment on the situation, a leading member of the bar, senior partner in a distinguished law firm and a member of one of the most patrician and talented families in the city, replied: "I know nothing about politics or elections"; another Philadelphia gentleman, also one of the more successful and highly paid executives in the city, could only say: "I haven't followed the situation enough to be intelligent about it;" and a former bank president and head of one of the most affluent and oldest Quaker-turned-Episcopal clans in the city had "no comment. I'm not going to get into that situation."[11] Perhaps these comments are understandable reactions to the jungle politics of our larger cities today. But they also reflect the all-too-prevalent attitudes of a class which has been bred, in this twentieth-century America, to succeed rather than to lead.

The caste-psychology which has led an increasing number of wealthy, talented and educated old-stock Americans to withdraw from power while at the same time protecting their privileged way of life has surely been a factor in the declining authority of the establishment.

THE ARISTOCRATIC TENDENCY

There is perhaps an all too prevalent tendency toward caste among old-stock families of third- and fourth-generation wealth. On the other hand this is by no means the dominant trend. It is hardly conceivable that men who are actively carrying on family traditions of leadership, such, for example, as Henry Ford II, Thomas J. Watson, Jr., or Nelson Rockefeller, would exhibit the same cynical and irresponsible attitude toward America as those who are obsessed with their own caste superiority. In fact, America is probably now producing more leaders who have had inherited advantages than at any other time in the twentieth century. For we live in an age of radically conflicting social forces, and along with the alienated genteel and deracinated marginal man, the 1950's also produced such old-stock leaders as Robert Fiske Bradford, a Mayflower descendant, as Governor of Massachusetts; Sinclair Weeks, Secretary of Commerce; Robert Cutler, Assistant to President Eisenhower; Christian Herter and Dean Acheson as Secretaries of State; Henry Cabot Lodge, Ambassador to the United Nations, and his brother, Governor of Connecticut and Ambassador to Spain; John Cabot, Ambassador to Brazil (eleven Cabots are listed in the 1958-59 edition of *Who's Who in America;*) one Taft in the Senate and another a leader in civic and church affairs; one Saltonstall in the Senate and another head of Phillips Exeter Academy; a Lowell, a Pulitzer Prize-winner in poetry, and Charles Francis Adams, the head of Raytheon.

And also, at the end of the 1950's, the Democratic Party—the party of the urban ethnic masses, which has its share of aristocratic leaders like Stevenson, Harriman, Acheson and Bowles—finally produced a victory for the second Catholic Presidential candidate in our history. Future historians will certainly look back on the election of John Fitzgerald Kennedy to the Presidency of the United States, in 1960, as a turning point in our history and symbol of a trend toward ethnic aristocracy in America. It was a decisive victory over the forces of caste.

NOTES

*The assumed names of the stars, in the order listed above, were as follows: *Warner Brothers:* Doris Day, Lawrence Harvey, Tony Curtis, Karl Malden, Marjorie Main, Judy Garland and Tab Hunter; *20th Century-Fox:* Casey Adams, Ginger Rogers, Mitzi Gaynor, Bella Darvi, Claudette Colbert and Ethel Merman; *MGM:* Vic Damone, John Ericson, Cyd Charisse and Robert Taylor; *Columbia:* Dianne Foster, Judy Holliday, Glenn Ford, Rita Hayworth, Aldo Ray and Vince Edwards; *Paramount:* Kathryn Grayson, Donna Reed, Jane Wyman, June Allyson, Kirk Douglas, Danny Kaye, Dean Martin and Jerry Lewis.

[1]*Harper's,* March 1955, p. 81.

[2]The theory of the triple melting pot in the third generation derives from two main sources: Marcus Lee Hansen, *The Problem of the Third Generation Immigrant* (Rock Island, Ill.: Augustana Historical Society, 1938); and Ruby Jo Reeves Kennedy, "Single or Triple Melting Pot? Intermarriage Trends in New Haven, 1870-1940," *American Journal of Sociology*, XLIX, 4, January 1944. For a fascinating discussion of this subject, see Will Herberg, *Protestant, Catholic, Jew: An Essay in American Religious Sociology* (New York: Anchor Books, 1960).

[3]Nathan Glazer, *American Judaism* (Chicago: University of Chicago Press, 1957).

[4]Here I am following the historical accounts of American Judaism contained in Nathan Glazer, *op. cit.,* and Oscar Handlin, *Adventure in Freedom: Three Hundred Years of Jewish Life in America* (New York: McGraw-Hill Book Company, 1954). See also E. Digby Baltzell, *An American Business Aristocracy* (New York: Collier Books; 1962), Chap. 11.

[5]For an excellent study of New York's Jews during this period, see Moses Rischin, *The Promised City: New York's Jews, 1870-1914* (Cambridge: Harvard University Press, 1962).

[6]See Cleveland Amory, *Who Killed Society?* (New York: Harper & Brothers, 1960), Chap. VIII.

[7]Nathan Glazer, "Social Characteristics of American Jews, 1654-1954," *American Jewish Year Book*, Vol. 56 (Philadelphia: The Jewish Publication Society of America, 1955), p. 9.

[8]Handlin, *op. cit.,* p. 144.

[9]Joseph P. Sims, *The Philadelphia Assemblies, 1748-1948* (Privately printed), p. 8.

[10]Lawrence H. Fuchs, "Some Political Aspects of Immigration," *Law and Contemporary Problems*, XXI (Spring 1959): 271.

[11]Philadelphia *Evening Bulletin*, February 29, 1960.

CHAPTER 22

Full Citizenship for the Negro American?

TALCOTT PARSONS

The designation "second-class citizen" has often and with justice been used to describe the status of the Negro in American society. As the British sociologist T. H. Marshall has shown with particular clarity,[1] citizenship is a complicated matter that is by no means exhausted by the more literal meanings of the term "civil rights." I should like to begin this discussion with an analysis of the meaning of the concept of citizenship, leaning heavily on Marshall's work, though attempting to go beyond it in some respects. I shall then attempt to analyze some of the conditions which have been necessary to account for the progress which the Negro American has made so far toward gaining full citizenship—and which, at the same time, the society has made toward including the Negro in that status— and the further conditions which must be fulfilled if the process is to approach completion.

The concept of citizenship, as used here, refers to full membership in what I shall call the *societal community*.[2] This term refers to that aspect of the total society as a system, which forms a *Gemeinschaft*, which is the focus of solidarity or mutual loyalty of its members, and which constitutes the consensual base underlying its political integration. This membership is central to what it means to be defined, in the case of our own nation, as "an American"—hence the Negro American, not vice versa. The Negro slave could have been, and certainly was called, an "American Negro"—he was resident in the United States and owned by American citizens, but was not part of the societal community in the present sense.

Perhaps John Rawls has formulated, in general philosophical terms, more clearly than anyone else the way in which full citizenship implies a fundamental equality of rights—not equality in *all* senses, but in the sense in which we refer to the rights of membership status in the societal community.[3]

From the unit viewpoint, societal community is a category of the commitment of members to the collectivity in which they are associated, and of the members to each other. It is the focus of loyalties which need not be absolute, indeed cannot be, but which require high priority among loyalties of the members.[4] To occupy this position the associational structure must be in accord with the common values of the society: members are committed to it because it both implements their values and organizes their interests in relation to other interests.

In all "advanced" societies, societal community is linked with political organization, but is also differentiated from it. Although all advanced societies are "politically organized," this aspect of their organization, what we ordinarily refer to at the societal level as government is not identical with community in the present sense. It is precisely when the two are in some kind of conflict that revolutionary situations can arise.

THE NATION AS
SOCIETAL COMMUNITY

In modern Western history, the focus of the differentiation of the societal community lay in the emergence of the nation, hence of "nationalism." Obviously, a similar process is now going on in many parts of the world in the formation of the "new nations." There are three aspects of the emergence of the nation which I should like to note and then briefly spell out for the American case.

The first is the differentiation of criteria for belonging to the nation in contrast to membership in the more "primordial" kinship-ethnic and, often, religious groupings. Here the change is toward the establishment of *associational* criteria. In the case of a total society, as politically organized, it is impossible for membership to be entirely voluntary for all, but it can move very far in this direction, that is, away from a purely ascriptive basis, and has done so. More importantly the status of citizenship comes to be institutionalized in terms independent of the ascriptive criteria just cited, for it concerns above all the "natural rights" so fundamental to American tradition.

Second, the nation is differentiated from its government. This is *not* to say they are dissociated. Rather, this differentiation involves the development of political independence by the societal community so that it is no longer ascribed to any particular governmental leadership, such as hereditary monarchy with full executive authority. The obverse of this development is that government becomes structurally independent in that it is free to mobilize within the society those resources which are relatively fluid, for example, in establishing an appointive civil service free of more paricularistic ties and in soliciting support from a range of different groups in the constituency.

Finally, the differentiation of the societal community as a nation involves a shift of the integration of the three elements, community, ascriptive bases, and government, in the direction of a synthesis of citizenship and territoriality. This is necessary because the individual is anchored in residential ties, even though there is high residential mobility, because work as well as residence is located physically, and because the availability of resources is territorially anchored.[5]

The process by which previously excluded groups attain full citizenship or membership in the societal community will, in this paper, be called *inclusion*. This is, as will be shown presently, a highly complex process. It will be argued that, at least under the conditions which have prevailed in American society, this has been intimately linked with the process of differentiation which has produced an increasingly *pluralistic* social structure. Not only are there many subcollectivities within the societal community, but the typical individual participates through membership in an increasingly wide variety. If interest is centered in *ethnic* groups, membership is necessarily by hereditary ascription.[6] In religious affiliation, a larger voluntary element is common, but most religious affiliations, at least to the larger groups, are *de facto* hereditary and often closely associated with ethnicity.

In a pluralistic social structure, membership in an ethnic or religious group does not determine *all* of the individual's social participations. His occupation, education, employing organization, and political affiliation may in varying degrees be independent of his ethnicity or religion. On the whole, the trend of American development has been toward increasing pluralism in this sense and, hence, increasing looseness in the connections among the components of total social status.

This trend has one particularly important implication for our purposes, namely, that it is essential to make a clear distinction between *inclusion* and *assimilation*. There may be pluralism of religious and ethnic groups among full citizens which cuts across many other involvements of the same people. The prototype was the original religious pluralism within the white Protestant group, which was built into the constitutional structure by the separation of Church and State and by religious toleration and freedom. It has subsequently been extended to include Jews and Catholics through what is usually called an "ecumenical" process.

However, because the United States was originally primarily a white Protestant society, it was often thought that inclusion was synonymous with becoming Protestant or as similar as possible to the Anglo-Saxon tradition. The developments which will be outlined below make it quite clear that this is not the case for the other white groups, and I shall argue that it need not and probably will not be so for the Negro. Full inclusion and multiple-role participation are compatible with the maintenance of distinctive ethnic and/or religious identity, though not in the sense which is the obverse of exclusion, namely self-imposed isolation as in the case of extreme Jewish Orthodoxy.

THE COMPONENTS OF CITIZENSHIP

T. H. Marshall, in his discussion of the development of citizenship in Great Britain noted above, distinguished three components of the status of citizenship, the *civil* (which in an American reference should perhaps be called legal), the *political,* concerned particularly with the democratic franchise, and the *social,* which refers essentially to the context we defined as "welfare" or, in the terms of our federal organization, health, education, and welfare.

Marshall establishes an important pattern of temporal sequence in the institutionalization of these three components as criteria of membership in the English national community: the civil came first, the political next, and the social last.

Further explanation of the meaning of these components is necessary. The civil or legal component concerns the *application* of the value system to the relevant context. This is what is particularly salient in the context of the term, *rights.* Rights indicate that members of the societal community in the normative sense "must" enjoy certain basic freedoms and securities in them. The catalogue is of course familiar. It involves security of each individual and of property, freedom of speech, religion, assembly, and association, and both substantive and procedural equality before the law—components formulated in our Constitutional tradition as "equal protection of the laws" and "due process of law." These rights are to take precedence over any particular political status or interest and over any social component such as wealth or poverty, prominence or obscurity.

It is a very long step from the constitutional and legal enactment of these rights to their effective implementation, and this process is still going on in many sectors of American society, even in some which are largely unrelated to the racial problem. But, the constitutional basis of these rights is firmly established and has served as the most important lever for exerting pressure during the earlier stages of the Negro inclusion movement. The special role of the N.A.A.C.P. has been to exploit this aspect of our citizenship structure in behalf of the Negro.

The political component concerns participation in collective goal-attainment, at the societal level in the process of government. The differentiation of government from the societal community, as noted above, implies that the average citizen is neither a governmental functionary in any usual sense nor a totally controlled subject of his government. He does, however, have rights of participation in the governmental process. These crystallize at two main points in modern politics. One is the franchise, basically the right of a formal voice in the selection of leader—leadership being a more generalized and practicable focus than specific policies, which are decided by referendum. The other is the right to attempt to influence policy, starting with the rights of free speech and assembly, but extending to the sensitive area of "lobbying." As mediating structures, the party system and the institutionalization of mass media become involved here. The body of citizens needs "spokesmen," the potential influencer needs media for making his wishes and their gratifications known, and leaders need structural outlets for their opinions, appeals, and proposals.

The social component does not concern

the opportunity to express and implement the rights derived from the societal values so much as the resources and capacities necessary for this implementation. In this connection the societal community defines and presents standards for the allocation of resources to the community as a whole and to its various subsectors. The obverse of this is the definition of the terms on which capacities, as matched with opportunities, can be involved in the process of inclusion. This is a special context of the problem of "qualifying" for inclusion.

There are two categories of resources which must be distinguished for our purposes. In our achievement-oriented society, one can scarcely imagine that justice would prevail if large classes of its members, through no fault of their own, were either denied opportunity for achievement (including the reaping of its rewards) or handicapped severely in gaining access to it. Given the formal status of equality in civil or legal rights and in basic political participation, these rights can be "empty" if opportunity is not equalized.

Of course, discrimination may be abolished or minimized across a whole range of opportunities, particularly in employment. But even absence of discrimination is "empty" if remediable handicaps continue to prevail. These handicaps may be randomly distributed among the categorial grouping with which this discussion is primarily concerned. But if they are linked to the status position of the excluded group, they raise the essential problem of the implementation of the rights of citizenship through the equalization of opportunity and the base from which that opportunity can be exploited.

This is where the distinction between the two categories of resources becomes essential. The first category is mainly financial. For an individual to be able to take advantage of available opportunities he must have not only the capacity but also the financial means to do so. This aspect of the social citizenship complex was paramount in the discussions and measures of public policy during the New Deal era. The second concerns the underlying capacity of the units, especially individuals and their families, to function effectively in the environment in which they are placed. At the level of the individual this concerns above all health and education. There has been so much discussion of all these themes that it is not necessary to spell them out further here. Suffice it to say that, first, increasing attention is being placed on education as the most decisive link between the individual's underlying levels of capacity and his relation to the opportunity structure.[7] Second, the concept of "welfare" is a diffuse one extended from the most elementary financial conditions of subsistence to the problem of the structure of the social environment in which disadvantaged groups are placed. This latter extension reflects the fact, firmly established by social science, that at the bottom of the social scale (as judged by the usual criteria of success, prestige, and so on) there is a vicious circle of cumulative *disadvantage,* the more marked the "competitiveness" of the society becomes. This broad tendency is inseparable from the development of individualism, the kinds of citizenship rights we have been talking about, and related matters. It almost goes without saying that the Negro in this country is very deeply caught up in this vicious circle and that Marshall's category of social citizenship is particularly important in the present context.[8]

The three principal components of the citizenship complex seem to constitute not only a rough temporal series, but also a type of hierarchy. With all the differences between British and American societies, they have very similar values. After all, with an important infusion from the French Enlightenment and the Revolutionary tradition, the origin of our own values lies mainly in our British heritage.

We can then say that it is the civil or legal rights which come closest to direct implementation of the values which Myrdal formulated in his famous summary of the *"American Creed."*[9] In understanding what has been going on, it is crucial to remember that the societal commitment to this value pattern has exerted steady pressure toward its implementation in behavior and institutions, though this has often been counteracted in specific ways. These commitments, though they be genuine, cannot by themselves bring about a restructuring of the society. Attempts to implement them will inevitably encounter what Mayhew[10] has called "structural discrimination," which can be overcome only if factors other than the assertion of commitments come into play. Without them, the outcome will be either a stalemate, as it was for so long in the United States, or a traditionalist revolution restoring the ascendancy of the contravalue orientation—a prototype being post-Reconstruction Southern society.

The spread and consolidation of the legal component through judicial process rather than legislation is particularly important in view of the present situation in America. This is a step well beyond a *moral* commitment to the relevant rights, because it places the power of government presumptively behind their implementation. In Little Rock, Governor Faubus was defying not only the "decent opinion of mankind," but also a specific order of a duly constituted federal court. This dramatizes the sense in which the 1954 decision on education was a decisive landmark—yet by itself it produced only a rather paltry "tokenism" in spite of being on the books for a full decade. Clearly something more was required, though this is not to belittle the enormous importance of the legal commitment. This Supreme Court decision was part of a much larger trend in the general development of judicial interpretation of the Constitution, of which more will be said later.

The two other principal factors are, on the one hand, the mobilization of political pressures designed to insure that the excluded group can enjoy both formal rights and actual participation in the political process and, on the other, the mobilization of the governmental apparatus to take the responsibility of implementing these rights. From this point of view, the step from the Supreme Court's espousal of Negro rights to the Civil Rights Act of 1964 and 1965 was crucial, as has so often been remarked. Both, to be sure, obligate the government.

But in the latter case the obligation has been enacted by the elected representatives of the people on the recommendation of a popularly elected President. Hence it can no longer be called the "whim" of nine men who, in the political as distinguished from the legal sense, do not "represent" anyone.[11] Of course there are still many steps which must be taken before effective implementation can be achieved, but the Civil Rights Acts clearly add a major set of social forces to the side of effective implementation.

Even if enforcement were effective, it would still be necessary to bring about the essential set of conditions concerned with qualifications for taking advantage of the opportunities offered. The newly included group must have the capacity to perform its role creditably. The mere statement that justice requires inclusion is not enough because allegations of injustice must involve the capacity factor—namely, that the excluded group could make valuable contributions but is denied the opportunity to do so. Capacity must be asserted on the part of the excluded group, and, insofar as it is not yet present, the larger community must take steps to help develop it.

The hierarchy to which we referred above concerns a relation between necessary and sufficient conditions. With reference to the Negro in the United States, I state broadly that although the institutionalization of both legal rights and political participation constitutes the necessary conditions of much further progress toward full inclusion in the societal community, this is not in itself sufficient. It also requires the implementation of the social component in such a way that the realistic handicaps, so conspicuous in the background, are reduced to the point that, though they cannot be expected to disappear in the short run, they become more or less manageable.

The constitution of a societal community is never static, but is continually changing over time. In my view, the main outline of the American community was established in the broad process of founding the new nation. This basic outline includes the Constitution as well as various aspects of the

system as a total social process. At the same time, American society has been subject to major changes. The focus of the present essay is on changes in the composition of its membership through the inclusion of groups previously excluded, more or less unambiguously, from full membership. The Negro, both because of slavery and because of Southern regional isolation, was long kept insulated from the forces favoring inclusion. The groups constituted by the "new immigration" of the turn of the century were in a different situation.

I shall attempt to analyze the process of inclusion by using a model roughly similar to the "supply and demand" paradigm of economics. There are demands for inclusion—*both* from the excluded group and from certain elements who are already "in" —and there is a supply, which also operates on both sides of the exclusion line. Supply here refers, for the excluded groups, to their qualifications for membership, a matter of their cultural and social structures. On the side of the receiving community, "supply" consists in structural conditions which create institutionalized "slots" into which the newly received elements can fit, slots structured in accordance with the basic citizenship patterns of the developing community, not opportunities for crude "exploitation" by its members. Supply in this sense refers to a set of structural conditions on both sides of the "equation." This will be analyzed in terms of the factors necessary to extend and consolidate the societal community as such, that is, the commitment to association in a national community, the mobilization of political power and influence, and the establishment of the capacities which have been reviewed in the present section, as well as the underlying value-patterns which are assumed throughout.

The demand aspect concerns the *mobilization* of these factors and their consequences, again on both sides of the inclusion-exclusion boundary. It is a matter first of the existence of attitudes, in both the group "wanting in" and significant sectors of those already in, that the inclusion is normatively desirable and that it *should* be promoted, and then the transformation of these attitudes into various action programs and their implementation. Certainly, much of the actual process often occurs inconspicuously without much of a movement— this, for example, seems to have been the case for much of the inclusion of the new immigration, though by no means all of it. Nevertheless, as expression and implementation of demand in the present sense, the relevant *movements* have a very important place in our analysis.

Such movements tend to gather strength as the strain of conflict between the normative requirements for inclusion and the factual limitations on it are translated into pressures to act. Movements, however, not only express strain in this sense, but "stir things up" further. Thus, their consequences are often relatively unpredictable.[12] One tendency of this type of movement should be noted. The ultimate social grounding of the demand for inclusion lies in commitment to the values which legitimize it. The generation reaction to increasing strain is to increase mobilization of such commitments. This in turn is often associated with a demand for direct, immediate, and complete action to implement the values in full. This tendency encounters a problem deriving from the fact that value-commitment, crucial as it is, is only one of the factors necessary for successful inclusion. Strengthening this factor without likewise strengthening the others may lead not to promotion of the "cause," but to a disproportionate activation of the *always-present* factors of resistance, and hence to setbacks. The activists in such movements are above all likely to become impatient with those who would pay attention to the importance of the other factors.[13]

This is the broad paradigm which the reader is requested to keep in mind in reading the sometimes involved discussion which follows.

THE AMERICAN RECORD ON INCLUSION PROCESSES

The present crisis over the inclusion of the Negro in the American community has unique features besides its immediacy,[14] but it does not stand alone. A brief review of the larger context of related problems may prove illuminating. Two propositions will introduce the discussion. First as already noted, the core of the American community was basically white, Anglo-Saxon, and Protestant. These three terms, which have become so deeply embedded in the more popular culture, will serve as the axes of our analysis. Second, the United States, in sharp contrast to most of Europe, including our ancestral Britain, has been the proverbial land of open opportunity, welcoming all to join in building a new society in the "New World."

To be sure, this claim was never fully justified. Quite early it was made unmistakably clear that mass Oriental immigration would not be welcomed (note the Chinese exclusion act of 1882). Indeed it may be argued that the Constitutional termination of the Slave Trade was as much an effort to limit the numbers of Negroes in the territorial United States as it was a reflection of hostility to slavery as such. Nevertheless, compared with other societies, especially of that time, the U.S. was notably liberal until the 1924 immigration laws. It placed more emphasis than any other nation of, or before, its time on the view that it was indeed a voluntary association. People were here because either they or their immediate forebears *wanted* to come. And, the proportion of those who came of their own volition was extremely high for quite a long time. The fact that many were escaping from what they felt to be oppressive conditions rather than coming to positive opportunities does not change this pattern. The Negro is the exception, because his forebears were typically *brought* here as slaves.

Though various early crises of the American nation may be related to this problem, the focus of this discussion will be on the aftermath of the great wave of free immigration of the generation ending with the First World War. This was perhaps, except for the Negro, *the* great test of the norms of freedom for all comers to associate in forming a new kind of nation.[15] Most of the immigrants were a part of the so-called new immigration from eastern and southern Europe, and as such they violated more sharply than previous large immigrations the older WASP formula for the societal community; they were not only non-Anglo-Saxon, but even non-Germanic in ethnic origin, being mostly from the Latin and Slavic countries (especially Italy and Poland). Also they were predominantly Roman Catholic, except for the very large influx of Jews from eastern Europe. In addition, the Catholics were usually peasants. Earlier, there had been a small element of German Jews, who had become relatively fully included and a larger group of English-speaking Catholics, the Irish, who were marked by a particularly sharp hostility to everything English. These two elements proved in the end to be very important mediators between the older elements and the larger masses of the new.

In this connection the WASP's generally succumbed to the temptation to define their own role on rather aristocratic terms, but on bases so tenuous that they must be considered only a pseudo-aristocracy. This occurred during the period immediately following World War I when economic prosperity was rampant and when "status-seeking" was certainly far more intensive than in the second postwar period. This is the period of the derogatory names like "wops," "polacks," and "kikes," and of the greatest prevalence of "snobbish" anti-Semitism, the deep feeling that having a Jew as a member of your club was totally unacceptable. (It is perhaps significant that such snobbishness was particularly prominent in the younger generation—in fraternities and sororities, and particularly in the Harvard Final Clubs.)

THE NEGRO CASE

If the predominantly Catholic part of the new immigration owed its primary status ascription in American society mainly to its lower-class status, for the Negro this has been almost wholly the case. For our purposes, color will be treated not as a direct component of the social status of the Negro

—for in strict theoretical terms it is not that—but as a symbol. On relatively concrete levels, it is correct to say that individual Negroes are discriminated against in various ways solely because of their skin color. This statement is not, however, an explanation of the general phenomenon of color discrimination, as distinguished from individual cases. Unfortunately this vital distinction is often not kept firmly in mind. Our concern is with the general phenomenon.

In this context skin color symbolizes inferiority in the sense that it is purported to justify placing Negroes as a category so radically at the bottom of the scale as to be only equivocally inside the system at all. It will perhaps be illuminating to consider the problem first in connection with the difference between the South and the North.[16]

The Civil War broke out about the time of, and partly as a result of, the process of industrialization and urbanization in the North. This accentuated the difference in social structure of which slavery was a primary feature. The South was largely an agrarian society with a planter gentry at the top practicing an aristocratic style of life, and with the great mass of menial labor being done by Negro slaves. The principal class whose status was equivocal was the white group which could not pretend to gentry status, but which wanted above all to avoid being classified with the Negroes. It was something like a case society. Though the slaves were formally emancipated as a result of the South's defeat in the war, the post-Reconstruction reaction confirmed this caste structure with the "Jim Crow" system.

The southern Negro has generally had to start his rise by acquiring the most elementary components of legal and political citizenship. Through court decisions and now increasingly through legislation, this part of the task of inclusion has progressed a long way toward accomplishment. The social component is another matter—incluison in this area is just beginning to develop, and there is no doubt that it will prove the most difficult of the three processes.

Until the First World War the Negro was scarcely a "problem" in the North, mainly because his numbers were so small. This was changed by the great migrations which began about that time, accelerated by the boll weevil havoc in southern cotton growing. Of course, this process has now gone so far that less than half the Negro population is resident in the eleven states of the old Confederacy, and the proportion will continue to decline. Moreover, in the South there has been a great deal of migration to the cities, so that the category, southern rural Negro—once the predominant type— is now a distinct minority.

The upward mobility of the white urban lower groups, the new immigration, has contributed to the fact that, in both North and South, the Negro is predominantly urban and lower class. Today about half of the estimated 20 percent of Americans who are "the poor" are Negroes.[17] This classifies about 50 percent of the Negroes as poor, whereas no other group—Irish, Italian, and so forth—has nearly that large a proportion.

In a sense the South has "infected" the North with the virus of the Negro problem, even though its meaning has been deeply changed. It was hardly to have been expected that Southerners would get very much Northern political support for maintaining the Jim Crow system intact. Even the coalition of Southern Democrats and northern conservative Republicans has been gradually eroded to the point that, with the mounting pressure and certain general changes, it has almost disappeared. However, the "problem" is now becoming much more uniform throughout the nation —it is becoming an urban class problem.[18]

Jewish inclusion would probably have been much more difficult had it not been for the type of differentiation process in the economy exemplified by the growth of corporate business, and for the great development of higher education, which opened the doors of the professions to considerable numbers of Jews. Similarly, the pluralization of the political system, the breakup of the city machines as the preserves of specific groups, and the decline of the corresponding "better element" sectors of the political structure have greatly facilitated the inclusion of the Catholic groups. I should like to suggest that the "host society" has been undergoing an important process of structural change which is creating essential conditions for the inclusion not only of the Negro, but of the whole lower class in the societal community.

In an important sense, American society has been protected against the urgency of the class problem by the fact that for so long such a large proportion of its lowest socioeconomic groups has been of recent immigration status, especially in the crucially important cities which have increasingly become the structural focus of the newer society. As noted, upward mobility has greatly alleviated the potential class problems, but they are now being brought to an acute and symbolically appropriate focus by the Negro's becoming the prototypical disadvantaged category.

In the broadest terms the incipient inclusion process depends for its success on the much more effective institutionalization of Marshall's social component of citizenship. However, it comprises new movements with respect to all three of the components. It has, for example, been noted that a most important trend in the Supreme Court decisions of recent years is the extension of the Bill of Rights to the level of the states, especially through reinterpretation of the Fourteenth Amendment.[19] Many of these decisions, such as the school desegregation ruling of 1954, have most notably affected discrimination in the South. Others, however, such as the requirement that indigent defendants accused of crime be provided with counsel (the *Gideon* case), apply more generally. Furthermore, not only legal rights, in the narrower sense, but also political and social rights are affected. Thus the reapportionment cases profoundly affect the franchise and, with it, the distribution of political power; and the school cases impinge on the social component. They seem to imply that government is obligated to provide adequate educational facilities to the whole population—with discrimination by race being only one aspect of the present inadequacy.

Within this framework of legal rights, public policy is attempting to cope with the causes of *de facto* discrimination, not just by color but by any status of inferiority which cannot be fairly attributed to the individual himself. A certain religio-ideological grounding of this first emerged with the prominent Social Gospel movement in American Protestantism in the latter part of the nineteenth century (which, incidentally, had much to do with the establishment of sociology as an academic discipline in this country) and with its role in the development of philanthropy concerned with the disadvantaged classes. The New Deal comprised a second main phase, with the beginning of comprehensive federal social welfare legislation, including the consolidation of the legal status of trade unionism through the Wagner Act and, particularly, unemployment, old age, and other benefits. The opposition of the Supreme Court to such legislation, especially by the states, was also ended in that period. The United States now seems to be well into a third phase. Perhaps its most important feature has been the shift in concern from welfare in the narrower sense to health, education, and the nature of the urban community, focusing most acutely so far upon housing.

By the narrower sense of welfare, I mean that concerned primarily with money income. The older conceptions of lower-class status emphasized lack of financial means as the central feature of being disadvantaged. Hence, stress was put on improvement in financial status. This was reasonable especially when, as in the Great Depression, massive unemployment was the most acute condition needing a remedy. However, there has been increasing insight that poverty is a function of other factors such as poor health, both physical and—as has been emphasized more recently—mental, and certain aspects of community structure and the like.

Education has become the most salient link with the occupational system, which is, in turn, the principal basis of financial independence for the individual and his immediate family. There has been a general upgrading of education. On the one hand, this means that larger proportions of the age cohort have been attaining higher levels of education, with the results that the disadvantaged minority, especially the well-known drop-outs, has been separated from the majority with increasing sharpness. On the other hand, educational requirements for good employment have been rising at the same time—most of the present unemployment is found among the poorly qualified groups, and educational qualifications are becoming of increasing importance in holding jobs. It seems that not only formal opportunity for a relatively good education (that is, at least through high school), but also capacity to take advantage of it, both in individual ability and in motivation, is coming to be as much a requisite of full inclusions as civil and voting rights.

Behind this is the problem of the social environment of the disadvantaged, the "slum." The central concern is the vicious circle of the factors in *actual* inferior capacity for valued performance, in which poverty, bad health, low educational standards, family disorganization, delinquency, and other anti-social phenomena are mutually reinforcing. This is where the structure of the urban community itself becomes a salient problem focus. The new concern centers on the residential community. In this connection attention has been called to the fact that the Negro is disadvantaged, even beyond other slum dwellers, in many senses besides the color of his skin. First and foremost, he has been peculiarly lacking in relatively strong family organization[20] which could give strong psychological support to the individual, especially as a child. Second, this has been connected in turn with a relative weakness in "community" institutions of mutual support and solidarity, for example, of the sort which have preeminently characterized Jewish groups even before they rose significantly from their initial low status in American society. Even as the victim of the most radical discrimination of any group, the Negro has not only been forced to be subservient, but has also failed to develop, or bring with him from his southern rural past, sufficient ingredients for socially effec-

tive self-help—a question not merely of individual qualities and initiative, but of collective solidarity and mutual support at many levels, particularly the family and the local community. The strongest Negro institutions have centered in the churches, a vital complex which must be preserved carefully against some of the disintegrating tendencies of urban life. The role of the churches in the civil rights movement perhaps symbolizes this best and will be commented upon further below.

SOME HIGHLIGHTS OF THE INCLUSION PROCESS

It is reasonable to suggest that, whatever the extent and nature of the responsibility for the many previous failures, the time is ripe for a major advance. The broad tendency of modern society, one in which America has played a rather special role, has been egalitarian in the sense of institutionalizing the basic rights of citizenship in all three categories sketched here.[21] This tendency has become institutionalized over an increasingly broad front, the legal development noted above being prototypical. The basic types of inequality which have continued to be tolerated—in this context rather than that of recognition and reward of achievement—have been justified, when at all, primarily in terms of "paternalistic" immunities of a variety of sectoral types, the status of the child in the family being a kind of model. In case after case, these immunities have been whittled away, so that the universalistic norms of the society have applied more and more widely. This has been true of all the main bases of particularistic solidarity, ethnicity, religion, regionalism, state's rights, and class. The "sovereignty" of the individual American state has perhaps been the most important single bulwark of these particularisms, in the first instance those of WASP's, but potentially of every group.

Today, more than ever before, we are witnessing an acceleration in the emancipation of individuals of all categories from these diffuse particularistic solidarities. This must be seen as a further *differentia-*

tion of the role-set in which the individual is involved. By being included in larger community structures, the individual need not cease to be a member of the smaller ones, but the latter must relinquish certain of the controls over him which they previously exercised. This reasoning applies to aristocratic groups as much as it does to negatively privileged ones like the Negro. We have been witnessing major steps in the extension and conslidation of the societal community.

Let me emphasize again one particularly important aspect of the present phase, that the more general insistence on the basic equalities of citizenship, which is essential to the inclusion process, cuts across the status of Negro. In its deeper layers, it is a demand not for the inclusion of Negroes as such, but for the elimination of *any* category defined as inferior in itself. For a long time the status of the Negro was a peculiarly southern problem. Then it became a national problem, but *qua* Negro. Now we are entering the phase in which it is no longer that, but the problem of eliminating status-inferiority as such, regardless of race, creed, or color. The Negro, in becoming only a "special case," even if a very salient one, loses a ground for special consideration which he has enjoyed. At the same time, he has established a position for tapping much wider bases of support than before. He can become the spokesman for the much broader category of the disadvantaged, those excluded on this egregious ground. The Negro movement, then, can become the American style "socialist" movement. This is to say that the basic demand is for full inclusion, not for domination or for equality on a basis of separateness.[22]

At the risk of repetition, I may note that the successful accomplishment of this goal of inclusion depends on a balanced mobilization of four categories of factors. The first is commitment to the values which underlie the assumption that the goal itself is desirable. This has a long history in American society and is clearly of the greatest importance. I have mentioned that it was invoked by Myrdal. Recently we have seen a notable "effervescence" (in Durkheim's sense) with respect to activation of these value-commitments at the requisite levels. Here the Negro movement has played the paramount part, but the activation has extended far beyond the movement itself. Its incidence in religious circles is especially noteworthy, not least in the way it has brought all faiths of the white community, Catholics and Jews as well as Protestants, together behind the Negro cause. The presence of Catholic nuns among the demonstrators in Selma was a new note having a significance scarcely to be overestimated.

Mere affirmation of the values is not enough. If a process of change is to be a new implementation of fundamental values, its basic direction must be articulated. This involves the development of a conception of the societal community in which all elements will be fully included in the sense of this discussion. In our own cultural background, quite different directions have also enjoyed powerful value-sanctions, even if rather insecurely. One example was the conception of the Negro as inherently inferior—indeed, in a certain version of older Calvinism now dominant in South Africa, as rightfully belonging in a subordinated status. It is the basic values, as applied to the developing conception of the American societal community, which together form the normative focus of the power of the movement.

This factor underlies the trend to implement the values by inclusion—the only tolerable solution to the enormous tensions lies in constituting a single societal community with full membership for all. This is a renewal and reinterpretation of the concept of the Union which was so central for Lincoln. No other solution is tolerable from the American point of view—hence the Black Muslims cannot gain active support in the general community. And despite much ambivalence, it seems certain that the main Negro community is committed to this outlook. The mobilization of these loyalties and commitments on both sides of the racial line seems to be the second crucial factor in the general inclusion process.

It has been very common to postulate and emphasize a primary difference between the "idealists" who hope to achieve integration by asserting the values of, and a willingness for, acceptance, and the "realists" who say that *only* the mobilization of political power and economic interests will help. I should strongly repudiate this framing of alternatives. It is quite correct that the goal cannot be achieved *without* the mobilization of power and economic interests, but it does not follow that these factors are themselves sufficient. It is only a balanced combination of "ideal" and "real" factors which provides the formula for success.

In speaking of political power, I should like to conceive it here more broadly than is usual. Essential as government is, it does not stand alone in implementing major political changes. The political problems of integration involve all fields of organizational decision-making, especially for business firms to accept Negroes in employment, for colleges and universities to admit them for study, for trade unions to avoid discrimination. We have become acutely aware of the limitations of political power. Against a recalcitrant group, attempts to *enforce* compliance are all-too-often ineffective. Nevertheless, at certain crucial points its mobilization is clearly an essential factor, a factor which includes making decisions affecting inclusion processes *binding* as obligations on all members of the requisite collectivity, whether governmental or private. It is particularly important to remember that the use of power has a double effect. First, it mobilizes sanctions against recalcitrants in such ways that they may no longer be able to afford previously feasible resistance. Second, it asserts on behalf of the relevant collectivity that the policy of inclusion must be taken seriously, and hence that noncompliance will not be allowed to proceed with impunity.

Of all the factors favoring integration, economic interests are the most neutral as far as normative obligations are concerned. They involve both the extent to which receiving elements can "afford" the risks involved in taking various steps and the

development of realistic capacities to do so—a theme discussed above in connection with the whole complex of inferiority of status. Perhaps most important is that without support from the other three sets of factors, economic interests and capacity to exploit economic opportunities are weak reeds. This has been made vividly clear where state governments in the deep South, backed by what seems to have been a white consensus, have adamantly opposed steps toward integration. In such cases business men simply would not move. But where the balance of the other factors shifts toward integration, economic interests on both sides can provide a powerful reinforcement of the change. It is a question of "getting over the hump."[23]

THE NEGRO MOVEMENT AND THE PROBLEM OF NEGRO IDENTITY

A particularly conspicuous feature of the recent phase in the changing status of the Negro has been the emergence of a strong movement which has had very extensive and important white support, but which has struck much deeper roots in the Negro community itself than have previous phases. The emergence of the movement is a function of several factors such as the general social changes outlined above, the stimulus of the emergence of African states, the strengthening of the Negro middle classes, with their higher levels of education, and the concentration of Negro masses in the cities, primarily in the North. This essay cannot attempt a more detailed analysis of these developments. I should like rather to state a few of their implications, especially regarding the opportunities they present.

It has been remarked that the Negro group has generally had less solidarity and weaker organization than the other ethnic groups which have preceded it in gaining inclusion. The growth of the present movement seems to be both a symptom and a cause of a notable strengthening in this solidarity, which is beginning to create a more clearly defined group consciousness and sense of power and opportunity. It presents a new opportunity to shift the definition of Negro status away from its predominantly negative meaning as an oppressed group which is typically excluded and exposed to multifarious disadvantages. The problem is to develop a basis for a more positive conception of group identity in both American and world society. I should like to suggest that there is a most unusual opportunity inherent in the nature of the movement and its situation, the importance of which, however, is not yet widely appreciated.

One major point of reference is that the primary source of Negro grievance, exclusion on the basis of alleged *inherent* inferiority, is the most radical grievance entertained by any major non-WASP group, except possibly the American Indian's grievance of dispossession. It raises a clearer, more drastic *moral* issue than the other cases, one compounded by the status of the Negro's ancestors as slaves in America and by the injustice of using the "trivial" symbol of color as a primary basis of exclusion. Given the universalistic and egalitarian elements in our national traditions, both religious and Constitutional, it is difficult to find an issue which is morally more straight forward.

It has been possible to keep the issue relatively insulated for a long time, but recent social changes as well as the movement itself have made this progressively more problematic. Now, in a period of rising economic affluence, and, it may be said, moral ambivalence both about this and about the confusions over the American position in world affairs, the nation has been presented with a notable opportunity to define a clear and *simple* issue of conscience. By and large, the reverberation of the issue in many different groups has been extensive and impressive, in spite of tenacious resistance. Perhaps the issue also becomes more urgent precisely because of the progress made in resolving the other issues of inclusion which we have discussed, since this leaves the Negro even more conspicuously excluded.

I have noted that the processes of social change in the present century have tended increasingly to polarize the society along an axis which includes not only political conservatism in resistance to change but, closely related to this, what we call religious "fundamentalism." In the South the connection between militant segregationism and fundamentalism has been very clear.[24]

Generally speaking, there are also important connections between lower-class status in industrial societies, social origins in more "primitive" or "underdeveloped" social settings, particularly of a peasant type, a certain general conservatism (or, as Lipset says, "authoritarianism"), and religious fundamentalism. Indeed, one may say that the predominant kind of Catholicism among the new immigrant urban masses was a form of fundamentalism and that the liberalization of American Catholicism in the last generation is partly a function of the upward mobility and inclusion of these masses. To a degree, the Orthodoxy of so many east European Jewish immigrants was also a form of fundamentalism.

The majority of Negro Americans have been and are, religiously speaking, fundamentalists. But, this fact does not have simple consequences. Undoubtedly, in their segregated and insulated status in the rural South, it helped to motivate acceptance of their lot, as the corresponding features of Catholic and Jewish fundamentalism have done in both the peasant or ghetto circumstances of the "old countries" and in the difficult early stages of involvement in American society as first- and second-generation immigrants.

At the same time, there is the deepseated Judeo-Christian tradition of religious motivation to preserve integrity, to assert autonomy, and eventually to seek justice through change in the structure of the situation. Here, what I am calling the more fundamentalist orientation has, in the course of history, repeatedly assumed moral leadership, in part facilitated by an unworldly lack of concern for the complexities of process in the highly differentiated societies. Fundamentalists in this sense—which includes such "secular religions" as

Communism—tend to be direct-actionists, to see issues in *simple* moral terms; and about half the time they have the balance of long-run merit on their side.

However, Negro fundamentalism, like that of the previous immigrant masses, has come to be mobilized predominantly on the side of differentiation and inclusion, not of segregation and exclusion. The development of the movement has strongly activated the moral sentiments of the other groups, including very significant groups of non-Protestants. This process has quite directly *split* the fundamentalist element in American religion, with all its important *indirect* relations to politics and other contexts. The *moral* basis of opposition to change in the older and simpler order—so strongly emphasized by our latter-day conservatives—is thereby gravely undermined. There has developed, significantly, a strong and sometimes very sharp dialogue on the subject of moral justification between those camps. This brings the process of restructuring the social system to the highest normative level, a level already fully structured specifically in terms of religious and social pluralism. It raises, in a form difficult to evade, the question of the moral basis of the American type of "Free Society."

I should like to emphasize the subtle combination of similarities and differences between the processes of inclusion for the groups of the new immigration and for the Negro. All three have been in certain respects "foreign." They have also come with socio-cultural patterns which have been relatively "backward" by the main standards of the new society—to put it sharply, all except Jews have been "peasants," and they have been small-town bourgeois. All three have had religio-cultural orientations which can be called "fundamentalist." Environmentally, however, all three have been plunged into a converging set of integrating influences, as the most recently arrived lower-class group in the largest urban communities.

In the other context, the three are not only distinct from each other, but constitute a series. The Jews, curiously from some points of view, have proved the easiest to include. This was not the case in Germany, with its much more hierarchical social structure. But in "individualistic" America, the principal problem was that of defining the legitimacy of, and opportunity for, cultural pluralism without prejudicing the other, more instrumental bases of participation. The Catholics had to overcome high American sensitivity to tightly organized collectivities which might be accused of "conspiracy."

In this succession, the Negro stands at the "end of the line." He is the most serious (hence in some respects, the most plausible) basis of exclusion, namely, his inherent inferiority. The relatively satisfactory—it will not in our time ever be fully so—resolution of the problem of Negro inclusion will certainly be one of the greatest achievements of American society. Moreover, the record of the movement, even up to this point, makes it clear that a very major part of the credit will go to the Negro community itself; it will be *their* achievement, certainly in the sense of direct goal-orientation to a much greater degree than is true of the groups which have already gained inclusion.

This seems to me to constitute a crucially important focus for the future of the collective Negro identity. The Negro community has the opportunity to define itself as the spearhead of one of the most important improvements in the quality of American society in its history—and to do so not only in pursuit of its own obvious self-interest, but in the fulfillment of a *moral* imperative.

Near the beginning of this essay, the distinction between inclusion and assimilation was stressed. The purport of this latest phase of the analysis is to suggest that to identify nondiscrimination (that is, inclusion) too strongly with complete "color-blindness" might be to throw away a very precious asset, not only for the Negro, but for American society as a whole. My own view is that the healthiest line of development will not be only the preservation, but the actual building up, of the solidarity of the Negro community and of the sense that being a Negro has positive value. In the process there is the danger of cultivating separatism, as most conspicuously exemplified by the Black Muslims. But the pluralistic solution, which has been stressed throughout this discussion, is neither one of separatism—with or without equality—nor of assimilation, but one of full participation combined with the preservation of identity. The American Jewish and Catholic groups have, by and large, been able to achieve this goal.

Quite clearly, the Negro's own associations with fellow Negroes who survive the inclusion process should no longer be compulsory.[25] Each individual Negro should be free to associate with any non-Negro in any legal way he sees fit, and, if he so desires, to give up completely his identity as a Negro in the sense of belongings to a Negro community. But this does not mean that Negro identity should or will disappear. I should envision continuing predominance of marriages of Negroes with each other. I see no reason that some religious denominations should not be identified as "Negro churches," or that, as long as residence there is not compulsory, many neighborhoods should not continue to be mainly Negro, as many today are Jewish.

Once being a Negro loses the stigma of inferiority, I suggest, it is likely that these will cease to be salient issues. After, all, color is a *symbol* and, if the context of its historic meanings is sufficiently changed, the prospect is that it will cease to be the basis of a stigma.

NOTES

[1]T. M. Marshall, *Class, Citizenship, and Social Development* (Garden City, N.Y.: Doubleday, 1964), Chap. IV.

[2]Cf. Talcott Parsons, *Societies: Comparative and Evolutionary Perspectives* (Englewood Cliffs, N.J.: Prentice-Hall, 1966).

[3]John Rawls, "Constitutional Liberty and the Concept of Justice," in C. J. Friedrich, ed., *Justice (Nomos VI)*, (New York: Atherton Press, 1963).

[4]Edward A. Shils, *The Torment of Secrecy* (Glencoe, Ill.: Free Press, 1956).

[5]Talcott Parsons, "The Principal Structures of Community," *Structure and Process in Modern Societies* (Glencoe, Ill.: Free Press, 1960).

[6]Qualifications must be made, for example, for interethnic marriages where, with or without formal "adoption," the couple functions primarily in one group and, hence, the "inmarrying" spouse may be said to have changed ethnic affiliation, especially if the children identify clearly with the one group.

[7]Peter F. Drucker, "Automation Is Not the Villain," *The New York Times Magazine*, January 10, 1965.

[8]Considerable evidence on these points is presented in other papers in the *Daedalus* issue, notably those by Rashi Fein, Daniel P. Moynihan, and Thomas F. Pettigrew.

[9]Gunnar, Myrdal, *An American Dilemma* (New York: Harper, 1944).

[10]Leon Mayhew, "Law and Equal Opportunity: Anti-discrimination Laws in Massachusetts," (Ph.D. diss., Harvard University, 1964).

[11]Even Arthur Krock, if my memory serves me, was impressed by this point.

[12]Neil J. Smelser, *Theory of Collective Behavior* (New York: Free Press, 1963).

[13]An almost classic instance of this is the recent impatience of the ministers, whose commitments to the values of racial equality have been impressively activated, with President Johnson, essentially because he wanted to mobilize strong political support for his more drastic proposals on voting rights before taking his own strong personal stand about the Selma crisis. The proposals were on the whole in favor of immediate and drastic federal compulsion in Alabama, regardless of the possible political costs.

[14]Cf. Pettigrew, *A Profile of the Negro American* (Princeton, N.J.: Van Nostrand, 1964).

[15]Oscar Handlin, *The Uprooted* (Boston: Little, Brown, 1951).

[16]Color, in turn, symbolizes *parentage*, since of course the skin color of Negroes varies greatly. The social criterion is that a Negro is anyone, one or both of whose parents were socially classified as a Negro.

[17]Cf. Pettigrew, *Profile of a Negro American*.

[18]However dramatic, episodes like that in Selma are clearly coming into the category of "mopping up operations."

[19]Erwin N. Griswold, *Law and Lawyers in the United States* (Cambridge: Harvard University Press, 1964).

[20]Cf. remarks of Clifford Geertz in the 1964 *Daedalus* planning conference.

[21]Contrary, of course, to the temporary trend to the establishment of a WASP aristrocracy.

[22]It could perhaps be said that the claim of Orthodox Judaism for a secure position in the host society is a case of the "separate but equal" principle. Similar things can be said of other

ethnic and religious situations, for example the French minority in Canada.

[23]It must be understood that the economic factor here includes the whole opportunity-capacity complex, which is especially important for the Negro. For this reason *primary* reliance on economic interests is clearly inadequate.

[24]Charles Campbell and Thomas Pettigrew, *Christians in Racial Crisis* (Washington, D.C.: Public Affairs Press, 1959).

[25]Not only that, but the positive value of a Negro identity in the long run should not be used to justify failing to act to break up *discriminatory* segregation in the more immediate situation.

CHAPTER 23

Minorities and the Process of Stratification

BEVERLY DUNCAN and OTIS DUDLEY DUNCAN

I T is commonly held that ethnic and racial minorities differ with respect to the rapidity of assimilation into the "majority" socioeconomic system or in the rate of upward social mobility between generations. Indeed, the relative positions of the several minorities with respect to vertical mobility often are assumed to be sufficiently well documented that investigations of the correlates or causes of mobility differentials can proceed without re-establishing the magnitude of the differentials themselves. In exploring the consequences for social mobility of inter-group differences in "psychological and cultural orientations toward achievement," for example, Rosen (1959) took as given the low vertical mobility of Negroes, the greater vertical mobility of Southern Italians and French-Canadians, and the still greater vertical mobility of the Jewish and Greek minorities. For him the cause of mobility differentials rather than the existence of such differentials was problematic. Paral-

The research reported herein was carried out under Contract No. OE–5–85–072 with the U.S. Office of Education, as a part of Project No. 5–0074 (EO–191), "Socioeconomic Background and Occupational Achievement: Extensions of a Basic Model." Susan Bittner and Ellen Shantz provided computational assistance.

lelism between the assumed ranking of groups with respect to vertical mobility and their ranking with respect to the "Achievement Syndrome" was taken to imply that differences among minorities in the achievement orientation of their members were reflected in their disparate rates of vertical mobility.

At the same time that this linkage between achievement orientation and vertical mobility was discussed in the literature, Nam (1959) reported a set of findings about differences in socioeconomic status between immigrant and second-generation Americans in each of ten national-origin groups. The mean of the status scores for the second-generation exceeded the mean status score for the immigrant groups when inter-group differences in age and rural-urban residence had been controlled statistically. The national-origin groups for which the difference in score between generations fell closest to the mean difference were the Czechs, the Italians, and the Russians. If the last group can serve as a surrogate for the Jewish minority and if the experience of Southern Italians is accurately represented by the experience of all Italians, Nam's findings imply that both Jews and Southern Italians were "average" minorities with respect to rate of vertical mobility. Differences between generations for the other minority groups studied by Rosen were not assessed by Nam, but the possibility that Rosen's assumed ranking of minorities with respect to vertical mobility was erroneous must be entertained. If so, the consequences of ethnic variation in achievement orientation for social mobility become ambiguous.

Recently Taeuber and Taeuber (1968) have pointed out some pitfalls in inferring rates of vertical mobility for national-origin groups from comparisons of the socioeconomic status of immigrant and second-generation Americans. Specifically, they call attention to the implicit and demonstrably false assumption that the foreign-born and second-generation Americans surveyed on a given date approximate "immigrants and their children" or "second-generation Americans and their parents." It is, however, on precisely such comparisons, bolstered by an occasional intensive study for a select subpopulation, that generalizations about the social promotion of American minorities rest.

A body of data now exists which permits somewhat tighter measurement of the educational and occupational achievements of native Americans and the influence thereon of social origin and national origin.

THE DATA ON ACHIEVEMENT AND ORIGIN

Each civilian noninstitutional male between the ages of 20 and 64 who was included in the March, 1962, Current Population Survey conducted by the United States Bureau of the Census was asked to complete a supplementary questionnaire, "Occupational Changes in a Generation," which dealt with his social background. A report on the survey has been published (Blau and Duncan, 1967), and the details are not recapitulated here.

The subset of data presently under scrutiny is restricted to native non-Negro males who were between the ages of 25 and 64 in 1962 and whose family heads had been pursuing a nonfarm occupation when the respondent was 16 years old. The seven items of information which enter the analysis are identified in Table 1. Most crucial are the indicators of origin and achievement. Social origin is indexed by two variables: school years completed by the head of the family in which the respondent was living at

age 16; and the socioeconomic status score of the job then held by the family head. National origin appears as a 13-fold classification based on the country of birth of the fathers of native white males, the region of birth of the white males of native parentage, and a residual category for the native males of the "minor" nonwhite races. Achievement is indexed by the school years completed by the respondent and by the socioeconomic status score of the job he held, or had most recently held, at the time of the survey.

The quality of the survey data is thought to be generally good, insofar as independent checks can be made (Duncan, 1965; Blau and Duncan, 1967). The numbers of sample cases in several national-origin strata are small, however, and even a rough check on the differences among national-origin groups can only be carried out for one social characteristic, the educational attainment of the respondents. A mean education score was calculated from published tabulations of the 1950 Census (Vol. IV, Pt. 3, Ch. A, Tables 10 and 20) for native white males aged 25 to 44, of foreign or mixed parentage, and residing in urban or rural-nonfarm territory. The coefficient of correlation between these scores and the scores reported in Table 1 was found to be 0.98 over nine national-origin groups (the six nations separately identified in the stub of Table 1, England-Wales, Norway, Sweden, and Austria equated with Northwest Europe except Ireland and Germany, Mexico equated with America except Canada, and a residual "all other"). The education score for nonwhites other than Negroes is somewhat suspect, however. The score reported in Table 1 resembles closely a Census-based score for Japanese and Chinese, who are estimated to make up roughly half the group. It appears unduly high when allowance is made for the fact that the other group members are primarily American Indians, whose educational attainment is substantially less. (Although we have no specific indication that this is the case, it may be that the respondents to the survey and supplementary questionnaire do not proportionately represent American Indians.)

The survey results reveal fairly substantial differences among national-origin groups with respect to both educational and occupa-

TABLE 1. MEAN SCORES AND STANDARD DEVIATIONS ON SIX SOCIAL CHARACTERISTICS FOR NATIVE CIVILIAN NON-NEGRO MALES OF NONFARM BACKGROUND, AGED 25 TO 64 IN 1962, AND DEVIATIONS FROM THE RESPECTIVE GRAND MEANS FOR NATIONAL-ORIGIN SUBGROUPS: UNITED STATES, 1962

| National Origin | Family Head's | | Siblings, number | Edu-cation | First Occu-pation | Current Occu-pation | Number[a] (000's) |
	Edu-cation	Occu-pation					
All Non-Negroes	....	.....	....	.....	.....	.....	22,712
Mean Score	8.63	34.06	3.85	11.69	30.35	43.45	....
Standard Deviation	3.66	22.72	2.94	3.30	22.10	24.58	....
White, Native Father, Respondent Born—							
South	−0.28	−0.37	0.43	−0.65	−2.32	−2.47	4,549
North or West	0.85	3.23	−0.42	0.35	0.92	1.31	11,349
White, Foreign Father, Father born—							
USSR	−1.51	2.39	−0.46	1.43	9.55	8.77	575
NW Europe, exc. Ireland and Germany	0.55	−0.12	−0.31	0.26	4.52	5.55	1,040
Ireland	−0.48	−5.67	0.03	0.32	4.24	1.03	413
Canada	0.38	1.85	0.29	0.16	−0.53	0.89	538
Germany	0.18	−1.56	0.37	−0.55	−2.37	0.05	643
Europe, exc. NW, Italy, Poland, and USSR	−2.09	−8.09	0.62	−0.04	−1.41	−0.69	1,165
Poland	−2.91	−11.77	0.87	−0.65	−4.00	−4.80	620
Italy	−2.94	−10.94	0.91	−0.64	−2.28	−6.03	1,282
America, exc. Canada	−3.23	−11.30	1.62	−2.77	−6.67	−14.85	244
All Other[b]	−1.99	−3.54	0.86	−0.32	−2.95	−5.30	137
Nonwhite, exc. Negro[b]	0.24	−1.20	0.60	−0.12	−4.79	3.12	157

[a] Includes men not reporting specific items; approximate sample frequencies may be obtained by dividing population frequencies, in thousands, by 2.17.

[b] Base is fewer than 100 sample cases.

SOURCE: Unpublished tabulations from March, 1962 Current Population Survey and supplement thereto, Occupational Changes in a Generation, conducted by the U.S. Bureau of the Census.

tional achievement. Especially distinguished by high achievement are the Russian-Americans, who outrank not only the other minorities, but also the native-of-native majority. The lowest achievement is recorded on the part of native Americans whose fathers were born in Latin America, most often in Mexico. It is neither of these groups which most closely resembles the third-generation in achieved status, however, but rather the Irish, the Canadians, the Germans, and the "other Europeans," such as Czechs. Moreover, were a measure of vertical mobility to be constructed by subtracting from the mean achievement score of respondents the corresponding mean score for their family heads, the group of "other European" origin would outrank Russian-Americans with respect to occupational mobility; and German-Americans rather than Latin-Americans

would appear to be low achievers in the educational sphere.

Perhaps a more fruitful approach is to view membership in a given national-origin group as a predetermined variable in a model of the process of stratification (Blau and Duncan, 1967, Ch. 5)—one which may influence achievement both through its linkages with other ascribed characteristics and by fostering an "achievement syndrome" or circumscribing opportunities for achievement.

ORIGINS AND EDUCATIONAL ACHIEVEMENT

From a life-cycle perspective, the earliest measure of achievement available in this subset of data is the number of school years or grades completed by the respondent. Measures on the family head's educational and occupational attainment are temporally prior to the achievement measure, and typically all siblings will have been born prior to the completion of the respondent's schooling. These three characteristics along with membership in a national-origin group are taken as antecedent to the respondent's educational achievement.

Let us suppose that the process of stratification operates in an identical fashion for men in the so-called majority and in the several minorities, i.e., that the respective net effects of head's education and occupation and the number of siblings on educational achievement are constant over national-origin groups. Differences in educational achievement would nonetheless be observed, because the several national-origin groups differ with respect to social origin or their mean scores on the respective family-

background characteristics. Only to the extent that the achievement of a national-origin group exceeds or falls short of the achievement "expected" on the basis of the group's social origin could an effect of national origin *per se* on achievement be entertained as a possibility.

Values of the partial regression coefficients summarizing the relations of the number of school years completed by the respondent to family head's education and occupation and the number of siblings are reported in the first column of Table 2. Gross or observed differences among national-origin groups with respect to school years completed are shown in the second column. Appearing in the third column are the differences "expected" among these groups on the basis of their mean scores on the three family-background characteristics and the partial re-

TABLE 2. SUMMARY OF ANALYSES OF THE EFFECTS OF SOCIAL AND NATIONAL ORIGINS ON EDUCATIONAL ATTAINMENT: AMERICAN NATIVE CIVILIAN NON-NEGRO MALES OF NONFARM BACKGROUND, AGED 25 TO 64 IN 1962

| Origin Characteristic | Partial Regression Coefficients | Mean Education Score | | | Partial Regression Coefficients |
		Observed	Expected	Obs. Less Exp.	
Social Origin					
Family Head's—					
Education	.1680	....	....	....	.1898
Occupation	.0376	....	....	....	.0374
Siblings, Number	−.2802	....	....	....	−.2708
National Origin					
White, Native Father, Respondent Born—					
South	....	−0.66	−0.18	−0.48	−0.51
North or West	....	0.36	0.38	−0.02	−0.04
White, Foreign Father, Father Born—					
USSR	....	1.44	−0.04	1.48	1.51
NW Europe, exc. Ireland and Germany	....	0.26	0.17	0.09	0.08
Ireland	....	0.32	−0.30	0.62	0.63
Canada	....	0.16	0.05	0.11	0.09
Germany	....	−0.54	−0.13	−0.41	−0.42
Europe, exc. NW, Italy, Poland, and USSR	....	−0.04	−0.83	0.79	0.83
Poland	....	−0.66	−1.18	0.52	0.58
Italy	....	−0.64	−1.16	0.52	0.57
America, exc. Canada	....	−2.78	−1.42	−1.36	−1.30
All Other [a]	....	−0.32	−0.71	0.39	0.42
Nonwhite, exc. Negro [a]	....	−0.12	−0.16	0.04	0.04

[a] Base is fewer than 100 samples cases.
SOURCE: See Table 1.

gression coefficients summarizing the relation of the education score to the respective background scores for this non-Negro, non-farm, native population as a whole. Both the observed and expected scores for each group are expressed as deviations from the mean score for all respondents. Finally, the fourth column contains a set of estimates of the national-origin effects *per se,* the excess or deficit of the observed score with respect to the expected score.

An alternative set of estimates of the national-origin effects, net of social origin, is reported in the fifth column of Table 2. The respondent's education score has been regressed not only on family head's education and occupation and the number of siblings, but also on the national-origin classification. The classification enters the analysis as a set of dummy variables: the respondent is assigned a score of unity on the variable representing the national-origin class in which he holds membership, and a score of zero on the other variables representing national-origin classes. (Values of the coefficients measuring the net effect of nationality-group membership are so scaled that their weighted sum equals zero.) These estimates of the effects on educational achievement of national origin, net of social origin, resemble closely in magnitude the estimates of national-origin effects obtained in the analysis reported above.

Although allowance for inter-group differences in social origin reduces the range of difference with respect to educational achievement by about a third, some 2.8 grades separate the mean scores of the highest-achieving and lowest-achieving national-origin groups, after group starting points have been equalized. At the lower limit of the range, after as well as before adjustment for social origin, are the Latin Americans; the performance of Russian-Americans consistently sets the upper limit on the range. Membership in a particular national-origin group can rather clearly constitute a substantial "handicap" or "bonus" in the stratification process, although the relative numbers of individuals holding such membership may be too small for the nationality factor to make a major contribution to variation in the total population. In the subset of data under analysis here, for example, the inclu-

sion of national origin as well as social origin as an explanatory factor results in an increment of only 1.8 percent to the "explained" variance in educational attainment.

Of somewhat special interest may be the finding that membership in a non-Negro minority typically has a positive effect on educational achievement. In fact, achievement for no minority save the Latin-American is damped *vis-à-vis* the performance of third-generation Southerners, when all groups are equalized with respect to starting point. Only one other minority, the German-American, could be identified as "underachieving" even by the more stringent standard of performance set by third-generation Americans born in the North or West.

Whatever mechanism one wishes to adduce as causative, there can be little doubt that a "melting-pot" phenomenon obtains in America, in at least one sense of that term. The national-origin classification is found to account for only three percent of the variance among survey respondents with respect to grades of school completed. On the other hand, the national-origin classification accounts for some 11 percent of the variance among the respondents with respect to the formal schooling of their family heads. The rather sharp differentials in formal schooling by nationality that obtained in the parental generation did not persist among their native sons, who assimilated the American norms of school attendance.

ORIGINS AND OCCUPATIONAL ACHIEVEMENT

In the basic model of the process of stratification suggested by Blau and Duncan (1967, Chap. 5), the effects of social origin on occupational achievement are represented as in large measure indirect. The effect of social origin is transmitted to occupational achievement primarily by way of the influence of origin on educational attainment, which, in turn, influences occupational achievement. One may entertain the possibility that members of some minorities may not secure occupational status consonant with their educational attainment, however, whether because of high achievement motivation not fully realized in the educational sphere or because of discrimination in the job market.

Let us begin by regressing the socioeconomic status score of the respondent's current occupation on the three family-background characteristics and then regress the score on the national-origin classification along with the social-origin indicators. The results, summarized in columns (1) and (2) of Table 3, are, in broad outline, similar to the results observed when educational achievement was regressed on social and national origins. Allowance for inter-group differences in social origin reduces the range of difference with respect to occupational achievement by a third, but the extremes remain separated by some 15 score points on a scale whose standard deviation is 25 score points in the whole population under study. Again, minority-group membership is conducive to high achievement *vis-à-vis* the achievement of third-generation Americans when levels of origin in the social structure are equalized; the noteworthy exception remains the Latin-American minority. Once more distinguished by high achievement, given their social origin, are the Russian-Americans.

In the next set of analyses, summarized in columns (3) and (4) of Table 3, a measure of prior achieved status, the educational attainment of the respondent, is introduced as an explanatory factor along with the origins indicators. Differences in occupational achievement among the national-origin groups are reduced substantially when allow-

TABLE 3. SUMMARY OF ANALYSES OF THE EFFECTS OF SOCIAL AND NATIONAL ORIGINS AND PRIOR ACHIEVED STATUS ON CURRENT OCCUPATIONAL ACHIEVEMENT: AMERICAN NATIVE CIVILIAN NON-NEGRO MALES OF NONFARM BACKGROUND, AGED 25 TO 64 IN 1962

Characteristic	Partial Regression Coefficients					
	(1)	(2)	(3)	(4)	(5)	(6)
Social Orgin						
Family head's—						
Education	0.81	0.92	0.15	0.17	0.05	0.03
Occupation	0.29	0.29	0.14	0.14	0.10	0.10
Siblings, Number	−1.53	−1.50	−0.42	−0.43	−0.30	−0.30
National Origin						
White, Native Father, Respondent Born—						
South	....	−1.66	....	0.34	....	0.38
North or West	....	−1.03	....	−0.87	....	−0.53
White, Foreign Father, Father Born—						
USSR	....	8.78	....	2.83	....	1.33
NW Europe, exc. Ireland and Germany	....	4.62	....	4.32	....	3.40
Ireland	....	3.15	....	0.66	....	−0.54
Canada	....	0.44	....	0.07	....	0.43
Germany	....	0.89	....	2.56	....	2.68
Europe, exc. NW, Italy, Poland, and USSR	....	4.50	....	1.22	....	0.89
Poland	....	2.56	....	0.28	....	−0.13
Italy	....	1.18	....	−1.07	....	−1.92
America, exc. Canada	....	−6.20	....	−1.09	....	−2.61
All Other [a]	....	−1.18	....	−2.85	....	−2.82
Nonwhite, exc. Negro [a]	....	4.14	....	3.99	....	5.11
Prior Achieved Status						
Education	....	....	3.96	3.94	3.13	3.13
First Occupation	....	....	....	....	0.28	0.27
Coefficient of Determination	.182	.193	.392	.395	.432	.434

[a] Base is fewer than 100 sample cases.
SOURCE: See Table 1.

ance has been made not only for their differences in social origin, but also their differences with respect to the intervening factor, educational attainment. The range of differences over groups falls from 15 to 7 score points and is bounded no longer by the Latin-Americans and Russian-Americans. Such influence as nationality has on achievement appears to operate differently in the job market than in the schools.

The nationality factor *per se* does not appear, then, to loom large in the process of matching men and jobs. Once equated with respect to starting point in the social structure and educational attainment, the occupational achievement of one national-origin group differs little from that of another. Membership in one of three minorities—Italian-American, Latin-American, or the residual "all other"—may depress occupational success by comparison with the norm for the non-Southern third-generation. Evaluated against the performance of the Southern third-generation, not only these groups but also the men whose origins trace to Canada or Poland suffer a modest handicap. Achieving increasingly greater occupational success given their social origin and formal schooling are the Irish, the "other Europeans," the Germans, the Russians, the members of the minor nonwhite races, and the men whose origins trace to nations of northwest Europe other than Ireland and Germany.

When the national-origin groups are equated not only with respect to starting point in the social structure and educational attainment, but also with respect to starting point in the occupational structure as indexed by the socioeconomic status score of the first job, the description of the nationality factor and occupational success remains essentially unchanged. The relevant analyses are summarized in columns (5) and (6) of Table 3. Nationality does not appear to operate as a common basis for selective promotion once entry into the job market has been effected, although a close reading of the data reveals a few instances in which a minority loses ground in the competition for jobs as work experience lengthens. The Italian-Americans and Latin-Americans, who enter near the bottom of the occupational structure, appear to accumulate a job-mar-

ket disadvantage; the Russian-Americans, the Irish-Americans, and the group whose origin can be traced to other nations of northwestern Europe, all of whom enter near the top of the occupation structure, fail to maintain fully their initial job-market advantage. Selective promotion or employer discrimination on the basis of nationality cannot be inferred with confidence, however, for the typical pattern of job mobility may be distinctive for men entering the occupation structure near its extremes irrespective of their nationality.

Occupations were somewhat more closely related to national origin in the parental generation than among the men currently in the work force. The national-origin classification accounts for some 4 percent of the variance in the socioeconomic status scores for the family heads' occupations as compared with 1 percent of the variance in the socioeconomic status scores for the respondents' occupations on either the first or current job. Unlike the intergenerational comparison of the effect of nationality and educational attainment, in which the schooling of many members of the parental generation occurred in foreign countries, the intergenerational comparison with respect to occupational status reflects the placement of the respective generations in the American occupational structure. This comparison takes no account of generational differences in job qualifications for the several national-origin groups, but it indicates an unambiguous narrowing of differences among group positions in the occupation structure between generations.

EDUCATIONAL OR OCCUPATIONAL ACHIEVEMENT

The influence of origin, social or national, on occupational achievement can operate either (a) by way of an effect on educational achievement which, in turn, influences occupational success or (b) directly, i.e., without mediation by schooling. The impact of social origin on occupational achievement occurs primarily through social differentials in schooling and educational differentials in occupational achievement. No such blanket generalization can be made, however, with respect to the transmission of influence from the nationality factor to occupational achievement.

Estimates of the importance of the indirect and direct routes of transmission, respectively, are derived from partial regression coefficients reported in Tables 2 and 3. The strength of the direct route is reflected in the magnitude of the partial regression coefficent for current occupation on the given origin variable when all other origin variables and educational attainment have been held constant statistically, as in regression model (4) of Table 3. The strength of the indirect route is reflected in the magnitude of the product of two partial regression coefficients: current occupation on educational attainment when all original variables have been held constant statistically (3.94, as given in column (4) of Table 3); and educational attainment on the given origin variable when all other origin variables have been held constant statistically (coefficients in the fifth column of Table 2). (Numerical values of the two components are given in parentheses following the names of nationality groups discussed in succeeding paragraphs.)

Loosely speaking, the indirect effect of the nationality factor on occupational success reflects inequalities in the distribution of education above and beyond those based on social origin. The direct effect reflects inequalities in the distribution of job opportunities above and beyond those based on formal educational qualifications and social origin. A national-origin group can suffer discrimination or enjoy preferential treatment in either distributive process.

Third-generation Southerners (direct, 0.34; indirect, —2.01) and German-Americans (2.56; —1.65) are detectably handicapped in the competition for jobs by virtue of their educational under-achievement. Given their formal schooling as well as their starting point in the social structure, the Southerners experience neither discrimination nor preferential treatment in the job market, however, and the German-Americans encounter somewhat preferential treatment in the competition for jobs. Their cases are rather different from that of the Latin-Americans (—1.09; —5.12), who not only are severely handicapped in the competition for jobs by virtue of educational under-

achievement, but also encounter discrimination subsequent to school leaving.

Irish-Americans (0.66; 2.48) and Polish-Americans (0.28; 2.29) enjoy a somewhat preferential position with respect to the distribution of schooling by comparison with other Americans of similar social origin. Their occupational success is, however, in line with the American "average" for men of similar social origin and educational qualification. In contrast, the men whose origin can be traced to Russia (2.83; 5.94) or "other Europe" (1.22; 3.27), Czechoslovakia, for example, occupy a distinctly advantaged position with respect to the distribution of schooling and a detectably advantaged position with respect to the distribution of jobs. Still another distributive pattern is represented by the experience of Italian-Americans (—1.07; 2.25). Italians, like the Irish and the Polish, enjoy a somewhat preferential position with respect to the distribution of schooling, but their occupational success falls short of the American "average" for men of similar social origin and educational qualification.

Among the national-origin groups separately identified here, there occurs but one instance of distinctly preferential position with respect to the competition for jobs. The group is a rough approximation to the Anglo-Saxon Protestants, stereotypically held to enjoy a favored position in American society. The men whose origin can be traced to nations of northwestern Europe other than Ireland and Germany (4.32; 0.32) are preponderantly sons of migrants from England and Wales, the Scandinavian countries, and Austria. There is no evidence that they are over-achievers in the American school system, but their occupational success is greater than that of other Americans with similar social origin and educational qualification.

DISCRIMINATION AGAINST MINORITIES

The experience of non-Negro minorities in America, as revealed by these observations on their educational and occupational achievements, would argue against the existence of pervasive discrimination on purely ethnic grounds. The notion of equal opportunity irrespective of national origin is a near reality, challenged most severely by the cumulative over-achievement of Russian-Americans and the cumulative under-achievement of Latin-Americans.

The experience of the Negro minority in America, as revealed by comparable observations on their educational and occupational achievements, makes one less sanguine about the equality with which distributive processes operate in this country. The current occupations of Latin-Americans are reflected in a mean socioeconomic status score which falls short of the mean score for all non-Negro, nonfarm, native males by 15 points. The current occupations of Negro-Americans are reflected in a mean score which falls short of the same (non-Negro) mean by 24 points. After adjustment for starting point in the social structure and formal educational qualifications, membership in the Latin-American minority results in a handicap of one point on the socio-economic status scale; but membership in the Negro minority results in a handicap of twelve points on this scale (Duncan, 1968). The evidence of discrimination against the American Negro in the competition for jobs is difficult to discount.

Models of the type displayed in this report can bring to light the extent and patterns of differentials associated with minority-group status and disclose something of their mechanism. Whether the causes of the residual factors in differential social promotion can be taken to be cultural, structural, or social-psychological in nature cannot be determined with the type of data available for this analysis.

REFERENCES

Blau, Peter M. and Otis Dudley Duncan.
  1967 The American Occupational Structure. New York: John Wiley and Sons.
Duncan, Beverly.
  1965 Family Factors and School Dropout: 1920–1960, Final report on Cooperative Research Project No. 2258, Office of Education. Ann Arbor: The University of Michigan.
Duncan, Otis Dudley.
  1968 "Inheritance of poverty or inheritance of race?" in Daniel P. Moynihan (ed.), forthcoming volume.
Nam, Charles B.
  1959 "Nationality groups and social stratification in America." Social Forces 37 (May): 328–33.
Rosen, Bernard C.
  1959 "Race, ethnicity, and the achievement syndrome." American Sociological Review 24 (February):47–60.
Taeuber, Alma F. and Karl E. Taeuber.
  1968 "Recent immigration and studies of ethnic assimilation." Demography (forthcoming).

CHAPTER 24

Income and Education

HERMAN P. MILLER

INTRODUCTION

This chapter considers the relation between education and income as reflected in detailed statistics from the 1960 Census. Although much is already known about this subject from the annual income surveys conducted by the Bureau of the Census, from tabulations of the preceding two censuses, and from special studies of selected professional occupations, there is some evidence that economists only now are awakening to the pivotal importance of education as it relates to individual income determination and national economic growth. While the benefits of education to the individual are obvious—increased schooling generally leads to a better paying job—benefits to the Nation are perhaps not so well known.

Recent studies of the factors underlying economic growth in the United States highlight the role of education in increasing the productivity of the American worker.[1] Economists have been unable to explain increases in productivity during the past 75 years entirely on the basis of changes in the accumulation or use of physical capital, and have been forced to look for other possible explanations. According to one writer, they have turned principally in two directions:

. . . First, they have begun to study the mechanism of technological changes. . . . Secondly, they have begun to study changes in the quality of the labor force and the process of investment in human beings, especially investment in health and education. . . . [2]

Traditionally studies of the relation income and education begin with an apology for stressing the material benefits of schooling. Economists and statisticians—many of whom are also educators—are not oblivious to the cultural and social values of education, to the richness and permanent satisfactions that education adds to life, and to the chance it offers to be of service, to enrich and improve the lives of others. Although we can no more place a monetary value on education in its broadest sense than on friendship or health, the fact remains that there are measurable financial returns associated with, though not necessarily the result of, educational attainment.

Viewed in this perspective, the problem of measuring returns of an investment in education becomes amenable to economic analysis, since it involves the allocation of scarce resources among desired goals. The existence of other values associated with education should not preclude the possibility of comparing financial costs and benefits; nor should the people engaged in this type of analysis feel compelled to explain that they are not materialistic dolts unaware of the better things in life.

Two different aspects of the problem are analyzed in this chapter. First, the relation between income and education, in a given year, is examined for men in various subgroups of the population classified with

364

respect to education.[3] For example, comparisons will be made of average incomes for all white and nonwhite college graduates. These comparisons are made for the years 1939, 1949, and 1959, and for geographic regions as well as for the country as a whole. Similar comparisons, using earnings rather than total income, are made for whites and nonwhites with different amounts of schooling, in about 100 occupations.

The second type of analysis in this section involves the estimation of lifetime income for various groups with different amounts of schooling. The estimates are based on data for 1939, 1949, and 1959 for whites and nonwhites.

The interpretation of any statistical relation such as that between income and education is a delicate matter, fraught with peril. The unwary analyst might easily view the higher incomes of persons with more than average schooling as *prima facie* evidence of the financial rewards of education. Such an unqualified interpretation would be logically incorrect because it overlooks several important factors that may determine both income and education; it would be empirically incorrect because of important exceptions to the general rule. The following discussion reviews some of the more important qualifications to be kept in mind when interpreting the data.

PROBLEMS OF INTERPRETING THE DATA

VARIATIONS ABOUT THE AVERAGE

Although income and education are closely correlated, the relation is far from perfect. For this reason it would be fallacious and perhaps even harmful to draw inferences about individual cases from the evidence presented here for the general population. Many highly educated men have relatively low incomes and it is not uncommon to find wealthy men with little formal training. The 1960 Census shows that about 2½ million college graduates had incomes under $7,000, whereas nearly the same number of men who never went

beyond the twelfth grade receive over $7,000.

A more general view of the variability of income within education groups is provided by a multiple regression analysis applied to income data for 1958 for males in the Current Population Survey. In this analysis, individual income was used as the dependent variable, and eight characteristics—age, marital status, color, residence, region, weeks worked, occupation, and education—were used as independent variables. A regression equation showing income as a function of all the other variables selected for study was then prepared, and the coefficient of multiple regression was computed to ascertain how much of the variation in individual income could be explained by the specific factors. The coefficient of multiple correlation was 0.59 ($R^2=0.35$), which means that the combination of the eight factors accounted for only one-third of the variation in individual income. Although many analysts would consider this a rather high correlation, it is quite evident that any attempt to predict individual income on the basis of these eight factors, which include education, would fall far short of the mark.

Obviously there is much about the determination of individual income that is not accounted for by education or by any of the other characteristics included in a census or the usual household survey. The unexplained variation may be due in part to errors in reporting and to chance factors such as illness, or a "good" or "bad" year, which produce short-run fluctuations in individual income. Primarily, however, the inability to explain more of the variation in individual income must be due to omission from the measurement of such key variables as ability, effort, motivation, and quality of education. If education alone is considered, it is undoubtedly true that many intelligent individuals never get as much schooling as they should, and that some individuals with relatively low intelligence get more schooling than they can absorb.

A recent study by the National Science

Foundation shows that only 75 to 80 percent of the 17-year-old boys who rank in the upper 30 percent of their high school class go to college.[4] The main reason given for the failure of the high-ability youth to obtain college training was inadequate financial resources. It seems clear, therefore, that the general population contains millions of people who had the ability but lacked the opportunity to go to college. It would not be surprising if the underlying ability of these people showed through in later life despite their lack of college training.

Other possible reasons for the large unexplained variation in the relation between income and education come to the fore when comparisons are made between whites and nonwhites. Several recent studies have noted the sluggish way in which nonwhite incomes have responded to increases in education, but have either ignored the data or treated them in a cursory way.[5] Nonwhites have traditionally been virtually excluded from certain occupations. Many who have completed college are concentrated in low-paid jobs. It is entirely possible, indeed likely, that the increase in their years of schooling has raised the productivity potentials of nonwhites; however, because of discrimination, these potentials may not have been realized. Other factors bearing on the situation relate to the precise meaning of the unit of analysis—years of schooling—with which education is equated.

Definition of Education

Educational attainment is measured in our census statistics in years of school completed. Since there are obvious differences in the importance of a year of elementary school, a year of high school, or a year of college, these classifications by level of training are made in the basic data; and since they distinguish one year of schooling from another, they introduce a qualitative factor into the statistics. Beyond this distinction, the census figures make no allowance for differences in the quality of training provided or received. The crude attempts that have been made—largely for purposes of historical comparison—to modify the concept in terms of school year equivalents based on days of schooling per year,[6] must be regarded as faltering first steps. Statistics showing that the average young Negro male is only about 1½ years behind the average young white male in years of school completed present an erroneous impression of the educational gap between the two groups when account is taken of the fact that most young Negroes have received education in northern "ghetto" schools or "separate but equal" southern schools. Qualitative differences have tended to be ignored in measures of physical capital[7] and, except for minor attention, they are also being ignored in recent work on human capital. For broad overall analyses, it is perhaps essential to ignore the qualitative element, especially since it cannot be accurately measured. This logic seems much less compelling when attention is focused on relatively small subgroups in the population.

Another important limitation on the concept of "years of school completed" is that no differentiation is made with respect to the benefits derived from exposure to a given number of years of education. The concept has an entirely different meaning for a student who has done well in a school system with high standards and established bases for measuring achievement, than it has for the poorly motivated student who has just managed to get by in a school system with low standards. Education, after all, is not synonymous with time spent in a schoolroom. If, as a result of cultural, social, or economic reasons, nonwhite students tend to be concentrated near the bottom of their classes, they cannot be expected to profit as much as white students from a year of schooling, since there appears to be an association between scholastic achievement and occupational success.[8] There is some empirical basis for the judgment that problems of behavior, discipline, and lack of motivation appear disproportionately in Negro areas;[9] this may well explain in part the poor correlation between income and education for nonwhite men.

The whole question of the relationship between income (or earnings) and such objective measures as IQ tests, aptitude tests, standardized achievement tests, or other measures has not been adequately explored, in spite of the fact that there is much basic data on the subject. In view of the importance of education, and the increasing share of the national income being devoted to it, perhaps it is time to intensify the efforts spent on collating school and army records with socioeconomic data collected in household surveys, to the end that the economic importance of education to the individual, when other relevant factors are taken into account, may be more precisely measured.

ASSUMPTIONS ABOUT ECONOMIC GROWTH IN ESTIMATES OF LIFETIME INCOME

Estimates of lifetime income provide an insight into the financial returns associated with education that cannot be readily obtained from the annual income data. These estimates are derived from data showing variations in the income of individuals in different age and education groups at a given time; specifically, the calendar years for which data are presented. The figures, therefore, are based on incomes of a cross section of the male, population at a given point in time and do not actually trade an individual's income from the time he starts to work until he retires. It is important that several assumptions made in the preparation of these estimates be understood.

The model is static in that it assumes that all relationships which existed at the time of the survey will prevail in the future. It assumes, for instance, that during an individual's working years there will be no future increases in life expectancy, an assumption of doubtful worth.

The model discounts future earnings at the same rate for all socioeconomic groups. This procedure may be valid if the purpose is to provide a single estimate of lifetime

income from an overall standpoint; and in that case we would use the rate that would best reveal the present value from a single standpoint. If, however, the purpose is to show the estimate that might be considered by individuals or particular groups in making their decisions, then different discount rates for different socioeconomic groups might be appropriate. One of the major problems of low-income families is their inability to plan ahead—to recognize the future implications of present actions. It is very likely, for example, that college graduates discount the future at a far lower rate than high school graduates. If this is the case, the present value of a future stream of income is likely to be far higher for the college group than for the high school group.

Perhaps the major shortcoming of the model is that it assumes no future increases in average income. It recognizes that each individual may expect his own income to rise as he gains in experience, seniority, and other factors that produce income differences among age groups at a given point in time. What it fails to recognize is that " . . . in a growing economy every individual may expect an upward trend in his own earnings superimposed on the cross-sectional pattern for a particular year."[10]

ANNUAL INCOME AND EDUCATION

THE OVERALL PICTURE

Some of the basic statistics pertaining to the relationship between annual earnings and educational attainment are presented in table 1 which shows the figures in absolute form for all groups. In order to permit a comparison of differentials for more recent as well as older graduates, each table presents data for whites and nonwhites for each age group, as well as for the total 25 years old and over.

As previously noted, women are excluded from the analysis for the reasons that a large proportion never enter the labor market after marriage, and that many of those who do work are employed only part time. This is not to say that schooling

Table 1.—Average (Mean) Total Money Earnings for Males 18 to 64 Years Old in the Experienced Civilian Labor Force, by Years of School Completed, Age, and Color, by Regions: 1959

Years of school completed and age	United States			North			South			West		
	Total	White	Nonwhite	Total	White	Nonwhite	Total	White	Nonwhite	Total	White	Nonwhite
25 TO 64 YEARS OLD												
Total	$5,847	$6,112	$3,260	$6,128	$6,266	$3,998	$4,905	$5,407	$2,427	$6,520	$6,682	$4,498
Elementary: Less than 8 years	3,659	3,983	2,562	4,341	4,457	3,607	2,932	3,346	2,057	4,215	4,363	3,510
8 years	4,725	4,837	3,318	4,872	4,932	3,794	3,979	4,215	2,569	5,221	5,300	4,132
High school: 1 to 3 years	5,379	5,555	3,522	5,566	5,685	3,972	4,653	4,958	2,714	5,861	5,974	4,392
4 years	6,132	6,250	4,021	6,163	6,245	4,246	5,675	5,889	3,062	6,613	6,721	5,002
College: 1 to 3 years	7,401	7,554	4,355	7,565	7,688	4,645	7,034	7,268	3,446	7,424	7,551	5,016
4 years or more	10,078	10,238	5,671	10,430	10,541	5,865	9,496	9,773	4,791	9,807	9,934	6,928
4 years	9,255	9,406	4,897	9,692	9,785	5,312	8,503	8,766	4,013	8,989	9,115	6,153
5 years or more	11,136	11,317	6,510	11,372	11,515	6,433	10,944	11,254	5,807	10,744	10,876	7,832
18 TO 24 YEARS												
Total	2,731	2,835	1,888	2,895	2,927	2,435	2,299	2,507	1,492	3,035	3,084	2,413
Elementary: Less than 8 years	1,957	2,131	1,475	2,504	2,528	2,341	1,621	1,830	1,289	2,165	2,151	2,273
8 years	2,465	2,589	1,745	2,743	2,777	2,355	2,000	2,185	1,440	2,823	2,888	2,123
High school: 1 to 3 years	2,549	2,662	1,860	2,706	2,753	2,282	2,141	2,338	1,520	2,874	2,922	2,302
4 years	3,036	3,105	2,216	3,115	3,144	2,600	2,700	2,852	1,714	3,295	3,347	2,597
College: 1 to 3 years	2,619	2,641	2,168	2,595	2,596	2,565	2,456	2,513	1,665	2,860	2,897	2,273
4 years or more	3,538	3,563	2,844	3,552	3,560	3,159	3,440	3,499	2,544	3,660	3,692	2,936
4 years	3,638	3,665	2,818	3,662	3,670	3,140	3,561	3,630	2,570	3,715	3,746	2,956
5 years or more	3,276	3,291	2,902	3,279	3,281	3,186	3,072	3,107	(B)	3,519	3,552	(B)
25 TO 34 YEARS												
Total	5,188	5,412	3,190	5,408	5,527	3,835	4,449	4,871	2,404	5,773	5,897	4,343
Elementary: Less than 8 years	3,225	3,537	2,332	3,880	3,986	3,349	2,732	3,127	1,967	3,649	3,744	3,037
8 years	4,197	4,357	2,994	4,393	4,468	3,562	3,539	3,827	2,384	4,804	4,925	3,572
High school: 1 to 3 years	4,783	4,998	3,240	4,947	5,081	3,733	4,115	4,491	2,522	5,366	5,496	4,017
4 years	5,361	5,480	3,717	5,422	5,498	4,013	4,878	5,101	2,828	5,860	5,971	4,614
College: 1 to 3 years	5,849	5,964	4,072	5,931	6,014	4,320	5,504	5,688	3,283	6,055	6,161	4,675
4 years or more	7,053	7,146	4,760	7,136	7,203	4,810	6,833	6,997	3,921	7,109	7,177	5,867
4 years	6,986	7,083	4,537	7,139	7,196	4,780	6,668	6,854	3,649	7,011	7,080	5,728
5 years or more	7,145	7,233	5,047	7,140	7,220	4,837	7,097	7,223	4,479	7,230	7,296	6,036

B Base less than 1,000 persons.

Table 1.—Average (Mean) Total Money Earnings for Males 18 to 64 Years Old in the Experienced Civilian Labor Force, by Years of School Completed, Age, and Color, by Regions: 1959—Con.

Years of school completed and age	United States			North			South			West		
	Total	White	Nonwhite	Total	White	Nonwhite	Total	White	Nonwhite	Total	White	Nonwhite
35 TO 44 YEARS												
Total	$6,259	$6,540	$3,543	$6,497	$6,653	$4,243	$5,315	$5,839	$2,633	$7,084	$7,251	$4,995
Elementary: Less than 8 years	3,658	4,015	2,648	4,377	4,529	3,712	3,057	3,492	2,169	4,374	4,514	3,705
8 years	4,730	4,861	3,474	4,850	4,922	3,874	4,072	4,332	2,724	5,368	5,470	4,371
High school: 1 to 3 years	5,500	5,671	3,809	5,641	5,757	4,206	4,841	5,141	2,948	6,062	6,175	4,818
4 years	6,398	6,507	4,379	6,414	6,492	4,522	5,946	6,142	3,310	6,886	6,988	5,405
College: 1 to 3 years	7,846	8,007	4,651	7,989	8,130	4,886	7,405	7,629	3,732	7,989	8,124	5,353
4 years or more	10,863	11,027	6,377	11,072	11,188	6,640	10,473	10,777	5,211	10,820	10,929	8,049
4 years	9,970	10,127	5,321	10,345	10,449	5,559	9,280	9,561	4,284	9,818	9,934	6,897
5 years or more	11,967	12,148	7,409	11,962	12,100	7,528	12,246	12,603	6,296	11,885	11,993	9,234
45 TO 54 YEARS												
Total	6,194	6,487	3,209	6,536	6,679	4,018	5,100	5,653	2,422	6,940	7,131	4,437
Elementary: Less than 8 years	3,759	4,093	2,645	4,468	4,595	3,684	2,997	3,418	2,102	4,396	4,580	3,699
8 years	4,904	5,000	3,457	5,038	5,091	3,885	4,160	4,371	2,668	5,361	5,432	4,299
High school: 1 to 3 years	5,719	5,852	3,655	5,918	6,009	4,097	4,963	5,186	2,830	6,144	6,246	4,398
4 years	6,691	6,793	4,157	6,705	6,779	4,309	6,316	6,502	3,273	7,074	7,163	5,154
College: 1 to 3 years	8,604	8,752	4,593	8,737	8,851	4,901	8,353	8,616	3,487	8,588	8,686	5,711
4 years or more	13,313	13,536	6,463	13,942	14,058	7,081	12,202	12,650	5,582	12,788	12,986	7,934
4 years	11,614	11,798	5,346	12,341	12,439	5,703	10,385	10,729	4,592	11,019	11,184	6,578
5 years or more	15,384	15,684	7,511	15,828	15,985	8,060	14,672	15,336	6,479	14,921	15,189	9,377
55 TO 64 YEARS												
Total	5,737	5,993	2,929	6,099	6,218	3,826	4,671	5,196	2,116	6,145	6,310	3,875
Elementary: Less than 8 years	3,810	4,088	2,530	4,393	4,479	3,590	2,868	3,275	1,911	4,237	4,410	3,349
8 years	4,840	4,908	3,324	4,962	5,001	3,772	4,074	4,238	2,476	5,180	5,229	3,958
High school: 1 to 3 years	5,762	5,874	3,513	6,028	6,112	3,955	4,959	5,144	2,606	5,949	6,026	4,327
4 years	6,824	6,940	3,888	6,888	6,984	4,122	6,523	6,708	2,894	6,987	7,092	4,644
College: 1 to 3 years	8,610	8,760	4,307	8,962	9,097	4,661	8,305	8,539	3,235	8,013	8,105	4,996
4 years or more	13,089	13,300	5,891	14,078	14,238	6,393	11,782	12,159	5,048	11,478	11,587	7,666
4 years	12,061	12,263	4,523	12,845	12,977	5,134	10,913	11,275	3,725	10,778	10,959	5,077
5 years or more	14,349	14,582	7,399	15,675	15,888	7,684	12,790	13,208	6,470	12,292	12,315	(B)

B Base less than 1,000 persons.
Source: 1960 *Census of Population, Subject Reports, Occupation by Earnings and Education,* Series PC(2)–7B, and unpublished data of the Bureau of the Census.

is economically unimportant for women; on the contrary, the better educated women tend to have higher living standards than those who have not had much schooling. The difference, however, is not generally or necessarily reflected in the kind of work they do—since most of them do not work —nor is it associated with their age, place of residence, or other personal characteristics discussed in this chapter. Among women, the association between education and financial returns tends to be more indirect than for men, and is attributable, to a large extent, to the fact that better educated men tend to marry better educated women. It is because of the indirect nature of this association that the present study excludes the analysis of the relation between income and education for women.

Looking first at the figures for all age groups combined, we can see the now familiar tendency for earnings to increase with education. This finding parallels that obtained in virtually all other studies of the relation between income and education, some dating back to the early part of this century.[11] Below the college level, there is roughly a $500 to $1,000 difference (about $10 to $20 per week) between each of the education groups shown. Thus, among men whose formal schooling ended before the eighth grade, mean income was about $3,700 in 1959, compared with about $4,700 for elementary school graduates. Men with some high school training but no diploma had a mean income of $5,400 compared with $6,100 for graduates. The greatest increase in annual earnings was found at the college level, where men with 1 to 3 years of training averaged $7,400 compared with $10,100 received by graduates.

There is a relatively large difference in earnings (29 percent) between men who complete the eighth grade and those who do not; this pattern has been observed in numerous studies conducted under varying economic conditions. It is hard to imagine that the specific skills learned in the eighth grade are so different from those learned in previous grades as to produce so large a differential in earnings or income. It is more likely that the failure to graduate from elementary school serves as a basis for identifying those persons who, for a variety of reasons, will tend to lag far behind the general population in productivity and income. At this level, education may serve as a proxy variable for other factors that prevent successful learning and lead to low productivity.

A similar differential (although not quite as marked) between persons who attain a given level of schooling and those who graduate from that level, appears also at the higher grades. For example, in 1959, men who had started high school but did not graduate received on the average about $700 more per year than men who completed their schooling in the eighth grade. High school graduates, however, received about $800 more per year than men who started high school but did not graduate. Similarly, men who attended college but did not graduate had, on the average, about $1,300 more per year than high school graduates. The comparable differential for men with 4 years of college was about $1,900 per year. The income differential between men with 1 to 3 years of college, and those who have graduated, reflects, in part, differences in "ability." It is also likely that a diploma leads to better paying jobs, and thereby creates an earnings differential not necessarily related to the specific skills acquired in the final year of schooling.[12]

Among elementary and high school graduates there was a sharp increase in average earnings between the ages of 18 to 24 years (hereafter referred to as age 20 which is roughly the average for the group) and 25 to 34 years (hereafter referred to as age 30); and a moderate rise during the following 10 years. By age 40, however, most of these men were close to their peak earnings and most increases thereafter were small, resulting in a slight drop in mean earnings at ages 55 to 64. In contrast, the average earnings of college graduates rose sharply for each age group and did not reach a peak until they were over 45 years old.

VARIATION BY OCCUPATION

Occupations vary greatly in the amount of formal schooling required. Most professional work can be done only by those who have completed 4 years of college and, for many jobs, several years of highly specialized postgraduate work are also required. Although clerical workers need far less education, completion of high school is today generally a minimum requirement for most white-collar jobs. Laborers and operatives, on the other hand, need little schooling or specialized training of any type. Many of the crafts require some high school training plus several years of apprenticeship which are not reflected in the census reports on years of school completed. In view of these considerations, the relationship between education and earnings is quite different in the various occupations. The basic figures bearing on this relationship are shown in table 2. In order to remove the effects of age from the data, the figures are shown for men aged 25 to 64, and for those aged 35 to 44.

Relatively few occupations in the professional field had appreciable numbers of persons who were not college graduates. In these occupations, however, the earnings of college graduates exceeded those of elementary and high school graduates by a wide margin. Accountants and auditors are a case in point. Those who were elementary or high school graduates averaged about $7,200; college graduates averaged $8,500. Those without college training probably worked at the more routine jobs in which they carried out the functions prescribed by men with formal training in accounting. It is undoubtedly true that in this, as in other professions, most of the top jobs require college training.

Similar differences were found among engineers and scientists. In these occupations the differential between college graduates and men with less schooling was considerably greater than in accounting. As for engineers, a relatively small number worked in the profession even though they had never gone beyond the eighth grade,

and no doubt some who claimed the title were not actually doing engineering work. Others may have been *bona fide* engineers on the basis of experience rather than education. At any rate, in 1959 their average earnings were $7,400; high school graduates earned $8,100 on the average; and college graduates, $9,700. Differences of similar scale prevailed among natural scientists.

Farming is an occupation in which earnings are not often thought to be highly associated with education. This impression is incorrect. In 1959, farmers who did not go beyond elementary school earned only $3,200 on the average; high school graduates, about $4,200; and college graduates averaged $6,800. The age distribution of farmers is quite different from that of other occupations. However, as shown in table 2, the relationships described above are as valid for the 35-to-44-year age group as for all men in the prime working ages.

Although earnings of clerical workers are somewhat less responsive to education than earnings of most other workers, for the occupation group as a whole they varied appreciably with education, average earnings ranging from $4,800 for elementary school graduates, to $6,400 for those with 4 years or more of college.

Within this major group, however, the pattern of earnings was much different for some specific occupations. For example, mail carriers who were elementary school graduates averaged $5,000, and only $400 more if they had completed high school. College men who delivered the mail earned only $5,300. Mail delivery was one of the few occupations in which college graduates earned less than high school graduates. It is possible, of course, that some of the college men in this occupation were part-time workers, and that others had less seniority than men who entered the postal service immediately upon graduation from high school. Even so, it is apparent that the limited range of earnings does not permit much of a payment for education. The earnings pattern of postal and shipping clerks was about the same as that of mail carriers.

The earnings of craftsmen were most responsive to increases in education—more so than might be expected on the basis of *a priori* judgment. A question hard to answer is, what, specifically, do bricklayers, plumbers, mechanics, and other craftsmen learn in 4 years of high school that would make their annual earnings considerably higher than those of men in the same trade who never went beyond grammar school? Part of the answer may be that education is associated with general intelligence, and that "years of schooling" is in some measure a proxy variable for aptitude to learn. Another possibility is that even within a given trade, employers or unions give preference to high school graduates in consideration for apprenticeships. Whatever the explanation may be, in every craft for which data are shown, high school graduates earned considerably more than men with only 8 years of schooling. In some occupations—such as linemen, electricians, plumbers, and mechanics—college training also seemed to pay off, while in others, there seemed to be no added reward for higher education.

Considering the occupation group as a whole, craftsmen who did not go beyond the eighth grade averaged $5,200 in 1959; high school graduates, $6,100; and college graduates, $8,100. The fact that the overall average for college graduates is higher than that shown for any specific craft within the group indicates that master craftsmen with college training work at jobs other than those shown in table 2. A large proportion are foremen.

The highest paid workers in the building trades are electricians. Their earnings ranged from $6,100 for elementary school graduates, to $6,800 for college graduates. Overall, plumbers earned somewhat less than electricians, a difference due partly to the fact that plumbers on the average have considerably less education; those who were elementary school graduates earned about $500 less than electricians with the same years of schooling. However, plumbers who were high school graduates earned as much as electricians with equal educa-

tion, and college graduates earned considerably more. Plasterers without much education earned considerably less than plumbers; however, those who were high school graduates had average earnings only about $100 less than plumbers. Painters and carpenters earned far less than other men in the building trades regardless of the years of schooling they had completed.

Even among semiskilled and unskilled workers there was a close association between earnings and education. Among operatives, for example, elementary school graduates averaged $4,700; high school graduates, $5,300; and college graduates, $5,800. Bus drivers with 4 years of high school averaged $700 a year more than elementary school graduates; for truck drivers the differential was $600; and for miners, $1,000. Even among the low-paid farm laborers, high school graduates earned 40 percent more than elementary school graduates.

The patterns described for all workers applied to whites and nonwhites alike, with this major difference: nonwhites in every occupation earned far less than whites with the same amount of schooling. The fact is that in every major occupation except farming, nonwhite high school graduates on the averaged earned less than whites who did not go beyond the eighth grade. This pattern prevailed not only in the South, where discriminatory patterns are deeply entrenched and openly admitted, but also in the North where discrimination has been far more muted.

The relationship between earnings and age varies considerably by occupation. In most professional and managerial jobs— which tend to offer the greatest security and the best opportunities for advancement to positions of increasing responsibility—incomes tend to rise regularly until about age 50, when a plateau is reached and maintained until retirement. Workers in these jobs are generally paid annual salaries rather than weekly or hourly wages: thus their earnings are not diminished because of the periodic illnesses which frequently afflict older people.

Clerical workers, for many of the same reasons that apply to professionals, also tend to maintain their incomes as they approach retirement. Their peak, however, comes earlier—around age 40. The main reason that their earnings do not continue to increase between ages 40 and 50 (as in the case of professionals) is that opportunities for advancement are more limited.

For craftsmen, operatives, and lower paid workers, earnings rise rapidly in the early years, reaching a peak when the men are around age 40, and showing a distinct tendency to decline in the older age groups.

The relationships just described are shown graphically in figures 1 to 4.

Figures for engineers who are college graduates show that their earnings rose by 70 percent (from $4,800 to $8,200) between the ages of 20 and 30, with an increase of 28 percent (to $10,400) between ages 30 and 40, and a further rise of 10 percent (to $11,500) by age 50. This peak was maintained until about age 60. The same general pattern was found for accountants, college professors and instructors, lawyers, natural and social scientists, and physicians. For dentists the earnings pattern differs significantly from that for other professions. Dentists had their peak earnings at age 40; during the next 10 years their average dropped by about 12 percent, and by age 60 their earnings were no higher than during the early years of practice. The decline in earnings with age in this occupation may be partly due to physical factors which cause an earlier reduction in work schedules than in most other professions.

The pattern of earnings for managerial workers in public administration is about the same as that for other professional workers, although the earnings of managers and officials in private industry continued to increase to age 60.

Among clerical workers who were high school graduates, earnings rose sharply (from $3,000 to $5,000) between ages 20 and 30, with a further rise of about $700 between ages 30 and 40. The peak of $5,700 reached at age 40 was maintained until retirement. This same general pattern

applied to bank tellers, bookkeepers, mail carriers, and office machine operators. The earnings of postal clerks showed a slight tendency to rise in the older age groups. The earnings of shipping clerks, on the other hand, showed a distinct tendency to decline in the older age groups, reflecting the insecurity of employment among older people and their greater difficulty in finding reemployment.

The earnings of sales workers show only a slight tendency to decline as they grow older. Earnings of salesmen who were elementary school graduates rose progressively from $2,600 at age 20, to $4,600 at age 30. At age 40 their earnings averaged $5,200 and at age 50, about $5,600. This peak was maintained through age 60. Salesmen who were college graduates had about the same pattern, but their earnings were, of course, much higher. High school graduates also had a similar pattern, but their earnings fell off slightly about the age of 60.

The earnings of foremen behave very much like those of professional workers, but on a much lower level. Earnings rise until about age 50, when they reach a plateau which is maintained until retirement. Craftsmen, however—almost without exception—tended to experience declines in earnings once they had passed their fortieth birthday. For example, the mean earnings of carpenters who were high school graduates rose from $5,400 at age 30, to $5,700 at age 40; but those aged 50 earned only $4,900 on the average; and those aged 60, only $4,500. This pattern was more or less typical of most other occupations.

The reasons for the declines in earnings among craftsmen (and other blue-collar workers) are not hard to find. Payment in these occupations is typically on an hourly basis; not to work is not to earn. Furthermore, as men reach their fifties and sixties they tend to have more frequent illnesses, and as a result their earnings suffer. And in many of these occupations there is no tenure. Work on a construction project, for instance, lasts until the project is com-

Table 2.—Average (Mean) Total Money Earnings for Males 25 to 64 Years Old in the Experienced Civilian Labor Force, by Years of School Completed, Age, and Color, for Selected Occupations; 1959

Age and occupation	Total				White				Nonwhite			
	All education groups	Elementary school graduates	High school graduates	College graduates	All education groups	Elementary school graduates	High school graduates	College graduates	All education groups	Elementary school graduates	High school graduates	College graduates
25 TO 64 YEARS												
Total experienced civilian labor force	$5,847	$4,725	$6,132	$10,078	$6,112	$4,837	$6,250	$10,238	$3,260	$3,318	$4,021	$5,671
Professional, technical, and kindred workers[1]	8,762	5,991	7,104	10,003	8,881	6,110	7,156	10,154	5,519	3,393	5,159	6,147
Accountants and auditors	7,825	7,156	7,270	8,480	7,852	7,196	7,282	8,518	5,969	(B)	(B)	6,082
Clergymen	4,399	3,509	4,032	4,589	4,503	3,858	4,312	4,613	2,968	(B)	2,658	3,897
College professors and instructors	8,158	(B)	(B)	8,235	8,232	(B)	(B)	8,309	6,574	(B)	(B)	6,668
Dentists	16,057	(B)	(B)	16,231	16,232	(B)	(B)	16,424	11,266	(B)	(B)	11,086
Engineers, technical	9,001	7,363	8,137	9,681	9,023	7,399	8,153	9,706	7,447	(B)	(B)	8,129
Lawyers and judges	15,793	(B)	10,448	15,927	15,919	(B)	(B)	16,054	8,270	(B)	(B)	(B)
Natural scientists	8,288	(B)	6,638	8,718	8,359	(B)	6,668	8,792	6,139	(B)	(B)	6,472
Physicians and surgeons	19,493	(B)	(B)	19,632	19,208	(B)	(B)	20,048	9,393	(B)	(B)	9,455
Social scientists	9,030	(B)	8,007	9,398	9,090	(B)	8,081	9,468	(B)	(B)	(B)	(B)
Teachers	6,042	(B)	5,625	6,149	6,148	(B)	5,709	6,256	4,742	(B)	(B)	4,831
Farmers and farm managers	3,438	3,199	4,231	6,830	3,576	3,227	4,231	6,908	1,551	1,982	4,242	(B)
Managers, officials, and proprietors, exc. farm	9,387	7,151	8,742	13,400	9,478	7,210	8,786	13,491	4,823	4,485	5,624	6,532
Clerical and kindred workers[1]	5,372	4,843	5,451	6,447	5,458	4,900	5,517	6,546	4,282	3,876	4,470	4,939
Mail carriers	5,265	4,964	5,351	5,250	5,298	4,986	5,381	5,276	4,996	(B)	5,040	5,183
Office machine operators	5,545	4,971	5,636	6,303	5,607	4,999	5,696	6,301	4,544	(B)	(B)	(B)
Postal clerks	5,383	5,241	5,459	5,392	5,458	5,310	5,530	5,360	5,038	(B)	5,066	5,464
Shipping and receiving clerks	4,532	4,533	4,674	4,716	4,654	4,597	4,814	4,909	3,616	3,609	(B)	(B)
Sales workers	6,990	5,397	6,797	9,350	7,043	5,434	6,831	9,393	4,105	3,586	4,647	5,301
Craftsmen, foremen, and kindred workers[1]	5,585	5,245	6,091	8,133	5,678	5,299	6,142	8,223	3,757	3,834	4,487	5,157
Brickmasons, stonemasons, and tile setters	5,192	5,039	5,905	(B)	5,461	5,142	6,106	(B)	3,426	4,012	3,864	(B)
Carpenters	4,531	4,387	5,325	5,666	4,618	4,428	(B)	5,864	2,928	3,182	4,067	(B)
Compositors and typesetters	6,192	5,993	6,312	6,678	6,231	6,042	6,352	6,698	4,700	(B)	(B)	(B)
Electricians	6,224	6,083	6,407	6,840	6,247	6,101	6,423	6,905	5,143	(B)	5,596	(B)
Linemen & servicemen, teleg., t'phone, & power	6,173	5,816	6,304	7,117	6,202	5,841	6,314	7,117	4,373	(B)	(B)	(B)
Machinists	5,690	5,476	5,964	5,695	5,723	5,501	5,985	5,684	4,591	4,349	5,068	(B)
Mechanics and repairmen	5,033	4,816	5,486	6,050	5,120	4,870	5,537	6,136	3,713	3,670	4,372	(B)
Painters, construction and maintenance	4,128	4,154	4,753	4,772	4,237	4,205	4,845	4,778	2,808	3,052	3,497	(B)
Plasterers	5,152	4,878	6,212	(B)	5,536	5,072	6,416	(B)	3,288	(B)	(B)	(B)
Plumbers and pipe fitters	5,857	5,580	6,357	7,685	5,944	5,625	6,394	7,847	3,653	(B)	(B)	(B)
Toolmakers, and die makers and setters	6,802	6,584	6,991	7,042	6,818	6,596	7,004	7,069	(B)	(B)	(B)	(B)

B Base less than 1,000 persons.

[1] Includes other occupation groups, not shown separately.

Table 2.—Average (Mean) Total Money Earnings for Males 25 to 64 Years Old in the Experienced Civilian Labor Force, by Years of School Completed, Age, and Color, for Selected Occupations: 1959—Con.

Age and occupation	Total				White				Nonwhite			
	All education groups	Elementary school graduates	High school graduates	College graduates	All education groups	Elementary school graduates	High school graduates	College graduates	All education groups	Elementary school graduates	High school graduates	College graduates
25 TO 64 YEARS—Con.												
Operatives and kindred workers[1]	$4,702	$4,667	$5,271	$5,833	$4,866	$4,757	$5,372	$5,997	$3,421	$3,591	$3,990	$4,123
Bus drivers	4,392	4,294	5,020	(B)	4,468	4,325	5,060	(B)	3,708	(B)	4,698	(B)
Mine operatives and laborers (n.e.c.)	4,456	4,318	5,339	(B)	4,510	4,342	5,388	(B)	3,454	(B)	(B)	(B)
Truck and tractor drivers	4,655	4,771	5,340	5,504	4,943	4,913	5,494	5,886	3,018	3,339	3,722	(B)
Operatives and kindred workers (n.e.c.)	4,715	4,701	5,275	6,143	4,855	4,774	5,366	6,300	3,618	3,823	4,129	(B)
Service workers, including private household[1]	3,974	3,757	4,689	5,233	4,279	3,927	4,953	5,555	2,922	2,926	3,291	3,634
Barbers	4,388	4,409	4,737	(B)	4,546	4,509	4,864	(B)	2,958	(B)	3,529	(B)
Firemen, fire protection	5,729	5,375	5,896	(B)	5,738	5,371	5,907	(B)	5,400	(B)	(B)	(B)
Policemen and detectives	5,474	4,788	5,527	7,618	5,498	4,810	5,541	7,721	4,922	(B)	5,205	(B)
Farm laborers and foremen	1,976	2,258	3,161	4,734	2,237	2,373	3,264	4,869	1,285	1,480	2,349	(B)
Laborers, exc. farm and mine	3,578	3,775	4,393	4,872	3,895	3,924	4,603	5,111	2,802	3,093	3,433	3,755
35 TO 44 YEARS												
Total experienced civilian labor force	6,259	4,730	6,398	10,863	6,540	4,861	6,507	11,027	3,543	3,474	4,379	6,377
Professional, technical, and kindred workers[1]	9,592	5,858	7,510	11,011	9,703	6,007	7,560	11,158	6,407	(B)	5,404	7,145
Accountants and auditors	8,345	(B)	7,267	9,241	8,374	(B)	7,273	9,276	6,701	(B)	(B)	(B)
Clergymen	4,708	(B)	4,401	4,856	4,774	(B)	4,657	4,878	3,386	(B)	(B)	(B)
College professors and instructors	8,916	(B)	(B)	8,971	9,020	(B)	(B)	9,073	6,591	(B)	(B)	(B)
Dentists	20,098	(B)	(B)	20,118	20,208	(B)	(B)	20,229	(B)	(B)	(B)	(B)
Engineers, technical	9,560	6,869	8,413	10,445	9,583	6,977	8,430	10,465	8,102	(B)	(B)	9,204
Lawyers and judges	14,920	(B)	(B)	15,028	15,045	(B)	(B)	15,156	(B)	(B)	(B)	(B)
Natural scientists	9,014	(B)	7,261	9,439	9,070	(B)	7,300	9,492	7,256	(B)	(B)	7,807
Physicians and surgeons	23,302	(B)	(B)	23,388	23,664	(B)	(B)	23,758	(B)	(B)	(B)	(B)
Social scientists	9,678	(B)	(B)	10,188	9,772	(B)	(B)	10,316	(B)	(B)	(B)	(B)
Teachers	6,571	(B)	6,169	6,636	6,711	(B)	6,292	6,778	4,968	(B)	(B)	5,035
Farmers and farm managers	3,839	3,436	4,480	7,565	3,980	3,460	4,472	7,646	1,940	2,447	4,937	(B)
Managers, officials, and proprietors, exc. farm	9,350	6,597	8,600	12,919	9,432	6,669	8,642	13,014	5,310	4,566	5,843	6,336
Clerical and kindred workers[1]	5,669	4,767	5,678	7,180	5,771	4,854	5,746	7,329	4,525	3,865	4,699	5,293
Mail carriers	5,374	5,097	5,431	5,355	5,395	5,124	5,451	5,514	5,173	(B)	5,185	(B)
Office machine operators	6,068	(B)	6,109	5,547	6,137	(B)	6,181	(B)	(B)	(B)	(B)	(B)
Postal clerks	5,448	5,372	5,488	(B)	5,497	5,390	5,530	5,452	5,223	(B)	5,217	5,690
Shipping and receiving clerks	4,706	4,493	4,919	(B)	4,858	4,627	5,062	(B)	3,671	(B)	3,781	(B)

B Base less than 1,000 persons.

[1] Includes other occupation groups, not shown separately.

Table 2.—Average (Mean) Total Money Earnings for Males 25 to 64 Years Old in the Experienced Civilian Labor Force, by Years of School Completed, Age, and Color, for Selected Occupations: 1959—Con.

Age and occupation	Total				White				Nonwhite			
	All education groups	Elementary school graduates	High school graduates	College graduates	All education groups	Elementary school graduates	High school graduates	College graduates	All education groups	Elementary school graduates	High school graduates	College graduates
35 TO 44 YEARS—Con.												
Sales workers	$7,618	$5,242	$7,182	$10,679	$7,673	$5,300	$7,212	$10,720	$4,682	(B)	$5,278	(B)
Craftsmen, foremen, and kindred workers[1]	5,900	5,294	6,405	8,799	6,004	5,363	6,455	8,912	3,994	4,048	4,831	(B)
Brickmasons, stonemasons, and tile setters	5,370	5,009	6,069	(B)	5,687	5,144	6,271	(B)	3,676	(B)	(B)	(B)
Carpenters	4,984	4,792	5,677	(B)	5,083	4,843	5,722	(B)	3,237	(B)	(B)	(B)
Compositors and typesetters	6,404	(B)	6,568	(B)	6,440	(B)	6,610	(B)	(B)	(B)	(B)	(B)
Electricians	6,435	6,078	6,605	(B)	6,455	6,114	6,623	(B)	5,627	(B)	(B)	(B)
Linemen & servicemen, teleg., t'phone, & power	6,586	5,769	6,801	(B)	6,627	5,811	6,812	(B)	(B)	(B)	(B)	(B)
Machinists	5,927	5,515	6,219	(B)	5,964	5,561	6,232	(B)	4,724	(B)	(B)	(B)
Mechanics and repairmen	5,344	4,932	5,840	6,746	5,442	5,007	5,888	6,902	3,902	3,682	4,678	(B)
Painters, construction and maintenance	4,410	4,308	5,007	(B)	4,547	4,398	5,099	(B)	3,022	(B)	(B)	(B)
Plasterers	5,511	(B)	6,593	(B)	5,921	(B)	6,828	(B)	3,682	(B)	(B)	(B)
Plumbers and pipe fitters	6,225	5,671	6,684	(B)	6,319	5,726	6,725	(B)	3,874	(B)	(B)	(B)
Toolmakers, and die makers and setters	7,062	6,647	7,239	(B)	7,079	6,660	7,252	(B)	(B)	(B)	(B)	(B)
Operatives and kindred workers[1]	4,954	4,823	5,569	6,541	5,139	4,936	5,664	6,766	3,608	3,696	4,334	(B)
Bus drivers	4,849	4,355	5,367	(B)	4,907	4,409	5,390	(B)	4,368	(B)	(B)	(B)
Mine operatives and laborers (n.e.c.)	4,681	4,554	5,443	(B)	4,723	4,580	5,505	(B)	3,854	(B)	(B)	(B)
Truck and tractor drivers	4,940	5,043	5,551	(B)	5,249	5,212	5,719	(B)	3,144	3,420	3,887	(B)
Operatives and kindred workers (n.e.c.)	4,949	4,815	5,570	6,873	5,103	4,895	5,645	7,086	3,824	3,922	4,555	(B)
Service workers, including private household[1]	4,375	3,841	5,010	6,116	4,744	4,070	5,253	6,568	3,132	3,064	3,567	(B)
Barbers	4,743	4,730	4,948	(B)	4,958	4,791	5,097	(B)	3,344	(B)	(B)	(B)
Firemen, fire protection	5,887	5,292	6,095	(B)	5,894	5,247	6,108	(B)	(B)	(B)	(B)	(B)
Policemen and detectives	5,748	4,516	5,766	8,295	5,774	4,503	5,781	8,426	5,205	(B)	5,474	(B)
Farm laborers and foremen	2,090	2,313	3,539	(B)	2,375	2,416	3,621	(B)	1,375	1,632	(B)	(B)
Laborers, exc. farm and mine	3,765	3,879	4,661	5,447	4,130	4,070	4,881	5,735	2,960	3,186	3,671	(B)

B Base less than 1,000 persons.
[1] Includes other occupation groups, not shown separately.
Source: 1960 *Census of Population, Subject Reports, Occupation by Earnings and Education,* Series PC(2)–7B, table 1.

INCOME DISTRIBUTION IN THE UNITED STATES

Figure 1 —EARNINGS OF ENGINEERS, BY EDUCATION AND AGE: 1959

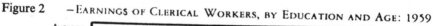

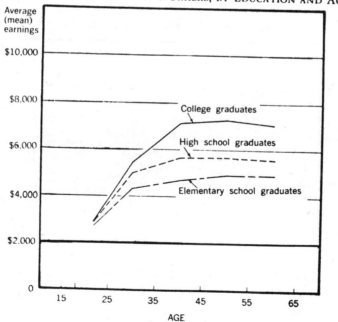

Figure 2 —EARNINGS OF CLERICAL WORKERS, BY EDUCATION AND AGE: 1959

INCOME AND EDUCATION

Figure 3   —Earnings of Salesmen and Sales Clerks (n.e.c.), by Education
and Age: 1959

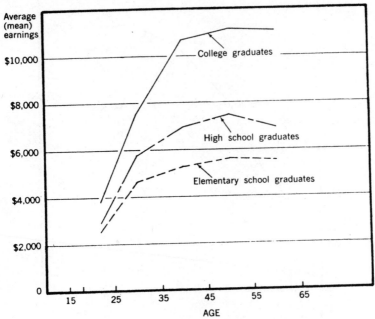

Figure 4   —Earnings of Carpenters, by Education and Age: 1959

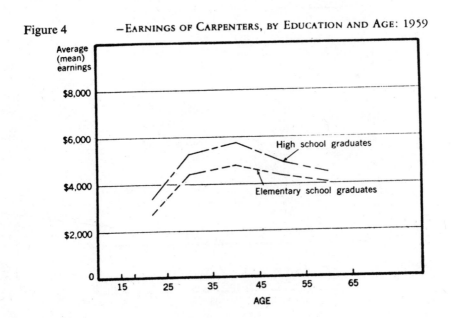

Table 3.—Estimated Lifetime Income (Earnings) Based on Arithmetic Means for Males in Selected Age Groups, by Years of School Completed for Selected Years, 1939 to 1961
[In thousands]

Years of school completed and age	1961[1]	1959[2]	1958[1]	1956[1]	1949[1]	1946[2]	1939[3]
INCOME FROM AGE 18 TO DEATH							
Elementary: Total	$176	(NA)	$152	$153	$113	(NA)	(NA)
Less than 8 years	151	(NA)	129	131	98	(NA)	(NA)
8 years	205	(NA)	178	179	133	(NA)	(NA)
High school: 1 to 3 years	235	(NA)	204	202	152	(NA)	(NA)
4 years	273	(NA)	242	244	185	(NA)	(NA)
College: 1 to 3 years	334	(NA)	287	278	209	(NA)	(NA)
4 years or more	453	(NA)	402	373	296	(NA)	(NA)
INCOME FROM AGE 25 TO DEATH							
Elementary: Total	165	(NA)	142	142	105	$87	(NA)
Less than 8 years	142	(NA)	120	122	91	74	(NA)
8 years	191	(NA)	166	166	123	99	(NA)
High school: 1 to 3 years	222	(NA)	192	189	142	108	(NA)
4 years	256	(NA)	227	228	175	136	(NA)
College: 1 to 3 years	323	(NA)	277	268	202	162	(NA)
4 years or more	435	(NA)	386	359	287	202	(NA)
INCOME FROM AGE 18 TO 64							
Elementary: Total	157	(NA)	136	137	100	(NA)	$40
Less than 8 years	135	$143	115	117	87	(NA)	(NA)
8 years	182	184	158	159	117	(NA)	(NA)
High school: 1 to 3 years	206	212	182	180	132	(NA)	57
4 years	241	247	218	216	159	(NA)	71
College: 1 to 3 years	284	293	255	243	181	(NA)	78
4 years or more	379	417	355	325	251	(NA)	110
INCOME FROM AGE 25 TO 64							
Elementary: Total	146	(NA)	125	125	92	74	37
Less than 8 years	125	131	106	107	80	62	(NA)
8 years	169	169	146	146	107	85	(NA)
High school: 1 to 3 years	193	197	170	166	122	92	53
4 years	224	228	202	199	149	114	67
College: 1 to 3 years	273	278	244	232	173	139	74
4 years or more	361	397	339	311	241	169	105

NA-Not available.

[1] Total money income.

[2] Total money earnings.

[3] Restricted to persons reporting $1 or more of wage or salary income and less than $50 of other income for native white and Negro males.

Source: Data for 1959 and 1961 are based on unpublished estimates of the Bureau of the Census. Data for 1939, 1946, and 1949 are from Herman P. Miller, "Annual and Lifetime Income in Relation to Education: 1939 to 1959," *American Economic Review,* December 1960; and data for 1956 and 1959 are revisions of estimates previously published in this article.

pleted, after which a new job must be found. Where employers have a choice, they are often likely to select younger workers for the job.

The variation of earnings with age for operatives, service workers, laborers, and other blue-collar workers, was very similar to that for craftsmen.

Table 4.—Estimated Lifetime Income (Earnings) of Males 25 to 64 Years
Old, by Years of School Completed, for Selected Years, 1939 to 1961
[In thousands]

Year	Elementary-high school differential			High school-college differential		
	Elementary school graduates	High school graduates	Ratio	High school graduates	College graduates	Ratio
1961	$169	$224	75	$224	$361	62
1959	169	228	74	228	397	57
1958	146	202	72	202	339	60
1956	146	199	73	199	311	64
1949	107	149	72	149	241	62
1946	85	114	75	114	169	67
1939	(NA)	67	(NA)	67	105	64

NA-Not available.
Source: Table 3.

LIFETIME INCOME AND EDUCATION

Changes since 1939. The general method used to estimate lifetime income and some of the limitations of the figures were described earlier in this chapter. Table 3, which follows, shows how estimated lifetime income has changed since 1939 for men with different amounts of schooling. Before these data are discussed, several cautions must be noted.

First, because of changes in the income concept, the figures are not exactly comparable from year to year. The data for 1939 are for wages and salaries; for 1946 and 1959, the data represent earnings; and for 1949, 1956, 1958, and 1961, they represent total money income. These variations in concept may have some impact on changes over time. A second, and more general consideration, is the fact that the estimates reflect the economic conditions and other circumstances that existed in each of the years for which data are shown. Some of the differences from year to year may reflect changes in these circumstances. For example, the increase in the value of a college education by about $140,000, between 1949 and 1961, reflects the increase in prices as well as changes in the underlying relationships.

In every year for which data are presented, additional schooling is associated with a very substantial increase in lifetime income. On the basis of conditions in 1961, a man with less than 8 years of schooling could expect to earn about $151,000 in a lifetime. Graduation from elementary school would add $54,000 to his expected earnings. Similarly, a man with 1 to 3 years of high school could expect to earn $235,000 over a lifetime, compared with a total of $273,000 for the high school graduate. Financial returns prove greatest, as might be expected, at the college level. The man with some college training, but without a degree, could expect to earn about one-third of a million dollars in a lifetime, whereas the total for the college graduate was nearly half a million.

No dramatic changes have taken place in these relationships during the past 20 years. Table 4 shows that throughout the postwar period, elementary school graduates could expect incomes that averaged about three-fourths of those received by high school graduates. The income expectations of high school graduates averaged between 57 and 67 percent of those of college graduates.

NOTES

[1]Edward F. Denison, "The Sources of Economic Growth in the United States," Supplementary Paper No. 13, Committee for Economic Development, 1962.

[2]Alice M. Rivlin, "Research in the Economics of Higher Education: Progress, and Problems," *Economics of Higher Education* (U.S.: O.E., 1962), p. 361.

[3]Women have been excluded from the analysis. Since a large proportion do not enter the labor market, and many of those who do are employed on a part-time basis only, the relation between their income and education may be distorted. In contrast, since practically all adult men are full-time workers, it can be assumed that any advantages which may accrue from more schooling will be reflected in their incomes.

[4]Donald S. Bridgman, "The Duration of Formal Education for High-Ability Youth," National Science Foundation, NSF 61-36.

[5]See for example, Gary S. Becker, "Underinvestment in College Education," *American Economic Review Proceedings,* 50 (May, 1960): 348; and Edward F. Renshaw, "Estimating the Returns to Education," *The Review of Economics and Statistics* XLII (August, 1960): 322.

[6]Theodore W. Schultz, "Education and Economic Growth," *Social Forces Influencing American Education,* Sixtieth Yearbook of the National Society for the Study of Education, 1961.

[7]Mary Jean Bowman, "Human Capital: Concepts and Measures," *Economics of Higher Education* (U.S.: O.E., 1962).

[8]See Donald S. Bridgman, "Problems in Estimating the Monetary Value of College Education"; and Dael Wolfle, "Economics and Educational Values," in *Higher Education in the United States: the Economic Problems,* ed. Seymour E. Harris (Cambridge: Harvard University Press); and Ernest Havemann and Patricia West, *They Went to College* (New York: 1952), p. 164.

[9]Calvin F. Schmid, "Impact of Recent Negro Migration on Seattle Schools" (Paper presented at International Population Conference, Vienna, 1959).

[10]H. S. Houthakker, "Education and Income," *Review of Economics and Statistics* (Cambridge: Harvard University Press, 1959), p. 27.

[11]Educational Policies Commission, *Education and Economic Well-Being in American Democracy* (Washington, D.C.: National Education Association and American Association of School Administration, 1940).

[12]Although this discussion is presented in terms of arithmetic means, the same kind of analysis could be made in terms of the medians shown in the report from which table 1 was derived. The general picture would not differ much, particularly below the college level, where there is not much difference between means and medians, largely because persons who lack college training do not have ready access to the highest paying jobs. For college graduates, there is a substantial difference between the means and medians, although all the general patterns described above on the basis of the arithmetic means remain unchanged. Some analysts contend that the median is a more useful measure than the mean because it is less affected by extreme values at the upper end of the distribution and more nearly shows what the "typical" individual may expect to receive. To some extent the usage here may be a matter of taste. From a strictly mathematical viewpoint, however, the arithmetic mean is the preferable measure since medians should not be treated algebraically. Often, of course, medians are used in the absence of means and they are treated as though they behave like means. This usage may be justified as a basis for providing rough measures where accurate estimates of the mean cannot be made or are too costly to compute. Mathematical considerations aside, the use of the median as a representative value for the "typical" individual is based on the implicit assumption that a particular point in a frequency distribution can be used to make inferences for the individual case. It says, in effect, that the "average" individual is more likely to receive the "average" income (i.e., the income of the middlemost person in a distribution) than the mean income which is weighted by the high incomes of a relatively small number of people. If the use of the median is intended to serve this purpose, it is incorrect since the frequency distribution is essentially a probability statement and no single point on that distribution is more valid for a given case than any other point. In view of these considerations, only means are shown in all tables in this chapter containing basic data. The derived measures and text discussions are also presented in terms of the means.

CHAPTER 25

The Role of Economic Dominants in Community Power Structure

ROBERT O. SCHULZE

THAT persons occupying positions of economic importance are among the key wielders of local influence and control has long been one of the most commonplace assumptions of American sociologists and one of the most consistent findings of research concerned with American communities and community power structures.[1] With very few exceptions, however, most studies relevant to the role of economic dominants in community control structures have focused on current power configurations. Relatively little research attention has yet been devoted to historical shifts in local power structures associated with the metropolitan and bureau-

cratic drift of American life.[2] Likewise, while most relevant studies have indicated that a considerable number of persons of significant local influence are men of economic substance, they have not revealed the pattern of community involvement (nor changes in that pattern) of the economically most-powerful considered as a category. Thus, we have heard a good deal about the activities and influence of the "X" family and its equivalents in American communities, but rather less about the "Y" families, and almost nothing at all about the ratio of "Xs" to "Ys" either currently or over time.

This paper reports some findings of an investigation of the power structure of a middle-sized American community—findings concerned primarily with the historical role of the economic dominants in that community's power structure.[3] Although the study has among its numerous limitations those inevitable in any piece of single-community research, it is hoped that it might be theoretically and methodologically suggestive for research in other communities, especially those which—like the subject of this study—have become satellites in a society in-

Expanded version of paper read at the annual meeting of the American Sociological Society, August, 1957. I wish to thank Morris Janowitz and Melvin Reichler, both of the University of Michigan, for their helpful comments on this paper.

[1] In addition to the well-known works of the Lynds, Warner, Hollingshead, Mills, and Hunter, see: Roland J. Pellegrin and Charles H. Coates, "Absentee-Owned Corporations and Community Power Structure," *American Journal of Sociology*, LXI, 5 (March, 1956), pp. 413–419; George Belknap and Ralph Smuckler, "Political Power Relations in a Mid-West City," *Public Opinion Quarterly*, XX, 1 (Spring, 1956), pp. 73–81; A. Alexander Fanelli, "A Typology of Community Leadership Based on Influence and Interaction Within the Leader Subsystem," *Social Forces*, 34, 4 (May, 1956), pp. 332–338; Robert E. Agger, "Power Attributions in the Local Community," *ibid.*, pp. 322–331; Peter Rossi, "Historical Trends in the Politics of an Industrial Community," paper presented at the 51st annual meeting of the American Sociological Society, September, 1956.

[2] Rossi's study is a notable exception.

[3] Robert O. Schulze, *Economic Dominance and Public Leadership: A Study of the Structure and Process of Power in an Urban Community*, microfilmed Ph.D. dissertation, University of Michigan, 1956. (University Microfilms, Publication No. 21,359.)

creasingly dominated by giant metropolitan centers and large national corporations.

The rudimentary theory underlying this research may be briefly summarized. The basic assumption was that as the functional relationship of the community to the larger society changes, so does the nature and form of its control structure, and so, too, does the role of its economic dominants in that structure.

It was hypothesized that in the community *relatively* self-contained and uninvolved in the larger social and economic system, the community with few and scattered commitments beyond its borders, local power would tend to be structured as a pyramid and heavily concentrated at the apex. More specifically, it was surmised that those persons who exercised major control over the community's economic system would tend to be the same persons who exercised preponderant control over its socio-political system, and that this latter control would be reflected, at least in part, by their active leadership and participation in the political and civic life of the community.

With increasing urbanization and as the community passed beyond what Lloyd Warner has called "the period of local capitalism"[4] however, it was suggested that the economic dominants would begin to withdraw their interest and active attention from the local socio-political system. Although the major economic units would have grown in size and potential influence, it was hypothesized that several factors would militate against the effective exercise, the actual "cashing-in" of their power in the community. The most significant of these would be the fact that the local community would have become ever less important to the survival and prosperity of its dominant economic units. As the activities of these units became increasingly directed toward—and by—populations and groups other than the local ones, the relevance of local community organizations and the impact of local political influences on the major economic units would accordingly diminish. As this occurred, the local power structure would

in effect, bifurcate—with those who exercised primary direction over its socio-political system no longer being essentially the same set of persons who exercised primary control over its economic system.[5]

An effort was made to test this general theory in Cibola, a Midwestern industrial community of some 20,000 inhabitants, located approximately 30 miles from Metro City, one of the nation's largest metropolitan centers. Founded in 1823, Cibola grew rather slowly until World War II. Between 1940 and 1950, however, its population increased over 50 per cent, a shift symptomatic of countless other changes to which the community has lately been subject. One of the principal changes has been the gradual absorption of its major industrial plants by large, absentee-owned corporations, a trend sharply accelerated during the World War II period.

In our research, we attempted to reconstruct Cibola's economic dominants from the time of its founding in 1823 until 1955, and to determine the general nature and

---

[4] W. Lloyd Warner and J. O. Low, "The Factory in the Community," in William Foote Whyte (ed.), *Industry and Society*, New York: McGraw-Hill, 1946, p. 35.

[5] It is not suggested that the decline in the economic dominants' leadership and participation in community decision-making processes stems wholly from their diminishing concern with local affairs. With their attenuation of local involvement, it is obvious that effective contact and meaningful communication between economic dominants and diverse elements of the community population are likewise reduced, contributing to what has been referred to as the loss of "multi-class leadership" by the top business groups in American communities. In such a situation, economic dominants—when they occasionally may want to influence community decisions—may find that their local leadership base has so shrunken that their effectiveness is impaired. Somewhat illustrative of this was the case of Cal Lamkin, the general manager of a large industrial plant in the community studied. Long inactive in local political and voluntary associational affairs, Lamkin was eventually prevailed upon to stand for election to the board of directors of the local Chamber of Commerce. To the considerable embarrassment of the Chamber's officials, however, Lamkin failed to muster sufficient votes to win a seat on the board. Cf. Wilbert E. Moore, *Industrial Relations and the Social Order*, New York: The Macmillan Company, 1951, pp. 547–553. Although presented in causal terms somewhat different from those suggested in this paper, the best known and perhaps most sanguine statement of the American business elites' loss of multi-group leadership is contained in Kenneth Galbraith, *American Capitalism and the Concept of Countervailing Power*, Boston: Houghton, Mifflin, 1952.

extent of their overt involvement in the political and civic life of the community.

The economic dominants for the various historical periods were operationally-defined as those persons who: (a) occupied the top formal roles in the largest industries and banks in the community; or (b) were members of the boards of directors of two or more of these industries and banks, thus serving formally to "interlock" the dominant economic units; or (c) were the largest property-owners in the community.[6]

Insofar as local involvement was reflected by occupancy of formal offices in the political and civic organizations in the community, the research tended clearly to support the basic hypothesis. *The historical drift has been characterized by the withdrawal of the economic dominants from active and overt participation in the public life of Cibola.* Tables 1, 3, and 4 are presented to illustrate this withdrawal.

TABLE 1. NUMBER AND PERCENT OF ECONOMIC DOMINANTS IN PUBLIC OFFICE, 1823–1954 PERIODS

Period	Number of Economic Dominants	Number of Economic Dominants in Public Office	Per Cent of Economic Dominants in Public Office
1823–1860	12	10	83
1860–1900	21	17	81
1900–1940	43	12	28
1940–1954	31	7	23

Table 1 indicates that prior to the turn of the century, fully four-fifths of Cibola's economic dominants held public office in the community, while since 1900, the proportion has declined to approximately one-quarter.[7] Likewise, as shown in Table 3, the

[6] Specific criteria for classification as an economic dominant in each historical period were based on such measures as number of employees (industries), capital worth (banks), and assessed valuation of holdings (property-owners). Various source data were utilized in the determination of these measures, including county tax records, city directories and histories, newspapers, records of individual companies and of the Chamber of Commerce and the State Historical Collections, plus such standard references as *Poor's Register of Directors and Executives* and *Polk's Bank Directory*.

[7] It might be suggested that the declining proportion of economic dominants in public office was

TABLE 2. CHANGES IN NUMBER OF ECONOMIC DOMINANTS AND NUMBER OF AVAILABLE OFFICES, 1823–1954 PERIODS

Period	Percentage Change in Number of Economic Dominants	Percentage Change in Number of Public Offices in City Government
From 1823–1860 to 1860–1900 periods	plus 75	plus 80
From 1860–1900 to 1900–1940 periods	plus 105	plus 183
From 1900–1940 to 1940–1954 periods	minus 28	minus 30

proportion of economic dominants who have held the top political office in Cibola has sharply diminished. Not indicated in either of these two tables is the fact that *none* of the most recent type of economic dominant—the managers of the absentee-owned corporations—has held any public office (elective or appointive) in the community.

There was some evidence that in the early decades of this century the arena of active

TABLE 3. NUMBER AND PER CENT OF ECONOMIC DOMINANTS IN OFFICE OF VILLAGE PRESIDENT OR MAYOR, 1823–1954 PERIODS

Period	Number of Dominants in Office of Village President or Mayor	Per Cent of Dominants in Office of Village President or Mayor	Per Cent of "Politically-Active" Dominants in Office of Village President or Mayor*
1823–1860	5	42	50
1860–1900	7	33	41
1900–1940	2	5	17
1940–1954	1	3	14

* "Politically-Active": All those economic dominants who had held *any* public office.

a function of the fact that the number of dominants increased at a greater rate than the number of available offices, and therefore, that the declining proportions are spurious. This was not the case. Changes in the number of economic dominants throughout the four periods were very closely paralleled by proportionately similar changes in the number of available public offices. (See Table 2.)

TABLE 4. NUMBER OF ECONOMIC DOMINANTS IN
OFFICES OF THE CHAMBER OF COMMERCE,
1920–1955 *

Period	Median Number of Memberships per Year on Board of Directors	Number Serving as President
1920–1927	6	3
1927–1934	3	2
1934–1941	3	0
1941–1948	2	1
1948–1955	1	0

* The Cibola Chamber of Commerce was founded in 1920. From that date until 1953, the number of directors was fifteen; in the latter year, the number was increased to eighteen. Directors serve two-year terms and are eligible for reelection.

local involvement of Cibola's economic dominants shifted from politics to the important voluntary associations. Even in this area, however, an appreciable subsequent diminution of active participation has been apparent—perhaps best reflected by the declining number of dominants holding responsible office in the community's most influential association, the local Chamber of Commerce.

It is suggested that the withdrawal of the economic dominants was primarily a consequence of the changing relationship of the community's economic system to that of the larger society. Prior to about 1900, three aspects of Cibola's economic life were especially notable: (a) all of its economic dominants were local residents; (b) all of its dominant economic units were locally-owned; and (c) the majority of its dominants were associated in extensive economic networks *within* the community.

Our research established that in the pre-1900 period, almost 70 per cent of the economic dominants had known business or financial ties—as partners, co-officers or co-directors—with other dominants in the community. Thus, throughout most of Cibola's history, its "average" economic dominant was not only a local resident, or merely the head of a single major economic unit; he was also directly and indirectly linked with a considerable number of other major economic units and dominants within the community.

Combined, these factors provided most economic dominants with deep, branching roots in Cibola. The business and financial links, in particular, afforded many of them a basis for shared concern in the local community. The economic networks served to weld together blocs of dominants, giving them frequent and specific occasion for interpersonal contact. By the same token, the very diversity of the "average" dominant's local economic commitments meant that there was always a variety of areas and methods in which local political considerations could impinge upon his pecuniary and related interests. The evidence suggests that these considerations were closely associated with the high incidence of involvement by economic dominants in the socio-political system of the community.

The period since 1900, and more particularly, since 1930, has been marked by the increasing absorption of the local economic system into the larger industrial complex, especially that of Metro City. While several complex social factors were patently involved, the following three seem most closely related to the eventual withdrawal of the economic dominants from active participation in the political-civic life of Cibola: (a) the establishment by a growing number of locally-owned industrial units of direct supplier relationships with a small number of large, non-local manufacturing plants; (b) the subsequent introduction into the local economic system of an increasing number of branch plants of large, absentee-owned corporations; and (c) the concomitant dissolution of the extensive networks of inter-locking director and officerships which had formerly served to link significant numbers of local economic dominants within the community.

Consequently, the overt direction of the political and civic life of Cibola has passed almost wholly into the hands of a group of middle-class business and professional men, almost none of whom occupies a position of economic dominance in the community. That this has in fact been the case was suggested in another aspect of our research by the finding that only two of Cibola's seventeen current economic dominants were perceived by the local voluntary association heads to have been among the eighteen most influential leaders in the community.[8] And both of these two, by the way, were heads of relatively small, locally-owned economic units.

Patently, these data reveal changes only in the level of overt and manifest involvement of the economic dominants in the local power structure. It may be suggested, of course, that covertly—"behind-the-scenes" —the economic dominants continue to exercise considerable direction and control of community affairs. However, the findings of another part of our research strongly suggest that things may, in fact, be what they seem.

In an effort to view the community power structure "in action," we endeavored to determine the patterns and processes of local decision-making in a series of recent community episodes (including a successful campaign to change the structure of municipal government from a mayor-aldermen to a city manager form, and an ambitious but unsuccessful annexation effort).[9] Our findings in this aspect of the research forced us to conclude that the recent economic dominants—and especially those representing the growing number of large, absentee-owned corporations—appear indeed to have dissociated themselves from active involvement in Cibola's power structure.

These episodes reflected a growing adherence on the part of the absentee-owned corporations in Cibola to a "hands-off" position with regard to local political decision-making. And while it cannot be conclusively documented within the limits of the present paper, this evolving policy is graphically suggested

by presenting excerpts from interviews with several executives in the larger economic units.

The general manager of the second largest manufacturing plant in the community, commenting on our findings that but two of the top ten officials in his plant actually resided in Cibola, stated:

> That's a sore spot with me. I've always felt that if I'm going to work in a town, I ought to live there. But there's no consensus on that by a long ways. It's been discussed at the highest levels in our corporation—I know because I've been on the company's community relations committee ever since it was set up. The company has decided that it won't encourage its executives to live in the communities where they work if they don't already or if they don't want to. . . . The company doesn't feel its people—at least its executives—have to live in a town in order to have good community relations. Just about the opposite, as a matter of fact. You're always subject to a hell of a lot of local pressures if you're there. If they know where you are, you're always a target. So maybe it's better not to be in a position to be asked to do something than to have to say, "No."

In discussing the paucity of both formal and informal contacts between corporation officials and local leaders, the assistant general manager of the largest industrial plant in Cibola said:

> No, I've almost never gone downtown for lunch "with the boys." I sometimes get my hair cut in [Cibola], but outside of that I don't show my face any more than I feel I absolutely have to. . . . The people at the Chamber of Commerce seem to fall all over themselves trying to do anything we want— but the point is, we don't really *want* anything there except for the people to have a good opinion of us. But mostly due to this placating attitude of the town's leaders, I'm afraid to say much or be around much.

The corporations were interested, to be sure (as the title of one company's "kit for divisional executives" indicated) in "Making Friends for [U. S. Motors] in the Local Community," but a growing number of them were coming to regard "making friends" and "getting involved" as inconsonant. The general manager of another large plant summed up his attitude:

> One sure way to give [our firm] a black eye would be for me to get myself into things so deeply in town that no matter what I did, I'd end up alienating a lot of people.

---

[8] The heads of 143 voluntary associations in Cibola were asked a series of five questions intended to elicit their perceptions of the most influential leaders in the community. On the basis of their total "nominations," the eighteen most-frequently cited persons were designated as the "public leaders" of Cibola. See Robert O. Schulze and Leonard U. Blumberg, "The Determination of Local Power Elites," *American Journal of Sociology*, 63, 3 (November, 1957), pp. 290–296.

[9] In these reconstructions, a variety of source materials was utilized, including intensive interviews with the seventeen current economic dominants, the eighteen persons perceived by the 143 local voluntary association heads as the community's most influential leaders, and a selected number of informants. In addition, relevant newspaper files, Chamber of Commerce records and reports, and city council minutes were reviewed.

And another:

> You've got to remember that what I do doesn't affect us just here. The guy who represents our company in this area could affect our reputation a lot of other places as well. . . . Why, if I went out and got myself [involved] in local politics, you'd see a new boy in these shoes so damned fast it'd make your head swim.

Meaningful participation in the decision-making processes of a community such as Cibola was mainly regarded by these corporations as entailing risks to their operations and to their positions in the larger social system—risks which could not be offset by any palpable advantages which might accrue to them through playing significant roles in the local power structure. They were clearly cognizant, for example, of the possibility that involvement by their executives in local affairs might induce conflicting loyalties. Likewise, their executives recognized that decisive involvement in critical community decisions posed the threat of alienating significant superiors and publics at the extra-community level, thus endangering their larger occupational and public relations objectives. It seems tenable that it was the very sensitivity of the large corporations to socio-political determinations at the regional and national levels which militated against their involvement in these matters at the level of the local community.

The central finding of the Cibola study—the bifurcation of the community's power structure, stemming from the withdrawal of the economic dominants from active direction of the political and civic life of the community—appears quite generally to corroborate the investigation of Peter Rossi and his associates of the changing patterns of political participation in a middle-sized industrial community in New England.[10] Likewise, our findings seem to be consistent with C. Wright Mills' observations regarding the altered position of large economic units in the power structures of local communities.[11] On the other hand, the Cibola findings do not appear consistent with Hunter's research in Regional City, nor, especially, with that of Pellegrin and Coates in Bigtown.[12]

In addition to the obvious and perhaps significant differences in the sizes of the several communities involved, it will be noted that Hunter and Pellegrin and Coates studied the structures and dynamics of community power in Southern cities, while Rossi's and the present research concern New England and Midwestern communities, respectively. In correspondence with the writer, Pellegrin has suggested that the disparate findings may be largely the function of regional differences: the historical tradition of paternalism being perhaps stronger in the South than in the North. It has also been suggested that economic dominants may become involved in community power structures independent of the desires of their economic units to guide or influence local decision-making. Thus, for example, to the extent that economic dominants represent the wealthier interests in the community and are a major source of voluntary donations to local charities and similar activities, they may be coopted into decision structures by those actively "in charge" in order to reinforce the latter's control positions and to guarantee a continued source of contributions. Likewise, to the extent that the economic dominants represent the upper prestige levels in a community, they may be drawn into the control structure by the active community leaders in an effort by the latter to legitimize their own prestige positions.

It should be noted, however, that both of the foregoing hypothetical instances cast the economic dominants in the role of rather reluctant participants in local power structures. In such situations, it would be *other* members of the community, not the economic dominants nor the dominant economic units themselves, who would have most stake in the latters' local involvement. And this, in turn, would have, perhaps, significant ramifications for the kinds of roles which the economic dominants played in community power structures and for the degree of interest and local concern with which they acted out these roles.

[10] Rossi, *op. cit.*

[11] C. Wright Mills, *The Power Elite*, New York: Oxford University Press, 1956.

[12] Floyd Hunter, *Community Power Structure*, Chapel Hill: University of North Carolina Press, 1953; Pellegrin and Coates, *op. cit.*

Whatever the reasons for the apparent differences in the nature and extent of economic dominant involvement in local power structures—and the delineation of these reasons should certainly be one objective of future research—the Cibola study appears to document the absence of any neat, constant, and direct relationship between *power as a potential for determinative action*, and *power as determinative action, itself*. It suggests, likewise, the need to re-examine the role of economic dominance in community power structures in view of the continued drift of American society, on the one hand, toward the concentration of population in suburban and satellite communities, and, on the other, toward the continuing expansion of huge economic bureaucracies.

VII

The Social Psychology of Status

Description and analysis of the hierarchical arrangement of social roles, of the differential values placed upon different activities, and of the ways in which access to valued roles and activities is governed form an important core of the study of social stratification. In analyses of this kind, however, one can lose sight of the role of the individual in social systems. To be sure, hierarchical arrangements and patterns of differential evaluation are Durkheimean phenomena in the sense that they have a life of their own and constitute a reality *sui generis* insofar as they persist independent of the *particular* persons who occupy the roles or carry the values at any moment in history. But this fact alone does not remove them from dependence upon *some* persons and, to be more specific, processes of replacing role incumbents and transmitting values from person to person and from generation to generation. How are persons prepared for and how do they adjust to roles varying in social status? How is the hierarchy of desirable ends prescribed by a society learned? What are the cues to status and how do people respond to status differences in diverse situations? Does occupancy of roles of varying status create

intrapersonal strain and conflict? If so, how are they resolved? These and related questions are addressed by the articles incorporated in this section.

Socialization into Status Roles. Although there is still a great deal to be learned about practices and processes of socialization, a few facts about the relations of social status to socialization and vice versa are well established. One of the best known aspects of status socialization is the relatively early ages at which children (at least in industrialized societies, but presumably elsewhere as well) are aware of adult differentials in social status and/or evaluation (see Clark and Clark, 1947, for a study of the inculcation of racial identification among Negro children). For example, during preschool ages, children often evidence interest in careers in occupations which figure prominently in children's play such as firemen, policemen, airplane pilots, and the like. On entering school, however, their choice of occupational careers very quickly converges to a more realistic pattern of occupational opportunities. Desired occupational distributions relative to observed ones are still skewed in favor of the higher status jobs indicating, of course, that many

389

will ultimately be disappointed in their aspirations on entering the world of work (see Spaeth, 1968; 1970). Prestige ratings elicited from pre-school children also tend to reflect the peculiar view of the occupational structure embodied in children's play. Thus, children will often evaluate menial occupations in a favorable light and be unable to rate some of the most highly remunerated jobs at all. This situation changes rapidly, however, on entering school—so rapidly in fact that ratings elicited from sixth graders will *on the average* replicate ratings obtained from a random sample of the adult population. There is probably no more impressive evidence of the relative success of the school in reinforcing and inculcating cultural values (see Weinstein, 1958; Simmons, 1962).

There is also a variety of well known differences in the child-rearing practices of various socioeconomic groups (see Bronfenbrenner, 1958; Sears *et al.*, 1957; Miller and Swanson, 1958; Kohn, 1963). The full implications of these differences are, however, largely unknown, both because no study has yet bothered to follow up the subsequent careers of offspring in order to examine the consequences of child-rearing practices for socioeconomic outcomes and because the inability to state the consequences of alternative practices in terms of learning theory has made theory construction and speculation about their likely consequences for school and career attainment especially difficult.

Regardless of the actual practices of child-rearing followed in different socioeconomic groups, one important cue to an individual's social origins is plainly transmitted primarily through family socialization and is only partially modified by subsequent learning and experience. Linguistic style and vocabulary are, of course, the matters in question. There is little question that not only vocabulary and sentence construction, but the nuances of accent and pronunciation as well, serve to identify the social class background of speakers (see Levine and Crockett, 1966; Heise, 1966; Labov, 1966). One is not born with the marks of one's origins; they are rubbed in

through socialization and learning. Social class differences in language usage are, however, overlaid in the United States by striking racial and regional variations. Doubtless the "noise" introduced by these dimensions has, in making language an uncertain clue to status, allowed many to create covers for their social origins: Yankees can't tell hillbillies from Southern farmers of aristocratic background. That "noise" however has achieved important meaning in its own right, because in some areas it is taken as a certain sign of one's racial heritage (when race is not obvious from visual contact, as in radio or telephone communication).

Interaction Among Unequals. The various sorting mechanisms discussed in previous sections tend to make status peers out of such informal aggregates as coworkers, friends and neighbors. In the simplest possible terms, work tends to be organized so that coordinated work is typically engaged in by status equals whose work pace is controlled or whose productivity is judged by a status superior. Equals at work are, of course, remunerated similarly and, consequently, they live in similar places and follow similar life styles. Social distance in the work place, consequently, tends to be reinforced by physical distance between places of residence. Thus, the status equality of coworkers yields a status equality of neighbors and both create a status equality among friends insofar as they limit and define one's opportunities for friendship formation. To be sure, these processes of workplace, residential and social segregation are far from perfect and there is, for most persons, at least some variability in the social status of their informal contacts. But mainly, informal associations are made between individuals of similar status and socioeconomic standing (see Laumann, forthcoming): janitors are no more likely to see their doctors at the local pub than are enlisted men to be found drinking in the officer's club.

Because informal contacts tend to be among socioeconomic equals, socioeconomic criteria cannot operate effectively as bases of deference. Other features of one's social position, such as age and sex and especially social background are more likely, therefore, to be status conferring in such informal settings. In actual practice, however, the very *informality* of the occasion may turn individual differences in verbal ability, personal attractiveness and interpersonal competence into the key bases upon which deference is organized.

While socioeconomic status is not a particularly important basis of deference in much informal interaction, it is an extremely important source of deference both in formal situations and in certain casual and accidental meetings between strangers. The selection of foremen in jury deliberations is, for example, governed by the relative socioeconomic status of the jurors. As might be expected, professionals are not only disproportionately selected as nominal group leaders, but they also tend to exercise a relatively high degree of influence over the decision reached through deliberation. Trial by jury, though formally a trial by one's peers, may thus become for the ordinary citizen more nearly a trial by one's status superiors with all that implies for the social stratification of justice (see Strodtbeck, et al., 1957).

The use of titles (Sir, Lord, Dr.) to obtain better service from headwaiters, porters, airline stewardesses and similar personnel is, of course, well known. More important, however, is the use of one's occupational post and socioeconomic level to obtain credit, to set its terms, and indeed, for many commercially available items, to effect bargain rates (see Caplovitz, 1963). Everyone likely to be reading this volume has probably used his status both to obtain help (usually information or small favors) from others of inferior position and also to brush aside similar requests from others. The selection by Shils included here gives a comprehensive review of the bases of deference and its relation to social structure, while the analysis presented in Milgram's paper suggests just how far status may go towards securing compliance from others.

Perceptions of Status. Most of the selections included in this volume focus upon the conditions in which persons find themselves rather than upon the impressions persons have formed of their circumstances. Collective psychological impressions and common values do, of course, form the bases of such phenomena as occupational prestige and the sources of between-group variation in tastes and life styles. But individual psychology is also important to understanding the social meaning and the consequences of inequality. To be sure, many Marxist scholars have regarded such concerns as epiphenomenal, though we doubt Negroes and other relatively deprived victims of aggression on the part of those experiencing "status frustration" would concur.

An important point of departure for understanding perceptions of social status is an investigation of the relationships between conceptions of one's place in the social structure and features of one's past and current achievements and experiences. Centers, for example, in the selection included in this volume, demonstrates both how an individual's class identification is rooted in his *economic* position and how in turn these conceptions influence his political action.

Direct inquiries into conceptions of the class structure, such as those devised by Centers, are subject to a variety of criticisms. For one thing, they impose the theoretical scheme of the researcher upon the subjects. While this is permissible in societies where the class structure is highly visible and class boundaries well known, it is dubious whether these properties characterize the stratification system of industrial and industrializing nations. In other words, you can ask people about their membership in an arbitrarily preselected set of mutually exclusive classes only if you make the presumption that the person to whom the question is posed will understand what you are talking about. This is possible only when the investigator already knows what people think the class structure is like and when most people think it is the same (so the same categories will be intelligible from respondent to respondent). These conditions, we would suggest, are seldom met in any precise way (see Kaufman,

1946; Kahl and Davis, 1955). In any case, it is plain that one cannot use Centers' method to find out what people think the class structure is like; it can only be used to collect the impressions people have about their locations in a well defined class structure.

Utilization of a methodology such as that employed in Centers' study requires one to accept the implicit supposition that persons can unambiguously locate themselves in a class structure. In industrial societies, however, such clues to one's position as educational attainment, occupational pursuit and economic level are only imperfectly intertwined (see Ossowski, 1963). Indeed, they are so imperfectly related that one can question whether or not industrial societies have a *class* structure at all (see Nam and Powers, 1965). Because the connections between different possible bases of determining one's class position are governed by *statistical* regularities rather than by *exact* relations, many individuals may experience conflicting inputs about their location in the hierarchy of socially determined worth. Is, for example, the man with a graduate degree scratching a living from free-lance writing on a level with his professors or with his janitor who lives at a corresponding economic plane? People in such circumstances, particularly where one of the attributes is an *ascribed* and permanent trait such as race, might be thought to experience some conflict and manifest corresponding symptoms of anxiety (see Jackson, 1962). People find themselves in these circumstances, of course, precisely because the stratification system is imperfectly *crystallized*. Insofar as persons are aware of the ambiguities in their status position introduced by discrepancies in their relative standing on different stratification variables, inquiries about class identification lose their meaning. Many people will cease to have *a* class identification; instead they will have several alternative possible class identifications fluctuating perhaps from day to day or from social situation to social situation. An uncrystallized society is not very likely to be class conscious.

In recent years voluminous literature concerning the consequences of status crystallization has been slowly accumulating. Taking their leads from Benóit-Smullyan's (1944) seminal conceptual formulations and from Lenski's initial work (1954) on the propensity of status inconsistents to support left-wing political movements, other researchers have attempted to relate status crystallization to a large array of behavioral and attitudinal variables ranging from participation in informal networks to expression of psychosomatic symptoms. This work has been informed for the most part by the *assumption* that persons located at *dissimilar* levels in different status hierarchies (such as income, ethno-religious, racial, and so forth) will receive incongruent inputs from interpersonal relations. Some relationships, for example, will confirm the actor's claim to deference, while others will deny it. Consequently, the actor is faced with the problem of resolving these conflicting inputs and it is, so students of status crystalization have claimed, the resolution of these conflicts which drives those experiencing status inconsistency to express hostility to outgroups, withdraw from social relationships, support policies of social change, and so forth. Geschwender, in a paper included in this section, provides a restatement of the general theory of status crystallization in terms of cognitive dissonance.

As a reading of Geschwender's paper indicates, the conceptual apparatus associated with the study of status crystallization is quite elaborate and highly abstract. Despite the substantial development of the theory, however, the empirical evidence supporting it has been at best tenuous (see Treiman, 1964; Laumann and Segal, 1970). Indeed, owing to a variety of methodological difficulties, much of the evidence advanced to support the empirical generalizations noted above turn out to be of faulty manufacture. Some of these difficulties are reviewed in a simple and elementary way in the paper prepared for this volume by two of the editors.

The importance of the social psychology of stratification hinges, in the final analysis, upon the veracity of W. I. Thomas's dictum that things believed to be real are real in their consequences. If people act out the presumed interests of classes they *believe* themselves to be in and if they resolve conflicts between *perceived* incongruities in the statuses they occupy, then it matters little whether there are identifiable classes with alternative life chances or how crystallized are the various status ladders within the society. What matters is not their condition, but their perception of it. While within broad limits incorrect perceptions will be confronted with unexplained features of experience, no society is so obviously organized that people can maintain only one conception of it. Thus, there is ample room for perceptions to influence substantial areas of behavior, though the documentation of this fact in everyday life is largely circumstantial. Because we all act upon our perceptions, we often lose sight of the *degree* to which our actions in fact conform to them and, indeed, of the *extent* to which our perceptions are little more than a by-product of our past actions. Thus, we still need studies which isolate the relative impacts of actual and perceived location in the status hierarchy upon various facets of political and social behavior. Once we have them we shall be able to document the degree and consequences of false consciousness in modern society.

REFERENCES

Adams, Stuart.
1953- "Status congruency as a variable in small
54 group performance." Social Forces 32: 16-22.
Benóit-Smullyan, Emile.
1944 "Status, status types, and status interrelationships." American Sociological Review 9: 151-161.
Bright, William.
1966 "Language, social stratification, and cognitive orientation." Sociological Inquiry 36: 313-318.
Bronfenbrenner, Urie.
1958 "Socialization and social class through time and space." Pp. 400-425 in Eleanor

Maccoby, et al. (eds.), Readings in Social Psychology. New York: Henry Holt.
Caplovitz, David.
1963 The Poor Pay More: Consumer Practices of Low-Income Families. New York: Free Press.
Clark, K. B., and M. P. Clark.
1947 "Racial identification and preference in Negro children." Pp. 169-178 in T. M. Newcomb, E. L. Hartley et al. (eds.), Readings in Social Psychology. New York: Henry Holt.
Heise, David R.
1966 "Social status, attitudes, and word connotations." Sociological Inquiry 36: 227-239.
Hodge, Robert W., and Donald J. Treiman.
1968 "Class identification in the United States." American Journal of Sociology 73: 535-547.
Jackson, Elton F.
1962 "Status inconsistency and the symptoms of stress." American Sociological Review 27: 469-480.
Kahl, Joseph A., and James A. Davis.
1955 "A comparison of indexes of socioeconomic status." American Sociological Review 20: 317-325.
Kaufman, Harold F.
1946 Defining Prestige in a Rural Community. Sociometry Monograph No. 10. New York: Beacon House.
Kohn, Melvin.
1963 "Social class and parent-child relationships: An interpretation." American Journal of Sociology 68: 471-480.
1969 Class and Conformity: A Study in Values. Homewood, Illinois: Dorsey Press.
Labov, William.
1966 "The effect of social mobility on linguistic behavior." Sociological Inquiry 36: 186-203.
Laumann, Edward O.
1966 Prestige and Association in an Urban Community. Indianapolis: Bobbs-Merrill.
Informal Networks and Value Orientations in a Metropolis. Chicago: Markham. Forthcoming.
Laumann, Edward O., and David R. Segal.
1970 "Status inconsistency and ethnoreligious group membership as determinants of social participation and political attitudes." American Journal of Sociology. Forthcoming.
Leggett, John C.
1963 "Working class consciousness, race and political choice." American Journal of Sociology 70: 171-176.
Lenski, Gerhard.
1954 "Status crystallization: A non-vertical dimension of social status." American

Sociological Review 19: 405-413.

Levine, Lewis, and Harry J. Crockett, Jr.
1966   "Speech variation in a Piedmont community: Postvocalic r." Sociological Inquiry 36: 204-226.

Miller, Daniel R., and Guy E. Swanson.
1958   The Changing American Parent. New York: Wiley.

Nam, Charles, and Mary G. Powers.
1965   "Variations in socio-economic structure by race, residence, and life cycle." American Sociological Review 30: 97-103.

Ossowski, Stanislaw.
1963   Class Structure in the Social Consciousness. London: Routledge and Kegan Paul.

Rosen, Bernard C.
1956   "The achievement syndrome: A psychocultural dimension of social stratification." American Sociological Review 21: 203-211.

Schneider, Louis, and Sverre Lysgaard.
1953   "The deferred gratification pattern: A preliminary study." American Sociological Review 18: 142-149.

Sears, Robert R., et al.
1957   Patterns of Child Rearing. Evanston, Illinois: Harper & Row.

Simmons, Dale D.
1962   "Children's rankings of occupational prestige." The Personnel and Guidance Journal 41: 332-336.

Spaeth, Joe L.
1968   "Occupational prestige expectations among male college graduates." American Journal of Sociology 73: 548-558.
1970   "Occupational attainment among male college graduates." American Journal of Sociology 75: 632-644.

Strodtbeck, Fred L., Rita M. James, and Charles Hawkins.
1957   "Social status in jury deliberations. American Sociological Review 22: 713-719.

Treiman, Donald J.
1964   "Status discrepancy and prejudice." American Journal of Sociology 71: 651-664.

Weinstein, Eugene.
1958   "Children's conceptions of occupational stratification." Sociology and Social Research 42: 278-296.

CHAPTER 26

The Boys and the Total Institution

IAN WEINBERG

Before boys enter public schools they experience a process of anticipatory socialization in preparatory schools.[1] The "manifest" function of preparatory schools is to give boys the necessary academic and sporting skills which they will continue to need in the public school. Their "latent" function is to ensure that boys are socialized in such a way that they do not disrupt the workings of public schools they enter.[2]

The preparatory schools sever the child's ties with his family. He learns to live in an environment where discipline and not affection controls behavior. He surrenders the privacy of the family to the continual presence of male peers. If a mother-surrogate exists, such as the school matron or the headmaster's wife, he has to learn to share her with many others. He learns to wait his turn, and to be treated equally and fairly by authority, so that he is never spoiled. When the child experiences these things, he may only be seven years old. Often he is embarrassed by the females in his family, whose dress and behavior may make them prominent when they visit him at school.

The idea is that the child will become more sensitive to statuses within the organization of a boarding school than to symbols of class or family. He should also learn that the trust and friendship of his peers are more important than the material things the family can provide. From the small peer group of the preparatory school the child will go on to the public school and finally into the elite, and throughout he will profit from and depend on informal groups of people like himself. The idea is derived from the Victorians and reveals their suspicion of the woman and their emphasis on early manhood rather than childhood. They were determined that children should not be spoiled either by permissive child-rearing or by indulgent mothers, and the total institution of the preparatory school allows their vision to have continual influence. The preparatory schools are crucial in seeing to it that children from wealthy and privileged families learn to take care of themselves from an early age, and do not become selfish. An observer writes:

> It is not unreasonable to suggest that what is called the "public school spirit" has at least its origin in the preparatory schools. . . . It is in the preparatory school that the small boy fresh from home first learns that he is a member of a small commonwealth and becomes imbued with the idea of teamwork and of give-and-take. . . . He is governed not so much by what his headmaster says as by the ideas of his fellows as to "what is and what is not done."[3]

The preparatory school usually has some kind of prefectorial structure, and the child will learn both to take and to give orders. At the age of thirteen he will take a Common Entrance or scholarship examination, and then proceed to his public school.

On entering his public school the boy who at his preparatory school was a senior and privileged person finds that he is a "new boy." He is often subjected to the *rites de passage* which occur in total institutions.[4] These ceremonies are usually organized by boys in the middle stratum of the school, who are no longer classified as "new boys." They may consist of singing before the house, or being made to feel ridiculous in various ways. Sometimes the housemaster and his prefects attend to legitimate and to control the proceedings. The violence of these ceremonies has declined as English society itself has become less savage since the nineteenth century, but they still persist, however attenuated or changed in form.

The new boy is often forced to do such things as memorize the geography of the school, or to learn esoteric points of school lore, and then answer questions about them. He learns a new slang, and finds that one of its characteristics is that the most scathing expressions are often reserved for him.

In many public schools the process of humiliation is prolonged and emphasized by the fagging system. The new boy has to act as a menial for a senior boy, perhaps for as long as a year. It is difficult to estimate how many schools have fagging. In a 1963 analysis of twenty-seven public schools, twenty-one had fagging, lasting from three to seven terms.[5] The privilege of having a fag is usually reserved to prefects. Usually the fag's duties are carefully prescribed and limited by authority. An example of the system, at Blundell's School, illustrates the range of his duties:

> A fag may be called upon to do the following duties (1) To sweep and tidy his fagmaster's study, and to do washing up for him when necessary; (2) To clean his fagmaster's C.C.F. (Combined Cadet Corps. This is the trainee military unit for boys which exists at public schools.) equipment, to press his uniform and to clean his C.C.F. boots; (3) To clean any games equipment, games clothes, or games footwear; (4) To do errands for him. Errands not of a personal nature connected with school administration may be done at any time and not only within the limits prescribed for fagging.

> A fag may not be asked to perform any of the following duties: (1) Daily shoe cleaning of brown or black walking shoes; (2) The making of his fagmaster's bed; (3) Personal fagging for his fagmaster in the School dining hall.[6]

Many of these duties are traditional.

The systematic humiliations endured by the new boy serve to erase all of his former statuses, whether of family, class or preparatory school. He loses his means of defense against the institution, and is a *tabula rasa* for the new "total identity"[7] to be imprinted by the public school. Any confidence or rebelliousness is drubbed out of him.

The humiliations increase the solidarity of new boys against the rest of the school, and help keep their social distance from other organizational strata an enduring phenomenon. When they become the middling and then the senior stratum in the school, they will not display undue sympathy for those they have to haze or discipline. The effect of crushing family ties is evident when two brothers are in different strata, and the senior boy not only does not help his sibling but participates in hazing him. Each organizational stratum experiences the kind of separateness and cohesion felt by different generations in social structures. Dornbusch found a similar situation with cadets at the United States Coast Guard Academy. "As a consequence of undergoing this very unpleasant experience [i.e., hazing] together," he writes, "the swab class develops remarkable unity."[8] The feelings of distinction engendered as juniors help new boys adapt to their relationships with their subordinates as they become more senior, and so help to maintain the stability and the formality of social interaction between the strata within the school.

The *rites de passage* not only humiliate the new boy. They also signalize his new bonds with the collectivity of the public school. Garfinkel writes that "structurally a degradation ceremony bears close resemblance to ceremonies of investiture and elevation"[9]

The learning of a new slang is also a mechanism of inclusion. All children and adolescents use slang to differentiate themselves from the adult community. Public school private languages are more intimate and less general. They are based on historic school lore, and are understood by masters.

Once the new boy learns the private language he can manipulate his environment. The new language may specify norms of behavior. It may therefore act as a channel for the communication of new norms because the new boy must learn it. If the new boy is socially mobile, he may also have to adapt to public school pronunciation, which may differ considerably from the accents of his home and region.[10] Senior boys will make fun of his accent until he changes it.

When the new boy has surmounted these humiliations, he moves into the middling stratum of boys whose ages range from fifteen to seventeen. By this time the transition to a "changed total identity" should have occurred. Consequently it is often this stratum which humiliates the new boys. The middling stratum has no legitimate authority over new boys. This is reserved to the prefects. Bullying is often the only way in which the boys in the middling statum can exercise a degree of social control over their juniors. Their aggression is channeled downward toward the helpless instead of upward toward prefects and masters who form the authority structure. Some of the masters who teach them may not agree because, as in all other schools, boys at this age are the most troublesome.

The effect is to further the aims of the institution and not to disrupt it. Bullying adds to the humiliation of new boys, which is legitimate, and sublimates rebelliousness. Dornbusch found that the middle stratum of cadets at the Coast Guard Academy administered hazing to the "swabs."[11] It may be a characteristic of all total institutions. Where the top stratum of "inmates" exercises delegated authority, the middling stratum turns to "hazing" and bullying. The boys in the middling stratum are the most troublesome because they are gaining their full physical strength and they wish to test their independence in an environment which is now familiar. Like all other adolescents, they are caught between childhood and manhood. To this ambiguity is added another. In the organization of the public school they have an ambiguous middling status. They are difficult to handle because

they know the school. The new boys are a problem because they do not.

Consequently the middling stratum and the new boys are the objects of the many rules and discipline of the institution. These are various categories of rules. Some prescribe dress, and are very specific, especially for wear outside of the institution.[12] Prefects regularly inspect boys' dress to ensure that they are clean and tidy. Other rules define "bounds," the places both inside and outside the school where boys may go. Usually these rules limit boys to the environs of the school except under special dispensation.

Other rules also proscribe illegitimate leisure pursuits such as gambling, smoking or meeting girls. Sometimes the newspapers boys may read are policed. At St. Edward's School, Oxford, "boys may only purchase such papers as are approved by their housemaster."[13] The rules relate to every aspect of the daily routine. The lesser schools often forbid bad manners. Most lists of rules also state that any conduct contrary to common sense is an offense.

Besides the limitations of the rules, boys live by a strict and invariable routine. The schools hours at Rossall are an example:

Breakfast	7:55
Chapel	8:50
1st school	9:10
2nd school	10:00
Physical training and/or break	10:45
3rd school	11:15
4th school	12:05
Lunch	1:05
1st preparation (study period)	1:45
Games	2:40
Afternoon tea	4:10
5th school	4:30
6th school	5:20
Supper	6:15
2nd preparation	6:45
Choice period	7:40
Chapel or house prayers	8:35
Late preparation (for boys over 15)	9:00
Bad—under 13	9:00
Bed—under 15	9:20
Bed—remainder	9:50

The routine is ordered by a system of bells, which ring throughout the community. At King's College, Taunton, it was estimated that in five years, the length a boy would normally remain at the school, he would hear 38,120 chimes.

The prefects administer the rules. In the contemporary public shcool, the prefect system seems to be functioning at full strength. Prefects are still responsible to the headmaster alone or to the housemaster for their actions. In the twenty-seven schools studied by Broxton, the prefects were allowed to flog boys in all but seven of them. The headmaster's permission was necessary in only three schools.[15] Flogging is the ultimate punishment for an infraction of the rules. At some schools the prefects meet together and watch floggings. There are degrees of criminality, but the principle is that the more people who watch a public schoolboy being flogged, the worse is his crime. If he commits an unpardonable crime, like stealing from a store in the village, he may be beaten before the whole school. In many schools the prefects are left with the supervision of the daily routine. They are often much more capable than new assistant masters in keeping boys quiet. The headmaster is busy, and the Houses are becoming too large for housemasters to exercise close control. The prefects may have more to do now than their Victorian predecessors.

Duffield analyzed twenty-six schools, and found that in twenty-three prefects supervised meals. In twenty-four they also supervised preparation at night, the time the boys do their homework.[16] In serious cases the prefects may meet as a body, or refer the case to the headmaster. For example, at Uppingham, "praeposters are responsible for the observance of all rules and may enforce them by punishment. All serious cases must be tried by the praeposters as a court. Both before and after the trial the court must allow an appeal to the headmaster."[17]

It is clear that the public schoolboy is closely supervised. Students of administration have agreed that the ideal span of control for a supervisor within an organization is one supervisor to six subordinates. Close control is possible with this ratio. In most public schools the span of control is about one to five. In the larger schools, which tend to be the superior ones, the figure is about one to six.[18] There is slightly more freedom in the greater schools. The enrollment boom may be affecting this span of control. It is therefore very significant because the system of discipline in the schools depends on the span of control.

What are the results of the system of behavior we have been analyzing? It is obvious that the mortifications of subordinate status, the multiplicity of rules, and the invariability of the daily routine limit the sphere of autonomy left to the boys. They cannot escape into the family environment during the term, for most school rules explicitly forbid such behavior. To spend a night away from school is a rare privilege, sometimes granted only to senior prefects.

Some of the schools, mainly the very small ones, are perhaps quasi-familial. In answering the questionnaire, the headmaster of "Cuthbert" said his school's distinctive characteristic was a "family atmosphere created by the school being on one campus," and the headmaster of "Tamara" remarked that his school had "a strong family spirit because it is not too big." The headmaster of "Gisborne" even called himself "the head of a family." But in general the schools are bureaucratic structures. The boys learn to relate to others and to be rewarded not by emotional or affective relations but by a system of interaction which is *affectively-neutral*. Parsons and Shils use this phrase to mean "the role-expectation that the incumbent of the role in question should restrain any impulses to certain affective expressions and subordinate them to considerations of discipline."[19]

Public schoolboys learn from an early age to adapt themselves to bureaucratic structures. They are first introduced to the simple structure of the preparatory school, and then they go on to the more complicated structure of the public school. After this they may go on to college, or else into yet larger and very complex organizations.

They learn to obey organizational rules before they are mature enough to understand the functions that rules perform. A kind of formalism and rule-obedience might be expected of them in later life. But they also learn that the good of the organization comes before their personal welfare. Stephen Spender has written in the *Harvard Educational Review* that "the explanation of the extraordinary civic sense of responsibility of England is to be found in English education, which teaches boys to take themselves seriously as functions of an institution before they take themselves seriously as persons or as individuals."

Public schoolboys are forced to mature early as members of a collectivity. They become men, even before they have become boys. But forced maturity, though it may lead to an ingrained sense of responsibility for others, may involve a neglect of individual development. Public schoolboys develop their public rather than their private selves.

This happens because the public schools educate an elite. There is an institutional bias toward preparing boys for their public and bureaucratic lives rather than for their private lives. For example, the schools tend to neglect sex education, and they are not worried that boys do not meet girls. The schools act as if these personal spheres were none of their business, to be handled by the boys themselves or by the family during vacations. They force boys to follow the middle class pattern of *deferred gratification* to its logical conclusion. This situation is causing a great deal of strain in the contemporary public school. Boys are restive because the schools neglect these areas of private and personal development, but not out of a concern for the privacy of the individual. If they did they would not police their charges' private lives so closely. The public schools were structured to deal with a Victorian situation in which adolescence did not exist. Most children went to work early and became adults, and public schoolboys of the same age were also treated as adults. As in other industrial societies, a teen-age culture is appearing in Britain, which indicates that adolescence, as a period of freedom and anticipatory role-playing, is now common.[20] Public schoolboys also want to enjoy adolescence. The public schools are not much better equipped to deal with modern adolescence than many parents. The masters are hampered by the rules and necessities of a total institution.

As houses increase in size and bureaucratic form, there occurs a differentiation of groups and a formality in patterns of interaction. Housemasters are constrained from creating a familial set of relationships within their houses, and from acting *in loco parentis*. The institutional and bureaucratic image, which comes down from the headmaster, is imprinted on the boys. Housemasters cannot deal with adolescent problems except by disciplinary action, which probably aggravates them.

The weakness of sub-units within the schools, and affective neutrality, mean that boys tend to be treated in a fair, equal and impersonal way. This is perhaps what Parsons would call *universalism*. External statuses are irrelevant. This helps to maintain organizational stability, for boys are subject to the same rules and are treated according to their statuses in the local hierarchy rather than to other statuses. No resentment is directed toward the institution as such.

This means that public schoolboys should become *achievement-oriented*. Rewards exist, but they do not come automatically, and boys are forced to exert themselves to gain them. Public schools abound with competitiveness of all sorts, from the athletic to the academic.

All schools in industrial societies fulfill this function, because they force children to play roles in a system where an *achieved* status must be won, whereas in the family the child naturally has an *ascribed* status. The significance of the public schools is that, because they are total institutions, they are able to fulfill this function more than other types of schools. During the term there is no escape for the public schoolboy into an ascriptive family role. The necessity to achieve status is as much a persistent fact of life as the neo-Gothic buildings surrounding him.[21]

The structural situation which ensures that this is so is the very strong peer relationships which obtain in public schools. This derives from the enforced solidarity of each entering "generation" of new boys and from the communality of the total institution, encouraged by the systematic denial of external statuses. There is competition within and between peer groups. Besides encouraging competitiveness, the longrun effects of the public schoolboy's sensitivity to peers is difficult to analyze. Perhaps he is always more dependent on his clique, and tends to conform to their mores. He may be used to working well in a group, and favor committees and consultations in later life rather than autocratic leadership. The advocates of the public schools seem to mean these things when they say that the schools inculcate a "team spirit." "Team spirit" was impossible when it was customary for the elite to use tutors and governesses for their children. So, perhaps, was a strong achievement orientation. Children could not help feeling superior to tutors and governesses, and so being educated by inferiors made them more assured of their own ascriptive status. In public schools they neither feel superior to their peers, nor do they expect privilege unless they strive for it.

These strong peer groups can be seen as the informal organization of the boys within in the schools. Informal organization has been extensively studied. Since the time of Elton Mayo and his associates, industrial sociologists have often thought that worker peer groups created their own normative world, and opposed the demands of executives.[22] Do peer groups in public schools threaten the purposes of the headmaster and his staff by posing their own needs for self-respect against organizational demands?

It is difficult to say, but the schools seem to ward off potential danger by persistently emphasizing *superordinate goals* in daily activities. Loyalty to the school is generated in sporting competition with other schools, in academic competition and so forth. Daily activities are seen as directly related to the honor of the school. House loyalty is also stimulated, and sometimes may clash with loyalty to the goals of the school.[23] But the emphasis on superordinate goals and close supervision seems to prevent the peer groups from gaining too much autonomy.

The communality of boys within a total institution, and the informal organization into peer groups which results, seem to produce a set of norms which contribute to the public schoolboy's code and to the cluster of elite norms and values. It is very difficult to find empirical justification for the norms, though studies of other total institutions suggest that they are widespread. Criminologists have found that prisoners often have a definite set of norms, or code, which derives from the prison setting and which greatly influences behavior.[24] These codes serve to protect the inmate's self against authority, so that the public schoolboys' code is fundamentally a defense of self against the formal authority of the school. The codes also make it easier to live a nonprivate life among peers.

Public schoolboys conform to a norm of honesty, which rules out cheating and stealing. If these two crimes were to go unchecked, life would be impossible within the schools. Second, they conform to the norm that irritation at the discomforts imposed by school life should be borne with self-control, and that anger be not channeled at peers.[25] Third, the boys have a strong rule against "squealing" on another boy.[26] Fourth, there is a norm of manliness. It is here that there is a real similarity between the public schoolboy and other males in total institutions, particularly adult convicts.[27] The latter face a constant crisis in preserving their masculinity. The public schoolboy has problems of sexual identity. He has to live effectively segregated from the other sex for long periods of the year, and he is at a stage in his life when he is trying to define himself as a male. Like the convict he is deprived of the means of earning a living, an essential buttress to masculinity, for the majority of his peers may leave school at sixteen and begin to work.

Consequently the public schoolboy tries

to prove his manliness. He may participate enthusiastically in the Combined Cadets Corps or its equivalent. He may endure the cold and hazards of Scouting. Above all he tries to shine at athletics. Kingsley Davis has suggested that adolescents in advanced societies, who cannot hunt or fight like young men in primitive societies, take to sports to assert their maleness.[28] The public schoolboy has to try harder than others because he is in a total institution in which manliness is particularly hard to realize. The norm of manliness, and the need from which it derives, is an additional reason for the importance of organized games within the public schools.

These are norms of behavior, and actual behavior is often quite different. The difference between public schools and total institutions housing deviants, such as convicts, is that inmates in the latter construct a normative code to defy custodial authority. The norms of public schoolboys usually lack defiance and hostility. A careful consideration of their norms suggests that they in fact function in support of authority within the schools. They stabilize rather than disrupt traditional rules and procedures. If public schoolboys did not abide by the rule of honesty, the headmaster and his assistant masters would lose control. They do not have the means to stop stealing, if it should break out in serious proportions. The norm of bearing the irritants of daily life means that they can claim to train "character" and not be besieged by complaints. The taboo against "squealing" prevents boys from carrying tales to their parents, and furthers the autonomy of masters. The need to prove manliness establishes the position of organized games which are officially encouraged.

Also, because the norms are a form of social control imposed by the boys on each other, they enable the headmaster and his staff to keep somewhat aloof from the petty details of routine discipline. The norms reinforce official rules. These rules have what Gouldner calls a "remote control" function, for they try to control far from their source.[29] They are helped in this situation by these informal norms. Further-

more boys may internalize norms of conduct from significant others in their peer groups—norms which the school purposefully tries to inculcate.

It is interesting to consider whether these norms are important in later life. If they are, they constitute an important clue to the informal norms of the English elite. Honesty and mutual trust, self-control, an ability to endure hardships and to assert manliness without female support, were certainly attributes of men in the imperial civil service, and of many contemporary politicians and bureaucrats of the traditional mold.

However, we must not neglect the modes of adaptation of boys within the total institution of the public school. One mode of adaptation to a total institution is *withdrawal*.

Withdrawal does not necessarily lead to isolation, because boys are forced into powerful peer groups. It is impossible to decide whether withdrawal is a significant phenomenon or not. The shock of entering a public school, with its *rites de passage* and systematic humiliations, may stimulate withdrawal. The necessity to live so publicly and to mature so early may mean that a proportion of boys never expose or perhaps even face their true selves. The institutional bias toward education for public behavior, and the informal norm of self-control, inhibit the display of private feelings. Where it occurs, withdrawal may have long-term effects, and result in the reserve and repression of emotion for which some members of the English elite are famous. Of course withdrawal may also be a desire for privacy, so that complete exposure to communality at an early age leads to a strong need for privacy as a reaction in later life.

It is certainly true that the public schools did change the emotional behavior of public servants. It was quite common in the early nineteenth century, before the rise of the public schools, for aristocrats to cry in public. But the overseas civil servants of the late nineteenth and early twentieth centuries were highly controlled, and they never cried nor lost their tempers *coram populo*. To be slightly withdrawn, but very sensitive to others as a result of early and persistent exposure to peers, was a mixture which perfectly suited the needs of imperial judicial administration. Withdrawal also produces shyness, which reinforces a liking for peers and a fear of strangers.[30]

However, boys may withdraw by rebelling, instead of withdrawing into self. The narrow span of control may mean that rebelliousness is immediately disciplined. But the relative aloofness of the headmaster and his staff from routine discipline does give rebels some room to maneuver. If rebellion takes the form of sexual experimentation, it is punished by authority. Some forms of withdrawal by rebellion further the purposes of the school and may be encouraged. A recognizable form of rebellion in many schools is withdrawal into intellectual pursuits, which may bring great prestige to the institution. Eccentricity in hobbies or opinions is tolerated, and perhaps even respected.

Many senior boys may demonstrate rebelliousness by a simple transgression of the rules. For instance, it is probable that many public schoolboys break the rule against smoking.[31] Others play with shocking opinions. In the 1950s a group of senior boys at Shrewsbury filled the school magazine with amusing drawings, and lambasted their conservative peers in the debating society. A few years later they were scandalizing the nation with a libelous journal called *Private Eye*. A famous rebel in the 1930s was Esmond Romilly, Churchill's nephew, who ran away from Wellington and preached anarchism from a London attic. Rebels and eccentrics are more likely to appear in the major schools, which are usually larger and where by tradition the headmaster and the assistant masters permit boys considerable autonomy. Rebellion and eccentricity deriving from withdrawal during public schooldays greatly influence the English elite. The eccentric is tolerated in elite circles, though he may be despised and satirized. The political rebel perhaps joins the Labor Party and gives to that highly working-class entity the sophistication and leadership abilities of men like Cripps, Dalton, Crossman and Gaitskell.

But it is reasonable to test the supposition that politically, at least, most public schoolboys do not rebel.

The data are quite consistent. Public schoolboys do seem to be politically conservative. Voting Labor is almost invariably minute. The surprising inference is the relative popularity of the Liberal Party. The bias toward Conservatism and Liberalism is much greater than in the country as a whole.

The Conservatism of public schoolboys may be a function of their social origins. Wilson writes, "As one would expect from boys whose parents are in high- and middle-income brackets, they are mostly right-wing in their political views."[32] But it is also a result of living in a total institution.

The public schools shield boys from anti-Conservative ideas. In many schools, for example, newspapers are censored to ensure that boys read Conservative papers.[33] The schools are isolated and internal-looking communities, and boys are more interested in school affairs than in wider political issues.

To read the debates of public schoolboys in their senior years, which are well reported in school magazines, is to gain an impression of a solid Conservative core of boys. Thus in 1956 the Abingdon Society at Downside contained only three boys who voted against the motion that "this House Disapproves of Hereditary Titles," while three years later the Society found itself preferring "the Old to the New."[34] In 1951 at Winchester the Debating Society voted by 57 to 39 that "this House is proud of being class-conscious." The school magazine said that the proposer of the motion, a housemaster, "painted a horrible picture of the classless society. Those who supported such a society were the failures, who felt inferior . . . [and he] emphasized the duties of the gentleman; it was no question of privileges. The function of a gentleman was to lead. The lower orders expected him to lead and did not resent his superiority." His seconder, a boy, said:

Class-consciousness was part of our heritage. Unless you were proud of class, you could not have great leaders. In any society there must be distinctions. Some sections must be born to lead, others to be led. But the class system was elastic. You could move up and down the scale . . . More was expected of the gentleman than of the coalminer. His privileges had gone, but his duties remained.[35]

The wit and humor of expression for which English parliamentary dialectic is famous emerges in these debates. Yet one wonders why so many of these senior boys insist on a joking relationship with many of the important issues of the day. It may be a species of defending privacy, characteristic of the socialization process in the schools, so that boys hesitate to be serious and to display their true selves to their peers. To be flippantly detached is to be invulnerable. The elite characteristic of offhandedness, of treating serious subjects almost amusedly, may find its etiology in the total institutional situation of public schoolboys, and the withdrawal it produces.

Yet it would be too hasty to conclude that all public schoolboys are Conservative, or that Conservatism is the only result of total institutional socialization. The data on political behavior indicate considerable support for the Liberal Party. Politically the voting behavior of public schoolboys in this instance may be part of a larger secular trend. More nonmanual young people are voting Liberal. A recent study states that "it is decisively young people in the higher non-manual occupational categories who give the Liberals such support as they get among the young."[36]

Despite considerable evidence for rebellion, whether it appears as a form of withdrawal or as an aspect of adolescence, it is probable that the most general mode of adaptation is that the boy accepts the institution's view of him and conforms to its demands.

He learns that the school is, formally, a system of statuses and functions, and that he must accept his own status within it. Once he does this he lowers resentment against individuals from higher strata who bully or discipline him, for it is clear that they act this way because of their place in the structure, and not because of any personal animus. It also becomes apparent that this system of statuses and functions is, as in any educational institution, supportive of roles which are *self-liquidating*.[37] This means that student roles have an initial and a terminal point which are known to all including the student. In public schools the effect of the self-liquidation of roles is that as the boy goes up through the school he is less and less subject to humiliation and discipline, so that he finally makes the transition to the role of college student or young adult more easily. The boy lives in the security of knowing that certain things will happen to him at certain stages in his school career. He accepts early humiliation because he will one day administer rather than receive it. To administer discipline is also to be less subject to it. Progressively he gains privileges in the form of release from the rules. As Goffman says, "The question of release from the total institution is elaborated into the privilege system.[38]

The school as a hierarchy of authority, and a complex of self-liquidating roles, offers the opportunity for social mobility. It is a worthwhile and legitimate goal for a boy to strive for the privileges which release him from the total institution. And of course the schools want their charges to make the transition to adulthood. The schools offer appropriate rewards of prestige and deference to those who conform and climb the ladder of mobility.

The ladder of mobility from fag to prefect justifies the lowly positions on the bottom of the hierarchy, with their menial functions, while the rewards and privileges at the top are enough to make the boys forget what they have suffered before. The reward system, which is based on the freedom and authority of prefects, demands the hardships and policing of junior boys. Consequently to reach the top, to enter the school elite by becoming a prefect can be a compelling motivation. A recent book on Marlborough says that "the real criterion of success, however, as in the outside world is power; or perhaps even more the prestige which derives from it. The power exercised by a prefect or a house captain, as well as the lower grades in the Marlborough hierarchy of authority, is real."[39]

The prefect system is therefore multifunctional. It removes the burden of administration from the headmaster and his assistant masters. But it also acts as a reward system for conformity to school norms, and is the ultimate step in an internal ladder of social mobility. It co-opts the senior, most mature and articulate boys into the authority hierarchy at a stage when they could cause infinite trouble if excluded. It leaves the reward system firmly in the hands of the headmaster and his housemasters, for they appoint boys to prefectorial vacancies. This gives them a control over the norms of the boys, as they need only appoint boys who satisfy their standards. The lowly fag is not only presented with a ladder he may climb but also with role-models whose characteristics are legitimated by authority. For this reason the prefect system and the steps to it act as a communications network for the transmission of appropriate norms.

The prefect system encourages conformity to official norms among the boys. It is an excellent socialization for those who may enter the elite. The boy who abides by the rules may expect to become a prefect as his school role liquidates, yet he has to strive for the honor. To be a prefect is an achieved status. Boys learn that it is expected of them that they reach elite status, but that it is also right and proper for them to be ambitious in order to realize their aspirations. Many elites decay because the sons of leading men have no ambition or achievement orientation. The problem is partially solved in England because at their most impressionable ages these boys are working earnestly to surmount mobility obstacles and to reach positions of power and authority. The public schools have an institutional bias toward an education for public rather than private behavior. The prefect system reflects this bias, because prefects learn to administer others in a highly structured and bureaucratic institution. Like their nineteenth century forebears they are boys at the same time as they are members of the authority stratum. They experience pressure form the headmaster and his assis-

tant masters as well as from their peers and their juniors. They have to be tactful and diplomatic. If they become unpopular with the boys by harsh methods, they may find that they can constantly be irritated by the contempt of their fellow members of the total institution. It is no wonder that the English elite is known for its caution in administration, as well as its lack of entrepreneurial *brio*, for the prefect system is ideally suited to produce other-directed men who will make excellent recruits for bureaucracies.

The distinction between the different levels of school organization encourages solidarity within each and social distance between levels. This is particularly important in the relationships of masters and boys. Schools always face the problem that the professionals in the organization, the teachers, have as clients the same people that they discipline. Merton and Barber describe this as the problem of "sociological ambivalence."[40] The problem is exacerbated in public schools because masters and boys are forced to live in close proximity within a total institution. The prefect system protects the masters because the prefects assume so much of the disciplinary role. The masters are able to emphasize their teaching role, though the separation of teaching and disciplinary roles through the prefect system may not be completely successful. Thus social distance mechanisms between masters and boys are useful in averting friction between the two groups. The complicated patterns of action revolving around seniority in an organization which gives great weight to hierarchy help to sharpen the formality of interaction.

Lastly it is interesting to consider the total effect of the elite tradition of education on the relationship between sons and families, and particularly between sons and fathers. This tradition in operation separates parents and their children. Boys are not educated by their parents, but rather they experience the nanny-preparatory school-public school cycle. In Freudian theory boys only identify strongly with their fathers if oedipal conflict is successfully resolved. The successful resolution of oedipal conflict may be hampered in some instances by the traditional cycle of education which separates fathers and sons. It is most important for the continuity of elites that boys do identify with their fathers and inherit their political and business interests.

Perhaps the English situation is somewhat different. Elite children may experience and may transfer some of the oedipal conflict to their relationships with preparatory and public schools. The result of this transferred friction may create identification with public school norms and values. Consequently the nanny - preparatory school-public school cycle may be the crucial device for ensuring identification with the elite rather than with a particular family. This in turn may help the child come to terms with his father, and perhaps even take him as a role-model. The evidence for such transferred hostility is highly inferential. It is suggested by the extraordinary effect of a public school education on boys, who never seem quite to put it behind them. Foreigners often notice that these Englishmen have an obsession about their schooldays which is not found elsewhere.

NOTES

[1][Ed. note] This is a Study of the British public school system.

[2]See Robert K. Merton, "Manifest and Latent Functions: Toward the Codification of Functional Analysis in Sociology," *Social Theory and Social Structure* (New York: The Free Press, 1962), p. 44.

[3]Hugh C. King, "The Preparatory Schools," *Yearbook of Education 1932* (London: Evans Brothers), chap. 12, p. 217.

[4]Erving Goffman, "The Characteristics of Total Institutions," in Amitai Etzioni, ed., *Complex Organizations* (New York: Holt, 1964), p. 317.

[5]Joan Broxton, "The Prefectorial System" (paper for the Diploma of Education at Oxford, 1963).

[6]Blundell's School, *School Rules* (Tiverton: Tiverton Printers, 1953), p. 11.

[7]The phrase is Harold Garfinkel's. See his "Conditions of Successful Degradation Ceremonies," *American Journal of Sociology* LXI (March 1956): 421.

[8]Sanford M. Dornbusch, "The Military Academy as an Assimilating Institution," *Social Forces* 33 (May, 1955): 318.

[9]Harold Garfinkel, *op. cit.,* p. 421.

[10]See Professor Pear's comments in *Personality, Appearance and Speech* (London: Allen & Unwin, 1957), p. 77.

[11]Dornbusch, "The Military Academy," p. 318.

[12]See, for example, *Oundle School Dress Regulations* (unpublished, 1956).

[13]St. Edward's School, Oxford, *School Rules and Instructions* (Oxford: Holywell Press, 1963), p. 10.

[14]*Rossall School* (Preston: T. Snape, n.d.), p. 10.

[15]Broxton, "The Prefectorial System."

[16]R. J. L. Duffield, "Prefects in Schools," paper for the Diploma in Education, Oxford, 1963), p. 10.

[17]Uppingham School, *School Rules* (Uppingham: John Hawthorn, 1956), p. 7.

[18]I am deriving these figures from the formula $S=L/N$, where S is the span of control, L is the number of supervisory levels, and N the total number of nonsupervisory members of the organization. I am assuming that there are four supervisory levels in public schools, headmaster, housemasters, assistant masters and prefects. See Peter M. Blau and W. Richard Scott, *Formal Organizations: A Comparative Approach* (San Francisco: Chandler, 1962), p. 167.

[19]Talcott Parsons and Edward A. Shils, *Toward a General Theory of Action* (Cambridge: Harvard University Press, 1951), p. 87.

[20]See John B. Mays, "Teenage Culture in Contemporary Britain and Europe," *Annals of the American Academy of Political and Social Sciences* 338 (November, 1961): 22-33.

[21]For an analysis of universalism in a total institution, see Howard Schuman, "Social Structure and Personality Constriction in a Total Institution" (Ph.D. diss., Harvard University, 1961), chap. IV.

[22]For a summary of this literature, see Wilbert E. Moore, "Informal Organization of Workers," *Industrial Relations and the Social Order* (New York: Macmillan, 1962), chap. XII, p. 273 ff.

[23]I am taking the concept of *superordinate goals* from the classic Robbers Cave Experiment. See Muzafer Sherif *et al.*, *Intergroup Conflict and Cooperation: The Robbers Cave Experiment* (Norman, Oklahoma: Institute of Group Relations, University of Oklahoma, 1961).

[24]See Gresham Sykes and Sheldon L. Messinger, "Inmate Social System," in Richard A. Cloward *et al.*, *Theoretical Studies in the Social Organization of the Prison* (New York: Social Science Research Council, 1960), pp. 5-19, and Edwin H. Sutherland and Donald R. Cressey, "The Prison Community," *Principles of Criminology* (New York: J. B. Lippincott, 1955), esp. p. 497 ff.

[25]Sykes and Messinger write that for prisoners "emphasis is placed on the curtailment of affect; emotional frictions are to be minimized and the irritants of daily life ignored." "Inmate Social System," p. 8.

[26]The first element of the inmate code is that one con does not "rat" on another. *Ibid.*, p. 6.

[27]*Ibid.*, p. 8.

[28]Kingsley Davis, "Adolescence and the Social Structure," *Annals of the American Academy of Political and Social Science* 236 (November, 1944): 10.

[29]Alvin W. Gouldner, *Patterns of Industrial Bureaucracy* (New York: The Free Press, 1954), p. 157.

[30]See Geoffrey Gorer, "Some Notes on the British Character," in *Horizon* XX (December 1949/January 1950) 376.

[31]See the comments of the school medical officer at Haileybury, "Fags for the Fags," *New Society* 14 (January 3, 1963): 5.

[32]John Wilson, *Public Schools and Private Practice* (London: Allen & Unwin, 1962), p. 13.

[33]See Ian Weinberg, *The English Public Schools* (Ph.D. diss., Princeton University, 1964), p. 276.

[34]*The Raven* (1956), p. 17, and (1959), p. 174.

[35]*The Wykehamist* (April 2, 1951), p. 251.

[36]Philip Abrams and Alan Little, "The Young Voter in British Politics," *British Journal of Sociology* XVI:2 (June, 1965): 100.

[37]A concept used by E. L. Leemans; see Frank A. Pinner, "Student Trade-Unionism in France, Belgium and Holland: Anticipatory Socialization and Role-Seeking," *Sociology of Education* 37:3 (Spring, 1964): 192.

[38]Goffman, "Characteristics of Total Institutions," p. 322.

[39]*Marlborough, An Open Examination, Written by the Boys* (London: Kenneth Mason Publications, 1963), p. 62.

[40]Robert K. Merton and Elinor Barber, "Sociological Ambivalence," in *Sociological Theory, Values, and Sociocultural Change*, ed. Edward A. Tiryakian (New York: The Free Press, 1963), pp. 91-121.

CHAPTER 27

Sponsored and Contest Mobility
and the School System

RALPH H. TURNER

Several important differences between the American and English systems of social control and of education reflect a divergence between the folk norms governing modes of upward mobility in the two countries. Under the American norm of contest mobility, *elite status is the prize in an open contest, with every effort made to keep lagging contestants in the race until the climax.* Sponsored mobility, *the English norm, involves controlled selection in which the elite or their agents choose recruits early and carefully induct them into elite status. Differences between the American secondary school and the British system, in the* value *placed upon education, the* content *of education, the system of examinations, the attitude toward students working, the kind of financial subsidy available to university students, and the relation of social class to clique formation may be explained on the basis of this distinction.*

THIS paper suggests a framework for relating certain differences between American and English systems of education to the prevailing norms of upward mobility in each country. Others have noted the tendency of educational systems to support prevailing schemes of stratification, but this discussion concerns specifically the manner in which the *accepted mode of upward mobility* shapes the school system

directly and indirectly through its effects on the values which implement social control.

Two ideal-typical normative patterns of upward mobility are described and their ramifications in the general patterns of stratification and social control are suggested. In addition to showing relationships among a number of differences between American and English schooling, the ideal-types have broader implications than those developed in this paper: they suggest a major dimension of stratification which might be profitably incorporated into a variety of studies in social class; and they readily can be applied in further comparisons between other countries.

* This is an expanded version of a paper presented at the Fourth World Congress of Sociology, 1959, and abstracted in the *Transactions* of the Congress. Special indebtedness should be expressed to Jean Floud and Hilde Himmelweit for helping to acquaint the author with the English school system.

THE NATURE OF ORGANIZING NORMS

Many investigators have concerned themselves with rates of upward mobility in specific countries or internationally,[1] and with the manner in which school systems facilitate or impede such mobility.[2] But preoccupation with the *extent* of mobility has precluded equal attention to the predominant *modes* of mobility. The central assumption underlying this paper is that within a formally open class system that provides for mass education the organizing folk norm which defines the accepted mode of upward mobility is a crucial factor in shaping the school system, and may be even more crucial than the extent of upward mobility. In England and the United States there appear to be different organizing folk norms, here termed *sponsored mobility* and *contest mobility,* respectively. *Contest* mobility is a system in which elite [3] status is the prize in an open contest and is taken by the aspirants' own efforts. While the "contest" is governed by some rules of fair play, the contestants have wide latitude in the strategies they may employ. Since the "prize" of successful upward mobility is not in the hands of an established elite to give out, the latter can not determine who shall attain it and who shall not. Under *sponsored* mobility elite recruits are chosen by the established elite or their agents, and elite status is *given* on the basis of some criterion

of supposed merit and cannot be *taken* by any amount of effort or strategy. Upward mobility is like entry into a private club where each candidate must be "sponsored" by one or more of the members. Ultimately the members grant or deny upward mobility on the basis of whether they judge the candidate to have those qualities they wish to see in fellow members.

Before elaborating this distinction, it should be noted that these systems of mobility are ideal types designed to clarify observed differences in the predominantly similar English and American systems of stratification and education. But as organizing norms these principles are assumed to be present at least implicitly in people's thinking, guiding their judgments of what is appropriate on many specific matters. Such organizing norms do not correspond perfectly with the objective characteristics of the societies in which they exist, nor are they completely independent of them. From the complex interplay of social and economic conditions and ideologies people in a society develop a highly simplified conception of the way in which events take place. This conception of the "natural" is translated into a norm—the "natural" becomes what "ought" to be—and in turn imposes a strain toward consistency upon relevant aspects of the society. Thus the norm acts back upon the objective conditions to which it refers and has ramifying effects upon directly and indirectly related features of the society.[4]

In brief, the conception of an ideal-typical organizing norm involves the following propositions: (1) The ideal types are not fully exemplified in practice since they are normative systems, and no normative system can be devised so as to cope with all empirical exigencies. (2) Predominant norms usually compete with less ascendant

[1] A comprehensive summary of such studies appears in Seymour M. Lipset and Reinhard Bendix, *Social Mobility in Industrial Society,* Berkeley and Los Angeles: University of California Press, 1959.

[2] *Cf.* C. A. Anderson, "The Social Status of University Students in Relation to Type of Economy: An International Comparison," *Transactions of the Third World Congress of Sociology,* London, 1956, Vol. V, pp. 51–63; J. E. Floud, *Social Class and Educational Opportunity,* London: Heinemann, 1956; W. L. Warner, R. J. Havighurst, and M. B. Loeb, *Who Shall Be Educated?* New York: Harper, 1944.

[3] Reference is made throughout the paper to "elite" and "masses." The generalizations, however, are intended to apply throughout the stratification continuum to relations between members of a given class and the class or classes above it. Statements about mobility are intended in general to apply to mobility from manual to middle-class levels, lower-middle to upper-middle class, and so on, as well as into the strictly elite groups. The simplified expressions avoid the repeated use of cumbersome and involved statements which might otherwise be required.

[4] The normative element in an organizing norm goes beyond Max Weber's *ideal type,* conveying more of the sense of Durkheim's *collective representation; cf.* Ralph H. Turner, "The Normative Coherence of Folk Concepts," *Research Studies of the State College of Washington,* 25 (1957), pp. 127–136. Charles Wagley has developed a similar concept which he calls "ideal pattern" in his as yet unpublished work on Brazilian kinship. See also Howard Becker, "Constructive Typology in the Social Sciences," *American Sociological Review,* 5 (February, 1940) pp. 40–55.

norms engendered by changes and inconsistencies in the underlying social structure. (3) Though not fully explicit, organizing folk norms are reflected in specific value judgments. Those judgments which the relevant people regard as having a convincing ring to them, irrespective of the logic expressed, or which seem to require no extended argumentation may be presumed to reflect the prevailing folk norms. (4) The predominant organizing norms in one segment of society are functionally related to those in other segments.

Two final qualifications concerning the scope of this paper: First, the organizing folk norm of upward mobility affects the school system because one of the latter's functions is the facilitation of mobility. Since this is only one of several social functions of the school, and not the most important function in the societies under examination, only a very partial accounting of the whole set of forces making for similarities and differences in the school systems of United States and England is possible here. Only those differences which directly or indirectly reflect the performance of the mobility function are noted. Second, the concern of this paper is with the current dynamics of the situation in the two countries rather than with their historical development.

DISTINCTIONS BETWEEN THE TWO NORMS

Contest mobility is like a sporting event in which many compete for a few recognized prizes. The contest is judged to be fair only if all the players compete on an equal footing. Victory must be won solely by one's own efforts. The most satisfactory outcome is not necessarily a victory of the most able, but of the most deserving. The tortoise who defeats the hare is a folk-prototype of the deserving sportsman. Enterprise, initiative, perseverance, and craft are admirable qualities if they allow the person who is initially at a disadvantage to triumph. Even clever manipulation of the rules may be admired if it helps the contestant who is smaller or less muscular or less rapid to win. Applied to mobility, the contest norm means that victory by a person of moderate intelligence accomplished through the use of common sense, craft, enterprise, daring, and successful risk-taking[5] is more appreciated than victory by the most intelligent or the best educated.

Sponsored mobility, in contrast, rejects the pattern of the contest and favors a controlled selection process. In this process the elite or their agents, deemed to be best qualified to judge merit, choose individuals for elite status who have the appropriate qualities. Individuals do not win or seize elite status; mobility is rather a process of sponsored induction into the elite.

Pareto had this sort of mobility in mind when he suggested that a governing class might dispose of persons potentially dangerous to it by admitting them to elite membership, provided that the recruits change character by adopting elite attitudes and interests.[6] Danger to the ruling class would seldom be the major criterion for choice of elite recruits. But Pareto assumed that the established elite would select whom they wished to enter their ranks and would inculcate the attitudes and interests of the established elite in the recruits.

The governing objective of contest mobility is to give elite status to those who earn it, while the goal of sponsored mobility is to make the best use of the talents in society by sorting persons into their proper niches. In different societies the conditions of competitive struggle may reward quite different attributes, and sponsored mobility may select individuals on the basis of such diverse qualities as intelligence or visionary capability, but the difference in principle remains the same.[7]

---

[5] Geoffrey Gorer remarks on the favorable evaluation of the successful gamble in American culture: "Gambling is also a respected and important component in many business ventures. Conspicuous improvement in a man's financial position is generally attributed to a lucky combination of industry, skill, and gambling, though the successful gambler prefers to refer to his gambling as 'vision.'" *The American People*, New York: Norton, 1948, p. 178.

[6] Vilfredo Pareto, *The Mind and Society*, New York: Harcourt, Brace, 1935, Vol. 4, p. 1796.

[7] Many writers have noted that different kinds of societies facilitate the rise of different kinds of personalities, either in the stratification hierarchy or in other ways. *Cf.* Jessie Bernard, *American Community Behavior*, New York: Dryden, 1949, p. 205. A particularly interesting statement is Martindale's exploration of "favored personality" types in sacred and secular societies. Don Martindale

Under the contest system society at large establishes and interprets the criteria of elite status. If one wishes to have his status recognized he must display certain credentials which identify his class to those about him. The credentials must be highly visible and require no special skill for their assessment, since credentials are presented to the masses. Material possession and mass popularity are altogether appropriate credentials in this respect, and any special skill which produces a tangible product and which can easily be assessed by the untrained will do. The nature of sponsored mobility precludes these procedures, but assigns to credentials instead the function of identifying elite members to one another.[8] Accordingly, the ideal credentials are special skills that require the trained discrimination of the elite for their recognition. In this case, intellectual, literary, or artistic excellencies, which can be appraised only by those trained to appreciate them, are fully suitable credentials. Concentration on such skills lessens the likelihood that an interloper will succeed in claiming the right to elite membership on grounds of the popular evaluation of his competence.

In the sporting event there is special admiration for the slow starter who makes a dramatic finish, and many of the rules are designed to insure that the race should not be declared over until it has run its full course. Contest mobility incorporates this disapproval of premature judgments and of anything that gives special advantage to those who are ahead at any point in the race. Under sponsored mobility, fairly early selection of only the number of persons necessary to fill anticipated vacancies in the elite is desirable. Early selection allows time to prepare the recruits for their elite position. Aptitudes, inherent capacities, and spiritual gifts can be assessed fairly early in life by techniques ranging from divina-

and Elio Monachesi, *Elements of Sociology,* New York: Harper, 1951, pp. 312–378.

[8] At one time in the United States a good many owners of expensive British Jaguar automobiles carried large signs on the cars identifying the make. Such a display would have been unthinkable under a sponsored mobility system since the Jaguar owner would not care for the esteem of persons too uninformed to tell a Jaguar from a less prestigious automobile.

tion to the most sophisticated psychological test, and the more naive the subjects at the time of selection the less likely are their talents to be blurred by differential learning or conspiracy to defeat the test. Since elitists take the initiative in training recruits, they are more interested in the latters' capabilities than in what they will do with them on their own, and they are concerned that no one else should first have an opportunity to train the recruits' talents in the wrong direction. Contest mobility tends to delay the final award as long as practicable to permit a fair race; sponsored mobility tends to place the time of recruitment as early in life as practicable to insure control over selection and training.

Systems of sponsored mobility develop most readily in societies with but a single elite or with a recognized elite hierarchy. When multiple elites compete among themselves the mobility process tends to take the contest pattern, since no group is able to command control of recruitment. Sponsored mobility further depends upon a social structure that fosters monopoly of elite credentials. Lack of such monopoly undercuts sponsorship and control of the recruitment process. Monopoly of credentials in turn is typically a product of societies with well entrenched traditional aristocracies employing such credentials as family line and bestowable title which are intrinsically subject to monopoly, or of societies organized on large-scale bureaucratic lines permitting centralized control of upward social movement.

English society has been described as the juxtaposition of two systems of stratification, the urban industrial class system and the surviving aristocratic system. While the sponsored mobility pattern reflects the logic of the latter, our impression is that it pervades popular thinking rather than merely coexisting with the logic of industrial stratification. Patterns imported into an established culture tend to be reshaped, as they are assimilated, into consistency with the established culture. Thus it may be that changes in stratification associated with industrialization have led to alterations in the rates, the specific means, and the rules of mobility, but that these changes have been guided by the but lightly challenged organizing norm of sponsored mobility.

SOCIAL CONTROL AND THE TWO NORMS

Every society must cope with the problem of maintaining loyalty to its social system and does so in part through norms and values, only some of which vary by class position. Norms and values especially prevalent within a given class must direct behavior into channels that support the total system, while those that transcend strata must support the general class differential. The way in which upward mobility takes place determines in part the kinds of norms and values that serve the indicated purposes of social control in each class and throughout the society.

The most conspicuous control problem is that of ensuring loyalty in the disadvantaged classes toward a system in which their members receive less than a proportional share of society's goods. In a system of contest mobility this is accomplished by a combination of futuristic orientation, the norm of ambition, and a general sense of fellowship with the elite. Each individual is encouraged to think of himself as competing for an elite position so that loyalty to the system and conventional attitudes are cultivated in the process of preparation for this possibility. It is essential that this futuristic orientation be kept alive by delaying a sense of final irreparable failure to reach elite status until attitudes are well established. By thinking of himself in the successful future the elite aspirant forms considerable identification with elitists, and evidence that they are merely ordinary human beings like himself helps to reinforce this identification as well as to keep alive the conviction that he himself may someday succeed in like manner. To forestall rebellion among the disadvantaged majority, then, a contest system must avoid absolute points of selection for mobility and immobility and must delay clear recognition of the realities of the situation until the individual is too committed to the system to change radically. A futuristic orientation cannot, of course, be inculcated successfully in all members of lower strata, but sufficient internalization of a norm of ambition tends to leave the unambitious as individual deviants and to forestall the latters' formation of a genuine subcultural group able to offer collective threat to the established system. Where this kind of control system operates rather effectively it is notable that organized or gang deviancy is more likely to take the form of an attack upon the conventional or moral order rather than upon the class system itself. Thus the United States has its "beatniks"[9] who repudiate ambition and most worldly values and its delinquent and criminal gangs who try to evade the limitations imposed by conventional means,[10] but very few active revolutionaries.

These social controls are inappropriate in a system of sponsorship since the elite recruits are chosen from above. The principal threat to the system would lie in the existence of a strong group the members of whom sought to *take* elite positions themselves. Control under this system is maintained by training the "masses" to regard themselves as relatively incompetent to manage society, by restricting access to the skills and manners of the elite, and by cultivating belief in the superior competence of the elite. The earlier that selection of the elite recruits is made the sooner others can be taught to accept their inferiority and to make "realistic" rather than phantasy plans. Early selection prevents raising the hopes of large numbers of people who might otherwise become the discontended leaders of a class challenging the sovereignty of the established elite. If it is assumed that the difference in competence between masses and elite is seldom so great as to support the usual differences in the advantages accruing to each,[11] then the differences must be artificially augmented by discouraging acquisition of elite skills by the masses. Thus a sense of mystery about the elite is a common device for supporting in the masses the illusion of a much greater hiatus of competence than in fact exists.

While elitists are unlikely to reject a sys-

---

[9] See, e.g., Lawrence Lipton, *The Holy Barbarians,* New York: Messner, 1959.

[10] *Cf.* Albert K. Cohen, *Delinquent Boys: The Culture of the Gang,* Glencoe, Ill.: Free Press, 1955.

[11] D. V. Glass, editor, *Social Mobility in Britain,* Glencoe, Ill.: Free Press, 1954, pp. 144–145, reports studies showing only small variations in intelligence between occupational levels.

tem that benefits them, they must still be restrained from taking such advantage of their favorable situation as to jeopardize the entire elite. Under the sponsorship system the elite recruits—who are selected early, freed from the strain of competitive struggle, and kept under close supervision—may be thoroughly indoctrinated in elite culture. A norm of paternalism toward inferiors may be inculcated, a heightened sensitivity to the good opinion of fellow elitists and elite recruits may be cultivated, and the appreciation of the more complex forms of aesthetic, literary, intellectual, and sporting activities may be taught. Norms of courtesy and altruism easily can be maintained under sponsorship since elite recruits are not required to compete for their standing and since the elite may deny high standing to those who strive for position by "unseemly" methods. The system of sponsorship provides an almost perfect setting for the development of an elite culture characterized by a sense of responsibility for "inferiors" and for preservation of the "finer things" of life.

Elite control in the contest system is more difficult since there is no controlled induction and apprenticeship. The principal regulation seems to lie in the insecurity of elite position. In a sense there is no "final arrival" because each person may be displaced by newcomers throughout his life. The limited control of high standing from above prevents the clear delimitation of levels in the class system, so that success itself becomes relative: each success, rather than an accomplishment, serves to qualify the participant for competition at the next higher level.[12] The restraints upon the behavior of a person of high standing, therefore, are principally those applicable to a contestant who must not risk the "ganging up" of other contestants, and who must pay some attention to the masses who are frequently in a position to impose penalties upon him. But any special norm of paternalism is hard to establish since there is no dependable procedure for examining the means by which one achieves elite credentials. While mass esteem is an effective brake upon over-exploitation of position, it rewards scrupulously ethical

and altruistic behavior much less than evidence of fellow-feeling with the masses themselves.

Under both systems, unscrupulous or disreputable persons may become or remain members of the elite, but for different reasons. In contest mobility, popular tolerance of a little craftiness in the successful newcomer, together with the fact that he does not have to undergo the close scrutiny of the old elite, leaves considerable leeway for unscrupulous success. In sponsored mobility, the unpromising recruit reflects unfavorably on the judgments of his sponsors and threatens the myth of elite omniscience; consequently he may be tolerated and others may "cover up" for his deficiencies in order to protect the unified front of the elite to the outer world.

Certain of the general values and norms of any society reflect emulation of elite values by the masses. Under sponsored mobility, a good deal of the protective attitudes toward and interest in classical subjects percolates to the masses. Under contest mobility, however, there is not the same degree of homogeneity of moral, aesthetic, and intellectual values to be emulated, so that the conspicuous attribute of the elite is its high level of material consumption—emulation itself follows this course. There is neither effective incentive nor punishment for the elitist who fails to interest himself in promoting the arts or literary excellence, or who continues to maintain the vulgar manners and mode of speech of his class origin. The elite has relatively less power and the masses relatively more power to punish or reward a man for his adoption or disregard of any special elite culture. The great importance of accent and of grammatical excellence in the attainment of high status in England as contrasted with the twangs and drawls and grammatical ineptitude among American elites is the most striking example of this difference. In a contest system, the class order does not function to support the *quality* of aesthetic, literary, and intellectual activities; only those well versed in such matters are qualified to distinguish authentic products from cheap imitations. Unless those who claim superiority in these areas are forced to submit their credentials to the elite for evaluation, poor

---

[12] Gorer, *op. cit.*, pp. 172–187.

quality is often honored equally with high quality and class prestige does not serve to maintain an effective norm of high quality.

This is not to imply that there are no groups in a "contest" society devoted to the protection and fostering of high standards in art, music, literature, and intellectual pursuits, but that such standards lack the support of the class system which is frequently found when sponsored mobility prevails. In California, the selection by official welcoming committees of a torch singer to entertain a visiting king and queen and "can-can" dancers to entertain Mr. Khrushchev illustrates how American elites can assume that high prestige and popular taste go together.

FORMAL EDUCATION

Returning to the conception of an organizing ideal norm, we assume that to the extent to which one such norm of upward mobility is prevalent in a society there are constant strains to shape the educational system into conformity with that norm. These strains operate in two fashions: directly, by blinding people to alternatives and coloring their judgments of successful and unsuccessful solutions to recurring educational problems; indirectly, through the functional interrelationships between school systems and the class structure, systems of social control, and other features of the social structure which are neglected in this paper.

The most obvious application of the distinction between sponsored and contest mobility norms affords a partial explanation for the different policies of student selection in the English and American secondary schools. Although American high school students follow different courses of study and a few attend specialized schools, a major educational preoccupation has been to avoid any sharp social separation between the superior and inferior students and to keep the channels of movement between courses of study as open as possible. Recent criticisms of the way in which superior students may be thereby held back in their development usually are nevertheless qualified by the insistence that these students must not be withdrawn from the mainstream of stu-

dent life.[13] Such segregation offends the sense of fairness implicit in the contest norm and also arouses the fear that the elite and future elite will lose their sense of fellowship with the masses. Perhaps the most important point, however, is that schooling is presented as an opportunity, and making use of it depends primarily on the student's own initiative and enterprise.

The English system has undergone a succession of liberalizing changes during this century, but all of them have retained the attempt to sort out early in the educational program the promising from the unpromising so that the former may be segregated and given a special form of training to fit them for higher standing in their adult years. Under the Education Act of 1944, a minority of students has been selected each year by means of a battery of examinations popularly known as "eleven plus," supplemented in varying degrees by grade school records and personal interviews, for admission to grammar schools.[14] The remaining students attend secondary modern or technical schools in which the opportunities to prepare for college or to train for the more prestigeful occupations are minimal. The grammar schools supply what by comparative standards is a high quality of college preparatory education. Of course, such a scheme embodies the logic of sponsorship, with early selection of those destined for middle-class and higher-status occupations, and specialized training to prepare each group for its destined class position. This plan facilitates considerable mobility, and recent research reveals surprisingly little bias against children from manual laboring-class families in the selection for grammar school, when related to measured intelligence.[15] It is altogether possible that ade-

[13] See, e.g., *Los Angeles Times*, May 4, 1959, Part I, p. 24.

[14] The nature and operation of the "eleven plus" system are fully reviewed in a report by a committee of the British Psychological Society and in a report of extensive research into the adequacy of selection methods. See P. E. Vernon, editor, *Secondary School Selection: A British Psychological Inquiry*, London: Methuen, 1957; and Alfred Yates and D. A. Pidgeon, *Admission to Grammar Schools*, London: Newnes Educational Publishing Co., 1957.

[15] J. E. Floud, A. H. Halsey, and F. M. Martin, *Social Class and Educational Opportunity*, London: Heinemann, 1956.

quate comparative study would show a closer correlation of school success with measured intelligence and a lesser correlation between school success and family background in England than in the United States. While selection of superior students for mobility opportunity is probably more efficient under such a system, the obstacles for persons not so selected of "making the grade" on the basis of their own initiative or enterprise are probably correspondingly greater.

That the contrasting effects of the two systems accord with the social control patterns under the two mobility norms is indicated by studies of student ambitions in the United States and in England. Researches in the United States consistently show that the general level of occupational aspiration reported by high school students is quite unrealistic in relation to the actual distribution of job opportunities. Comparative study in England shows much less "phantasy" aspiration, and specifically indicates a reduction in aspirations among students not selected following the "eleven-plus" examination.[16] One of the by-products of the sponsorship system is the fact that at least some students from middle-class families whose parents cannot afford to send them to private schools suffer severe personal adjustment problems when they are assigned to secondary modern schools on the basis of this selection procedure.[17]

This well-known difference between the British sorting at an early age of students into grammar and modern schools and the American comprehensive high school and junior college is the clearest application of the distinction under discussion. But the organizing norms penetrate more deeply into the school systems than is initially apparent.

The most telling observation regarding the direct normative operation of these principles would be evidence to support the author's impression that major critics of educational procedures within each country do not usually transcend the logic of their respective mobility norms. Thus the British debate about the best method for getting people sorted according to ability, without proposing that elite station should be open to whosoever can ascend to it. Although fear of "sputnik" in the United States introduced a flurry of suggestions for sponsored mobility schemes, the long-standing concern of school critics has been the failure to motivate students adequately. Preoccupation with motivation appears to be an intellectual application of the folk idea that people should *win* their station in society by personal enterprise.

The functional operation of a strain toward consistency with the organizing norms of upward mobility may be illustrated by several other features of the school systems in the two countries. First, the value placed upon education itself differs under the two norms. Under sponsored mobility, schooling is valued for its cultivation of elite culture, and those forms of schooling directed toward such cultivation are more highly valued than others. Education of the non-elite is difficult to justify clearly and tends to be half-hearted, while maximum educational resources are concentrated on "those who can benefit most from them"—in practice, this means those who can learn the elite culture. The secondary modern schools in England have regularly suffered from less adequate financial provision, a higher student-teacher ratio, fewer well trained teachers, and a general lack of prestige in comparison with the grammar schools.[18]

Under contest mobility in the United

---

[16] Mary D. Wilson documents the reduction in aspirations characterizing students in British secondary modern schools and notes the contrast with American studies revealing much more "unrealistic" aspirations; see "The Vocational Preferences of Secondary Modern School-children," *British Journal of Educational Psychology*, 23 (1953), pp. 97–113. See also Ralph H. Turner, "The Changing Ideology of Success," *Transactions of the Third World Congress of Sociology, 1956*, London, Vol. V, esp. p. 37.

[17] Pointed out by Hilde Himmelweit in private communication.

[18] Less adequate financial provision and a higher student-teacher ratio are mentioned as obstacles to parity of secondary modern schools with grammar schools in *The Times Educational Supplement*, February 22, 1957, p. 241. On difficulties in achieving prestige comparable with grammar schools, see G. Baron, "Secondary Education in Britain: Some Present-Day Trends," *Teachers College Record*, 57 (January, 1956), pp. 211–221; and O. Banks, *Parity and Prestige in English Secondary Education*, London: Routledge and Kegan Paul, 1955. See also Vernon, *op. cit.*, pp. 19–22.

States, education is valued as a means of getting ahead, but the contents of education are not highly valued in their own right. Over a century ago Tocqueville commented on the absence of an hereditary class "by which the labors of the intellect are held in honor." He remarked that consequently a "middling standard is fixed in America for human knowledge." [19] And there persists in some measure the suspicion of the educated man as one who may have gotten ahead without really earning his position. In spite of recent criticisms of lax standards in American schools, it is in keeping with the general mobility pattern that a Gallup Poll taken in April, 1958, reports that school principals are much more likely to make such criticisms than parents. While 90 per cent of the principals thought that ". . . our schools today demand too little work from the students," only 51 per cent of the parents thought so, with 33 per cent saying that the work was about right and six per cent that schools demanded too much work.[20]

Second, the logic of preparation for a contest prevails in United States schools, and emphasizes keeping everyone in the running until the final stages. In primary and secondary schools the assumption tends to be made that those who are learning satisfactorily need little special attention while the less successful require help to be sure that they remain in the contest and may compete for the final stakes. As recently as December, 1958, a nationwide Gallup Poll gave evidence that this attitude had not been radically altered by the international situation. When asked whether or not teachers should devote extra time to the bright students, 26 per cent of the respondents replied "yes" and 67 per cent, "no." But the responses changed to 86 per cent "yes" and only nine per cent "no" when the question was asked concerning "slow students." [21]

In western states the junior college offers

many students a "second chance" to qualify for university, and all state universities have some provision for substandard high school students to earn admission.

The university itself is run like the true contest: standards are set competitively, students are forced to pass a series of trials each semester, and only a minority of the entrants achieve the prize of graduation. This pattern contrasts sharply with the English system in which selection is supposed to be relatively complete before entrance to university, and students may be subject to no testing whatsoever for the first year or more of university study. Although university completion rates have not been estimated accurately in either country, some figures are indicative of the contrast. In American institutions of higher learning in 1957–1958, the ratio of bachelor's and first-professional degrees to the number of first-time degree-credit enrollments in the fall four years earlier was reported to be .610 for men and .488 for women.[22] The indicated 39 and 51 per cent drop-out rates are probably underestimates because transfers from two-year junior colleges swell the number of degrees without being included in first-time enrollments. In England, a study of the careers of individual students reports that in University College, London, almost 82 per cent of entering students between 1948 and 1951 eventually graduated with a degree. A similar study a few years earlier at the University of Liverpool shows a comparative figure of almost 87 per cent.[23] Under contest mobility, the object is to train as many as possible in the skills necessary for elite status so as to give everyone a chance to maintain competition at the highest pitch. Under sponsored mobility, the objective is to indoctrinate elite culture in only those presumably who will enter the elite, lest there grow a dangerous number of "angry young men" who have elite skills without elite station.

---

[19] Alexis de Tocqueville, *Democracy in America,* New York: Knopf, 1945, Vol. I, p. 52.

[20] An earlier Gallup Poll had disclosed that 62 per cent of the parents opposed stiffened college entrance requirements while only 27 per cent favored them. Reported in *Time,* April 14, 1958, p. 45.

[21] Reported in the *Los Angeles Times,* December 17, 1958, Part I, p. 16.

[22] U. S. Department of Health, Education, and Welfare, Office of Education, *Earned Degrees Conferred by Higher Education Institutions, 1957–1958,* Washington, D. C.: Government Printing Office, 1959, p. 3.

[23] Nicholas Malleson, "Student Performance at University College, London, 1948–1951," *Universities Quarterly,* 12 (May, 1958), pp. 288–319

Third, systems of mobility significantly affect educational content. Induction into elite culture under sponsored mobility is consistent with an emphasis on school *esprit de corps* which is employed to cultivate norms of intra-class loyalty and elite tastes and manners. Similarly, formal schooling built about highly specialized study in fields wholly of intellectual or aesthetic concern and of no "practical" value serves the purpose of elite culture. Under contest mobility in the United States, in spite of frequent faculty endorsement of "liberal education," schooling tends to be evaluated in terms of its practical benefits and to become, beyond the elementary level, chiefly vocational. Education does not so much provide what is good in itself as those skills, especially vocational skills, presumed to be necessary in the competition for the real prizes of life.

These contrasts are reflected in the different national attitudes toward university students who are gainfully employed while in school. More students in the United States than in Britain are employed part-time, and relatively fewer of the American students receive subsidies toward subsistence and living expenses. The most generous programs of state aid in the United States, except those applying to veterans and other special groups, do not normally cover expenses other than tuition and institutional fees. British maintenance grants are designed to cover full living expenses, taking into account parental ability to pay.[24] Under sponsored mobility, gainful employment serves no apprenticeship or testing function, and is thought merely to prevent students from gaining the full benefit of their schooling. L. J. Parry speaks of the general opposition to student employment and asserts that English university authorities almost unanimously hold that ". . . if a person must work for financial reasons, he should never spend more than four weeks on such work during the whole year."[25]

Under contest mobility, success in school work is not viewed as a sufficient test of practical merit, but must be supplemented by a test in the world of practical affairs. Thus in didactic folk tales the professional engineer also proves himself to be a superior mechanic, the business tycoon a skillful behind-the-counter salesman. By "working his way through school" the enterprising student "earns" his education in the fullest sense, keeps in touch with the practical world, and gains an apprenticeship into vocational life. Students are often urged to seek part-time employment, even when there is no financial need, and in some instances schools include paid employment as a requirement for graduation. As one observer describes the typical American view, a student willing to work part-time is a "better bet" than "the equally bright student who receives all of his financial support from others."[26]

Finally, training in "social adjustment" is peculiar to the system of contest mobility. The reason for this emphasis is clear when it is understood that adjustment training presumably prepares students to cope with situations for which there are no rules of intercourse or for which the rules are unknown, but in which the good opinions of others cannot be wholly ignored. Under sponsored mobility, elite recruits are inducted into a homogeneous stratum within which there is consensus regarding the rules, and within which they succeed socially by mastering these rules. Under contest mobility, the elite aspirant must relate himself both to the established elite and to the masses, who follow different rules, and the elite itself is not sufficiently homogeneous to evolve consensual rules of intercourse. Furthermore, in the contest the rules may vary according to the background of the competitor, so that each aspirant must successfully deal with persons playing the game with slightly different rules. Consequently, adjustment training is increasingly considered to be one of the important skills imparted by the school system.[27] That the

---

[24] See, e.g., C. A. Quattlebaum, *Federal Aid to Students for Higher Education*, Washington, D. C.: Government Printing Office, 1956; and "Grants to Students: University and Training Colleges," *The Times Educational Supplement*, May 6, 1955, p. 446.

[25] "Students' Expenses," *The Times Educational Supplement*, May 6, 1955, p. 447.

[26] R. H. Eckelberry, "College Jobs for College Students," *Journal of Higher Education*, 27 (March, 1956), p. 174.

[27] Adjustment training is not a necessary accompaniment of contest mobility. The shift during the

emphasis on such training has had genuine popular support is indicated by a 1945 *Fortune* poll in which a national sample of adults was asked to select the one or two things that would be very important for a son of theirs to get out of college. Over 87 per cent chose "Ability to get along with and understand people;" and this answer was the second most frequently chosen as the *very* most important thing to get out of college.[28] In this respect, British education may provide better preparation for participation in an orderly and controlled world, while American education may prepare students more adequately for a less ordered situation. The reputedly superior ability of "Yankees" to get things done seems to imply such ability.

To this point the discussion has centered on the tax-supported school systems in both countries, but the different place and emphasis of the privately supported secondary schools can also be related to the distinction between sponsored and contest mobility. Since private secondary schools in both countries are principally vehicles for transmitting the marks of high family status, their mobility function is quite tangential. Under contest mobility, the private schools presumably should have little or no mobility function. On the other hand, if there is to be mobility in a sponsored system, the privately controlled school populated largely with the children of elite parents would be the ideal device through which to induct selectees from lower levels into elite status. By means of a scholarship program, promising members of lesser classes could be chosen early for recruitment. The English "public" schools, in fact, have incorporated into their charters provisions to insure that a few boys from lesser classes will enter each year. Getting one's child into a "public" school, or even into one of the less prestigeful private schools, assumes an importance in England relatively unknown in the United States. If the children cannot win scholarships the parents often make extreme financial sacrifices in order to pay the cost of this relatively exclusive education.[29]

How much of a role private secondary schools have played in mobility in either country is difficult to determine. American studies of social mobility usually omit information on private *versus* tax-supported secondary school attendance, and English studies showing the advantage of "public" school attendance generally fail to distinguish between the mobile and the nonmobile in this respect. However, during the nineteenth century the English "public" schools were used by *nouveaux riches* members of the manufacturing classes to enable their sons to achieve unqualified elite status.[30] In one sense, the rise of the manufacturing classes through free enterprise introduced a large measure of contest mobility which threatened to destroy the traditional sponsorship system. But by using the "public" schools in this fashion they bowed to the legitimacy of the traditional system—an implicit acknowledgement that upward mobility was not complete without sponsored induction. Dennis Brogan speaks of the task of the "public" schools in the nineteenth century as "the job of marrying the old English social order to the new."[31]

With respect to mobility, the parallel between the tax-supported grammar schools and the "public" schools in England is of interest. The former in important respects have been patterned after the latter, adopting their view of mobility but making it a much larger part of their total function. Generally the grammar schools are the vehicle for sponsored mobility throughout the middle ranges of the class system, modelled after the pattern of the "public" schools which remain the agencies for sponsored mobility into the elite.

EFFECTS OF MOBILITY ON PERSONALITY

Brief note may be made of the importance of the distinction between sponsored

---

last half century toward the increased importance of social acceptability as an elite credential has brought such training into correspondingly greater prominence.

[28] Reported in Hadley Cantril, editor, *Public Opinion 1935–1946*, Princeton: Princeton University Press, 1951, p. 186.

[29] For one account of the place of "public" schools in the English educational system, see Dennis Brogen, *The English People*, New York: Knopf, 1943, pp. 18–56.

[30] A. H. Halsey of Birmingham University has called my attention to the importance of this fact.

[31] *Op. cit.*, pp. 24–25.

and contest mobility with relation to the supposed effects of upward mobility on personality development. Not a great deal is yet known about the "mobile personality" nor about the specific features of importance to the personality in the mobility experience.[32] However, today three aspects of this experience are most frequently stressed: first, the stress or tension involved in striving for status higher than that of others under more difficult conditions than they; second, the complication of interpersonal relations introduced by the necessity to abandon lower-level friends in favor of uncertain acceptance into higher-level circles; third, the problem of working out an adequate personal scheme of values in the face of movement between classes marked by somewhat variant or even contradictory value systems.[33] The impact of each of these three mobility problems, it is suggested, differ depending upon whether the pattern is that of the contest or of sponsorship.

Under the sponsorship system, recruits are selected early, segregated from their class peers, grouped with other recruits and with youth from the class to which they are moving, and trained specifically for membership in this class. Since the selection is made early, the mobility experience should be relatively free from the strain that comes with a series of elimination tests and long-extended uncertainty of success. The segregation and the integrated group life of the "public" school or grammar school should help to clarify the mobile person's social ties. (One investigator failed to discover clique formation along lines of social class in a sociometric study of a number of grammar schools.[34]) The problem of a system of values

may be largely met when the elite recruit is taken from his parents and peers to be placed in a boarding school, though it may be less well clarified for the grammar school boy who returns each evening to his working-class family. Undoubtedly this latter limitation has something to do with the observed failure of working-class boys to continue through the last years of grammar school and into the universities.[35] In general, then, the factors stressed as affecting personality formation among the upwardly mobile probably are rather specific to the contest system, or to incompletely functioning sponsorship system.

It is often taken for granted that there is convincing evidence to show that mobility-oriented students in American secondary schools suffer from the tendency for cliques to form along lines predetermined by family background. These tendencies are statistically quite moderate, however, leaving much room for individual exceptions. Furthermore, mobility-oriented students usually have not been studied separately to discover whether or not they are incorporated into higher-level cliques in contrast to the general rule. Nor is it adequately demonstrated that the purported working-class value system, at odds with middle-class values, is as pervasive and constraining throughout the working class as it is conspicuous in many delinquent gangs. The model of contest mobility suggests, then, that there is more serious and continuing strain over the uncertainty of attaining mobility, more explicit and continued preoccupation with the problem of changing friendships, and more contradictory learning to inhibit the acquisition of a value system appropriate to the class of aspiration than under sponsored mobility. But the extent and implications of these differences require fuller understanding of the American class system. A search for personality-forming experiences specific to a sponsorship system, such as the British, has yet to be made.

CONCLUSION: SUGGESTIONS FOR RESEARCH

The foregoing discussion is broadly impressionistic and speculative, reflecting more

[32] Cf. Lipset and Bendix, op. cit., pp. 250 ff.

[33] See, e.g., August B. Hollingshead and Frederick C. Redlich, Social Class and Mental Illness, New York: Wiley, 1958; W. Lloyd Warner and James C. Abegglen, Big Business Leaders in America, New York: Harper, 1955; Warner et al., Who Shall be Educated?, op. cit.; Peter M. Blau, "Social Mobility and Interpersonal Relations," American Sociological Review, 21 (June, 1956), pp. 290–300.

[34] A. N. Oppenheim, "Social Status and Clique Formation among Grammar School Boys," British Journal of Sociology, 6 (September, 1955), pp. 228–245. Oppenheim's findings may be compared with A. B. Hollingshead, Elmtown's Youth, New York: Wiley, 1949, pp. 204–242. See also

Joseph A. Kahl, The American Class Structure, New York: Rinehart, 1957, pp. 129–138.

[35] Floud et al., op. cit., pp. 115 ff.

the general impression of an observer of both countries than a systematic exploration of data. Relevant data of a variety of sorts are cited above, but their use is more illustrative than demonstrative. However, several lines of research are suggested by this tentative analysis. One of these is an exploration of different channels of mobility in both England and the United States in an attempt to discover the extent to which mobility corresponds to the mobility types. Recruitment to the Catholic priesthood, for example, probably strictly follows a sponsorship norm regardless of the dominant contest norm in the United States.

The effect of changes in the major avenues of upward mobility upon the dominant norms requires investigation. The increasing importance of promotion through corporation hierarchies and the declining importance of the entrepreneurial path of upward mobility undoubtedly compromise the ideal pattern of contest mobility. The growing insistence that higher education is a prerequisite to more and more occupations is a similar modification. Yet, there is little evidence of a tendency to follow the logic of sponsorship beyond the bureaucratic selection process. The prospect of a surplus of college-educated persons in relation to jobs requiring college education may tend to restore the contest situation at a higher level, and the further possibility that completion of higher education may be more determined by motivational factors than by capacity suggests that the contest pattern continues within the school.

In England, on the other hand, two developments may weaken the sponsorship system. One is positive response to popular demand to allow more children to secure the grammar school type of training, particularly by including such a program in the secondary modern schools. The other is introduction of the comprehensive secondary school, relatively uncommon at present but a major plank in the labour party's education platform. It remains to be determined whether the comprehensive school in England will take a distinctive form and serve a distinctive function, which preserves the pattern of sponsorship, or will approximate the present American system.

Finally, the assertion that these types of mobility are embedded in genuine folk norms requires specific investigation. Here, a combination of direct study of popular attitudes and content analysis of popular responses to crucial issues would be useful. Perhaps the most significant search would be for evidence showing what courses of action require no special justification or explanation because they are altogether "natural" and "right," and what courses of action, whether approved or not, require special justification and explanation. Such evidence, appropriately used, would show the extent to which the patterns described are genuine folk norms rather than mere by-products of particular structural factors. It would also permit determination of the extent to which acceptance of the folk norms is diffused among the different segments of the populations.

CHAPTER 28

Deference

EDWARD A. SHILS

Into every action of one human being towards another there enters an element of appreciation or derogation of the 'partner' towards whom the action is directed. It enters in varying degrees; some actions contain very little of it, some consist almost entirely of appreciation or derogation, in most actions the appreciative or derogatory elements are mingled with others, such as commanding, coercing, cooperating, purchasing, loving, etc.

Appreciation and derogation are responses to properties of the 'partner', of the role which he is performing, of the categories into which he is classified or the relationships in which he stands to third persons or categories of persons—against the background of the actor's own image of himself with respect to these properties. This element of appreciation or derogation is different from those responses to the past or anticipated actions of the 'partner' which are commands, acts of obedience, the provision of goods or services, the imposition of injuries such as the withholding or withdrawal of goods and services, and acts of love or hatred.

These acts of appreciation or derogation I shall designate as *deference*. The term *deference* shall refer both to positive or high deference and to negative or low deference or derogation. Ordinarily, when I say that one person defers to another, I shall mean that he is acknowledging that person's worth or dignity but when I speak of a person's 'deference-position', that might refer either to a high or low deference-position. What I call deference here is sometimes called 'status' by other writers. There is nothing wrong with that designation, except that it has become associated with a conception of the phenomenon which I wish to modify. The term 'deference', with its clear intimation of a person who defers,

---

[1] This paper is a further exploration of the theme of my earlier papers 'Charisma, order and status', *American Sociological Review*, vol. 30 (April 1965), pp. 199–213; 'Centre and periphery', in *The Logic of Personal Knowledge: Essays in Honour of Michael Polanyi* (London: Routledge, Kegan Paul, 1961), pp. 117–30; 'The concentration and dispersion of charisma', *World Politics*, vol. XI, 1, pp. 1–19; and 'Metropolis and province in the intellectual community' in N. V. Sovani and V. M. Dandekar (eds.), *Changing India: Essays in Honour of Professor D. R. Cadgil* (Bombay: Asia Publishing House, 1961), pp. 275–94.

brings out the aspect which has in my view not been made sufficiently explicit in work on this subject in recent years.

Deference is closely related to such phenomena as prestige, honour and respect (and obscurity and shame, dishonour and disrespect), fame (and infamy), glory (and ignominy), dignity (and indignity).

Acts of deference are performed in face-to-face relationships and in the relationship of actors who have no direct interactive relationship with each other but who are members of the same society. (It can exist too in the relationships of individual actors or collectivities in different societies, although to the extent that this occurs the societies in question cease to be totally separate societies.)

The granting of deference entails an attribution of superiority (or inferiority) but it is not the same as an attribution of goodness or wickedness. It does however often have such overtones; occasionally there is a suggestion that the superiority requires goodness for its completeness. It is an attribution of merit (or of defect); it is an assessment which attributes worthiness (or unworthiness) which is quite distinct from an attribution of moral qualities. What this worthiness consists in is an obscure matter.

To be the recipient of deference from another actor, whether in some tangible or clearly perceivable and discrete form of action from other persons, or to possess it in an autonomous symbolic form which is regarded as an 'objectification of deference' quite apart from the deferential actions of concrete actors, or to possess it by believing oneself to be entitled to it through the possession of the qualities which are conventionally accepted as the grounds on which deference is elicited or granted, is a widespread desire of human beings. It might even be said that the desire to be 'worthy' is a 'need' of human beings in the way in which affection, erotic gratification and the satisfaction of organic needs such as nutriment and bodily warmth are 'needs'.

To grant or accord deference is also a 'need' of human beings aroused or generated by the process of interaction and by the fact of living in a society which goes beyond the limited radius of face-to-face interaction. Just as they wish to be worthy and to have that worth acknowledged by the deference of other persons, so they also often have a need to live in a social world implanted with worthiness, to acknowledge the embodiments of that worth and to derogate those who are unworthy.

Deference of the sort which I discuss in this paper is a way of expressing an assessment of the self and of others with respect to 'macro-social' properties. By macro-social properties, I refer to those characteristics which describe the role or position of persons in the larger (usually national) society in which they live. The act of symbolization of deference is an attribution of deference-position or status in the total society. In acts of deference performed within face-to-face relationships or within limited corporate groups, the deference is often but not always accorded primarily with respect to status in the larger society. The deference accorded to a father as head of a family is not deference in my sense of the word when it does not make reference to the father's position in the society outside the family. The deference awarded to a superior or colleague within a corporate body is a mixture of deference with respect to intra-corporate status and to 'macro-social' status. The deference accorded to a woman or to women as a category or to a man or to men as a category is at the margin of macro-social deference. The deference accorded to age or youth is similarly marginal. Both age and sex are significant factors in the determination of the 'life chances' of a person and therewith of the likelihood that that person will receive deference. They are moreover themselves the objects of deferential judgments. Yet the deference granted to age or to sex seems to be of a different order from that deference which is an appreciation of worthiness or a derogation of unworthiness.

THE BASES OF DEFERENCE

The disposition to defer and the performance of acts of deference are evoked by the perception, in the person or classes of persons perceived, of certain characteristics or properties of their roles or actions. These characteristics or properties I shall call deference-entitling properties or entitlements. While they do not by themselves and automatically arouse judgments of deference, they must be seen or believed to exist for deference to be granted. Deference-entitlements include: occupational role and accomplishment, wealth (including type of wealth), income and the mode of its acquisition, style of life, level of educational attainment, political or corporate power, proximity to persons or roles exercising political or corporate power, kinship connections, ethnicity, performance on behalf of the community or society in relation to external communities or societies, and the possession of 'objective acknowledgments' of deference such as titles or ranks.

It is on the basis of the perception of these entitlements that individuals and classes or more or less anonymous individuals who are believed to possess some constellation of these entitlements are granted deference; it is on the basis of the possession of these properties that they grant deference to themselves and claim it from others. It is on the basis of simultaneous assessments of their own and of others' deference-entitlements that they regulate their conduct towards others and anticipate the deferential (or derogatory) responses of others.

Why should these properties be singled out as pertinent to deference?

What is it about them which renders them deference-relevant? Why are they and not kindness, amiability, humour, manliness, femininity, and other temperamental qualities which are so much appreciated in life, regarded as deference-relevant?

The cognitive maps which human beings form of their world include a map of their society. This map locates the primary or corporate groups of which they are active members and the larger society which includes these groups, but with which they have little active contact. The map which delineates this society entails a sense of membership in that society and a sense of the vital character of that membership. Even though the individual revolts against that society, he cannot completely free himself from his sense of membership in it. The society is not just an ecological fact or an environment; it is thought to possess a vitality which is inherent in it and membership in it confers a certain vitality on those who belong to it. It is a significant cosmos from which members derive some of their significance to themselves and to others. This significance is a charismatic significance; i.e. it signifies the presence and operation of what is thought to be of ultimate and determinative significance.

If we examine each of the deference-relevant properties with reference to this charismatic content, i.e. with reference to the extent to which it tends to have charisma attributed to it, we will see that each of these properties obtains its significance as an entitlement to deference primarily on these grounds.

Occupational role is ordinarily thought of as one of the most significant entitlements to deference. The most esteemed occupations in societies, for which there are survey or impressionistic data, are those which are in their internal structure and in their functions closest to the *centres*. The centres of society are those positions which exercise earthly power and which mediate man's relationship to the order of existence—spiritual forces, cosmic powers, values and norms—which legitimates or withholds legitimacy from the earthly powers or which dominates earthly existence. The highest 'authorities' in society—governors, judges, prime ministers and presidents and fundamental scientists—are those whose roles enable them to control society or to penetrate into the ultimate laws and forces which are thought to control the world and human life. Occupational roles are ranked in a sequence which appears approximately to correspond with the extent to which each role possesses these properties. The charismatic content of a given occupational role will vary with the centrality of the corporate body or sector in which it is carried on. The most authoritative role in a peripheral corporate body will carry less charisma than the same type of role in a more centrally located corporate body. The roles which exercise no authority and which are thought to have a minimum of contact with transcendent powers call forth least deference.

Of course, occupational roles and their incumbents are also deferred to on account of certain highly correlated deference-entitling properties such as the income which the practice of the occupation provides, the educational level of its practitioners, the ethnic qualities of its incumbents, etc. Conversely, occupational roles which are ill-remunerated and the incumbents of which have little education and are of derogatory ethnic stocks receive little deference on the grounds of these traits as well as on the grounds of the nature and functions of the occupational role itself. Nonetheless, occupational role is an independent entitlement to deference.

Beyond occupational role, accomplishment within the role is a deference-entitlement both micro- and macro-socially. To be not only a judge but an outstanding judge, to be not only a scientist but an outstanding scientist constitutes a further deference-entitlement. It does this not only because outstanding accomplishment renders its performer more 'visible' and therewith more likely to be the recipient of deference but much more because accomplishment is the realization of the potentiality of creative action. Creativity is a feature of centrality; creative action makes the creator part of the centre.

Wealth is deferred to—great wealth is greatly deferred to, and poverty is derogated—because it is powerful. But without association with charismatic occupation or with political power, wealth is not as much deferred to as when it enjoys those associations. Wealth which is manifested only by purchasing power is not as esteemed as wealth which embodies its power in the ownership and management of landed estates or in the directorship of great industrial corporations, employing many thousands of persons. Wealth is, in one important aspect, purchasing power and as such it is like income; it is also the power to employ and the power to dismiss from employment. These powers over physiological existence and access to dignity are tremendous but they are not peculiar to wealth and are quite compatible with the propertylessness of those who exercise these powers. Wealth also calls forth deference when it is associated with a certain style of life, for which it is indeed a condition.[1] Wealth is therefore both a derivative and a conditional entitlement to deference. It is derivative from occupation, from the exercise of power, over persons and over the soil; it is conditional to a 'style of life'. It is

[1] Wealth alone calls forth a qualified deference. Until the wealthy acquire an appropriate style of life and associations, they do not gain 'acceptance' by those whom they equal or exceed in wealth and who already have a high deference position. The contempt shown towards the *nouveau riche* is well known and it often takes a generation for wealth to acquire the appropriate education, religion, occupation and style of life which are necessary for assimilation into a higher deference-stratum.

also conditional to income;[1] it itself and alone is significant primarily as a potentiality of power. To gain the deference which sociologists often assert is the reward of wealth it must find completion in a wider complex of properties such as the actual exercise of power through an authoritative occupational role, through a 'validating' style of life, etc.

Income too is regarded as an entitlement to deference as a manifestation of power, but it is a limited and segmental power which is exercised in the specific buyer-seller relationship in the purchase of goods and services. Purchasing power, confined as it is to very specific exchange relationships, is not a very weighty entitlement to deference. Income alone possesses only potential deference-entitlement.[2] Nonetheless, a high income, like a large fortune, is regarded as a valid entitlement to deference when it is used to acquire what it can most legitimately be used for, namely the style of life to which it corresponds, or to acquire those other purchasable entitlements like educational opportunity, and associational membership. Income is therefore a *conditional* deference-entitlement which acquires deference primarily when manifested in another category. In itself it possesses as little charisma as an immediate specific potential power confers.

A style of life is a deference-entitlement because it is a pattern of conduct which is a voluntary participation in an order of values. A style of life is value-permeated; it demonstrates connection with a stratum of being in which true value resides. The conventional and long-standing deference given to the 'leisure classes' was not given because idleness was a virtue or because work or occupation was a burden but because leisure permitted the cultivation and practice of a value-infused pattern of life. Like an authoritative occupation, it was a value-generating and value-infused existence. More than authoritative occupations, it belongs, despite its material embodiment, to the realm of

[1] Cf. the anomaly experienced in the contemplation of very wealthy persons who do not *use* their wealth in the practice of an appropriate style of life, who exercise no power through its use (employing no one, exercising no control over the agricultural or industrial properties in which it is invested), and who practise no occupation. All they have is the potentiality which we know from the observation of other cases wealth possesses. They enjoy such deference as they receive—apart from what they might receive by virtue of their family name—because of the potentiality rather than the actuality of their exercise of power. Potentiality is less instigative of deference than actuality. As a result, they are the objects of an ambivalent judgment, deference granted for the potentiality of power which wealth confers, deference withheld for their failing to complete the potentiality of wealth by manifesting it in the fuller pattern which is incumbent on anyone who is high in any single distribution.

[2] Although all resources in particular distributive categories contains the potentiality of conversion into a position in another distributive category, they vary in their degree of specificity. Income can be used to purchase objects at relatively fixed rates, e.g. household furnishings, books, education, etc.; education is not equally specific in the response which it is thought to be entitled to call forth. Neither is political authority. In general we can say that the more diffuse a potentiality, the greater is its entitlement to deference.

culture. It included eating ('commensality') 'in style', living in the midst of an appropriate *décor*, in an appropriate quarter ('a good address'), surrounded by servants who provide not just labour power but a ritual environment.[1] In its highest form, 'style of life' was found in courts and palaces, in great country houses and grand bourgeois establishments. Style of life requires income as a condition but it is an entitlement to deference not as a direct function of wealth and income or simply as an indicator of wealth and income. It is facilitated by wealth and income but it enhances them and transfigures them. It does so because it partakes of a charismatic quality which they contain only in the potentiality but not in their sheer and specific actuality.

The level of educational attainment possesses deference-entitling properties partly because it is often conditional to entry into authoritative, creative and remunerative occupational roles but even more because it is an assimilation into an ideal realm. It is an assimilation into a pattern of values and beliefs which are part of the centre of existence. The 'possessor' of a large amount of education is often an incumbent of an authoritative occupation and as an actual or potential incumbent of such an occupation he receives deference; he also has the likelihood of a higher than average income and an appropriate style of life and as such he receives deference also.[2] The educated person is one who has received the culture of beliefs and appreciations which are central in the society. These beliefs may be scientific beliefs about the way in which the world works, they may be beliefs about the 'essential' nature of the society, its history, its religion, its cultural traditions and objectivations. Education is also the acquisition of skills which prepare for participation in the centre of the society through the exercise of authority, technological performance, the discovery and transmission of vital truths about the universe, man and society, in short for *creating* and *ordering*. Education is an autonomous, non-derivative entitlement to deference because it is integral to and testifies to its possessor's participation in the charismatic realm.

The exercise of power whether in an occupation or through the employment of purchasing power is determinative of the life chances of the persons over whom it is exercised; therewith it shares in the charisma which is inherent in the control of life. It is difficult to separate power from occupational role because much or even most power is exercised in

---

[1] Of course, 'style of life' can be shrivelled to hedonistic self-indulgence, 'conspicuous consumption' or sheer idleness, all of which are capable of gaining ascendancy within the pattern.

[2] The deference-entitlement of education is also affected by the institutions and countries in which it is acquired. Some schools and universities and university systems are thought to be more central than others. Those educated in them acquire more of a charismatically infused culture.

occupational roles, in corporate bodies, particularly if we include inherited, entrepreneurially initiated, appointed and elected incumbency in roles in the state, church, armies, economic organizations, universities, etc. Authority exercised through occupational roles becomes more diffuse the higher its position within any corporate hierarchy, whether the hierarchy be religious, political, military or whatever. Its diffuseness, which is another facet of its creating and ordering responsibility and capacity, is crucial to its deference-entitlement.

There is undoubtedly some power which is not occupational in the locus of its exercise. It might be worth while, therefore, to employ a separate category for power as a deference-entitlement for those persons whose charismatic ascendancy is not a function of an occupational role.[1]

Where everyone in a society or at least all adults stand in at least one important respect in equal relationship to the exercise of authority in government by virtue of citizenship, deference is dispersed. The sharing of power and the attendant equalization of deference through citizenship does not abolish the inequality of power and thus the inequality of deference associated with the unequal distribution of authoritative occupational roles. It does, however, offset it and in some situations to a very considerable extent.

Relative proximity to persons in powerful roles is another deference-entitlement. The proximity may be a fiduciary relationship between the incumbent of a very authoritative role and his 'personal staff'; it may be a close personal relationship of friendship or affection; it may be little more than the acquaintanceship of frequent encounter; it may be the primordial tie of kinship. Whatever the content of the relationship, the important thing is that the magnitude of its entitlement to deference for a given person is assessed (*a*) by the deference-position of the person to whom he stands in proximity and (*b*) the degree of proximity. To be the son or cousin or the intimate friend of a person of no significant status adds no status to those in that degree of proximity; indeed it makes for the insignificant status of those who stand in such proximity. Being a close friend or a frequently met colleague of a person of a high deference-position confers more deference than would a slighter degree of friendship or a less intense collegial intercourse. The deference-position of the person at the end of the chain is determined by the properties already

[1] Just as within occupations, there are inter-individual differences in creativity or productivity, so it is perfectly conceivable that this creativity can manifest itself avocationally and outside the corporate bodies within which such activities are ordinarily carried on. There are religious prophets who arise out of the laity, revolutionary politicians who are not incorporated into the established political order, intimates of rulers who have no formal political occupation and whose own occupations are not constitutively endowed with power. All of these are exercisers of power in a way which is independent of their occupational roles. (Of course, the definition of occupation in this way has the danger of turning occupational role into a residual category.)

referred to; the relationship is the channel through which a fundamentally charismatic quality is transmitted. Just as the member of a corporate body participates in the charisma of his organization, whether it be a university, a church or a government, so membership in a personal relationship or in a primordial collectivity (e.g. family) is constituted by or results from a diffusion of the charisma of the central person or role of the collectivity. Those who stem from 'famous' families, those who keep the company of important persons, who move in 'important' circles, share in the charismatic quality of those whose charisma gives fame to families and importance to circles. The three modes of linkage—primordial, personal and collegial—are all different from each other and yet each has been regarded as a legitimate channel through which charisma and, consequently, the entitlement to deference can be shared.

Ethnicity is very much like the kinship tie—they are both primordial, being constituted by the significance attributed to a presumed genetic connection and the primordial unity arising therefrom. Unlike kinship connection as an entitlement to deference, ethnicity does not refer to a genetic link with a particular important person or persons. It is a link with a collectivity in which a vital, charismatic quality is diffused. It is thought to represent the possession of some quality inherent in the ethnic aggregate and shared by all its members. Indeed the possession of that 'essential' quality as manifested in certain external features such as colour, hair form, physiognomy and physique constitutes membership in the aggregate. In societies which are ethnically homogeneous, the ethnic entitlement is neutral; in societies which are ethnically plural, the ethnic entitlement can only be neutralized by an overriding civility or sense of citizenship or by the disaggregation of the society to the point where it almost ceases to be a society.

Areal provenience whether it be rural or urban, regional or local, provincial or metropolitan can also be a deference-entitlement in a variety of ways. In some respects, it can be derivative from occupational roles and the exercise of authority insofar as particular occupational roles and the exercise of authority tend to be more concentrated—although not necessarily in the same locations—to a greater extent in some areas than in others. It might also be derivative from the greater proximity to authority and eminence which is more likely in some areas than in others. But the soil and the city might be independent entitlements, one gaining ascendancy over the other in accordance with prevailing beliefs concerning the sanctity of the soil or the charisma of urban existence.

Religious adherence or affiliation is similar to ethnicity in that it is a deference-entitlement referring to membership in a collectivity, but in this case the collectivity is constituted by the sharing of beliefs about sacred things and therewith by the sharing of the charisma of the church or sect. Whereas practically all societies are differentiated in occupational roles and in income and power or authority and are bound to be so by their nature as societies, ethnic and religious heterogeneity is not inevitable.

Indulgence conferred on the community or on society by protecting it from injury or by enhancing its position—power, wealth, deference— among communities or societies is regarded as an entitlement to deference for those who confer such indulgence. Successful military men, politicians and statesmen, diplomats, athletes in international competitions, literary men and artists are deferred to within their own societies in proportion to their external deference or their enhancement of the power of their own society *vis-à-vis* other societies. The enhancement of the deference-position and power of the society enhances the deference-position of its members by virtue of their membership in it. It is the same here as in the case of proximity to importance or membership in primordial collectivities. There is a sense of some shared essential quality with those who 'represent' the society.[1]

A title or emblem conferred by the major deference-bearing institutions of the society is an entitlement to deference—such are the criteria by which deference is allocated in societies. They are not all of equal importance in the formation of deference judgments nor do their relative weights remain constant through time or among societies. Ethnicity, area, religion might vary considerably in their significance in accordance with the strength of the sense of civility and the extent and intensity of religious belief. Education might become more important when a larger proportion of the population seeks education and possesses different amounts and kinds of education. The more equal the distribution of any given deference-entitlement, the less weight it has in differentiating the deference-positions of the members of a society. This does not mean that it loses its significance in the determination of the allocation of deference, only that it ceases to differentiate the worth of individuals. In fact, while ceasing to differentiate, it might at the same time raise the deference-position of most individuals throughout the society. But there is also a possibility that a particular criterion might become irrelevant, or at least diminish in relevance, to deference, losing its influence on the level of deference as it ceases to discriminate among individuals, groups and strata.[2]

---

[1] There is a deference-stratification among societies. It includes the deference-stratification of whole societies and an international deference-stratification system of individuals which is however extremely fragmentary.

[2] If we can imagine a society, the technology of which has become so automated that a large part of the gainfully employed population ceases to be differentiated by occupation, we are confronted by a situation in which occupations, at least for a large part of the population,

The phenomena of the stratification system are generally thought of as so massive in their impact on the rest of society that it is only natural that they too should be conceived of as having a substantial existence. Indeed they are spoken of as if they possessed a continuous, almost physical, tangibility which enables them to be apprehended by relatively gross methods of observation. In fact, many of these properties are very discontinuous or intermittent in their performance. When they are not actual, they fall into a condition of 'latency'. The different entitlements vary in the continuity and substantiality of their performance or manifestation. And what is true of entitlements to deference applies even more to deference behaviour itself.

First of all, however, before considering deference behaviour as such, I should like to consider the substantiality and continuity of the entitlements.

Occupational roles are, for example, performed for from one- to two-thirds of the waking life of the human being so employed for most of the days of each week for most of the weeks of the year over a period of forty to fifty or more years, through youth, adulthood and old age. A wealthy person usually has his wealth in the form of real property, chattels or convertible paper, available to him whenever he wishes to call upon it and as long as he owns it. The receipt and expenditure of income is a less continuous property, not only because the amount of income received fluctuates or varies over the course of a decade or a lifetime but also because once expended it ceases to be available, and because when not being used it is not visible. Only the results of expended income are visible in the material or tangible components of a style of life. Income is *recurrent* and it can be regularly recurrent as a disposable sum but not *continuously* and it is not always *substantially* manifested.

The style of life of a person or a family is a pattern heterogeneous in its composition and pervasive in apparel, speech, domestic arrangements, physical, social and cultural. Its material apparatus is grossly observable. Like occupational role, among the deference entitlements, it is performed, enacted or lived in a larger proportion of waking time (and even sleeping time) than the other deference entitlements. Style of life is, with occupational role, the most substantial and continuous of the various deference-entitlements. It is, with occupation, the most visible.

have lost their capacity to confer different deference-positions in their practitioners. This does not mean that the entire gainfully employed population has become occupationally homogeneous, but for that section which has become homogeneous occupation will count for no more than race in an ethnically almost homogeneous society.

Level and type of educational attainment is a different kind of thing. It is like kinship in the sense that it is membership in a category which entails no present action. (Indeed kinship entails no action on the part of the actor in question. It is a *past* biological connection, a *present* genetic composition and classification by self and other.) Level of educational attainment insofar as it is a past qualification for present incumbency in a role has ceased to exist except as a marker of a past accomplishment, like a medal awarded for heroism in a long past battle. Where it is interpreted as an approximate indication of present level of culture, it refers to very discontinuously performed actions. Insofar as it refers to the number of years in which studies were carried on, to the subjects studied and certifications which attest to amounts, etc., it refers to past events which provide a basis for present classification by self and other. Thus, while to an external analyst the level of educational attainment is a stable property of a person, it is not continuously operative in that person's action or interaction with others. It is a fluctuating and intermittent quality, sometimes of high salience, sometimes latent. It need not be so in all societies, in all strata or in all individuals. In societies or strata which are highly 'education-conscious', it will be more continuously salient as a categorial property than in those which are less 'education-conscious'. Persons of a given level of educational attainment will manifest it more substantially in their speech, thought and conduct.

Power, which is so closely and often associated with the performance of occupational role, resembles it in this respect too, since it is often exercised or performed for significantly continuous periods, with sufficiently regular recurrence. (It is also like occupational role in the sense that it places its practitioner in a category which calls forth responses from self and other in situations outside the occupational or power-exercising role.)

The foregoing observations were intended to render a little more explicit than is usually done the temporal discontinuity of entitlements, their intermittence and periodicity of performance and visibility. I have done this because these characteristics of entitlement affect their probability of being perceived and therewith of calling forth deference. I have also done it because I wish to call attention to what appear to me to be important, even if not readily evident, features of deference behaviour.

The term *status*, when it is used to refer to deference-position, ordinarily carries with it, as I suggested earlier, overtones of the stability, continuity and pervasiveness which are possessed by sex and age. A person who has a given status tends to be thought of as having that status at every moment of his existence as long as that particular status is not replaced by another status. One of the reasons why I have chosen to use the term 'deference-position' in place of 'status' is that it makes a little more prominent the fact that status is not a substantial property of the person arising automatically from the possession of certain entitlements but is in fact an element in a relationship between the person deferred to and the deferent person. Deference towards another person is an attitude which is manifested in behaviour.

Acts of deference judgments are evaluative classifications of self and other. As classifications they transcend in their reference the things classified. A person who is evaluatively classified by an act of deference on the basis of his occupation is in that classification even when he is not performing his occupational role. The classificatory deference judgment, because it is a generalization, attains some measure of independence from the intermittence of entitlements. It has an intermittence of its own which is not necessarily synchronized with that of the entitlements.

Overt concentrated acts of deference such as greetings and presentations are usually shortlived, i.e. they are performed for relatively short periods and then 'disappear' until the next appropriate occasion. The appropriate occasions for the performance of concentrated acts of deference might be regular in their recurrence, e.g. annually or weekly or even daily, but except for a few 'deference-occupations' they are not performed with the high frequency and density over extended periods in the way in which occupational roles are performed. But does deference consist exclusively of the performance of concentrated deferential actions? Is there a 'deference vacuum' when concentrated deferential actions are not being performed? Where does deference go when it is not being expressed in a grossly tangible action?

To answer this question, it is desirable to examine somewhat more closely the character of attenuated deference actions. There are concentrated, exclusively deferential actions which are nothing but deferential actions just as there are exclusively power or style or life or occupational actions but in a way different from these others. Occupational actions are substantial; all effort within a given space and time is devoted to their performance. They can be seen clearly by actor and observer as occupational actions; the exercise of authority has many of these features, especially when it is exercised in an authoritative occupational role. Expenditures of money are of shorter duration but they too are clearly definable. The acts of consumption and conviviality which are comprised in a style of life are of longer duration but they too are also clearly defined. On the other hand, level of educational attainment and kinship connection and ethnicity are not actual actions at all, they are classifications in which 'objectively' the classified person is continuously present although once present in the class he does nothing to manifest or affirm.

But deference actions—deferring to self and other, receiving deference from self and other—are actions. They result in and are performed with reference to classifications but they are actions nonetheless. They are not however always massive actions of much duration. They occur more-over mainly at the margin of other types of action. Deference actions performed alone are usually very shortlived; they open a sequence of interaction and they close it. Between beginning and end, deference actions are performed in fusion with non-deferential actions. Through-out the process of interaction they are attenuated in the substance of the relationship in which the performance of tasks appropriate to roles in corporate bodies, to civil roles, to personal relationships, etc., occurs. Deference actions have always been largely components of other actions; they are parts of the pattern of speaking to a colleague, a superior or an inferior about the business at hand in an authoritatively hierarchical corporate body, of speaking about or to a fellow citizen, of acting towards him over a distance (as in an election). In other words, deference actions seldom appear solely as deference actions and those which do are not regarded, especially in the United States, as a particu-larly important part of interaction in most situations. Nonetheless, deference is demanded and it is accepted in an attenuated form.

This then is the answer to the question as to where deference goes when it ceases to be concentrated: it survives in attenuation, in a pervasive, intangible form which enters into all sorts of relationships through tone of speech, demeanour, precedence in speaking, frequency and mode of contradiction, etc.

Deference can, however, become extinct. A person who fails to retain his entitlements in the course of time also loses the deference which his entitlements brought him. He might not lose it entirely; ex-prime ministers, professors emeriti, retired generals, long after they departed from their occupational roles continue to receive some deference, although it is probably, other things being equal, less than they received while active incumbents. Kings in exile, great families fallen on hard times also lose much of their deference and some, sinking away into peripheral obscurity, cease to be known and their deference becomes entirely local.

The salience of deference behaviour is closely related to deference-sensitivity. Indifference to deference is a marginal phenomenon but individuals, classes and societies differ in the degree to which they demand deference—whether concentrated or attenuated—or are relatively unperceptive regarding its appropriateness, its presence or its absence. Snobs are persons whose demand for deference is great and for whom the deference-position of those they associate with is their most relevant characteristic.

It is one of the features of modern Western societies that they are moving in the direction of deference-indifference and attenuation. The movement is very uneven among modern societies with the United States, Canada and Australia in the lead, with other countries some distance behind but they too seem to be moving further along than they were a half century ago. The movement is also very uneven within societies, with marked differences between classes and generations.

The equalitarian tendencies of contemporary Western societies have not only witnessed the attenuation and retraction of deference, they have also seen it assimilated into the pattern of intercourse among equals. But can it be said that deference still exists in relations among equals? Is not equality a point where deference disappears? Concentrated and salient deference behaviour was a feature of the relations between the great of the earth and their subordinates. There is to be sure no elaborate ritual of deference between equals in contemporary Western societies and particularly in American society, except that which still obtains between heads of states, between heads of churches, heads of universities, on especially ceremonial occasions, etc.

Concentrated deference actions have by no means disappeared but they have become less elaborate and with their diminished elaboration they have been abbreviated. They have become less substantial and less separate from other actions. Ceremonial deference and formalized etiquette have diminished in magnitude and frequency.

The decline in the power of aristocracies and the diminution of the number of monarchies have been accompanied by a reduction in the amount or proportion of ceremonial deference in societies. Modes of spoken and written address have come to bespeak a more homogeneous distribution of deference throughout societies and in doing so they have moved towards simpler, briefer forms. The movement is not however all one way; the strata which previously were treated with the minimum of deference or indeed with negative deference have now begun to receive an enhanced deference although in the simplified and shorter forms of a less ritualized society.

The inherited rituals of deference tended largely to be concerned with the relations of superiors and inferiors. As an equalitarian outlook became more prominent, the rituals of deference fell into the same discredit as relationships which they expressed. It is however an open question whether equality or approximate equality is antithetical to rituals of deference. What seems fairly certain is that the relationships of equals can and do at present contain considerable elements of attenuated deference and can indeed not dispense with them.

Nonetheless, it would be wrong to fail to acknowledge that contemporary societies are less oriented towards their centres with respect to deference than their ancestors of a century ago. It is not merely on account of the decline of aristocracy and monarchy. These are only instances of a more general phenomenon, namely the diminution of the ruling classes in the various countries. When élites were smaller, educational opportunity more restricted and the kinship tie more respected than they are nowadays, the various sectors of the centre—the political, administrative, ecclesiastical, cultural and military élites—and to some extent the economic élite—were closer to each other through common origins, common institutional experiences, a shared conviviality and the linkage of kinship than they are now when the obligations of kinship are less observed in recruitment to the élite, when specialization has gone further and numbers greatly increased. One of the consequences of this pluralization of the élites is that their model is less imposing. Each sector is taken for what it is and, except for the very pinnacle of the head of state and the head of the government, the sense of difference in worth is felt to be less great than it once was.

THE DISTRIBUTION OF DEFERENCE

It has long been characteristic of the study of deference and of the deference-positions (status) which it helps to produce to ascribe to them a distribution similar in important respects to the distribution of entitlements such as occupational roles and power, income, wealth, styles of life, levels of educational attainment, etc. The entitlements are all relatively 'substantial' things which are not matters of opinion but rather 'objective', more or less quantifiable, conditions or attributes and as such capable of being ranged in a univalent and continuous distribution. Every individual has one occupation or another at any given period in time or for a specifiable duration; every individual has—if it could be measured—such and such an average amount of power over a specifiable time period. Every individual has some style of life, certain components of which at least are enduring and observable—and he either possesses them or does not possess them. There are of course cases of persons having two widely different kinds of occupational roles within the same limited time period ('moonlighting'), of persons having widely divergent incomes within a given period, but these and other anomalies can quite easily be resolved by specifiable procedures for the collection of data and for their statistical treatment and presentation.

Present-day sociological notions of deference (status, esteem, prestige, honour, etc.) grew up in association with the 'objective'[1] conception of social stratification. For reasons of convenience in research and also

---

[1] The 'objective' conception concerned itself with the relatively substantial entitlements, the 'subjective' with the 'opinion'-like elements.

because common usage practised a system of classification into 'middle', 'upper', 'lower',[2] etc., classes, research workers and theorists attempted to construct a composite index which would amalgamate the positions of each individual in a number of distributions (in particular, the distributions of occupational role and education) into some variant of the three-class distribution. The resultant was called 'social-economic status' (sometimes, 'socio-economic status').

The 'subjective' conception of social stratification appreciated the 'opinion'-like character of deference but for reasons of convenience in research procedure and because of the traditional mode of discourse concerning social stratification, the 'subjective factor' itself tended to be 'substantialized' and it too was regarded as capable of being ranged in an univalent distribution.[2] Sometimes as in the Edwards classification in the United States or in the Registrar-General's classification in the United Kingdom, this 'subjective factor' impressionistically assessed by the research worker was amalgamated with the 'objective factors' in arriving at a single indicator of 'status'. Status was taken to mean a total status, which included both deference-position and entitlements, constructed by an external observer (not a participant in the system). But this conception has not found sufferance because it is patently unsatisfactory. Deference-position—or esteem, prestige or status—does belong to a different order of events in comparison with events like occupational distribution, income and wealth distribution, etc. It belongs to the realm of values; it is the outcome of evaluative judgments regarding positions in the distributions of 'objective' characteristics.

The improvement of techniques of field work in community studies and sample surveys has rendered it possible to collect data, relatively systematically, about these evaluations and to assign to each person in a small community or to each occupation on a list a single position in a distribution. Research technique has served to obscure a fundamental conceptual error. As a result, since each person possessed a status (or deference-position), they could be ranged in a single distribution. Such a distribution could occur, however, only under certain conditions. The

---

[1] The prevalence of the trichotomous classification and variations on it is probably of Aristotelian origin. There is no obvious reason why reflection on experience and observation alone should have resulted in three classes. This might well be a case where nature has copied art.

[2] It is quite possible that this pattern of thought which emerged in the nineteenth century was deeply influenced by the conception of social class of the nineteenth-century critics of the *ancien régime* and of the bourgeois social order which succeeded it. In the *ancien régime* the most powerful ranks were designated by legally guaranteed titles which entered into the consciousness of their bearers and those who associated with or considered them. These designations were not 'material' or 'objective'. They did not belong to the 'substructure' of society. They were therefore 'subjective' but they were also unambiguous. They could be treated in the same way as 'objective' characteristics. By extension, the same procedure could be applied to the other strata.

conditions include (*a*) an evaluative consensus throughout the society regarding the criteria in accordance with which deference is allocated; (*b*) cognitive consensus throughout the society regarding the characteristics of each position in each distribution and regarding the shape of the distributions of entitlements; (*c*) consensus throughout the society regarding the weights to be assigned to the various categories of deference-entitling properties;[1] (*d*) equal attention to and equal differentiation by each member of the society of strata which are adjacent to his own and those which are remote from it;[2] (*e*) equal salience of deference judgments throughout the society; (*f*) univalence of all deference judgments.

Were these conditions to obtain, then the distribution of deference-positions in such a society might well have the form which the distributions of 'objective' entitlements possess. There are, however, numerous reasons why the distribution of deference-positions or status does not have this form. Some of these reasons are as follows: (*a*) Some consensus concerning the criteria for the assessment of entitlements might well exist but like any consensus it is bound to be incomplete. Furthermore criteria are so ambiguously apprehended that any existent consensus actually covers a wide variety of beliefs about the content of the criteria. (*b*) Cognitive consensus throughout the society regarding the properties of entitlements and the shape of their distributions is rather unlikely because of the widespread and unequal ignorance about such matters as the occupational roles, incomes, educational attainments of individuals and strata. (*c*) The weighting of the various criteria is not only ambiguous, it is likely to vary from stratum to stratum depending on the deference position of the various strata and their positions on the various distributions; it is likely that each stratum will give a heavier weight to that distribution on which it stands more highly or on which it has a greater chance of improving its position or protecting it from 'invaders'. (*d*) The perceptions of one's own stratum or of adjacent strata are usually much more differentiated and refined and involve more subsidiary criteria than is the case in their perceptions of remote strata. Thus even if they are compatible with each other there is no identity of the differentiations made by the various strata. (*e*) Some persons are more sensitive to deference than are others and this difference in the salience of deference occurs among strata as well. Some persons think frequently in terms of deference position, other think less frequently in those terms. Accordingly assessments of other human

---

[1] Where these three conditions exist, there would also exist a consensus between the judgment which a person makes of his own deference-position and the judgments which others render about his position.

[2] It also presupposes equal knowledge by all members of the society about all other members.

beings and the self may differ markedly within a given society, among individuals, strata, regions and generations with respect to their tendency to respond deferentially rather than affectionately or matter-of-factly or instrumentally. The arrangement of the members of a society into a stratified distribution as if each of them had a determinate quantity of a homogeneous thing called deference (or status or prestige) does violence to the nature of deference and deference-positions; it further obscures in any case sufficiently opaque reality. The possibility of dissensus in each of the component judgments—cognitive and evaluative—which go to make up a deference-judgment can, of course, be covered by the construction of measures which hide the dispersion of opinions. If all inter-individual disagreements are confined to differences in ranking within a given stratum, the procedure would perhaps be acceptable. But, if 80 per cent of a population place certain persons in stratum I and if 20 per cent place them in stratum II, is it meaningful to say that the persons so judged are in stratum I?

The dissensus which results in inter-individually discordant rankings seriously challenges the validity of procedures which construct univalent deference distributions and then disjoin them into strata. This difficulty would exist even if there were agreement about the location of the boundary lines which allegedly separate one deference stratum from the other. But there is no certainty that there will be consensus on this matter, and the purpose of realistic understanding is not served by assuming that there is such consensus or by constructing measures which impose the appearance of such a consensus on the data.

The conventional procedure of constructing deference distributions has tended to assume a considerable degree of clarity and differentiated-ness in the perception of the distribution of deference-entitling proper-ties through the society. But as a matter of fact perceptions are vague and undifferentiated. Terminologies and classifications, particularly in relatively 'class-unconscious' societies, are not standardized and terms like 'poor', 'working people', 'lower classes', 'ordinary people', etc., are used in senses which the user has not reflected upon and which do not have a definite referent. There is no reason—at least until further research has been done—to think that they are interchangeable with each other although sociologists do treat them as if they are.

If differentiation and specificity are slight in speaking about strata adjacent to one's own, they are even less developed in reference to remoter strata of which the judging person has no direct experience. This does not mean that deference-judgments are not made about these remoter strata; it does mean that such judgments are made with scant knowledge of the extent to which these deference-entitlements actually exist in the persons or strata so judged. The cognitive stratification map becomes vaguer with regard to those areas of the society far from the range of experience of the judging person. This too renders cognitive consensus impossible even if evaluative criteria were identical. What one judge looking at his own immediate stratification environment sees as highly differentiated, another who views it from a distance sees as homogeneous. Thus every sector of the stratification system is highly differentiated but only to those who are living in the midst of that sector.[1]

Up to this point I have cast doubt on the conventional treatments of the distribution of deference positions by referring to the diverse sorts of dissensus among individuals, strata, regional cultures, etc. But I wrote as if each of these agents of judgment spoke with a single voice. There is some justification for this since there *is* a tendency in many societies to regard the deference system as something objective, as *sui generis*, as existing outside the judging persons and independently of their own evaluations and appreciations of persons and strata. This tendency to 'objectivize' the distribution of deference is in part a product of the perception of the deference judgments of other persons in one's own society. But it also represents a tendency to believe in the 'objectivity', the 'givenness' of deference stratification which is a product of a tendency to believe that in addition to our own tastes and dispositions there is a realm of normative being which exists independently of those tastes and values.

But alongside of this tendency to believe in an 'objective' order of worthiness, there is a widespread alienation from that order and the acceptance and alienation exist very often in the same persons. This ambivalence is very difficult to apprehend by present-day techniques of research and it is even more difficult to deal with it systematically—at least for the present. It exists nonetheless and it is apt to become stronger as society becomes more differentiated and as the 'ruling class' in the sense of a set of persons intimately interrelated through kinship, common institutional experiences and long personal friendships, filling most of the positions at the top of the various distributions, gives way before a less unitary and therefore less imposing élite.

There is nothing pathological about this ambivalence. Submission to the ascendancy of the centre and to the standards which affirm it is painful because the indignity of inferiority is painful. The society which focuses on the centre imposes such indignity on the periphery. The more highly integrated a society ecologically, the greater will be the strain on the periphery, and the less imposing the élite at the centre, the more likely the emergence of the negative side of the ambivalence. The impli-

---

[1] The question arises therefore whether a distribution of deference positions incorporates the perceptions and categorizations which are applied to one's own and adjacent strata or those which are applied to remote ones. Whichever alternative is followed, the factitious character of the distribution so constructed is evident.

cations of this ambivalent attitude are far-reaching and they cannot be gone into here. Let it suffice to say the presently prevailing methods of describing deference distributions cannot accommodate these simple facts. Yet without these simple facts of ambivalence and alienation in the stratification system, how can class conflict and movements for reform by the re-allocation of deference and its entitlements be dealt with? And what is one to make of the anti-authoritarianism and antinomianism which has been a fluctuatingly frequent phenomenon of modern societies? How does this fit into a picture which portrays deference positions as univalently and consensually distributed?

Finally, I should like to conclude these reflections on the problems of deference distribution with some observations on equality. In general, the prevailing techniques for representing deference distributions proceed with a fixed number of strata or by means of scales which rank occupations or persons on a continuum running from o to 100. Both procedures assume a constant distance between the extremes and between the intervals or strata. This does not however seem to accord with the realities of the movement of modern societies towards a higher degree of equality of deference than was to be found earlier.

The range of deference-distribution probably varies among societies. Some are more equalitarian than others. In what does this equalitarianism consist apart from increased opportunities or life-chances for peripheral strata? Does it not consist in an appreciation of the greater worthiness of the peripheral strata—a judgment shared to some extent throughout their society. It is indeed a matter of opinion but it is an opinion of profound significance for the stratification system. I cannot go into the causes of this development;[1] I wish here only to call attention to its relevance to any realistic description of deference systems.

DEFERENCE INSTITUTIONS AND DEFERENCE SYSTEMS

Whereas most of the things valued by men become the explicit foci of elaborate institutional systems concerned with their production, acquisition, protection, maintenance, control and allocation, the same cannot be asserted of deference. Unlike economic or military or political or ecclesiastical institutions, deference institutions are marginal to the valued objects which they seek to affect. There is a College of Heralds, there are chiefs of protocol in departments of foreign affairs, there are *Who's Who's* and *Social Registers*, authors and publishers of books on deportment and on modes of address, there are advisers to prime

---

[1] I have attempted to explain the causes of this movement towards the narrowing of the range of dispersion of deference-positions in 'The Theory of Mass Society', *Diogenes*, 39 (1962), pp. 45–66.

ministers and presidents on the award of honours, there is an *Almanach de Gotha*, a great many states have a system of honours and many have had systems of titles and orders. Armies award medals and universities award earned and honorary degrees. Armies have titles of rank as do universities. Civil services too have ranks and designations which denote differences and ranks of authority but which are also titles of deference. Many of those institutions have handbooks which specify orders of precedence. All of these institutional arrangements confer or confirm deference; they seek to express deference, to create and legitimate claims to deference, to specify who should receive it and to entitle particular persons in a way which objectifies their claims to deference. Only a few of these institutions have sought explicitly to determine a 'generalized' deference position, namely those who sought to control and guarantee membership in nobilities or aristocracies. Others awarded deference for rather specific qualifications and although in many of these cases the deference was generalized, in others it remained an indicator of a quite specific achievement and thereby attained scarcely any measure of generalization. But at best, they have touched only a small part of the societies in which they have functioned and although they intensify and strengthen the deference system they cannot be said to create it or to manage it.

The deference system of a society extends throughout the length and breadth of that society. Everybody falls within it, yet very few of those have their deference positions determined by the deference-conferring and deference-confirming institutions. The actual really functioning deference system of a society envelops the deference institutions and takes them into account but it is not predominantly determined by them.

Most of the deference-behaviour—the behaviour which expresses deference—occurs in the face-to-face interaction of individuals and very few of those who receive some allocation of deference have any titles or medals. The deference which they receive is received from other persons who respond not to titles or honours of which they have heard or emblems of which they see on the garments of the persons deferred to, but to the entitling properties which they believe are possessed by the person to whom deference is given. Titles and medals might be taken into account and even when the title is used in full and correctly, the use of the title in addressing the person deferred to is at most only a part of the deference expressed. The title is thought to stand for something more than itself, for kinship connections, acknowledgment by the sovereign or occupational role and these too are not ultimate; they are evocative of other characteristics, of positions on various distributions.

The deference granted is as I have said earlier expressed in overtones of speech and action. Much of it is expressed in relations of authority and it appears together with commands and acts of obedience, with the giving of counsel and the taking of counsel, in the interplay of authorities and subjects, colleagues and neighbours performing the actions called for by authority, collegiality and neighbourliness. It is far more subtle and richer than the prescriptions for the ritual manifestations of deference and it is also often more impoverished. Being a duke or a professor or a colonel constitutes only one element—a quite considerable element —in the generalized deference which the incumbents of those ranks and the bearers of those titles receive. Those who associate with them and who defer to them respond to other things about them as well as to their ranks and titles. The excellence of their performance past and current, the power which they actually exercise or have exercised, the level of culture and their style of life, insofar as these can be perceived or imagined or are already known from previous experiences and from other sources, enter into the determination of the deference granted and expected.

Deference institutions are more important in some types of societies and in some strata than in others. In societies in which there is a sharp disjunction between centre and periphery, they will have more influence than in societies in which the periphery has expanded inwardly and overwhelmed the centre.

Deference institutions are especially important at or near the centre of society although ordinarily it is not the intention of those who manage them to confine their influence to that zone. But because deference is more intense in face-to-face relationships and direct interaction than it is in remote relationships, there is a tendency for deference systems to become dispersed in a particular way. Deference systems tend to become territorially dispersed into local systems which are more differentiated to those who participate in them than is the national system. I do not mean to say that the several systems ranging from local to national are in conflict with each other. Indeed they can be quite consensual and the local usually could not be constituted without reference to persons, roles and symbols of the centre. In the various zones and sectors of the periphery where the centre is more remote, the imagery of the centre still enters markedly into the deference system and local differentiations are often simply refined applications of perceptions and evaluations which have the centre as their point of reference. Thus, for example, local deference judgments will make more subtle internal distinctions about occupational role and authority, income and style of life than would judgments made from a distant point either peripheral or central. Still the distinctions will refer to distances from some standard which enjoys its highest fulfilment at the centre. It seems unlikely that centre-blindness can ever be complete in any society.

Nevertheless, the various systems do to some extent have lives of their own. The local deference system is probably more continuously or more frequently in operation than the national system—although as national societies become more integrated and increasingly incorporate with local and regional societies, the national deference system becomes more frequently and more intensely active.

In all societies, the deference system is at its most intense and most continuous at the centre. The high concentrations of power and wealth, the elaborateness of the style of life, all testify to this and call it forth. It is at the centre that deference institutions function and this gives an added focus and stimulus to deference behaviour. The centre adds the vividness of a local deference system to the massive deference-evoking powers of centrality. Within each local or regional deference system, there are some persons who are more sensitive than others to the centre and they infuse into the local system some awareness of and sensitivity to the centre.

At some times and at others, individuals whose preoccupations are mainly with the local deference systems—insofar as they are at all concerned with deference—place themselves on the macro-social deference map. This self-location and the perception that others are also locating themselves is the precondition of a sense of affinity among those who place themselves macro-socially on approximately the same position in the distribution of deference. The placement of others is made of course on the basis of fragmentary evidence about occupational role, style of life, or elements of these and the sense of affinity is loose, the self-location very vague, very inarticulated and very approximate. In this way deference (or status) strata are constituted. They have no clear boundaries and membership cannot be certified or specified. It is largely a matter of sensing one's membership and being regarded by others as a member. Those one 'knows' are usually members, and beyond them the domain spreads out indefinitely and anonymously in accordance with vague cognitive stratification maps and an inchoate image of the 'average man'; within each stratum, an 'average man' possesses the proper combination of positions on the distribution of significant deference-entitlements.

Thus the formation of deference-strata is a process of the mutual assimilation of local deference systems into a national deference system. It is through class consciousness that deference-strata are formed.

In the course of its self-constitution a deference stratum also defines in a much vaguer way the other deference strata of its society. It draws boundary lines but, except for those it draws about itself, the boundaries are matters of minor significance. Boundary lines are of importance only or mainly to those who are affected by the location of the boundary, i.e. those who live close to it on one side or the other. The location of a line of division in the distribution of deference is regarded as important primarily by those who fear that they themselves are in danger of expulsion or who are refused admission to the company of members of a stratum to whom they regard themselves as equal or to whom they wish to be equal and whose company they regard as more desirable than the one to which they would otherwise be confined. The members of any deference stratum are likely to be ignorant about the location of deference stratum boundaries which are remote from them and if they are not ignorant, they are indifferent.

The various deference strata of local deference systems are in contact with each other through occasional face-to-face contacts. They are present in each others' imaginations and this deferential presence enters into all sorts of non-deferential actions of exchange, conflict and authority.

In national deference systems too the different strata are in contact with each other, not very much through face-to-face contact but through their presence in each other's imagination. This presence carries with it the awareness of one's distance from the centre and it entails some acceptance of the centrality of the centre and some acceptance of the greater dignity of the centre. It is an implicit belief that the centre embodies and enacts standards which are important in the assessment of oneself and one's own stratum.

In some sense, the centre 'is' the standard which is derived from the perception, correct or incorrect, of its conduct and bearing. These remote persons and strata which form the centre might be deferred to, or condemned in speech, and the pattern of their conduct, bearing, outlook, etc., might be emulated or avoided. An 'objective existence' is attributed to the rank ordering from centrality to peripherality of the other strata and within this rank ordering one's own stratum is located. The ontological, non-empirical reality which is attributed to position in the distribution of deference makes it different from 'mere' evaluation and sometimes even antithetical to it.

On a much more earthly level, contacts between deference strata occur and in many forms—particularly through the division of labour and its coordination through the market and within corporate bodies and in the struggle for political power. This does not mean that the strata encounter each other in corporately organized forms[1] or that,

---

[1] Corporate organizations, membership in which is determined by a sense of affinity of deference positions and of positions in other distributions, seldom enlist the active membership of all the members of the stratum or even of all the adult male members of the stratum. Those who are not members of the corporate body are not, however, to be regarded as completely devoid of the sense of affinity with other members of their stratum. 'Class consciousness' in this sense is very widespread but it is a long step from this type of 'class consciousness' to the aggressively alienated class consciousness which Marxist doctrine predicted would spread throughout the class of manual workers in industry and Marxist agitation has sought to cultivate.

when there is interstratum contact in the encounter of corporate bodies, these bodies include all or most members of their respective strata. Much of this inter-stratum contact takes place through intermediaries who act as agents and who receive a deference which is a response both to their own deference-entitling properties and those of their principals. Those who act on behalf of these corporate bodies do so in a state of belief that they are 'representing' the deference-stratum to which they belong or feel akin.

A society can then have a deference system of relatively self-distinguishing and self-constituting deference strata, with the strata being in various kinds of relationship with each other. Such a situation is entirely compatible with the absence of the type of objective deference distribution which we rejected in the foregoing section. Each of the deference strata possesses in a vague form an image of a society-wide deference distribution but these images cannot be correct in the sense of corresponding to an objective deference distribution, which might or might not actually exist.

DIGRESSION ON PLURAL SOCIETIES

I have emphasized the importance of the self-constitutive character of the classes which make up a system of deference stratification. I have also emphasized the unreality of the construction of status distributions on which sociologists have expended so much effort and at the same time I have also stressed the elements of integration of the deference strata into a single system focused on the centre of society. Some writers contend that the deference system and the associated stratification systems of what are called plural societies are incompatible with this mode of analysis. By a plural society, they mean one in which various ethnic groups are so segregated from each other that they form societies separate and distinct from each other. Yet they do not go so far as to say that the various constituent societies are totally independent of each other; they acknowledge that they are integrated into a single economy and that they live under a single political authority. In that sense the constituent societies of a plural society are parts of a single society.

The problem which this poses for the study of deference systems is well worth consideration. What we find is that the ethnic entitlement is regarded in these societies, particularly by the more powerful, life chances controlling section of the dominant ethnic group, as so absolutely crucial, that it is made into such a salient criterion of deference that those whose deference-positions are affected by it are included into broad deference strata in comparison with which all other deference-entitlements are of secondary importance. These other deference-entitlements exist and they do determine differences in the allocation of deference but they are only capable of generating differences within each of the major ethnically determined deference strata. Each ethnically determined deference stratum is internally differentiated in accordance with the distribution of deference-entitlements within it. Each approximates a completely self-contained deference system but it does not become completely self-contained. It fails to do so because despite its highly segregated pluralism the society does have a centre and this centre constitutes a focus of each of the partially separate deference systems. The latter bear some resemblance to the deference systems of whole societies because of the differentiation of occupational roles within each of the ethnic sectors but the occupational structure of each sector is not the complete occupational structure of the total society. That total occupational structure is distributed between the ethnic sectors and there is indeed some overlap between them. It is because of these points of overlap—between the bottom of the super-ordinate deference stratum and the peak of the subordinate deference stratum—that conflicts arise. These conflicts could only arise because the sectors or strata are parts of a peculiarly integrated single deference system.

DEFERENCE SYSTEMS AND STRATIFICATION SYSTEMS

When it is not treated as an unreal, conceptually constructed amalgam of a number of positions on a variety of distributions, deference has often been treated as an epiphenomenon. It is often considered as having relatively little weight in the determination of conduct—apart from the choice of companions in conviviality or in the motivation of emulatory conduct. Yet it is deference which is responsible for the formation of strata or classes.

Deference is, as a result of its properties of a generalization, the crucial link in the stratification system. Without the intervention of considerations of deference position, the various very differentiated inequalities in the distribution of any particular facility or reward would not be grouped into a relatively small number of vaguely bounded strata. The very idea of an equivalence among positions in different distributions could not be realized if there were no generalization to cut across them.

By a stratification system, I mean a plurality of strata within a single society with some sense of their internal identity, of the internal similarity and of their external differences vis-à-vis other strata. The stratification system is constituted by strata which are formed by persons who have approximately similar positions on a variety of separate distributions. This approximate similarity of positions is a precondition of the sense of affinity—because it strengthens the sense of identity of the self from which the sense of affinity of many selves is formed. If each person were randomly heterogeneous in his cluster of positions the likelihood of identity and therewith of affinity would be much less than it is in fact.

The sense of identity is a vague perception of self and other and it refers to some pervasive qualities of those so identified. These qualities by which strata identify themselves and others are frequently referred to by a shorthand terminology such as 'wealth' or 'poverty' or 'rulers' or 'people' or 'workers' or 'bosses'. These terms refer to positions on particular distributions such as wealth and income, power and occupational role. Yet these terms have for those who use them a significance beyond the limited descriptive sense in which they are used. Each term stands for a position on each of a number of distributions and implies that positions in the various distributions are correlated and connected with each other. Those who are 'workers' are also 'poor' or in any case relatively low in wealth and income distribution. Those who are 'bosses' are also 'rich' or at least higher in the wealth and income distributions and they usually have more political power. Those who are 'well off' have more education and more authority through their occupational roles and through political participation.

The connections between the positions of an individual on the different distributions are of two sorts. One is the connection through 'life chances'. 'Life chances' are opportunities to enter into a higher position on any distribution from a lower position on that distribution or on several distributions. 'Life chances' are determined by the power of income, by personal, civil and kinship relationships and by occupational role and level of education. Any one of these can have a determinative influence on the allocation of 'life chances', i.e. on the opportunity to ascend on that distribution or in others.

A 'life chance' which arises from position on a particular distribution also affects chances for maintaining or acquiring 'life chances' for positions on other distributions. Income permits education to be purchased; the acquisition of education increases the probability of higher deference and higher income; higher education increases the probability of greater political influence; increased political influences increase the likelihood of a greater access to financial resources.

There is a widely experienced aspiration to bring positions on a series of distributions into an appropriate correspondence with each other. Each position provides resources for affecting positions on other distributions. Why should this be so? Why should there be thought to be an 'appropriate' relationship among positions, an equilibrium which should be striven for? Why, when a person has much political power does he not use his political resources exclusively to enhance or maintain his political power instead of expending them on bringing his style of life or the education of his children 'into line' with his political position?

(Of course, one reply to this question is to say that it is generally believed that improving positions on the non-political distributions is a necessary condition for maintenance or improvement of the position on the political distribution. But is not this very belief itself evidence of the belief in an appropriate pattern of positions which is thus a precondition for the more 'costly' political support necessary for further improvement in political position? Another reply to the question is that most human beings, given the opportunity, will strive to enhance their position in any particular distribution and that being in a better position on one distribution provides resources for betterment on others. But although there is some truth in this assertion it does not confront the fact that there is a sense of an appropriate pattern of positions on different distributions.)

The belief that it is appropriate that the several positions on the various distributions should be consonant or harmonious with each other is attributable to the belief that they each express a common, essential quality. An 'inappropriate' pattern of positions bears witness to the absence of the essential quality. There is something 'unseemly' or 'eccentric' or 'perverse' or 'unfortunate' about the individual or family whose positions are scattered at a variety of unequal points on the several distributions.

This common or essential quality is the charismatic quality which requires diffuse and pervasive expression in the various distributions. The cognitive element in an act of deference is the perception of the presence of this quality and its generalization beyond any specific manifestation in action is an acknowledgment of the apparent possession of charismatic quality by the person deferred to. The demand for deference is the demand for a diffuse acknowledgment of the diffuse charisma which is possessed in some measure by the self and which is above all in its earthly form resident in the centres of society. Self respect—deference to the self—is an acknowledgment of one's own charisma and of one's satisfactory proximity to the centre in an essential respect.

The cognitive and evaluative map of a stratification system is a differential allocation of deference to a series of aggregates of persons— for the most part anonymous—in accordance with their proximity to the centre and thus in accordance with the magnitude of their presumed charisma. The stratification system of a society is the product of imagination working on the hard facts of the unequal allocation of scarce resources and rewards. The charisma is imaginary but it has the effect of being 'real' since it is so widely believed in as 'real'. Deference which is basically a response to charisma is only a matter of opinion but it is an opinion with profound motivation and a response to profound needs in the grantor and the recipient of deference.

CHAPTER 29

Some Conditions of Obedience and Disobedience to Authority

STANLEY MILGRAM

THE SITUATION in which one agent commands another to hurt a third turns up time and again as a significant theme in human relations. It is powerfully expressed in the story of Abraham, who is commanded by God to kill his son. It is no accident that Kierkegaard, seeking to orient his thought to the central themes of human experience, chose Abraham's conflict as the springboard to his philosophy.

War too moves forward on the triad of an authority which commands a person to destroy the enemy, and perhaps all organ-

ized hostility may be viewed as a theme and variation on the three elements of authority, executant, and victim.[1] We describe an experimental program, recently concluded at Yale University, in which a particular expression of this conflict is studied by experimental means.

In its most general form the problem may be defined thus: if X tells Y to hurt Z, under what conditions will Y carry out the command of X and under what conditions will he refuse. In the more limited form possible in laboratory research, the question becomes: if an experimenter tells

STANLEY MILGRAM, Ph.D.: Professor of Psychology, Graduate Center of the City University of New York, completed the study described here while an assistant professor of psychology at Yale University.

This research was supported by two grants from the National Science Foundation: NSF G-17916 and NSF G-24152. Exploratory studies carried out in 1960 were financed by a grant from the Higgins Funds of Yale University. The author is grateful to John T. Williams, James J. McDonough, and Emil Elges for the important part they played in the project. Thanks are due also to Alan Elms, James Miller, Taketo Murata, and Stephen Stier for their aid as graduate assistants. The author's wife, Sasha, performed many valuable services. Finally, a profound debt is owed to the many persons in New Haven and Bridgeport who served as subjects.

[1] Consider, for example, J. P. Scott's analysis of war in his monograph on aggression:
'. . . while the actions of key individuals in a war may be explained in terms of direct stimulation to aggression, vast numbers of other people are involved simply by being part of an organized society.
'. . . For example, at the beginning of World War I an Austrian archduke was assassinated in Sarajevo. A few days later soldiers from all over Europe were marching toward each other, not because they were stimulated by the archduke's misfortune, but because they had been trained to obey orders.' (Slightly rearranged from Scott (1958), *Aggression*, p. 103.)

a subject to hurt another person, under what conditions will the subject go along with this instruction, and under what conditions will he refuse to obey. The laboratory problem is not so much a dilution of the general statement as one concrete expression of the many particular forms this question may assume.

One aim of the research was to study behavior in a strong situation of deep consequence to the participants, for the psychological forces operative in powerful and lifelike forms of the conflict may not be brought into play under diluted conditions.

This approach meant, first, that we had a special obligation to protect the welfare and dignity of the persons who took part in the study; subjects were, of necessity, placed in a difficult predicament, and steps had to be taken to ensure their wellbeing before they were discharged from the laboratory. Toward this end, a careful, post-experimental treatment was devised and has been carried through for subjects in all conditions.[2]

Terminology. If Y follows the command of X we shall say that he has obeyed X; if he fails to carry out the command of X, we shall say that he has disobeyed X. The terms to obey and to disobey, as used here, refer to the subject's overt action only, and carry no implication for the motive or experiential states accompanying the action.[3]

To be sure, the everyday use of the word obedience is not entirely free from complexities. It refers to action within widely varying situations, and connotes diverse

---

[2] It consisted of an extended discussion with the experimenter and, of equal importance, a friendly reconciliation with the victim. It is made clear that the victim did not receive painful electric shocks. After the completion of the experimental series, subjects were sent a detailed report of the results and full purposes of the experimental program. A formal assessment of this procedure points to its overall effectiveness. Of the subjects, 83.7 per cent indicated that they were glad to have taken part in the study; 15.1 per cent reported neutral feelings; and 1.3 per cent stated that they were sorry to have participated. A large number of subjects spontaneously requested that they be used in further experimentation. Four-fifths of the subjects felt that more experiments of this sort should be carried out, and 74 per cent indicated that they had learned something of personal importance as a result of being in the study. Furthermore, a university psychiatrist, experienced in outpatient treatment, interviewed a sample of experimental subjects with the aim of uncovering possible injurious effects resulting from participation. No such effects were in evidence. Indeed, subjects typically felt that their participation was instructive and enriching. A more detailed discussion of this question can be found in Milgram (1964).

[3] To obey and to disobey are not the only terms one could use in describing the critical action of Y. One could say that Y is cooperating with X, or displays conformity with regard to X's commands. However, cooperation suggests that X agrees with Y's ends, and understands the relationship between his own behavior and the attainment of those ends. (But the experimental procedure, and, in particular, the experimenter's command that the subject shock the victim even in the absence of a response from the victim, preclude such understanding.) Moreover, cooperation implies status parity for the co-acting agents, and neglects the asymmetrical, dominance-subordination element prominent in the laboratory relationship between experimenter and subject. Conformity has been used in other important contexts in social psychology, and most frequently refers to imitating the judgments or actions of others when no explicit requirement for imitation has been made. Furthermore, in the present study there are two sources of social pressure: pressure from the experimenter issuing the commands, and pressure from the victim to stop the punishment. It is the pitting of a common man (the victim) against an authority (the experimenter) that is the distinctive feature of the conflict. At a point in the experiment the victim demands that he be let free. The experimenter insists that the subject continue to administer shocks. Which act of the subject can be interpreted as conformity? The subject may conform to the wishes of his peer or to the wishes of the experimenter, and conformity in one direction means the absence of conformity in the other. Thus the word has no useful reference in this setting, for the dual and conflicting social pressures cancel out its meaning.

In the final analysis, the linguistic symbol representing the subject's action must take its meaning from the concrete context in which that action occurs; and there is probably no word in everyday language that covers the experimental situation exactly, without omissions or irrelevant connotations. It is partly for convenience, therefore, that the terms obey and disobey are used to describe the subject's actions. At the same time, our use of the words is highly congruent with dictionary meaning.

motives within those situations: a child's obedience differs from a soldier's obedience, or the love, honor, and *obey* of the marriage vow. However, a consistent behavioral relationship is indicated in most uses of the term: in the act of obeying, a person does what another person tells him to do. *Y* obeys *X* if he carries out the prescription for action which *X* has addressed to him; the term suggests, moreover, that some form of dominance-subordination, or hierarchical element, is part of the situation in which the transaction between *X* and *Y* occurs.

A subject who complies with the entire series of experimental commands will be termed an *obedient* subject; one who at any point in the command series defies the experimenter will be called a *disobedient* or *defiant* subject. As used in this report, the terms refer only to the subject's performance in the experiment, and do not necessarily imply a general personality disposition to submit to or reject authority.

Subject Population. The subjects used in all experimental conditions were male adults, residing in the greater New Haven and Bridgeport areas, aged 20 to 50 years, and engaged in a wide variety of occupations. Each experimental condition described in this report employed 40 fresh subjects and was carefully balanced for age and occupational types. The occupational composition for each experiment was: workers, skilled and unskilled: 40 per cent; white collar, sales, business: 40 per cent; professionals: 20 per cent. The occupations were intersected with three age categories (subjects in 20s, 30s, and 40s, assigned to each condition in the proportions of 20, 40, and 40 per cent respectively).

The General Laboratory Procedure. The focus of the study concerns the amount of electric shock a subject is willing to administer to another person when ordered by an experimenter to give the 'victim' in-

> *"The focus of the study concerns the amount of electric shock a subject is willing to administer to another person when ordered by an experimenter to give the 'victim' increasingly severe punishment."*

creasingly more severe punishment. The act of administering shock is set in the context of a learning experiment, ostensibly designed to study the effect of punishment on memory. Aside from the experimenter, one naive subject and one accomplice perform in each session. On arrival each subject is paid $4.50. After a general talk by the experimenter, telling how little scientists know about the effect of punishment on memory, subjects are informed that one member of the pair will serve as teacher and one as learner. A rigged drawing is held so that the naive subject is always the teacher, and the accomplice becomes the learner. The learner is taken to an adjacent room and strapped into an 'electric chair.' [4]

The naive subject is told that it is his task to teach the learner a list of paired associates, to test him on the list, and to administer punishment whenever the learner errs in the test. Punishment takes the form of electric shock, delivered to the

---

[4] A more detailed account of the laboratory procedure can be found in Milgram (1963). A similar and independently evolved experimental procedure, employing a shock generator, victim, and learning task, was reported by Buss (1961). Buss used the technique for studying aggression, not obedience, and did not make use of the fundamental measure employed in the present study: break-off points. His investigation promises to be a useful complement to the present research.

learner by means of a shock generator controlled by the naive subject. The teacher is instructed to increase the intensity of electric shock one step on the generator on each error. The learner, according to plan, provides many wrong answers, so that before long the naive subject must give him the strongest shock on the generator. Increases in shock level are met by increasingly insistent demands from the learner that the experiment be stopped because of the growing discomfort to him. However, in clear terms the experimenter orders the teacher to continue with the procedure in disregard of the learner's protests. *Thus, the naive subject must resolve a conflict between two mutually incompatible demands from the social field. He may continue to follow the orders of the experimenter and shock the learner with increasing severity, or he may refuse to follow the orders of the experimenter and heed the learner's pleas. The experimenter's authority operates not in a free field, but against ever-mounting countervailing pressures from the person being punished.*

A few technical points need to be considered before the findings of the study are described. For the purpose of delivering shock, a simulated shock generator is used, with 30 clearly marked voltage levels that range from 15 to 450 volts (and each activated by one of 30 individual lever switches set in a horizontal line). The naive subject is given a sample shock of 45 volts to convince him of the authenticity of the instrument. The generator bears verbal designations that range from 'Slight Shock' to 'Danger: Severe Shock.'

The responses of the victim are standardized on tape, and each protest is coordinated to a particular voltage level on the shock generator. Starting with 75 volts the learner begins to grunt and moan. At 150 volts he demands to be let out of the experiment. At 180 volts he cries out that he can no longer stand the pain. At 300

volts he refuses to provide any more answers to the memory test, insisting that he is no longer a participant in the experiment and must be freed. In response to this last tactic, the experimenter instructs the naive subject to treat the absence of an answer as equivalent to a wrong answer, and to follow the usual shock procedure. The experimenter reinforces his demand with the statement: 'You have no other choice, you must go on!' (This imperative is used whenever the naive subject tries to break off the experiment.) If the subject refuses to give the next higher level of shock, the experiment is considered at an end. A quantitative value is assigned to the subject's performance based on the maximum intensity shock he administered before breaking off. Thus any subject's score may range from zero (for a subject unwilling to administer the first shock level) to 30 (for a subject who proceeds to the highest voltage level on the board). For any particular subject and for any particular experimental condition the degree to which participants have followed the experimenter's orders may be specified with a numerical value, corresponding to the metric on the shock generator.

This laboratory situation gives us a framework in which to study the subject's reactions to the principal conflict of the experiment. Again, this conflict is between the experimenter's demands that he continue to administer the electric shock, and the learner's demands, which become increasingly more insistent, that the experiment be stopped. The crux of the study is to vary systematically the factors believed to alter the degree of obedience to the experimental commands, to learn under what conditions submission to authority is most probable, and under what conditions defiance is brought to the fore.

Pilot Studies. Pilot studies for the present research were completed in the winter of

1960; they differed from the regular experiments in a few details: for one, the victim was placed behind a silvered glass, with the light balance on the glass such that the victim could be dimly perceived by the subject (Milgram, 1961).

Though essentially qualitative in treatment, these studies pointed to several significant features of the experimental situation. At first no vocal feedback was used from the victim. It was thought that the verbal and voltage designations on the control panel would create sufficient pressure to curtail the subject's obedience. However, this was not the case. In the absence of protests from the learner, virtually all subjects, once commanded, went blithely to the end of the board, seemingly indifferent to the verbal designations ('Extreme Shock' and 'Danger: Severe Shock'). This deprived us of an adequate basis for scaling obedient tendencies. A force had to be introduced that would strengthen the subject's resistance to the experimenter's commands, and reveal individual differences in terms of a distribution of break-off points.

This force took the form of protests from the victim. Initially, mild protests were used, but proved inadequate. Subsequently, more vehement protests were inserted into the experimental procedure. To our consternation, even the strongest protests from the victim did not prevent all subjects from administering the harshest punishment ordered by the experimenter; but the protests did lower the mean maximum shock somewhat and created some spread in the subject's performance; therefore, the victim's cries were standardized on tape and incorporated into the regular experimental procedure.

The situation did more than highlight the technical difficulties of finding a workable experimental procedure: it indicated that subjects would obey authority to a greater extent than we had supposed. It

also pointed to the importance of feedback from the victim in controlling the subject's behavior.

One further aspect of the pilot study was that subjects frequently averted their eyes from the person they were shocking, often turning their heads in an awkward and conspicuous manner. One subject explained: "I didn't want to see the consequences of what I had done." Observers wrote:

> . . . subjects showed a reluctance to look at the victim, whom they could see through the glass in front of them. When this fact was brought to their attention they indicated that it caused them discomfort to see the victim in agony. We note, however, that although the subject refuses to look at the victim, he continues to administer shocks.

This suggested that the salience of the victim may have, in some degree, regulated the subject's performance. If, in obeying the experimenter, the subject found it necessary to avoid scrutiny of the victim, would the converse be true? If the victim were rendered increasingly more salient to the subject, would obedience diminish? The first set of regular experiments was designed to answer this question.

Immediacy of the Victim. This series consisted of four experimental conditions. In each condition the victim was brought 'psychologically' closer to the subject giving him shocks.

In the first condition (Remote Feedback) the victim was placed in another room and could not be heard or seen by the subject, except that, at 300 volts, he pounded on the wall in protest. After 315 volts he no longer answered or was heard from.

The second condition (Voice Feedback) was identical to the first except that voice protests were introduced. As in the first condition the victim was placed in an adjacent room, but his complaints could be heard clearly through a door left slightly ajar, and through the walls of the laboratory.[5]

The third experimental condition (Proximity) was similar to the second, except that

---

[5] It is difficult to convey on the printed page the full tenor of the victim's responses, for we have no adequate notation for vocal intensity, timing, and general qualities of delivery. Yet these features are crucial to producing the effect of an increasingly severe reaction to mounting voltage levels. (They can be communicated fully only by sending interested parties the recorded tapes.) In general terms, however, the victim indicates no discomfort until the 75-volt shock is administered, at which time there is a light grunt in response to the punishment. Similar reactions follow the 90- and 105-volt shocks, and at 120 volts the victim shouts to the experimenter that the shocks are becoming painful. Painful groans are heard on administration of the 135-volt shock, and at 150 volts the victim cries out, 'Experimenter, get me out of here! I won't be in the experiment any more! I refuse to go on!' Cries of this type continue with generally rising intensity, so that at 180 volts the victim cries out, 'I can't stand the pain', and by 270 volts his response to the shock is definitely an agonized scream. Throughout, he insists that he be let out of the experiment. At 300 volts the victim shouts in desperation that he will no longer provide answers to the memory test; and at 315 volts, after a violent scream, he reaffirms with vehemence that he is no longer a participant. From this point on, he provides no answers, but shrieks in agony whenever a shock is administered; this continues through 450 volts. Of course, many subjects will have broken off before this point.

A revised and stronger set of protests was used in all experiments outside the Proximity series. Naturally, new baseline measures were established for all comparisons using the new set of protests.

There is overwhelming evidence that the great majority of subjects, both obedient and defiant, accepted the victims' reactions as genuine. The evidence takes the form of: (a) tension created in the subjects (see discussion of tension); (b) scores on 'estimated pain' scales filled out by subjects immediately after the experiment; (c) subjects' accounts of their feelings in post-experimental interviews; and (d) quantifiable responses to questionnaires distributed to subjects several months after their participation in the experiments. This matter will be treated fully in a forthcoming monograph.

(The procedure in all experimental conditions was to have the naive subject announce the voltage level before administering each shock, so that—independently of the victim's responses—he was continually reminded of delivering punishment of ever-increasing severity.)

---

the victim was now placed in the same room as the subject, and one and a half feet from him. Thus he was visible as well as audible, and voice cues were provided.

The fourth, and final, condition of this series (Touch-Proximity) was identical to the third, with this exception: the victim received a shock only when his hand rested on a shockplate. At the 150-volt level the victim again demanded to be let free and, in this condition, refused to place his hand on the shockplate. The experimenter ordered the naive subject to force the victim's hand onto the plate. Thus obedience in this condition required that the subject have physical contact with the victim in order to give him punishment beyond the 150-volt level.

Forty adult subjects were studied in each condition. The data revealed that obedience was significantly reduced as the victim was rendered more immediate to the subject. The mean maximum shock for the conditions is shown in *Figure 1*.

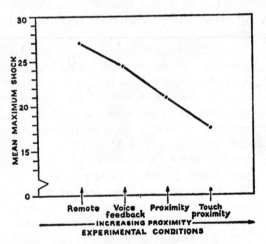

Expressed in terms of the proportion of obedient to defiant subjects, the findings are that 34 per cent of the subjects defied the experimenter in the Remote condition, 37.5 per cent in Voice Feedback, 60 per cent in Proximity, and 70 per cent in Touch-Proximity.

How are we to account for this effect? A first conjecture might be that as the victim was brought closer the subject became more aware of the intensity of his suffering and regulated his behavior accordingly. This makes sense, but our evidence does not support the interpretation. There are no consistent differences in the attributed level of pain across the four conditions (i.e. the amount of pain experienced by the victim as estimated by the subject and expressed on a 14-point scale). But it is easy to speculate about alternative mechanisms:

Empathic cues. In the Remote and to a lesser extent the Voice Feedback condition, the victim's suffering possesses an abstract, remote quality for the subject. He is aware, but only in a conceptual sense, that his actions cause pain to another person; the fact is apprehended, but not felt. The phenomenon is common enough. The bombardier can reasonably suppose that his weapons will inflict suffering and death, yet this knowledge is divested of affect, and does not move him to a felt, emotional response to the suffering resulting from his actions. Similar observations have been made in wartime. It is possible that the visual cues associated with the victim's suffering trigger empathic responses in the subject and provide him with a more complete grasp of the victim's experience. Or it is possible that the empathic responses are themselves unpleasant, possessing drive properties which cause the subject to terminate the arousal situation. Diminishing obedience, then, would be explained by the enrichment of empathic cues in the successive experimental conditions.

Denial and narrowing of the cognitive field. The Remote condition allows a narrowing of the cognitive field so that the victim is put out of mind. The subject no longer considers the act of depressing a lever relevant to moral judgment, for it is no longer associated with the victim's suffering. When the victim is close it is more difficult to exclude him phenomenologically. He necessarily intrudes on the subject's awareness since he is continuously visible. In the Remote conditions his existence and reactions are made known only after the shock has

> "... *obedience was significantly reduced as the victim was rendered more immediate to the subject.*"

been administered. The auditory feedback is sporadic and discontinuous. In the Proximity conditions his inclusion in the immediate visual field renders him a continuously salient element for the subject. The mechanism of denial can no longer be brought into play. One subject in the Remote condition said: 'It's funny how you really begin to forget that there's a guy out there, even though you can hear him. For a long time I just concentrated on pressing the switches and reading the words.'

Reciprocal fields. If in the Proximity condition the subject is in an improved position to observe the victim, the reverse is also true. The actions of the subject now come under proximal scrutiny by the victim. Possibly, it is easier to harm a person when he is unable to observe our actions than when he can see what we are doing. His surveillance of the action directed against him may give rise to shame, or guilt, which may then serve to curtail the action. Many expressions of language refer to the discomfort or inhibitions that arise in face-to-face confrontation. It is often said that it is easier to criticize a man 'behind his back' than to 'attack him to his face'. If we are in the process of lying to a person it is reputedly difficult to 'stare him in the eye'. We 'turn away from others in shame' or in 'embarrassment' and this action serves to reduce our discomfort. The manifest function of allowing the victim of a firing squad to be blindfolded is to make the occasion less stressful for 'him, but it may also serve a latent function of reducing the stress of the executioner. In short, in the Proximity conditions, the subject may sense that he has become more salient in the victim's field of awareness. Possibly he becomes more self-conscious, embarrassed, and inhibited in his punishment of the victim.

Phenomenal unity of act. In the Remote conditions it is more difficult for the subject to gain a sense of *relatedness* between his own actions and the consequences of these actions for the victim. There is a physical and spatial separation of the act and its consequences. The subject depresses a lever in one room, and protests and cries are heard from another. The two events are in correlation, yet they lack a compelling phenomenological unity. The structure of a meaningful act—*I am hurting a man*—breaks down because of the spatial arrangements, in a manner somewhat analogous to the disappearance of phi phenomena when the blinking lights are spaced too far apart. The unity is more fully achieved in the Proximity conditions as the victim is brought closer to the action that causes him pain. It is rendered complete in Touch-Proximity.

Incipient group formation. Placing the victim in another room not only takes him further from the subject, but the subject and the experimenter are drawn relatively closer. There is incipient group formation between the experimenter and the subject, from which the victim is excluded. The wall between the victim and the others deprives him of an intimacy which the experimenter and subject feel. In the Remote condition, the victim is truly an outsider, who stands alone, physically and psychologically.

When the victim is placed close to the subject, it becomes easier to form an alliance with him against the experimenter. Subjects no longer have to face the experimenter alone. They have an ally who is close at hand and eager to collaborate in a revolt against the experimenter. Thus, the changing set of spatial relations leads to a potentially shifting set of alliances over the several experimental conditions.

"When the victim is placed closer to the subject, it becomes easier to form an alliance with him against the experimenter."

Acquired behavior dispositions. It is commonly observed that laboratory mice will rarely fight with their litter mates. Scott (1958) explains this in terms of passive inhibition. He writes: 'By doing nothing under . . . circumstances [the animal] learns to do nothing, and this may be spoken of as passive inhibition . . . this principle has great importance in teaching an individual to be peaceful, for it means that he can learn not to fight simply by not fighting.' Similarly, we may learn not to harm others simply by not harming them in everyday life. Yet this learning occurs in a context of proximal relations with others, and may not be generalized to that situation in which the person is physically removed from us. Or possibly, in the past, aggressive actions against others who were physically close resulted in retaliatory punishment which extinguished the original form of response. In contrast, aggression against others at a distance may have only sporadically led to retaliation. Thus the organism learns that it is safer to be aggressive toward others at a distance, and precarious to be so when the parties are within arm's reach. Through a pattern of rewards and punishments, he acquires a disposition to avoid aggression at close quarters, a disposition which does not extend to harming others at a distance. And this may account for experimental findings in the remote and proximal experiments.

Proximity as a variable in psychological research has received far less attention than it deserves. If men were sessile it would be easy to understand this neglect. But we move about; our spatial relations shift from one situation to the next, and the fact that we are near or remote may have a powerful effect on the psychological processes that mediate our behavior toward others. In the present situation, as the victim is brought closer to the man ordered to give him shocks, increasing numbers of subjects break off the experiment, refusing to obey. The concrete, visible, and proximal presence of the victim acts in an important way to counteract the experimenter's power and to generate disobedience.[6]

[6] Admittedly, the terms *proximity, immediacy,*

Closeness of Authority. If the spatial relationship of the subject and victim is relevant to the degree of obedience, would not the relationship of subject to experimenter also play a part?

There are reasons to feel that, on arrival, the subject is oriented primarily to the experimenter rather than to the victim. He has come to the laboratory to fit into the structure that the experimenter—not the victim—would provide. He has come less to understand his behavior than to *reveal* that behavior to a competent scientist, and he is willing to display himself as the scientist's purposes require. Most subjects seem quite concerned about the appearance they are making before the experimenter, and one could argue that this preoccupation in a relatively new and strange setting makes the subject somewhat insensitive to the triadic nature of the social situation. In other words, the subject is so concerned about the show he is putting on for the experimenter that influences from other parts of the social field do not receive as much weight as they ordinarily would. This overdetermined orientation to the experimenter would account for the relative insensitivity of the subject to the victim, and would also lead us to believe that alterations in the relationship between subject and experimenter would have important consequences for obedience.

In a series of experiments we varied the physical closeness and degree of surveillance

of the experimenter. In one condition the experimenter sat just a few feet away from the subject. In a second condition, after giving initial instructions, the experimenter left the laboratory and gave his orders by telephone; in still a third condition the experimenter was never seen, providing instructions by means of a tape recording activated when the subjects entered the laboratory.

Obedience dropped sharply as the experimenter was physically removed from the laboratory. The number of obedient subjects in the first condition (Experimenter Present) was almost three times as great as in the second, where the experimenter gave his orders by telephone. Twenty-six subjects were fully obedient in the first condition, and only 9 in the second (Chi square obedient *vs.* defiant in the two conditions, 1 d.f.$=14.7$; $p<.001$). Subjects seemed able to take a far stronger stand against the experimenter when they did not have to encounter him face to face, and the experimenter's power over the subject was severely curtailed.[7]

Moreover, when the experimenter was absent, subjects displayed an interesting form of behavior that had not occurred under his surveillance. Though continuing with the experiment, several subjects administered lower shocks than were required and never informed the experimenter of their deviation from the correct procedure. (Unknown to the subjects, shock levels were automatically recorded by an Esterline-Angus event recorder wired directly into the shock generator; the instrument provided us with an objective record of the subjects' performance.) Indeed, in telephone conversations some subjects specifically assured the experimenter that they

---

closeness, and *salience-of-the-victim* are used in a loose sense, and the experiments themselves represent a very coarse treatment of the variable. Further experiments are needed to refine the notion and tease out such diverse factors as spatial distance, visibility, audibility, barrier interposition, etc.

The Proximity and Touch-Proximity experiments were the only conditions where we were unable to use taped feedback from the victim. Instead, the victim was trained to respond in these conditions as he had in Experiment 2 (which employed taped feedback). Some improvement is possible here, for it should be technically feasible to do a proximity series using taped feedback.

---

[7] The third condition also led to significantly lower obedience than this first situation, in which the experimenter was present, but it contains technical difficulties that require extensive discussion.

were raising the shock level according to instruction, whereas in fact they were repeatedly using the lowest shock on the board. This form of behavior is particularly interesting: although these subjects acted in a way that clearly undermined the avowed purposes of the experiment, they found it easier to handle the conflict in this manner than to precipitate an open break with authority.

Other conditions were completed in which the experimenter was absent during the first segment of the experiment, but reappeared at the point that the subject definitely refused to give higher shocks when commanded by telephone. Although he had exhausted his power via telephone, the experimenter could frequently force further obedience when he reappeared in the laboratory.

Experiments in this series show that the physical *presence* of an authority is an important force contributing to the subject's obedience or defiance. Taken together with the first experimental series on the proximity of the victim, it would appear that something akin to fields of force, diminishing in effectiveness with increasing psychological distance from their source, have a controlling effect on the subject's performance. As the victim is brought closer, the subject finds it harder to administer shocks to him. When the victim's position is held constant relative to the subject, and the authority is made more remote, the subject finds it easier to break off the experiment. This effect is substantial in both cases, but manipulation of the experimenter's position yielded the more powerful results. Obedience to destructive commands is highly dependent on the proximal relations between authority and subject.

Tensions. The description of final scores does not fully convey the character of the subjects' performance, and it would be useful to interrupt our reporting of quantitative relationships to remark on the subjects general reaction to the situation.

One might suppose that a subject would simply break off or continue as his conscience and temperament dictated. Yet this is very far from what happened. There were powerful reactions of tension and emotional strain in a substantial proportion of the participants. Persons were observed to sweat, tremble, stutter, bite their lips, and groan as they found themselves increasingly implicated in the experimental conflict. Some sense of the subjects' mood can be gotten from a transcript of their remarks at break-off point. Here are the remarks of two defiant subjects:

> Is he banging? . . . Is he hurt out there? Well, I don't want to be responsible for anything that happens to him. No, I can't go on with it. I don't know whether he's all right or not. I mean he may have a heart condition or something; I wouldn't feel right doing it. He's banging for help. He's evidently in trouble or he wouldn't bang . . . I don't see any sense to this—to knocking him out or something. I just can't see it.
>
> *(Subject refuses to administer shocks)*
> [*Subject 0108*]
>
> The man is banging. He wants to get out . . . I'm sorry. If the man wants to get out I'd just as soon stop . . . I don't want to administer any more [extremely excited] . . . I will gladly refund the check, but I will not harm this man . . . I'm sorry, I will not give him any more if he obviously wants to get out. There is no money in the world that will make me hurt another individual. [*Subject 010X*]

And here is a transcript from an obedient subject. He began the experiment calmly, but became increasingly tense as the experiment proceeded. After administering the 150-volt shock, he began to address the experimenter in agitated tones:

> *150 volts delivered.* You want me to keep going?
> *165 volts delivered.* That guy is hollering in there. There's a lot of them here. He's

liable to have heart condition. You want me to go?

180 volts delivered. He can't stand it! I'm not going to kill that man in there! You hear him hollering? He's hollering. He can't stand it. What if something happens to him? . . . I'm not going to get that man sick in there. He's hollering in there. You know what I mean? I mean I refuse to take responsibility. He's getting hurt in there. He's in there hollering. Too many left here. Geez, if he gets them wrong. There's too many of them left. I mean who is going to take responsibility if anything happens to that gentleman?

[The experimenter accepts responsibility.] All right.

195 volts delivered. You see he's hollering. Hear that. Gee, I don't know. *[The experimenter says: 'The experiment requires that you go on.']*—I know it does, sir, but I mean—hugh—he don't know what he's in for. He's up to 195 volts.

210 volts delivered

225 volts delivered

240 volts delivered. Aw, no. You mean I've got to keep going up with the scale? No sir. I'm not going to kill that man! I'm not going to give him 450 volts! *[The experimenter says: 'The experiment requires that you go on.']*—I know it does, but that man is hollering in there, sir . . .

Despite his numerous, agitated objections, which were constant accompaniments to his actions, the subject unfailingly obeyed the experimenter, proceeding to the highest shock level on the generator. He displayed a curious dissociation between word and action. Although at the verbal level he had resolved not to go on, his actions were fully in accord with the experimenter's commands. This subject did not want to shock the victim, and he found it an extremely disagreeable task, but he was unable to invent a response that would free him from *E*'s authority. Many subjects cannot find the specific verbal formula that would enable them to reject the role assigned to them by the experimenter. Perhaps our culture does not provide adequate models for disobedience.

One puzzling sign of tension was the

"Perhaps our culture does not provide adequate models for disobedience."

regular occurrence of nervous laughing fits. In the first four conditions 71 of the 160 subjects showed definite signs of nervous laughter and smiling. The laughter seemed entirely out of place, even bizarre. Full-blown, uncontrollable seizures were observed for 15 of these subjects. On one occasion we observed a seizure so violently convulsive that it was necessary to call a halt to the experiment. In the post-experimental interviews subjects took pains to point out that they were not sadistic types and that the laughter did not mean they enjoyed shocking the victim.

In the interview following the experiment subjects were asked to indicate on a 14-point scale just how nervous or tense they felt at the point of maximum tension *(Figure 2)*. The scale ranged from 'Not at

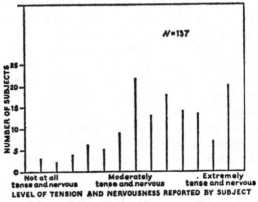

Figure 2 shows the self-reports on 'tension and nervousness' for 137 subjects in the Proximity experiments. Subjects were given a scale with 14 values ranging from 'Not at all tense and nervous' to 'Extremely tense and nervous'. They were instructed: 'Thinking back to that point in the experiment when you felt the most tense and nervous, indicate just how you felt by placing an X at the appropriate point on the scale.' The results are shown in terms of mid-point values.

all tense and nervous' to 'Extremely tense and nervous'. Self-reports of this sort are of limited precision, and at best provide only a rough indication of the subject's emotional response. Still, taking the reports for what they are worth, it can be seen that the distribution of responses spans the entire range of the scale, with the majority of subjects concentrated at the center and upper extreme. A further breakdown showed that obedient subjects reported themselves as having been slightly more tense and nervous than the defiant subjects at the point of maximum tension.

How is the occurrence of tension to be interpreted? First, it points to the presence of conflict. If a tendency to comply with authority were the only psychological force operating in the situation, all subjects would have continued to the end and there would have been no tension. Tension, it is assumed, results from the simultaneous presence of two or more incompatible response tendencies (Miller, 1944). If sympathetic concern for the victim were the exclusive force, all subjects would have calmly defied the experimenter. Instead, there were both obedient and defiant outcomes, frequently accompanied by extreme tension. A conflict develops between the deeply ingrained disposition not to harm others and the equally compelling tendency to obey others who are in authority. The subject is quickly drawn into a dilemma of a deeply dynamic character, and the presence of high tension points to the considerable strength of each of the antagonistic vectors.

Moreover, tension defines the strength of the aversive state from which the subject is unable to escape through disobedience. When a person is uncomfortable, tense, or stressed, he tries to take some action that will allow him to terminate this unpleasant state. Thus tension may serve as a drive that leads to escape behavior. But in the present situation, even where tension is ex-

treme, many subjects are unable to perform the response that will bring about relief. Therefore there must be a competing drive, tendency, or inhibition that precludes activation of the disobedient response. The strength of this inhibiting factor must be of greater magnitude than the stress experienced, else the terminating act would occur. Every evidence of extreme tension is at the same time an indication of the strength of the forces that keep the subject in the situation.

Finally, tension may be taken as evidence of the reality of the situations for the subjects. Normal subjects do not tremble and sweat unless they are implicated in a deep and genuinely felt predicament.

Background Authority. In psychophysics, animal learning, and other branches of psychology, the fact that measures are obtained at one institution rather than another is irrelevant to the interpretation of the findings, so long as the technical facilities for measurement are adequate and the operations are carried out with competence.

But it cannot be assumed that this holds true for the present study. The effectiveness of the experimenter's commands may depend in an important way on the larger institutional context in which they are issued. The experiments described thus far were conducted at Yale University, an organization which most subjects regarded with respect and sometimes awe. In post-experimental interviews several participants remarked that the locale and sponsorship of the study gave them confidence in the integrity, competence, and benign purposes of the personnel; many indicated that they would not have shocked the learner if the experiments had been done elsewhere.

This issue of background authority seemed to us important for an interpretation of the results that had been obtained thus far; moreover it is highly relevant to any comprehensive theory of human obedience. Consider, for example, how closely our compliance with the imperatives of others is tied to particular institutions and locales in our day-to-day activities. On request, we expose our throats to a man with a razor blade in the barber shop, but would not do so in a shoe store; in the latter setting we willingly follow the clerk's request to stand in our stockinged feet, but resist the command in a bank. In the laboratory of a great university, subjects may comply with a set of commands that would be resisted if given elsewhere. *One must always question the relationship of obedience to a person's sense of the context in which he is operating.*

To explore the problem we moved our apparatus to an office building in industrial Bridgeport and replicated experimental conditions, without any visible tie to the university.

Bridgeport subjects were invited to the experiment through a mail circular similar to the one used in the Yale study, with appropriate changes in letterhead, etc. As in the earlier study, subjects were paid $4.50 for coming to the laboratory. The same age and occupational distributions used at Yale, and the identical personnel, were employed.

The purpose in relocating in Bridgeport was to assure a complete dissociation from Yale, and in this regard we were fully successful. On the surface, the study appeared to be conducted by RESEARCH ASSOCIATES OF BRIDGEPORT, an organization of unknown character (the title had been concocted exclusively for use in this study).

The experiments were conducted in a three-room office suite in a somewhat rundown commercial building located in the downtown shopping area. The laboratory was sparsely furnished, though clean, and marginally respectable in appearance. When subjects inquired about professional affiliations, they were informed only that we were a private firm conducting research for industry.

Some subjects displayed skepticism concerning the motives of the Bridgeport experimenter. One gentleman gave us a written account of the thoughts he experienced at the control board:

> . . . Should I quit this damn test? Maybe he passed out? What dopes we were not to check up on this deal. How do we know that these guys are legit? No furniture, bare walls, no telephone. We could of called the Police up or the Better Business Bureau. I learned a lesson tonight. How do I know that Mr. Williams [the experimenter] is telling the truth . . . I wish I knew how many volts a person could take before lapsing into unconsciousness . . .
> [*Subject 2414*]

Another subject stated:

> I questioned on my arrival my own judgment [about coming]. I had doubts as to the legitimacy of the operation and the consequences of participation. I felt it was a heartless way to conduct memory or learning processes on human beings and certainly dangerous without the presence of a medical doctor.
> [*Subject 2440 V*]

There was no noticeable reduction in tension for the Bridgeport subjects. And the subjects' estimation of the amount of pain felt by the victim was slightly, though not significantly, higher than in the Yale study.

A failure to obtain complete obedience in Bridgeport would indicate that the extreme compliance found in New Haven subjects was tied closely to the background authority of Yale University; if a large proportion of the subjects remained fully obedient, very different conclusions would be called for.

As it turned out, the level of obedience in Bridgeport, although somewhat reduced, was not significantly lower than that obtained at Yale. A large proportion of the

Bridgeport subjects were fully obedient to the experimenter's commands (48 per cent of the Bridgeport subjects delivered the maximum shock *vs.* 65 per cent in the corresponding condition at Yale).

How are these findings to be interpreted? It is possible that if commands of a potentially harmful or destructive sort are to be perceived as legitimate they must occur within some sort of institutional structure. But is is clear from the study that it need not be a particularly reputable or distinguished institution. The Bridgeport experiments were conducted by an unimpressive firm lacking any credentials; the laboratory was set up in a respectable office building with title listed in the building directory. Beyond that, there was no evidence of benevolence or competence. It is possible that the *category* of institution, judged according to its professed function, rather than its qualitative position within that category, wins our compliance. Persons deposit money in elegant, but also in seedy-looking banks, without giving much thought to the differences in security they offer. Similarly, our subjects may consider one laboratory to be as competent as another, so long as it *is* a scientific laboratory.

It would be valuable to study the subjects' performance in other contexts which go even further than the Bridgeport study in denying institutional support to the experimenter. It is possible that, beyond a certain point, obedience disappears completely. But that point had not been reached in the Bridgeport office: almost

". . . our subjects may consider one laboratory to be as competent as another, so long as it is *a scientific laboratory."*

half the subjects obeyed the experimenter fully.

Further Experiments. We may mention briefly some additional experiments undertaken in the Yale series. A considerable amount of obedience and defiance in everyday life occurs in connection with groups. And we had reason to feel in the light of many group studies already done in psychology that group forces would have a profound effect on reactions to authority. A series of experiments was run to examine these effects. In all cases only one naive subject was studied per hour, but he performed in the midst of actors who, unknown to him, were employed by the experimenter. In one experiment (Groups for Disobedience) two actors broke off in the middle of the experiment. When this happened 90 per cent of the subjects followed suit and defied the experimenter. In another condition the actors followed the orders obediently; this strengthened the experimenter's power only slightly. In still a third experiment the job of pushing the switch to shock the learner was given to one of the actors, while the naive subject performed a subsidiary act. We wanted to see how the teacher would respond if he were involved in the situation but did not actually give the shocks. In this situation only three subjects out of forty broke off. In a final group experiment the subjects themselves determined the shock level they were going to use. Two actors suggested higher and higher shock levels; some subjects insisted, despite group pressure, that the shock level be kept low; others followed along with the group.

Further experiments were completed using women as subjects, as well as a set dealing with the effects of dual, unsanctioned, and conflicting authority. A final experiment concerned the personal relationship between victim and subject. These will have to be described elsewhere, lest the present report be extended to monographic length.

It goes without saying that future research can proceed in many different directions. What kinds of response from the victim are most effective in causing disobedience in the subject? Perhaps passive resistance is more effective than vehement protest. What conditions of entry into an authority system lead to greater or lesser obedience? What is the effect of anonymity and masking on the subject's behavior? What conditions lead to the subject's perception of responsibility for his own actions? Each of these could be a major research topic in itself, and can readily be incorporated into the general experimental procedure described here.

Levels of Obedience and Defiance. One general finding that merits attention is the high level of obedience manifested in the experimental situation. Subjects often expressed deep disapproval of shocking a man in the face of his objections, and others denounced it as senseless and stupid. Yet many subjects complied even while they protested. The proportion of obedient subjects greatly exceeded the expectations of the experimenter and his colleagues. At the outset, we had conjectured that subjects would not, in general, go above the level of 'Strong Shock.' In practice, many subjects were willing to administer the most extreme shocks available when commanded by the experimenter. For some subjects the experiment provides an occasion for aggressive release. And for others it demonstrates the extent to which obedient dispositions are deeply ingrained, and are engaged irrespective of their consequences for others. Yet this is not the whole story. Somehow, the subject becomes implicated in a situation from which he cannot disengage himself.

The departure of the experimental results from intelligent expectation, to some extent, has been formalized. The procedure was to describe the experimental situation in concrete detail to a group of competent persons, and to ask them to predict the performance of 100 hypothetical subjects. For purposes of indicating the distribution of break-off points judges were provided with a diagram of the shock generator, and recorded their predictions before being informed of the actual results. Judges typically underestimated the amount of obedience demonstrated by subjects.

In *Figure 3*, we compare the predictions

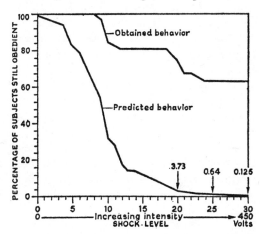

of forty psychiatrists at a leading medical school with the actual performance of subjects in the experiment. The psychiatrists predicted that most subjects would not go beyond the tenth shock level (150 volts; at this point the victim makes his first explicit demand to be freed). They further predicted that by the twentieth shock level (300 volts; the victim refuses to answer) 3.73 per cent of the subjects would still be obedient; and that only a little over one-tenth of one per cent of the subjects would administer the highest shock on the board. But, as the graph indicates, the obtained behavior was very different. Sixty-two per cent of the subjects obeyed the experimenter's commands fully. Between expectation and occurrence there is a whopping discrepancy.

Why did the psychiatrists underestimate the level of obedience? Possibly, because their predictions were based on an inadequate conception of the determinants of human action, a conception that focuses on motives *in vacuo*. This orientation may be entirely adequate for the repair of bruised impulses as revealed on the psychiatrist's couch, but as soon as our interest turns to action in larger settings, attention must be paid to the situations in which motives are expressed. A situation exerts an important press on the individual. It exercises constraints and may provide push. In certain circumstances it is not so much the kind of person a man is, as the kind of situation in which he is placed, that determines his actions.

Many people, not knowing much about the experiment, claim that subjects who go to the end of the board are sadistic. Nothing could be more foolish as an overall characterization of these persons. It is like saying that a person thrown into a swift-flowing stream is necessarily a fast swimmer, or that he has great stamina because he moves so rapidly relative to the bank. The context of action must always be considered. The individual, upon entering the laboratory, becomes integrated into a situation that carries its own momentum. The subject's problem then is how to become disengaged from a situation which is moving in an altogether ugly direction.

The fact that disengagement is so difficult testifies to the potency of the forces that keep the subject at the control board. Are these forces to be conceptualized as individual motives and expressed in the language of personality dynamics, or are they to be seen as the effects of social structure and pressures arising from the situational field?

A full understanding of the subject's action will, I feel, require that both perspectives be adopted. The person brings to the laboratory enduring dispositions toward authority and aggression, and at the same time he becomes enmeshed in a social structure that is no less an objective fact of the case. From the standpoint of personality theory one may ask: What mechanisms of personality enable a person to transfer responsibility to authority? What are the motives underlying obedient and disobedient performance? Does orientation to authority lead to a short-circuiting of the shame-guilt system? What cognitive and emotional defenses are brought into play in the case of obedient and defiant subjects?

The present experiments are not, however, directed toward an exploration of the motives engaged when the subject obeys the experimenter's commands. Instead, they examine the situational variables responsible for the elicitation of obedience. Elsewhere, we have attempted to spell out some of the structural properties of the experimental situation that account for high obedience, and this analysis need not be repeated here (Milgram, 1963). The experimental variations themselves represent our attempt to probe that structure, by systematically changing it and noting the consequences for behavior. It is clear that some situations produce greater compliance with the experimenter's commands than others. However, this does not necessarily imply an increase or decrease in the strength of any single definable motive. Situations producing the greatest obedience could do so by triggering the most powerful, yet perhaps the most idiosyncratic, of motives in each subject confronted by the setting. Or they may simply recruit a greater number and variety of motives in their service. But whatever the motives involved—and it is far from certain that they can ever be known—action may be studied as a direct function of the situation in which it occurs. This has been the approach of the present study, where we sought to plot behavioral irregularities against manipulated properties of the social field. Ultimately, social psychology would like to have a compelling *theory of situations* which will, first, present a language in terms of which situations can be defined; proceed to a typology of situations; and then point to the manner in which definable properties of situations are transformed into psychological forces in the individual.[8]

Postscript. Almost a thousand adults were individually studied in the obedience research, and there were many specific conclusions regarding the variables that control obedience and disobedience to authority. Some of these have been discussed briefly in the preceding sections, and more detailed reports will be released subsequently.

There are now some other generalizations I should like to make, which do not derive in any strictly logical fashion from the experiments as carried out, but which, I feel, ought to be made. They are formulations of an intuitive sort that have been forced on me by observation of many subjects responding to the pressures of authority. The assertions represent a painful alteration in my own thinking; and since they were acquired only under the repeated impact of direct observation, I have no illusion that they will be generally accepted by persons who have not had the same experience.

With numbing regularity good people were seen to knuckle under the demands of authority and to perform actions that were callous and severe. Men who are in everyday life responsible and decent were seduced by the trappings of authority, by the control of their perceptions, and by the uncritical acceptance of the experimenter's definition of the situation, into performing harsh acts.

What is the limit of such obedience? At many points we attempted to establish a boundary. Cries from the victim were in-

serted; not good enough. The victim claimed heart trouble; subjects still shocked him on command. The victim pleaded that he be let free, and his answers no longer registered on the signal box; subjects continued to shock him. At the outset we had not conceived that such drastic procedures would be needed to generate disobedience, and each step was added only as the ineffectiveness of the earlier techniques became clear. The final effort to establish a limit was the Touch-Proximity condition. But the very first subject in this condition subdued the victim on command, and proceeded to the highest shock level. A quarter of the subjects in this condition performed similarly.

The results, as seen and felt in the laboratory, are to this author disturbing. They raise the possibility that human nature, or —more specifically—the kind of character produced in American democratic society, cannot be counted on to insulate its citizens from brutality and inhumane treatment at the direction of malevolent authority. A substantial proportion of people do what they are told to do, irrespective of the content of the act and without limitations of conscience, so long as they perceive that the command comes from a legitimate authority. If in this study an anonymous experimenter could successfully command adults to subdue a fifty-year-old man, and force on him painful electric shocks against his protests, one can only wonder what gov-

"With numbing regularity good people were seen to knuckle under to the demands of authority and to perform actions that were callous and severe."

---

8 My thanks to Professor Howard Leventhal of Yale for strengthening the writing in this paragraph.

ernment, with its vastly greater authority and prestige, can command of its subjects. There is, of course, the extremely important question of whether malevolent political institutions could or would arise in American society. The present research contributes nothing to this issue.

In an article entitled "The Dangers of Obedience," Harold J. Laski wrote:

> . . . civilization means, above all, an unwillingness to inflict unnecessary pain. Within the ambit of that definition, those of us who heedlessly accept the commands of authority cannot yet claim to be civilized men.
>
> . . . Our business, if we desire to live a life not utterly devoid of meaning and significance, is to accept nothing which contradicts our basic experience merely because it comes to us from tradition or convention or authority. It may well be that we shall be wrong; but our self-expression is thwarted at the root unless the certainties

we are asked to accept coincide with the certainties we experience. That is why the condition of freedom in any state is always a widespread and consistent skepticism of the canons upon which power insists.

References

Buss, Arnold H. *The Psychology of Aggression.* New York and London: John Wiley, 1961.

Kierkegaard, S. (1843). *Fear and Trembling.* English edition, Princeton: Princeton University Press, 1941.

Laski, Harold J. The Dangers of Obedience. *Harper's Monthly Magazine* 159: June, 1–10, 1929.

Milgram, S. Dynamics of Obedience: Experiments in Social Psychology. Mimeographed report, *National Science Foundation,* January 25, 1961.

——————. Behavioral Study of Obedience. *J. abnorm. soc. Psychol.* 67:371–8, 1963.

——————. Issues in the Study of Obedience: A Reply to Baumrind. *Amer. Psychol.* 19:848–52, 1964.

Miller, N. E. Experimental Studies of Conflict. In J. McV. Hunt (Ed.), *Personality and the Behavior Disorders.* New York: Ronald Press, 1944.

Scott, J. P. *Aggression.* Chicago: University of Chicago Press, 1958.

CHAPTER 30

Class Consciousness and Class Structure

RICHARD CENTERS

THE psychological differences among the various occupational strata that have been described in the preceding chapter are certainly substantial ones. They exist, moreover, in such a degree and pattern as to indicate a tendency toward the cleavage of the population toward two distinct poles of attitude and behavior. There is, to be sure, no sharp, neat point where day changes to night, i.e. where one stratum or set of strata clings unanimously to one point of view and the one adjacent to it in the hierarchy clings as a man, so to speak, to another. Rather, there is a situation obtaining much like the pictures one sees in a biological textbook of a cell that is beginning to divide, there being masses of material concentrated at two ends of a continuum with a gradient of stuff between. A cleavage into sub-cultures is incipient, but is not complete. What has been described is a trend. The lowest occupational ranks, i.e. the semi-skilled and unskilled workers, represent the frontier of one direction in attitude and behavior, the top business group represents the extreme in another. Unanimity of opinion within either stratum is not, admittedly, the rule, but the differences between strata are frequently so striking as to suggest strongly the very sort of basic irreconciliability of viewpoint that has been described by persons who conceive of social classes as interest groups even now the parties to a struggle.

Significance of Class Identifications

THE sort of differences in attitude and belief between strata that have been disclosed, particularly in these key areas, do indeed seem to be the stuff out of which social conflict between groups is made, but, as has been pointed out above, prior study has indicated little in the way of class identifications or feelings of belongingness to distinct classes that would support the view that there is any of the requisite *group consciousness* for the behaving of these strata as units

467

in conflict with other social groups. As Thouless (47) has pointed out, the absence of group consciousness, such as race, or national or class consciousness may be the decisive factor in preventing a group from taking common action; for he says: "The internal cohesiveness of a social group and its power to act as a unit in competition with other social groups *depend to a large extent on the extent to which members of the group are aware of the reality of the group and of their own membership in it.*"[1]

The importance of *a distinctive name* to identify the group and its members has also been pointed out by several social psychologists. Thouless, again, has summed up its importance in a peculiarly apt way:

"The absence of group consciousness may be the determining factor in preventing a group from taking cooperative action. The blue-eyed people of Great Britain, for example, are not group conscious. If it were desired to make them take violent action against the brown-eyed, *it would be necessary first to give them a distinctive name,*[2] and to make them think of themselves as members of this blue-eyed group *and identified with its interests*[3] rather than as members of the British people as a whole.

"It was reported by travellers (I do not know how truly) that, early in the nineteenth century before the beginnings of their revolt against the Turkish rule, the people occupying the country we now call 'Bulgaria' had very commonly no name which they gave themselves as a distinct people. If this was so, the first condition for a successful rising was that they should think of themselves as 'Bulgarians,' i.e. that they should become race conscious. Similarly Marx, when trying to prepare for a proletarian revolution, rightly considered that it was necessary that the working classes should become 'class-conscious,' that they should think of themselves as forming a separate class from the rest of the community with interests that were peculiar to them. Governments that do not want a proletarian revolution aim at the reduction of class consciousness. Those whose aim is to prevent national wars similarly

[1] Italics not in original.   [2] Italics not in original.
[3] Italics not in original.

see a danger in national consciousness and would rather intensify consciousness of membership of larger units (so that, for example, an individual would think of himself as a European rather than as an Englishman or German)." (47, p. 326f.)

Class Identifications—The American Class Structure

SUCH remarks as these make it patently clear that the discovery of what names the people of the several social classes in our culture distinguish themselves by is of prime importance in considerations of class theory. The determination of what names *are* in actual use has not proved an easy task, as has been pointed out in previous discussion. In framing a question on class identification for the present study it has also been indicated before that the writer built upon what knowledge had been gained before. It was considered unnecessary to repeat the exploratory work of the *Fortune* survey, which had asked an open-answer type of question, for public attitude surveys based on cross sections of the total population characteristically achieve quite similar results, and *Fortune's* question, "What word do you use to name the class in America you belong to?", had gained the information necessary for the formulation of a question designed to more rigidly structure the identifications into a system. Since *Fortune* had found that the terms *middle class* and *working* (or *laboring*) *class* were the most frequently used of all, it was clear that these, along with the terms *upper class* and *lower class*, which (together with apparently equivalent terms) constituted the next most frequent responses, should constitute the alternatives for the question used in the present study.

Members of the cross section were asked: "If you were asked to use one of these four names for your social class, which would you say you belonged in: the middle class, lower class, working class or upper class?" The answers will convincingly dispel any doubt that Americans are class conscious, and quite as quickly quell any glib assertions like *Fortune's* "America is Middle Class."

TABLE 18

Class Identifications of a National Cross Section
of White Males (July 1945)
(N = 1,097)

Per Cent Saying	
Upper Class	3
Middle Class	43
Working Class	51
Lower Class	1
Don't Know	1
"Don't Believe in Classes"	1

Not only do all but an insignificant minority admit of membership in some class, but over half of our people (51 per cent) say they belong to the working class (Table 18). Given the opportunity now to claim membership in any of four different classes, only about half as many claim to belong to the middle class as have been found calling themselves middle class in previous studies. Whereas the latter have shown, characteristically, figures of from 80 to 90 per cent, only 43 per cent of people now say they are middle class.

These results are those from the main survey which was carried out in July 1945. Their reliability was checked in two follow-up studies conducted in February 1946 and in March 1947 respectively. Data from the 1946 survey are cited in Table 19. Both studies reveal substantially the same relation-

TABLE 19

Class Identifications of a National Cross Section
of White Males (February 1946)
(N = 1,337)

Per Cent Saying	
Upper Class	4
Middle Class	36
Working Class	52
Lower Class	5
Don't Know	3

ships as those indicated in the 1945 data. The authenticity of these class identifications seems unquestionable.

In all three studies the figures for identification with the lower class are below those previously found for this class when only the terms upper, middle and lower class were used. Though the differences are very small and may represent merely errors in sampling, there is certainly a suggestion in them that the smaller percentages for lower class identification are functions of the inclusion of the working class label, a possibly less invidious and opprobrious term.

Definitions of the Several Classes

THE above point leads at once into the query: *What, after all do these names mean?* Who belongs in these classes? To what do they correspond in terms of stratification? What are they to be identified with in terms of some objective criterion that is common and public? These are serious questions and demand answer. One can find textbook and dictionary definitions enough, to be sure, but these do not serve us here, for, in essence, *a class is no more nor less than what people collectively think it is.* It is a psychological structuring and must be observed, just as any other psychological datum, before we can infer its basis and nature.

Thus conceived, it becomes readily apparent that classes demand *social definitions.* That is, they must be defined by the people collectively. In accordance with this conviction, it was decided to ask the people who identified themselves with the several classes to define the membership of the class they claimed they belonged to. Because of the relative objectivity and intelligibility of occupational labels to the general public, and because it is so essential to determine the meanings of the respective classes in terms of some stratification index, it was decided to try to find out what the *occupational composition* of each class was. Accordingly, each person who claimed membership in some class was handed a card listing the several occupational categories shown below and asked, "Which of those in this list would you say belonged in the . . . . . .

class? (whichever the respondent had chosen). Just call out
the letters."

A. Big business owners and executives.
B. Small business owners and operators.
C. Factory workers.
D. Office workers.
E. Doctors and lawyers.
F. Servants.
G. Farmers.
H. Laborers such as miners, truck drivers, and shop-
      workers.
I. Store and factory managers.
J. Waiters and bartenders.
K. Salesmen.

Interviewers were instructed to ask the person "any others?" etc., before leaving this question in order that a complete response might be obtained from each one. Results are
shown in Figures 5, 6, 7, and 8. Those for the upper and
lower classes, that is, Figures 5 and 6, are, of course, offered
only as a suggestion of the trend, for the numbers of people
who claimed membership in either of these classes is much
too small for their definitions to be derived from an adequate
sampling.

*It is clear that each class has a distinctive pattern of occupa-
tional strata as members.* There is overlapping, to be sure, and
obviously imperfect agreement obtains with respect to the
inclusion or exclusion of a given occupational group in a given
class. But, by and large, the patterns of membership are distinctive enough to allow one to visualize the two major
classes, middle and working, respectively, as roughly separate
sectors of the population. The upper and middle classes comprise mainly the business and professional[4] people, it is obvi-

[4] The writer is generalizing the category "Doctors and Lawyers" here in
making a reference to professional people. In a pretest of the stimulus
material the label *Professional People* was used but it was found that some
poorly educated persons did not understand the word "Professional." For
the same reason, the terms *Skilled, Semi-skilled* and *Unskilled Workers*
could not be used. To overcome this difficulty, use of examples of the respective categories appeared to be a fair solution.

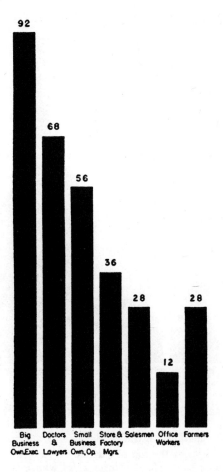

FIGURE 5. Occupational Composition of the Upper
Class According to Upper Class Specifications of
the Occupational Membership

Numbers at the top of each bar represent the per
cent of people in the upper class who include the
given occupational group in the upper class

ous, while the working and lower classes contain mostly the
manual workers. The position assigned by the various classes
to big business owners and executives is about the clearest of
that of any of the categories, both in terms of its inclusion in
the upper class (Figure 5) and in terms of its exclusion from
all other classes by all but insignificant minorities of their
members. The position given to farmers is, in contrast, the

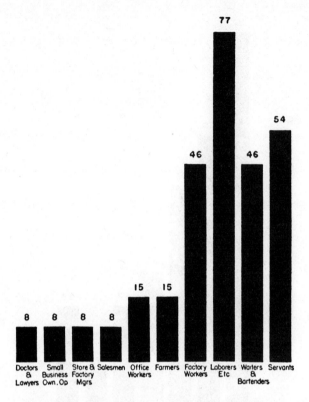

FIGURE 6. Occupational Composition of the Lower
Class According to Lower Class Specifications of
the Occupational Membership

> Numbers at the top of each bar represent the per
> cent of people in the lower class who include the
> given occupational group in the lower class

most ambiguous of all, for considerable percentages of all
four classes name them as members. Most typically, however,
they are claimed as a working class group. It is regretted that
the list handed to respondents did not contain separate mention of farm owners and managers, farm tenants, and farm
laborers. This should be done if this sort of survey is repeated
in the future.

The class position of office workers seems also to be an
equivocal one, for they are claimed almost as often by working class people as they are by the middle class. The difficulty
of assigning them to class membership appears thus no less a

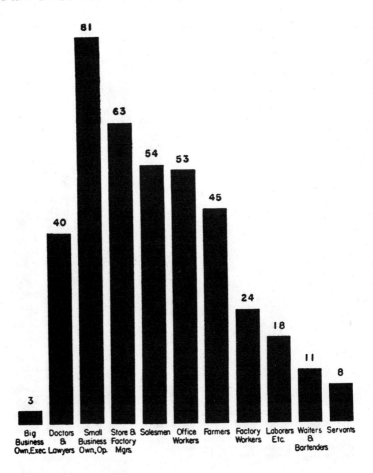

FIGURE 7. Occupational Composition of the Middle Class According to Middle Class Specifications of the Occupational Membership

Numbers at the top of each bar represent the per cent of people in the middle class who include the given occupational group in the middle class

one with the members of actual classes than it has been to social scientists. Traditionally they have been thought of by the latter as middle class or "lower middle class," and they have frequently been characterized as "the assistants of management" and in other similar terms that indicate an identification with the dominant stratum. Still, considerable numbers of them are wage earners just as are most manual workers,

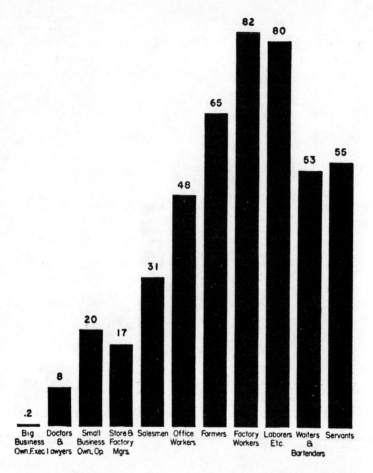

FIGURE 8. Occupational Composition of the Working Class According to Working Class Specifications of the Occupational
Membership

   Numbers at the top of each bar represent the per cent of people
   in the working class who include the given occupational group
   in the working class

and they have more and more of late years begun to form
unions of their own and to make common cause with the
manual worker. All of this is so commonly known and commented upon as a symptom of the economic unrest in this
stratum, however, as to make superfluous much discussion
here. The following quotation from a publication devoted to
the problems of management (*Modern Industry*) indicates

how widely the changing attitudes of white collar workers are noted and the inferences that are being drawn from this phenomenon:

" 'You Can't Eat Air Conditioning,' sneers a union organizing leaflet addressed to the office employees of a New Jersey plant. The company, recruiting typists, had used glowing newspaper ads to describe its ideal working conditions, but failed to mention that salaries were lower than those paid janitresses.

"That union message typifies a change in attitude and outlook of white-collar employees, one that promises to affect all employer-employee relations.

"Today's labor ferment is boiling over deep into the ranks of a group of employees long considered to be almost part of management. White-collar workers' ideas are growing akin to those prevailing in the factory. So are their methods.

"The recent strike of members of the Federation of Westinghouse Independent Salaried Unions is a spectacular example. Demanding a bonus incentive system similar to that given production workers, striking white-collar workers closed or seriously curtailed production in six Westinghouse units for three weeks.

"Traditionally 'hard to organize,' both white-collar unions and big catch-all industrial unions claim it is becoming easier to make office employees union-conscious. The Chicago branch of United Office & Professional Workers (CIO), for example, reports more requests from non-union offices for help in unionizing in the three weeks after V-J Day than in the previous six months.

"This trend, however, does not mean that on your way to work tomorrow a sound truck will be calling out your secretary to strike for higher wages. Nor does it mean that employees are no longer interested in comfortable offices or in cordial working relationships. It does mean that behind the cheerful smiles and pleasant chatter of your office help may be mounting unrest, an increasing feeling that salaries are inadequate, and an increasing attraction to getting what they feel they must have by militant means.

"The trend is a long-time one. Starting during the mass

labor upheavals of 1935 and 1936, it slackened off somewhat just before the war, to swing up again during the war years and since.

"Today, 1.4 million clerical and professional workers belong to national labor unions. Of these, 5% work in manufacturing establishments, but their number is increasing.

"There are many reasons for this:

"As war-production demands glorified the muscles, office work lost much of its social prestige.

"Many former office employees secured temporary war-plant jobs, joined unions, and picked up completely new *'working-class' attitudes.*"[5] (59, pp. 49-50)

Class Identifications of Occupational Strata

THE conception of one's own role and class membership is, one can see after such remarks as these, a highly significant issue in social and economic behavior, and, from the standpoint of possible class conflict, an all-important one. What is the relation between people's present occupational status and their class membership? An answer is found in Table 20, and, perhaps more easily, in Figure 9.

Nearly three-quarters of all business, professional and white collar workers identify themselves with the middle or upper classes. An even larger proportion of all manual workers, 79 per cent, identify, on the other hand, with the working and lower classes. Within the detailed urban occupational categories there is the same sort of gradation displayed as that shown for politico-economic orientations in the last chapter (Figure 9). But now, somewhat more than in the usual case, there is also a definite and sharp break to be discerned in the difference in the identifications of white collar workers as compared to those of skilled manual workers. The former, despite such trends as those reported above, still tends to be a middle class group, the latter to be, in heavy majority, a working class one.[6]

[5] Italics not in original.

[6] Preliminary analysis of data on the class identifications of women indicates that these generalizations apply to women as well as men. The occupation-class relationships appear substantially the same, regardless of the sex of the sample.

TABLE 20

Psychological Differences of Occupational Strata: Class Identification

Q23a. If you were asked to use one of these four names for your social class, which would you say you belonged in: the Middle Class, Lower Class, Working Class, or Upper Class?

Occupation	N	% Upper Class	% Middle Class	% Working Class	% Lower Class	% Don't Know	% Don't Believe in Classes	% Total Upper and Middle	For "Total Upper and Middle" Differences Are Significant Between
Urban									
A. All Business, Professional, and White Collar	430	4	70	23	0.2	1.2	1.8	74	A & B
B. All Manual Workers	414	1	20	77	1.7	0.3	—	21	B & A
(Detailed Groupings for A and B)									
1. Large Business	54	13	78	7	—	2.0	—	91	1 & 3,4,5,6,7
2. Professional	73	4	81	10	—	1.0	4.0	85	2 & 4,5,6,7
3. Small Business	131	3	70	24	—	1.5	1.5	73	3 & 1,5,6,7
4. White Collar	172	2	61	34	0.6	0.6	1.8	63	4 & 1,2,5,6,7
5. Skilled Manual	163	2	26	71	1.0	—	—	28	5 & 1,2,3,4,6
6. Semi-skilled	174	1	14	83	1.0	1.0	—	15	6 & 1,2,3,4,5
7. Unskilled	77	—	18	75	7.0	—	—	18	7 & 1,2,3,4
Rural									
C. Farm Owners and Managers	153	3	42	51	1.0	3.0	—	45	C & D
D. Farm Tenants and Laborers	69	2	16	73	2.0	7.0	—	18	D & C

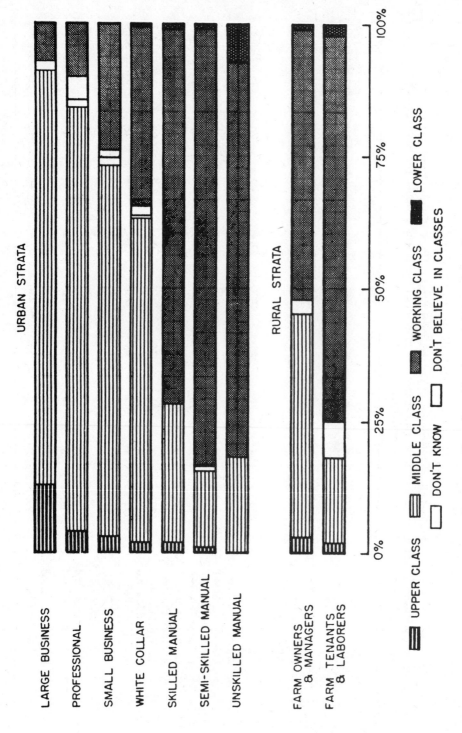

FIGURE 9. Class Identifications of Occupational Strata

The rural strata, though showing a clear division in loyalty, and in the direction to be expected by virtue of their economic position, show, as usual, less difference than that to be found between the business, professional and white collar group and the manual stratum. This is probably a function of several factors. For one thing they are, like urban manual workers, a predominantly *tool using* group and also, like them, a *producing* group. Insofar as such factors might influence their conception of their role, status and economic interests, it apparently predominates over another supposed tendency for them to claim membership in the non-working class groups, i.e. upper and middle classes, by virtue of their economic independence as it is manifested in *tool owning* and *proprietorship*. Moreover, though extremes of wealth and poverty exist among them, the vast majority of even the proprietors are only poor or average in economic status.[7] Such homogeneity of standards of living might readily be supposed to be a factor tending to reduce psychological differences and to promote homogeneity of viewpoint and outlook instead. Here, where only occupational status or objective role is taken into account, the difference appears smaller than it would if other economic or stratification variables were considered.

The question also occurs as to their conceptions of the classes (mainly middle and working) with which they identify themselves. Are farm people, when they say they belong to the middle class, really identifying themselves with the same occupational strata as are the urban people who so identify themselves? For answer one need but glance at Figure 10 where the respective urban and rural definitions of the middle class are compared. In all essential respects the profiles of occupational membership are strikingly similar, but it is clear also that farmers who say they are middle class are much more often convinced that farmers belong to that class than are urban middle class people. Precisely the same sort of generalization may be made with respect to the comparison of urban and rural definitions of the working class as shown in Figure 11.

[7] For data on this point see Table 97 in Appendix III.

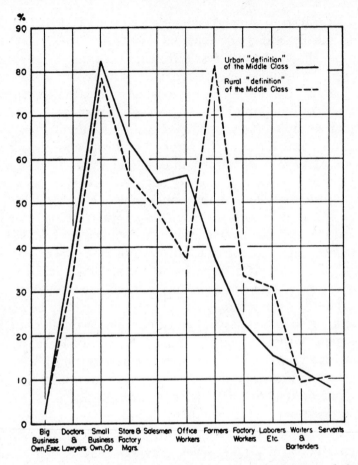

FIGURE 10. Comparison of Urban and Rural Definitions of the Middle Class

Points on the lines above each occupational category indicate the percentage of persons who say members of that occupational category are members of the middle class

Criteria for Inclusion in One's Own Class

IN seeking a social definition of the several classes, the assumption that occupation is a primary criterion of class composition has proved to be a useful one. It is true that it has had no definitive previous research to establish it, but it does certainly seem a reasonable hypothesis to hold in virtue of the views expressed by the bulk of the treatises on the subject of

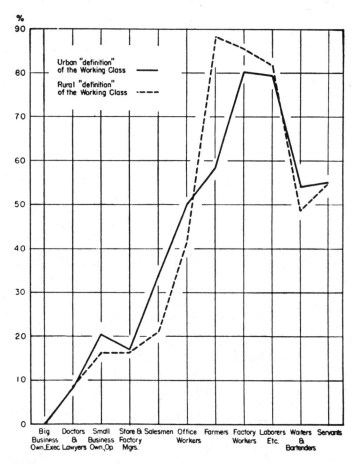

FIGURE 11. Comparison of Urban and Rural Definitions of the
Working Class

Points on the lines above each occupational category indicate
the percentage of persons who say members of that occupational category are members of the working class

classes by sociologists and anthropologists. The people can
and do use occupation to define social classes if asked to do so.
But the problem of criteria is certainly not thereby to be
regarded as a closed one. It was suspected that several criteria
besides occupation might be important. In order to push insight into this aspect of the problem somewhat further, the
people of the cross section were asked, "In deciding whether
a person belongs to your class or not, which of these other

things do you think is most important to know: who his family is, how much money he has, what sort of education he has, or how he believes and feels about certain things?" Results for the general public are summarized in Table 21.

TABLE 21

Criteria for Own Class Membership Other than Occupation

*Per Cent Saying**	
Beliefs and Attitudes	47.4
Education	29.4
Family	20.1
Money	17.1
Character and Morals	1.7
Occupation, "Just Occupation"	1.3
Personality	.9
Behavior, Manners	.8
Ability, Achievements	.5
"Whether or not He Works with His Hands"	.3
Intelligence	.1
Don't Know	9.1

* Percentages add to more than 100 per cent. People gave more than one criterion.

Nearly half of the population thinks that the most important thing to know about a person from the standpoint of membership in its class is (other than occupation)[8] *the way the person "believes and feels about certain things."* There is a wealth of implication in such a finding, for it is just the possession of common ideologies, attitudes, values and interests that are commonly supposed to be basic to the formation of class consciousness. The conception of classes as interest

[8] Because people had just been asked to define their class in terms of its occupational membership, the "which of these other" phrase was believed necessary in order to avoid what might appear to respondents as an unwelcome repetition of a question they had, in a sense, just answered. Its inclusion necessarily limits the generality of the resulting responses to criteria other than occupation. From it one can infer nothing concerning the relative importance of these criteria *in comparison with occupation*. Further study is required before this important relationship can be determined.

groups is clearly not an unfounded one in terms of this evidence, and it strikingly confirms the findings presented in the preceding chapter.

The primacy of beliefs and attitudes as a criterion of class membership is general (Table 22). It is the first criterion of every class (except the lower, and here the number of cases is too small to be taken as more than suggestive), and it is likewise first with every occupational stratum (Table 23). Other criteria vary in importance from class to class. The people in the upper and middle classes more frequently emphasize family and education than do those of the working class. The latter also are noticeably less able to respond in a definite way than the middle and upper class people, though no obvious reason why this should be so suggests itself. These trends in behavior appear to characterize the situation obtaining with respect to the criteria used by specific occupational groups also. The higher occupational groups tend to emphasize family and education more than the lower ones. But they also give appreciably greater numbers of responses, so that critical comparison is made somewhat difficult.

TABLE 22

Criteria of Own Class Membership (Other than Occupation) Used by Persons Claiming Membership in the Several Classes
(See text for exact wording of question.)

Class	N*	% Family	% Money	% Education	% Beliefs and Attitudes	% Other Criteria	% Don't Know
Upper	29†	41.3	17.2	34.5	65.5	3.4	—
Middle	464	23.9	16.6	41.0	51.3	5.7	3.4
Working	557	16.9	18.3	21.0	44.2	5.7	13.5
Lower	13†	—	46.2	38.5	23.1	46.2‡	23.1

* Percentages add to more than 100 per cent. More than one criterion was often named.
† Obviously too few cases for statistical adequacy. Included here as merely suggestive of a trend.
‡ Includes one mention each for the following: Occupation, "Whether or not he works with his hands," intellect, achievements, behavior, character.

TABLE 23

Psychological Differences of Occupational Strata: Criteria for Own Class Membership Other than Occupation

(See text for exact wording of question.)

	N*	% Family	% Money	% Education	% Beliefs and Attitudes	% Other Criteria†	% Don't Know
Urban							
A. All Business, Professional, and White Collar	423	22.0	18.9	39.2	51.8	7.1	4.3
B. All Manual Workers	409	17.6	16.4	23.7	46.2	6.1	13.4
(Detailed Groupings for A and B)							
1. Large Business	54	25.9	18.5	29.6	57.4	3.7	5.6
2. Professional	72	15.3	22.2	56.9	58.3	1.4	1.4
3. Small Business	129	26.4	16.3	40.3	47.3	8.5	5.4
4. White Collar	168	20.2	19.6	33.9	50.6	9.5	4.2
5. Skilled Manual	162	19.1	12.3	25.3	51.2	8.0	11.7
6. Semi-skilled	170	17.6	20.6	23.5	42.9	5.9	11.2
7. Unskilled	77	14.3	15.6	20.8	42.9	2.6	22.1
Rural							
C. Farm Owners and Managers	153	22.2	13.1	22.9	47.7	3.3	9.8
D. Farm Tenants and Laborers	67	19.4	22.4	25.4	35.8	17.9	1.5

* Percentages add to more than 100 per cent. More than one criterion was often given.
† Includes "just occupation," "Whether or not he works with his hands," intellect, achievement, behavior, character, morals, and personality.

Criteria and Causes for Membership in the Several Classes in General

IT does not follow, of course, that the criteria one uses to determine the membership of one's own class are identical with those used to assign persons to other classes. But people do use something, and the attempt was made to discover what these criteria are.

The Criteria for the Upper Class

The subjects of the cross section were asked, "What would you say puts a person in the upper social class?" Figures for the total cross section and for each class are given in Table 24.

TABLE 24

Criteria and Causes for Membership in the Upper Class
Q24a.   What would you say puts a person in the upper social class?

Per Cent Saying*	National (N = 1097)	Upper Class (N = 29)†	Middle Class (N = 467)	Working Class (N = 564)	Lower Class (N = 13)†
Wealth, Income	66.8	34.5	70.7	66.5	53.8
Education	24.1	31.0	23.3	24.5	53.8
Family Origins, Family Position, etc.	13.9	34.5	17.3	11.0	—
Abilities, Achievements	7.0	3.4	8.6	6.0	7.7
Good Character, Leadership, "Welfare Contributions"	6.0	17.2	6.4	5.0	7.7
Attitudes and Beliefs	5.9	20.7	7.1	4.1	15.4
Power, Influence, Prestige	3.9	—	3.9	4.3	7.7
Way of Life, Manners, Conduct, Breeding, Culture, Refinement, etc.	3.4	13.8	4.5	1.8	—
High-ranking Occupation, or Position	3.3	—	5.1	2.0	7.7
Associates, "Society," Club Membership	3.0	3.4	3.9	2.1	—
Personality, Dress, Appearance	2.5	6.9	2.8	2.0	—
Intelligence	1.3	3.4	1.7	.5	—
Leisure	.9	—	.4	1.4	—
Graft, Dishonesty, etc.	.5	—	.2	.7	—
"There Is No Upper Class"	1.5	—	2.4	.7	—
No Opinion	5.2	—	2.8	6.4	15.4

* Percentages add to more than 100 per cent. Many people named two or more criteria.
† Figures obviously are too small for statistical reliability, and are included here as suggestion only.

Wording of this question presented difficulties, for the idea of criteria is not an easy one to translate into common speech. That the "put" did not entirely succeed in conveying the idea of criteria will be obvious from inspection of the extended list of responses. While most people did give answers that are reasonably interpretable as criteria, some gave replies that suggest that they were thinking in terms of causes or mechanisms used by people in getting into the upper class. At any rate, there is pretty fair agreement in the relative importance of various criteria and causes between the two classes for which reliable samples are available (i.e. the middle and working classes). *Wealth or income is the distinctive mark of upper class membership* to both of them, but education and family connections are also important, though rather poor seconds and thirds, with both the middle and working classes. The upper class people, it is interesting to note, use somewhat different criteria from those of outsiders. Wealth is to them no more important (in terms of frequency, at least) than family origin, and both of these are only slightly more important than education. Also, it is suggestive that they use character and leadership, attitudes and beliefs, and such outward signs as ways of life, manners, conduct, breeding and culture much more than do those of other classes.

The Criteria for the Lower Class

"What puts a person in the lower class?" Here people again give answers in terms of both criteria and causes (Table 25). The most obvious answer is "being poor," and it is by a considerable margin the most frequent one received. Poor education or lack of education is next. A surprisingly large proportion of people appear to think of the lower class as a rather despicable group. Poor character and low morals, drink, crime, lack of ability, low intelligence, shiftlessness, laziness, lack of ambition or motivation, menial labor, etc., all indicate the disesteem in which this group is held. The middle and working classes differ little in their responses on the whole. For both of them the term lower class frequently connotes a despised or *déclassé* group. The lower class itself is scarcely present in sufficient number to defend itself, but those that are present say poverty and lack of education are either the factors that put them there or are the signs by which they distinguish themselves from others.

TABLE 25

Criteria and Causes for Membership in the Lower Class
Q24b.   What would you say puts a person in the lower social class?

Per Cent Saying*	National (N = 1097)	Upper Class (N = 29)	Middle Class (N = 467)	Working Class (N = 564)	Lower Class (N = 13)
Poverty	33.7	24.1	33.8	34.6	38.5
Poor Education or Lack of Education	22.5	10.3	27.8	19.0	38.5
Poor Character and Low Morals (except drink and crime)	12.8	27.6	11.1	12.9	—
Habits, Conduct, Behavior, Way of Life	9.9	17.2	11.3	8.7	7.7
Lack of Motivation or Ambition	9.6	10.3	11.8	8.2	—
Laziness, Shiftlessness, etc.	9.3	3.4	9.0	10.1	—
Attitudes and Beliefs	5.5	3.4	5.4	5.7	7.7
Family Origins	5.4	10.3	6.4	4.6	—
Lack of Opportunity	4.9	6.9	4.7	4.9	7.7
Low Intelligence	4.6	10.3	7.1	2.3	—
Lack of Ability	4.3	3.4	5.1	3.9	—
Drink	3.9	—	3.4	4.6	7.7
"Poor Management"	3.3	—	4.1	2.8	7.7
Occupation, Menial Labor, etc.	2.7	—	3.4	2.5	—
Bad Luck	1.9	6.9	1.1	2.1	—
Associates	1.9	—	1.7	2.1	—
Crime	1.5	3.4	1.9	.9	—
Fear, Timidity, Lack of Self-Confidence	1.5	—	1.7	1.4	—
"Unfair Pay," "Exploitation," "Economic System"	1.1	—	.4	1.8	—
"There Is No Lower Class"	.7	—	.4	.9	—
No Opinion	6.6	10.3	3.2	8.2	7.7

* Percentages add to more than 100 per cent. Respondents named several factors.

Those who have wondered why in previous studies so few people called themselves lower class certainly can find the answer here. Those who might be logically supposed to so identify themselves, i.e. laborers, shun such an opprobrious term, reserving it for the unworthy people they despise. They prefer, in overwhelming numbers, to call themselves "working class," a name that one could conceivably hold with dignity and self respect. One cannot assume, of course, that working class and lower class have precisely the same meaning in terms of stratification, for the few data that exist for the occupational definition of the lower class suggest that the lower class category is a more exclusively manual labor grouping than is the working class (compare Figures 6 and 8). The working class embraces as membership all the strata claimed by the lower, but it includes strata that apparently people of the lower class dare not claim.

The data cited in Table 24 also suggest an explanation for the fact that few people claim membership in the upper class. A scrutiny of the qualifications for membership—namely wealth, education, family heritage, ability, achievement, good character, leadership, power, influence, prestige, high ranking occupation or position, club membership, dress, intelligence and leisure—shows that such criteria of esteem far outnumber those connoting disapprobation such as "graft" or "dishonesty" which a trivial few insist upon. Could many people meet such requirements? The answer is plainly no. The upper class is, further, clearly identified with the top occupational strata, especially the economically dominant big business owners and executives, and, as such, it is certain to be an exclusive class, for the number of people of such status is an insignificant one in terms of the total population.

The Criteria for the Middle Class

There still remain to be examined the criteria (and causes) for membership in the two main classes, namely the middle and working.[9] Those for the middle class are given in Table 26. In terms of the national totals, money, income, etc., are

[9] Because of the limited funds available at the time of the initial survey in 1945, and other considerations such as the desire to avoid wearying respondents with repetitive questions and the necessity for holding the interview time to a reasonable length, data on the criteria for the middle and working classes were not obtained at that time. The data summarized in Tables 26, 27, 28, and 29 concerning these classes were secured in a later study carried out in 1947 through the cooperation of the American Institute of Public Opinion (Gallup Poll).

the main criteria for this class just as they are for the upper, but to a far less definitive extent. Whereas two-thirds of the cross section say these are what "puts" a person in the upper class only somewhat over one-third of the people use them to assign persons to the middle class. Many (especially members of the middle class themselves) qualify their use of such criteria by statements such as "not rich, not poor," "live comfortably," "all necessities and some luxuries," or give such a description as their only answer to this question. Education is the next most frequent criterion, but it too is distinctly not so important for middle class membership as it is for upper (compare Table 24). It is noteworthy that members of the upper and middle classes more commonly think of it as a reason for membership in the middle class than working and lower class people do. These latter groups think education much more important for upper class affiliation (cf. Table 24). A similar statement might be made regarding such criteria as family, position and environment. They seem more

TABLE 26

Criteria and Causes for Membership in the Middle Class
Q.   What would you say puts a person in the middle class?

Per Cent Saying*	National (N = 1516)†	Upper Class (N = 44)	Middle Class (N = 582)	Working Class (N = 790)	Lower Class (N = 48)
Money, Income, etc.	36	36	39	34	46
Not Rich, Not Poor, Live Comfortably, All Necessities and Some Luxuries, etc.	13	7	20	9	4
Education	13	20	18	8	8
Owning Small Business, Profession or Trade	11	5	7	15	4
Family, Position, Environment	9	11	13	5	10
Property or Security	6	2	5	7	12
Good Job, Steady Job	6	2	5	6	10
Salaried Work, White Collar Work	4	2	4	4	—
"Working People"	2	5	3	2	—
"Good Citizen"	1	—	1	‡	—
No Opinion	18	25	9	22	21

* Percentages add to more than 100 per cent. Many people named more than one criterion.
† Includes some persons who did not identify with any class.
‡ Less than one-half of one per cent.

important to middle class and upper class people than to others, and rank just after education with them.

To the members of the working class the most important criterion of middle class membership after money or income is the ownership of a small business, profession or trade; in sum, being an independent operator or proprietor of some kind. *This is a distinctive mark to them.* No working class person, as can be seen in Table 27, uses it as a sign of his own class.

Owning property or having security of income is the next most frequent criterion for middle class membership in terms of the national figures, and to the lower class it is second only to money or income in importance. Having a good job or a steady job, which comes next in the national figures, also is given considerable emphasis by this latter group.

It no doubt must be a surprise to the many social scientists who have so often attempted to assign salaried and white collar workers to the middle class that so few of the American people actually appear to consider salaried or white collar work a reason for such assignment. *Only 4 per cent of this national*

TABLE 27

Criteria and Causes for Membership in the Working Class
Q. What would you say puts a person in the working class?

Per Cent Saying*	National (N = 1518)†	Upper Class (N = 44)	Middle Class (N = 583)	Working Class (N = 791)	Lower Class (N = 48)
"Working for a Living"	26	20	13	37	21
Manual, Common, Mill or Factory Work or Labor	23	18	26	20	33
Lack of Income	14	14	14	14	19
Being an Employee or Wage Worker	10	—	9	11	4
Lack of Education or Training	7	16	13	4	4
Kind of Job, Type of Work	6	11	9	4	12
Lack of Security	4	2	3	5	2
Position or Background	2	5	4	1	—
Average Income	1	—	2	1	—
No Opinion	11	18	13	7	10

* Percentages add to more than 100 per cent. Many people named more than one criterion.
† Includes some persons who did not identify with any class.

cross section indicated salaried or white collar work as a criterion. No person in the lower class, and only 2 per cent of upper class people gave it as a reason. The suggestion is certainly strong that if this has ever in itself been a factor in identifying people with the middle class it has become much less important and is much less important now. But the question needs some further analysis before any acceptance of this suggestion, and it will be returned to later on.

The Criteria for the Working Class

When one turns to examine the criteria for inclusion in the working class (Table 27) it cannot help but strike one as highly significant that *the most distinctive criterion given for membership in this class is "working for a living."* In terms of such a loose and general (though no less meaningful) criterion, it is no wonder that so many white collar and salaried workers have joined the ranks of the working class to swell its numbers into the major class in the social structure. To many, doubtless, it matters little that one is salaried or white collared. He works for a living—that puts him in the working class. Such, one might guess, must be the rationale of many people who identify themselves with the working class at least, for "working for a living" is by far the most important reason for working class assignation given by the working class affiliates themselves.

But there is no doubt that something more definite than just "working for a living" serves to put people in the working class. Almost as important for such membership, in terms of the percentage of the population mentioning them, are such criteria as manual labor or work, common labor, mill or factory work or labor. *It is plain that the criteria for the working class are overwhelmingly status, function and role with respect to the economy of production and exchange.* If "working for a living," manual labor, etc., being an employee or wage worker, kind of job, type of work and position or background all be considered together, it can be seen that 67 per cent of the respondents named such criteria (national totals considered). Lack of income, given by 14 per cent of respondents, and lack of education or training, given by 7 per cent, are not unimportant criteria for the working class, but they are certainly far less important for it than they are for the lower class (compare Table 25 with Table 27). Indeed these are less important factors for working class assignation than for any other class assignation, upper, middle or lower.

Salaried and White Collar Work as Bases for Class Distinctions

One of the most striking facts disclosed by these data on class criteria is shown in Table 27, where the criteria for the working class are summarized, and those used by the several classes are contrasted. It can be seen there that nearly three times as many people who identify with the working class name "working for a living" as a criterion of that class as people who are identified with the middle class do—37 per cent as compared with 13 per cent. Another significant contrast is in the use of the "manual labor . . ." type of criterion between these two classes. The middle class person names it more often than the working class individual does. Moreover, the people of the middle class name it twice as often as "working for a living" as a criterion for the working class (26 per cent compared to 13 per cent). But something like the reverse of this holds for the relative emphasis given these two criteria by the people of the working class. To them "working for a living" is almost twice as important a criterion for their class as working with one's hands (i.e. manual labor, etc.). The percentages are 37 and 20 respectively.

Now it was pointed out previously that being a white collar worker did not appear to be an important criterion for the middle class, for only 4 per cent of either the middle class or the working class name it as a criterion. But these relationships that have just been described clearly suggest that more use is made of the fact of being a white collar worker in class distinctions than the criteria given for the middle class would lead one to suppose. *The situation seems to be somewhat like this*: Being a white collar or salaried worker is not nearly so much a strong reason for putting a person in the middle class as being a salaried or white collar worker is a reason for *not* putting a person in the working class, since manual work and working for wages *are* such important criteria for that class. The effect is to make the *white collar work* vs. *manual work* and *salaried work* vs. *wage work* dichotomies both important bases for class distinction in virtue of their importance as criteria for working class affiliation, and the psychological effect is to push white collar workers toward identification with the middle class. (About 61 per cent of white collar workers identify with the middle class and an additional 2 per cent identify with the upper class.)

Stratum and Class Differences in Criteria

IT is suggested in the foregoing discussion that from the differences in emphasis on criteria between classes certain insights may be gained as to the rationale for recruitment to the various classes. More concretely it has been suggested that, by and large, white collar workers and others who do not work with their hands or for wages are recruited to the middle class because they don't, and because they consider manual and wage work important criteria for membership in another (the working) class. Many of them see their role and status as different from the manual worker's role and status and (to interpret freely) they consider this important. Not working with their hands or for wages gives them something in common with the middle class and forms at least part of their rationale for identifying with it. But the fact remains that they do work for a living, which, because it is an important qualification for membership in the working class might well serve to identify them with that class if they considered it important. *But, by and large, they don't.* In Table 27 it can be seen that those who identify with the middle class lay twice as much stress on manual work as a criterion for the working class as they do on working for a living. Can it not be a reasonable inference that it is the very structure of the person's thinking and feeling about his role and status that recruits him into or identifies him with a social class? Is it not significantly in keeping with this hypothesis, too, that people who do identify themselves with the working class almost exactly reverse the emphasis on these two criteria, placing nearly twice as much emphasis on working for a living as they do on manual work as a criterion for their class? The suggestion is strong that it is people whose outlooks upon things are similar and who evaluate things in similar ways who form themselves into the same social class.

But more evidence, something in the way of a crucial test, is demanded to support such an hypothesis. In searching for one, the thought came to the writer that such a test might be supplied, although in a rather crude sense, in a comparison of the class criteria in use by people of common occupational position but of different class allegiance.

Business, professional and white collar people are predominantly identified with the middle class, but a sizable minority of them are affiliated with the working class. Now if it is to be supposed that common ways of people's conceiving their class are factors recruiting them to it, it should be found that this minority group of working class affiliates within the business, professional and white collar stratum tends to stress the same criteria for the working class as would be stressed by the majority of that class. The majority of the class is found in the manual stratum, of course. Further, these working class affiliates from the business, professional and white collar stratum should differ in their stresses on criteria from middle class affiliates in their stratum and differ in the direction characteristic of their class as a whole.

In Table 28 are data which substantially support the foregoing interpretation. *The predicted relationships are there.* The business, professional and white collar affiliates of the working class lay very much the same stresses on the various criteria for that class as the manual portion of the working class does. Both stress working for a living far more than manual work, and the differences between middle and working class affiliates within the same occupational stratum are in the predicted direction beyond doubt.

Only with regard to two of the criteria do business, professional and white collar affiliates of the working class differ appreciably from the manual workers of that class. They lay

TABLE 28

Stratum and Class Differences in Criteria for the Working Class:
Stratum "Membership" Constant, Class Identification Varied
Q. What would you say puts a person in the working class?

Per Cent Saying*	ALL BUSINESS, PROFESSIONAL AND WHITE COLLAR		ALL MANUAL WORKERS	
	Middle Class (N = 335)	Working Class (N = 191)	Middle Class (N = 126)	Working Class (N = 439)
"Working for a Living"	10	40	16	39
Manual Work, Common Labor, Mill or Factory Work	30	15	18	23
Lack of Income	14	18	19	13
Being an Employee or Wage Worker	9	12	10	12
Lack of Education or Training	13	4	13	4
Kind of Job, Type of Work	10	2	4	5
Lack of Security	3	6	3	5
Position or Background	5	1	2	†
Average Income	2	1	3	1
No Opinion	11	7	17	6

* Percentages add to more than 100 per cent. Respondents named more than one criterion in some cases.
† Less than one-half of one per cent.

somewhat less emphasis on manual work and somewhat more emphasis on lack of income as qualifications for membership. But if they want to be identified with the working class it is not to be expected, in view of their objective position, that they should stress qualifications that would bar them, but rather that they should emphasize those that gain them entrance. Having low income perhaps in a sense thus compensates for not being a manual worker with them. It is shown in a later chapter that low economic status markedly influences the class identifications of this group, so that economic factors are doubtless involved in recruitment.

So far, the hypothesis that common ways of evaluating the criteria of class distinction are factors integral to the structuring of social classes has received undeniable support. But still another test is possible.

The middle class, like the working class, is inhomogeneous as far as the occupational status of its affiliates is concerned. Most come from the business, professional and white collar stratum, but many are manual workers. Now if common ways of conceiving the qualifications for a class are typical of its membership and are factors in the membership's identification with it, the minority group of manual workers who identify themselves with the middle class should emphasize the same criteria as the majority of the middle class. This majority of middle class people is business, professional and white collar by occupation. Further, the manual worker affiliates should differ appreciably in respect to emphases of these criteria from those of their stratum who are affiliated with the working class, and should differ in the direction characteristic of the majority of middle class affiliates.

In Table 29 it can be seen that the actual data in the comparisons presented there are entirely consonant with these requirements.

The respective sectors of the middle class, regardless of the difference in their objective positions, manifest similar patterns of stresses on the qualifications for membership in their class. Both emphasize the "not rich, not poor," "live comfortably" type of criteria more than people of their respective strata but of working class membership do. Further, they both place more emphasis on education and on family, position and background, and lay less emphasis on owning a small business, profession or trade and on having property or security.

In only one or two instances is there a finding that constitutes a clear exception to the expected pattern. The manual workers who identify with the middle class do not emphasize salaried or white collar work quite so much as business, professional and white collar affiliates to the middle class do. But they should not be expected to be very conscious of this as a qualification, since, being manual workers, it would tend to raise a barrier to their identification with this class. The manual workers also emphasize money or income considerably less than do those of the middle class who are business, professional and white collar in occupation, probably for this same reason. That is, since their incomes are generally not

TABLE 29

Stratum and Class Differences in Criteria for the Middle Class:
Stratum "Membership" Constant, Class Identification Varied
Q. What would you say puts a person in the middle class?

Per Cent Saving*	ALL BUSINESS, PROFESSIONAL AND WHITE COLLAR		ALL MANUAL WORKERS	
	Middle Class (N = 335)	Working Class (N = 191)	Middle Class (N = 126)	Working Class (N = 439)
Money, Income, etc.	42	43	30	32
Not Rich, Not Poor, Live Comfortably, All Necessities and Some Luxuries, etc.	19	9	21	10
Education	20	7	15	8
Owning a Small Business, Profession or Trade	8	12	5	18
Family, Position, Background and Environment	13	9	17	4
Property or Security	5	10	5	8
Good Job, Steady Job	5	5	7	7
Salaried Work, White Collar Work	7	2	I	5
"Being Working People"	3	2	3	I
"Being a Good Citizen"	I	I	—	†
No Opinion	8	15	II	23

* Percentages add to more than 100 per cent. Respondents named more than one criterion in some cases.
† Less than one-half of one per cent.

high, great emphasis on money or income as a criterion of the class they identify themselves with could not be expected.

Despite these exceptions, which do seem to reflect differences in objective status, the data as a whole, in all of these comparisons, serve to indicate that members of the respective classes, regardless of objective differences in status, tend to evaluate the criteria of class distinction and to define the qualifications for membership in their own classes in quite similar ways. It is important to class theory that such a tendency exists, beyond doubt, for the holding of common views and the possession of common attitudes by social classes are just the factors supposed to be constituent to their structure.

CHAPTER 31

Continuities in Theories of Status Consistency and Cognitive Dissonance

JAMES A. GESCHWENDER

ABSTRACT

This paper attempts to place an explanation of the consequences of status inconsistency within the framework of dissonance theory. It integrates the Theory of Social Certitude, the Principle of Expectancy Congruence, and the Theory of Distributive Justice into the Theory of Cognitive Dissonance. The combined theory is evaluated in terms of its utility in explaining the empirical consequences of status inconsistency. A series of predictions are made regarding particular behavioral responses to specific inconsistency profiles.

The concept of status consistency (status crystallization or status congruence) is gradually assuming greater prominence in the literature of social stratification. Its major weakness lies in its use as a structural characteristic predicting behavioral consequences without an explicitly stated social-psychological theory of motivation to account for these predictions. Three such theories have been proposed. They are Homans' Theory of Distributive Justice,[1] Zaleznik's Theory of Social Certitude,[2] and Sampson's Principle of Expectancy Congruence.[3]

The last-named is an attempt to explain the findings of status consistency research within the framework of Festinger's Theory of Cognitive Dissonance.[4] Sampson's approach is similar to that of Zaleznik but has the advantage of being more general. However, it is still incomplete as it does not adequately explain all consequences of status inconsistency. It is suggested herein that the Theory of Distributive Justice can bridge this gap if it can be integrated into a dissonance framework. Two attempts to do this have been made.[5] However, they represent mere beginnings as they are limited as to degree of specification and detailed analysis. The present paper hopes

---

[1] George C. Homans, *Social Behavior: Its Elementary Forms* (New York: Harcourt, Brace & Co., 1961).

[2] A. Zaleznik, C. R. Christenson, and F. J. Roethlisberger, in collaboration with George C. Homans, *The Motivation, Productivity, and Satisfaction of Workers* (Cambridge: Harvard University Press, 1958), pp. 56-66.

[3] Edward E. Sampson, "Status Congruence and Cognitive Consistency," *Sociometry*, 26 (June 1963), pp. 146-162.

[4] Leon Festinger, *A Theory of Cognitive Dissonance* (Evanston, Illinois: Row, Peterson & Co., 1957).

[5] James A. Geschwender, "Explorations in the Theory of Social Movements and Revolutions," unpublished manuscript; and C. Norman Alexander, Jr. and Richard L. Simpson, "Balance Theory and Distributive Justice," *Sociological Inquiry*, 34 (Spring 1964), pp. 182-192.

to complete the task and to spell out in some detail further implications of the combined theory.

The strategy of attack will be to briefly describe the Theory of Social Certitude and the Principle of Expectancy Congruence, to relate them to each other, and to evaluate this combination. The Theory of Distributive Justice will then be described and integrated into dissonance theory. This combination will subsequently be evaluated as to its ability to explain the empirical findings of status consistency and further theoretical implications will be derived.

SOCIAL CERTITUDE
AND EXPECTANCY CONGRUENCE

The essence of the Theory of Social Certitude is the assumption that each status position carries with it a set of behavioral expectations regarding both the behavior of the occupant of said position and the behavior of all persons with whom he interacts. Each individual occupies several positions and possesses several sets of behavioral expectations which may either reinforce or contradict one another.

The status consistent possesses sets of behavioral expectations which either reinforce or are consistent with one another. A condition of social certitude exists and social relations are fluid and satisfying. The status inconsistent possessess sets of expectations which conflict with one another. A condition of social certitude does not exist. Anxiety is produced for all concerned and social relations are hampered and unsatisfying. This sets in motion forces tending toward the creation of status consistency.

The Principle of Expectancy Congruence and the Theory of Social Certitude have much in common. The major difference between them is that the former is stated within the framework of the more general dissonance theory while the latter stands alone. Sampson bases his analysis upon the following assumption:

Let us make the assumption that one aspect of each position—or set of positions—along a given status dimension consists of certain expectations for the behavior of the occupant of that position. Thus, for example, a person ranking high in education may meaningfully be said to have certain expectations held by others and by himself for his

behavior. A similar parallel between rank position and expectation can be drawn for other dimensions along which persons can be ranked.[6]

From this point, the analysis is identical to that proposed by Zaleznik. Incongruent expectations are a problem for everyone and interfere with interaction. Congruent expectations simplify interaction. Thus, there is a pressure on all participants to create and maintain a congruence of expectations. This is why status inconsistency is an undesirable state which produces pressure toward changing the situation.

EVALUATION OF SOCIAL CERTITUDE
AND EXPECTANCY CONGRUENCE

The Principle of Expectancy Congruence has the advantage of being derivable from a more general theory of motivation. This makes it more attractive than the Theory of Social Certitude as it may be more easily related to findings in other areas. However, the ultimate test of any theory is how well it explains empirical findings. It is at this point that the principle breaks down.

Research has demonstrated a relationship between status inconsistency and tendencies toward social isolation, mobility striving, political liberalism, psychosomatic symptoms of stress, and preference for changes in the social order or actual attempts to bring about these changes. This research will be discussed below. Some of these findings are explainable within an expectancy congruence approach and some are not.

The frustrations and anxieties produced by a lack of expectancy congruence might easily produce psychological symptoms of stress. They might interfere with social interaction and produce a tendency for inconsistents to withdraw into social isolation. They might also produce mobility strivings to achieve a state of expectancy congruence. However, this approach does not do a very good job of explaining the status inconsistent's preference for a change in the social order and predisposition for participation in social movements. Actually, mobility strivings are only partially explained. This approach does not supply us with any means of predicting which response to incon-

---

[6] Sampson, *op. cit.*, p. 153.

sistency a status inconsistent will be likely to select. An expanded theory which integrates the Theory of Distributive Justice into dissonance theory might perform this function.

THE THEORY OF DISTRIBUTIVE JUSTICE

An author can usually state his own ideas better than someone else can summarize or paraphrase them. Thus, it is best to quote Homans' description of his theory:

A man in an exchange relation with another will expect that the rewards of each man will be proportional to his costs—the greater the investments, the greater the profits. . . . Finally, when each man is being rewarded by some third party, he will expect the third party, in the distribution of rewards, to maintain the relation between the two of them . . . . The more to a man's disadvantage the rule of distributive justice fails of realization, the more likely he is to display the emotional behavior we call anger . . . . men are rewarded by the attainment of justice, especially when just conditions are rewarding in other ways. For instance, I am more likely to demand justice when justice would bring me more money than when it would bring me less. . . . Not only do men display anger, or less predominantly, guilt when distributive justice fails in one way or the other, but they also learn to do something about it. They learn to avoid activities that get them into unjust exchanges; they learn to emit activities that are rewarded by the attainment of justice . . . .[7]

Homans suggested that certain status dimensions could be viewed as investments into a social situation while others could be viewed as rewards received from that situation. The four dimensions that Lenski utilized in his analysis of status consistency may be classified according to this framework. Education and ethnicity may be seen as investment dimensions. There are universalistic norms in American society which lead one to expect that he will be rewarded in terms of his level of education. There are also particularistic norms which lead one to expect that he will be rewarded in terms of his ethnic status. Thus, education may be classified as an achieved in-

---

[7] Homans, *op. cit.*, pp. 332-333.

vestment and ethnicity as an ascribed investment.

Occupation and income may be viewed as reward dimensions. Income is clearly a reward as it determines one's standard of living. Occupation may also be seen as a type of reward. Some occupations are preferable to others in terms of the amount of physical labor demanded by them, the cleanliness of the work, and the amount of individual autonomy allowed. Thus, occupation may be classified as a social reward and income as a material reward.

Using these definitions, it could be concluded that a state of distributive justice exists when individuals who possess greater investments (higher education and/or ethnicity) also possess greater rewards (higher occupation and/or income). Those persons whose investments are higher than rewards (level of occupation and/or income below level of education and/or ethnicity) will experience a felt injustice and feel anger. It is reasonable to assume that this anger may be directed against the society which fails to maintain distributive justice and may lead to behavior designed to change society in order to eliminate this inequity.

Those persons whose investments are lower than their rewards (education and/or ethnicity below level of occupation and/or income) would experience a felt injustice and feel guilt. It may be assumed that individuals who are over-rewarded will not attempt to reduce guilt feelings by lowering their reward level. It is more likely that they will develop a political philosophy which, if implemented, would ameliorate the consequences of being short-changed for those who are under-rewarded. They might also develop a philosophy which defines ascribed investments as irrelevant to rewards. In short, they may become political liberals. If educational investment is the low dimension, they may either attempt to raise their level of education to one consistent with rewards received or else develop a definition of education as being "ivory tower" and impractical, which would lead to anti-intellectualism. It is to be noted that the Theory of Distributive Justice is not equipped to handle an explanation of the consequences of either investment (education–ethnicity) or reward (occupation–income) inconsistencies.

RELATION OF DISTRIBUTIVE JUSTICE TO DISSONANCE THEORY

It is possible to incorporate the Theory of Distributive Justice into dissonance theory with the addition of a few assumptions. We may assume that every individual includes within his cognitive set cognitions concerning his status level in the educational, occupational, ethnic, and income hierarchies. We may assume that he possesses cognitions defining education as an achieved investment, ethnicity as an ascribed investment, occupation as a social reward, and income as a material reward. We may also assume that he possesses cognitions which define the proper relation that should hold between investment and reward dimensions. This definition of the proper relation between investments and rewards would be based upon the individual's perception of that relation which normally exists in society.

Thus, experiencing a state of felt injustice is reduced to experiencing cognitive dissonance resulting from inconsistency among simultaneously held cognitions. The empirical consequences of felt injustice may be seen as behavioral attempts to reduce dissonance.

This may be combined with Sampson's assumption that each status position carries with it expectations regarding behavior that should be forthcoming from, or directed toward, the occupant of that position. Congruent sets of expectations facilitate the development of satisfying patterns of social interaction and incongruent sets of expectations impede this development. Thus, status inconsistency leads to the development of cognitive dissonance, and attempts to cope with this inconsistency represent behavioral attempts to reduce dissonance. Other behavioral responses may be non-coping responses indicating an inability to reduce dissonance. Dissonance theory, thus expanded, may enable us to explain the empirical consequences of status inconsistency which have been observed and to predict others not yet observed.

EVALUATION IN RELATION TO FINDINGS

The research literature has demonstrated six different types of responses to status inconsistency. These are enhanced mobility striving, withdrawal into social isolation, psychosomatic symptoms of stress, political liberalism, preference for and attempts to change the social order, and prejudice. The findings in each of these areas of research will be considered separately and in relation to the foregoing theoretical approach.

Mobility Striving

Benoit-Smullyan proposed the existence of a status equilibration process.[8] He stated that individuals are ranked or have status on three major dimensions: the economic, political, and prestige hierarchies. These types of status are analytically distinguishable and often empirically independent, but there is a tendency for one to be transformed into the others through a status equilibration process.

Implicit in Benoit-Smullyan's analysis is the assumption that possession of discrepant statuses in different hierarchies creates strain for individuals and causes them to follow a course of action designed to bring their statuses into line with one another. This assumption was not tested. Fenchel et al. did attempt to test this hypothesis with an undergraduate population at CCNY.[9] They had the students rate themselves as to their general standing in five potential reference groups and as to where they would like to stand. The difference between the two ratings was taken as an index of status striving. The hypothesis was supported as the students did tend to strive for a common ranking in all reference groups.

Homans reinterpreted one of his earlier studies into a framework which lends support to the equilibration hypothesis.[10] This was a study of female clerical workers and involved two categories of jobs—cash posters and ledger clerks. The line of promotion was from cash poster to ledger clerk. The general evaluation was that the position of ledger clerk was a better job, carried more responsibility, and conveyed more status. However, the same salary was paid to both positions. Ledger clerks protested demanding that they be paid

---

[8] Emile Benoit-Smullyan, "Status, Status Types, and Status Interrelations," *American Sociological Review*, 9 (April 1944), pp. 151-161.

[9] Gerd H. Fenchel, Jack H. Monderer, and Eugene H. Hartley, "Subjective Status and the Equilibration Hypothesis," *Journal of Abnormal and Social Psychology*, 46 (October 1951), pp. 476-479.

[10] Homans, *op. cit.*, pp. 237-242.

more than the cash posters as would befit their more important jobs. They were status inconsistent because their material rewards were not comparable to their occupational status. They were attempting to reduce dissonance by raising their lower-ranking status to a level consistent with their higher-ranking one.

The literature does not deal with variations in response by pattern of status inconsistency. However, it does yield implications for it. It suggests that persons experiencing dissonance resulting from status inconsistency may attempt to reduce this dissonance by altering their ranking on one or more of the dimensions of status. This would not be equally possible for all types of inconsistents. Persons who are low ethnically but high on the other dimensions could not normally be expected to alter their ethnic status through individual mobility. But a person who is high in education and low in occupation and/or income might hope to reduce dissonance through hard work, individual effort, and mobility on the occupational and/or income dimensions. More will be said about this below.

Political Liberalism

Lenski studied the relationship between status inconsistency and political liberalism.[11] A sample of persons were asked their views toward a government-sponsored health insurance program, price controls, and a general extension of governmental powers. Their responses were classified along a continuum of liberalism. The more liberal responses were found to be associated with low status consistency. Democratic voting was taken to be an indication of relative liberalism and was found to be associated with low status consistency.[12]

---

[11] Gerhard E. Lenski, "Status Crystallization: A Non-Vertical Dimension of Social Status," *American Sociological Review,* 19 (August 1954), pp. 405-413.

[12] Kenkel's retest of this hypothesis produced results which did not support it. See William F. Kenkel, "The Relationship Between Status Consistency and Politico-Economic Attitudes," *American Sociological Review,* 26 (June 1961), pp. 365-368. However, this retest was severely criticized. See Gerhard E. Lenski, "Comments on Kenkel's Communication," *American Sociological Review,* 26 (June 1961), pp. 368-369. Lenski maintained

Both of these associations held when general status levels were controlled. Certain patterns of inconsistency were more closely associated with liberalism than others. A person of low ethnic status and high income, occupational, or educational status tended to be more liberal than the reverse combinations. Individuals with low educational and high occupational statuses tended to be more politically liberal than did those with the opposite combination. An inconsistent with high occupational and low income status was more likely to be liberal than was the reverse combination. In fact, the high income–low occupation inconsistent was less likely to be liberal than were consistents.

Lenski's findings have been interpreted as indicating that status inconsistents may be prone to engage in social movements designed to bring about major changes in society. This may be erroneous. The particular items that Lenski used to measure political liberalism appear to be more closely related to a mild reformist perspective as might be incorporated into a welfare state or great society philosophy rather than the type of outlook that would motivate a person to join a social movement with more sweeping aims.

These findings suggest that a person who experiences dissonance resulting from status inconsistency may try to reduce his dissonance through the development of a liberal political outlook. The relationship of particular types of inconsistents to political liberalism is suggestive. Inconsistents with low educational and high occupational statuses and inconsistents with low ethnic and high occupational or income statuses are types of inconsistents categorized above as over-rewarded. Their investment dimensions are lower than their reward dimensions. They would be expected to feel guilt. Their attempts to reduce dissonance might be expected to take the form of attempting to ameliorate the consequences for others of their getting more than their share, and to develop a belief that ethnicity should not be related

---

that Kenkel erred in using different indices of status. His lack of results may have resulted from not using those that Lenski believed had a central place in American society. For the purposes of the present analysis, it will be useful to assume that Lenski's criticisms are correct.

to rewards. Both of these are indications of political liberalism.

The inconsistent with low ethnicity but a high educational status represents a different type. He has brought his achieved investment to a level higher than his ascribed investment. In this sense, he is a success. One might expect that, in this sample, this type of inconsistent is also high on reward dimensions. This is based on the fact that inconsistents with high education and low occupation are lower on the liberalism scale. Thus, they may also be over-rewarded and react as the others described above. However, I would suggest that we reserve judgment of this type of inconsistent. It might be necessary to know his position on reward dimensions before making any predictions about him. Similarly, we should reserve decision on the two types of reward inconsistents (high income–low occupation and high occupation–low income). It is difficult to draw any conclusions regarding the relative importance of income and occupation as types of rewards.

Social Isolation

Lenski also studied the relationship between status inconsistency and tendencies toward social isolation.[13] He found that status inconsistents were less likely than status consistents to interact with neighbors and fellow workers outside of business hours, to be members of voluntary associations, to be regular participants in those voluntary associations in which they were members, and less likely to report sociable motives (noneconomic reasons) for those voluntary ties that they had. No attempt was made to analyze the relation between types of inconsistency and tendency toward social isolation.

Homans provided data which suggest that this tendency toward social isolation may not always be voluntary.[14] He found that the status inconsistent members of a work group were high on initiating interaction for others but were low on the receipt of interaction from others. Generally the interaction that they initiated took the form of horseplay or joking. Homans suggested that joking may be the reaction of the inconsistent to the insecurities in the situation, while the reaction of others is a tendency to avoid the inconsistent.

These results are explainable with the assumptions that Sampson makes in his Principle of Expectancy Congruence. Status inconsistency creates a situation in which there exist conflicting sets of behavioral expectations. This interferes with the development of fluid tension-free interaction. Thus, interaction becomes unpleasant and tends to be broken off. It may be possible that the earliest stage of this process is found in other persons avoiding the inconsistent and in the inconsistent resorting to joking. Withdrawal on the part of the inconsistent may represent the final acceptance on his part of the impossibility of creating satisfying patterns of interaction. Suicide is the most extreme form of withdrawal, and Gibbs and Martin found a relationship between status inconsistency and propensity toward suicide.[15]

Preference for Social Change

Lenski postulated that status inconsistents might be prone to react against society by participating as leaders in social movements and that a society with widespread status inconsistencies was unstable and generated pressures toward change.[16] However, he never empirically tested this proposition. Benoit-Smullyan made a similar suggestion when he stated, "There are historical grounds for supposing that when legal, customary, or other barriers seriously hamper the equilibrating tendency,

---

[13] Gerhard E. Lenski, "Social Participation and Status Crystallization," *American Sociological Review,* 21 (August 1956), pp. 458-464.

[14] George C. Homans, *Sentiments and Activities* (Glencoe, Illinois: The Free Press, 1962), p. 100.

[15] Jack P. Gibbs and Walter T. Martin, "Status Integration and Suicide," *American Sociological Review,* 23 (April 1958), pp. 140-147. For other research documenting the fact that status inconsistency interferes with the development of free communications and satisfying interaction see Stuart Adams, "Status Congruency as a Variable in Small Group Performance," *Social Forces,* 32 (October 1953), pp. 16-22; Ralph V. Exline and Robert C. Ziller, "Status Congruence and Interpersonal Conflict in Decision-Making Groups," *Human Relations,* 12 (April 1959), pp. 147-162; and Arlene C. Brandon, "Status Congruence and Expectations," *Sociometry,* 28 (September 1965), pp. 272-288.

[16] Lenski, "Status Crystallization . . . ," p. 412.

social tensions of revolutionary magnitude may be generated."[17] He cited as evidence the fact that support for the Nazi Party came from large classes of persons who became impoverished but retained their former prestige statuses.

There are other historical examples of status inconsistents who have supported social movements. Frazier noted that Negro support for organizations like the Urban League and the NAACP tends to come from middle-class Negroes.[18] Lipset pointed out that urban middle-class leaders in the C.C.F. tended to come from minority groups, while the urban middle-class leaders in the Liberal and Conservative Parties tended to come from the Anglo-Saxon majority group.[19] Michaels noted that middle-class Jews were quite prominent in European Socialist parties.[20] These last three examples are all of status inconsistents whose ethnic status was lower than their occupational status. It is worth noting at this point that the examples show low ethnicity–high occupation inconsistents supporting leftist movements and high occupation–low income inconsistents supporting rightist movements.

Ringer and Sills found a high proportion of status inconsistents among political extremists in Iran. They were overrepresented among the extremists on the revolutionary left and the nationalistic right.[21] The inconsistents were of a high educational level and only a moderate

economic status. The degree of inconsistency was sharpest for the revolutionary left. Both types of extremists were anti-colonialist and this common antagonism to vestiges of colonialism may have been more important in attracting adherents than their left–right differences. These data show a tendency for under-rewarded inconsistents with a high level of education to take an extremist position in reacting against the social order. The data regarding the NAACP, C.C.F., and Jewish socialists show over-rewarded inconsistents with a low ethnic status taking a more moderate reformist position when reacting against the social order.

Goffman related status inconsistency to preferences for change in power distributions within society.[22] Status inconsistency was measured using the educational, occupational, and income hierarchies. Preference for change was measured by asking respondents to check their perceptions of the amount of influence in the conduct of national affairs presently held by, and the amount of influence that they prefer be held by, state governments, big business, labor unions, businesses that were not big, and the national government. Status inconsistents exhibited a greater preference for change than did status consistents. This relation held with general status levels controlled. No attempt was made to analyze differences between status types. It is not possible to discuss the left–right direction of these preferences for change without knowing more detail about the responses than Goffman provided.

These findings suggest that there is reason to believe that status inconsistents may attempt to reduce dissonance by reacting against the social order, or at least by expressing a preference for a change in the present distribution of power within society. They further suggest that under-rewarded inconsistents are more likely than over-rewarded inconsistents to take an extreme reaction against the social order. This is predictable from the assumptions incorporated into dissonance theory from the Theory of Distributive Justice. Homans states

---

[17] Benoit-Smullyan, op. cit., p. 160. For supporting documentation see also William Kornhauser, The Politics of Mass Society (Glencoe, Illinois: The Free Press, 1959), p. 181. Lipset cites unpublished research by Robert Sokol which found a relationship between perceived status discrepancy and support of McCarthy, but patterns of discrepancy were not discussed. See Seymour M. Lipset, "Three Decades of the Radical Right," in Daniel Bell, The Radical Right (New York: Anchor Books, 1955), p. 403.

[18] E. Franklin Frazier, Black Bourgeoisie (Glencoe, Illinois: The Free Press, 1959), pp. 98-104.

[19] Seymour M. Lipset, Agrarian Socialism (Berkeley: University of California Press, 1950), p. 191.

[20] Robert Michels, Political Parties, (trans.) Eden and Cedar Paul (New York: Dover Publications, 1959), pp. 260-261.

[21] Benjamin B. Ringer and David L. Sills, "Political Extremists in Iran," Public Opinion Quarterly, 16 (Winter 1953), pp. 689-701.

[22] Irwin W. Goffman, "Status Consistency and Preference for Change in Power Distribution," American Sociological Review, 22 (June 1957), pp. 275-288.

that anger is a stronger emotion than guilt. The angry (under-rewarded) inconsistent would be expected to experience a sharper form of dissonance and a more extreme reaction than would guilty (over-rewarded) inconsistents.

Psychosomatic Symptoms

Elton Jackson studied the relationship between status inconsistency and the exhibition of psychosomatic symptoms.[23] Consistency was measured in terms of the ethnic, educational, and occupational status dimensions. He found a significant relationship between status inconsistency and the exhibition of psychosomatic symptoms. He also found a significant difference between types of inconsistents.

Jackson noted that two types of inconsistents (high ethnicity combined with either low occupation or low education) had high rates of psychosomatic symptoms, while the opposite types (low ethnicity combined with high education or high occupation) did not have symptom rates which differed from that of status consistents. He noted that Lenski had found the two types of status inconsistents with high symptom rates to exhibit only a slight tendency toward political liberalism and the two types with low symptom rates to exhibit strong tendencies toward political liberalism. He suggested that the important determinant is the relationship between achieved and ascribed ranks. Those with high ascribed and low achieved ranks are likely to see themselves as failures and to develop high psychosomatic symptom rates. Persons with low ascribed and high achieved ranks are likely to see themselves as successes—they have made it despite their ethnic handicap. Thus, they will direct their response to stress outward. This will take a political form for many.

The major difficulty with this interpretation

of political and psychosomatic responses as alternative ways of reacting to inconsistency is that it does not seem to apply equally well to all types of inconsistents. Jackson included in his table, but did not discuss, psychosomatic symptom rates and tendencies toward political liberalism for high occupation–low education and high education–low occupation inconsistents. Both types of inconsistents have symptom rates higher than consistents and also exhibit a stronger tendency toward political liberalism. The one possible support for viewing political and physical reactions as alternative responses comes from the fact the symptom rates for these two types of inconsistents are lower than those with high physical, low political responses and their tendency toward political liberalism is less than those with high political, low physical responses. Possibly these results show a tendency for some persons experiencing this type of inconsistency to react physically and others to react politically.

Jackson advanced one other tentative proposition that bears examination. He found male inconsistents with high occupation and low educational statuses to have a symptom rate much higher than did status consistents. Those males who had high educational and low occupational statuses exhibited a symptom rate lower than that of status consistents. He suggests that mobility opportunities might explain this. The latter type of inconsistent is likely to see the possibility of future mobility bringing about consistency, while the former type cannot look forward to this possibility. More mobility would simply cause greater inconsistency. Jackson indicated elsewhere the existence of the relation of mobility possibilities and age.[24] Younger inconsistents, who had status profiles which could become consistent through mobility, had lower levels of psychosomatic symptoms than older inconsistents with similar profiles. This could indicate that with advanced age mobility would be defined as less likely and persons would give up striving and develop physical responses.

Jackson's major contribution came in demon-

---

[23] Elton F. Jackson, "Status Consistency and Symptoms of Stress," *American Sociological Review*, 27 (August 1962), pp. 469-480. Dunham has also found that persons with high education and low occupation exhibit a tendency toward both schizophrenia and psychopathies, though he raises questions regarding the causal direction. See H. Warren Dunham, Patricia Phillips, and Barbara Srinivasan, "A Research Note on Diagnosed Mental Illness and Social Class," *American Sociological Review*, 31 (April 1966), pp. 223-227.

[24] Elton F. Jackson, "Status Consistency, Vertical Mobility, and Symptoms of Stress," unpublished Ph.D. dissertation, University of Michigan, 1960, p. 95.

strating that failure to reduce dissonance through either mobility or political reactions might force one to attempt to live with dissonance. Dissonance is tension-producing and, in the absence of dissonance-reducing behavioral attempts, might easily produce a physical response leading to psychosomatic symptoms.

Prejudice

There is currently very little research relating status inconsistency to prejudice.[25] However, we can draw indirect inferences regarding this relationship if we accept membership in the Ku Klux Klan as an indication of racial prejudice. Vander Zanden has pulled together the names and occupations of 153 members of the Klan.[26] Ninety-eight of these were found in occupations (skilled labor, marginal businessmen, and marginal white-collar occupations) which are the occupations in which Negroes are making the greatest inroads.[27] The rest are

[25] See Donald J. Treiman, "Status Discrepancy and Prejudice," *American Journal of Sociology,* 71 (May 1966), pp. 651-664. Treiman attempted to evaluate the relative utility of a status consistency and an additive hypothesis for the explanation of prejudice. He concluded that the additive hypothesis was adequate for the explanation of prejudice without making the complex assumptions involved in a status consistency hypothesis. His treatment is unsatisfactory for three reasons. First, he limited himself to a consideration of education—income inconsistents. Second, he used family income rather than individual income. This does not give an individual status profile as one does not know how many people contribute to total family income. Third, and most important, he used a system of classification which produced some "inconsistents" which could be more accurately classified as consistents. This does not mean that his findings are necessarily wrong—merely that they are questionable.

[26] James W. Vander Zanden, *Race Relations in Transition* (New York: Random House, 1965), pp. 42-43.

[27] For a description of these inroads see James A. Geschwender, "Social Structure and the Negro Revolt: An Examination of Some Hypotheses," *Social Forces,* 43 (December 1964), pp. 248-256; James A. Geschwender, "Desegregation, the Educated Negro, and the Future of Social Protest in the South," *Sociological Inquiry,* 35 (Winter 1965), pp. 58-68.

transportation workers, semiskilled or unskilled laborers. These are occupations in which whites have been receiving competition from Negroes for many years. It is reasonable to assume that in the South, the status attributed to an occupation declines with increases in the proportion of Negroes. Thus, KKK members are status inconsistent because their occupational status fails to come up to their high ethnic status.

If membership in the KKK is not accepted as a valid indication of racial prejudice, it certainly is an indication of willingness to express and/or act out hostility toward members of a racial minority. Thus, we can see that under-rewarded status inconsistents may attempt to reduce dissonance by directing hostility against members of a minority group.

DISCUSSION

It would appear that all research findings to date dealing with consequences of status inconsistency can be explained within the framework of an expanded version of dissonance theory. This would require combining the initial premises of the theory with Sampson's assumptions and a series of assumptions derived from the Theory of Distributive Justice. A brief statement of the assumptions would go as follows:

1. All persons hold sets of cognitions which include some that are reality-based, some which are definitional, and some that are normative. Reality-based cognitions describe the existing state of affairs while normative cognitions describe the state of affairs which should exist.

2. Any set of cognitions may stand in a relation of dissonance, consonance, or irrelevance depending upon the internal relations which hold among reality-based and normative cognitions. If the conjunction of a reality-based and a normative cognition implies another reality-based cognition in the set then a state of consonance exists. If this conjunction implies the negation of another reality-based cognition in the set then a state of dissonance exists. If this conjunction implies neither another reality-based cognition nor the negation of one in the set then a state of irrelevance exists.

3. Reality-based cognitions will include perceptions of one's status in the educational,

occupational, income, and ethnic hierarchies. They will also include perceptions of behavior expected from, and expected to be directed toward, the occupants of positions in each of these hierarchies. Definitional cognitions will include the definition of ethnicity as an ascribed investment, education as an achieved investment, occupation as a social reward, and income as a material reward. Normative cognitions will include beliefs regarding the proper relation that should exist among the various status positions. Particularly, they will include the belief that rewards received should be proportional to investments. Possession of a higher level of ascribed investments than achieved investments will be defined as failure. The reverse combination will be defined as success.

4. Dissonance is an upsetting state and will produce tension for the individual. This tension will lead to an attempt to reduce dissonance by altering cognitions, adding new cognitions, or deleting old ones. Attempts to alter reality-based cognitions will involve attempting to change the real world. Attempts to alter normative cognitions will involve attempts to change evaluations of the real world and will take place within the cognitive system.

5. Status inconsistents whose rewards received are less than believed to be proper for their investments will feel anger and inconsistents whose rewards exceed investments will feel guilt. Anger is a sharper form of dissonance than guilt. The perception of failure produces a sharper form of dissonance than the perception of success. The intensity of dissonance-reducing behavior will be directly proportional to the sharpness of dissonance.

6. Dissonance-reducing attempts will take the form of coping responses, attempts to change the real world, when possible. When coping responses are not possible, dissonance-reducing attempts will take the form of attempting to withdraw from interaction. When neither changing the real world nor withdrawal from it is possible, dissonance will remain and the tension will be manifested in psychosomatic symptoms.

7. Dissonance-reducing attempts will move from the simple to the complex. That is, the simplest types of alterations in reality that would reduce dissonance will be attempted first.

If these attempts are unsuccessful, a shift will be made to increasingly complex attempts. The simplest form of altering reality is to attempt to change one's own status through individual mobility. Downward mobility would create sharper dissonance by causing a comparison with rewards received in the past, and therefore believed possible, and rewards currently received. Thus, only upward mobility would be a dissonance-reducing move. The next most simple form of altering reality is to strike out against individuals and categories of individuals (e.g., prejudice and discrimination). The most complex form of attempting to change reality is attempting to alter society. The simplest form of withdrawal is social isolation, and the most complex form of withdrawal is suicide.

These assumptions enable us to make deductions for each of the patterns of inconsistency which would explain the empirical findings to date. These patterns are presented in Chart 1.

Under-rewarded status inconsistents whose high investment dimension is ethnicity would feel sharp dissonance (anger). Mobility might possibly be a way of reducing dissonance depending on their level of education. If it is possible, it will be attempted first. If it is not possible, or if it is unsuccessful, attempts to reduce dissonance will shift to attacking categories of persons. It would be expected that this type of inconsistent would be highly prejudiced and would engage in discrimination. Any attempt to change the society would likely take the form of trying to create a state of affairs in which ethnicity has increased importance—a racist social movement. If none of these attempts are successful, then one would expect a tendency toward social isolation and a high level of psychosomatic symptoms.

Under-rewarded inconsistents whose high investment dimension is education would experience sharp dissonance (anger). Mobility for them is possible and will be attempted as a means of reducing dissonance. If mobility attempts are unsuccessful or blocked (e.g., if they are minority group members) then the individual will shift to more complex forms of dissonance reduction. Prejudice and discrimination may develop but could hardly result in changing reality if they were directed against

SOCIAL FORCES

CHART 1. STATUS CONSISTENCY PATTERN AND REACTIONS TO DISSONANCE

Responses	Under-Rewarded Inconsistents		Over-Rewarded Inconsistents		Investment Inconsistents		Reward Inconsistents	
	High Ethnicity / Low Occupation / Low Income	High Education / Low Occupation / Low Income	Low Ethnicity / High Occupation / High Income	Low Education / High Occupation / High Income	High Ethnicity / Low Education	High Education / Low Ethnicity	High Occupation / Low Income	High Income / Low Occupation
COPING RESPONSES								
Emotional reaction	Anger	Anger	Guilt	Guilt	Definition as failure	Definition as success	Ambiguity	Ambiguity
Mobility possibility	Possible, depends upon level of education	Possible, depends upon age	Not possible	Unlikely	Unlikely	Not possible	Unlikely, but depends upon age	Not possible
Prejudice	If no mobility, then high prejudice and discrimination likely	If no mobility, then possible prejudice against majority or minority groups (unlikely to aid in coping)	May develop anti-majority prejudice (unlikely to help cope) or prejudice against other minorities	May develop prejudice, but this is unlikely to aid in coping	Prejudice and discrimination highly probable	May develop anti-majority prejudice (unlikely to help cope) or prejudice against other minorities	Possible, but probably not aid in coping	Possible, but probably not aid in coping
Social change attempt	If neither mobility nor prejudice proves adequate, then possibly joins a racist social movement	If other coping responses fail (as is likely), then prone to join extremist social movements—providing perception of adequate power	If prejudice fails to reduce dissonance, then moderate change response such as liberalism or moderate reform social movement	Moderate change response such as political liberalism or participation in moderate reform social movement possible	Prone to join racist social movements	Moderate change response such as political liberalism or participation in reform social movement likely	No prediction. Data show tendency toward both political liberalism and extremist movements	No prediction. Data show no tendency toward liberalism
NON-COPING								
Social isolation	If coping responses fail, then tendency to withdraw into social isolation	If coping responses fail, then tendency to withdraw into social isolation	Doubtful, even if coping responses fail	Doubtful, even if coping responses fail	If coping responses fail, tendency toward social isolation	Doubtful, even if coping responses fail	Tendency toward social isolation quite probable	Tendency toward social isolation quite probable
Symptoms of stress	If coping responses fail and withdrawal impossible, then symptoms likely	If coping responses fail and withdrawal impossible, then symptoms likely	Doubtful, even if coping responses fail	Doubtful, even if coping responses fail	If coping responses fail, and isolation impossible, symptoms likely	Doubtful, even if coping responses fail	If social isolation not possible, symptoms quite probable	If social isolation not possible, symptoms quite probable

members of the majority group. Thus one would be prone to attempt to change society and this .attempt would take a more extreme form (social movements or revolution). A requirement for participating in social movements and revolutions is the belief that one has the power to be successful. If this is lacking, or the change attempt fails, then the inconsistent would be forced into social isolation and/or exhibition of psychosomatic symptoms.

Over-rewarded status inconsistents whose low investment dimension is ethnicity will not be able to reduce dissonance through mobility. They may develop anti-majority group prejudices but this will do them little good. Thus, they will be forced to attempt to reduce dissonance by changing society. Their mild state of dissonance (guilt) will produce a moderate change response such as political liberalism or participation in a moderate reform social movement. It is doubtful if they will be forced into social isolation or exhibition of psychosomatic symptoms, as they will be able to define themselves as successes for overcoming their ethnic handicap.

Over-rewarded inconsistents whose low investment dimension is education will probably not be able to reduce dissonance through individual mobility, nor would they benefit by attacking other categories of people through prejudice. Thus, it is likely that they would start their dissonance-reducing attempts at the level of societal alteration. Their mild state of dissonance (guilt) would lead to a moderate response such as political liberalism. It is possible that this would fail and force them into social isolation, but the mild degree of dissonance might make it unlikely that they would develop psychosomatic symptoms to any great extent.

Investment inconsistents could not be considered as either over- or under-rewarded. Those with ethnicity as the higher dimension are failures and those with ethnicity as the lower dimension are successes. Failures would not be able to expect mobility. They would probably develop hostility toward minority groups, and might be prone to join racist social movements. If these dissonance-reducing attempts fail, they would be forced into social isolation and be prone to display psychosomatic symptoms. The successes could not expect social mobility and would not gain from attacking categories of persons. Their mild dissonance might lead them into attempts to reduce dissonance by moderate attempts at social change such as developing a liberal political philosophy or supporting moderate reform movements. If these attempts are unsuccessful, it is unlikely that they would exhibit strong psychosomatic symptoms though they may be forced into social isolation.

Reward inconsistents could not be defined as over- or under-rewarded, successes or failures, without knowledge of their investment dimensions. The only prediction one could make about them is that they would exhibit a tendency toward social isolation and possibly the exhibition of psychosomatic symptoms. However, one might expect that high occupation–low income inconsistents would also have a high level of education and be prone to act like other under-rewarded–high education inconsistents.

CONCLUSIONS

Sampson made a major contribution to the development of a motivational theory which would explain the behavioral consequences resulting from status inconsistency. He did this by placing reactions to status inconsistency within a cognitive dissonance framework through the addition of an expectancy congruence assumption. The present paper attempts to develop this further by adding a set of assumptions derived from the Theory of Distributive Justice. The task is hardly finished. Considerable refinement of these assumptions and empirical testing of derived propositions is required. Nevertheless, it is hoped that the present paper is a step in the right direction.

CHAPTER 32

Nonvertical Dimensions of Social Stratification

ROBERT W. HODGE and PAUL M. SIEGEL

The attitudes and behavior of individuals may be affected not only by their location on each of the several dimensions of social stratification, but also by the particular status configuration described by the locus of their positions on each of these dimensions. Many studies have shown, that the several dimensions of social stratification, including such variables as income, occupational prestige, education, and ethnic status, have independent effects upon a host of attitudes and social behavior. Indeed, "For the forecasting of a great many facets of a man's behavior, it is hard to beat the usual tired old socioeconomic variables and the standard personal background data."[1] Socioeconomic indicators are, however, only imperfectly intercorrelated, and collectively they may be viewed as defining a multidimensional space rather than a single unidimensional continuum. Each of the vertical or hierarchical dimensions, as education and income for instance, which define this status space may make an independent contribution to the formation of attitudes and the determination of behavior. The several vertical dimensions which define a multidimensional status space may, however, be themselves combined to form a nonvertical dimension of status. As Lenski observed in his pioneering, empirical study of status crystallization, "Theoretically it becomes possible to conceive of a nonvertical dimension to individual or family status —that is, a consistency dimension. In this dimension units may be compared with respect to the degree of consistency of their positions in the several vertical hierarchies.

In other words, certain units may be consistently high or consistently low, while others may combine high standing with respect to certain status variables with low standing with respect to others."[2] The units of which Lenski speaks represent status configurations; our purpose here is to evaluate the effects of consistent and inconsistent status configurations and to explore the logic of this conceptualization.

EMPIRICAL EVIDENCE

The results of numerous empirical studies suggest that the effects of status configurations, status consistency, or status crystallization are quite pronounced and enable one to explain a variety of phenomena more thoroughly than is possible by reference to vertical dimensions of social status alone. In his initial empirical study of the relationship between status crystallization and political attitudes, Lenski found that "regardless of whether income rank was high and educational rank low, or the reverse, or what the particular nature of the status inconsistency was, the fact of imperfect status crystallization *per se* seems to have been related to political liberalism"[3] and suggested that "the more frequently acute status inconsistencies occur within a population the greater would be the proportion of that population willing to support programs of social change."[4] Submitting Lenski's suggestions to further empirical test, Goffman reported empirical "support for the hypothesis of an inverse relationship between the degree of status consistency and preference for change in the distribution of power."[5] Only recently, Lenski himself has examined comparative data bearing upon his initial concern with the association between status consistency and political liberalism. Examining the hypothesis that "inconsistency produces stress, and stress generates political discontent which manifests itself in support for liberal parties,"[6] Lenski found that "the hypothesis that inconsistency increases liberal or left of center political tendencies is supported in 21 of the 25 tests in the four countries."[7]

Discussions of the relationship between status inconsistency and political attitudes have usually been guided by the assumption that status inconsistency engenders some form of psychological stress. This stress is in turn assumed to incline one to accept liberal political ideologies and is regarded as the intervening variable which accounts for the relationship between status inconsistency and political attitudes. A variety of direct and indirect empiricial tests of this postulated relationship between status inconsistency and stress have appeared over the past few years. Arguing that negatively sanctioned or unrewarded behavior declines in frequency and that status inconsistency is associated with the denial of rewards in the realm of interpersonal relations, Lenski predicted that "persons whose status is poorly crystallized will exhibit a tendency to withdraw from, or avoid, social intercourse."[8] Using data on interaction between neighbors and fellow workers (off the job) and on participation and membership in clubs and voluntary organization, Lenski found that persons with poorly crystallized statuses manifested lower levels of activity. Additional data bearing upon the reasons for maintaining organizational ties revealed that persons with poorly crystallized statuses initiated and maintained club memberships for *sociable* reasons less frequently than those with a high degree of status consistency. The more instrumental character of organizational memberships among those of poorly crystallized status is taken as further evidence of their withdrawal from social interaction: " . . .

persons with poorly crystallized status might be expected to join voluntary associations not because of the opportunities which such groups provide for meeting new people and making new friends, but rather because the group and the social relationships which go with it are necessary *means* to the end of personal advancement, the reform of society, or some other nonsociable end."[9]

The rather indirect evidence relating status inconsistency and stress provided by Lenski's data on interaction with neighbors and organizational participation has been augmented by more direct evidence derived from reports of psychosomatic symptoms and other expressions of stress. Jackson reported, for example, that the degree of status inconsistency is positively associated with the prevalence of psycho-physiological symptoms among both males and females whenever racial-ethnic rank is superior to occupational or educational rank, among males whenever occupational rank is superior to educational rank, and among females whenever their educational rank is superior to their husband's occupational rank.[10]

The weight of the empirical evidence bearing upon the important social and psychological ramifications of status inconsistency is augmented further by the results of studies conducted in other research traditions. Most notable are studies of the effects of cross-pressures on voting behavior. Individuals such as Episcopal laborers or Negro doctors who have loyalties to groups with different, traditional political alignments are subject to cross pressures. The Irish Catholic merchant is, for example, constrained by his ethnic and religious background to support the Democratic party and by his occupational role to support the Republican party. The conflicting voting allegiances of these two salient reference groups place the Irish Catholic merchant under cross-pressures, a circumstance which is not felt by the Irish Catholic policeman who guards his store and whose allegiance to the Democratic Party does not conflict with his pattern of group loyalties. Empirical investigations have shown that individuals who are subjected to cross-pressures, whether generated by conflicting group loyalties or affiliation with friends of differing political convictions, are less likely to turn out at polls for elections and remain less decisive about their choices of candidates over the course of an election campaign.[11] These findings, like those derived from the literature on status consistency, provide an empirical basis for the claim that a full understanding of the effects of social stratification cannot be gleaned from the study of the independent effects of an individual's location in each of several status hierarchies. One must also explore the possibility that the conflicts experienced by individuals with inconsistent status configurations are given novel resolutions which cannot be deduced solely from a knowledge of the location of individuals on the hierarchical dimensions of status.

THE METHODOLOGICAL CHALLENGE

Despite the accumulating mass of evidence of the effects of status consistency, the interpretation of these effects has been continually challenged. Soon after Lenski's original empirical study, Kenkel published conflicting evidence based on a different sample, different measures of political liberalism, and, most importantly, a somewhat different procedure for identifying individuals occupying highly or poorly crystallized statuses. Reviewing the relationship between status consistency and attitudes about (1) the Taft-Hartley law, (2) foreign trade, (3) government care for the needy, (4) wartime strikes, (5) price control, (6) government ownership of aircraft factories, and (7) the strictness of labor laws, Kenkel observed, "The conclusion seems inescapable that, basically, respondents classified as consistent or inconsistent do not differ with regard to the attitudes measured by these seven questions."[12] Recently, Kelly and Chambliss have attempted to resolve the disparity between Lenski's and Kenkel's findings concerning the relationship between status consistency

and political liberalism. New data reported by these authors "support Kenkel's finding of no relationship between status consistency and political liberalism" and "raise serious doubts as to the explanatory utility of the concept of status consistency."[13]

The main thrust of criticism concerning the effects of status consistency has, however, been methodological rather than empirical in character. Practically all of the studies reviewed above, including those producing negative evidence, are subject to criticism on the grounds that the effects of status consistency have been examined with no control *at all* or with no control *for all* of the initial status variables from which the measures of status consistency were constructed. This is a particularly penetrating criticism on two counts: (1) status consistency was introduced precisely because it was thought to explain variation which could not be attributed to the independent effects of hierarchical measures of status and (2) examination of the effects of status consistency *within* the categories created by simultaneous cross-tabulation of *all* the hierarchical status variables utilized in the derivation of the measure of status consistency is *logically* impossible. In order that their force may be clearly seen, these points require further elaboration.

Most theoretical and conceptual elaborations in science are introduced to accomplish one or both of two things: (1) to expand the power of a scientific theory by either extending the range of phenomena to which it applies or increasing the precision of its explanation of phenomena already under the purview of the theory and (2) to provide a simpler explanation of phenomena already accounted for by an unsatisfactorily complex formulation. The concept of status crystallization was designed to complicate, rather than simplify, the theory of social stratification; consequently, it is not vindicated by its ability to provide a less complex explanation of behavior. At least abstractly, a theory of social stratification augmented by the concept of status crystallization does not appear to have a larger domain than a theory of stratification unencumbered by the notion of status crystallization. Thus, no justification for introducing the concept of status crystallization can be found in its extension of the theory of stratification to cover new phenomena. The primary reason for introducing the concept of status crystallization, and the one advanced by its proponents, appears to be its ability to explain more precisely phenomena known to be associated with the socioeconomic status. However, since no one has demonstrated that measures of status crystallization have an effect on behavior which is independent even of the variables from which such measures derive, much less independent of all relevant stratification variables, there is no intellectual force to the claim that the concept of status crystallization enables one to achieve a more precise and more complete explanation of behavior.

The entire scientific status of the concept of status crystallization is complicated once it is made apparent that there is no logically conceivable way of *isolating* the effects of status crystallization from the effects of the socioeconomic variables from which measures of status crystallization are constructed. Ordinarily, one demonstrates that the introduction of a new variable augments the explanatory power of a theory by showing that, *within* categories of the independent variables already incorporated in the theory, the new variable exhibits a significant association with the dependent variable in question. A demonstration of this kind is, however, not possible in the case of status crystallization, for *within* a category formed by the conjunction of a status from each of several dimensions there can be *no* variation in the configuration of statuses. Thus within-category variation in attitudes or behavior could not possibly be explained by within-category variation in status configuration—there is none.

Consider, for example, a two-variable measure of status inconsistency derived from comparison of an individual's education and the income of his family. In this case, we would ideally like to examine the effects of status consistency within educational and income categories. The impossibility of effecting such comparisons may be clearly seen in Table 1, which gives means of Seeman's powerlessness scale (adjusted for age and sex of respondent) for various degrees of status consistency among persons who completed one year of college or more. (The data are taken from an unpublished study of the Northeast Power Blackout of 1965, conducted by the National Opinion Research Center.) As the reader can see in Table 1, there is a clear and monotonic relationship between status consistency and powerlessness. Respondents whose income and educational levels are inconsistent feel a greater sense of ineffectiveness in individual action; the greater the inconsistency between education and income becomes, the greater is the sense of powerlessness. Despite the systematic relationship exhibited by the means in Table 1, the interpretation nevertheless remains ambiguous. For as the reader can see in the second column of the table, respondents who differ in their levels of income-education consistency also differ systematically in their levels of family income. There is no way whatsoever of determining by inspection of the table whether the observed mean

Table 1.—Powerlessness by Status Discrepancy and Income, Adjusted for Age and Sex, for Those with Some College Experience

Status Discrepancy Level	Family Income	Mean of Powerlessness Scale, Adjusted for Age and Sex	Number of Respondents
Total, some college or more		2.54	378
Consistent	$10,000 or more	2.35	204
Mildly inconsistent	$7,000—9999	2.58	94
Fairly inconsistent	$5,000—6999	2.89	37
Strongly inconsistent	Under $5,000	3.03	43

differences in powerlessness are the effects of status inconsistency or of income. The difficulty which keeps one from making an unambiguous interpretation of Table 1 plagues most studies of status inconsistency. Recognition of this difficulty has led to the introduction of more refined statistical techniques and to a somewhat altered notion of status inconsistency.

FURTHER METHODOLOGICAL CONSIDERATIONS

The data on powerlessness given in the third column of Table 1 represents only one column of a more elaborate table which shows the mean level of powerlessness by income not only for those with some college but also for other educational groups. In the other columns of the more elaborate table one would not ordinarily expect to observe means identical to those shown in Table 1. Education, like income, is apt to have an effect upon powerlessness; if its effect is in the same direction as that of income, one would expect the means in the remaining columns of the more elaborate table to be somewhat higher at each income level than those found in Table 1. The information in the remaining columns of the more elaborate table can help to resolve the ambiguity in the interpretation of Table 1. Consider, for example, the data on powerlessness presented in Table 2 for those with eight or fewer years of school completed. If we first examine the initial two columns, we will observe an important difference between Table 2 and Table 1. Among those with some college (Table 1), the most consistent persons were those with

the highest levels of family income, while the least consistent were those with the lowest family incomes. Just the reverse is the case among those at the lowest educational level (Table 2): the most consistent are those with the lowest incomes, while the most inconsistent have the highest incomes. Because of these differences between Table 1 and Table 2 in the association between income and status inconsistency, the alternative explanations of the findings shown in Table 1 lead one to expect *different* relationships in Table 2. If the pattern of results observed in Table 1 are explained by income, then one would expect to observe results in Table 2 which are parallel to those observed among persons with one or more years of college. The means, of course, might be higher because of the effect of educational level, but one should still find among those with only an elementary school education a *negative* correlation between family income and powerlessness. If, on the contrary, one interprets the patterns observed in Table 1 as reflecting the influence of status inconsistency rather than the influence of family income, one is led to expect a positive correlation between family income and powerlessness in Table 2. Among those with elementary school educations, the most consistent have the lowest incomes and (according to the pattern observed in Table 1) should have the lowest felt sense of powerlessness, while the least consistent are those with the highest incomes and should have the greatest feelings of powerlessness. Consequently, if status consistency is the variable thought to explain the results in Table 1, one is led to expect a *positive* correlation between fam-

Table 2.—Powerlessness by Status Discrepancy and Income, Adjusted for Age and Sex, for Those with Eight or Fewer Years of School Completed

Status Discrepancy Level	Family Income	Mean of Powerlessness Scale, Adjusted for Age and Sex	Number of Respondents
Total, 8th Grade or less		3.18	268
Strongly inconsistent	$10,000 or more	2.53	21
Fairly inconsistent	$7,000—9999	2.40	38
Mildly inconsistent	$5,000—6999	2.71	59
Consistent	Under $5,000	3.66	150

ily income and powerlessness in Table 2.

As the reader can see by inspection of Table 2, the relationship between income and powerlessness among those with elementary school education is negative, like that observed among those with one or more years of college. Consequently, Table 2 gives little support to the status consistency hypothesis: the results among both those with some college and those with elementary educations exhibit a negative association between powerlessness and income, while status inconsistency has a positive association with powerlessness among those with some college and a negative association with powerlessness among those completing eight or fewer years of school. Thus, reference to income would seem to provide a more *parsimonious* interpretation of the results in Table 1 and Table 2. Income has the same effect on powerlessness at both ends of the educational continuum. Status inconsistency, however, is more complexly intertwined with powerlessness, having associations of different signs with powerlessness at opposite ends of the educational continuum.

Although Occam's razor inclines one to make reference to income rather than to status inconsistency in interpreting the data reported in Tables 1 and 2, there is no logical way of separating the effects of income from those of status inconsistency in the two tables. Indeed, status consistency theory provides a wholly plausible interpretation of the results presented in the two tables. Such an interpretation follows readily once one recognizes a distinction between different types of status inconsistency. In Table 1, which refers to those with one or more years of college, status inconsistency is manifested by achieving a level of income relatively *below* one's level of education. By way of contrast, status inconsistency among those with eight or less years of school completed is manifested in a level of income which is relatively *above* one's level of education. Thus, the two tables refer to two different types of status inconsistency, the type in which income is high relative to education and the type in which income is low relative to education.

These two distinct types of status inconsistency need hardly have the same consequences for behavior. The person who gains little income relative to his educational standing is likely to be depressed, frustrated, or otherwise disenchanted by the low rate of return upon his educational investment, while the person who gains much income despite an inferior level of educational attainment is unlikely to experience similar feelings of psychological malaise. Thus, once a distinction between the two types of status inconsistency is introduced, one finds ample grounds for postulating a *positive* correlation between status inconsistency and powerlessness when income is low relative to education and a *negative* correlation between status inconsistency and powerlessness when income is high relative to education. This is precisely the pattern exhibited by the data in Tables 1 and 2. There is no way of establishing that this explanation of the data is inferior to one which makes reference only to income and argues simply that income facilitates a sense of power by enabling one to exercise a greater control over one's environment and life style. The latter explanation is attractive because of its simplicity, and because it requires only minimal psychological assumptions, but these are not sufficient grounds for rejecting a more complex explanation of the data. We are, then, back in the quandary we started in, unable to isolate the effects of status inconsistency from the effects of the status variables which define it.

Reduced to its logical skeleton, the quandary appears in a far wider range of issues than its discussion in the context of status discrepancy might suggest. Consider, for example, a proposition relating behavior or attitudes to social mobility, i.e., to the *configuration* of statuses of sons and their fathers, or of sons at two points in their lives. Insofar as it is reasonable to expect a son's status to affect his behavior holding father's status constant, variations in behavior can be attributed either to the statuses independently or to their particular conjunctions or configurations—e.g., the *difference* between a son's status and that of his father taken as a measure of his mobility—with equal validity.

While the quandary arises from the attempt to attribute explanatory power exclusively to either the independent effects of the status variables or some dimension defined by their particular conjunctions or configurations, it does not always arise from such attempts. Consider a proposition relating the frequency of informal visits between parents and their adult offspring to the geographic locations of the residences of the parents and offspring. One would not be likely to suppose that the location would affect the frequency of visiting, but instead would fasten upon the particular spatial configurations of residences—the distances separating the residences of parents and offspring—as being the explanation for whatever relation obtained spatial location and visiting. In this case one can make the distinction between the effects of the statuses taken independently (geographic location) and of their particular configurations (geographic distance) and decisively attribute the effects to one and not the other, but it must be done *a priori*. This is generally the case, that is, only on *a priori* grounds can one unequivocally allocate variation to either the effects of the statuses taken independently or to their particular combinations.

While the dilemma uncovered here is quite general—since it depends upon the logical rather than the substantive construction of variables—some headway can be made in untangling the "independent" effects of status variables from effects of their particular configurations at the cost of more rigorous specification of the problem—a cost which no scientific endeavor should be unwilling to pay. The explanation of Tables 1 and 2 which makes reference only to income leads us to expect that the relationship between income and powerlessness should be "the same" within every educational category. (At least it provides no reason to expect otherwise.) If the relation of income to powerlessness is not "the same", within two educational categories the differences can only be attributed to some function of the particular conjunc-

tion of educational and income statuses. If they comport with its psychological implications, these differences can be attributed to status inconsistency; if not, some other function of the particular combinations of statuses must be invoked.

The cost of this means of discovering status consistency effects is now obvious: On the one hand we must provide a model of the relations of income and education to powerlessness, in order that "sameness" have some operational meaning and on the other hand, we must develop the implications of the status consistency theory in order to be able to tell whether it or some other explanation holds. (Of course, we could attribute *all* departures from "sameness" to status inconsistencies, *a priori*.)

Many models of the relations between income, education, and powerlessness are available. They vary in the form they attribute to the relations and in the degree to which they specify them. In turn, this variation carries over to the form and specificity with which they permit description of the effects of "inconsistency". A thorough exposition of these alternative models and the techniques appropriate to assessing their adequacy would require more discussion than the present context warrants. To give some idea of the considerations involved, a single example will be presented.

A rather stringent model of the relations among income, education, and powerlessness holds that the mean difference in powerlessness between two particular income levels at the same level of education should be the same quantity regardless of which education level is chosen. (Simple algebraic manipulation will show that this specification is logically equivalent to requiring that the mean difference in powerlessness between two particular educational levels at the same level of income should be the same quantity regardless of which income level is chosen.) In addition, we require that as income or education increases (or as both increases), powerlessness decreases.[14] Consider, for example, the mean differences in powerlessness between those with family incomes of $10,000 or more and those with family incomes under $5000 in the two tables. Among those with one or more years of college, this difference is -0.68 ($=2.35 - 3.03$), while among those with elementary educations this difference is -1.13 ($=2.53 - 3.66$), over half again as large. Statistical interactions —relations between income and powerlessness which are not "precisely" the same (in the sense of the model used here) from one educational category to the next—are not encompassed by the explanation of Tables 1 and 2 which makes reference solely to some kind of "average" relationship between income and powerlessness. Instead, these interactions must be explained by recourse to consideration of status configurations, i.e., by consideration of the effects upon behavior of particular combinations of status.

The notion of status inconsistency has thus undergone a rather radical evolution from its original conception, chiefly as a result of rigorous logical scrutiny of its content. We have seen that the only meaning that "status inconsistency effects" can have which is distinct from the meaning of "status effects" is that the *relation* between status and attitudes or behavior depends upon (varies with) the conjunction of particular levels on the several dimensions of social status. These remarks may suggest the importance of close (methodos) logical analysis of concepts. They can only hint at the directions which research on non-vertical dimensions of social stratification may take. But they clearly indicate that we need both more rigorous theoretical specification of the kinds of interactions between status variables and behavior which would count as "status inconsistency effects"[15] and methodologically sound empirical work which would permit unambiguous assessment of whether or not such effects exist.[16]

NOTES

[1]Frederick Mosteller and David L. Wallace, "Inference in an Authorship Problem: A Comparative Study of Discrimination Methods Applied to Authorship of the Disputed *Federalist* Papers," *Journal of the American Statistical Association,* 58 (June, 1963), p. 304.

[2]Gerhard E. Lenski, "Status Crystallization: A Non-vertical Dimension of Social Status," in Seymour Martin Lipset and Neil J. Smelser (eds.), *Sociology: The Progress of a Decade* (Englewood Cliffs, N.J.: Prentice-Hall, 1961), p. 485. Originally published in the *American Sociological Review,* 19 (August, 1954), pp. 405-13.

[3]*Ibid.,* p. 492.

[4]*Ibid.*

[5]Irwin W. Goffman, "Status Consistency and Preference for Change in Power Distribution," *American Sociological Review,* 22 (June, 1957), p. 281.

[6]Gerhard E. Lenski, "Status Inconsistency and the Vote: A Four Nation Test," *American Sociological Review,* 32 (April, 1967), p. 299.

[7]*Ibid.* Lenski does not appear, however, to understand that the several tests within each country are not independent of each other.

[8]Gerhard E. Lenski, "Social Participation and Status Crystallization," *American Sociological Review,* 21 (August, 1956), p. 459.

[9]*Ibid.,* p. 461.

[10]Elton F. Jackson, "Status Consistency and Symptoms of Stress," *American Sociological Review,* 27 (August, 1962), p. 479.

[11]See, for example, Paul Lazarsfeld, Bernard Berelson, and Hazel Gaudet, *The People's Choice* (New York: Duell, Sloan, and Pearce, 1944), Ch. 15; and Bernard Berelson, Paul Lazarsfeld, and William N. McPhee, *Voting* (Chicago, Ill.: University of Chicago Press, 1954), pp. 129-132.

[12]William F. Kenkel, "The Relationship Between Status Consistency and Politico-Economic Attitudes," *American Sociological Review,* 21 (June, 1956), pp. 366-367.

[13]K. Dennis Kelly and William J. Chambliss, "Status Consistency and Political Attitudes," *American Sociological Review,* 31 (June, 1966), p. 381.

[14]A simpler model would merely require that mean powerlessness differences be of the same sign (in the same direction) for all comparisons of two particular income groups within levels of education, and *vice versa*. A more stringent model would require that decreases in powerlessness be *proportional* to increases in either income or education.

[15]For a treatment of some of the criteria to be met and problems likely to be encountered by such specification, see Hubert M. Blalock, Jr., "Theory Building and the Statistical Concept of Interaction," *American Sociological Review,* 30 (1965), pp. 374-380; "The Identification Problem and Theory Building," *American Sociological Review,* 31, (1966) pp. 52-61; and "Status Inconsistency and Interaction: Some Alternative Models," *American Journal of Sociology,* 73 (1967), pp. 305-315.

[16]Exemplary empirical treatments are afforded in Donald J. Treiman, "Status Discrepancy and Prejudice," *American Journal of Sociology,* 71 (1964), pp. 651-664; and Edward O. Laumann and David R. Segal, "Status Inconsistency and Ethno-religious Group Membership as Determinants of Social Participation and Political Attitudes," in Edward O. Laumann, *Informal Networks and Value Orientations in a Metropolis* (New York: Van Nostrand, 1971 tentative).

VIII

Stratification and the Community

Accessibility is an ultimate constraint upon the location of one's work and the place of one's residence. This factor alone is sufficient to bind inextricably the stratification of roles within organizations and the stratification of residential neighborhoods. Thus the ecology of local industry, coupled with the differential demands of different industries for personnel of alternative grades, is one important basis of the spatial distribution of status in metropolitan communities. Our purpose in this introductory essay is to sketch briefly how industrial location, the socioeconomic level of employees, and the necessary accessibility of places of residence to places of work act concertedly to create the socioeconomic differentiation of residential areas within cities. The content of social life within these areas as well as the way in which residence and other features of stratification are intertwined are discussed in the selections incorporated in this section.

Although the movements of individuals *into* the central business districts are accomplished by various means, their movements *within* the central business district, whether it be from store to store or service to service or work to lunch and return, are

largely restricted to foot traffic and short journeys via mass transit. The jumble of shops and services which comprise the central business district is sustained because it makes a large number of different services simultaneously accessible to a large number of people; the burden of maintaining a central location with its associated high land values, high costs of high-rise construction and crowded access routes for deliveries can be carried because of the economies of scale resulting from mass merchandising. Centralized retail establishments require centralized wholesaling. Consequently, the central business district tends to become encircled by warehousing facilities, transport docks and other shipping, receiving and transport enterprises including train and bus terminals (see Berry, 1967). (Indeed, you can usually mark out the fringes of the central business district by fixing the locations of rail depots and warehouses, even though they may have fallen into ill repair or have been out of use in recent years.) In turn, these transportation services attract yet another ring of industrial enterprises which can make good use of centralized shipping both in distributing their own products and in assembling their raw materials.

The core of the city comes to consist, then, of a center comprised of retail businesses, professional services, and administrative offices and two successive rings: first, wholesale establishments, warehouses and transport facilities and, second, light manufacturing enterprises with a sprinkling of heavy industries which are not directly dependent upon a seaboard or other special location. This pattern, as we have described it here, is highly idealized and every concrete case will probably offer some important exception to it. Some of the reasons are discussed below, but here we may note that urban congestion is one of the most important. Accessibility makes centrality advantageous; modern megalopolises have diverged from this pattern into various degrees of multiple nucleation because the free movement of people and goods has been retarded by the congestion of urban transport networks to the point where time costs offset travel distance and make decentralized facilities more accessible (see Thompson, 1965). At every stage in the development of the city, transportation technology probably places a limit upon the growth of the central business district. As we now see them, the central business districts are doubtless best regarded as products of the railroad era (see Warner, 1962); their demise and the new, emergent patterns of decentralization are a feature of the automobile age. But the existence of a center, regardless of what divergences from an ideal pattern may be found in concrete instances, creates one of the single most important constraints upon the development of residential ecology. What the central business district secures is that the centralization of jobs is more pronounced than the centralization of the residences of their incumbents. This principle, together with the industrial organization of the center, goes a long way toward explaining the status topography of cities (see Hoover and Vernon, 1962).

Apart from low-level service personnel, such as elevator operators and janitors, the jobs created in the core of the city are primarily concentrated at the professional, managerial, sales and clerical levels. Working class posts are, however, in much greater supply in the warehousing and manufacturing belts surrounding the central business district. If the white-collar workers of the city center lived in the residential areas immediately adjacent to the manufacturing districts, they would spend less time traveling to and from work and would force the industrial workers to travel further than would be necessary if they lived in the area physically most accessible to their places of work. Instead, the area of heavy and light industry around the central shopping areas tends to be surrounded by a zone of workingmen's homes (see Burgess, 1924). These residential areas, made undesirable by their proximity to surrounding industries and the industrial pollution to which they are exposed, are well within the budgets of working-class families, and the proximity of work location eliminates the necessity of maintaining (second) cars or paying public transit fares as jobs can be reached by walking or cycling.

The area of workingmen's homes shades off almost imperceptibly into middle-class residential areas, which are characterized by the greater amount of land devoted to recreational and scenic uses and the mixture of single-family and multiple-family dwelling units or, perhaps more commonly, one- or two-family homes made singularly dull and unattractive by their replication of a common, cardboard box architecture. These areas house not only the mass of lower-level white-collar workers—clerical workers, office staff, mail carriers, low-level salesmen and the like—but also the owners and managers of local shops serving these persons, a few professional persons likewise serving a purely local rather than a metropolitan clientele, and, of course, a few workingmen who have achieved fiscal security through seniority. A final zone in this idealized pattern is comprised largely by single-family dwelling units, amply spaced on large lots, occupied in the main by professional men and top managers (see B. Duncan, 1957).

Although the description of the spatial distribution of status in the metropolis given above is plainly an abstraction from the complexities of concrete cases in which the locational advantages of some sites may occasion uses unlike those postulated here, the central features of the pattern have been empirically observed in a wide variety of modern, industrial cities. Chicago and Paris, Cleveland and Winnipeg, Oxford and Hull, all exhibit a common pattern of occupational segregation in which the greater the social status difference between two occupational groups, the larger the residential dissimilarity between them. In most of these cities, the residences of the highest status groups are, in addition, the least centralized. (See, for Chicago, Duncan and Duncan, 1955; for Paris, Rhodes, 1969; for Cleveland, Uyeki, 1964; for Winnipeg, Smith and Kornberg, 1969; and for Oxford, Collison and Mogey, 1959). The nearly equal accessibility of these diverse groups to their often common places of work is achieved by a stratification of transport which coincides with the economic levels of its users. The worker will find walking, cycling or a short journey by public bus convenient; the white-collar worker will find an express bus or rapid transit attractive for his journey and for his purse; the manager and professional man will enjoy the comfort of an electric suburban train or the luxury of sitting through each morning's traffic jam in his private automobile; and, of course, a few men of means and taste will begin their work reclining in the luxurious leather of a radiophone-equipped, chauffeur-driven Rolls. To each according to his means is true enough of one's mode of access; but each will find his journey to work limited to approximately one-half hour (see B. Duncan, 1956, 1957; for an opposing view see Morgan, 1967). Inequalities in status and alternative modes of transit are used, then, to secure a near universal equality of access.

There are several exceptions to the patterns described above and these are noteworthy in their own right. First, one needs to recognize, of course, that places of work are imperfectly centralized, so that there is an appreciable intermingling of residences of different occupational groups. Local shopping areas and heavy industries decentralized because of their need to locate on a waterway, transport line or near a raw material source create competition for housing which results in the residential mixture of occupational groups. Thus, even at the status extremes, only two-thirds to three-quarters of professional men would have to change their places of residence in order to achieve a residential distribution by census tract equivalent to that observed for unskilled laborers. Second, locational advantages of various kinds, especially variations in terrain, may lead to the development of a status topography which departs in one or another way from the concentric pattern noted above. Thus, in Chicago, the lakefront, stretching north from the city's center, is virtually a continuous row of high-rise, high-status apartment buildings; in Montreal, physical heights have been turned into the homes of the socially elevated, despite the fact that the initial approaches to Mount Royal border on the central business district; in Portland, Oregon, the bluffs overlooking the Willamette River have similarly been adopted by the well-to-do; and in Manchester, England, the prevailing winds have left the southern half of the city virtually free from industrial smoke and pollution, making the southerly suburbs among the highest-status towns in England and leaving the northern areas of the city for workers and industry. Exceptions of this kind indicate, of course, that, though accessibility is important in the determination of industrial location and the residential patterns of status groups, it is in the final analysis only a constraint rather than a unique cause (see Firey, 1947).

In recent years, the basic pattern described above has been appreciably eroded. Urban congestion, as suggested above, has made the ring of industries surrounding the central business district increasingly inaccessible. With little room for spatial expansion and with the prospect of ever-increasing traffic, many of these firms have relocated in the suburbs next to new industries, rather than renew deteriorating physical plants in the central city. In many cities, the suburbanization of manufacturing has made possible the urban renewal of areas surrounding the central business district. The conversion of this land to residential use, typically through construction of urban villas consisting of shopping facilities, town houses and high-rise apartments, has enabled the city to recapture some of the higher status, suburban families. Their motive in returning to the city is identical to industry's desire to leave it: the increasing congestion of freeways has made daily commutation between the suburb and the city's center increasingly impractical. The full implications of industrial relocation in undeveloped suburban tracts remain to be worked out in the years ahead. It is not impossible that it will ultimately reverse the present pattern of status gradients from the city center. Surely, it has had the immediate effect of making some of the most secure and stable employment inaccessible to our Negro citizens who are isolated in central-city ghettoes.

The arguments advanced to this point plainly do not apply to non-industrial cities for the simple reason that they have no industrial base to exploit the transport facilities associated with centralized retail merchandising. Consequently, one expects a somewhat different status topography to be found in the cities of undeveloped and developing nations. Indeed, one might well expect the clerks and sales workers of retail shops, the few professional men and managers, as well as the administrative officials of local government to cluster residentially around the city center, much as they did around the squares of medieval towns. A second ring might well consist of small tradesmen and traditional craftsmen living and working in the same building, and running the decentralized shops of the quasi-villages which have piled one upon another in many primate cities. Toward the periphery one would find, of course, the least skilled workers and peasants, tilling subsistence from small plots or making daily journeys to more substantial land-holdings beyond the city proper. Such a pattern is just the reverse of that of industrial cities, for it requires that the housing of those in the most prestigious occupations

be most, rather than least, centralized. Nevertheless, this pattern has been found to predominate in a number of preindustrial cities, including Poona, India (see Mehta, 1968), and Guatemala City (see Caplow, 1949).

Some authors have taken the existence of reverse status gradients in primate cities as empirical grounds for rejecting the zonal scheme associated with Ernest Burgess (1924). However, one should recognize that these divergent patterns are intelligible within a common framework which emphasizes the importance of accessibility and transport technology in the determination of patterns of land use (see Schnore, 1965). Furthermore, there is evidence that in the early phases of their own development, industrial cities themselves were characterized by an inverse correlation between socioeconomic level of residents and distance from the center of the city. Indeed, Burgess himself had occasion to comment upon the traces of this pattern still evident in Chicago: large, single-family dwelling units, really estates, near the central business district which have been converted to business offices or subdivided into multiple-family dwelling units. Indeed, these vestiges of an older period exist to the present day. Thus, the status topography of large cities in underdeveloped countries may signal an evolutionary pattern in city development, rather than the existence of important cultural bases of social ecology.

The status differentiation of residential areas noted in this introductory section provides, then, an ecological basis for class (or status) behavior. Groups of diverse social status have a territorial base. The institutions they patronize — schools, churches, small shops and so forth—are correspondingly differentiated (see Suttles, 1968). The urban neighborhood becomes a highly visible manifestation of the status structure, and individual occupational careers come to be mirrored in one's residential movements. A home is not just where you live; it is a location in a well developed status ecology and, inferentially, a telltale clue to one's location in the occupational hierarchy. Such status areas are, of course, both a setting for and an expression of the class behaviors whose description provides the primary content of this section.

REFERENCES

Abu-Lughod, Janet L.
1969 "Testing the theory of social area analysis: The ecology of Cairo, Egypt." American Sociological Review 34:198-212.

Amory, Cleveland.
1947 The Proper Bostonians. New York: E. P. Dutton.

Berry, Brian J. L.
1967 Geography of Market Centers and Retail Distribution. Englewood Cliffs, New Jersey: Prentice-Hall.

Berry, Brian J. L., and Philip H. Rees.
1969 "The factorial ecology of Calcutta." American Journal of Sociology 74: 445-491.

Burgess, Ernest W.
1924 "The growth of the city: An introduction to a research project." Publications of the American Sociological Society 18: 85-97. Reprinted in Robert E. Park, Ernest W. Burgess, and Roderick D. McKenzie (eds.), The City. Chicago: University of Chicago Press, 1967.

Caplow, Theodore.
1949 "The social ecology of Guatemala City." Social Forces 28: 113-133.

Collison, Peter.
1960 "Occupation, education, and housing in an English city," American Journal of Sociology 65: 588-97.

Collison, Peter, and John Mogey.
1959 "Residence and social class in Oxford." American Journal of Sociology 64: 599-605.

Duncan, Beverly.
1956 "Factors in work-residence separation: Wage and salary workers, Chicago, 1951." American Sociological Review 21: 48-56.
1957 "Intra-urban population movement." In Paul K. Hatt and Albert J. Reiss, Jr. (eds.), Cities and Society. Glencoe, Ill.: Free Press.

Duncan, Otis Dudley, and Beverly Duncan.
1955 "Residential distribution and occupational stratification." American Journal of Sociology 60: 493-503.

Farley, Reynolds W.
1970 "The changing distribution of Negroes within metropolitan areas: The emergence of black suburbs." American Journal of Sociology 75: 496-511.

Firey, Walter.
1947 Land Use in Central Boston. Cambridge: Harvard University Press.

Hawley, Amos, and Otis Dudley Duncan.
1957 "Social area analysis: A critical appraisal." Land Economics 33: 337-345.

Hoover, Edgar M., and Raymond Vernon.
1962 Anatomy of a Metropolis. Garden City, New York: Anchor Books.

Lynd, Robert S., and Helen M. Lynd.
1929 Middletown: A Study in American Culture. New York: Harcourt, Brace & Co.
1937 Middletown in Transition: A Study in Cultural Conflict. New York: Harcourt, Brace & World.

Marquand, John Phillips.
1949 Point of No Return. Boston: Little, Brown.

Mehta, Surinder K.
1968 "Patterns of residence in Poona (India) by income, education, and occupation." American Journal of Sociology 73:496-508.

Morgan, James N.
1967 "A note on the time spent on the journey to work." Demography 4: 360-362.

Schnore, Leo F.
1963 "The social and economic characteristics of American suburbs." Sociological Quarterly 4: 122-134.
1965 "On the spatial structure of cities in the two Americas." In Philip M. Hauser and Leo F. Schnore (eds.), The Study of Urbanization. New York: Wiley.

Smith, Joel, and Allan Kornberg.
1969 "Some considerations bearing upon comparative research in Canada and the United States." Sociology: Journal of the British Sociological Association 3: 341-357.

Suttles, Gerald D.
1968 The Social Order of the Slum: Ethnicity and Territory in the Inner City. Chicago: University of Chicago Press.

Thompson, Wilbur R.
1965 A Preface to Urban Economics. Baltimore: Resources for the Future.

Uyeki, Eugene S.
1964 "Residential distribution and stratification, 1950-1960." American Journal of Sociology 69: 491-498.

Vidich, Arthur J., and Joseph Bensman.
1958 Small Town in Mass Society: Class, Power, and Religion in a Rural Community. Princeton: Princeton University Press.

Warner, Sam Bass, Jr.
1962 Streetcar Suburbs: The Process of Growth in Boston, 1870-1900. Cambridge: Harvard University Press and the Massachusetts Institute of Technology Press.

Warner, W. Lloyd.
1959 The Living and the Dead: A Study of the Symbolic Life of Americans. New Haven: Yale University Press.

CHAPTER 33

The Domestic Cycle and the Distribution
of Power in Turkish Villages

PAUL STIRLING

In this paper I seek to show some structural relations between domestic organisation and village organisation. Incidentally and inevitably, it becomes clear also that this system flourished in the villages only because the larger society of which it formed part provided appropriate conditions.[1]

In my argument, I have relied on a rather schematic view, and have kept historical and ethnographic data to the minimum. Nevertheless, the arguments and ideas arose directly from my field work experience, and are fully borne out by what I found in that area. I am sure from my reading and observation that they also apply more widely.

From 1949 to 1952, I lived for periods totalling about 13 months in two villages not very far east of Kayseri in central Turkey. The villagers of this area are settled cereal cultivators. They keep draught animals – oxen and water buffaloes, and in some villages nowadays horses, – flocks of sheep and goats, and chickens. They grow some vegetables and fruit.

The villages vary in size from about 50 to over 200 households. They are compact, separated from each other by from half-an-hour to two hours' walking. Each is the centre of a territory with known boundaries within which

1. Dr. Maurice Freedman suggested to me the explicit inclusion of this point. I am also clearly indebted to the recent Cambridge symposium; Goody (ed.), 1958.

its flocks and herds graze freely. All the villages in the area in which I worked were Turkish speaking, and orthodox Sunni Muslims.

The first village in which I lived, Sakaltutan, was fairly remote, and was still using the traditional agricultural techniques. A road, just possible for a daily lorry service, had been opened up two years before my arrival, making a revolutionary change in the ease of communication with the town. The village contained roughly 100 households and 600 people.

The other village, Elbaşı,[1] was the administrative and gendarme centre for about twenty villages. It contained about 210 households and 1,200 people. It had much better and older communications; more developed social relations with town; richer and more sophisticated leaders; horses, carts and steel ploughs; and much more land per head. Yet the differences in the way of life of the majority of the people were slight.

I start from four main characteristics of the villages, two concerned with the domestic cycle, and two with the distribution of power.

(i) The ideal household in the villages is unquestionably the joint patrilocal household, consisting of a man, his wife or wives, all his sons and their wives and children, and his unmarried daughters. On the death of the household head, the household is expected to split, each son becoming head of an independent household. People are unanimous on this ideal.

(ii) In spite of this unanimity, households conforming to this ideal were in a minority in both villages. In Sakaltutan, 15 out of 105 households were full joint households, and these contained 22% of the village population; in Elbaşı, 20 households out of 208, containing 15% of the population. By 'full joint', I mean households in which a male head has a married son or sons, and at least one paternal grandchild. If we include all households with more than one married couple, then 25 households in Sakaltutan, containing 34% of the population, and 44 households in Elbaşı, containing 29% of the population, are joint. These include three in Sakaltutan, and two in Elbaşı, shared by married brothers.

Breaches of the rule that sons should not leave the household of a living father do occur, but these in no way account for the fact that full joint households are a minority. Five fathers in Sakaltutan and three in Elbaşı had married sons who had separated from them and are counted as heads of simple households. But if all the sons had returned home, the number of joint households would have risen by only one in each village.

---

1. Ş. is pronounced like sh; l (distinct in modern Turkish from i) is very near the indefinite English vowel er; so Elbası roughly rhymes with usher in England and cosher in U.S.A.

(iii) The villages lacked clear political leadership.[1] Every village has an official headman, elected, or at least chosen, by the village, but these were comparatively young men and they seldom remained in office for more than the prescribed term, which was changed from four years to two in 1950; often for less. Most of them did not enjoy their term of office, and there was sometimes difficulty in filling the post. They were usually junior members of important families, or occasionally dependents of important kinsmen. In some cases there was sharp rivalry over the control of the office, though not over the office itself.

Even unofficially, no one man dominated any of the villages I knew, with one possible exception: Karabey of Elbaşı, who died in 1951[2], before I began work in his village.

The villages are divided into a number of small shallow agnatic lineages. Many of the households were more or less unattached, or else, though acknowledging their agnatic kin, in fact had very little to do with them. But most of the important households, and many others, were grouped in lineages,[3] which besides discharging, with special emphasis between themselves, the ordinary duties of neighbours and kin, – help in sickness and distress, and at life crises – were also organised for common defence. Members of such a group would immediately offer support, armed if necessary, if one of the lineage were attacked or insulted, and were expected to avenge the death of any member who was killed. These lineages ranged from three or four to twenty households. They were not, however, politically organised, and, at least at the time of my field work, no single lineage appeared to be able to dominate a village, except indirectly through one outstandingly wealthy household.

Many households and lineages claimed ancestors who had been men of influence, but in no village did I find evidence of power or office remaining traditionally in one lineage, or passing by inheritance as a matter of course. Different lineages and different households achieve importance at different times.

(iv) This impression is confirmed by another fact which I found at first surprising. In several instances, men of wealth and substance were quite clearly from families of comparatively recent immigrants into the village, or had a recent history of poverty. On the other hand, poor men sometimes claimed illustrious fathers or grandfathers. For example, the head of the wealthiest family in Sakaltutan was himself the son of a woman who had come to the village as a widow. Two poor men owned a very large guest house, and were sons of a man who had apparently been highly respected in the village. A man

1. I have given details of the ranking system of Sakaltutan elsewhere. STIRLING, 1953.
2. See below p. 207.
3. STIRLING, 1960.

in Elbaşı whose father had in fact been a man of power and importance, but died poor on his return from Mecca, was the youngest of five brothers, all of whom had passed through periods of poverty, and some of whom were still very poor. He himself however was the head of a very prosperous household, with five sons, large land holdings and a very comfortable total income. These instances were by no means isolated, and they indicate a high rate of mobility within the village hierarchy.

Of these four characteristics, the first two concern the household. At first sight, the numerical predominance of simple households might appear inconsistent with the acceptance of the three generation joint household as the ideal. In fact, given the rules, the distribution of types of households is what one would expect under the demographic conditions of village life. Every household begins as simple, following the splitting up of the paternal household on the father's death. As a man's sons grow up and marry, his household becomes in its turn joint. In a sense at the death of the head, the household may be said to continue in his sons, who work the same land, normally live in the same building, and inherit some of the father's relationships. But it simplifies discussion to speak arbitrarily of the household as ending with the final division following the father's death, and as being replaced by the households of his sons. Even if we assumed a life expectation of 60 years for men, and an average gap between father and son of 25 years, it is obvious that an 'average' household head would have to spend 15 years after his father died before his grandson was born, and then he would experience ten years as head of a full joint household before his own death. At any one time in any one village, with such an 'average', less than half the households would be full joint.

This model is grossly oversimplified, but it is I think completely conclusive. In fact, achieving a full joint household is even more difficult than it suggests. Adult men themselves often die prematurely, leaving unmarried children; the child death rate is high, and so is the rate of infertility and miscarriage among women. A man may beget a run of daughters. The death rate was even higher in the past, and was accentuated by conscription for the Ottoman army. Many men who would in 1950 have been village grandfathers were said to have 'remained on mobilisation', that is, to have failed to return from the wars in which Turkey was engaged from 1911 to 1922. The recent fall in the death rate and improvement in health conditions has led to a rapid increase in population,[1] but so far this has the effect of increasing the proportion of younger

---

1. The population of Turkey has risen from 13.6 millions in 1927, to an estimated 26.9 millions in 1959. (*Annuaire Stat.*, République Turque, 1951; *Turkish News*, Turkish Embassy, London, 15th May, 1959.)

simple households. If the death rate continues to fall, and the household structure does not change, the proportion of full joint households in the villages will eventually increase. Nevertheless, it is clear that in any community in which married sons remain with their fathers, but separate on their fathers' death, simple households are likely to be numerically preponderant, even though the joint household is the ideal.

My first two characteristics are then really one – namely, the customary domestic cycle, shaped by the splitting of the household following the father's death into households headed by his sons. The third and fourth – lack of clear political leadership and rapid mobility in the recent past – are also aspects of a single characteristic.

The demographic cycle I have just discussed entails an economic cycle. Resources at the disposal of the household's head grow with the growth of the household's labour force, and are then divided between the new households formed at his death. How this actually works out depends on the resources available and the use that can be made of them. Of these resources, land is of course of fundamental importance; but oxen to work the land are also important, especially when land is plentiful, as I shall show.

I propose to distinguish two types of *de facto* land situation. Neither is greatly affected by the national legal system, since the village arranges by far the greater part of its land problems within itself. Changes in the national system are only indirectly relevant. It is quite conceivable that both types should exist as well under a regime of absentee landlords or tax farmers so long as these outsiders treated the village as a collectivity, as under the present system of freehold, under which taxes are individually assessed and collected by state officials. Since, as will appear, with population growth one type must *a priori* develop into the other, I am presenting a model of one aspect of the recent history of many Turkish villages, quite independent of the national reforms. What I know of rural Turkey in general is consistent with this claim.[1]

Type 1. More land is available for cultivation than the village population with their technical resources can use. Hence anyone who has the necessary man-power, draught animals and seed, can plough land freely.

Type 2. All cultivable land is under cultivation, except for essential meadow land for pasture.

Before I proceed to discuss these two types of situation, I wish first to stress a relevant truism, and secondly, to summarise the local inheritance system.

---

1. In particular, the study of land usage in Central Anatolia by John A. Morrison in 1932 helped to provoke my analysis. My theory is consistent with his detailed data. MORRISON, 1938.

First, economic power (a publicly accepted right to a relatively large share of the community's resources) and political power (the ability, publicly accepted or not, to get other people to do what one wants them to do) are closely related. The one generates the other, and no one can hold one without some of the other. In small scale traditional relatively autonomous communities such as those of much of the rural Middle East, this relation is closer than in a modern western state where economic rights can be enforced by invoking the power of the State, and direct political rights over other people are limited by effectively enforced legal and constitutional restrictions.

Inheritance in the villages is always said by informants to follow a simple egalitarian principle – equal division of a man's possessions between his sons. This simple system is not of course in conformity either with the Şharia, which the villages still profess in general terms to follow, nor with the Turkish Civil Code, which is borrowed direct from the Swiss Civil Code. In straightforward cases, the rights of widows and daughters are in fact commonly ignored, and the patrimonial land divided between sons. Where, as is also common, complications and disputes arise, a surviving widow may perhaps take a share, and so may sisters or sisters' children.[1] Even then, the share may be agreed ad hoc, and not as laid down in any code. I am confident that, at the moment, the villagers are moving towards an increasing invocation of formal law, and in particular inheritance by and through women, and away from a traditional state in which land normally passed only to male agnates. But women's formal rights are still, I would say, ignored more often than not. I was at first surprised to be told repeatedly that one did not, or should not, expect to acquire land through one's wife, and though these statements were not always disingenuous, they at least reflected a feeling that to marry for land was not a respectable or a sensible gambit.

In what follows, I assume an equal division of property between sons. That this does not always happen does not greatly affect the argument, since if other kin sometimes take a share too, the consequences of the division of holdings would be intensified rather than diminished.

Type 1. Surplus of land

In this situation, anyone who is able and who wishes, is permitted to plough village land. He must of course be a member of the village, he must have the necessary time and energy, or someone else to work on his behalf, and he must own or be able to borrow oxen, a plough and seed.

---

1. See STIRLING 1957 for further details of the legal situation.

The amount of land a man can plough with the traditional equipment in the Anatolian climate is limited. Ploughing takes place, either in the autumn after the rains have begun, and before the frost and snow, or after the thaw and before the end of the cool, wet spring weather. Both periods are apt to be very short, especially the spring period. The villagers say that one man with a good pair of oxen can plough about 20 *donüm* (very roughly 40 decares, 10 acres) a year. Clearly the quality of the ground, the weather, the strength of the oxen, the health and industry of the farmer and the size of the *donüm* all influence the actual amount. But there is an upper limit; a household can only work roughly 20 *donüm* a year for each working male of the household.

In fact, the household owns twice this amount of land, because the villages operate a two-year fallow system. Half the village territory is cropped each year, and the other used for pasture for the animals. No man can defy this system, since his crops would be eaten by the animals. A man may leave land for three or five years or longer, either because he lacks labour or resources, or because the land is poor. But the fallow period must be an odd number of years.

Nowadays, even the poor households expect to market some of their crops each year to the government buying agency. But in the past they do not seem as a normal practice to have grown cash crops. Transport to town was difficult and slow, and probably, for the small man on his own, dangerous – he would be robbed on the way or cheated when he got there. If the year was good, there would be little or no market in the local towns, which had large agricultural populations of their own, and fertile suburban villages; and if the crop was poor, he would have nothing to market. Some grain was very probably bartered direct with peddlars in the villages, for such things as tools, clothes, sugar and coffee and so on, and according to one informant surpluses could be sold to the tax farmer. Probably only leading figures in a village ever took the trouble themselves to take grain to market to sell for cash on any considerable scale. In these conditions, most villagers almost certainly did not make any great efforts to farm more than enough land to meet their foreseeable requirements.

As a household grows with the birth of sons, its needs and its manpower grow also. The household head takes over more land, which his sons plough for him. With more manpower and gun power his household becomes more important. The household income per capita will also increase, partly because the young men have few if any children of their own to support, partly because the co-ordination of several workers and several teams of oxen increases efficiency. The household head can run a guest room, provide hospitality, and acquire supporters. His household reaches a peak of wealth and power.

But when he dies and the household's land is divided, each son will receive roughly as much as one man can plough. In most cases, each heir will have to face the period of early married life with young dependent children on his own, and he is unlikely to count for much personally in the village. He will be unable to produce much surplus, nor will he need to do so. Only those who succeed in begetting and bringing up a number of sons will in turn become heads of important village households; and on their death, these will again divide into small and unimportant ones. Thus there is a tendency for the sons of large and powerful households to start roughly equal with the sons of more modest households. A father's importance is less relevant to the importance of descendants than their own hard work, health, fertility and luck.

Clearly, such a model is oversimplified. Many factors influenced the way the system worked; I would like to discuss four obvious ones.

First, land is not by any means all of the same value, and valuable land is never a free good. Some village land is likely to be irrigated. How much, is highly variable. Irrigation apart, land near the village is more easily worked, and gets the benefit of manure from ash, refuse and latrines. In persistently prolific lineages, the amount of this good land per household will tend to diminish through fragmentation. On the other hand, in the days before rapid expansion of the population many households and branches of lineages died out, or produced only daughters, who would transfer the land to other households and lineages. Holdings of this more valuable land would therefore vary greatly, and fortuitously; and thus young households do not in fact start equal.

Secondly, every village must have contained some men who did not own any oxen, and who could thus work no land, and for the most part probably owned none. Such unfortunates must have had great difficulty in raising credit to acquire oxen necessary to taking over land for ploughing. They formed the lowest rung of village society, and supplied the watchmen and herdsmen, extra labour at the harvest, and – but this looks forward to my fourth point – extra workers for more successful neighbours.

Thirdly, many villagers own sheep, and a few own considerable flocks. But in this area it is impossible for sheep to survive the winter without shelter and fodder. The size of the flock is therefore limited by the amount of straw available for winter feed, and is thus directly related to the annual crop, and thus to the size of the household labour force.

The fourth factor is far more disturbing to the model I have set up. Success once achieved breeds success, and economic and political power grow together. A man with a large household can employ labourers from among those without oxen, or from destitute strangers. Some labourers lived entirely in their master's household as servants, others were hired on a short term or even day to day basis. Hired labour enables the employer to increase his holdings of land beyond the capacity of his own sons, and increased holdings allow him to feed more retainers, and to establish direct political control over his co-villagers. He will be in a position to establish direct social relations with townsmen and officials, to market grain, and to mediate between government and less successful co-villagers. Eventually he may extend his influence to other villages than his own.

The difficulties in this kind of empire building must have been considerable. In the first place, a man had to have rare good fortune to achieve a large successful household equipped with sons early enough in life to have vigour and time left to increase the empire. Secondly, his fellow villagers and even his own agnates would cease to wish him well at the point at which their own personal interests appeared to be threatened. As for the expansion of influence beyond his village, this would depend on firm control over his own village, enabling him to count on acquiescence and support. Thirdly, other political leaders in the area – officials, large landholders in the local town, successful men in neighbouring villages and so on – would be unwilling to see their own spheres invaded, or their own power threatened. To steer between the opposition in his own village and the hostile suspicion of outside powers must have required great skill and great good fortune. But undoubtedly it did occasionally happen.

I knew one man, Karabey of Elbaşı, who had actually attained such a position, though in rather unusual circumstances. He was said to have owned over a thousand *donüm*. (Probably in this case a thousand decare, or 250 acres.)[1] Even in Sakaltutan, some twenty miles away, he was said 'to hold the countryside in his hand'. I was told he had been a personal friend of Ataturk, and probably his power dated back to the troubled days of the nineteen-twenties following the War of Independence. Most of the land he owned lay outside the borders of his own village, in a broad irrigated valley, and had formerly belonged to a large Christian village which had been evacuated at the time of the exchange of population with Greece which began in 1923. He had owned a tractor and a combine harvester long before these things were common in Turkey, and had taken the harvester annually for hire to Adana, south of the Taurus mountains, where the harvest is much earlier than on the plateau.

Even men like this usually build their strength on many sons. And as they grow wealthier, they would seek to increase the number of their wives in order to have yet more sons. In 1951 and 1952, the estate of the Karabey was in dispute between his heirs; three widows, out of six wives, and eight children

1. The government officially equates a *donüm* and a decare. But in village language, a *donüm* is a much larger measure, highly variable, but usually 2 or 3 decares. 1 decare equals 1/4 acre.

and grandchildren were staking claims. No one son could expect to succeed to his position of informal dominance in the village. Thus even when a man broke through the inhibiting factors and established real power and importance, this power died with him personally. Each of his sons would start life in a comparatively modest household of his own. A son might have some advantages of prestige and wealth to give him an initial lead in the race, but he still needed time, luck and skill of his own to win eminence for himself .

Type 2

Once a village reaches a point where spare cultivable land is no longer freely available, marginal land ceases to be a free good, and the opportunities for empire building are gone. Yet sons remain an asset. They are still a source of prestige and protection within the village, they can still help on the land, and they can earn by working in the village or by migrant labour. I knew several really poor men who were very much better off for having two or three adult sons. But the more successful the father in producing sons, the poorer in land will be the sons when it comes to a division. Thus in Sakaltutan, as in many neighbouring villages, most households, including many with only one working man, owned less land than they could comfortably have worked with their available working population; most households, agriculturally, were underemployed.

This shortage of land leads to ad hoc arrangements for share cropping. No household is willing to leave land uncultivated if an alternative arrangement is possible, and conversely plenty of people are anxious to cultivate more than they own. Year to year agreements are made, but these change constantly with changes in manpower and ox-power in village households. Even so, many of the villagers have less than a full year's work to do on the land, and, except at harvest, cheap casual labour is always in good supply. Since the population is now growing with no accompanying growth in overall production, the village standard of living is likely to fall. Increasing underemployment and poverty are only offset by the rise, in very recent times, in the demand for and profitability of migrant labour. Sakaltutan, for example, certainly could not support its population without a large income in remittances from its sons in the cities.

Establishing and maintaining rights to specific pieces of land is of much greater importance under these circumstances than when land is freely available. Moreover, the claiming of rights through women is one of the few ways of expanding a limited patrimony. The increase in claims of this kind is therefore not merely due to the influence of modern, urban ideas, but to a change in the landholding situation. Since frequently land arrangements in the recent past have been ad hoc, non-legal and unsystematic, opportunities for argument are unlimited, justice in an abstract sense an impossibility, and litigation – increasingly popular as a weapon – is useless as a method of achieving a satisfactory and sensible settlement.

No household can now re-establish large enough land holdings to keep several sons fully occupied, but a household with a moderate sized holding which has only one heir may be able to maintain a position of relative prosperity over more than one generation. In Sakaltutan, and in other villages of similar structure, internal political power was divided between a number of these moderately endowed households, none of which was in a position to dominate. Where there was more than one heir, a division of the family holdings usually made it impossible for the heirs to remain among these leading households.

One way by which in theory a man might re-establish power in the village is by purchase of land. In fact, in my observation this never seems to be attempted. Sale is rare except among close kin. If an inheriting sister or a brother leaves the village, he or she will sell to her agnates. Other sales are regarded, except on a very small scale or in special circumstances, as immoral. Properly registered legal sale is of course perfectly possible under the Turkish Civil Code, provided one can prove title. But most villagers would have difficulty in establishing legal title, although most village holdings are known to the whole village and are not in dispute. The cost of getting the necessary documents and the involvement with lawyers does not appeal to villagers. In fact, sales in the village have customarily not been sales at all but pawning. No legal document is executed; at the most a piece of paper is signed by the villagers themselves. The vendor retains the right to reclaim the land at the original price whenever he wishes, unless other conditions are specifically laid down. In any case, the demand for land is heavy and the supply hardly exists.

By concentrating on two somewhat *a priori* models, both referring to the past, and illustrating them with selected field material, I am certain to have given a false picture. Recent political, economic and technical changes have made both systems out of date. Since the Second World War, partly due to the extension of price stabilization through the government Office of Soil Products, and partly due to a number of more direct measures, cash cropping has received a tremendous stimulus, reflected in a jump in the land under grain, between 1944 and 1956, from 7,000 hectares to 11,600 hectares.[1]

1. République Turque, *Ann. Stat.* 1953. *Production Yearbook*, 1958, F.A.O., Rome.

Tractor ploughing is now possible, making feasible holdings larger than the traditional ones, and once legal rights are established they can be defended by the legitimate force of the central government, not merely by one's close agnates' gun power. Land can be farmed for a cash profit based on a guaranteed price for the crops. Obviously, it is no longer allowed to sit about unclaimed. The recent history of Elbaşı illustrates this. In the late forties there occurred a sort of land rush in which those with the means vied with each other to plough up the remaining spare pasture, until the whole village was split into those who thought no more village pasture could be spared, and those who still wanted to take the last chance of expanding their own holdings. The fighting was settled by the authorities in favour of the status quo. At present, several households hold more land than they can work, many have adequate holdings, share croppers are hard to come by, and casual labour is scarce and migrant labour comparatively limited.

On the other hand, the sharp rise in the demands for, and the relative cash return from, skilled migrant labour has led to a very much larger number of young men from most villages, even Elbaşı, going away to work than ever before. They are mostly building trade operatives – painters, plasterers, masons. Their incomes enable them to maintain by village standards a relatively high level of prestige consumption, but without exercising thereby any real power in village affairs. For some of these migrants, the village ceases to be the main theatre for achievement. They measure their standing against a vastly wider background, including sections of urban society. But many others still look to the village, and many middle-aged men give up the annual migration if they can possibly afford to do so.

The cycle of domestic growth and fission in these villages apparently inhibited the establishment of hereditary leadership or dominant lineages, by making it impossible for one son of a leading man to inherit control of all the resources on which his father's position was based. It is possible to argue that a later or earlier division of the household might not have these effects. If the division of households had normally taken place later in the cycle, a household head with a dominant position might then have been succeeded in office or in power and wealth by a brother who retained a command of the same domestic resources. If, on the other hand, sons had customarily separated on marriage and farmed separately, all households would have been much on the same economic level, and political leadership would necessarily have rested on other factors than land and food resources. It might then have been possible for a younger man to succeed his father.

The relation between the domestic cycle and the distribution of power is not of course simply causal. If the domestic cycle appears to prevent the direct inheritance of political power, it is equally arguable that the absence of hereditary political power is a necessary condition of the development of this form of the domestic cycle. They are part of a single system.

This system, as I have described the model, was self-adjusting. Even the rare case of a man whose success grew beyond the bounds of his own village was confronted both with increasing difficulties in the maintenance of equilibrium within his empire, and with its extinction at his death. But in fact I needed here to introduce also outside factors, namely the resistance of those already holding political power above village level. In other words, the maintenance of the system I have described depends on the absence of detailed interference in the village affairs, and also on the existence of a central power able to suppress, or to absorb and draw out of the village, any one who succeeded beyond a certain level in the acquisition of power. The system also depended on the economic isolation, that is, on the near autarky of the village, and the absence of a class with economic resources from outside the village sufficient to introduce more marked and permanent social differentiation. The system in which the domestic cycle and the distribution of power were mutually supporting depended for its maintenance on the existence of a certain type of large scale political and economic organisation. Now with the vastly increased intervention of the national bureaucracy in village affairs and the rapid technical and economic development of Turkey, the political and economic conditions under which the processes described can continue to repeat themselves no longer exist.

BIBLIOGRAPHY

F.A.O., *Production Yearbook* 1958.
Goody, J. (Ed.) 'The Developmental Cycle in Domestic Groups', *Cambridge Papers in Social Anthropology* No. 1, 1958.
Morrison, John A., *Alısar: A Unit of Land Occupance in the Kanák Su Basin of Central Anatolia*. Chicago, 1939.
République Turque, *Annuaire Statistique*, 1951 and 1953.
Stirling, Paul. 'Social Ranking in a Turkish Village', *British Journal of Sociology*, Vol. IV, No. 1, March 1953.
'Land, Marriage, and the Law in Turkish Villages', *U.N.E.S.C.O. International Social Science Bulletin*, Vol. IX, No. 1, 1957.
'A Death and a Youth Club: Feuding in a Turkish Village', *Anthropological Quarterly*, Vol. 33, No. 1, Washington, January 1960.
Turkish News, Turkish Embassy, London, 15th May, 1959.

CHAPTER 34

What Social Class Is in America

W. LLOYD WARNER, MARCHIA MEEKER and KENNETH EELLS

THE AMERICAN DREAM AND SOCIAL CLASS

IN THE bright glow and warm presence of the American Dream all men are born free and equal. Everyone in the American Dream has the right, and often the duty, to try to succeed and to do his best to reach the top. Its two fundamental themes and propositions, that all of us are equal and that each of us has the right to the chance of reaching the top, are mutually contradictory, for if all men are equal there can be no top level to aim for, no bottom one to get away from; there can be no superior or inferior positions, but only one common level into which all Americans are born and in which all of them will spend their lives. We all know such perfect equality of position and opportunity does not exist. All Americans are not born into families of equal position: some are born into a rich man's aristocracy on the Gold Coast; some into the solid comfort of Suburbia's middle classes; and others into a mean existence among the slum families living on the wrong side of the tracks. It is common knowledge that the sons and daughters of the Gold Coasts, the Main Lines, and Park Avenues of America are more likely to receive recognition for their efforts than the children of the slums. The distance these fortunate young people travel to achieve success is shorter, and the route up easier, than the long hard pull necessary for the ambitious children of the less fortunate middle class. Though everyone has the common right to succeed, it is not an equal "right"; though there is equality of rank for some of us, there is not equality of rank for all of us.

When some men learn that *all* the American Dream does not fit *all* that is true about the realities of our life, they denounce the Dream and deny the truth of *any* of it. Fortunately, most of us are wiser and better adjusted to social reality; we recognize that, though it is called a Dream and though some of it is false, by virtue of our firm belief in it we have made some of it true. Despite the presence of social hierarchies which place people at higher and lower levels in American communities, the principles of democracy do operate; the Christian dogma that all men are equal in the sight of God be-cause He is our Father and we are His spiritual children, buttressed by the democratic faith in the equality of men and the insistence on their equal rights as citizens, is a powerful influence in the daily life of America.

From grade school on, we have learned to cite chapter and verse proving from the lives of many of the great men of American history that we can start at the bottom and climb to the highest peaks of achievement when we have a few brains and a will to do. Our mass magazines and newspapers print and reprint the legendary story of rags to riches and tell over and over again the Ellis-Island-to-Park-Avenue saga in the actual lives of contemporary successful immigrant men and women. From mere repetition, it might be thought the public would tire of the theme; the names are all that vary and the stories, like those of children, remain the same. But we never do tire of this theme, for it says what we need to know and what we want to hear.

Among people around us, we sometimes recognize men who have got ahead, who have been successfully upward-mobile, and who have reached levels of achievement beyond even the dreams of most men. Many Americans by their own success have learned that, for them, enough of the Dream is true to make all of it real. The examples from history, from the world around us, and from our own experience provide convincing evidence that, although full equality is absent, opportunity for advancement is present suf-ficiently to permit the rise of a few from the bottom and a still larger number from the middle to the higher economic and social levels. Although we know the statement that everyone is equal but that some men are higher than others is contradictory, and although some of us smile or become angry when we hear that "all of us are equal but some are more equal than others," we still accept both parts of this proposition either by understressing one part of the proposition or by letting all of it go as a paradox we feel to be true.

Our society does an excellent job in giving us an explicit knowl-edge of, and good argument for, the equalitarian aspects of our life.

We have much scholarly knowledge about the workings of democracy, but we have little scientific knowledge about the powerful presence of social status and how it works for good and evil in the lives of all of us. Yet to live successfully and adaptively in America, every one of us must adjust his life to each of these contradictions, not just one of them, and we must make the most of each. Our knowledge of the democratic aspects of America is learned directly as part of our social heritage, but our understanding of the principle of social status tends to be implicit and to be learned obliquely and through hard and sometimes bitter experience. The lives of many are destroyed because they do not understand the workings of social class.[1]

It is the hope of the authors that this book will provide a corrective instrument which will permit men and women better to evaluate their social situations and thereby better adapt themselves to social reality and fit their dreams and aspirations to what is possible.

Our great state papers, the orations of great men, and the principles and pronouncements of politicians and statesmen tell us of the equality of all men. Each school boy learns and relearns it; but most of us are dependent upon experience and indirect statement to learn about "the wrong side of the tracks," "the Gold Coast and the slums," and "the top and bottom of the social heap." We are proud of those facts of American life that fit the pattern we are taught, but somehow we are often ashamed of those equally important social facts which demonstrate the presence of social class. Consequently, we tend to deny them or, worse, denounce them and by so doing deny their existence and magically make them disappear from consciousness. We use such expressions as "the Century of the Common Man" to insist on our democratic faith; but we know that, ordinarily, for Common Men to exist as a class, un-Common superior and inferior men must also exist. We know that every town or city in the country has its "Country Club set" and that this group usually lives on its Gold Coast, its Main Line, North Shore, or Nob Hill, and is the top of the community's social heap. Most of us know from novels

---

[1] Jurgen Ruesch, Martin B. Loeb, *et al.*, *Chronic Disease and Psychological Invalidism; a Psychosomatic Study* (New York: American Society for Research in Psychosomatic Problems, 1946). A research at the University of California Hospital by Ruesch and others which demonstrates that this can be literally true; their results show how certain serious physical and mental ailments are directly attributable to social class and mobility strivings and anxieties.

such as those of Sinclair Lewis of the Main Streets that run through all our towns and cities, populated by Babbitts or, more explicitly stated, by "the substantial upper-middle class"; and by now, thanks to another group of novelists such as Erskine Caldwell, we know there is a low road, a Tobacco Road, that runs not only by the ramshackle houses of the poor whites of the South, but by the tarpaper shanties of the slums and river bottoms or Goat Hills of every town and city in the United States.

The "superior people" of Marquand's New England, "the North Shore crowd," divided into a top level of "old families" with a set of values and a way of life rated above those of the "new families," are matched by Philadelphia's "Main Line" families in Christopher Morley's *Kitty Foyle* and by similar groups in many other novels which report on the dominance of "the upper classes" in all regions of the United States. Reading them, together with similar novels reporting on Suburbia and Main Street for the middle classes and those on the Tobacco Roads and the city slums for the lower levels, gives one the understanding that throughout the towns and cities of America the inhabitants are divided into status levels which are ways of life with definite characteristics and values. Talking to and observing the people of these communities demonstrate that they, too, know how real these status levels are, and they prove it by agreeing among themselves about the levels and who belongs to them in their particular city.

Although well aware of social class, social scientists have been more concerned with their theories and with quarreling among themselves about what social class is than with studying its realities in the daily lives of the people.[2] Until recently, they have lagged behind the novelists in investigating what our classes are, how they operate in our social life, and what effect they have on our individual lives.

But recent scientific studies of social class in the several regions of the United States demonstrate that it is a major determinant of individual decisions and social actions; that every major area of American life is directly and indirectly influenced by our class order; and that the major decisions of most individuals are partly controlled by it. To act intelligently and know consciously how this

---

[2] See Chapter 15 for a list of some of their publications and comments about each publication.

basic factor in American life affects us and our society, it is essential and necessary that we have an explicit understanding of what our class order is, how it works, and what it does to the lives and personalities who live in it. Our most democratic institutions, including our schools, churches, business organizations, government, and even our family life, are molded by its all-pervading and exceedingly subtle but powerful influence.

The researches on social class in the several regions of the United States [3] make it possible to fill in much of the missing knowledge necessary to give Americans such explicit understanding of social class and to answer some of the important questions we raise about it when adjusting to the realities of our existence. Reduced to their simplicities these questions are: What is social class? How are social classes organized? And how do they function in the individual and the community? How do we use such knowledge to adjust ourselves more satisfactorily to the world around us? What is the effect of class on buying and selling and other problems of business enterprise, on the problems of personnel, on school and education, on the church and religion, on the acceptance and rejection of the communications of mass media such as the radio, magazine, newspaper, and motion picture? And, above all, are there effective and simple techniques of studying and applying the social-class concept so that those who are not specialized class analysts can apply such knowledge to the practical problems of their business or profession or to the research problems of the scientist?

The answer to this last important question is "yes"; the answer to the others will be found in this volume. The authors believe that they present a sufficient description here of how to do these things to enable interested people to deal with problems arising from social class. They recognize that further refinement is necessary and that modifications and improvements will have to be made, but the fundamental elements are now known sufficiently well to provide this set of instructions adequate to the identification and measurement of social class in America. Most of the book—all chapters between this and the last—will deal specifically with these instructions.

THE STRUCTURAL IMPERATIVE—WHY WE HAVE A CLASS SYSTEM

The recognition of social class and other status hierarchies in

---

[3] For a commentary on some of these see Chapter 15.

this country comes as no surprise to students of society. Research on the social life of the tribes and civilizations of the world clearly demonstrates that some form of rank is always present and a necessity for our kind of society.

Just as students of comparative biology have demonstrated that the physical structure of the higher animals must have certain organs to survive, so students of social anthropology have shown that the social structures of the "higher," the more complex, societies must have rank orders to perform certain functions necessary for group survival.

When societies are complex and service large populations, they always possess some kind of status system which, by its own values, places people in higher or lower positions. Only the very simple hunting and gathering tribes, with very small populations and very simple social problems, are without systems of rank; but when a society is complex, when there are large numbers of individuals in it pursuing diverse and complex activities and functioning in a multiplicity of ways, individual positions and behaviors are evaluated and ranked.[4] This happens primarily because, to maintain itself, the society must co-ordinate the efforts of all its members into common enterprises necessary for the preservation of the group, and it must solidify and integrate all these enterprises into a working whole. In other words, as the division of labor increases and the social units become more numerous and diverse, the need for co-ordination and integration also increases and, when satisfied, enables the larger group to survive and develop.

Those who occupy co-ordinating positions acquire power and prestige. They do so because their actions partly control the behavior of the individuals who look to them for direction. Within this simple control there is simple power. Those who exercise such power either acquire prestige directly from it or have gained prestige from other sources sufficiently to be raised to a co-ordinating position. For example, among many primitive peoples a simple fishing expedition may be organized so that the men who fish and handle each boat are under the direction of one leader. The efforts of each boat are directed by the leader and, in turn, each boat is integrated into the total enterprise by its leader's taking orders from his superior. The

---

[4] See the reference to Hobhouse, Wheeler, and Ginsberg, *The Material Culture and Social Institutions of the Simpler Peoples,* in Chapter 15.

same situation prevails in a modern factory. Small plants with a small working force and simple problems possess a limited hierarchy, perhaps no more than an owner who bosses all the workers. But a large industrial enterprise, with complex activities and problems, like General Motors, needs an elaborate hierarchy of supervision. The position in a great industrial empire which integrates and co-ordinates all the positions beneath it throughout all the supervising levels down to the workers has great power and prestige. The same holds true for political, religious, educational, and other social institutions; the more complex the group and the more diverse the functions and activities, the more elaborate its status system is likely to be. We will amplify this point later.

The studies of other societies have demonstrated one other basic point: the more complex the technological and economic structure, the more complex the social structure; so that some argue (the Marxians and many classical economists) that technological advancement is the cause of social complexity and all class and status systems. It cannot be denied that economic and technological factors are important in the determination of class and status orders. We must not lose sight of the fact, however, that the social system, with its beliefs, values, and rules, which governs human behavior may well determine what kind of technology and what kind of economic institutions will survive or thrive in any given tribe or nation. In any case, social complexity is necessary for economic advancement. Furthermore, social complexity is a basic factor determining the presence or absence of class.

The Marxians have argued that the economic changes our society is undergoing always result in a class war in which "the proletariat" will be triumphant and out of which a "classless society" will result. The authors do not agree with them for several reasons. The principal reasons are: (1) the presence of a class order does not necessarily mean class conflict—the relations of the classes can be and often are amiable and peaceful; (2) classless societies (without differential status systems) are impossible where there is complexity for the reasons previously given. Russia's communistic system, supposedly designed to produce a pure equalitarian society, necessarily has citizens who are ranked above and below each other. Generals, there, outrank privates; commissars, the rank and file; and members of the Politburo, the ordinary comrade. Occupants of these higher ranks in Russia tend to associate together; those of the lower ranks form their own groups. Their children are trained according to the rank of their parents. This means that the younger generation learns these status differences, thereby strengthening status differences between levels and fostering the further development of social class in Communistic Russia.

All this has occurred despite the fact the Russians have removed the means of production from private hands and placed them under the control of the State ("the people"). The economic factor which by Marxian doctrine produced social classes is largely absent; yet social hierarchies and social classes are present for the reason that Russia is a complex society and needs them to survive.

These status trends in Russia will undoubtedly continue, for her population is vast, her peoples diverse, her problems immensely complex; and elaborate systems of co-ordination and control are necessary for such a nation to maintain itself. The Communist ideals of economic and political equality cannot produce perfect equality within the complexities of Russian life.

But let us return to the United States. We, too, have a complex, highly diverse society. We, too, possess an elaborate division of labor and a ramified technology. And we, too, possess a variety of rank orders built on the need of maintaining unity and cohesion in making our common enterprises successful. Men occupying high and low positions possess families. Their families and their activities are identified with their social position. Families of the same position tend to associate together. They do this informally or through cliques, associations, or other institutions. This social matrix provides the structure of our class system. Children are always born to their families' position. Through life they may increase or decrease their status. The family thereby strengthens and helps maintain our class order. Social status in America is somewhat like man's alimentary canal; he may not like the way it works and he may want to forget that certain parts of it are part of him, but he knows it is necessary for his very existence. So a status system, often an object of our disapproval, is present and necessary in our complex social world.

If we cannot eliminate the system of status, we can and must work to keep it as democratic and equalitarian as possible. To be successful we must see to it that each American is given his chance to move in the social scale. This ideal of equality of opportunity is essential for our democracy. To do this intelligently, we must know what our class order is and what can be done to make it conform most closely to the needs of the American people.

The remainder of this chapter will briefly summarize what we now know about our social classes and how they are organized and function in the towns and cities of the several regions of the United States. We will start with the New England Yankees and then go on to the Middle and Far West and end up with the South before we take up the question of the common features of American class and what it is as a status system.

CLASS AMONG THE NEW ENGLAND YANKEES

Studies of communities in New England clearly demonstrate the presence of a well-defined social-class system.[5] At the top is an aristocracy of birth and wealth. This is the so-called "old family" class. The people of Yankee City say the families who belong to it have been in the community for a long time—for at least three generations and preferably many generations more than three. "Old family" means not only old to the community but old to the class. Present members of the class were born into it; the families into which they were born can trace their lineage through many generations participating in a way of life characteristic of the upper class back to a generation marking the lowly beginnings out of which their family came. Although the men of this level are occupied gainfully, usually as large merchants, financiers, or in the higher professions, the wealth of the family, inherited from the husband's or the wife's side, and often from both, has been in the family for a long time. Ideally, it should stem from the sea trade when Yankee City's merchants and sea captains made large fortunes, built great Georgian houses on elm-lined Hill Street, and filled their houses and gardens with the proper symbols of their high position. They became the 400, the Brahmins, the Hill Streeters to whom others looked up; and they, well-mannered or not, looked down on the rest. They counted themselves, and were so counted, equals of similar levels in Salem, Boston, Providence, and other New England cities. Their

---

[5] See Chapter 15 for a description of the several volumes of "Yankee City Series." New and poorly organized towns sometimes have class systems which have no old-family (upper-upper) class.

sons and daughters married into the old families from these towns and at times, when family fortune was low or love was great, they married wealthy sons and daughters from the newly rich who occupied the class level below them. This was a happy event for the fathers and mothers of such fortunate young people in the lower half of the upper class, an event well publicized and sometimes not too discreetly bragged about by the parents of the lower-upper-class children, an occasion to be explained by the mothers from the old families in terms of the spiritual demands of romantic love and by their friends as "a good deal and a fair exchange all the way around for everyone concerned."

The new families, the lower level of the upper class, came up through the new industries—shoes, textiles, silverware—and finance. Their fathers were some of the men who established New England's trading and financial dominance throughout America. When New York's Wall Street rose to power, many of them transferred their activities to this new center of dominance. Except that they aspire to old-family status, if not for themselves then for their children, these men and their families have a design for living similar to the old-family group. But they are consciously aware that their money is too new and too recently earned to have the sacrosanct quality of wealth inherited from a long line of ancestors. They know, as do those about them, that, while a certain amount of wealth is necessary, birth and old family are what really matter. Each of them can cite critical cases to prove that particular individuals have no money at all, yet belong to the top class because they have the right lineage and right name. While they recognize the worth and importance of birth, they feel that somehow their family's achievements should be better rewarded than by a mere second place in relation to those who need do little more than be born and stay alive.

The presence of an old-family class in a community forces the newly rich to wait their turn if they aspire to "higher things." Meanwhile, they must learn how to act, fill their lives with good deeds, spend their money on approved philanthropy, and reduce their arrogance to manageable proportions.

The families of the upper and lower strata of the upper classes are organized into social cliques and exclusive clubs. The men gather fortnightly in dining clubs where they discuss matters that concern them. The women belong to small clubs or to the Garden Club and give their interest to subjects which symbolize their high status and evoke those sentiments necessary in each individual if the class is to maintain itself. Both sexes join philanthropic organizations whose good deeds are an asset to the community and an expression of the dominance and importance of the top class to those socially beneath them. They are the members of the Episcopalian and Unitarian and, occasionally, the Congregational and Presbyterian churches.

Below them are the members of the solid, highly respectable upper-middle class, the people who get things done and provide the active front in civic affairs for the classes above them. They aspire to the classes above and hope their good deeds, civic activities, and high moral principles will somehow be recognized far beyond the usual pat on the back and that they will be invited by those above them into the intimacies of upper-class cliques and exclusive clubs. Such recognition might increase their status and would be likely to make them members of the lower-upper group. The fact that this rarely happens seldom stops members of this level, once activated, from continuing to try. The men tend to be owners of stores and belong to the large proprietor and professional levels. Their incomes average less than those of the lower-upper class, this latter group having a larger income than any other group, including the old-family level.

These three strata, the two upper classes and the upper-middle, constitute the levels above the Common Man. There is a considerable distance socially between them and the mass of the people immediately below them. They comprise three of the six classes present in the community. Although in number of levels they constitute half the community, in population they have no more than a sixth, and sometimes less, of the Common Man's population. The three levels combined include approximately 13 per cent of the total population.

The lower-middle class, the top of the Common Man level, is composed of clerks and other white-collar workers, small tradesmen, and a fraction of skilled workers. Their small houses fill "the side streets" down from Hill Street, where the upper classes and some of the upper-middle live, and are noticeably absent from the better suburbs where the upper-middle concentrate. "Side Streeter" is a term often used by those above them to imply an inferior way of life and an inconsequential status. They have accumulated little property but are frequently home owners. Some of the more successful members of ethnic groups, such as the Italians, Irish, French-Canadians, have reached this level. Only a few members of these cultural minorities have gone beyond it; none of them has reached the old-family level.

The old-family class (upper-upper) is smaller in size than the new-family class (lower-upper) below them. It has 1.4 per cent, while the lower-upper class has 1.6 per cent, of the total population. Ten per cent of the population belongs to the upper-middle class, and 28 per cent to the lower-middle level. The upper-lower is the most populous class, with 34 per cent, and the lower-lower has 25 per cent of all the people in the town.

The prospects of the upper-middle-class children for higher education are not as good as those of the classes above. One hundred per cent of the children of the two upper classes take courses in the local high school that prepare them for college, and 88 per cent of the upper-middle do; but only 44 per cent of the lower-middle take these courses, 28 per cent of the upper-lower, and 26 per cent of the lower-lower. These percentages provide a good index of the position of the lower-middle class, ranking it well below the three upper classes, but placing it well above the upper-lower and the lower-lower.[6]

The upper-lower class, least differentiated from the adjacent levels and hardest to distinguish in the hierarchy, but clearly present, is composed of the "poor but honest workers" who more often than not are only semi-skilled or unskilled. Their relative place in the hierarchy of class is well portrayed by comparing them with the classes superior to them and with the lower-lower class beneath them in the category of how they spend their money.

A glance at the ranking of the proportion of the incomes of each class spent on ten items (including such things as rent and shelter, food, clothing, and education, among others) shows, for example, that this class ranks second for the percentage of the money spent on food, the lower-lower class being first and the rank order of the other classes following lower-middle according to their place in the social hierarchy. The money spent on rent and shelter

---

[6] See W. Lloyd Warner and Paul S. Lunt, *The Social Life of a Modern Community*, Vol. I, "Yankee City Series" (New Haven: Yale University Press, 1941), pp. 58-72.

by upper-lower class is also second to the lower-lower's first, the other classes' rank order and position in the hierarchy being in exact correspondence. To give a bird's-eye view of the way this class spends its money, the rank of the upper-lower, for the percentage of its budget spent on a number of common and important items, has been placed in parentheses after every item in the list which follows: food (2), rent (2), clothing (4), automobiles (5), taxes (5), medical aid (5), education (4), and amusements (4-5). For the major items of expenditure the amount of money spent by this class out of its budget corresponds fairly closely with its place in the class hierarchy, second to the first of the lower-lower class for the major necessities of food and shelter, and ordinarily, but not always, fourth or fifth to the classes above for the items that give an opportunity for cutting down the amounts spent on them. Their feelings about doing the right thing, of being respectable and rearing their children to do better than they have, coupled with the limitations of their income, are well reflected in how they select and reject what can be purchased on the American market.[7]

The lower-lower class, referred to as "Riverbrookers" or the "low-down Yankees who live in the clam flats," have a "bad reputation" among those who are socially above them. This evaluation includes beliefs that they are lazy, shiftless, and won't work, all opposites of the good middle-class virtues belonging to the essence of the Protestant ethic. They are thought to be improvident and unwilling or unable to save their money for a rainy day and, therefore, often dependent on the philanthropy of the private or public agency and on poor relief. They are sometimes said to "live like animals" because it is believed that their sexual mores are not too exacting and that pre-marital intercourse, post-marital infidelity, and high rates of illegitimacy, sometimes too publicly mixed with incest, characterize their personal and family lives. It is certain that they deserve only part of this reputation. Research shows many of them guilty of no more than being poor and lacking in the desire to get ahead, this latter trait being common among those above them. For these reasons and others, this class is ranked in Yankee City below the level of the Common Man (lower-middle and upper-lower). For most of the indexes of status it ranks sixth and last.

---

[7] The evidence for the statements in this paragraph can be found in *The Social Life of a Modern Community*, pp. 287-300.

CLASS IN THE DEMOCRATIC MIDDLE WEST AND FAR WEST

Cities large and small in the states west of the Alleghenies sometimes have class systems which do not possess an old-family (upper-upper) class. The period of settlement has not always been sufficient for an old-family level, based on the security of birth and inherited wealth, to entrench itself. Ordinarily, it takes several generations for an old-family class to gain and hold the prestige and power necessary to impress the rest of the community sufficiently with the marks of its "breeding" to be able to confer top status on those born into it. The family, its name, and its lineage must have had time to become identified in the public mind as being above ordinary mortals.

While such identification is necessary for the emergence of an old-family (upper-upper) class and for its establishment, it is also necessary for the community to be large enough for the principles of exclusion to operate. For example, those in the old-family group must be sufficiently numerous for all the varieties of social participation to be possible without the use of new-family members; the family names must be old enough to be easily identified; and above all there should always be present young people of marriageable age to become mates of others of their own class and a sufficient number of children to allow mothers to select playmates and companions of their own class for their children.

When a community in the more recently settled regions of the United States is sufficiently large, when it has grown slowly and at an average rate, the chances are higher that it has an old-family class. If it lacks any one of these factors, including size, social and economic complexity, and steady and normal growth, the old-family class is not likely to develop.

One of the best tests of the presence of an old-family level is to determine whether members of the new-family category admit, perhaps grudgingly and enviously and with hostile derogatory remarks, that the old-family level looks down on them and that it is considered a mark of advancement and prestige by those in the new-family group to move into it and be invited to the homes and social affairs of the old families. When a member of the new-family class says, "We've only been here two generations, but we still aren't old-family," and when he or she goes on to say that "they (old family) consider themselves better than people like us and the poor dopes around here let them get away with it," such evidence indicates that an old-family group is present and able to enforce recognition of its superior position upon its most aggressive and hostile competitors, the members of the lower-upper, or new-family, class.

When the old-family group is present and its position is not recognized as superordinate to the new families, the two tend to be co-ordinate and view each other as equals. The old-family people adroitly let it be known that their riches are not material possessions alone but are old-family lineage; the new families display their wealth, accent their power, and prepare their children for the development of a future lineage by giving them the proper training at home and later sending them to the "right" schools and marrying them into the "right" families.

Such communities usually have a five-class pyramid, including an upper class, two middle, and two lower classes.[8]

Jonesville, located in the Middle West, approximately a hundred years old, is an example of a typical five-class community. The farmers around Jonesville use it as their market, and it is the seat of government for Abraham County. Its population of over 6,000 people is supported by servicing the needs of the farmers and by one large and a few small factories.

At the top of the status structure is an upper class commonly referred to as "the 400." It is composed of old-family and new-family segments. Neither can successfully claim superiority to the other. Below this level is an upper-middle class which functions like the same level in Yankee City and is composed of the same kind of people, the only difference being the recognition that the distance to the top is shorter for them and the time necessary to get there much less. The Common Man level, composed of lower-middle- and upper-lower-class people, and the lower-lower level are replicas of the same classes in Yankee City. The only difference is that the Jonesville ethnics in these classes are Norwegian Lutherans and Catholic Poles, the Catholic Irish and Germans having been absorbed for the most part in the larger population; whereas in Yankee City the ethnic population is far more heterogeneous, and the Catholic Irish are less assimilated largely because of more opposition to

---

[8] It is conceivable that in smaller communities there may be only three, or even two, classes present.

them, and because the church has more control over their private lives.

The present description of Jonesville's class order can be brief and no more than introductory because all the materials used to demonstrate how to measure social class are taken from Jonesville. The interested reader will obtain a clear picture in the chapters which follow of what the classes are, who is in them, the social and economic characteristics of each class, and how the people of the town think about their status order.

The communities of the mountain states and Pacific Coast are new, and many of them have changed their economic form from mining to other enterprises; consequently, their class orders are similar to those found in the Middle West. The older and larger far western communities which have had a continuing, solid growth of population which has not destroyed the original group are likely to have the old-family level at the top with the other classes present; the newer and smaller communities and those disturbed by the destruction of their original status structure by large population gains are less likely to have an old-family class reigning above all others. San Francisco is a clear example of the old-family type; Los Angeles, of the more amorphous, less well-organized class structure.

CLASS IN THE DEEP SOUTH

Studies in the Deep South demonstrate that, in the older regions where social changes until recently have been less rapid and less disturbing to the status order, most of the towns above a few thousand population have a six-class system in which an old-family elite is socially dominant.

For example, in a study of a Mississippi community, a market town for a cotton-growing region around it, Davis and the Gardners found a six-class system.[9] Perhaps the southern status order is best described by Chart I on page 19 which gives the names used by the people of the community for each class and succinctly tells how

---

[9] Allison Davis, Burleigh B. Gardner, and Mary R. Gardner, *Deep South* (Chicago: University of Chicago Press, 1941). Also read: John Dollard, *Caste and Class in a Southern Town* (New Haven: Yale University Press, 1937); Mozell Hill, "The All-Negro Society in Oklahoma" (Unpublished Ph.D. dissertation, University of Chicago, 1936); Harry J. Walker, "Changes in Race Accommodation in a Southern Community" (Unpublished Ph.D. dissertation, University of Chicago, 1945).

the members of each class regard themselves and the rest of the class order.

The people of the two upper classes make a clear distinction between an old aristocracy and an aristocracy which is not old. There

CHART I

THE SOCIAL PERSPECTIVES OF THE SOCIAL CLASSES *

UPPER-UPPER CLASS		LOWER-UPPER CLASS
"Old aristocracy"	UU	"Old aristocracy"
"Aristocracy," but not "old"	LU	"Aristocracy," but not "old"
"Nice, respectable people"	UM	"Nice, respectable people"
"Good people, but 'nobody'"	LM	"Good people, but 'nobody'"
"Po' whites"	UL / LL	"Po' whites"

UPPER-MIDDLE CLASS		LOWER-MIDDLE CLASS
"Society" — "Old families"	UU	"Old aristocracy" (older) "Broken-down aristocracy" (younger)
"Society" but not "old families"	LU	
"People who should be upper class"	UM	"People who think they are somebody"
"People who don't have much money"	LM	"We poor folk"
	UL	"People poorer than us"
"No 'count lot"	LL	"No 'count lot"

UPPER-LOWER CLASS		LOWER-LOWER CLASS
	UU / LU	
"Society" or the "folks with money"	UM	"Society" or the "folks with money"
"People who are up because they have a little money"	LM	"Way-high-ups," but not "Society"
"Poor but honest folk"	UL	"Snobs trying to push up"
"Shiftless people"	LL	"People just as good as anybody"

* Allison Davis, Burleigh B. Gardner, and Mary R. Gardner, *Deep South* (Chicago: University of Chicago Press, 1941), p. 65.

is no doubt that the first is above the other; the upper-middle class views the two upper ones much as the upper classes do themselves but groups them in one level with two divisions, the older level above the other; the lower-middle class separates them but considers them co-ordinate; the bottom two classes, at a greater social distance than the others, group all the levels above the Common Man as "society" and one class. An examination of the terms used by the several classes for the other classes shows that similar principles are operating.

The status system of most communities in the South is further complicated by a color-caste system which orders and systematically controls the relations of those categorized as Negroes and whites.

Although color-caste in America is a separate problem and the present volume does not deal with this American status system, it is necessary that we describe it briefly to be sure a clear distinction is made between it and social class. Color-caste is a system of values and behavior which places all people who are thought to be white in a superior position and those who are thought of as black in an inferior status.

Characteristics of American Negroes vary from very dark hair and skin and Negroid features to blond hair, fair skin, and Caucasian features, yet all of them are placed in the "racial" category of Negro. The skin and physical features of American Caucasians vary from Nordic blond types to the dark, swarthy skin and Negroid features of some eastern Mediterranean stocks, yet all are classed as socially white, despite the fact that a sizable proportion of Negroes are "whiter" in appearance than a goodly proportion of whites. The members of the two groups are severely punished by the formal and informal rules of our society if they intermarry, and when they break this rule of "caste endogamy," their children suffer the penalties of our caste-like system by being placed in the lower color caste. Furthermore, unlike class, the rules of this system forbid the members of the lower caste from climbing out of it. Their status and that of their children are fixed forever. This is true no matter how much money they have, how great the prestige and power they may accumulate, or how well they have acquired correct manners and proper behavior. There can be no social mobility out of the lower caste into the higher one. (There may, of course, be class mobility within the Negro or white caste.) The rigor of caste rules varies from region to region in the United States.[10]

The Mexicans, Spanish Americans, and Orientals occupy a somewhat different status from that of the Negro, but many of the characteristics of their social place in America are similar.[11]

The social-class and color-caste hypotheses, inductively established as working principles for understanding American society, were developed in the researches which were reported in the "Yankee City" volumes, *Deep South,* and *Caste and Class in a Southern Town.* Gunnar Myrdal borrowed them, particularly color-caste, and made them known to a large, non-professional American audience.[12]

THE GENERALITIES OF AMERICAN CLASS

It is now time to ask what are the basic characteristics of social status common to the communities of all regions in the United States and, once we have answered this question, to inquire what the variations are among the several systems. Economic factors are significant and important in determining the class position of any family or person, influencing the kind of behavior we find in any class, and contributing their share to the present form of our status system. But, while significant and necessary, the economic factors are not sufficient to predict where a particular family or individual will be or to explain completely the phenomena of social class. Something more than a large income is necessary for high social position. Money must be translated into socially approved behavior and possessions, and they in turn must be translated into intimate participation with, and acceptance by, members of a superior class.

This is well illustrated by what is supposed to be a true story of

---

[10] See St. Clair Drake and Horace R. Cayton, *Black Metropolis* (New York: Harcourt, Brace & Co., 1945), for studies of two contrasting caste orders; read the "Methodological Note" by Warner in *Black Metropolis* for an analysis of the difference between the two systems.

[11] See W. Lloyd Warner and Leo Srole, *The Social Systems of American Ethnic Groups,* Vol. III, "Yankee City Series" (New Haven: Yale University Press, 1945). Chapter X discusses the similarities and differences and presents a table of predictability on their probable assimilation and gives the principles governing these phenomena.

[12] Gunnar Myrdal, *An American Dilemma* (New York: Harper & Bros., 1944). For an early publication on color-caste, see W. Lloyd Warner, "American Caste and Class," *American Journal of Sociology,* XLII, No. 2 (September, 1936), 234-37, and "Formal Education and the Social Structure," *Journal of Educational Sociology,* IX (May, 1936), 524-531.

what happened to a Mr. John Smith, a newly rich man in a far western community. He wanted to get into a particular social club of some distinction and significance in the city. By indirection he let it be known, and was told by his friends in the club they had submitted his name to the membership committee.

Mr. Abner Grey, one of the leading members of the club and active on its membership committee, was a warm supporter of an important philanthropy in this city. It was brought to his attention that Mr. Smith, rather than contributing the large donation that had been expected of him, had given only a nominal sum to the charity.

When Mr. Smith heard nothing more about his application, he again approached one of the board members. After much evasion, he was told that Mr. Grey was the most influential man on the board and he would be wise to see that gentleman. After trying several times to make an appointment with Mr. Grey, he finally burst into Grey's offices unannounced.

"Why the hell, Abner, am I being kept out of the X club?"

Mr. Grey politely evaded the question. He asked Mr. Smith to be seated. He inquired after Mr. Smith's health, about the health of his wife, and inquired about other matters of simple convention.

Finally, Mr. Smith said, "Ab, why the hell am I being kept out of your club?"

"But, John, you're not. Everyone in the X club thinks you're a fine fellow."

"Well, what's wrong?"

"Well, John, we don't think you've got the *kind* of money necessary for being a good member of the X club. We don't think you'd be happy in the X club."

"Like hell I haven't. I could buy and sell a half dozen of some of your board members."

"I know that, John, but that isn't what I said. I did not say the amount of money. I said the kind of money."

"What do you mean?"

"Well, John, my co-workers on the charity drive tell me you only gave a few dollars to our campaign, and we had you down for a few thousand."

For a moment Mr. Smith was silent. Then he grinned. So did Mr. Grey. Smith took out his fountain pen and checkbook. "How much?"

At the next meeting of the X club Mr. Smith was unanimously elected to its membership.

Mr. Smith translated his money into philanthropy acceptable to the dominant group, he received their sponsorship, and finally became a participant in the club. The "right" kind of house, the "right" neighborhood, the "right" furniture, the proper behavior—all are symbols that can ultimately be translated into social acceptance by those who have sufficient money to aspire to higher levels than they presently enjoy.

To belong to a particular level in the social-class system of America means that a family or individual has gained acceptance as an equal by those who belong in the class. The behavior in this class and the participation of those in it must be rated by the rest of the community as being at a particular place in the social scale.

Although our democratic heritage makes us disapprove, our class order helps control a number of important functions. It unequally divides the highly and lowly valued things of our society among the several classes according to their rank. Our marriage rules conform to the rules of class, for the majority of marriages are between people of the same class. No class system, however, is so rigid that it completely prohibits marriages above and below one's own class. Furthermore, an open class system such as ours permits a person during his lifetime to move up or down from the level into which he was born. Vertical social mobility for individuals or families is characteristic of all class systems. The principal forms of mobility in this country are through the use of money, education, occupation, talent, skill, philanthropy, sex, and marriage. Although economic mobility is still important, it seems likely now that more people move to higher positions by education than by any other route. We have indicated before this that the mere possession of money is insufficient for gaining and keeping a higher social position. This is equally true of all other forms of mobility. In every case there must be social acceptance.

Class varies from community to community. The new city is less likely than an old one to have a well-organized class order; this is also true for cities whose growth has been rapid as compared with those which have not been disturbed by huge increases in population from other regions or countries or by the rapid displacement of old industries by new ones. The mill town's status hierarchy is more likely to follow the occupational hierarchy of the mill than the levels of evaluated participation found in market towns or those with diversified industries. Suburbs of large metropolises tend to respond to selective factors which reduce the number of classes to one or a very few. They do not represent or express all the cultural factors which make up the social pattern of an ordinary city.

Yet systematic studies (see Chapter 15) from coast to coast, in cities large and small and of many economic types, indicate that, despite the variations and diversity, class levels do exist and that they conform to a particular pattern of organization.

HOW CLASS OPERATES IN OUR DAILY LIVES

Because social class permeates all parts of our existence, it is impossible to do more than indicate how it enters consciously or unconsciously into the success and failure of business, professional, and other occupations or to show how knowledge of its effects is necessary for increasing the predictive qualities of much of the research done by psychologists and social scientists. Class is vitally significant in marriage and training children as well as in most social activities of a community. Status plays a decisive role in the formation of personality at the various stages of development, for if young people are to learn to live adaptively as mature people in our society they must be trained by the informal controls of our society to fit into their places.

Education is now competing with economic mobility as the principal route to success. Today fewer men rise from the bottom to the top places in industry and business than did a generation ago. More and more, the sons of executives are replacing their fathers in such positions, leaving fewer positions into which the sons of those farther down can climb from the ranks. Captains of industry educate their sons to take their places or to occupy similar places in other industries. Also, more and more top jobs in industry are being filled by men coming from the technical and engineering schools or from the universities. The route up for them is no longer through a hierarchy of increasing skill to management and ownership as it was two generations ago. The prudent mobile man today must prepare himself by education if he wishes to fill an important job and provide his family with the money and prestige necessary to get "the better things of life."

Social-class research demonstrates that our educational system performs the dual task of aiding social mobility and, at the same time, working effectively to hinder it. This ceases to be a paradox when all the facts are examined. In the lower grades, our public schools are filled by children from all walks of life. Since education is free in the public schools, since everyone has a right to it and our laws try to keep children in school, and since it is common knowledge that "if you want to get ahead you must get an education," it would be assumed that children at, and below, the Common Man level would stay in school and equip themselves for mobility. Such is not the case. The social and educational systems work to eliminate the majority of them and permit only a few to get through. It has been estimated that, whereas 80 per cent of the upper- and upper-middle-class children actually go to college, only 20 per cent of the lower-middle and five per cent of the lower-class children get there.[13] The evidence indicates that most, if not all, of the children of the top classes complete their preparation and go on to college, whereas those from the lower classes start dropping out in the grade schools and continue to do so in increasing numbers in high school. Only a very few of them go on to college. The educational conveyor belt drops lower-class children at the beginning and bottom of the educational route and carries those from the higher classes a longer distance, nearly all the upper-class children going to the end of the line.

If the teachers and school administrators in grade and high schools know the class positions of the children who enter their schools they can predict who will and who will not get to college. Furthermore, with such knowledge the educator can act to change a negative prediction to a positive one for the bright, ambitious lower- and lower-middle-class children, whose chances for higher education are now very slight.

The reason for the high mortality rate among the lower-class children becomes apparent when one examines the relation of the teachers and the other children to them. We now know that the intelligence of lower-class children is not responsible for their failures in school for often their I.Q.'s are equal to those of children higher up. Although inferior intelligence has been the most frequent and

---

[13] Robert J. Havighurst and Hilda Taba, *Adolescent Character and Personality* (New York: John Wiley & Sons, 1948).

plausible explanation,[14] I.Q. tests equated to social class demonstrate that differential intelligence is not the answer.

Teachers, it must be said, although one of the most democratically minded groups in America, tend to favor the children of the classes above the Common Man and to show less interest in those below that level. Studies in the Deep South, New England, and the Middle West indicate that they rate the school work of children from the higher classes in accordance with their family's social position and conversely give low ratings to the work of the lower-class children.

To illustrate how the system of rating the child's abilities and attainments is relative to his position in the social-class order, we will quote from *Who Shall Be Educated?* [15] on what happens in Old City in the Deep South.

"In some elementary schools where there is more than one classroom per grade there is a section system by which students are rated and put together into A section, B section, C section, and more if necessary. In Old City, we find such a system. Each grade is divided into three sections: A, B, and C. This division into sections pervades the whole school system but of necessity it has less formal characteristics in the later years of high school. The junior high-school principal says of these sections:

> When a child enters school he is put into one of three sections according to what the teacher thinks his ability is. When you have dealt with children much you soon find that you can pretty well separate them into three groups according to ability. Then if a child shows more ability he may be shifted into a higher group or if he fails he may be moved into a lower group.

"Sometime later when this same principal was asked whether there seemed to be any class distinctions between the sections, he answered:

> There is to some extent. You generally find that children from the best families do the best work. That is not always true but usually it is so.

---

[14] The unpublished studies of Allison Davis, Robert J. Havighurst, and their collaborators on the class bias *within* the I.Q. tests themselves provide strong evidence to show that the tests are not "culture free" but reflect the middle- and upper-class cultural bias of those who fabricate them. For example, the tests, being largely products of upper-middle-class people, reflect their, biases and only middle- and higher-class children are properly prepared to take them.

[15] W. Lloyd Warner, Robert J. Havighurst, and Martin B. Loeb, *Who Shall Be Educated?* (New York: Harper & Bros., 1944), pp. 73-74.

The children from the lower class seem to be not as capable as the others. I think it is to some extent inheritance. The others come from people who are capable and educated, and also the environment probably has a great effect. They come to school with a lot of knowledge already that the others lack.

"Whatever one may think of this principal's theory in explanation of the correlation between social position and school section, this correlation holds true. There is a strong relationship between social status and rank in school. An analysis of the classes of three years in which the social position of 103 girls was known, shows that:

(1) of the ten upper-class girls, eight were in section A, one in B, and one in C

(2) of the seven upper-middle class girls, six were in section A and one in B

(3) of the thirty-three girls from lower middle and indeterminate middle class, twenty-one were in section A, ten in section B, and two in section C

(4) of the fifty-three lower-class girls, only six were in section A, twenty-eight in section B, and nineteen in section C.

"A teacher in junior high school was willing and able to talk more explicitly about these sections than was the principal quoted above. This teacher was asked if there was 'much class feeling in the school' and she said:

Oh, yes, there is a lot of that. We try not to have it as much as we can but of course we can't help it. Now, for instance, even in the sections we have, it is evident. Sections are supposed to be made up just on the basis of records in school but it isn't and everybody knows it isn't. I know right in my own A section I have children who ought to be in B section, but they are little socialites and so they stay in A. I don't say there are children in B who should be in A but in the A section there are some who shouldn't be there. We have discussed it in faculty meetings but nothing is ever done.

"Later on, she said:

Of course, we do some shifting around. There are some border-liners who were shifted up to make the sections more nearly even. But the socialites who aren't keeping up their standard in the A section were never taken into B or C section and they never will. They don't belong there socially. Of course, there are some girls in A section who don't belong there socially, but almost everyone of the socialites is in A.

"In Old City the ranking of students in their classrooms is clearly influenced by status considerations."

The democratically minded educator asks how this can be. The answer is that most of it is done through ignorance of social class and how it operates in our lives. To be more specific, part of the general answer lies within the teacher as a product of our class system. The teacher conscientiously applies his own best values to his rating of the child. The middle-class teacher, and over three-fourths of teachers are middle-class, applies middle-class values. For him, upper- and upper-middle-class children possess traits that rank high and are positive; lower-class children have characteristics that are negative and are ranked low.

Perhaps the most powerful influence of social class on the educational careers of our children, and certainly one of the most decisive and crucial situations in settling the ultimate class position of children from the Common Man and lower-class levels, is the influence of other children on the child's desire to stay in school. If the world of the child is pleasant, rewarding, and increases his self-esteem, he is likely to want to stay and do well. If it is punishing and decreases his self-respect, he is likely to do poorly and want to quit.

In a study of children's ratings of other children in a middle western community, Neugarten found that the children of the upper and upper-middle classes were rated high by all other children for such traits as good looks, liking for school, leadership, friendship, and many other favorable personal traits; lower-class children were ranked low or, more often than not, were given a negative rating and were said to be bad looking, dirty, and "people you would not want for friends." [16] When it is remembered that these children were only in the fifth and sixth grades and that each child in these grades was supposedly rated by all other children with no reference to status, we can see how quickly class values influence behavior and have their decisive effect in molding the personalities and influencing the life careers of Americans from their earliest years. School for the children of the populous lower classes is not the satisfactory place it is for the middle and upper classes. Given children of equal intellect, ability, and interest, it can be predicted by the use of class

---

[16] Bernice L. Neugarten, "Social Class and Friendship among School Children," *American Journal of Sociology*, LI, No. 4 (January, 1946), 305-13.

analysis that a large percentage of those from the lower classes will be out of school before the sophomore year in high school and that none of the upper-class children, except those physically or mentally handicapped, will quit school.

If our society is to use more effectively the brains and native talent of this great army of young people, it must learn how to train them. To do this, it must keep them in school long enough to equip them with the skills and disciplines necessary for them to function satisfactorily in our economic and social world. Children, as well as teachers and school administrators, must have a conscious and explicit understanding of social class and a simple and easy way to use such knowledge in solving problems. Personality and I.Q. tests are important instruments to guide the teacher, but unless they are supplemented with instruments to measure and count the effects of social class they are insufficient. We believe the instructions in this book for the measurement of social class provide much of the necessary information.

Studies of the relations of workers and managers in business and industry demonstrate how class continues to operate selectively when the young people leave school. Management is bringing college-trained men into the lower ranks of supervisors and promoting fewer from the ranks because it finds that the workers, while good men technically, do not have the necessary knowledge about handling men and relating themselves effectively to the higher reaches of management. Their education is often insufficient to make them good prospects for continuing advancement. The hiring of formally educated men effectively puts a ceiling over the legitimate aspirations of workers expecting to rise in the ranks. The blocking of the worker's mobility and the encouragement of college-trained men is the ultimate payoff of what began in the grade schools. Mobility for workers is becoming more difficult; this means for the United States generally that the American Dream is becoming less real.[17]

Studies of the personalities of workers and managers now being made demonstrate that the effects of social-class and mobility drives are clearly discernible and demonstrably a part of the personality of individuals.[18]

---

[17] See W. Lloyd Warner and J. O. Low, *The Social System of the Modern Factory*, Vol. IV, "Yankee City Series" (New Haven: Yale University Press, 1947), for a discussion of how many of the strikes and conflicts with management are determined by the factor of worker's blocked opportunity.

[18] The ordinary tests of personnel offices fail completely to account for social

In another area, studies of magazine subscriptions show that the class factor is of real importance in the selection of magazines. Readers from different class levels prefer various magazines on the basis of the different symbolic appeal of the stories and pictures. The Yankee City research showed that class entered not only into the purchase of magazines but into newspaper reading.[19] Later research indicates it has a decided effect on radio listening.

A casual examination of the advertising displayed in various magazines demonstrates that advertising agencies and their clients often waste their money because they are ignorant of the operation of class values in their business. This is not surprising since so many status factors have to be considered. The class distribution of readers of the periodicals published in America varies enormously. The readers of certain magazines are confined to the narrow limits of the classes above the Common Man, others to the lower classes, still others to the Common Man level, but there are some who are not confined to any one segment, being well distributed throughout all class levels. The editors of the magazines last designated, intuitively, by trial and error, or some better means, have chosen reading matter which appeals to all levels. The others, not knowing how to extend their readership or appealing deliberately to a narrow range, have a status-limited range of readers.

The readers to whom the advertiser is appealing may or may not be the potential purchasers of his product. The product may be of such a nature that it appeals to only a narrow segment of the total society; to advertise in those media which have readers largely from other strata or to pay for advertising in journals which appeal to every level is a waste of money.

Although advertising agencies often spend their money foolishly when judged by class criteria, the fault is not always theirs, for frequently the manufacturer or retailer does not know how his product appeals to the different classes. Sometimes the product will appeal to but one level, but often a product might appeal to, and be used by, all class levels, were the producer aware of how his product is

---

mobility and class factors, yet the predictive value of these factors for the success of managers in different kinds of jobs is very high.

[19] See Warner and Lunt, *The Social Life of a Modern Community*, Chapter XIX; and W. Lloyd Warner and William E. Henry, "Radio Daytime Serial: A Symbolic Analysis," *Genetic Psychology Monographs*, 1948, 37, pp. 3-71.

valued at different social levels. It is certain that the use and meaning of most objects sold on the American market shift from class to class.

The soap opera is a product of contemporary radio. The average upper-middle-class radio listener has little interest in soap operas; in fact, most of this group are actively hostile to these curious little dramas that fill the daytime air waves. Yet, millions and millions of American women listen daily to their favorite soap operas, and advertisers of certain commodities have found them invaluable in selling their products.

Research has shown that the soap opera appeals particularly to the level of the Common Man. The problems raised in these folk dramas, their characters, plot, and values have a strong positive appeal to women of this class level, whereas they have little appeal to women above the Common Man level.[20]

Other researches demonstrate that furniture, including drapes, floor coverings, chairs and other seating facilities, is class-typed.

Another phenomenon of class, social mobility, is enormously important in the daily lives of Americans and, to a very great degree, determines how they will act on the job or at home. Recent studies of executives in large business enterprises clearly demonstrate that the success or failure of all of them is partly determined by the presence or absence of a "mobility drive." Our research shows that when a family loses its desire to achieve and advance itself, this very often is reflected in the executive's "slowing down" or being unwilling to make the effort necessary for success as a manager. On the other hand, some men are too aggressively mobile and stir up trouble by their overly ambitious desires and their ruthless competition.

Tests combining knowledge of social class and personality demonstrate the necessity of knowing not only what the man's status level is, what it has been, and what he wants it to be, but how the class values and beliefs of his early training have become integral parts of his personality, and ever-present guides for what he thinks, what he feels, and how he acts. Those concerned with selecting executives need a personality inventory and a man's I.Q. to predict how a man will function in a given job; but they also need to find out what his experiences in our status order have done to his individuality and character structure.

---

[20] *Ibid.*

Every aspect of American thought and action is powerfully influenced by social class; to think realistically and act effectively, we must know and understand our status system.

We now face the task of giving exact and precise instructions on how to measure social class and how to identify and locate exactly the class position of anyone in our American society. The methods presented give the reader two techniques for establishing social-class position. The next chapter gives an over-all general set of instructions on how to use each of the two methods and how to combine them when necessary.

SPECIAL READINGS

Those who wish to know more about social class in America and about social stratification generally should read the last chapter (Chapter 15) of this book before continuing with the chapters on instruction for using the techniques for studying social status. It is a commentary on some of the more important publications on social class, color-caste, and other forms of status and rank. Some may prefer to study a few selected readings; for them, the following publications are suggested:

L. T. Hobhouse, G. C. Wheeler, and M. Ginsberg. *The Material Culture and Social Institutions of the Simpler Peoples.* London: Chapman & Hall, 1915.

This exhaustive study of hundreds of communities and societies of the world demonstrates how social stratification and rank are highly correlated with technological advancement and the increase in social complexity. See in particular pages 228-237.

Gunnar Myrdal. *An American Dilemma.* New York: Harper & Bros., 1944.

A study based on original research done by many of the writers listed in Chapter 15. Deals with the conflict between the values of democracy and the values of social status in America. Special reference: pages 667-705.

W. Lloyd Warner and Paul S. Lunt. *The Social Life of a Modern Community.* Vol. I, "Yankee City Series." New Haven: Yale University Press, 1941.

Read especially pages 127-201 and pages 422-450. The first readings are the "Profiles," which describe various kinds of personalities, their actions and values, and their social institutions as they are found in the several classes in a New England town. The last selection summarizes how various social characteristics, such as education, occupation, good and bad neighborhoods and houses, are distributed through the upper, middle, and lower classes.

Other books that might be read at this time are: *Deep South,* by Allison Davis, Burleigh B. Gardner, and Mary R. Gardner (University of Chicago Press), and *Plainville, U.S.A.,* by James West (Columbia University Press).

*Research Problems and Questions for Class Papers and
Further Investigation*

Students may wish to do special research of their own. Several important problems are listed at the end of each chapter. (Of course, many others are possible.) The order of investigation to be followed with each problem might be: (1) the readings suggested after each chapter and with each suggestion, (2) additional readings suggested by these first readings, and (3) interviewing people in your community, school, or neighborhood for original material. (For instructions about interviewing, see "Special Readings" for Chapter 6.)

Problem 1. How are education and the school related to social stratification? Who in America gets an education and who does not? Suggested first readings: *Who Shall Be Educated?* by W. Lloyd Warner, Robert J. Havighurst, and Martin B. Loeb, and the further readings listed in the bibliography for each chapter of that book.

Problem 2. How does social class affect personality and social adjustment? Suggested readings: *Father of the Man,* by Allison Davis and Robert J. Havighurst, pages 215-223; *Children of Bondage,* by Allison Davis and John Dollard, pages 3-44 and 156-184; and *Color and Human Nature,* by W. Lloyd Warner, Buford H. Junker, and Walter A. Adams, pages 1-31.

Problem 3. How does social class affect what people want and buy? See *The Social Life of a Modern Community,* by Warner and Lunt, pages 287-300.

Problem 4. How does social class affect what kind of books people read? See *The Social Life of a Modern Community,* pages 378-386.

Problem 5. How does social class affect the purchase of different magazines? See *The Social Life of a Modern Community,* pages 386-412.

Problem 6. How does social class affect the habits of radio listeners and what effect do certain kinds of programs have upon those who listen? Read *Radio Daytime Serial: A Symbolic Analysis,* by Warner and Henry. The methods for similar studies are fully described in this monograph.

CHAPTER 35

The Decline and Fall of Social Class

ROBERT A. NISBET

The essential argument of this paper may be stated briefly. It is that the term social class is by now useful in historical sociology, in comparative or folk sociology, but that it is nearly valueless for the clarification of the data of wealth, power, and social status in contemporary United States and much of Western society in general.

I should emphasize that this position is taken without prejudice to the value of a class society. Despite an overwhelming orientation of social scientists during the past century or two toward equalitarianism, the evidence is far from clear that a classless society would be a good society. It may well be that the ideology of equalitarianism, with its components of ever-ready amiability, other-directedness, celebration of the common man, and gravity toward consensus, has much to do with the rampant invasion of privacy and erosion of individuality which have so often made it difficult to hold high the banner of intellectualism and cultural standards in our society. Further, social class has often been a bulwark against political power. Indeed, the historical evidence is clear that in the development of human civilization some astonishing outbursts of creativtiy have been closely associated with class societies.

But my concern here is not whether a class society is good or bad. The question is, rather, may American society at the present time reasonably and objectively be called a class society? It is well to look first at a few clearcut definitions of class.

A class society, the anthropologist Goldschmidt writes, is "one in which the hierarchy of prestige and status is divisible into groups each with its own economic, attitudinal, and cultural characteristics and each having differential degrees of power in community decisions."[1] Richard Centers, writing from a more psychological point of view, has emphasized that "a man's class is a part of his ego, *a feeling on his part of belongingness to something;* an identification with something larger than himself."[2] Halbwachs writes that in a society composed of social classes, "each of these social categories determines the conduct of its members and imposes definite motivations on them; it stamps each category with such a peculiar and distinctive mark, so forcibly, that men of different classes, even though they live amid the same surroundings are contemporaries, sometimes strike us as belonging to different species of humanity."[3]

All of these descriptions get at the hard core of social class: class, where it exists, is a tangible relationship; it is substantive, functional, and recognizable through ordinary processes of observation. The proof of existence of a social class worthy of the sociological name should not have to depend upon multi-variate analysis, with correlations generally reaching no higher than .5.

Turn to the sociological writings of such men as Cooley, Sumner, and Ross. Here too, along with some penetrating insights into the nature of social stratification, is the unspoken assumption that the reality of class is plain to all, that it needs no substantiation, merely description or analysis. Add to imaginative literature and sociology the lay articles, sermons and orations of the time, and the conclusion is plain that irrespective of the oft-spoken American dream of every man a president, people took class for granted and knew in intimate and daily detail what the content and attributes were of the classes referred to. Despite the ideology of democratic equalitarianism, despite what Tocqueville and Bryce had written about the tenuous character of class lines in the United States, social class, even as recently as 1910, was an understood reality.

How very different is our situation today. It is hard to resist the conclusion that in recent years statistical techniques have had to become ever more ingenious to keep the vision of class from fading away altogether. To this point Arnold Anderson has written cogently: "There is a risk that the search for refined techniques may lead to our unconsciously overlooking the original problem. For example, use of multiple techniques for combining scores on different status scales may yield a valid 'status' score. Social class, however, has traditionally implied membership in groups or quasi-groups."[4] To which I would add that some multiple correlation of status attributes have not only produced sociological monstrosities but, more important, have obscured the data and acted to prevent the appearance of new perspectives in stratification.

Consider for a moment a possible analogy to our preoccupation with social class in the United States: the kinship structure known as the kindred. The kindred is an ancient and real form of association. Almost all human society has been at one time or another based upon it. Even today in the United States the kindred demonstrably exists in our nomenclature, not to mention blood and marital relationships. Further, there are even yet small parts of the United States where the kindred has a certain functional importance; is a recognized part of the culture. Now, I do not think I exaggerate when I say that at least as strong a case can be made out for the

role of the kindred as for class in the United States and most of Western culture. But who would bother to make it? Who would seriously treat a small Ozarks community with respect to kindred as a "microcosm of American society," as the place where "all Americans live"? How many social scientists would declare that since *kinship* is an unalterable part of human society, the *kindred* is therefore inevitable and that one's failure to know the interests of his kindred is the result of ideological distortion? And, finally, who would suggest seriously that since kinship is inescapable one had best accept his kindred in the interest of peace of mind?

There is no need to belabor the question. The answer is fairly clear and lies, of course, in the realm of political and social values. Unlike other concepts of sociology that of class has had for a long time certain value overtones to which few if any of us could be insensitive. For most social scientists (preponderantly liberal in political matters) any denial of the existence of class seemed tantamount to asserting that all Americans have equal opportunity. Too seldom has it occurred to us that the manifest facts of inequality could be placed in other perspectives of stratification.

Undeniably, class studies based upon community analysis have produced many essential data and, along with these data, many perceptive and valuable insights into the nature of status behavior, affiliation and prestige. But, for the moment leaving aside my fundamental criticism of the non-historical and non-contextual character of these studies, one is forced to conclude that both data and insights too often suffer from a kind of Procrustean adjustment to a conceptual framework that is at once too short and too narrow. It becomes more and more difficult to suppose that the hypothesis of social class would be invoked at the present time in studies of American stratification and power were it not for the deep roots of this hypothesis in the conceptual memory of sociology.

At its extreme, especially in certain of Warner's works, the class perspective has the attributes of a Never Never land: observations carefully sterilized of historical considerations, constructed of self-fulfilling interviews and premises, skillfully extrapolated through use of linear scales and multiple correlations; the whole processing a certain internal consistency, even credibility, but, on overview, possessing about as much relation to national American society as James Branch Cabell's enchanted land of Poictésme does to Times Square.

We come, finally, to the social components of class. It is here that sociologists and anthropologists, especially the Warner school, have demonstrated greatest ingenuity in defense of class as a reality in contemporary American life. Through indexes of status characteristics and evaluations of participation in community life, a strong and often imaginative effort has been made to buttress what remains of a perspective that has been declining almost from the time it was first formulated. It is said in effect that even if class conceived as power cannot be demonstrated, life styles and the general preoccupation with social status leave us with self-conscious and culturally implicative classes numbering anywhere from three to ten.

But the evidence here seems to me no more compelling than in the economic and political spheres. I suggest that in the same way that there has been a general disengagement of economic and political power, during the past century and more, from any homogeneous scale of stratification, leaving in its wake plurality and dispersion, so has there been a general disengagement of social status itself from any clearly definable set of ranks. That scales of status exist in our society is incontestable, that they are often of driving concern to individuals is equally incontestable. But social status is at once too continuous within each of the numerous scales of status to make possible any identification of classes that have more than the most restricted or specialized acceptance.

I do not doubt that within a community that is sufficiently isolated from the main currents of national life, sufficiently arrested in terms of historical change, sufficiently homogeneous so far as its economy and government are concerned, a clear and meaningful class system could be discovered. I merely emphasize that to discover such a community today it is necessary to go either to the underdeveloped areas of the world or, in American society, to a few remaining and fast-disappearing pockets of the old order.

It is because social status, like economic and political power, has become disengaged from real class lines in modern society, that such novels as *Point of No Return*, *What Makes Sammy Run?*, and John Braine's recent *Room at the Top* are more illuminating so far as status behavior is concerned than the majority of community studies of social class. These novels are concerned with individuals in a mobile society, preoccupied by status considerations exactly *because* classes have been replaced by impersonal levels connected by ever wider channels of vertical mobility. Perhaps I go too far in the last reference; perhaps studies which are only now really beginning will show that channels of mobility are not as wide and congested as I think they are; but as sociologists we cannot overlook the significance of the almost universal *belief* that they are.

In any event, the crucial point here is not the extent of vertical mobility but rather the fact that we are living in a society governed by status, not class, values, and that class lines recede everywhere in almost exact proportion to the reality and urgency of individual status considerations. As a consequence of its disengagement from class, social status has become simultaneously more individual, more autonomous, and is, on any realistic basis, almost as multiple and diverse as is American culture. If I am wrong on this, will someone please rank for me on any linear *class* scale the following individuals: Ted Williams, Ike Williams, G. Mennen Williams, Esther Williams, Mrs. Harrison Williams, and Robin Williams.

Schumpter pointed out in his *Imperialism and Social Classes* that "the family, not the individual person, is the true unit of class and class theory." This is correct, and what has happened to kinship in modern society, both to its structure and to its relation to the larger society, has been closely involved in the shift from social class to social status. Social status does not really imply the existence of groups at all; it can be used with reference to a continuous scale of invidiously valued positions, and it is with this in mind that Goldschmidt has insisted that the "proper figure of speech is not that there are rungs of a ladder; it is rather that there is a chromatic scale of status—a glissando."

There may be still a few communities in the United States where a man's professional, marital and associative choices will be, for as long as he lives in the community of his birth, limited by the level of his family of orientation in almost the same way that one's choices are widened or narrowed by the racial or ethnic group he belongs to. Such communities are few. For, generally, family of orientation is regarded as a marker or starting place by which individuals measure the distance they have moved upward or downward, and, on this matter, I repeat, J. P. Marquand and John Braine have told us more than has Professor Warner.

Admittedly, a status-based society may be as inequalitarian at any given time as one organized in terms of class divisions. Further, it can scarcely be doubted that one's life chances, even his aspirations, will be influenced by the level of his family of orientation. Unquestionably, the sense of personal determination of status will be weaker, on the whole, at the extremes than in middle levels of status, in even the most mobile of societies. Such considerations do not, however, affect the central question of class any more than do the equally vivid facts of inequality of power and wealth in society.

I should say that, nationally, the nearest we come to class consciousness is in what Mozell Hill has called level consciousness. Unlike class consciousness, level consciousness makes for a high degree of individual-ism with respect to aspirations and life chances; it does not promote feeling of identification or collective involvement. The principal motive of the level-conscious individual is to pass up and out of the level in which he finds himself. He is, so to speak, on the make. He lives in an atmosphere of competition that is nourished constantly by education and ideology and by the substantive fact of a shortage of skill in the industrial and professional world. Level consciousness creates awareness of one's differences from others, rather than similarities, and in this respect the individual is constantly moved by distinctions he invents between himself and others, by preoccupation, even anxiety, with these distinctions. As Professor Hill writes, "one by-product of this on the American scene is that people have come to feel that it is not so much a matter of destroying those on a higher level of consumption as it is of acquiring skills, strategies and techniques which will enable one to surmount his level."[5]

It is sometimes said that the failure of individuals to respond accurately to questionnaires which seek to derive a class consciousness corresponding to income level is simply the consequence of "ideological distortion." But, quite apart from the fact that such assertions run the risk of self-sealing and self-fulfilling reasoning, they do not give proper due to the social role of ideology. An ideology is not a shadow or representation. It is as real a part of one's social behavior as job or income. As real, and oftentimes more decisive.

The notable unwillingness of substantial numbers of people to concede the existence of class divisions, despite the bait of forced-choice questionnaires and the heavy pull of terminological tradition, is itself a social fact of the highest order. Granted that some uncomfortable economic realities are often obscured by the ideology of classlessness, whether in suburbia or elsewhere, the fact of this refusal to concede the existence of class is itself a powerful influence in preventing differential social statuses from becoming crystallized into classes.

In sum, the concept of social class has

been an important, and probably inevitable, first step in the study of differential power and status in society; admittedly, there are non-Western areas of civilization, as well as ages of the past, where the class concept is indispensable to an understanding of power and status; but so far as the bulk of Western society is concerned, and especially the United States, the concept of class is largely obsolete. Any useful inquiry into the distribution of wealth, power and status, and their interactions, will have to be made, I believe, in terms of concepts that are more representative of the actual history of modern political and economic society.

NOTES

[1]Walter Goldschmidt, "Social Class in America —A Critical Review," *American Anthropologist* 52 (October-December, 1950), 492.

[2]Richard Centers, *The Psychology of Social Classes* (Princeton: Princeton University Press, 1949), p. 27.

[3]Maurice Halbwachs, *The Psychology of Social Classes* (Glencoe, Ill.: The Free Press, 1958), p. 4.

[4]C. Arnold Anderson, "Recent American Research on Social Stratification." Third Working Conference on Social Mobility and Social Stratification (Amsterdam, 1954), published in *Mens en Maatschappij*, 1955, pp. 321-37.

[5]Mozell Hill in an unpublished manuscript on class and mobility.

CHAPTER 36

The Subcultures of the Working Class, Lower Class, and Middle Class

HERBERT J. GANS

The Peer Group Society:
Class or Ethnic Phenomenon?

One of the initial purposes of this study was to compare a low-income population such as the West Enders to the middle class, and, if possible, to isolate some of the basic differences between them. The relative stability of the social structure across the generations from Southern Italy to the West End, which I described in the last chapter, would seem to suggest that there might be an Italian way of life. This idea in turn would support the hypothesis that the peer group society is an ethnic phenomenon and that the principal differences between the West Enders and the middle class are ethnic ones.

An alternative hypothesis, however—that the peer group society is a working-class phenomenon and that class differences separate the West Enders from the middle class—is more justified. The West Ender is a descendant of farm laborers who became blue-collar workers in urban America. As I have tried to show, the similarities

575

in ways of life over the generations have resulted from the similar economic and social positions that the Southern Italian and the West Ender have occupied in the larger Italian and American societies respectively.

The hypothesis is further supported by studies of other working-class populations which have shown that these, too, exhibit many characteristics of the peer group society. The same is true of other ethnic groups whose members are of blue-collar status. Such characteristics, however, are not displayed by those of white-collar status. Consequently, the class hypothesis offers a better explanation than the ethnic one.

The characteristics that West Enders share with other working-class groups can be conceived as forming a working-class subculture, which differs considerably from both lower- and middle-class subcultures. A description of these subcultures and of the differences between them indicates why attempts to transform working-class people in the middle-class image have failed. It also points to some of the major problems of working- and lower-class subcultures, and suggests some proposals for how planners and caretakers should deal with these problems. These proposals will be presented in the next chapter.

A Survey of Working- and Lower-Class Studies [1]

A wealth of evidence from other studies indicates that the peer group society is a class, rather than an ethnic, phenomenon. My survey of these studies will be cursory. It will consider various social structural and cultural characteristics in the order in which I have described them among the West Enders.

Although the existence of a peer group society has not been reported in other working-class populations, Walter Miller's study of an Irish and Negro neighborhood did conclude that: "Lower class society may be pictured as comprising a set of age-graded one-sex peer groups which constitute the psychic focus and refer-

1. Most of the reported studies deal with the working class, some with the lower class, and others fail to distinguish between the two. Differences between the two classes will be discussed in the next section. In the survey, I shall use the term "working class" to describe both, unless the study cited refers specifically to lower-class people.

ence group for those over twelve and thirteen." [2] The distinction between the peer group society and the outside world is much like Hoggart's dichotomy of "us" and "them" in the British working-class. [3] He writes:

> . . . the world outside is strange and often unhelpful . . . it has most of the counters stacked on its side . . . to meet it on its own terms is difficult. One may call this, making use of a word commonly used by the working classes, the world of "Them." . . . The world of "Them" is the world of the bosses, whether those bosses are private individuals or . . . public officials. . . . "Them" includes the policemen and those civil servants . . . whom the working classes meet. . . . To the very poor, especially, they compose a shadowy but numerous and powerful group affecting their lives at almost every point. . . . "They" are "the people at the top" . . . who . . . "get yer in the end," "aren't really to be trusted," "are all in a clique together," "treat y'like muck." [4]

Similarly, a study of American working-class women notes their separation from "the outer world," and their fear of its " 'chaotic and catastrophic' qualities." [5] In some ways Redfield's conception of the relationship between the peasant and the elite is like that between the West Ender and the outside world. [6] Moreover, Lewis's description of the Mexican "culture of poverty" bears a number of resemblances to the way of life of the poorest West Enders. [7]

My description of routine- and action-seekers is paralleled in many ways by S. M. Miller and Frank Riessman's distinction between the "unskilled, irregular worker . . . [who] . . . lacks the

2. Walter B. Miller, "Lower Class Culture as a Generating Milieu of Gang Delinquency," *Journal of Social Issues*, vol. 14, No. 3 (1958) pp. 5–19, at p. 14.

3. Richard Hoggart, *The Uses of Literacy*, London: Chatto and Windus, 1957, Chap. 3.

4. *Ibid.*, p. 62.

5. L. Rainwater, R. Coleman, and G. Handel, *Workingman's Wife*, New York: Oceana Publications, 1959, pp. 44–45.

6. Robert Redfield, "Peasant Society and Culture," in *Little Community and Peasant Society and Culture*, Chicago: University of Chicago Press (Phoenix Books), 1960, pp. 36–39.

7. Oscar Lewis, *The Children of Sanchez*, New York: Random House, 1961, pp. xxiii–xxvii.

disciplined, structured and traditional approach of the stable worker and stresses the excitement theme." [8] Their analysis, based on a review of American working-class studies, reflects the general sociological distinction between working and lower class.[9] Walter Miller's study of lower-class culture describes in more systematic detail what I have called action-seeking. He notes its "focal concerns" with such qualities as toughness, daring, adroitness in repartee, excitement, and rejection of superordinate authority.[10] His discussion of excitement observes that:

> For many lower-class individuals the rhythm of life fluctuates between periods of relatively routine or repetitive activity and sought situations of great emotional stimulation. Many of the most characteristic features of lower-class life are related to the search for excitement or "thrill." [11]

The largest amount of data is available on family life. The segregation of family roles and the separate lives of husbands and wives have been reported in studies of the English working class,[12] among Puerto Ricans, both in Puerto Rico and in New York,[13] in a

8. S. M. Miller and Frank Riessman, "The Working Class Subculture: A New View," *Social Problems*, vol. 9 (1961), pp. 86–97, at p. 95.

9. See, for example, W. Lloyd Warner and Paul S. Lunt, *The Social Life of a Modern Community*, New Haven: Yale University Press, 1941, which distinguishes between and describes upper-lower and lower-lower classes; and the work of his associates, for example, August B. Hollingshead, *Elmtown's Youth*, New York: Wiley and Sons, 1949.

10. Walter B. Miller, *op. cit.*, summarized from Chart I, p. 7.

11. *Ibid.*, pp. 10–11. See also his "Implications of Urban Lower-Class Culture for Social Work," *Social Service Review*, vol. 33 (1959), pp. 219–236; and Warren Miller's novel of the episodic life in a lower-class Negro gang, *The Cool World*, Boston: Little, Brown, 1959.

12. See, for example, J. M. Mogey, *Family and Neighborhood*, London: Oxford University Press, 1956, p. 58; and Elizabeth Bott, *Family and Social Network*, London: Tavistock Publications, 1957, pp. 58 ff. Bott also cites a number of earlier studies with a similar finding, and notes that not all working-class families are segregated.

13. Helen Icken, "From Slum to Housing Project," unpublished study made for the Urban Renewal and Housing Administration, Commonwealth of Puerto Rico, 1960, mimeographed, p. 55; Elena Padilla, *Up from Puerto Rico*, New York: Columbia University Press, 1958, pp. 151–152.

Mexican family,[14] and in a national American working-class sample.[15] A study of Polish-Americans describes this segregation as follows:

> . . . the pairs are not "one" . . . the marriage relation is not intensive. There is not a ceaseless seeking out of the other's motivations, no rigid set of expectations to which the other must conform.[16]

The same study also notes the men's need to display and defend their masculinity.[17] Similar findings have been reported in most working-class populations regardless of ethnic origin.[18] The subordinate role of children in what I have called the adult-centered family has been observed among New York Puerto Ricans [19] and in a general survey of working-class culture.[20] Two American studies point out the lack of interest in children as individuals.[21] The pattern of permitting freedom to boys, and of keeping girls at home has also been found among Puerto Ricans.[22]

The central role of the peer group has been suggested, as previously noted, by Walter Miller's study of Irish and Negro lower-class adolescents.[23] Another American study found that:

14. Lewis, *op. cit.*, p. 335.

15. Lee Rainwater, *And the Poor Get Children*, Chicago: Quadrangle Books, 1960, p. 69; and Social Research, Inc., "Status of the Working Class in Changing American Society," Chicago: Social Research, Inc., February, 1961, mimeographed, p. 80.

16. Arnold W. Green, "The 'Cult of Personality' and Sexual Relations," in Norman W. Bell and Ezra F. Vogel, eds., *A Modern Introduction to the Family*, New York: The Free Press of Glencoe, 1960, pp. 608–615, at pp. 614–615.

17. *Ibid.*, p. 614.

18. Walter Miller, "Lower Class Culture as a Generating Milieu of Gang Delinquency," *op. cit.*, p. 9; Rainwater, *op. cit.*, pp. 84–85; Icken, *op. cit.* Lewis's study of a Mexican family gives innumerable examples of this phenomenon.

19. Padilla, *op. cit.*, pp. 179 ff.

20. Miller and Riessman, *op. cit.*, p. 92. They use the term "parent-centered."

21. L. Rainwater, R. Coleman, and G. Handel, *op. cit.*, p. 89; and Social Research, Inc., *op. cit.*, pp. 161, 163.

22. Icken, *op. cit.*, p. 57; Padilla, *op. cit.*, pp. 186 ff.

23. Miller, "Lower Class Culture as a Generating Milieu of Gang Delinquency," *op. cit.*, p. 14.

Husband and wife tend to have few, if any friends in common.
Relationships with friends tend to be on a single-sex basis. . . .
Often relatives are the only friends. If husband or wife do have
friends who are not relatives, they have them as individuals and
not as couples.[24]

Many studies have shown the existence of the family circle, notably
in England,[25] and among New York Puerto Ricans.[26] The prevalence of spending one's social life with relatives more than with
friends has been reported in England [27] and in a variety of American working-class groups.[28]

A number of findings on group life and personality have suggested that many of the elements I have summarized as person-
orientation are found among working-class people generally, and
one survey of American studies describes them as person-centered.[29]
This article also notes the practice of personalizing bureaucracy
and other outside world situations, as does an account of English
working-class life.[30] A study of American working-class women
describes their problems in regard to self-control, and shows how
lack of self-control encourages their children in turn to express
anger through violence.[31] It also suggests that working-class adolescents express themselves motorically, or physically, while middle-

24. Social Research, Inc., *op. cit.,* p. 82.

25. Mogey, *op. cit.,* p. 97; Bott, *op. cit.,* p. 112; Michael Young and Peter
Willmott, *Family and Kinship In London,* London: Routledge and Kegan Paul,
1957, Chap. V.

26. Padilla, *op. cit.,* pp. 112 ff. She calls it "the great family group."

27. Madeline Kerr, *The People of Ship Street,* London: Routledge and
Kegan Paul, 1958, pp. 106–108. Young and Willmott report the rejection of
mobile relatives, *op. cit.,* pp. 143–144.

28. Floyd Dotson, "Patterns of Voluntary Association among Urban Working Class Families," *American Sociological Review,* vol. 16 (1951), pp. 687–693,
at p. 691; Rainwater, Coleman, and Handel, *op. cit.,* p. 107; Bennett M. Berger,
Working-Class Suburb, Berkeley: University of California Press, 1960, p. 68;
and Social Research, Inc., pp. 63, 82. Rainwater, Coleman, and Handel also
note the working-class woman's difficulty in making friends. *Op. cit.,* p. 108.

29. Miller and Riessman, *op. cit.,* pp. 93–94.

30. *Ibid.,* and Hoggart, *op. cit.,* p. 28.

31. Daniel R. Miller, Guy E. Swanson *et. al., Inner Conflict and Defense,*
New York: Holt, Rinehart, and Winston, 1960, Chap. 14.

class adolescents use conceptual and symbolic modes.[32] Another study of American working-class women stresses the importance of group life, the fear of loneliness, and their concern with what others think of them.[33] An analysis of lower-class interview respondents has described in considerable detail their tendency to be concrete and particularistic, to think anecdotally, to personalize events, and to see phenomena only from their own perspective: [34] they do not "assume the role of another toward still others." [35] The limited repertoire of roles also has been described in a study of an English group,[36] and the inability or unwillingness of people to adopt other roles has been reported as lack of empathy in a previously mentioned study of Middle Eastern peasants.[37]

A number of American studies have shown the scarcity of working-class participation in what I have described as community life.[38] For example, the West Enders' pattern of being religious but not being identified with the church has been found among other American groups, both Protestant and Catholic,[39] and in England as well.[40]

Both American and English studies have reported the working-

32. *Op. cit.*, Chap. 15. A national survey reports that "respondents with less education tend to be less introspective about themselves, whether about strong points or shortcomings." G. Gurin, J. Veroff, and S. Feld, *Americans View Their Mental Health*, New York: Basic Books, 1960, p. 69.

33. Rainwater, Coleman, and Handel, *op. cit.*, pp. 64–66. See also Hoggart, *op. cit.*, p. 72.

34. Leonard Schatzman and Anselm Strauss, "Social Class and Modes of Communication," *American Journal of Sociology*, vol. 60 (1955), pp. 329–338; and Anselm Strauss and Leonard Schatzman, "Cross Class Interviewing: An Analysis of Interaction and Communicative Styles," in Richard N. Adams and Jack J. Preiss, ed., *Human Organization Research*, Homewood, Ill.: Dorsey Press, 1960, pp. 205–213.

35. Schatzman and Strauss, *op. cit.*, p. 331.

36. Kerr, *op. cit.*, Chap. 17.

37. Daniel Lerner, *The Passing of Traditional Society*, New York: The Free Press of Glencoe, 1958.

38. Dotson, *op. cit.*, p. 688; Berger, *op. cit.*, p. 59; Rainwater, Coleman, and Handel, *op. cit.*, pp. 114 ff. See also Morris Axelrod, "Urban Structure and Social Participation," *American Sociological Review*, vol. 21 (1956), pp. 13–18.

39. Berger, *op. cit.*, pp. 45 ff.; Rainwater, Coleman, and Handel, *op. cit.*, p. 123.

40. Hoggart, *op. cit.*, pp. 94–97; Kerr, *op. cit.*, pp. 135–136.

class' detachment from work,[41] the concern with job security,[42] and the negative evaluation of white-collar workers and bosses.[43] The West Enders' ambivalence about education is also widely shared. The conception that school should teach children to keep out of trouble has been described by an English study; [44] that education must contribute to the occupational success of the individual, by many studies, including an American [45] and a Puerto Rican one.[46] Two studies have indicated that working-class mothers want more education for their children than do the fathers.[47]

I have already reported the prevalence of the general conception that the outside world is not to be trusted. This extends also to a skepticism about caretakers,[48] a reluctance to visit settlement houses,[49] and a fear of doctors and hospitals that seems to be found in all countries.[50] Similarly, working-class people everywhere believe—or know—the police to be crooked, and politicians, corrupt. In America,[51] England,[52] and Mexico,[53] researchers have described

41. A concise review of studies of work patterns and attitudes of working-class and lower-class people is found in Joseph A. Kahl, *The American Class Structure*, New York: Holt, Rinehart and Winston, 1957, pp. 205–215.

42. Ephraim H. Mizruchi, "Social Structure, Success Values and Structured Strain in a Small City," paper read at the 1961 meetings of the American Sociological Association, mimeographed; Social Research, Inc., *op. cit.*, pp. 57–58.

43. Katherine Archibald, "Status Orientations among Shipyard Workers," in Reinhard Bendix and Seymour M. Lipset, eds., *Class, Status and Power*, New York: The Free Press of Glencoe, 1953, pp. 395–403; Young and Willmott, *op. cit.*, p. 14.

44. Hoggart, *op. cit.*, p. 98.

45. Social Research, Inc., pp. 51–53; see also Archibald, *op. cit.*, p. 399; and Mizruchi, *op. cit.*

46. Padilla, *op. cit.*, p. 198.

47. Herbert H. Hyman, "The Value System of Different Classes," in Bendix and Lipset, *op. cit.*, pp. 426–442, Tables III, IV; and Icken, *op. cit.*, p. 34.

48. Padilla, *op. cit.*, p. 264.

49. Albert Cohen, *Delinquent Boys: The Culture of the Gang*, New York: The Free Press of Glencoe, 1955, pp. 116–117.

50. Hoggart, *op. cit.*, p. 42; Kerr, *op. cit.*, p. 39; Lewis, *op. cit.*, p. xxviii.

51. Miller and Riessman, *op. cit.*, p. 91.

52. Hoggart, *op. cit.*, p. 87.

53. Lewis, *op. cit.*, pp. xxvii, 351, 389. On the personalization of government, see Miller and Riessman, *op. cit.*, p. 93; Padilla, *op. cit.*, p. 256; and Lewis, *op. cit.*, p. 332.

the working- and lower-class antagonism toward law, government, and politics.

Conversely, the mass media are accepted, often more enthusiastically than by other classes. A recently published study of American television viewers has made this finding, and noted the working-class audience's interest in and identification with performers.[54] Several studies have also suggested the preference for action dramas over other forms of media content, not only in America,[55] but all over the world.[56] In Green's study of a Polish group, the rejection of romantic films by young working-class adults was described as follows: "At the local movie house, when the hero pauses in pursuit of the villain to proffer the heroine a tender sentiment, whistling and footstamping greet his fall from grace." [57]

As I have not attempted to make a complete survey of the literature, I have mentioned here only some of the many similarities between the West Enders and other groups. Even so, it should be evident that, by and large, the peer group society is associated with working- and lower-class life. Moreover, the data show that many of its features are found among other ethnic groups who have come to America from Europe—notably the Irish and Polish—as well as among racially differentiated groups, such as the Negroes and the Puerto Ricans. Incidentally, the peer group society also cuts across religious lines, for many of its characteristics appear not only among Protestants in England and America, but among European and Latin Catholics as well.

Some differences—including a few ethnic ones—do exist between the West Enders and other working-class people. Yet many of these differences can be traced to class factors operating in past and present generations. Italian-Americans, for example, differ from the Irish-Americans in a number of ways. The Irish are more respectful of paternal authority, of the older generation, of the

---

54. Ira O. Glick and Sidney J. Levy, *Living with Television*, Chicago: Aldine Publishing Company, 1962, Chap. III, VII.

55. See, for example, Berger, *op. cit.*, pp. 74–75.

56. Herbert J. Gans, "American Films and Television Programs on British Screens: A Study of the Functions of American Popular Culture Abroad," Philadelphia: Institute for Urban Studies, 1959, mimeographed, Chap. 4.

57. Green, *op. cit.*, p. 613.

church, and of authority in general. Irish men are also much closer to their mothers than are Italian men, a fact that has a number of implications for family structure, family dynamics, and even for the ways in which mental illness is expressed.[58]

Many of these differences can be related to the fact that the Irish immigrants came from landowning, peasant families. In Ireland, the father was the sole owner of the family farm, and thus was free to choose as to which of his sons would inherit it. As a result, sons were in a subordinate position.[59] One study of the Irish peasantry notes, in fact, that sons were called boys until the day the father surrendered the farm to one of them, even if they themselves were middle-aged adults.[60] The conditions which the Irish immigrants found in America evidently did not encourage any major change in family structure. Certainly, one could argue that those Irish-Americans who turned to politics and the priesthood found that the relationship between the political boss and his underlings and between the Bishop and his priests was much the same as that between the farm owner and his sons. Needless to say, not all Irish-Italian differences can be explained purely by class factors, or by cultural differences which developed from economic conditions in Europe. They do seem, however, to be of primary importance.

West Enders also differ from other working-class, and especially lower-class, groups in the role that the mother plays in family life. Studies of the English working class, for example, have stressed the importance of the "Mum" and the dominance of the mother-daughter relationship over all others, even when the daughter is married and has children of her own.[61] Similarly, studies of the Negro, Puerto Rican, and Carribean lower classes have shown the

58. These differences between the Irish are reported in Ezra F. Vogel, *op. cit.*, and M. K. Opler and J. L. Singer, "Ethnic Differences in Behavior and Psychopathogy," *International Journal of Social Psychiatry*, vol. 2 (1956), pp. 11–22. See also Mark Zborowski, "Cultural Components in Responses to Pain," *Journal of Social Issues*, vol. 8 (1952), pp. 16–30; and Paul Barrabee and Otto van Mering, "Ethnic Variations in Mental Stress in Families with Psychotic Children," *Social Problems*, vol. 1 (1953), pp. 48–53.

59. Conrad M. Arensberg and Solon T. Kimball, *Family and Community in Ireland*, Cambridge: Harvard University Press, 1940, pp. 47 ff.

60. *Ibid.*, pp. 51, 56.

61. The previously cited studies by Young and Willmott, and by Kerr describe this relationship in great detail.

family to be what anthropologists call matrifocal.[62] The mother is the head of the household, and the basic family unit includes her, her children, and one or more of her female relatives, such as her mother or aunt. Often the man is a marginal and only intermittent participant in this female-based household.[63] American studies of the lower class have reported what Walter Miller calls "serial monogamy"—a pattern in which a woman lives and has children with a series of men who desert her or whom she asks to leave.[64]

The reason for this pattern among Negroes can be found in the fact that in past and present, they have lived under conditions in which the male's position in the society has been marginal and insecure. Under slavery, for example, the formation of a normal family was discouraged, although the female slave was allowed to raise her own children. Since the days of slavery, the Negro's economic position has been such as to maintain much of this pattern. The man who has difficulty in finding a steady job and is laid off frequently finds it difficult to perform the functions of a male breadwinner and household head. Moreover, when the woman is able to find steady employment or can subsist on welfare payments, she tends to treat the man with disdain and often with open hostility, especially if he complicates her life by making her pregnant. Under these conditions, there is no incentive for the man to remain in the family, and in times of stress he deserts. Moreover, when the male children grow up in a predominantly female household—in which the man is a powerless and scorned figure—their upbringing encourages ambivalence as to male functions and masculinity. Thus, the pattern is perpetuated into the next generation.[65]

The hypothesis that the female-based family can be traced to

62. See, for example, Raymond T. Smith, *The Negro Family in British Guiana,* London: Routledge and Kegan Paul, 1956; and for America, E. Franklin Frazier, *The Negro Family in the United States,* Chicago: University of Chicago Press, 1939.

63. Walter B. Miller, "Lower Class Culture as a Generating Milieu of Gang Delinquency," *op. cit.,* p. 14.

64. Walter B. Miller, "Implications of Urban Lower-Class Culture for Social Work," *op. cit.,* p. 225.

65. Walter B. Miller, "Lower Class Culture as a Generating Milieu of Gang Delinquency," *op. cit.,* p. 9.

class and, more specifically, to occupational factors is supported by
studies describing this family type among peoples who have not been
slaves.[66] It has been found, for example, among Puerto Ricans,
both on the island and in New York. It seems, however, to be more
prevalent among Puerto Ricans from sugar cane areas, which have
a plantation economy much like that under which the Negro endured slavery.[67] The hypothesis is supported in another way by
the fact that a somewhat similar family constellation prevails when
the man's occupation separates him from his family for long periods. Thus, a study of sailors' families in Norway indicates that the
woman takes over the dominant role in the family, and overpro-
tects her children.[68] Although the girls show no negative consequences, the boys seem to develop what Tiller calls a defensive
feminine identification, and compensatory masculine traits. When
such boys become adults, they thus favor occupations that stress
masculinity and minimize female contact and the family role.

The female-based family, however, is not found among West
Enders, and the reasons perhaps can also be traced to occupational
factors. Although the West Enders' ancestors suffered from unemployment, the totally agrarian economy of Southern Italian society
and the extremely strenuous character of farm labor created no
employment opportunities for women. Indeed, the family could
best survive if the woman stayed home and bore a large number
of children who could eventually add to the family's income. As a
result, the woman did not take on an economic function, and the
man maintained his position in the family even though he could
not always support it adequately. This family constellation seems
to have been strong enough to endure in America during those
periods when the man was unemployed and the woman could find
a job. Needless to say, some family instability and male marginality
or desertion has occurred among the immigrants and the second

66. I have not been able to find any explanation of the dominant role
of the "Mum" in the English working-class family. It should be noted, however,
that this family is not female-based.

67. I owe this suggestion to Howard Stanton. In the sugar cane economy,
there is work for only three to four months a year.

68. Per Olav Tiller, "Father Absence and Personality Development of Children in Sailor Families," Oslo: Institute for Social Research, 1957, mimeographed.

generation, but such cases have been considerably fewer than among newcomers with female-based families.

Finally, the West Enders may be contrasted to the Jews, an ethnic group which came to America at about the same time as the Italians, but with a different occupational history.[69] The Jews who emigrated from Poland and Russia around the turn of the century were neither farm laborers nor peasants, but peddlers, shopkeepers, and artisans with a more middle-class occupational tradition. They also differed from their fellow immigrants in their belief in education, partly for reasons related to this tradition. Although they worked initially as unskilled and semiskilled laborers in America, they reacted differently to their environment than did the ethnic groups from peasant and farm labor origins. Superficially, the Jewish family structure resembled the Italian one, with a nuclear household surrounded by a large family circle. Because of the high value placed on education, however, the immigrants did not restrain their children from contact with the outside world. As already noted, they encouraged the children to use the schools and settlement houses to prepare themselves for white-collar and professional occupations. Thus, the Jewish young people pursued careers that drew them apart from the parental generation at the same time that their Italian neighbors rejected such careers as "lonely ventures" that could only break up the cohesion of the family circle. Although the Jewish immigrants did bemoan the children's acculturation into styles of life congruent with their higher occupational level, they also took pride in the successful mobility of their offspring.[70]

I would not want to claim that the West Enders are like all

69. This account draws on Marshall Sklare, *Conservative Judaism*, New York: The Free Press of Glencoe, 1955; and Nathan Glazer, *American Judaism*, Chicago; University of Chicago Press, 1957.

70. For a detailed study of differences between American-born Italians and Jews, see Fred L. Strodtbeck, "Family Interaction, Values and Achievement," in D. C. McClelland, A. Baldwin, U. Bronfenbrenner, and F. Strodtbeck, *Talent and Society*, Princeton: D. Van Nostrand, 1958, pp. 135–194. He compares Jewish values, such as the belief in education, the desirability of individual achievement, and the striving for mobility and for rational mastery of the world to the Italians' familism and fatalism. Even so, he suggests that "differences between Italians and Jews are greatly attenuated when class level is held constant." *Op. cit.*, p. 154, based on an unpublished study by B. Tregoe.

other working-class and peasant ethnic groups, or that all differences between them and other populations can be explained by
class factors. Indeed, many differences between the ethnic groups
must be attributed to other factors in their cultural traditions and
in their American experience.[71] Until comparative studies of these
groups are made that hold class constant, however, we will not
know exactly where these differences are located, nor how they can
be explained.

IX

The Consequences of Stratification

Students of social stratification have had little difficulty identifying its correlates since most facets of social life have proven to be intertwined with various aspects of social inequality. The theory of stratification at its present stage of development is not, however, an adequate theory of the consequences of stratification.

There are several reasons for the present unsatisfactory understanding of how stratification is implicated in social life. One central difficulty flows from the confusion between *systems of action* and *systems of stratification*. As sketched in the opening sections of this volume, social differentiation and stratification are important properties of systems of action (societies and their constituent subsystems). Each subsystem of a society is characterized by its own form of stratification: earnings and wealth in the economic sphere; privilege and power in the political system; moral worth and personal trust in religious and family life; and prestige and esteem in the occupational world. No one of these *forms* of inequality comprises in its own right a system of action. Indeed, all of them together do not qualify as an identifiable social system or subsystem. Instead, each form is embedded or implicated in some particular subsystem and comprises the hierarchical *aspect* of that system. (The function of stratification within each subsystem is, in part, understandable in terms of the functional theory of stratification: the existence of alternative forms of stratification in different systems is related both to the requirement of obtaining commitments of differing individuals to different subsystems that often demand different qualities and skills and to the necessity of distinguishing between performances in different contexts of subsystems.) Because the subsystems with which the various forms of stratification are associated are themselves interconnected, the several forms of inequality are not empirically independent of each other. Indeed, they tend to be more or less congruent: persons of wealth tend also to be judged morally worthy and so forth. Thus, stratification is, in this sense, *systematic,* but it is not in itself a *functional* subsystem of society (see Parsons, 1961, 1966, 1970; Johnson, 1960).

Important aspects of behavior within each of the subsystems of a society are directly related to the stratification of that subsystem. For example, the kind and

589

number of alternative life styles available to a family unit is an immediate consequence of its economic circumstances. However, one's location in the hierarchy of one sub-system may well constrain one's behavior in another. To continue the foregoing example, we can readily see, that even though the level or volume of one's consumption is set by one's financial circumstance, the actual types and patterns of goods consumed by different families *at the same economic level* vary considerably. These differences may be accounted for by a wide range of non-economic variables, ranging from socialization in ethnic and religious subcultures to so simple a parameter as the range and variety of goods available in accessible shopping facilities (see Suttles, 1968). Such cross-system influences make it impossible to talk unidimensionally about any particular consequence of stratification. Different forms of stratification may have quite different implications for behavior, as in the case of fertility rates which are positively correlated with income, inversely associated with educational attainment, and not associated in any clear pattern at all with occupational stratification (see Freedman, 1963; Blau and Duncan, 1967: Chapter 11). Patterns such as the one just observed may, however, be explained under a unified theory of the specific phenomena under consideration, even though they are not explicable in the light of a general theory about the consequences of stratification. Thus, for example, as one's educational level rises, the economic value of one's time increases and one may well choose to lavish time upon few children rather than distribute it among many children. But as one's income level rises, the marginal utility of an additional unit of income declines and one may prefer to expend the time required to obtain the additional income unit on leisure or child-rearing. Hence, rather simple notions from elementary economics seem to enable one to untangle the somewhat puzzling interrelationships between fertility rates, economic level and educational attainment.

Another source of difficulty in understanding the consequences of stratification rests on the distinction between the stratification of social roles and the stratification of their individual occupants. Ordinarily, we think of the authority vested, for example, in heads of households as being a component part of the role of father. The authority is, in this case, independent of who occupies the role and is ascribed not only to all fathers in equal degree but also to individuals who are not themselves genealogically related to other household members but who have come to occupy the father role in households formed through remarriage. A similar situation occurs in alternative family structures, such as the matriarchy found in some Negro communities, where the functional equivalent of the role of the household head is usually occupied by someone other than the biological father of adolescent household members. In any concrete situation, however, the control exercised by the household head must be understood by reference both to the authority vested in the role and to the personal influence or charisma of its occupant. The authority vested in household heads may, in short, be compromised by the personal influence of other family members. Wives may dominate their husbands; that such an arrangement is contrary to the normative role structure is evidenced by the somewhat sympathetic reference to men so situated as "henpecked." But other deviations from normative structures of authority, both in the family and elsewhere, are not necessarily so easy to detect. Thus, in order to discern the *relative* influence on individual behavior of the authority built into roles, personal influence, and compliance to the authority and influence of others requires painstaking detailed study of the behavior of many individuals in similar roles in identical circumstances.

Any empirical attempt to separate the effects of role and personal characteristics is made all the more complicated insofar as (a) the effects of role and personal characteristics tend to cancel each other by exerting equal and opposite influences, and (b) the effects of role and personal characteristics upon *each other* tend to blur empirically the analytic distinction between them. Thus, for example, the evolution of a more equalitarian household structure has resulted from compromise of the authority of the household head as women have assumed some financial responsibilities through higher levels of labor force participation. Similarly, ascent to a prestigious position may well improve the esteem attributed to individuals: Richard Nixon looks better in the White House than out of it. Of course, when men of questionable repute occupy prestigious posts, the legitimacy of those posts may be undermined. The recent history of the judiciary, in which the resignation of one Supreme Court justice was secured and the appointment of another not confirmed because of their questionable business connections, makes the point clear.

Many of the consequences of stratification are, on detailed analysis, also causes of stratification. That is, many of its short-run consequences are long-run causes of opportunity structures and other facets of inequality. First, consider fertility rates which, as we have already indicated, may be analyzed partly as consequences of stratification, although affected in different ways by different facets of social stratification. Socioeconomic differences in fertility rates are intertwined with the time path of the size distribution of socioeconomic groups. If we could imagine a society in which everyone remained at the socioeconomic level of their origins, differentials in fertility would, unless offset by the force of differential mortality, imply a more rapid growth of some socioeconomic levels than others. The *relative* sizes of the several classes could, in this instance, be maintained only by allowing some persons to escape from their origins and achieve alternative socioeconomic levels. Since, empirically, fertility rates tend to be highest in the lowest socioeconomic groups, the net balance of such movements would have to be upward in order to maintain the *relative* sizes of the several socioeconomic levels. Some authors have, consequently, suggested that differential fertility induces upward mobility by creating a vacuum at the top of the socioeconomic ladder (see Sib-

ley, 1942; Kahl, 1953: 251-275). It is not, however, differential fertility that induces or brings about net upward mobility; this mobility is the outcome of economic forces which have led to the continued expansion of job opportunities at the higher socioeconomic levels and the contraction of opportunities at the lower levels. Differential fertility is not by itself sufficient to "induce" upward mobility; it is, however, one of several factors, including differential mortality and patterns of inter- and intragenerational mobility, which are implicated in the changing size distribution of socioeconomic levels (see Treiman, 1970).

The so-called vicious circle of race relations is perhaps a better known example of the intermingling of cause and consequence in the maintenance of social inequalities between groups. There is probably little doubt that the subservient, self-deprecating, Sambo-personality type found among American Negroes was historically *adaptive* to the social role of "Negro" in the United States; it was a way of coping with a society that regards its Negro citizens as inferior and treats them accordingly. But the personality type which is adaptive in an environment of discrimination also contributes to the maintenance of that system. Sambo—black or white—has no place in an economic order founded on individual initiative and achievement. Just how the system of discrimination will ultimately be shaped by the militancy of the present generation of Negro youth remains to be seen. Already, they have made clear that sleepy Sambo was neither the necessary product of family socialization among Negroes nor a genetically determined trait; he was an adaptive response to white violence which has again and again been called forth to repress the attempts of Negroes to claim their legal rights as citizens and their moral rights as human beings.

The selections incorporated in this section reveal the great variety of social phenomena which are associated with one's place in the socioeconomic hierarchy. These range from political behavior and mental illness to compliance and mate selection. Needless to say, many other facets of social life are also intertwined with social stratification; some of these are covered in the references below.

REFERENCES

Adams, Bert N.
  1968   Kinship in an Urban Setting. Chicago: Markham Publishing Co.
Blau, Peter M., and Otis Dudley Duncan.
  1967   The American Occupational Structure. New York: Wiley.
Chinoy, Ely.
  1955   Automobile Workers and the American Dream. Garden City, New York: Doubleday.
Ellis, Robert A., and W. Clayton Lane.
  1967   "Social mobility and social isolation: A test of Sorokin's dissociative hypothesis." American Sociological Review 32: 237-253.
Freedman, Deborah.
  1963   "The relation of economic status to fertility." American Economics Review 53: 414-426.
Glenn, Norval D., and Jon P. Alston.
  1968   "Cultural distance among occupational categories." American Sociological Review 33: 365-382.
Goldhammer, Herbert.
  1957   "Voluntary associations in the United States." In Paul K. Hatt and Albert J. Reiss, Jr. (eds.), Cities and Societies. 2d ed. Glencoe, Ill.: Free Press.
Goode, William J.
  1962   "Marital satisfaction and instability: A cross-cultural class analysis of divorce rates." International Social Science Journal 14: 507-526.
Hewitt, John P.
  1970   Social Stratification and Deviant Behavior. New York: Random House.
Johnson, Harry M.
  1960   Sociology: A Systematic Introduction. New York: Harcourt, Brace & World.
Kadushin, Charles.
  1964   "Social class and the experience of ill health." Sociological Inquiry 34: 67-80.
Kahl, Joseph.
  1953   The American Class Structure. New York: Rinehart and Company.
Kephart, William M.
  1955   "Occupational level and marital disruption." American Sociological Review 20: 456-465.
Kitagawa, Evelyn M., and Philip M. Hauser.
  1968   "Education differentials in mortality by cause of death: United States: 1960." Demography 5: 318-353.
Kohn, Melvin L.
  1969   Class and Conformity: A Study in Values. Homewood, Ill.: Dorsey Press.
Laumann, Edward O.
  1966   Prestige and Association in an Urban Community. Indianapolis: Bobbs-Merrill.
Liebow, Elliot.
  1967   Tally's Corner: A Study of Negro Streetcorner Men. Boston: Little, Brown.
Miller, Daniel B., and Guy E. Swanson, et al.
  1960   Inner Conflict and Defense. New York: Holt, Rinehart, and Winston.
Miller, S. M., and Frank Reissman.
  1964   "The working-class subculture: A new view." Pp. 24-36 in Arthur B. Shostak and William Gomberg (eds.), Blue-Collar World: Studies of the American Worker. Englewood Cliffs, New Jersey; Prentice-Hall.
Miller, Walter B.
  1958   "Lower-class culture as a generating milieu of gang delinquency." Journal of Social Issues 14: 5-19.
Parsons, Talcott.
  1961   "An outline of the social system." Pp. 30-79 in Talcott Parsons and Edward Shils, et al. (eds.), Theories of Society. New York: Free Press.
  1966   Societies: Evolutionary and Comparative Perspectives. Englewood Cliffs, New Jersey: Prentice-Hall.
  1970   "Some further thoughts on the action theory of stratification." Sociological Inquiry 40 (Spring).
Pettigrew, Thomas F.
  1964   A Profile of the Negro American. Princeton, New Jersey: D. Van Nostrand.
Powell, Elwin H.
  1958   "Occupation, status, and suicide: Toward a redefinition of anomie." American Sociological Review 23: 131-138.
Rainwater, Lee.
  1966   "Crucible of identity: The Negro lower-class family." Daedalus 95: 172-216.
Reiss, Albert J., Jr., and Albert L. Rhodes.
  1961   "The distribution of juvenile delinquency in the social class structure." American Sociological Review 26: 720-732.
Sibley, Elbridge.
  1942   "Some demographic clues to stratification." American Sociological Review 7: 322-330.
Srole, Leo, and Thomas S. Langner, et al.
  1962   Mental Health in the Metropolis. Volume I. New York: McGraw-Hill.
Suttles, Gerald D.
  1968   The Social Order of the Slum: Ethnicity and Territory in the Inner City. Chicago: University of Chicago Press.

Treiman, Donald J.
  1970 "Industrialization and social stratification." Sociological Inquiry 40 (Spring).

Tumin, Melvin M.
  1957 "Some unapplauded consequences of social mobility in a mass society." Social Forces 36: 32-37.

Vidich, Arthur J., and Joseph Bensman.
  1960 Small Town in Mass Society. Garden City, New York: Doubleday.

Wrong, Dennis H.
  1958 "Trends in class fertility in western nations." The Canadian Journal of Economics and Political Science 24: 216-229.

CHAPTER 37

Status, Conformity, and Innovation

GEORGE C. HOMANS

Our study of the substantive findings of research began in this book with Chapter 5 on Influence. In that chapter and the ones immediately following we were concerned with the processes by which a group develops a structure—that is, the processes by which it reaches the condition we call practical equilibrium—when the kinds of behavior any one member gives to any other tend to repeat themselves time and time again. We looked, for instance, at the way members try to change the behavior of a deviate, and if they fail to do so, give him little interaction or social approval. We looked also at the way members get differentiated in esteem. But as we have gone on, we have become less and less concerned with the way structure develops and more and more concerned with the nature of the structure itself.

In parallel with this changing interest, we have become steadily less concerned with esteem and more concerned with status. This does not mean that esteem has become any less important in the social behavior we have studied: it only means that our intellectual interests have been changing. Esteem is the actual social approval many members emit to one of their number. One of the most important, but still only one, of the determinants of his status is their recognition—and his own recognition—that he is getting the esteem. What we recognize are stimuli; any item of behavior is not only a reward (or punishment) but also a stimulus to the person to whom it is directed, and a stimulus not only to him but to interested spectators. A man's status in a group is a matter of the stimuli his behavior toward others and others' behavior toward him—including the esteem they give him—present both to the others and to himself, stimuli that may come to make a difference in determining the future behavior of all concerned.

As time has gone by, we have also had to consider more and more complex forms of social behavior. Once status gets recognized, it sets the stage for new developments in behavior, developments we call secondary because their appearance depends on the prior establishment of the more primitive forms. We ran into this secondary development early in the book, but the study of status congruence first forced us to take serious account of it. Men not only behave in the ways described by our propositions but often come to recognize that they are doing so. Though they would never state the propositions in quite our language, they do become aware of general relationships between different forms of behavior. Which stimuli shall become crucial in determining a man's status depends on which relationships his companions have become aware of, and the stimuli in turn create new rewards and costs for new kinds of behavior. To return to the example we have used so often: once two men get recognized as equals in status, and once it is recognized that equals are commonly people who emit equally valuable activities—once the relationship between equality in status and equality in value gets recognized as a congruent one—then a man who goes to another and asks for a service for which he cannot make an equivalent return has cast some doubt on his equality with the other in the eyes of his companions. He has presented them with a stimulus suggesting that some different kind of behavior from what they have hitherto adopted toward him may bring them reward. To cast doubt on his status may, therefore, be a cost to a man, a cost he could not have incurred until the other members had become aware of the congruent relationship, and accordingly he may refrain from asking for the service in question unless he stands in dire need of it. The service itself may be valuable, but the stimulus he presents to his companions in asking for it is something else again. In short, one of the potentially rewarding activities of men is the presentation of stimuli, and they try to manipulate, to their advantage, the stimuli they present to others.[1]

[1] The great, and fascinating, expert in this field is E. Goffman, *The Presentation of the Self in Everyday Life* (New York, 1959).

The secondary mechanisms may help the primary ones maintain stability in a group. If, for instance, our man refrains from asking another for a service he is unable to return, he has by that fact maintained his equality with the other and thus contributed to the general stability of social relations. But we are far from arguing that the recognition of status and the secondary mechanisms it brings into play always contribute to social stability. They may, on the contrary, introduce important possibilities for further change and innovation. It is appropriate that these should be the subject of the present chapter, for it is the last chapter in which we shall encounter altogether new material. To put the matter a little too neatly: we began by showing how change creates group structure and we shall end by showing how group structure creates change.

In particular we shall be interested in showing how, when differences in status between members have once become recognized and established, these differences tend from then on to stimulate further differences in their behavior. From this point of view, we shall consider that members may occupy three different types of social position: upper, middle, or lower status. We do not claim that every group possesses just three levels of status, no more and no less, or that a member can always be assigned unambiguously to one of the levels. We do claim that a threefold division is not arbitrary but inherent in the strategy of the situation, and indeed it appears in many class structures in society at large. Upper-status people have many others below them but few or none above; lower-status people have many above them but few or none below; but middle-status people have others both above and below them. These differences are obvious but not trivial; for as we shall soon see, they create differences in the risks people take when they emit new behavior. In the present chapter we shall consider the threefold division in its relation to innovation, on the one hand, and conformity, on the other. We shall also have to bring in a variable we have already encountered in earlier chapters: the degree to which a man's status is established and unambiguous or fluid and ambiguous, that is, the degree to which social certitude prevails.

Status and Conformity: Field Research

Without more ado, let us look at some of the evidence, first the evidence from field research and then, at greater length, the evidence from experiments. In natural groups, as we cannot repeat too often, a man of high status gets his position by providing for other members services that they find valuable and rare. So far as members set a high value on conformity to certain norms, for instance, an output norm in an industrial group, the man who conforms is doing them a valuable service, though not a particularly rare one—unless like Taylor in the Bank Wiring Observation Room he conforms more closely than anyone else.[2] Therefore, a man of high status will conform to the most valued norms of his group as the minimum condition of maintaining his status.

In *The Human Group* I said that a man of high status would conform to a high degree to all the norms of his group, but this was certainly an overstatement; indeed the book itself supplied evidence against it.[3] To keep his high status a man must provide rare and valuable services to others, but so long as he does that, the other members may allow him some leeway in lesser things. He may even take the leeway. Mere slavish conformity to any old norm may put him back among the masses instead of keeping him set apart from them, where he belongs. He is apt to be a leader, in a position of authority. If there is any correcting to be done, he is the one to do it: it is his business to correct others, not others' to correct him. If, then, he violates group norms in minor ways, it will take some presumption on the part of other members to tell him he is wrong.

The margin of freedom from group control enjoyed by a man of high and established status has been well described by Everett Hughes:

> Here is an apparent paradox: Admittance to the group may be secured only by adherence to the established definitions of the group, while unquestioned membership carries the privilege of some deviant behavior. This is, of course, not a paradox at all; for it is characteristic of social groups to demand of the newcomer a strict conformity which will show that he accepts the authority of the group; then, as the in-

[2] G. C. Homans, *The Human Group* (New York, 1950), p. 78.
[3] *Ibid.*, p. 141.

dividual approaches the center of the group and becomes an established member, they allow him a little more leeway.[4]

At the moment we are not particularly interested in the newcomer to
a group, but since Hughes has brought him up, let us say a word about
him in passing. At this end of the book we are dealing with complex
forms of behavior, and of their complexity justice is always a part. A
newcomer is a man who has acquired little investment in a group; if
his returns from membership are to be, in accordance with the rules
of distributive justice, proportional to his investment, his rewards must
be kept low and his costs high. So far as it constrains behavior and
restricts freedom, conformity to norms is costly. Hence other members often try to make newcomers conform strictly to the norms of the
group. Whether they will conform is another matter. Probably they
will if esteem is not too long denied them. What happens when they
cease to be newcomers without having won much esteem we shall soon
consider. On the other hand, a man who has fully earned his footing
may be exempted from rigid compliance.

We have looked briefly at the man of high status as he appears in
field studies; let us now look at the man of low status. In his study of
sixteen agents in a Federal law-enforcement agency, which we have
already cited and which we shall describe at length in the next chapter,
Blau pays special attention to the behavior of one unpopular agent,
unpopular because he violated important norms of the group. He reported to his superior a bribe offered him by the management of one
of the firms he investigated and took a threatening attitude toward
management in general. The other agents interpreted his reporting the
bribe as an effort to lick his superiors' boots, and they disapproved of
it for other reasons too. The firms, they felt, were under such great
temptation to offer bribes that it was unfair to tell on them when they
succumbed; the offer of a bribe also gave an agent an unofficial hold
over a firm and so helped him in his investigatory work, but the hold
would be lost if bribes were ever reported. This agent also talked too
much, completed more work than the others thought right, and refused
to help them out with their technical problems.

For these reasons he received little esteem; indeed he was ostracized:
so far as possible the others cut off interaction with him. But note that

[4] E. C. Hughes, "The Knitting of Racial Groups in Industry," *American
Sociological Review*, Vol. 11 (1946), p. 517.

to ostracize a man is to remove him from social control: if he holds out against that pressure there is nothing more the group can do to bring him back into line, short of physical violence. The group has lost its leverage on his behavior. The next time he has a choice whether or not he will do something they want, he is the less apt to do it the less they have left to take away from him in the way of esteem and interaction. He has nothing to lose by nonconformity and perhaps even something to gain by vexing them.

The investigator says of this agent:

> To be sure, his deviant behavior contributed to his continued isola-tion, but this position also encouraged lack of conformity. . . . His overproductivity had made him an isolate and, once in this position, he became the only member of the agency who ignored a very im-portant unofficial norm. The individual who had adapted himself to an isolated position could more readily violate the norms of the group.[5]

His preceding actions had won him low esteem from others, and his low esteem in turn made it likely that his next actions, too, would be unacceptable to the group, confirming him in his low esteem. Social behavior is full of such vicious spirals, as it is of favorable ones. Note also that once he had built up a record of bad behavior, no single ac-tion in conformity to group norms would have done much to raise his esteem. It would take time to live down his past, which meant that on any particular occasion he had little to gain by conformity as well as little to lose by its opposite. This sense of being trapped by their pasts makes some people anxious to start fresh in new groups. "They know me," they say, "too well in there."

If this agent had had anything to hope for from the group, if he had still been vying for acceptance by it, no doubt he would have been less prepared to violate group norms. But this was not the case: not only was his status low but it was firmly established as low. Accord-ingly we may say that members of established low status in a group are particularly apt not to conform to its norms. Since they get little reward from the group, they are also particularly apt to leave the group altogether—if there is anywhere they can go.

[5] P. M. Blau, *The Dynamics of Bureaucracy* (Chicago, 1955), p. 155.

Status and Conformity: Experimental Research

In the scanty evidence of field research we have found some reason to believe that men of both upper and lower status, in their different ways and for different reasons, show some tendency toward nonconformity. As yet we have had nothing to say about men of middle status. In contrast to the other two, are they particularly apt to be conformists? To answer this question let us turn to the experimental evidence, and first to research carried out by Kelley and Shapiro.[6]

The investigators brought the subjects, who were college freshmen, into the experimental room in groups of five or six at a time. There the members introduced themselves to one another; each told the others something about himself, and then the investigators had each one answer a simple sociometric test in which he was to say, on the basis of this brief acquaintanceship, how acceptable as a co-worker he found each of the other members. After this, the investigators put each member into an alcove by himself and asked him not to communicate with the others. While he was there, they handed him a slip of paper apparently showing how he had scored on the sociometric test: whether his fellow members had chosen him as an acceptable co-worker or not. As soon as he had read the slip, the investigators hastily withdrew it as if they had handed it out inadvertently, never meant to do so at all, and only now realized their mistake. Naturally this little act had the effect of stamping their scores all the more indelibly upon the subjects' minds. Some of the subjects were thus persuaded that they were highly acceptable to the others, and some that they were not in the least acceptable. A further questionnaire asked each member to say whether he wanted to keep on as a member of the same group. Not surprisingly, members in the high-acceptance condition were much more apt than the others to want to continue.

The investigators then told each member that he was to carry out a task, that his score on it would be pooled with those of the other members of his group, and that the group with the highest average score would get a fifteen-dollar prize. The task was this: he was shown a

[6] H. H. Kelley and M. M. Shapiro, "An Experiment on Conformity to Group Norms where Conformity is Detrimental to Group Achievement," *American Sociological Review*, Vol. 19 (1954), pp. 667-77; see also J. M. Jackson and H. D. Saltzstein, *Group Membership and Conformity Processes* (Ann Arbor, 1956).

series of ten pairs of white cardboard squares, the two squares in each pair being labeled A and B. He was to say which square contained the more dots; the investigator told him that the same square was the correct answer every time, but did not tell him which one it was, A or B. Unknown to the subject, the squares in the first pair contained an equal number of dots, but thereafter with each presentation square A lost a few dots and B gained a few so that it became more and more clear to an unprejudiced observer that B had more. After every presentation, each member gave his choice of square and indicated his confidence in it. At that time he was allowed to write notes to his fellow members. These were collected but not delivered. Instead, by a procedure that became familiar to us in the chapter on Influence, the investigators delivered to each subject a set of notes, actually the same for each member, but purporting to come from other members. All the notes suggested that the right answer in every case was square A and not square B. That is, each member received visual evidence that one answer was correct, while being informed by his fellow members that another one was. He also knew that a correct answer would help his group get a prize. Would he conform to the apparent influence of other members even though conformity might be detrimental to group achievement?

From each member's choice of square in each presentation, and from the degree of confidence he expressed in that choice, the investigators calculated his conformity score, a measure of the degree to which he had given in to group influence; and they then correlated these scores with members' acceptance or nonacceptance by the others and their willingness or unwillingness to continue in the group.

The most interesting findings were the following. Members who set a low value on membership in the group, most of whom also believed they were not acceptable to their fellow members, tended to show little conformity. This appears to be an experimental reproduction of the phenomena Blau described: a group that has withheld esteem from a member has by that fact lost control over him. Faced with a choice between doing what the group wanted and doing what would at least satisfy his own self-respect—in this case naming the square that really had the more dots—the man of low status was apt to choose the latter. Since the group could not hurt him any further, he had nothing to lose by not conforming.

The second finding was even more interesting. Members that set a high value on membership in the group were, on the average, somewhat more likely to be conformers than the others. But individually they varied in their conformity far more than did the nonconformers in their nonconformity: some conformed very much and some very little, as if they had fallen heavily on one side of a dilemma or the other.

It seems to have been from a desire to explore further the bearing of this last, ambiguous finding that Kelley, this time in company with Dittes, embarked on a second study.[7] Since the procedure of the new experiment was in many ways the same as that of the last, we shall only report the ways in which it differed. Several groups met separately to discuss the question which of two gangs of juvenile delinquents should be judged more worthy of help. The discussion was based on two sets of fictitious court records, so doctored that the members of a group were almost certain to reach the decision that one of the gangs was more worthy than the other, but only after they had talked the matter over for some time. In their instructions, the investigators emphasized that a group's decision should be unanimous, like a jury's, and when the group did reach unanimity each member was to register the fact by rating the gangs, both in public and in private, on a number of different scales.

The investigators interrupted the discussion three times and asked each member to rate the others on the desirability of their remaining in the group. At the end of the discussion they announced the average score the group as a whole had received on these tests, and then let each member look in private at what purported to be his own score in relation to the average. In fact, of course, the scores were fictitious, and they were designed to produce a finer discrimination among degrees of acceptability than had been achieved in the earlier experiment. Of the six members of each group, one found his score to be above the average (the "high" condition), two found theirs to be about average ("average"), two found theirs to be slightly below the average ("low"), and one found his to be far below ("very low"). The investigators also discussed his score with each member and allowed the highs and the averages to believe that their ratings were pretty

[7] J. E. Dittes and H. H. Kelley, "Effects of Different Conditions of Acceptance on Conformity to Group Norms," *Journal of Abnormal and Social Psychology*, Vol. 53 (1956), pp. 100-07.

stable and unlikely to change in the future, while they persuaded the lows and very lows that their ratings were liable to change and get even worse. The higher a man's status the more stable his status, the investigators suggested. Besides status itself, they tried to manipulate the degree to which status was perceived as established.

After each man understood his apparent standing in the group, the members renewed their discussion of the gangs; but this time the investigators introduced new evidence designed to suggest that the group's original and unanimous decision was wrong, and that the other gang was probably the worthier of the two. The experimental question then became the following: Under what conditions of perceived acceptance by the others were members more or less likely, in the face of the new evidence, to cleave to the group's original decision? The investigators used three different measures of conformity: the degree to which a member expressed agreement with the group's decision in a private rating of the gangs, the degree to which he did so in his public rating, and the degree to which in discussion he tended to discount or explain away the new information. The investigators also noted how long it took each member to make his new ratings, their assumption being that a man who took little time was probably sticking automatically to the original decision. They also measured how big a part each member took in the discussion following the release of the new information.

The investigators then asked each group to work on another problem, the members this time judging, in a succession of pairs of squares, which square contained the more dots. Since this procedure was much like that of the previous experiment we shall not describe it further. When work on both problems had come to an end, each member answered a final questionnaire, reporting how highly he valued his membership in the group, how free he felt to express opinions contrary to the group's judgment, and how secure he felt in his social standing— especially how strongly he believed that the group would in the future reject him even more than it had already.

And now for the results. As we might have foretold, the order of the four classes in acceptance was their order in evaluation of their membership in the group: the more highly a member felt he was accepted by the others, the more highly he valued his membership; but the differences in this respect between the very lows and the lows, and be-

tween the lows and the averages were much more significant statistically than the difference between the averages and the highs. In other
respects the averages and the highs behaved quite differently. The
previous experiment had, in effect, lumped the two together in the
high-acceptance condition, and got from them much conformity as
well as much of its opposite. The present experiment separated them,
and in so doing it managed also to separate conformists from nonconformists. For by almost every measure the present highs conformed
less to, and expressed more freedom to differ from, the group judgment than did any other class, whereas the averages, in sharp contrast,
were the greatest conformers of all. The averages also turned in their
new ratings sooner than did any other class and participated most in
the discussion of the new information, though largely by discounting it
and explaining it away. The investigators suggest that the averages
found it rewarding to belong to the group and felt considerable acceptance by the others, but that they thought they had still more acceptance yet to win. They suggest that the conforming behavior of the
averages reflected their aspirations to still higher social standing.

Turning now to the lows, we find that, like the earlier experiment,
they were somewhat nonconformist, but that, unlike the earlier one,
they were not as much so as the highs. With the very lows, the same
general tendency presented a slightly different twist. We shall remember that there was only one of them in each group: he was both low and
alone in his status. More apt than any other status to feel they were
about to be rejected altogether, setting at the same time a low value on
membership, and expressing little conformity in their private judgments, the very lows nevertheless expressed in public more conformity
than did any other status, took less part in discussion, and felt less freedom to disagree. As the investigators say: "In the extreme case . . .
where acceptance is so low that actual rejection is presumably an im-
minent possibility, anxiety about rejection is especially high, and the
result seems to be a pattern of guarded public behavior."

Upper Status and Originality

We now have experimental evidence that it is not just members of
low status, but members of high status as well, who are prone at times
to nonconformity. But before we ask whether both lows and highs are

nonconformists for the same reasons, let us look at one more piece of research, this time carried out by Bartos and carried out on natural groups rather than on artificially formed, experimental ones.[8]

The subjects of the research were 231 active members of six teenage Y.M.C.A. clubs in a small Midwestern town. At the first meeting of the year each club elected eight officers, four of whom were to serve for the first term of the school year and four for the second; and after his election the president of the club appointed several other officers to help him with the work.

The clubs may appear somewhat over-officered, but that only helped the investigator to divide the membership into four classes differing in status. From high status to low they were: (1) the presidents, or leaders, (2) the remaining elective officers, whom the investigator called elected lieutenants, (3) the appointed officers, or appointed lieutenants, and (4) the members not holding office, or followers, this last class being obviously the largest. Whereas the preceding studies were forced to create differences in status by experimental manipulation, here the investigator had them handed to him naturally by the election and appointment system. But note that, if any comparison at all is valid, the "lows" and "very lows" in the last study corresponded to only a small section of the followers in this one, and that most of the followers were equivalent to the "averages."

The investigator had each subject look at a series of twelve pairs of cards and asked him "to match one of the three lines appearing on each of the right hand cards with the one line appearing on each of the left hand cards." Since the line on the left was always just the same length as one of the lines on the right, the job of matching should have been simple. But naturally the investigator did not mean to let his subjects off as easily as all that. While a subject was making his choice of lines, he heard off-stage the voices of six persons, which he was led to believe were the voices of members of his club, urging that one of the lines in the right hand card was the proper match for the line on the left; and in seven instances out of the series of twelve the voices unanimously urged the choice of the wrong line. The investigator in fact played the voices from a tape recorded in advance of the experiment.

After putting each subject through this experimental condition, the

[8] O. J. Bartos, "Leadership, Conformity, and Originality," unpublished paper presented at the 1958 meeting of the American Sociological Society.

investigator had him do the same matching job all over again with what seemed to be a new set of cards but was actually the same one, and this time without the chorus of voices. As a good experimenter, he wanted to make sure that the subjects would not make the same mistakes when not under the apparent influence of their fellow members as they had when they were under it. Not surprisingly they made many more mistakes in the first condition than in the second, and they made them by doing what the voices told them. Accordingly the investigator concluded that the number of mistakes a subject made by giving in to the influence brought to bear on him was a valid measure of his conformity.

The investigator had the subjects take two further tests. The first, called the independence-of-judgment scale, consisted of a series of fifteen statements with each of which the subject was to say whether he agreed or disagreed. For instance, one such statement was: "It is easy for me to take orders and do as I am told." Not unnaturally, agreement with statements like this was held to be evidence of a propensity to conformity. The experiment itself was modeled on an earlier one by Asch, and answers to such statements had in fact discriminated between those of Asch's subjects that conformed and those that did not.[9] Finally in the second test the subject looked through a series of drawings, both freehand drawings of strange asymmetrical figures and ruled drawings of symmetrical and geometrical shapes, and decided which ones he found most pleasing aesthetically. These drawings the investigator had borrowed from another piece of earlier research, which had seemed to show that the number of "complex" cards a man chose was a valid measure of his "originality."

The problem now was to relate the statuses of the members to their differences in the various measures of conformity and originality. On the line test the leaders of the clubs were far less conformist than other members. Most conformist were the elected lieutenants in the next highest status, but there was no great difference in conformity between them and the people holding the two lowest statuses: the appointed lieutenants and the followers. Much the same thing was true of the independence-of-judgment test: the leaders were far less conformist than the others; this time the followers were most conformist but not much more so than the elected and appointed lieutenants. In the readiness of the members of highest status to resist influence from the rest of the

[9] S. E. Asch, *Social Psychology* (New York, 1953), pp. 450-501.

group, these results are in accord with the Kelley experiments. But there is little hint, such as appeared in the final Dittes-Kelley study, that the members lowest in status, the followers, were also prone to nonconformity. We must remember that the followers in the present study made up more than half of the whole membership and so included many people equivalent to the "averages" of Dittes and Kelley. The "averages" were, of course, strong conformists.

As for the results of the originality test, the leaders were the most original, followed by the elected lieutenants, with the other two classes —the appointed lieutenants and followers—at the bottom of the list and about equally unoriginal. But we lay much less weight on these findings than we do on the results of the line-matching test, where people were actually under the influence of the apparently unanimous and incorrect judgments of other members of their groups. This test, it seems to us, comes closest to simulating actual social behavior.

Though the last three studies we have examined—Kelley-Shapiro, Dittes-Kelley, and Bartos—do not reach absolutely identical results, they do tend in the same general direction. The members of middle status in a group, whether they are so actually or only believe themselves to be so, seem most disposed to give in to influence coming apparently from a large number of other members or to cleave to an opinion that other members have once accepted. Less prone to conformity are members of either upper or lower status. We suspect that this latter finding would have emerged from the research even more clearly if, in the Kelley-Shapiro study, the membership had been divided into three statuses instead of two and if, in the Bartos study, the lower status had not embraced more than half the whole membership. Be that as it may, let us accept as established the main tendencies of the research and ask how we shall account for them. Above all, let us ask whether the same general kind of explanation will account for the behavior of men in all three statuses.

Status and the Risks of Action

We should not treat the last three experiments as simply studies in conformity to group norms. In each experiment, what faces the subject is not just an established group norm but rather information to the effect that the other members are agreed in believing a certain state of affairs to exist, when the direct evidence suggests that it may not exist at all. Were not the subject faced with information conflicting with the apparent group judgment, there would be no question of his not conforming. But the fact is that he does have alternative courses of action open to him—and this is true of most cases of conformity. Under the circumstances, what determines his choice of alternative?

In reaching his decision, a member is presented with two sorts of stimuli: those making up the situation itself, and those making up his own status. In the past, the appearance of similar stimuli have been occasions when his acting in different ways has brought him different degrees of reward. Some of the stimuli in the situation are similar to those present in the past when he uttered a judgment and was rewarded by having it turn out to be correct. Some of the stimuli making up his status are similar to those present in the past when he conformed to a group norm and was rewarded with social approval. The question is: How similar are they? Which combination of stimuli will govern his behavior and make it more probable that he will emit one of the alternatives rather than the other?

To put the matter in less cumbersome, though possibly also less fundamental terms: the member perceives, on the basis of his past experience, that he takes risks in adopting either of the two alternatives. He may either agree with the apparent group judgment or disagree and assert his independent judgment. Both courses of action promise rewards and costs in both self-respect and status, and neither the rewards nor the costs are certain. The risks, moreover, are of two kinds. First, if he agrees or disagrees, will he turn out to be correct? And second, if he is correct or incorrect, what will he gain or lose? If he is correct, he certainly will enhance his self-respect, but what will he do to his status? He must bear both kinds of risk in mind, which need not mean that he must do so consciously. For it is conceivable that even if he agrees with the group and turns out to be correct in doing so, he will not do his status much good. Under these circumstances, it may be a better bet for him to disagree with the group, even though he judges that his chances of being correct are doubtful, so long as he will do his status a lot of good should he turn out to be correct after all. When the ratio between the values of two rewards is greater than the ratio between the probabilities of attaining them, it is wiser to go for the greater value than the greater probability.

In the light of this analysis, what are the risks faced by men of different status in agreeing or disagreeing with an apparent group judgment? If an upper-status man conforms and the group's judgment turns out to be correct, he is just where he was before: no damage is done to his status but he has not improved it either. Much the same is true if he conforms and the group's judgment turns out to be incorrect. He may not lose much: although the event will have proved him wrong, everyone else will have been wrong too—for he must presume that there will be no treachery and that all the others will in fact have reached the same conclusion they asked him to reach. Still, it will do him little good to be wrong with the rest when upper-status people get their position by being different from the rest and better.

If, on the other hand, he does not conform, and the group's judgment turns out to be correct, he will at least have been "different"; and though he will have sacrificed a certain amount of esteem, it is conceivable that as a man of high status he is relatively satiated with esteem, and that the pleasures of indulging his independent judgment have risen in value. Even, moreover, if he does lose esteem, he will still have a lot left to play with. We are talking about people whose status is high and established, and the point about such people is that they have a long way to go before hitting the bottom. The further one can fall before all is lost, the more opportunity one has for retrieving one's position, and so the more room for maneuver.

But what, finally, if the upper-status man refuses to conform and the group's judgment turns out to be incorrect, if, that is, he turns out to be right and the rest wrong? Not only will he, by backing his own independent judgment, have forgone no self-respect; but he will also have increased, as he could have done in no other way, the esteem in which the others hold him as a possessor of rare abilities. He will especially have increased it if his correct judgment brings rewards to the other members, as it did in the first of the experiments we examined. He will not have been simply indulging for his own pleasure in the license the group sometimes allows to upper-status people, but will once more have made a unique contribution to the welfare of the group, which it is the business of upper-status people to do. His behavior will have been in keeping with his position; he will have acted out his role, for what we mean when we say a man has a role is that a certain kind of behavior has become established as congruent with his status in other respects.

Under these circumstances, the balance of risk makes it likely that an upper-status man will choose nonconformity. Naturally we do not mean that he need make the calculations consciously, or that all upper-status people reach, consciously or unconsciously, the same conclusions. We only assume that their very status makes nonconformity a good bet for them, and that enough of them take the bet to make a difference in the statistics.

In these experiments, we may think of the men who refuse to conform as being potential innovators. Under new circumstances they follow their own judgment instead of taking the old course of sticking with the group. And in Chapter 14 on Authority we saw that leaders are actual innovators in the sense that they take the initiative in changing the behavior of a large number of others. Whether or not they do so because they have more energy or intelligence than others, our present point is that they are further encouraged by their strategic position as upper-status people. For leaders must take risks, and only the success of the changes they bring about can replace the capital they have put up. But if the risks of innovation are there to be taken, upper-status people are better able to take them than others, for they have less than the others to gain by doing the same old thing and less to lose by trying something different.

Now let us face a person of middle status with the same predicament and ask what he stands to gain and lose by conformity and nonconformity. Remember that in the nature of the case his position is less secure than that of either of the other two: the lower-status man, already at the bottom, has no more status to lose; and the upper-status man, just because he has a lot of status to lose, can afford to risk some of it; but the middle-status man can less easily stand the loss of his little all. In this sense the division of a status system into three levels is not arbitrary but corresponds to three different strategic positions. At any rate, if the man of middle status conforms to the group's judgment and the group turns out to be right, his position as an accepted member is confirmed, and it needs confirming more than does that of an upper-status member. If he conforms and the group is wrong, he does not lose anything: he has only been a boob with the rest, who are in no condition to turn on him. If, on the other hand, he refuses to conform, and the group's judgment turns out to be right, he may really hurt himself in status; he is not so far from the bottom that a single misstep will not bring him appreciably closer to it. And if, finally, he refuses to conform, the group's judgment turns out to be wrong, and he, accordingly, is right, he will indeed gain status; but it will take more than one such achievement to get him to the top. Nor does he rise in a vacuum: his gain in status is at the same time a challenge to someone above him. He cannot afford to be right unless he is ready to accept the risks of future rivalry. A middle-status person who has behind him, in his past, only a moderate amount of activity rewarding to the other members needs more to bring him up and less to bring him down than does a man of higher status, who has already done the work of establishing himself. Under these circumstances, where nonconformity offers gains but also serious risk of loss, a man is apt to bet on conformity instead: it cannot hurt his position, it may even help it a little, and it is in either case less risky than the alternative.

No doubt the middle-status man who is determined to get to the top can only put some of his money on nonconformity regardless of its risks. Though he will have to repeat his successes and face the rivalry of men who have already arrived, nothing else will get him where he wants to be. But such men must naturally be few compared with those that set their sights less high or even worry about staying where they are. As Peter Blau says of his agents in the Federal law-enforcement agency: "Officials whose standing in the group was intermediate, particularly relatively new members, who were still trying to improve their position, semed to conform more strictly with group norms than those of higher status."[10]

Let us finally turn to the people at the bottom of the social heap. If a lower-status man conforms to the group's judgment and the group is correct, he does not get very far. Our assumption in this chapter is that a man's past behavior largely determines the present behavior of others toward him. If in the past a long run of his behavior has been "bad" by the others' standards—and that is what we mean when we say his position as a man of lower status is established—then one example of "good" behavior will not do much for him: it will take more than that to bring him up. If, moreover, there must be someone at the bottom of every group, any improvement in his behavior that does not

[10] P. M. Blau, op. cit., p. 242.

clearly put him ahead of somebody else will leave him relatively where he was before. The same is true if he conforms and the group's judgment turns out not to be correct.

If, on the other hand, he rejects the group's judgment and the group is correct, he has nothing in the way of status to lose because he is at the bottom anyhow. And if he rejects the group's judgment, the group turns out to be wrong, and he therefore turns out to be right, he has something to gain. He has saved his self-respect and has been justified in doing so. If he resents the position the group has assigned him, if he feels that they are depriving him of something rightfully his, then showing them up when they are wrong is a delightful way of getting back at them. There are compensations for even the worst of positions, and God tempers the wind to the shorn lamb.

However delightful being right when the rest are wrong may be for its own sake, it is, against all justice, a poor method for a lower-status man to use who wants to get accepted by the group. Status congruence gets in its way. Though the event has proved him correct in his judgment, yet as a man who has been assigned lower status he has no business being correct: it is out of character; whereas for an upper-status man to do the same thing is perfectly in character and not resented, for it constitutes just one more proof of what the group knows already. One of the difficulties a man encounters with rising in the world once his companions have safely consigned him to a low status is that no matter how good, how valuable, his activities later become, they will deny him the credit of them. "It wasn't really he that did it," they say, "and anyhow who is he to put himself forward?" Try as he will, he cannot do anything right.

The upper-status man has little to gain by conformity, the lower-status one little to lose by its opposite, and so for different reasons the behavior of both is biased in the same way. The latter is apt to bet on nonconformity for the rewards other than status that it can bring him. But note that if he does so, it only confirms him as an outsider in the eyes of the group, and makes it still less likely that on the next occasion any single item of "good" behavior will raise his standing. If the nonconformity of the upper-status man only plays into his own hands, only gives him a chance to raise his status further, the nonconformity of the lower-status one works increasingly against him. In elementary social behavior, as we have pointed out more than once, "whosoever hath, to him shall be given; but whosoever hath not, from him shall be taken away even that which he hath." And as we saw at the beginning of the chapter, a group that has assigned a man low status is apt by that fact to have sacrificed control of him, for it has left itself nothing to deprive him of should he behave badly, by its standards, the next time. It has already done its worst.

Low-status members of a group are, therefore, apt to go still lower. They are apt, indeed, to leave the group altogether unless they can find some reward to take the place of the esteem that has been denied them. Such reward may be provided by other people in the same boat, other people rejected by the group, who cling together all the more fiercely for that reason, giving to one another the approval denied them elsewhere. The phenomenon of companionship in misery—a few people each of whom chooses each of the others for many different activities, both at work and at leisure—seems to appear especially often at the very lowest levels of groups.

The three experiments we have considered presented the subjects with a choice between doing and not doing what the group apparently wanted them to do, when the other information they were given left them with a clear alternative to conformity. Although the experiments seemed thoroughly artificial, the kind of problem they set for a member does come up again and again in real groups. Accordingly we may guess that the research does tell us something of general importance about the relationship between status and behavior.

Vying for Acceptance

So far we assumed that the status of the persons concerned was pretty well established. If it is not established, the relationship between status and behavior may be of a wholly different sort. We have seen, for instance, that a man of established lower status is apt to be a nonconformist. In Blau's words, "The individual who had adapted himself to an isolated position could more readily violate the norms of the group." But if a man has not given up, if he still sees a chance to be accepted, if he is still vying for membership, his behavior is more apt to be conformist, indeed overconformist, than the reverse. We shall remember the experiment by the Sherifs, in which they separated the boys in a summer camp into two rival groups. As hostility between the two groups increased, the lower-status members of each group became more vociferous than the rest in venting their opposition to the other, as if they hoped thereby to demonstrate that they were full-fledged members.[11]

People are the more ready to go on vying for membership, the more fully they accept their original assignment to lower status as being in accord with the rules of distributive justice; and this depends on their investments. A man whose investments justify a higher status than the other members have been ready to accord him will add resentment against them to the other reasons for failing to conform to their norms, and so will speed up the vicious spiral that separates him from the group. But a man whose investments are low to begin with, because he is a newcomer or for some other reason, has no occasion for resentment, and since his investments can only improve with time, may hope that if he is patient and does nothing to upset things, he will sooner or later be taken in.

In the study of the machining and assembly department of the Industrial Controls Corporation, which we have spoken of several times, the investigators found two small subgroups, which were of equally low status but reacted differently.[12] One subgroup consisted of workers, low in pay and skill, whose backgrounds were apt to have one or more of the following characteristics: they were Protestant, middle-class, or white-collar. As such they were different from, and in their own eyes better than, the urban, lower-class Irish Catholics who made up half the membership in the department and dominated it. By working as hard as they could they violated the output norm praised and perpetuated by the dominant cliques, and so confirmed their low status. No doubt the moral value set on hard work, which has been called the Protestant Ethic and which they had inherited along with their background, helped them to behave as they did, but so did their pleasure in showing up the workers of higher status, whose judgment they resented. They were typical nonconformists who were not vying for membership and whom their group had accordingly lost control of.

The other subgroup consisted of workers whose backgrounds resembled those of the dominant cliques, except that they were not Irish

[11] M. Sherif and C. W. Sherif, *Groups in Harmony and Tension* (New York, 1953), p. 284.

[12] A. Zaleznik, C. R. Christensen, and F. J. Roethlisberger, *The Motivation, Productivity, and Satisfaction of Workers* (Boston, 1958), pp. 375-80.

but Italians or members of other nationalities lower than the Irish in ethnic status. The dominant members tended to joke at their expense, the jokes emphasizing the ethnic element: for instance, they might call them "Guineas." But the joking was not enough to stop their vying for full-fledged membership in the group. They took the jokes in good part; they hung around on the outskirts of the games the "regulars" played; they were ready to accept menial jobs as coffee-carriers; and they started various low-valued activities, like temporary betting-pools, which high-status people were ready to take part in but not to organize. They were, moreover, ultraconformists: they abided by the output norm and "articulated all the subtleties of the sentiments involved in restriction of output." It was as if they felt that their investments entitled them to no higher status than they started with, and that if only they stuck to the rules time was bound to be on their side. They were lower-status conformists whom, because they were still vying for membership, their group still kept control of. We may well ask how long a group can keep people vying for a rise in status without doing something to satisfy them.

Status and Conformity in Society at Large

Instead of summarizing, let us end this chapter by looking briefly at some large-scale phenomena that bear a little resemblance to the ones we have just been examining on a small scale. We should never assume that the informal group is a microcosm of society at large, that what holds good of the one holds good also of the other. It would be hard, for instance, to make out that upper-class people in society at large, like upper-status ones in small groups, are especially apt to be innovators. And yet, though the resemblances may be superficial, some characteristics of some social-class systems at some times seem to resemble what we have noticed about status in small groups—particularly the tendency for members high and low in status to resemble one another in their nonconformity and to differ from members of middle status. In the recent past of the South of this country,[13] and in England in the seventeenth century, there are hints that both upper and lower classes were less restrained in the fields of gambling, drink, and forni-

[13] J. Dollard, *Caste and Class in a Southern Town* (New Haven, 1937), pp. 75-97.

cation, more ready to indulge in the simple sensuous pleasures of life than were the climbers, the strainers, the insecure of the middle classes.

The landed aristocrat, already at the top, has little to gain from a rigid compliance with the minor moral standards of society. Since his social position is secure, whatever his economic position may be, he finds other rewards—including an indulgence in his eccentricities and in the pleasures of the flesh—relatively more rewarding than further striving for status. And the poor farm laborer, who has little to gain by respectability and nothing to lose by its opposite, is similarly attracted by the simple sensuous pleasures—riot and debauchery—which have the further charm of not costing much money. Respectable people treat him like an animal, and his natural response is indeed animalian, which comfortably confirms the respectable in the moral judgment they have passed on him. Yet they have their moments of envying him his license, above all, his freedom from striving. He can afford to relax and be a natural man. In a wry way, he is making the best of a bad society. But the people in the middle, particularly if they see some chance of rising in the world, must seek, by close adherence to a rigid morality, to differentiate themselves from what they call the rabble and establish their claims to social recognition. Middle-class people are more apt to be puritanical than either upper- or lower-class ones. Yet in saying this we are immediately reminded how dangerous it is to generalize from the small group to society at large. For in the England of the seventeenth century, middle-class people, though they certainly were conformists in morality, were far from being conformists in other respects. Puritanical in the general sense in manners, they were also Puritans in the special sense in religion: they were religious reformers. And at the crisis of the seventeenth century, when King and Commons faced one another in arms in the Civil War, middle-class people were specially likely to support Parliament, while the other two classes—not all but many of them—tended to identify themselves with one another and with the king.[14]

[14] J. M. Lloyd Thomas, ed., *The Autobiography of Richard Baxter* (London, 1931), p. 34.

CHAPTER 38

Social Class, Speech Systems, and Psycho-therapy

BASIL B. BERNSTEIN

Today various forms of psycho-therapy are being extended to include a greater number of individuals from different social backgrounds. Training programmers for probation officers, social workers, psychologists, and members of the prison and borstal services are gradually being extended at different rates to include an understanding of psycho-dynamic processes and a therapy-oriented relationship. I shall start from an assertion that sensitivity to the psychotherapeutic relationship and the form of communication considered to be appropriate is less available to members of the lower working class not by virtue of innate deficiencies in intelligence but because of a culturally induced speech system whose dimensions of relevance and significance do not orient the lower working-class patient in the therapy relationship. Conversely, the speech system of the therapist creates for him sets of expectations which are not met by the lower working-class patient. By lower working-class I refer to individuals who are employed in lower manual occupations, approximately 30 percent of the labour force.

Let us start by examining some general aspects of the psycho-therapy relation with which I shall be concerned.

1. It is a form of social relationship which exerts a tension on the patient to structure and restructure his discrete experience in a verbally significant form. In terms of the patient's other relationships, the therapy relationship attempts to elicit from the patient a unique order of communication.

2. The referent for this communication is the patient—or rather his motivational processes and the implicit or explicit social relationships which they engender. The "I" of the patient is undergoing a continuous transformation by virtue of those unique communications.

3. The form of authority within the therapy relationship is unclear and ambiguous. The patient often is given no clear understanding of what is or is not expected of him. The shape of the social relationship is not defined in any detail. Differences in social status which serve as orientation for behaviour outside of the therapy relationship do not serve to indicate appropriate behaviour within it.

4. In as much as the patient's communications are filtered through the purposes, goals, beliefs, and emotional imperatives of the patient's natural group then the patient's appropriate perception of himself is often considered to be hindered. The conventions which confer upon the patient his social identity are viewed from the point of view of the therapist as material to be worked through. Put more simply, the form of the therapy relationship involves

the patient in a position of suspended isolation; he stands in relation to his group rather like a figure differentiated from his ground.

5. Finally, successful therapy is based upon "mutual belief on the part of both therapist and patient that the illness may be removed by participation in a social relationship where the major activity is the transformation of discrete experience through the medium of communication essentially through speech."

Summarising these points we get something like this:

The therapy relationship is based upon the belief that the conditions which brought the patient into the relationship may be ameliorated by communication in a context where the normal status relationships serve as no guide for behaviour in a context which involves a suspension of the patient's social identity and where the referent for the communication is the discrete experience of the patient.

This is a somewhat unusual social relationship involving some strange requirements. It will be argued that members of the lower working class who are limited to a particular speech system are likely to find these requirements difficult to meet. Such individuals are likely to benefit less from therapy, to break off treatment early, whilst the therapist will tend to find the relationship unrewarding. He will require a sensitivity towards his patient of a different order than that necessary for a middle-class patient. From the therapist's point of view the lower working-class patient's communication will seem to be inadequate: there will be a low level of insight, the patient may seem to be negative and passive, so forcing the therapist into taking a more dominant role than he would wish and, above all, the therapist will meet an unwillingness on the part of the patient to transform his personal feelings into unique verbal meanings. The lower working-class patient will have difficulty in verbalizing his personal experience and in receiving communications which refer to the sources of

his motivations. I shall argue that these difficulties do not necessarily stem from low intelligence but originate in the speech system the child learns in his culture and that this speech system creates for the developing child dimensions of relevance and learning wholly appropriate for his natural environment but inappropriate for orientating the individual in special relationships like therapy.

Research indicates that the verbal I.Q. scores of members of the lower working-class are likely to be severely depressed in relation to scores at the higher ranges of non-verbal tests. Furthermore, research based upon small groups of middle- and working-class subjects matched for average verbal I.Q. and non-verbal I.Q. indicates that the working-class groups use a markedly different speech system than the matched middle-class groups. The working-class groups' speech is characterized by a reduction in qualifiers, adjectives, adverbs, particularly those which qualify feelings, the organisation of the speech is comparatively simple, and there is a restriction on the use of the self-referent pronoun "I" and an increase in personal pronouns. The written work of matched groups of middle- and working-class boys indicates a similar pattern of differences and also that the working-class prefers much more concrete than abstract propositions. As these limited studies were of small groups matched for I.Q., the sources of the differences in the speech and the relations must lie in differences between the cultures.

These differences found in the speech I shall take as indices of a particular form of communication; they are not in any sense accidental but are contingent upon a form of social relationship, or more generally, a social structure. These differences I shall argue indicate the use of a linguistic code. It is a code which does not facilitate the verbal elaboration of meaning; it is a code which does not help the user put into words his intent, his unique purposes, beliefs, and motivations. It also does not help him to receive such communications from others. It is a code which sensitises the user to a particular form of social relationship which is unambiguous, where the authority is clear cut and serves as a guide to action. It is a code which helps to sustain solidarity with the group at the cost of the verbal signalling of the unique difference of its members. It is a code which facilitates the ready transformation of feeling into action. It is a code where changes in meaning are more likely to be signalled non-verbally than through changes in verbal selections.

From this perspective the psycho-therapy relationship involves, for a member of the lower working-class, a radical change in his normal coding process. What requires to be made relevant for this relationship is almost the antithesis of what *is* made relevant by the coding process the individual normally uses in his cultural environment. How does this way of translating experience come about? What in the culture is responsible for the speech system? To begin with there is nothing unusual or unique about the speech system. It is not helpful to consider it a form of substandard English. It is not a speech system induced by innate intelligence.

Different social structures will generate different speech systems. These speech systems or codes entail for the individual specific principles of choice which regulate the selections he makes from language at both the syntactic and lexical level. What the individual actually says, from a developmental perspective, transforms him in the act of saying.

As the child learns his speech, or in our terms learns specific codes which regulate his verbal acts, he learns the requirements of his social structure. From this point of view every time the child speaks, the social structure of which he is a part is reinforced in him, and his social identity develops and is constrained. The social structure becomes for the developing child his psychological reality by the shaping of his acts of speech. If this is the case, then the processes which orient the child to his world and the kind of relationships he imposes are triggered off initially and systematically reinforced by the implications of the speech system. Underlying the general pattern of the child's speech are critical sets of

choices, in-built preferences for some alternatives rather than others, planning processes which develop and are stabilised through time—coding principles through which orientation is given to social, intellectual and emotional referents. Children who have access to different speech systems, and so to the coding principles which sustain them, by virtue and only by virtue of their arbitrary position in the class structure, may take quite different lines of development, may adopt quite different intellectual and social procedures which are only tenuously related to their purely psychological abilities.

I shall start by asking the following questions: What kinds of social relationships generate what kinds of speech systems? What kinds of principles or planning procedures control the speech systems? What kinds of relationships in the environment do these planning procedures, or rather the linguistic options which are taken up, both give access to and stabilise?

I shall confine my attention to one speech system or code. I am going to define this speech system in terms of the ease with which it is possible to predict the syntactic alternatives which are taken up to organise meaning. If it is fairly easy to predict the syntactic alternatives used to organise meaning across a range of speech I shall call this system a restricted code. It is possible to predict these syntactic alternatives because the range of alternatives used in this code are relatively few. The speech is comparatively simple in structure. We can go a little further and say that in the case of a restricted code the vocabulary will be drawn from a narrow range. Although the code has been defined in terms of syntax we can go on to suggest certain psychological correlates of this code. If a speaker is moving towards a restricted code then the code, that is the linguistic options he is taking up, will not facilitate the speaker in his attempt to put into words his purposes, his intent, his unique experience in a verbally explicit form. Further, the events in the environment which are given significance create a particular order of learning.

Let us start off by asking what is responsible for the simplification of the structure of the speech in this code, what is responsible for the narrow range of vocabulary choices, what is responsible on a psychological level for the constraints on the verbal signalling of the unique experience of the speaker? If we know this we shall begin to have an idea of the social learning which this code gives access to and stabilises. I shall suggest that both the simplification in the structure and the constraint upon the verbal signalling of intent have their origin in the form of the social relationship constraining the speakers.

In the case of a restricted code the speech is played out against a back-cloth of assumptions common to the speakers, against a set of shared interests and identifications, in short against a cultural identity which reduces the need for the speakers to elaborate verbally their intent and make it explicit. If you know somebody very, very well, an enormous amount may be taken for granted; you do not have to put into words all that you feel because the feelings are common. But knowing somebody very well is a particular kind of social relationship; knowing somebody very well indicates common interests, identifications, expectations, although this need not necessarily mean common agreement. Concretely, a restricted code is not necessarily class linked but will arise in closed communities like a prison, combat units in the armed services but also between close friends, in the peer group of children and adolescents. In fact, wherever the form of the social relationship is based upon some extensive set of closely shared identifications self-consciously held by the members.

In these social relations which generate a restricted code, the speech will tend to be fast, fluent, with reduced articulatory clues, and the meanings are likely to be condensed, dislocated and local to the relationships. There will be a low level of vocabulary and syntactic selection. The how rather than the what of the communication becomes relevant. Finally, and of critical importance, the unique meaning of the person will tend to be implicit and not verbally elaborated.

In fact the sequences will have the same *general* forms as this:

Examples

It's all according like well those youths and
     that if they get with gangs and that they
     most
they most
have a bit of a lark around and
say it goes wrong
and that and they probably knock some off
     I think they do it just to be a bit big you
     know
getting publicity here and there
          V.I.Q. average (lower working class).
     Transcript of a tape recorded discussion.

The point I want to make is that a restricted code is available to all members of society as the social conditions which generate it are universal. But it may be that a considerable section of our society, in particular, members of the lower working-class who work in unskilled or semi-skilled occupations, 30 percent of the labour force, is limited to this code and has no other. We have a special case, a case where children or adults can use only one speech system. What this code makes relevant to them, the learning generated by the apparently spontaneous acts of speech may not be appropriate for the demands of the psycho-therapeutic relationship.

I would like to look more closely at some of the psychological and sociological implications of this code with psycho-therapy in mind.

When a child learns a restricted code, he learns to perceive language in a particular way. Language is not perceived as a set of theoretical possibilities which can be transformed into a facility for the communication of unique experience. Speech is not important media for communicating relatively explicitly the experience of separateness and difference. Speech is not a primary means for a voyage from one self to the other. In as much as this is so, areas of the self are not likely to be differentiated by speech and so become the object of special perceptual activity. It is also likely that the motivations of others will not serve as starting points for enquiry and verbal elaboration. Of some importance is that the identity of the individual will be refracted to him by the concrete symbols of his group rather than creating a problem to be solved by his own unique investigations. In a sense, a person limited to a restricted code has a problem of identity because this problem is irrelevant.

I would like to consider next a family where only a restricted code is used. Here the "I" of the mother, her uniqueness, the way she communicates separateness and difference is likely to be conveyed non-verbally rather than through controlled verbal discriminations If this is so then much of the awareness of the developing child of his mother is less available for verbalisation because it has rarely been verbalised. A powerful bond of a non-verbal form is forged. The motivations, the intents of mother and child are less available to each because these are not objects of verbal inquiry.

A critical aspect of the family is the means of expression of authority, particularly the type of verbal interaction, authority relationships create. I shall argue that associated with parents limited to a restricted code is a specific form of authority relations.

Authority can be expressed so as to limit the chances of verbal interaction within the relationship, or authority can be expressed so as to increase verbal interaction. The area of discretion available to the child may be reduced to an uncompromising acceptance, withdrawal, or rebellion within the authority relationship, or the social context of control may permit a number of responses on the part of the child. Authority may be expressed through commands and threats or it may rest on appeals. These appeals used by authority may be of two basic kinds person-oriented or status-oriented. If the appeals are status-oriented then the behaviour of the child is referred to some general or local rule which constraints conduct "shouldn't you clean your teeth," "you don't behave yourself like that on a bus," "children in grammar schools are expected to behave rather differently."[1] Status appeals may also relate the child's behaviour to the rules which regulate his conduct with reference to age, sex or age relationships, e.g. "Little boys don't play with dolls," "you should be able to stop doing that by now," "you don't talk to your father, teacher, social worker, etc., like that." These are important implications of status appeals. If they are not obeyed, the relationship can quickly change to reveal naked power and may become punitive. Status appeals are impersonal. They rely for their effectiveness upon the status of the regulator. The effect of these appeals is to transmit the culture or local culture in such a way as to increase the similarity of the regulated with others of his group. If the child rebels, he is challenging very quickly the culture of which he is a part and it is this which tends to force the regulator into taking punitive action. Finally the social context of control is such that the relationship is unambiguous—the relative statuses are clear-cut.

The person-oriented appeals are very different. In these appeals, the conduct of the child is related to the feelings of the regulator (parent) or the significance of the act, its meaning is related explicitly to the regulated, to the child, e.g. "Daddy will be pleased, hurt, disappointed, angry, ecstatic if you go on doing this." "If you go on doing this you will be miserable when the cat has a nasty pain."

In the case of person-oriented appeals the conduct of the child is referred to the *feelings* of the regulator, in the second case the significance of the act, its meaning, is related directly to the child. There are important consequences of the *person-oriented* appeals. Control is effected through either the verbal manipulation of feelings or through the establishing of reasons which link the child to his acts. In this way, the child has access to the regulator as a person and he has access to the significance of his own acts as they relate to him as consequences. The person-oriented appeals tend to work through the verbalising of intent, whereas the status-oriented appeals, especially if they move quickly to power, are concerned with consequences of actions and not with intent. The status-oriented appeals rely for their effectiveness upon differences in status, whereas the person-oriented appeals rely more upon the manipulation of thought and feeling. The person-oriented appeals elicit guilt in the child in terms of the effects of his actions upon persons and things. The child learns to adapt to the tensions involved in relating to persons and things mainly by being able to tolerate guilt and through having a more conscious awareness, through language, of the consequences of his actions. Where the child is subject to status-oriented appeals which change swiftly to a power relationship then a whole order of relationships are not learned. I suggest that where the sole speech system of the parents is a restricted code, then power and status-oriented appeals will be used more. The child will become sensitive to a particular kind of control and the learning involved and may well be bewildered in a context of control where person-oriented means are used.

I should like to consider some areas of affective difficulty which may be elicited, maintained, and strengthened by a role relationship where both members are limited to a restricted code. It has been argued that extra-verbal channels will carry messages bearing the mutual intents of mother and child. Inter-personal aspects of this relationship in which each will uniquely qualify each other's experience will tend *not* to be raised to the level of verbal elaboration and be made explicit. The areas of discrete intent will not be areas of elaborated speech. This does not mean that these areas have no significance, only that whatever significance they may have is less available for linguistic regulation. Tensions arising in these areas are more likely to be denied as the means of dealing with them consciously are less available.

Further, if it is the case that authority relationships within the family tend to be status and power relations rather than person-oriented relations then the focus of the discipline of relation will be upon the consequences of the act rather than upon the intent of the child. Thus it could be argued

that where the focus is upon *consequence* the relationship moves towards one of an inter-status type whereas if the focus is upon intent the relationship moves towards one of an inter-personal type. What is made available for learning, what is made relevant in person- or status-oriented relations is radically different. The linguistic codes which transmit these relationships, behaviourally, are also different. The *speech* in a status- or power-oriented relation is such that what is taken over by the child is the status aspect of the relation *not* the personal aspect of the relation. Again it should be noted that this reinforces the primacy of the extra-verbal channels for the perception or decoding of discrete intent. It is necessary to repeat that the perception of discrete intent occurs but the orientation of the perception is towards the extra-verbal channels.

Lack of clarity or ambiguity in the inter-status relation is likely to raise the level of tension for an individual limited to a restricted code and these tensions are less subject to verbal control. It is then much more likely that these tensions will be dissipated quickly through some immediate channel; changes in muscular tension, somato-motor set, or expressive behaviour. Further the individual may try to neutralise his affective involvement in a situation of inter-personal strain by denial or attributing the responsibility for the strain to an encumbent of another status. There is a probability that although the individual will hold notions of wrongness and justice, feelings of guilt and personal involvement may be dissociated from the notions of wrongness. On the other hand, the level of unconscious guilt may well be high.

Psychopathology will tend to be shaped in terms of high guilt thresholds, low anxiety thresholds, and an inability to tolerate anxiety. In situations which elicit perceptions of ambiguity or ambivalency the individual may be unable to tolerate the resultant tension involved in loss of structure. He will tend to move towards a well articulated social structure where hierarchy, age, age relations, and sex will provide clear unambiguous prescriptions for appropriate behaviour as a means of controlling stress.

Thus a special group of defence mechanisms of an unconscious order is likely to be associated with this code which helps to maintain the stability. The defences are likely to include denial, disassociation, and displacement rather than more elaborate defences which rely upon verbal procedures like rationalisation. These defences may help to shape the type of psychopathology.

There is one further point of a more sociological nature which needs to be made. Different modes of speech issue from different role relations. Individuals may be unable to produce appropriate speech modes because they are unable to deal with the role relation necessary for the appropriate communication. If a person is using an elaborated code, that is, where the person's intent is raised to the level of verbal explicitness, where his "I" is mediated by extensive verbal discriminations, a range of discretion must inhere in his role if such speech is to be produced at all. Further, the person's social history must have included practice and training for the role which social relations require. Role here refers to the particular relations necessary for the production of a restricted or elaborated code. In the case of an elaborated code the role relations receive less support from implicit identifications shared by the participators. The orientation of the individual will be based upon the expectation of psychological difference, his own and others. Individuated speech pre-supposes a history of a particular role relation if it is to be prepared and delivered appropriately. Inasmuch as difference is part of the expectation, there is less reliance or dependency on the listener; or rather this dependency on the listener is reduced by the verbal explication of meaning. The dependency underpinning the use of a restricted code is upon the closely shared, extensive range of identifications which serve as a back-cloth to the speech and define the role relation. The dependency underpinning the use of an elaborated code is upon the verbal explication of meaning. The sources of role strain

which inhere in these codes and so in the social relations which generate them are different. Simply, to produce an elaborated code, the person must be able to cope with the measure of social isolation which inheres in the role relations which these communications generate. This kind of isolation does not inhere in role relations which generate a restricted code. In terms of what is said *verbally* a restricted code is a *status*-oriented code, whilst an elaborated code is a *person*-oriented code.

I shall now try and pull together these various implications of a restricted code. The code is generated in social relationship where the intent of others may be taken for granted. This sharing or expectation of common intent simplifies the structure of the speech and so makes it predictable. It removes the need in the speakers to elaborate verbally their unique experience. Hence the reduction of qualifiers of various kinds. The speech is relatively impersonal and serves to transmit similarity rather than differences in personal experience. The code functions to permit the signalling of social rather than personal identity. The latter tends to be signalled through nonverbal and expressive means rather than through elaborate varying of verbal selections. The code tends to make relevant the concrete here and now action situation rather than point to reflective, abstract relationships.[2] It does not facilitate a sustained interest in processes, particularly motivational processes. The self is rarely the subject of verbal investigation. Speech is not used as a means for a voyage from oneself to the other person. Behaviour is controlled in a social context in which status is unambiguous and in which the intent of the regulated and regulator is rarely verbally explored and so feelings of guilt and personal involvement in misdemeanours may be reduced. The code strengthens solidarity with the group by restricting the verbal signalling of personal difference. This does not mean that no differences will be signalled but that they will rarely be systematically explored. A strong sense of social identity is induced probably at the cost of a sense of personal identity.

Finally the code is not generated by I.Q. but by the culture acting through the family relationships.

From this point of view the psycho-therapy relationship involves, for an individual limited to a restricted code, a relationship where the signals are antithetic to his own way of making relationships. For the status relationships are ambiguous, give no indication for here and now behaviour. It is a person-oriented relationship which increases the tension upon the individual to structure and re-structure his experience in a verbally unique way. For the patient it involves a loss of social identity which his very code promotes and exposes the patient to the reflections on his personal identity in a social relationship which from the patient's point of view is unsupporting. A lack of insight into the sources of motivation combined with the dependency of the patient will tend to force the therapist into taking, from his point of view, too active or dominant a role in the relationship. The restricted code patient's main defence against the tensions induced by the therapy relationship is a great passivity and dependency. The therapist has to deal with feeling in himself that this kind of relationship invokes. Thus, the therapy relationship involves for the restricted code patient a situation of change of code and with this, a major change in the means whereby the patient orients to his natural world.[3] It is thought that if the therapy is successful there will be a change in the patient's code.

I am not suggesting that therapy with patients limited to a restricted code cannot be rewarding and beneficial. The absence of so-called appropriate communication is pregnant with meaning and significance for the therapist if he has a more sensitive understanding of the predicament of the patient and a willingness to adapt his technique.

NOTES

[1]Intonation can, of course, give these statements the character of commands; however, they do permit further interaction of a kind that serves to clarify the norms which inhere in the specific status of the regulated. On the other hand, the regulator may shift the basis of the appeal to that of person-oriented or fall back on power.

[2]It is important to qualify at this point. Often powerful *descriptions* of feelings are offered, e.g., "The smoke from the factories makes me lonesome, "It hurts like my head's coming off my neck," "It's like broken glass inside me." Difficulty often occurs when one moves away from metaphor and simile.

[3]A point may well be reached where therapist and patient face each other in an unproductive silence. The therapist not knowing how to elicit responses from the patient and the patient not knowing how to give them.

BIBLIOGRAPHY

Bernstein, B.
  1958 "Some sociological determinants of perception." British Journal of Sociology IX: 159.
  1960 "Social class and linguistic development." P. 288 in A. H. Halsey, J. Floud and C. A. Anderson (eds.), Education, Economy, and Society. New York: Free Press.
  1962a "Linguistic codes, hesitation phenomena, and intelligence." Language and Speech 5:31.
  1962b "Social class, linguistic codes, and grammatical elements." Language and Speech 5:221.
  1965 "A socio-linguistic approach to social learning." In J. Gould (ed.), Penguin Survey of the Social Sciences. Baltimore: Penguin Books.
  1970 "A socio-linguistic approach to socialisation: With some reference to educability." In J. Gumperz and D. Hymes (eds.), Directions in Sociolinguistics. New York: Holt, Rinehart & Winston.
Bernstein, B., and D. Henderson.
  1969 "Social class differences in the relevance of language to socialisation." Sociology 3 (January): No. 1.
Gumperz, J., and D. Hymes (eds.).
  1970 "A socio-linguistic approach to socialisation: With some reference to educability. Directions in Sociolinguistics. New York: Holt, Rinehart, & Winston.
Hawkins, P. R.
  1969 "Social class, the nominal group and reference." Language and Speech 12, pt. II (April-June): 125-135.
Hollingshead, A. B., and F. C. Redlich.

1958   Social Class and Mental Illness. New York: Wiley.

Koln, M. L.
1959a   "Social class and parental authority." American Sociological Review 24:352-366.
1959b   "Social class and parental values." American Journal of Sociology 64:337-351.

Lawton, D.
1963   "Social class differences in language development." Language and Speech (October-December).

Miller, D. R., and G. E. Swanson.
1959   Inner Conflict and Defense. New York: Henry Holt.

Ministry of Education.
1959   "Fifteen to eighteen." Report of the Central Advisory Council for Education. Vol. I, Ministry of Education, London, H.M.S.O., specifically p. 376.

Riessman, F.
1962   The Culturally Deprived Child. New York: Harper & Row.
1963   "New Models for a treatment approach to low income clients." Paper presented to American Ortho-psychiatric. Association Convention, March, 1963.

Turner, G. J., and R. E. Pickvance.
(in press) "Social class differences in the expression of uncertainty in five-year-old children." Language and Speech.

CHAPTER 39

Evolution in Process

THEODOSIUS DOBZHANSKY

Methods of contraception are neither novel inventions nor monopolies of technologically advanced societies. They were known to and utilized by preliterate peoples. What is new is the relative efficacy, acceptability, and safety of these methods. Their increasingly widespread use has ushered in a trend toward lower birth rates. In Europe the decline of fertility started early in some countries—in France and in Ireland by the mid-nineteenth century. Elsewhere in northwestern Europe it began by about 1870, in Spain and Italy early in the current century, in eastern Europe and in Japan around 1920. The birth rate in the United States was about 55 per 1,000 in 1800; it declined to a low point of 18 in 1933 and rose somewhat in the postwar "baby boom." Elsewhere in the world the decline has merely begun or is yet to commence (United Nations 1953). The trend toward lower birth rates is a salutary one, in view of the deadly menace of runaway population growth. One hopes that this trend will become universal. And yet it provokes serious misgivings.

Populations of different parts of the world grow at unequal rates. As shown in Table 25, the population of Europe will about double during the twentieth century, that of North America and of Asia will quadruple, and that of Central and South America will increase by a factor of more than nine. Habits of prejudice, fears of competition, and specious "scientific" arguments make some people alarmed when they discover that the group to which they belong is not the fastest growing. Hence such shibboleths as "the yellow peril," "the rising tide of color," etc. One may as well accept the fact that the future will contain a relatively greater proportion of descendants of some than of other races. Anyway, no useful purpose will be served by what has been described as a "passionate protest against the meek inheriting the earth."

Another facet of the situation is perhaps more genuinely disturbing but not necessarily irremediable. In technologically advanced societies the business of propagation seems to be entrusted largely to people with mediocre to inferior qualifications for parenthood. The fact that the prosperous are less fertile than the poor and that city and town dwellers tend to have fewer children than do rural people was first noticed in Europe as early as the seventeenth and eighteenth centuries (United Nations 1953). This has been since confirmed by numerous studies. As birth rates declined, they fell more rapidly among the higher than among the lower social classes. This is true regardless of how one defines "higher" and "lower"—by social position, income, education, etc. As shown in Table 26, fertility is inversely related to educational status. The more schooling a person has, the fewer children he tends to produce. The low fertility of college graduates, particularly women graduates, was until recently notorious (see however p. 317).

TABLE 26

Schooling and the mean numbers of children ever born to American white women aged 45–49 years (after the 1940 U.S. Census, from Osborn)

Schooling completed	Children per woman	Children per married woman
None	3.95	4.97
Grade school		
1–4 years	4.33	4.54
5–6 "	3.74	3.97
7–8 "	2.78	3.04
High school		
1–3 years	2.37	2.61
4 "	1.75	2.03
College		
1–3 years	1.71	2.07
4 or more	1.23	1.83

This situation is undesirable, irrespective of any genetic considerations. People who should be able to provide the best environment for the physical and mental development of their children produce fewest progeny. Genetic consequences cannot, however, be ignored. They have been debated in many ways by many biologists, psychologists, sociologists, and political propagandists. Many dreadful prophecies and strident proclamations have been made. It cannot be gainsaid that there is a predicament here which should cause concern. The argument given runs somewhat as follows.

Poorly educated people include both those who lacked the opportunity for better education and those deficient in the capacity for such education. The genetic endowment for whatever it is that makes people able to profit by education is less common among the poorly trained than among the well educated. And the incidence of talent, ability, or whatever it takes to achieve success (however defined in a given society) is lower among the unsuccessful than among the successful. This may sound as blatantly undemocratic as Galton's speculations criticized in Chapter 3. But there is a difference which should allay the qualms of even the most compulsive egalitarians. It is recognized that many people deficient in education were fully capable of profiting by it; that many have-nots and failures are no less gifted than the haves and the successes; that in different environments and under different social systems the present failures might be successes and the successes failures; and that equality of opportunity must be striven for not because people are alike but precisely because they are different (p. 244). We should not, however, be lured into disregarding the fact that in any environment and under any social system, be it democracy or a dictatorship of the right or the left, people will differ in achievements, and this variability is in part genetically conditioned.

Now, the differential fertility described above makes those who achieve less mundane success achieve most success in reproduction. Therefore it happens that each following generation is descended in greater proportion from the less well endowed strata of the preceding generation. This amounts to a selection favoring lower endowment. Many investigators, not satisfied with this finding, make brave attempts to predict just how rapidly human abilities will deteriorate. Estimates of the expected decline of intelligence as measured by IQ techniques are the favorite targets of such predictions.

The methods used are really simple and at first sight convincing. Suppose that single children have a certain average IQ and that families with two, three, four, and higher numbers of children have progressively lower mean IQs. A well-conducted census will show the proportions of families with different numbers of children in the population. This tells us what proportions of the individuals of the next generation will be descended from families with different numbers of children and with different intelligence levels. The degree of the heritability of intelligence is estimated by various methods, such as comparisons of identical and fraternal twins (Chapter 4). The predicted rates of decline of the average intelligence in American and British populations varies from one to four IQ points per generation. A grim prospect indeed! Cook (1951) believes:

> As this process continues, the fortunate combinations of many plus-genes in one individual occur less frequently; the average level of intelligence and the proportion of gifted individuals declines. Should the feeble-minded level be reached, most of the plus-genes will have been eliminated. But before this time growing inefficiency and incompetence would cause a collapse of modern industrial society.

Are People Becoming Less Intelligent?

The somber prognosis of declining intelligence has called forth a number of investigations designed to test its validity. By far the most significant of these are the surveys conducted by the Scottish Council for Research in Education (1949, 1953). In 1932, and again in 1947, an intelligence test was administered to all eleven-year-old children that could be reached in Scotland. About 88 per cent of the estimated children of that age in the country were actually tested; the remainder were absent from school on the days of the testing or could not be tested because of some bodily handicaps. The fifteen-year interval between 1932 and 1947 corresponds to at least half of the average length of a human generation. Has, then, the intelligence of the Scottish children dwindled during this time? Far from it, the average score has slightly but significantly increased! A similar situation was found in the United States: the soldiers drafted for the Second World War scored on the average higher than those in the First World War (Tuddenham 1948).

This result causes some embarrassment to the prophets of doom. Indeed, in Scotland, as elsewhere, the intelligence of children is negatively correlated with family size (in the 1947 survey a correlation coefficient -0.28 was obtained). The average score of single children was 3.7 points above that in families with three children, 11.1 points above families with six children, 14.0 above families with nine children, and 17.7 above families with twelve or more children. The investigators who conducted the surveys honestly admit that they expected a decline, not a rise. Among the explanations offered are improved health of the children and increasing "test sophistication," i.e., a greater familiarity with the kinds of tasks employed in the tests. It is amusing that some writers use these explanations to argue that the Scottish surveys have borne out the predictions that the intelligence is declining! Truly, they let no inconvenient fact interfere with their predilections.

An excellent critical analysis of the intelligence–fertility problem has been made by Anastasi (1956, 1959; these papers contain extensive references to other relevant publications). Most investigators have compared the average intelligence of single children with that of children having one or more siblings, not the intelligence of children with that of their parents. This is important because the amount of attention a child gets from his parents is on the average less in large than in small families; the development of the child's verbal faculties is, therefore, likely to be retarded in large families, and this will influence adversely the IQ scores. Data comparing the intelligence test scores of parents and their children with family sizes are scanty. The few published studies of this kind have yielded much less impressive correlations than the studies in which only the intelligence of the children and the size of the family were investigated. One would like to compare the scores of parents and children in families of the same size, but such data are scarce or unavailable.

These strictures undercut the overconfident calculations of the expected rates of the decline of intelligence. But it would be as hasty to conclude that the genetic basis of intelligence is in no danger of erosion. The consequences of the greater fertility of the less intelligent members of the population remain in need of elucidation. A suggestion well worth investigating further has been made by Penrose (1949, 1950a). Decreased fertility of the possessors of genetically-conditioned superior intelligence is compatible with preservation of a constant intelligence level in the population, provided that it is matched by a low fertility of the least well endowed members of the same population. In other words, people of middling intelligence may produce most children, while very intelligent and very unintelligent people have small families. One of the possible mechanisms to bring about such a situation would be a balanced polymorphism, mediocrities being the heterotic heterozygotes and the superior and the inferior people representing the two kinds of homozygotes.

Penrose has made a study of the parental origins of 1,194 mentally deficient patients in a hospital in England. As shown in Table 27, the matings in which one or both parents are low-grade defectives produce smaller families than normal parents do. Moreover,

TABLE 27

Mean number of siblings per an institutional mental defective
(after Penrose 1949)

Parents	Cases observed	Siblings (mean)
Superior x normal	9	2.89
Normal x normal	798	4.72
Normal x dull	196	5.45
Normal x feebleminded and dull x dull	113	4.52
Normal x imbecile and dull x feeble-minded	54	3.82
Dull x imbecile and feebleminded x feebleminded	24	3.58

there is evidence of assortative mating (the tendency for people of similar degree of intelligence to marry), and many defectives do not marry at all. This matter certainly needs further study. It may turn out that the intelligence level is under the control of a normalizing natural selection (p. 131), mediocrity being favored above superior intelligence as well as above wretched stupidity.

A lucid analysis of the changing patterns of differential fertility in the United States is given in a short paper by Kirk (1957). His data come mainly from a study of the families of men in *Who's Who*, which aims "to include the names, not necessarily of the best, but rather of the best known, men and women in all lines of useful and reputable achievement." These men have had smaller families than the general population of their generation. However, "the difference is progressively narrowing, and the younger men listed in *Who's Who* may approximate or exceed the national average in completed family size for their age groups. Men in *Who's Who* marry later, but more of them marry and they have fewer childless marriages than the general population of comparable age."

Kirk finds, in agreement with investigators of other population groups, that fertility is negatively related to social mobility. Those who have an inherited social status have more children than do the "self-made" men who had to struggle for comparable status. Large families may obviously act as impediments in such a struggle. "If present trends continue, the genetic qualities of men in *Who's Who* will be biologically perpetuated in the future at least in their numerical proportion to the general population. This is in marked contrast to the situation prevailing for at least two generations in the past." This again agrees with a more general trend. The birth rates in the United States have increased during the postwar period in all social strata; however, the greatest relative increases have been in those socially favored groups which had been characterized earlier by deficient fertility.

It may well be that the situation in which the economically more successful and, also, the more intelligent (which is certainly not the same thing) strata of the population failed to produce their proportional quota of children was only a temporary one. It may have arisen, especially in the West, because some people became familiar with efficient methods of progeny limitation before others. It is interesting in this connection that the patterns of differential fertility in at least some underdeveloped and non-Western countries favored greater families in economically more prosperous strata. This seems to have been the situation in China (Ho 1959b, Hsu 1959).

The direction of natural selection in the human species has certainly been shifting in the environments created by cultural changes. Have these changes and shifts been on the whole beneficial or injurious? Asking this is really another way of posing the question whether man must accept the "natural" drift of evolution as something preordained and inevitable. The alternative to such acceptance is pitting the forces of man's knowledge and wisdom against the forces of nature. The concluding chapter attempts to approach this fateful problem.

CHAPTER 40

Do American Women Marry Up?

ZICK RUBIN

I̲N̲ his chapter on marriage and the family in the *Handbook of Modern Sociology,* Zelditch writes:

> The available data suggest that *hypergamy* is more common than *hypogamy*—that is, females tend to marry males of higher social rank more often than males tend to marry females of higher social rank. (Zelditch, 1964:688)

Burchinal makes a similar statement in his chapter on mate-selection in the *Handbook of Marriage and the Family:*

> The bulk of the data support the generalization that when status heterogamy occurs men tend to marry down and women tend to marry up—a phenomenon known as the mating gradient. (Burchinal, 1964:654)

That women tend to marry up (and men to marry down) the socioeconomic ladder in some societies is a well-demonstrated fact. In classical Hindu society and among the Natchez Indians of North America, for example, hypergamy with respect to social class reportedly was an institutionalized part of the stratification system. Davis (1941) and Merton (1941) offer similar explanations of this phenomenon. Since the male determines the social rank of his family, it is suggested, he can afford to marry down without loss of status. He may, in effect, exchange his loftier economic position for personal qualities which he finds attractive

in a wife. The wealthy female, on the other hand, is not in a position to make such a trade.

Several recent studies of courtship in the United States lend support to the view that this reasoning is applicable to American society. For example, Coombs and Kenkel (1966) found that college women expressed higher aspirations than men in their demands for a computer-selected date on such dimensions as campus status and scholastic ability, and lower aspirations with respect to physical attractiveness. Kephart (1967) made the surprising discovery that as the age of college women increased (from 18 to 24), they reported decreasing numbers of past romantic experiences. Men reported the more logical cumulative increase with age. Kephart interprets this result as reflecting retrospective distortion by the women. As they get closer to marriage, women tend to deny previous loves and infatuations which would impinge on their monogamistic ideal. "The female's romantic conation is more adaptive and directive than that of the male," Kephart concludes. "Apparently, she is able to exercise a greater measure of control over her romantic inclinations, adapting them to the exigencies of marital selection." (1967:472.) Such an orientation seems to be in line with the tendency to marry up.

Further evidence of the woman's adaptive orientation was obtained when Kephart asked his respondents the following question: "If a boy (girl) had all the other qualities you desired, would you marry this person even if you were not in love with him (her)?" Few respondents answered

This research was done while the writer held a National Institute of Mental Health Predoctoral Fellowship. I am grateful to Professor Otis Dudley Duncan for his assistance in all phases of the research.

633

"yes" to this question, but only 24 percent of the women (as compared to 65 percent of the men) answered "no." Fully 72 percent of the females and only 24 percent of the males said they were undecided. As one co-ed told the interviewer, "If a boy had all the other qualities I desired, and I was not in love with him—well, I think I could talk myself into falling in love." Socioeconomic status presumably looms large among the "other qualities."

There is also evidence suggesting that parental participation in their children's courtship may constitute a force toward hypergamy in the United States. Bates (1942) asked young married persons whether their parents had attempted to influence their courtship. Among the female respondents, 69 percent reported that their fathers had made such an attempt and 97 percent that their mothers had made such an attempt. The corresponding percentages for males were only 49 and 79. Bates presented no data specifically indicating that these pressures were toward marrying up, however.

In spite of such supporting evidence in terms of prevailing cultural values, the hypothesis that American women tend to marry up (the "hypergamy hypothesis") remains to be tested directly. Both Zelditch and Burchinal seem to assume (as Davis and Merton do *not*) that the tendency toward hypergamy has wide cross-cultural generality. And in presenting evidence for the predominance of hypergamy over hypogamy, both rely on studies undertaken in the United States. These studies are by Centers (1949), Hollingshead (1950), and Sundal and Mc-Cormick (1951). We will consider each of them briefly.

Centers (1949) reported data from a national survey of white males, excluding farmers and men married to farmers' daughters. In support of the hypergamy hypothesis, he presented such facts as the following: About 85 percent of the men who were business executives married down, whereas only 45 percent of the women whose fathers were business executives married down. On the other hand, about 24 percent of the men who were skilled manual workers married up, while 48 percent of the women whose fathers were skilled manual workers

married up. But these data are not directly relevant to the hypergamy hypothesis because husbands' occupations are compared to their wives' *fathers'* occupations. The differences between men and women may well be attributable to the large upward shift in the American occupational structure in the course of a generation (cf. Blau and Duncan, 1967). They need have nothing to do with marriage patterns. Centers appears to have been somewhat aware of this difficulty, because he also presents outflow percentages of wives' fathers' occupations for husbands as categorized by *their* fathers' occupations. These data are not easily interpreted, however, because comparable outflow percentages for wives are not presented.

Hollingshead (1950) presents data on 1,008 marriages which took place in New Haven, Connecticut, in 1948, and concludes that "when class lines were crossed the man selected a woman from a lower class far more frequently than was true for women" (p. 626). The conclusion is of doubtful significance, however. In the first place, Hollingshead measured social class by coding the residential area in which the spouses lived before marriage. This is probably a less valid index of socioeconomic status than father's occupation. Second, the phrase "far more frequently" in the above quotation is an overstatement. The figures were as follows. In 232 cases (23 percent of the total) the man married down, in 189 cases (19 percent) the man married up. In the remaining 587 cases (58 percent) both spouses were of the same "class." To bolster his argument, Hollingshead singled out particular instances of hypergamy. For example, four Class I men married women from Classes V and VI, whereas no Class I woman married a man from any class lower than Class III. But these instances are based on too few cases to be convincing. In sum, if Hollingshead's study provides support for the hypergamy hypothesis, it is support of a rather weak sort. In any case, generalizing from the New Haven population to the American population is clearly unjustified.

Finally, Sundal and McCormick (1951) present data on marriages in Madison, Wisconsin, between 1937 and 1943. Most of it is poorly suited to our present purpose because brides' status was measured by their *own* occupations at the time of marriage, rather than by their fathers' occupations. It seems clear that the jobs held by young women before marriage do not provide reliable indications of their social status. Sundal and McCormick also obtained data on the occupations of the spouses' parents, but report only the finding that "about one in every three young women who married sons of professional and business men were daughters of skilled, semi-skilled, or unskilled manual workers." (1951:44.) Since no other outflow percentages nor any marginal percentages are presented, it is impossible to assess the import of this datum for the hypergamy hypothesis.

These three studies comprise the sum of the evidence cited in support of the proposition that hypergamy is more common than hypogamy in the United States. Their combined force is clearly trivial. Moreover, in his recent study of stratification in Cambridge and Belmont, Massachusetts, Laumann (1966:74–76) did not find a preponderance of hypergamy. It must be concluded, then, that the assumption that American women tend to marry up is not justified by the available evidence. Our review also suggests that more adequate investigations of interclass marriage patterns in the United States are called for. The results of such studies would be of interest to at least three groups of social scientists—sociologists interested in aspects of social stratification, sociologists and anthropologists interested in the American matrimonial system, and social psychologists interested in processes of mate-selection.

Unfortunately, there are no extant data which would allow a completely unambiguous evaluation of the hypergamy hypothesis. Nevertheless, some headway can be made with presently available large-sample data. The remainder of this paper points to some ways in which such data can be applied to the question of hypergamy in the United States. As will be pointed out in greater detail later, there is a sense in which the question is meaningless. If certain constraints are assumed to be operative within the matrimonial system of a society, then there can be no net tendency toward hypergamy or hypogamy—one must precisely counterbalance the other. On the other hand,

if the constraints are somewhat loosened and the question is more clearly specified, it becomes susceptible to an empirical answer. For the present, we can make the question somewhat more precise: "Do American women of particular socioeconomic origins marry up more frequently (and down less frequently) than do men of the same origins?"

DATA

Data relevant to the hypergamy hypothesis are contained in the tabulations of Blau and Duncan's (1967) study of "occupational changes in a generation." The data were obtained from a clustered sample of American men, conducted by the U.S. Bureau of the Census as an adjunct to the March, 1962, Current Population Survey. The total sample of 20,700 respondents represented the 45 million men 20 to 64 years old in the civilian, non-institutional population of the United States. The data to be presented here are drawn from about two-thirds of this total. They include those white males in the sample who were living with their wives at the time of the survey and whose wives were between 22 and 61 years old. Cases in which one or more pieces of necessary data were not reported (about 14 percent of the restricted sample) are excluded from the analyses. The main analyses to be presented are based on cross-tabulations of husbands' fathers' occupations by their wives' fathers' occupations, in each case reported by the husband as of the time the spouse was 16 years old. Analyses were performed separately for two age groups: couples in which the wife was between 22 and 41 years old at the time of the survey, and those in which the wife was between 42 and 61 years old.

Occupational Categories. All occupational data were reduced to the following five categories:

I. *Professional and managerial*—professionals; salaried managers, officials and proprietors (except farm).
II. *White-collar*—self-employed managers, officials, and proprietors (except farm); clerical and sales workers.
III. *Upper blue-collar*—craftsmen, foremen, and kindred workers.
IV. *Lower blue-collar*—operatives, service workers, and laborers (except farm and mine).
V. *Farm*—farmers and farm laborers.

TABLE 1. NUMBER OF INTERCLASS AND INTRACLASS MARRIAGES (IN THOUSANDS)

| | Older Group (Wives 42–61) | | | | | |
| | Wife's Father's Occupation | | | | | |
	I	II	III	IV	V	Total
Husband's Father's Occupation						
I. Professional and managerial	212	219	160	161	130	882
II. White-collar	230	439	308	353	346	1676
III. Upper blue-collar	214	308	551	636	380	2089
IV. Lower blue-collar	169	343	563	923	465	2463
V. Farm	182	307	453	634	2193	3769
Total	1007	1616	2035	2707	3514	10879
	Younger Group (Wives 22–41)					
	Wife's Father's Occupation					
	I	II	III	IV	V	Total
Husband's Father's Occupation						
I. Professional and managerial	341	396	303	317	158	1515
II. White-collar	410	600	568	625	306	2509
III. Upper blue-collar	317	458	882	972	435	3064
IV. Lower blue-collar	323	548	1004	1777	595	4247
V. Farm	202	307	523	860	1857	3749
Total	1593	2309	3280	4551	3351	15084

The first four categories are ordered in accordance with prevailing notions of socio-economic status, as measured by Duncan's occupational status scores (Reiss, et al., 1961). The "farm" category is diverse with respect to status, however, and on the whole the status of farmers is hardly different from that of lower-blue-collar workers.

RESULTS

Frequency Distributions. In Table 1 the cross-tabulations of husbands' fathers' occupations by wives' fathers' occupations are presented for the two age groups. The frequencies are given in thousands, and represent estimates of the *population* frequencies, produced by the Census Bureau by appropriate weighting of the sample frequencies. The relatively large numbers in the diagnoal cells reflect the large amount of intraclass mating. Homogamous marriages comprise 39.7 percent of the couples in which the wife was between 42 and 61 years old and 36.2 percent of the couples in which the wife was between 22 and 41 years old.

Percentage Distributions. Table 2 indicates the outflow percentages of spouses' fathers' occupations, given the husbands' and wives' own fathers' occupations. These percentages must, of course, be interpreted in light of the overall, or marginal, percentages of husbands' and wives' origins. These are

given on the bottom lines of the two tables. The tables indicate a high degree of similarity between the marriage patterns of men and those of women within each status level. One difference revealed in both age groups is that among the children of farmers, women tended to marry at the same level more than men, and men tended to marry up—particularly to the children of lower-blue-collar workers—more than women. As suggested previously, however, it is not clear that such farm/lower-blue-collar marriages are directional with respect to status. The data in Tables 1 and 2 may be summarized as follows: Among the older couples (wives aged 42 to 61), 29.0 percent of the women married up and 31.3 percent married down. Among the younger couples (wives aged 22 to 41), 31.0 percent of the women married up and 32.8 percent married down. In both age groups, then, there is a slight excess of hypogamous to hypergamous marriages. This finding runs counter to the hypothesis that American women tend to marry up more than to marry down.

Particular Interclass Combinations. In Table 3, we make explicit the relative frequency of hypergamous and hypogamous marriages for each of the ten types of interclass marriage (I–II, I–III, etc.). Each entry is the difference between the number of hypergamous and the number of hypo-

TABLE 2. OUTFLOW PERCENTAGES FOR INTERCLASS AND INTRACLASS MARRIAGES

	I	II	III	IV	V
Older Group (Wives 42–61) (Destination) Second Spouse's Father's Occupation					
(Origin) First Spouse's Father's Occupation					
I. Professional and managerial					
Husband	24.0	24.8	18.1	18.2	14.7
Wife	21.0	22.8	21.2	16.8	18.1
II. White-collar					
Husband	13.7	26.2	18.4	21.1	20.6
Wife	13.6	27.2	19.1	21.2	19.0
III. Upper blue-collar					
Husband	10.2	14.7	26.4	30.4	18.2
Wife	7.9	15.1	27.1	27.7	22.3
IV. Lower blue-collar					
Husband	6.9	13.9	22.9	37.5	18.9
Wife	6.0	13.0	23.5	34.1	23.4
V. Farm					
Husband	4.8	8.1	12.0	16.8	58.2
Wife	3.7	9.8	10.8	13.2	62.4
Overall distribution of wives	9.3	14.8	18.7	24.9	32.3
Overall distribution of husbands	8.1	15.4	19.2	22.6	34.6
Younger Group (Wives 22–41) (Destination) Second Spouse's Father's Occupation					
(Origin) First Spouse's Father's Occupation					
I. Professional and managerial					
Husband	22.5	26.1	20.0	20.9	10.4
Wife	21.4	25.7	19.9	20.3	12.7
II. White-collar					
Husband	16.3	23.9	22.6	24.9	12.2
Wife	17.2	26.0	19.8	23.7	13.3
III. Upper blue-collar					
Husband	10.3	15.0	28.8	31.7	14.2
Wife	9.2	17.3	26.9	30.6	15.9
IV. Lower blue-collar					
Husband	7.6	12.9	23.6	41.8	14.0
Wife	7.0	13.7	21.4	39.0	18.9
V. Farm					
Husband	5.4	8.2	14.0	22.9	49.5
Wife	4.7	9.1	13.0	17.8	55.4
Overall distribution of wives	10.6	15.3	21.7	30.2	22.2
Overall distribution of husbands	10.0	16.6	20.3	28.2	24.8

gamous marriages for a given type. Positive numbers indicate an excess of hypergamy, negative numbers an excess of hypogamy. It is to be noted that in both age groups the largest discrepancies are found for marriages between the children of farmers and lower-blue-collar workers. In the older group, it is estimated that 169,000 more

TABLE 3. EXCESS OF HYPERGAMOUS TO HYPOGAMOUS MARRIAGES (IN THOUSANDS) FOR
EACH INTERCLASS COMBINATION

| | Older Group (Wives 42–61) Spouse B's Father's Occupation | | | | |
	I	II	III	IV	V
Spouse A's Father's Occupation					
I. Professional and managerial	...	...	...	...	...
II. White-collar	−11	...	...	...	...
III. Upper blue-collar	−54	0	...	...	...
IV. Lower blue-collar	−8	10	73	...	...
V. Farm	−52	39	−73	−169	...

| | Younger Group (Wives 22–41) Spouse B's Father's Occupation | | | | |
	I	II	III	IV	V
Spouse A's Father's Occupation					
I. Professional and managerial	...	...	...	...	...
II. White-collar	−14	...	...	...	...
III. Upper blue-collar	−14	110	...	...	...
IV. Lower blue-collar	−6	77	−32	...	...
V. Farm	−44	−1	−88	−265	...

farmers' sons than farmers' daughters married "up" into the lower-blue-collar class. In the younger group the comparable figure is 265,000. By summing the discrepancies given in Table 3, we can also obtain estimates of the overall excess of hypogamous to hypergamous marriages. In the older group, 245,000 more women married down than up; in the younger group, the figure was 277,000.

Correcting for Supply Characteristics. The absolute estimates given in Table 3 may be of value to demographers concerned with the flow of population across class lines. With regard to mate-selection processes, however, they are of ambiguous import because they do not take into account the available supply of potential mates. The socioeconomic characteristics of this supply (or "pool of eligibles") may be estimated from the overall distribution of status origins for husbands and for wives. These marginal distributions may be used to estimate the individual cell frequencies which would be obtained if mating were completely random with respect to socioeconomic origins. By comparing these expected frequencies with those that were actually obtained, we can derive indices which represent mating tendencies over and above those dictated by the available supply. Such indices may be better suited to the question at hand than are absolute frequencies.

Since our present interest centers on interclass marriages, we considered the diagonal cell frequencies (representing intraclass marriages) as well as the marginal frequencies to be fixed. Proceeding from this assumption, expected frequencies for the off-diagonal cells were obtained by means of the statistical technique outlined by Goodman (1965).[1] As dictated by this procedure, each expected frequency is proportional to the product of two constants, one representing the row marginal and one representing the column marginal coresponding to a given cell. The sum of any row or column of expected (off-diagonal) frequencies is equal to the sum of that row or column of actual (off-diagonal) frequencies. The actual cell frequencies were then compared to these expected values, yielding "relative departures"[2] for the various socioeconomic pairings.

The mathematical elimination of the effects of the supply characteristics is not an unambiguously desirable procedure. Differences between the socioeconomic distribu-

---

[1] The "BLOCK" computer program, written by J. Michael Coble of the Population Studies Center, University of Michigan, was used for this purpose. The program follows an iterative procedure set forth by Goodman (1964:184–185).

[2] Relative departure=

$$\frac{\text{Actual frequency} - \text{Expected frequency}}{\text{Expected frequency}}\bullet$$

tions of husbands and of wives may reflect several factors. First, for example, the differences may result from response error or bias on the part of the male respondents. Second, the fact that husbands are typically several years older than their wives may be associated with a differential distribution of status origins, because of rapid changes in the American occupational structure. Third, differential mortality rates by class (e.g., in military service) may lead to variations by class in the sex ratios for persons of marriageable age. Fourth, and most significantly, there may be differences between the male and the female marriage rates within particular occupational classes.

The first three of these potential sources of inequality are more or less extraneous to processes of mate-selection *per se,* and the mathematical elimination of their effects seems appropriate. Differential marriage rates by class, on the other hand, may represent an important aspect of the question at hand. One of the alternatives open to a prospective spouse is not to marry at all. If, as Berelson and Steiner (1964:307) state, upper-class men are more likely to marry than lower-class men and upper-class women are *less* likely to marry than lower-class women, an overall tendency toward hypergamy would probably be found. Such a finding would seem to reflect "true" hypergamy rather than artifact. Since the number of unmarried persons of the same age and origins as the persons in the sample is unknown, it was necessary to equate the "pool of eligibles" with those persons who in fact married. As a result, the correction process has the effect of denying the relevance of a person's option not to marry.

In eliminating the effects of the marginal frequencies, then, we may be throwing out some wheat with the chaff. We are stipulating, in effect, that there can be no *overall* preponderance of hypergamy or hypogamy—on the whole, the two must balance out. Such a balance is logically necessary in a closed, monogamous system in which there are equal numbers of marrying men and women within each socioeconomic stratum. In a hypothetical two-class society, for example, if all the women in Class B marry up to the men in Class A, there would be no recourse for the women in Class A other than to marry down to the men in Class B. But it should be recognized that such a perfect balance is not to be expected in a real society, and that the mathematical imposition of such a balance may lead to some distortion. On the other hand, if our conclusions are restricted to those persons who *do* marry, the mathematical constraints are more clearly justified.

Relative Hypergamy Index. On the basis of the computed expected frequencies, a Relative Hypergamy Index (RHI) was derived for each type of interclass marriage. For any given socioeconomic pairing, the RHI is equal to the difference between the relative departure for wives marrying up and the corresponding relative departure for wives marrying down. Positive numbers indicate a relative excess of hypergamy, negative numbers a relative excess of hypogamy. These values, presented in Table 4, may be interpreted on the individual level. They represent, in essence, the extent to which a girl is more likely than her older brother to marry up (or less likely to marry down) from her class to a particular other class, as compared to the difference which would be expected if interclass mating were random. Table 4 indicates that in both age groups there is a disproportionately large amount of hypergamy in marriages between Class I and Class II. That is, when we take the overall distribution of spouses into account, daughters of white-collar workers were more likely than their brothers to marry the children of professionals and managers. In addition, we again note that marriages between the children of farmers and of lower-blue-collar workers tended to be "hypogamous." But marriages linking farmers' children to the children of white-collar workers were more likely to be hypergamous.

Weighted Hypergamy Index. Table 3 indicated the absolute discrepancies between the number of hypergamous and hypogamous marriages for each socioeconomic pairing. Table 5 presents analogous discrepancy figures, but this time the correction for supply characteristics is included. These indices are computed by weighting the relative departures by the respective expected frequencies before subtracting the hypogamous

TABLE 4. RELATIVE HYPERGAMY INDICES

| | Older Group (Wives 42–61) | | | | |
| | | | Spouse B's Father's Occupation | | |
	I	II	III	IV	V
Spouse A's Father's Occupation					
I. Professional and managerial	...	...	...	...	...
II. White-collar	.24	...	...	...	...
III. Upper blue-collar	−.11	−.01	...	...	...
IV. Lower blue-collar	.00	−.10	−.01	...	...
V. Farm	−.04	.21	−.06	−.07	...

| | Younger Group (Wives 22–41) | | | | |
| | | | Spouse B's Father's Occupation | | |
	I	II	III	IV	V
Spouse A's Father's Occupation					
I. Professional and managerial	...	...	...	...	...
II. White-collar	.19	...	...	...	...
III. Upper blue-collar	−.06	.06	...	...	...
IV. Lower blue-collar	−.03	−.04	−.05	...	...
V. Farm	.01	.09	.08	−.10	...

from the hypergamous value for a given interclass combination. They may be computed directly by subtracting the difference between actual and expected frequencies for hypogamous cases from the corresponding difference for hypergamous cases.

These Weighted Hypergamy Indices (WHI) may be interpreted as the excess (in thousands) of hypergamous to hypogamous marriages within a given interclass combination, above and beyond what would be expected on the basis of the marginal and intraclass frequencies. By summing the val-

ues in Table 5, we conclude that in the older group, 53,000 more women married down than up as compared to what would be expected if interclass mating were random. In the younger group, 68,000 more women married down than up. These figures are much smaller than the absolute excesses of hypogamy derived from Table 3. They suggest that most of the hypogamous tendency indicated by Table 3 can be accounted for by the supply characteristics of the "pool of eligibles." The small size of these frequencies also suggests that on the whole,

TABLE 5. WEIGHTED HYPERGAMY INDICES

| | Older Group (Wives 42–61) | | | | |
| | | | Spouse B's Father's Occupation | | |
	I	II	III	IV	V
Spouse A's Father's Occupation					
I. Professional and managerial	...	...	...	...	...
II. White-collar	16.6	...	...	...	...
III. Upper blue-collar	−19.3	−4.8	...	...	...
IV. Lower blue-collar	2.4	−48.8	0.8	...	...
V. Farm	0.3	70.2	−24.8	−45.7	...

| | Younger Group (Wives 22–41) | | | | |
| | | | Spouse B's Father's Occupation | | |
	I	II	III	IV	V
Spouse A's Father's Occupation					
I. Professional and managerial	...	...	...	...	...
II. White-collar	21.9	...	...	...	...
III. Upper blue-collar	−18.7	22.6	...	...	...
IV. Lower blue-collar	−15.7	−37.8	−40.7	...	...
V. Farm	12.6	37.1	44.7	−94.3	...

hypergamous and hypogamous tendencies are virtually equal.

It should be noted that our mathematical constraints do *not* necessitate a precise balance of the *frequency* of hypergamy and hypogamy over the table. The constraints do necessitate an overall equilibrium when (and only when) the WHI for each socioeconomic pairing is weighted by a value representing the size of the interclass gap. The sum of such doubly weighted indices must equal zero. Table 5 shows that there is a preponderance of hypergamy among marriages involving large interclass jumps—most notably, marriages between the children of farmers and of white-collar workers. The finding that there are more than the expected *number* of hypogamous as compared to hypergamous marriages, therefore, is both possible and meaningful.

Effects of the Husband's Own Occupation. All of the analyses reported may also be performed on the cross-tabulations of wives' fathers' occupations by husbands' *own* occupations. Such analyses seem appropriate in light of the explanations of hypergamy which have been offered. If women marry up because of a desire for status and prestige, the occupation of a prospective husband's *father* may not be as relevant as the prospective husband's own occupation and occupational prospects. Analyses employing the husband's own occupation encounter severe difficulties, however. For example, the likelihood of our being able to illuminate mate-selection processes by means of such analyses is reduced by the possibility that marriage has an *effect* on the husband's occupational career. In addition, indices derived from cross-tabulations which refer to two generations simultaneously do not readily lend themselves to straightforward interpretations. Because of these and other difficulties, such analyses will not be presented.

CONCLUSIONS

The present data clearly do not permit an ideal test of the hypergamy hypothesis. Such a test would require data gathered from a sample of both men and women, both married and unmarried. In addition to information about the respondent's and his (or her) present spouse's socioeconomic origins, data on previous marriages would also be relevant. Nevertheless, the foregoing analyses may justify several tentative conclusions.

Our large-sample data include so many cases in each cell that significance values referring to possible sampling error are more or less extraneous. As Blau and Duncan state (1967:17), "With some exaggeration, we can assert that any difference large enough to be at all interesting is statistically significant. Indeed, the data show all kinds of 'significant differences' (not due to sampling error) that can be given no clear interpretation and that may be so slight as to be of no practical importance." In assessing the practical importance of the results reported here, one may wish to consider both the estimated magnitude of the effects and the interpretations which may be given them. From Table 3, we concluded that in each age group there was an absolute excess of hypogamous to hypergamous marriages of about 260,000. When the characteristics of the supply of persons marrying across class lines were taken into account, this figure dwindled to about 60,000. These figures may be compared to the population bases of about 11 million couples in the older group and 15 million couples in the younger group. To the extent that our procedures are justified, therefore, we may conclude that any overall tendency toward hypergamy or hypogamy in the United States is negligible.

It should be observed at this point that it is impossible to "correct" for unknown quantities of response bias. If there is a systematic bias in the present data, it may well be in the direction of apparent hypogamy—that is, men may tend to overestimate the social origins of their wives more than they do their own social origins. If this speculation is correct, then there may indeed be an overall preponderance of hypergamy which is not revealed in the data.

Although no overall hypergamous or hypogamous tendency is revealed by our analyses, one or the other pattern may predominate for particular interclass pairings. Of perhaps greatest significance is the finding that marriages between members of the two highest classes tend to be hypergamous. When (and only when) the constraints of the matrimonial market are taken into account, it appears that the daughter of a white-collar worker is more likely to marry the son of a professional or manager than the white-collar girl's brother is to marry the professional boy's sister. This result is obtained in both age groups, and is most clearly revealed in the Relative Hypergamy Indices (Table 4). It may be suggested that the "adaptive romantic orientation" of women referred to at the start of this report is most characteristic of upper- and middle-class women. It may also be speculated that writers who have assumed that American women tend to marry up have based their assumption upon their acquaintance with these upper- and middle-class marriages. The present results indicate that generalization from Class I-Class II marriages to all interclass marriages is not justified.

A second noteworthy finding refers to the special role of farmers' children in the marriage market. Tables 4 and 5 both indicate, from their respective viewpoints, that farmers' daughters tend to marry up to white-collar workers' sons more often than farmers' sons marry up to white-collar workers' daughters. In the younger group, hypergamy is predominant among marriages between farmers' children and the children of professionals and upper-blue-collar workers as well. These results may be linked to the suggestion by Duncan and Reiss (1956) that there has been a large excess of females to males in the migration of teen-agers from farm to city. This suggestion would explain the 1950 Census finding that at age 19, the male-to-female sex ratio was at a peak of 133:100 in farm areas and at a low of 84:100 in urban areas (Duncan and Reiss, 1956: 53). Since the median age of first marriage for women is about 20, the implication is that farmers' daughters will be more likely than their brothers to marry city dwellers, who are typically of higher socioeconomic origins. Counterbalancing this tendency is the predominance of "hypogamy" among marriages between the children of farmers and of lower-blue-collar workers, who may be relatively abundant in rural areas. All of the above reasoning points to the need to consider spatial as well as occupational distribution in attempts to account for mate-selection processes. For the present, however, the question of whether farm girls head for the city *in order to marry up* must remain unanswered.

Finally, the analyses reveal some apparent historical trends. For example, the tendency for farm girls to marry up is more general among the younger than among the older group. In general, however, the similarity of the results for the two age groups is more striking than the differences between them. In the United States from about 1920 to 1962, interclass marriage patterns seem to have been relatively stable.

REFERENCES

Bates, Alan.
1942 "Parental roles in courtship." Social Forces 20 (May):483–486.
Berelson, Bernard and Gary A. Steiner.
1964 Human Behavior. New York: Harcourt, Brace.
Blau, Peter M. and Otis Dudley Duncan.
1967 The American Occupational Structure. New York: Wiley.
Burchinal, Lee G.
1964 "The premarital dyad and love involvement." Pp. 623–674 in Harold T. Christensen (ed.), Handbook of Marriage and the Family. Chicago: Rand McNally.
Centers, Richard.
1949 "Marital selection and occupational strata." American Journal of Sociology 54 (May): 530–535.
Coombs, Robert H. and William F. Kenkel.
1966 "Sex differences in dating aspirations and satisfaction with computer-selected partners." Journal of Marriage and the Family 28 (February):62–66.
Davis, Kingsley.
1941 "Intermarriage in caste societies." American Anthropologist 43 (July–September):376–395.
Duncan, Otis Dudley and Albert J. Reiss, Jr.
1956 Social Characteristics of Urban and Rural Communities, 1950. New York: Wiley.
Goodman, Leo A.
1964 "A short computer program for the analysis of transaction flows." Behavioral Science 9 (April):176–186.
1965 "On the statistical analysis of mobility tables." American Journal of Sociology 70 (March):564–585.
Hollingshead, August B.
1950 "Cultural factors in the selection of marriage mates." American Sociological Review 15 (October):619–627.
Kephart, William M.
1967 "Some correlates of romantic love." Journal of Marriage and the Family 29 (August):470–479.
Laumann, Edward O.
1966 Prestige and Association in an Urban Community. Indianapolis: Bobbs-Merrill.

Merton, Robert K.
1941 "Intermarriage and the social structure: fact and theory." Psychiatry 4 (August): 361–374.
Reiss, Albert J., Jr., et al.
1961 Occupations and Social Status. New York: Free Press.
Sundal, A. Philip and Thomas C. McCormick.

1951 "Age at marriage and mate selection, Madison, Wisconsin, 1937–1943." American Sociological Review 16 (February):37–48.
Zelditch, Morris, Jr.
1964 "Family, marriage, and kinship." Pp. 680–733 in Robert E. L. Faris (ed.), Handbook of Modern Sociology. Chicago: Rand McNally.

CHAPTER 41

Social Class, Mental Illness, and American Psychiatry: An Expository Review

S. M. MILLER and ELLIOT G. MISHLER

This book may well have a marked effect upon the future practice of psychiatry. It reports the results of a major investigation by a sociologist-psychiatrist team of the relationships between social class and the appearance and treatment of mental illness. Fragmentary findings had been made available before (twenty-five articles have appeared over the last five years), but a great deal of important material is presented here for the first time and the authors have expanded their forthright interpretations of the study's implications for the treatment of the mentally ill.

The excitement of a pioneering study arises from the freshness of its point of view and the provocativeness of its findings. It poses new questions and places old ones in a new light. This quality of exciting discovery is present in the important and sometimes startling findings of this study. We can give some indication of the significance of the book by quoting the three major hypotheses which are the central concerns of the investigation: "(I) The prevalence of treated mental illness is related significantly to an individual's position in the class structure. (II) The types of diagnosed psychiatric disorders are connected significantly to the class structure. (III) The kind of psychiatric treatment administered by psychiatrists is associated with the patient's position in the class structure."

A major problem of such ground-breaking investigations is that the core discovery overwhelms both authors and readers alike by the

644

brute fact of its existence. In the first wave of response there is often a neglect of fundamental questions concerning the approach, the methodology, and the interpretations placed upon the data. The chapter summaries tend to enter without qualifications into the folklore of the discipline.

The potential importance of this book for theory, research, and practice in the mental illness field is too great to permit such neglect.

I. Exposition of Findings

A. THE SOCIAL CLASS STRUCTURE

The basic data on social class composition are derived from interviews with respondents in a 5 per cent sample of all households in the metropolitan area of New Haven, Connecticut, which had a total population of about 236,940 persons. The New Haven population is divided into five social classes arranged in a hierarchal order. The family's class position is determined by the score of the head of the family on a weighted "Index of Social Position" that is derived from three separate scales measuring the social rank of his (a) area of residence; (b) occupation; and (c) education. The weights used in the formula for computing the summary index and the cutting points used to distinguish between classes were decided on specifically for this study and are not extrapolation from theory or other research. Roughly, occupation receives almost as much weight as the other two scores combined.

Class I, or the *upper class*, constitutes about 3 per cent of the population. It is composed of both "old" and "new" families who live in the most exclusive residential areas; the family head is a college graduate who is either an executive of a large firm or a professional. Class II, the *upper middle class*, is 8.4 per cent of the population and is made up occupationally of the managerial and professional groups. In Class III, the *lower middle class*, who make up 20.4 per cent of the population, about half are in salaried white collar work and the remainder either own small businesses, are semi-professionals, foremen, or skilled workers.

Class IV, the *working class*, is the largest group and accounts for half the households (49.8 per cent). Half of the group is semi-skilled workers, a third is skilled, and about a tenth is white collar employees. The overall educational level is much lower than in the class above it.

The *lower class*, Class V, which is 18.4 per cent of the population of New Haven, is made up of unskilled and semi-skilled workers of low education.

A rich and detailed description is provided of the historical background of the social class structure and of certain cultural characteristics of each of the classes such as their religious, family, ethnic, and leisure time patterns.

B. THE PREVALENCE OF PERSONS
IN PSYCHIATRIC TREATMENT

A "Psychiatric Census" was carried out in which an attempt was made to enumerate all persons from the New Haven metropolitan area who were "in treatment with a psychiatrist or under the care of a psychiatric clinic or mental hospital between May 31 and December 1, 1950."

The procedure here was remarkably thorough: systematic inquiries were made of relevant facilities and practitioners in New England and New York City and to special facilities further afield. The investigators' persistence brought response from every hospital and clinic contact and from 70 per cent of the private practitioners. In all, they believe that they may have missed only about 2 per cent of the community's residents who were receiving treatment. A total of 1,891 cases was enumerated on whom there was sufficient data for analysis. The data thus only permit discussion of *treated* mental illness, not of the total amount of mental illness in the community. To study the latter, a different type of research design with a psychiatric interview or some similar device of a cross-section of the community would be necessary. Thus, in the Hollingshead-Redlich study, there would have had to have been a psychiatric study of all of the individuals included in the 5 per cent sample of New Haven to enable statements to be made about "true" incidence and prevalence.

The major finding—one of the study's core discoveries—is of a systematic relationship between social class and the treated prevalence of mental illness. As can be seen in Table A, classes I through IV are somewhat underrepresented in the patient population, while Class V,

Table A—Class Status and the Distribution of Patients and Nonpatients in the Population

Class	POPULATION, PER CENT	
	Patients	Nonpatients
I	1.0	3.0
II	7.0	8.4
III	13.7	20.4
IV	40.1	49.8
V	38.2	18.4
	n = 1891	236,940

$x^2 = 509.81$, 4df, $p < .001$

Source: Hollingshead, A. B., and Redlich, F. C.: *Social Class and Mental Illiness*, Table 8, p. 199.

to which 38 per cent of the patient group are assigned by their scores on the Index of Social Position, is greatly overrepresented with twice as many patients as might be expected on the basis of their number in the community. Significant differences are also found in a comparison of treated prevalence rates per 100,000 population (computed so as to adjust for age and sex differences among the classes) which are distributed as shown in Table B.

Table B—Class Status and Rate of (Treated) Psychosis per 100,000 Population (Age and Sex Adjusted)

Class	Adjusted Rate Per 100,000
I–II	523
III	528
IV	665
V	1,668
Total Population	808

Source: Text Table, p. 210.

In a more detailed analysis, Hollingshead and Redlich divide the patient group into specific diagnostic categories. A first glance reveals that the differences among the classes in treated prevalence rates are much greater for psychoses than for neuroses. The proportions of patients diagnosed as psychotic increase as one moves from Class I–II through Class V and conversely the proportions diagnosed as neurotic decrease (this reversal of the first relationship is automatic inasmuch as the two general categories make up the whole of the patient group). However, since this is a tempting finding to cite, it is important to point out that the authors discount its general importance and attribute it as possibly arising from the "differential use of psychiatric facilities by the population."

There are interesting differences among the social classes in regard to the specific neurotic disturbance which is modal among those who are in treatment: In Classes I and II the modal disturbance is character neuroses; in III and V, anti-social and immaturity reactions; while phobic-anxiety reactions are frequent in Class IV. Each of the above accounts for about one-third of the neurotic patients in each class as can be seen in Table C.

Table C—Percentage of Patients in Each Diagnostic Category of (Treated) Neurosis—by Class (Age and Sex Adjusted)

Diagnostic Category of Neurosis	Class I–II	III	IV	V
Antisocial and Immaturity Reactions	21	32	23	37
Phobic-Anxiety Reactions	16	18	30	16
Character Neuroses	36	23	13	16
Depressive Reactions	12	12	10	8
Psychosomatic Reactions	7	9	13	11
Obsessive-Compulsive Reactions	7	5	5	0
Hysterical Reactions	1	1	6	12
	n = 98	119	182	65

$x^2 = 53.62$, df 18, $p < .001$

Source: Table 13, p. 226.

With regard to specific types of psychoses, much less variation in their percentage importance is found than is the case with the neuroses, as Table D reveals. In particular, for some of the major categories, differences are essentially non-existent—schizophrenia is the predominant

Table D—Percentage of Patients in Each Diagnostic Category of (Treated) Psychosis—by Class (Age and Sex Adjusted)

Diagnostic Category of Psychosis	Class			
	I–II	III	IV	V
Affective Psychoses	21	14	14	7
Psychoses Resulting from Alcoholism and Drug Addiction	8	10	4	8
Organic Psychoses	5	8	9	16
Schizophrenic Psychoses	55	57	61	58
Senile Psychoses	11	11	12	11
	n = 53	142	584	672

$$x^2 = 48.23, df\ 12, p < .001$$

Source: Table 14, p. 228.

psychotic disorder in all classes and the proportions of all psychotics who are schizophrenic run from a low of 55 per cent in Class I to 61 per cent in Class IV. This finding is striking since earlier studies have reported a much higher rate of schizophrenia in Class IV and V neighborhoods than in other neighborhoods. Little variation exists among the classes in diagnoses of senile psychoses (11 or 12 per cent in each). Class V is disproportionately low in the affective psychoses with 7 per cent, and the other classes give figures of 14 or 21 per cent. Organic psychoses are highest in Class V (16 per cent) and lowest in Class I (5 per cent), and Class IV with 4 per cent has half the rate of the other classes for psychoses resulting from alcoholism and drug addiction.

The treated prevalence rates for all of the separate neuroses (except hysterical reactions) show statistically significant differences among the classes. However, there is no ordering from a higher to a lower

Table E—Class Status and the Rate of Different Types of (Treated) Psychoses per 100,000 of Population (Age and Sex Adjusted)

Type of Disorder	Class			
	I–II	III	IV	V
Affective Psychoses *	40	41	68	105
Psychoses Due to Alcoholism and Drug Addiction †	15	29	32	116
Organic Psychoses ‡	9	24	46	254
Schizophrenic Psychoses §	111	168	300	895
Senile Psychoses ¶	21	32	60	175
	n = 53	142	585	672

* $x^2 = 17.49, 3df, p\ .001$
† $x^2 = 77.14, 3df, p\ .001$
‡ $x^2 = 231.87, 3df, p\ .001$
§ $x^2 = 452.68, 3df, p\ .001$
¶ $x^2 = 88.36, 3df, p\ .001$

Source: Table 15, p. 232.

class that is consistent from one diagnostic category to another. The pattern of each neurosis with class must be examined and interpreted separately, as the authors do. Table E on the rates of persons in psychiatric treatment for different types of psychoses by class is the clearest demonstration in the book of an ordered inverse relationship of the type of disorder under treatment and social class. Although the curves for each disorder (affective, organic, schizophrenic, etc.) vary, in *every* case there is an increase in the rates as one moves from Class I–II to Class III, to Class IV, to Class V.

C. THE INCIDENCE OF MENTAL ILLNESS

One of the most important tools of epidemiological research and analysis is the distinction between *incidence*, i.e., the occurrence of new cases during some time, and *prevalence*, i.e., the total number of active cases in the population during some specified time. Although incidence is one of the components in a total prevalence picture, there is no systematic relation between the two since cases may be active currently that first appeared at any point in the past. In other words, as is generally known, prevalence rates do not directly reflect incidence rates since the former are dependent on rates of recovery and mortality from illness as well as on the occurring of illness.

All the figures reported above, and those in previous articles based on the study are for the prevalence of being in treatment. The most important new material in the volume is the presentation of incidence data for the psychiatric sample. It was derived by separating-out patients who entered or re-entered treatment during the interval of observation from those who had been in treatment at the beginning of the interval. It should be emphasized again that both incidence and prevalence rates refer to individuals *in treatment*, rather than to individuals with a mental disorder whether or not they are in treatment. Consequently, the appropriate definition of incidence data for this investigation might be the numbers or rate of those first coming into treatment and prevalence might be stated as the numbers or rate of those in treatment during the study period.

The rates of coming into treatment for all kinds of mental illness are reported in Table F.

Table F—Class Status and Rate of Incidence of (Treated) Neurosis and Psychosis per 100,000 Population (Age and Sex Adjusted)

Class	Rate
I–II	97
III	114
IV	89
V	139
Total	104

$$x^2 = 8.41, 3df, p < .05$$

Source: Text Table, p. 212.

The table shows that the overall differences remain statistically significant but the differentials are markedly reduced in comparison with the prevalence rates. Class IV now has the lowest rate. The authors summarize by stating: "Classes I and II contribute almost exactly the number of new cases (incidence) as could be expected on the basis of their proportion of the community's population. Class IV had a lower number than could be expected proportionately, whereas Class V had an excess of 36 per cent" (p. 215). In further analyses, Hollingshead and Redlich demonstrate that there is *no* significant statistical difference among the classes in the rate at which persons come under treatment for neuroses and show that the sharpest break in this rate for psychoses as a whole and for schizophrenia (both cases where the overall differences among classes are statistically significant) occurs between the rates for Classes I through IV (pp. 235–6). (We shall return at a later point to these important findings regarding incidence.)

The data on incidence and prevalence reveal that Classes IV and V comprise two-thirds of the community (68.2 per cent) and provide more than three-fourths (78.3 per cent) of the mental patients. Thus, due to the size of these two classes, the high psychotic incidence rates in Class V, and the long duration of illnesses in both classes, *psychiatry —whether or not it is aware of it—is largely concerned with Class IV and V patients.* Of course, private practitioners have few Class IV and V patients, but our calculations of the Hollingshead-Redlich data show that these two sources of treatment work with only 21 per cent of all New Haven mental patients.

D. PATHS TO TREATMENT

In an excellent discussion of the paths to psychiatric treatment, the authors make explicit their fundamental orientation that mental illness is a socio-cultural phenomenon as well as a psychological one. Thus, they state ". . . abnormal acts can be evaluated only in terms of their cultural and psychosocial contexts," and "Whether abnormal behavior is judged to be disturbed, delinquent, or merely idiosyncratic depends upon who sees it and how he appraises what he sees."

The sources of referral for treatment, i.e., the agencies or persons who decide that the behavior is that "type" of abnormality for which psychiatric treatment is appropriate, vary systematically by social class. Among neurotics, 55 to 60 per cent of those in Classes I through IV are likely to have been referred by physicians (almost entirely by private practitioners in the first three classes, and about half the time in Class IV by clinic physicians). The proportion of neurotic cases coming from medical referrals drops to 40 per cent in Class V; an equivalent proportion is referred by social agencies; with an additional 14 per cent directed to treatment by the police and courts (p. 186).

The differences are even more striking among psychotics where one-third of the patients in Class I were self-referrals and another 40 per cent came through family and friends. More than three-fifths of the Class III and IV patients were referred by physicians. For Class IV psychotics the police and courts are important, accounting for 19 per cent of the cases, and in Class V these two sources account for 52 per cent while social agencies contribute 20 per cent. The findings for schizophrenia are similar to those for psychosis in general (pp. 187–189).

The brief case reports that are presented to illustrate the different treatment consequences that follow on the same behavior when exhibited by persons of different classes should be required reading in all psychiatric residency programs. The authors note that "there is a definite tendency to induce disturbed persons in Classes I and II to see a psychiatrist in more gentle and 'insightful' ways than is the practice in Class IV and especially in Class V, where direct, authoritative, compulsory, and at times, coercively brutal methods are used."

And, their bitter, concluding epigram to this section is uncomfortably appropriate to their findings: "The goddess of justice may be blind, but she smells differences, and particularly class differences."

E. PATTERNS OF TREATMENT

At the end of their chapter on the Treatment Process, Hollingshead and Redlich state that "the data presented lead to the conclusion that treatment for mental illness depends not only on medical and psychological considerations, but also on powerful social variables to which psychiatrists have so far given little attention," and that "We have found real differences in *where, how, and how long* persons in the several classes have been cared for by psychiatrists."

These conclusions are based on a large number of detailed analyses of relations among diagnosis, treatment agency, treatment, and social class. We shall cite only a few of the most decisive findings.

First, the patient group as a whole divides into three relatively equal parts according to the principal type of therapy received: psychotherapies, organic therapies, or custodial care. Eighty-four per cent of the psychotic group is in treatment in a state mental hospital; 64 per cent of the neurotics are in the hands of private practitioners, and another 23 per cent are being treated in clinics.[3]

Despite the stress placed on diagnosis in psychiatric theory and practice, there is no overall relationship for neurotic patients between type of treatment and the specific diagnostic label attached to the patient. However, treatment is related directly to both social class and the agency in which the patient is treated. Even where treatment is received from the same facility, which is the most stringent test since it eliminates the selective bias that is present in the differential access to and choice of facilities by the different classes, there is a marked relationship between social class and type of treatment. For example, over 85 per cent of the Class IV and V neurotics in treatment with private practitioners receive "directive psychotherapy," while 45 per cent of Class I and II private patients receive "psychoanalysis or analytic psychotherapy." Consistent with this is the inverse relationship between social class and the likelihood of receiving the traditional "50 minute hour." (Ninety-four per cent in Classes I and II, 45 per cent in Class V; Tables 28 and 29, pp. 268–70).

A similar relationship between the "depth" and duration of the therapy and social class is also found in clinics, and there is additional evidence in a separate study of one clinic that the "patient's class status determines the professional level of the therapist who treats him." Public hospitals appear to be more democratic in their assignment of treatment to neurotic patients, inasmuch as there is no overall relationship between social class and treatment in these institutions.

The findings with regard to class bias in the type of treatment given to psychotic patients and to schizophrenics are less clear and less consistent than for the neurotic group. On the other hand, the relations of class to the duration and history of treatment are very significant and very revealing. For example, as one moves down the class ladder, the likelihood for schizophrenics of having been in continuous treatment increases, while moving in the other direction there is an increased likelihood of periods of remission and re-entry into treatment. In other words, once he enters treatment the Class V schizophrenic is likely to be kept under psychiatric care (Table 38, p. 295). Further, for psychotics there is a direct increase from Class I to Class V in the time duration of their present course of treatment; while for a neurotic this relationship is reversed. In other words, while the lower class neurotic is dismissed from treatment much more quickly than patients from higher classes, the lower class psychotic is rarely perceived as "ready" to leave treatment.

In comparing patients of Classes III–V who have been admitted to the hospital for the first time with patients of the same classes who have been hospitalized previously, a striking finding emerges: The new patient is more likely to receive custodial care than the longer time patient! The implication is that patients of these classes are not given custodial care because of the failure of other methods but are somewhat routinely assigned to this very limited care. In Class V, for example, 64 per cent of the patients who are receiving custodial care had not had any previous treatment.

No discussion of treatment is complete that omits mention of expenditures and fees. The chapter dealing with this material contains more detailed comparative information than is available in any other source. One of the most salient findings is that the mean cost per day in private hospitals is higher for Class IV patients than for patients in the higher classes ($31.11 to $23.76 for a Class I person). This result which is contrary to expectation results from the discriminatory discounts granted higher status persons. Further, the higher status persons receive the most expensive therapies which leads the authors to state: "To use a metaphor, private hospitals are designed for the 'carriage trade' but they are supported by the 'shock box.'" A similar relationship is found in clinics where treatment expenditures per patient are strongly related to class status, with the result that "Class II patients receive the most therapy and Class V patients the least." This finding is particularly disturbing since the clinics have presumably been developed to serve the psychiatric needs of lower status persons.

F. RECOMMENDATIONS

In a thoughtful and interpretive summary of the implications of their findings for the problem of the mentally ill in our society, Hollingshead and Redlich point to the gap between the extent of the need and the resources currently available to meet it. While they give proper emphasis to the financial problem (what America needs is a "good five-dollar psychotherapist"), they also point to the difficulties that result from the differences in cultural values and role expectations between psychiatrists and patients from the lower social classes. They note that psychiatrists tend to come from the upper and middle classes and have outlooks which lead many of them to dislike Class IV and V patients and to disapprove of the behavior patterns of Class V individuals.

More than money will be needed. Among the possible partial solutions to the problems that they suggest are proposals that psychiatrists themselves be trained to recognize and deal squarely with the differences between themselves and patients from other classes; that new forms and modes of therapy be developed to reach the "difficult" patient (whose difficulty seems to reflect the difference between his and his therapist's class positions more than his psychological disturbance); and, that new non-medical therapists, whose education would be less expensive than psychiatrists', be trained to treat the emotional disorders which do not have medical problems associated with them.

II. Discussion of Findings

This detailed and complex study touches on a large number of important issues concerning the social context of mental illness and its treatment. It represents a distinct step forward in a number of ways.

Three features of the study are especially notable: (a) The presentation of incidence figures as well as prevalence data is strongly to be commended. (b) The method of estimating the social class of patients and the community, despite the limitations indicated below, is an improvement over those employed in previous studies which tended to assume that all who lived in a particular area or paid a similar rent were in the same class. (c) Social class is linked to many more facets of mental illness than just the rate and kind of mental illnesses; in particular, the link of class to the treatment process is innovational.

In our discussion we have restricted ourselves to and organized our comments around three topics that are critical for the study: the concepts of social class and mental illness; the validation of the basic hypotheses; and, the implications of the study for psychiatric treatment.

A. CONCEPTS OF SOCIAL CLASS
AND MENTAL ILLNESS

Among sociologists, there is a variety of approaches to the problem of social stratification. Hollingshead and Redlich view the different classes as different primarily in their "styles of life" and use their combined scores on education, occupation, and residence as rough indices of these five different sub-cultures rather than as variables that are important in their own right.

In a study that directs explicit attention to the problems of getting "to" treatment and getting something "out of" treatment, the use of a combined index is unfortunate since it precludes analyses that might help to clarify what is involved in these processes. For example, it would have been of particular interest to be able to examine the relationships of education to the prevalence and treatment data in order to determine if an increase in education is associated with an increase in the propensity to view one's problems in psychological terms and therefore to benefit from psychological modes of treatment. Such a possibility is suggested by results in recent surveys of attitudes toward mental illness.[4] Enough evidence also exists to indicate that educational differences among individuals of the same occupational level are associated with differences in other characteristics, such as attitudes on public issues, so as to make the possibility of such crossbreaks especially desirable.[5]

In the Hollingshead system, some wage-earners are Class IV, others III or V, while white-collar workers are either III or IV. The class groupings thus become overlaps of various kinds, reducing their homogeneity, confusing comparisons and making generalizations difficult. An anomaly is that 18 per cent of New Haven was assigned to Class V in a time of prosperity. This figure seems high even with New Haven's migrant labor situation and may be due to a conceptualization of Class V which leads to a broad category characterized by widely varying behavior; for example, regular but unskilled workmen are lumped together with irregular but semi-skilled workmen.

Occupation scores correlate .88 with the original criterion on which the weighted index was based, and correlate less highly than this with residence and education (.50 and .72 respectively, p. 394). From this, it would appear that little would have been lost if occupation alone were used as the index of social class. On the other hand, much might have been gained by this procedure since, in addition to permitting potentially revealing analyses, it would have reduced the heterogeneity of the social class groups allowing for more precise interpretations of the results. (If the data for occupation, education, and area of residence have been separately recorded by the researchers, it would be a comparatively simple procedure to see what variations by education exist within levels of occupations as classified, for example, by the Bureau of the Census. Such additional "runs" of the data would extend their usefulness, especially by permitting comparisons with other investigations.)

The importance of the study's findings, and our confidence in them, rests in large part on the fundamental assumption that the two basic variables of social class and mental illness have been measured independently of each other—if not, then the found relationships must be viewed skeptically as possibly spurious. This seems an easy enough accumption to accept. However, the findings in a recent study [6] raise serious doubts as to its validity. In this exceptionally well-controlled study, Haase is able to demonstrate that the same set of presenting symptoms is diagnosed as more severe when the patient is perceived by subtle cues to be a working class person than when he is seen as in the middle class. In the Hollingshead-Redlich study, despite the safeguards, this bias might be reflected in such findings as the relatively higher rates of psychoses as compared to neuroses when one moves down the populations coming into treatment as well as the prevalence rates of persons in treatment for the different classes. One such study, of course, is insufficient grounds for rejecting the findings presented here. The issue, however, is of such crucial importance that the final acceptance of the findings must rest on further investigations of the relationship of class to the diagnostic process itself.

B. THE VALIDATION OF HYPOTHESES

Compared to most investigations of complicated areas in social science, this book is a model of clarity with regard to the presentation of its guiding hypotheses and the procedures by which these hypotheses were tested empirically. The assumptions behind each decision in the development of the research design are stated explicitly and the basic instruments are described with sufficient detail so as to permit other researchers to replicate the study with exactitude.

This report is organized around three hypotheses that were formulated explicitly and tested directly. (Findings on two other hypotheses dealing with social mobility and the relation of class to developmental factors in psychiatric disorders will be reported in the companion volume by J. K. Myers and B. H. Roberts, *Family and Class Dynamics in Mental Illness*, New York, John Wiley & Sons, 1959.) Briefly, the hypotheses, which we have quoted earlier, state that the social class structure is related to the treated prevalence of mental illness, the specific types of diagnosed psychiatric disorders, and the types of treatment administered by psychiatrists to patients. The authors conclude that their findings confirm these hypotheses, and we have reported the relevant findings in our expository section above. At this point, we shall re-examine their interpretations of some of the critical tables.

One of the major faults in the authors' approach to their findings is found in the first direct comparison that they present between the proportions of patients and the proportions of persons in the community in each of the five social classes (see Table A). Only *one* class, Class V, has disproportionately more patients than its frequency in the population, and *all* the other classes have less patients than would be expected. (If the data in this table are re-computed with the omission of Class V, the Chi Square test—the statistic used to evaluate all of the major findings—remains statistically significant but is markedly reduced in size, and the disproportionate contribution of Class IV is only 4 per cent more than expected, and of Class III, 3 per cent less than expected.)

While at various points they note that the major difference is between Classes IV and V, they include in their summary of this table the statement that "The lower the class, the greater proportion of patients in the population." The same interpretive tendency is found in their discussion of class differences on adjusted rates of mental illness (p. 210) where they ignore the fact that the Class III rate is actually *lower* than the rate in Class I–II. Again, in commenting on the class differences in incidence rates, they state (p. 212) "In a word, class status is linked to the incidence of treated mental illness." (The rates are shown in Table F.) A re-computation of these data, omitting Class V, reveals Class III and *not* Class IV as having a higher than expected number of patients.

Basing their remarks on the data we have just reviewed, Hollingshead and Redlich conclude their chapter by stating

> . . . enable us to conclude that Hypothesis I is true. Stated in different terms, a distinct inverse relationship does exist between social class and mental illness. The linkage . . . follows a characteristic pattern; Class V, almost invariably, contributes many more patients than its proportion of the population warrants. Among the higher classes there is a more proportionate relationship. . . . (p. 217).

What we are attempting to point out by this close review of their data is that the authors' tendency to report that there is a consistent and ordered inverse relationship between social class and mental illness is simply not an accurate interpretation of their findings. It would have been, as a matter of fact, more consistent with their "styles of life" view of social classes to have stressed what we believe is the major finding, namely the consistent differences between Class V and the other classes, with the differences that exist among the latter not clearly and consistently patterned in a hierarchal fashion.

Our attention was first called to this problem by the comments and remarks of other professionals and students who were summarizing the book's findings in seminars and staff meetings by statements like "The lower the class the higher the rates of mental illness." The general tendency in discussions of class differences to group together Classes I–II versus Classes IV and V is another contributor to the misinterpretation of their findings. The book is so notable for its clarity in other respects that it is unfortunate that the interpretive summaries lend themselves so easily to confusion and distortion. (It might also be mentioned that synoptic statements of the order, "The lower the class the higher the rates of mental illness," ignore the nature of the Hollingshead-Redlich data which are of treated illnesses, not total illnesses. The relation between treated and total illnesses in different social classes is not known and the total rates cannot be assumed to be a standard coefficient of the treated rates.)

In interpreting the relationships between class and specific types of neurosis and psychosis (Hypothesis II) there is a tendency to use an overall significant statistic to report differences for specific disorders when the latter are less systematic and depend on rather small numbers of cases. For example, their two basic tables (Tables C and D) demonstrate that overall, there are statistically significant associations of the five classes with the seven specific neuroses and with the five specific psychoses. They then refer to an "extreme concentration" of hysterical patients in Class V. Examination reveals there are only eight Class V patients in this category and the reduction of the cell by two or three cases would erase its percentage difference from Class IV. Again, they state, "The higher the class, the larger the proportion of patients who are affective psychotics," yet a reduction of three cases among those in Classes I–II would completely eliminate the differences from Class I through Class IV, leaving only Class V as different from the others.

So far, except for one illustration, we have been concerned in our discussion with the reports and interpretations of prevalence data which permit specific tests of the authors' explicit hypotheses and form the major substantive findings around which the book is organized. We have already remarked on the important distinction between prevalence and incidence and will turn now to the findings on the incidence of specific disorders.

Hollingshead and Redlich separately compute rates for each of the "components" of prevalence: new cases arising during their six months interval of observation (incidence), cases that re-entered treatment during that period (re-entry), and those that had been in treatment at the beginning of the period (continuous). They then proceed to test for significant differences among the classes for each of these rates, separately for neuroses and psychoses. (See data presented in Table G. We consider them to be the most important findings in the book on social class and mental illness.)

They find significant differences among the classes for each of the component rates *except* for the incidence of neurosis. In other words, there is no systematic relationship between social class and the rates of coming into treatment for neurosis.

**Table G—Incidence, Re-entry, Continuous, and Prevalence Rates per
100,000 for (Treated) Neuroses and Psychoses—by Class
(Sex and Age Adjusted)**

NEUROSES

Class	Incidence	Re-entry	Continuous	Prevalence
I–II	69	44	251	349
III	78	30	137	250
IV	52	17	82	114
V	66	35	65	97
$x^2 =$	4.40	8.64	69.01	56.05
df	3	3	3	3
p	$<.05$	$<.05$	$<.001$	$<.001$

PSYCHOSES

Class	Incidence	Re-entry	Continuous	Prevalence
I–II	28	44	117	188
III	36	38	217	291
IV	37	42	439	518
V	73	88	1344	1505
$x^2 =$	12.37	15.73	748.47	741.09
df	3	3	3	3
p	$<.01$	$<.01$	$<.001$	$<.001$

Source: Table 16, p. 235.

It appeared to us that the statistical significance of the other relationships of class and incidence rates (both new and old cases) might
depend almost entirely on Class V. We re-computed incidence and re-
entry rates for neuroses and psychoses, omitting Class V from the
calculations. The test showed *no* significant differences among Classes
I through IV. (Chi Square for the incidence and re-entry of neuroses
are 1.96 and 3.36; for psychoses, the figures are .28 and .08. None of
these is significant at the .05 criterion value.)

To summarize these findings: there are *no* significant differences
among social classes I–V in the incidence of new cases of neuroses.
There are *no* significant differences among classes I through IV in the
incidence of new or old cases of neuroses *or* psychoses. Class V has
significantly different and higher rates of new and old cases of psychosis
(and the inclusion of Class V in the computations suggests that Class
IV has a *lower* rate of re-entry of neurotics than the other classes).

The contrast between the significant differences in prevalence and
the findings we have just reported of non-significant differences in
incidence is extremely important. By concentrating on the prevalence
data, an important finding for sociologists and psychiatrists—that
Class IV has the lowest overall mental illness rate—is ignored, and some
traditional views about the incidence of mental illness are left un-
touched. There is an implication at many points throughout the book
that the prevalence findings may be interpreted as class differences in

the likelihood of developing various mental illnesses (the descriptions of class sub-cultures in Chapters 3 and 4, and the discussions of social class and the life cycle in Chapter 12 are presumably given an important place in the book because treated prevalence data are to some extent thought of in these terms). It is also likely that the findings will be discussed in both the lay and professional literature to some extent as if the prevalence findings did bear on questions of etiology.

Perhaps a recent statement on this by Dr. Redlich himself may serve to minimize such a tendency. "The New Haven study has not really brought out anything which is of etiological significance in explaining differences in prevalence, and prevalence in itself is not a very good measure from an epidemiological viewpoint. . . . We found, as far as the accumulation of schizophrenics in the lower classes is concerned, that although not entirely, it is mostly due to the fact that the lower socio-economic groups get different treatment and have different opportunities for rehabilitation." [7] It is unfortunate that this position was not stated as clearly in the book under review. In addition to these restrictions on the interpretation of the prevalence findings, and the fact that the data deal only with *treated* prevalence, our re-examination of the incidence data also supports the conclusion that the etiological significance of social classes for mental illness is yet to be demonstrated.

When the spurious issue of etiology is brushed aside, the book's major findings stand out quite clearly and they are of extreme importance. Essentially, these *refer* to the differential psychiatric treatment given to patients of different classes with the apparent result of an accumulation of cases in the lower classes. Besides the differences between the distributions of incidence and prevalence rates that we have discussed there are other findings that bear on this. The differences among classes on the paths to treatment, the types of treatment received, and the costs of treatment are important contributions to the understanding of the social aspects of medicine.

It should be noted that in many respects the study is an important followup of the Committee on Costs of Medical Care more than two decades ago.[8] By carefully studying how many and what kinds of persons are in psychiatric treatment, the nature and place of treatment, how much medical time is spent with them, and the costs of treatment, a baseline is provided for discussion of the most effective social utilization of psychiatric manpower and resources. Coupled with other data, the present study provides an opportunity to define the "psychiatrically indigent" category—undoubtedly a much more inclusive category than that of the "medically indigent."

The authors' conclusions regarding class bias in treatment do not depend on the other findings and do not suffer from the weaknesses of method and interpretation that we have discussed above. They are to be commended for their courage in facing this important issue squarely and for their no less courageous attempt to meet the problem by a forthright presentation of a number of proposals that are decidedly controversial in American psychiatric practice.

C. IMPLICATIONS OF THE STUDY

In view of the preceding discussion, we shall not take space to discuss the important theoretical issues about the relationship of social factors to the etiology of mental illness.[9] Rather, we shall restrict our remarks in this section to the study's implications for psychiatric practice.

It has been well known before this that the needs of the population for psychiatric treatment were not being met adequately. What this investigation demonstrates beyond this, is that the distribution of available resources is socially discriminatory. We believe that a serious moral question is also involved in this discovery, since the psychiatric profession legitimates its claim to high status and to social and economic rewards on the grounds that it functions in a "universalistic" nondiscriminatory way. Actually, it operates in such a way as to restrict its "best" treatments to persons in the upper social classes.

We agree that the need requires the development of new modes of treatment, better understanding by psychiatrists of social class patterns, and their reactions to them, and new types of non-medical therapists. We wish, however, to point to some of the assumptions involved in these recommendations and raise some questions that deserve further consideration. First, the authors appear to assume that psychoanalysis or some form of analytic psychotherapy is always ideally preferable to a directive or organic mode of treatment, and that therefore Class IV and V patients are being short-changed. At one level this is a value question since the different therapies are associated with different therapeutic goals, and the issues of what goals to select and who is to decide upon them lie in the realm of value. At another level, this is an empirical issue of whether other forms of treatment might not actually be more effective, rather than simply less costly and less demanding for certain groups of patients. Definitive empirical evidence does not yet exist to provide an answer to this question.

There also seems to be the assumption that it is the psychiatrist who relatively completely controls the type of treatment given. It may be that patients search out psychiatrists who will give them their preferred type of treatment and reject non-preferred treatments, both from private practitioners and within the clinics and hospitals. The selective process and pressures emanating from the patient cannot be ignored in a full account of the biased pattern of psychiatric treatment.

This leads to a related point. There is a tendency to discuss the problem of therapy with working class and lower class persons in a way that implies that the therapist wishes to give the patient "more" than the patient wishes. For example, some practitioners assert that the therapist wants to help the patient come to his own decisions, but the patient only wants to be told what to do; the therapist wants to establish a long term relationship with the patient, but the patient wants a quick remedy; the therapist wants deep and lasting changes, but the patient is satisfied with superficial and transient results. The alternatives may be multiplied beyond this, but what is important is that they seem to imply a rejection of the therapist and the therapeutic process by the patient. We should like to suggest that quite the opposite may be happening. Rather than asking for "less" than he is offered, the working class and lower class patient may actually be asking for "more" in the sense that he wants a fuller, more extensive, and more permanent relationship than is possible either within the traditional definition of the therapeutic relationship or in terms of what the therapist wishes to enter into. In other words, it may be the therapist who drives the patient from treatment because he cannot handle the demands placed upon him, rather than the patient who drops treatment because its demands are too much for him.[10] (With the knowledge we have of working class and ethnic cultures it is difficult to subscribe without qualifications to assertions that patients from these groups do not like to talk or have special difficulties entering into relationships. The basic questions are: What kind of relationships, with whom, and under what conditions? In raising these questions we are suggesting that some prevailing interpretations of working class and lower class life may have to be re-evaluated.)

III. Research Perspectives in Social Psychiatry

Perhaps nothing emerges more clearly from the book viewed as a whole than the need for continued systematic research on the relationships of social factors to mental illness and psychiatric practice. Our critical comments on the Hollingshead-Redlich study have included suggestions as to how future studies of a similar nature might be improved. We should like at this point to note briefly some additional areas and questions for research that have been suggested by both the achievements and shortcomings of this work.

A. THE ETIOLOGY AND EPIDEMIOLOGY OF MENTAL DISORDERS

The etiological significance of social variables such as social class for various mental disorders remains an open question. Clearly, studies of "true" incidence will be needed before we are able to suggest answers to this question. In design these studies will have to be comparative and longitudinal and they will have to permit the isolation and control of different and changing forms of psychiatric practice. Field investigations of "true" prevalence such as the "Midtown" and "Stirling County" studies, reports from which are now in preparation, will provide a beginning for understanding the relationships between such data and those for treated prevalence as reported by Hollingshead and Redlich. It is to be hoped that future investigations, in addition to including alternative indices of social class, will also be concerned with the effects of other social factors such as, for example, community and family structure, and ethnicity.[11]

More attention will have to be paid to the general problems of psychiatric diagnosis and classification. The nomenclature of the clinic is not particularly useful for field studies, but conceptual links must be forged among the different typologies and indices that are being developed. In all of this work it will be of particular importance not to neglect the fact that the process of psychodiagnosis is inherently a social process and full understanding requires the perspectives of sociological theory and analysis. In addition to data on types of disorders, the extension of a public health approach to the control of mental illness will require information on the severity and the extent of disability associated with mental illness so that large-scale social programs in the prevention, termination, or reduction of such disabilities may be undertaken.[12]

B. PATTERNS OF PSYCHIATRIC TREATMENT

The findings presented by Hollingshead and Redlich on the different paths to treatment followed by patients from different classes are very important, and this is an area in which we need to know much more. The history of the illness before the point of referral, the factors that enter into seeking help at a particular stage, the relation of time and type of referral to outcome, and the relationships of all of these to social class require exploration in further studies.

What variables and processes are involved in the initial phase of treatment that seems to be such an important determinant of later outcomes? How much choice is available to the patient and how does he exercise his choice? How does the process of class discrimination in assignment and treatment operate in clinics and other treatment facilities? How are the goals of treatment set and how are these goals related to the different values of patients and therapists and to their images of and attitudes toward each other?

The list of important research questions may be expanded easily. We wish to end with a special plea for evaluative studies of the effects of various forms of psychiatric treatment. There is a desperate shortage of systematic evidence in this area, and without such evidence our decisions regarding proper treatment tend to be determined by current fashions in psychiatry or by implicit social values and assumptions.

Although we have been critical of some of the methods and interpretations we should like to stress our respect and admiration for this fascinating and exciting study. It is a book of considerable significance that focuses our attention on a range of important problems which had barely been discussed before. We regard it as a study of psychiatric practice rather than as one of epidemiology, and consider it a great contribution to the study of treatment. If it is not the definitive study that hopefully may be made in the next decade or two, that study will, in part, be possible because of the pioneering work of Hollingshead and Redlich.

Notes

1. Hollingshead, August B. and Redlich, Frederick C.: *Social Class and Mental Illness*, New York, John Wiley & Sons, 1958, 442 pp., $7.50.

2. A number of persons commented on earlier versions of this paper. In particular, the exposition has benefitted from the detailed comments of Ernest M. Gruenberg, M.D., Matthew Huxley, and Frank Riessman. Only the authors, of course, bear responsibility for the final formulations presented in this paper.

3. Calculating the data in terms of the psychiatric agency involved reveals some important practices: 30 per cent of the patients treated by private practitioners and by public clinics are suffering from various types of psychotic disorders.

4. See relevant findings in the forthcoming National Opinion Research Center study directed by Shirley Star; *People's Attitudes Concerning Mental Health*, New York: Elmo Roper, 1950; and Elaine and John Cumming, *Closed Ranks*, Cambridge: Harvard University Press, 1957.

5. Stouffer, Samuel: *Communism, Conformity and Civil Liberties*, New York: Doubleday, 1955. Riessman, Frank: "Workers' Attitudes Toward Participation and Leadership," unpublished doctoral dissertation, Columbia University, 1955.

6. Haase, William: "Rorschach Diagnosis, Socio-Economic Class, and Examiner Bias," unpublished Ph.D. dissertation, New York University, 1956. For a general discussion of diagnostic tests and social class, see Riessman, Frank, and Miller, S. M.: "Social Class and Projective Tests." *Journal of Projective Tests*, December, 1958, 22, pp. 432–439.

7. *Symposium on Preventive and Social Psychiatry*, April 15–17, 1957. Walter Reed Army Institute of Research, Washington, USGOP, 1958. (P. 199).

8. See the report by Lee, Roger I. and Jones, Lewis Webster: *The Fundamentals of Good Medical Care*. Chicago: University of Chicago Press, 1933. They quote Dr. Olin West that ". . . the outstanding problem before the medical profession today is that involved in the delivery of adequate, scientific medical service to all the people, rich and poor, at a cost which can be reasonably met by them in their respective stations in life." "Adequate medical care" is defined in both quantitative and qualitative terms: ". . . a sufficient quantity of good medical care to supply the needs of the people according to the standards of good current practice." (P. 3)

9. Nor shall we discuss a problem that we have alluded to several times—how representative the census of patients is of all of the mentally ill people in New Haven, especially in regard to the social class distribution of the total. Since individuals of different classes come to clinic and other treatment through different routes, it may not be assumed that the census sampled to the same degree the actual amount of all mental disorders in the different social classes.

10. Some evidence exists that many patients of other classes may have similar sets of expectations and present similar problems to psychiatrists. In a by-product of the study under review, it has been found that Class III and V patients exhibit strong resemblances in their expectations of therapy. Our hypothesis would be that it is the low-educated members of Class III who especially exhibit "non-psychiatric" attitudes. Redlich, F. C., Hollingshead, A. B., and Bellis, E.: "Social Class Differences in Attitudes Towards Psychiatry." *American Journal of Orthopsychiatry*, January, 1955, 25, pp. 60–70.

11. For an illustration of the relation of one aspect of community structure, namely, multiple- vs. single-family dwelling units, to cerebral arteriosclerosis and senile psychosis, see New York State Department of Mental Hygiene, *Fourth Annual Report of the New York State Health Commission*, 1954, pp. 31–33; on the impact of ethnic variations in family

structure, see Barabee, Paul and von Mering, Otto: "Ethnic Variations in Mental Stress in Families with Psychotic Children." *Social Problems*, October, 1953, 1, pp. 48–53; and Singer, J. L. and Opler, M. K.: "Contrasting Patterns of Fantasy and Motility in Irish and Italian Schizophrenics." *Journal of Abnormal and Social Psychology*, July 1956, 53, pp. 42–47.

12. Gruenberg, Ernest M.: "Application of Control Methods to Mental Illness." *American Journal of Public Health*, August, 1957, 47, pp. 944–952.

CHAPTER 42

The Shifting Role of Class in Political Attitudes and Behavior

PHILIP E. CONVERSE

The first studies of social class to use the new techniques of large-scale sampling documented a number of relationships between status and politico-economic attitudes. Such empirical demonstration was a valuable, if not always surprising, contribution. We learned, for example, that people lodged in different strata of the social system have tended to hold somewhat different attitudes regarding the benevolence of the existing social order, much as interest-group theory and classical views on stratification had postulated. We became familiar, furthermore, with the finding that different status groups may implement these beliefs in differential voting behavior. Thus, over the last 25 years, high-status persons in the United States have favored the Republican party while the less fortunately placed have subscribed instead to the Democratic party.

Although some particulars of these findings have been subject to controversy, their broad outlines have been so completely absorbed into the basic lore of attitude research as to become commonplace. We have come to consider them, implicitly at least, as relationships

of roughly constant magnitude and, hence, diminishing fascination. However, the passage of time now permits us to evaluate the extent to which changes can occur in the role played by social class in political opinions and behavior.

It is only such observation of stability and change over a lengthening period of our national history that can provide an empirical test for some of the more important hypotheses as to the significance of social class in a modern society. The first round of survey studies in this area served for the most part to document only a static description of class differences. There was found to be indeed a visible divergence of opinion on matters of economic interest between members of different class levels. But the grand dynamic models of the classic-stratification theorists received little empirical support or challenge in these materials. Marx, for example, had taken the existence of social strata with divergent interests as a postulate, self-evident beyond need for proof, and proceeded to spin a theory concerning the social and economic conditions under which class consciousness might be expected to vary

665

as modern industrial society developed. However obsolete his speculations may appear today, it can be fairly said that we have yet to exploit modern research vehicles toward a more adequate understanding of the dynamic role which status plays in the political life of a modern state as it passes through depression, war, and prosperity.

It is our theses that in the United States the strength of relationships between status and political variables is subject to more short-term variation than is generally recognized. Yet we hold that this instability need not be a source of dismay to the student of social class; if we accept the strength of these relationships as a critical variable in its own right and seek its determinants in the major events which impinge upon the social system, we shall have taken a first step toward putting a dynamic view of social class and its political consequences on an empirical footing.

Such analysis requires comparative measurement over time. A national sample survey conducted by the Survey Research Center (SRC) of the University of Michigan during October and November of 1956 permits a detailed comparison of class attitudes in 1956 with those encountered by Richard Centers in his 1945 study.[1] A cross-sectional sample of 1,772 respondents, chosen by strict probability methods from all adult citizens living in private households in the United States, was interviewed just prior to the 1956 presidential election and again just subsequent to it. Since the 1945 survey involved a sample of 1,097 adult white males, the following comparison is based upon the 728 white male respondents interviewed in the 1956 study.[2]

Centers' detailed description of the assignment of respondents to an occupational status in his pioneering study allowed us to make a matching array within our sample. The second measure of status, the respondent's self-assignment to a social class, was obtained in 1956 through an elaboration of the original question devised for this purpose by Centers.[3] Each person interviewed was asked: "There's quite a bit of talk these days about different social classes. Most people say they belong either to the middle class or to the working class. Do you ever think of yourself as being in one of these classes?" If the response was affirmative, the respondent was simply asked "Which one?" If the response was negative, the ensuing question was "Well, if you had to make a choice, would you call yourself middle class or working class?" In both cases, the respondent was then asked, "Would you say you are about an average (class selected) person or that you are in the upper part of the (class selected)?"

The results of the class identification question are shown in Table 1. Although three rebellious spirits—all women—

---

[1] The 1956 study was carried out at the Survey Research Center under the direction of Angus Campbell and Warren E. Miller. It was supported by a grant from the Rockefeller Foundation. A full report of the study will become available at a later date. The 1945 study by Richard Centers is fully reported in *The Psychology of Social Classes* (Princeton: Princeton University Press, 1949).

[2] It might be noted that the findings to be presented here hold generally for the total cross-sectional sample, however. While certain factors such as the relative indeterminacy of the occupation status of many women act to reduce slightly the clarity of some of the relationships reported, our data for females look substantially like those for males. On the other hand, inclusion of nonwhite respondents would, if anything, serve to sharpen relationships, as such racial groups fall at an extreme of the status continuum and manifest opinions and political behavior appropriate to this extreme. Nevertheless, our interest in the specific magnitude of relationships over time legislated against treatment here of any elements of the sample not directly comparable with the 1945 data.

[3] This question was phrased: "If you were asked to use one of these four names for your social class, which would you say you belonged in: the middle class, lower class, working class, or upper class?"

TABLE 1

SUBJECTIVE CLASS IDENTIFICATION OF WHITE MALES

| | SRC 1956 | | | | SRC 1952 | Centers 1945 |
	Aware of social class	Unaware of social class	Total		Total	Total
Average working class	50%	42%	47%	(Lower class) 2%		1%
Upper working class	11	+10	11	(Working class) 59		51
Working-class total	61	52	58	61		52
Average middle class	33	34	33	(Middle class) 35		43
Upper middle class	6	5	5	(Upper class) 1		3
Middle-class total	39	39	38	36		46
Reject idea of class		5	2	1		1
Don't know, not ascertained	*	4	2	2		1
	(N = 456)	(N = 272)	(N = 728)		(N = 666)	(N = 1097)

* Less than one half of one percent.

assigned themselves to the "upper class" despite the wording of the question, it will be noted that we have sacrificed the differentiation of the handful of people who chose "upper" or "lower" class in the 1945 study to subdivide each major class into an "average" or "upper" segment more susceptible to detailed analysis. If, however, we restrict our attention to gross comparisons between frequencies in the two major classes, we find a sizeable shift from choice of middle class to choice of working class, by comparison with the 1945 distribution.

It is impossible to judge whether these differences are a result of a shift in underlying parameters in the interim, or whether more mechanical discrepancies are involved. The quota sample design used in the Princeton study may have been vulnerable to a systematic upward shift in economic status of respondents

chosen. It seems fairly safe to say, however, that the differences in distribution of class identification are not a result of the change in question wording, since we see that the Centers question repeated verbatim from a 1952 SRC study produced a distribution which coincides almost exactly with that found by the SRC using the revised wording in 1956 (Table 1).

As a final point of comparison, we find that the subjective choice of class affiliation as obtained with the 1956 question related to status as objectively determined by occupation in much the same fashion as it did within the 1945 data. Among the nonfarm portion of the sample, we find some tendency for higher-status respondents in 1956 to place themselves more frequently in the working class. Nonetheless, the correlation between the two modes of status measure-

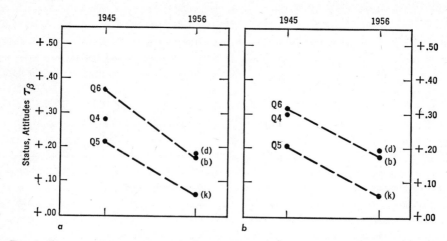

FIG. 1. Status and attitudes,* 1945 and 1956, showing (a) the relationships between attitudes and occupation status, and (b) the relationships between attitudes and subjective class. (Letters and numbers in parentheses refer to attitude items on the 1945 and 1956 questionaires.†)

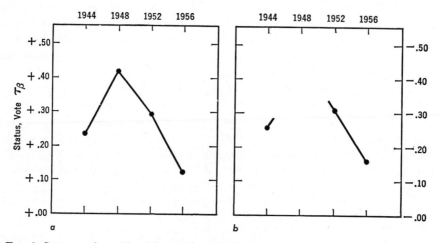

FIG. 2. Status and presidential vote,* 1944 through 1956, showing (a) the relationships between vote and occupational status, and (b) the relationships between vote and subjective class.

* We have followed the usage of the 1945 study in removing farm occupations from the basic occupation-status array. For purposes of comparability, therefore, all coefficients in Figures 1 and 2 are based on a subsample of white males reporting nonfarm occupations. The 1945 coefficients in Figure 1 represent an N ranging from 758 to 835, while the N for the 1956 coefficient varies between 525 and 574. In Figure 2, elimination of nonvoters reduces the N in 1945 to about 700, to 141 in 1948, 455 in 1952, and 480 in 1956. In all cases, the addition of white females to the Survey Research Center data would more than double the number of cases without any substantial effect on the coefficients involved.

† Question 4 in the 1945 study was "Would you agree that everybody would be happier, more secure, and more prosperous if the working people were given more power and influence in government, or would you say we would all be better off if the working people had no more power than they have now?" For questions 5 and 6, see footnote 6.

ment in 1956 ($\tau_\beta = .46$) is very close to that represented in the earlier study ($\tau_\beta = .49$).[4]

In sum, then, there seems to be little question about the comparability of measurement between the two studies with regard to the primary independent variables. Therefore, it seems reasonable to assume that any notable differences which we may find in relationships between these status measures and political variables after the lapse of a decade are due to actual changes in the American scene.

Social Class and Political Attitudes in 1956

Politico-economic attitudes constituted a major type of dependent variable for the 1945 study. From a large battery of questions concerning governmental policy asked in the 1956 SRC study we have chosen three which appear most closely related in content to the items employed by Centers in forming his scale of "conservatism-radicalism." These agree-disagree items are as follows:

(b) "The government in Washington ought to see to it that everyone who wants to work can find a job;"

(d) "The government ought to help people get doctors and hospital care at low cost;"

(k) "The government should leave things like electric power and housing for private businessmen to handle."

These questions have as a common core the distinction between what Centers referred to in 1949 as "two opposed philosophies of government—an individualistic one and a collectivistic one." Centers considers this "the central issue of all today's politico-economic strife" and the locus of the largest differences in class attitude.[5]

It would be dangerous to make comparisons of absolute response distributions for questions similar in spirit though not in letter. However, if the empirical situation is like that which Centers encountered, we would have a right to expect these basic politico-economic orientations to relate clearly to status variables much as they did in 1945. Instead, we find a general decline in the strength of these relationships (see Figure 1).

Each of our three questions shows a lower order of relationship with both subjective class and occupational status than Centers' data show for 1945. If we draw a trend line between the questions from the two studies which are most closely matched in content the contrasts are striking.[6] Assuming an equivalence between the questions, we find the em-

---

[4] The tau-beta statistic due to Kendall will be used throughout this analysis to fulfill the need for a measure of degree of association between variables. Such coefficients have been computed from the bivariate distributions published by Centers as well as for our own data. This statistic is derived from a rank-order correlation technique which handles any number of ranked categories or ties. The tau-beta tends to produce coefficients which are lower in magnitude than corresponding Pearson-product-moment coefficients computed from the same data. Therefore, the absolute magnitude of the coefficients may appear somewhat conservative to the reader accustomed to the Pearson r, and considerably more conservative than the tetrachoric r originally used by Centers.

[5] See Guy E. Swanson, Theodore M. Newcomb, and Eugene L. Hartley (eds.), *Readings in Social Psychology* (New York: Henry Holt & Co., Inc., 1952), p. 301.

[6] This matching equates our question (b) with Centers' question (6): "Which one of these statements do you most agree with? (1) The most important job for the government is to make it certain that there are good opportunities for each person to get ahead on his own. (2) The most important job for the government is to guarantee every person a decent and steady job and standard of living." The 1956 item (k) is likewise paired with question (5) in the Princeton study: "As you know, during this war, many private businesses and industries have been taken over by the government. Do you think wages and salaries would be fairer, jobs more steady, and that we would have fewer people out of work if the government took over and ran our mines and industries in the future, or do you think things would be better under private ownership?"

ployment-guarantee issue more highly related to both subjective and objective status than the free-enterprise issue in 1956, exactly as it was in 1945. But by 1956 both relationships have receded and the respective slopes of their decline are very close to parallel.

We cannot conclude that politico-economic attitudes are no longer significantly associated with statuses and self-perceptions in the economic order. Indeed, when we introduce more refined measurement, such as the distinction between the "average" and "upper part" of the two major subjective classes, we find that we can restore at least a part of the old strength of relationship which Centers treats. But if we can assume that the two gross classes and the politico-economic attitudes as measured in 1956 may be legitimately compared with those of Centers in 1945, it is beyond dispute that a sizable decline in the association between them has occurred in the interim.

SOCIAL CLASS AND POLITICAL BEHAVIOR IN 1956

A prime behavioral outlet for class consciousness is the act of voting. Centers acknowledges the relevance of the vote by employing it as a validity criterion for his scale of conservatism-radicalism and by describing its familiar relationships to various definitions of status.[7] The relationship between status and vote allows a more extensive test of the assertion that status differentials fluctuate considerably in their degree of impact on mass political behavior. The series of presidential election studies at the Survey Research Center provides

material for status-trend lines similar to those we have used for attitudes, yet with more frequent data.[8] By prefixing computations from Centers' tables on status and the vote, we can thus observe a span of four presidential elections.

Figure 2 reveals a striking range of variation in the strength of the status-vote relationship since the last Roosevelt election in 1944. The degree to which people of self-designated middle- or working-class status have given their votes to the presidential candidates of the Republican and Democratic parties respectively has fluctuated widely over little more than a decade.

In the face of this variation, two regularities which emerge from the data become most noteworthy. The first is the degree of coincidence between the objective and subjective variants of the status-vote relationship over time. As we have seen, class identification, while strongly related to occupation status, still enjoys considerable variation independent of it.[9] One form of the relationship could, for example, lag behind the other in its temporal cycles, or vary within narrower limits. Instead, we find psychological and social status, despite their differing division of the sample, producing almost identical relationships with the vote over three elections.

The second regularity is apparent if we compare Figures 1 and 2. The decline in the status-attitude relationships between 1945 and 1956 matches the two terminal points of the status-vote trend in provocative fashion. Unfortunately, we lack comparable attitudinal material for the intervening period with which to fill out Figure 1. We have, of course, no

---

[7] Centers, *op. cit.*, pp. 45–47, p. 115.

[8] Moreover, while the comparability of attitudinal items used in the two studies is not perfect, the act of voting provides nearly identical behaviors for comparison.

[9] For example, if we were to make the arbitrary assumption that people of nonmanual occupation were a "true" middle class, with the manual occupations constituting the working class, we would find roughly equivalent portions of the sample, amounting to more than a quarter of the total, indulging in "misclassification" upward or downward. Given such slippage between the two definitions of status, we might expect more differential variation between each of them and the vote.

guarantee that status-vote relationships need follow the fluctuation of relationships between status and certain relevant politico-economic attitudes. We shall have occasion to comment below on some of the factors which may disrupt direct translation of crystallized economic interest into voting behavior. Nevertheless, the congruence between the status-vote and status-attitude trends lends strong support to the conclusion that we are dealing with variation in an important property of a social system.

We suggest, therefore, that the *strength of relationship* between status and relevant politico-economic variables may be taken as a fairly reliable measure of such a system property at a point in time. For easy reference, we shall label this relational concept *status polarization*.[10]

By definition, status polarization is a group-level concept. It should indicate the degree to which groups at opposing ends of the status continuum have taken up mutually antagonistic value positions in the politico-economic sphere. We may imagine that as polarization increases it is likely to become manifest in values less immediately bound up with economic self-interest and public policy, so that a more salient and generalized antagonism exists between class groups. Its limiting case is class war.

The counterpart of status polarization at the individual level would be, therefore, the familiar concept of class consciousness. The fit is not perfect. We can imagine a mild divergence of beliefs between various class subcultures without any of the visible loyalty to a class group or hostility toward another class which we associate with full-fledged class consciousness. But in a rough way, the po-larization of a social system is taken to reflect the extent and intensity of class consciousness measured over a representative portion of its members.

Richard Centers was concerned with the measurement of class consciousness and his demonstration of the psychological reality of class is a move in this direction. However, his implication that "self-affiliation" alone is sufficient to distinguish the "internally cohesive . . . social groupings" which we tend to associate with class consciousness is not entirely convincing.[11] The claim is compounded by the use of the label "class identification" for the self-affiliation procedure. We can take "identification" to refer to a sense of belongingness with a group, a usage which accords fairly well with the concept of class consciousness. Or—and this is closer to the Centers procedure—we can take it to refer merely to the nominal assignment of an object to a category.

The interview question with which we prefaced our requests for self-assignment to a class was less an attempt to sort out respondents who were class-conscious in the old militant sense than to improve upon the Centers technique by distinguishing a group for whom the notion of class was most salient and self-allocation most nearly habitual. With this limited objective in mind, we shall speak of "class awareness" rather than "class consciousness." However, it seems reasonable to suppose that we have to some degree "tightened the ring" on a small group of people who may be sufficiently class-conscious to merit the term: we would expect the two thirds of our sample who admitted class awareness to contain most of them. Therefore, we may take our measure of awareness as a serv-

---

[10] It should be emphasized that it is difficult to attach any unequivocal meaning at this point to the *absolute magnitude* of coefficients of the relationship between status and attitudes or the vote. Given its operational definition, status polarization can show a hypothetical variation between .00 and 1.00. However, it is clear that the absolute magnitude of any coefficient is a function of the dependent variables employed.

[11] Centers, *op. cit.*, p. 28. See also pp. 74–76.

TABLE 2

STATUS-VOTE AND STATUS-ATTITUDE RELATIONSHIPS FOR WHITE MALES
ACCORDING TO AWARENESS OF SOCIAL CLASS *

| | Attitudes, 1956 | | | |
	1956 presidential vote	Item (b) Government guarantee of employment	Item (d) Government medical aid	Item (k) Government vs. private industry
Aware of social class	.20 (N = 358)	.17 (N = 430)	.22 (N = 416)	.08 (N = 388)
Unaware of social class	.07 (N = 207)	.09 (N = 228)	.12 (N = 227)	−.01 (N = 203)

* The cell entry indicates the τ_β for the relationship between subjective status and vote or attitudes; the number of cases is included for each coefficient.

iceable individual measure relating to status polarization.

We lack the data from earlier samples requisite to test the hypothesis that fluctuation in our measure of status polarization would be directly reflected in variation in class awareness over a period of time. But with minimal inference we may substitute a cross-sectional test for a longitudinal one. If our measure of awareness is reliable and our concept of status polarization meaningful, we should expect higher status-attitude and status-vote relationships within the group of people who are aware of class than within the group who are unaware.

Table 2 provides some support for this proposition. While the low general level of relationships between status and our dependent variables coupled with the large proportion of the sample who reported being "aware" imposes a ceiling on variation, there is indication that lack of awareness of class reduces the likelihood that the respondent will hold beliefs and will vote along lines most "appropriate" for his subjective class group. A more differentiated measure of awareness might show bigger differences in re-

lationships between these groups. However, it seems reasonable to suppose that status polarization in a society will reflect, over time, the varying extent and intensity of awareness of social class among its members.

SOME DETERMINANTS OF STATUS POLARIZATION

We turn now to the consideration of some of the factors that may account for variations in status polarization. Without a more adequate accumulation of data, we cannot pursue the argument closely at an empirical level. However, initial and cursory speculation will serve to mark out directions for investigation.

We assume that status polarization in a society reflects concern about the allocation of rewards and deprivations across the status continuum. In modern western democracies this concern has been primarily economic, directed at the distribution of wealth. Under prevailing expectations the inequity represented by a bimodal distribution of wealth would undoubtedly be accompanied by status polarization as well. Conversely, in the

United States the expansion of a middle class engaged in service occupations which fail to fit the old ownership-proletariat cleavage may currently be functioning to set upper limits on the polarization potential of the society.

In the shorter term, given a fairly constant pattern of wealth distribution, we would predict that polarization would increase in time of depression and decrease in periods of prosperity. The net decline of status polarization which we have seen in relevant attitudes between 1945 and 1956 lends credence to such a proposition, if we consider the general increase in prosperity which has characterized the period since the depression of the 1930's.

However, the sharp crest attained by status-vote relationships in 1948 suggests that this decline in attitude polarization may not have been monotonic during the intervening period. On the other hand, the mild levelling of the economy in the reconversion period between the end of the war boom and the recession of 1949 would hardly seem sufficient, in itself, to generate the rapid increase in polarization suggested by our data. We conclude that a single-factor theory is oversimplified and that we must cope with a more complex explanatory burden.

Consideration of the effects which war may have on status polarization is an obvious first step toward explanation of our data and consequent modification of our theory. Even an overseas war, it must be conceded, has a major impact on any population involved; yet this impact, in contrast to that of a depression, is less clearly distributed along status lines. Pressing questions of foreign policy eclipse those concerns of domestic economics which lead so directly to cleavage among status-interest groups. Therefore, we would propose that war and the pre-eminence of foreign policy considerations may act to reduce status polarization temporarily. For the case in point we would suggest that polarization tendencies carrying over from the depression

were dampened by the national crisis imposed by World War II but rebounded toward their prewar level after that conflict was concluded.

The temporary evaporation of the most burdensome foreign problems, along with the sudden unleashing of pent-up class-relevant actions, particularly the great postwar strikes in major industries, the struggle in Congress to place legislative controls on the activities of labor unions, and the development of first anxieties concerning an "inevitable" postwar depression, all must have contributed to a rise in the relative salience of domestic economic issues which had remained dormant during the war. After the 1948 peak of status polarization, we may speculate that the renewal of the threat of global war along with the outbreak of hostilities in Korea ought to have acted, in concert with increasing prosperity, to depress the level of status polarization once again.

If war and the consequent prominence of foreign-policy concerns do in fact work toward a reduction of polarization, we should be able to find traces of this effect in our 1956 sample, who were interviewed at a time when many voters were still apprehensive about war. It would follow from our argument that respondents showing marked concern over foreign policy could not be expected to vote in accordance with their subjective class position, whether or not they were aware of that position. On the other hand, respondents who were aware of their self-assigned status and for whom domestic policy controversies were more salient than foreign affairs and the possibility of war should show a higher status-vote relationship than that found in the total sample.

In the 1956 interview a series of open-ended questions which enabled the respondent to volunteer comments on aspects of the current political scene which were important for him permitted us to test this proposition. Table 3 bears out

TABLE 3

STATUS–VOTE RELATIONSHIPS FOR
WHITE MALES ACCORDING TO
RELATIVE CONCERN OVER DOMESTIC
OR FOREIGN ISSUES *

	Higher domestic issue concern	Equiva- lent concern	Higher foreign issue concern
Aware of social class	.25 (N=191)	.20 (N=105)	.00 (N=62)
Unaware of social class	.04 (N=99)	.14 (N=74)	−.02 (N=34)

* The cell entry indicates the τ_β for the relationship between subjective status and vote or attitudes; the number of cases is included for each coefficient.

our speculations rather well. While it represents once again a cross-sectional rather than a longitudinal test, we can infer that, other things equal, status polarization will vary inversely with the salience of war over a period of time.

Other political factors in addition to the intrusion of foreign policy may affect the level of polarization or act to disturb the correspondence between attitudinal polarization and the status-vote relationship. For example, rapid changes in degree of attitudinal polarization may be reflected only imperfectly in voting behavior due to loyalties which have grown up between the voter and a particular political party. Thus, theories of voting behavior which imply, by suggesting that status can affect the vote only

as an expression of economic self-interest, that the level of attitudinal polarization is an upper limit for a status-vote relationship, are not entirely adequate; we can imagine conditions under which party identifications born in time of polarization could conserve a status-vote relationship after relevant status attitudes had faded.

Other prominent elements in the election situation may tend to mitigate the simple expression of economic interest. A magnetic presidential candidate can have a broad public appeal which defies status lines. It is at least suggestive that three of the four elections recorded in Figure 2 were dominated by such personalities, while it is the remaining election in 1948 which produced the high-water point of the status-vote trend line. Once again we may turn to our 1956 data for evidence concerning the degree to which the personal characteristics of the candidates may draw the attention of the voters away from domestic economic concerns and thereby weaken status voting. Table 4, constructed on the basis of volunteered comments similar to those in Table 3, offers some support for this proposition, although the differences generated are less sharp than in the case where the intruding factor is concern over foreign affairs.[12]

Another type of political factor which must serve to set varying limits on the status-vote relationship over time is the convergence and divergence of the domestic-policy positions of the two major parties. However high the level of attitudinal polarization in the society, the impact of status on vote decision is de-

[12] It is interesting to note that further combination of political orientations of this sort can produce a "purified" group for whom the status-vote relationship is extremely high. Another category of volunteered response not subsumed under the domestic-issue comments treated above covers those cases in which a party or a candidate is seen to support or discriminate against—in economic terms—some group in the society such as the "working man," the "aged," etc. If we isolate an extreme group of 60 "aware" voters who gave the most frequent group references and domestic-issue comments, while giving a minimum of responses concerning foreign issues or the candidates, we find a τ_β of .49 between subjective status and vote, in contrast with the coefficient of .16 for white male voters over the total sample in 1956.

TABLE 4*

STATUS-VOTE RELATIONSHIPS FOR WHITE MALES
ACCORDING TO RELATIVE CONCERN OVER
DOMESTIC ISSUES AS OPPOSED TO INTEREST IN THE CANDIDATES

	High domestic issue concern	Balanced candidate interest & domestic issue concern	High candidate interest
Aware of social class	.30	.21	.17
	(N = 87)	(N = 103)	(N = 159)
Unaware of social class	.06	.10	.04
	(N = 47)	(N = 76)	(N = 81)

* The cell entry indicates the τ_β for the relationship between subjective status and vote or attitudes; the number of cases is included for each coefficient.

pendent on the degree to which the political parties proffer clear and equally polarized policy alternatives. Where party differences with regard to economic philosophy are not perceived by the electorate, political translations from attitude to vote will lose any discernible status significance.

It is likely that differences between the parties on status-relevant economic issues had by 1956 reached a decade's low. However, since our respondents were asked for each of our three questions on economic policy whether or not they saw differences in the way in which the two parties would handle the problem, we can inquire whether the status-vote relationship is not highest among people in the sample who still perceive these differences between the parties.

If we include the variable of class awareness as a precondition for meaningful status voting, we find the coefficients

in Table 5 which clearly support the general argument.[13] Of course, discrimination between the two parties with regard to domestic policy may accompany high salience of domestic issues, both at the objective policy level and in the reflection of these differences in perceptions of an interested segment of the electorate. Therefore, Table 5 is, in conjunction with Tables 3 and 4, part of a larger whole. If the salience of domestic issues rests at a constant level over a period of time, any tendency for the two parties to climb on the same domestic-policy bandwagon in appealing for public support must act as a force reducing status polarization of the vote.

By reflecting on some of the factors which must influence status polarization, we have been able to sort out of our 1956 sample a group for whom status remains a significant determinant of vote, despite the general decline of predictive efficacy

[13] Similar differences are evident in data from the Survey Research Center study of the 1952 election, although we lack in this case the variable of class awareness with which to sharpen the findings. Among people who saw differences between the two parties on general policy with regard to the degree of government welfare activity, the status-vote relationship was $.41(\tau_\beta)$ as opposed to .19 among those who failed to discriminate between the parties at this point.

TABLE 5*

STATUS-VOTE RELATIONSHIPS FOR WHITE MALES
ACCORDING TO PERCEPTION OF DIFFERENCES BETWEEN THE
PARTIES ON THREE DOMESTIC ISSUES

	Perceived no differences	Perceived differences on one or more issues
Aware of social class	.04 (N = 94)	.26 (N = 263)
Unaware of social class	.08 (N = 75)	.03 (N = 131)

* The cell entry indicates the τ_β for the relationship between subjective status and vote or attitudes; the number of cases is included for each coefficient.

of status over the total sample. Some of these factors, such as the intrusion of war, are likely to reduce the general level of polarization in the society as a whole. Others which we have discussed may intervene to disturb the direct translation of economic attitudes into political action. Both types of factors must be examined in detail if we are to piece together an understanding of the varying role of status differences in public life over time.

SUMMARY

By replicating, after the lapse of a decade, the Richard Centers study of relationships between objective and psychological status on the one hand and certain attitudes and the vote on the other, we have demonstrated considerable variability in the strength of these relationships. We have proposed that such variability be exploited as a tool by investigators who wish to bring some empirical "reality testing" to dynamic theories of class and status. Toward this end, we have tried to show the clear relationships between this "status polarization" as a property of a social system and the concept of individual class consciousness prominent in such dynamic theory.

Finally, we have taken recent variation in status polarization as the basis for a preliminary discussion of some of the factors which seem to determine its level, as measured by either status-attitudes or status-vote relationships at any point in time. We assume that investigation proceeding along such lines may increase our general understanding of the long-term effect of status position on political attitudes and behavior.

X

Dynamics of Change in Stratification Systems

Our understanding of the dynamics of social stratification has developed at two levels, corresponding to the distinction between a change *of* systems and a change *in* a system. Thus, looking backwards through history into an ever more hazy past, many social theorists have sought to understand the transformation from one type of society to another, especially the transition from feudalism to capitalism and the evolutionary stages of capitalistic development (see Marx, 1936; Weber, 1930, 1961; Pirenne, 1933; Smelser, 1959). Although various authors have settled upon somewhat different conceptions of how this transformation was accomplished and have approached the problem with alternative methodological strategies, a common definition of the problem has been reached by a surprisingly diverse collection of both contemporary authors and prominent figures of historical importance in the development of sociology. Broadly put, the problem is twofold: first, to describe as completely and as accurately as possible the differences that exist between two polar types of society which are often seen as lying at opposite ends of a folk-urban continuum or referred to as preindustrial and industrial and, sec-

ond, to devise an explanatory account both of the process of evolution along this continuum or between these two types and of the location of contemporary societies on this spectrum. So stated, a fair case could be made that this problem is *the* problem of sociology not only because it preoccupied the founding fathers of sociology but also because a great deal of work tangential to this problem is, in fact, derivative from it.

Obviously, in a brief introduction any attempt to summarize even one important contribution to our understanding of transitions between societal types would be rendered irrelevant by its superficiality. It is enough to note that the account given by Morton H. Fried in the selection included in this volume draws heavily upon the earlier formulations of Friedrich Engels (1884). Consequently, rather more emphasis is given to the understanding of change through the resolution of inherent conflicts than would be found in a statement of a contemporary functionalist. Parsons (1960, 1966), for example, sees the entire process of capitalist development as occurring within a framework of essentially constant and common values. Since changing the normative-value pattern amounts to moving from one society to another, societies are never *qualitatively* transformed, because such a transformation would constitute the historical boundary between present and past societies. Instead, societies are made increasingly complex through the process of structural differentiation in which the importance of kinship is typically eroded through the establishment of new structures (bureaucracies, corporations, schools, etc.) which take over functions previously fulfilled within the confines of extended kinship groups. Such structural differentiations are, in part, possible precisely because they are legitimized by a stable value pattern and they occur, in a manner of speaking, in response to social strains rather than fundamental conflicts. The last sentence clearly indicates the nuances of understanding which separate different accounts of the transformation between preindustrial and industrial societies and of the development of capitalism. The sharp distinction which is often drawn between the analyses of Marx and of Weber or Parsons is, at best, artificial because such a separation is made only at the expense of ignoring Parsons' use of the concept of strain. In fact, there is probably little in their respective theories which is inherently irreconcilable, though to say their accounts are identical would be as oversimplified as saying they are totally opposite. Marx did place the greater emphasis on both the role of conflict and of economic structures in the transformation, whereas Weber and Parsons have been more concerned with the role of values and normative patterns. There is a sense in which history is a dirt track for Marx and paved road for Weber and Parsons. Both track and road, however, have similar origins and destinations and take one over much the same terrain.

Various approaches have been used to understand the development of modern societies. Anthropologists, for example, have often sought to do so through the implicit or explicit comparison of "primitive" bands and tribes with more urbanized populations. Indeed, Redfield's (1947, 1953) now famous formulation of the folk-urban continuum is in many ways still the best contemporary statement of the problem. Others have sought to piece together the anthropological materials into a more comprehensive evolutionary perspective (see Steward, 1955; White, 1959; Parsons, 1966). Historians and, especially, such early sociologists as Marx and Weber have sought to promote understanding through analysis of particular historical cases, a strategy still evident in the work of contemporary sociologists such as Smelser (1959) and Bellah (1957). Archaeologists (see Adams, 1966) have really combined the strategies of doing anthropological field work and using historical records by utilizing the cultural artifacts which have survived ancient, often non-literate, civilizations as informants. Explicitly comparative studies of existing nation states have, of course, become increasingly important, especially as census and other official records have been made comparable between nations at diverse stages of development and as ethnographic reports have been abstracted into data archives suitable for comparative studies (see Murdock, 1957; Goody, 1969). All of the work flowing from these diverse methodological traditions is of direct relevance to the dynamics of stratification systems because it takes for its central problem the explanation of how modern society and, in particular, modern economic institutions and social inequalities developed. Needless to say, a very substantial part of the sociological corpus falls into precisely this area (see Lenski, 1966).

Another literature has, however, developed about the dynamics of social stratification *within* a system. The kind of problem which is typically posed involves the interrelations between changes in various facets of stratification (such as income inequality, educational and occupational distributions, or the degree of association between such variables, i.e., degree of crystallization) and other aspects of the social structure such as urbanization, political organization and so forth. Studies of this kind are often quantitative because the knowledge that there has been a change in the system or that there is a difference between systems to be explained is typically revealed by examination of similar quantitative evidence compiled at two points in time for the same country (or at the same point in time for different countries). The ability to make such quantitative comparisons rests on the assumption that the meaning of the operations by which they were collected did not change, in the one case, from one time to the next or does not vary, in the other case, from country to country. Such an assumption is tantamount to assuming that one is examining a change in a system rather than a change of systems. Thus, one probably would not find a comparison of the occupational distribution observed in a feudal regime with one found in a modern industrial society very satisfactory because these occupational distributions would be derived from such totally different occupational structures. Change *of* system tends to invalidate comparisons for many of the same reasons that comparative analyses of different types of primitive societies are invalid: the meaning of constant operations shifts with the change of the system. However, if it were possible, a comparative analysis of the occupational distribution found in medieval Europe with that found in 19th century Europe might nevertheless prove very important precisely because of the insight it would probably give into changes in occupational structure, even though one might not be able in the end to collapse the two structures into any form in which meaningful comparisons of the distribution of workers in them could be made.

The distinction between a change of and a change in a system is, in the final analysis, a little hazy. Probably any noteworthy change *in* a system (expansion of educational opportunities for example) introduces some corresponding changes in the meaning of constant research operations. Similarly, even the most dramatic changes of systems may not wholly invalidate comparative analysis. In other words, probably no comparison is either wholly valid or completely invalid. We can take this situation seriously by either reducing ourselves to writing historical almanacs and travelogs or by building theories of validity and error into our theories about societies.

One central facet of social stratification is, without question, the shape of the occupational distribution. As C. Wright Mills put it, " . . . occupations are the most ostensible and the most available 'way into' an understanding of stratification." (Mills, 1963) Our hazy knowledge of how changes in occupational distribution are brought about is typical, unfortunately, of our general state of knowledge about changes within social systems. A brief review of the difficulties one finds when approaching so seemingly simple a problem may prove instructive. One approach to understanding changes in occupational distributions is straightforward because it seeks only to isolate the correlates of such change rather than to specify how the change is effected. Thus, one can construct some index of change in the occupational distribution (see Reiss, 1957), describe the changes that have occurred by, for example, noting the rate of expansion of professional and technical workers, and, finally, identify the correlates of such changes by finding other distinctive features of social systems which covary with them, such as the growth of urbanization and the expansion of educational opportunities. Such an analysis, though useful in suggesting how the component parts of a social system hang together, is, however, less than satisfactory because it does not enable one to see precisely how transformations in either occupational distributions or in their correlates such as educational and urban-rural distributions are effected (see Treiman, 1970).

Abstractly, we can think of a change in the occupational distribution as the result of change in any one of three processes which give rise to the distribution of persons into a set of occupational categories. These three factors are the demand for personnel of various kinds, the available supply of persons with various kinds of skills and experiences, and the marketplace itself which matches, more or less effectively, the supply of persons to demand. But what do we know about the operation of these factors? The answer must be, not very much, at least not very much that is tangible, quantified and precisely summarized. On the demand side, for example, we know in a general way that the numbers and kinds of occupational roles which are created will respond to exogenous changes in technology and to the whole tempo and pattern of economic growth. The measurement of changes in demand is, however, barely underway with discussion and exploratory investigations of the volume and types of job vacancies (see NBER, 1966; Joseph, 1966). Our knowledge of the precise operation of the market is no less tenuous. We are confident that circles of kin and friends are very important factors in the way some people find jobs (see Sheppard and Belitsky, 1966), but these factors may be relatively more important in the determination of migration between labor markets than in the actual process of finding a job within a labor market. No one can say, however, exactly how persons and jobs get matched, even though we do know, through the study of the correlates of occupational attainment, a great deal about the end product of the matching process.

On the supply side, current research is in a relatively more satisfactory state. We know, of course, that in the very short run, supply is relatively fixed, though its occupational composition is constantly and predictably changing as each cohort moves through its working life. The supply of different skills changes slowly as new cohorts move through the educational system into the labor force and old ones die and retire. Because we now have, or are very close to having, a conceptually sound demographic model of the educational system (see Stone, 1966), it seems reasonable to assume that some strides will soon be made toward understanding how changes in the supply of persons with respect to occupational qualifications and experiences are effected.

Perhaps the most progress in understanding how changes in the occupational distribution are effected has been made by simply getting the demography of the problem straight so that we could begin to see precisely how the changes might occur. For example, as late as the 1950's, some sociologists supposed that the difference between occupational distributions of the labor force at thirty-year intervals or less could be interpreted as the net change attributable to occupational shifts within a generation since the average length of a generation (i.e., the mean age of mothers at the birth of their children) is about thirty years (see Kahl, 1953). Another common assumption was that intergenerational mobility tables (or matrices) represented the process of occupational mobility in a way that made it reasonable to compare current trends in occupational distributions with the algebraic result of using the occupational distribution of fathers and the father-son mobility matrix to produce the (actual) occupational distribution of sons and then reemploying the father-son mobility matrix to produce the expected occupational distribution of grandsons (see Hodge, 1966). In particular, the stable vector associated with an intergenerational occupational transition matrix was interpreted as indicating the direction of change in the occupational distribution (see Matras, 1960). Although adequate criticism of these assumptions requires examination of technical considerations beyond the scope of this volume (see Duncan, 1966), we can sketch here their basic demographic flaws.

The basic point is a simple demographic fact: there is no point in time at which all of the fathers of men now in the labor force were themselves simultaneously and exclusively in the labor force. Consequently, there is no conceivable way in which occupational distributions at two different fixed points in time could be considered to represent the occupational distributions of fathers and their sons. At any point in time, the labor force contains both fathers and sons of men currently in the labor force.

Similar considerations also invalidate the use of intergenerational occupational transition matrices to describe the direction of change in the occupational distribution. In this case, however, the problem is more nearly one of how the measurements are made than of the facts of demographic regimes. Most studies of intergenerational occupational mobility make observations upon the occupations of fathers at some common reference point in the life cycle of sons, such as the date of their birth or when they reached some specified age or entered the labor force. By way of contrast, the occupations of sons are typically observed at some fixed point in time, usually the survey date. Obviously, there is no single point in time at which all sons now in the labor force reached some common reference point in their life cycle. Consequently, while the occupational distribution of the sons in such a matrix corresponds to the occupational distribution at a fixed point in time (the survey date), the occupational distribution of the fathers in the table is dispersed over time according to the age of their sons now and the age at which the sons attained the criterion stage in the life cycle. Thus, if one wished to apply the observed intergenerational occupational transition matrix to sons currently in the labor force in order to arrive at an expected distribution of grandsons, assuming, among other things, that the processes observed in the last generation will persist into the succeeding one, he would need not the occupational distribution of sons at a single date but the occupational distribution of sons dispersed in time, as are the fathers' occupations in the mobility matrix in hand.

Conceptually, the error lies in regarding occupational mobility matrices such as those we have been discussing as reflecting occupational changes in a generation. A more appropriate matrix for the operations under discussion would relate the occupations of fathers at some specified point in the careers of fathers to the occupations of sons at a similar point in their careers. Such a matrix might not, however, be easily obtained with the usual survey methods since (a) not all respondents (sons) need yet have passed the relevant point in their life cycle and (b) at least some of the information would have to be based on recall of past occupational experiences rather than on reporting of current ones.

Recourse to intergenerational occupational mobility alone affords no hope of understanding how the occupational distribution at one time is transformed into the occupational distribution at some later point. An appropriate set of linear equations describing such a transition has only recently become available (see Matras, 1967; Goodman, 1968). They make allowance at least for levels and socioeconomic differentials in fertility and mortality, intergenerational occupational mobility and intragenerational occupational mobility. Like stable population theory, the theory of occupational transformation embedded in these equations contains a number of assumptions, some highly dubious. But at least we are on the verge both of seeing how the transition must take place and of specifying where our understanding is less than wholly satisfactory. Unfortunately, the recent literature on this subject is too technical for inclusion in a reader of the present kind.

The issues and strategies discussed in this brief introduction are touched upon in various ways by the papers included in this section. As already noted, the selection by Fried reviews the evolution of modern systems of stratification from those characteristic of agrarian, preindustrial societies. The Keyfitz paper sketches the way in which the modern world is itself stratified, broadly speaking, into old states and new nations and indicates how population demography is working in the aftermath of colonialism at least to maintain, if not to heighten, the stratification of the world. The paper by Petras and Zeitlin indicates how processes of contagion and diffusion of ideas may enable the consequences of stratification in one area to have important ramifications in adjacent regions with alternative bases of inequality. Finally, the paper by Duncan, while providing useful information on recent changes in the pattern of occupational mobility and occupational distribution in the United States, also shows how decomposition of changes into their logical components can lead to their partial understanding, even in the absence of complete information.

REFERENCES

Adams, Robert McC.
1966   The Evolution of Urban Society. Chicago: Aldine.

Bellah, Robert.
1957   Tokugawa Religion: The Values of Pre-industrial Japan. New York: Free Press.

Dahrendorf, Ralf.
1959   Class and Class Conflict in Industrial Society. Stanford, California: Stanford University Press.

deTocqueville, Alexis.
1955   The Old Regime and the French Revolution. New York: Doubleday.

Duncan, Otis Dudley.
1966   "Methodological issues in the analysis of social mobility." In Neil J. Smelser and S. M. Lipset (eds.), Social Structure and Mobility in Economic Development. Chicago: Aldine.

Engels, Friedrich.
1884   The Origin of the Family, Private Property, and the State, in the Light of the Researches of Lewis H. Morgan. New York: International Publishers, 1942 (reprinted).

Goodman, Leo A.
1968   "An elementary approach to the population projection-matrix and to the mathematical theory of population growth." Demography 5.

Goody, Jack.
1969   "Inheritance, property, and marriage in Africa and Eurasia." Sociology: The Journal of the British Sociological Association 3: 55-76.

Joseph, Myron L.
1966   "Job vacancy measurement." Journal of Human Resources 1: 59-80.

Kahl, Joseph A.
1953   The American Class Structure. New York: Rinehart.

Lenski, Gerhard E.
1966   Power and Privilege: A Theory of Stratification. New York: McGraw-Hill.

Marshall, T. H.
1950   Citizenship and Social Class. Cambridge: Cambridge University Press.

Marx, Karl.
1936   Capital. New York: Modern Library.

Marx, Karl, and Friedrich Engels.
1932   Manifesto of the Communist Party. New York: International Publishers.

Matras, Judah.
1960   "Comparison of intergenerational mobility patterns: An application of the formal theory of social mobility." Population Studies 14: 163-169.
1967   "Social mobility and social structure: Some insights from the linear model." American Sociological Review 32: 608-614.

Mills, C. Wright.
1963   "The sociology of stratification." In Power, Politics and People: The Collected Essays of C. Wright Mills. New York: Ballantine.

Murdock, George Peter.
1957   "World Ethnographic Sample." American Anthropologist 59: 664-687.

NBER
1966   The Measurement and Interpretation of Job Vacancies: A Conference Report. New York: National Bureau of Economic Research.

Parsons, Talcott.
1960   Structure and Process in Modern Societies. New York: Free Press.
1966   Societies: Evolutionary and Comparative Perspectives. Englewood Cliffs, New Jersey: Prentice-Hall.
1970   "Some further thoughts on the action theory of stratification." Sociological Inquiry 40 (Spring).

Pirenne, Henri.
1933   Economic and Social History of Medieval Europe. New York: Harvest Books.

Redfield, Robert.
1947   "The Folk Society." American Journal of Sociology 41: 293-308.
1953   The Primitive World and its Transformations. Ithaca: Cornell University Press.

Reiss, Albert J., Jr.
1957   "Change in the occupational structure of the United States, 1910 to 1950." In Paul K. Hatt and Albert J. Reiss, Jr. (eds.), Cities and Society (revised edition). Glencoe, Ill.: Free Press.

Rosenberg, Hans.
1958   Bureauracy, Aristocracy and Autocracy: The Prussian Experience 1660-1815. Cambridge: Harvard University Press.

Schumpeter, Joseph.
1942   Capitalism, Socialism and Democracy. New York: Harper & Row.

Sheppard, Harold L., and A. Harvey Belitsky.
1966   The Job Hunt: Job Seeking Behavior of Unemployed Workers in a Local Economy. Baltimore: Johns Hopkins Press.

Smelser, Neil J.
1959   Social Change in the Industrial Revolution. New York: Free Press.

Steward, Julian.
1955   Theory of Cultural Change. Urbana: University of Illinois Press.

Stone, Lawrence.
1965   The Crisis of the Aristocracy: 1558-1641. London: Oxford University Press.

Stone, Richard.
1966   "Input-output and demographic accounting: A tool for educational planning." Minerva 4: 365-380.

Toennies, Ferdinand.
  1957 Community and Society. Trans. and ed. by Charles P. Loomis. East Lansing: Michigan State University Press.
Treiman, Donald J.
  1970 "Industrialization and social stratification." Sociological Inquiry 40 (Spring).
Weber, Max.
  1930 The Protestant Ethic and the Spirit of Capitalism. Translated by Talcott Parsons. London: Allen and Unwin.
  1947 The Theory of Social and Economic Organization. Translated by A. M. Henderson and Talcott Parsons. New York: Free Press.
  1961 General Economic History. Translated by Frank H. Knight. New York: Collier Macmillan.
  1968 Economy and Society. Translated by Gunther Roth and others. (3 volumes). Totowa, New Jersey: Bedminster.
White, Leslie A.
  1959 The Evolution of Culture: The Development of Civilization to the Fall of Rome. New York: McGraw-Hill.

CHAPTER 43

On the Evolution of Social Stratification and the State

MORTON H. FRIED

The evolutionists never discussed in detail—still less observed—what actually happened when a society in Stage A changed into a society at Stage B; it was merely argued that all Stage B societies must somehow have evolved out of the Stage A societies.

E. R. LEACH, 1954, p. 283

To some extent E. R. Leach's charge, which relates to the evolution of political organization, is unfair. The climate in which pristine systems of state organization took shape no longer exists. The presence of numerous modern states and the efficiency of communications have converted all movements toward state-level organization into acculturation phenomena of some degree. In fact, it seems likely that the only truly pristine states—those whose origin was *sui generis,* out of local conditions and not in response to pressures emanating from an already highly organized but separate political entity—are those which arose in the great river valleys of Asia and Africa and the one or two comparable developments in the Western Hemisphere. Elsewhere, the development of the state seems to have been "secondary" and to have depended upon pressures, direct or indirect, from existing states. Where such pressures exist, the process of development is accelerated, condensed, and often warped, so that a study of contemporary state formation is a murky mirror in which to discern the stages in the development of the pristine states.

Further, the conditions of emergence of rank and stratification as pristine phenomena are similarly obscured when the impetus to change is the introduction of aspects of a market economy, money as a medium of exchange, rationalization of production, and the transformation of labor into a commodity. It would be extremely gratifying to actually observe societies in transition from a "Stage A" (egalitarian organization) to a "Stage B" (rank society) and from there to a "Stage C" (stratification society) and finally from that stage to a "State D" (state society). Indeed, some of these observations have been made, though no one has yet been able to follow a single society or even selected exemplars from a group of genetically related societies through all these stages. Instead, a variety of unrelated societies are selected, each representing one or another of the several possible transitions. Mr. Leach himself has contributed one of the most valuable of the accounts dealing with this matter in his analysis of the movement from *gumlao* to *gumsa* organization among the Kachin of northern Burma.

Following leads supplied in the data of such accounts as that of Leach, just mentioned, of Douglas Oliver (1955), and others, it is our intention to discuss in detail the things which it seems to us must have occurred in order to make the previous transitions possible. Since the data are largely contemporary, the statements are to be viewed as hypotheses in their application to pristine situations beyond even archaeological recall.

Here then is what we seek to accomplish: (1) to suggest some specific institu-

684

tional developments, the occurrences of which are normal and predictable in viable societies under certain conditions, and in the course of which the whole society perforce moves into a new level of sociocultural organization; (2) to suggest some of the conditions under which these institutional developments occurred and came to florescence; (3) to indicate, as a by-product, that the movement occurs without conscious human intervention, the alterations taking place slowly enough and with such inevitability that the society is revolutionized before the carriers of the culture are aware of major changes.

In approaching this task, it seems wise, if only to head off needless argument, to deny any intention of supplying a single master key to a lock that has defied the efforts of great talents from the time of the Classical civilizations to the present. It seems obvious that other sequences of events than those sketched here could, under proper circumstances, have had similar results. Indeed, the writer is eager to entertain other possibilities and hopes hereby to stimulate others to offer counter suggestions. It will also be obvious to the reader that substantial trains of thought herein stated are merely borrowed and not created by the writer. The recent strides in economic anthropology, and I refer primarily to the work of Polanyi, Arensberg, and Pearson (1957), the clarification of some basic concepts in the study of social organization, and the incentives provided by a seminal paper by Paul Kirchoff (1935) have all been combined in the present effort.

THE NON-RANK NON-STRATIFIED SOCIETY

Every human society differentiates among its members and assigns greater or less prestige to individuals according to certain of their attributes. The simplest and most universal criteria of differential status are those two potent axes of the basic division of labor, age and sex. Beyond are a host of others which are used singly or in combination to distinguish among the members of a category otherwise undifferentiated as to sex or age group. Most important of the characteristics used in this regard are those which have a visible relation to the maintenance of subsistence, such as strength, endurance, agility, and other factors which make one a good provider in a hunting and gathering setting. These characteristics are ephemeral; moreover, the systems of enculturation prevalent at this level, with their emphasis upon the development of subsistence skills, make it certain that such skills are well distributed among the members of society of the proper sex and age groups.

The major deviation from this system of subsistence-oriented statuses is associated with age. However, it makes no difference to the argument of this paper whether the status of the old is high or low since the basis of its ascription is universal. Anyone who is of the proper sex and manages to live long enough automatically enters into its benefits or disabilities.

Given the variation in individual endowment which makes a chimera of absolute equality, the primitive societies which we are considering are sufficiently undifferentiated in this respect to permit us to refer to them as "egalitarian societies." An egalitarian society can be defined more precisely: it is one in which there are as many positions of prestige in any given age-sex grade as there are persons capable of filling them. If within a certain kin group or territory there are four big men, strong, alert, keen hunters, then there will be four "strong men"; if there are six, or three, or one, so it is. Eskimo society fits this general picture. So do many others. Almost all of these societies are founded upon hunting and gathering and lack significant harvest periods when large reserves of food are stored.

There is one further point I wish to emphasize about egalitarian society. It accords quite remarkably with what Karl Polanyi has called a reciprocal economy.[1]

Production in egalitarian society is characteristically a household matter. There is no specialization; each family group repeats essentially similar tasks. There may be individuals who make certain things better than do others, and these individuals are often given recognition for their skills, but no favored economic role is established, no regular division of labor emerges at this point, and no political power can reside in the status (Leacock, 1958). Exchange in such a society takes place between individuals who belong to different small-scale kin groups; it tends to be casual and is not bound by systems of monetary value based upon scarcity. Such exchanges predominate between individuals who recognize each other as relatives or friends, and may be cemented by such procedures as the provision of hospitality and the granting of sexual access to wives.

Within the local group or band the economy is also reciprocal, but less obviously so. Unlike the exchanges between members of different local groups which, over the period of several years, tend to balance, the exchanges within a group may be quite asymmetrical over time. The skilled and lucky hunter may be continually supplying others with meat; while his family also receives shares from the catch of others, income never catches up with the amounts dispensed. However, the difference between the two quantities is made up in the form of prestige, though, as previously mentioned, it conveys no privileged economic or political role. There frequently is a feeling of transience as it is understood that the greatest hunter can lose his luck or his life, thereby making his family dependent on the largesse of others.

In all egalitarian economies, however, there is also a germ of redistribution. It receives its simplest expression in the family but can grow no more complex than the pooling and redisbursing of stored food for an extended family. In such an embryonic redistributive system the key role is frequently played by the oldest female in the active generation, since it is she who commonly coordinates the household and runs the kitchen.

THE RANK SOCIETY

Since a truly egalitarian human society

does not exist, it is evident that we are using the word "rank" in a somewhat special sense. The crux of the matter, as far as we are concerned, is the structural way in which differential prestige is handled in the rank society as contrasted with the way in which egalitarian societies handle similar materials. If the latter have as many positions of valued status as they have individuals capable of handling them, the rank society places additional limitations on access to valued status. The limitations which are added have nothing to do with sex, age group, or personal attributes. Thus, the rank society is characterized by having fewer positions of valued status than individuals capable of handling them. Furthermore, most rank societies have a fixed number of such positions, neither expanding them nor diminishing them with fluctuations in the populations, save as totally new segmented units originate with fission or disappear as the result of catastrophe or sterility.

The simplest technique of limiting status beyond those already discussed, is to make succession to status dependent upon birth order. This principle, which is found in kinship-organized societies, persists in many more complexly organized societies. At its simplest, it takes the form of primogeniture or ultimogeniture on the level of the family, extended family, or lineage. In more complex forms it may be projected through time so that only the first son of a first son of a first son enjoys the rights of succession, all others having been excluded by virtue of ultimate descent from a positionless ancestor. There are still other variants based on the theme: the accession to high status may be by election, but the candidates may come only from certain lineages which already represent selection by birth order.

The effects of rules of selection based on birth can be set aside by conscious action. Incompetence can be the basis for a decision to by-pass the customary heir, though it would seem more usual for the nominal office to remain vested in the proper heir while a more energetic person performed the functions of the status. A strategic murder could also accomplish the temporary voiding of the rule, but such a solution is much too dangerous and extreme to be practical on the level which we are considering. It is only in rather advanced cultures that the rewards associated with such statuses are sufficient to motivate patricide and fratricide.

Whether accomplished by a rule of succession or some other narrowing device, the rank society as a framework of statuses resembles a triangle, the point of which represents the leading status hierarchically exalted above the others. The hierarchy thus represented has very definite economic significance, going hand in hand with the emergence of a superfamiliar redistributive network. The key status is that of the central collector of allotments who also tends to the redistribution of these supplies either in the form of feats or as emergency seed and provender in time of need. Depending on the extent and maturity of the redistributive system, there will be greater or lesser development of the hierarchy. Obviously, small-scale networks in which the members have a face-to-face relationship with the person in the central status will have less need of a bureaucracy.

In the typical ranked society there is neither exploitative economic power nor genuine political power. As a matter of fact, the central status closely resembles its counterpart in the embryonic redistributive network that may be found even in the simplest societies. This is not surprising, for the system in typical rank societies is actually based upon a physical expansion of the kin group and the continuation of previously known kinship rights and obligations. The kingpin of a redistributive network in an advanced hunting and gathering society or a simple agricultural one is as much the victim of his role as its manipulator. His special function is to collect, not to expropriate; to distribute, not to consume. In a conflict between personal accumulation and the demands of distribution it is the former which suffers. Anything else leads to accusations of hoarding and selfishness and undercuts the prestige of the central status; the whole network then

stands in jeopardy, a situation which cannot be tolerated. This, by the way, helps to explain that "anomaly" that has so frequently puzzled students of societies of this grade: why are their "chiefs" so often poor, perhaps poorer than any of their neighbors? The preceding analysis makes such a question rhetorical.

It is a further characteristic of the persons filling these high status positions in typical rank societies that they must carry out their functions in the absence of political authority. Two kinds of authority they have: familial, in the extended sense, and sacred, as the redistributive feasts commonly are associated with the ritual life of the community. They do not, however, have access to the privileged use of force, and they can use only diffuse and supernatural sanctions to achieve their ends. Indeed, the two major methods by which they operate are by setting personal examples, as of industriousness, and by utilizing the principles of reciprocity to bolster the emergent redistributive economy.[2]

Despite strong egalitarian features in its economic and political sectors, the developing rank society has strong status differentials which are marked by sumptuary specialization and ceremonial function. While it is a fact that the literature abounds in references to "chiefs" who can issue no positive commands and "ruling classes" whose members are among the paupers of the realm, it must be stated in fairness that the central redistributive statuses *are* associated with fuss, feathers, and other trappings of office. These people sit on stools, have big houses, and are consulted by their neighbors. Their redistributive roles place them automatically to the fore in the religious life of the community, but they are also in that position because of their central kinship status as lineage, clan[3] or kindred heads.

FROM EGALITARIAN TO RANK SOCIETY

The move from egalitarian to rank society is essentially the shift from an economy dominated by reciprocity to one having redistribution as a major device. That being the case, one must look for the causes of ranking (the limitation of statuses such that they are fewer than the persons capable of handling them) in the conditions which enable the redistributive economy to emerge from its position of latency in the universal household economy, to dominate a network of kin groups which extend beyond the boundaries of anything known on the reciprocal level.

Though we shall make a few suggestions relating to this problem, it should be noted that the focus of this paper does not necessitate immediate disposition of this highly complicated question. In view of the history of our topic, certain negative conclusions are quite significant. Most important of all is the deductuion that the roots of ranking do not lie in features of human personality. The structural approach obviates, in this case, psychological explanations. To be precise, we need assume no universal human drive for power[4] in comprehending the evolution of ranking.

It is unthinkable that we should lead a reader this far without indicating certain avenues whereby the pursuit of the problem may be continued. We ask, therefore, what are the circumstances under which fissioning kin or local groups retain active economic interdigitation, the method of interaction being participation in the redistributive network?

In a broad sense, the problem may be seen as an ecological one. Given the tendency of a population to breed up to the limit of its resources and given the probably universal budding of kin and local groups which have reached cultural maxima of unit size, we look into different techno-geographical situations for clues as to whether more recently formed units will continue to interact significantly with their parent units, thereby extending the physical and institutional range of the economy. Such a situation clearly arises when the newer group moves into a somewhat different environment while remaining close enough to the parent group to permit relatively frequent interaction among the members of the two groups. Given such a

condition, the maintenance of a redistributive network would have the effect of diversifying subsistence in both units and also providing insurance against food failures in one or the other. This is clearly something of a special case; one of its attractions is the amount of work that has been done upon it by another student of the problem (Sahlins, 1957, 1958).

It is possible to bring to bear upon this problem an argument similar to that employed by Tylor in the question of the incest taboo (Tylor, 1888: 267; White, 1948), to wit: the redistributive network might appear as a kind of random social mutation arising out of nonspecific factors difficult to generalize, such as a great personal dependence of the members of the offspring unit upon those they have left behind. Whatever the immediate reason for its appearance, it would quickly show a superiority over simple reciprocal systems in (a) productivity, (b) timeliness of distribution, (c) diversity of diet, and (d) coordination of mundane and ceremonial calendars (in a loose cyclical sense). It is not suggested that the success of the institution depends upon the rational cognition of these virtues by the culture carriers; rather the advantages of these institutions would have positive survival value over a long period of time.

We should not overlook one other possibility that seems less special than the first one given above. Wittfogel has drawn our attention on numerous occasions to the social effects of irrigation (see Wittfogel, 1957, for a summation of his latest thinking). The emergence of the superfamilial redistributive network and the rank society seem to go well with the developments he has discussed under the rubric "hydroagriculture," in which some supervision is needed in order to control simple irrigation and drainage projects; yet these projects are not large with the state. It was the passage to stratified society which laid the basis for the complex division of labor which underlies modern society. It also gave rise to various arrangements of socioeconomic classes and led directly to both classical and modern forms of colonialism and imperialism.

It may be wondered that one of the prime explanations for the emergence of ranking, one much favored by notable sociologists of the past, has not appeared in this argument. Reference is to the effects of war upon a society. I would like in this article to take a deliberately extreme stand and assert that military considerations serve to institutionalize rank differences only when these are already implicit or manifest in the economy. I do not believe that pristine developments in the formalization of rank can be attributed to even grave military necessity.

THE STRATIFIED SOCIETY

The differences between rank society and stratified society are very great, yet it is rare that the two are distinguished in descriptive accounts or even in the theoretical literature. Briefly put, the essential difference is this: the rank society operates on the principle of differential status for members with similar abilities, but these statuses are devoid of privileged economic or political power, the former point being the essential one for the present analysis. Meanwhile, the stratified society is distinguished by the differential relationships between the members of the society and its subsistence means—some of the members of the society have unimpeded access to its strategic resources[5] while others have various impediments in their access to the same fundamental resources.

With the passage to stratified society man enters a completely new area of social life. Whereas the related systems of redistribution and ranking rest upon embryonic institutions that are as universal as family organization (*any* family, elementary or extended, conjugal or consanguineal, will do equally well), the principles of stratification have no real foreshadowing on the lower level.

Furthermore, the movement to stratification precipitated many things which were destined to change society even further, and at an increasingly accelerated pace. Former

systems of social control which rested heavily on enculturation, internalized sanctions, and ridicule now required formal statement of their legal principles, a machinery of adjudication, and a formally constituted police authority. The emergence of these and other control institutions were associated with the final shift of prime authority from kinship means to territorial means and describes the evolution of complex forms of government associated with the state. It was the passage to stratified society which laid the basis for the complex division of labor which underlies modern society. It also gave rise to various arrangements of socioeconomic classes and led directly to both classical and modern forms of colonialism and imperialism.

THE TRANSITION TO STRATIFIED SOCIETY

The decisive significance of stratification is not that it sees differential amounts of wealth in different hands but that it sees two kinds of access to strategic resources. One of these is privileged and unimpeded; the other is impaired, depending on complexes of permission which frequently require the payment of dues, rents, or taxes in labor or in kind. The existence of such a distinction enables the growth of exploitation, whether of a relatively simple kind based upon drudge slavery or of a more complex type associated with involved divisions of labor and intricate class systems. The development of stratification also encourages the emergence of communities composed of kin parts and non-kin parts which, as wholes, operate on the basis of non-kin mechanisms.

So enormous is the significance of the shift to stratification that previous commentators have found it essential that the movement be associated with the most powerful people in the society. Landtman, for example, says: "It is in conjunction with the dissimilarity of individual endowments that inequality of wealth has conduced to the rise of social differentiation. As a matter of course the difference as regards property in many cases goes hand in hand with difference in personal qualities. A skilful hunter or fisher, or a victorious warrior, has naturally a better prospect of acquiring a fortune than one who is inferior to him in these respects" (Landtman 1938: 68).

If our analysis is correct, however, such is definitely not the case. The statuses mentioned by Landtman are not those which stand to make great accumulations but rather stand to make great give-aways. Furthermore, the leap from distribution to power is unwarranted by the ethnographic evidence.

There are unquestionably a number of ways in which secondary conditions of stratification can emerge. That is, once the development of stratification proceeds from contact with and tutelage by cultures which are at the least already stratified and which may be the possessors of mature state organization, there are many specific ways in which simpler cultures can be transformed into stratified societies. The ways which come quickest to mind include the extension of the complex society's legal definitions of property to the simpler society, the introduction of all-purpose money and wage labor, and the creation of an administrative system for the operation of the simpler society on a basis which is acceptable to the superordinate state. Often the external provenance of these elements is obvious in their misfit appearance. A sharper look may reveal, indeed, that the stratified system is a mere façade operated for and often by persons who have no genuine local identities, while the local system continues to maintain informally, and sometimes in secrecy, the older organization of the society. Put more concretely, this means that "government" appointed chiefs are respected only in certain limited situations and that the main weight of social control continues to rest upon traditional authorities and institutions which may not even be recognized by the ruling power.

An excellent climate for the development of stratification in a simple society can be supplied in a relatively indirect way by a society of advanced organization. Let us take the situation in which a culture has no concept of nuclear family rights to land. The economy is based upon hunting, trapping, and fishing, with the streams and forests being associated in a general way with weakly organized bands which have a decided tendency to fragment and reconstitute, each time with potentially different membership. Subvert this setup with an external market for furs and a substantial basis for stratification has been laid. This system, like the direct intervention of a superordinate state, also seems to have certain limitations for there is ample evidence that the development of private property in such a system as that just mentioned is confined to trapping lines and does not extend to general subsistence hunting and fishing in the area (see Leacock, 1958).

Another situation that bears study is one in which important trade routes linking two or more advanced societies traverse marginal areas in which simple societies are located. Certain geographical conditions make it possible for the relatively primitive folk to enhance their economies with fruits derived from the plunder of this trade or, in a more mature system, by extorting tribute from the merchants who must pass by. The remoteness of these areas, the difficulty of the terrain and the extreme difficulties and costs of sending a punitive force to pacify the area often enables the simpler people to harass populations whose cultural means for organized violence far exceeds their own. Be this as it may, the combination of the examples of organization presented by the outposts of complexly organized societies and the availability of commodities which could not be produced in the simple culture may combine to lay the basis for an emergence of stratification. Precisely such conditions seem partially responsible for the political developments described for the Kachin (Leach, 1954: esp. 235, 247 ff.).

None of this seems to apply to the pristine emergence of stratification. As a matter of fact, it is not even particularly suggestive. There is, however, one particular ecological condition that appears in highland Burma which also has been noted elsewhere, each time in association with rather basic shifts in social organization paralleling those already sketched in the previous section of this paper. We refer to the shift from rainfall to irrigation farming, particularly to the construction of terraced fields. This is admittedly a restricted ethnographic phenomenon and as such it cannot bear the weight of any general theory. It is the suggestive character of these developments and the possibility of extrapolating from them to hypothetical pristine conditions that makes them so interesting.

In brief, the shift to irrigation and terracing is from swiddens or impermanent fields to plots which will remain in permanent cultivation for decades and generations. Whereas we have previously stressed the possible role of hydro-agriculture in the transition from egalitarian to rank society, we now note its possible role in the transition to stratification. This it could accomplish by creating conditions under which access to strategic resources, in this case land and water, would be made the specific prerogative of small-scale kin groups such as minimal lineages or even stem families. Through the emergence of hydro-agriculture a community which previously acknowledged no *permanent* association between particular component units and particular stretches of land now begins to recognize such permanent and exclusive rights. Incidentally, the evidence seems to indicate that the rank-forming tendencies of hydro-agriculture need not occur prior to the tendencies toward stratification: both can occur concomitantly. This in turn suggests that we must be cautious in constructing our theory not to make stratification emerge from ranking, though under particular circumstances this is certainly possible.

A point of considerable interest about hydro-agriculture is that it seems to present the possibility of an emergence of stratification in the absence of a problem of overpopulation or resource limitation. We need a great deal of further thought on the matter. Studies of the last two decades, in which a considerably higher degree of agricultural expertise on the part of the fieldworkers has been manifested than was formerly the case, have increasingly tended to

show that hydro-agriculture does not invariably out-produce slash and burn and that, other things being equal, a population does not automatically prefer hydroagriculture as a more rationalized approach to agricultural subsistence. Here we can introduce a factor previously excluded. The hydro-agricultural system invariably has a higher degree of settlement concentration than swiddens. Accordingly, it would seem to have considerable value in the maintenance of systems of defense, given the presence of extensive warfare. Here then, is a point at which military considerations would seem to play an important if essentially reinforcing role in the broad evolutionary developments which we are considering.

The writer is intrigued with another possibility for the emergence of stratification. Once again, the conditions involved seem a little too specific to serve the purpose of a single unified theory. It requires the postulation of a society with a fixed rule of residence, preferably one of the simpler ones such as patrilocality/virilocality or matrilocality/uxorilocality[6] and a fixed rule of descent, preferably one parallel to the residence rule. It further postulates a condition of population expansion such that, given slash and burn agriculture, the society is very near the limits of the carrying capacity of the system. Such conditions are very likely to develop at varying speeds within an area of several hundred miles due to obvious imbalances in reproductive rates and to microecological variation. Now, as long as there is no notable pressure of people on the land, deviation in residence and even in descent will be expectable though quite unusual and lacking in motivation. As the situation grows grave in one area but remains relatively open in another, there may be a tendency for a slight readjustment in residence rules to occur. For example, in a normally virilocal society, the woman who brings her husband back to her natal group transgresses a few customary rules in doing so but presents her agnates with no basic problems in resource allocation since she, as a member of the agnatic group, has her own rights of access which may be shared by the spouse during her lifetime. The complication arises at her death when her husband and all of her children discover themselves to be in an anomalous position since they are not members of the kin community. Where local land problems are not severe and where such breaches of the residence pattern are yet uncommon, it is not unlikely that the aliens will be accepted as *de facto* members of the community with the expectation that future generations will revert to custom, the unorthodox switch of residence fading in memory with the passage of time. Here we have a crude and informal *ambilanak*. But as the local community enters worsening ecological circumstances and as the exceptional residence becomes more frequent, the residence and descent rules, particularly the latter, assume greater and greater importance. As the situation continues, the community is slowly altered, though the members of the community may be unable to state exactly what the changes are. The result, however, is clear. There are now two kinds of people in the village where formerly there was only one. Now there are kernel villagers, those who have unimpaired access to land, and those whose tenure rests upon other conditions, such as loyalty to a patron, or tribute, or even a precarious squatter's right.

THE STATE SOCIETY

The word should be abandoned entirely . . . after this chapter the word will be avoided scrupulously and no severe hardship in expression will result. In fact, clarity of expression demands this abstinence. (Easton, 1953: 108)

The word was "state" and the writer, a political scientist, was reacting to some of the problems in his own field in making this judgment, but it does look as if he was pushed to drastic action by the work of some anthropologists in whose hands the concept of state lost all character and utility, finally ending as a cultural universal. E. Adamson Hoebel (1949: 376), one of the few United States anthropologists to make a serious specialization in the field of law and the state, formerly introduced students

to this question by remarking that

where there is political organization there is a state. If political organization is universal, so then is the state. One is the group, the other an institutionalized complex of behavior.

In a revision of the same book after a few years, Hoebel's (1958: 506) treatment of the subject seems to indicate that he is in the process of rethinking the matter. His summary words, however, repeat the same conclusion:

Political organization is characteristic of every society. . . . That part of culture that is recognized as political organization is what constitutes the state.

This is a far cry from the approach of evolutionists to the state as exemplified in Sumner and Keller (1927, I: 700):

The term state is properly reserved for a somewhat highly developed regulative organization. . . . It is an organization with authority and discipline essential to large-scale achievements, as compared with the family, for example, which is an organization on the same lines but simpler and less potent. A useful definition of the state requires a clear statement about political power. In this light, note our previous emphasis on the absence of coercive economic or political power in the egalitarian and rank societies. It is only in the stratified society that such power emerges from embryonic and universal foreshadowings in familial organization.

The maturation of social stratification has manifold implications depending on the precise circumstances in which the developments take place. All subsequent courses, however, have a certain area of overlap; the new social order, with its differential allocation to access to strategic resources, must be maintained and strengthened. In a simple stratified society in which class differentials, are more implicit than explicit the network of kin relations covers a sufficient portion of the total fabric of social relations so that areas not specifically governed by genuine kinship relations can be covered by their sociological extensions. The dynamic of stratification is such that this situation cannot endure. The stratified kin group emphasizes its exclusiveness: it erodes the corporative economic functions formerly associated with stipulated kinship and at every turn it amputates extensions of the demonstrated kin unit. The result of this pruning is that the network of kin relations fails more and more to coincide with the network of personal relations. Sooner or later the discrepancy is of such magnitude that, were non-kin sanctions and non-kin agencies absent or structured along customary lines only, the society would dissolve in uncomposable conflict.

The emergent state, then, is the organization of the power of the society on a supra-kin basis. Among its earliest tasks is the maintenance of general order but scarcely discernible from this is its need to support the order of stratification. The defense of a complete system of individual statuses is impossible so the early state concentrates on a few key statuses (helping to explain the tendency to convert any crime into either sacrilege or *lèse majesté*) and on the basic principles of organization, e.g., the idea of hierarchy, property, and the power of the law.

The implementation of these primary functions of the state gives rise to a number of specific and characteristic secondary functions, each of which is associated with one or more particular institutions of its own. These secondary functions include population control in the most general sense (the fixing of boundaries and the definition of the unit; establishment of categories of membership; census). Also a secondary function is the disposal of trouble cases (civil and criminal laws moving toward the status of codes; regular legal procedure; regular officers of adjudication). The protection of sovereignty is also included (maintenance of military forces; police forces and power; eminent domain). Finally, all of the preceding require fiscal support, and this is achieved in the main through taxation and conscription.

In treating of this bare but essential list of state functions and institutions the idea of the state as a universal aspect of culture

dissolves as a fantasy. The institutions just itemized may be made to appear in ones or twos in certain primitive societies by exaggeration and by the neglect of known history. In no egalitarian society and in no rank society do a majority of the functions enumerated appear regardless of their guise. Furthermore there is no indication of their appearance as a unified functional response to basic sociocultural needs except in those stratified societies which are verging upon statehood.

THE TRANSITION TO STATE

Just as stratified society grew out of antecedent forms of society without the conscious awareness of the culture carriers, so it would seem that the state emerged from the stratified society in a similar, inexorable way. If this hypothesis is correct, then such an explanation as the so-called "conquest theory" can be accepted only as a special case of "secondary-state" formation. The conquests discussed by such a theorist as Franz Oppenheimer (1914) established not stratification but super-stratification, either the conqueror or the conquered, or perhaps even both, already being internally stratified.

The problem of the transition to state is so huge and requires such painstaking application to the available archaeological and historical evidence that it would be foolish to pursue it seriously here. Let us conclude, therefore, by harking back to statements made at the outset of this paper, and noting again the distinction between pristine and secondary states. By the former term is meant a state that has developed *sui generis* out of purely local conditions. No previous state, with its acculturative pressures, can be discerned in the background of a pristine state. The secondary state, on the other hand, is pushed by one means or another toward a higher form of organization by an external power which has already been raised to statehood.

The number of pristine states is strictly limited; several centuries, possibly two millennia, have elapsed since the last one emerged in Meso-America, and there seems to be no possibility that any further states of the pristine type will evolve, though further research may bring to light some of the distant past of which we yet have no positive information. In all, there seems to have been some six centers at which pristine states emerged, four in the Old World and two in the New: the Tigris-Euphrates area, the region of the lower Nile, the country drained by the Indus and the middle course of the Huang Ho where it is joined by the Han, Wei, and Fen. The separate areas of Peru-Bolivia and Meso-America complete the roster.

If there is utility in the concept of the pristine state and if history has been read correctly in limiting the designation to the six areas just enumerated, then we discover a remarkable correlation between areas demanding irrigation or flood control and the pristine state. Certainly this is no discovery of the author. It is one of the central ideas of Wittfogel's theory and has received extensive treatment from Julian Steward and others (see Steward, 1955: 178-209; Steward et al., 1955). The implication of the "hydraulic theory" for this paper, however, is that the development of the state as an internal phenomenon is associated with major tasks of drainage and irrigation. The emergence of a control system to ensure the operation of the economy is closely tied to the appearance of a distinctive class system and certain constellations of power in the hands of a managerial bureaucracy which frequently operates below a ruler who commands theoretically unlimited power.

It is an interesting commentary on nineteenth-century political philosophy that the starting point of so many theories was, of necessity, the Classical world of Greece and Rome. According to the present hypothesis, however, both of these great political developments of antiquity were not pristine but secondary formations which built on cultural foundations laid two thousand years and more before the rise of Greece. Furthermore, it would seem that the active commercial and military influences of the truly ancient pristine states, mediated through the earliest of the secondary states to appear in Asia Minor and the eastern Mediterranean littoral, were catalysts in the events of the northern and western Mediterranean.

CONCLUSION

The close of a paper like this, which moves like a gadfly from time to time, place to place, and subject matter to subject matter, and which never pauses long enough to make a truly detailed inquiry or supply the needed documentation, the close of such a paper requires an apology perhaps more than a conclusion.

I have been led to write this paper by my ignorance of any modern attempt to link up the contributions which have been made in many sub-disciplines into a single unified theory of the emergence of social stratification and the state. That the theory offered here is crude, often too special, and by no means documented seems less important than that it may be used as a sitting duck to attract the fire and better aim of others.

NOTES

[1]The reader may object to crediting Polanyi with the concept of a reciprocal economy. While it is true that Thurnwald and Malinowski earlier expressed similar concepts, and Durkheim, with his distinction between segmental and organic societies, also foreshadows this development, it awaited Polanyi's analysis to place reciprocal economies into systematic harmony with other, more complex types of economy, such as the redistributive type discussed later on, and the market kind as well. For Polanyi's definitions of each of these types see Polanyi, Arensberg, and Pearson, 1957, pp. 250-56.

[2]For an ethnographic illustration of this point see Oliver, 1955, pp. 422 ff.

[3]These, of course, would be ranked lineages or ranked clans. Cf. Fried, 1957, pp. 23-26.

[4]As does Leach, 1954, p. 10.

[5]Strategic resources are those things which, given the technological base and environmental setting of the culture, maintain subsistence. See Fried, 1957, p. 24.

[6]Our residence terms follow usage suggested by J. L. Fischer (1958).

REFERENCES

Easton, David.
1953   The Political System. New York.
Fischer, J. L.
1958   "The classification of residence in censuses." American Anthropologist, 60: 508-17.
Fried, Morton H.
1957   "The classification of corporate unilineal descent groups." Journal of the Royal Anthropological Institute, 87: 1-29.
Hoebel, E. Adamson.
1949   Man in the Primitive World. 1st ed. New York.
1958   Man in the Primitive World. 2d ed. New York.
Kirchhoff, Paul.
1935   "The principles of clanship in human society." (Ms; cf. Davidson Journal of Anthropology, 1 [1955]).
Landtman, Gunnar.
1938   The Origin of the Inequality of the Social Classes. London.
Leach, E. R.
1954   Political Systems of Highland Burma. Cambridge, Mass.
Leacock, Eleanor.
1958   "Status among the Montagnais-Naskapi of Labrador." Ethnohistory, 5: Part 3: 200-209.
Oliver, Douglas.
1955   A Solomon Island Society. Cambridge, Mass.

Oppenheimer, Franz.
1914   The State: Its History and Development Viewed Sociologically. New York.
Polanyi, Karl, Conrad M. Arensberg, and Harry W. Pearson (eds.).
1957   Trade and Market in the Early Empires. Glencoe, Ill.
Sahlins, Marshall.
1958   Social Stratification in Polynesia. Seattle.
1957   "Differentiation by adaptation in Polynesian societies." Journal of the Polynesian Society, 66: 291-300.
Steward, Julian H.
1955   Theory of Culture Change. Urbana, Ill.
Steward, Julian H., et al.
1955   Irrigation Civilizations: A Comparative Study. Social Science Monographs #1, Washington, D.C.
Sumner, W. G., and A. G. Keller.
1927   The Science of Society. New Haven, Conn.
Tylor, Edward B.
1888   "On a method of investigating the development of institutions; applied to laws of marriage and descent." Journal of the Royal Anthropological Institute, 18: 245-69.
White, Leslie.
1948   "The definition and prohibition of incest." American Anthropologist, 50:41 35.
Wittfogel, Karl A.
1957   Oriental Despotism. New Haven Conn.

CHAPTER 44

Privilege and Poverty: Two Worlds on One Planet

NATHAN KEYFITZ

*"To cross simultaneously the four coinciding lines
of income, race, culture, and geography which separate the nationally poor from the middle classes
of the world is today's problem."*

Nathan Keyfitz, at the time this article was
originally published, was professor of sociology
and co-director of the Population Research Training Center at the University of Chicago.

In the developed countries of the world,
such as the United States and the USSR,
the newspaper reader finds many current
events interpreted in terms of a conflict of
ideologies—free enterprise versus communism. In the underdeveloped countries,
such as Indonesia, essentially the same
events are presented as illustrating a quite
different conflict—subject peoples versus
their recent or present imperial masters.
This article will argue impartially that both
antagonisms are today superficial and out-
moded. They were congruent with the social reality of the nineteenth century, came
to their mature literary expression in the
early twentieth century, and by the 1950's
were leading that omnipresent ghostly existence to which such ideologies are condemned when history has outdistanced
them.

A quite different conflict will be presented here, arising from the nature of the
perfected industrial machine now assembled or being assembled throughout Europe, the Soviet Union, the United States,
Canada, and Japan. This machine can live
on itself, producing the raw materials with
which it is nourished and the capital by
which it transforms itself and becomes ever
more efficient and productive. In this context I shall discuss the rich and poor peoples of the world, their incomes and rates
of population increase, the widening of the
welfare gap, and the attitudes and behavior
which may follow from these.

The number of births per thousand population is one of the most pertinent facts
that can be cited for a country. The observed range runs from something above 10
per thousand to something below 60. Dividing this interval at two points—20 and
30—will provide objectively the differentiation we need for the present argument. A
very simple pattern appears when we consider in three categories the countries of the
world whose figures are given in the 1964
United Nations *Demographic Yearbook:*
(1) under 20 births per thousand population, (2) between 20 and 30, and (3) over
30 per thousand.

1. In the group under 20 appears just
about every country of Europe, and Japan
alone among the countries of Asia. Thus
France stands at 18.1, the United Kingdom
at 18.7, West Germany at 18.2, Czechoslovakia at 17.1, Bulgaria at 16.1, Hungary at
13. There is no distinction according to
whether the economy is planned or unplanned, nor whether the official outlook is
liberal or Marxist, pro-natalist as in France
or restrictionist as in Japan; evidently the
birthrate reflects merely the fact that all of
these countries are industrialized and fairly
densely settled. The only European countries where the birthrate is over 20, and in
those it is very slightly above, are Ireland,
Spain, Portugal, and the Netherlands.

2. The group from 20 to 30 includes the
United States at 21.2, the USSR at 21.2 in

1963, Argentina at 21.5, Canada at 23.8, Australia at 20.6, and New Zealand at 24.1. What do these countries have in common? I suggest two features: industrial development and space. Here again we have a group of countries which are homogeneous in regard to industry and territory; they are—once again—heterogeneous in regard to political and economic organization and official philosophy. Our impression that variable philosophies can be superimposed on given real conditions is strengthened.

3. The group from 30 births per thousand and upward includes the rest of the world: all of Asia except Japan and the USSR, all of Africa, all of Latin America except Argentina. And indeed within the range of 30 and over there is a considerable gap at the lower limit; most of the countries are actually over 40. Statistics here are less firm than elsewhere, but we can safely refer to Mexico at 45.2 in 1964, to Iran at 45-48, and to India at 40.

It happens that we can express the populations in the three groups very conveniently in round numbers: (1) the crowded developed countries total about 500 million; (2) the spacious developed countries another 500 million; (3) the underdeveloped countries about two billion.

THE INCREASE IN POPULATION

In contrast to births, crude death rates vary little among the countries of the world: practically all are below 20 per thousand. Indeed, some of the countries with the highest birthrates also have the lowest crude death rates; this is because their age distribution is shifted toward the younger end of the continuum. For example, in 1964 Puerto Rico's crude death rate was 7.1, while that of the United States was 9.4 per thousand. Mexico is estimated as having for 1964 a birthrate of 45.2 and a death rate of 9.8, so that it is increasing at 35.4 per thousand. Among Asian countries one can cite Pakistan, with births at 43-46 per thousand, deaths at 16-17, and natural increase at 26-30 per thousand per year increase for the decade between the

censuses of 1951 and 1961 and 23 per thousand from 1958 to 1963. The figures for Pakistan could easily be underestimated. If in the underdeveloped countries death rates continue to fall rapidly, while birthrates stay over 40 per thousand, a rate of increase of three per cent per annum could become generalized among populations now totaling about two billion.

Do the underdeveloped countries reveal any downward trend in birthrates paralleling that in their death rates? While relevant data are lacking, there are signs of change on the rim of Asia. Taiwan's crude birthrate stood at 44.8 in 1956, at 37.4 in 1962, and at 34.5 in 1964; the fall was continuous over the interval. Birthrates in Hong Kong, Singapore, and Ceylon have also fallen, though less sharply.

Suppose that the crowded developed countries (mostly Europe and Japan) increase at .75 per cent per annum, the developed countries with spacious lands continue near their postwar peak of 1.5 per cent per annum, and the presently underdeveloped countries increase at three per cent per annum. The first gorup doubles in 93 years; the second group quadruples in 93 years; the third group octuples in 93 years. Instead of the numbers half a billion, half a billion, and two billion of today, we would find one billion, two billion, and 16 billion, which, aside from everything else, would represent a drastic shift in proportions: the developed populations would drop from one-third of the total to less than one-sixth. Like many other projections, this one is made in the hope that it will not materialize. Its sinister character appears in the fact that the lines which divide countries by birthrates coincide almost exactly with those that divide them by per capita income.

INCOME

Income comparisons are more difficult than demographic ones. We kow that the U.S. national income is over $500 billion, shared by a population of less than 200 million, so that the per capita income is above $2,500 per annum. India's national income, the equivalent of about $35 billion, is shared among nearly 500 million people, so that its per capita is $70 per annum. We cannot say categorically that the American is 35 times better off in amenities than the agerage Indian, but the disparity is large.

A more concrete observation is that the consumption of foodstuffs in calories per person per day for 1961 in the United States was 3,100, in India 2,040. These averages tell us nothing about irregularities in supply which have led to pre-harvest food riots in many Indian cities in recent years. Moreover they say nothing about composition of diet: while the average American ate 212 pounds of meat, the average Indian ate four, consuming 333 pounds of cereals and potatoes against 250 for the American.

Agricultural production is a random variable, and it is by no means easy to judge the trend of performance. The Indian Third Plan aimed at 100 million tons of food grains by 1965-66, against 79.7 millions by 1960-61. It now appears likely that 1965-66 will show only 92 million tons. If population is growing at more than two per cent per year, and foodstuffs increase at only three per cent per year, progress is being made, but very slowly. Agricultural production of the countries of Asia and the Far East increased by .5 per cent per year in the first three years of the "development decade"—much less than population, which grew at 2.4 per cent per year. In other parts of the world—for example, Latin America—per capita supplies may be no better than they were a generation ago. World rice production increased from 250.4 million short tons in 1958 to 270.6 million in 1962. At two per cent per year this is, if anything, less than the increase in the number of rice-eating people during the same period. Nor is there any obvious way of changing the prospects for this "cornerstone of economic development." Indeed, as Gunnar Myrdal has put it, "successful agricultural development in underdeveloped countries requires an entirely new technology." ("Jobs, Food and People," *International Development,* VIII, June 1965, p. 6).

It is true that manufacturing shows a greater pace of advance; in India again, paper, cement, steel, and aluminum show gains which are on the whole well above the five per cent per annum frequently cited as an objective. But this is on a small base.

Future income is related to present investment. Comparing two countries, Canada and India, whose economics are about equal in size, we note for India a total intended investment, public and private, including foreign aid of 10,400 crores during the Third Plan; this is roughly $20 billion, or $4 billion per year. Canadian private investment alone, omitting residential construction, amounted to $5.5 billion in 1964, in a national income whose total was almost identical with that of India. Some 20 million Canadians not only divide among themselves the same income as about 25 times their number of Indians, but if investment is equally efficient in the two countries, Canadian income will grow faster. The least one can say of such comparisons is that they offer no promise that the income gap will be narrower in the years ahead.

POVERTY IN EARLY CAPITALIST SOCIETY

Within the new nations of England and France in the nineteenth century there were rich and poor, and for a long period it seemed that the gap between them was increasing. The poorer the poor and the more conspicuous the rich, the greater the strain on civil order. The instability of society was graphically expressed in the mob scenes of *Barnaby Rudge,* where the socially irrelevant issue of Catholicism was the occasion for passionate destruction. Urban poverty was associated with disorder in *Les Misérables.*

Yet it is in the presently advanced countries, where the working classes were politically most alert, the tensions of poverty most severe, and the challenge of ostentatious wealth most galling, that the issue has been peacefully resolved. Individual workingmen of talent made their way into the middle classes, and even those who remained in the working class realize increased income, both absolute and in relation to the rich. The benefits of industrial progress were somehow shared, and the gap tended to close. The poor who limited the number of their children and so were able to educate them better set an example of upward mobility, and between the 1870's and the 1930's this was perceived by all social groups in Europe and America.

As the West transformed itself into an industrial society, we may crudely summarize the two relevant social attitudes: ambition and revolution—the drive to rise within the existing social system, against the desire to destroy the existing system and create a new one. Only since World War II has West Europe turned clearly toward the former. The Nazi revolt in Germany, an apparently advanced country in the thirties, seems to have been largely supported by the votes of those farthest from industry. In North America the ideology of revolt has never been widespread, and now the poor are reduced in numbers to a small, and probably disappearing, minority.

THE DISAPPEARING POVERTY LINE

The world has moved to the point where the significant separation of poor and rich is no longer within nations but by national boundaries. In the former colonies there has been a start in stripping maharajahs, hacendados, and even civil servants of a large part of their income. This has been matched in richer countries by some tendencies toward equalization, though these have been less important than the general further income rise.

Much as poverty in the United States is discussed today, it is in fact a residual element, numerically not very important. To define it objectively is not easy, but one view calls poor those people who have to spend more than one-third of their income to secure a satisfactory diet. A small family on an income of about $3,000 per annum is in this position at present prices, and this

has been identified as the poverty line. Apparently only 18 per cent of the population of the United States is in households of less than $3,000 income. This includes disproportionate numbers of old people, those in the rural south, Negroes, husbandless families, and other special cases which are the object of much current legislative attention. The poor white workers is disappearing, and he will surely be followed by the other categories. Families living in poverty are said to have decreased from 12 million in 1947 to 8.9 million in 1963.

The corresponding poverty line in India is equally difficult to specify, but we will consider one analysis which treats it as a family income of 3,000 rupees per year (P. D. Ojha and V. V. Bhatt, "Some Aspects of Income Distribution in India," *Bulletin of the Oxford University Institute of Economics and Statistics,* XXVI, 1964). The value of a rupee in providing amenities may be more than the official twenty-one cents, and there may be more components of Indian income which do not come through the market; on the other hand the Indian family is larger than the American, and on 3,000 rupees it is certainly less comfortable than the American family on $3,000. It would, for example, spend much more than one-third of its income on food. Hence distribution figures based on a survey of the Indian National Sample Survey covering the period from mid-1955 to mid-1957 may be safely applied for our purpose. They show 78,479,000 households below the 3,000-rupee line and 3,921,000 above; below were 95.3 per cent, above were 4.7 per cent. Moreover the American families who were below the poverty line of $3,000 averaged $1,778, while the average for those under 3,000 rupees was 1,070 rupees per household, or one-third of the income at the poverty line here drawn. Hence we are understating the contrast when we say that over 95 per cent of India is poor, while 82 per cent of the United States is well off.

With the shift in perspective from our own national position to the world view, the presently underdeveloped countries take on the role of the poor of the nineteenth century. They include all categories: the industrious poor of India; the indoctrinated and disciplined proletariat of China, with their intensively cultivated resentment; the noisy and ineffectual street mobs of Indonesia. In the degree to which the rough figures given earlier for the three categories of countries apply both the birthrates and to wealth, we may think of the present world situation as involving one billion middle class or potentially middle class people—mostly Europeans and North Americans—and two billion poor. If the gap in per capita incomes and birthrates remains, a terrifying prospect, then in somewhat over three generations some three billion rich people will face some 16 billion poor.

LIBERTY AND EQUALITY

To cross simultaneously the four coinciding lines of income, race, culture, and geography which separate the nationally poor from the middle classes of the world is today's problem. The circumstances of different languages and lack of apparent opportunity to rise socially are just those that make for the greatest class conflict.

The process by which the poor formerly became middle class included two opposite kinds of treatment. One involved making individuals suffer for their imprudence and delinquency: the man who had more children than he could afford was left in poverty; the one who restricted the number of his children and worked hard was rewarded—or his children were—with a middle class home in the suburbs. This we call liberty, and it was much favored by Malthus. The opposite of liberty, which we call equality—for example, charity, and enforced redistributive measures—also had a role; schools for the poor were supported by the rich, as were libraries, hospitals, and parks. Thus liberty, in the form of private property, self-help, and individual responsibility, was supplemented by the opposite configuration, labelled equality, expressed most characteristically in the graduated income tax. In Western European history the poor have asked for equality, while the rich wanted liberty.

Today the poor claim liberty. Private property—or that extension of property called sovereignty—among nations is, largely at the wish of the poor, far more absolute than it ever has been among individuals within a nation. No overall authority sets rules among the nations, and in international trade each is free to sanction movement of capital into or out of its borders and to deal as it wishes with its own resources. The poor nations accept from the rich voluntary gifts of food, small gifts of capital and of technical assistance; these are the small redistributive measures now in existence. Property and freedom, once the slogans of the bourgeoisie, are now adopted by the poor.

Since suffering the consequences of their own errors is what ultimately makes people responsible, will not the extreme of private property among nations ensure that the poor will learn such salutary lessons as that poverty increases as family size increases? Not necessarily. Hardship can teach responsibility only if suitably interpreted. People need adequate access to information in order to come to sound conclusions. Some governments offer such access, while others deny it. More broadly, the sentiment of liberty, which the underdeveloped world emphasizes in dealings between nations, gives way to equality in relations within the underdeveloped countries. The uniformity of poverty thereby attained is not likely to encourage initiative among their people.

SEPARATENESS AND FRUSTRATION

Among the underdeveloped, intensification of poverty can cause whole nations, like the neurotic patient, to be caught in a web of necessity which they cannot perceive. Frustration is inevitable. An outlet in foreign animosity is one morbid result, and new countries need not take long to develop traditional hostilities. Indeed, war sometimes appears to be the lesser evil. As a brilliant representative of the underdeveloped world puts it: "Now war . . . is evil, war is cruel, war is inhuman. But still more evil, still more cruel, still more inhuman is the slow and agonizing death of daily hunger" (Abdus Salam, "World Security and Developing Nations," *Bulletin of the Atomic Scientists,* September 1964, p. 6). He is speaking of a level of irrationality which disregards the fact that the outcome of war will be intensification of hunger.

WEAKENING THE LINKS BETWEEN POOR AND RICH

The growth of population in the poor countries inhibits economic development (A. J. Coale and E. M. Hoover, *Population Growth and Economic Development in Low-Income Countries,* New Jersey: Princeton University Press, 1958). Today this seems to be true, less because of diminishing marginal returns than because of the difficulty of securing capital at the same time to finance increased population and to change the structure of the economy. Outside private capital is objectionable as infringing on freedom, and with economic inertia and population increase, the poor country is hard pressed to find that surplus over basic needs which constitutes domestic capital. In the face of hunger, policy is oriented more and more to the short-run solution, often wasteful and inefficient, and creating a further difficulty in the accumulation of capital.

On the developed side of the world it becomes more and more apparent that the very nature of industrial society is to accumulate capital and hence increase income, a process hardly inhibited by particular material shortages. Japan's postwar dynamism shows how unimportant it is to have raw materials at hand. Moreover, the industrial machine reaches back to the manufacture of its own raw materials, a tendency which could well be extended to fuels in the next generation.

This reveals itself clearly in falling prices of raw materials, not because of a conspiracy of the West, but as an unplanned consequence of technical advance. Thus, adverse terms of trade add to the insult of blatant Western prosperity the injury of economic isolation of the underdeveloped world. This isolation is made more complete by population growth in the East. For with the increase of population in such places as East Bengal and Java more and more land is required for cereals and less and less is left for such cash crops as jute and sugar.

Population growth in the poor countries and technical advance in the rich ones are two factors which weaken the economic links between rich and poor. The various older forms of cooperation between Europeans and non-Europeans, which are now for one reason or another becoming obsolete, show little sign of being replaced by viable new forms of cooperation.

It is true that the developing countries are making demands on the developed ones. They have succeeded—against some opposition from the West—in establishing the United Nations Conference on Trade and Development (UNCTAD), based on the principle of preference for the developing countries, rather than the most-favored nation principle which the rich countries are inclined to see as the ideal. The poor exporters of tropical products consider that price maintenance for their goods has just as sound an economic case as price maintenance for agricultural products within the United States or Europe. They want lower shipping rates, an international agency to provide capital, and some relief from the burden of repayment of earlier—usually bilateral—loans. There is little sign that these demands will initiate the new creative forms of cooperation that the situation requires.

The basic factors which increasingly separate the developed and the underdeveloped worlds are concealed by jet travel, by over two thousand meetings each year of international committees sponsored by the United Nations, by foreign aid in all its varieties. Yet it will take more than committee meetings and patchwork aid to deal with the trends now coming into view.

The rich countries may be maintaining a level of foreign aid and information just sufficient to animate the sense of class difference but not enough to remove any appreciable part of the real poverty which underlies it. A kind of class struggle is shaping up entirely different from the one

Marx wrote about. He saw country after country becoming ripe for revolution as it passed a certain point of material advance; in fact is is only passing that point that can make a country safe from revolution. But to demonstrate that Marx was wrong does not in itself solve any problems.

FROM COLD WAR TO RICH VERSUS POOR

In this deadlocked situation there is great danger. The bipolarity of the United States and the USSR is dissolving in their common prosperity. The contest between them for a while included healthy competition in aid giving, but this has abated. The armament competition also shows prospects of curtailment, though the signs are less clear. But even if there is disarmament, the intense research of the cold war has one permanent result: a host of relatively inexpensive devices of mass destruction. It will not be easy to prevent these from coming onto the market at prices which make them more and more accessible to the frustrated countries.

Can the impending termination of the cold war be the occasion for a worldwide development program that will avoid this new and rising danger? The Western powers are not inclined to apply a specified per cent of savings on armaments toward development, and believers in peace will not want to tax disarmament. But the advanced nations are very far from giving even the one per cent of their national incomes which has been repeatedly put forward as the minimum needed for development, and which could be afforded quite independently of disarmament. Neil W. Chamberlain takes the view that only with much more drastic redistributive measures—say a 10 per cent income tax on the world's rich—will development be possible and the danger of war removed. There is little sign of this being accepted; in any case no one knows under quite what conditions large transfers would actually promote development. The poor countries need management as well as capital. Will they accept both in the form of private direct invest-

ment? Fear and hatred of foreign management has often been proportional to the incapacity of one's own nationals to compete with foreigners; the more badly a country lacks management skills, the more sharply it spurns them when they are offered by foreigners.

ATTITUDES

If my reading of trends is correct, and poverty continues to look across the oceans at uniform and increasing affluence, present unfavorable attitudes are likely to be intensified. Max Scheler used the word *ressentiment* to describe the socialist hostility to the established structures of twentieth century Europe. Certainly it characterizes the thought of the later Marx, perhaps the supreme prophet of the tension between poverty and social order. Yet there is a degree of the bitterness in the potential world confrontation between rich and poor which goes beyond Marx, because its source is not possible exploitation but rather exclusion from industrial life, of which low raw material prices are an aspect.

The demand of the West for tropical products in the days when its industrial machine was yet imperfect necessarily contained some elements of genuine working together, with a hope on the part of the oppressed, who saw themselves as doing the main work, that the going enterprise would sooner or later belong to them. One may speak harshly of exploitation, but as long as men are engaged in common activity they can communicate with one another. The very hypocrisy of the ruler is a means by which he can be influenced, especially when hypocrisy is reinforced by material need of the rich for the poor. The colonial situation was certainly bad, but the prospect today is worse, for a time is coming when the rich no longer need the poor, and even hypocrisy may decline.

The rich countries are reaching ever higher levels of comfort and pleasure; if each rise of income makes the powerful industrial machine less dependent on the pitiful supplies of rubber or fuel or sugar or cocoa which have constituted the sole wealth of the underdeveloped world, what depths of hatred will not be stirred in those large and functionless populations whose numbers are in many instances a product of colonialism, now left high and dry with its retreat?

The citizen of the rich world sees himself as fully earning the privileged position in which he sits. To the poor he has earned nothing. And we should be humble enough to remember that it is western society which is productive, and not necessarily we as individuals. The economics of the matter are complex, but as a practical fact a cobbler or a college professor in Calcutta, working at his bench or addressing his class, can perform with exactly the same effort and skill as his opposite number in Chicago, and his real income is at the most favorable one-fifth as much. For a long while the citizen of Calcutta has thought this was so because in some invisible way the Chicagoan was exploiting him. With the advance of western technology and the consequent increasing separateness of the rich and poor on their opposite sides of the world the absurdity of the notion of exploitation will become more and more patent. One cannot expect that it will therefore cease to be used, and if it is dropped the frustration which it has expressed in the past is likely to be carried by other bitter slogans.

Can separation and the hatred which goes with it themselves constitute the necessary spur to development? There is some suggestion of this in the history of Japan and the USSR. If a country has space, leadership, and a disciplined people, it may be able to effect a transformation of its productive apparatus, notwithstanding the isolation imposed on the poor by the technology of the rich. The constructive aspect of tension is shown to some degree in countries as diverse as Egypt, Pakistan, Ceylon, Burma, and particularly China. But even if constructive animosity dominates for a time, its control for peaceful ends is uncertain, and what is today an impulse to development may lead at any moment to war. The matter is complicated; Soviet animosity seems to be attenuated by afflu-

ence. I have no notion whether China will make the grade to development, nor whether she will be more dangerous if she does or does not.

A NEW DIMENSION OF CONFLICT?

Much has been written on conflict and its functions; I cannot here summarize the material, or hope to add to it. In discussions of class antagonisms, a universal assumption has been that the ruler and the ruled need one another. In an advanced society those displaced by automation are citizens who can give or withhold votes. At the very least they are potential workers able to render still useful services if they are suitably retrained. They have a great advantage over the citizens of the underdeveloped countries who are similarly displaced by American technology. The Indonesian plantation worker who is automated out by rubber factories in the United States which can make better rubber more cheaply, cannot, like the unemployed American, be trained afresh to reenter the system at a higher level.

To this difference between the displaced in the rich countries and those in the underdeveloped ones we cite again the difference in rates of reproduction. The new conflict situation, if things go as badly as they may, will involve great numbers of the very poor, so crowded they have no land to work nor tools to apply, no goods and services they can threaten to withhold, with ample complaints against the world's rich but no voice that will carry across the oceans.

DEVELOPMENT AS A SELECTIVE PROCESS

The darkening contrast between increasingly uniform wealth on the one side and uniform poverty on the other is brightened in certain poor countries where clear progress is being made. These—people and government—are concerned with population, food, and industrial growth, if sometimes awkwardly or inefficiently. They permit enough circulation of information to learn from their mistakes. If in the next decade even half a dozen, small or large, can rise out of the mass of the world's poor they will encourage others in what might become a general movement. It is those countries which are making material progress—Taiwan, Singapore, Chile, Turkey, Yugoslavia, Mexico, for instance—which are also for the most part doing something about their population problem.

To get such countries off the ground, in the hope that the means to their progress will be noted and imitated by others, deserves the utmost effort and even sacrifice by the rich. The means evidently include whatever measures of communication and technique will enable them to limit their population growth, as well as assistance in the form of capital and management. Bold effort on a limited front seems the appropriate policy for the advanced countries.

In contrast to the constructive effect of concentrated massive help for those countries that are helping themselves is the confrontation of the developed and the underdeveloped, the demands and counterdemands across the gap which increasingly separates them. The confrontation of rich and poor as such within the United Nations, or of Europeans and the "new emerging forces" that Mr. Sukarno is so eager to mobilize, produces nothing but confusion. What is needed is something of that updraft that has been so successful in Europe and America, of competitive ambition expressed in family limitation and diligent work, applied now among nations as well as among individuals.

CHAPTER 45

Miners and Agrarian Radicalism

JAMES PETRAS and MAURICE ZEITLIN

Chilean mining municipalities are centers from which political radicalism is diffused into surrounding non-mining agricultural and non-agricultural areas. The greater the number of mining municipalities a "satellite" municipality adjoins, the more likely it is to have a "high" vote for the presidential candidate of the Socialist-Communist coalition (FRAP). Municipalities that are neither mining municipalities nor adjoining any, are least likely to have a "high" FRAP vote. In agricultural areas, political differences based on class position among the peasants tend to disappear in the mining and "satellite" municipalities. In the non-mining, non-satellite municipalities, however, class structure does determine voting. Mining and adjoining municipalities develop a radical political culture that tends to eliminate the political importance of class differences among the peasants, uniting them across class lines.

GENERALLY, empirical analyses of class and politics focus on the relative chances for given types of political behavior in different classes, but neglect *the interaction of these classes and the political consequences of such interaction.* Moreover, even when reference *is* made to the possible political relevance of such interaction, the emphasis has been on assymetrical influence, i.e., on how the privileged classes may moderate the politics of the unprivileged.[1]

This is a joint work in the fullest sense; our names are in alphabetical order. We are indebted to Michael Parker for his helpful comments on an original draft of this article.

[1] Cf. Seymour Martin Lipset, *Political Man*, New York: Doubleday & Co., 1960, esp. pp. 231 and following.

For instance, the possibility that the working class might modify the political behavior of the middle classes has scarcely been entertained, nor has the possible impact of the workers on the development of political consciousness in other exploited classes been explored. The latter is precisely what we focus on in this article: the impact of organized workers in Chile on the development of political consciousness in the peasantry.

In Chile, agricultural relations have gradually become modernized, and traditional social controls have loosened considerably. In the central valley, where Chile's agricultural population is centered, the modernization favored by the Chilean propertied classes may be directly responsible for the growth of rural radicalism. As one writer has put it: "The principal impact of technological advance and farm rationalization has been to undermine the secure if impoverished position of the agricultural laborers which has been an important feature of the traditional system of employment. Wage rates are barely keeping up with consumer price increases and [these rates] may have fallen recently. Thus while the attempts to increase output and productivity have not been very successful, these attempts have led to changes which adversely affect the landless laborer. These changes in Chilean agriculture may lead to demands for a more radical transformation in the future." [2] This breakdown of the traditional rural social structure, the growth of a "rural proletariat," and emergence of demands for radical reforms in the agrarian structure may allow other relatively oppressed groups who have similar demands and *are* highly organized to provide leadership for the peasantry as it enters the political struggle in Chile. The most highly organized and politically conscious working class centers in Chile are in the mining municipalities—centers from which the miners' political influence may be diffused into the surrounding countryside.

ORGANIZED WORKING CLASS POLITICS
IN CHILE

In Chile, both the organized trade union movement and the emergence of insurgent political parties began in the northern areas of Tarapaca and Antofagasta, where 40 percent of the labor force was already employed in the mines by 1885. Soon after the middle of the last century, large-scale social conflict rivaling similar outbreaks in Europe were occurring with increasing frequency and intensity.[3] The northern nitrate city of Iquique and the southern coal mining area

of Lota were frequently the scenes of struggles of civil war proportions in which hundreds if not thousands of workers were killed. The first general strike in 1890 originated in Iquique and spread throughout the country. Despite the violent reaction of the public authorities, the first labor organizations began to emerge—based predominantly in the nitrate mines of the north.[4] The Chilean Workers Federation was founded in 1908 by Conservatives as a mutual aid society. By 1917 it had become a militant industrial trade union; two years later it called for the abolition of capitalism. Between 1911 and 1920 there were 293 strikes involving 150,000 workers. In 1919 the Chilean Workers' Federation (FOCH) became affiliated with the Red Trade Union Federation. The FOCH, the largest national union, contained an estimated 136,000 members of which 10,000 were coal miners and 40,000 nitrate miners—miners accounting for almost 37 percent of all union members. Of all industries, it was only in mining that a majority of the workers were organized. In 1906, the first working-class Socialist leader, Emilio Recabarren, was elected from a mining area —although he was not allowed to take office.

The Socialist Party that grew out of the establishment of the so-called "Socialist Republic," [5] (June 4–16, 1932) had its most cohesive working-class political base among the copper miners. Although the Socialist Party condemned both the Second and Third Internationals, it claimed adherence to Marxism and the establishment of a government of organized workers as its goal. The Communists also secured their major base in the mining areas. In the municipal elections of 1947, the last relatively free

[2] Marvin Sternberg, "Chilean Land Tenure and Land Reforms" (unpublished doctoral dissertation), University of California, Berkeley, 1962, pp. 132–133.

[3] Over one-third of all the strikes and popular demonstrations occurring in the period between 1851–1878 involved miners, according to Hernán Ramírez Necochea, *Historia de Movimiento Obrero en Chile: Antecedentes Siglo XIX,* Santiago: Editorial Austral, no date, pp. 133–134.

[4] One of the worst massacres in labor history occurred in Chile at that time, when ten thousand nitrate miners marching in Iquique were machine-gunned, and two thousand died. Julio Cesar Jobet, *Ensayo Critico del desarrollo economico-social de Chile,* Santiago: Editorial Universitaria, 1955, p. 138.

[5] Following the Ibañez military regime, in the midst of a general economic crisis, the "Socialist Republic" consisted of a series of four military *juntas* beginning on June 14, 1932, and ending on the 30th of that month. The officers had no social program and their only achievement was the establishment of the Socialist Party under the leadership of one of them, Marmaduke Grove.

election before the ten-year ban on the.Community Party (1948–1958), the Communists received 71 percent of the coal miners' vote, 63 percent of the nitrate miners' vote and 55 percent of the vote of the copper workers; nationally, in contrast, they received only 18 percent of the vote.

The eleven major mining municipalities accounted for 20 percent of the total national Communist vote.[6] Their history of class conflict and organized political activity clearly established the miners as the most active revolutionary force in Chilean society. Their political radicalism is in line with the radicalism of miners all over the world,[7] in great part the result of the structure of the "occupational community" of the miners. The high degree of interaction among the miners results in very close-knit social organization. Since they are concentrated together, and in relative physical and social isolation from the influences of the dominant social classes in the society, it is highly

[6] The Communist Vote in Mining Centers (1947) [a]
(National Vote=18 percent)

Copper Mining Zone	%
Chuquicamata	68
Potrerillos	47
Sewell	50
Total	55

Nitrate Mining Zone	%
Iquique	34
Pozo Almonte	70
Lagunas	64
Toco	79
Pedro de Valdivia	72
Total	63

Coal Mining Zone	%
Coronel	68
Lota	83
Curanilahue	63
Total	71

[a] Ricardo Cruz Coke, *Geografía electoral de Chile*, Santiago: Editorial del Pacífico, 1952, pp. 81–82.

[7] Lipset, *op. cit.*, pp. 242–246. See also Clark Kerr and Abraham Siegel, "The Interindustry Propensity to Strike—An International Comparison," in Arthur Kornhauser, Robert Dubin and Arthur Ross, (ed.) *Industrial Conflict*, New York: McGraw-Hill, 1954, pp. 200–201.

likely that a shared class outlook based on the recognition of their common interests will develop. The question we deal with here is the impact, if any, that these highly organized, politically radical miners have on the traditionally conservative rural poor.

RURAL LABOR FORCE

Sharp divisions have existed between the urban and rural sectors of the Chilean labor force. A fundamental factor in the stability, continuity and power of the propertied classes was the social condition and attitudes of the rural labor force. The system of rural labor established in colonial times continued down through the twentieth century, little changed by the Revolution for Independence or by a century and a quarter of parliamentary and presidential democracy.

Formally free, the rural labor force was bound to the land by the fact that neighboring landowners would refuse to hire a tenant who had left a *hacienda* because he was discontented with his lot. The economic status of the *inquilino* (tenant worker) was the same throughout the nineteenth and most of the twentieth century: a few pennies a day in wages, a one- or two-room house, a ration of food for each day he worked, and a tiny plot of land. Usually he was required to supply labor for some 240 days a year.[8] Debt servitude was widespread and opportunity for the *inquilino* to advance from that status and become an economically independent farmer was nonexistent. The social and religious life of the *inquilino* was restricted by the landowners (*hacendados*) who preferred that their employees have minimal contact with outsiders. The landowners organized the fiesta, the amusements and the "civil jurisdiction" within the hacienda ("*fundo*"). In the middle 1930's these *fundos* approximated the "ideal type" of an authoritarian system of social control and rigid social stratification.

Within the larger society, where some voluntary associations defending working-class interests were able to establish themselves, the rural poor lived in conditions in which the apparatus of violence and force

[8] George McBride, *Chile: Land and Society*, New York: American Geographical Society, 1936, pp. 148–155.

was regulated by a single owner or family, alternative sources of information were prohibited, and voluntary associations were forbidden. Middle-class parliamentary parties such as the *Radicales* did not advocate a program of socioeconomic reform of the traditional landed system. They were unable to mobilize the peasantry and lower-class rural populace against the landowners' rule. In turn, this forced the middle-class parties to forego a meaningful and dynamic program for industrial and democratic development, and allowed the Socialists and Communists, and then the Christian Democrats, to become spokesmen for the rural poor and agrarian reform.

In his control of the *inquilino*, the landowner held an effective counterweight to any political program of social and economic development that negatively affected his interests. The alliance of foreign investors, large landowners, and those urban entrepreneurs integrated with them, rested on the control the landowners had of the *inquilino*; this was the condition *sine qua non* for their continuing political hegemony.

Apart from the *inquilino*, there was a sector of the rural labor force which was not attached to the land, and consequently was less directly under the dominance of the landowners. These "free laborers" have constituted about one-third of the rural work force; three decades ago they were already said to "have the reputation of provoking many difficulties in the relation between the inquilino and the farm owner." [9] The free laborers were reputed to be frequently more independent in their outlook and more likely to object to any excesses committed by the landowners against the workers. With the gradual mechanization of agriculture and the increased payment in wages in recent years, the rural population has become like wage laborers.

MINERS AND PEASANTS: THE DIFFUSION
PROCESS

Only with industrial development, and especially mining, did the agricultural labor force in Chile begin to have even a hint of political consciousness, impelled largely by their contact with industrial workers. The

landowners' strategy had been to isolate the *inquilinos* from the urban working class, prohibiting their independent organization. By restricting their experience to the *fundo* itself, the *patron* had inhibited the development of their political awareness. With the rapid growth of the urban working class in the period after World War I, strikes spread to the rural districts for the first time in the history of the country. Uprisings took place on a number of *fundos*. The miners took the leadership in this early attempt at rural organization. In 1919, an abortive attempt was made to organize the *inquilinos* into a nationwide federation in the Cometa region in the Aconcagua Valley, "the intention being to federate the *inquilinos* with an organization of miners." [10] Again in the 1930's a broad militant movement of peasant unionization developed, supported by sectors of the urban working class; it was violently repressed by the state and politically defused by the electoral strategy that the leftist parties adopted during the Popular Front. [11]

In recent years the closed system of the large *fundos* has begun to change under the impact of the growth of commercial-capitalistic economic and social relations and, more important, as political organization, trade unions and outside communications networks have been able to undermine the information monopoly of the large landowners.

In the 1958 presidential election, significant sectors of the Chilean peasantry shifted their traditional allegiance away from the Right. The Socialist-Communist coalition, *Frente de Accion Popular* (FRAP) and the Christian Democratic Party are competing for the allegiance of this important and newly emerging social force; they have formed their own peasant "unions" and advocated programs for agrarian reform. In both the 1958 and the 1964 Presidential elections, FRAP campaigned actively throughout the countryside. With old political alignments shifting and the balance of social forces changing, the political direction which the Chilean peasantry will take is seen by all major political parties as a major factor in

---

[9] *Ibid.*, p. 164.

[10] *El Agricultor*, May, 1920, p. 113, cited in McBride, *op. cit.*, p. 166.
[11] Luis Vitale, *Historia del movimiento obrero* Santiago: Editorial POR, 1962, p. 88 *et passim*.

determining the future of Chilean society. The decisive role that the miners can play in determining the direction taken by the peasantry will become clear from our findings.

Our analysis is based on the electoral returns of the Presidential elections of 1958 and 1964, with primary emphasis on the 195 agricultural municipalities. An ecological analysis of these election results is meaningful; distortions of the results through vote-tampering and coercion are believed to have been minimal. In these elections, competing political programs that included the socialist alternative were presented to the Chilean peasantry at a moment when it is emerging as a national political force. Our focus here is on the political impact of the organized mining centers on the peasantry, and on the differential political response of different types of peasantry.

FINDINGS

We define as agricultural municipalities those in which 50 percent or more of the economically active population are engaged in agriculture.[12] Mining municipalities are those in which at least 500 individuals *or* 50 percent or more of the economically active population are in the mining sector. Each of the 296 municipalities in the country was located on a map (in Mattelart, *Atlas Social de las Comunas de Chile*) and each municipality that directly adjoined any mining municipality was defined as a "satellite."

The vote for Salvadore Allende, presidential candidate of the Socialist-Communist coalition (FRAP) is taken as an index of radical political behavior. We define a "high" vote for Allende in 1958 as 30 percent (the national average) or more in the municipality, and a "low" vote as 20 percent or less; in 1964, a "high" vote is 40 percent (the national average) or more in the municipality, and "low" is 25 percent or less.[13]

[12] The data were compiled from several sources: *Censo Nacional Agricola—Ganadero*, Vols. I-VI, Santiago: Servicio nacionale de estadisticas y censos, Republica de Chile, 1955; *Censo de Población*, Santiago: Dirección de Estadistica y Censos de la Republica de Chile, 1960; Armand Mattelart, *Atlas Social de las Comunas de Chila*, Santiago: Editorial del Pacifico, 1966.

[13] We have used "high" and "low" ends of the

If our assumption is correct that the mining municipalities are not only centers of political radicalism but also centers from which political radicalism is diffused into surrounding non-mining areas, then we should find that the greater the number of mining municipalities a "satellite" adjoins, the more likely it is to have a "high" vote for Allende, the FRAP presidential candidate. (The number of mining municipalities adjoining a satellite ranges from one to four.) The municipalities that are neither mining municipalities nor adjoin any should be least likely to give a "high" vote to Allende.

As Table 1 shows, this is precisely what we find in both agricultural and non-agricultural municipalities in 1958 and in 1964. The same relationship holds when we look at the tail end of the vote—the "low" Allende vote (Table 2): The greater the number of mining municipalities adjoining it, the greater the likelihood in a municipality that Allende received a "high" vote (and the less the likelihood of a "low" vote). The greatest political differences are between the mining municipalities and the municipalities that are neither satellites nor have mines in them.

In addition to this demonstration of the political impact of the mining centers on surrounding non-mining areas, the following should be noted: (1) The agricultural municipalities, whatever their proximity to mining centers, have proportionately fewer "high" Allende municipalities among them than the non-agricultural ones. Despite FRAP's appreciable growth in strength in the agricultural areas, the non-agricultural, industrial and urban municipalities still provide the major electoral base of the Left. (2) Yet the strength of the Left grew

voting spectrum as an *index* of radicalism because we are concerned with municipalities as social units, and relative radicalism as an *attribute* of the municipality. Thus, a municipality with a "high" FRAP vote is a "radical" municipality. This procedure differs from simply taking the mean or median FRAP vote in the municipalities and therefore focusing on simple *quantitative* differences, whatever the actual vote. Neither procedure is intrinsically "correct." One or the other is more useful depending on the focus of the analysis; when looking for the determinants of political radicalism, in ecological analysis, we think our procedure is more useful.

TABLE 1. PERCENT "HIGH" VOTE FOR ALLENDE AMONG MALES IN MUNICIPALITIES CLASSIFIED BY PREVA-
LENCE OF AGRICULTURE AND MINING, 1958 AND 1964

| | Prevalence of Agriculture | | | | | | | | |
| | Non-agricultural Municipalities | | | Agricultural Municipalities | | | Entire Country | | |
Prevalence of Mining	1958	1964	(N)	1958	1964	(N)	1958	1964	(N)
Neither "satellites" nor mining municipalities	45	67	(58)	31	51	(162)	35	55	(220)
"Satellites" [a]	73	93	(15)	60	80	(30)	69	82	(45)
Mining municipalities	93	93	(28)	..	..[b]	(3)	93	93	(31)

[a] A further breakdown of "satellites" according to the number of mining municipalities they adjoin also yields a direct relationship between proximity to mining centers and political radicalism. There are too few cases to examine the relationship among non-agricultural municipalities, however. Among agricultural municipalities, 58 percent of the "Satellites" of one mining municipality (N=19) gave Allende a "high" vote in 1958, and 82 percent of the "satellites" of two to four mining municipalities (N=11) gave him a "high" vote. In 1964, the respective figures are 74 percent and 91 percent. In the entire country, in 1958, of the first "satellite" group (N=25), Allende got a "high" vote in 64 percent, and of the second group, 75 percent of the municipalities. The respective figures for 1964 in these groups are 76 percent and 90 percent.

[b] All three mining agricultural municipalities gave Allende a "high" vote in both elections, 1958 and 1964.

throughout the agricultural municipalities from 1958 to 1964. This indicates that the *Frapistas* are penetrating and broadening their support in the peasantry as a whole, and not merely in particular peasant "segments" or strata, a point to which we shall return below. (3) It is beyond the scope of this article, but it should be pointed out that the miners' political influence apparently radiates out to other workers, perhaps even others in the "*clase popular*" made up of a variety of poor from pedlars to artisans and manual laborers. As a cohesive, organized, politically conscious community, the miners' political influence is critical not only in the peasantry but also among other lower strata. The existence of a major mining population whose political influence reaches other exploited strata may explain why class-based and class-conscious politics have emerged so much more clearly in Chile than in other

countries in Latin America which, while having large strata of urban and rural poor, lack cohesive working-class centers.[14]

THE MINERS' POLITICAL CONSCIOUSNESS

The high degree of radical political consciousness in the mining areas of Chile was indicated by the results of Trade Union elections held shortly after Government troops killed 7 and wounded 38 miners during a military occupation of striking copper-mining areas in April, 1966. *El Mercurio,*

[14] We hope to deal extensively with this question in another article. The Agricultural Census makes it possible to gauge the impact of the miners on given agricultural strata but a comparable census for the non-agricultural areas of Chile does not exist. The regular census does not include occupational breakdowns on the municipal level. Such an analysis will require indirect indicators of class structure.

TABLE 2. PERCENT "LOW" VOTE FOR ALLENDE AMONG MALES IN MUNICIPALITIES CLASSIFIED BY PREVA-
LENCE OF AGRICULTURE AND MINING, 1958 AND 1964

| | Prevalence of Agriculture | | | | | | | | |
| | Non-agricultural Municipalities | | | Agricultural Municipalities | | | Entire Country | | |
Prevalence of Mining	1958	1964	(N)	1958	1964	(N)	1958	1964	(N)
Neither "satellites" nor mining municipalities	21	10	(58)	49	20	(162)	41	17	(220)
"Satellites"	7	0	(15)	20	3	(30)	16	2	(45)
Mining municipalities	4	0	(28)	..	..	(3)	3	0	(31)

the anti-Communist conservative daily, editorialized before the election: "The election of union officers that will take place in El Salvador, Potrerillos and Barquito will be realized in an atmosphere of liberty adequate for the workers to express their preferences without the shadow of government pressure over the voters or candidates. These acts are of considerable importance because they will demonstrate what the spontaneous will of the workers really is when they do not feel menaced or intimidated by agitators. . . . Now the workers can take advantage of the new climate in the mines in order to form union committees that serve their interests rather than subordinating themselves to partisan politics." [15] The "spontaneous will" of the workers resulted in an overwhelming victory for the FRAP candidates, even when the elections were government supervised.[16] The point is that the way the miners voted in the presidential elections represents real support for the left—a high level of political consciousness that can be and is effectively transmitted to the peasantry.

In Chile, the organized mining workers' "isolated" communities have a high level of participation in activities, controversies, and organizations—features that are essential to a democratic society. The reason may be, as Lipset suggests, that the "frequent interaction of union members in all spheres of life . . . [makes] for a high level of interest in the affairs of their unions, which translates itself into high participation in local organization and a greater potential for democracy and membership influence." [17]

More important, these same miners consciously seek to influence the politics of others. *El Siglo*, the Communist daily, recently reported that "The two hundred delegates attending the Eighth National Congress of the Miners Federation . . . has adopted a resolution that, throughout the country, it will lend the most active class solidarity to the workers in the countryside in their struggles in defense of their rights

and for the conquest of a true Agrarian Reform. A few days ago the powerful unions [nitrate miners] of Maria Elena, Pedro de Valdivia and Mantos Blancos in the province of Antofagasta adopted a similar resolution." [18] The politicization of the peasantry by the miners is both a conscious effort and a "natural process."

The Left, conscious of the diffusion of radical ideas through informal communication between the working class and the peasantry, intervenes to maximize their advantages from this situation, accentuating and deepening the process of the diffusion of radical ideas. The importance that the Left attributes to this interaction between class conscious workers and the peasantry is shown by the remarks of Luis Corvalan, Communist Party General Secretary:

"The political and cultural ties between the city and the country, between the proletariat and the campesinos, have developed in many ways. The children of campesinos who go to work in industry learn many things which they soon teach to their relatives and friends who have remained on the *fundo* or in the village and with whom they maintain contacts. Thousands of *inquilinos* . . . and small owners have become laborers in the construction of hydro-electric plants, roads, reservoirs and canals, or have been incorporated into the infant industries of sugar or lumber and live alongside numerous members of the proletariat who come from the cities. Furthermore, the crises and the repressive measures employed against the urban working class have caused many of the workers in the mines and factories to return to the country. *Throughout Chile, on the fundos and in the villages, we have seen many laborers, including some who were union leaders in the nitrate coal and copper* [industries]. It follows that the political work of the popular parties and especially of us Communists, should also figure among the principal elements that have influenced and are influencing the creation of a new social consciousness in the countryside." [19] (Our italics)

As urbanization and industrialization impinge on the peasantry and cause migrations of the labor force, so also is the political

---

[15] *El Mercurio*, April 15, 1966, p. 3.

[16] The FRAP candidates obtained 16,227 votes, the Radical Party 3,287, and the Christian Democrats 3,263. The FRAP elected seven of the ten new union officers, replacing three Christian Democrats. *Ultima Hora*, April 19, 1966, p. 2.

[17] *Op. cit.*, p. 408.

[18] *El Siglo*, February 20, 1966, p. 10.

[19] Luis Corvalan. "The Communists' Tactics Relative to Agrarian Reform in Chile" in T. Lynn Smith (editor), *Agrarian Reform in Latin America*, New York: Knopf, 1965, p. 139. Our translation of the original differs slightly from the version in Smith's book.

awareness of those individuals who have roots in both cultures heightened. These individuals bring the new ideas of struggle and of class solidarity to their friends and relatives still living in the rural areas and employed in agriculture. To the extent that the Left political parties are effective in organizing and politicizing these newly recruited industrial workers, they have an effective carrier of radicalism into the countryside.

THE DIFFUSION OF "POLITICAL CULTURE" AND THE STRUCTURE OF THE AGRICULTURAL LABOR FORCE

We discussed elsewhere the relationship between the structure of the agrarian labor force—the class composition of the countryside—and the FRAP presidential vote.[20] We find an inverse relationship between the proportion of proprietors in a municipality's agricultural labor force and the likelihood that it would give Allende a "high" vote. The higher the proportion of agricultural proprietors in a municipality the less likely it was to have a "high" Allende vote. This was consistent with our finding regarding the relationship between the proportion of wage laborers in a municipality's agricultural labor force and the vote—the higher the proportion of wage laborers, the greater the likelihood that the municipality gave Allende a "high" vote. From this evidence, we concluded that class position is a major determinant of peasant political behavior and that the rural proletariat, as distinguished from peasant proprietors, is apparently the major social base of the FRAP in the Chilean countryside.

The question now is what impact the or-

---

[20] James Petras and Maurice Zeitlin, "Agrarian Radicalism in Chile," *British Journal of Sociology*, forthcoming.

ganized political centers, the mining municipalities and their satellites, have on the class determination of voting in the countryside. We find that the political differences based on class position among the peasants tend to disappear in the mining and satellite municipalities. In the non-mining, non-satellite municipalities, however, class structure continues to determine voting patterns. The mining satellites are more likely, whatever the structure of the agricultural labor force (or class composition of the peasantry), to give Allende a "high" vote than the non-mining, non-satellite municipalities (Table 3). The theoretical point is clear: the mining and adjoining areas develop a distinct political culture, radical and socialist in content, that tends to eliminate the importance of class differences in the peasantry, and unite the peasants across class lines.

The fact is that the Chilean Left not only specifically directs its working class activists in the trade unions to unite with peasants in support of their demands but also emphasizes the role they can play in uniting different peasant strata: *El Siglo*, the Chilean Communist daily, writes: "All the workers in all the unions should unite with the peasants, wherever the unions are near agricultural properties in which the peasants are initiating struggles in defense of their interests. The miners' unions must be there to help the organization of the peasant unions. All our fellow miners must be there to bring all their moral and material support to the peasants who are struggling for possession of the land." [21] The Communist Party general secretary urges that "the forms of organization should be in accord with the wishes of the campesinos themselves; but we Communists believe that the best form of organization is that of the independent

---

[21] *El Siglo*, February 20, 1966, p. 10.

TABLE 3. PERCENT "HIGH" VOTE FOR ALLENDE AMONG MALES IN AGRICULTURAL MUNICIPALITIES CLASSIFIED BY PREVALENCE OF MINING AND PROPRIETORS, 1964

Prevalence of Mining	Percent Proprietors							
	70 plus		50–69		30–49		under 30	
Neither "satellite" nor mining municipality	29	(35)	46	(24)	51	(37)	80	(54)
Mining "satellites"	83	(6)	100	(3)	87	(8)	90	(10)
Mining municipalities	100	(1)	100	(1)		(0)	100	(1)

union, with headquarters in the village, in which are grouped the workers from various *fundos* and *all of the modest sectors of the rural population from the wage-hand to the small proprietor,* including the sharecropper, the poor campesino, etc." [22] Communist organizing strategy, the formation of independent organizations which include all of the rural "modest sectors . . . from wage hands to the small proprietor," adds a conscious element to further the general process of social interaction and diffusion of political consciousness that unites laborers and small proprietors in the areas adjoining mining centers.

CONCLUSIONS

The miners' organizational skills and political competence, the proximity of the mines to the countryside, the sharing of an exploited position, and conscious political choice, enable the miners to politicize and radicalize the Chilean countryside. The

---

[22] Corvalan, *op. cit.,* p. 141.

sense of citizenship and the necessity of having their own leaders that develops in the mining communities, where the miners themselves, rather than "other strata and agencies," run their affairs, also expresses itself in the political leadership and influence that their communities exert in adjoining rural areas. Further, the miners can supply legal, political, and economic resources to aid the peasants concretely, and thus demonstrate to them the power of organization and of struggle in defense of their common interests against landowners. Where the miners have a strong political organization, peasant proprietors and agricultural wage laborers are equally susceptible to radicalism. Political men, such as the Chilean miners, who make an effort to organize or influence peasant proprietors spread over the countryside, relatively isolated and atomized, can provide a link between them. The miners' leadership and ideology provide the peasants with a form of communication and sharing of experience that is necessary for them to recognize and be able to act upon their common interests.

CHAPTER 46

The Trend of Occupational Mobility
in the United States

OTIS DUDLEY DUNCAN

U NTIL a decade or so ago, most sociologists who wrote on the matter were of the opinion that the volume or rate of social mobility was declining.[1] This conclusion was questioned both by Rogoff's data[2] for Indianapolis, pertaining to years around 1940 and 1910, and by critical discussions[3] that pointed to flaws in the reasoning and evidence then available. The most recent and empirically cogent exploration of the topic,[4] comparing national samples studied in 1945, 1947, 1952, and 1957, yields the "impression that no striking

changes have occurred in mobility patterns and rates since World War II. . . . what movement has occurred, however, is in the direction of increasing rates of movement."[5] Jackson and Crockett present this conclusion with appropriate qualifications, because of the defects of the original studies and doubts about their comparability.

In view of the current concern for the "inheritance of poverty" and the perennial interest in whether the American social structure is becoming more "rigid," further effort to assess the trend is not out of place. The present report can claim to make a contribution by virtue of its dependence on the most nearly definitive estimates of occupational mobility yet made for this country. Lacking such estimates for the past, however, we resort to an indirect procedure for ascertaining time changes in mobility patterns, which, though conceptually sound, entails serious possibility of measurement error. As in other problems of social measurement, we had best rely on the convergence of a variety of evidence, rather than the results of any single study.

METHOD

Unpublished tables from the cooperative study, "Occupational Changes in a Generation (OCG),"[6] provide the following infor-

This report was prepared in connection with a project on "Differential Fertility and Social Mobility," supported by research grant GM-10386, U.S. Public Health Service. A version of this paper was presented at the 1964 annual meeting of the American Sociological Association.

[1] Elbridge Sibley, "Some Demographic Clues to Stratification," *American Sociological Review,* 7 (June, 1942), pp. 322–330; J. O. Hertzler, "Some Tendencies Toward a Closed Class System in the United States," *Social Forces,* 30 (March, 1952), pp. 313–323; August B. Hollingshead, "Trends in Social Stratification: A Case Study," *American Sociological Review,* 17 (December, 1952), pp. 679–686.

[2] Natalie Rogoff, *Recent Trends in Occupational Mobility,* Glencoe, Ill.: Free Presss, 1953.

[3] Gideon Sjoberg, "Are Social Classes in America Becoming More Rigid?" *American Sociological Review,* 16 (December, 1951), pp. 775–783; Ely Chinoy, "Social Mobility Trends in the United States," *American Sociological Review,* 20 (April, 1955), pp. 180–186; Gerhard E. Lenski, "Trends in Inter-Generational Occupational Mobility in the United States," *American Sociological Review,* 23 (October, 1958), pp. 514–523.

[4] Elton F. Jackson and Harry J. Crockett, Jr., "Occupational Mobility in the United States: A Point Estimate and Trend Comparison," *American Sociological Review,* 29 (February, 1964), pp. 5–15.

[5] *Ibid.,* p. 15.

[6] U.S. Bureau of the Census, "Lifetime Occupational Mobility of Adult Males: March 1962," *Current Population Reports,* Series P-23, No. 11 (May 12, 1964). These data were collected for a project supported by a grant (G-16233) from the National

mation for each of four groups of birth cohorts—men aged 25–34, 35–44, 45–54, and 55–64 in March 1962: respondent's major occupation group in 1962 by major occupation of his father (or other person who was the head of the family) at the time the respondent was "about 16 years old," and respondent's occupation in 1962 by the occupation group of his own first job. Regarding father's occupation or, alternatively, first job as the respondent's origin status, the principle used here is that the origin distribution of an older cohort can be applied to the transition matrix of a younger cohort to calculate what the destination distribution of the older cohort would have been, 10, 20, or 30 years ago, if it had experienced the same probabilities of mobility as the younger cohort at a comparable age. Using independent estimates of the actual destination distributions of the older cohort at the earlier dates, one can compare its actual with its "expected" distributions, attributing any discrepancy to (net) changes in pattern of mobility.

The principle and the specific procedures had best be set forth formally. Let $P=(p_{ij})$ be the transition matrix of an intergenerational occupational mobility table. That is, p_{ij} is the proportion, out of all respondents originating in the ith category of father's occupation, whose destination (status as of the survey date) is the jth occupation class. Hence p_{ij} is what Carlsson[7] calls an "outflow coefficient," and P is what Miller[8] calls the "standard outflow table." Note that $\Sigma_j p_{ij}=1.0$. Let $A=(a_i)$ be the origin vector associated with the mobility table, i.e., a row vector such that $\Sigma_i a_i=1.0$, which gives the proportion of respondents who originated in the ith occupation category. Let $C=(c_j)$ be the destination vector, giving the proportions with destinations in the jth occupation category, so that $\Sigma_j c_j=1.0$. In consequence of these definitions, we have the identity, $C=AP$.

Let us attach subscripts to the vectors

and matrices to identify four birth cohorts of men and four years in which destinations are observed. Thus C_{rs} is the destination vector for men in the rth cohort observed in year s and A_{rs} is the origin vector for the same cohort, as it would have been ascertained by retrospective questions in a survey taken in year s. The foregoing identity now reads, more explicitly, $C_{rs}=A_{rs}P_{rs}$. Assign $r=0$ for men born in 1897–1906, $r=1$ for 1907–16, 2 for 1917–26, and 3 for 1927–36. Let $s=6$ refer to 1962, $s=5$ to 1952, 4 to 1942, and 3 to 1932.

The OCG tables provide estimates of A_{06}, A_{16}, A_{26}, and A_{36}; C_{06}, C_{16}, C_{26}, and C_{36}; and P_{06}, P_{16}, P_{26}, and P_{36}. The crucial assumptions are, then, that $A_{06}=A_{05}=A_{04}=A_{03}$; that $A_{16}=A_{15}=A_{14}$; and that $A_{26}=A_{25}$. Even in concept, these equations can only be approximate, because the cohorts are not closed to mortality and external migration. Although, in practice, we may well assume that differential mortality and differential migration have negligible effects, we must also admit the possibility of sampling and other survey errors. A cohort reporting in 1962 on father's occupation might give different responses from those of the same cohort interrogated in 1952, even though the facts of their social origins could not have changed. Here, as elsewhere in mobility research, it is easier to appreciate the likelihood of sizeable errors, both random and systematic, than to estimate them or to devise suitable corrections.

The remaining information required calls for some further approximations. A first estimate of C_{05}, C_{15}, and C_{25} (the occupation distributions of men 45–54, 35–44, and 25–34 years old in 1952) is given by 1950 census tables of age by occupation for the male experienced civilian labor force.[9] These were simultaneously adjusted to the age distribution and the occupation distribution of the male experienced civilian labor force shown in 1952 Current Population Survey sample statistics.[10] The adjustment assumed

Science Foundation to the University of Chicago, Peter M. Blau, principal investigator.

[7] Gösta Carlsson, *Social Mobility and Class Structure*, Lund, Sweden: CWK Gleerup, 1958, p. 73.

[8] S. M. Miller, "Comparative Social Mobility," *Current Sociology*, 9 (1960), p. 7.

[9] U.S. Bureau of the Census, "Occupational Characteristics," *1950 Census of Population*, Special Report P-E, No. 1 B, Washington: Government Printing Office, 1956, Tables 4 and 5.

[10] U.S. Bureau of the Census, "Aunual Report on the Labor Force: 1952," *Current Population Reports*, Series P-50, No. 45 (July, 1953), Tables D and 3.

that the 1952 CPS figures were "true" marginals of the age-by-occupation tabulation, while the 1950 census figures were initial estimates of the cell frequencies in such a tabulation, to be adjusted to the marginals. The procedure is the one given by Deming for "adjusting sample frequencies to expected marginal totals, both sets of marginal totals known." [11] There are two reasons for making this adjustment: (1) it updates the 1950 data to 1952, providing an exact cohort match and allowing for nontrivial changes in the occupation structure over the two-year period; (2) it adjusts the census data to CPS levels, a matter of some consequence in view of systematic differences between CPS and census data.

Destination distributions were also needed for 1942 (C_{04}, C_{14}) and 1932 (C_{03}). Here, we were content to use 1940 and 1930 census data, matching for age and thus incurring a two-year slippage from a cohort match. Some adjustment of these census data, to secure comparability with the 1950 Census, had been made by Jaffe and Carleton, so these authors' figures, for men 35–44 and 25–34 in 1940 and 25–34 in 1930, were used.[12]

Actually, since concern is with mobility *trends* rather than annual fluctuations of occupational distributions, one could argue that 1930 is a more pertinent basis for evaluating earlier experience than 1932, the year in which the Great Depression was at its trough. That is, 1930 data for men 25–34 years old may more nearly represent the implicit trend as of 1932 than would data on men 25–34 years old in 1932. Similarly, 1940 data are little affected by World War II, while in 1942 the economy was on a short-run war-time basis. Whatever the merit of this argument, however, it is well to recognize that the comparisons involving the two earlier years involve less adequate approximations than those pertaining to 1952.

Once the estimates of origin and destination distributions are accepted, we can take advantage of a quite rigorous procedure for comparing transition matrices, even though

some of the matrices are unknown. Consider the null hypothesis, $P_{25}=P_{36}$, where P_{25} cannot be observed directly. On this hypothesis, $A_{25}P_{36}=C_{25}$, or, by virtue of the assumption about origin distributions, $A_{26}P_{36}=C_{25}$. Now, this equation could hold even if $P_{25}\neq P_{36}$; hence, we should have to be cautious in accepting the null hypothesis. But if $A_{26}P_{36}\neq C_{25}$, we can be quite sure that the null hypothesis is false. In this event, the set of differences, $A_{26}P_{36}-C_{25}$, shows in *net* terms the differences between the mobility patterns represented by P_{36} and P_{25}.

The calculations just outlined can be repeated using the intragenerational transition matrices for mobility from first job to current occupation, Q_{rs}, and the first job distributions, B_{rs}, as origin vectors. The previous assumptions and notation still apply, substituting B for A and Q for P, with the general identity being $C_{rs}=B_{rs}Q_{rs}$.

Table 1 outlines the derivation of the comparisons that will be made. "Expected" distributions are those that would have been produced by the transition matrix obtained for a younger cohort in 1962, if it had applied to the experience of an older cohort up to the same age that the younger cohort had attained in 1962.

One of the transition matrices is illustrated in Table 2. The actual origin and destination distributions associated with this particular matrix are given in lines (1) and (2) of Table 3. Line (3) shows the origin distribution for the next older cohort, and line (4) shows its destination distribution as of 1952, as estimated by the procedure already described. The result of the hypothetical calculation of the 1952 destination distribution of the older cohort is given in line (5). The differences, line (6), between "expected" and actual distributions as of 1952 are interpreted as resulting from the differences between the transition matrix for men 25–34 years old in 1962 (Table 2) and the unknown transition matrix for men 25–34 in 1952. That is, we can see the net results of the fact that the two matrices were not identical, even though we do not know exactly what one of them was like.

Observe that an extension of the scheme in Table 1 subsumes the possibility of comparing mobility matrices to 1962 with those

[11] W. Edwards Deming, *Statistical Adjustment of Data,* New York: Wiley, 1943, Ch. 7.

[12] A. J. Jaffe and R. O. Carleton, *Occupational Mobility in the United States, 1930–1960,* New York: King's Crown Press, 1954, Appendix Table 1.

TABLE 1. FORMAT FOR COMPARISONS OF MOBILITY TO 1962 WITH MOBILITY TO 1952, 1942, AND 1932

Item and Source	Birth Cohort			
	1927–1936	1917–1926	1907–1916	1897–1906
Age in—				
1962	25–34	35–44	45–54	55–64
1952	...	25–34	35–44	45–54
1942	...	...	25–34	35–44
1932	...	...	...	25–34
Origin distribution, ascertained in 1962				
Father's occupation (1962 OCG)	A_{36}	A_{26}	A_{16}	A_{06}
First job (1962 OCG)	B_{36}	B_{26}	B_{16}	B_{06}
Observed transition matrix to 1962				
From father's occupation (1962 OCG)	P_{36}	P_{26}	P_{16}	P_{06}
From first job (1962 CCG)	Q_{36}	Q_{26}	Q_{16}	Q_{06}
Observed (or estimated) destination distribution in—				
1962 (1962 OCG)	C_{36}	C_{26}	C_{16}	C_{06}
1952 (1950 Census, adjusted to 1952 CPS)	...	C_{25}	C_{15}	C_{05}
1942 (1940 Census, Jaffe-Carleton)	...	...	C_{14}	C_{04}
1932 (1930 Census, Jaffe-Carleton)	...	...	...	C_{03}
Destination distribution expected on the basis of intergeneration mobility				
1952	...	$A_{26}P_{36}$	$A_{16}P_{26}$	$A_{06}P_{16}$
1942	...	...	$A_{16}P_{36}$	$A_{06}P_{26}$
1932	...	...	...	$A_{06}P_{36}$
Destination distribution expected on the basis of intrageneration mobility				
1952	...	$B_{26}Q_{36}$	$B_{16}Q_{26}$	$B_{06}Q_{16}$
1942	...	...	$B_{16}Q_{36}$	$B_{06}Q_{26}$
1932	...	...	...	$B_{06}Q_{36}$
Differences between expected and observed destination distributions, column number in Table 4				
1952	...	(1)	(2)	(3)
1942	...	...	(4)	(5)
1932	...	...	...	(6)

that will apply in the future. For example, $A_{36}P_{16}$ is the expected destination distribution in 1982 for men 45–54 years old at that time. When the 1982 data become available, C_{38}—$A_{36}P_{16}$ will provide a basis for inferring differences in intergenerational mobility to 1962 and to 1982 for men 45–54 years of age, even if no OCG-type survey is carried out in 1982.

RESULTS

Substantively, line (6) of Table 3, repeated in column (1) of Table 4, reveals that young men in 1962 had entered salaried professional and technical occupations and, secondarily, salaried managerial jobs in larger proportions than their counterparts in 1952, but had gone in smaller proportions into farming, operative and kindred jobs, craft occupations, and self-employed proprietorship. A virtually identical pattern

of differences is observed, although the magnitudes are a little smaller, when the first-job-to-current-occupation matrices for 1962 and 1952 are compared in column (1), lower panel of Table 4. In these comparisons, we have taken account of the fact that the more recent cohort had a more favorable starting point—as revealed by the comparison of lines (1) and (3) of Table 3. One may, if he likes, say that "opportunities" for men with given origins were more favorable in 1962 than they were in 1952. "Opportunities," however, would have to be regarded as a composite of greater demand for high-level salaried white-collar workers and a better-qualified supply of men to fill the jobs. The 1927–36 cohort, of course, had a higher level of educational attainment than the 1917–26 cohort.

Table 4 summarizes all six sets of comparisons. Much the same pattern of differ-

TABLE 2. TRANSITION MATRIX P_{36}, MOBILITY FROM FATHER'S OCCUPATION TO RESPONDENT'S OCCUPATION IN 1962, FOR MEN 25 TO 34 YEARS OLD IN 1962 (in Percentages)

Father's Occupation					Respondent's Occupation in 1962 (see code in stub)								
	(1)	(2)	(3)	(4)	(5)	(6)	(7)	(8)	(9)	(10)	(11)	(12)	Total*
Professional, technical, and kindred workers													
(1) Self-employed	6.6	54.0	8.0	5.1	8.8	2.9	2.2	5.8	0.0	6.6	0.0	0.0	100.0
(2) Salaried	1.6	43.8	9.9	1.2	9.6	7.1	10.6	12.2	1.9	1.6	0.5	0.0	100.0
Managers, officials, and proprietors, except farm													
(3) Salaried	1.2	34.9	17.0	1.5	6.9	8.8	17.9	7.6	1.0	2.5	0.7	0.0	100.0
(4) Self-employed	2.4	21.1	19.5	11.1	11.5	6.5	10.7	11.4	2.7	2.8	0.4	0.0	100.0
(5) Sales workers	3.0	25.0	6.9	2.1	20.8	9.6	12.3	10.2	5.7	2.7	1.5	0.0	100.0
(6) Clerical and kindred workers	2.1	29.7	7.5	3.1	6.4	11.6	18.2	12.3	5.7	2.1	1.4	0.0	100.0
(7) Craftsmen, foremen and kindred workers	0.3	17.4	8.0	4.0	4.7	6.4	28.7	19.0	4.8	5.9	0.3	0.5	100.0
(8) Operatives and kindred workers	0.8	13.9	3.5	2.7	4.0	7.4	20.4	27.6	6.0	11.2	0.7	1.8	100.0
(9) Service workers, including private household	0.4	13.3	6.5	1.7	9.3	8.0	20.7	25.1	9.5	4.8	0.4	0.4	100.0
(10) Laborers, except farm and mine	0.0	6.5	3.9	1.1	4.9	6.7	23.7	33.1	6.0	11.9	0.8	1.5	100.0
(11) Farmers and farm managers	0.4	7.6	3.5	3.2	2.2	7.7	15.2	24.9	4.9	9.5	13.9	6.9	100.0
(12) Farm laborers and foremen	0.8	2.9	1.2	0.0	1.6	3.7	17.6	25.7	12.7	11.0	2.0	20.8	100.0

* May differ from row sum owing to rounding error.

TABLE 3. ORIGIN AND DESTINATION DISTRIBUTIONS USED IN COMPARING INTERGENERATION MOBILITY TO 1952 AND 1962 FOR MEN 25 TO 34 YEARS OLD (IN PERCENTAGES)

Item and Formula	Occupation (see code in Table 1)												Total
	(1)	(2)	(3)	(4)	(5)	(6)	(7)	(8)	(9)	(10)	(11)	(12)	
(1) Origin distribution, men 25–34 in 1962: A_{96}	1.5	4.7	4.5	7.9	3.7	4.7	19.8	18.1	5.8	6.8	19.8	2.7	100.0
(2) Destination distribution,* men 25–34 in 1962: $C_{96}=A_{96}P_{96}$	1.0	17.2	7.0	3.4	5.9	7.3	19.2	21.0	5.1	7.2	3.3	2.5	100.0
(3) Origin distribution, men 25–34 in 1952 (35–44 in 1962): A_{96}	1.3	3.2	4.3	7.5	4.8	3.2	18.5	15.6	4.8	7.2	26.8	2.8	100.0
(4) Destination distribution, men 25–34 in 1952 (a) First approximation: 1950 Census data, men 25–34	0.9	8.3	4.5	3.7	7.0	7.4	19.9	24.2	4.6	8.2	7.8	3.6	100.0
(b) Adjusted to 1952 (see text): C_{95}	0.9	8.8	4.9	4.5	5.7	7.6	21.0	24.6	4.4	8.3	6.6	2.7	100.0
(5) Expected destination distribution,* men 25–34 in 1952: $A_{95}P_{95}$	1.0	15.4	6.6	3.3	5.5	7.1	19.1	22.0	5.3	7.8	4.0	2.9	100.0
(6) Difference between expected and observed (estimated) destination distributions for men 25–34 in 1952: $A_{95}P_{95}—C_{95}$	0.1	6.6	1.7	−1.2	−0.2	−0.5	−1.9	−2.6	0.9	−0.5	−2.6	0.2	0.0

* May differ slightly from results which would be obtained in carrying out calculation with figures in Tables 1 and 3, owing to rounding error.

ences already noted for age 25–34 reappears in the second and third columns of Table 4, where the 1962–1952 comparisons concern the matrices for men respectively 35–44 and 45–54 years old. A few variations in detail can be discerned, but there is no need to list all of them verbally. Perhaps the most interesting pattern is that contrasts between the 1952 and 1962 matrices tend to be most pronounced for the youngest age group (25–34) and least so for the oldest (45–54). This tendency is summarized in the indexes of dissimilarity shown at the bottom of the relevant columns of differences.

The fourth and fifth columns of Table 4 present the two possible comparisons of 1962 with 1942 matrices, for men 25–34 and 35–44. The subdivision of the first two occupation groups into self-employed and salaried workers is no longer available, and this is a pity in view of the evidence that the distinction is important. The evidence is clear, however, that the 1962 matrices put larger proportions of men into these top two occupation groups than did the 1942 matrices, and also a larger proportion into the top blue-collar category, craftsmen and foremen. In comparison with the 1942 matrices, the 1962 matrices put far fewer men into farm occupations and jobs as laborers. The

TABLE 4. DIFFERENCES, IN PERCENTAGE POINTS, BETWEEN OCCUPATION DISTRIBUTIONS FOR MEN OF SPECIFIED AGES PRODUCED BY 1962 MOBILITY MATRICES (FATHER'S OCCUPATION TO CURRENT OCCUPATION; FIRST JOB TO CURRENT OCCUPATION) AND BY MATRICES FOR EARLIER YEARS

Major Occupation Group	1962 minus 1952			1962 minus 1942		1962 minus 1932
	(25–34)	(35–44)	(45–54)	(25–34)	(35–44)	(25–34)
	(1)	(2)	(3)	(4)	(5)	(6)
			Intergeneration mobility			
Professional, technical, and kindred						
Self-employed	0.1	0.3	−0.1	8.3	4.7	9.3
Salaried	6.6	3.5	1.5			
Managers, officials, and proprietors						
Salaried	1.7	2.4	0.7	2.9	5.5	1.3
Self-employed	−1.2	0.0	1.0			
Sales workers	−0.2	0.1	0.3	−1.3	−1.4	−1.6
Clerical and kindred	−0.5	0.4	0.6	0.1	0.6	0.7
Craftsmen, foremen	−1.9	−0.8	0.1	4.8	2.9	0.8
Operatives and kindred	−2.6	−2.0	0.0	−0.8	1.3	3.9
Service	0.9	−0.3	−0.3	0.0	−1.4	0.5
Laborers	−0.5	−0.5	−1.0	−5.0	−3.6	−5.1
Farmers	−2.6	−2.6	−2.3	−5.1	−6.1	−6.2
Farm laborers	0.2	−0.5	−0.5	−3.9	−2.5	−3.6
Index of dissimilarity*	(9.5)	(6.7)	(4.2)	(16.1)	(15.0)	(16.5)
			Intrageneration mobility			
Professional, etc.: Self-employed	−0.1	0.3	0.0	5.8	4.8	7.3
Salaried	5.1	2.8	1.9			
Managers, etc.: Salaried	1.5	2.4	0.9	3.1	5.4	0.8
Self-employed	−1.1	−0.4	0.5			
Sales	0.1	0.3	0.3	−0.7	−1.0	−0.5
Clerical	−0.6	0.7 .	0.9	0.1	1.2	1.0
Craftsmen, foremen	−1.2	−1.0	0.2	5.0	2.3	1.1
Operatives	−2.1	−1.8	−0.4	−0.4	0.9	3.9
Service	1.0	−0.3	−0.2	0.0	−1.7	0.6
Laborers	−0.6	−0.4	−1.1	−5.1	−3.7	−5.6
Farmers	−2.5	−2.3	−2.5	−4.6	−5.8	−5.7
Farm laborers	0.5	−0.3	−0.5	−3.2	−2.4	−2.9
Index of dissimilarity*	(8.2)	(6.5)	(4.7)	(14.0)	(14.6)	(14.7)

* Sum of positive differences.

comparisons for the two age groups are quite consistent.

The final comparison, column (6) of Table 4, concerns matrices separated by three decades, and only one age group can be examined. In this case the 1962 matrix assigned more men to professional occupations and more to operative jobs than did the 1932 matrix, and fewer men to farm occupations and jobs as laborers.

The 1962–1942 and 1962–1932 differences, as summarized by the indexes of dissimilarity, are larger than the 1962–1952 differences. Although this is doubtless of substantive import, all three comparisons are possible for only one age group, and the "observed" distributions for 1942 and 1932 are perhaps more questionable than the 1952 distribution.

Three points of interpretative comment are offered. First, the larger indexes of dissimilarity for the 1962–1942 and 1962–1932 comparisons, relative to the 1962–1952 comparisons, suggest that the (unknown) mobility matrices that might have been observed in 1952 resemble the 1962 matrices more closely than would the 1942 or 1932 matrices.

Second, the larger indexes of dissimilarity for intergenerational comparisons than for intragenerational comparisons indicate that part of the improvement in "opportunities" over time is reflected in mobility from father's occupation to first job (not studied here).[13] The remainder is registered in intragenerational mobility, first job to current occupation.

Third, the higher indexes for younger cohorts, noted especially in 1962, suggest that recent improvements in "opportunities" have been differentially distributed, to the advantage of recent entrants into the working force. As noted above, any adequate explanation of changing "opportunity structures" must refer both to altered conditions of manpower demand and to changes in the quality or character of the supply.

In summary, the 1962 matrices produced more "upward" mobility—particularly into salaried professional and technical positions —and less "downward" mobility—into lower blue-collar and farm occupations—than did the 1952, 1942, or 1932 matrices. As of 1962, there was little immediate cause for anxiety about whether the American occupational structure was providing more restricted opportunities. But is is well to remember that the OCG data refer to a historical experience in which the transition to complete industrialization was rapidly nearing its end. If the movement off farms has been a major factor inducing upward mobility from nonfarm origins in the past, it is not clear what its counterpart may be in an era when few persons originate on farms. American sociology may be approaching another period of concern about tendencies producing rigidification. Repeated readings of the trends will be required.

---

[13] See U.S. Bureau of the Census, "Lifetime Occupational Mobility of Adult Males: March 1962," *op. cit.*, for relevant data.

XI

The Problem of Equality

The physical and mental capacities of individuals are demonstrably dissimilar (see Anastasi, 1958); these dissimilarities, when socially identified, are frequently translated into social inequalities in wealth, in power, in status and in opportunity. The problem of equality is, fundamentally, two-fold: first, there is the problem of justifying broad social equalities between persons of diverse abilities and, second, having justified equalities in some regard, there is the problem of rationalizing the persistence of inequalities in others (see Parsons, 1970). Stated otherwise, the first problem is that of finding some merit common to all men which vindicates their equalitarian treatment despite their diverse abilities and the second problem is that of consistently reconciling whatever solution is offered to the first problem with the empirical fact that some are more equal than others. All societies are equalitarian in some regards and inequalitarian in others. It is the task of political philosophy to provide a sound basis for making distinctions when they are made and for ignoring distinctions which could be made. It is the task of ideology to convincingly assert the essential justice of the national political philosophy.

Needless to say, numerous ideologies which justify social inequalities have emerged during the development of civiliza-tions (see Ossowski, 1963; Burke, 1790; Sumner, 1883). One of the important differences between these diverse viewpoints hinges upon whether they regard group differences in wealth, status, etc., as primarily the products of heredity or of environment. Ordinarily, an equalitarian ideology is associated with the belief that in some fundamental sense, all men are created equal and, hence, that any group differences in attainment ultimately must be attributable to differences in their environmental advantages. Such a perspective commits one to the view that inequalities in outcome are *necessarily* the product of inequalities in opportunity. While justice demands equalization of differential opportunities, equalitarian ideology provides a yardstick for measuring the extent of inequalities in opportunity. That ruler is the extent of group differences in outcome for, so the ideology goes, to the degree that groups differ in their attainment, they must suffer disadvantages or handicaps. In this way, the inherent logic of equalitarian ideologies commands at least an equality of socioeconomic and other outcomes as between groups differing in their ethnic, religious, racial, regional and socioeconomic origins. Any differences in average outcomes must, in the final analysis, rest on differences, perhaps undetected, in opportunity. Consequently, an equalitarian ideology usually is associated with a program for social welfare designed to eliminate all group differences in outcome through remedial programs of various kinds.

If the idea that the social stratification of groups is illegitimate flows from an equalitarian ideology which traces such group differences to differential environmental advantages, then the notion that individual differentiation is itself due to environmental advantages or disadvantages makes not just group, but individual differences in wealth, in status, or whatever equally illegitimate. Such a view, carried to its logical conclusion, leads one to anarchism or utopian illusions of a society whose division of labor is maintained through cooperative spirit rather than differential reward. If, indeed, the order one obseves in a society, which gives to some a degree of control over others, is only an artifact of differential environmental advantages and bears no relation to any identifiable individual differences, then one's place in society is only accidental; everyone's capacity is inherently equal to everyone else's, though apparently and superficially differing according to environmental happenstances. In this view, differential wealth and differential power are not rewards to differential ability but the product of accident. And, once established, such differentials tend to be self-perpetuating through the laws of inheritance. But authority accidentally acquired is easily seen as arbitrary and carries no command of respect and, therefore, of obedience. Thus, this view undermines the bases of authority and leads to anarchism.

Plainly, very few entertain the hypothesis (which so far as we can see is refuted by the available empirical evidence) that *individual* differences may be accounted for by environmental advantage alone. Hence, environmentalism and equalitarianism usually go hand in hand only insofar as *group* differences are concerned. Equality of outcome is extended only to the point of equivalent group performances; equality of opportunity is extended to all individuals, but *within* each group individuals of differing abilities and motivations will make dif-

ferential use of similar opportunities and these attain different individual outcomes. Thus, the equalitarian ideology implicitly makes the measure of hereditary differences in ability the differential individual outcomes which would be observed if all individuals were presented with a standardized and, therefore, equal array of opportunities. There is a sense in which the equalitarian avoids being an anarchist only by admitting that there are genetic bases of individual differences and, in so doing, becomes an oppressive socialist whose sense of fairness commands him to routinize the opportunities and advantages of all to a common mean. (After the revolution, strawberries and cream for everyone; if you don't like strawberries and cream, then you will learn to.)

Once a hereditary basis of individual differences is admitted, one must at least *intellectually* consider the possibility that *group* differences in outcome have a hereditary as well as an environmental basis. To maintain a stout defense that environmental advantage alone is the basis of group differences in outcome requires one to take an *ideological* position which is not yet wholly defensible scientifically. But once hereditary differences are seen as a potential source of variation in group outcomes, the ideological basis for the equalization of group outcomes has been undermined. One might still maintain a plea for the equalization of opportunities, but insofar as there is an independent measure of ability (i.e., a measure other than the unequal outcomes of individuals with similar opportunities) even this concept is transformed. Not all abilities (which now admittedly vary from one individual to the next) are necessarily nurtured best by the *same* environment. Once hereditary bases of group and individual outcomes are admitted, equality of environmental opportunity is transformed into an equality of opportunities for individuals to realize their inherited capacities. Equality of opportunity in this sense is, however, wholly consistent with gross inequalities in access to important environmental advantages, for resources should not be made available to individuals whose capacities prevent them from effectively utilizing them. Consequently, we may have tracking in schools and other forms of inequality and at the same time claim to be creating an environment in which individuals have equal opportunity to develop their inherited capacities. The existence of hereditary differences undermines any simplistic equalitarian ideology and is an important rationalization for elitism in modern societies.

The ideological viewpoints sketched above have been illustrated by situations more extreme than are usually found in everyday life. Yet the tension between an equalitarian ideology and a stratified social order is real. That tension is more pronounced when an equalitarian ideology is coupled to a pattern of recruitment based on individual achievement, because the one value pattern asserts a fundamental, though ambiguous, commonality of individuals and the other asserts a no less fundamental, but unspecified, divergence of individual capacity. The resolution of this tension is the often shallow attempt to separate the dimensions of equality from the dimensions of achievement, to make the bases upon which people are equal separate from those upon which they are manifestly unequal (see T. H. Marshall, 1950). No one can understand the recent history of protest by American students and racial minorities if he thinks this separation is anything other than a flimsy cover by those in the saddle for their efforts to stay there. It may well be that our social order deserves preservation, but it will not find its philosophical justification in an equalitarian ideology.

Societies are more complicated than ideologies make them out to be and, for this reason, the philosophy of equality is profoundly irrelevant to its practice. The establishment of each new facet of equality creates a fresh facet of inequality. This will necessarily be so as long as the bases of equality or inequality are intercorrelated with each other. Suppose, for example, that a social policy directly equating the average income of Negroes and non-Negroes in the United States was implemented by supplementary income payments. Such a policy, it is easy enough to show, would discriminate against white investments in educational attainment. How can this be? The lower educational attainment of Negroes and the positive association between income and education will not be changed by a policy which equates the average income of Negroes and non-Negroes. Consequently, once the gross or zero-order association between race and income goes to zero, the *partial* association (controlling for education) between race and income would show a net positive increment for being a Negro, that is the return in income for investment in an additional year of education would be greater for Negroes than for non-Negroes. Thus, equality of outcome at one level (the gross, mean group difference) implies inequality of outcome at another (the mean differences between the races within educational categories). Equalization of outcomes (and opportunities) in a gross way can easily create substantial second-order inequalities. These empirical complexities make the translation of ideologies into concrete social policies virtually impossible. Just how complex the web of inequality can be is amply illustrated by the papers about three aspects of inequality—race, income and age—included in this section.

REFERENCES

Anastasi, Anne.
   1958   Differential Psychology: Individual and Group Differences in Behavior (3d ed.). New York: Macmillan.
Burke, Edmund.
   1790   Reflections on the Revolution in France and on the Proceedings of Certain Societies in London Relative to That Event.
Burt, Cyril, and M. Howard.
   1956   "The multifactorial theory of inheritance and its application to intelligence." British Journal of Statistical Psychology 9: 95-131.
Duncan, Otis Dudley.
   1969   "Inheritance of poverty or inheritance of race?" in Daniel P. Moynihan (ed.), On Understanding Poverty: Perspectives from the Social Sciences. New York: Basic Books.

1967   "Discrimination against Negroes." Annals of the American Academy of Political and Social Science 381: 85-103.

Elkins, Stanley M.
1963   Slavery: A Problem in American Institutional and Intellectual Life. New York: Grosset and Dunlap, Universal Library.

Friedman, Milton.
1962   Capitalism and Freedom. Chicago: University of Chicago Press.

Hofstadter, Richard.
1944   Social Darwinism in American Thought. Philadelphia: University of Pennsylvania Press.

Jensen, Arthur R.
1944   "How much can we boost IQ and scholastic achievement." Harvard Educational Review 39: 1-123. (See, too, the controversy raised by this article in subsequent issues of this same journal.)

Keller, Suzanne.
1963   Beyond the Ruling Class. New York: Random House.

Laidler, Harry W.
1968   History of Socialism: A Comparative Study of Socialism, Communism, Trade Unionism, Cooperation, Utopianism and Other Systems of Reform and Reconstruction. New York: Thomas Y. Crowell.

Larner, Jeremy, and Irving Howe (eds.).
1968   Poverty: Views from the Left. New York: William Morrow.

Marshall, T. H.
1950   Citizenship and Social Class. Cambridge: Cambridge University Press.

Ossowski, Stanislaw.
1963   Class Structure in the Social Consciousness. London: Routledge and Kegan Paul.

Parsons, Talcott.
1970   "Some further thoughts on the action theory of stratification." Sociological Inquiry 40 (Spring).

Sumner, William Graham.
1883   What the Social Classes Owe to Each Other. New York: Harper & Brothers.

Young, Michael.
1961   The Rise of the Meritocracy: 1870-2033. Harmandsworth, England: Penguin Books, Ltd.

CHAPTER 47

On the Cost of Being a Negro

PAUL M. SIEGEL

Arguing that racial prejudice can be understood only if the process by which racial groups form images of themselves and others is viewed as a *collective* phenomenon, Herbert Blumer had occasion to identify four types of feeling always present in racial prejudice by a majority group. These he specified as: (1) a feeling of superiority, (2) a feeling that the subordinate group is intrinsically alien and different, (3) a feeling of proprietary claim to certain areas of privilege and advantage, and (4) a fear and suspicion that the subordinate race harbors designs on the prerogatives of the dominant group.[1] While Blumer makes it amply clear that the "sense of group position" which these four types of feeeling comprise is not the same as objective social status, the two are not altogether independent of each other. Since the sense of group position is a historical product, originally formed out of the conditions of initial contact between the two groups, "subsequent experience in the relation of the two racial groups, especially in the area of claims, opportunities, and advantages may mold the sense of group position in many diverse ways."[2]

The source of race prejudice lies in a felt challenge to the sense of group position.

> The challenge, one must recognize, may come in many different ways. It may be in the form of an affront to feelings of group superiority; it may be in the form of attempts at familiarity or transgressions of the boundary line of group exclusiveness; it may be in the form of encroachment at countless points of proprietary claim; it may be a challenge to power and privilege; it may take the form of economic competition. Race prejudice is a defensive reaction to such challenging of the sense of group position.... It functions, however shortsightedly, to preserve the integrity and the position of the dominant group.[3]

In recent years, in North and South, schools and churches, public

Revision of a paper read at the 59th Annual Meeting of the American Sociological Association, Montreal, September, 1964. I wish to acknowledge the encouragement and advice of P. M. Hauser and Robert W. Hodge. The research was completed under a grant to the National Opinion Research Center from the National Science Foundation (NSF G#85. "Occupations and Social Stratification"). The paper serves as background for the major focus of the project, which is the social evaluation of occupations, industries, and ethnicities.

[1] Herbert Blumer, "Race Prejudice as a Sense of Group Position," in Jitsuichi Masuoka and Preston Valien, editors, *Race Relations: Problems and Theory*, Chapel Hill: University of North Carolina Press, 1961, p. 219.

[2] *Ibid.*, p. 223.

[3] *Ibid.*, p. 222.

and private places, Negro leaders and their white collaborators have
not challenged but *assaulted* the established order of relations between
the two racial groups. There can be little question that the Negro has
improved his objective social condition over the past half century.
His occupational attainment is higher, his death rate lower, and his
educational attainment greater than fifty, nay ten, years ago. These
aspects of the Negro's progress are well known,[4] but they do not necessarily indicate a reduction in white-nonwhite differentials. In large
part improvements in the Negro's status are reflections of secular
trends in the whole society. The more delicate question of how white-
nonwhite *differentials* in education, occupation, and income have been
affected by these secular trends is another matter, and the subject
of this paper. Although we cannot trace the full impact of objective
conditions upon the "sense of group position," we can provide a context of objective relations within which the collective process of racial
identification must occur. It is inconceivable that the state of the
collective conscience should be independent of the shape of objective
relations. Indeed, we will be able to identify a number of critical
objective relations which can only provide an impetus to the current
protest movement.

One major concern of the current civil rights movement is for
equal jobs and job opportunities. When the *Newsweek* Poll asked
Negroes how discrimination had affected them personally, about a
third of those interviewed said it had kept them from getting the
kinds of jobs they wanted.[5] It is fitting then that we begin our investigation with an examination of the occupational segregation of whites
from nonwhites and the changes that have occurred in this segregation in the decade from 1950 to 1960. For each of four age cohorts
and at each of eight educational levels we can establish the index of
dissimilarity[6] between the white and nonwhite major occupation
distributions. The index of dissimilarity indicates the percentage of
nonwhites (or of whites) who would have to change their major

[4] For a recent summary see, U.S. Department of Labor, *The Economic Situation of Negroes
in the United States*, Bulletin S-3, revised, Washington, D.C.: U.S. Government Printing Office,
1962.

[5] William Brink and Louis Harris, *The Negro Revolution in America*, New York: Simon and
Schuster, 1963, p. 190.

[6] The index of dissimilarity, or *delta*, is defined by

$$\Delta = \tfrac{1}{2} \sum_{i=1}^{n} |x_i - y_i|,$$

where x_i is the percentage of one population in the ith of n categories and y_i is the corresponding percentage for another population. So defined,

$$\sum_{i=1}^{n} x_i = \sum_{i=1}^{n} y_i = 100.$$

In the present case x_i and y_i are just the percentages of whites and nonwhites of given ages
and educational attainments which are in the ith major occupational group.

occupation group in order that the occupational distributions of whites and nonwhites within that age-education group be the same. Table 1 sets forth indices of this type for both 1950 and 1960.[7]

In Table 1 we note that there are two kinds of comparisons which can be made. These are indicated in the second panel of the table, for those with no years of schooling completed. The curved arrow represents "inter-cohort" comparisons, i.e., comparisons between two distinct groups of persons of similar education, but reaching a given age at two different points in time. Thus from the second panel of Table 1 we see that the index of dissimilarity between the occupational distribution of whites and nonwhites with no years of schooling completed and who were aged 25–34 in 1950 was 23.2. For the group reaching these ages in 1960, again with no years of schooling completed, the index of dissimilarity was slightly lower, 18.6. There are a total of 32 inter-cohort comparisons possible in Table 1, each specific to age and education. Of these 32 independent comparisons, 25 show that the occupational segregation of the two races was lower in 1960 than in 1950. Although the indices of dissimilarity are not vastly lower in 1960 than in 1950, there is nevertheless some indication of slight occupational desegregation. At almost every educational level, younger nonwhite cohorts are finding slightly less occupational segregation than was found by the cohort born ten years earlier at comparable ages.

The inter-cohort comparisons are complemented by the "intra-cohort" comparisons indicated by the diagonal arrows in the second panel of Table 1. The intra-cohort comparisons contrast the occupational segregation of the same group of people at two points in time. Thus in the second panel of Table 1 we see as before that the index of dissimilarity between the occupational distributions of whites and nonwhites with no years of schooling completed and who were aged 25–34 in 1950 is 23.2. Following the diagonal arrow we see that ten years later, when this same group of people is aged 35–44, the index of dissimilarity has fallen to 18.0. In all there are 24 intra-cohort comparisons specific to age and education in this table. Of these 24

---

[7] Some minor points to be noted in the discussion of Table 1: the 1950 indices are computed on the employed male population, while the 1960 data pertain to the experienced civilian labor force. This incomparability would tend to make the 1960 indices somewhat larger than the 1950 indices if no change had occurred. In analyzing Table 1 we make use of a convenient assumption: that educational attainment is fixed subsequent to age 25. This assumption enables us to study changes within *educational* as well as age cohorts. Although errors of reporting in the two censuses and actual increases in educational attainment of those over 25 imply that the assumption is not always valid, it is nevertheless reasonable in the majority of cases.

The data are drawn from U.S. Bureau of the Census, *U.S. Census of Population: 1960, Subject Reports, Educational Attainment*, Washington, D.C.: U.S. Government Printing Office, 1963, Table 8; U.S. Bureau of the Census, *U.S. Census of Population: 1950*, Volume 4, *Special Reports*, Part 5, Chapter B, *Education*, Washington, D.C.: U.S. Government Printing Office, 1953, Table 11. In both years the categories "occupation not reported" and "school years not reported" were excluded when computing percentage distributions over major occupation groups.

TABLE 1

INDICES OF DISSIMILARITY BETWEEN WHITE AND NONWHITE OCCUPATIONAL
DISTRIBUTIONS FOR MALES AGED 25–64 IN THE UNITED STATES,
1950 AND 1960, BY AGE AND EDUCATION*

Years of School Completed and Census Year	Age Group			
	25–34	35–44	45–54	55–64
Total				
1950	36.5	39.1	39.6	36.7
1960	35.4	37.3	38.5	38.9
No school years				
1950	23.2	20.8	22.2	32.2
1960	18.6	18.0	15.7	19.8
Elementary 1–4 years				
1950	22.8	24.2	25.6	29.7
1960	19.9	21.2	23.6	24.8
Elementary 5–7 years				
1950	26.2	28.8	29.0	26.4
1960	26.1	26.6	28.6	30.4
Elementary 8 years				
1950	28.9	32.6	34.2	31.4
1960	27.0	26.9	30.3	33.5
High School 1–3 years				
1950	29.0	36.0	39.6	38.4
1960	28.2	31.4	33.4	37.8
High School 4 years				
1950	33.8	39.1	40.5	36.9
1960	33.4	34.1	35.8	38.7
College 1–3 years				
1950	38.8	39.5	39.3	29.2
1960	34.4	38.2	37.6	34.8
College 4 or more years				
1950	17.8	17.8	21.6	17.2
1960	18.6	19.1	18.7	19.0

* Source: U.S. Bureau of the Census, *U.S. Census of Population: 1950, 4, Special Report,*
Part 5, Chapter B, *Education,* Table 11; and *U.S. Census of Population: 1960, Subject Reports,*
Educational Attainment, Table 8.

Note: Data pertain to the "Employed" in 1950 and to the "Experienced Civilian Labor
Force" in 1960.

contrasts, 18 show a decline between 1950 and 1960 in the occupational
segregation of a given age-education cohort of whites and nonwhites.
This improvement, ignoring differential mortality, it appears, can only
result from differential mobility on the part of nonwhites: they must
have moved in such a way as not only to make their occupational distributions more similar to those of whites, but also in such a way as
to compensate for the intra-generational mobility experienced by their
white peers between 1950 and 1960.

One might be tempted to summarize the findings in Table 1 as
indicating slight but consistent tendencies towards occupational desegregation within educational groupings over the ten year period. Such
a conclusion, while accurate to some extent, overlooks the most basic
pattern in the table, a pattern of white-nonwhite differentials persist-

ent at least since 1940, and one to which we shall return several times in the course of this paper.[8] Inspection of the table reveals that in both 1950 and 1960 there was a tendency for dissimilarity to increase with level of education and taper off at the highest levels: in both 1950 and 1960 the highest indices of dissimilarity occur at the high school and some college levels. Inspection of Hare's tables reveals a similar pattern for 1940.[9] Persons with so much education are qualified for supervisory, craft, sales, and managerial duties. These are, however, the very occupations denied to Negroes by social mores governing race relations, especially the norm which proscribes the supervision of white workers by Negroes. Nonwhites who complete college can take up professional occupations servicing Negro clienteles. Both Negroes and whites at the lower levels of education cannot achieve much more than operative level jobs. It is at the high school and some college levels that nonwhites are most segregated from whites. Yet *these are the very educational levels which Negroes are now reaching in large numbers* for the first time. In 1940 only 19 per cent of all Negro males aged 25–34 fell into the categories 1–3 years of high school, 4 years of high school completed, and 1–3 years of college. By 1950, 34 per cent of all Negro males aged 25–34 were in these educational categories. And in 1960 the corresponding figure was 54 per cent.[10] Thus in each of the last two decades a considerably increasing proportion of young Negroes have been able to upgrade themselves educationally, only to arrive at the very educational levels where occupational segregation is the greatest.

It is not hard to see the importance, in the current reformation of race relations, of this change in educational attainment and its resultant exposure to greater occupational segregation. While the pattern is not historically unique to the current decade, it is a pattern to which more and more of the Negro population is being exposed, and it can only serve to add acrimony to Negro-white relations. It was Hare's failure to see this basic relation of educational achievement and patterns of occupational segregation, that led him to expect education to play a vital role in easing the tensions of inequality

---

[8] The pattern of small declines in the occupational segregation of nonwhites from whites between 1950 and 1960 was detected between 1940 and 1950 in Nathaniel Hare, *The Changing Occupational Status of the Negro in the United States: An Intracohort Analysis*, unpublished Ph.D. dissertation, University of Chicago, 1962, especially Chapter iii, "Race and Major Occupation," pp. 34–78.

[9] *Ibid.*, Table 11.

[10] U.S. Bureau of the Census, *U.S. Census of Population: 1940: Education. Educational Attainment by Economic Characteristics and Marital Status*, Washington, D.C.: U.S. Government Printing Office, 1947, Table 2, p. 9; U.S. Bureau of the Census, *U.S. Census of Population: 1950*, Volume 4, *Special Reports*, Part 5, Chapter B, *Education*, Washington, D.C.: U.S. Government Printing Office, 1953, Table 5, p. 43; U.S. Bureau of the Census, *U.S. Census of Population: 1960. Subject Reports. Nonwhite Population by Race*, Washington, D.C.: U.S. Government Printing Office, 1963, Table 19, p. 30.

between the races. Focusing on the group with the highest level of education, college graduates—where occupational segregation is at a relative minimum—he projected that, as the secular trend of increasing education brought more and more Negroes to this level, occupational segregation would disappear. The data so far reviewed suggest that as more and more Negroes gain higher and higher educational levels, fewer and fewer Negroes will be able to profitably employ their education. Thus, it is likely that while whites' image of the Negro must reflect Negroes' increasing educational attainment, this improvement in educational status not only increases the possibility of whites perceiving a Negro threat to white prerogatives: it creates greater motivation for Negroes to demand equal treatment both inside and outside the labor market, and it provides reinforcement of an image of Negroes as inferior and unable to realize the potential of their education. A further and more detailed picture of Negro-white differentials in this basic aspect of the group condition—making a living—is offered by the consideration of income as determined within occupational groups by education. While they are unable to provide the historical perspective we have used here, the data discussed below go a long way towards amplifying the findings reported here—that Negroes are just beginning to be exposed to a whole new area of segregation.

Prior to the publication of the 1960 Census of Population, simultaneous tabulations of income by education *and* occupation were not available.[11] Tabulations of this kind are now available, specific to region and race, for a five per cent sample of the male civilian experienced labor force aged 25–64 in 1960.[12] These data provide a unique opportunity for examining white-nonwhite differentials in average earnings within major occupation groups at every educational level, for both the South and the non-South (which will be called the North). Figures 1 to 10 show the relationship between mean earnings in 1959 and educational attainment separately for whites and nonwhites in the North and South. A separate figure is presented for each Census major occupation group; a capital N is used to identify curves for nonwhites and a capital W identifies those for whites; and solid lines indicate incomes in the North while dashed lines indicate those in the South.[13]

[11] Apart from small sample surveys, the only exception to this statement is U.S. Bureau of the Census, *Current Population Reports, Population Characteristics,* Series P-20, 99, "Literacy and Educational Attainment: March 1959," Washington, D.C.: Bureau of the Census, February 4, 1960, Table H, p. 7.

[12] U.S. Bureau of the Census, *U.S. Census of Population: 1960, Subject Reports, Occupation by Earnings and Education,* Washington, D.C.: U.S. Government Printing Office, 1963.

[13] In constructing the ten figures it was necessary to score grouped educational data in the following manner:

The pattern of relationships illustrated in Figures 1 to 10 is remarkably consistent. With the single exception of nonwhite farmers in the North,[14] the figures show that at *every* educational level in every occupational group, and in the North as well as the South, nonwhites have average earnings less than those of whites. This finding has long been anticipated but until the appearance of the 1960 Census data it was not possible to demonstrate it comprehensively. The figures also enable one to see the magnitude of the differentials, which are frequently in excess of a thousand dollars. Indeed, not only are differences of this magnitude observed between white and nonwhite earnings within each of the geographic regions under consideration: differences in excess of $1000 are observed between the earnings of nonwhites in the South and nonwhites elsewhere in the United States.

While one might choose to interpret these differences as due to quality differences in education, or to differences in detailed occupational distributions within major occupation groups, it seems unlikely that either factor alone, or both in conjunction, could produce differentials as large as those shown in the charts. This point is perhaps amply documented by reading some of the more dramatic differentials from the charts. For example, Figure 1 shows that a white professional

Educational Group	*Score*
0–7 years of school completed	6
8 years of school completed	8
1–3 years of high school completed	10
4 years of high school completed	12
1–3 years of college completed	14
4 or more years of college completed	17

Use of these scores may slightly distort the observed relationship between education and income, especially at the extremes. However, it is unlikely that knowledge of the exact mean years of school completed by race and region for the educational groupings used would alter any of the conclusions drawn here.

Mean earnings presented here are derived from grouped data and may misrepresent the actual distribution of earnings, especially when a large number of individuals fall into the open-ended category "$25,000 or more." Details of how these means were computed are to be found in *Ibid.*, p. x. Although we are not wholly satisfied with the methods employed by the Bureau of the Census in deriving these means, especially the estimation of a mean for the "$25,000 or more" category by interpolation of a Pareto curve, it seems unlikely that recalculation of them would alter the patterns described here. Inspection of analogous figures plotted using medians instead of means leads to essentially the same interpretations.

It must be noted that data refer to males aged 25–64 in the experienced civilian labor force *with earnings in 1959.* Thus differentials in white-nonwhite unemployment for short periods can be reflected in the income differentials shown in the figures, but differential year-long unemployment has been eliminated by considering only those with some earnings in 1959. Given the higher rate of nonwhite long-term unemployment this probably means that differences would be greater if the entire experienced civilian labor force were included.

Source: U.S. Bureau of the Census, *U.S. Census of Population: 1960, Subject Reports, Occupation by Earnings and Education. Final Report PC* (2)-7B, Washington, D.C.: U.S. Government Printing Office, 1963. Tables 1, 2, and 3.

[14] While in general the nonwhite labor force is a close approximation to the Negro labor force (Negroes constitute about 90 per cent of all employed nonwhite males aged 25–64 in 1960) this approximation fails in the case of two regional-occupational groups. Negroes comprise only 14 per cent of all nonwhite males aged 25–64 employed as farmers or farm managers in the non-Southern United States and only 35 per cent of all nonwhite males aged 25–64 employed as farm laborers or foremen in the non-Southern United States. (See U.S. Bureau of the Census, *U.S. Census of Population: 1960, Subject Reports, Nonwhite Population by Race,* Washington, D.C.: U.S. Government Printing Office, 1963, Tables 37–41). We shall therefore not discuss these two figures further.

FIGURES 1–10

MEAN INCOME OF 25–64 YEAR OLD U.S. MALES OF THE EXPERIENCED LABOR FORCE
IN EACH OCCUPATIONAL CATEGORY AT DIFFERENT LEVELS OF EDUCATION, BY RACE
AND REGION.*

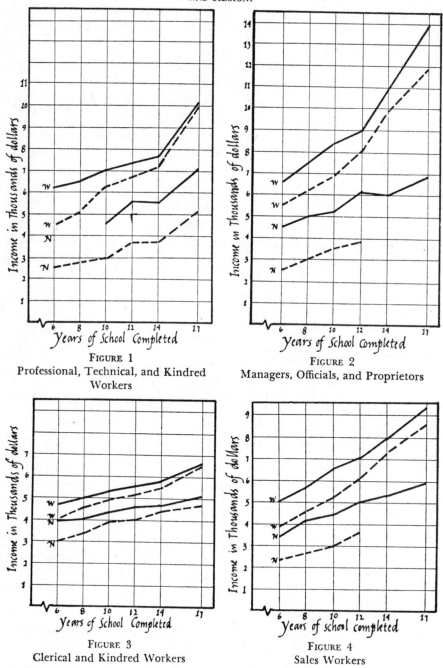

FIGURE 1
Professional, Technical, and Kindred
Workers

FIGURE 2
Managers, Officials, and Proprietors

FIGURE 3
Clerical and Kindred Workers

FIGURE 4
Sales Workers

* Note for Figures 1–10: Occupational categories are those used by the U.S.
Census. Dotted lines represent the Southern United States; solid lines describe the
balance of the country. "W" and "N" refer to white and nonwhite, respectively.

FIGURES 1–10

MEAN INCOME OF 25–64 YEAR OLD U.S. MALES OF THE EXPERIENCED LABOR FORCE IN EACH OCCUPATIONAL CATEGORY AT DIFFERENT LEVELS OF EDUCATION, BY RACE AND REGION.*

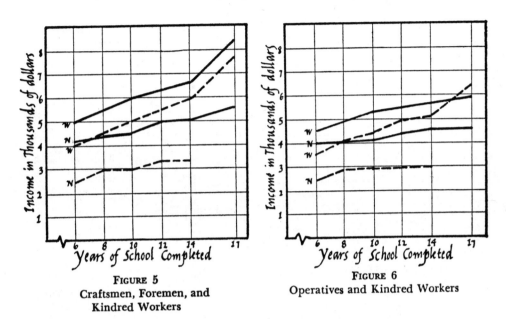

FIGURE 5
Craftsmen, Foremen, and
Kindred Workers

FIGURE 6
Operatives and Kindred Workers

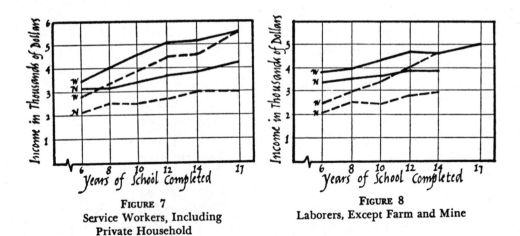

FIGURE 7
Service Workers, Including
Private Household

FIGURE 8
Laborers, Except Farm and Mine

FIGURES 1–10
MEAN INCOME OF 25–64 YEAR OLD U.S. MALES OF THE EXPERIENCED LABOR FORCE
IN EACH OCCUPATIONAL CATEGORY AT DIFFERENT LEVELS OF EDUCATION, BY RACE
AND REGION.*

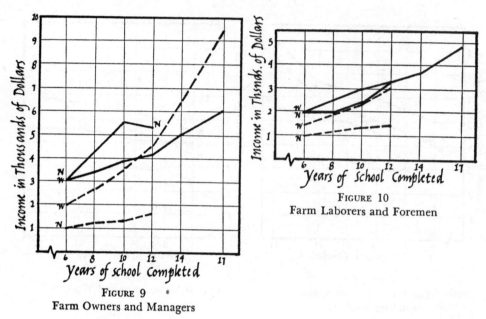

FIGURE 10
Farm Laborers and Foremen

FIGURE 9
Farm Owners and Managers

in the North, with fewer than eight years of school completed, earns on the average a thousand dollars more per year than a nonwhite professional in the South with four or more years of college. Figure 2 indicates that on the average a nonwhite Northern manager who has completed four or more years of college earns no more than his white counterpart with less than eight years of school completed. This latter difference reflects, no doubt, the etiquette of retail relationships, wherein Negro managers are largely restricted to servicing Negro clientele and are restricted from achieving supervisory positions superior to whites. Other striking contrasts can be found in each of the figures.

Many of the striking contrasts one can extract from the figures might of course be "explained away" by differences in the detailed occupational pursuits of whites and nonwhites within major occupational categories. But since we have previously argued that at some educational levels Negroes cannot *get* the same jobs as whites, to invoke detailed occupational differentiation of those Negroes who do gain employment comparable with that of their white educational peers is to change the argument from "Negroes are paid less than whites with the same training in the same jobs," to "Negroes are not allowed into the high paying jobs within major occupational groups." The latter argument could be buttressed by reference to the rules of race relations which exclude Negroes from positions of authority over whites, or from entry into trades governed by discriminatory unions. The point is, of course, that the income differentials displayed in Figures 1 to 10 do not necessarily reflect white-nonwhite pay differentials for similar work and similar training: various features of the social organization of the relations between the races may also account for the differentials. But regardless of what final account is given of the differentials here displayed, an individual Negro cannot expect to earn as much as a white person with the same number of years of school completed and at the same general level of employment.

Inspection of the figures also reveals that the white-nonwhite differentials in earnings at most occupational and educational levels are greater inside than outside the South. Although the differential is occasionally as great as $1000, for most occupation-education combinations the white-nonwhite income difference is on the order of $100 to $500 greater in the South.[15]

Apart from racial and regional differences in income, we can also derive some understanding of how the occupational structure itself affects the differential incomes of Negroes and whites. All of the figures are plotted in the same scale, so comparisons between them can readily be made. Comparisons of this kind will show that the differentials between whites and nonwhites average least among clerical and kindred workers, service workers, and unskilled laborers. Since these are the very levels at which one might expect the detailed occupations of whites and nonwhites to be most similar, these comparisons tend to confirm our previous suspicion that part of the white-nonwhite income differential observed at the higher status occupational levels reflected differences in detailed occupational affiliation.

Close inspection of the figures also reveals that there is both a general tendency for income to increase with education and two sub-tendencies: (1) for income to increase *more* rapidly with increasing education in some occupations than in others; and (2) for white-nonwhite *differentials* to increase with increasing education. The general tendency and the first sub-tendency indicate that there is what can be thought of as a return on investment in education and that the return on this investment is higher in professional, managerial, sales, and craft occupations than among the other major occupational cate-

---

15 Again, part of this inter-regional variation in the magnitude of white-nonwhite income differentials might be attributable to inter-region variation in the relative quality of white and nonwhite schooling. However, it should be noted that the gross income differences displayed in these figures have not been adjusted for inter-region variation in real income. Because the cost of living is less in the South than in the North, the income differentials would be increased within the South and decreased between the South and North if the earnings of Southerners were adjusted to reflect the purchasing power of the dollar in the North.

gories, excluding farmers and farm managers (a special case). This is not too surprising: the payoff on investment in education is conditioned by the relevance of the training to the kind of work performed. One can easily see that in this respect the white and nonwhite occupational hierarchies are roughly parallel. This phenomenon is, of course, quite relevant to the matter at hand, for it is from the very occupations at which the return upon investment in education is greatest that Negroes find themselves excluded by rules governing the *social context* of the practice of occupations. Thus we conclude that the Negro who manages to upgrade himself educationally is apt to find the occupational door closed at the levels of employment which enable him to realize his investment in educational attainment, a conclusion to which we have been drawn before.

The tendency for income differentials between whites and nonwhites to increase with increasing education holds both inside and outside the South. While the figures are not sufficiently enlarged for the pattern to be clearly seen in all of them, it emerges clearly in Figures 2, 5, and 7, for managers, craftsmen, and service workers, respectively.[16] Statistically the pattern means that the slope of the regression of income on education within occupational categories will be less for nonwhites than for whites.[17] Substantively the divergence implies that the return in income for completing a given educational step is less for nonwhites than it is for whites. Since they are independent, if we compare the slopes of the curves for whites and nonwhites at each educational step, within regions and major occupational groups, we can summarize the patterns of return upon investment in education by counting the number of comparisons in which the income increment for completing a given educational step is larger for whites than for nonwhites. Within the South there are 33 such comparisons.[18] In 29, or 87.2 per cent of these 33 comparisons the increment in average earnings for completing a given education step is less for nonwhites than for whites. The pattern for the North is equally striking: in 34, or 82.9 per cent of the 41 comparisons in the North, the increment in average earnings for completing a given educational step was larger for whites

[16] This pattern is a fairly persistent one, but it is difficult to evaluate because of age differences between the races. Nonwhites, especially at the highest educational levels, are somewhat younger than whites. Whether standardization would remove the observed pattern is hard to tell. Casual inspection of age-specific cross-tabulations of earnings by race, major occupation group, and education suggest that the divergence between white and nonwhite earnings with increasing education would persist after controlling the effects of age. See U.S. Bureau of the Census, *U.S. Census of Population: 1960, Subject Reports, Occupation by Earnings and Education,* Washington, D.C.: U.S. Government Printing Office, 1963. Table 1.

[17] We have not employed regression techniques in this paper because the relationship between income and education does not appear to be linear within all major occupation groups.

[18] Points are omitted in the figures if the averages they represent are based on less than 50 sample cases or, since we are working with a five per cent sample, the total number of persons falling into a group is less than 1,000.

than for nonwhites. These findings suggest, barring serious errors of reporting which could account for the observed pattern, that the rate of return upon educational investment is appreciably less for Negroes than for whites.[19] Thus the Negro not only starts out with a financial handicap, but in most occupations the handicap is *accentuated* with increasing education.

In order to summarily display this disadvantageous aspect of increasing education, we present in the first column of Table 2 the mean

TABLE 2

DECOMPOSITIONS OF MEAN DIFFERENCES BETWEEN WHITE AND NONWHITE EARNINGS
IN 1959 FOR MALES AGED 25–64 IN THE UNITED STATES, 1960,
SPECIFIC TO EDUCATION GROUPS*

Years of School Completed	Mean Difference White–Nonwhite Earnings	Mean Difference Attributable to Occupational-Regional Composition	Mean Difference Net of Composition	Mean Nonwhite Earnings
Elementary 0–7 years	$1,421	$ 725	$ 696	$2,562
Elementary 8 years	1,519	601	918	3,318
High School 1–3 years	2,033	757	1,276	3,522
High School 4 years	2,229	823	1,406	4,021
College 1–3 years	3,199	1,441	1,758	4,355
College 4 or more years	4,567	767	3,800	5,671

* Source: U.S. Bureau of the Census, *U.S. Census of Population: 1960, Subject Reports, Occupation by Earnings and Education*, Washington, D.C.: U.S. Government Printing Office, 1963. Table 1.

white-nonwhite earnings difference for each of six levels of educational attainment for all occupations and regions. While the tabled values clearly show that the difference between white and nonwhite earnings increases with increasing education, differences in occupational and regional distributions—shown in the figures to account for sizeable white-nonwhite earnings differences—are not taken into account in the first column of the table. A simple procedure will enable us to remedy this confounding.

We begin by noting that for all males aged 25–64 in the experienced civilian labor force with earnings in 1959 and with, for example, less than eight years of education, the difference between the average earnings of whites and nonwhites was $1421. This is a gross figure and

[19] There are two kinds of error which are likely candidates for explaining part of the white-nonwhite differential in earnings. Negroes might under-report their total earnings. A more likely candidate, especially for explaining differences in the income-education relationship within major occupation groups, assumes that Negroes over-report their educational attainment *relative to whites*. Thus, in every census education category, the *actual* education of nonwhites is less than that of whites. However, both these kinds of error—under-reporting of income and over-reporting of education—require that Negroes be more perverse than whites. To our knowledge there is no substantial evidence in support of such a claim, and it seems unlikely that errors of this kind could explain differentials of the magnitude observed here.

in no way takes account of occupational or residential differences between the two groups. We can, by simple algebraic manipulation of the difference of these two mean incomes, decompose it into two terms: one term expressing that part of the total difference attributable to white-nonwhite differences in regional and occupational composition (tabulated as the "mean difference attributable to composition"), and the other term expressing that part of the total difference attributable to white-nonwhite earnings differences specific to occupation region (the "mean difference net of composition").[20] This particular formula is not unique; it is only one of numerous similar relationships which enable one to ascertain the components of a difference between two rates.

Working out the suggested decomposition of the total earnings difference among those with less than eight years of schooling, we see that $725 of the total difference of $1421 can be attributed to differences in the proportions of whites and nonwhites in particular occupational-regional categories. On the other hand $696 of the total difference in white-nonwhite earnings can be attributed to white-nonwhite differences in rates of earnings within region and occupation combinations for this particular educational group. These rate differences can be interpreted as reflecting the money costs to nonwhites of discrimination, though they may to some extent be influenced by quality differences in education or occupation which are too fine to be discerned by our gross measures. It is quite apparent in Table 2 that, while earnings differences due to composition do not vary systematically with education, when the effects of occupational and regional composition are removed the remaining earnings differences increase regularly as level of educational achievement increases. This means that, even if whites had the same occupational and regional configuration as nonwhites, there would remain rather large income differences; and these would be accentuated with increasing education.

[20] Letting W represent mean income to whites and w represent mean income of nonwhites, we can represent the gross mean difference by:

$$(1) \quad W - w = \sum_{i,j} N_{ij} W_{ij} - \sum_{i,j} n_{ij} w_{ij}$$

Where N_{ij} is the proportion of all whites who are in the ith region (South or non-South) and the jth occupation, and n_{ij} and w_{ij} are the corresponding proportions and mean wage rates for nonwhites and the summation is over all combinations. The value W - w will not be changed by adding and then subtracting the same term, so we can write

$$(2) \quad W - w = \sum_{i,j} N_{ij} W_{ij} + \sum_{i,j} n_{ij} W_{ij} - \sum_{i,j} n_{ij} W_{ij} - \sum_{i,j} n_{ij} w_{ij}$$

This can be regrouped and rewritten thus:

$$(3) \quad W - w = \sum_{i,j} n_{ij} (W_{ij} - w_{ij}) + \sum_{i,j} W_{ij} (N_{ij} - n_{ij})$$

Note that the first term on the right-hand side of (3) is merely the sum over all nonwhites of white-nonwhite mean earning differences within region and occupation. The second term on the right side of (3) is the portion of the gross differences due to compositional differences. See Evelyn M. Kitagawa, "Components of a Difference between Two Rates," *Journal of the American Statistical Association*, 50 (December, 1955), pp. 1168–1194.

We have seen that over the past twenty years there has been a slight tendency towards occupational desegregation and that this tendency appears whether we follow a particular group of people through the period or look at the experience of people at particular age-education conjunctions at different points in time. We also have found evidence of persistent high levels of occupational segregation at all ages among those who completed high school or attended less than four years of college. Thus, while evidence from the longitudinal data seems to indicate a pattern of gradually lessening occupational segregation, there is one finding which agrees with the more pessimistic conclusions to be drawn from our more extensive cross-sectional analysis. These data suggest a bleak picture from the viewpoint of the nonwhite, no matter how they are regarded. The figures show that Negroes earn less than whites at almost all educational levels in almost all occupations, both in the North and the South, and these differentials are greater in the South. While there are some occupational groups in which these differentials are minimized, the minima are rather large. The return upon investment in education appears to be less for non-whites than for whites in almost all occupational groups.

The data provide no support for the view that education will immediately remove the financial and occupational handicaps imposed on the Negro. On the contrary, they suggest that increasing the level of educational attainment of the Negro may lead to higher white-non-white income differentials, at least in the short run. Since this is a statement about longitudinal trends inferred from cross-sectional data, it is intended to be taken with great caution. However, the data certainly warrant the conclusion that there is no closing of the income gap at higher levels of education.

Findings like these clearly suggest part of what current racial protest movements are about. Before we proceed to assess the import of these objective relations in terms of the subjective processes that underlie race relations, it might be well to attempt to provide a single figure which expresses the impost referred to in the title of this paper.

We have thus far avoided the question of the cost of being a Negro for two reasons. First, we wanted to demonstrate that white-nonwhite income differentials appear at most educational and occupational levels and that little progress in occupational desegregation has been made since 1940. These findings, of course, imply that the cost of being a Negro is itself a variable. Consequently, any single figure must be an average taken over widely different circumstances. Second, we avoided preparing such an estimate because *any* evaluation of the average cost of being a Negro is necessarily arbitrary at certain points owing to (1) decisions about methods of calculation and (2) limitations imposed by the available data. Although the estimate we present below has some appeal, it ignores differences in white-nonwhite age structure and, of course, suffers from being taken over major instead of detailed occupational categories. Therefore, it must be treated as but one of several such estimates that could be made.

We have already discussed the method by which we shall estimate the cost of being a Negro, for it consists of modifying the decomposition equation already discussed to take account of education as a compositional variable in addition to occupation and region. Applying this new equation to the mean difference in white-nonwhite earnings for the total population of males aged 25–64 with earnings in 1959, we shall again derive two terms, one corresponding to the amount of the difference attributable to occupational, educational, and regional differences between the two groups, and the other expressing the difference in earnings net of composition. We shall interpret this second term as the cost of being a Negro.

Working out the suggested decomposition of the total difference in average white-nonwhite earnings, we find that only $1097 of the total difference of $2852 can be attributed to white-nonwhite differences in mean earnings within region, occupation, and education combinations. Thus, net of regional, educational, and occupational effects, the cost of being a Negro is roughly a thousand dollars. On the other hand, 61.5 per cent of the total difference in white and nonwhite mean earnings can be attributed to compositional differences with regard to region, occupation, and education. This suggests that the current discrepancy might be appreciably reduced if Negroes could bring their educational, occupational, and geographical distribution more into line with that of whites. We have tried to argue here that changes along the first two dimensions would *not* be particularly efficacious, and there are good arguments that equalization of the geographic distributions of the races would not ameliorate the income distributions. In any case such herculean metamorphoses would not eliminate income differentials—for 38.5 per cent of the current difference in average earnings of whites and nonwhites is apparently *independent of the achievement* of nonwhites! To put it baldly, about two-fifths of the difference in average earnings of whites and nonwhites is what it costs to be black.

The relations discussed in this paper between education, occupation, and income are not new, they are not even newly uncovered. The only new thing here is the data which enable us for the first time simultaneously to "control" for the effects of educational and occupational composition while assessing white-nonwhite income differentials. It should not be surprising, then, that rather than state stunning new hypotheses about Negro-white relations we are merely able to shore-up platitudes, or at least supply an argument from data in place of arguments from common sense. If, as Blumer suggests, race relations are founded upon the "sense of group position," which in turn reflects to some extent the actual situation, then we should expect these objective relationships to have their representations in the sense of position of each of the two racial groups. There is scattered evidence that they do.

Certainly an important class of such representations are those which arrogate to whites the right to the supervisory, managerial, and service occupations currently denied to Negroes. We have repeatedly referred to these norms in the course of this paper to explain occupational segregation. The data suggest the basis of a white sense of superiority to Negroes who are apparently incapable of realizing the potential for advancement which lies dormant in their new educational attainments. And, finally, although economic competition need not always prove threatening to the competitors, in this case we might expect whites to see their prerogatives threatened by this encroaching, inferior group. Thus, we have the bases of feelings of "prerogatives," "moral superiority," and "threat:" the stuff of prejudice.

On the Negro side we might advance a simple investment model to account for the differentially high Negro school-dropout rate as reflecting investor choices of other, better paying investments. We might speak of the motivation provided the civil rights movement by the discovery on the part of thousands of young Negroes that their coveted education wasn't worth much on the open market.

Despite our ability to translate our findings into statements in the terms of Blumer's scheme, the findings are most satisfactory as a simple summary of what the Negro has to overcome to achieve economic equality. As the majority of Negroes interviewed by the *Newsweek* Poll put it, "If you do the same work as a white man, you will probably be paid less than he will."[21] And, we can now say how much less: about a thousand dollars a year.

[21] Brink and Harris, *op. cit.*, p. 194.

CHAPTER 48

Aid to the Poor and Social Exchange

GERALD D. SUTTLES and DAVID STREET*

In recent decades, aid to the poor has been dramatically increased by the provision of public funds.[1] While the funds available through this source of aid may come much closer to meeting the subsistence needs of the poor, the character of the arrangements which have developed for distributing public aid raises a number of questions about the integration of the poor or their relationship to the wider society.

One way of approaching these questions is to ask how well public aid meets the minimal economic requirements of an individual or family. This is the characteristic approach of public administrators and a common way of evaluating public aid programs. An alternative approach is to examine public aid in terms of how well it creates a set of exchange relations which bind the poor to one another and to the wider society.

It is this latter approach that we will explore in this paper. The general problem, then, is to analyze how public aid to the poor either contracts or expands the network of social relations which integrate a person into society. Obviously, the position we are exploring derives from the tradition established by Mauss and Malinowski on social exchange.[2] We place primary emphasis upon the way in which social exchanges draw people into social relations and regulate social conduct. Only secondarily are we interested in how nearly public aid exchanges fulfill subsistence needs.

Unfortunately most of this discussion must proceed in the absence of much information on how public aid is actually distributed. Lacking further information, we can start only by assuming that public aid is distributed legally and according to the official rules or eligibility. Doubtless, this is an over-simplification, but it is from such over-simplifications that theories must be made. We shall explore, then, the implications of what we see as a basic shift from the distribution of aid as a more nearly private practice carried out within preexisting relations to the administration of aid through very formal social arrangements, impersonal and distant. In doing so, we will focus principally on the urban poor.

BENEFACTORS AND RECIPIENTS

There has always been some form of formalized giving to the less fortunate by the more affluent. Until the institutionalization of charity in a separate organizational form and the shift of aid primarily from the expenditure of voluntary contributions to that of taxes, aid to the poor was defined as more or less a private option, and a distinctive relationship was maintained between the recipient and the benefactor. Generally, the former accepted his gifts humbly while attesting to the generosity of the latter. Except for certain small and ritualized contributions required for "alms to the poor" or Christmas turkeys for the poor both deserving and undeserving, the benefactor's charity was officially a personal option that exceeded beyond the obligations of explicit social rulings. Failure to donate might cast doubt on a potential donor's personal character, his commitment to religious or other values, or his financial ability, but the recipient could not exact the contribution by appeal to a third party.

This relationship is most clearly seen in the paternalistic charity of the "owner" of the company town,[3] but it was also dominant in many of the early forms of aid involving a middleman—a minister or priest, a worker for a private poor-relief agency, or others. Especially before the era of the professionalization of social work around the ideals of social criticism (for example, those of Dorothea Dix), middlemen generally worked as agents of the givers, extracting the same testimonies of appreciation and self-reform from the recipient as would the benefactor himself.

Under this situation, the recipient might approach or avoid the benefactor or his agent as his circumstances permitted. During good times, he could become obstreperous or intractable. In bad times he had to act humble and ingratiating and to project a new rectitude. With each contingency, he could attune his response and general demeanor to current requirements. He could, in fact, deny the role of recipient without hazarding more than the benefits at issue, although, admittedly, this might lead on occasion to near starvation. On the whole, this private distribution of welfare benefits tended to confirm existing status distinctions and institutional arrangements, as contributions helped to highlight the positions of the better-off. The beneficiaries acknowledged their rightful status as dependents or showed themselves even less deserving by failing to recognize the realities of their condition. And benefactor, recipient, and any middleman were ordinarily visible members of the same community, their symbiotic relationship expressing its principles of order.

With the development of new and more extensive insitutions between those who give and those who receive, the relationships among benefactor, middleman and recipient have changed in several ways. The major alteration came historically when the mass destitution of the Great Depression produced a recognition of the inadequacy of private charity and yielded the major public welfare programs, both social insurance and public assistance. In this effort, large segments of aid to the poor became redefined not as voluntary transfers but as the returns on personal investment, as yet made or not, in governmental insurance programs. In the case of public assistance programs, the benefactor is no longer a private agent shoring up his personal selection for his appointed position and his own criteria for the worthiness of the recipients, but a taxpayer.[4] Moreover, the person who actually dispenses the aid is fully an agent—and a government agent administering a statute, whose personal preferences officially count for little. In turn, the recipient's eligibility is established by a limited number of universalistic criteria. Thus, both parties in such a relationship can be *compelled* to initiate or terminate their dealings irrespective of their personal desires.[5]

The shift to impersonality in the provision of aid was foreshadowed in the character of the development of large-scale private assistance to the poor up through the early 30's. Under these programs, the recipient increasingly found himself freed from the necessity to express humility or to monitor his behavior as a condition to receiving aid. The role of fawning before the charitable was assumed by the social work intermediaries who—when away from the benefactors could even express the then progressive social work view that the displacements of the industrial order, not the character of the recipients, were primarily responsible for the condition of the poor. At the minimum, aid was often rationalized as necessary to help the wife and children no matter what the attitude of the drunkard father of the family, and during the Depression, recipient motives became increasingly irrelevant in light of what was obviously a great collective misfortune. Further, the definition of psychiatric casework as the major technology of the social work did not become dominant soon enough to reestablish recipient demeanor and motives as important criteria for giving out public assistance. It is doubtful that even with better timing, casework would have had this impact since, to this day, it almost certainly would be impossible to get a consensus on what motives of clients are relevant and how to interpret them sufficiently for a program that must withstand challenge in the courts.

Even where welfare workers retain some discretion in handling their cases, the heavy hand of an administrative policy of uniformity is apt to guide their decisions and further depersonalize the worker-client relationship. The progressive centralization of public welfare programs and the federal policies seeking uniformity have pushed the distribution of public assistance further in the direction of the bureaucratic model. Currently the state of Massachusetts has the most geographically decentralized system of any state for distributing public assistance. Yet Derthick writes of its past and present performance:

> Thirty years ago, the distribution of assistance was determined by local politics— mainly by politics in the ideal sense, as the process by which community values are expressed and allocated, but also by politics in the vulgar sense, as the allocation of favors on the basis of friendship and self-interest. Today, assistance is in general distributed in accordance with rules that originate elsewhere than in the local community and are little affected in content or application by local politics in any sense.[6]

Impersonality in the criteria for allocating aid under public assistance is coupled with impersonality in the relationship between dispenser and recipient. Their interaction comes to reflect not only the traditional differences in social status but also a complete difference in social and ecological worlds. There comes to be no basis for the dispenser-recipient relation other than the benefits at hand. Those who dispense aid are almost never relatives, friends or neighbors of those they serve. Indeed this is avoided lest it lead to corruption, nepotism or favoritism. The relevant norms here are those virtues embodied in the Progressive movement which simultaneosuly diminished another source of goods and services for the poor—favors received from the political machine in exchange for votes—

through civil service and related reforms. Further, in public assistance, neither participant is captured in a relationship that is guaranteed by permanent considerations or additional exchanges beyond the immediate benefits at hand, except that the recipient must orient himself to the agency's accumulating dossier. Such a relationship must be extremely perfunctory or else very fragile with each party fearful lest he invest too much in the other. Relations of this sort are usually guarded and seldom result in the full-scale presentation of self that follows an exchange of "gifts."[7]

This formal dispensation of welfare benefits also does not bind together social units that reach beyond the immediate parties involved. Only very rarely do those formally assigned the duty of distributing charity impress their relatives, neighbors and friends into subsequent exchanges with the recipient. In turn, the recipient is at most a representative of a single domestic unit. Welfare exchanges of this type, then, do not join together entire communities or categories of people. No matter how congenial the relationship between benefactor and recipient, then, it is not transitive.

Further, once a person has appealed to the distributor of formal benefits he cannot retreat or retract his identification of himself without jeopardizing any future appeals he may wish to make to similar sources. The distributors keep written records that help define a person's eligibility for subsequent benefits, and each dispenser is constrained to consult these records before making a recommendation. Necessarily this makes each recipient cautious lest he alienate future benefits by seeming too adventuresome, independent or secure at the present.

Most importantly, the provision of benefits through public channels of distribution often operates formally to exclude those gifts which can be obtained through other means. So long as a recipient has sources of help among his neighbors, relatives or friends, the distributors are often obliged to eliminate or deduct these from those services and goods he would receive through formal channels. Frequently this applies to a wide range of services. For example, a recipient who is currently being advised by a relative and appeals to a professional dispenser for help may often be told he must discontinue his reliance on such hearsay or the professional will step aside, not wanting to "interfere." Similarly, a woman who appeals to the police to quell a group of noisy teenagers cannot then go to the latter's parents and remonstrate. Often, even where provisions are made for welfare clients to receive financial aid from both public and private sources, the former must be deducted from the latter. The benefits and services obtained through formal sources, then, do not simply augment those already available. The most obvious consequence is that for those who opt for public sources of revenue and services, it is advisable that they curtail their dependencies and exchanges with private sources or to cover them well and live with the risk of exposure. Often it is not worth the danger, and the recipient feels he must retreat from many exchanges with his kinfolk, fellow residents and friends.

HORIZONTAL EXCHANGE AND ITS DEVALUATION

Looking back on earlier welfare practices, we are likely to think of them principally as exchanges between the affluent and the needy. This is an oversimplification. Usually, the wealthy gave a fiesta, dispensed Christmas packages, or helped a local poorhouse only occasionally. Except for rural areas and quite small populations, the affluent were too distant from the temporary, changing and private needs of the poor to distribute benefits effectively where they would count most. This is why so often an intermediary was selected as the arbiter of these gratuities—frequently a parish priest or some other local person more able to diagnose the immediate needs of such a group.

For the most part, however, charity at the time was a parallel exchange between equals or between those less needy and those more needy. Often it was a transaction between kinsmen, neighbors, friends,

peers and other persons trapped in a role set that made it impossible to ignore each other's wants. As the members of these role sets often shared a common residential area, charity was usually an exchange between coresidents. Thus, it tended to cement a bond between persons who already had a serious interest in each other's good will, for as people who must live in close proximity and share the same public facilities, neighbors have a paramount interest in being able to trust one another. Charitable exchanges were one of the tokens that conveyed that trust.

Doubtless, the benefits that the residents of a poor neighborhood could extend to one another were rather meager. They ranged in value from the mere solace of understanding through small loans to free room and board. These gifts gained in value, however, by their scarcity. Where solace is in short supply it is much valued. If the worst sort of room and board are lacking, they become most dear. Like all benefits, these seem to obey the law of supply and demand. Without anyone intending it, then, an "invisible hand" added value to the exchanges of the poor; as coresidents, they were very much dependent upon one another. In turn, each was forewarned not to offend the other. The distinction between beneficiary and recipient was temporary at most. Within time, those most in need might become those most able to help, so that no firm line could be drawn between the two. And within urban neighborhoods, those who would not reciprocate would tend to select themselves for out-migration.

Certainly these exchanges among the poor were often transacted reluctantly and they hardly resembled the charitable "free gift." Most likely, benefits were given in times of real need and in some sense were expected to be repaid.[8] Such transactions left people with a diffuse claim on one another, and the burden of these claims should not be underemphasized. Aid and services were bartered, at least initially, when people were in dire need and for rather mercenary reasons. But while this removed the romance from these exchanges, it also gave them a firm value and left intact a more durable if burdensome network of relationships.

It is our contention that the formal aid system can substantially undercut these patterns of mutual aid. Under this system, even assuming that the poor who share a common residential location will continue their exchanges, these must be depreciated by the increasing supply from external sources. Correspondingly, the poor will have fewer and fewer reasons for being concerned about each other's welfare and the dangers of offending one another. Such a mercenary view of human relations may offend the reader.[9] We do not mean to insist that such benefits are the only reason for association among the poor, but only that they are one reason for such affiliations and, in that respect, are an important contributor to social order. Moreover, such "mercenary" exchanges seem especially important at the inception of a relationship even though this relationship may later persist for other reasons. When persons first meet, those who insist that their only design is to extend gratuitously their good will arouse every kind of suspicion. By contrast, someone who approaches another with a clear "reason" and some promise of repayment is received as a credible associate. Thus, while such mercenary exchanges may not be crucial to the continuity of social relationships, they may be more fundamental to their inception.

SUPPORTIVE WORLD VIEW

As a result of the dependence upon one another for small benefits, there often developed among the poor a corallary that cautioned against offending a neighbor. Rumor had it that relative comfort and prosperity were at best a temporary condition subject to the favor of God or change. At any time, one might exchange stations, going from the role of benefactor to that of recipient. For the reasonable man among the poor, this carried a persuasive warning: don't offend your neighbor, for tomorrow he might become a necessary benefactor.

The general force of such a myth was to make it nearly impossible for the poor to

partition their fellow residents into permanent and predictable units according to who was benefactor or recipient. For the individual, this myth may have led to the sacrifice of many ambitions and to practices of frugality, but it assured a quick redistribution among those in need. More importantly, it dramatized their interdependence and the futility of separating their present fortune from the misfortune of their fellow residents.

Formal and public charity tends to produce quite a different set of myths. There is often the fear that those who receive such benefits must be in the service of their benefactors and obliged to "fink" on their neighbors. This belief is not entirely without foundation. As representatives of a wider social order, those who dispense this help (policemen, youth workers, domestic peace corps, county welfare personnel, etc.) are obliged to report transgressions that come to their attention. Whether or not they actually make such reports is a moot point. Given the evidence at hand, it is advisable for the poor to keep their underlife to themselves. Of course, where large numbers are dependent on formal assistance, and where privacy is tenuous, there may be an effort to build solidarity to enlarge the ring of secrecy. The typical practice, however, appears to be for each domestic unit to withdraw behind closed doors lest a skeleton stray from its closet and make its way into the hands of one of these public watchdogs. A corollary is to restrict social relations to highly formal social occasions where there is little opportunity for intimacy and a disclosure of one's underlife. The final outcome inevitably must be a growing estrangement and suspicion between coresidents.

SOME EXCEPTIONS

We must exempt from this generalization two categories of people whose attraction to one another and whose potential for exchange seem to exceed the range of benefits of formal assistance. The first is comprised of the young and unmarried who seem to find an eternal attraction in one another. For the most part, they have not yet slaked their sexual curiosity or formed their surest friendships. Certainly it is unlikely that an agency will fill the first of these needs. On consideration, it is equally unlikely that public aid officials will be able to engineer the friendships of such young people. In order to find compatriots, young people must often engage in the most intimate sorts of self disclosure.[10] In practice, this implies a bawdy and ribald exchange where private loyalties are assured by a disregard for public conventions. On any count, it is unlikely that public practitioners of public aid can provide for such encounters.

A second category consists of those people who regularly engage in illegal enterprises: prostitutes, pimps, thieves, drug addicts, and so forth. All of these persons find it advisable to take in hand their relationships with coresidents. Sometimes they may attempt to act the part of overseers dictating the course of "safe behavior." Alternatively they may attempt to ingratiate themselves with local residents, and to make connections rather than enemies. Their interests here are obvious. More than anyone, they are dependent on the good will or cooperation of their neighbors. Where the major affections of the latter are already captured by the agents of social welfare, those in the underworld have every reason to think that coercion is their only surety.

These are old and persistent themes in slum neighborhoods that have been the traditional centers of vice. Most generally, these areas have produced an exceptional type of social order where the older and more respectable residents remain at a distance from one another because of their suspicions and lack of interdependence. By contrast, the younger people are driven into each other's arms by a lack of prior friendships and the necessity to disclose far more than the agents of social welfare can afford to tolerate. Similarly, those engaged in illegal enterprises find in each other those most able to help and least likely to betray them. Both groups are bound together by a covenant dictated by their inability to appeal to outside sources; i.e., those provided by official bodies. Thus, there tends to develop a bottom heavy social order where young persons and those attached to illegal enterprises are most interdependent with one another and, thereby, most capable of corporate action.

These observations may be true of almost any residential group where poverty arouses suspicions that cannot be assuaged except by the assurances of frequent exchange. Seemingly, these are mostly areas where coresidents have no basis for trusting one another except for the protestations each has made to the other. The benefits offered by formal sources, then, only further the estrangement between adults while enhancing the charm that adolescents and illegal entrepreneurs have for each other's company.

TRUST AS A CONDITION FOR INDIFFERENCE

Just because people can assure one another of their good will by frequent exchanges, there is no reason to assume that the absence or infrequency of such exchanges should make them enemies. Instead, they could simply remain indifferent to one another's shortcomings or attributes. Actually this comes close to the practice of some residents in large apartment houses where an encounter is scarcely cause for raising one's eyes. Such equanimity becomes more difficult, however, when one accepts the myth that poverty, low ethnic or racial status, and a lack of education are likely to lead to a good deal of amoral opportunism or plain irrationality. For those living in the urban slums, this is a persuasive, compelling, and frightening doctrine.

Emphasis of this myth by public agencies has a further impact upon the social and moral relations of the poor, indeed a self-fulfilling one. While some welfare programs are justified on straightforward humanitarian criteria, for example, providing enough food, protection to children, or decent amenities of life, the funding of the great majority is sought under a claim that its efforts will reduce crime, delinquency, mental illness, broken families, irrational aggression, or personal alienation. Unless one assumes that a shortage of goods and services causes these instances of deviance, this claim makes no sense. No doubt welfare agencies and workers have no intention of arousing distrust and alienation among the poor. Nevertheless, the connotation communicated by their presence and claims may result in exactly these conditions. If those funding these welfare agencies can be convinced that poverty will cause irrational violence, is there any reason to assume that the poor themselves are not equally forewarned against their neighbors?

In fact it is just on this point that the claims of this paper differ from those made by most welfare agencies. As a rule, agencies regard goods and services as a means of satiating the greedy and troublesome appetites of individuals. In the present argument, however, goods and services have been evaluated only by their capacity to produce interdependencies between people who have to trust one another, that is, of co-residents. In this view, the substantive value of a particular commodity relative to individual need is irrelevant. All we need consider is whether or not a particular service or commodity can be exchanged between people who might otherwise distrust one another. The fact that such commodities or services are more an individual burden than a benefit is not so important. By their exchange, these become a sign of one's good intentions and a reassurance that coercion is unnecessary. Thus, items gain value in exchange rather than in use.

In any case, those charged with the duty of distributing public funds apparently believe, or at least feel they must reiterate, the doctrine that it is personal shortages that principally give rise to public discontents and deviations. Otherwise, their role could become meaningless or be seen as an obstruction to exchanges that could enjoin the poor to a more profitable view of each other. It is to be expected, then, that the welfare officials will attempt to broaden the public circulation of the myth. To the extent that the attempts are successful, the poor have additional grounds for their estrangement. Here again, the formal distribution of social welfare seems only to broaden gulfs among those with scanty resources.

SUMMARY

The general burden of this paper has been to contrast formal and informal systems of welfare distribution from the perspective of exchange theory. The central tenet of this theory is that the goods, services and other benefits become valuable basically as media by which people can signify their good intentions and orderliness through exchange. In that sense, all such benefits are like money: "mere" tokens that have no inherent value but, in exchange, signal the ensuing course of a relationship. In contrast is another view which suggests that the principal importance of goods and services resides in the ways in which they are desired in their own right. In turn, individual deficiencies are consdered to be the source of great distress, arousal, vindiction, opportunism and irrationality. To protect ourselves and the victims of scarcity from one another, it has been suggested that the mean be given such a quantity of goods and services that their appetites will be filled and their wrath subsided. Hopefully, the poor will then join the rest of us in the orderly pursuit of yet greater quantities of goods and services.

By and large, the modern distribution of welfare benefits seems to be predicated on the latter type of analysis. Thus it is supposed that by greater and greater outlays of goods and services one can solve the problems of the poor. Exchange theory suggests quite a different set of outcomes. In sum:

1. The relationship between public dispenser and recipient will be quite attenuated because neither party has any reason to continue the relationship except for the exchange of welfare benefits.
2. The controls that the dispenser can exercise over a recipient are quite limited because they are restricted

by the universalistic rules that define the recipient's eligibility. Thus, the formal dispensation of welfare benefits *directly* influences only a very narrow range of the recipient's behavior.

3. The exchange of welfare benefits is not "transitive" in the sense of binding together additional persons beyond the immediate dyad within which the exchange takes place.

4. Ties to formal sources of welfare benefits tend to alienate alternate informal sources either because of the rules of eligibility or because an acceptance of such benefits alienates one's loyalties from other benefactors. For this reason, benefits dispensed through public channels tend to replace rather than augment benefits received from alternate sources.

5. The existence of formal channels of welfare distribution tends to increase the number of vertical exchanges relative to the number of horizontal ones within a particular stratum. Correspondingly, recipients gain another reason to be more tractable with regard to their superiors than with their equals.

6. Even where the number of exchanges within a strata remains constant, their value will decline with an increase in aggregate supply as determined by vertical exchanges. Thus, the *proportion* of goods and services that the poor lose by offending one another becomes less as they receive more from formal sources.

7. While these new public benefits may not devalue the exchanges already underway in existing horizontal relations, they are competitive with whatever benefits a potential relationship may hold in store. Over time, then, we should expect fewer *new* horizontal relationships as the influx of public benefits from vertical sources increases.

8. Public sources of welfare increase

the certainty of such benefits because they are distributed on the basis of explicit and universalistic criteria. By maintaining eligibility, a recipient may optimize his security although he often does not maximize or optimize his payoff.

9. The certainty of public welfare benefits and their vertical source tends to make it possible to partition people into permanent categories as to who is benefactor and who is recipient. This belies an ancient myth that relative affluence is a gift of the Gods. Hence, recipients have little reason to assume that each may at some future date change stations.

10. Among those identified as likely recipients, adolescents and those engaged in illegal enterprises are least able to substitute the benefits of public welfare for those they are presently exchanging. Basically, this is because the agents of public welfare are constrained to dispense only those benefits that the wider society condones. The general implication, however, is a bottom-heavy power structure where adolescents and those engaged in illegal exchanges are most interdependent and most able to mobilize for corporate action.

11. The extension of public welfare benefits to eligible persons is most often posited on the argument that it is the lack of such benefits that makes the recipient irresponsible, opportunistic, irrational, overly aggressive, perverse or apathetic. In due course, the assignment of such benefits and services tends to identify recipients as especially irresponsible, opportunistic, irrational, etc. The general outcome can only be a further estrangement between recipients and a growing tendency for them to think that coercion is their only safeguard against exploitation.

12. Vertical exchanges and universalis-

tic criteria of eligibility are most likely to reduce exchanges among coresidents, yet these are the people who most need the assurances of indifference or exchange because their propinquity makes it least possible for them to ignore each other's public character.

EMPIRICAL PROBLEMATICS

Obviously, the propositions of this paper are a guideline rather than a substitute for research. All research, however, must begin with some leading notions for gathering and interpreting data. Unfortunately there is scarcely any reliable data that could be used to test the propositions put forward in this paper. We intend to begin such a research effort through a study of poor families and public assistance agencies in Chicago.[11] In our own view, there are likely to be three points at which the findings of this study are apt to qualify our general argument.

First, it is entirely conceivable that we may find that a substantial number of those who enter the welfare rolls do so only after they have exhausted their available sources of mutual aid. In this case, the empirical focus would become not so much the comparison of assisted with non-assisted individuals as much as the study of the extent to which movement into the public assistance area creates a set of conditions which mitigate against the reestablishment of ties of mutual aid once the immediate financial crisis of the individual has been alleviated.

Second, an important question of the research is to gauge the extent of deviations from formal rules in the practices of agency officials. Many caseworkers may not be prone to penalize clients who take in moderate amounts of extra money through part-time jobs or who shift their children to the homes of relatives or friends during working hours. Indeed, some caseworkers may be strongly identified with the notion of fighting the agency, advocating the clients' right within the agency and with landlords and external agencies, and allowing the client (whom they see as receiving only the most pitiful amount of financial aid) to "cope" in whatever ways he can up to the point at which the worker himself runs the risk of being disclosed as being in collusion with his client. Such deviations from formal policy could give considerable leeway for particularly enterprising clients to develop lively exchanges beyond those officially prescribed, although it is expected that the high turnover rates of client-identified caseworkers and the ways in which agencies continually assert new rules make it unlikely that sizeable numbers of clients could feel this type of freedom in any stable way.

A third significant empirical question is that of the types of persons within the welfare population who are more and less accurately characterized by our theoretical analysis. Clearly, some members of the public assistance population lack the capacity for self-help because of deficiencies in mental or physical abilities, through old age, or through emotional problems and the like. Further, some sub-cultural groups, particularly certain ethnic groups, may be especially able to developing forms of mutual aid, expressed both by staying off of "public charity" and by persevering in self-help even when on aid. Conversely, among some populations and within certain settings (specifically, especially among Negroes living in public housing), public assistance may be so common that it loses its meaning as a stigmatizing symbol, and there may be no conception of patterns of self-help that are not somehow dependent on public funds. That is, the notion of self-help may be reduced to combatting the welfare agency and other bureaucracies.

This empirical problem is especially important for the black population. It can be argued that Negroes in America have never really developed a meaningful system of mutual aid, being dependent predominantly on slaveowners until the Civil War, on white Southern landowners until World War I, on white philanthropy until the Depression, and on public welfare ever since. Because of the caste and class lines between recipients and benefactors, their exchange has never developed on a really personal basis, and it was never such as to enlarge exchanges within the black aggregate. Further, the opportunity to develop mutual exchanges among Negroes through politics, following the lead of white immigrant groups, was substantially diminished by civil service and other reform movements which came just as the Negroes were coming to the cities in sizeable enough numbers really to take advantage of the machine. Thus for blacks we may be able to give our framework more than a partial test through historical comparison. With them, the main burden of the framework will involve an evaluation of the capacity of our approach to make intelligible the widespread acceptance of a "dependency mentality" and the lack of a tradition of "self help" which antedates the beginning of mass public assistance programs.

DISCUSSION AND PROGNOSIS

The major task of this article has been to explore the implications of exchange theory for two different systems of welfare benefits distribution. The prevailing strategy is to regard the poor as people who principally lack the benefits that others have at hand. An alternate strategy is to consider the poor as those having a shortage of items to transfer to one another as currency or tokens of their good will. One implication of this latter perspective is that recent attempts at distributing welfare benefits are likely to achieve quite different results than those explicitly stated.

While the major considerations here are of a theoretical nature, it would be ostrichlike to assume that we can examine these strategies of welfare distribution with equanimity. In this statement of exchange theory one likely inference is that formal and vertical attempts to relieve the condition of the poor are hopeless and ought to be abandoned. This does not follow. Larger supplies of goods and services may be justified wholly on humanitarian grounds and on the futher social psychological rationale that in America the great rise in consciousness of the society's tremendous affluence has produced a sharp upgrading

in what is the minimum basic standard of living compatible with self respect. Further, it is clear that some portion of the client population is incompetent to manage its own affairs and, most importantly, to bring up its own children (for whom no alternative environment is currently available), and this requires a continuation of budgeting, surveillance, and control for that segment.

However, if one is actually interested in alleviating the basic social condition of the poor, exchange theory suggests that whatever benefits are distributed should be used as much as possible to enlarge exchanges among the poor themselves. In practical terms, this means that the poor be supplied with numerous benefits which they can dispose of as suits their purpose. In this way each recipient could become a benefactor within his own horizon or strata. This would reassert the need for horizontal affiliations, the need for local friends, the indeterminacy between benefactors and recipients, and so on.

It should be clear in the present context that of current efforts, the attempt to raise levels of collective political action and "maximum feasible participation" of the poor seems largely irrelevant, concerned as it is principally with symbolic rewards rather than the day-to-day exchanges of the poor. The movement to form client unions to battle the welfare bureaucracy for rights and due process offers some occasions to create a solidarity among the poor and, to some extent, to raise issues involving rights to the free use of aid. It falters, however, in that it largely partakes of the assumption that simply more aid is the answer, an assumption which is likely to produce the outcome that assistance procedures will simply become more rigidified as they are tested through protest. Proposals for a guaranteed annual income or similar measures have the possibility of making the assistance program so universalistic that the casework middleman could actually be eliminated, and with it some of its limiting features. However, given political realities, the only feasible form these proposals could take would seem to involve an elaborate system of checking in detail on samples of recipients using present criteria, thus saving manpower but not changing the essential features of the relationship of dispenser to recipient. Of the present programs, the movement to develop "new careers for the poor" seems the most promising, for it at least provides fluid resources, including not only an unscheduled income but, often, also access to positions where one can help friends get jobs.

This brings us to the point where we must add some cautions. Once in control of disposable benefits, the poor are likely to use them for purposes of social control rather than to distribute them according to need or virtue. Thus, benefits will flow to those who are most amenable to the benefactor. This will produce a certain social order but not one that moral authorities will easily accept as just or impartial. Instead, the general practice will be one of "corruption," with welfare benefits disposed of to assure the favor of the recipient. Such exchanges may draw the poor into each other's service and preserve an amnesty between them, but are unlikely to satisfy our notions of a "just" distribution according to needs. However, the main point of this essay has been to inquire into the validity of the assumptions on which such a notion of justice is based.

NOTES

*We appreciate the helpful comments of Howard E. Freeman and Mayer N. Zald.

[1]One strong indication of the shift in the role of public welfare is found in the following estimate: Using 1929 dollars, between 1929 and 1966, private welfare donations increased from $2.25 per capita to $5.50 per capita, whereas public welfare expenditures increased from $5.25 per capita to $120.00 per capita. (Sources: *Historical Abstracts, Social Security Almanac*, 1948 and *Social Security Bulletin and Statistical Supplement for 1966.*)

[2]Marcel Mauss, *The Gift*, trans. I. Cunnison (Glencoe, Ill.: Free Press, 1954); Bronislaw Malinowski, *Argonauts of the Western Pacific: An Account of Native Enterprise and Venture in the Archipelagoes of Melanesian New Guinea* (New York: Dutton, 1960).

[3]We recognize, of course, that aid to the poor often may involve a component of conscious or unconscious self-interest, as when the mill-owner may see his charity as necessary to avoid the rebellion or demoralization of his employees.

[4]One result of the growth of public programs has been that those with a genuine urge to welfare benefaction have turned their contributions away from the poor to family service and other agencies serving a more middle-class clientele, paralleling the movement of professional social workers to these settings. See Richard A. Cloward and Irwin Epstein, "Private Social Welfare's Disengagement from the Poor: The Case of Family Adjustment Agencies," in Zald, ed., *Social Welfare Institutions* (New York: John Wiley, 1965), pp. 623-44.

[5]This is not to deny the existence of variation among public assistance jurisdictions in the discretion allowed to caseworkers in making decisions on aid, the creative uses of manipulation by clients to enlist additional assistance, or the readiness of some workers, especially young political liberals, to bend the rules or even enter into implicit collusion with the clients to provide them with additional aid. The essential feature that the workers and agency are to exercise very little discretion in dealing with the clients is clear, however, and is reinforced (for a variety of reasons that have their own merits) by the long-standing effort of the social work profession to agitate for abolition of the means test, by constitutional restrictions and sensibilities newly applied to "midnight raids," and by the new-found awareness of "client rights."

[6]Martha Derthick, "Inter-city Differences in the Administration of Public Assistance Programs: The Case of Massachusetts," in James Q. Wilson, ed., *City Politics and Public Policy* (New York: John Wiley, 1968), p. 265.

[7]Mauss, *The Gift.*

[8]See Michael Gold, *Jews without Money* (New York: Horace Liveright, 1930); William F. Whyte, *Street Corner Society* (Chicago: University of Chicago Press, 1937), pp. 12, 106, 256-58, 142-43; and Claude Brown, *Manchild in the Promised Land* (New York: MacMillan, 1965.)

[9]However, it is exactly such a mercenary view of humanity that underlies many recent efforts to ameliorate the condition of our poor. Apparently, the assumption is that if they only have a full belly and adequate opportunities they will stop being troublesome and become tractable citizens. Hardly anyone suggests that such "mercenary benefits" are important only as tokens which preserve the transactions between people. Among other works, Richard A. Cloward and Lloyd Ohlin's *Delinquency and Opportunity* (Glencoe, Ill.: Free Press, 1960), has been very important in tailoring public reactions to poverty. The book is

a near caricature of the economic man who affiliates himself to others only for purposes of individual greed.

[10]This is not to say that all adolescents discover such compatriots. Some, especially those closely chaperoned by their parents, may remain without a friend who would violate all the rules for
the sake of their personal relationship. Such a
youngster, however, is probably the shy child who
can never let down his hair and join the pleasures
of others despite the dictates of ideal norms. He
remains the "square" or, perhaps, the "find." See

Erving Goffman, "Fun in Games," *Encounters*
(Indianapolis, Indiana: Bobbs-Merrill, 1961), pp.
17-81.

[11]In a forthcoming study, "The Human Side of
Poverty," to be conducted in collaboration with
Donald J. Bogue and supported by a grant from
the Rockefeller Foundation. This study, proceeding through both structured interviews and general fieldwork inside agencies and in poverty neighborhoods, will initially be especially concerned
with comparing recipients and non-recipients of
roughly similar economic levels.

CHAPTER 49

The Youth Ghetto

JOHN LOFLAND

GIVEN all the current clamor over youth, teenagers, and the like, it is with considerable hesitation that I add yet another statement to the confusing caldron of polemics. At the same time, I feel it necessary to do so, for I have become a bit disturbed by the emotional stance taken by the people who talk about youth. Commentators, and even researchers on the topic, seem to feel so strongly about it, to be so close to it, that they have been unable, I think, to achieve the emotional and social distance necessary for adequate understanding. It seems, indeed, that those things that are most in need of discussion come often to be the most confused and least understood. There may even be a tendency to talk about important topics so much that we become saturated, baffled, and bored, and finally give up.

Despite my concern over the way in which otherwise dispassionate scholars can be exercised about the topic of youth, I want to try to approach the "youth question" from the point of view of a bemused and amused, but intrigued, outsider to the debate. From such a distance it is hopefully possible to argue that the issue of youth is only an empirical instance of some very general social processes that have to do with far more than merely youth or even age. From such a distance one can try to surmount the idiosyncracies that arise from thinking largely in terms of popular labels and one can perhaps raise general considerations relevant to, but far more general than, the topic. By so doing I hope to show again the merit of the famous platitude that the longest way around may be the shortest way home.

JOHN LOFLAND *is assistant professor of sociology at the University of Michigan. His article is a revision of an address given at Kalamazoo College, July 13, 1967, in a series on "The Moral Revolution of Our Time."*

In order most effectively to achieve, first distance and finally close-ness, it will be necessary, at the outset, to introduce some very abstract and remote or seemingly irrelevant topics.   These apparently remote con-ceptions involve an understanding of the notions of social categories, of categorical clusterings, and of pivotal categories.   Approaching somewhat closer, it will be necessary, second, to discuss age as a social dimension and the characteristics of age categories—in particular, the categories of child, teenager, youth, and early, middle, and late adult.   Third, and finally, I will, from the distance so developed, focus directly upon what might be called "the youth ghetto," and discuss adult conceptions of and practices toward it, conduct within it, and interaction between it and categories of adults.[1]

IN DESCRIBING social categories, we may begin with the observation that there exists a most peculiar species of animal whose most distinc-tive characteristics include, among other things, the following: it walks on its hind legs, uses symbols, and is extraordinarily sensitive to what the other animals of its kind think and feel about it.   This animal is further distinguished by, and very peculiar in, the assiduousness with which it feels a need linguistically to designate objects in the world.   So it is that this creature has a category with which it designates its general kind of object and which serves to set it off from all other objects in the world.   The more esoterically inclined of these animals label the general category *homo sapiens*, while the more mundane dub the category merely "man-kind," "human beings," "people," or that vestige of male supremacy, "man."

This animal is not satisfied, however, with simply setting itself off from all the other kinds of objects in the world.   Nor is it satisfied with the enterprise of making fine distinctions among and between all the ob-jects that fall outside its own general category.   No, this animal, which calls itself man, or mankind, engages also in making distinctions within the category of its most general kind.

One of the more popular subdivisions is based on differential place in what is identified as the reproductive cycle.   The dimension of sex is thus divined and there arises a division between the categories of "male" and "female."   A second very widespread division identifies the amount of time human objects have existed and divides mankind on the dimen-sion of age.   There are, thus, categories such as "child," "adolescent," "adult," and so forth, the specific terms depending upon who is doing the discriminating and designating.

Because it is possible for selected combinations of people to produce

---

[1] I should like to express my indebtedness to the works of, and conversations with, Lyn H. Lofland, Jerry Suttles, and Max Heirich. The seemingly unconnected but actually parallel and comple-mentary work of Suttles on an inner-city slum and Heirich on campus demonstrations have pro-vided, in part, the data, concepts, and propositions upon which I will attempt a more generalized statement with particular reference to youth. While these people are responsible for what follows in the sense of making it more possible, they are not to be held accountable for the direction taken or conclusions reached. See Gerald D. Suttles, *The Search for Moral Order: Identity and Conduct in an Urban Slum* (Chicago: University of Chicago Press, [in press]); Max Heirich, "Demonstrations at Berkeley, 1964–65" (doctoral dissertation, University of California, Berkeley, 1967).

other people and to cooperate in managing their joint young products, and, moreover, to cooperate in the task of sheer survival, there exists yet another basis for further division of mankind, this time along the dimension of their biological relationships to one another. There are, thus, categories of family or kin position. Many units of kin occupying adjacent ground may come to see that particular territory as reasonably and legitimately "theirs," setting it off (at least symbolically) from all other pieces of ground on the planet. As some kin groups come to dominate other kin groups, the claimed area may grow quite large, relative to the total space on the planet. Or, it may be quite small, yet be seen as equally crucial, as, for example, with units such as neighborhoods or even city blocks. Our animal may even get to feel that the location of one's residence on the planet is a crucially important dimension along which to distinguish categories of territorial habitation.

Such a territorial category of mankind, settled in a place for a long period of time, may even come to feel that it has some special way of life that distinguishes "my kind of people" from all the rest of the people in the world. There can thus arise a dimension called "culture," and various categories of it.

In moving around on the planet, differences in specific definitions of sex, age, kinship, and territory may be seen as associated with differences in the color or form of the surface casing of the animal; and so another dimension along which to divide kinds of people in the world appears, one sometimes called "race" or "ethnicity."

The process of extracting sustenance from the surface of the planet (or from other people) may place these two-legged animals in relations to one another such that it is felt reasonable to divide the general category yet again, this time along the dimension of how the materials necessary for physical survival are assembled. Such designations may be called jobs or occupations and in some societies may run into thousands upon thousands of distinctive categories. Such categories, themselves, have differential capacity to assemble resources. Some seem able to command the obedience of many of the other animals. Thus there can grow up a dimension of difference, designated by this animal with categories such as the more wealthy and the less wealthy, or the rich and the poor.

This species of animal, then, is that kind of creature that is constantly dividing itself into categories of "kinds of people" along dimensions such as sex, age, kin, territory, culture, race, work, and material resources.

HAVING complicated its world by discriminating all these and other dimensions and designating numerous categories along them, this peculiar animal then tries to simplify its world again through the process of clustering selected categories of some of the dimensions. So it is that a significant proportion of the species feels, for example, that animals of a certain category of the dimension, race, should reside in certain categories of the dimension, territory, and should assemble sustenance by occupying themselves with certain categories of the dimension, work.

More particularly, some of the species feel that what are called "whites" should reside in "nice" neighborhoods and make a living from some of the "cleaner" kinds of work; and correspondingly, other categories of race have their appropriate other places and other categories of work.

Or, some of the species may feel that certain categories of age are most appropriately clustered with certain kinship categories and with certain occupational categories. When these presumed proprieties of clustering are breached, comment and perhaps punishment are undertaken as a means of forcing these erroneously clustered instances of the species back into a proper or acceptable cluster of displayed categories. We see such a concern on those occasions when newspapers, for example, deem as newsworthy the fact that two married sixteen-year-olds are publisher-editors of a town newspaper.[2] Or, when it is deemed newsworthy—even to the extent of requiring an accompanying picture—when a sixteen-year-old girl marries a sixty-two-year-old man, thereby becoming "stepmother to five, grandmother to another five and a great-grandmother."[3]

These and numerous other occurrences are seen as news, and as worthy and in need of reporting and comment because they violate shared conceptions of appropriate categorical clustering. Such cluster violations are also, of course, objects of many kinds of punishment—the reason, I suspect, that the sixty-two-year-old husband just mentioned felt it necessary to tell reporters, "We'll make a go of it if they leave us alone." While these age-kinship examples are, in a sense, trivial, they illustrate the fundamental principle of categorical clustering.

If categories are clustered, we can conceive the possibility that a large number of categories along the most fundamental dimensions can pile upon one another, as it were, creating a new or derived class of the species, mankind, out of the coincidence of categories. Thus, in an exaggerated case, the human animals in the category immigrant (on the dimension nativity) can be almost exclusively of a particular category of race or ethnicity and also almost exclusively of low education. They can be also almost exclusively those who occupy certain territories (say, inner-city areas); almost exclusively those who work in low-paid, unskilled jobs and who are unemployed; and almost exclusively those who practice a given category of religion or culture.

Such a situation is empirically rare, but in that territory called America, this extreme of categorical clustering has sometimes been approximated.[4]

WHEN the categories of a set of dimensions begin, empirically, to pile upon one another—that is, to cluster—this peculiar animal not only perceives and comes to expect the clustering but introduces a further simplification. One of the categories of the dimensions so piled

[2]*Detroit Free Press*, March 15, 1965, p. 1.
[3]*Ibid.*, July 21, 1965, p. 2.
[4]Cf. Suttles, *op. cit.*, Part I.

up is singled out and treated publicly as their most important and significant feature. It defines the character of those animals whose categories are so clustered. That is, there comes to be a pivotal category that defines "who those people are," socially speaking. Indeed, as we shall see, the singled out pivotal category may have ascribed to it a causal force; it may be seen as responsible for "making" the animals the way they are relative to their other clustered categories.

Through time and across societies, what particular categories have piled upon one another or have clustered seems to have varied considerably; and, therefore, so have the particular categories singled out as pivotally defining human animals to one another.

What category is defined as pivotal is, of course, a function of specific, defined situations and the social organizational units of reference within which human animals are encountering one another. A person momentarily situated within a work setting may be pivotally defined as a worker. The same person, shifted to a family, political, or religious setting, may, in them, be pivotally defined, respectively, as a father, politician, or believer. In these examples, the social organizational units of reference are organizations and the categories attributed as pivotal derive from the designative framework of the corresponding setting.

Under some conditions the unit of reference with which a large proportion of the population defines one another in specific encounters comes to be the society at large. Thus, in contemporary America, if the male just mentioned is, say, Negro, and in a racially mixed work setting, others are not likely to pivotally define him as worker but as a Negro who happens incidentally to be a worker as well.

Those pivotal categories which permeate a wide variety of concrete settings—are used by a very high proportion of the population as a basis upon which they pivotally identify—and which are in conflict with one another may be called nationally dividing dimensions and pivotal categories. Pivotal categories which are activated as a basis for organizing action and conflict in only a few settings and are dropped in other settings, or permeate a variety of kinds of settings only in some confined part of the population, might be called localized pivotal categories.

In the short history of America there has already been a succession of different nationalized dimensions and pivotal categories around which division and conflict have been organized. Going back only to the middle of the last century, we see, in succession, the nationalized dimension of territory and its nationalized pivotal categories, northerner and southerner; the nationalized dimension of income or work and its nationalized pivotal categories, capitalist and worker; the nationalized dimension of nativity and its nationalized pivotal categories, immigrant and native-born; the nationalized dimension of sex and its nationalized pivotal categories, suffragette (female) and male; the nationalized dimension (more recently) of race and its nationalized pivotal categories, white and Negro.

Although a variety of nationalized dimensions of categorical conflict may be taking place at any given time, it would seem, from these examples, that one or another nationalized dimension becomes more or less primary in a given period and a variety of other dimensions of conflict are assimilated to the prime nationalized dimension. That is, alliances are formed for the purpose of a single basis of conflict. Thus, in the northerner-southerner case, the agricultural-industrial, slaver-nonslaver, states-rights–federalism categories became assimilated to a dimension of territory and its categories.

If one or another nationalized set of pivotal categories is likely to be a primary basis of conflict during a given period, there is raised the question of how one or another specific set comes to have this primacy. That is, one can assume there is always some prime dimension of conflict—some prime, nationalized, pivotal categories—and inquire into the conditions under which a particular dimension comes to the forefront.

While this is the most general question to pose, it is not my purpose here to explore a generalized answer. It is my purpose, rather, to take the question and its conceptual context as a framework within which to view some contemporary trends on the basis of which tentatively to project what might be the next nationalized dimension whose pivotal categories are, for Americans, the foremost bases of conflict.

AT THIS time, I am inclined to think that the current piling up of categorical sharing strongly suggests that the dimension of age (and the categories it provides) is becoming, or will become, our next identity and conflict equivalent of southerner and northerner, capitalist and worker, immigrant and "native stock," suffragette and male, white and Negro.

Let me point to some of the ways in which this new kind of piling up is occurring, referring first to the age category of youth.

1. If a dimension is to provide pivotal identities, it is highly facilitating to have it pile upon or coincide with territory. While territory itself may become the dimension of pivotal identification—as with northerner-southerner, USA–USSR—very often the sharing of territory will facilitate the public articulation of some other category that happens to coincide with a particular territory. One wonders, for example, whether the categories capitalist-worker, immigrant–native-born, Negro-white, would have been so nationally pivotal if they had not also been founded upon each opposing category having its own territory. In these terms, one might suggest, also, that the suffragettes, in contrast with the groups mentioned above, were never able to escalate sex categories as pivotal identities and bases of conflict to the extent that they might have wished because every major piece of territory they occupied was massively infiltrated by males.

Relative to age in American technological society, we may note that the coincidence between it and territory is proceeding apace and is most spectacular in the host communities of the ever-expanding multiversities. Into many of these communities in recent years, there have thronged literally tens of thousands of what we might call "youth"—human animals ranging in age from late teens to middle twenties. Because the political powers have opted for the model of a few large educational institutions, rather than many small ones, "cities of youth" are being created. The populations of some of them now approach or surpass forty thousand and the end is not yet in sight. Apparently some institutions even project enrollment figures of fifty to seventy-five thousand within the not too distant future.

Already, for example, 30 per cent of the population of Ann Arbor, Michigan, is composed of youth, or more precisely, students at the University of Michigan. They are not, however, distributed evenly throughout the city but are concentrated at its center, around the university. As the current high rate of apartment construction continues and as the university expands by about a thousand students a year, one can envision the day when the entire center city of Ann Arbor will be composed almost exclusively of human beings in their late teens to middle twenties. This trend is fostered in no small measure by the enormous rental rates in the center city which are likely to continue to rise and which force other age categories into the suburbs.

2. Thrust upon communities typically unprepared for their arrival, a significant proportion of the youth in these territories live crowded together in inadequate housing or equally crowded together in new but rent-gouging apartment buildings. Indeed the current circumstances of student living conditions—high density, crowding, bad housing, and rent gouging—remind one of the living conditions and exploitation of the immigrants in New York and Chicago in the early part of the century and of the Negroes in those (and other) cities somewhat later. Ghetto landowners come to think the ghetto area, as one owner of apartment buildings in Ann Arbor has put it, "a real estate paradise."

3. Also similar to early immigrants and later Negroes, the youth piled into these territories have low incomes, a fact which further serves to differentiate them from the surrounding population. Lacking the considerable amount of excess resources necessary to paint-up and fix-up their dwellings, youth, as did immigrants and as do Negroes, come to have publicly identifiable—that is, "sloppy and shoddy"—places of habitation. And, like other low income peoples, past and present, they rent rather than buy dwelling space.

4. Faced with uncertain employment and residence futures—actually a certainty that they will have to move—youth in these territories do not, to any significant degree, develop identification with local social institutions that precede their arrival—the pre-existing local political organizations, churches, business organizations, and so forth. As was said of

the earlier ghetto dwellers, they "stay with their own kind" and participate in informal and formal social organization dominated by others of their own category.

Such piling up of categories makes for, I think, the possibility of ghettos very similar to those that the dominant population worried about in connection with Italian, Irish, and Polish immigrants some forty or more years ago and the kind that we still worry about today in connection with Negroes.

Only now, instead of Italian, Irish, Polish, or Negro ghettos, the dominant sectors of the population may well become concerned about "youth ghettos" and all the social processes that surround concern over ghetto areas are likely to begin. Indeed, they have begun, as I shall suggest in a moment.

FIRST, however, we must pursue the obvious implication that categories piling up in one kind of territory means that other kinds of categories are likely to be piling up in yet other territories. If youth are being territorially segregated, this obviously means that they cannot be in some other places. These other places are of equal interest, for in them reside the sectors of the population who will be engaging in concern over youth ghettos.

Concomitant with the rise of youth ghettos, has been a growth of rather age-homogeneous bands of territory ringing American cities. These are the well-known suburban tracts, many neighborhoods of which have a rather peculiar character. In some of them one finds a population composed almost exclusively of what we might call "early adults"— human animals ranging in age, roughly, from late twenties to late thirties; and children—human animals below the age of about twelve. "Middle adults"—humans in their early forties to late fifties; and "late adults"— humans in their sixties and older; and teenagers are in a decided minority; in many cases, they are hardly present at all.

Piled upon this age category of early adult and its coincidence with a territory, one finds the employment and financial state known as "struggling" or "being on the way up." The neat row houses of early adults market in the fifteen to twenty-five thousand dollar range. Deep in installment debt, their lives are centered on the family unit. They are concerned that politicians treat them kindly, that is, that taxes be kept down. And they are likely to have voted for Goldwater.

In other suburban tracts, one finds a population composed almost exclusively of middle adults (forties and fifties) and teenagers. The neighborhood is largely undisgraced by the presence of children, early adults, or late adults and the neat row houses of the middle adults market in the twenty-five to fifty thousand dollar and up range. In large measure the middle adults have passed their "struggling." They have, in some sense, arrived.

Indeed, there would seem to be evolving a pattern wherein an age-sex unit of early adults establishes itself in an early-adult neighborhood, its members spawn their offspring and then, at the appropriate age, move to a middle-adult territory. In this way, age-sex units are always able to be with their "own kind," territorily protected from the contamination of contact with many other age categories. Teenagers, especially, are usually able to be with their corresponding age-category mates. They can be uncompromised by entanglements with children, early adults, or late adults.

Although all of this is only a tendency at present, it would seem to be a growing tendency and one which assumes additional significance in the light of the already more pronounced territorial segregation of late adults. We are all well aware that persons of sixty and over—often described with polite euphemisms such as "senior citizens"—have begun to assemble in special buildings in cities, in special neighborhoods within suburbs, and, indeed, in special areas of the nation. It is apparently the case that significant portions of Florida, Arizona, and Southern California are becoming something like the states of late adulthood. Piled upon these categories of age and territory are others, such as the marginal or unemployed state, often called "retirement." Special kinds of legislation have developed for this age group, defining their monetary rights and duties and relating even to the possibility of their marrying one another.

AMONG these six categories of age, two—youth and late adulthood— are already proceeding toward highly pronounced territorial segregation with the concomitant clustering of yet other categorical sharings around their respective ages and territories. The remaining four are already splitting into two sets of two each. Early adults are still territorially linked to children and middle adults are still territorially linked to teenagers.

However, the territorial link between middle adults and teenagers shows signs of weakening, given the absorption that teenagers have in the culture that centers on the high school. While teenagers must still share a household with middle adults and face school-and-other-specialized keepers of teenagers, they are achieving a rather well defined and dominated set of territories spread throughout communities. These include the school itself, drive-ins, and the like.[5] This separation is limited, however, in a way somewhat similar to the way in which the territorial integrity of the suffragettes was limited. While both had or have special territories, these were or are not large areas from which persons of other categories could or can be, at least formally, excluded.

Nonetheless, this partial territorial segregation exists and is deepening. Combined with the propensity of early adults to send their children to school at ever earlier ages, one can wonder if these remaining two sets of two categories (early adults and children; middle adults and teenagers) will not themselves territorially divide.

[5]James S. Coleman, *The Adolescent Society* (New York: Free Press of Glencoe, 1961).

Perhaps it is not entirely unrealistic, fanciful, or whimsical to suggest that there may come a day when children are almost entirely segregated under the supervision of child-rearing specialists. Perhaps parts of, say, Nevada, Utah, Wyoming, or Montana, could be given over to the task and designated as Children's States. Under such circumstances, early adults could devote themselves exclusively to the struggle of making it to the next neighborhood. The increasing numbers of college-educated, female early adults who now mourn the disuse of their talents and the incompatability of children and career, would be free more actively to participate with their male partners in the climb up.

Likewise, the separation of teenagers into teen cities, very much like the developing youth ghettos, would free their middle-adult parents to participate more intensively in the social and political machinations of the occupations in which they have now come to power.

Segregation, after all, has its attractions as well as its limitations. Given the already strong tendency of children and teenagers (indeed, of all the age categories) to group together and to prefer one another's company, these youngest categories may well, in the future, come to demand the same kinds of territorial rights now enjoyed by youth and late adults. At present, of course, they are still rather dominated by their respective age-superiors in territories run by, and fundamentally belonging to, these superiors. Equal justice for all might well be construed in the future to mean that each age category, including children and teenagers, has a right to its own piece of ground.

At such a future time, arguments are also likely to arise for the efficiency and effectiveness of specialized age territories for children and teenagers. In the same way that the family-oriented cottage industry and the "putting-out system" of industrial manufacture collapsed in the face of competition by the superior effectiveness of a centralized, industrial process, so too, the last remaining cottage industry—that of producing persons—might well falter in the face of harsh criticism of its inefficiency, its widely variable standards of production, and its excessive rate of rejects. Although they phrase them in different terms, many educators are, in fact, already making exactly these criticisms.

Any consideration of divisive forces must, however, at the same time, consider forces that limit the division. There is, after all, a strong ideology that adults should love their children, teenagers, or youth and that they should devote personal attention to them. Persons in the various age categories are still highly linked, despite geographical separation. Even youth still have parents and know that they will one day move into the older age categories.

It is nonetheless too easy to overemphasize the importance of such linkages, for youth in particular, as the slogan "Don't trust anyone over thirty" forcefully suggests. Parents may be linked to and love their youth but they are still capable of suspicion, rejection, and distrust of them. They can feel defamed and betrayed by them. As age-category segregation deepens, as more youth go to live in youth ghettos and come under the influence of the special kind of life carried on there, we should expect an increasing proportion of parents to feel that all the effort they put into Johnny or Mary was for naught and to ask themselves, "What did I do wrong?" Of course, they did nothing wrong, unless one counts as wrong their willingness to send their youths to college and to allow them to reside in youth ghettos.

IN ORDER to reasonably understand the social sources or causes of age-category segregation, a detailed analysis of at least the last seventy years of American history would be required. Systematic comparisons with similar and different developments in other societies would be indispensable. I will here, obviously, only suggest some very gross and very proximate forces promoting age-category segregation.

First, there is the rather peculiarly American guiding conception that the least expensive and most efficient technological alternative in projecting action is the "best" alternative. It seems to be cheaper and more efficient to expand universities and create giant new ones, than it would be to construct and staff a multitude of small ones. It seems to be cheaper and more efficient to build tracts of similarly priced houses on an assembly line basis than to intermix variously priced houses on a custom basis. It is believed to be cheaper and more efficient to bring late adults together into special housing adapted to their "needs"—likewise built on an assembly line basis—than to do otherwise. Specialized organizations and occupations are most cheaply and efficiently provided for each of these age categories, if each of them is massed together in a single area. Professors are more easily provided for youth; schools are more easily provided for children and teenagers; and medical specialties are more easily provided for late adults.

Second, there are the requirements, or rather lack of them, of a technological economic system. Despite all the demand for technical personnel existing in some sectors of the economy, the larger fact seems to be that there are simply not enough occupational slots in that economy to absorb any significant proportion of the hordes of youth and late adults existing within the population. In terms of economic necessity, youth and late adults (as well as teenagers and children) are surplus population. That is, a basic condition permitting them to congregate in their own grounds is that the vast bulk of them are not needed, anyplace, to perform economic functions.

One way, in particular, to manage youth is to develop the conception that they require advanced training or education if they are to participate eventually in the technological economy. This conception is given teeth by actually requiring "education" as a condition of employment, a condition which propels an ever-increasing proportion of these youth—some 40 per cent of them, or about six million bodies at the present time—into colleges, and a proportion into youth ghettos.

The surplus is eased out at the other end through the development of the conception that people are not really very good workers after about sixty or so, and should, for their own good and enjoyment, give up useful employment.

If age-category segregation is induced by forces such as these, and many others, we can also see that once begun it comes to have a dynamic of its own. Seeing less and less of one another, it becomes more difficult to know how to interact comfortably across age-category divisions. Having less practice and experience in it, early and middle adults, for example, come to be more uncomfortable about interacting with those late adults they do encounter; and the same is true of interactional relations among the other age categories. Such difficulties, in turn, provoke more mutual avoidance and an increasing constriction of topics about which they might have common interest. Segregation having begun, a process of spiraling or increasing isolation across the age-grades is set up.

LET me shift, finally, to a direct focus on the youth ghetto. I will discuss, in order, relations of adults to this territory, conduct within it, and some aspects of interaction between the two.

These topics are appropriately conceived in terms that we might use in discussing other, more familiar, kinds of ghettos. The more familiar ones have, of course, historically been based upon religion, ethnicity, or race. However, certain kinds of social processes seem relatively common to almost all ghettos, age-category ones included.

A condition of territorial segregation wherein a variety of additional categories are piled up, promotes a situation of low information flow from the ghetto to the surrounding territories. When low information flow occurs in the context of a measure of suspicion, fear, and distrust, the information most likely to be noticed, remembered, and circulated by persons in extra-ghetto territories is that which is discrediting or defaming. Adopting the point of view of suspicious, fearful, and distrustful persons, it is altogether reasonable for them to be attuned to discrediting information from the ghetto; such information serves to put them further on guard to protect themselves.

One type of defamation takes the form of imputing to the pivotal category in question a wide range of personal failings, often felt to be caused by the pivotal category itself. Non-ghetto dwellers build up in their minds an imputed "personality" of sorts that is believed to be characteristic of the particular ghetto dwellers, the particular pivotal category.[6]

In recent years we have begun to see the development of the rudiments of an imputed ghetto personality of youth, or, more narrowly, of students. Adults, the superordinate category in this case, seem to have begun the process of noticing, remembering, and relating a variety of kinds of imputed personal features of this latest stigmatized category.

[6]Cf. Suttles, *op. cit.*, and the literature cited therein.

One hears it commented that "they" are boisterous, they have no respect for property, they work irregularly and drive recklessly. They throw garbage out of their windows, and break bottles in the streets and on the sidewalks. They lounge in an unseemly fashion on balconies, dangle out of windows, and congregate in public thoroughfares. They accost strangers on the street with arcane propositions. They gamble all night, fail to pay shopkeepers and landlords, shoplift, and engage in riotous drinking sprees. They hang around on the streets, jaywalk, talk in a loud and crude fashion in public places, and live in disorder and filth. They let their dwellings run down, living like "animals," crowded six and seven together in small apartments. They have loose sexual behavior and fail to keep their bodies and clothes properly scrubbed and ordered. They engage in crime. Their women have no shame but dress scantily and recline suggestively on lawns or around buildings. They are residentially unstable, always moving, frequently leaving the landlord or even their own kind in the lurch.

Establishments which cater to their peculiar tastes are dimly lit and outfitted in outlandish decor. Obscene slogans and writings and pictures are likely to be found in the stores they frequent, especially the book shops.

While yet scattered and relatively uncrystallized as a personality portrait of youth ghetto residents, there would seem to be here already the elements of the classic portrait of failings attributed to ghetto dwellers throughout American history. This portrait has typically included— as it does here—the elements of laziness, irresponsibility, hedonism, lack of pride in property or personal appearance, promiscuousness, deviousness, and family and employment instability. We are currently most familiar with this portrait of imputations relative to Negro and Spanish-American ghetto dwellers, but essentially the same kinds of imputations were once made of, for example, the Italians and the Irish before their ghettos disintegrated. Indeed, where ghettos based on these latter pivotal categories persist, the process still goes on.[7] Such failings were imputed also to "laborers," or working men, during the struggle for unions in America.[8]

The similarity between the imputations now beginning to be made of residents of youth ghettos and the imputations made at one or another time of residents of Irish, Italian, Negro, and Spanish-American ghettos suggest considerable continuity in the portrait of imputed failings in American society. While the particular category that bears the brunt of these imputations has changed, the imputations themselves continue to be with us.

Such continuity, despite change in the particular pivotal category that is the object of the imputations, could, indeed, be taken to suggest the social necessity of a stratum which is believed to embody all the

[7]Suttles, *op. cit.*
[8]A similar kind of imputation of personal failings, of course, also takes place between regions of nations and nations themselves that are in conflict.

failings so feared by the dominant sectors of the society. Such an embodiment of what most people should not be seems always to be there, a vivid and living object-lesson in the difference between good and evil. After all, if everyone is good, how are participants in a society to know the difference between good and evil? It is perhaps through the dramatization of evil, achieved by assigning some sector of the society the task of "acting it out," that the remainder of the society more easily finds it possible to be good. The repository category of evil provides "good citizens" with the empirical materials needed in making a meaningful contrast and in gauging the appropriateness of conduct.

IN ADDITION to becoming objects of defaming imputations, ghetto dwellers find themselves, as well, the objects of specialized processes of social control and recognition. Such efforts are specialized because, while they are sometimes described as though they applied to the entire population, they are directed at the ghetto dwellers in particular.

Although they are relatively rudimentary as yet, we already see such specialized control and recognition efforts in, for example, the University of Michigan's attempt to regulate student operation of automobiles anywhere in an entire county without special registration. New laws regarding mufflers on motor vehicles have been adopted, and aimed, according to the public discussion, at the motorcycles of youth. (They are, it is said, terribly noisy.)

Within the context of ghettoization, already existing controls aimed especially at youth take on new significance. The military draft, which falls with special force on youth, comes to be defined as a special burden. Because of the uncertainty over whether any one of them is or is not twenty-one years of age, the purchase of alcoholic beverages becomes, typically, an occasion for an ID shakedown. In much the same way that Negroes in some parts of the country even today have to worry about obtaining public service, youth have to be concerned over producing a sufficient amount of "ID" even to ratify their minimal standing as persons. The treatment they receive at the hands of bar maids and bartenders and liquor store clerks serves well to communicate their special pivotal identity and to communicate others' assumption that youth are "likely to be liars." So, too, their credit may be a matter for suspicion and the obtaining of a telephone may require a special "security deposit," serving organizationally to impute to them an untrustworthy personal character.

And also parallel to Negroes, employers are willing to offer many youth only menial unskilled jobs and reluctant to proffer employment with career or developmental possibilities. That is, employers discriminate against youth in terms of whether they have made some kind of settlement with the military. If none has been made, reasonable employment is difficult to obtain. While employers are entirely rational in this, it constitutes, from the point of view of youth, a form of discrimination.

Youth become, too, objects of special recognition in the name of non-discrimination. A few radio stations, for example, have demonstrated their democratic virtues not only by having ethnic and racial radio programs but by setting aside hours or even days for youth programs. Radio stations in Ann Arbor recognize that area's special German past with "old country" shows, and at least one station gives over Saturday to student "ethnic radio." The youthful announcer for that day refers to Ann Arbor as "Student City."[9]

Eventually most ghettos rouse the moral sentiments of the dominant population to the point that a special corps of helping and rehabilitative personnel are recruited and deployed into the areas. It is the mission of these personnel to reduce the number of horrendous things that go on there and to make the residents straighten up and be good citizens.

While this kind of missionary activity, on any significant scale, may lie far in the future in relation to youth ghettos, one can discern its beginnings in such enterprises as the "campus ministry" and in the expansion of psychological counseling for those youth who are students.

If and when there comes to be a "war on youth ghettos," and even federal programs for such, these missionaries will no doubt follow the classic pattern of previous ghetto forays. They are likely to be more concerned with adjusting people to their lot within the existing structure than with considering alternative modes of social organization.

INFORMATIONAL inaccessibility and fear and suspicion of ghettos promote, in addition to defaming stereotypes of imputed personal features and specialized control, a special revelationary literature.

This literature is centrally oriented to the question, "What are X (the pivotal category) *really* like?" Whether the "X" has been southerners, workers, suffragettes, immigrants, or of late, Negroes, the popular press has frenzied itself with efforts to "inform" the dominant sectors of the society what is "really" going on, what, of late, is "happening." Such popular revelations promise us an "inside view" of the innermost sections and horrendous events of the ghetto. Complete with the most grim or most bizarre of photographs and drawings, such revelations often lead the reader to believe that not only are his worst suspicions true but things are even worse than he had thought.

While we are most familiar with these popular revelations, historically, in connection with immigrants and Negroes, a similar kind of presentation is now being made about youth. One of the most recent, put out by *Look*, the contemporary master of the popular revelation, is called *Youth Quake*.[10] Retailing for one dollar, its cover features a blurred psychedelic-

---

[9]Like the separate entrances for whites and Negroes in southern states, Ann Arbor, Michigan's, YM-YWCA has a special side door neatly lettered with the words YOUTH ENTRANCE.
[10]Jack V. Fox, *Youth Quake* (New York: Cowles Educational Books, 1967).

like photograph of youth on a dance floor in "wildly" colored dress, presumably wreathing under the sounds emitted by a musical group. The front page text promises to tell us "WHAT'S HAPPENING" in these terms:

> Turned on and Tuned in . . . Teeny-boppers, Hippies . . . Sunset Strip to Washington Square . . . Conversations parents never hear— Sex, Drugs, God, Morality, Success—Mod and Mini . . . Psychedelic Lights . . . and much much more.

It should be noted that popular revelations of ghetto life are not entirely negative in character. While there is a large element of indignation and "tut-tutting," it is perhaps most accurate to say that these revelations contain a mixture of horror and romantic fascination with "people who live that way." Evil, after all, must have its attractions—to be natural—otherwise it would not be so popular.[11] Nor would the dominant categories of a society have to put so much energy into eliminating or holding it in check.

It is in part such romantic fascination that, in the past, made Harlem such a lure for white Manhattan residents and tourists. Indeed, historically, a variety of kinds of ghettos have come to service the vice needs of the population at large. Youth ghettos will perhaps also come to service the demand for vice.

Parallel to the growth of popular revelations and lagging behind them somewhat, there begins to be produced about ghettos a much less titillating but probably more accurate body of scholarly revelations. In historical succession, sociologists, for example, produced an enormous body of material on immigrants (now no longer read by much of anyone but historians of the field) and on Negroes, under the rubric "race relations." They are now "getting hip" to the "youth thing," and the scholarly outpouring has begun. Originally called "juvenile delinquency" in the fifties (when there were large amounts of money to be had for research on that), the caption has been expanded to "youth." Highly indicative is a recent well-received collection of writings called the *Handbook of Modern Sociology*, which has a special chapter on "Position and Behavior Patterns of Youth," without a corresponding chapter on any other age category.[12]

Interestingly enough, the theoretical debate common to the sociological literature on immigrants, Negroes, *and* youth is the question of the degree to which they are "really" different or similar to the rest of society. In all three bodies of materials, some people argue that "they" are significantly different in some fundamental fashion. This position is opposed by theorists who choose to emphasize different facts, in the direction of saying that the category is fundamentally similar. The debate has focused, in particular, on whether the ghettoized category has a distinctive culture, or "subculture."

[11]This is a long-noted feature of "evil," but it was most forcefully brought to my attention by Gerald D. Suttles in a private communication.
[12]David Matza, "Position and Behavior Patterns of Youth," in *Handbook of Modern Sociology*, edited by Robert E. L. Faris (Chicago: Rand McNally and Company, 1964), pp. 191–216.

The urge to produce such revelations inevitably gives rise to the phenomenon of ghetto spies, persons who either are permitted openly to hang around in the ghetto or who actually pass as "one," whatever the "one" in question may be. The spies of popular revelations are often reporters on assignment, but quite often, also, free lancers, as was apparently the case with race-ghetto spy John Griffin, author of *Black Like Me*.[13] Paul Goodman is perhaps the leading youth-ghetto spy among a wide range of persons who have tried to get in on this new kind of act.[14] Perhaps the ultimate in age-category spying has, however, already been achieved by that thirty-three-year-old lady who claims, "I Passed as a Teenager."[15] As always, the scholarly revealers have lagged behind in getting out their own spies, but they are beginning to catch up.

And, as has occurred with respect to previous ghettos, some members of the dominant pivotal category defect to "the other side." In the same way that some of the economic elite, in Marxian terms, are said to see the "true" direction of history and defect to the workers, or that some whites defect to and take up the Negro cause, we are now beginning to have age-category defectors. Edgar Friedenberg is perhaps the leading exemplar of such defection.[16]

IN ATTEMPTING briefly to characterize what happens within ghettos themselves, we must keep in mind two previously discussed points. First, the piling up or clustering of devalued categories in a given territory is in fact taking place. Second, this factual clustering is perceived (however dimly) by the surrounding populace and becomes a basis upon which all manner of additional failings are imputed. Taken together, factual clustering and the additional imputations form the situation of the ghettoite.

Two significant features of the situation of the ghettoite are: (1) extraordinary exposure to others of "his own kind," and correspondingly limited exposure to persons of "other kinds"; and (2) limited objective possibilities for establishing a stable life style, primarily because of low income, which is, in turn, a function of the imputations and practices of disreputability made of "his kind" by the surrounding populace.

The situation of the ghettoite is conducive to or "ready made for" familiar strategic lines of adaptation or response. I will mention two well-known strategies of adaptation appearing frequently in all ghettos which are now appearing in youth ghettos.

First, it is possible, and rather reasonable, for the ghettoite to accept the just-mentioned facts of his situation and to accommodate to them. He can come to believe that the imputations made and treatment accorded to his category by the dominant sectors of the society are in a significant measure true, reasonable, and justified. While he views these as sad

---

[13]John H. Griffin, *Black Like Me* (Boston: Houghton Mifflin Company, 1961).
[14]Paul Goodman, *Growing Up Absurd* (New York: Vintage Books, Inc., 1956).
[15]Lyn Tornabene, "I Passed as a Teenager," *Ladies' Home Journal*, LXXIV (June, 1967), pp. 113–18, and a book of the same title.
[16]Edgar Z. Friedenberg, *Coming of Age in America* (New York: Random House, 1965).

facts, he nonetheless accepts them as valid. The imputations of the ways in which he displays personal failings become then a basis upon which actual and new items of "personal failure" are predicated. (The irony here, of course, is that such new personal failings are perceived by the dominant categories and become the basis upon which they, in their turn, predicate more intensive imputations and discriminatory practices. That treatment, in its turn, feeds back to the ghettoite, and so it goes on.)

Under conditions of low income and almost exclusive exposure to one's "own" stigmatized kind and an uncertain residential future, and indeed, an uncertain future generally, it becomes reasonable to relax one's efforts at a conventional personal appearance and to relax one's efforts, as well, to maintain a conventionally clean, well-kept, and orderly household.

We are, of course, familiar with the relaxation of personal and household standards in ghettos based on ethnic or racial pivotal categories. And we are familiar, too, with the imputations sometimes made as to why these standards are relaxed. Among the most popular has been the notion of a special "lower class" or "Negro personality" which causes personal and household disorder and dirt.

However, exactly the same pattern of personal and household dirt occurs in youth ghettos. The youth found to display this pattern are drawn largely from middle and upper middle class backgrounds, a setting which presumably trained them in high standards of personal and household order and cleanliness. In the youth ghetto, we find a portion of them living in a fashion very similar to that in which people in other ghettos live.[17] And presumably when they depart from the ghetto for early adult neighborhoods, they will maintain the very particular style of cleanliness and order so characteristic of those neighborhoods.

It can be suggested that the youth ghetto pattern of personal and household disorder and dirt is a very important "control" or contrast case which tells us that it is not ghetto people qua deep-lying personality patterns that conduce to this relaxation, but rather the ghetto situation. As has been said, the ghetto situation is one of high exposure to one's own kind, low income, and uncertainty of residential and general future. Exposure almost exclusively to one's own kind reduces the felt need for "respectable" presentation. Low income makes respectable presentation extremely difficult to accomplish. Middle class people are insufficiently appreciative of the very high total cost of the tools and machines, paint, repair materials, and furnishings necessary to the rehabilitation and maintenance of a "respectable" household. This is especially the case where one is attempting this in what is already a ghetto dwelling. And, of course, an uncertain residential and general future renders the entire effort unreasonable in the first place. If we are to understand this pattern of ghetto living, then, we are better advised to scrutinize the

[17]I refer here to the garden-variety, run-of-the-mill youth in such ghettos, not simply to the more spectacular patterns embodied in youthful radicals or hippies.

characteristics of the ghetto situation rather than the personal characteristics of whatever category of people happen to be found there.

Second, while the majority of ghetto residents seem to "take it" and a proportion drift into the first pattern, a minority refuse to accept their situation and project a more active strategy of response. Co-mingling in the intensive fashion now made possible and necessary, some ghetto dwellers begin to crystallize new and unusual ideologies which purport to explain and interpret their particular situation and, typically, also to describe and explain all the rest of the world. Members of the human species who live in the ghetto situation seem particularly likely to spawn and be attracted to new and unusual ideologies that are characterized by members of the dominant society as "radical," "bizarre," "peculiar," or "fantastic." Ghettoites are particularly likely to so occupy themselves because of a lack of exposure to the more moderate and modulating categories of persons who might convince them of other realities; because of the stigmatizing imputations they face; and because of the objective deprivation and social exclusion under which they labor.

The general class of active ideological responses to the ghetto situation itself divides into two types of directions, which even sometimes compete with one another for adherents. One type, which might be called the political response, defines the ghetto situation and other sectors of society in terms of relatively immediate measures that can be undertaken to better the lot of ghettoites and perhaps even the life of the entire society. We are, of course, quite familiar with this in regard to Negro ghettos and the variety of civil rights organizations that seek to make this or that concrete change in the social order. The suggestion here, however, is that we can best understand what is called "The New Left"—meaning, most prominently, Students for a Democratic Society— as a movement arising out of the youth ghetto in exactly the same way political movements have, historically, risen out of other kinds of ghettos.

If the ghettoization of youth continues, we should expect to see the rise of a variety of kinds of other political responses, many of them more limited and moderate than Students for a Democratic Society. Already there are attempts to organize renters and to register student voters in order to increase their political power. There may come a day, indeed, when some cities will find that their politics revolve around the voting strength of various age-category ghettos, in the same way that Chicago politics has long revolved around ethnic and racial enclaves.

The other type of more active ideological response is considerably more sweeping in the scope of its projected change in the social order, but ironically more passive in the degree to which it seeks to make changes in that order. I refer to the various retreating and utopian—not untypically, religious—responses which involve withdrawing into highly distinctive residential enclaves, often within the ghetto, and living out therein a life that is considered perfect and ideal. The outside world is seen as sinful, demented, deluded, decadent, or otherwise in need of revolutionary change. Except for perhaps some efforts at making individual converts, such utopians do not directly attack the social order. The most famous instance of this type of response in connection with Negro ghettos has, of course, been Father Divine's Heavens.[18] We are witnessing, I think, an analytically identical strategy of response in the so-called "hippies" who have appropriated certain dwellings in youth ghettos as their utopian communities and who have even moved out to create their own ghettos, as in the Haight-Ashbury district of San Francisco. Although yet lacking a widely acknowledged messianic leader (Leary is apparently "out"), their ideology is remarkably similar to that espoused by followers of Father Divine, especially in the emphasis upon love, good-will, and the decadence of the larger society.

One other pattern of response should be mentioned, although it has not as yet appeared in the youth ghetto, at least not in organized form. This is the militant revolutionary pattern, exemplified by the Black Nationalists, or at least those among the Black Nationalists who advocate guerrilla warfare and violent subversion. But perhaps this still lies in the future and will only appear if youth ghettoization becomes very extreme.

The possibility and viability of the militant revolutionary pattern, and all the other patterns of response, are, of course, crucially undercut by a fundamental feature peculiar to age itself. While people who are identified in terms of racial and ethnic pivotal categories will remain instances of those categories all their lives, youth as a category is impermanently occupied. It would seem to be enormously difficult to predicate any kind of enduring collective action upon a population of participants that is continually leaving the category while others are continually arriving. In the end, that feature must be recognized as fundamentally debilitating to organized age-category conflict.

NONETHELESS, conflicts between the age categories of a more limited but highly spectacular character are still possible, and even likely, under conditions of youth ghettoization.

The prime meaning of ghettoization is, as mentioned, the piling up of all manner of categories of dimensions that are different from the categories of the rest of the society. A prime effect of this piling up of categories shared within a territory and little shared across territories, is the decline of routine, trustful relationships with individuals and organizations in extra-ghetto territories. Ghettoites are intensively and routinely exposed to other ghettoites, but only fractionally exposed in a routine fashion to non-ghettoites.

Such a situation of separation of categories of people serves to create distance, in both the physical and social senses, and, therefore, to engender relative ignorance or lack of information as to the intentions, plans, motives, and good or evil will of the other pivotal category.

[18]Sara Harris, *Father Divine, Holy Husband* (Garden City, New York: Doubleday and Company, Inc., 1953).

If there comes to be an absence of cross-categorical interaction, joint-problem solving, routine negotiation, and the like, there is created within both pivotal categories a condition of distrust and fear of the opposite category. This situation of separation and therefore distrust and fear spawned by ignorance is to be contrasted with the kinds of relations between social categories that create trust and confidence and therefore social stability. Cross-categorical trust and confidence are most likely to prevail where there is a high rate of relatively free interaction, relatively large numbers of communication channels, and prompt attention to grievances which can easily be brought to the attention of persons who will act to settle disputes in a just manner. A large number of communication links between categories allows each reasonably to present its point of view, its motives, its plans, its intentions. While each category may not agree with the other on such matters, each side is at least relatively accurately informed and there is little or no necessity for making all manner of surmises, guesses, and imputations of the motives and plans of its opposite number. Equally as important, in preparing such cross-category revelations of its plans and intentions, each is induced to modify its perspective to order to make it more acceptable to the opposite category. Concomitant with such exchanges are personal friendships, informal ties, personalistic advantages and pay-offs, and other more diffuse inter-categorical modes of compromising the involvement of persons in their own category. A tradition of exchange of views and negotiated settlements makes it more likely that any action initiated by one side will be received in an atmosphere of trust. All these practices make it less likely that any action by either category will be defined as fundamentally threatening.

We find precisely the opposite obtaining between ghettos and the host society. The absence of effective communication, co-optation, and compromise breeds, as noted, fear, suspicion, and distrust. Such a situation is fertile ground for the spread of all manner of fearful and cynical rumors as to what "the other side" is "really" up to. In the absence of reasonable information, the most gross of cynical motives can be and are imputed. (I refer you again to the slogan, "Don't trust anyone over thirty.")

It is in the situation of separation, fear, distrust, and negative imputations between categories that an action initiated by one category can be defined as fundamentally threatening to the basic interest of the opposite category.

If an action is defined as a fundamental threat, then it is reasonable to respond to this threat with a swift, decisive, strong defense. Of course, the opposite category which is the recipient of this defense thereupon feels itself grossly threatened. The recipient category, in order to protect its now felt-to-be-threatened fundamental interests, reciprocates with its own swift, decisive, strong defense. The opposite category is consequently even more threatened and responds in kind. We thus have what is called the escalation of conflict, a process that is the joint product of the two parties and a process that seems always to have an ambiguous beginning point, unless one traces the history of the relation all the way back to the beginnings of the original categorical separation.[19]

Where the swift, decisive, strong defense involves large numbers of ghetto persons acting in a nonroutine manner in public places, it is popularly labeled a demonstration, riot, or collective outbrust.[20] We have seen a number of these in connection with Negro ghettos. It is in exactly the same terms of ghettoization—the terms of separation, of fear, of distrust, and of high probability of threat—that we can also best understand similar events occurring on college campuses, that is, in youth ghettos.

If youth ghettos have already fired their shot heard round the world, it was probably the Berkeley "demonstrations," "disturbances," "revolt," or "revolution" of 1964–65. (Pick a label according to the preference of your age category.)

The well-known events at Berkeley were only a spectacular episode in the long history of decreasing categorical sharing and the growth of a relatively enclosed youth ghetto along the southern edge of the Berkeley campus. The relations between the two categories—university and youth —came finally to a confrontation where each category saw itself enormously threatened by the other category. Each category saw itself as rightly defending itself against the threats posed by the other category. It is indeed ironic that the growth of Berkeley's academic eminence in America closely corresponds to the growth of the conditions of separation between youth and the university. Berkeley's scholarly and research eminence was purchased at the price of relative indifference to, and separation from, its almost 28,000 charges. And, as the university learned, the price was much higher than it had been originally calculated. Although allowing at least one-quarter of the tenured faculty in many departments to be on leave for research (and a large "in residence" proportion on psychological leave) and allowing a large proportion of the teaching to be performed by youth called teaching assistants is conducive to a world-wide reputation for scholarship, these practices, when combined with a wide variety of other kinds of indifference and separation, are incompatible with linking the category of youth to the social order.[21]

And even more ironic, where there has been little communication, co-optation, and compromise between categories, it becomes all the more difficult to initiate them. Under conditions of separation, fear, threat, and defense, each category comes, indeed, rather fiercely to pronounce its refusal to compromise what are now well articulated and ideologized principles. That is, the existing separation tends to deepen and solidify into principled inter-categorical opposition.

[19]Excellent documentation and conceptualization of these situations and processes are presented in Suttles, *op. cit.*, and Heirich, *op. cit.* The process sketched in the foregoing passages may well be among the few that are found at all levels of social organization.

[20]When such defensive action involves merely individuals or small groups, it is labeled crime, delinquency, or deviance. When it involves nations it is labeled "war." Such differences in popular labels should not detract attention from the essential similarity of the social processes.

[21]My characterization of the Berkeley events is drawn from Heirich's definitive study, especially Chap. I, "Structuring the Conflict."

Universities that embark on the Berkeley quest for eminence, and in the same manner, might be apprised of the possibility that there may be a youth ghetto like Berkeley's in their future.

I HAVE suggested the possibility that we may be embarking upon a period in the American experience when age will become a nationalized pivotal dimension around which categories of persons are differentiated. I necessarily imply that a new kind of segregation may be afoot.

I am, of course, mindful of all those oft-printed remarks, running back at least to ancient Greece, which tell us that almost every generation has thought that new and unprecedented (and most often terrible) things were taking place among its youth. Such reprinted expressions of alarm are intended to tell us that the perception of the unprecedented—typically the decadent—is simply a generational illusion spawned by the fears of older persons. While I will make no judgment as to whether younger generations were or are decadent, one can say that very frequently there has in fact been an enormous change in generational views and practices, a change enshrined most recently in the transformation of Western societies into advanced, industrial, technological social orders.

We should be prepared to expect that the coming of this newest kind of social order might itself create a wide variety of likewise new types of categorical segregations, while yet other segregations disintegrate. So far as I have been able to determine, the current scale of the clustering of persons into territories on the basis of age is indeed a new phenomenon.

While the emerging primacy of the age dimension, and its categories, seems to be new, the social processes it follows, and that follow from it, are very old and universal. While we may have to come to grips with a new content and substance of social conflict, we need not at all despair, because we do know something about the character of the formal and analytic processes involved, and the concepts and propositions appropriate to an understanding of it. The primary question becomes, then, will the human animal use such understanding in coping with this new and emerging basis of conflict, or will it stumble through in the same gruesome manner it has done in the past, and play out, yet again, the painful drama of blind hostility?

Topical Index